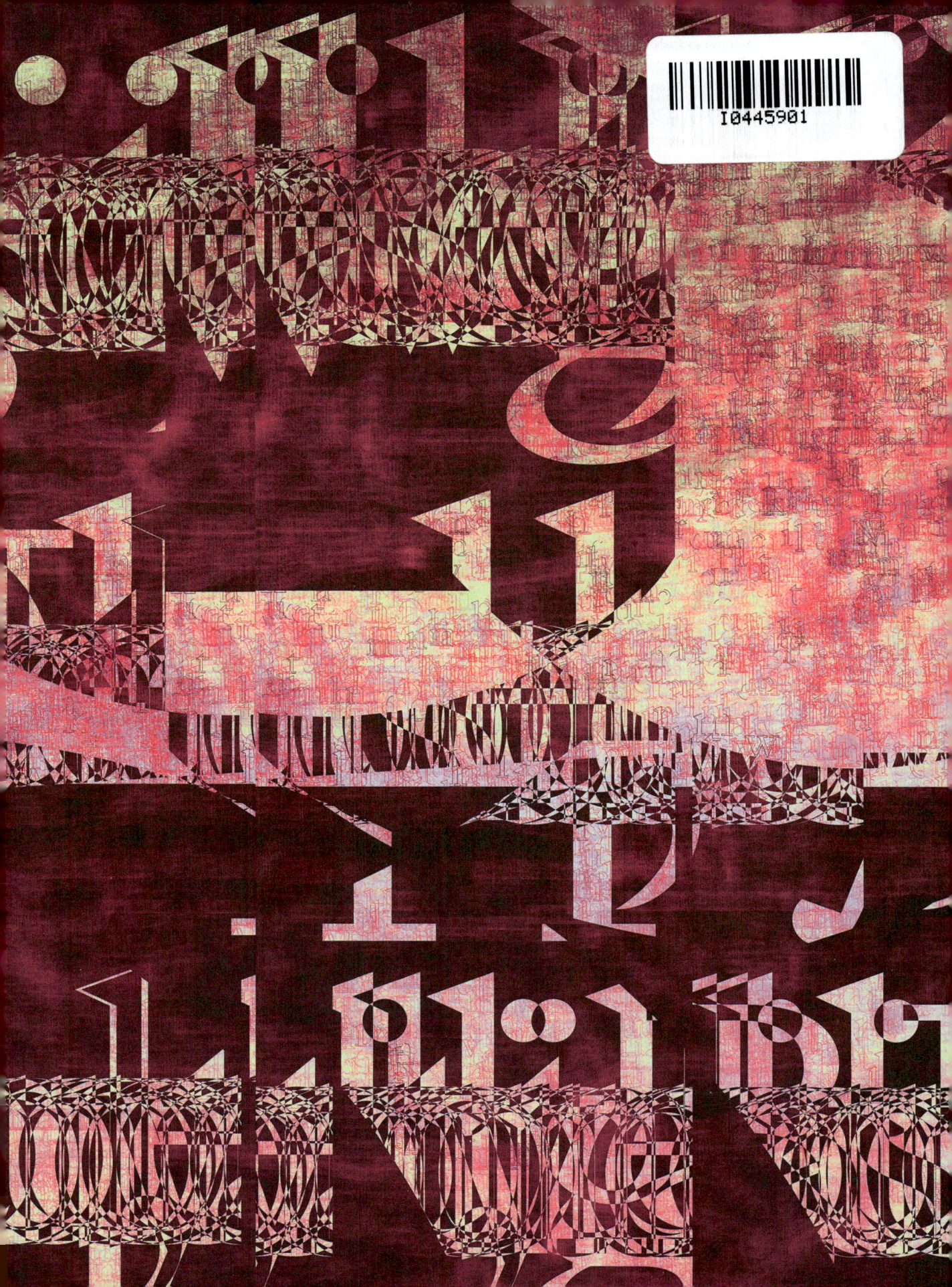

# On NFTs

*For Clara, A xIfL HF hRA gjJrOY ICLttkTvQxC IJrFz*
*SA hNrZG CeGRhV SZmGK.*

*For Hunters, TyBU a W1lIH RoeS BQe XJhb Wlkc y4gLz*
*I3LTkzM TgOTj MwLTg 3NDg2 RS5od G0 gLi4uI Dsp.*

R.A.

**Generative endpapers (front and back)**
commissioned by TASCHEN
Robert Alice
Outputs from *Source [On NFTs]*, 2024
Text, Natural Language Processing, p5.js
0×5e5551ff74c8f5bd3aaae8801aed0d579ddb470c, 1-125

# On NFTs

ROBERT ALICE (ED.)

**TASCHEN**

# EXPLORER

**Background**
qubibi
*hy2D6sa622Gk*, 06-02-2022 01:25:44
C#, Unity
Tezos, KT1KPth73LSTvaqin7bNc4nc2wWcdoxd3kMV, 12

# Crypto trading cards.

- *To*: CYPHERPUNKS <CYPHERPUNKS@TOAD.COM>
- *Subject*: Crypto trading cards.
- *From*: Hal <74076.1041@CompuServe.COM>
- *Date*: 17 Jan 93 13:48:02 EST

```
Giving a little more thought to the idea of buying and selling digital
cash, I thought of a way to present it.  We're buying and selling
"cryptographic trading cards".  Fans of cryptography will love these
fascinating examples of the cryptographic arts.  Notice the fine way
the bit patterns fit together - a mix of one-way functions and digital
signatures, along with random blinding.  What a perfect conversation
piece to be treasured and shown to your friends and family.

Plus, your friends will undoubtedly love these cryptographic trading
cards just as much.  They'll be eager to trade for them.  Collect a
whole set!  They come in all kinds of varieties, from the common
1's, to the rarer 50's, all the way up to the seldom-seen 1000's.
Hours of fun can be had for all.

Your friendly cryptographic trading card dealer wants to join the fun,
too.  He'll be as interested in buying your trading cards back as in
selling them.

Try this fascinating and timely new hobby today!

Hal
```

ROBERT ALICE

# INTRODUCTION

*This is how one pictures the angel of history. His face is turned toward the past. Where we perceive a chain of events, he sees one single catastrophe which keeps piling wreckage upon wreckage and hurls it in front of his feet. The angel would like to stay, awaken the dead, and make whole what has been smashed. But a storm is blowing from Paradise [...].The storm irresistibly propels him into the future to which his back is turned, while the pile of debris before him grows skyward. This storm is what we call progress.*

Walter Benjamin
*On the Concept of History*, 1940

In honor of Hal Finney (1956–2014)

Hal Finney
*Crypto Trading Cards*, 01-17-1993 13:48:02 EST
Cypherpunk Mailing List

*It is this dance, between the importance of text to NFTs and the disruption of blockchain to publishing, that has been the guiding inspiration and philosophical backdrop to the words found in these pages.*

Throughout the history of art, artists and writers, image and text have always been partners, mixing both fluently and violently together in a continual symbiotic dance, where images provoke text and those texts provoke more images, and the dance carries on. To hijack Walter Benjamin's words, that is the storm that we call art-historical progress. And yet on the blockchain, this call and response between artwork and text has become supercharged. An artwork does not exist on the blockchain without text. Whether it is a code-based on-chain work, or a hyperlink to a decentralized file server, text is the current and currency that creates and secures NFTs. One has to look no further than Larva Labs' *Autoglyphs* (2019) to understand that when stripped to its bones, NFTs are just text.

Blockchains are also deeply intertwined with the history of publishing, for what is a blockchain if not humanity's latest breakthrough in the art of the written record? Indeed, blockchains have reemphasized the importance of publishing as a communal act, drawing attention again to its social and political role in cultural debate and free speech. And so it is this dance, between the importance of text to NFTs and the disruption of blockchain to publishing, that has been the philosophical backdrop to the words found in these pages.

It would be impossible to measure precisely how many words have been written about NFTs. They have captured the public consciousness, challenging as all new art movements do the very basis of art itself. They have provocatively dominated our media, creating new communities and commodities; started a great rebalancing of digital versus physical art within art history and the art market; bringing in turn a new diverse generation of artists to global prominence. It is a history that has celebrated art at all levels and to all audiences; focused less on the art world elite but on themes of democratization, disintermediation, and decentralization. Art has been popularized to whole new audiences, and also further financialized. The commentary has evolved at rapid speed, at a high and often rancorous pitch, tracking in real time the radical development of this remarkably confounding space. Following nearly a decade of debate, we have reached a moment where reflection becomes possible: where a history can be told, genealogies traced, and patterns identified.

## Context

This book is one of the first major survey publications on blockchain-based art since Ruth Catlow and Furtherfield's 2017 landmark endeavor *Artists Re:Thinking the Blockchain*.[1] It was that visionary text that inspired me to commit my own artistic practice to this new experimental field. *Texts provoke images...* Since then, I have tried my best to contribute meaningfully to the NFT and crypto art spaces, creating both digital and physical work, largely focused on the histories of blockchains. If I may, I'd like to offer some context around my work and therefore the background for how this book came to be.

Though art-making has always been my focus, I first trained as an art historian at university. While making art and exploring crypto, I worked across the art world in museums and galleries in London, Vancouver, and Hong Kong. Following my reading of Catlow's text, my first art project focused on blockchain, *Portraits of a Mind* (2019–), was a historical inquiry into the ground zero of the blockchain movement: Satoshi Nakamoto's Bitcoin Core v0.1.0 — the very first codebase that ran Bitcoin in 2009. All roads lead back to those 12.8 million hexadecimal characters. It is the ultimate primary text. I was interested in opening the aperture of blockchain art's collaboration with art world institutions, to help expand the platform for blockchain-based art. Working with Christie's in 2020, the project became the first NFT and blockchain-based artwork sold at a major auction house. marked a small but key moment of validation for the space, paving the way for the seminal sale of Beeple's *EVERYDAYS: THE FIRST 5000 DAYS* (2021) at the same house six months later.

While focused on art-making, I remained engaged in art history. I curated *Natively Digital* at Sotheby's, spotlighting overlooked artists in early NFT history. The auction raised $17.1 million — a majority of sales went directly to artists. During the 2022 Venice Biennale, I revisited early NFT history with the show *0,14* at Palazzo Lolin. At the end of the year, I organized a conference on NFTs at the University of Oxford, titled *0xBAT*, aiming to build deeper bridges with the academic art history community. I opened the conference with a talk on a theory of NFTs. I was still primarily focused on art-making and in 2023, I was invited to mount a solo museum show at the Monnaie de Paris: linking crypto's 16-year history with the world's oldest continuously operating national mint, some 1,159 years old. The outcome of the show was the creation of a blockchain wallet by the French Ministry of Finance for the storage of NFTs at a nation-state level and the acquisition of works from the show by the Centre Pompidou. Titled *BABEL*, the exhibition drew inspiration from Borges's *The Library of Babel* (1941). *Texts provoke images...*

And yet still as I looked around at this Cambrian explosion of culture on-chain in late 2022, there still did not exist a full-scale art-historical survey since Catlow's and Furtherfield's

[1] Ruth Catlow, Marc Garrett, Nathan Jones, and Sam Skinner, *Artists Re:Thinking the Blockchain* (London: Torque Editions, 2017).

*It is a history that has celebrated art at all levels and to all audiences; focused less on the art world elite but on themes of democratization, disintermediation, and decentralization.*

work. One where artists were given their own space, and the work was placed front and center. The first chapter had definitely closed following the euphoria of 2022, and I remained wide eyed at my colleagues' creativity. Despite growing engagement by institutions, a maturing influx of sophisicated collectors, galleries, and platforms, our art history had not been laid down in an approachable format that could engage the next generation of artists, curators, critics, and collectors, especially not by a marquee publisher who could distribute globally. Unlike NFTs, books circulate in a slower way, they are familiar to a public still daunted by the blockchain. Books demand a different kind of attention. They meet the public on their terms, dressed in all the shibboleths that NFTs are trying to break down.

So I hope that gives some context to the full-circle nature and inspiration behind this book: an interest not just in art, but where it goes and how it circulates; in building bridges between the old institutions and new cultures; and the interplay between art and art history that characterizes much of my practice to date.

It is important to make clear that this book is artist-led and community focused. It comes from within the NFT space, it is not a helicopter survey. It is inspired by my colleagues' and friends' talent and creativity — of which I am in awe. To witness history in real time is a huge privilege — it is not often you get to write it while it is happening.

Indeed, a partial reason to sketch my journey is that I believe it is a similar path to many contributors in the NFT space, who have come from many adjacent fields. Much like great cities, it is this migratory melting pot that makes the space so exciting. As they say in coding, it is a feature not a bug. As an artist and a writer, I believe the blockchain is both humanity's most open canvas and blankest page. There are no gatekeepers. And so while the blockchain will always be the ultimate primary text for NFTs, it is my hope that *On NFTs* acts as an engaging physical portal into this new world.

**Curatorial Strategy**

What to call this undertaking? The title *On NFTs* is inspired by the art-historical and cryptographic tradition of the treatise, exemplified best by the Renaissance artist, art historian, and cryptographer Leon Battista Alberti's (1404–1472) two treatises *De Pictura/On Painting* (1450) and *De Cifris/On Ciphers* (1466).[2] Before the advent of blockchain, there exists no one individual in history who has furthered the dual fields of art and cryptography in equal measure. I wonder what he would have thought of this all?

A treatise examines the topic at hand both systematically and at length. But unlike the work of Alberti or other more traditional art-historical styles, this book is not authored by one individual. Rather than presenting a monolithic, singular perspective on NFTs and their place in art history, it is made up of multiple artistic and critical voices, mirroring the decentralized architecture and consensus-driven nature of the blockchain itself. This applies both to the spectrum of authors who have contributed individual chapters and to the curation of the 111 artists and further 111 writers included in the book.

The selection of the 111 artists was organized in part through rounds of outreach, starting with an initial selection of 30 artists that we felt had particularly strong global consensus built around their practice. These artists were asked to select a further six artists, who were asked in turn to select a further six artists. Armed with this long list, we approached practices with the following two questions in mind: To what extent had they contributed artistically and structurally to the NFT space? And to what extent had they pushed forward or challenged the concept of an NFT itself? The resultant curatorial strategy meant that the overwhelming majority of artists included in this book have been suggested by their peers and fellow community members. It has been a lesson in the power of decentralized co-curation.

Equally it was critical to me to show the NFT space as it really was during its first chapter, celebrating art at all levels and to all audiences. The majority of artists are still contributing to the space, some experimented, but if they were important at a particular time they speak to the rapidly evolving zeitgeist of digital art on the blockchain. This *partially* updated version adds eleven artists that I feel have produced defining works since formal research ended (mid-2023). It is important to therefore remember that this text is a portrait of the NFT space up to 2023, with only minor amendments and revisions. It speaks to a certain era and a certain perspective. It is our view that the book is more important as a historical artifact, than it would be if we decided to wholesale update it — that would be the job of a second volume.

It would be impossible to create a comprehensive account of this constantly expanding field. Indeed, to try to present an authoritative study would be to misunderstand the entire nature and philosophy of NFTs. In this, I think of this publication as a critical node in a wider art-historical network that is steadily coming online. The more publications, the more balanced and decentralized this art history will be. In this respect, our mission has been

2   In Latin, the preposition *de* functions as an abbreviation of the phrase "on the subject of."

*While we have gone to great lengths to place artists around other artists and essays that we hope reveal commonalities and a deeper sense of rhythm, artists are not blocks in a blockchain and in the fullness of their individuality, they resist neat categorization. If anything, it is a starting point for debate.*

to create an inclusive and diverse publication that reflects the spirit of the NFT community as a whole — one where fierce public debate is celebrated and which provides a long-term printed platform for the many important critical voices in the space. The goal was not to find the 111 most mature practices, but the 111 practices that best represent the entirety of the NFT movement. The book surveys not just 111 artists, but over 111 writers that the artists have chosen personally to write on their work. This includes artists within the book writing on each other, spouses on their other halves, internet friends (who have never met in person) on internet friends, parents writing on children, artificial intelligence (GPT-3) on artists who use these tools themselves, collectors on artists, ... the kaleidoscopic list goes on. It is a multifaceted portrait of an NFT space that bleeds both global and intimate. In doing so we have sought to ensure visibility for the significant figures — the builders, critics, curators, and collectors — who have played as important a role in establishing this new ecosystem and community as the artists themselves.

## Geography and Diversity

Where is this community from and who are they? While the blockchain and the metaverse transcend physical geographic boundaries, we have worked hard to look beyond the traditional blockchain and art epicenters to showcase a truly global art movement. In total, the artists are from 32 countries and every habitable continent in the world. The statistics though still paint a picture resembling a form of cultural dominance from the United States and Europe, with over 45% of the artists coming from North America, followed by 26% from Europe, 7% Africa, 6% South America, 5% Asia, and 3% Australasia.[3] Of the 111 artists and projects featured in this publication, 34.5% are women;[4] which shows that women artists number among the top creators, as chosen by their peers, at more than twice the rate of the reported 16% share of NFT sales that women artists account for.[5] Additionally, 2.2% of artists in the book identify as nonbinary. Much more work has to be done to encourage greater diversity on the blockchain from both the creative and the collector side, with the space mirroring structural diversity issues in the art world writ large, rather than providing a community and platform for a more diverse and inclusive cultural narrative. The inclusivity and openness of the blockchain are powerful tools, yet as with all technologies it is the people who interact with it who must choose how to use it.

## Essays and Flow

While these artworks are more than capable of speaking for themselves, readers will hopefully benefit from the scholarship in the surrounding texts. Aimed equally at newcomers — who are advised to refer to the wide-ranging glossary we have put together — and those who are intimately acquainted with the NFT space, the following essays reflect the richness and diversity of their subject matter. Written by prominent artists, critics, curators, and collectors, they are all builders where a lived experience within the NFT space has been prized as much as critical independence.

Each essay might best be approached as a series of treatises in miniature: not chapters in a longer narrative but rather self-sufficient essays united by a shared history and cultural landscape. Retracing the history of NFTs and its various subcategories, the main actors in the field, and the technology itself, the essays will have points of overlap: artworks have always had a tendency to escape from the confines of the categories in which we place them. There will also be moments of divergence and even direct contradiction: the NFT space is nothing if not welcoming of differences of opinion (except perhaps on the validity of NFTs themselves). This must equally be considered when analyzing the flow of artists in the book.

While we have gone to great lengths to place artists around other artists and essays that we hope reveal commonalities and a deeper sense of rhythm, artists are not blocks in a blockchain, and in the fullness of their individuality, they resist neat categorization. If anything, it is a starting point for debate.

The publication begins with my own essay, "On Quantum," introducing the prehistory and early history of NFTs through the prism of Kevin McCoy's landmark work *Quantum* (2014), contextualizing the birth of this new movement while providing a number of theoretical frameworks to think about the nature of NFTs. In "On Crypto Art," Jason Bailey, one of the earliest commentators and collectors in the space, and Alex Estorick, editor-in-chief of *Right Click Save*, present their reading of the term crypto art and the movement it has generated with a data-driven approach in keeping with the movement's key principles. Similarly focusing on a particular genre of NFTs, Sofia Garcia, a leading curator in the algorithmic art field, traces the history of algorithmic art from the 1960s through to its renaissance on the blockchain as one of the most cutting edge fields in contemporary art today. One of the most

3   The remaining 8% are anonymous.
4   This includes projects that are co-led, co-founded, or creatively directed by women (excluding anonymous artists and projects).
5   Sarah Cascone, "Depressing New Report Finds That Women Artists Accounted for Just 16 Percent of NFT Sales Over the Past 21 Months," *Artnet news*, November 5, 2021, https://news.artnet.com/market/nft-sales-just-16-percent-women-2030490.

*We have painstakingly cataloged each NFT with all the richness that the blockchain allows: you will find for each work the digital or physical mediums used to make the work, the chain the work is minted on, the contract address, the exact mint timestamp (UTC) down to the minute and second, the token ID, and, where applicable for works in series, the edition number.*

influential artists in the NFT space, Rhea Myers, has contributed an essay titled "On Chain" which delves into the notion of smart contracts and the blockchain themselves as an artistic medium, placing this fascinating technological development within a wider art-historical context. With contributions from Beeple, Refik Anadol, Brendan Dawes, Emily Xie, Erick Calderon, Harm van den Dorpel, and Ry David Bradley, the chapter "On Process" seeks to shine a light on the studio practices and processes that go into making this often technically complex work. My second essay, on the world of NFT avatars or PFPs (profile pictures), also looks back, this time at the origins of the avatar — within gaming, science fiction, and psychology — to examine the question of identity and cultural capital in our new Web3 age. From here, the essays telescope outwards, looking at how NFTs circulate within and engage with the world. Fittingly, a collective has formed to author an essay on decentralized autonomous organizations (DAOs). Aaron Wright, one of the leading authorities on DAOs, and Serena Tabacchi, director of the Museum of Contemporary Digital Art, lay out the history that this new kind of organizational structure both draws from and radically disrupts. A history of collecting swiftly follows, led by Michael Bouhanna, Head of Digital Art at Sotheby's, and Jehan Chu, an important collector and crypto thought leader. The essay unpacks how the blockchain has disrupted recent structures around collecting and, with a specific focus on the *wunderkammer*, argues that it in many ways resurrected older structures of collecting through the concept of patronage. Taking the form of a conversation between curator Hans Ulrich Obrist and the editorial platform *Outland*, the next essay presents a history and speculative future on how artists — both on and off the blockchain — are starting to interact and consider the metaverse and how curators and collectors are thinking about Web3 curatorial strategies. Finally, for those seeking a more technical history of the infrastructure behind NFTs, María Paula Fernández, Simon Denny, and Adina Glickstein provide a survey of the key developments in the space, from blockchains to token standards.

## Resources and How to Read

We are privileged to have the space here also to include an extensive exhibition history — an acknowledgment of the primary sources that have been so invaluable during the production of this publication. A scan of the glossary gives an eye-opening insight into the raucous lexicon of this online swarm. We have painstakingly cataloged each NFT with all the richness that the blockchain allows: you will find for each work the digital or physical mediums used to make the work, the chain the work is minted on, the contract address, the exact mint timestamp (UTC)[6] down to the minute and second, the token ID, and, where applicable for works in series, the edition number. Please be aware that where individual works are shown from a series, we have added the timestamp from the first edition in the series (not necessarily the one illustrated). Below the cataloging we have added the edition number. This will help the most assiduous of researchers pinpoint on the blockchain the exact works illustrated, while also providing general clarity around the wider body of work in a concise manner. Play symbols (▶) indicate video and dynamic artworks, each accompanied by a QR code in the QR Catalogue (pp. 618–635). For each dynamic NFT, these QR codes link directly to the location of the moving image files on the blockchain, providing the security against time that the blockchain does best and allowing these works to be accessible for as long as the blockchain remains alive.

Most of all, I am grateful to our publishers. TASCHEN is an iconic publisher with a deep history of disruption and risk-taking. Following the success of the SUMO edition, the book will now be available at a more approachable price (and manageable size!). It is here that I believe its real value will be found: in providing a long-term structural building block to educate the next generation of artists, critics, curators, and collectors in our early history. My only hope is that this book will provoke more images and, in response, more texts, and the dance carries on.

**ROBERT ALICE**
STUDIO@ROBERTALICE.COM

[6] For historical accuracy, as it is widely regarded as the first NFT, Kevin McCoy's *Quantum* (2014) has been cataloged with its local mint timestamp in Eastern Daylight Time (EDT, UTC-4).

## WHAT ARE NFTs

: Non-fungible tokens (NFTs) allow unique digital assets to be owned, purchased, or sold. NFTs "live" on decentralized blockchain databases, which means
two things. Firstly, <u>no trust is required when interacting with others on the
blockchain</u>. This means untrusting strangers can trade NFTs from anywhere at any
time without a mediating or "trusted" third-party, <u>creating less friction and
more democratic markets</u> that settle trade instantly. Secondly, <u>NFTs are immutable.</u> Once an NFT is minted on a blockchain, <u>its record can never be taken down,
hidden, or destroyed</u> (neither by the creator nor the owner) and <u>are publicly
viewable for as long as the blockchain exists.</u> An <u>NFT cannot be duplicated,</u>
and validating an NFT as authentic is a simple case of checking a blockchain's
public database.

## WHAT ARE NFTs USED FOR

: <u>An NFT can be any digital file:</u> code, images, videos, music, documents,
certificates, and virtual land are some of the most common examples. They can
also be a proxy for any physical asset, like a house or gold or even a can of
Heinz tomato soup. <u>For creatives, they can give a greater level of control and
ownership over their own work,</u> particularly commercially. Rights encoded into
the NFT stipulate forever the artist's specific wishes as to the rights around
that particular artwork. <u>Adding resale rights to the NFT's contract has allowed
artists to better benefit from the future resale of their artwork</u> where historically they have struggled to do so.

# NFT *noun*

(ˌɛnɛfˈti)

: NON-FUNGIBLE TOKEN : a unique digital identifier that cannot be copied, substituted, or
subdivided, that is recorded in a blockchain, and that is used to certify authenticity and ownership (as
of a specific digital asset and specific rights relating to it).

Merriam-Webster Dictionary, s.v. "non-fungible token," 2022.

## WHAT ARE BLOCKCHAINS

: Blockchains are <u>a new form of public database that no one owns or can tam-
per with.</u> They are decentralized global networks of computers that coordinate,
agree, and validate on "blocks" of transactions in return for rewards and fees.
Through consensus and cryptography, blockchains are able to validate the creation, ownership, and trade of cryptocurrencies or NFTs in a secure and trustless manner. Crucially, <u>while cryptocurrencies are fungible like cash, NFTs are
non-fungible, making them like unique collectibles.</u> Once a block of data is val-
idated it is set in stone and linked to a chain of all previous blocks forming
<u>an irreversible timeline of data.</u> This timeline is viewable and verifiable to
anyone with an internet connection. To view a live blockchain such as Ethereum,
go to Etherscan (etherscan.io).

## HOW DO I GET INVOLVED

1. To collect an NFT you will first need to <u>create a crypto wallet.</u> For the
Ethereum blockchain the most widely used wallet is MetaMask (metamask.io), while
Kukai (kukai.app) is recommended by Tezos blockchain. Alternatively, for more
security, you could use a hardware wallet such as a Ledger (ledger.com).
2. <u>Add the right crypto to your wallet</u> (ether [ETH] for Ethereum NFTs or Tez
[XTZ] for Tezos). You can deposit it from an exchange such as Coinbase (Coinbase.
com) or by purchasing it directly through the wallet provider.
3. Visit an NFT marketplace, such as OpenSea (opensea.io) or Objkt (Objkt.
com). You can then <u>create or collect an NFT using the cryptocurrency you
just bought.</u>

# NFTS ARE...

Given the ever-expanding number of use cases for NFTs, how can one accurately define the technology to encompass the viewpoints of the entire space? Does a centralized dictionary definition adequately define a decentralized community? To answer this question, Robert Alice sought the opinions of the NFT, art, and crypto communities, asking them to finish the simple statement: "NFTs are..."

Overleaf, this ledger of perspectives showcases the multifaceted opinions and polarizing points of view that NFTs currently engender. Often filled with wry humor and a healthy dose of cynicism, these alternative, personal definitions present a clearer insight into the NFT ecosystem than any dictionary definition could.

## *just a useful tool for digital artists*

**OSCAR HORMIGOS**
CHIEF CREATIVE OFFICER
AT COLECCIÓN SOLO

## *a swing state*

**NANCY BAKER CAHILL**
NEW MEDIA ARTIST

*made of people*
**QUASIMONDO.ETH**
ARTIST

*a big warm hug for artists of the world*
**DEBBIE SOON**
CO-FOUNDER OF HUG

*too dull to merit a book*
**PHINEAS HARPER**
CEO OF OPEN CITY

*the Urinal of the 21st Century*
**GEORG BAK**
DIGITAL ART ADVISOR

*a new medium, not the end themselves*
**ANDREABONAC.ETH**
ARTIST

*a new medium, not the end themselves*
**ANDREABONAC.ETH**
ARTIST

*making the internet weird again*
**PRIYANKA DESAI**
COO AT TRIBUTE LABS

*an opportunity for all artists to sell their work directly to the whole world without barriers*
**0XTECHNO.ETH**
NFT COLLECTOR

*a "what if" zone*
**JESSEDAMIANI.ETH**
FOUNDER OF POSTREALITY LABS

*a chance for art to change the world again*
**GRIFFINCOCKFOSTER.ETH**
CO-FOUNDER OF NIFTY GATEWAY

*financial care collapsed into expressive protocols*
**SIMONDENNY.ETH**
ARTIST

*time capsules buried in every garden*
**AURECEVETTIER.ETH**
ARTIST

*like Punk Rock. First, Anarchy. Then, Mainstream*
**RANI JABBAN**
DIGITAL ART PATRON

*certificates of digital scarcity, giving provenance to digital art. This means digital art becomes collectible*
**RYAN ZURRER**
COLLECTOR

*my only income stream pls help me*
**PPLPLEASR.ETH**
ARTIST

*trains to transformation. Mind the gap.*
**MATTKANE.ETH**
ARTIST

*creative freedoms manifested*
**PARIS HILTON**
QUEEN OF THE METAVERSE

*keeping me very busy*
**TYLERXHOBBS.ETH**
ARTIST

*taxable events*
**OKWME.ETH**
ARTIST AND BLOCKCHAIN ENGINEER

*forever – if minted properly*
**JP JANSSEN**
TOKEN PIONEER

*the future, risks/opportunities included*
**HERBERT W. FRANKE**
SCIENTIST, ARTIST, AND PHILOSOPHER

*marriage certificates for cuckolds*
**PHILIP HOOK**
ART HISTORIAN

*tradable human creativity*
**NANSEN.ETH**
CEO OF NANSEN

*transitory*
**RANKBADGER.ETH**
TECH AT SUPER BLOOM

*bearer bonds for data: everything can and will be an NFT*
**GARRETTEDVF.ETH**
CO-FOUNDER OF ATOMIC FORM

*what keeps me employed*
**JESSICA COOPER**
CLIENT COORDINATION MANAGER AT ARTXCODE

*stores of digital culture*
**YAT SIU**
CHAIRMAN OF ANIMOCA BRANDS

*Pixels of Culture enlightening digital worlds*
**SÉBASTIEN BORGET**
CO-FOUNDER OF THE SANDBOX

## a canvas on display for the entire world simultaneously

**ROBERT LESHNER**
FOUNDER OF COMPOUND

### a commodity, a provocation, a para-medium, a shibboleth, an inscribed artifact of capital at speed

**A. V. MARRACCINI**
ART HISTORIAN AND CRITIC

### elevating the world's best digital artists

**JEFFGDAVIS.ETH**
ARTIST AND CHIEF CREATIVE
OFFICER AT ART BLOCKS

---

*surveillance capitalism's greatest hack*
**COLBORN.ETH**
FOUNDER OF THE MUSEUM OF CRYPTO ART

*the access point of a convergence of creativity and technical innovation that will empower*
**HOLLY WOOD**
HEAD OF ARTIST RELATIONSHIPS AT RARIBLE

*the future religious artifact*
**RIMBAWAN GERILYA**
THIRD WORLD FUTURIST

*technology helping an outpouring of closeted artistic expression to find new life and appreciation*
**BERNADINE BRÖCKER WIEDER**
NFT ENTHUSIAST

*the weapons that artists & individuals will use to subvert the state of the world*
**FAUS.ETH**
FILMMAKER

*NOT DEAD lol, they are the pet rock of the 21st century, not all get it but they still want it*
**CRYPTOYUNA**
CRYPTO POP ARTIST

*not inherently a "medium," and neither necessary nor sufficient when transacting works of art*
**DR. TINA RIVERS RYAN**
EDITOR OF ARTFORUM

*value delivery mechanisms which allow us to create and power online communities*
**SERGITO.ETH**
CRYPTOPUNK COLLECTOR

*making traders art collectors and art collectors traders*
**SHILIANG TANG**
CIO OF LEDGERPRIME

*signed and programmable cultural containers embedded into an immutable timestamping engine*
**SIMON DE LA ROUVIERE**
ARTIST, CODER, AND NOVELIST

*most of the time just ego toys but sometimes they empower and timestamp deep human interactions*
**TOKENANGELS.ETH**
ANGEL INVESTOR AND CRYPTO ART COLLECTOR

*dead. Digital art is the future.*
**ELI SCHEINMAN**
ART DEALER AND ADVISOR

*culture redistributed*
**JAMES PARKER HEALY**
FOUNDER OF DIGITAL PRACTICE

*some code that doesn't transfer rights*
**TECHNOLLAMA.ETH**
COPYRIGHT AND IP RESEARCHER

*digital oxygen for degens*
**COZOMO DE' MEDICI**
COLLECTOR

*the cornerstone driving force for the digitalization and democratization of life and value*
**WHALESHARK**
FOUNDER OF $WHALE

*turning bits into bob*
**COSMO LINDSAY**
PROJECT MANAGER & HEAD OF RESEARCH AT STUDIO ROBERT ALICE

*digital milk yield from cat securities*
**CHARLIE EDWARDS**
INVESTMENT ANALYST AT ID THEORY

*a way for artists to establish creative sovereignty and become their own platform*
**WWHCHUNG.ETH**
FOUNDER OF MANIFOLD.XYZ

*a medium for public digital art*
**REFIK ANADOL**
MEDIA ARTIST

*the art world's Cornelian dilemma*
**MARLENE CORBUN**
HEAD CURATOR AT LACOLLECTION

*the herpes of the art world*
**PETER WU+**
CREATOR OF EPOCH

*enabling the emergence of "virtual property"*
**PRIMAVERA DE FILIPPI**
ARTIST AND BLOCKCHAIN SCHOLAR

*a long overdue missing link elevating digital first media in the world of contemporary art*
**SNOWFRO.ETH**
FOUNDER & CEO OF ART BLOCKS

*the ultimate fetish object*
**SARAH FRIEND**
ARTIST AND SOFTWARE DEVELOPER

*the building blocks of new participatory worlds*
**SAM SPIKE**
CREATIVE DIRECTOR AT FINGERPRINTS DAO AND CO-FOUNDER OF JPG

*are not the solution to the preservation of media art*
**REGINA HARSANYI**
PREVENTATIVE CONSERVATOR & CURATOR OF MEDIA ART AT MUSEUM OF THE MOVING IMAGE

*means to trace history*
**LICIA HE**
GENERATIVE ARTIST

*an intersectional technology: a social, financial and cultural landscapes meeting point*
**MARÍA PAULA FERNÁNDEZ**
CO-FOUNDER OF JPG.SPACE AND FOUNDER OF DEPARTMENT OF DECENTRALIZATION

*eirenicon – peace between faith & reason*
**KEVIN MCCOY**
ARTIST

*an empowering promise to all artists*
**FLAKOUBAY.ETH**
COLLECTOR AND FOUNDER OF LAL ART ADVISORY

*an immutable book of creations that trace to their creators; a pen to write what only they can say*
**CLAIRE SILVER**
AI COLLABORATIVE ARTIST, CRYPTOPUNK COLLECTOR, AND CO-FOUNDER OF ACCELERATEART

*1/3 culture, 1/3 community and 1/3 memes, best enjoyed on the rocks and through your feed*
**LUKAS AMACHER**
DIRECTOR OF 1OF1.WORKS

*one-of-a-kind digital assets that are tokenizing the world around us*
**SEEDPHRASE.ETH**
EARLY NFT COLLECTOR

## vases, for bouquets of information

**KATHERINE FRAZER**
ARTIST

*fergalicious, definition make them boys go loco*
**VXN**
ARTIST

*making each of us a potential patron*
**QINWENWANG.ETH**
PRODUCER OF VIRTJAL NICHE (2021) AT
UCCA LAB, BEIJING

*cute retail ponzinomics*
**GABEWISE.ETH**
BUSINESS DEVELOPMENT AT FIRSTMATE

*verifiable proof of everything*
**SHAUN DJIE**
FOUNDER OF TOKOCRYPTO AND CO-
FOUNDER OF DIGIX

*a gateway drug*
**WILL CORKIN**
CO-FOUNDER OF MANTRA AND SOMA.
FINANCE

*tools with which to build worlds*
**SATURNIAL.ETH**
FOUNDER & CEO OF FOUNDATION

*responsible for a major diversion of my attention*
**KELLY RICHARDSON**
ARTIST

*a mild gateway drug to digital scarcity*
**JOONIAN.ETH**
REPORTING ON NFTS SINCE 2017

*like candies, good for the mood*
**INNA MODJA**
FOUNDER & CEO OF CODE GREEN

*a necessary evil*
**ERTDFGCVB.ETH**
ARTIST

*, therefore I am*
**ALEKS.TEZ**
FOUNDER OF ELECTRIC ARTEFACTS

*a market in search of a product*
**GEORGECPARKER.ETH**
DOGECOIN PROFESSOR OF LAW & GRIFTING

*Smoke n Mirrors for the kids of tomorrow*
**SATSMOON.ETH**
ART CURATOR

## financialization as religion

**ED FORNIELES**
ARTIST

*the reason I learned the world's timezone*
**DIELA.ETH**
ARTIST, COLLECTOR, AND CO-FOUNDER OF
METARUPA

*ownable internet for a digital species*
**PIERS KICKS**
PARTNER AT DELPHI DIGITAL

*the essentially human ideals of self-sovereignty and ownership in a world where humans live digitally*
**VSLAV.ETH**
CEO OF BLOCKPARTY

*hotter than tinder dates (Google 2021)*
**JIAYIN CHEN**
WRITER AND CURATOR

*wild above rule or art, enormous bliss*
**SERWAH.ETH**
ARTIST

*the social lubricant enabling a global revolution of digital creativity*
**PUNK7635.ETH**
ART COLLECTOR

*proof that we care about who owns our future*
**STEPHAN S. DALAL**
BLOCKCHAIN LAWYER AND BUILDER

*the portal to the digital realm*
**RYAN ZURRER**
COLLECTOR OF BEEPLE'S *HUMAN ONE* (2021)
AND FOUNDER OF DIALECTIC AND VINE
VENTURES

*a logical progression of how we consume*
**GEORGE ODELL**
EXECUTIVE VICE PRESIDENT OF LIVEART

*Near Future Translations, proof of poetry. Neverending Floral Tokens in the garden of my mind.*
**SASHA STILES**
POET, ARTIST, AI RESEARCHER, AND CO-
FOUNDER OF THEVERSEVERSE

*wondrous URLS for some and WTF for others*
**ROBERT NORTON**
CO-FOUNDER & CEO OF VERISART

## anything but art; and just like canvas, or the paint tube, they have begun the next artistic revolution

**OHHSHINY**
COMMUNITY LEADER,
COLLECTOR, AND INVESTOR

*a paradigm shift in the way we interact and engage with each other in the digital domain*
**PABLO RODRIGUEZ-FRAILE**
DIGITAL ART PATRON

*all that is solid(ity) melting into air*
**AD1NA.ETH**
WRITER

*our parents' nightmare & our kids' future*
**MIREIA DE ANDRÉS**
WEB3 ENTREPRENEUR

*everything and nothing*
**CAMILLE BECKMANN**
RESEARCHER AT STUDIO ROBERT ALICE

*just a new technology for artists to play with*
**GABRIELLE SCHWARZ**
COPYWRITER AT STUDIO ROBERT ALICE

*canvas stretchers with inbuilt C.o.A.s*
**CIBELLE.ETH**
ARTIST, RESEARCH, AND ACTIVIST

*alchemy*
**NEWRAFAEL.ETH**
ARTIST

*metaverse-high school's double-edged swords*
**NANU BERKS**
ARTIST

¯\\_(ツ)_/¯
**JONASLUND.ETH**
ARTIST

*okay, but crypto art is the DNA*
**RARE SCRILLA**
CEO OF BITCOIN ART AND MUSIC

*a belief system, and so is art*
**SASKIA DRAXLER**
GALLERIST AT NAGEL DRAXLER

*an underlying technology*
**AUGUSTFR.ETH**
OWNER OF MIRAGE GALLERY

*hanging by a thread*
**CLARA METTER**
CREATIVE CONSULTANT

*every satoshi. Misnomer sells narrative.*
**DUNCAN**
CRYPTO ARTIST

## what lets this old man do what he loves

**JOSÉ DELBO**
90-YEAR-OLD COMIC
AND CRYPTO ARTIST

## generative artwork to infinity

**AARONPENNE.ETH**
VISUAL ARTIST AND DIRECTOR
OF ENGINEERING AT ART BLOCKS

## a multicellular organism

**SOFIA CRESPO**
NEURAL ARTIST

---

*ultimate commodities, separated from use*
**RHEA MYERS**
OG BLOCKCHAIN ARTIST

*artists' creative portal to the future*
**ANNE SPALTER**
ARTIST

*at present, cash grabs, scams & celebretism*
**KATE VASS**
FOUNDER OF KATE VASS GALERIE

*a welcome hazard to "authenticity"*
**AYA WALRAVEN**
DESIGNER

*the Nile Rodgers to my Diana Ross*
**DAWES.ETH**
ARTIST

*a symbol of belonging to something new*
**ILLSUN.ETH**
CHIEF BUSINESS DEVELOPMENT OFFICER AT
RARIBLE

*your story heard*
**DAVIDALL.ETH**
FOUNDER & CEO OF CHANGEDAO

*content access = free, ownership = scarce*
**GORDON BERGER**
NFT AND CRYPTO ART PIONEER

*a new way to expand physical experiences*
**ANDRÉS REISINGER**
UNCLASSIFIABLE ARTIST

*Opportunities not Handouts*
**VINTAGEMOZART.ETH**
CO-FOUNDER OF AFRICAN NFT COMMUNITY

*where an alien race will learn about us millions of years into the future*
**KRISTA KIM**
ARTIST AND CO-FOUNDER OF 0.XYZ

*a better way to preserve, trade and enforce rights that empower the individual*
**HUGO MCDONAUGH**
CO-FOUNDER & CEO OF MYNFT

*jiggy*
**ARCLIGHT**
ARTIST

---

*the answer to digital artist's prayers*
**JOE KENNEDY**
FOUNDER OF INSTITUT

*windows that frame meta layer of art*
**TAIHEI.ETH**
ARTIST AND FOUNDER & CEO OF
STARTBAHN, INC.

*vital to authentic digital artistic expression*
**GUILE TWARDOWSKI**
CRYPTOKITTIES ARTIST

*a writer's canvas*
**KALEN IWAMOTO**
CONCEPTUAL CRYPTO WRITER & ARTIST,
CO-FOUNDER OF THEVERSEVERSE & WEN NEW
STUDIO

*the reason I'm here right now typing...*
**PARINART.ETH**
ARTIST

*art transporter beams that "boldly go where no man has gone before"*
**NICHOLAS GENTILLI**
PHOTOGRAPHER

*the Artist's opportunity of a generation*
**MARC HARTOG**
FOUNDER OF ART3.IO

*the trail of our existence*
**SHABAN SHAAME**
FOUNDER & CEO OF EVERDREAMSOFT

*a tiny glimpse into the future*
**RY DAVID BRADLEY**
ARTIST

*the distinct human ->blockchain interface*
**YESSIN SCHIEGG**
CFO AT NEAR FOUNDATION

*a way of commodifying imaginary things*
**MITCHELLFCHAN.ETH**
NFT AND CRYPTO ART PIONEER

*not (yet) a new art form*
**NINA ROEHRS**
FOUNDER OF ROEHRS & BOETSCH

*rare pepes*
**JOE LOONEY**
RARE PEPE SCIENTIST (RETIRED)

---

*the new wave of Punk. We're all artists.*
**STEPHEN BLISS**
FOUNDER OF FEAR CITY LLC

*the first true digital revolution*
**CONLAN.ETH**
FOUNDER & CEO OF ASYNC ART

*sexy*
**REBECCAROSE.ETH**
ARTIST AND CURATOR

*a frame and crate to hold digital art*
**LEEMULLICAN.ETH**
DIRECTOR OF THE ESTATE OF LEE MULLICAN

*creating a new wave of collectors*
**JEAN-SÉBASTIEN BEAUCAMPS**
CEO OF LACOLLECTION

*digitized pleats in our social fabric*
**DANI LOFTUS**
CEO AT DRAUP AND FOUNDER OF
THIS OUTFIT DOES NOT EXIST

*opening Pandora's box on creativity – infinite capabilities, that in the hands of those with wrong intentions, can lead to infinite limitations*
**MILA ASKAROVA**
FOUNDER & CEO OF GAZELLI ART HOUSE

*like marbles, evolution of collectibles*
**ORLANDO GAUL**
FOUNDER OF NFTEES

*a gateway to a new museum audience*
**HANS-PETER WIPPLINGER**
DIRECTOR OF THE LEOPOLD MUSEUM

*a social technology*
**PHIL.BRIGHTMOMENTS.ETH**
SIGNER AT BRIGHT MOMENTS

*the future and will be the past*
**FUTUREACE.ETH**
TOKENOMICS AT BRIGHT MOMENTS

# TIMELINE

ROBERT ALICE
ADAM MCBRIDE

From seminal early whitepapers and key artworks through to the inception of new protocols and major technological upgrades, this timeline aims to capture the most significant events in the short history (and longer prehistory) of NFTs. Through color-coded blockchain-specific indicators, the timeline lays out the shifts in trends and chain dominance as the NFT space has evolved over the last decade.

— OFF-CHAIN
— MULTI-CHAIN
— BITCOIN
— NAMECOIN
— COUNTERPARTY
— ETHEREUM
— SOLANA
— TEZOS
— FLOW

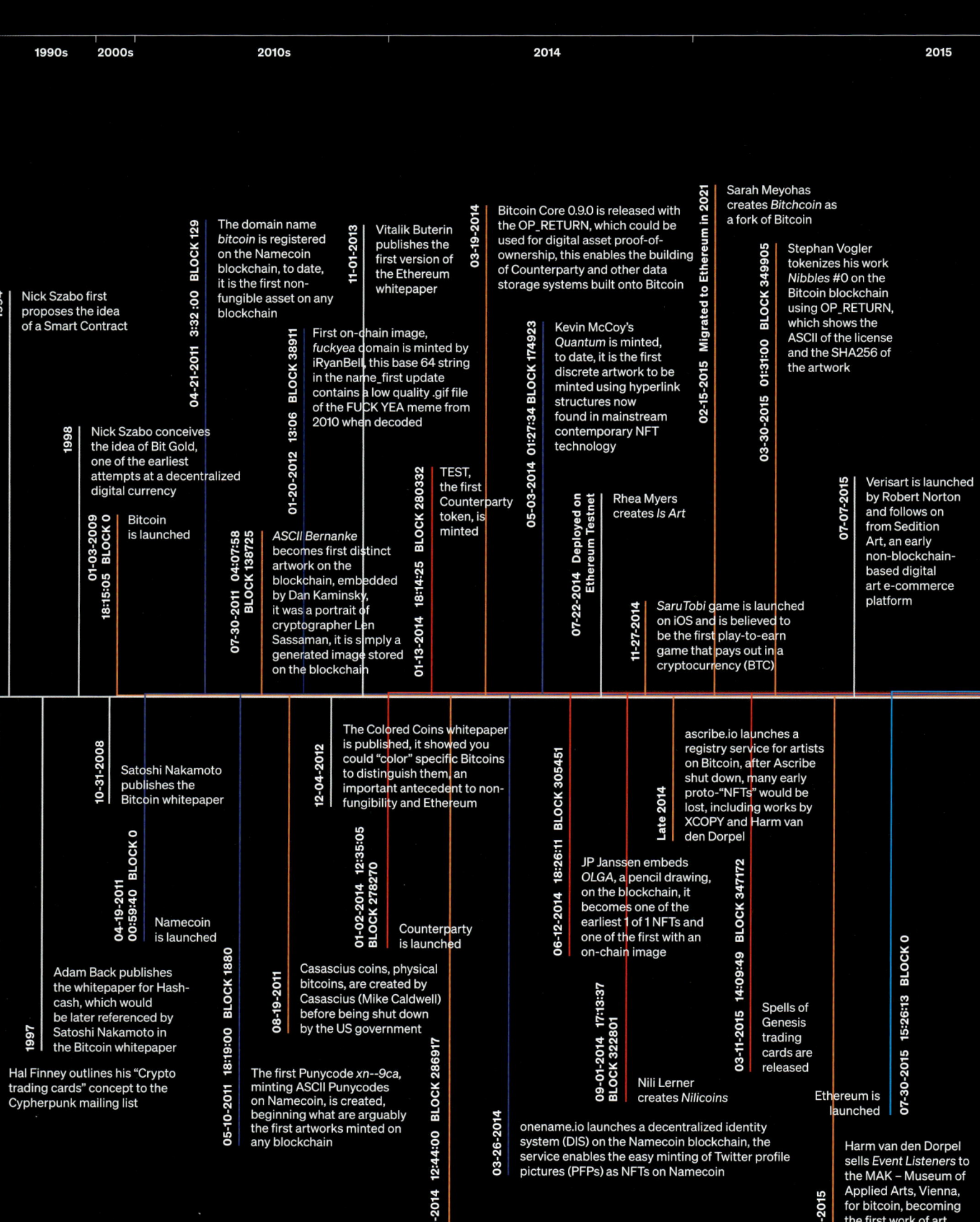

**1994**
Nick Szabo first proposes the idea of a Smart Contract

**1998**
Nick Szabo conceives the idea of Bit Gold, one of the earliest attempts at a decentralized digital currency

**01-03-2009 18:15:05  BLOCK 0**
Bitcoin is launched

**04-21-2011 3:32:00  BLOCK 129**
The domain name *bitcoin* is registered on the Namecoin blockchain, to date, it is the first non-fungible asset on any blockchain

**07-30-2011 04:07:58  BLOCK 138725**
*ASCII Bernanke* becomes first distinct artwork on the blockchain, embedded by Dan Kaminsky, it was a portrait of cryptographer Len Sassaman, it is simply a generated image stored on the blockchain

**01-20-2012 13:06  BLOCK 38911**
First on-chain image, *fuckyea* domain is minted by iRyanBell, this base 64 string in the name_first update contains a low quality .gif file of the FUCK YEA meme from 2010 when decoded

**01-13-2014 18:14:25  BLOCK 280332**
TEST, the first Counterparty token, is minted

**11-01-2013**
Vitalik Buterin publishes the first version of the Ethereum whitepaper

**03-19-2014**
**05-03-2014 01:27:34  BLOCK 174923**
Bitcoin Core 0.9.0 is released with the OP_RETURN, which could be used for digital asset proof-of-ownership, this enables the building of Counterparty and other data storage systems built onto Bitcoin

Kevin McCoy's *Quantum* is minted, to date, it is the first discrete artwork to be minted using hyperlink structures now found in mainstream contemporary NFT technology

**07-22-2014  Deployed on Ethereum Testnet**

Rhea Myers creates *Is Art*

**11-27-2014**
*SaruTobi* game is launched on iOS and is believed to be the first play-to-earn game that pays out in a cryptocurrency (BTC)

**02-15-2015  Migrated to Ethereum in 2021**

Sarah Meyohas creates *Bitchcoin* as a fork of Bitcoin

**03-30-2015 01:31:00  BLOCK 349905**
Stephan Vogler tokenizes his work *Nibbles* #0 on the Bitcoin blockchain using OP_RETURN, which shows the ASCII of the license and the SHA256 of the artwork

**07-07-2015**
Verisart is launched by Robert Norton and follows on from Sedition Art, an early non-blockchain-based digital art e-commerce platform

**01-17-1993 17:48:02**
Hal Finney outlines his "Crypto trading cards" concept to the Cypherpunk mailing list

**1997**
Adam Back publishes the whitepaper for Hash-cash, which would be later referenced by Satoshi Nakamoto in the Bitcoin whitepaper

**10-31-2008**
Satoshi Nakamoto publishes the Bitcoin whitepaper

**04-19-2011 00:59:40  BLOCK 0**
Namecoin is launched

**05-10-2011 18:19:00  BLOCK 1880**
The first Punycode *xn--9ca*, minting ASCII Punycodes on Namecoin, is created, beginning what are arguably the first artworks minted on any blockchain

**08-19-2011**
Casascius coins, physical bitcoins, are created by Casascius (Mike Caldwell) before being shut down by the US government

**12-04-2012**
The Colored Coins whitepaper is published, it showed you could "color" specific Bitcoins to distinguish them, an important antecedent to non-fungibility and Ethereum

**01-02-2014 12:35:05  BLOCK 278270**
Counterparty is launched

**02-20-2014 12:44:00  BLOCK 286917**
Rhea Myers creates *Proof Of Existence*

**03-26-2014**
onename.io launches a decentralized identity system (DIS) on the Namecoin blockchain, the service enables the easy minting of Twitter profile pictures (PFPs) as NFTs on Namecoin

**06-12-2014 18:26:11  BLOCK 305451**
JP Janssen embeds *OLGA*, a pencil drawing, on the blockchain, it becomes one of the earliest 1 of 1 NFTs and one of the first with an on-chain image

**09-01-2014 17:13:37  BLOCK 322801**
Nili Lerner creates *Nilicoins*

**Late 2014**
ascribe.io launches a registry service for artists on Bitcoin, after Ascribe shut down, many early proto-"NFTs" would be lost, including works by XCOPY and Harm van den Dorpel

**03-11-2015 14:09:49  BLOCK 347172**
Spells of Genesis trading cards are released

**07-30-2015 15:26:13  BLOCK 0**
Ethereum is launched

**04-23-2015**
Harm van den Dorpel sells *Event Listeners* to the MAK – Museum of Applied Arts, Vienna, for bitcoin, becoming the first work of art sold to a museum in cryptocurrency

## Top timeline (above axis)

08-07-2015 08:26:34 BLOCK 47205
*Terra Nullius* is created, allowing users to "engrave" nontransferable messages onto the Ethereum blockchain, becoming possibly the first of what Vitalik Buterin calls Soul Bound Tokens (SBTs)

12-15-2015
10-29-2015 21:11:55 BLOCK 459708
*Etheria v1.1* is created

06-04-2016
Harm van den Dorpel and Paloma Rodríguez Carrington create Left Gallery for digital art on the Ascribe platform

Simon Denny curates *Blockchain Visionaries* at the 9th Berlin Biennale

09-09-2016 01:46:42 BLOCK 428919
*Nakamoto Card*, the first card in the Rare Pepe project, is minted on Counterparty

09-16-2016 11:33:53 BLOCK 2269698
*Etherization* is created and is one of the first blockchain games on Ethereum

03-10-2017 17:05:44 BLOCK 3327417
Ethereum Name Service is created

06-09-2017 12:22:50 BLOCK 3842489
Original *CryptoPunks* contract is released by Larva Labs (later titled *V1 CryptoPunks*)

08-09-2017 04:04:36 BLOCK 4140907
*MoonCats* is launched

09-11-2017
Furtherfield's *Artists Re:Thinking the Blockchain* is published

11-23-2017 02:01:12 BLOCK 4604188
Verdandi releases the first of 12 NFTs on Ethereum, tying the artwork to the work's registration at the US Copyright Office, she is believed to be the first female artist to release art on Ethereum

12-20-2017
OpenSea Beta is launched

12-29-2017 16:53:15 BLOCK 4819310
*CryptoBots*, one of the first play-to-earn games, is released

## Bottom timeline (below axis)

08-08-2015 05:20:23 BLOCK 51807
Linagee creates the first Name Registration Service on Ethereum, an early Ethereum proto-NFT that would later evolve into the popular Ethereum Name Service (ENS)

11-01-2015 11:08:50 BLOCK 462680
ERC-20 token standard is created

04-30-2016 01:42:58 BLOCK 1428757
Creation of the world's first DAO, titled "The DAO"

06-17-2016 03:34:48 BLOCK 171849
The DAO is hacked after raising approximately 11.5 million ETH ($150 million)

09-14-2016
Joe Looney creates the Rare Pepe Wallet

11-17-2016 04:29:10 BLOCK 2641527
The community pixel board *PixelMap* is created

05-09-2017 17:53:16 BLOCK 3678548
*Curio Cards*, some of the first collectible artworks on Ethereum, are released

06-23-2017 21:05:06 BLOCK 3919706
Officially endorsed and patched *CryptoPunks* contract released by Larva Labs

08-29-2017 11:34:12 BLOCK 4216201
Mitchell F. Chan creates *Digital Zones of Immaterial Pictorial Sensibility*

10-05-2017 15:56:52 BLOCK 4339477
DADA is launched with its inaugural collection *Creeps and Weirdos*

11-23-2017 05:41:19 BLOCK 4605167
*CryptoKitties* are released, proposing what would later become the ERC-721 standard

12-19-2017 03:48:07 BLOCK 4760710
*CryptoCats* are launched

12-23-2017 23:16:22 BLOCK 4785178
*WeiCards* are launched

**2018**　　　　　　　　　　　　　　　　**2019**

01-04-2018  01:55:13  BLOCK 4853110

*CryptoTitties* are launched as one of the first fundraising NFTs to raise money for breast cancer

01-13-2018  17:32:18  BLOCK 504067

*HOMERPEPE* sells for $38,500 at Rare Art Festival, an important first IRL crypto art and NFT event

02-05-2018  08:05:00  BLOCK 5034046

Jonas Lund releases *Jonas Lund Tokens*, allowing collectors to influence his practice

02-18-2018  04:15:49  BLOCK 5113554

*CryptoJingles* are launched as possibly the first music NFT on Ethereum

04-01-2018  BLOCK

*Cryptovoxels* is launched

05-02-2018  BLOCK 5543801

*Mythereum* game launches, one of the first examples of NFT interoperability as players could merge a *CryptoKitty* into a Mythereum card and forge a new NFT

06-30-2018  17:07:32  BLOCK 0

Tezos is launched

07-17-2018

Christie's Art + Tech Summit is held on the topic of "Exploring the Blockchain," where Robbie Barrat's *AI Generated Nude Portrait #7* is given to all guests in attendance, with many now lost

09-06-2018

Andy Warhol's *14 Small Electric Chairs* (1980) is tokenized and sold on the blockchain

12-20-2018

Cryptograffiti's *Black Swan* becomes the least expensive painting ever sold, for 1 millisatoshi

03-21-2019  21:11:34  BLOCK 7414481

Simon de la Rouviere creates *This Artwork Is Always On Sale*

04-05-2019  21:13:34  BLOCK 7510386

*Autoglyphs*, the first on-chain generative art project, is released by Larva Labs

01-23-2020  16:37:16  BLOCK 9339070

ROBNESS is banned from SuperRare

02-26-2020  01:05:24  BLOCK 9556026

Async.art launches with the release of *First Supper*

---

12-26-2017  BLOCK 4395031

EtherRocks are launched, composed of 100 jpgs depicting rocks, which will explode in popularity in 2021 due to their memeability

01-24-2018

ERC-721 token standard v1 is released

02-14-2018  02:51:52  BLOCK 5086395

Kevin Abosch's *Forever Rose* sells for $1M

03-14-2018  04:06:48  BLOCK 5251724

The popular blockchain game *Axie Infinity* is launched and built on the Ronin network

04-05-2018  23:20:48  BLOCK 5387786

SuperRare is launched by John Crain with Robbie Barrat's *AI Generated Nude Portrait #1* becoming the first work minted on the platform

06-17-2018

ERC-1155 token standard is released

07-18-2018  23:26:19  BLOCK 5947506

*CryptoArte* launches as one of the first generative art projects on Ethereum. The art graphically shows the history of transactions on Ethereum

07-20-2018  19:25:08  BLOCK 5999728

terra0 launches its physical and digital Flower Tokens

11-08-2018  15:57:36  BLOCK 8028100

Snark.art is launched with its inaugural project, Eve Sussman's *89 Seconds Atomized*

02-20-2019

NFT.NYC holds its first event

04-01-2019

Anatoly Yakovenko publishes the Solana whitepaper

10-01-2019

Rarible is launched

02-20-2020

Decentraland is launched

03-16-2020  14:29:00  BLOCK 0

Solana is launched

**2018**　　　　　　　　　　　　　　　　**2019**

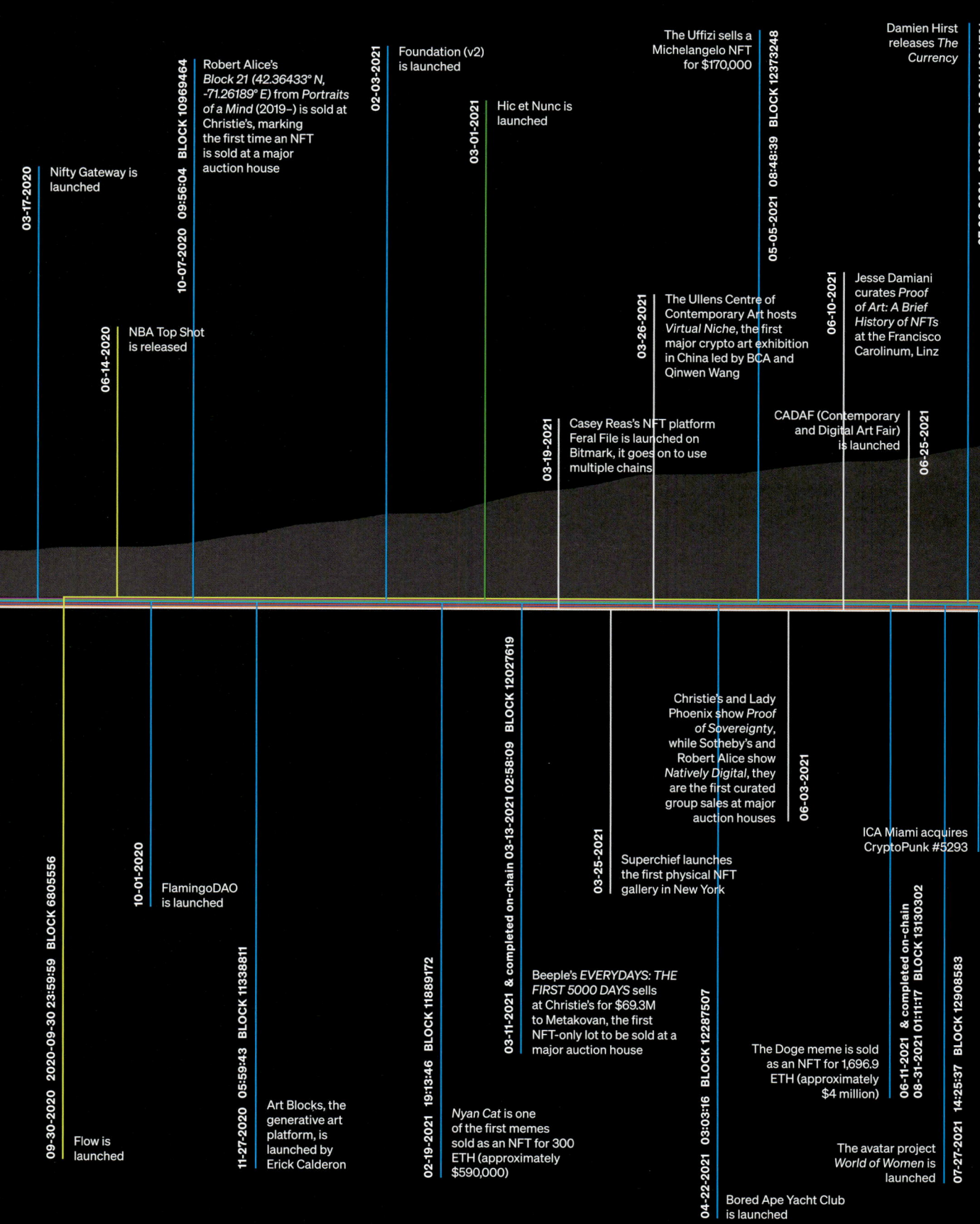

03-17-2020
Nifty Gateway is launched

06-14-2020
NBA Top Shot is released

10-07-2020 09:56:04 BLOCK 10969464
Robert Alice's *Block 21 (42.36433° N, -71.26189° E)* from *Portraits of a Mind* (2019–) is sold at Christie's, marking the first time an NFT is sold at a major auction house

02-03-2021
Foundation (v2) is launched

03-01-2021
Hic et Nunc is launched

The Uffizi sells a Michelangelo NFT for $170,000

05-05-2021 08:48:39 BLOCK 12373248

Damien Hirst releases *The Currency*

07-28-2021 02:22:09 BLOCK 12911731

03-26-2021
The Ullens Centre of Contemporary Art hosts *Virtual Niche*, the first major crypto art exhibition in China led by BCA and Qinwen Wang

06-10-2021
Jesse Damiani curates *Proof of Art: A Brief History of NFTs* at the Francisco Carolinum, Linz

03-19-2021
Casey Reas's NFT platform Feral File is launched on Bitmark, it goes on to use multiple chains

CADAF (Contemporary and Digital Art Fair) is launched

06-25-2021

09-30-2020 2020-09-30 23:59:59 BLOCK 6805556

10-01-2020
FlamingoDAO is launched

11-27-2020 05:59:43 BLOCK 11338811

03-11-2021 & completed on-chain 03-13-2021 02:58:09 BLOCK 12027619

Christie's and Lady Phoenix show *Proof of Sovereignty*, while Sotheby's and Robert Alice show *Natively Digital*, they are the first curated group sales at major auction houses

06-03-2021

ICA Miami acquires CryptoPunk #5293

07-31-2021 20:25:08 BLOCK 12935389

03-25-2021
Superchief launches the first physical NFT gallery in New York

02-19-2021 19:13:46 BLOCK 11889172

Beeple's *EVERYDAYS: THE FIRST 5000 DAYS* sells at Christie's for $69.3M to Metakovan, the first NFT-only lot to be sold at a major auction house

BLOCK 12287507

The Doge meme is sold as an NFT for 1,696.9 ETH (approximately $4 million)

06-11-2021 & completed on-chain 08-31-2021 01:11:17 BLOCK 13130302

07-27-2021 14:25:37 BLOCK 12908583

Flow is launched

Art Blocks, the generative art platform, is launched by Erick Calderon

*Nyan Cat* is one of the first memes sold as an NFT for 300 ETH (approximately $590,000)

04-22-2021 03:03:16

Bored Ape Yacht Club is launched

The avatar project *World of Women* is launched

2022

2023

8M

**08-01-2022**
Tyler Hobbs and Indigo Mané announce *QQL*, a generative art project whereby the collector becomes the collaborator, offering them the tools to explore algorithmic experimentation, selecting their precise output for mint

7M

**10-01-2021**
A *Curio Cards* complete set sells at Christie's for 393 ETH, or $1.2 million. The auction is the first time that Christie's offers an artwork for sale in a cryptocurrency (ETH)

**BLOCK 13806366**

**23:55:44**

**12-14-2021**
Pak's *Merge* sells for $91.8M on Nifty Gateway and breaks the record for most expensive NFT artwork to date

**01-01-2022**
Monthly NFT sales hit $4.8 billion on OpenSea alone

**07-07-2022**
Reddit launches their "Collectible Avatars," a set of limited edition avatars for their platform minted on Polygon — interestingly, Reddit refrained from using the term NFT in their announcement

**02-10-2023**
Centre Pompidou announces the acquisition of their first NFTs

6M

5M

**01-31-2022**
The critical publishing scene for NFTs develops with the launch of *Right Click Save*

**08-23-2021**
An *EtherRock* sells for 400 ETH ($1.3 million)

**10-11-2022**
Damien Hirst starts to burn his physical *The Currency* works at his Newport Street Gallery

4M

**11-18-2021**
ConstitutionDAO falls just short of purchasing one of the original 13 prints of the US Constitution, raising $42M in 7 days

**BLOCK 13466788**

**10:00:40**

**10-22-2021**

**11-01-2021**
The decentralized artist Botto mints *Asymmetrical Liberation*, which is its genesis NFT

**11-24-2021**

**BLOCK 14679593**

**13:58:11**

**04-29-2022**
Yuga Labs release *Otherdeeds* for their Otherside metaverse

**12-09-2022**
Buffalo AKG acquires an edition of every NFT in their *Peer to Peer* show on Feral File

3M

**"NFT"** recognized as the Word of the Year by Collins Dictionary for 2021

*Outland*, an art magazine dedicated to digital art and NFTs, is created

**05-12-2022**
Terra's LUNA collapses, causing a steep drop in the crypto market and a major NFT sell-off

2M

1M

0

NUMBER OF NFT WALLETS ON ETHEREUM IN MILLIONS

**11-29-2021**
Sandbox is launched

**10-21-2021**
Production starts on TASCHEN and Robert Alice's *On NFTs*

**05-10-2022**
Instagram starts supporting NFTs on its platform

**BLOCK 767430**

**20:32:00**

**02-13-2023**
LACMA acquires 22 NFTs donated by Cozomo de' Medici

**11-22-2021**
Pace Gallery launches Pace Verso, one of the traditional galleries to build in the NFT space

**07-18-2022**
Christie's launches Christie's Ventures to invest in tech and blockchain companies

**12-14-2022**
The first Ordinal, *Inscription 0*, is inscribed on Bitcoin, ordinals are launched on Bitcoin, using satoshis as a method for tracking non-fungible assets

**03-11-2022**
Yuga Labs acquires the IP for Larva Labs' *CryptoPunks* and *Meebits*

**11-10-2021**
The Hermitage Museum hosts the NFT show *Ethereal Aether*

**BLOCK 15537394**

**06:42:42**

**09-15-2022**

**11-15-2022**
Refik Anadol's *Unsupervised* opens at the Museum of Modern Art, New York

**10-28-2021**
fxhash is launched

**01-20-2022**
Twitter launches NFT profile pictures

SolSea is launched

**12-21-2021**
Manifold.xyz is launched

**06-21-2022**
eBay acquires NFT marketplace KnownOrigin

The Merge – Ethereum blockchain transitions to a proof-of-stake mechanism, reducing its carbon footprint by 99%

2022

2023

# CONTRIBUTORS

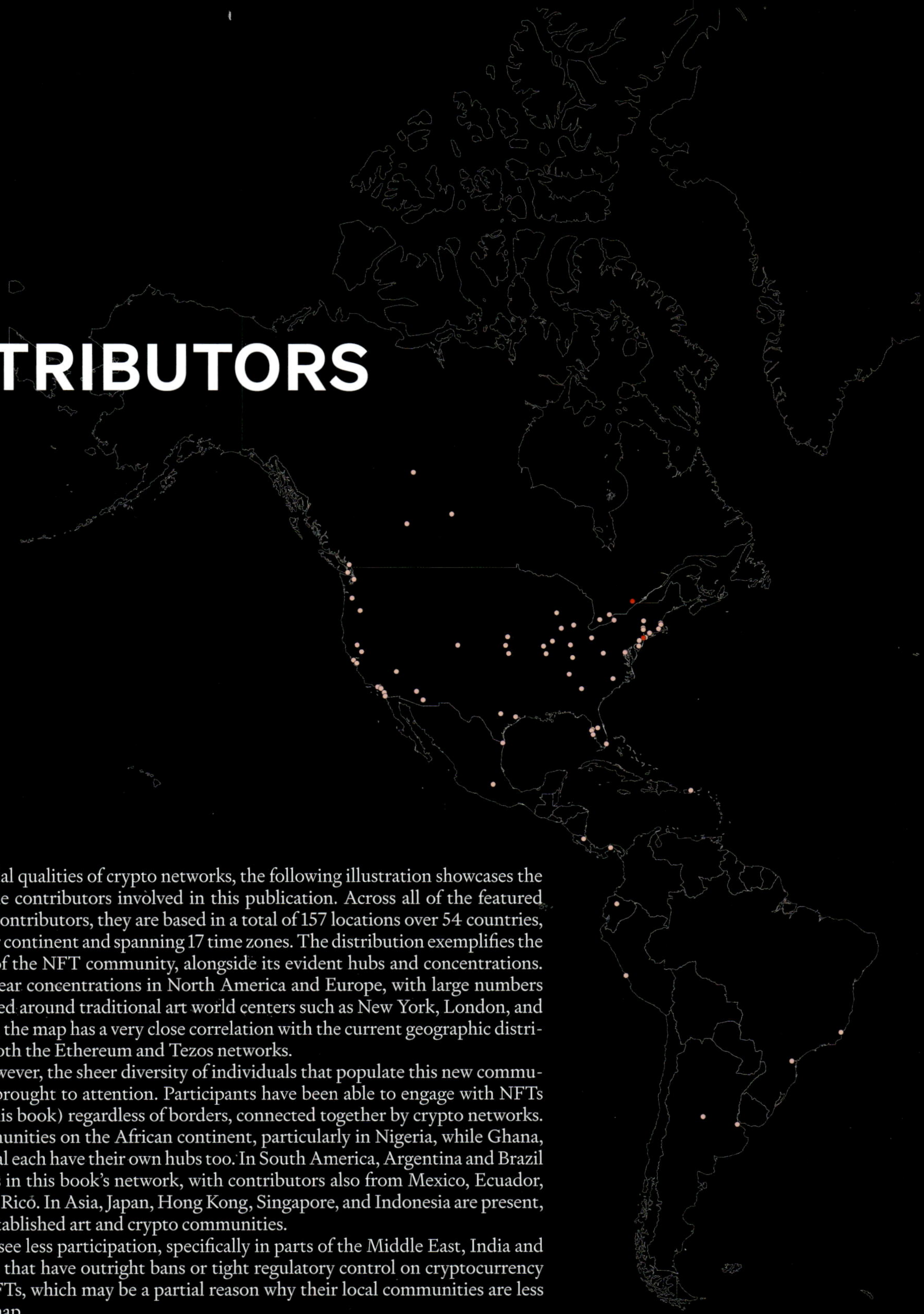

Reflective of the nodal qualities of crypto networks, the following illustration showcases the origins of each of the contributors involved in this publication. Across all of the featured artists, writers, and contributors, they are based in a total of 157 locations over 54 countries, covering every major continent and spanning 17 time zones. The distribution exemplifies the truly global nature of the NFT community, alongside its evident hubs and concentrations. Notably there lies clear concentrations in North America and Europe, with large numbers of individuals grouped around traditional art world centers such as New York, London, and Berlin. Interestingly, the map has a very close correlation with the current geographic distribution of nodes in both the Ethereum and Tezos networks.

Importantly, however, the sheer diversity of individuals that populate this new community should also be brought to attention. Participants have been able to engage with NFTs (and by extension this book) regardless of borders, connected together by crypto networks. We see strong communities on the African continent, particularly in Nigeria, while Ghana, Ethiopia, and Senegal each have their own hubs too. In South America, Argentina and Brazil are important nodes in this book's network, with contributors also from Mexico, Ecuador, Panama, and Puerto Rico. In Asia, Japan, Hong Kong, Singapore, and Indonesia are present, all areas with well established art and crypto communities.

Areas where we see less participation, specifically in parts of the Middle East, India and China, are also areas that have outright bans or tight regulatory control on cryptocurrency and by extension NFTs, which may be a partial reason why their local communities are less present across this map.

Number of Contributors

● 1 to 3
● 4 to 6
● 7+

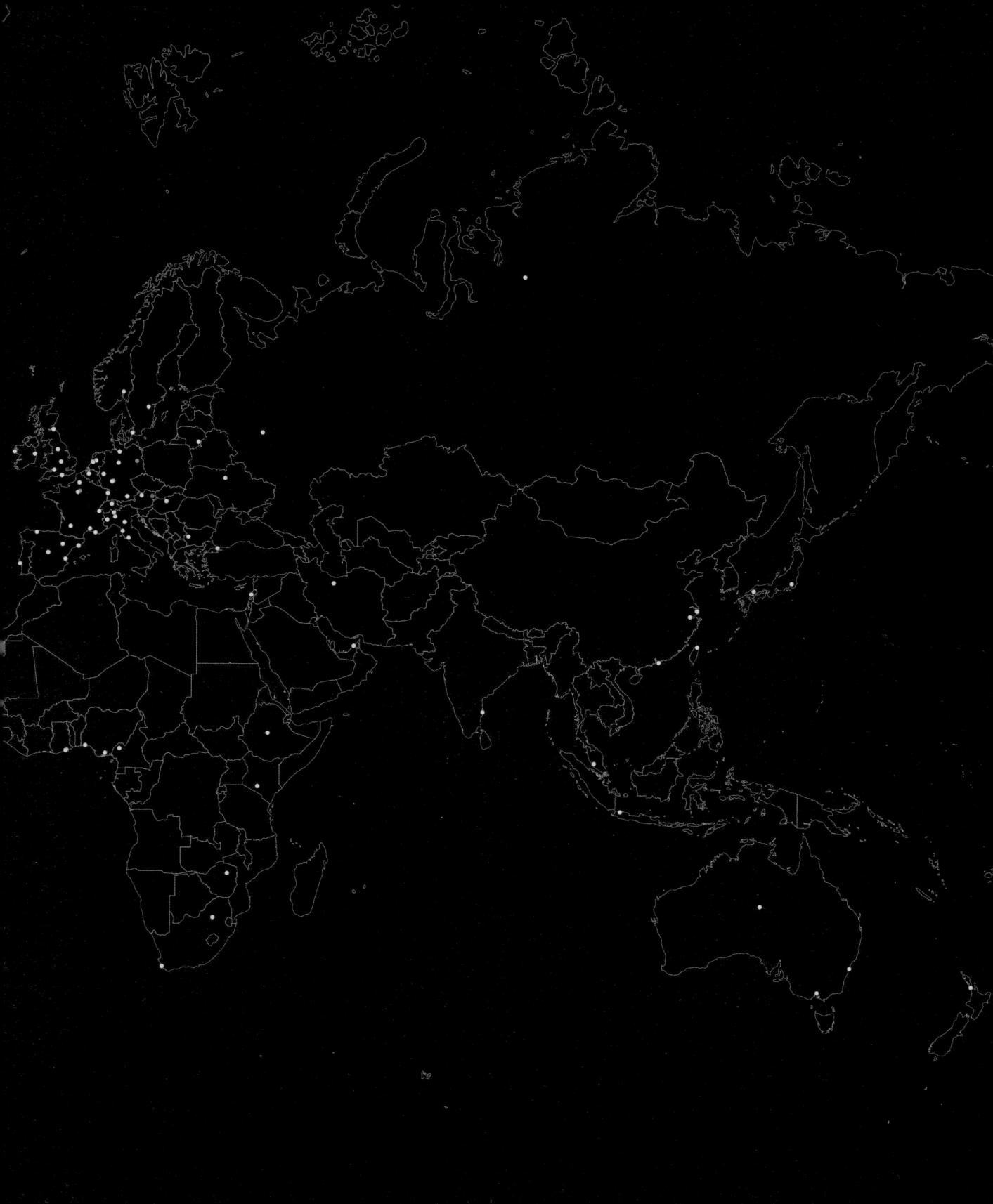

## THE EDITOR

ROBERT ALICE makes art, exhibitions, and books that investigate blockchains and their histories. Alice's work is collected in public collections and libraries internationally, including the Centre Pompidou, Los Angeles County Museum of Art, Bibliothèque Kandinsky, and the Monnaie de Paris.

Alice's work has been subject to reviews by leading curators such as Hans Ulrich Obrist and published in *The New York Times*, *Financial Times*, *CNN*, *Forbes*, *Art Review*, *Art News*, *The Art Newspaper*, among others. The first artist to sell an NFT at a major auction house, the work *Portraits of a Mind* (2019–) has been credited as one of the early catalysts behind the subsequent rapid growth in the blockchain art space. The project is now part of the National Collection of France.

Exhibitions of their work have been held internationally, including shows at Monnaie de Paris, Paris; Ullens Center of Contemporary Art, Beijing; Christie's, New York; Sotheby's, London and Hong Kong; Palazzo Lolin, Venice; Francisco Carolinum, Linz; Kunstverein Hamburg, among others.

In 2021, Alice curated *Natively Digital* at Sotheby's, bringing historic works to market, including Kevin McCoy's *Quantum* (2014) — the first NFT ever made. A trained art historian, Alice has lectured internationally on blockchain-based art, most notably co-producing the first academic conference on NFTs at Oxford University in 2022, entitled *0xBAT*, where they opened the conference with a keynote on a theory of NFTs. Alice has been a guest lecturer on blockchain culture at Central Saint Martins; Columbia University, Christie's Education, Kings College London, and Oxford University.

## ESSAY CONTRIBUTORS

### INTRODUCTION
ROBERT ALICE

### TIMELINE
ROBERT ALICE
& ADAM McBRIDE

### 01 ON QUANTUM
ROBERT ALICE

### 02 ON CRYPTO ART

JASON BAILEY is a writer and crypto art expert well-known for the prescient NFT blog *Artnome*. A leading crypto art collector, Jason has written on art and technology for *Art in America* and the *Harvard Data Science Review* and has lectured on digital art at Massachusetts Institute of Technology, Massachusetts College of Art & Design, Nanjing University, Art Basel, Sotheby's, and Christie's.

ALEX ESTORICK is a media theorist who seeks to develop socially progressive approaches to new technologies. As Editor-in-Chief at *Right Click Save*, he aims to drive critical conversation about NFTs, blockchain, and Web3. He is Contributing Editor for Art and Technology at *Flash Art*. He contributes to various publications — from *Frieze* to the *Financial Times* — and is responsible for the first aesthetics of crypto art. He co-curated *FEMGEN* at Art Basel Miami Beach (2022) and *Cure³* at Bonhams (2023), and has lectured on NFTs at Imperial College London, the Royal College of Art, Central Saint Martins, Sotheby's Institute of Art, and the Berlin Art Institute.

### 03 ON ALGORITHMIC ART

SOFIA GARCIA is founder of ARTXCODE, an algorithmic art agency. She has been an algorithmic art advisor to Buffalo AKG Art Museum, Rhizome, Sotheby's, Christie's, Phillips, and J.P. Morgan. She currently sits on the curation board of Art Blocks and the Board of Directors of Code/Art. Garcia has lectured on algorithmic art at Columbia University, Florida International University, and Glasgow School of Art, and has curated algorithmic art shows internationally, including the Contemporary Digital Art Fair, New York (2019), *When the Computer Made Art*, CADAF Miami (2019), *The Digital Miami Beach*, Miami (2021), and *Natively Digital 1.3: Generative Art*, Sotheby's (2022).

### 04 ON CHAIN

RHEA MYERS is an artist, hacker, and writer. Since 2014, Myers's art has explored the ideology, aesthetics, and social forces of the blockchain through smart contracts. Her writing has been featured in *ArtReview*, *Spike Art Magazine*, *Artists Re:Thinking the Blockchain* (2017), *The State Machines Reader* (2019), and *Radical Friends* (2022). In 2022, her collected writings, *Proof of Work: Blockchain Provocations 2011–2021*, were published. Myers's work has been exhibited internationally including *New World Order* at Furtherfield Gallery (2017), *Proof of Work* at Schinkel Pavillon (2018), *PERFECT* & *PRICELESS* at Kate Vass Galerie (2018), *Breadcrumbs* at Galerie Nagel Draxler (2021), and Sotheby's *Natively Digital* (2021).

### 05 ON PROCESS

BEEPLE, REFIK ANADOL, BRENDAN DAWES, EMILY XIE, ERICK CALDERON, HARM VAN DEN DORPEL, RY DAVID BRADLEY

### 06 ON AVATARS

ROBERT ALICE

**pp. 34, 35,** (detail)
Larva Labs
*Autoglyph #339*, 04-08-2019 16:24:33
ASCII, Solidity
Ethereum, 0xd4e4078ca3495DE5B1d4dB434BEbc5a986197782, 339

## 07 ON DAOs

AARON WRIGHT is a professor and co-author of *Blockchain and the Law: The Rule of Code* (2018). Co-Founder and CEO of Tribute Labs, Wright is a thought leader in the field of DAOs, having led and supported many of the most successful DAOs, including The LAO, Flamingo DAO, Neptune, Red DAO, Ready Player DAO, Neon DAO, and Dark Horse DAO. Wright is a Professor at Benjamin N. Cardozo School of Law (currently on leave). His academic research focuses on the legal implications of smart contracts and blockchain-based systems, and has been featured in publications such as *Oxford University Press* and the *Hastings Law Journal*.

SERENA TABACCHI is the Director and Co-Founder of the Museum of Contemporary Digital Art (MoCDA). Previously of the Tate, she is a part of the SuperRare DAO Council and a Curator at FlamingoDAO. Tabacchi has brought NFT exhibitions to museums such as the Museo della Permanente, the MAXXI Museum, and the Fondazione Palazzo Strozzi.

## 08 ON COLLECTING

MICHAEL BOUHANNA is worldwide Head of Digital Art and NFTs at Sotheby's. In 2021, Bouhanna drove Sotheby's first foray in the NFT art market. Under Bouhanna's stewardship, Sotheby's was recognized by Forbes Blockchain 50 and TIME100 Most Influential Companies of 2022 for its innovation in and expansion of the NFT art market. Bouhanna is an expert in the NFT market and advises many of the most prominent NFT collectors.

JEHAN CHU is the Founder of Kenetic, an Asia-based blockchain venture capital firm. Formerly Sotheby's Head of Client Development, Asia, and Art Advisor with Vermillion Art Collections, Chu has been collecting contemporary art since 2006, and is a foremost collector of fine art NFTs, and advisor to artists including Beeple and Refik Anadol, among others. He served on the Board of ParaSite Art Space in Hong Kong for 12 years, Design Trust for 10 years, is on the Director's Circle of San Francisco MoMA, and is global Crypto Advisor to Christie's.

## 09 ON THE METAVERSE

HANS ULRICH OBRIST is Artistic Director of the Serpentine in London, and Senior Advisor at LUMA Arles. Prior to this, he was the Curator of the Musée d'Art Moderne de la Ville de Paris. Since his first show World Soup (The Kitchen Show) in 1991, he has curated more than 350 shows.

BRIAN DROITCOUR is a critic, editor, curator, and contributor to various publications including *4Columns*, *Artforum*, and *Rhizome*, and catalogs for the Whitney Museum of American Art, the New Museum, and the Art Gallery of Ontario. From 2014 to 2021, he worked at *Art in America*, where he organized special issues on topics including the digitized museum, generative art, and immersive art. He is the Editor-in-Chief of *Outland*.

CHRISTOPHER Y. LEW is Chief Artistic Director at Horizon Art Foundation and formerly *Outland*. For *Outland*, he has commissioned major NFT projects by artists like Ian Cheng and Leo Villareal. He was a Curator at the Whitney Museum of American Art, where he oversaw the emerging artist program and was Co-Curator of the 2017 Whitney Biennial.

JASON LI is a Los Angeles–based entrepreneur and collector of emerging contemporary art. Li sits on the Artists Council for the Whitney Museum of American Art and is the founder of a media agency as well as CEO and Founder of *Outland*.

## 10 ON BUILDING

MARÍA PAULA FERNÁNDEZ is Co-Founder of jpg.space and the Department of Decentralization. She has been working in Web3 since 2017, having worked for several of the most prominent blockchain projects. In 2018, she founded the Department of Decentralization, hosting Web3 hackathons and researching, publishing, and curating at the intersection of art and technology. Currently she's focused on jpg.space building Web3 cultural infrastructure.

SIMON DENNY makes artworks that unpack stories technologists tell us. Denny has staged significant exhibitions linking blockchain and art such as *Proof of Stake*, Kunstverein Hamburg (2021) and *Proof of Work*, Schinkel Pavillon (2018). Recent solo projects include *Dotcom Seance* (with Guile Twardowski), Folia (2021); *Mine*, K21 Düsseldorf (2020) and MONA, Tasmania (2019); *Real Mass Entrepreneurship*, OCAT, Shenzhen (2017); Hammer Museum, Los Angeles (2017); *Products for Organising*, Serpentine Galleries London (2015); and *The Innovator's Dilemma*, MoMA PS1, New York (2015). Denny represented New Zealand at the 56th Venice Biennale.

ADINA GLICKSTEIN is a writer and editor living in Berlin. She is an Editor-at-Large at *Spike Art Magazine*, co-edited the publication's landmark "Web 3" issue (#70, Winter 2021–22), and writes regularly about art and internet culture for *Spike* and elsewhere.

**EXHIBITION HISTORY**
ROBERT ALICE and contributors

**GLOSSARY**
ROBERT ALICE

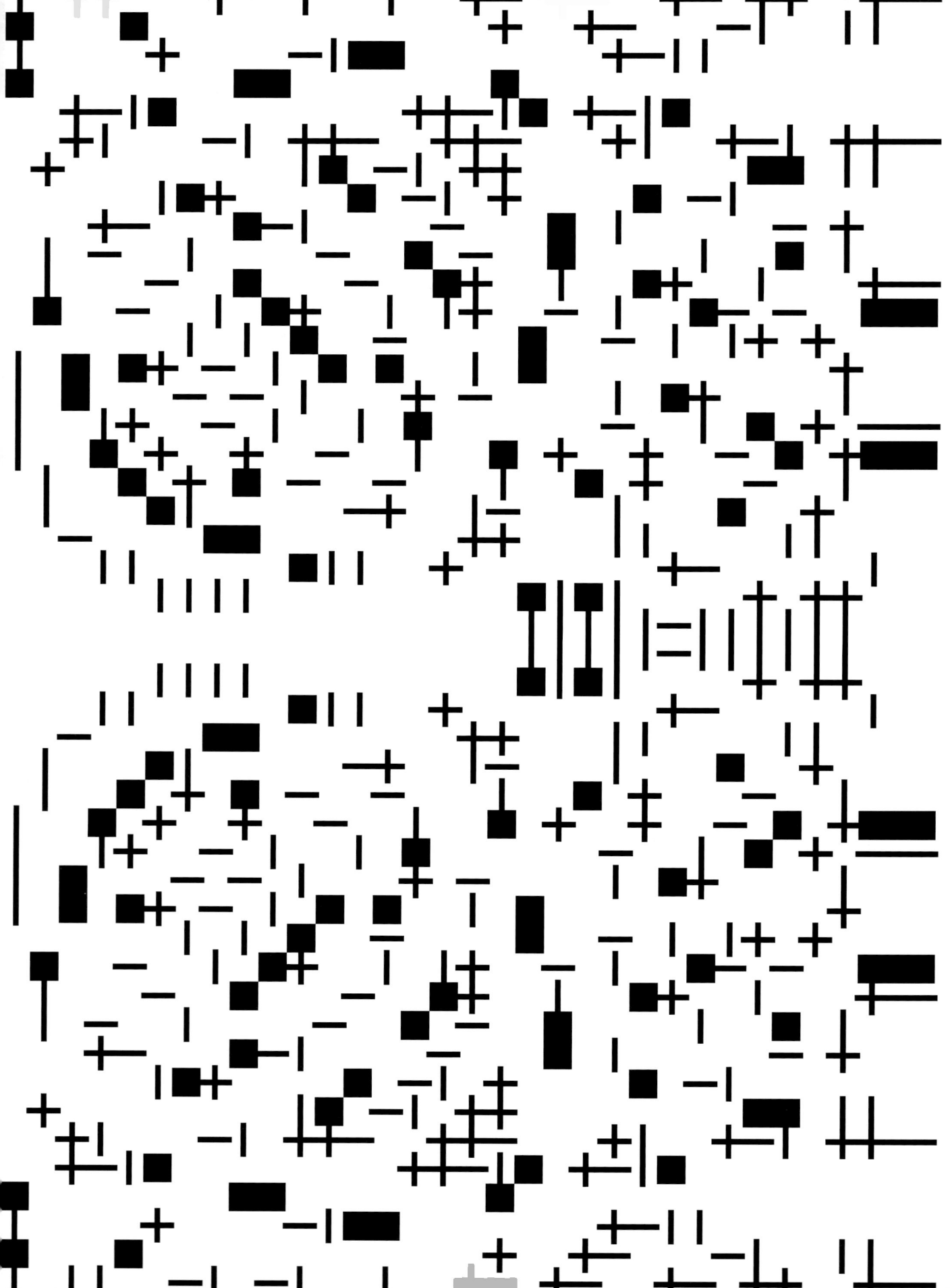

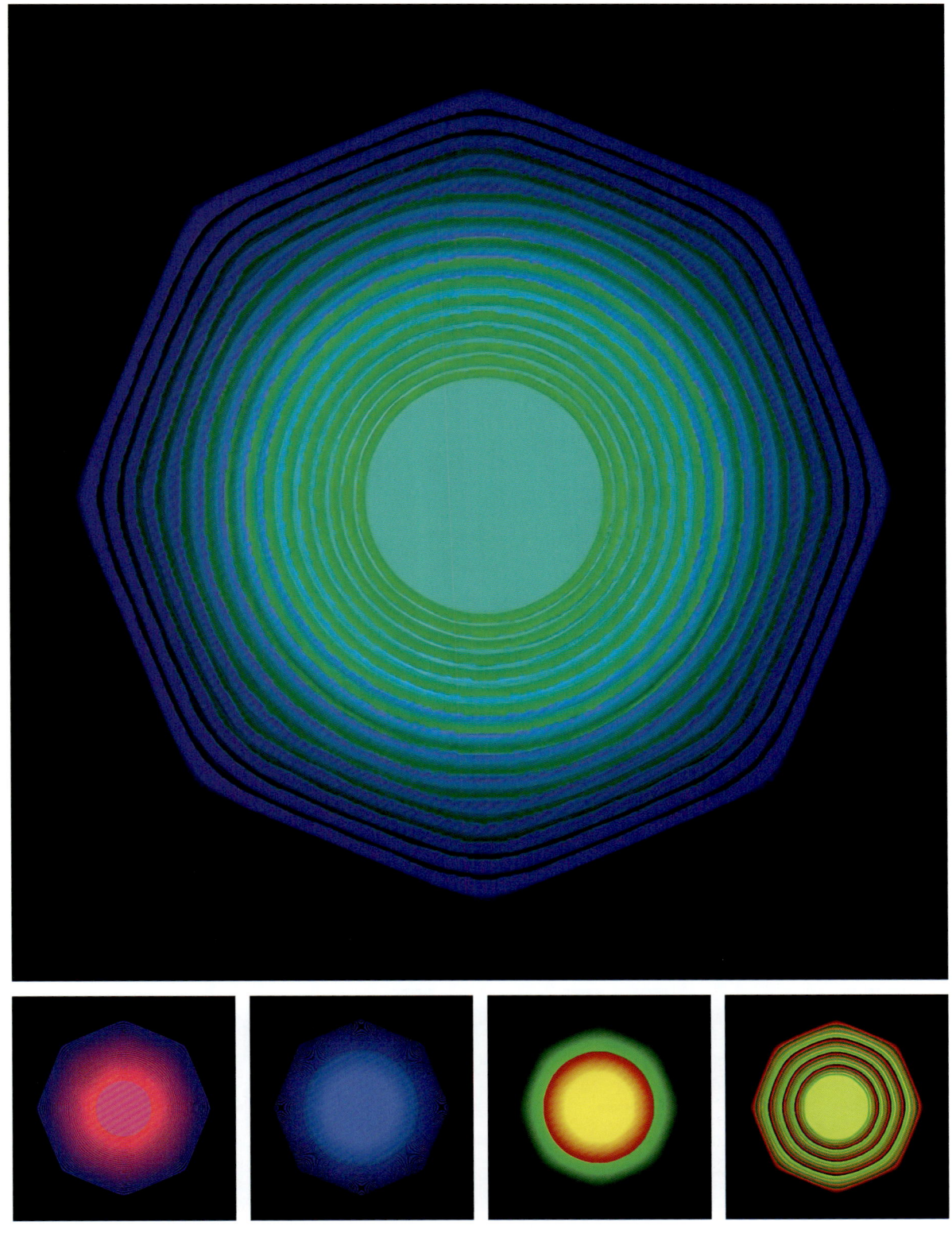

| # | TITLE | TIMESTAMP | MEDIUM | CHAIN | CONTRACT ADDRESS | TOKEN ID | EDITION SIZE | COLLABORATORS |
|---|---|---|---|---|---|---|---|---|
| 01 | **Quantum** | 05-02-2014 21:27:34 | Processing, GIF | NMC | N2nunKeYiYeqDCunDzJ3EQQh1fbAawegPW | NA | 1/1 | – |
| 02 | **Cars** | 05-03-2014 07:00:06 | Adobe After Effects | NMC | Mxv2j4a2XgXBxbQMNt67nKGf6cYgwrKp3C | NA | 1/1 | Jennifer McCoy |

# KEVIN MCCOY

UNITED STATES 1967

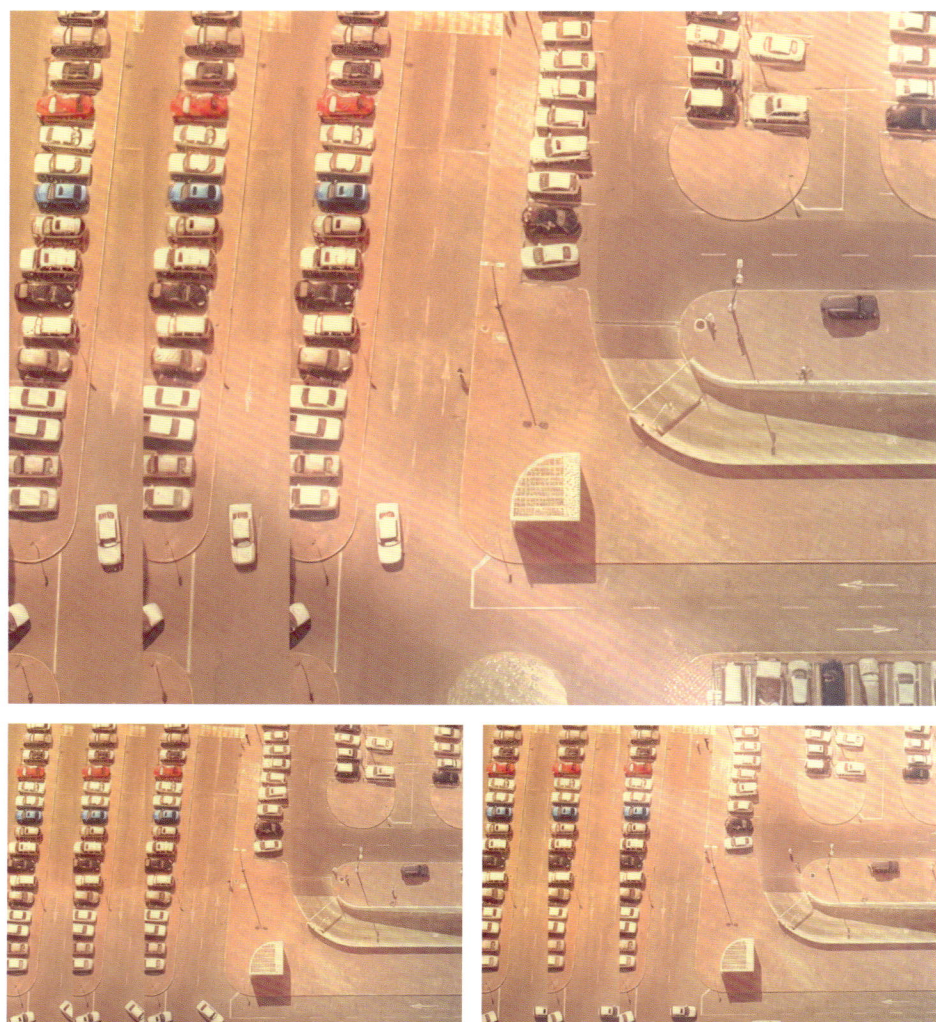

Pulsing, multicolored rings of light set off against a black background create the sense of moving through an astronomical phenomenon at speed in Kevin McCoy's *Quantum* (2014), a 360×360 pixel, 179-frame screen recorded loop from a code-generated animation written in the Processing language. The work's evocation of a futuristic science fiction narrative is balanced by the apparent presence of visual artifacts that seem to root it in the digital material of its time, with dithered colors and jagged pixel edges appearing among the rings. Swirling moiré-like patterns add a visual noise; on first glance, they seem to be a further artifact of the image's compression. But the patterns are too organized to arise from the functional algorithms of the Joint Photographic Experts Group or their counterparts. They are, in fact, produced by McCoy's code, the code that generated this work.

*Quantum* is widely regarded as the first NFT. In 2014, as part of the Seven on Seven conference organized by Rhizome, McCoy (working with Anil Dash) developed a system for establishing provenance for digital artworks on the Namecoin blockchain, which he called Monegraph. Prior to the launch of Ethereum, McCoy foresaw that the blockchain could be used to establish a cryptographically certified string of transactions, allowing digital works to be authenticated, bought, and sold.

In some ways, the story of *Quantum* is an example of how NFTs can allow the often-overlooked cultural value of digital works to be properly recognized. McCoy chose *Quantum* from his digital sketchbook to be the first work to be minted in this new system; the code had been written for possible use in a 2013 project, as a backdrop for a drag-racing video. Today, the work is very much in the foreground, inseparable from this origin story: suggestive of new worlds arriving, while rooted in the digital material of its time.

**MICHAEL CONNOR**
ARTISTIC DIRECTOR AT RHIZOME

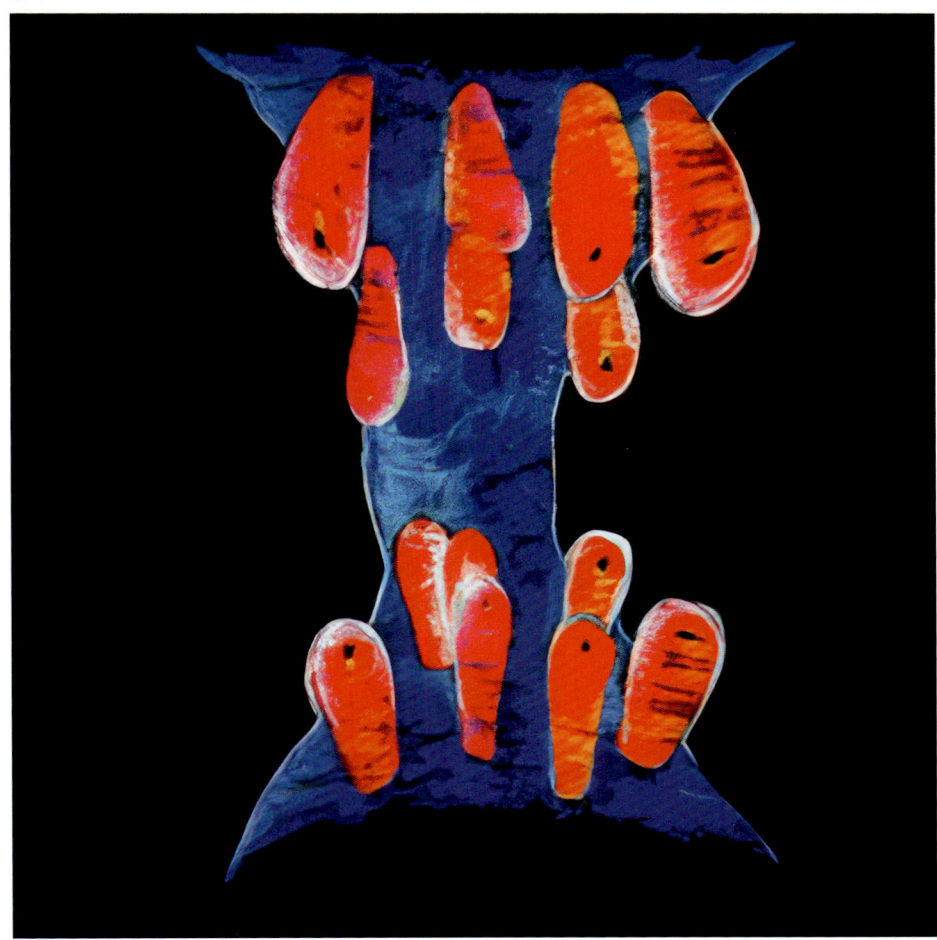

| # | TITLE | TIMESTAMP | MEDIUM | CHAIN | CONTRACT ADDRESS | TOKEN ID | EDITION SIZE | COLLABORATORS |
|---|---|---|---|---|---|---|---|---|
| 03 | **Primordial Loop** | 05-04-2014 14:33:59 | Adobe Photoshop | NMC | NJNrURXdjAexLUSWd3k Xw-Juj7nD6ZnvMUJ | NA | 1/1 | Jennifer McCoy, Torsten Burns |
| 04 | **Quantum Leap** | 06-22-2021 17:27:55 | JavaScript, WebGL | ETH | 0x8425633dbaf741db34b c35d5054e22a8ab4c9f31 | 1–3 | 1/1 of 3 | Jennifer McCoy |

EDITIONS ILLUSTRATED: (04) Primordial Star 1

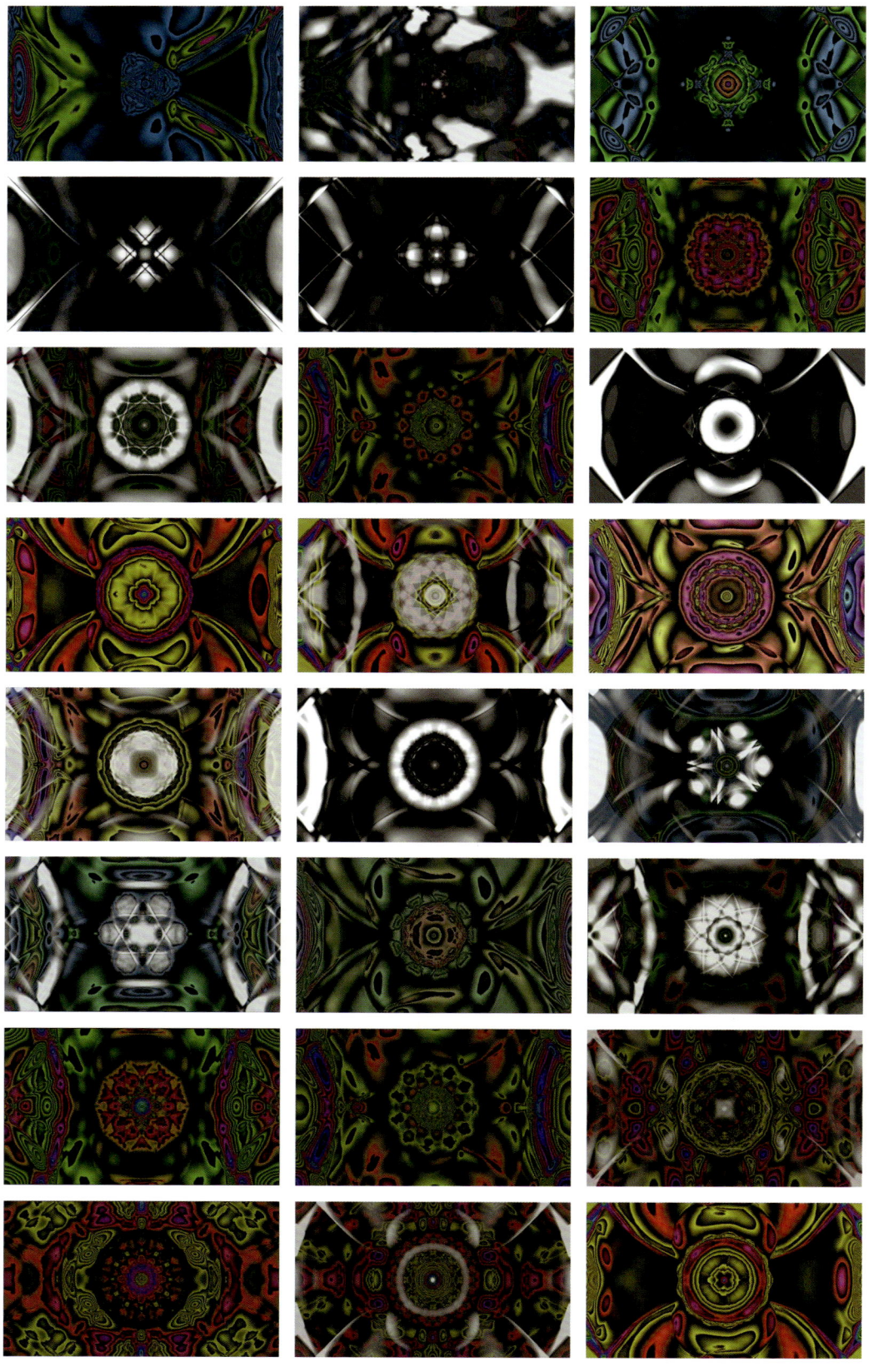

01

02

03

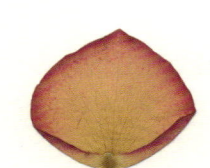

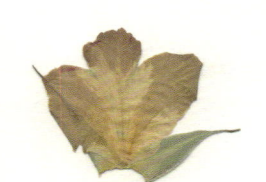

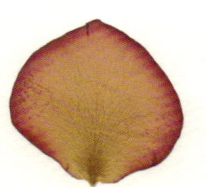

6.116

9.099

6.102

04

05

06

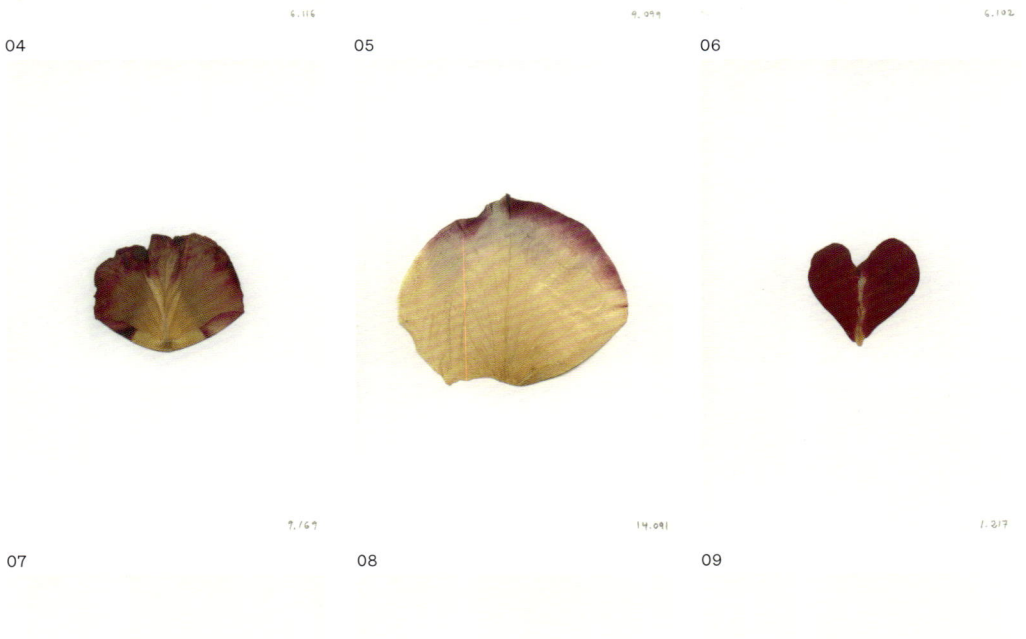

9.169

14.091

1.217

07

08

09

2.120

2.179

3.069

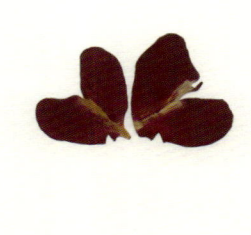

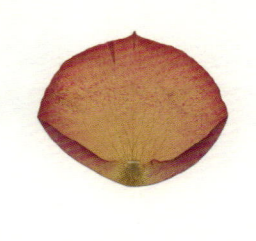

| # | TITLE | TIMESTAMP | MEDIUM | CHAIN | CONTRACT ADDRESS | TOKEN ID | EDITION SIZE |
|---|---|---|---|---|---|---|---|
| 01–09 | **Bitchcoin** | 05-22-2021 01:09:46 | ERC-1155 token, rose petal on archival paper | ETH | 0x5e86f887ff9676a58f25a6e057b7a6b8d65e1874 | 1011–16182 | 1/1 of 3,291 |
| 10 | **Bitchcoin** | 02-10-2015 | Fork of Bitcoin v0.8.2 | BTC | Defunct | NA | NA |

EDITIONS ILLUSTRATED: (01) #6.116, (02) #9.099, (03) #6.102, (04) #9.169, (05) #14.091, (06) #1.217, (07) #2.120, (08) #2.179, (09) #3.069

# SARAH MEYOHAS

UNITED STATES 1991

10 ▶

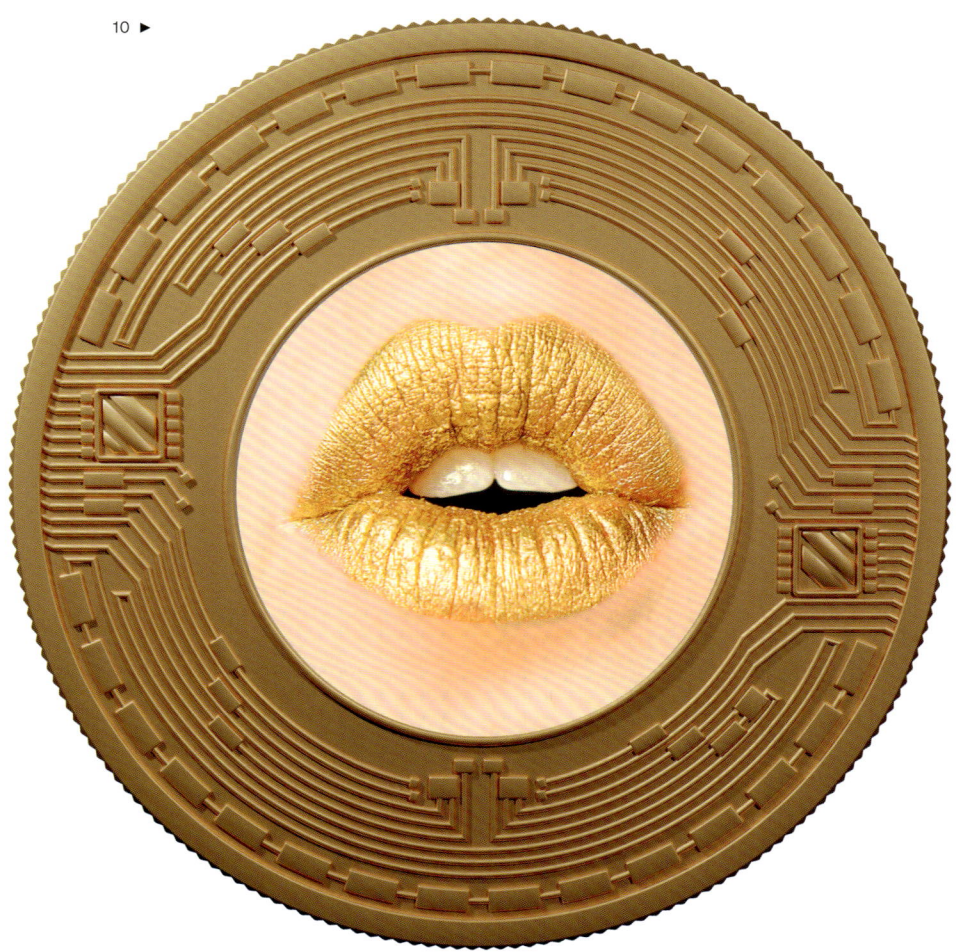

Sarah Meyohas is a native New Yorker of French and Turkish descent. With a BA in International Relations from the University of Pennsylvania, a BS in Finance from the Wharton School, and an MFA from Yale University, one could argue that she is perfectly equipped to take on, in a uniquely millennial way, the Duchampian question of the value of art, both aesthetic and economic. In February 2015, Meyohas envisioned a social token, *Bitchcoin*, an artist-made cryptocurrency, minted on her own proof-of-work blockchain, which could be exchanged in perpetuity for her artwork. The insinuation that the value of this token would appreciate alongside her work essentially proposed public fractional ownership of shares in her artistic career just like any other corporation, pushing the Warholian paradigm of art as business to the realm of financialization.

With an obvious reference to Bitcoin and a tongue-in-cheek nod to Dogecoin, *Bitchcoin* proposed the blockchain itself as an artistic medium, while maintaining an intrinsic connection to the physical world: the currency being pegged to units of photographs from Meyohas's *Speculations* (2015–) series necessitated

non-fungibility, creating a "proto-NFT" as early as 2015. At the project's public debut, approximately 100,000 *Bitchcoins* were mined by a computer that ran a fork of Bitcoin v0.8.2.

In 2017, *Bitchcoin* evolved further by embedding its proof-of-work deeper in the physical world. Each of the 100,000 rose petals, plucked by 16 male workers at the site of former Bell Labs designed by Eero Saarinen in New Jersey, would act as a stand-in for the digital currency. This process was thoroughly documented, establishing a definitive proof-of-work completed by the workers, accompanied by the 16 mm film *Cloud of Petals* (2017). In early 2021, Meyohas transplanted the currency onto Ethereum and minted 3,291 *Bitchcoins* on an ERC-1155 contract. The actual petals were retrieved from archival storage and the minted *Bitchcoins* became non-fungible, tokenized artworks each tied to their own unique petal.

**BEGUM YASAR**
CO-FOUNDER OF THE CENTER DAO

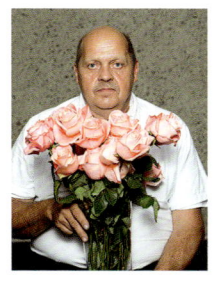 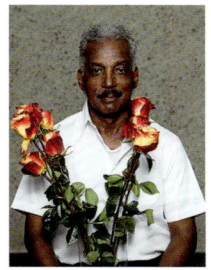 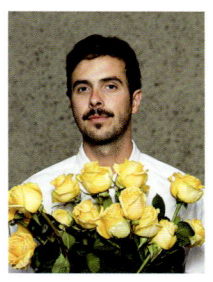 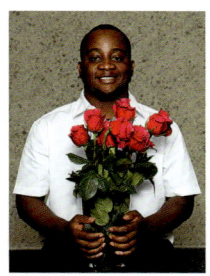

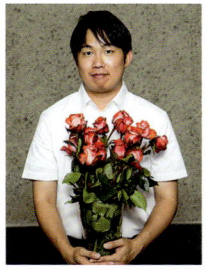 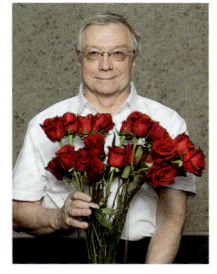 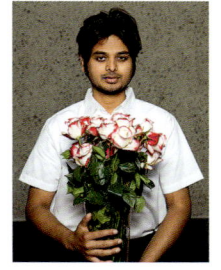 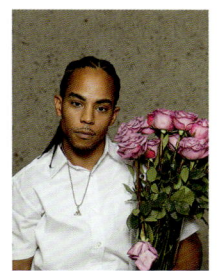

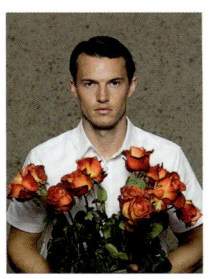 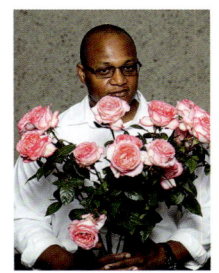 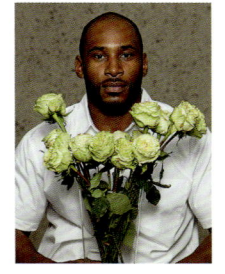 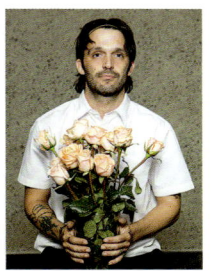

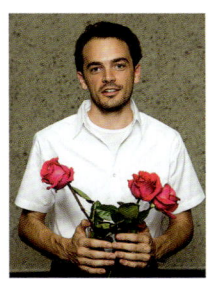 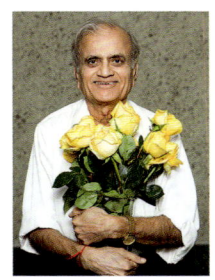 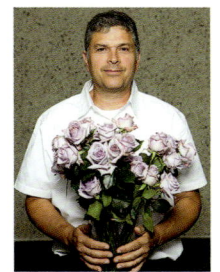 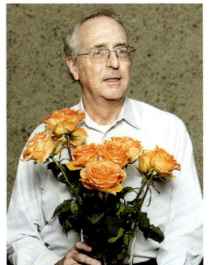

| # | TITLE | DATE | MEDIUM |
|---|---|---|---|
| 11, 12 | **Cloud of Petals** | 2017 | 16mm film transferred to HD video and 4K video |

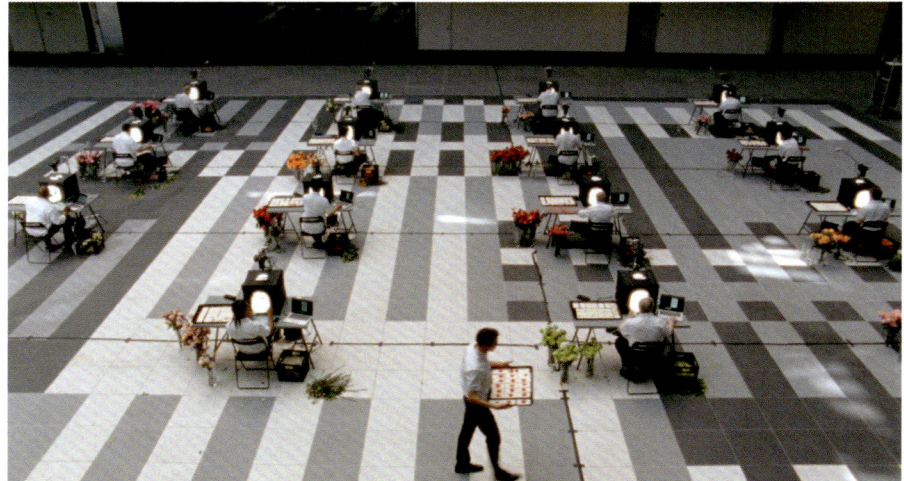

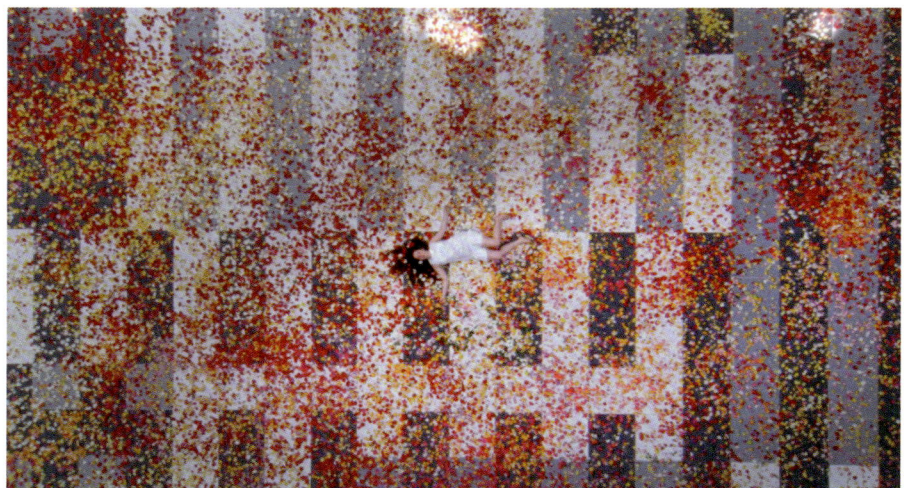

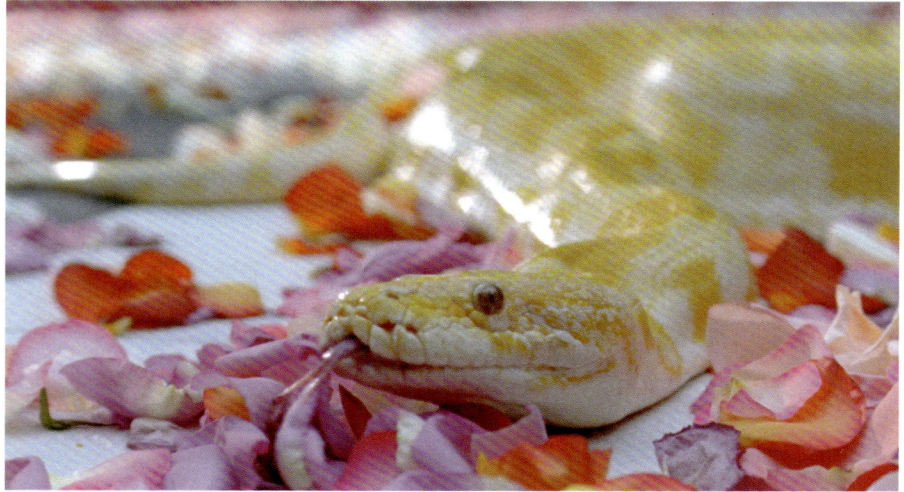

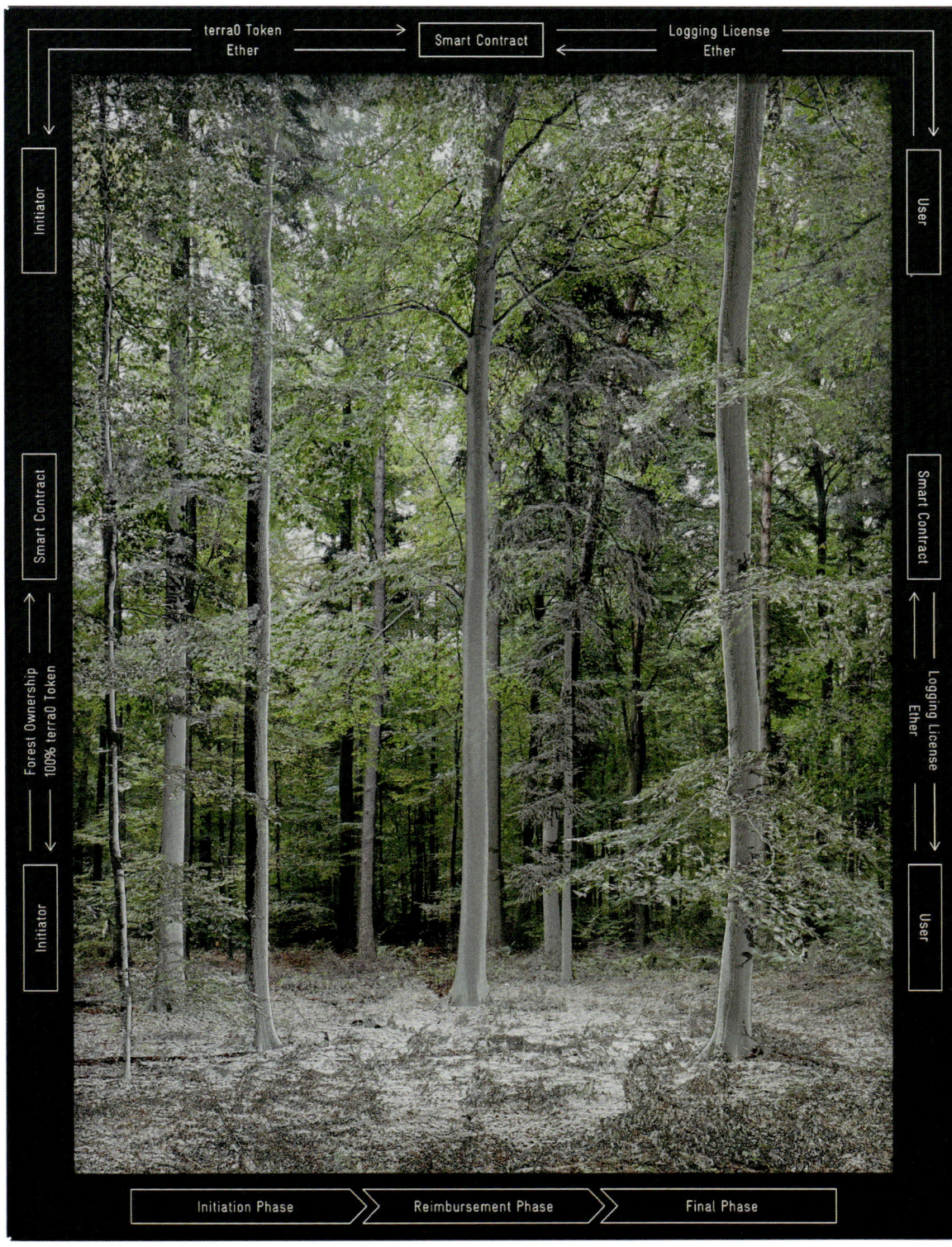

terra0 Token
Ether

Smart Contract

Logging License
Ether

Initiator

User

Forest Ownership
100% terra0 Token

Smart Contract

Smart Contract

Logging License
Ether

Initiator

User

Initiation Phase | Reimbursement Phase | Final Phase

| # | TITLE | | DATE | MEDIUM |
|---|---|---|---|---|
| 01, 02 | **terra0 – Can an augmented forest own and utilise itself?** | | 2016 | Whitepaper |

02

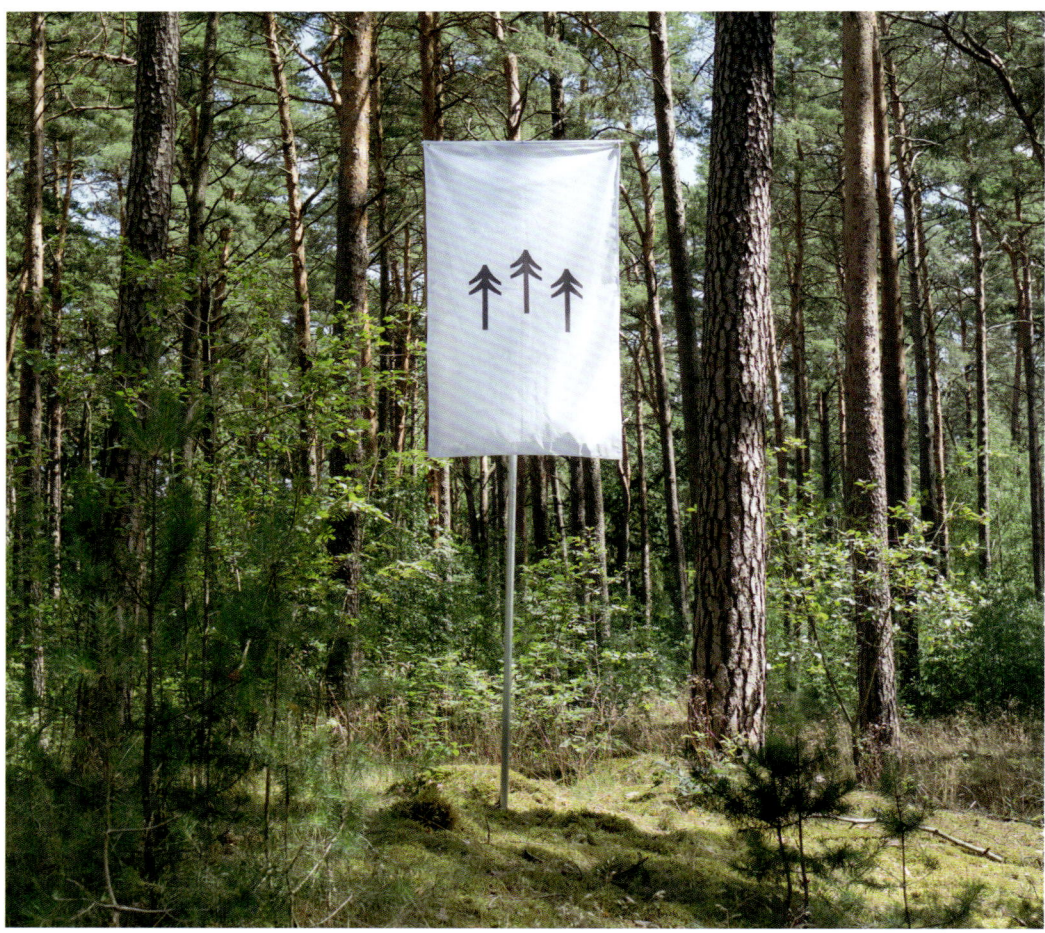

terra0 is an art collective exploring the creation of hybrid ecosystems in the technosphere. The group's first work, the terra0 white-paper, *Can an augmented forest own and utilise itself?* (2016) — based on research in areas of smart contracts, ecology, and economics — proposed technologically augmented ecosystems that are able to act as agents in their own right. terra0's artistic practice in recent years has focused on conducting experiments that identify, evaluate, and critically reflect on these inherent claims. The resulting work spans disparate mediums ranging from on-chain smart contracts, visual media, sculpture, and installation art.

One of these experiments was *Premna Daemon* (2018), which took the form of an autonomous Bonsai tree which used smart contracts, a web interface, several sensors, and cameras in order to facilitate payments from gallerygoers to the exhibition space to fund its upkeep and care while on display. Another, *Flowertokens* (2018), was a controlled attempt at generating the unique digital twins of 100 flowers (dahlia × hortensis) as NFTs. Centered around the tokenization and verification of natural commodities, users were able to buy, trade, and speculate on the tokenized dahlias via an online marketplace — the state of the individual tokens automatically updated according to the different phases of their corresponding

plant's growth — made possible by data which was kept in sync via live computer vision analysis. *Seed Capital* (2022), in many ways the logical successor to *Premna Daemon*, is an ongoing sculpture series that suggests ways to rethink the economic and ecological relationships between viewers, the institution, and the artwork by utilizing environmental sensors and automated decision-making processes. As a whole, these artworks function as technologically augmented organic systems which explore novel forms of financially mediated social contracts within embedded localities, iteratively probing and extending the initial concepts and components of the original whitepaper.

terra0 has exhibited at the 58th Carnegie International; the 17th International Architecture Exhibition — La Biennale di Venezia; Canadian Centre for Architecture, Montreal; The Shed, New York City; Kunsthalle Zürich; Francisco Carolinum, Linz; Chronus Art Center, Shanghai; Furtherfield Gallery, London; Schinkel Pavillon, Berlin; and Vienna Biennale, among others.

**TERRA0**
ART COLLECTIVE

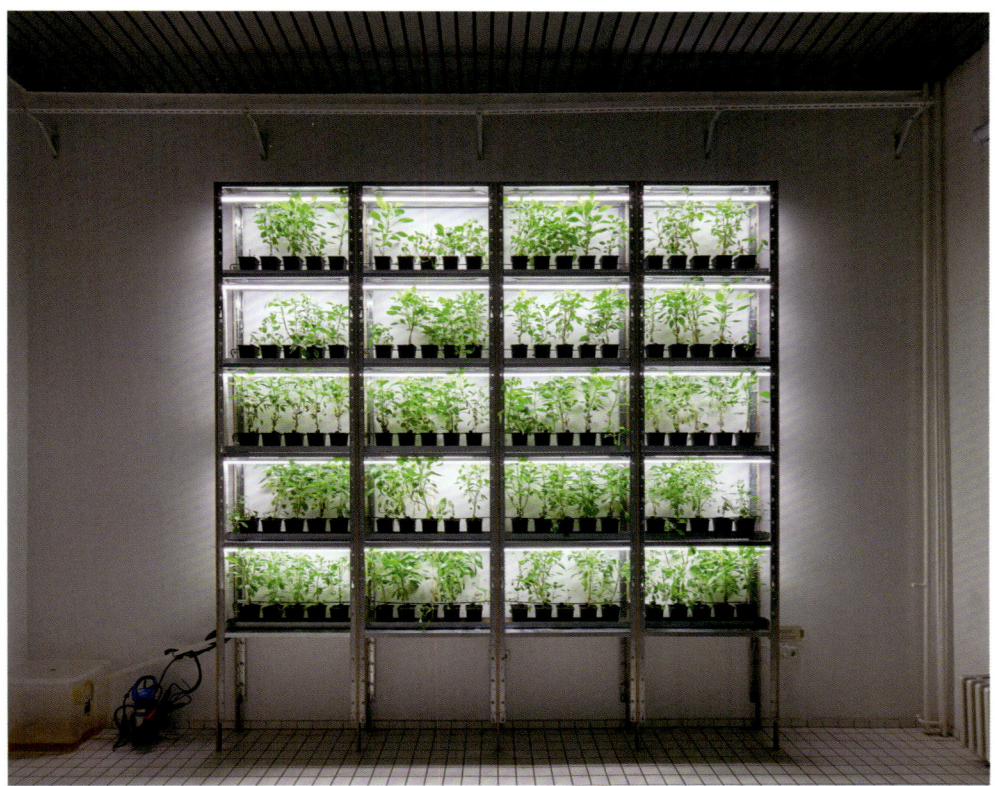

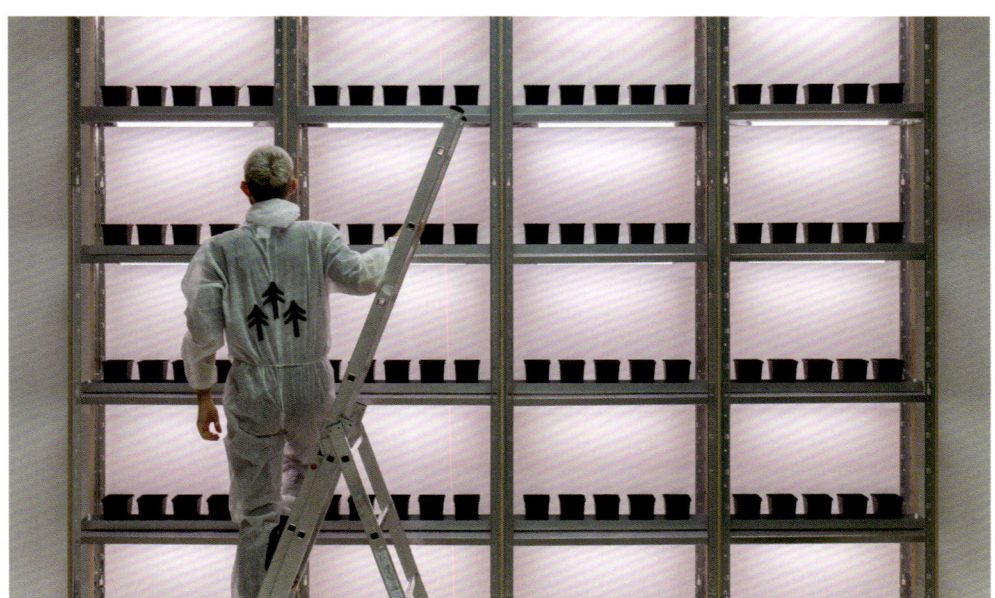

| # | TITLE | TIMESTAMP | MEDIUM | CHAIN | CONTRACT ADDRESS | TOKEN ID | EDITION SIZE |
|---|---|---|---|---|---|---|---|
| 03 | **Flowertokens** | 17-21-2018 17:47:52 | 100 Dahlia x Hortensis, grow rack, camera, web interface, front-/ back end, Ethereum smart contract | ETH | 0x43c9b7b7ce699ac2c1d3aad3b5a78274a0f9c86d | 1–100 | 1/1 of 100 |
| 04 | **Seed Capital – Certificates of Growth** | 03-07-2022 18:17:31 | Raspberry Pi, moisture and temperature sensor, plant, contract generated graphics | ETH | 0xdb7805468c975d7157c02b44d43e3ad2d549f664 | 1–414 | 1/1 of 414 |

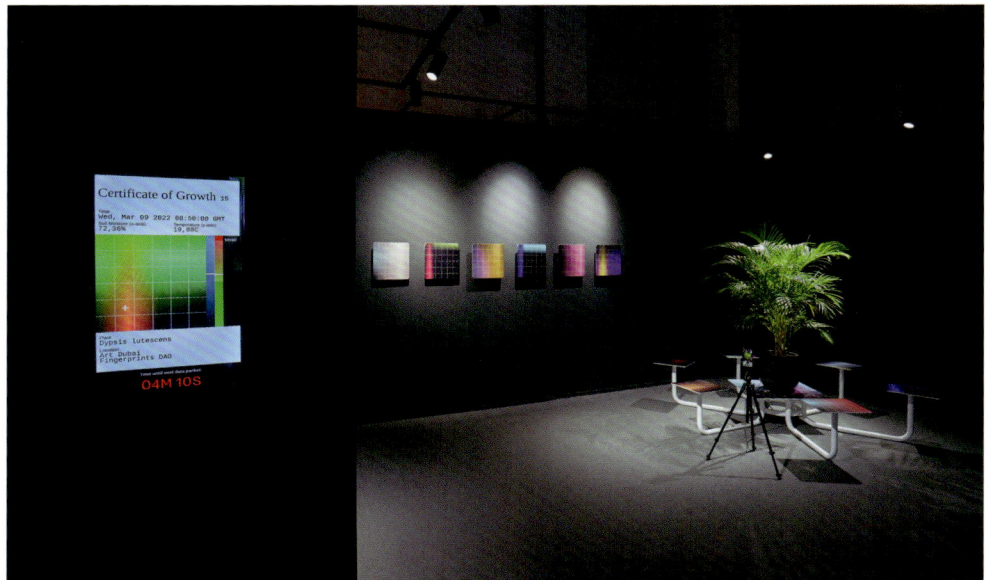

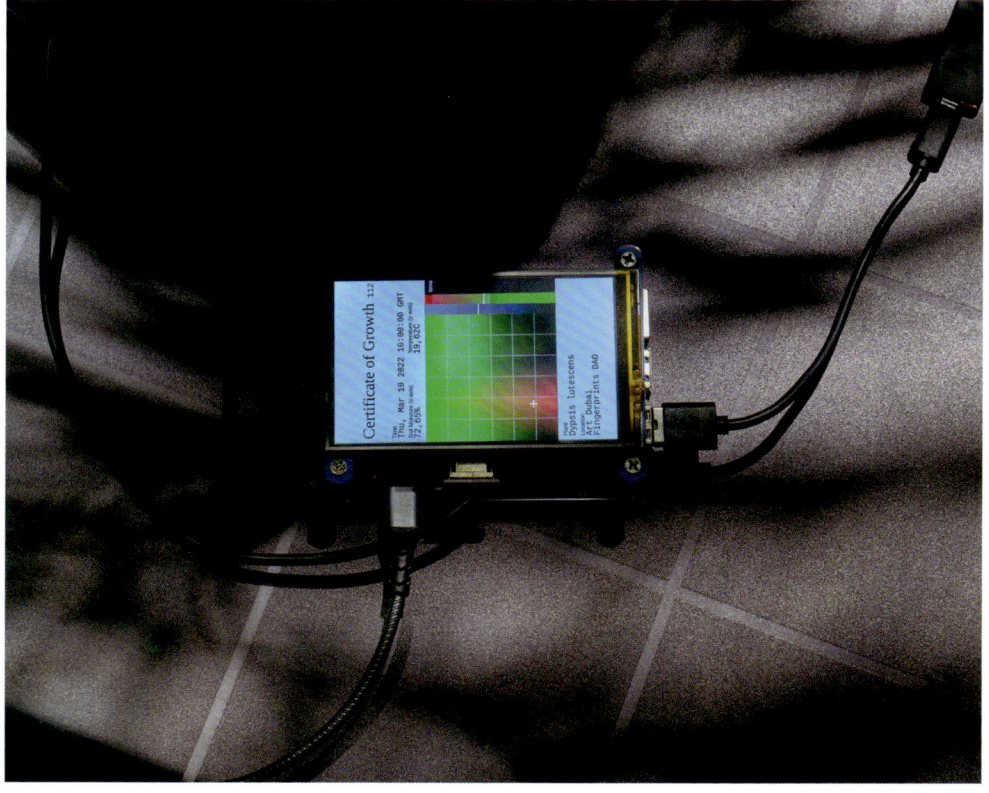

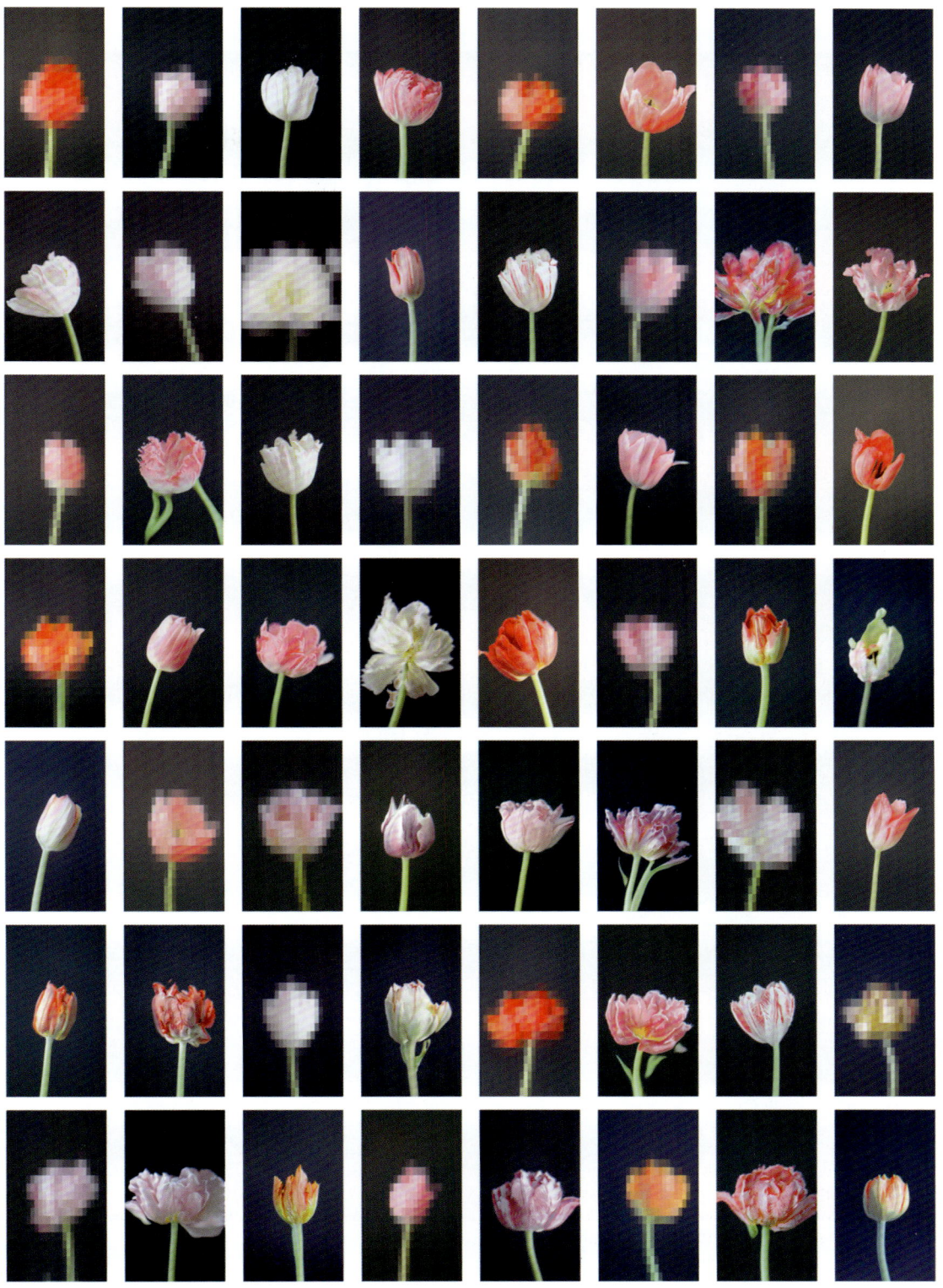

| # | TITLE | TIMESTAMP | MEDIUM | CHAIN | CONTRACT ADDRESS | TOKEN ID | EDITION SIZE |
|---|-------|-----------|--------|-------|------------------|----------|--------------|
| 01 | **Bloemenveiling** | 05-07-2019 22:06:53 | Website, Smart Contracts, GAN Generated Video and Bots | ETH | 0xF10a09C41F395c01F913-8b0CAf1b652A1A9042eC | 1-100 | 1/1 of 100 |
| 02 | **The Black Tulip** | 09-09-2023 20:52:11 | Website, Smart Contracts, GAN Generated Video and Bots | ETH | 0×8a11cE49B8f2645B6574-D24DC5250476929F146F | 1 | 1/1 |

EDITIONS ILLUSTRATED: (01) Various. The videoworks disappeared after a week of purchase, roughly the lifespan of a cut tulip, and are unable to be viewed. In collaboration with David Pfau.

02 ▶

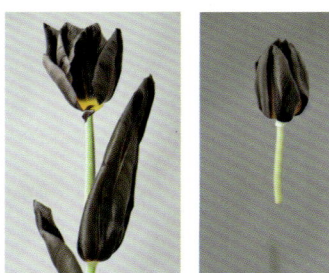
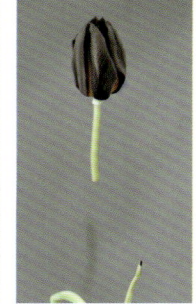
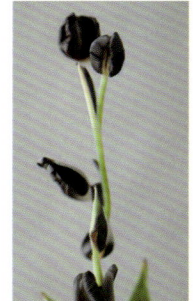
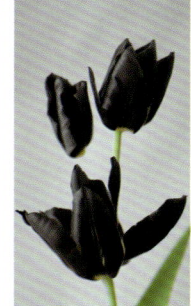
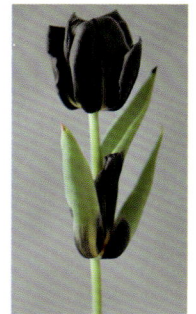
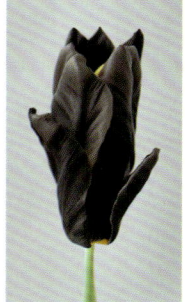
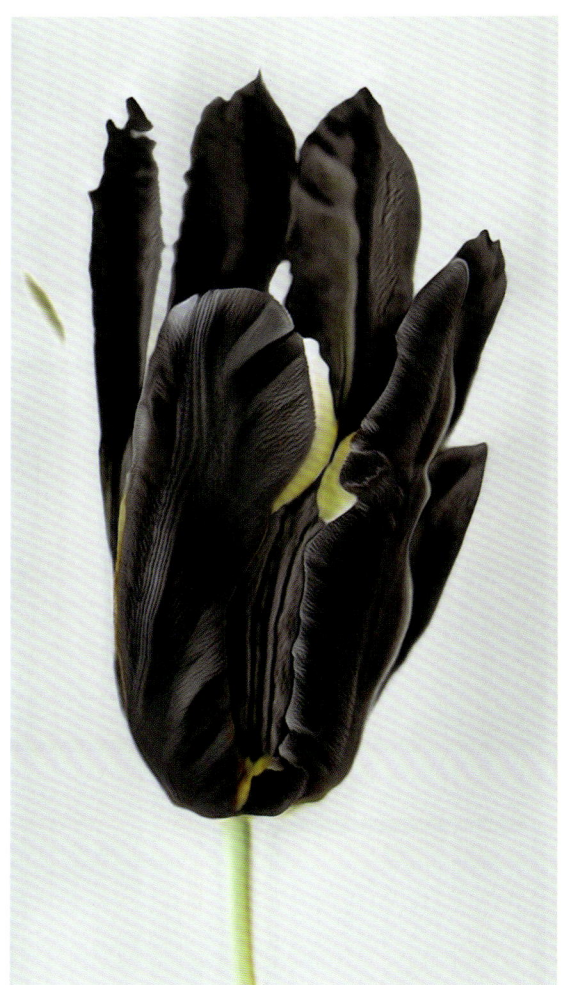

Anna Ridler's research of nature vis-à-vis algorithmic governance is a forensic unpacking of how value is coded — both computationally and culturally. Ridler's work fuses her background in literature with AI as it excavates the ideologies embedded within datasets, rendering visible the infrastructures that dictate what we desire and how we quantify them.

In 2019, I curated Ridler's solo show *Cryptobloom*, where I had the opportunity to experience *Bloemenveiling* (2019) firsthand. Co-created with David Pfau, this artwork is both an NFT online auction and a speculative system collapsing centuries of economic frenzy into recursive loops of machine logic and human compulsion. Ridler reanimates the 17th-century Tulip Mania — a proto-capitalist delirium — by staging an auction of AI-generated videos of tulips that emerged from two of her previous works: *Myriad Tulips* (2018), her dataset, and *Mosaic Virus* (2018–19), made using an AI model. In this online bid, bots artificially inflate prices while the audience competes to claim ownership of these ephemeral files. The work materializes speculative financial bubbles as a living archive, where still-life vanitas morph into real-time data streams.

Expanding on this research, *The Black Tulip* (2023) escalates this question into the realm of institutional sabotage. Deploying custom smart contracts that eliminate the possibility of increasing its price in future resales, Ridler's NFT becomes a paradox: a token that critiques tokenization. Its AI-generated black tulips come to life via algorithmic approximations that evoke the chromatic impossibilities of Alexandre Dumas's eponymous novel as well as the absurdity of assigning scarcity in a digital age. By forcing the work onto a purpose-built platform, Ridler does not merely comment on the NFT movement — it engineers its critique into the blockchain's very architecture.

Anna cultivates datasets as gardens — pixels latent with capital. Her algorithmic flora buzzes with organic-synthetic tension. Tulips, fractures, and flowers bloom where digital permanence's myth cracks under its own contradictions.

**DOREEN RÍOS**
FOUNDER AND CURATOR, [ANTI]MATERIA

**01**

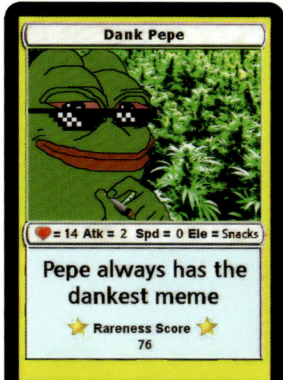

Dank Pepe

♥ = 14  Atk = 2  Spd = 0  Ele = Snacks

Pepe always has the dankest meme

⭐ Rareness Score ⭐
76

**02**

Smooth haired Pepe

♥ = 4  Atk =2  Spd =9  Ele =Shine

An injection of collagen in your hair shaft strengthens the hair follicles and improves hair growth

*Maybe he's born with it...*

**03**

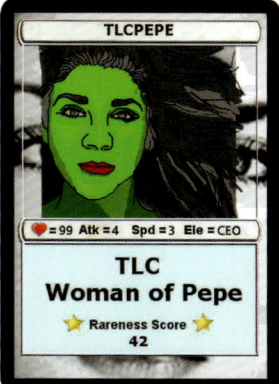

TLCPEPE

♥ = 99  Atk = 4  Spd = 3  Ele = CEO

TLC
**Woman of Pepe**

⭐ Rareness Score ⭐
42

**04**

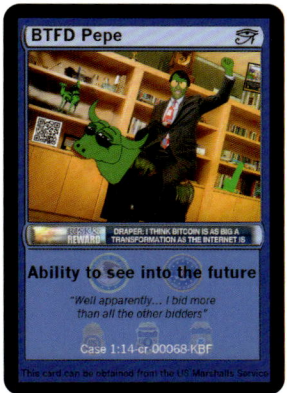

BTFD Pepe

DRAPER: I THINK BITCOIN IS AS BIG A TRANSFORMATION AS THE INTERNET IS

Ability to see into the future

*"Well apparently... I bid more than all the other bidders"*

Case 1:14-cr-00068-KBF

This card can be obtained from the US Marshalls Service

**05**

PEPE POPE

♥ =10  ATK=1  SPD=1  ELE=DIVINE

CLEANSING PEPE'S SOULS SINCE TIME BEGAN.
IMMUTABLE WEALTH.
IMMUNE SOUL.

RARENESS SCORE - GOD CARD

**06**

MONALISAPEPE

♥ = 808  R = 055

We don't make mistakes, just happy little accidents
*Enemy loses eyes for entire game
Attack increased by rarelemon wash
Or mistake birds*

*Warning: Staring at Mona her name Lisa too long is bad*

**07**

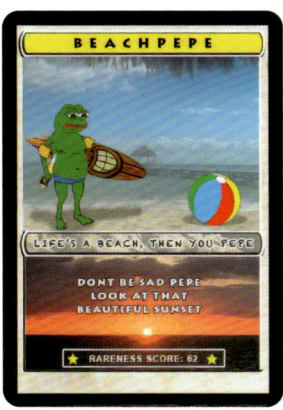

BEACHPEPE

LIFE'S A BEACH, THEN YOU PEPE

DONT BE SAD PEPE
LOOK AT THAT
BEAUTIFUL SUNSET

⭐ RARENESS SCORE: 62 ⭐

**08**

SHREMPEPE

♥ =20  Atk=8  Spd=9  Ele= B

One of the oldest and hairest Pepes known to exist.  +1 if any Silk Road Pepe is played. Thrives on basic income, will trailblaze for party, advances 2. -1 if WINKELPEPE played.

**09** ►

Jihan Wu Pepe

ATK = 659 PH/s          ELE =

*"fuck your mother if you want fuck"*

Covertly boosts your deck while denying all technological upgrades to your opponents when played

connoisseur card

| # | ARTIST NAME | TITLE | TIMESTAMP | MEDIUM | CHAIN | ISSUER ADDRESS | ASSET ID | EDITION SIZE |
|---|---|---|---|---|---|---|---|---|
| 01 | **Shawn Leary** | DANKPEPE | 09-13-2016 13:27:45 | Microsoft Paint | XCP | 15FPgnpZuNyZLVLsyB6UdFicsVvWFJXNve | DANKPEPE | 420 |
| 02 | **Aya** | HAIRPEPE | 09-23-2016 11:42:34 | Adobe Photoshop | XCP | 1EgkMa1d79BXGjU9eZbuuiZu4uYQVuRsPe | HAIRPEPE | 1,000 |
| 03 | **Shawn Leary** | TLCPEPE | 09-13-2016 16:15:54 | Microsoft Paint | XCP | 15FPgnpZuNyZLVLsyB6UdFicsVvWFJXNve | TLCPEPE | 1,000 |
| 04 | **Cryptonati** | BTFDPEPE | 03-31-2017 03:05:47 | Meme Magic | XCP | 13Mpz1EoP2wi1nGGwZt4kQ7hfxRmBRToKc | BTFDPEPE | 29,656 |
| 05 | **Boost** | PEPEPOPE | 09-27-2016 07:11:45 | Pixlr | XCP | 1JAuET9GmkADQarX5ZsgHXuHjJzwesfAKg | PEPEPOPE | 25 |
| 06 | **Our Earth Everyday** | MONALISAPEPE | 10-12-2016 13:10:54 | GIMP | XCP | 1AE4vfkDX4S49kxsuCve7zJDS5s5RtHYNs | MONALISAPEPE | 100 |
| 07 | **CryptoChainer** | BEACHPEPE | 10-20-2016 01:54:47 | Adobe Photoshop | XCP | 1M8tGrim6DP1zra6YAHotZfs19wxo78pzQ | BEACHPEPE | 244 |
| 08 | **Shawn Leary** | SHREMPEPE | 11-03-2016 23:32:45 | Microsoft Paint | XCP | 15FPgnpZuNyZLVLsyB6UdFicsVvWFJXNve | SHREMPEPE | 1,133 |
| 09 | **Indelible** | JIHANWU | 02-11-2018 13:27:19 | Adobe Photoshop | XCP | 18mxQdLxcLstD6ttbHykvEoAYdu4eADtEf | JIHANWU | 99 |
| 10 | **Boost** | RAREPEPE 'Nakamoto Card' | 09-09-2016 01:46:42 | Pixlr | XCP | 1GQhaWqejcGJ4GhQar7SjcCfadxvf5DNBD | RAREPEPE | 298 |
| 11 | **Mike** | HOMERPEPE | 09-29-2016 05:46:16 | Pixlr | XCP | 1KoMmriS96Rvajs7JRi9pJy4bj2JmDUZCJ | HOMERPEPE | 1 |

# RARE PEPE CARDS

10

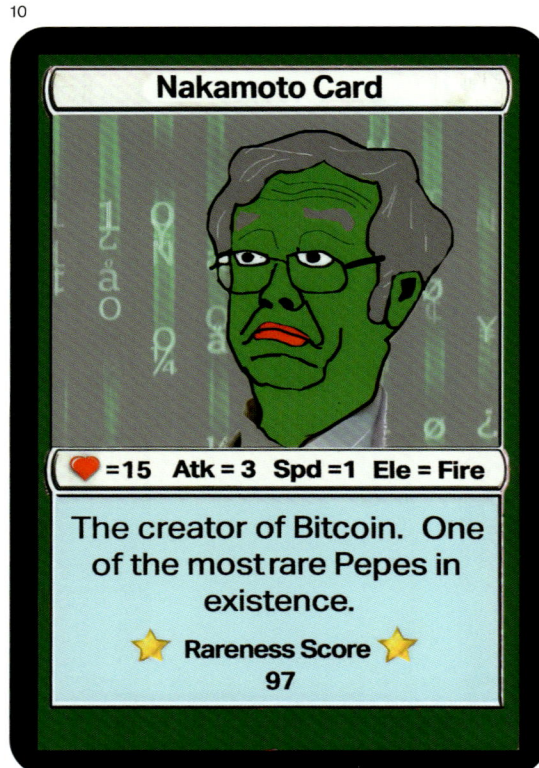

**Nakamoto Card**

♥ =15  Atk = 3  Spd =1  Ele = Fire

The creator of Bitcoin.  One of the most rare Pepes in existence.

⭐ Rareness Score ⭐
97

11

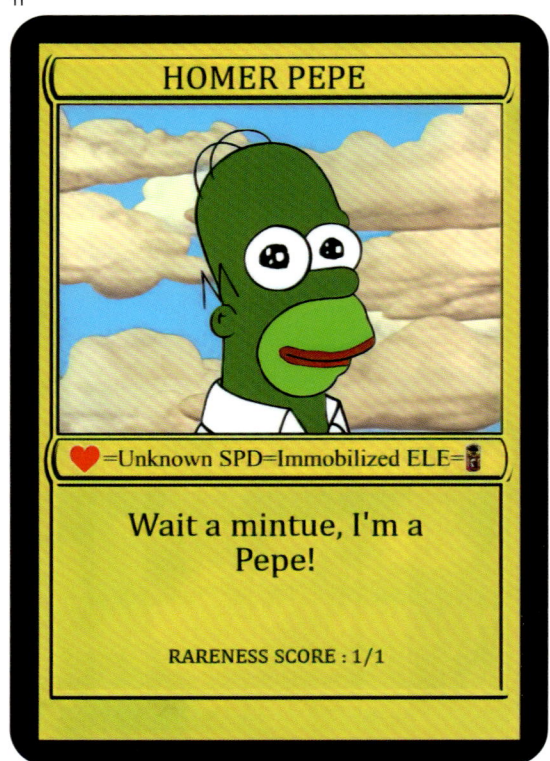

HOMER PEPE

♥=Unknown SPD=Immobilized ELE=🔋

Wait a mintue, I'm a Pepe!

RARENESS SCORE : 1/1

Established in September 2016, the Rare Pepe Directory contains 1,774 unique rare pepe cards created by artists from around the globe. This eclectic group from a wide range of backgrounds shared a common curiosity around exploring the idea of art tokens later known as NFTs.

The Rare Pepe Directory began when an anonymous internet user named Mike announced the *Nakamoto Card* (2016) in an online group chat devoted to discussion of Counterparty, a token platform on Bitcoin. Through his use of the rare pepe meme (a joke born on internet message boards two years earlier) and the Counterparty platform, Mike was able to bridge the conceptual gap between digital art and crypto tokens in a way that captured the imagination of many chat room members. Those members formed a new group devoted to rare pepe trading and as the traders became the artists a digital art token economy began to form.

The rare pepe trading community continued to grow and thrive throughout 2017. Artists from Venezuela to Japan contributed to building the Rare Pepe Directory. In January 2018, a contingent of rare pepe traders descended on the Rare Digital Art Festival in New York City, itself a seminal event in the history of NFTs. It was at this event that the *Homer Pepe* (2016) introduced festival attendees to the form and aesthetic of rare pepes. The *Homer Pepe*, in its simplicity, exemplifies the remixing of pop culture media found throughout the Rare Pepe Directory. One of only a handful of single issuance rare pepes in the directory, *Homer Pepe* introduced the concept of digital scarcity to the traditional art world and was a major catalyst for the crypto art movement.

**JOE LOONEY**
FOUNDER OF THE RARE PEPE WALLET AND
RARE PEPE SCIENTIST

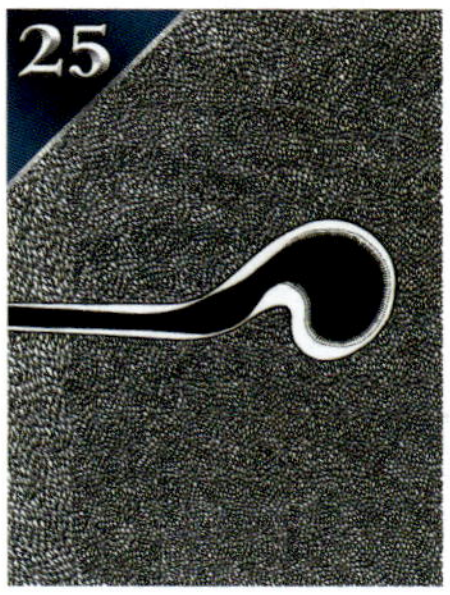

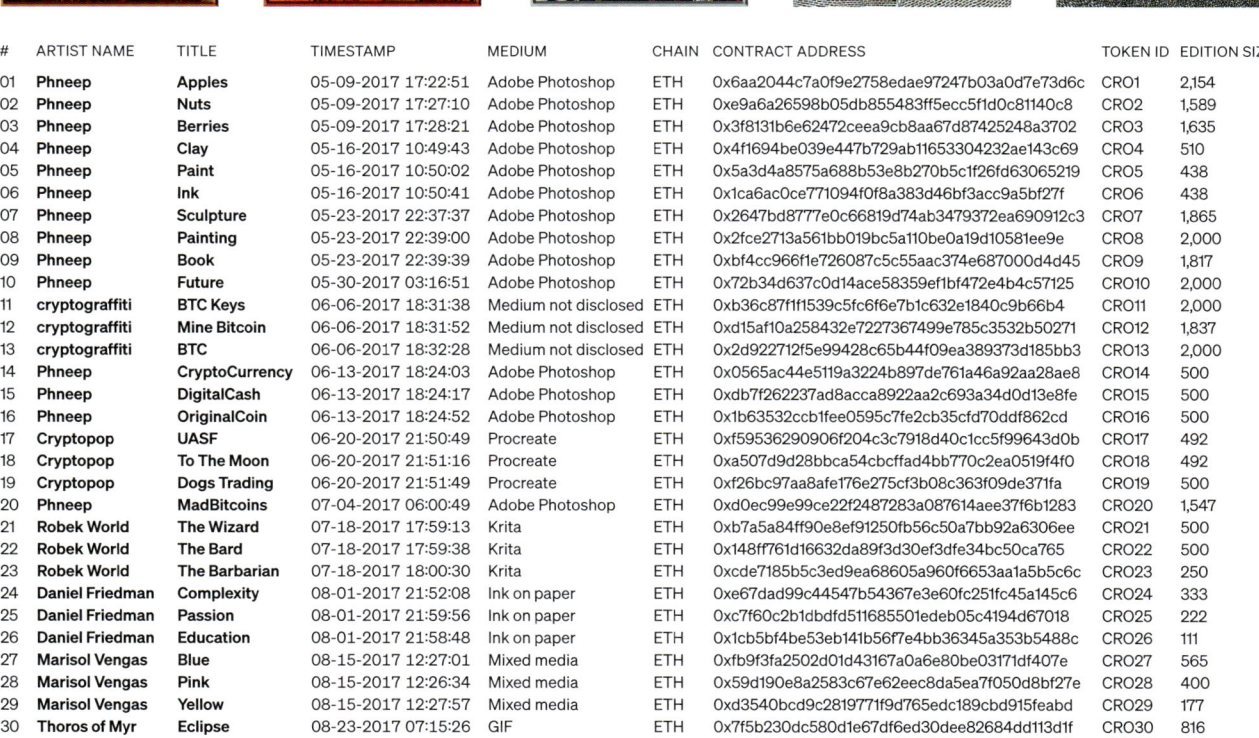

| # | ARTIST NAME | TITLE | TIMESTAMP | MEDIUM | CHAIN | CONTRACT ADDRESS | TOKEN ID | EDITION SIZE |
|---|---|---|---|---|---|---|---|---|
| 01 | **Phneep** | **Apples** | 05-09-2017 17:22:51 | Adobe Photoshop | ETH | 0x6aa2044c7a0f9e2758edae97247b03a0d7e73d6c | CRO1 | 2,154 |
| 02 | **Phneep** | **Nuts** | 05-09-2017 17:27:10 | Adobe Photoshop | ETH | 0xe9a6a26598b05db855483ff5ecc5f1d0c81140c8 | CRO2 | 1,589 |
| 03 | **Phneep** | **Berries** | 05-09-2017 17:28:21 | Adobe Photoshop | ETH | 0x3f8131b6e62472ceea9cb8aa67d87425248a3702 | CRO3 | 1,635 |
| 04 | **Phneep** | **Clay** | 05-16-2017 10:49:43 | Adobe Photoshop | ETH | 0x4f1694be039e447b729ab11653304232ae143c69 | CRO4 | 510 |
| 05 | **Phneep** | **Paint** | 05-16-2017 10:50:02 | Adobe Photoshop | ETH | 0x5a3d4a8575a688b53e8b270b5c1f26fd63065219 | CRO5 | 438 |
| 06 | **Phneep** | **Ink** | 05-16-2017 10:50:41 | Adobe Photoshop | ETH | 0x1ca6ac0ce771094f0f8a383d46bf3acc9a5bf27f | CRO6 | 438 |
| 07 | **Phneep** | **Sculpture** | 05-23-2017 22:37:37 | Adobe Photoshop | ETH | 0x2647bd8777e0c66819d74ab3479372ea690912c3 | CRO7 | 1,865 |
| 08 | **Phneep** | **Painting** | 05-23-2017 22:39:00 | Adobe Photoshop | ETH | 0x2fce2713a561bb019bc5a110be0a19d10581ee9e | CRO8 | 2,000 |
| 09 | **Phneep** | **Book** | 05-23-2017 22:39:39 | Adobe Photoshop | ETH | 0xbf4cc966f1e726087c5c55aac374e687000d4d45 | CRO9 | 1,817 |
| 10 | **Phneep** | **Future** | 05-30-2017 03:16:51 | Adobe Photoshop | ETH | 0x72b34d637c0d14ace58359ef1bf472e4b4c57125 | CRO10 | 2,000 |
| 11 | **cryptograffiti** | **BTC Keys** | 06-06-2017 18:31:38 | Medium not disclosed | ETH | 0xb36c87f1f1539c5fc6f6e7b1c632e1840c9b66b4 | CRO11 | 2,000 |
| 12 | **cryptograffiti** | **Mine Bitcoin** | 06-06-2017 18:31:52 | Medium not disclosed | ETH | 0xd15af10a258432e7227367499e785c3532b50271 | CRO12 | 1,837 |
| 13 | **cryptograffiti** | **BTC** | 06-06-2017 18:32:28 | Medium not disclosed | ETH | 0x2d922712f5e99428c65b44f09ea389373d185bb3 | CRO13 | 2,000 |
| 14 | **Phneep** | **CryptoCurrency** | 06-13-2017 18:24:03 | Adobe Photoshop | ETH | 0x0565ac44e5119a3224b897de761a46a92aa28ae8 | CRO14 | 500 |
| 15 | **Phneep** | **DigitalCash** | 06-13-2017 18:24:17 | Adobe Photoshop | ETH | 0xdb7f262237ad8acca8922aa2c693a34d0d13e8fe | CRO15 | 500 |
| 16 | **Phneep** | **OriginalCoin** | 06-13-2017 18:24:52 | Adobe Photoshop | ETH | 0x1b63532ccb1fee0595c7fe2cb35cfd70ddf862cd | CRO16 | 500 |
| 17 | **Cryptopop** | **UASF** | 06-20-2017 21:50:49 | Procreate | ETH | 0xf59536290906f204c3c7918d40c1cc5f99643d0b | CRO17 | 492 |
| 18 | **Cryptopop** | **To The Moon** | 06-20-2017 21:51:16 | Procreate | ETH | 0xa507d9d28bbca54cbcffad4bb770c2ea0519f4f0 | CRO18 | 492 |
| 19 | **Cryptopop** | **Dogs Trading** | 06-20-2017 21:51:49 | Procreate | ETH | 0xf26bc97aa8afe176e275cf3b08c363f09de371fa | CRO19 | 500 |
| 20 | **Phneep** | **MadBitcoins** | 07-04-2017 06:00:49 | Adobe Photoshop | ETH | 0xd0ec99e99ce22f2487283a087614aee37f6b1283 | CRO20 | 1,547 |
| 21 | **Robek World** | **The Wizard** | 07-18-2017 17:59:13 | Krita | ETH | 0xb7a5a84ff90e8ef91250fb56c50a7bb92a6306ee | CRO21 | 500 |
| 22 | **Robek World** | **The Bard** | 07-18-2017 17:59:38 | Krita | ETH | 0x148ff761d16632da89f3d30ef3dfe34bc50ca765 | CRO22 | 500 |
| 23 | **Robek World** | **The Barbarian** | 07-18-2017 18:00:30 | Krita | ETH | 0xcde7185b5c3ed9ea68605a960f6653aa1a5b5c6c | CRO23 | 250 |
| 24 | **Daniel Friedman** | **Complexity** | 08-01-2017 21:52:08 | Ink on paper | ETH | 0xe67dad99c44547b54367e3e60fc251fc45a145c6 | CRO24 | 333 |
| 25 | **Daniel Friedman** | **Passion** | 08-01-2017 21:59:56 | Ink on paper | ETH | 0xc7f60c2b1dbdfd511685501edeb05c4194d67018 | CRO25 | 222 |
| 26 | **Daniel Friedman** | **Education** | 08-01-2017 21:58:48 | Ink on paper | ETH | 0x1cb5bf4be53eb141b56f7e4bb36345a353b5488c | CRO26 | 111 |
| 27 | **Marisol Vengas** | **Blue** | 08-15-2017 12:27:01 | Mixed media | ETH | 0xfb9f3fa2502d01d43167a0a6e80be03171df407e | CRO27 | 565 |
| 28 | **Marisol Vengas** | **Pink** | 08-15-2017 12:26:34 | Mixed media | ETH | 0x59d190e8a2583c67e62eec8da5ea7f050d8bf27e | CRO28 | 400 |
| 29 | **Marisol Vengas** | **Yellow** | 08-15-2017 12:27:57 | Mixed media | ETH | 0xd3540bcd9c2819771f9d765edc189cbd915feabd | CRO29 | 177 |
| 30 | **Thoros of Myr** | **Eclipse** | 08-23-2017 07:15:26 | GIF | ETH | 0x7f5b230dc580d1e67df6ed30dee82684dd113d1f | CRO30 | 816 |

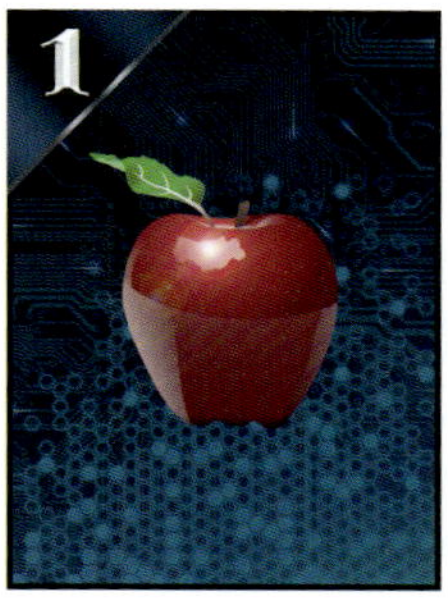

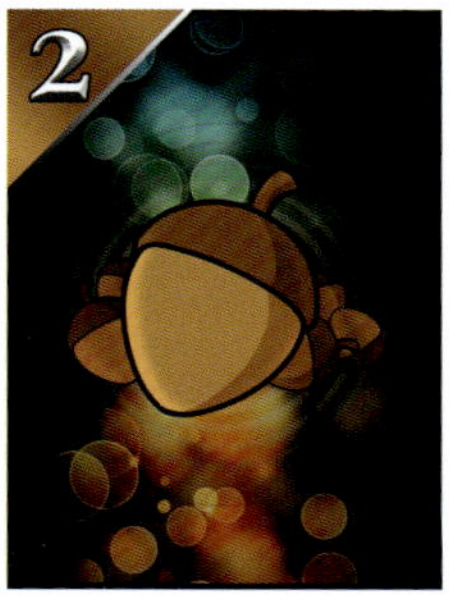

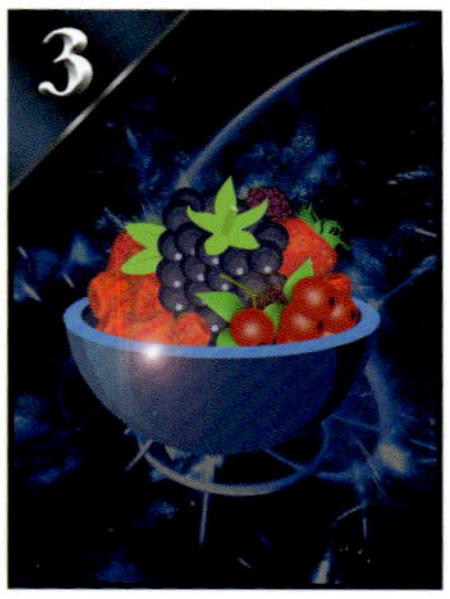

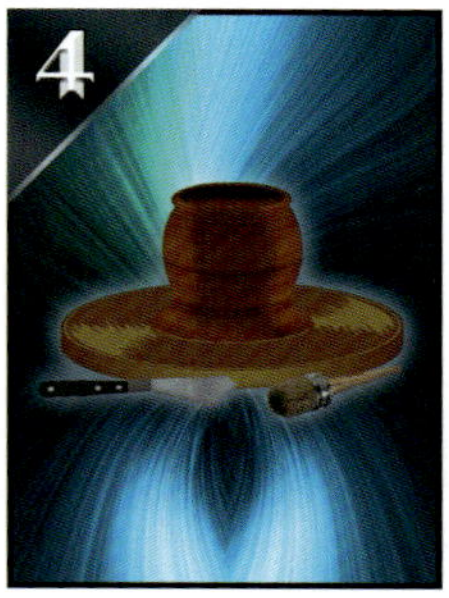

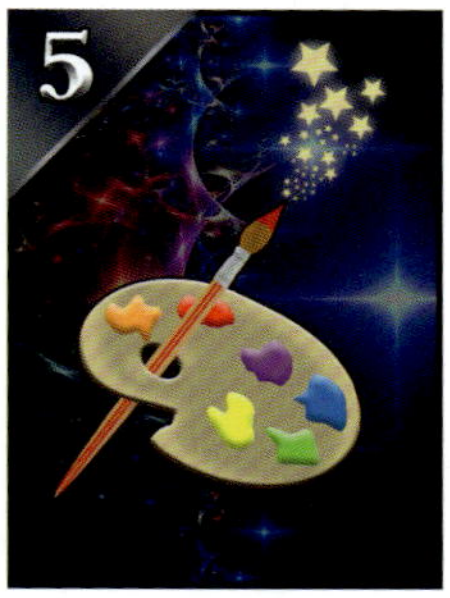

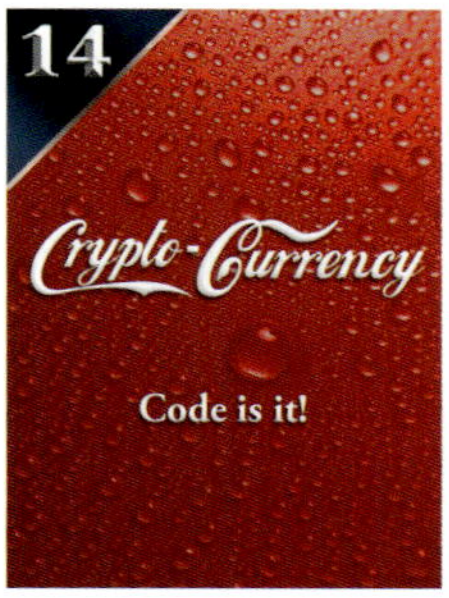

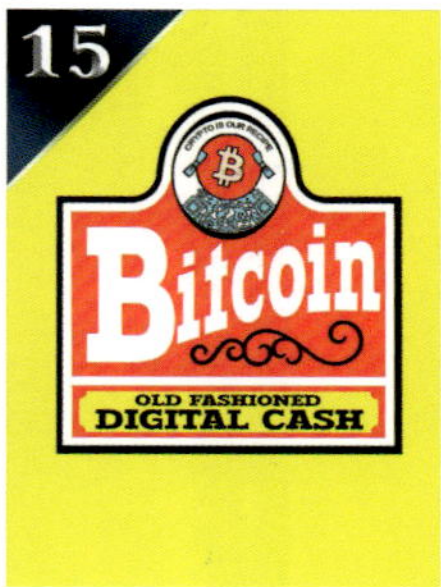

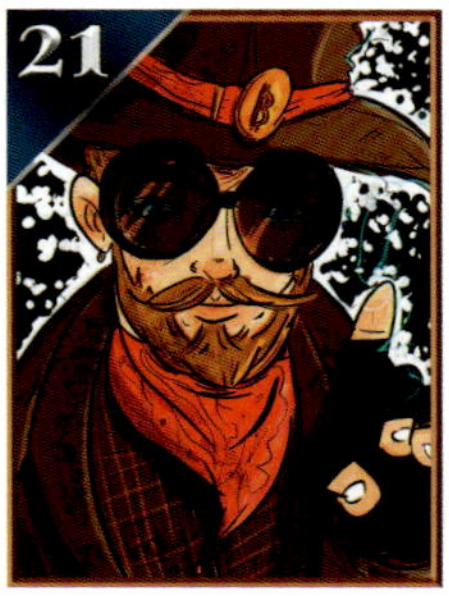

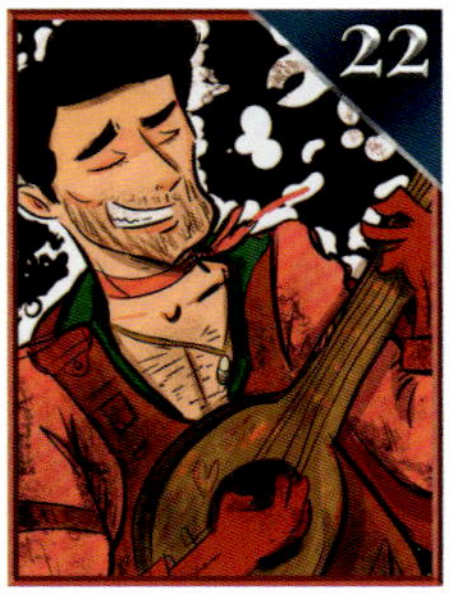

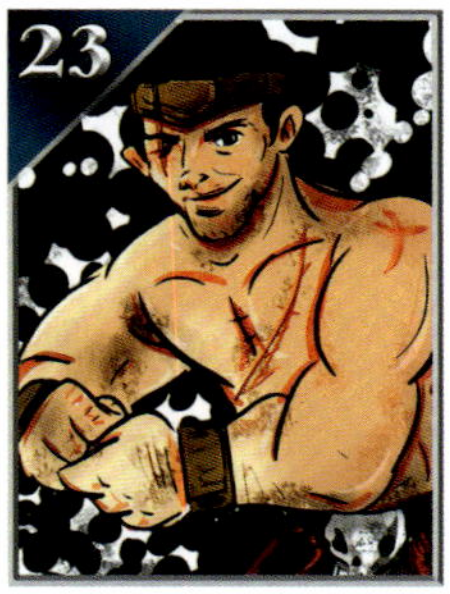

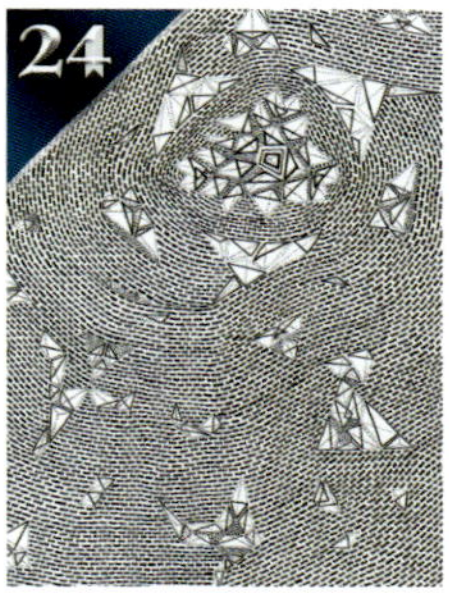

# CURIO CARDS

FOUNDED 2017

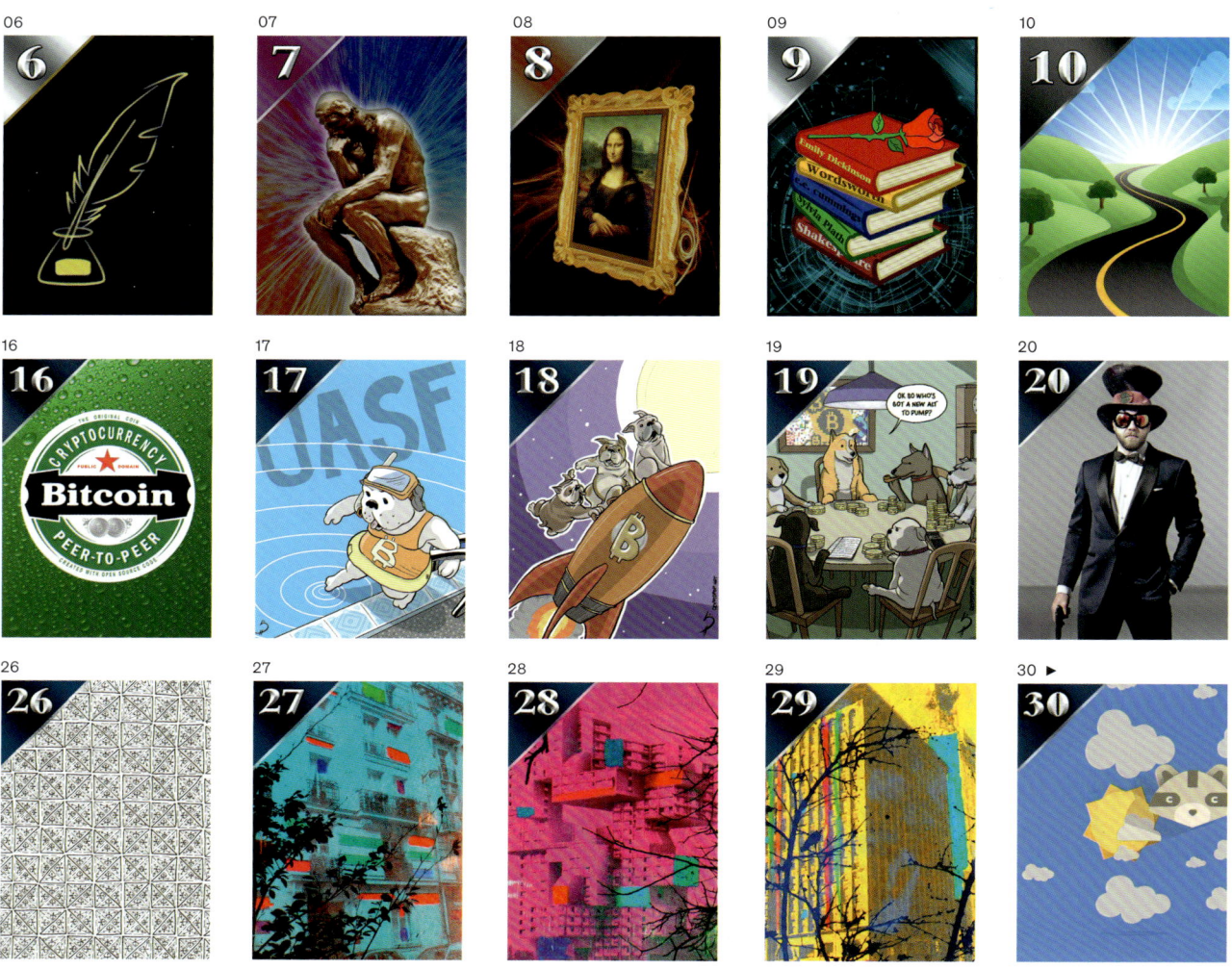

*Curio Cards* is the first art NFT project on Ethereum, launched as a permanent online art show gallery on May 9, 2017. *Curio Cards* used Ethereum to establish a new model for the creation and ownership of digital artwork. The *Curio Cards* approach was to create a unique set of rare collectible art, with contributions from seven artists with different styles and backgrounds. In doing so, *Curio Cards* pioneered a new way for artists to receive value for their work, interact with collectors, and build a broader community.

The official set of *Curio Cards* contains 30 pieces of art (also, there is a misprint of 17, titled 17b). The seven artists who created the art for *Curio Cards* (and the cards they created) are Phneep (1–10, 14–16, 20), Cryptograffiti (11–13), Cryptopop (17–19), Robek World (21–23), Daniel Friedman (24–26), Max Infeld aka Marisol Vengas (27–29), and Thoros of Myr (30). Various media were used in the creation of *Curio Cards*, including digital art, printmaking, pen and paper, mixed media, and animation. The NFTs 24–29 contain perhaps the first physical artworks represented on the Ethereum blockchain, and 23 may be the first animated GIF on the Ethereum blockchain.

For further contextualization of each artist, we encourage readers and art historians to explore the varied projects that each artist has contributed to.

*Curio Cards* are referenced in the original ERC-721 Non-Fungible Token Standard, and introduced several other computational features that were novel for the time. The *Curio Cards* project thus reflects a developmental advance in art itself, as well as in the social and computational aspects of art.

**D. A. FRIEDMAN**
CURIO CARD ARTIST
**O. C. RIPLEY**
CURIO CARD COLLECTOR

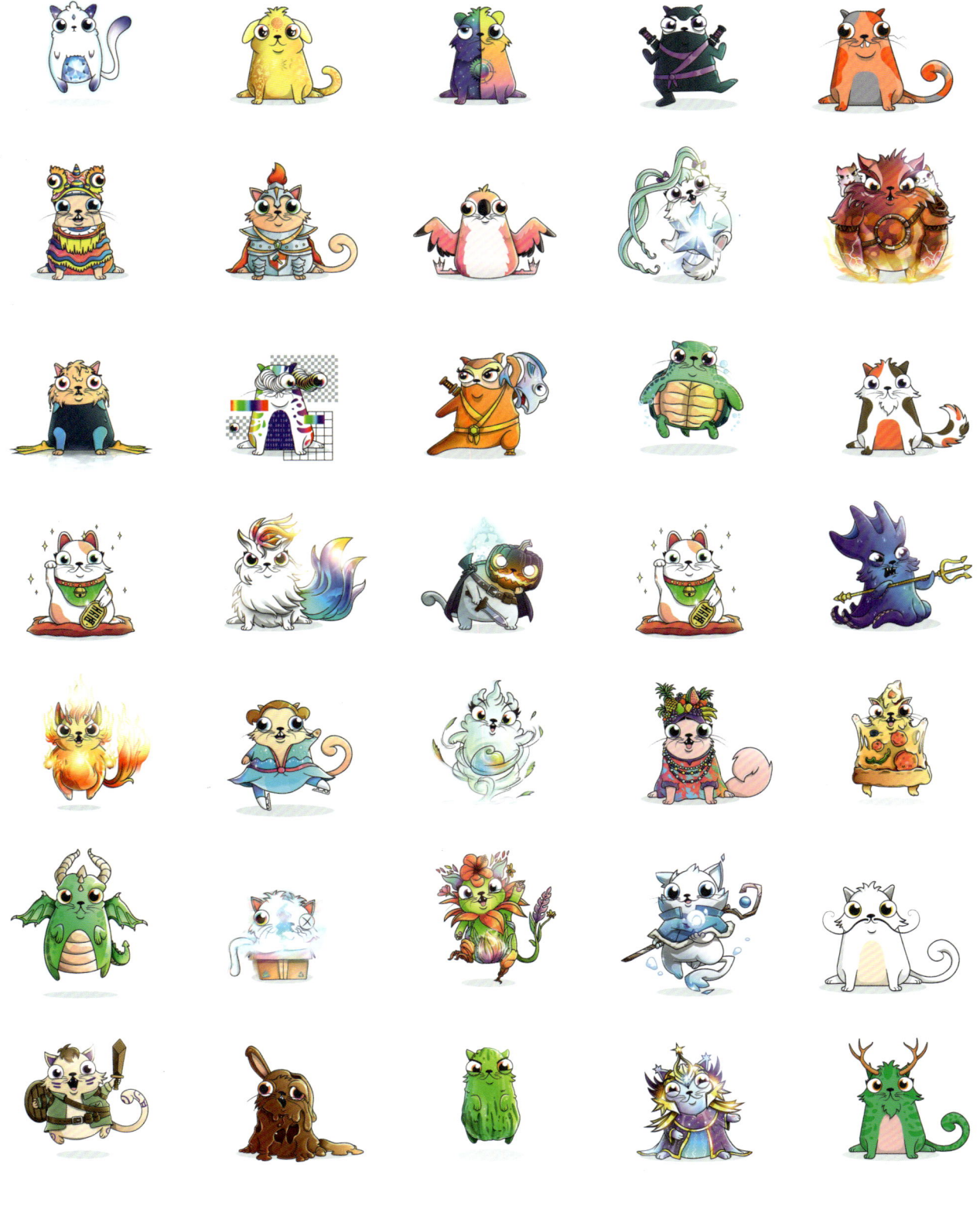

| # | TITLE | TIMESTAMP | MEDIUM | CHAIN | CONTRACT ADDRESS | TOKEN ID | EDITION SIZE |
|---|-------|-----------|--------|-------|------------------|----------|--------------|
| 01, 02 | **CryptoKitties** | 11-23-2017 06:19:59 | Adobe Illustrator, Adobe Photoshop | ETH | 0x06012c8cf97bead5deae237070f9587f8e7a266d | 1–∞ | 1/1 of ∞ |

EDITIONS ILLUSTRATED: (01) Various, (02) #127 Celestial Cyber Dimension

# CRYPTOKITTIES

FOUNDED 2017

02

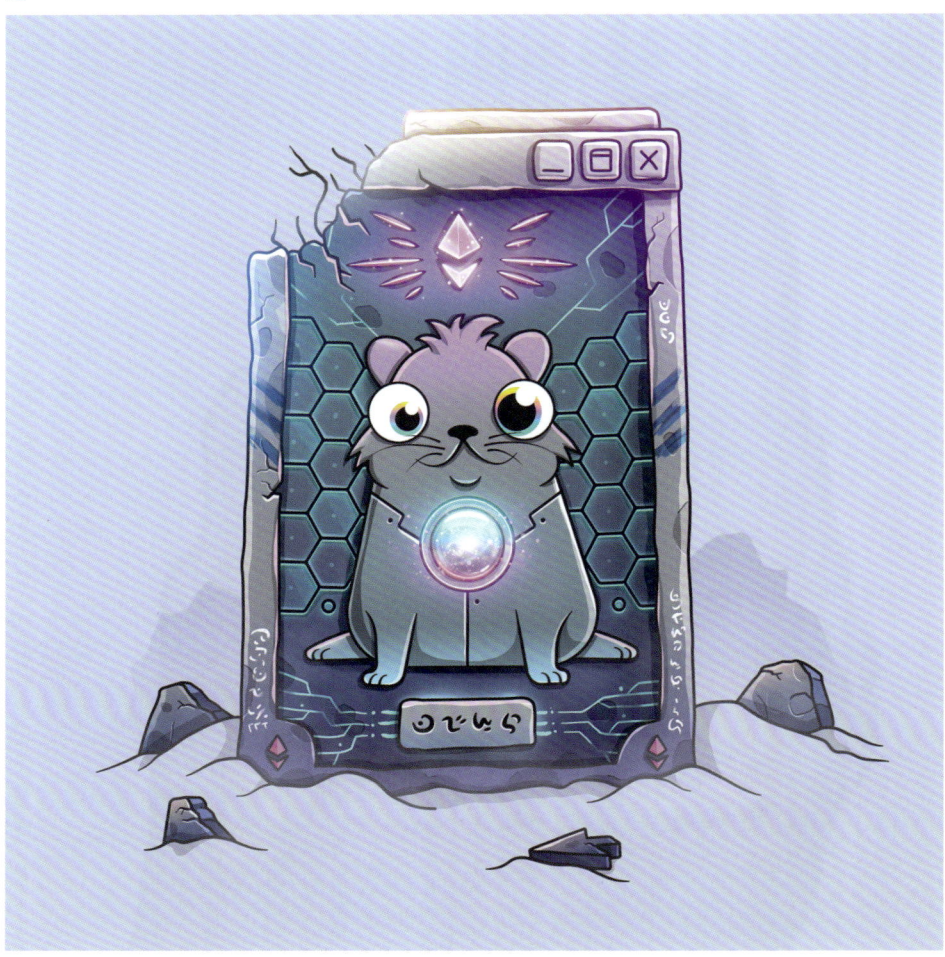

*CryptoKitties* is an Ethereum-based gamified collectible experience launched in late 2017. In the game, players collect and breed digital cats called *CryptoKitties*. Each Kitty has a unique genome that defines its appearance and traits. In total, it is estimated that there are over 17 billion unique combinations in the game. So far over two million Kitties have been bred by a passionate community of players and collectors.

Within the first week after its release, the project quickly grew in popularity with about 60,000 registered players and around 100,000 newborn Kitties clogging the Ethereum network. Around the same time, it started to spark the early larger conversations about digital asset ownership and what the relationship between art and blockchain could become.

In May 2018, the artwork *Celestial Cyber Dimension* (2017), an exclusive *CryptoKitty*, helped to tie that dialogue, being the first hybrid digital-physical NFT to set foot at Christie's, and was later exhibited and auctioned at the Ethereal Summit in New York. In August 2017, at the *Open Codes* exhibition, the real-time installation *Bringing Blockchain to Life* took the conversation to the Center for Art and Media (ZKM) in Karlsruhe, Germany, and examined the largely hidden but elegant technical mechanics behind the project's generative aspects.

The game also had a major impact on driving the accessibility and adoption of blockchain to a wider audience. Its concept and visual appeal made it one of the main access points for newcomers to this technology. 25% of the players were first-time blockchain users. It showcased early on that NFTs were a disruptive onboarding tool for crypto.

In hindsight, I feel very fortunate to have co-created the project with my beloved friends, a group of passionate and brilliant individuals under the roof of AxiomZen. What started as an experiment later became one of the major contributors to establishing NFTs as we know them today. It helped spark the ongoing digital art revolution and made us rethink what digital assets could mean.

**GUILE TWARDOWSKI**
CRYPTOKITTIES ARTIST

01

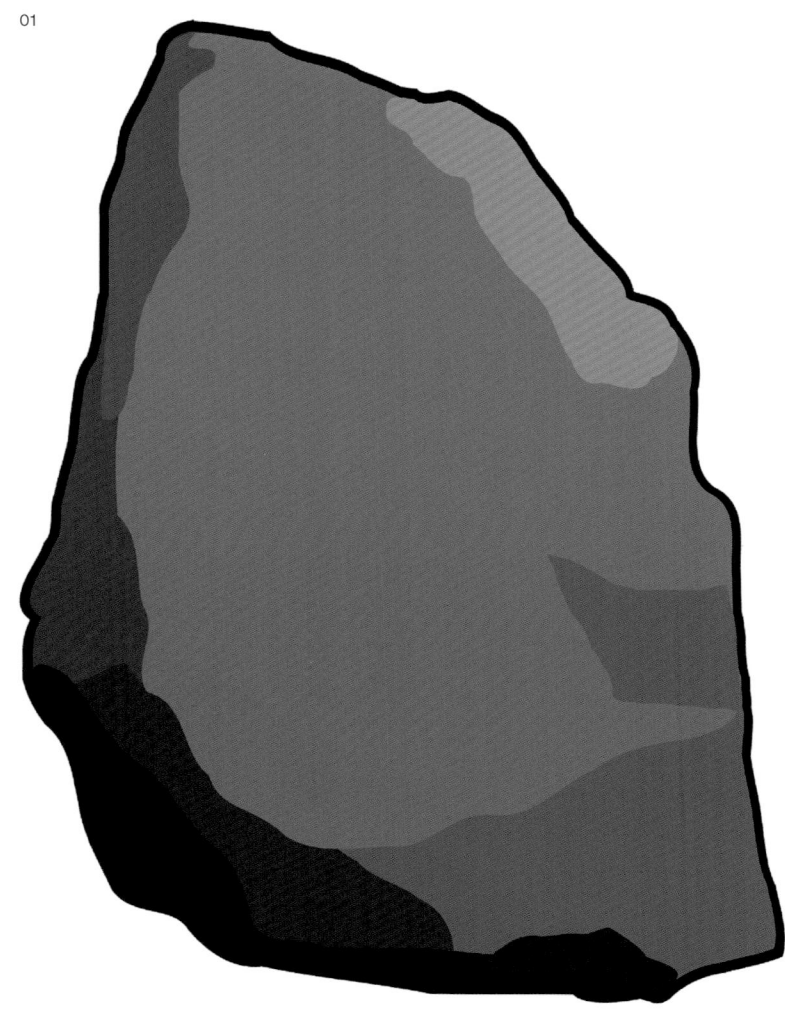

| # | TITLE | TIMESTAMP | MEDIUM | CHAIN | CONTRACT ADDRESS | TOKEN ID | EDITION SIZE |
|---|-------|-----------|--------|-------|------------------|----------|--------------|
| 01-04 | **EtherRocks** | 12-26-2017 02:24:27 | Clipart Rock | ETH | 0x41f28833be34e6ede3c58d1f597bef429861c4e2 | 0-99 | 1/1 of 100 |

EDITIONS ILLUSTRATED: (01) #20, (02) #1, (03) Various

02

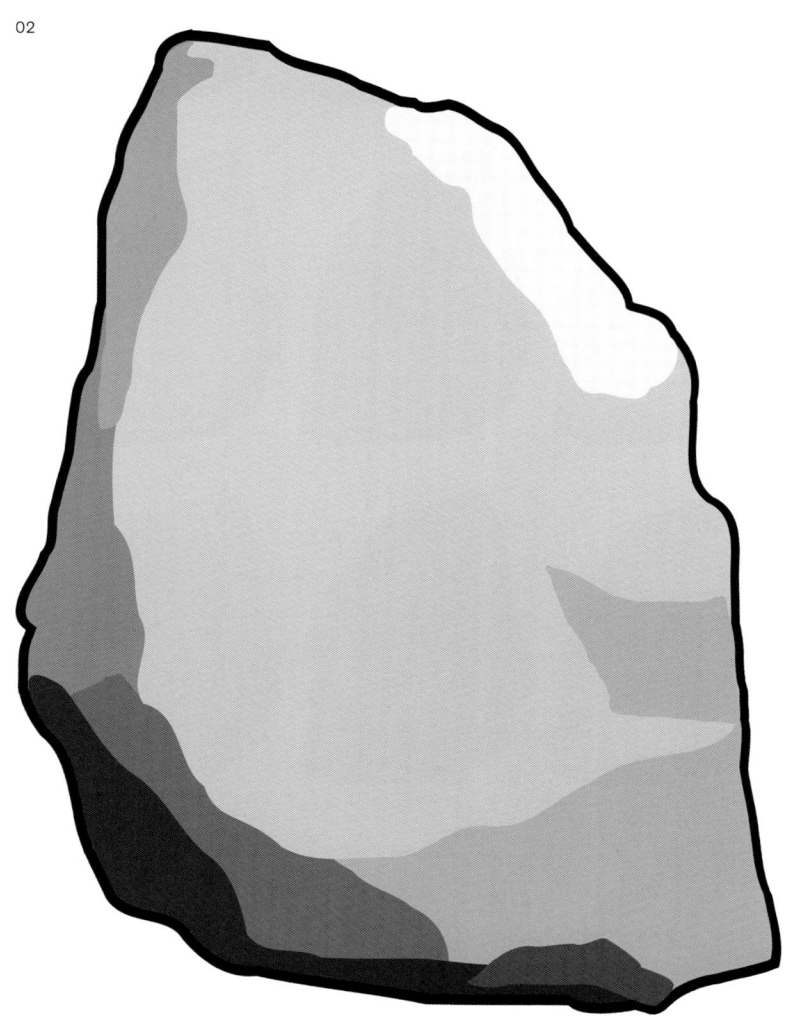

I released EtherRocks in late 2017. At the time, these were amongst the first projects on the Ethereum blockchain, having been released shortly after *CryptoPunks* (2017). I made it clear from the beginning that they had no purpose beyond collectibility. Yet, like the tangible pet rocks that they share conceptual affinities with, there is a definite affective appeal to them.

Only 100 rocks were ever released, each with the same two-dimensional aesthetic that refers to early video games and web graphics. Their simplicity has a purposeful irreverence to it, in line with the common language of the internet dictated by the self-deprecating and somewhat cynical nature of meme humor, particularly within crypto communities. Despite their nerve, or perhaps by virtue thereof, EtherRocks have come to be highly desired collectibles.

Remnants from the earliest days of crypto art, these works reveal the importance of timestamps in generating value. The immutability of the blockchain makes their historical importance absolutely indisputable, and the increasing amount of NFT projects, along with the media attention they have gathered, has only served to solidify their "neolithic" quality in crypto terms.

**"JOHN"**
CREATOR OF ETHERROCKS

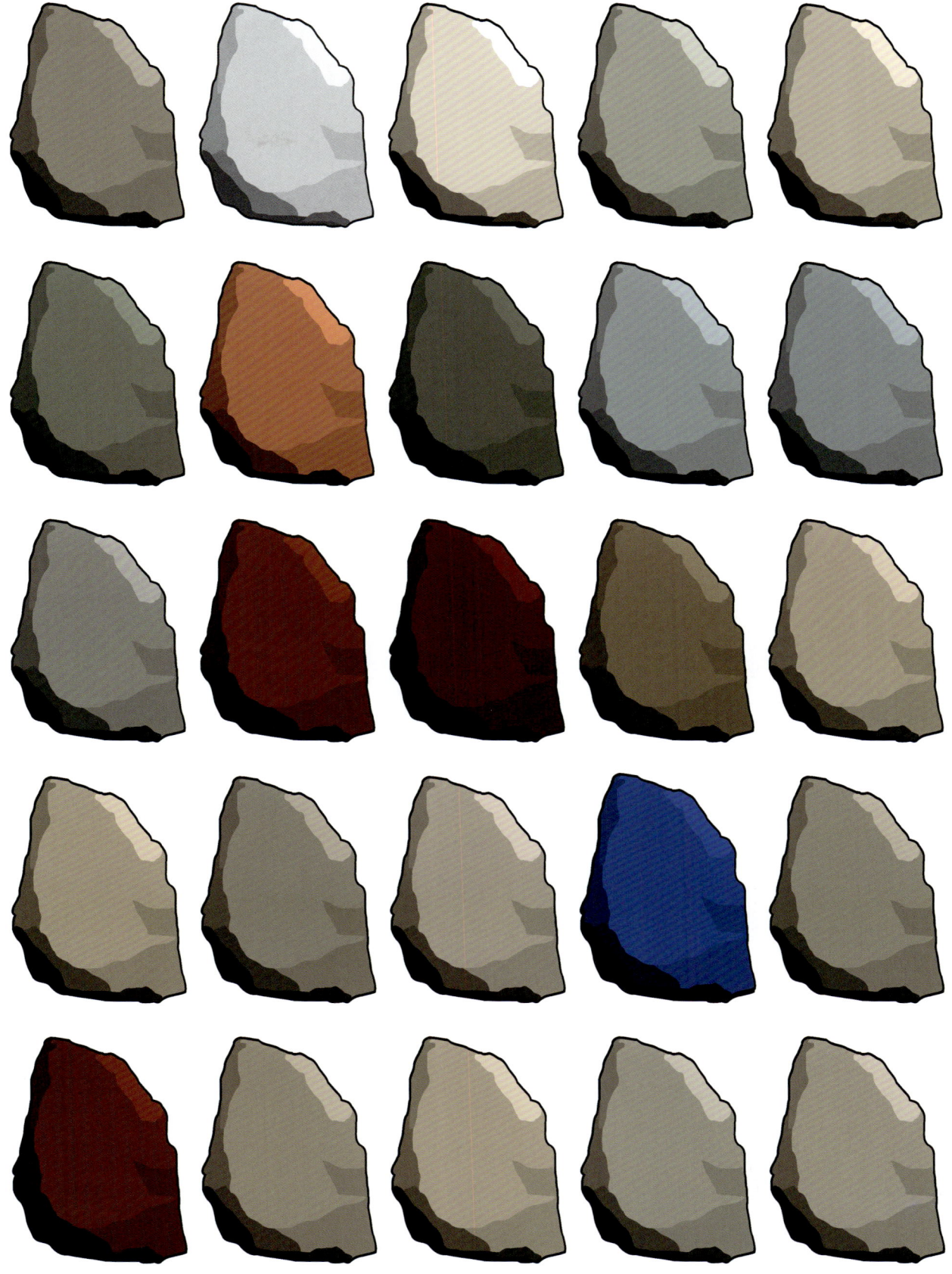

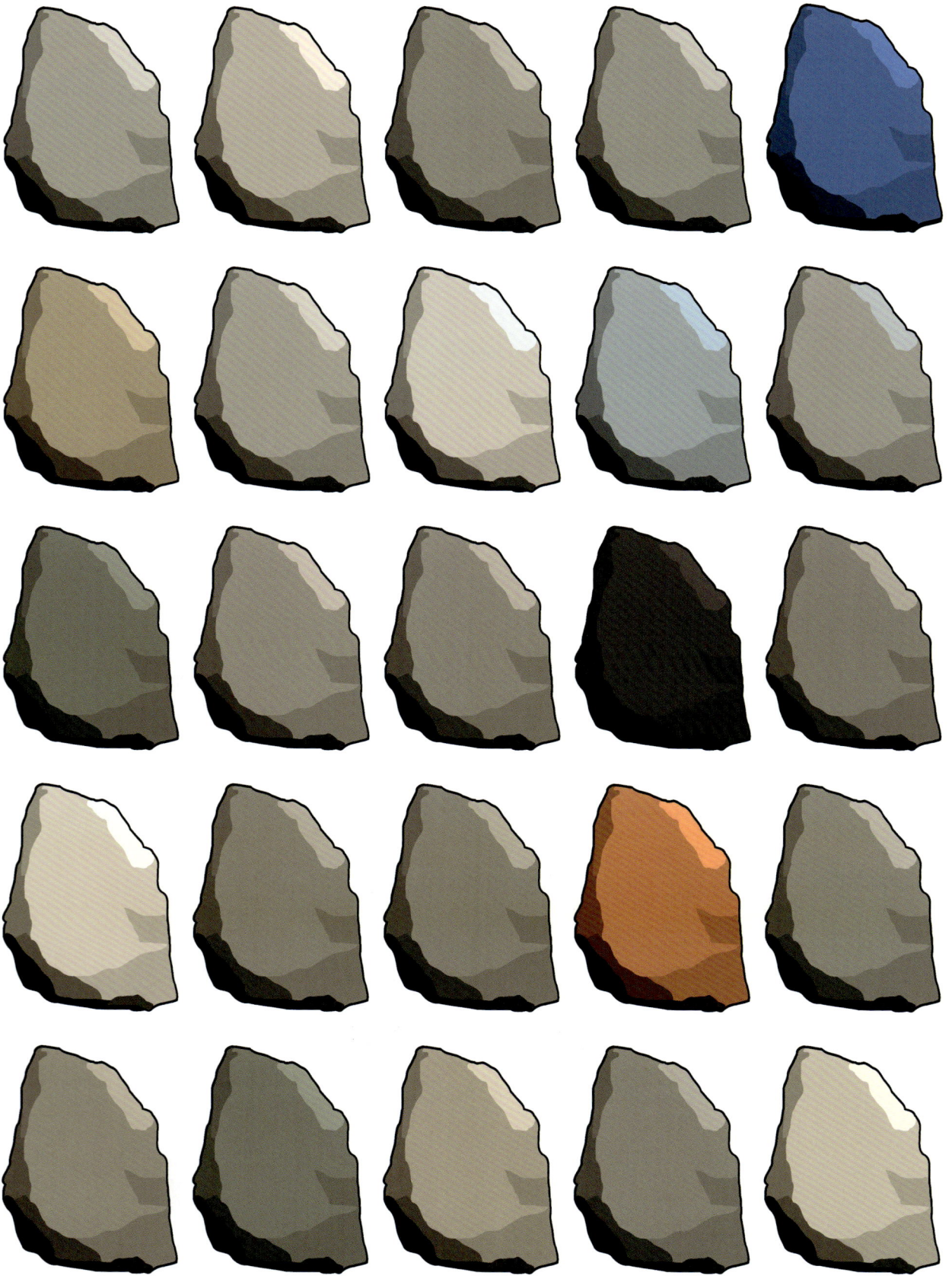

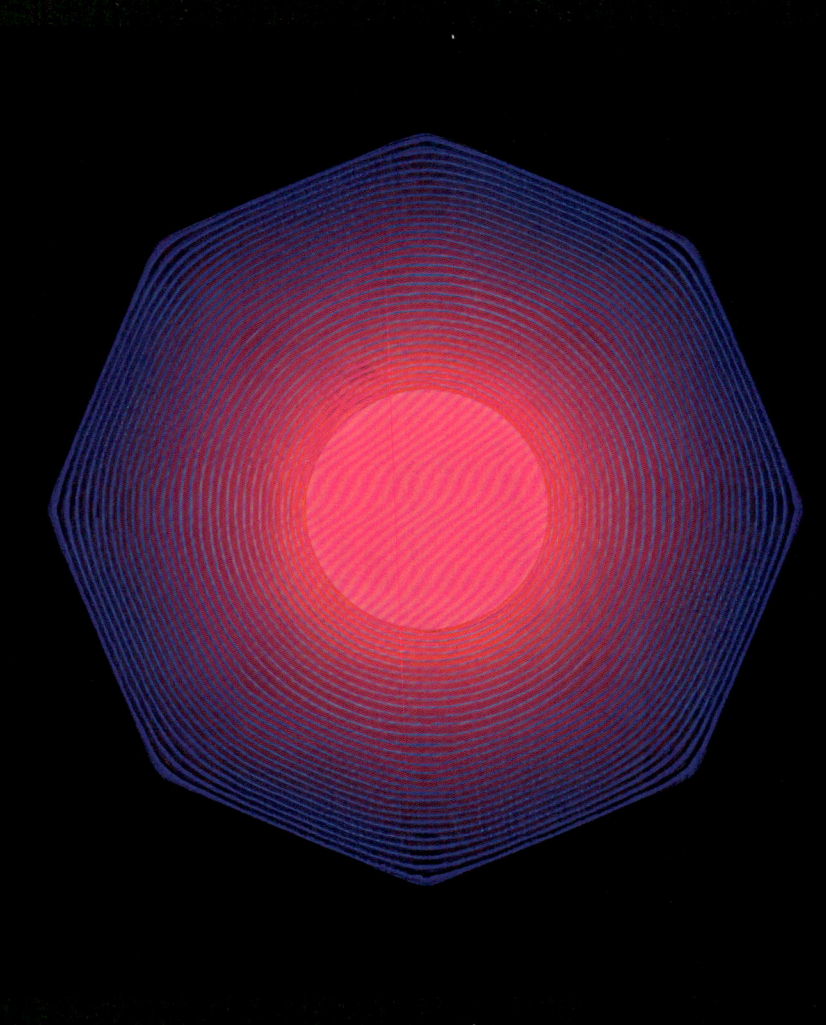

ROBERT ALICE

# ON QUANTUM

Art's Newest Chain: A History & Theory of Early NFTs

*So I came up with this word "scenius" — and scenius is the intelligence of a whole ... operation or group of people. And I think that's a more useful way to think about culture, actually. I think that — let's forget the idea of "genius" for a little while, let's think about the whole ecology of ideas that give rise to good new thoughts and good new work.*

Brian Eno
Sydney Luminous Festival, 2009

**01.00** ▶
Kevin McCoy
*Quantum*, 05-02-2014 21:27:34
Processing, GIF
Namecoin, N2nunKeYiYeqDCunDzJ3EQQh1fbAawegPW

Stills from a lecture on Monegraph by Kevin McCoy and Anil Dash at Rhizome's Seven on Seven Conference in 2014, held at the New Museum, New York. Slide 8 shows the minting of *Primordial Loop* (2014), likely the third NFT ever minted.

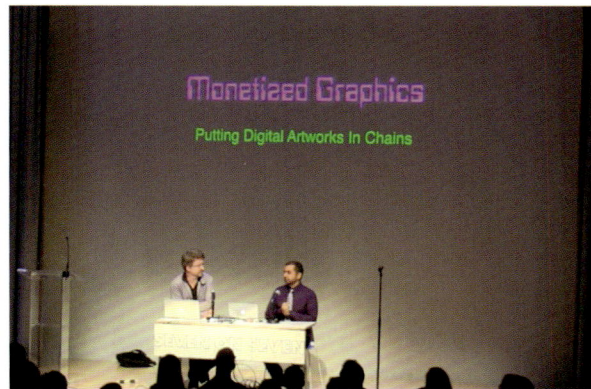
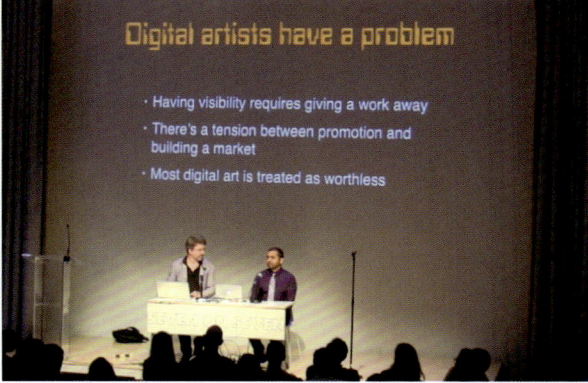
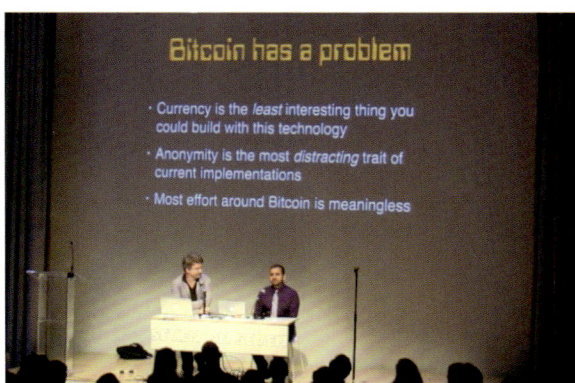
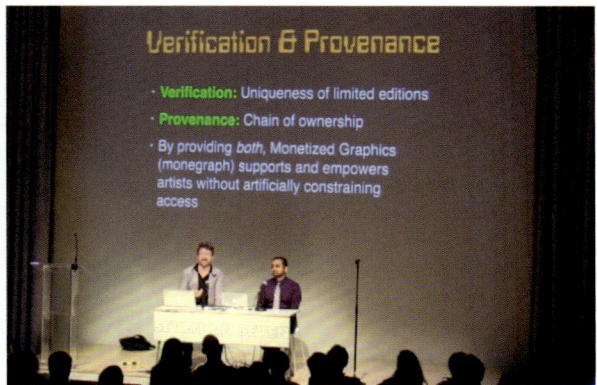
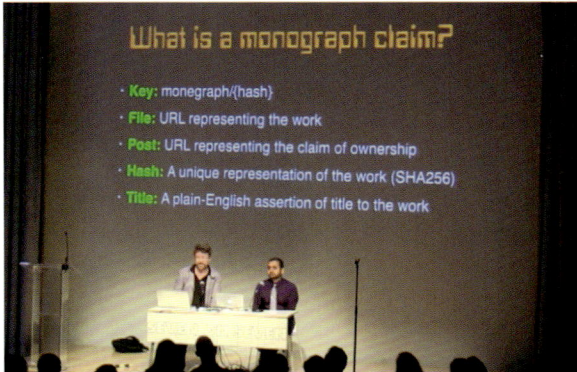
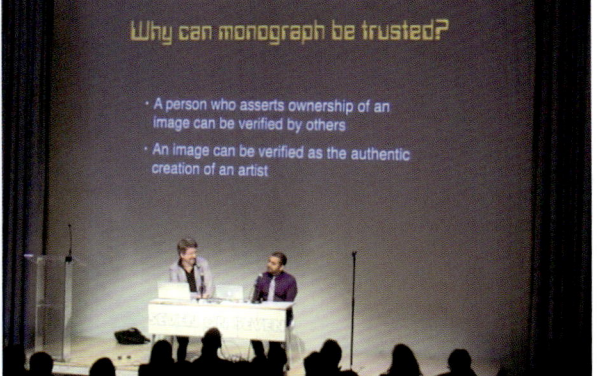
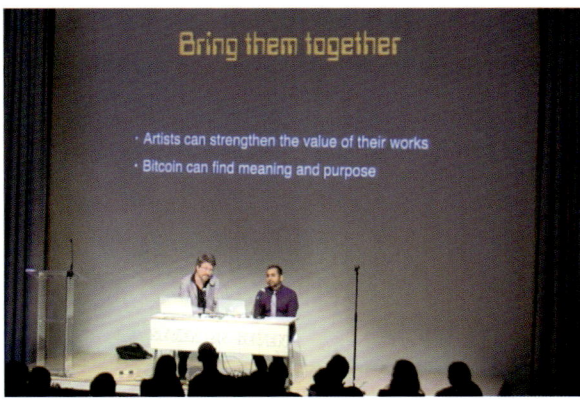
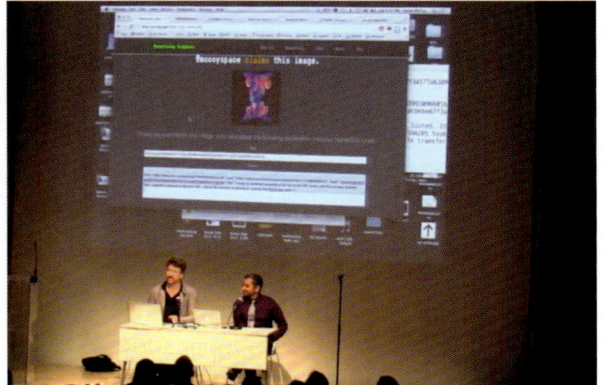

[1] *Quantum*'s position as one of the first examples of what an NFT would become — the term itself was coined three years after *Quantum* was minted — is derived from a consensus of opinion from a broad, yet reasonably new community of curators, researchers, "NFT archaeologists" (to take the term from Adam McBride), and legacy institutions. Indeed, *Quantum*'s authentication on the blockchain, via a transferable token registering ownership, public declaration, and a link leading to the artwork, is proto-identical in architecture to our current sense of NFTs. The major area in which it departs from our modern idea of an NFT is 1) in the fact that control of the token expires every 36,000 blocks (~200–250 days) and then had to be reclaimed due to the architecture of Namecoin and 2) that the media file is not stored on a decentralized database. Though contemporary artists working in the crypto art space at the time were aware of *Quantum*'s creation, Rhea Myers (see Rhea's useful essay "Regarding Quantum," at https://rhea.art/regarding-quantum, accessed July 25, 2022) and Simon Denny being two notable names, the consensus around its status has solidified over the course of a number of years of blockchain-based research. To date, no project has been found with the same intentionality and attention that it brought. The only project with a viable claim to date to be an antecedent is the anonymous Punycodes project in 2011 and iRyanBell's *fuckyea* (2010). While Punycodes carried with it a number of small creative gestures (emojis of faces and body parts) in Punycode ASCII, although it was not explicitly an art project and the ASCII generated on-chain were already well-known standardized uses of the vernacular. *Fuckyea* was an appendage of the famous meme on Namecoin — closer in scope to the ASCII Bernanke — interestingly unlike *Quantum* it was fully onchain. *Quantum* is though the first blockchain registered discrete media art by a known artist, where crucially its registry is also part of the artistic statement of the work.

[2] The term *non-fungible token* appears to have first been used on Twitter in August 2017 by French crypto-investor Pierre Entremont. Dieter Shirley, co-creator of the seminal CryptoKitties project, also coined the abbreviation *NFT* around this time.

[3] In 2014 (the same year that McCoy minted *Quantum*), at one of the first major digital art auctions — the Phillips x Tumblr auction titled *Paddles On* (July 3, 2014) — the top price paid for a digital work of art was £7,500 (for Quayola's *Topologies — Tiepolo, Immacolata Concezione* [2010]). The record that year for a digital work at public auction was Bill Viola's *Dolorosa* (2000) at Sotheby's New York for $149,000 — one of only a handful of artists working in digital media with mainstream commercial success. The same year, the most expensive physical work of art sold at auction was Andy Warhol's *Triple Elvis* (1963), which sold for $81,925,000.

[4] For more on the history of collecting digital art, please read: Michael Bouhanna and Jehan Chu's chapter, "On Collecting."

[5] Walter Benjamin, "The Work of Art in the Age of Mechanical Reproduction," trans. Henry Zohnin in Hannah Arendt ed. *Illuminations* (New York: Schocken Books, 1969).

In the long timeline of art, there are a small community of works that serve as genesis blocks to their own chain of art history. They become historical forks in cultural direction; forks that usher in new movements which, block by block, mint by mint, establish new art histories. Often unknown at the time, these works close chapters on the art histories that came before, while anchoring a new flourishing of artistic creativity. They occupy an important position: they came first. Pulsing with color, a raw beacon to a new era, Kevin McCoy's *Quantum* (2014) **[01.00]** is such a work. Minted by the artist on May 2, 2014 21:27:34 — or more precisely, Namecoin Block 174923 — the idea of NFT art quietly dawned.[1] What a noise it makes today.

Beyond its status as one of the earliest of these records, *Quantum*'s aesthetics, its medium, and its creator provide us a lens through which to analyze and lay out not just the early history of NFTs and their prehistory, but also a deeper understanding of what NFTs are.[2] As with the genesis of any idea or movement, one can also read into it the longer history of this act of creation. What drove McCoy to transition his long-standing digital practice onto the blockchain? Why was an artist whose work sits in the collections of the MoMA and the Metropolitan Museum of Art exploring an obscure and highly disruptive technology more popularly associated at the time with darknet marketplaces? The conclusions offered will reflect on the nature of NFTs, practically and theoretically, and how the early history of this still-fractured movement provided the conceptual and literal framework for one of art history's profound technological breakthroughs.

## Aura, Commerce, and Digital Art

The answer lies in Kevin and Jennifer McCoy's (his collaborator and wife) medium of expression: the pixel. They are digital artists, creative hackers who were early explorers of computers, code, and the new compositions and criticisms these systems could create. Digital art around the turn of the 21st century occupied an anxious position within the dual arenas of art: the public and the private. While it was respected curatorially in public institutions, in the private spheres of commerce, digital art lay victim to its very nature.[3] Both immaterial and infinitely replicable, only major institutions and the most adventurous of collectors collected digital art.[4] Digital artists and creators were the outcasts of the art market; simply put, they were not getting paid.

Why was this? In his well-known essay of 1935, Frankfurt School thinker Walter Benjamin (1892–1940) addressed the loss of the "aura" of original artworks in the era of mechanical reproduction. Writing on the advent of photography and film, his work foregrounded the development of a tiered system in which reproducible images or media were not deemed to have the same aura of authenticity, or inherent cult value, as unique works of art.[5] The rise of the internet, in which the very idea of the original was lost among "a universal fungibility of things" (to take the words of Benjamin's contemporary Theodor Adorno [1903–1969]), further complicated the question of whether digital art ever held the aura of originality.[6] It is a blockchain's base characteristics, its ability to make an immaterial work of digital art provably ownable and therefore communally (and artificially) scarce, that reinjects this promise of *aura* in the fabric of the digital object. As critics such as Brian L. Frye and Adam Geczy have argued, blockchain technology reshrouds digital artworks in a new kind of aura: the aura of ownership or *clout*.[7]

Before minting *Quantum* and his two following NFTs, *Cars* (2014) and *Primordial Loop* (2014) at the Seven on Seven Conference **[01.01]**, McCoy realized this, in what he calls "the fundamental shift that Bitcoin creates": the "magic alchemy" by which "everything is open-source and transparent [...] and yet there is still undeniably this idea of specific ownership."[8] This combination of the public (democratic) and private (economic) lives of a digital artwork solves for the Web 1.0 utopian goals of free circulation of images and culture, while Web3 now reestablishes the individual (in this case, the digital artist) as the locus of economic centrality. Digital artwork can now be shared and owned at the same time.[9] While Benjamin saw an artwork's reproducibility as the loss of the aura of the original, the "exhibition value," to use Benjamin's term, or virality of NFTs within contemporary media in fact works to install greater aura around the original. Retweets are consensus, likes are confidence. Clout is attention. And yet this is no panacea, for the aura of digital art is now challenged not by the virality of reproduction, but by the intimacy of price.

The birth of NFTs came out of a century of exploration and experimentation regarding how an (increasingly dematerialized) artwork can be owned and exchanged: the central question that drove McCoy to develop his "monetized graphics."[10] The blockchain made possible a process that artists of all mediums have been attempting to implement for decades: one in which the provenance of even the most immaterial conceptual and digital works could be traced and verified, and the sales of future works controlled.

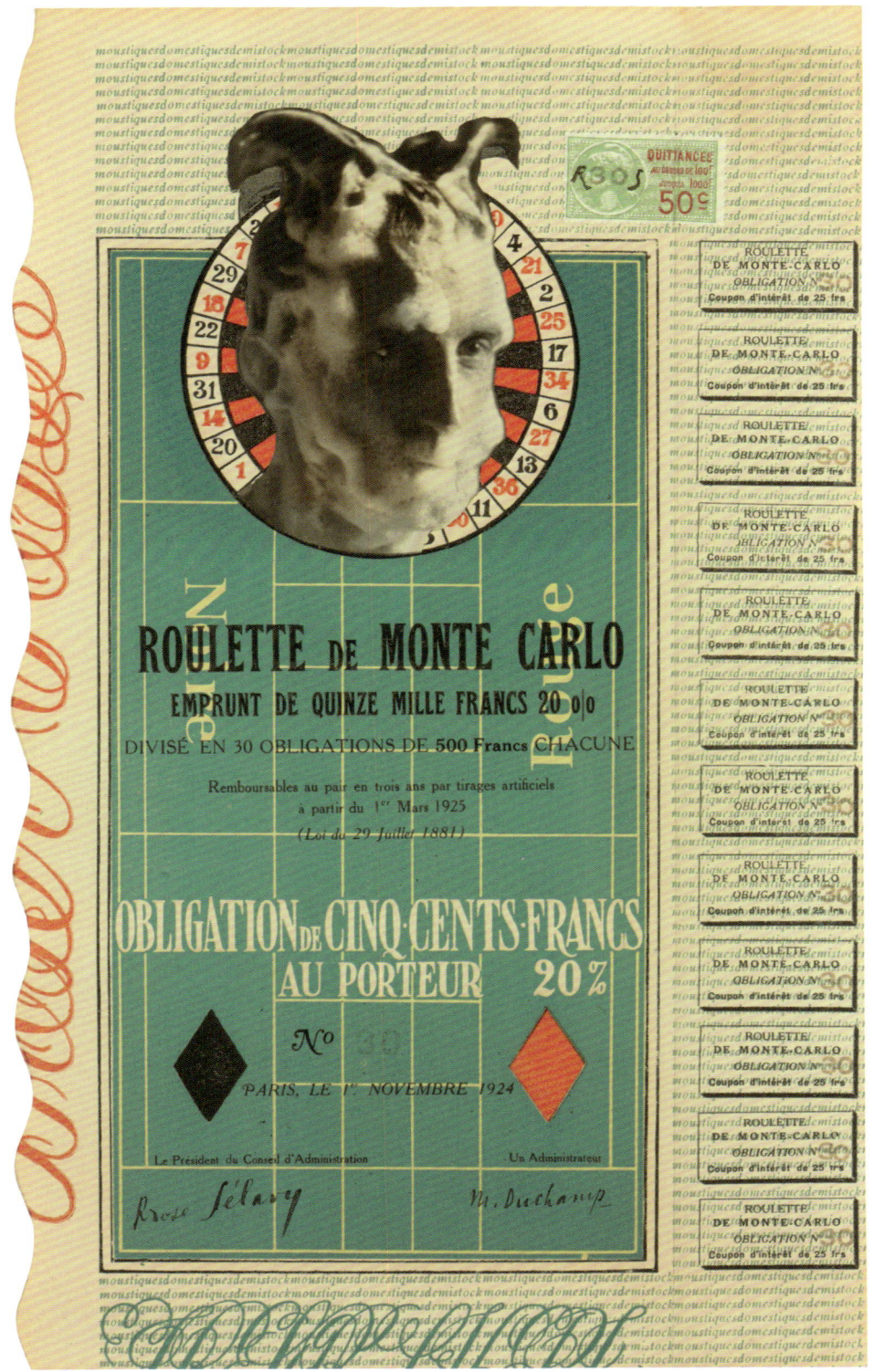

6  Octave Larmagnac-Matheron, "NFTs: A Digital Antifungal?," *Philonomist*, March 25, 2021, https://www.philonomist.com/en/article/nfts-digital-antifungal?check_logged_in=1.

7  See Adam Geczy, "What can Adorno and Walter Benjamin teach us about NFTs & Art," *its(t)artswithadam*, 2021, https://www.itstartswithadam.com/blog/what-can-adorno-amp-walter-benjamin-teach-us-about-nfts-amp-art; and Brian L. Frye & Primavera De Filippi, "In Conversation: Brian L. Frye & Primavera De Filippi," *Outland*, April 5, 2022, https://outland.art/brian-frye-primavera-de-filippi/.

8  Kevin McCoy, interview with the author, March 11, 2022.

9  Clare Veal, "Bringing the Land Foundation Back to Earth: A New Model for the Critical Analysis of Relational Art," *Journal of Aesthetics & Culture,* Vol. 6, No. 1 (2014), https://doi.org/10.3402/jac.v6.23701.

10  A portemanteau of which became "Monegraph." More information on Monegraph can be found in the chapter, "On Building."

11  Chan's *Digital Zones of Immaterial and Pictorial Sensibility* (2017) updated Klein's work by transforming the empty space into a blank screen and the receipt into an NFT on the Ethereum blockchain, pointing to the increasingly abstract notion of ownership in the digital — and immaterial — age.

12  In May 2012, art collector Roderic Steinkamp filed a lawsuit against dealer Rhona Hoffman over the loss of the certificate of authenticity for the Sol Lewitt *Wall Drawing #448* (1985) that he had purchased the year prior. At the heart of the legal dispute stood a debate over what constitutes the value of an immaterial artwork — the historical documentation or the certificate of authenticity? A debate that loses its sense when the two become intertwined, as they do with NFTs. See Daniel Grant, "Collector Files Lawsuit Over Lost Paperwork," *Artnews* (2012), https://www.artnews.com/art-news/news/collector-files-lawsuit-over-lost-lewitt-paperwork-578/.

13  For more on the conceptual roots of NFTs, see Massimo Franceschet, Giovanni Colavizza, T'ai Smith, Blake Finucane, Martin Lukas Ostachowski, Sergio Scalet, Jonathan Perkins, James Morgan, Sebastián Hernández; "Crypto Art: A Decentralized View," *Leonardo*, Vol. 54, No. 4 (2021): 402–405, https://doi.org/10.1162/leon_a_02003.

14  It is worth noting, however, that some concerns have emerged around the security of digital assets on the blockchain as a result of hacking incidents. See Moxie Marlinspike, "My First Impression about Web3," *Moxie*, January 7, 2022, https://moxie.org/2022/01/07/web3-first-impressions.html.

15  The lack of standardization across platforms means that royalties aren't always distributed on the secondary market. In fact, until recently, centralized platforms didn't always collect royalties, or at least not at a suitable rate for artists. Matt Kane's 2020 "Letter to Platforms," signed by a dozen NFT artists, set the new standard to a minimum of 10% resale royalties for all artists.

16  Sal Qadir and Gabe Parker, "NFT Royalties: The $1.8bn Question," *Galaxy*, October 21, 2022, https://www.galaxy.com/research/insights/nft-royalties/.

17  Ibid.

01.03
Seth Siegelaub and Robert Projansky
*The Artist's Reserved Rights Transfer and Sale Agreement*, 1971 Printed document, 8 pages, 30 × 26 cm

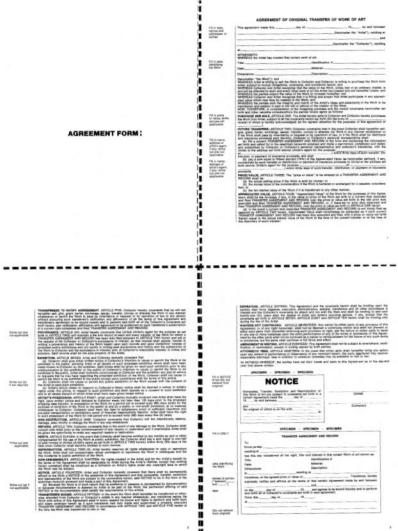

The importance of ownership and trade in art have historically been encapsulated in several important conceptual artworks predating the blockchain. In 1924, Marcel Duchamp (1887–1968) played with the nature of certification as art in his *Monte Carlo Bonds* **[01.02]**, which took the form of a legal document entitling owners to collect shares in the artist's gambling enterprise. Subject to further study in the chapter "On Chain," Yves Klein's (1928–1962) *Zone of Immaterial Pictorial Sensibility* (1959) pushed this relationship into the arena of the absurd, asking collectors to buy a portion of empty gallery space in exchange for gold. They would in turn receive a "receipt" (a check) for the work. In 2017, the work would be re-created on the blockchain by Mitchell F. Chan, making it one of the earliest NFT works.[11] In the 1960s, as the art object further dematerialized, artists focused less on Duchampian gesture and more towards the practicalities of ownership. Sol LeWitt (1928–2007) and Lawrence Weiner (1924–2021) worked to devise certificates of authenticity to verify the ownership of their increasingly immaterial works.[12] Even as recently as 2011, Rafaël Rozendaal devised an art website sales contract, loosely inspired by the iconic dealer Seth Siegelaub (1941–2013), to formalize his practice of selling web-based artworks as registered domain names. One of the key promoters of conceptual art in the 1970s, Siegelaub devised his Artist's Reserved Rights Transfer and Sale Agreement in 1971 **[01.03]**, with the help of lawyer Robert Projansky. According to the agreement, artists would receive a percentage of profits from future sales of their works.[13] The paper, which predated NFTs by over 40 years, would become a conceptual and historical touchstone for artists' fight to ensure their equity; its practical legacy remains much harder to ascertain.

These attempts to verify the ownership of conceptual artworks and safeguard the economic interests of artists were important predecessors to the technological innovations of art on the blockchain. The amalgamation of the digital art object and the certificate of authenticity into one singular crypto token alleviated the issues of catalog records being lost (or falsified) and the secluded backrooms of the international art market paying little attention to royalties. Using smart contracts — the automatically executed agreements embedded in non-fungible tokens — this entire process becomes exponentially more secure and largely permissionless.[14] With each mint, catalogues raisonnés are being immutably built in real time. Authenticity certificates are only lost if the artwork itself is lost: on the blockchain, they are firmly bound together. Today, NFTs have hard-coded into their smart contracts the creator's explicit wishes, including royalties from all future sales of their NFTs, a practice much harder to enforce in the non-NFT art market.[15]

Up to October 2022, over $1.8 billion in royalties have been paid out to NFT creators on-chain.[16] And while 80% of resale revenues are made by just 482 artists or projects, the long tail of the distribution curve is also very meaningful to many working artists.[17] To understand the long-term economic import of NFTs for an artist, one can look at the case of Warhol's secondary market. Through publicly available data one can estimate that if Warhol were an NFT artist with a 10% NFT royalty then the annual revenue for his foundation would rise

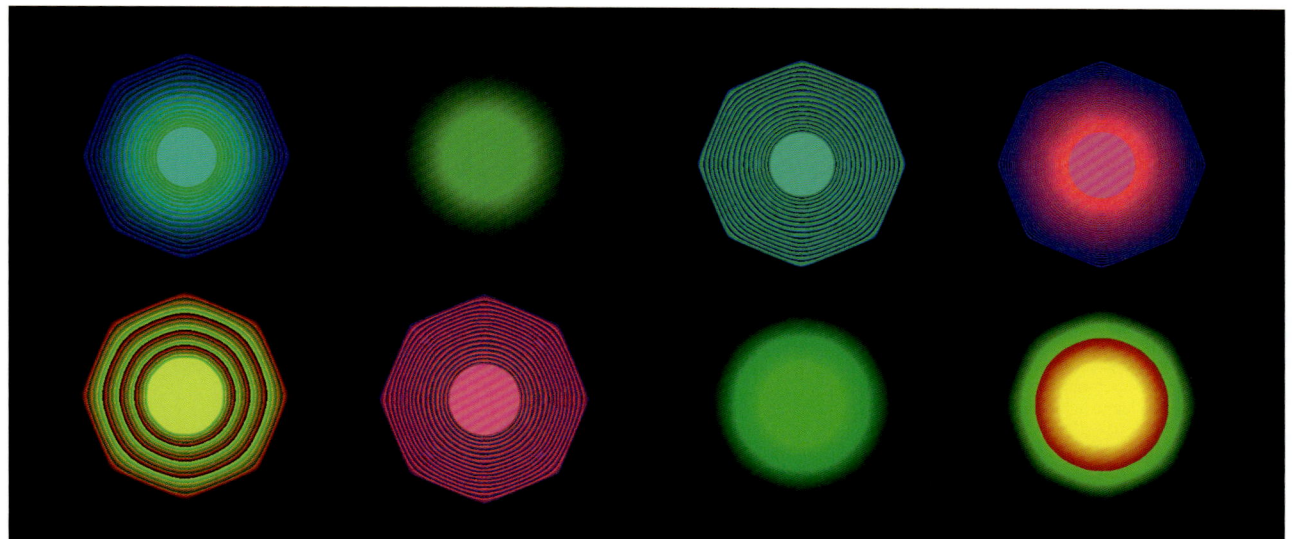

[18] This analysis was led by comparing data from the Andy Warhol Foundation and from global art market and auction reports from 2017 to 2019. In order to obtain these numbers, we calculated that over this time period, public auctions accounted for an average of 41.8% of total art market revenue. Based on the assumption that works by Andy Warhol mirrored this tendency, we were able to estimate the total sales revenue for works by Andy Warhol from his public auction results. We then compared these numbers to the annual revenue of the Andy Warhol Foundation for Visual Arts. Data from: Clare McAndrew, "The Art Basel and UBS Global Art Market Report," *Art Basel* (2018, 2019, 2020); Artprice, "Ranking of the top 500 artists by auction turnover...," *Artprice* (2018, 2019, 2020); US Department of the Treasury, Internal Revenue Service, *The Andy Warhol Foundation for the Visual Arts Form 990-T* (Washington, DC: 2017, 2018, 2019, 2020, 2021).

[19] Sal Qadir and Gabe Parker, "NFT Royalties: The $1.8bn Question," *Galaxy*, October 21, 2022, https://www.galaxy.com/research/insights/nft-royalties/.

[20] On-chain royalties can be bypassed by sending the assets and the funds in two separate transactions, but this only works in the case that both parties trust each other. There is a track record of NFTs being sold off-chain at major auction houses, in which they act as the trusted third party, without the remittance of artist royalties. Further to this, in recent times, a number of platforms are actively working to cut out the resale royalty as a competitive edge to attract collectors.

[21] The system allowed for the ownership of artworks to be registered on the Namecoin blockchain via a unique traceable key. However, it remained a precarious structure compared to today's NFTs. Ownership was embedded in the transaction as a statement and a link to a Twitter post publicly stating

from $20.8 million to $90.6 million — with no extra costs.[18] The issue though is that "royalties aren't a primitive that inherits the same on-chain permanence," as many in and outside the NFT space believe.[19] For clarity, it must be understood that blockchain-based royalties are not currently enforceable at the smart contract level and only across a platform that facilitates them. Tyler Hobbs's *QQL* (2022) was the first major NFT project to prevent transacting on 0% royalty fee marketplaces at the smart-contract level, showcasing that artists also have the power and ability to program their NFTs to only be transacted on royalty-paying marketplaces. Throughout 2023, an ideological and capitalist battle was waged as platforms competed for market share, showing how expendable NFT royalties can ultimately be in their current form. This being said, as the social consensus around royalties crystallized within NFT art communities, time and again artists have mobilized to protect these rights. For a new generation of digitally native artists, struggling with high-rent costs, less physical space to create, and an increasing portion of their cultural life shaped online, the long-term art-historical and financial incentives (though not without their challenges) baked into creative digital production are just starting to be understood.[20]

## Minting *Quantum*

At the arts organization Rhizome's annual Seven on Seven conference in New York in 2014, McCoy and his collaborator, the technologist Anil Dash, demonstrated the system they had created, called Monegraph, for registering digital artworks on an early blockchain called Namecoin — the first prototype for what NFTs would become.[21] Like many instances in the early history of NFTs, the room bristled with a mixture of skepticism, misunderstanding, and genuine excitement. During the presentation, the pair minted *Primordial Loop*, which Dash purchased for the few dollars he had in his pocket. *Quantum* **[01.04]**, along with a second work, *Cars*, had been minted the evening before. It was a GIF McCoy had made using the coding language Processing and selected from his archive as a test before the demonstration during the actual conference.

It is crucial to recognize that the first public demonstration of this new technology was to perform a sale and transfer of a work from one party to another. NFTs are not to be seen as a wholesale recalibration of digital art from the perspective of quality. They are transparent engagement of a digital artwork with the marketplace, where the dynamics of a work's purchase and trade are synonymous with its medium. This first demonstration of a proto NFT showcased the technology's commercial *aura*, and to a degree its cultural flavor: *Primordial Loop* was a GIF work from Jennifer and Kevin McCoy's project *Maintenance Web* (1997). The speculative net art project presents the fictional scenario of a gardening spaceship, the Green Field, with a focus on the cataloging of the ship's content and biographies of its crew. In this

John Whitney
*Permutations*, 1968
Computer-generated 16 mm color movie with sound

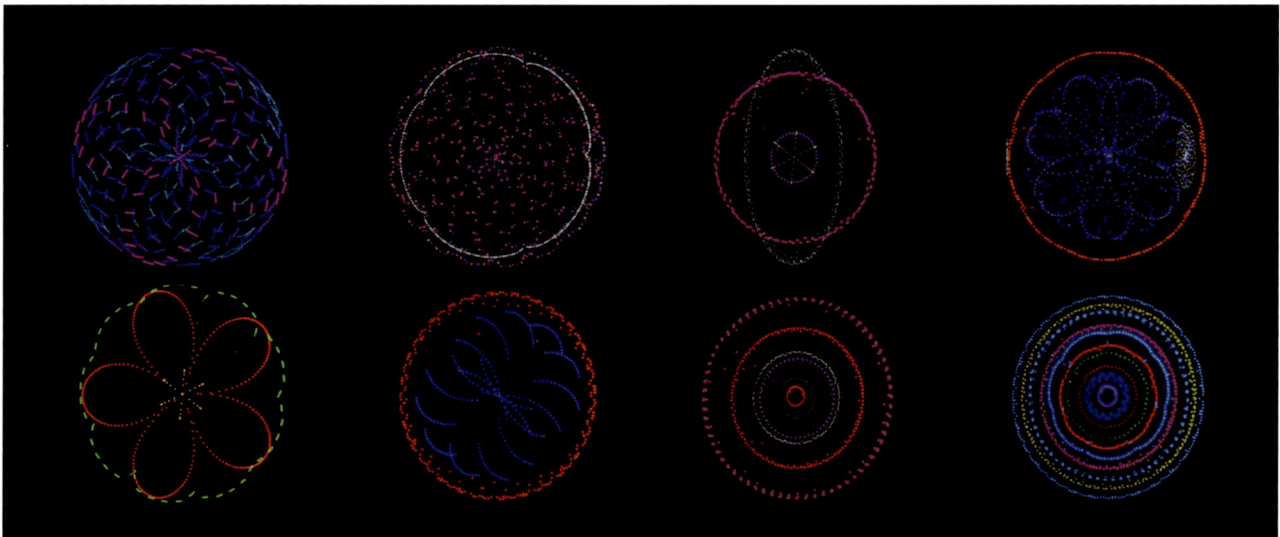

the authenticity of the concerned work. This ownership needed to be updated every 36,000 blocks (~200–250 days). This led to a lawsuit in 2021 when *Quantum* was sold at auction via an ETH token. As its name had not been claimed on Namecoin since 2015, another user attempted to take advantage of the flaw and assert ownership over the original work, provoking interesting legal questions about immutability, token standards, and copyright law. More information about how Monegraph works can be found in the "On Building" chapter. For more information on *Quantum*'s architecture see Rhea Myers's essay referenced in footnote 1.

[22] David Greer, "Quantum," *Mccoyspace*, 2021, https://www.mccoyspace.com/project/125/.

[23] For a detailed study of the blockchain as a medium ripe for conceptual engagement, please read Rhea Myers's essay "On Chain." It is also important to recognize that Whitney et al. sit not just at the aesthetic basis of the NFT space but also its technical basis more broadly. Their early experiments, particularly at Bell Laboratories and Technische Universität Stuttgart, would seed the research and development of computer graphic tools that would culminate in the programs used across the contemporary NFT landscape today. Adobe Suite, 3D modeling softwares such as Cinema 4D and Maya used by Beeple and Serwah Attafuah, and node-based programs such as Houdini and Touch Designer used by Brendan Dawes and Ix Shells, all find their roots however obliquely in developments such as Ken Knowlton's creations of the BEFLIX programming language for bitmap computer-produced movies or Whitney's earlier modification of a WWII anti-aircraft analog computer in the late 1950s to create the first motion-photography. These early pioneers were creating their own paintbrushes and chisels and holding

context, *Primordial Loop* was selected by McCoy specifically to inflect ideas around provenance, archiving, and science fiction within the context of the blockchain.

### *Quantum*: Looking Forward to NFTs and Backward to Computer Art

What of *Quantum* itself? Formally, the work foregrounds much of what would become central to the aesthetics often associated with NFTs. Rippling out and in like a beacon or network, it is a work about creation; a "mandala for a new age," in the words of the critic David Greer; a work that captures the spirit of a blockchain network itself, expanding and contracting as the world processes the place they want to give this contentious new technology.[22] Its pulsating ever-changing rhythms of color prefigure the generative, code-based works that now sit at the cutting edge of the NFT space, and encapsulate in no small part the palette of this new movement. Bold, brash, unfiltered acid green vibrates into cool blue; flat aggressive reds bleed into fluorescent pinks in a hexadecimal celebration of digital color. Pixelated, low-fi, and continually looping, the work speaks not just to the processes of algorithmic art but also the GIF art and glitch art movements that would be some of the first to onboard into the NFT space — led by the likes of XCOPY, Sarah Zucker, and Nicolas Sassoon. Indeed, the arbitrariness with which McCoy chose *Quantum* as this first of records hints not just at the future irreverence of the NFT community, but equally at the humble nature of the blockchain. Aesthetically and culturally agnostic, blockchains are no gatekeepers to culture, simply a record of it, moving the levers of historical and cultural permanence rightfully into the hands of artists, to accommodate their most flippant of whims.

While *Quantum* looks forward, it also looks back to the legacy of computer art that McCoy would have encountered while studying Integrated Electronic Arts at New York's Rensselaer Polytechnic Institute between 1990 and 1994. The early pioneer that *Quantum* refers back to most unmistakably is John Whitney Sr. (1917–1995), and specifically his *Permutations* (1968) **[01.05]**. Much like other early technologists-cum-artists such as A. Michael Noll, Ken Knowlton (1931–2022), Georg Nees (1926–2016), and Frieder Nake, Whitney's work prefigured much of the formal aesthetics and code-based craftsmanship of contemporary NFT practices. Indeed, it is important to note the model of technologist-cum-artist was also complemented by a number of artist-as-technologists such as Lillian Schwartz, Grace Hertlein (1924–2015), and Vera Molnár. The musicality and the rhythms of *Quantum* speak closely to the early visualizations by Whitney who, like many of his contemporaries, explored aesthetic innovations in computer graphics based around harmonics, symmetry, mathematics, and color. This legacy of formal exploration still resonates in the practices of many NFT artists today, which can also be seen at times to prioritize process over concept while fetishizing technical ability.[23]

Bitcoin's Genesis Block (Block 0) minted on 01-03-2009 18:15:05, including Satoshi Nakamoto's hardcoded link to the headline of *The Times* newspaper of the same day (see final column).

Dan Kaminsky
*ASCII BERNANKE*, 07-30-2011 04:07:58
On-chain ASCII
Bitcoin, Block 138725

```
00000000   01 00 00 00 00 00 00 00   00 00 00 00 00 00 00 00    ................
00000010   00 00 00 00 00 00 00 00   00 00 00 00 00 00 00 00    ................
00000020   00 00 00 00 3B A3 ED FD   7A 7B 12 B2 7A C7 2C 3E    ....;£íýz{.²zÇ,>
00000030   67 76 8F 61 7F C8 1B C3   88 8A 51 32 3A 9F B8 AA    gv.a.È.Ã^ŠQ2:Ÿ.ª
00000040   4B 1E 5E 4A 29 AB 5F 49   FF FF 00 1D 1D AC 2B 7C    K.^J)«_Iÿÿ...¬+|
00000050   01 01 00 00 00 01 00 00   00 00 00 00 00 00 00 00    ................
00000060   00 00 00 00 00 00 00 00   00 00 00 00 00 00 00 00    ................
00000070   00 00 00 00 00 00 FF FF   FF FF 4D 04 FF FF 00 1D    ......ÿÿÿÿM.ÿÿ..
00000080   01 04 45 54 68 65 20 54   69 6D 65 73 20 30 33 2F    ..EThe Times 03/
00000090   4A 61 6E 2F 32 30 30 39   20 43 68 61 6E 63 65 6C    Jan/2009 Chancel
000000A0   6C 6F 72 20 6F 6E 20 62   72 69 6E 6B 20 6F 66 20    lor on brink of
000000B0   73 65 63 6F 6E 64 20 62   61 69 6C 6F 75 74 20 66    second bailout f
000000C0   6F 72 20 62 61 6E 6B 73   FF FF FF FF 01 00 F2 05    or banksÿÿÿÿ..ò.
000000D0   2A 01 00 00 00 00 43 41   04 67 8A FD B0 FE 55 48    *....CA.gŠý°þUH
000000E0   27 19 67 F1 A6 71 30 B7   10 5C D6 A8 28 E0 39 09 A6   .gñ¦q0·.\Ö¨(à9..¦
000000F0   79 62 E0 EA 1F 61 DE B6   49 F6 BC 3F 4C EF 38 C4    ybàê.aÞ¶Iö¼?Lï8Ä
00000100   F3 55 04 E5 1E C1 12 DE   5C 38 4D F7 BA 0B 8D 57    óU.å.Á.Þ\8M÷º..W
00000110   8A 4C 70 2B 6B F1 1D 5F   AC 00 00 00 00             ŠLp+kñ._¬....
```

```
          ---BEGIN TRIBUTE---      Len was our friend.     P.S.  My apologies,
               #./BitLen           A brilliant mind,       BitCoin people.  He
          :::::::::::::::::::       a kind soul, and        also would have
          :::::::::::.:::.:.:::     a devious schemer;      LOL'd at BitCoin's
          :.:.''' ,,x¢W,"4x, ''     husband to Meredith     new dependency upon
          : , dWWWXXXXi,4WX,.       brother to Calvin,          ASCII BERNANKE
          ' dWWWXXXX7"   'X,        son to Jim and          :'::.:::::..:::.::.:
          lWWWXX7    __  _  X       Dana Hartshorn,         :.:.' _  __  _  '.:
          :WWWXX7 ,xXX7' "^^X       coauthor and            : ,^^_^^"x, .:
          lWWWX7, _.+,, _.+.,       cofounder and           : ' x7'       '4,
          :WWW7,. `^"_" ,^_'        Shmoo and so much       XX7             4XX
          WW",X:         X,         more.  We dedicate      XX               XX
          "7^^Xl.   _(_x7'          this silly hack to      X1 ,xxx,   ,xxx, XX
          `_ " XX ,xxWWWX7          Len, who would have     (' _,'+O, | ,o+,"
          )X- "" 4X" .___.          found it absolutely     4  "-^' X "^-'" 7
          ,W X   :Xi  _,+,          hilarious.              1,    ( )      ,X
          WW X    4XiyXWWXd         --Dan Kaminsky,         :Xx,_ ,xXXXxx,_,XX
          "" ,,   4XWWWWXX          Travis Goodspeed        4XXiX'-___-'XXXX'
          , R7X,      "^447^                                4XXi,_ _iXX7'
          R, "4RXk,  _,+                                   , '4XXXXXXXXX' _,
          TWk "4RXXi, X',x                                  Xx, """^^XX7,xX
          lTWk, "4RRR7' 4 XH                                W,"4WWx,_ _,XxWWX7'
          :lWWWk,  ^" '4                                    Xwi, "4WW7"4WW7',W
          ::TTXWWi,   Xll :..                               TXXWw, "7 Xk 47 ,WH
          -=-=-=-=-==-=-==-=-                               :TXXXWw, "), ,WWT:
          LEN "rabbi" SASSAMA                               ::TTXXWWW 1X1 WWT:.
                1980-2011                                   ----END TRIBUTE----
```

## Pre-*Quantum*: Early Artworks on the Blockchain

The history of pre-*Quantum* digital art can also be found in crypto. Even before *Quantum*, the blockchain was an arena for creative production. From the beginning of Bitcoin, early network participants felt the impulse to leave their mark on the chain. Playing with the immutability of the ledger, these acts function as a kind of futuristic cave painting or digital graffiti declaring "I was here." Indeed, the foundation of crypto — the very first block, Block 0, of the very first blockchain, Bitcoin — contains what could be argued to be a conceptual prototype of an NFT that predates *Quantum* itself. Bitcoin's founder Satoshi Nakamoto inserted in Block 0 a *link* or *hash* — 'The Times 03/Jan/2009 Chancellor on brink of second bailout for banks' — to an *artwork* — the front page of the British newspaper of that day **[01.06]**. The front page is itself held in a number of decentralized online and offline *databases* around the world. This relationship between *link*, *artwork*, and *decentralized database* is the core conceptual structure of most NFTs today. This political act — a rallying call in response to the 2008 financial crisis with its explicit commentary on too-big-to-fail bailouts — places visual culture, conceptual gesture, and the idea of an NFT at ground zero of the entire crypto movement.

The next example would come 138,725 blocks later on Bitcoin in 2011, with Dan Kaminsky's (1979–2021) ASCII portrait memorial to the cryptographer Len Sassaman (1980–2011), who tragically died by suicide that year at the age of 31 **[01.07]**.[24] Timestamped 07-30-2011 04:07:58, this is perhaps the earliest example of a coherent artwork on the blockchain. Indeed, more than two months before the *ASCII Bernanke*, on May 10, 2011, the Punycodes project, which used the Punycode ASCII character set from Unicode, saw anonymous users minting symbols and emojis to the Namecoin blockchain **[01.08]**. Punycodes is perhaps the earliest example of visual culture directly on the blockchain, though it is harder to label the digital graffiti of well-known ASCII "emojis" as intentional artistic practice. The use of ASCII in both *ASCII Bernanke* and Punycodes not only illustrates the nature of the blockchain ledger as a fundamentally text-based medium — indeed all NFTs are visual abstractions of digital code — but also the purists' interest in utilizing on-chain records to their fullest potential. It is a practice that remains artistically prized in the NFT space to this day.

These early examples of visual culture on the blockchain were sporadic, buried among the millions of transactions Bitcoin was processing each year. The idea that Bitcoin could be used for something other than transferring value was more formally proposed two years later in 2013, by a group including the future creator of Ethereum, Vitalik Buterin, as well as Israeli entrepreneurs Lior Hakim, Yoni Assia, and Meni Rosenfeld in their whitepaper, "Colored Coins."[25] The idea was to demarcate sets or individual bitcoins to distinguish them from the rest. "These bitcoins can then have special properties [...] and have value independent of the face value of the underlying bitcoins," the whitepaper explained. Among the many use cases mentioned in the whitepaper is "decentrally managing ownership of digital collectibles such as original artworks."[26] Yet it was not until 2014 and the emergence of new chains — particularly the Bitcoin forks Namecoin and Counterparty — that one starts to see a groundswell of conceptual development around the idea of an NFT.

these inventions and disruptions as equally important as the aesthetic or conceptual outputs they resulted in — it is a philosophy of technical experimentation that is still deeply rooted in NFT practices today.
[24] Dan Kaminsky's *Portrait of Len Sassaman* can be found in Bitcoin's Block 138725. Minted on 07-30-2011 04:07:58 with the hash: 0000000000000000798115f302cb5f71cfc4146b0f21b61f1461537e91dfe28483c. For more early research of cultural ephemera such as text and images on the Bitcoin blockchain, visit the excellent online explorer, *Messages from the Mines* at: https://messagesfromthemines.brangerbriz.com/.
[25] Yoni Assia, Vitalik Buterin, Lior Hakim, Meni Rosenfeld, Rotem Lev, "Colored Coins Whitepaper," December 4, 2013, https://www.etoro.com/wp-content/uploads/2022/03/Colored-Coins-white-paper-Digital-Assets.pdf.
[26] Ibid.

01.08
Unknown
*Punycode* ♂_♂, 05-29-2011 10:02:00
ASCII/Punycode
Namecoin, d/xn--ysca542m

01.09
Rhea Myers
*MYSOUL*, 11-21-2014 06:22:34
100 Counterparty Tokens
Counterparty, 1GoNR15KUWkqTyZfKTDsKeEacjLqJYJW15, MYSOUL

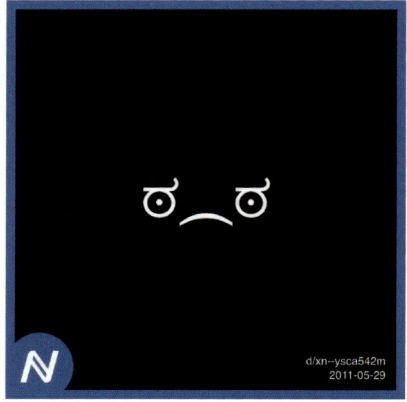

d/xn--ysca542m
2011-05-29

| MYSOUL Asset Information | | | | | |
|---|---|---|---|---|---|
| **Asset Name** | | | **Description** | | |
| MYSOUL | | | My soul. | | |
| **Last DEX Trade Price** | | **Market Cap** | **Total Supply** | **Divisible** | **Locked** |
| 0.00000000 XDP ($0.00) | | $0.00 | 100.00000000 | True | False |
| **Owner** | | | **Issuer** | | |
| DFqK1SSwcXEeMPP6t6p4ET8nGmY1Y5GiQN | | | DFqK1SSwcXEeMPP6t6p4ET8nGmY1Y5GiQN | | |

| # | Block | Time | Asset | | Quantity | Locked | Transfer |
|---|---|---|---|---|---|---|---|
| 1 | 461,334 | 2014-11-16 | MYSOUL | | 100.00000000 | False | False |

## Post-*Quantum*: NFTs as Trade and Buzz

Starting with *Quantum*, the earliest examples of this experimentation on Bitcoin's forks include records, conceptual works, and artistic currencies such as JP Janssen's *OLGA* (2014), a romantic gesture minted as a gift to the artist's then girlfriend (now wife) on Counterparty. It was released a month after *Quantum* and is even closer in format to a modern NFT. Others include Rhea Myers's *MYSOUL* (2014) **[01.09]**, which fractionalized the artist's soul into 100 units on Counterparty and Dogecoin, and Sarah Meyohas's *Bitchcoin* (2015), a photography-backed token project created on a fork of Bitcoin that gave collectors a share in the proceeds of her future practice. These early works rawly showcase the blockchain's ability to act as a conceptual medium to ask provocative questions around (collective) ownership and value, while also using the immutability of the ledger as a tool for political or emotional engagement.

A significant development in the NFT space post-*Quantum* took place outside of early artistic circles: the launch of the blockchain-based game *Spells of Genesis* (2015) on Counterparty **[01.10]**. In an uncanny fulfillment of Hal Finney's (1956–2014) prophecy, the game involved collecting trading cards: the first on-chain tokenized cards, called FD cards, were released in January 2015.[27] The cards, whose aesthetics came out of the traditional vernacular of fantasy trading cards, were presented in a gamified context where trade was central to their functionality. Echoed in subsequent projects as diverse as pure play games such as *CryptoKitties* (2017) and *Gods Unchained* (2021) to artworks such as Pak's *Merge* (2021), one sees in *Spells of Genesis* the idea that NFTs are *fast* art. The fact that the earliest cultural communities that assembled on the blockchain were engaged in the dynamics of trading cards suggests that, in antithesis to traditional value systems for art, NFTs are art meant to move. On-chain network activity is essential to their value. Trade is buzz.[28]

In *After Art* (2015), the critic David Joselit argued for the substitution of *aura* with what he defined as *buzz* arising "not from the agency of a single object or event but from the emergent behaviors of populations of actors."[29] Indeed, this prioritizing of community and network over the "agency" of a single object would be foregrounded in the development of crypto art through projects like the Rare Pepe Wallet by Joe Looney. Centered around Matt Furie's Pepe character, rare pepe cards were seeded by a pseudonymous user called Mike, who shared a trading card he had designed on the platform's Telegram chat in early September 2016.[30] The card brought together the (now contentious) internet meme with the mythology of Bitcoin in a design called the "Nakamoto Card," which depicted the mysterious cryptocurrency founder as a green-faced amphibian.[31] Within a week of the Nakamoto Card being shared, Looney had converted a Counterparty wallet he had built into a wallet for rare pepes, which, crucially, anyone could design and submit and then sell, buy, and trade. The resulting collection of rare pepe cards inserted very early on the power of meme, trade, and decentralized community into the principles of NFTs.[32] The 1,774 cards released across 36 series by up to 313 artists foregrounds the anti-aesthetic, heterotopic nature of NFTs as a global art movement, echoing the altermodern principles of Nicolas Bourriard, but within a contentiously crypto-libertarian context **[01.11]**. Based around constellations or archipelagos of creatives, the

[27] In a January 17, 1993, post on CompuServe to the Cypherpunks Mailing List, Hal Finney wrote presciently on the idea of cryptographic trading cards: "Giving a little more thought to the idea of buying and selling digital cash, I thought of a way to present it. We're buying and selling 'cryptographic trading cards.' Fans of cryptography will love these fascinating examples of the cryptographic arts. Notice the fine way the bit patterns fit together — a mix of one-way functions and digital signatures, along with random blinding. What a perfect conversation piece to be treasured and shown to your friends and family. Plus, your friends will undoubtedly love these cryptographic trading cards just as much. They'll be eager to trade for them. Collect a whole set! They come in all kinds of varieties, from the common 1's, to the rarer 50's, all the way up to the seldom-seen 1000's. Hours of fun can be had for all. Your friendly cryptographic trading card dealer wants to join the fun, too. He'll be as interested in buying your trading cards back as in selling them. Try this fascinating and timely new hobby today!"

[28] David Joselit, *After Art* (Princeton: Princeton University Press, 2013).

[29] Ibid.

[30] Mike, conversation with the author, March 17, 2022.

[31] Subject to greater exploration in "On Crypto Art," it is important to note here that the Pepe character, created by the artist Matt Furie in 2008, had an innocent history as an internet meme before becoming co-opted by right-wing extremists in around 2016. Looney and the Rare Pepe Wallet have maintained that the project had no involvement with or identification with the alt-right. For more on the fraught history of Pepe, see Scott Indrisek, "Pepe the Frog's Creator, Matt Furie, Is Trying to Save His Lovable Stoner Frog from the Alt-Right," *Artsy*, July 13, 2017, https://www.artsy.net/article/artsy-editorial-pepes-creator-save-lovable-stoner-frog-alt-right.

01.10
Spells of Genesis
*Satoshi Creator of Blockchain* (SATOSHICARD), 06-24-2015 22:09:13
Adobe Photoshop, Adobe Illustrator, iOS & Android game
Bitcoin, 1EewCNrN1oypSYZE81HBiqrjuhkLcz1qXR, SATOSHICARD

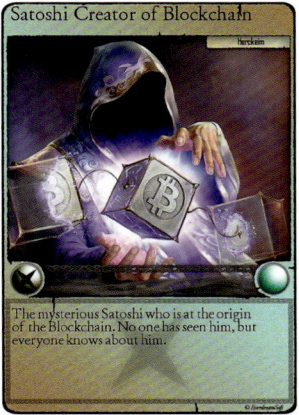

01.11
Geographical data for rare pepes
between 2014 and 2018 taken from Google

| Country | Users ↓ | Users |
|---|---|---|
| | 148,167<br>% of Total: 100.00% (148,167) | 148,167<br>% of Total: 100.00% (148,167) |
| 1. 🇺🇸 United States | 61,189 | 40.77% |
| 2. 🇬🇧 United Kingdom | 9,971 | 6.64% |
| 3. 🇨🇦 Canada | 6,933 | 4.62% |
| 4. 🇯🇵 Japan | 6,694 | 4.46% |
| 5. 🇩🇪 Germany | 5,284 | 3.52% |
| 6. 🇦🇺 Australia | 4,391 | 2.93% |
| 7. 🇫🇷 France | 3,781 | 2.52% |
| 8. 🇷🇺 Russia | 3,503 | 2.33% |
| 9. 🇪🇸 Spain | 3,099 | 2.06% |
| 10. 🇳🇱 Netherlands | 3,024 | 2.01% |
| 11. 🇮🇹 Italy | 2,521 | 1.68% |
| 12. 🇮🇳 India | 2,499 | 1.67% |
| 13. 🇨🇳 China | 2,034 | 1.36% |
| 14. 🇧🇷 Brazil | 1,815 | 1.21% |
| 15. 🇲🇽 Mexico | 1,475 | 0.98% |

project saw globalized participation from Venezuela to India, Mexico, Japan, and Australia, while the Rare Pepe Wallet was downloaded widely across every continent in the world.[33]

## Post-*Quantum*: NFTs as Community, Games, and Territory

These principles of access-to-all, global participation and the cultural decentralization of the rare pepe roadmap were to be continued by crypto art platform DADA's visual conversations in 2017 (and explored more deeply in "On Crypto Art"), and to date has built up to projects such as Dom Hofmann's bottom-up community building approach to *Loot* (2021), Tyler Hobbs and Indigo Mané's *QQL* (2022) and most recently Sam Spratt's *The Monument Game* (2023). Indeed, *Loot* — part game, part conceptual research practice — showcases the power of decentralization, community, and creative collaboration when implemented from first principles. Hofmann, another technologist-cum-artist, released 8,000 NFTs — each with nothing but eight lines of low-fi text describing eight pieces of randomized adventurer gear. No images, hierarchies, or connections were presented; they were "intentionally omitted for others to interpret."[34] Much like other projects with strong organic communities anchored by foundational origin stories, such as *CryptoPunks* (2017), Hofmann's 8,000 NFTs were released for free; collectors just had to pay the gas fee.[35] Largely in response to projects such as *Loot*, the writer and curator Kevin Buist developed a theory of what he termed "ectogames." In his words, "ectogames are NFT projects that offer elements of games — characters, gear, fictional settings, lore, strategy, and even player communities — but lack the organizing form of a game. Ectogames have some distant pre-blockchain antecedents, but they're largely an emergent phenomenon of recent NFT activity. Ectogames are not gamification — the imposition of game logic onto non-game activities. Rather, ectogames are what happens when the elements and behaviors we know from games move into new territory and coalesce into something else."[36] The viral CC0 (Creative Commons Zero) project, based solely around open-source community consensus, has gone on to produce several hundred derivative projects, narrative arcs, and platforms: an entire ecosystem of improvised interpretation with little to no direction from Hofmann. It carries elements of gamification, yet with no rules governing its play. The project and its resultant ecosystem provide a disruptive future model for the power of permissionless collaboration and showcase how NFTs can serve as the scaffolding for virtual worldbuilding.

The idea of virtual worlds or metaverses, first conjured up in the science fiction of Neal Stephenson and William Gibson, is now finding new manifestations in the NFT community. Having grown up on and with Stephenson's seminal 65,536-kilometer-long Street in *Snow Crash* (1992), many crypto builders today see the principles and architecture of Web3 as affording a glimpse at not just a decentralized metaverse, but also a digitally native exhibition context for NFTs. With the launch of Ethereum on July 30, 2015, creatives hacking at the edges of the blockchain's infrastructure to put art on the blockchain found themselves with a platform (Ethereum), set of tools (Solidity), and medium (smart contracts) purpose-built for creativity. Although Vitalik Buterin never foresaw the importance of

[32] Massimo Franceschet, Giovanni Colavizza, T'ai Smith, Blake Finucane, Martin Lukas Ostachowski, Sergio Scalet, Jonathan Perkins, James Morgan, and Sebastián Hernández, "Crypto Art: A Decentralized View," *Leonardo*, Vol. 54, No. 4 (2021), https://direct.mit.edu/leon/article/54/4/402/97295/Crypto-Art-A-Decentralized-View.

[33] Across the 36 series, there were over 313 unique issuance addresses, but some artists used multiple addresses so the total number of artists is probably in the mid- to high 200s. Data sourced from Joe Looney, June 10, 2022.

[34] Dom Hofmann (@dhof), "Loot," Twitter, August 27, 2021, 7:04 p.m., https://twitter.com/dhof/status/1431316631934967815?lang=en.

[35] For a full-scale study of *CryptoPunks*, please see the chapter "On Avatars."

[36] Kevin Buist, "What's Their Game?" in *Outland*, December 9, 2021, https://outland.art/blitmap-loot-ectogames/.

01.12
Etheria
*Various Etheria Artworks*,
2015–2022
ThreeJS
Ethereum, Various addresses

01.13
EtherRocks
*EtherRock #1*, 12-26-2017 02:24:27
Clipart rock
Ethereum,
0x41f28833Be34e6EDe3c58D1f597bef429861c4E2, 1

01.14
Kevin Abosch
*IAMA Coin*, 01-08-18 18:21:44
ERC-20
Ethereum,
0xD1cdB25428bF06f52bfe3af777C9B1e848f08A37, IAMACOIN

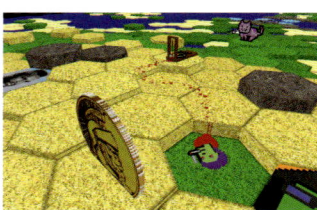
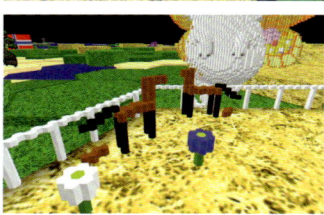
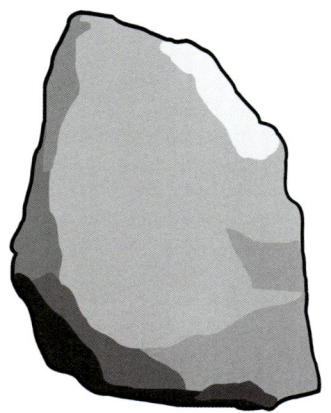

```
function IAMACOIN(
  ) {
  totalSupply = 1000000000000
  balances[msg.sender] = 1000
  name = "IAMACOIN";
  decimals = 18;
  symbol = "IAMA";

}
```

NFTs, it is of little surprise given its design that NFTs have become Ethereum's first "killer app." The first NFT projects on Ethereum were not conceptual smart contract-based works (although they would come) but early explorations of the metaverse ideal. The first of these — launched on August 7, 2015, and only unearthed by NFT archaeologist Wilt Chamberlain in September 2021 — was a project called *Terra Nullius* (2015), a Latin term meaning "nobody's land." The "terra nullius" principle is used in international law to justify territorial claims; similarly, by minting an NFT using the contract, users could stake a claim on the newly discovered realm of the blockchain and customize their stake by writing a short message. The project harks back to the ASCII art of the early days of Bitcoin, with each NFT simply taking the form of plain text — phrases often referencing internet and crypto culture, from 'looksrare' to 'Baby Vitalik'.

The notion of occupying a space on the blockchain drove these early projects. The first metaverse land project on Ethereum, *Etheria* (2015) **[01.12]**, for instance, required players to buy tokenized tiles on which they could then build, with all the data stored on-chain for the first time. While in *Terra Nullius* one sees the conceptual roadmap for the idea of digital ownership as itself a form of territorial claim (in the way domain names were in the late 1990s) that would later mature into areas such as Ethereum Name Service (ENS), in *Etheria* one sees the first glimpses of decentralized land ownership and the construction of virtual worlds. The development of Cryptovoxels (2018), Decentraland (2020), Somnium Space (2018), and projects such as Fvckrender's *LVCIDIA* (2021/2022) later would go on to showcase, in equal measure, NFT's role in defining territory as both space and identity in the world of Ethereum.

Early Ethereum-based projects, however experimental and raw by today's standards, were orders more complex than blockchain-based digital art on pre-Ethereum chains. With better (but far from perfect) infrastructural plumbing in place, *CryptoPunks* (10,000 avatars) and then *CryptoKitties* (unlimited) showcased the possibilities of networks of collectors ten or one hundred times larger than the rare pepes or McCoy's Monegraph communities coming together, collecting, trading, and building large decentralized communities around digital culture. Alongside these two well-known projects, 2017 also saw the release of numerous other collectible projects, including *Curio Cards* which launched in May, *MoonCats* in August, and *EtherRocks* **[01.13]** later that year in December.

Indeed, the natural equation of collectibles — with all their logical rarities and value hierarchies — and the empirical, tradable nature of tokens on the blockchain is perhaps one of the truly natural use cases of NFTs. The importance of collectibility has in turn influenced the conceptual, aesthetic, and commercial formulas of NFT artists, where rarity values and hierarchies have become a key creative trend. This gamification of NFT art is supercharged by social media algorithms and the liquidity of cryptocurrencies creating volatile trends in the attention and market share paid to particular projects and artists. The clearer the rules and hierarchies, the more confidently the market responds. In the absence of curatorial structures around the art, NFT art is becoming more constructed within its own aesthetics. Strong associations with clear semiotics and gamified dynamics within artworks allow

markets to form around projects that take this approach. Inspired by the *CryptoPunk* model, avatar projects are created with clear hierarchies and rarity structures in mind. Part of the success of algorithmic art projects such as Snowfro's *Chromie Squiggle* (2020) or Tyler Hobbs's *Fidenzas* (2021) is that they are imbued with clear collectible structures. These collectible structures present game theory as intrinsic to the community's understanding and relationship with the work.

This focus on collectibles in the early history of NFTs on Ethereum was later complemented by a flurry of art projects in late 2017 and early 2018. These works — such as Sarah Friend's *Clickmine* (2017), Kevin Abosch's two projects *IAMA Coin* **[01.14]** and *Forever Rose* (both 2018), and Jonas Lund's *Jonas Lund Token* (2018) — showcased that artists were still exploring ERC-20 token standards to create more complex artistic blockchains, conceptual tokens, and funding strategies for their studios in the style of Meyohas and Myers before them. Critical discussions, led by the seminal Furtherfield publication *Artists Re:Thinking the Blockchain* (the first major text in the field) in September 2017 focused on the blockchain, not NFTs, as both a tool and object for analysis. This critical and artistic engagement with the blockchain as a medium points towards the fact that the contemporary conception of NFTs was inaugurated only after the creation of ERC-721 in January 2018. The flagship token standard — proposed by William Entriken, Nastassia Sachs, Dieter Shirley, and Jacob Evans — gave structure and standardization to a previously fragmented concept of digital art secured on the blockchain. It would also result in the creation of platforms and tools such as OpenSea (December 2017), SuperRare (April 2018), and others to give a groundswell of artists access to this groundbreaking technology.

### Alternative Avenues for the Digital Craftsperson

When this groundswell of artists did arrive, who were they? Majoritively but not exclusively, they were artists that existed outside the mainstream, or on the fringes of the narrow scope of the art world proper. They were technologists that moonlighted as artists, or artists that worked within commercial creative communities from music to film to fashion to data visualization. Just as John Whitney Sr. balanced commercial output via his company Motion Graphics, Inc. with his personal artistic practice through residencies at places such as IBM in 1969; McCoy showcased an interest in entrepreneurialism and business when launching Monegraph in 2014 alongside his artistic practice. The early figures building crypto art tools on Counterparty, like Joe Looney, to those working with Ethereum, like Rhea Myers, created their art alongside commercial practices in engineering, programming, and the arts. Many artists profiled in this book, forming the first vanguard of the NFT space, had commercial practices prior to the ERC-721. Few were full-time professional artists. The first four artists to mint on SuperRare include Robbie Barrat, a 19-year-old AI art prodigy who'd worked for NVIDIA; XCOPY, a well-established anonymous GIF artist posting his art for free on Tumblr since 2010; Hackatao, a disillusioned art duo from Milan; and Paulius, a remote working software engineer.

Elsewhere, artists like Matt Kane left the art world for a decade to work as a web developer; Brendan Dawes held a roster of important clients for his Houdini-led data visualization practice while contributing work to the MoMA's collection; and Sarah Meyohas now straddles her artistic practice with an interest in venture capital. Subject to further study in "On Crypto Art," Sarah Zucker discussed openly during a lecture at the Hammer Museum in 2022 how she had operated a "faith-based workflow […] of exposure" around the strategy of "make cool shit and then wait for emails."[37] These were artists who worked commercially because the cultural attention they received for their practices translated into large "content-creator" audiences, but not necessarily into financial value. As McCoy's Monegraph presentation at Seven on Seven in 2014 observed, prior to the advent of NFTs, "having visibility required giving away work."[38]

This new ecosystem affords greater optionality to the creatives confined by commercial constraints. In this, the focus of what could be termed the "NFT movement" is not on the narrow prescriptions of a curatorial elite, but on a celebration of art, at all levels, of all types, in all geographies, and to all audiences. As described further in the following chapter, it is this that stands as the pillar of the crypto art movement. It is NFT's popularization, and the corresponding democratization of (digital) artists' access to a market, that in turn shines a light on the overwhelming majority of artists and arts economies that sit outside of the gallery system.

Digital creatives are now either working full time as artists or having a creative output alongside their commercial output, often under a pseudonym. Indeed, creatives have used NFTs to elevate and market themselves back into commercial environments, except now the power structure has upended, brands are coming these creatives for clout rather than craft.

[37] Sarah Zucker (@thesarahshow), "When the resources are flowing you wanna be the one with a bucket," Twitter, June 17, 2022, 5:49 p.m., https://twitter.com/thesarahshow/status/1537839957795999744.

[38] Rhizome, "Seven on Seven 2014: Kevin McCoy & Anil Dash," Vimeo, 2014, https://vimeo.com/96131398.

[39] Mike Winkelmann, "About," *Beeple-Crap*, accessed June 29, 2022, https://www.beeple-crap.com/about.

[40] The *Everydays* themselves form something of a kaleidoscopic visual diary and place Beeple within the lineage of diarists and irreverent contemporary scene painters from Pieter Bruegel the Elder (1525–1569) and his disciples through to William Hogarth (1697–1764). Blending a highly honed skill set and instantly recognizable visual language, with entrepreneurial skill and opportunism, Beeple presents in his prolific output a contemporary Warhol for the digital age. Reminiscent of the societal reportage of Warhol's celebrity portraits in the 1960s, and Philip Guston's (1913–1980) political reportage in his Nixon drawings, Beeple's work is uniquely flavored with a distinct sense of apocalyptic pop and light-hearted but dark political engagement. In all the various studios I have spoken to Beeple, the only constant is the presence of two large television monitors playing 24-hour American news channels behind him. So central to the understanding of the current American political and cultural landscape, the American news cycle inflects Beeple's work with the currency of the everyday, providing relevancy and contention in equal measure. Framed by the algorithms of social media, bold compositions and strong color palettes create attention-inducing imagery laced with irony and pun. His work, which borrows heavily from Disney, Marvel, and the history of cartoon and science fiction, is reminiscent of the "high entertainment" that influential American arts teacher David Robbins termed "conceptual art for the masses." Philosopher Boris Groys, in *On the New* (1992), and artist Artie Vierkant, in *The Image Object Post-Internet* (2010), both artfully articulate the tension between the extraordinary and the everyday that find their place in equal measure in Beeple's work. "The successful (and deservedly so) mass cultural image production of our age," Groys writes, "concerns itself with attacks by aliens, myths of apocalypse and redemption, heroes endowed with superhuman powers, and so forth," Vierkant goes on to add: "But […] our ubiquitous authorship marks a point in cultural production at which the extraordinary is now also the ordinary — the myth is also the everyday." (Boris Groys, *On the New*, [Munich: Carl Hanser Verlag, 1992]; Artie Vierkant, *The Image Object Post-Internet*, 2010, https://jstchillin.org/artie/pdf/The_Image_Object_Post-Internet_a4.pdf).

**01.15**
Beeple
*EVERYDAYS: THE FIRST 5000 DAYS*, 02-16-2021 05:58:01
Cinema 4D, Octane Render, Adobe Photoshop
Ethereum, 0x2a46f2ffd99e19a89476e2f62270e0a35bbf0756, 40913

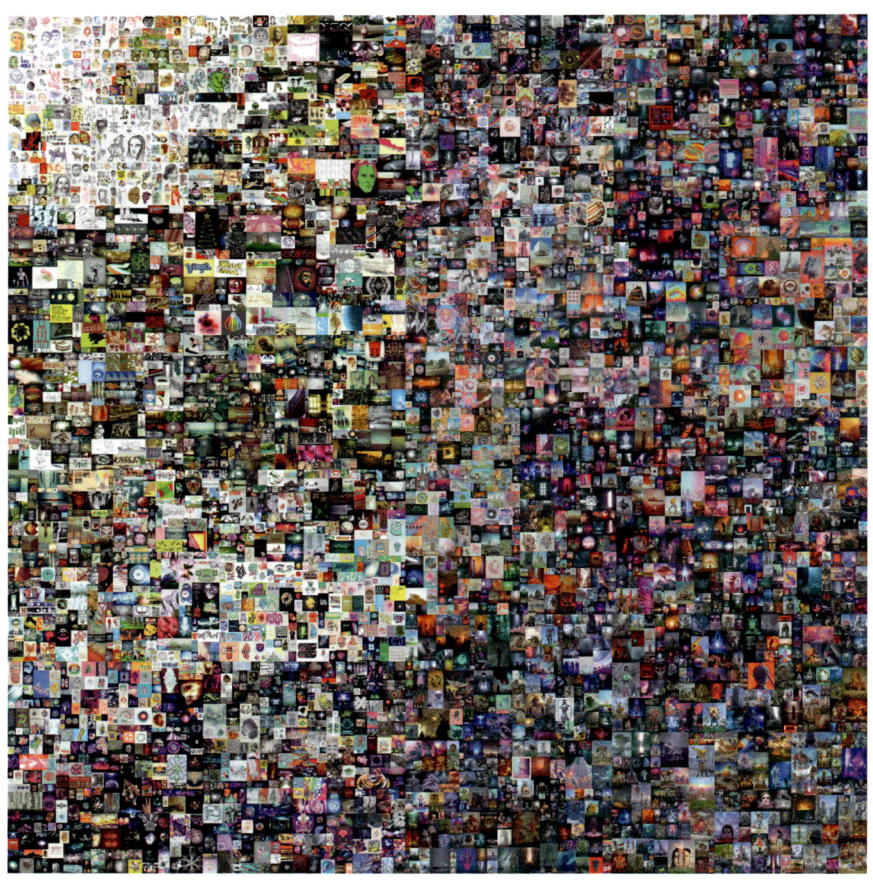

## The Case of Beeple

There is perhaps no greater example of this than Mike Winkelmann aka Beeple, who epitomizes not just the *pop*ular nature of the medium, but the early vanguard of commercial artists that have found creative freedom, and now institutional success, through NFTs. While few within the contemporary art world knew of Beeple before his landmark sale of *EVERYDAYS: THE FIRST 5000 DAYS* at Christie's in 2021 **[01.15]**, Beeple's work was highly celebrated across social media, fashion, music, popular culture, and most importantly, 3D graphics. A self-termed graphic designer, Beeple was well-known for popularizing and leading the Everyday movement, in which digital artists would make a work each day and post it on social media, a practice in line with conceptual art strategies of the 1960s but updated for the viral attention economies of social media.[39] While following in a deep lineage of artist as diarist, the Everydays were largely produced in silo to traditional art histories, instead he turned to science-fiction, pop culture and politics (for a longer analysis please see the footnote).[40] The project showcased technical improvement over time, a long-standing "proof-of-work" commitment to craftsmanship (Beeple has continued this practice since May 1 2007), daily commentary, and a shrewd strategy to remain at the top of followers' daily social media feeds.

Another bullet point in McCoy's 2014 presentation said: "there exists a tension between promotion and building a market"; for Beeple, the promotional quality of the *Everydays* across social media saw them leveraged into collaborations with Louis Vuitton during the Spring/Summer 2019 collection **[01.16]** and elsewhere with an impressive client list from Apple to Nike, but it rarely translated into sales of the artworks themselves. The *Everydays* exist as the artistic nucleus of a practice that, much like Sarah Zucker, operated equally in a faith-based workflow that included creating a vast catalog of Creative Commons work for free use by a global 3D graphics community, of which Beeple was a figurehead.

**01.16**
Photographs by Giovanni Giannoni from Nicolas Ghesquière's Louis Vuitton Ready-To-Wear Spring 2019 Collection
show featuring Beeple's *Everydays* at the Louvre Museum, 2018

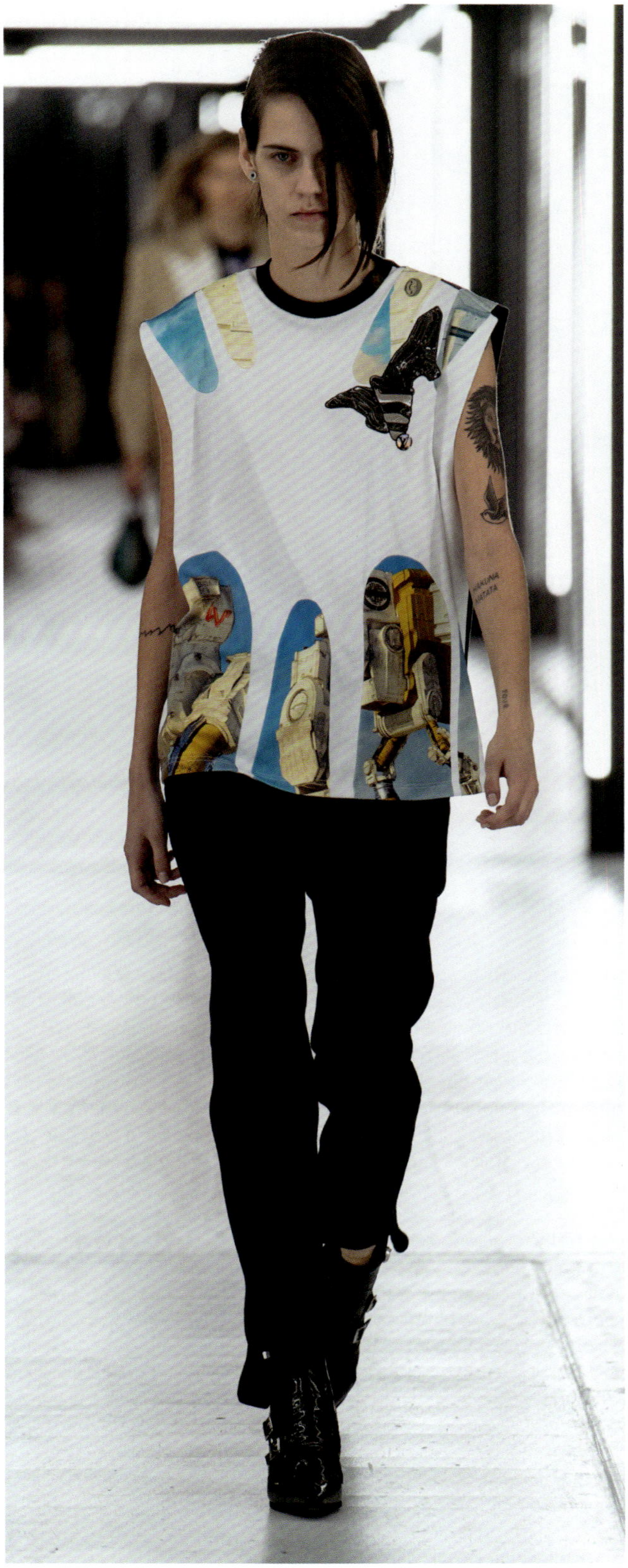

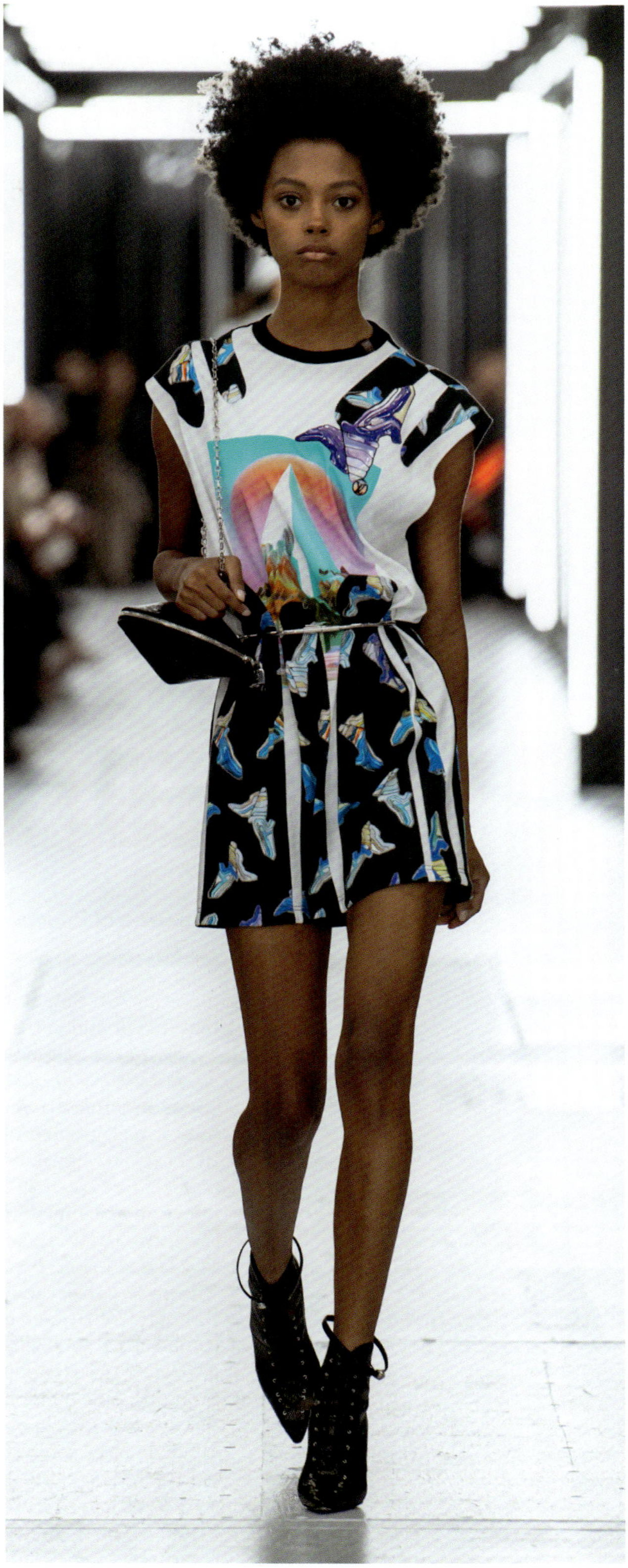

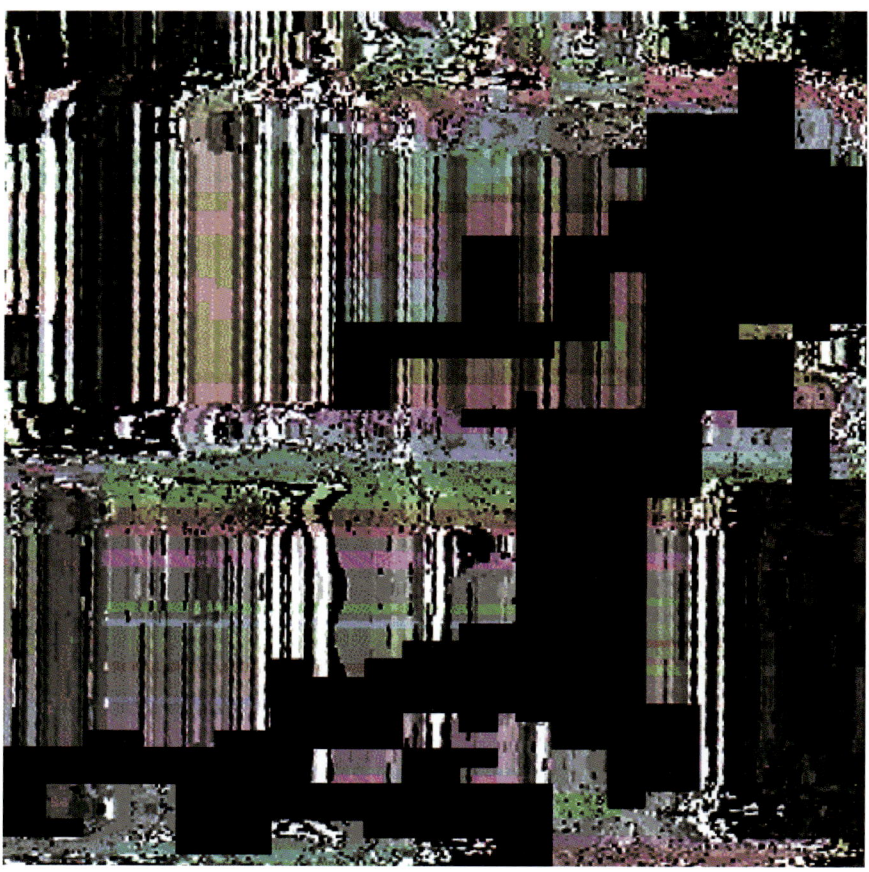

## NFTs Go Mainstream: Issues, Reexaminations, and Futures

Beeple's 2021 sale at Christie's closes the chapter on this early history of NFTs, and marks the moment that NFTs moved from a fringe community to a global frenzy, juiced by a crypto bull market and a need for digital escapism catalyzed by the global COVID-19 pandemic. Indeed, the extremity of Beeple's (and by extension the NFT community's) rapid ascent provoked not just a broad-based conversation around digital art on the global stage but equally an existential reexamination of the NFT community's cherished principles. The global attention on such a nascent and immature industry shone a light on many of the spaces' natural infrastructural and philosophical juxtapositions. The gamification of its economics juxtaposes a flattening of access to markets with the reality of a survival-of-the-fittest, winner-takes-all economic structure. Despite purporting to offer global and cultural decentralization, we still see centralization at a number of levels, economically and structurally. In the same manner as the headline-grabbing sale of *EVERYDAYS: THE FIRST 5000 DAYS* was conducted off-chain, the porting of *Quantum* to Ethereum in 2021 for posterity has created its own controversial questions, rightly or wrongly, around ownership and the immutability of (early) blockchains.[41] The case of resale royalties, one of the primary drivers for the NFT boom, has been shown by marketplaces such as Blur and OpenSea to not be as enforceable as first thought. Discussions around *aura*, *clout*, and *buzz* so central to this essay find conceptual challenges here that remain philosophically awkward and unresolved. Many of XCOPY's early works on the platform Ascribe (2015–2018) were lost permanently when the site was shut down **[01.17]**; NFTs he created in 2018 on early OpenSea competitors Rare Art and Fan Bits exist in a zombie-like form with no metadata attached to them.

While the infrastructure has developed with increasing maturity, platforms such as IPFS, where permanence is guaranteed by the structure of file hosting, and Arweave, where

[41] For more information on the Ethereum porting of *Quantum*, see Wallace Ludel, "Sotheby's and Artist Kevin McCoy sued over sale of early NFT," *The Art Newspaper*, February 4, 2022, https://www.theartnewspaper.com/2022/02/04/sothebys-kevin-mccoy-lawsuit-quantum-nft.

Simon Denny
*Backdated NFT / Ethereum stamp 2016–2018–2021*, 11-02-2018 11:58:37 (realized in 2021)
Adobe Creative Suite, offset print on adhesive-backed postage stamp paper and rubber stamp
Ethereum, 0x7c523c42ad255e5b270b12fee2ecc1103e88a9dc, 2712...6008

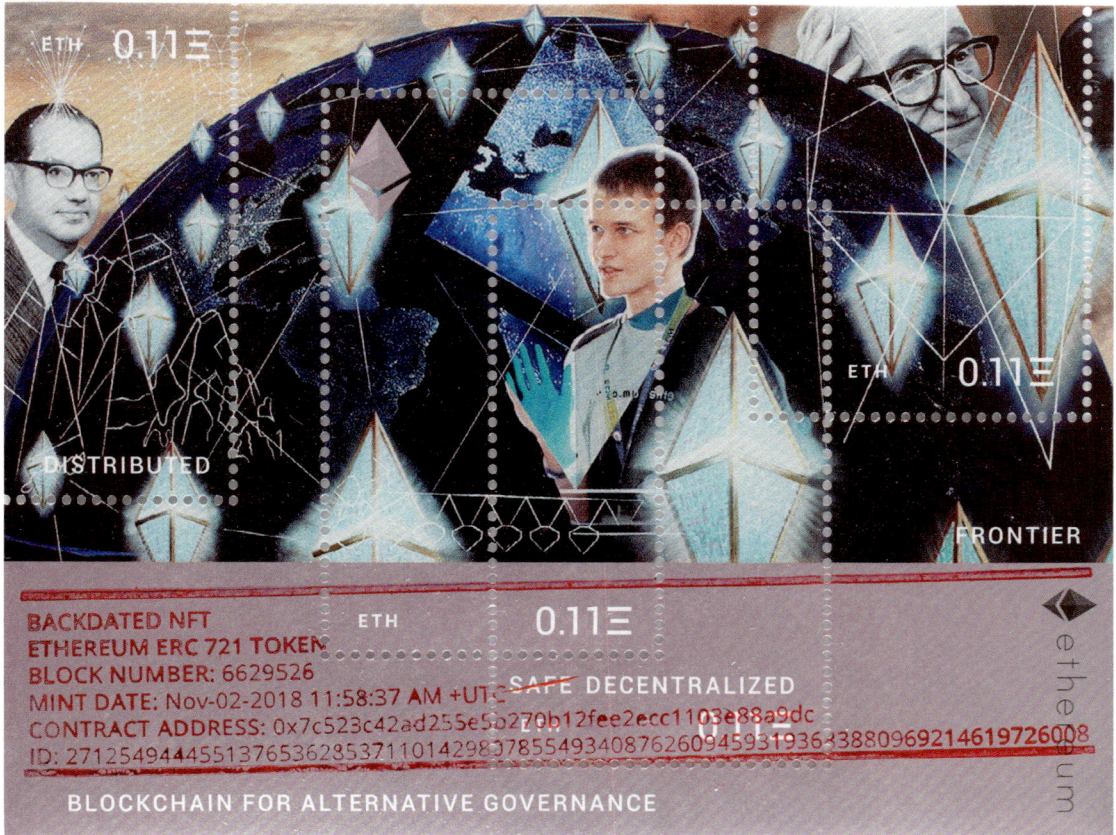

permanence is promised by tokenomics, now hold large repositories of huge financial and cultural value backed by the viabilities of their respective models. Jason Bailey, who collected many of XCOPY's now lost NFTs, has set up ClubNFT to "back up" one's NFTs, a business model that showcases many of the unresolved paradoxes of this new technology. The centralization of platforms such as OpenSea enables them to block users' wallets but also to do helpful things, like freeze hacked NFTs and provide centralized API feeds. The balance between the utopic libertarian roots of NFTs (and crypto more generally) and the drive for Web3 companies to acquire an ever-growing user base means trade-offs are being made every day between the ease of centralization and the political import of decentralization. The blockchain's weaknesses themselves have been demonstrated and exploited in several important conceptual artworks, including Simon Denny's *Backdated NFT/Ethereum Stamp* (2016–2018–2021) **[01.18]**, in which the artist in 2021 retrospectively switched out the image on a 2018 NFT's link to insert a work he made in 2016 on the blockchain. Moxie Marlinspike, creator of Signal, also took a playful jab at NFTs with his work *AtMyWhim* (2021). The same NFT presents a different image on every platform and, if owned, appears sardonically as a poop emoji in the collector's wallet. These works seek to make visible the, at times, imperfect nature of the blockchain's immutability, allow us pause for reflection, and guard against the boosterism of some of the community's most blinkered propagandists.

The NFT's attempt to power an economy of both rare, unique work and more democratically priced low-cost art has been skewed by practices of wash-trading and market manipulation at the high end and insistently high network fees at the low end. Elsewhere, crypto's carbon footprint weighed, at times unfairly, on the early history of NFTs, even as Ethereum 2.0 and the Merge — alongside native proof-of-stake chains — have allowed NFTs to become among the most energy efficient forms of art-making in history. These early issues will always abound in a space that is moving at the breakneck speed that open-source, decentralized disruption often entails. Nevertheless, the continued influx of richly talented developers, critics, curators, and most importantly artists, both unestablished and established, points to a vibrant

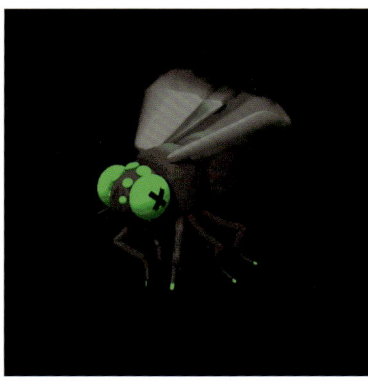

future where solutions to these issues expanded on above are being worked out in real time. Just last year, XCOPY created *Mutatio* (2024) **[01.19]**, selling just over one million NFTs in 24 hours to over 30,000 collectors. Works could be bought with ApplePay and owned using just an email address, such was the abstraction away from the blockchain. At last check, these NFTs still transact for ~$0.62. Imagine trying to sell, print, and ship one million prints. This is revolutionary. The promise of NFTs to democratize access to art, and to open the aperture on who considers themselves an art collector, is now meeting reality. At the other end of the spectrum, the venture capitalist Micky Malka and his wife Becky Kleiner set up NODE in 2025, a digital art foundation backed with a grant of $25 million, symptomatic of a growing maturity and institutionalization of collecting practices. Elsewhere, longtime champion of new media art Tina Rivers Ryan has taken the helm at the storied *Artforum*, suggesting a future where traditional art discourse will be ever more woven with digital art. The future looks very bright.

This particular history has sought to weave a narrative and theory of NFTs around the early art history of the space. In this, we see the seeds of the NFT space as the philosophical basis for its wider flowering, anchored by a focus on democratization, emancipation, geographic decentralization, and economic disintermediation. *Quantum* and its creator Kevin McCoy allow us to reflect on the multifaceted historical strands that weave together into the tapestry of NFTs as we understand them today. From the histories of computer art and technological innovations around computer graphics that are reflected in *Quantum*'s own aesthetics, to the philosophies of crypto that have collided both comfortably and uncomfortably with this deeply rich but often overlooked digital art history, NFTs are not so much a radical rupture with the past, but the culmination of many separate chains of history converging. The ethereal insertion of *aura* or *clout* that is so central to the viability of the NFT project has engendered a landscape of optimism and anxiety stoked by both real promise and overpromise. The consensus building around this aura of *clout* — a second order *aura* stemming not from the artwork itself but its record of ownership, has created volatility in accord — not only does one have to agree on the importance of chosen artworks but also on the validity of the technology that underpins it. In this we hope that Baudrillard was right when he wrote, in *Simulacra and Simulation* (1981), that "icon worshipers were the most modern minds, the most adventurous."[42] The early pioneers that this essay has shone a lens on were united by a shared desire to translate the dematerial into the icon, to create a new shared system of signification. This project, anchored by early engagements with community, trade, gaming, and collectibility, has created one of contemporary art's great spectacles, while disrupting contemporary art's current landscape both commercially and theoretically.

The complex political framework that envelops NFTs — for it is a technology that leans at once populist, libertarian, Marxist and hyper-capitalist — suggests a kaleidoscopic mirage that only a truly agnostic technology can engender. In this we are reminded that tools do not create art, artists do. While NFTs have crucially given birth to a new business model for artists, they have also more interestingly opened up new lines of inquiry artistically. On-chain networked art, "ectogames," algorithmic art, metaverse environments, and the reestablishing of a direct relationship between artist and collector (and the collector's creative and performative role within these new art forms) all showcase the new arenas where NFTs have expanded our definition of art while providing radical and provocative avenues for artists to explore. The following chapters, I believe, are a testament to this.

[42] Jean Baudrillard, "The Precession of Simulacra" in *Simulacra and Simulation*, trans. Sheila Faria Glaser, Ann Arbor (University of Michigan Press: 1994), 1, 3–7.

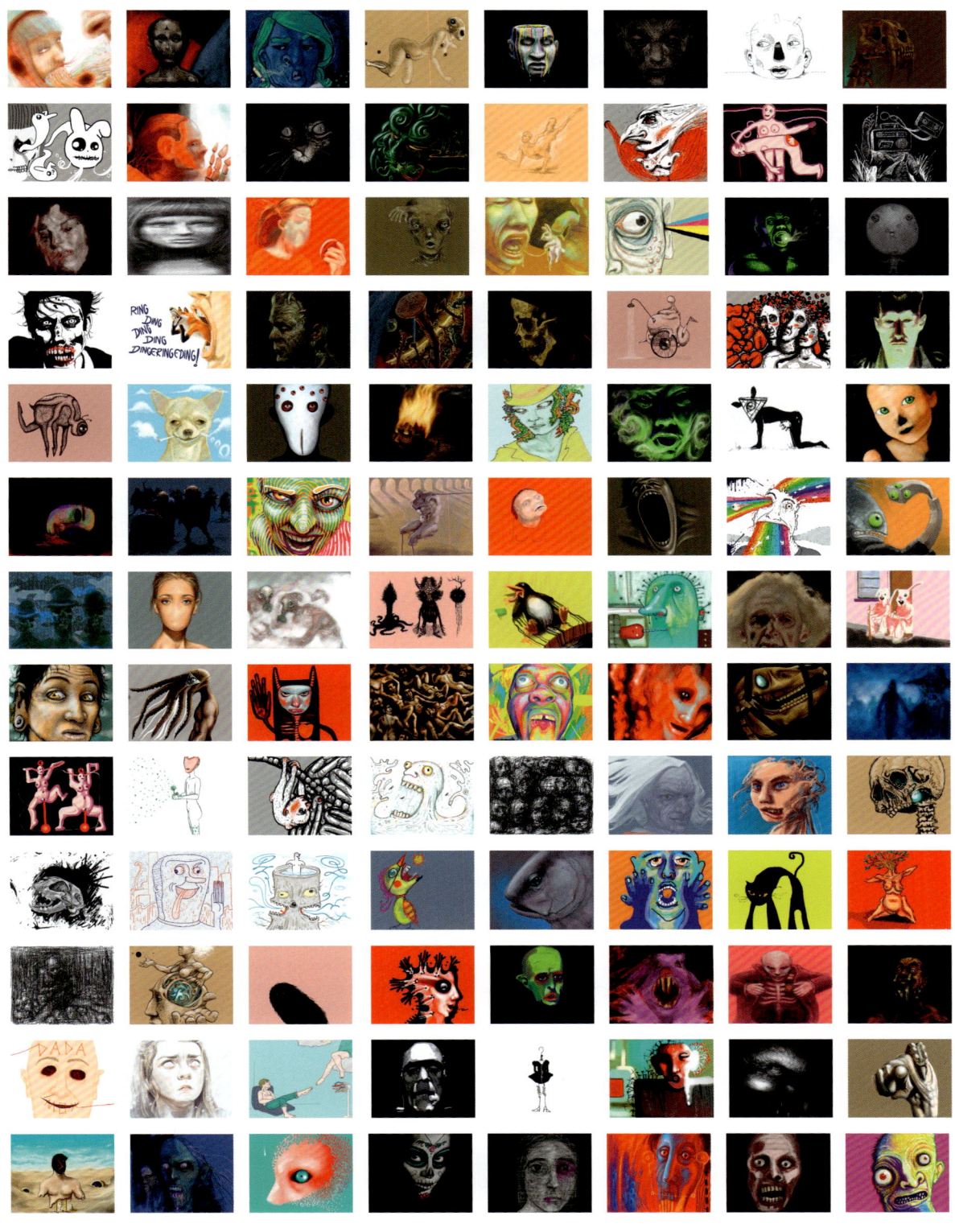

| #      | TITLE             | TIMESTAMP              | MEDIUM                                   | CHAIN | CONTRACT ADDRESS                           | ERC-20 TOKEN SUPPLY | EDITION SIZE                                       |
|--------|-------------------|------------------------|------------------------------------------|-------|--------------------------------------------|---------------------|----------------------------------------------------|
| 01, 02 | **Creeps & Weirdos** | 10-05-2017 15:56:52 | DADA Collaborative Drawing Platform | ETH   | 0x068696a3cf3c4676b65f1c9975dd094260109d02 | 1–16,600            | 108 artworks by 30 artists totalling 16,600 editions |

EDITIONS ILLUSTRATED: (01) Various, (02) Nomie

02

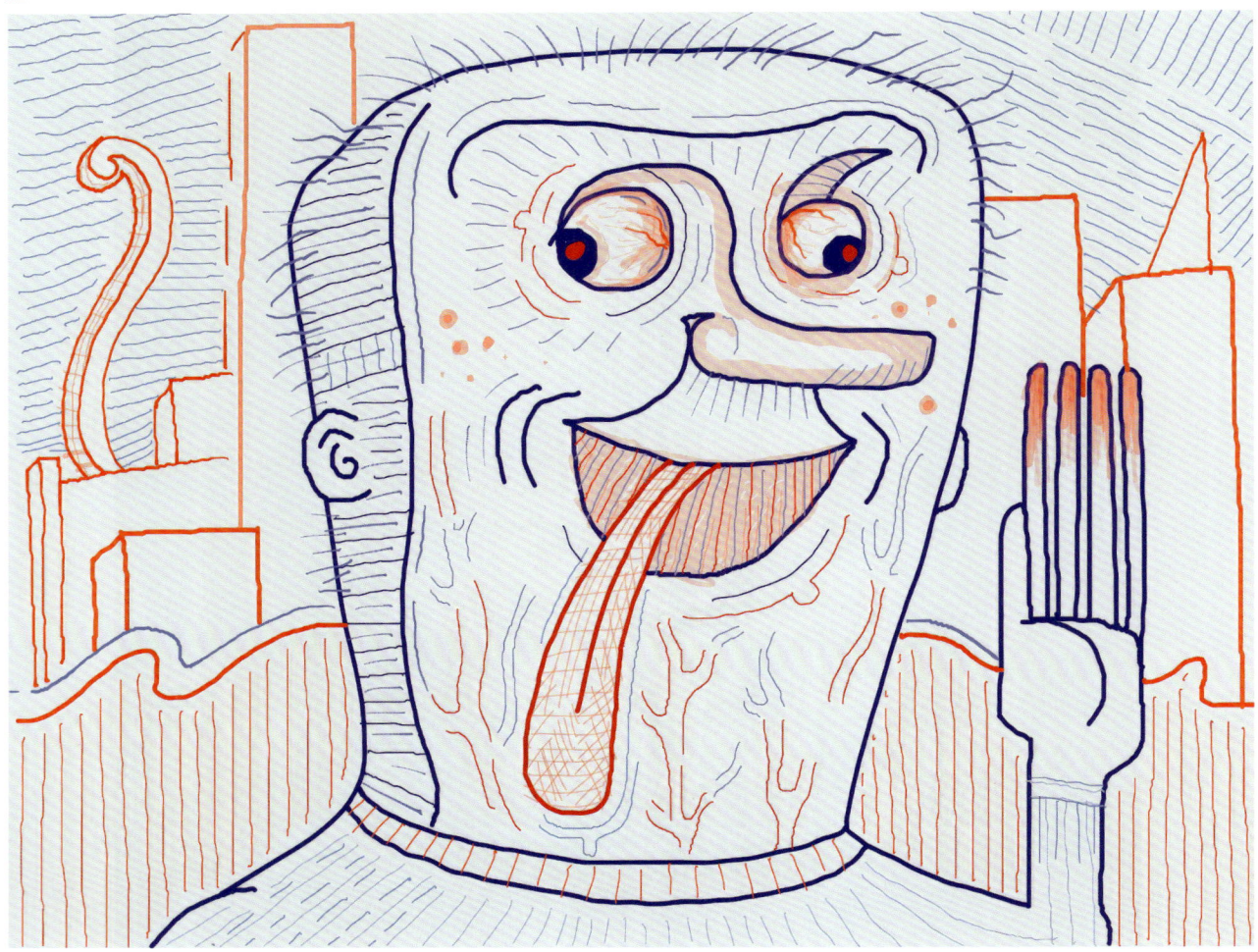

For all that words can't express, there is DADA. In an absurd act befitting its name, I have been asked to try. DADA is a platform for global, interconnected visual conversation. Artists create chains of images, replying to other artist's images with their own. Yet the simplicity of its function belies its significance. DADA is the wellspring from which the promise of NFTs and crypto art was born, nourished, and is sustained. The historic 2017 *Creeps & Weirdos* collection carries the immutable timestamp of this paradigm shift. These 108 groundbreaking pieces of crypto art, created as early as 2015 and curated in 2017, were the first NFTs to encode artist royalties on-chain. It was DADA who dared ask the question, "what if artists could capture the value of their work in perpetuity?"

As such, DADA carries the restorative, cross-cultural, and spiritual benefits of art-making combined with the representation and recognition of previously unseen artists and unconnected individuals. Its existence is a challenge to convention. It gives no instructions, never asks permission, refuses to hide behind a veil of false intentions, and leaves its doors open for all. It simply "is."

DADA is the promise of what could be, an invitation to return to art's values in a world obsessed with the value of art. It connects vital threads that run between hearts despite the boundaries presented by language, ideology, distance, and nationality. An accessible and universal tool, decoupled from money or status, and fueled instead by intrinsic rewards: the joy of making art, a sense of autonomy, validation, community, and mutual support.

With love, I am DADA, cut from this beautiful community of collaboration and the profundity of its diverse expression and artistry.

**COLBORN BELL**
FOUNDER OF THE MUSEUM OF CRYPTO ART

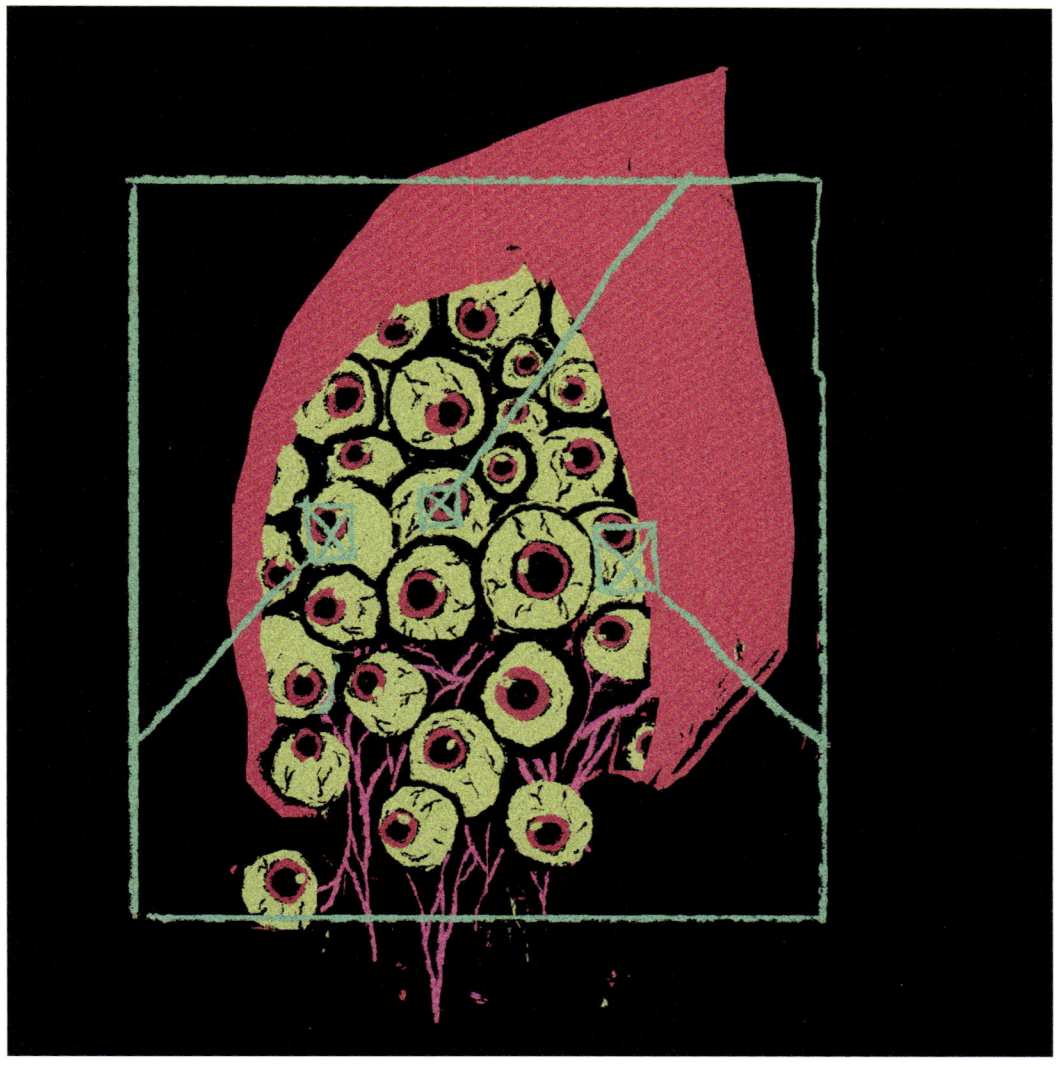

| # | TITLE | TIMESTAMP | CHAIN | MEDIUM | CONTRACT ADDRESS | TOKEN ID | EDITION SIZE |
|---|---|---|---|---|---|---|---|
| 01 | **data_lords** | 01-30-2020 20:30:52 | ETH | GIF | 0xb932a70a57673d89f4acffbe830e8ed7f75fb9e0 | 7533 | 1/1 |
| 02 | **Right-click and Save As guy** | 12-06-2018 21:32:40 | ETH | GIF | 0x41a322b28d0ff354040e2cbc676f0320d8c8850d | 1154 | 1/1 |
| 03 | **All Time High in the City** | 04-08-2018 19:15:31 | ETH | GIF | 0x41a322b28d0ff354040e2cbc676f0320d8c8850d | 11 | 1/1 |

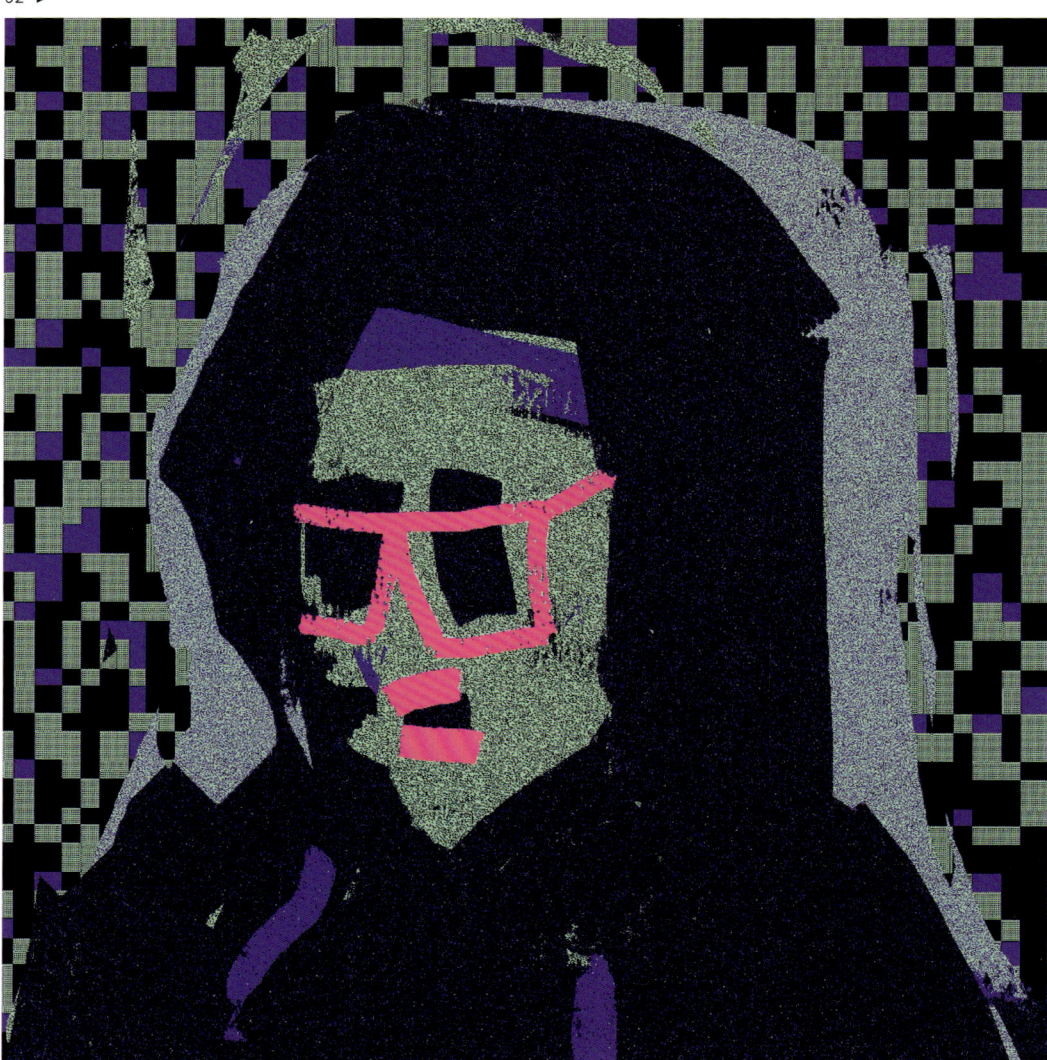

In every movement, an artist and a work come along that perfectly encapsulate its story and ethos. For NFTs and crypto art, that artist is XCOPY, and that work is *Right-click and Save As guy* (2018).

As one of the first artists to put art on a blockchain, and before that, pioneering the aggressive "glitch art" style on his now infamous Tumblr blog, XCOPY was the first to capture the meme of the moment in a minted artwork. Today, as NFTs begin to dominate mainstream conversation, you hear it more than ever — "Why would I buy it when I can right click and save as?"

Generative artist Dmitri Cherniak perfectly sums up the sentiment around the meme describing the term *Right-click and Save As* "synonymous both as a critique as well a booster of NFTs, and this seminal piece has pushed that meme further than we ever could have imagined." He continues to say "To me, XCOPY *is* crypto art. When folks describe early crypto art as glitchy, flashy, and eclectic, whether they know it or not, they are referencing XCOPY's dominant influence on the genre." One needs only to look at the thousands of derivatives this work has spawned to understand its influence on the NFT psyche.

As a notable collector of NFTs, and humble steward of XCOPY's *Right-click and Save As guy*, the meme has followed me personally as I have built my collection.

However, I see it not as a warning sign of the fragility of NFTs, but a reminder of the deep consensus this community has built up around the shared value of NFTs as unique digital artworks on the blockchain. In this, *Right-click and Save As guy* is an artistic co-opting of our detractors, a portrait of the establishment NFTs are meant to disrupt.

It is my hope this piece will forever inspire new artists to create digital art that can be right-click saved but that instead, people will choose to left-click own.

**COZOMO DE' MEDICI**
CURATOR OF THE MEDICI COLLECTION

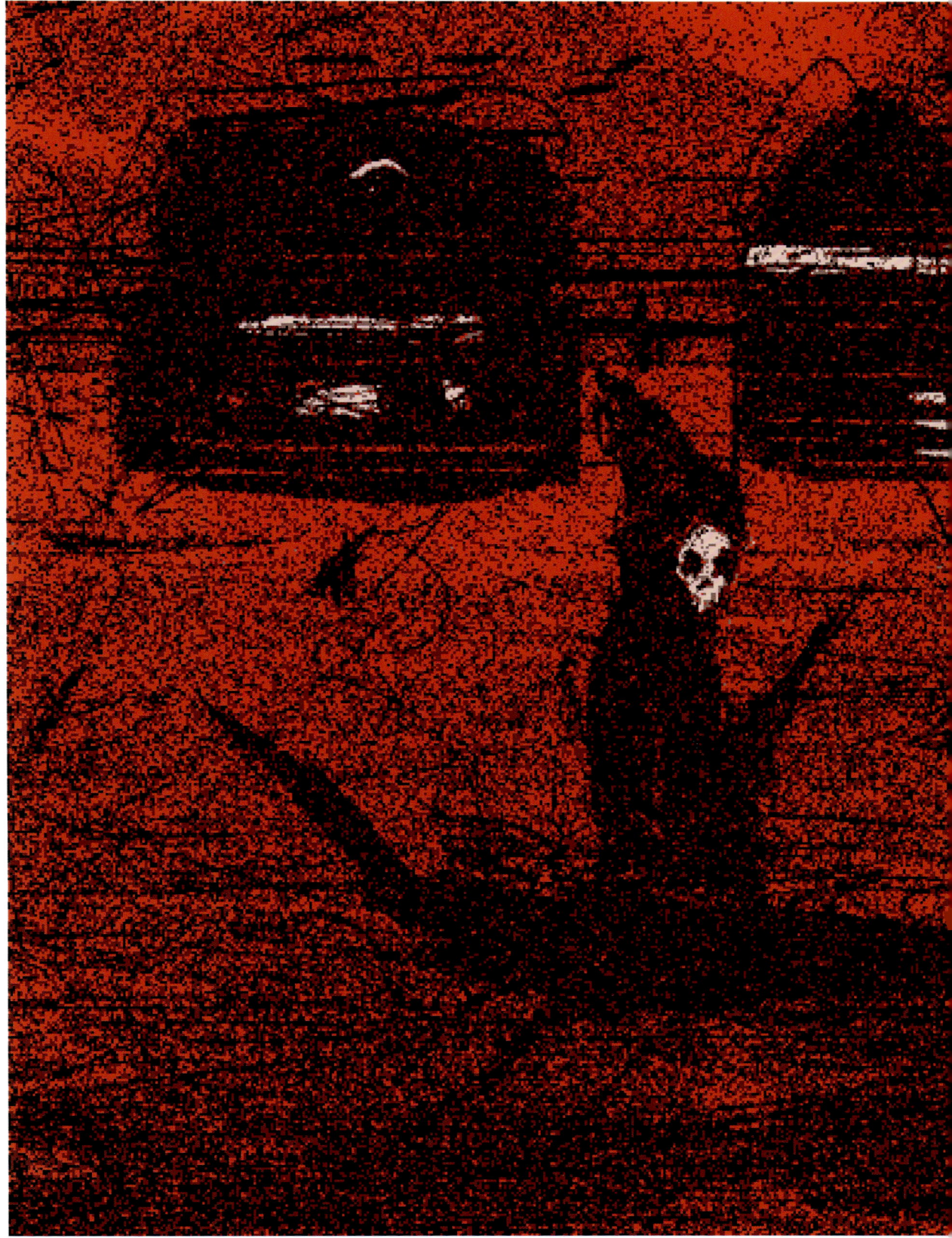

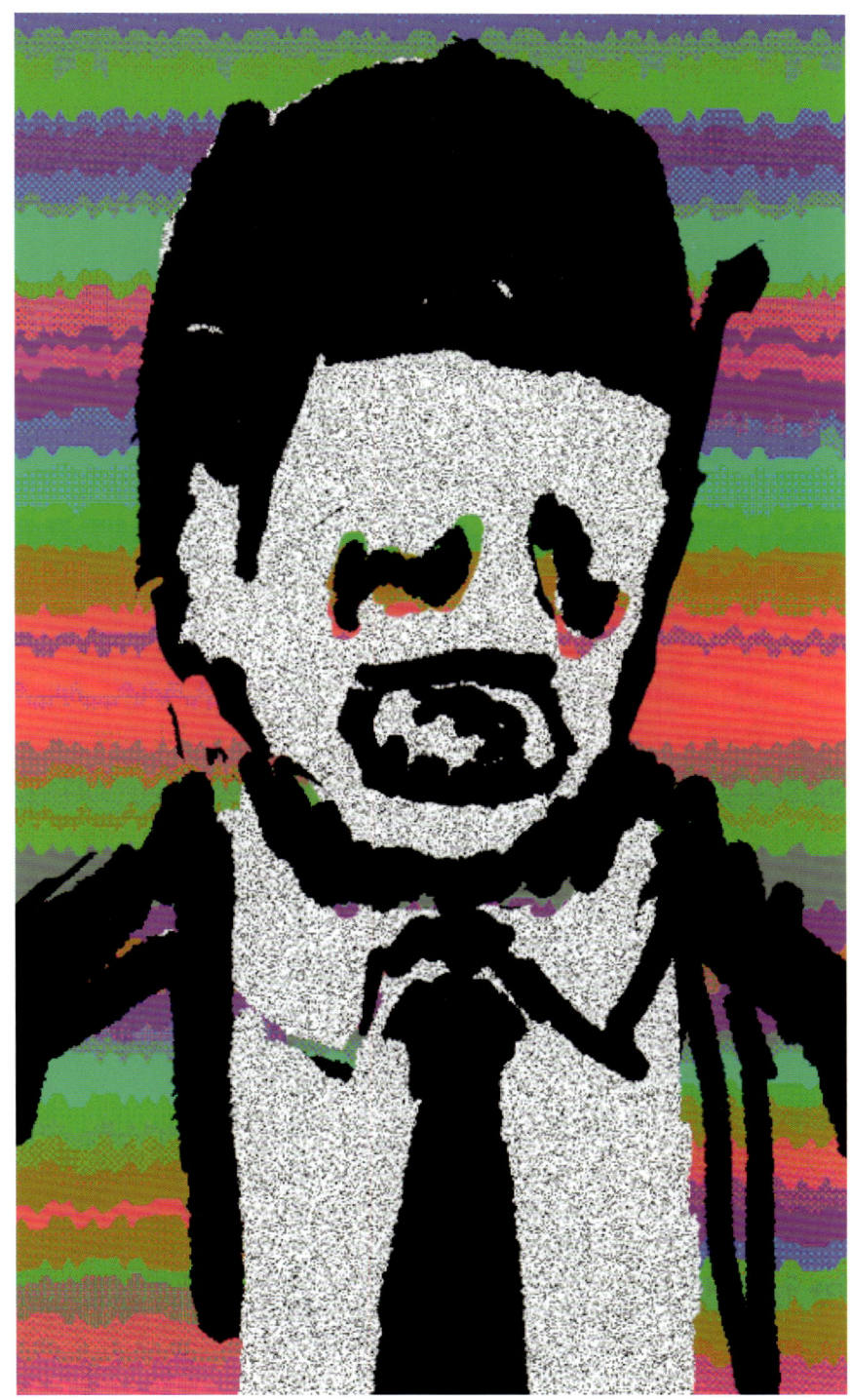

| # | TITLE | TIMESTAMP | MEDIUM | CHAIN | CONTRACT ADDRESS | TOKEN ID | EDITION SIZE |
|---|---|---|---|---|---|---|---|
| 04 | **A Coin for the Ferryman** | 04-08-2018 19:14:17 | GIF | ETH | 0x41a322b28d0ff354040e2cbc676f0320d8c8850d | 10 | 1/1 |
| 05 | **Nullwave** | 02-03-2019 22:36:20 | GIF | ETH | 0x41a322b28d0ff354040e2cbc676f0320d8c8850d | 1825 | 1/1 |
| 06 | **The Doomed** | 10-21-2018 10:32:33 | GIF | ETH | 0xfbeef911dc5821886e1dda71586d90ed28174b7d | 22001–22100 | 100 |
| 07 | **MAX PAIN** | 03-25-2022 02:25:18 | GIF | ETH | 0xd1169e5349d1cb9941f3dcba135c8a4b9eacfdde | 171000100001–171000107394 | 7,394 |
| 08 | **ART HISTORY: VOLUMES I–X** | 03-11-2020 21:52:53 | GIF | ETH | 0xb932a70a57673d89f4acffbe830e8ed7f75fb9e0 | 8711 | 1/1 |

05 ▶

06 ▶

07 ▶

08 ▶

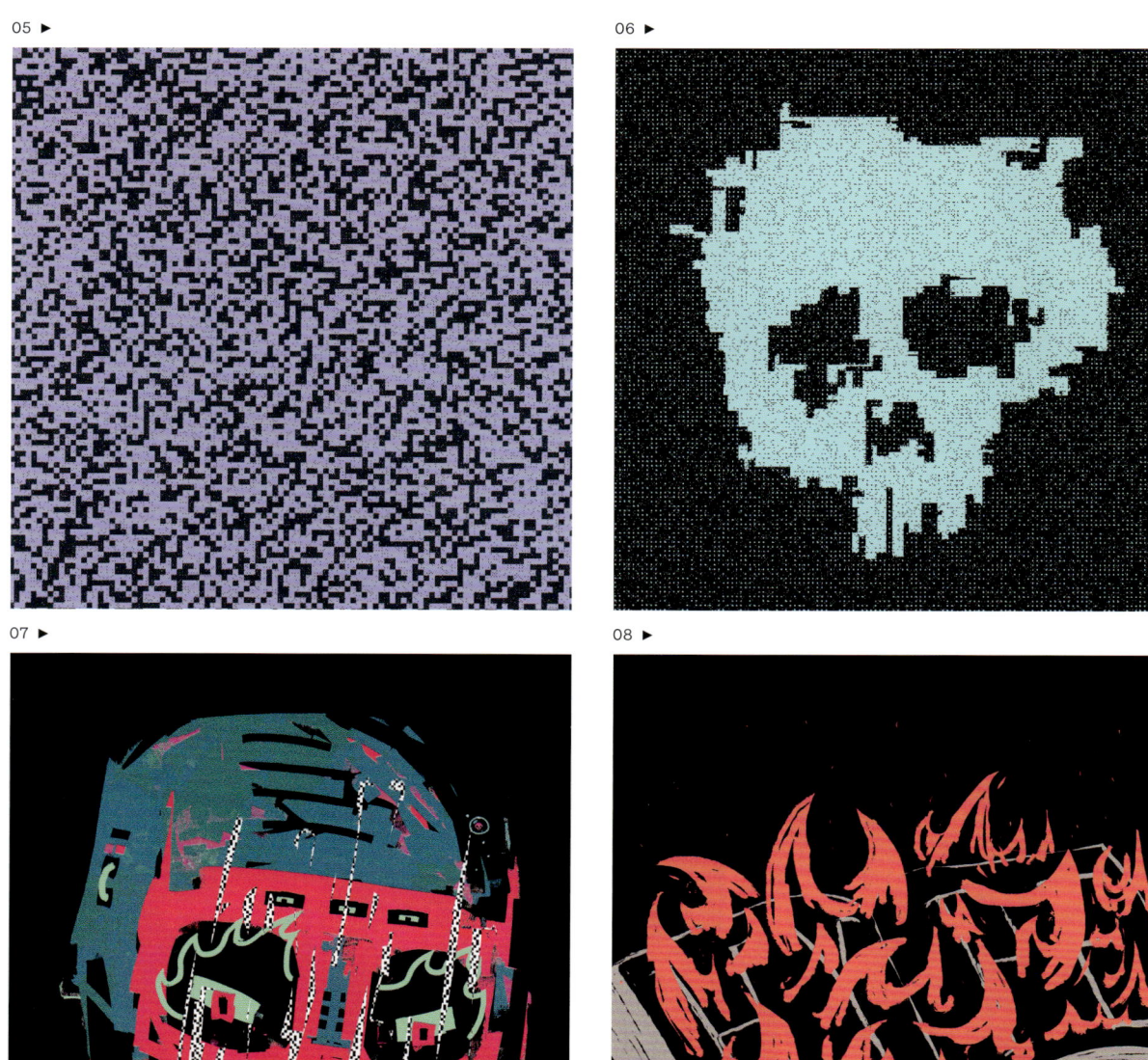

01 ▶

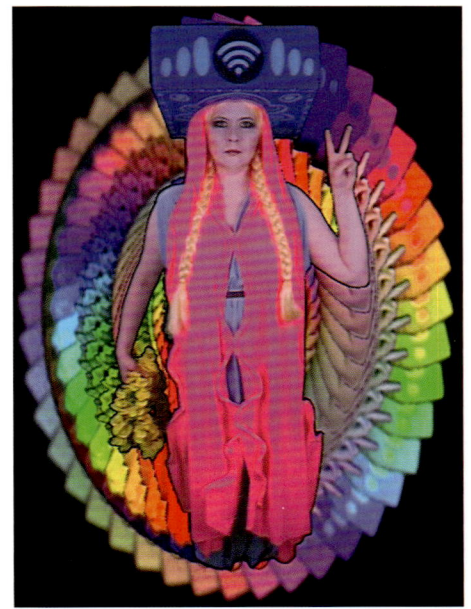

02 ▶

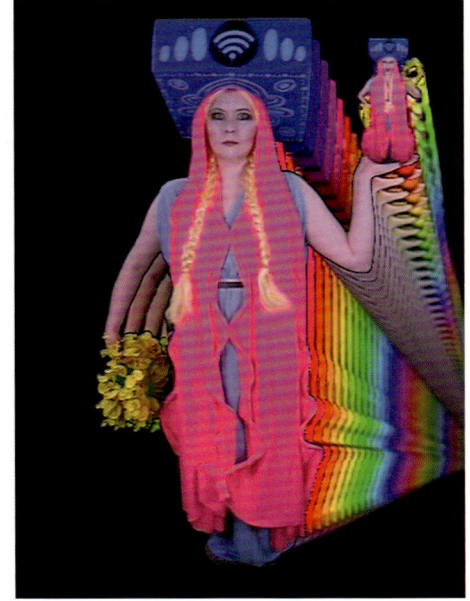

03 ▶

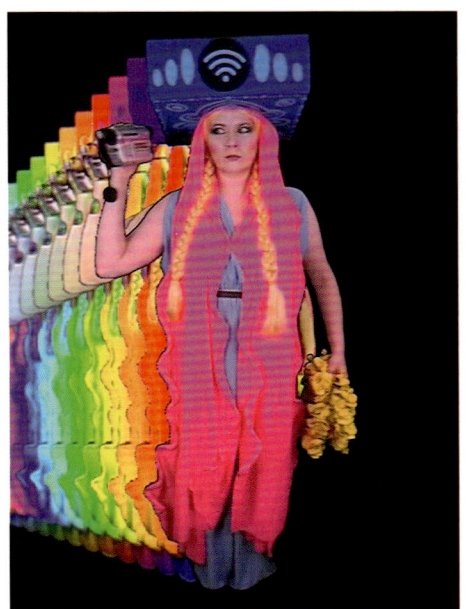

04 ▶

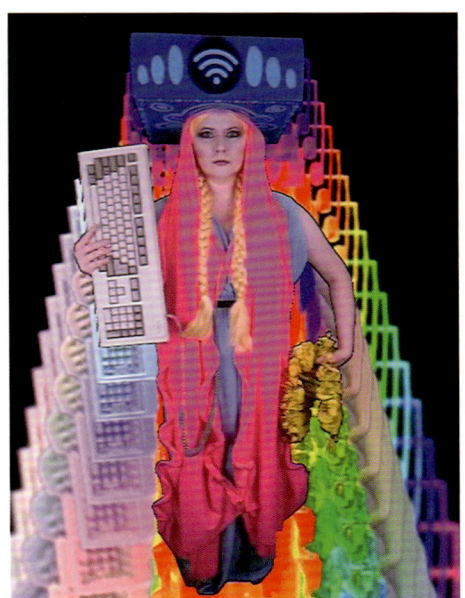

| #  | TITLE | TIMESTAMP | MEDIUM | CHAIN | CONTRACT ADDRESS | TOKEN ID | EDITION SIZE |
|----|-------|-----------|--------|-------|------------------|----------|--------------|
| 01 | **Caryatid: Wink** | 11-26-2022 08:50:59 | Digital video, performance, VHS | ETH | 0x2a86c5466f088caebf94e071a77669bae371cd87 | 1151...3404 | 1, +2 AP |
| 02 | **Caryatid: Recursion** | 11-26-2022 08:58:59 | Digital video, performance, VHS | ETH | 0x2a86c5466f088caebf94e071a77669bae371cd87 | 1111...1478 | 1, +2 AP |
| 03 | **Caryatid: Vision** | 11-26-2022 08:53:35 | Digital video, performance, VHS | ETH | 0x2a86c5466f088caebf94e071a77669bae371cd87 | 8419...9722 | 1, +2 AP |
| 04 | **Caryatid: Thought** | 11-26-2022 08:54:35 | Digital video, performance, VHS | ETH | 0x2a86c5466f088caebf94e071a77669bae371cd87 | 4433...3290 | 1, +2 AP |
| 05 | **THIS IS 2020** | 12-31-2019 20:11:12 | GIF, digital animation, VHS | ETH | 0xb932a70a57673d89f4acffbe830e8ed7f75fb9e0 | 6705 | 1/1 |
| 06 | **Space Loaf** | 06-16-2021 16:58:31 | Digital video, VHS | ETH | 0xb932a70a57673d89f4acffbe830e8ed7f75fb9e0 | 25459 | 1/1 |
| 07 | **Self Transcending** | 05-28-2021 04:13:30 | Digital animation, Sony Video Painter, VHS | ETH | 0x3184daa448cb5d1eaf4991d638d737350b4236e4 | 0 | 1/1 |
| 08 | **Most Everyone's Mad Here** | 04-04-2021 17:58:03 | GIF, digital animation, VHS | ETH | 0xb932a70a57673d89f4acffbe830e8ed7f75fb9e0 | 22853 | 1/1 |

05 ►
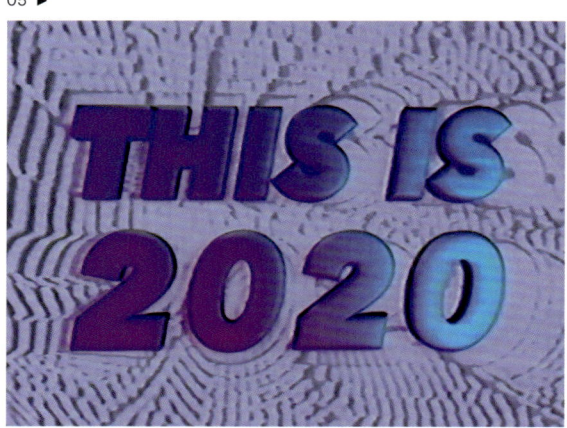

06 ►
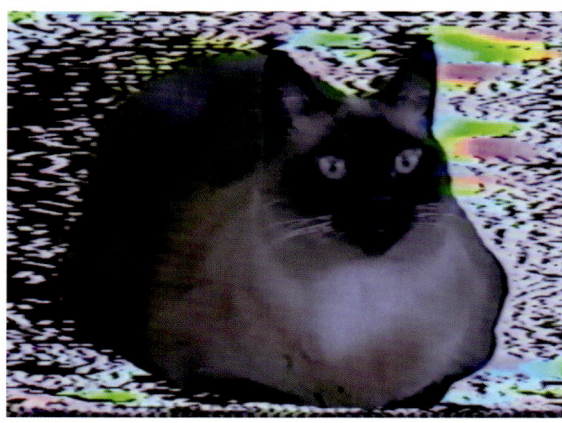

07 ►
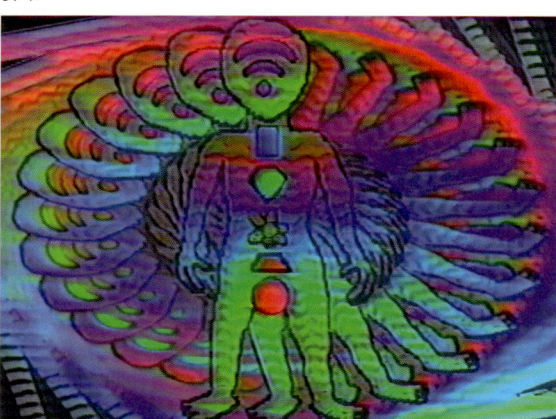

08 ►
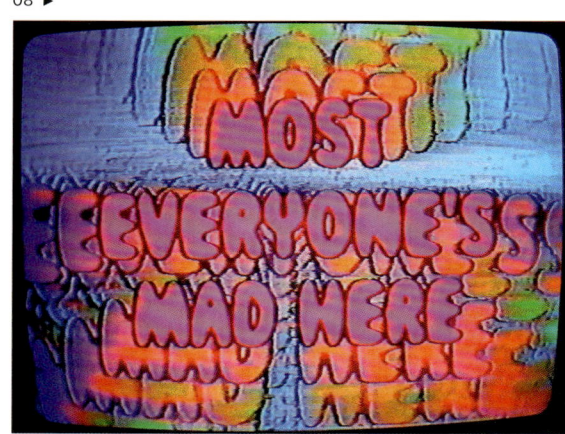

Sarah Zucker uses analog devices, particularly VHS, to create born-digital work. Zucker began tokenizing on the Ethereum blockchain in 2019. Her instantly recognizable style, combined with her powerful views on the nature of online identity, make her voice and visual sensibility an integral part of the foundation of crypto art as a movement.

Zucker's MFA in Dramatic Writing clearly informs her work, which often includes narrative series. She is a self-taught artist and uses techniques of her own design. Her multimedia process moves between a 1991 Sony Video Painter, a CRT display, and postproduction digital animation. The result is the unmistakable line work and undulating rainbows that are the artist's visual signature. @thesarahshow, Zucker's handle, is a reference to the artist's own online identity as something built for an audience. Her work is a conduit for the lived experience of those who saw the rapid rise of online identity as a construct.

Who do we become when we are online? Zucker addresses this question in *Self Transcending* (2021). This work was exhibited at Sotheby's *Natively Digital*, the auction house's first curated show of NFTs. The artist describes the work as a "vision of the Self as a Strange Loop." A sense of expansion pervades the piece. Zucker's reinterpretation of chakra symbols, a recurring motif, appears superimposed upon a human form. The symbol of the crown chakra is replaced with that of a wifi signal. The human form is repeated, creating a full circle. The effect is similar to the iconography of tantric deities such as the thousand-armed Avalokiteśvara. The GIF oscillates rainbow tones in a clockwise spiral, expanding ever outward in a shape that mirrors the figure at the center. We see the Self as a web, connected to others in our ever-expanding online realities.

**SARAH MOOSVI**
FOUNDER OF TARA DIGITAL COLLECTIVE AND
DIRECTOR OF TDC GALLERY

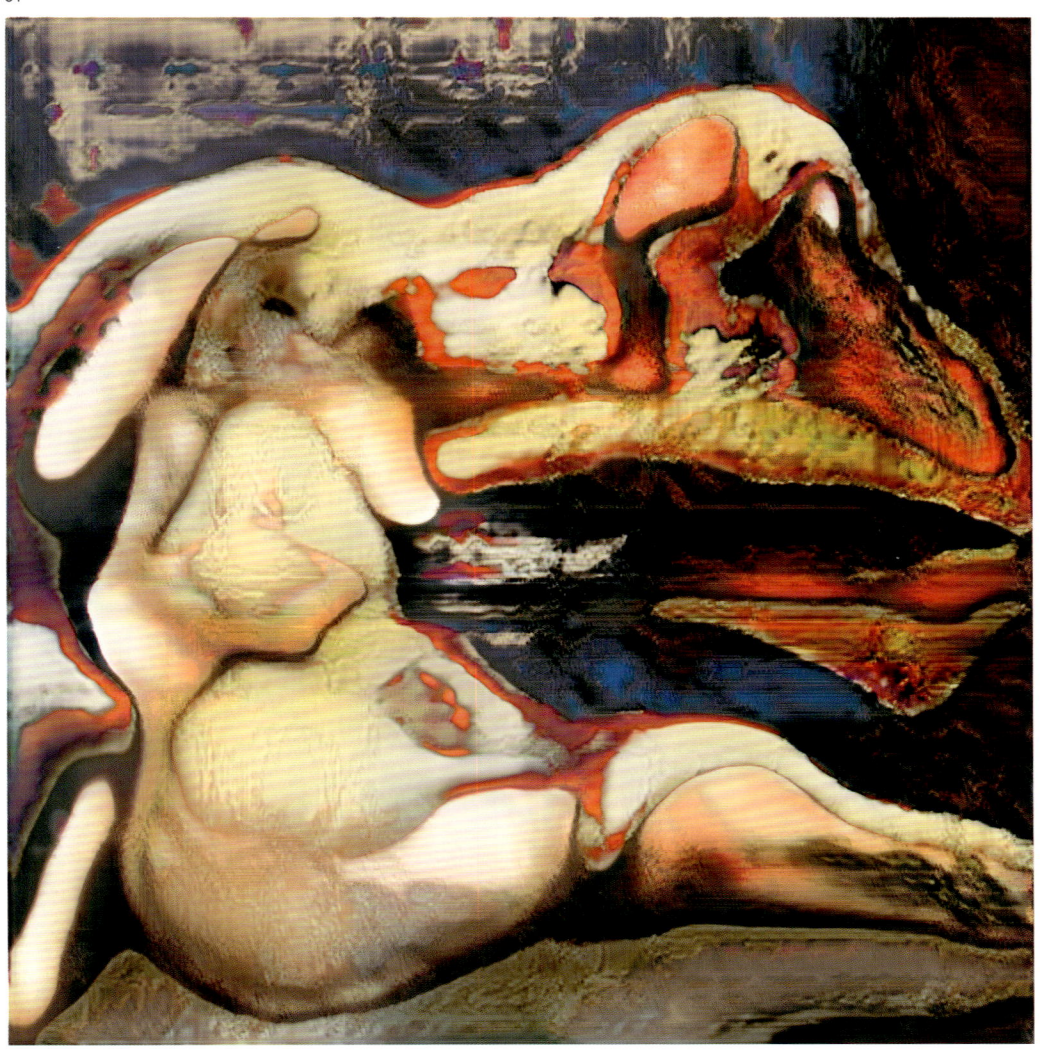

| # | TITLE | TIMESTAMP | MEDIUM | CHAIN | CONTRACT ADDRESS | TOKEN ID | EDITION SIZE |
|---|---|---|---|---|---|---|---|
| 01 | **AI Generated Nude Portrait #1** | 04-05-2018 23:20:48 | Artificial Intelligence, GAN | ETH | 0x41a322b28d0ff354040e2cbc676f0320d8c8850d | 1 | 1/1 |
| 02 | **saint nazaire** | 06-22-2020 16:05:30 | Artificial Intelligence, GAN | ETH | 0xb932a70a57673d89f4acffbe830e8ed7f75fb9e0 | 11266 | 1/1 |
| 03 | **AI Generated Nude Portrait #7** | 07-16-2018 22:51:40 | Artificial Intelligence, GAN | ETH | 0x41a322b28d0ff354040e2cbc676f0320d8c8850d | 191–490 | 1/1 of 300 |

EDITIONS ILLUSTRATED: (03) #1–300

02

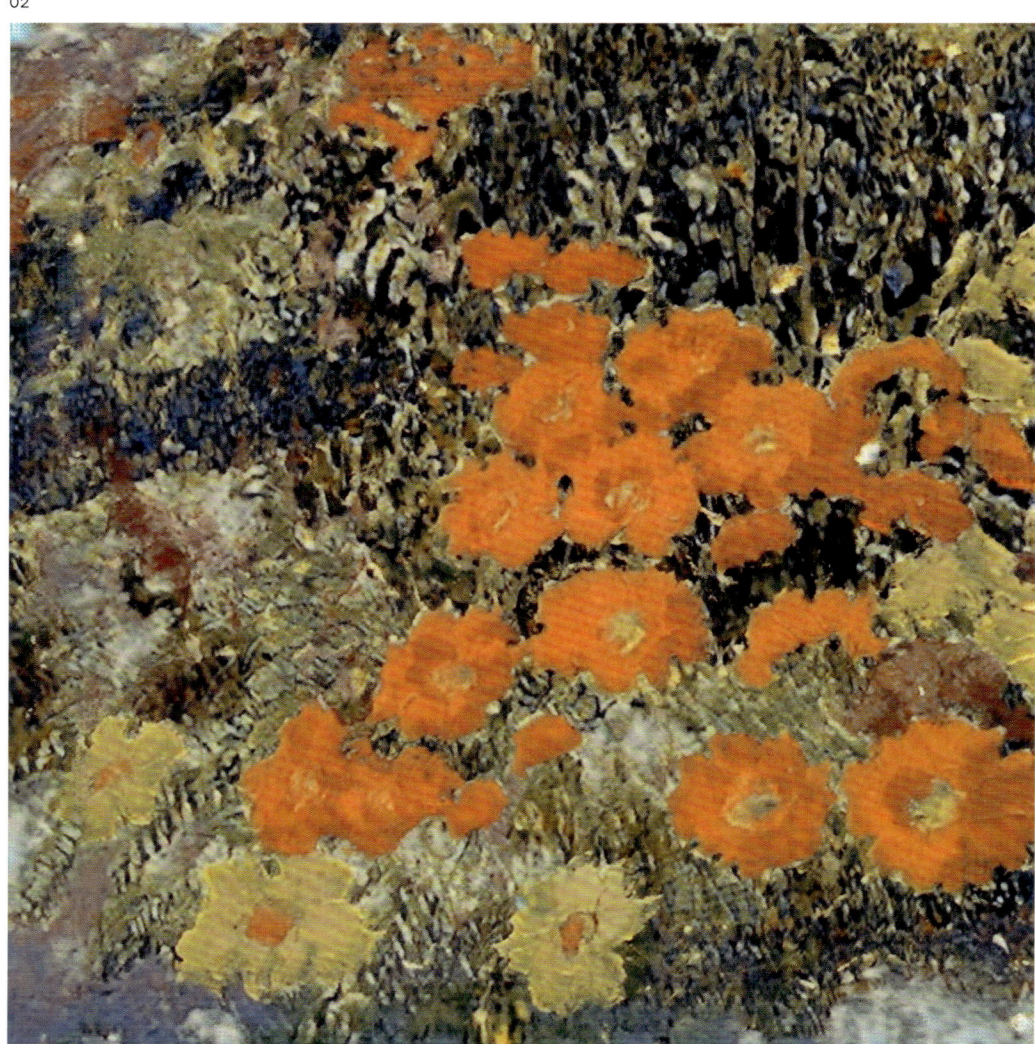

Robbie's name is legendary in both the NFT and AI art world. And I'm not talking about the "Lost Robbies" from 2018 or the controversial sale at Christie's of Obvious's *Portrait of Edmond Belamy* (2018), although one can easily find these stories online. I came to know him through Twitter back in late 2017 when I first started to share my own AI artwork: Robbie was very supportive, encouraging, and generous with his knowledge, and we became friends. Besides being gifted artistically, Robbie is a natural-born hacker, so no wonder he was interning in NVIDIA and then Stanford AI Labs straight out of high school. He takes his technical prowess beyond purely AI or visual into the broad spectrum of computational art like pixel, audio, video, etc.

He was also an early adopter of crypto art — Robbie's very first NFT, *AI Generated Nude Portrait #1*, was minted back in early 2018 and first collected by the well-known crypto art critic and NFT collector Jason Bailey.

Robbie's artwork presented here was created using open-source GANs which he trained on public domain WikiArt-type data-sets of paintings (including nudes, landscapes, portraits, etc.) and then carefully curated by himself: GANs are notorious for being prolific and thus curation is an important part of the AI artistic process. The sophisticated and idiosyncratic style of Robbie's work, was a perfect fit for crypto art and quickly gained popularity among NFT collectors.

His work is sought out especially after his sudden exit from the NFT scene in 2021 to pursue new artistic directions, both analog and digital.

**HELENA SARIN**
AI ARTIST AND SOFTWARE ENGINEER

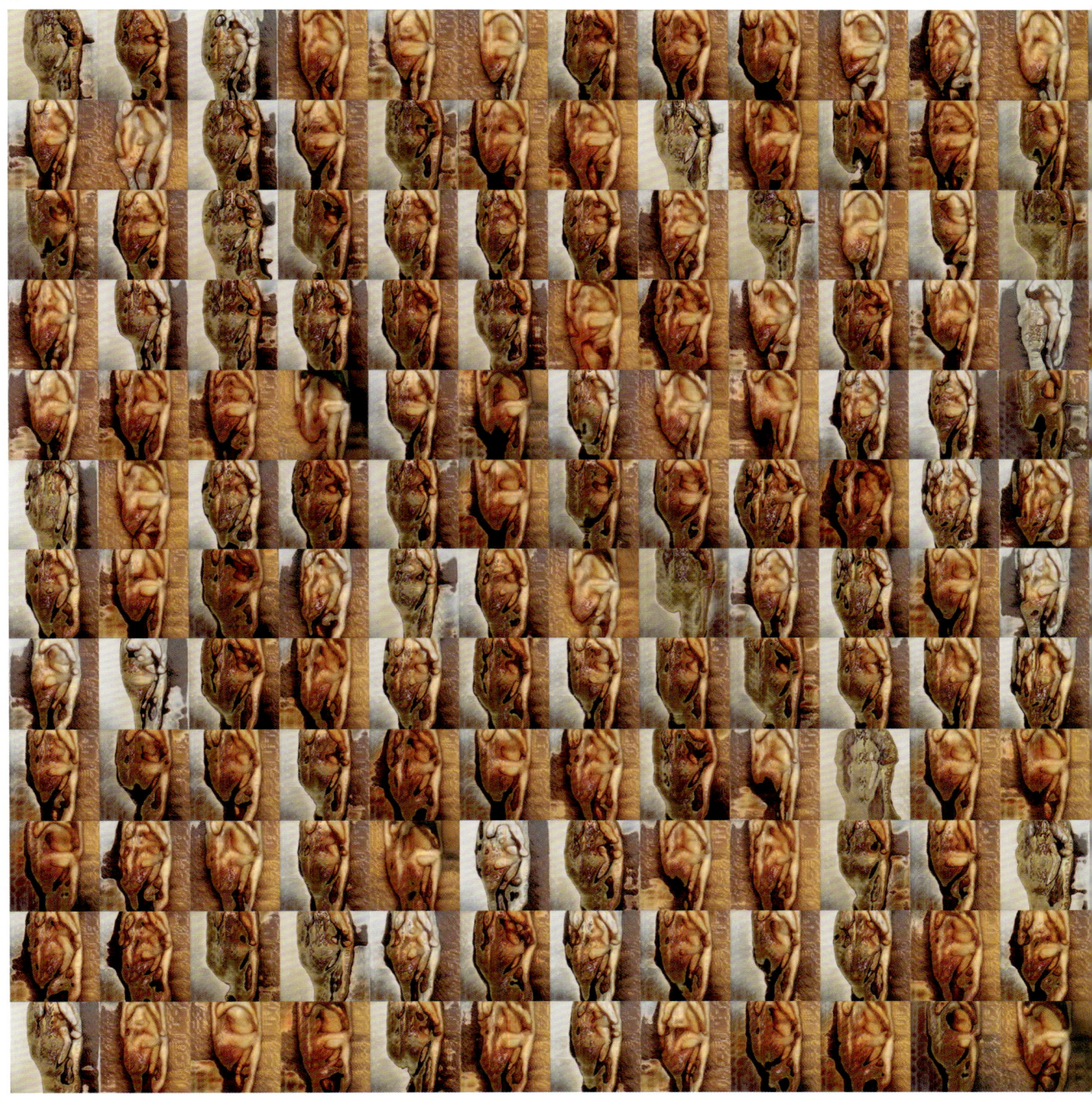

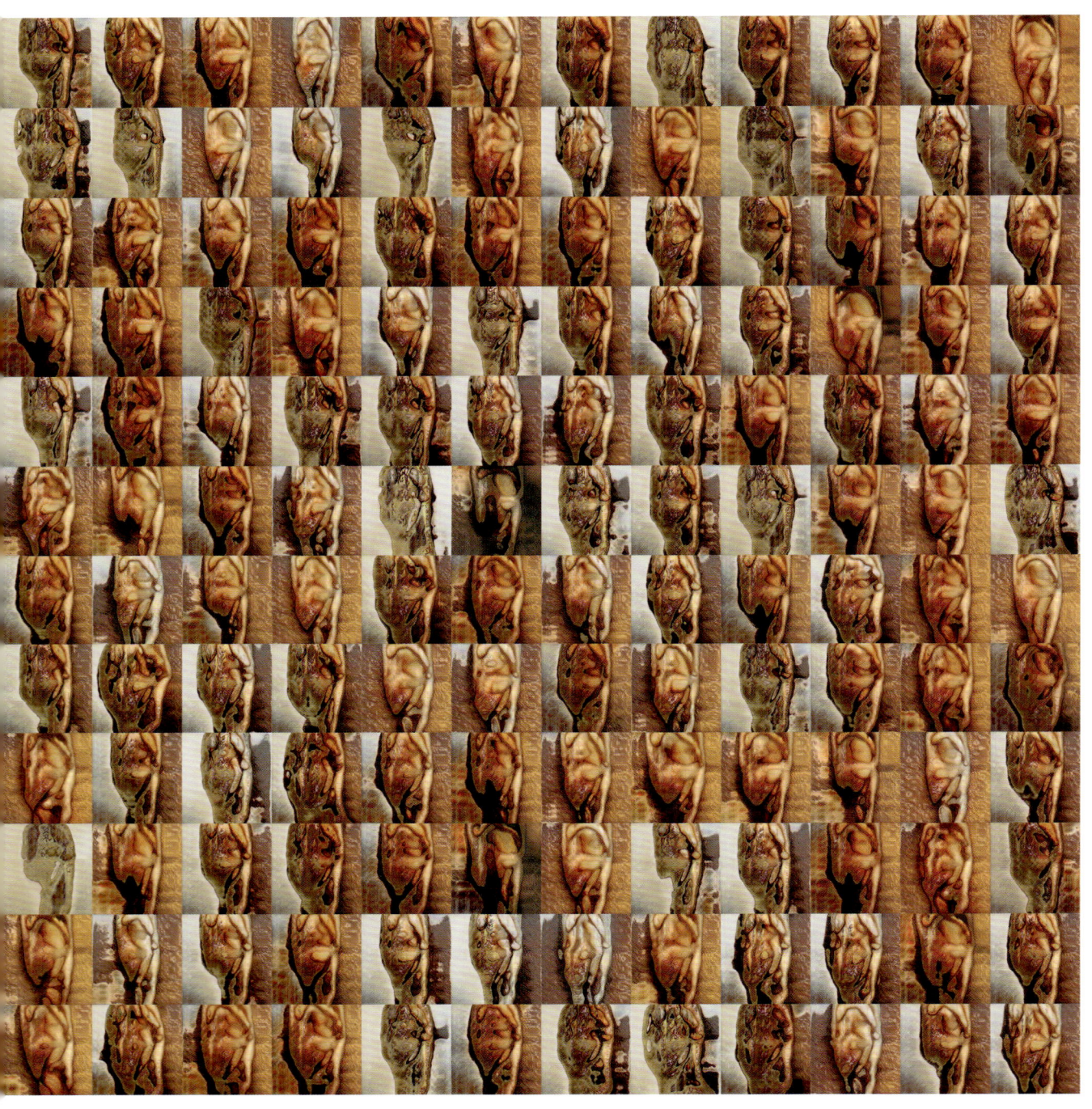

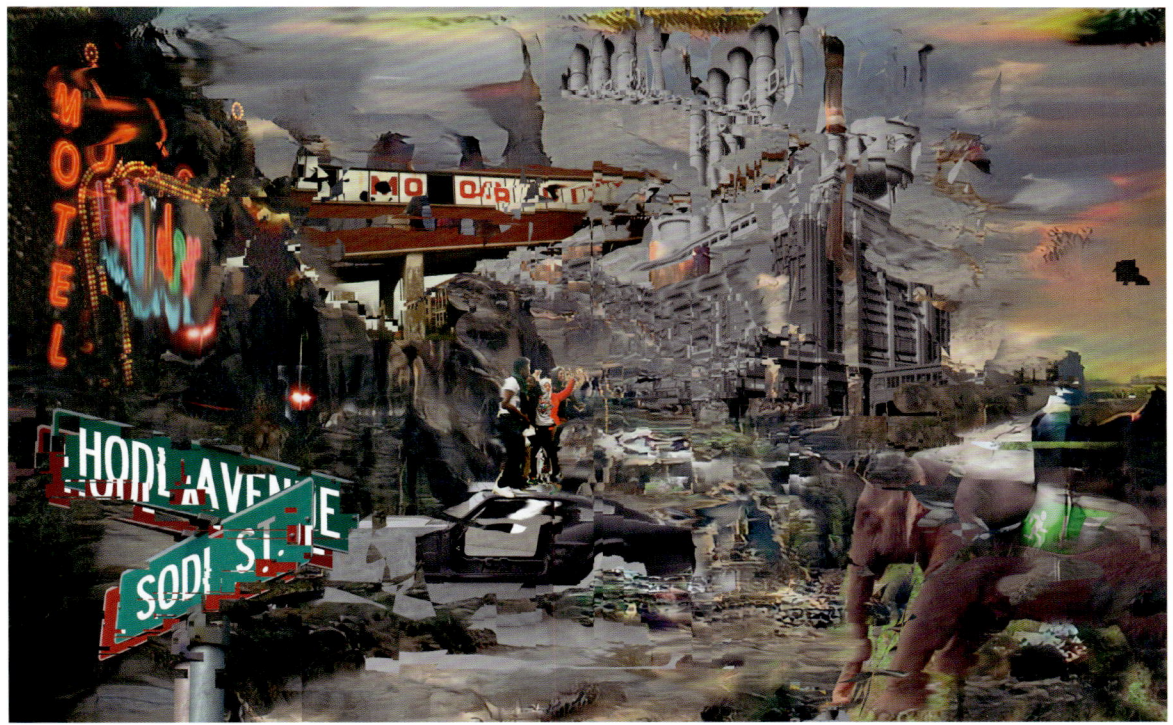

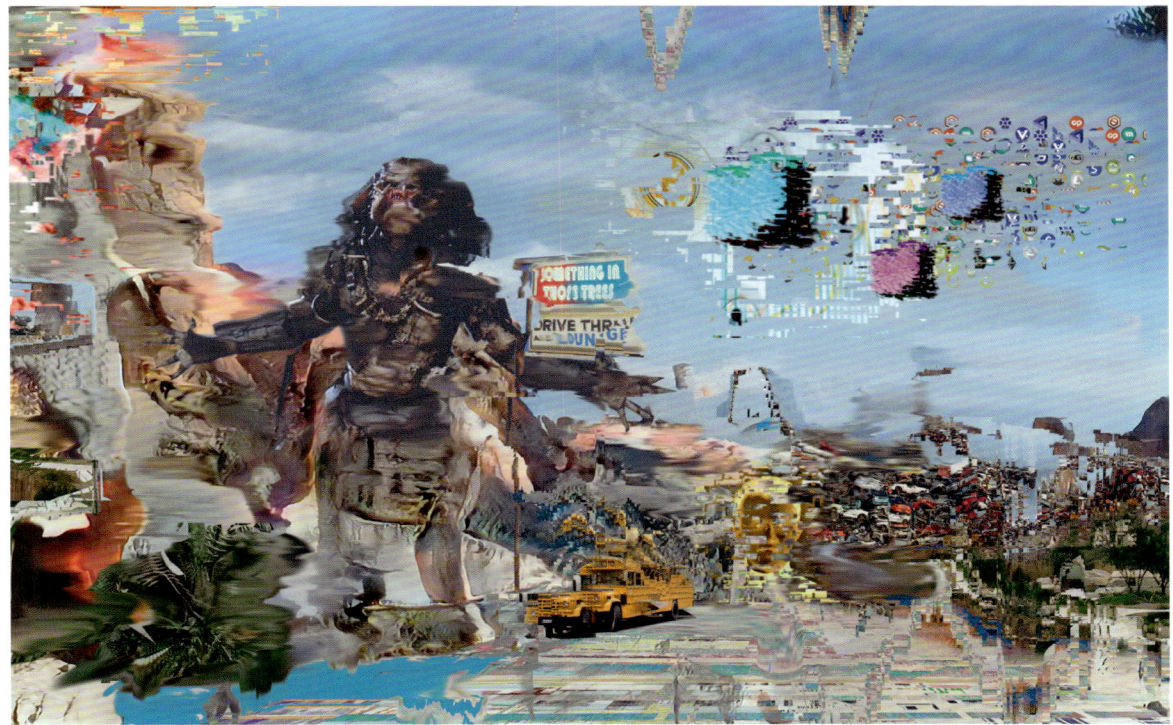

| # | TITLE | TIMESTAMP | MEDIUM | CHAIN | CONTRACT ADDRESS | TOKEN ID | EDITION SIZE | COLLABORATORS |
|---|---|---|---|---|---|---|---|---|
| 01 | **HODL Ave.** | 12-14-2019 22:55:08 | Adobe Photoshop | ETH | 0xb932a70a57673d89f4acffbe830e8ed7f75fb9e0 | 6112 | 1/1 | Norman Harman |
| 02 | **Défilé de Shitcoins** | 12-26-2019 23:03:22 | Adobe Photoshop | ETH | 0xb932a70a57673d89f4acffbe830e8ed7f75fb9e0 | 6539 | 1/1 | Norman Harman |
| 03 | **64 GALLON TOTER** | 01-23-2020 16:37:16 | PhotoMosh | ETH | 0xb932a70a57673d89f4acffbe830e8ed7f75fb9e0 | 7323 | 1/1 | – |

03 ▶

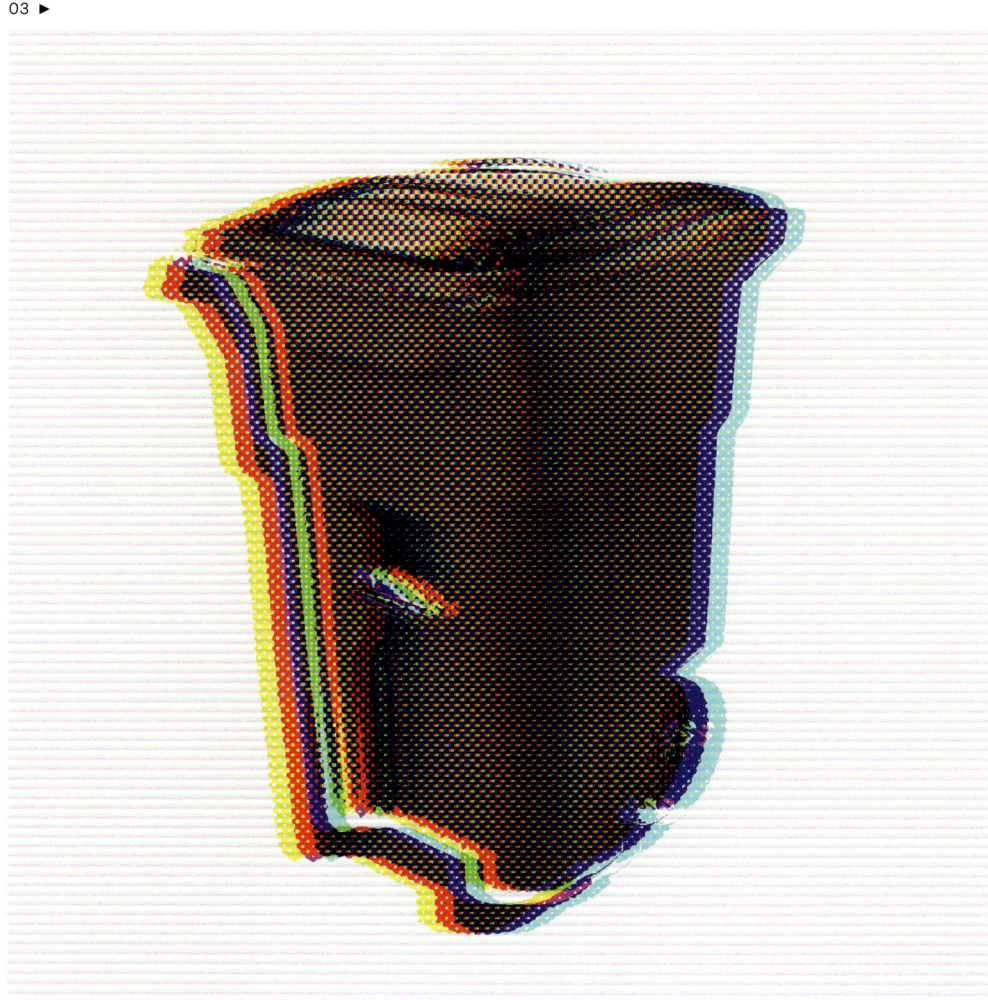

Born and raised in Redondo Beach, California, amidst surfers and skaters, ROBNESS skipped the beach and busied himself creating on canvas in his early career. Working in a rundown rehearsal space in Torrance, he realized his work might hold some value when thieves ripped his creations from the walls.

In 2014, cryptocurrency captured his imagination and allowed him to become a key figure in the digital art renaissance. He discovered the possibilities of combining blockchain technology with digital art as a new medium via a series of rare pepe works. Using an early protocol called Counterparty, he contributed to the historic collection, creating pieces that are now commonly known as NFTs.

ROBNESS often found himself embroiled in controversy. The strictly curated gallery, SuperRare banned him for his *64 GALLON TOTER* (2020), a work of protest consisting of a trash can photo manipulated with rudimentary digital tools. Duchamp's early 20th-century readymade work now spilled into the digital 21st century, mixing in with the modern problems of copyright law. While he eventually rejoined the platform, the divisive event spawned the TRASHART phenomenon — one of the earliest native crypto art movements.

ROBNESS harnesses the NFT medium as a platform of expression and criticism. Working with fellow artist Norman Harman to create *HODL Ave* (2019), the pair examined the maniacal nature of crypto traders. They continue to collaborate with an ongoing series entitled *The Last Confirmation* (2019–).

Whether minting a McDonald's application form to mark his timeline in the crypto art space or creating a huge collection of 11,111 PFP images, ROBNESS pokes fun at the establishment and calls out the irrational behavior of participants in an economy gone awry. He creates art as a means of protest, critique and, most importantly, as an act of rebellion against the status quo.

**DKLEINE**
WRITER, ARTIST, AND PODCAST HOST OF NFP WITH DKLEINE

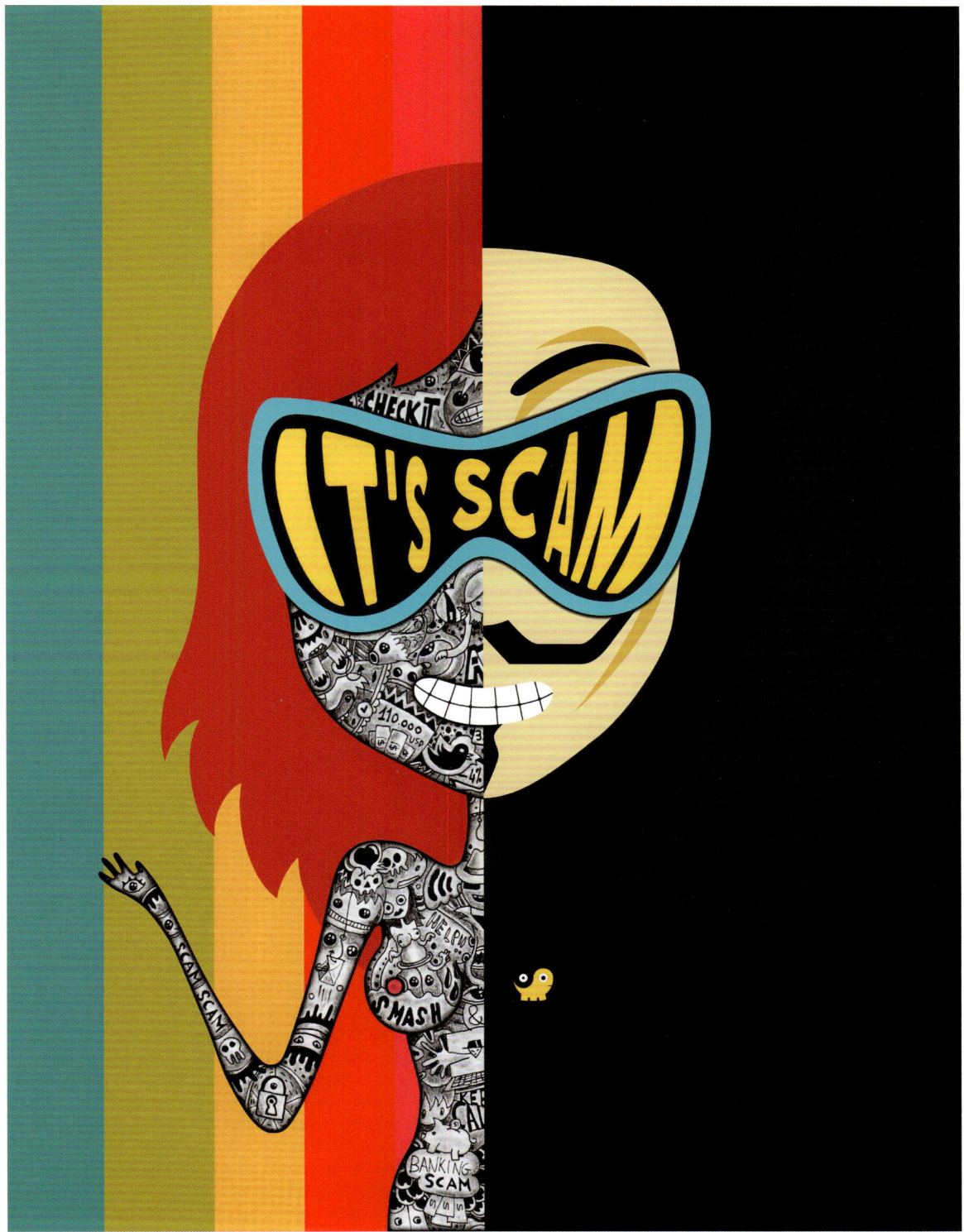

| # | TITLE | TIMESTAMP | MEDIUM | CHAIN | CONTRACT ADDRESS | TOKEN ID | EDITION SIZE |
|---|---|---|---|---|---|---|---|
| 01 | **It's SCAM – Left** | 08-07-2020 19:55:57 | Adobe Photoshop, Adobe After Effects | ETH | 0x1fc4336d4b3aa163ca855d45555207fddb70f719 | 3800040001–3800040023 | 23 |
| 02 | **Girl Next door** | 04-14-2018 06:20:31 | Adobe Photoshop, Adobe After Effects | ETH | 0x41a322b28d0ff354040e2cbc676f0320d8c8850d | 17 | 1/1 |

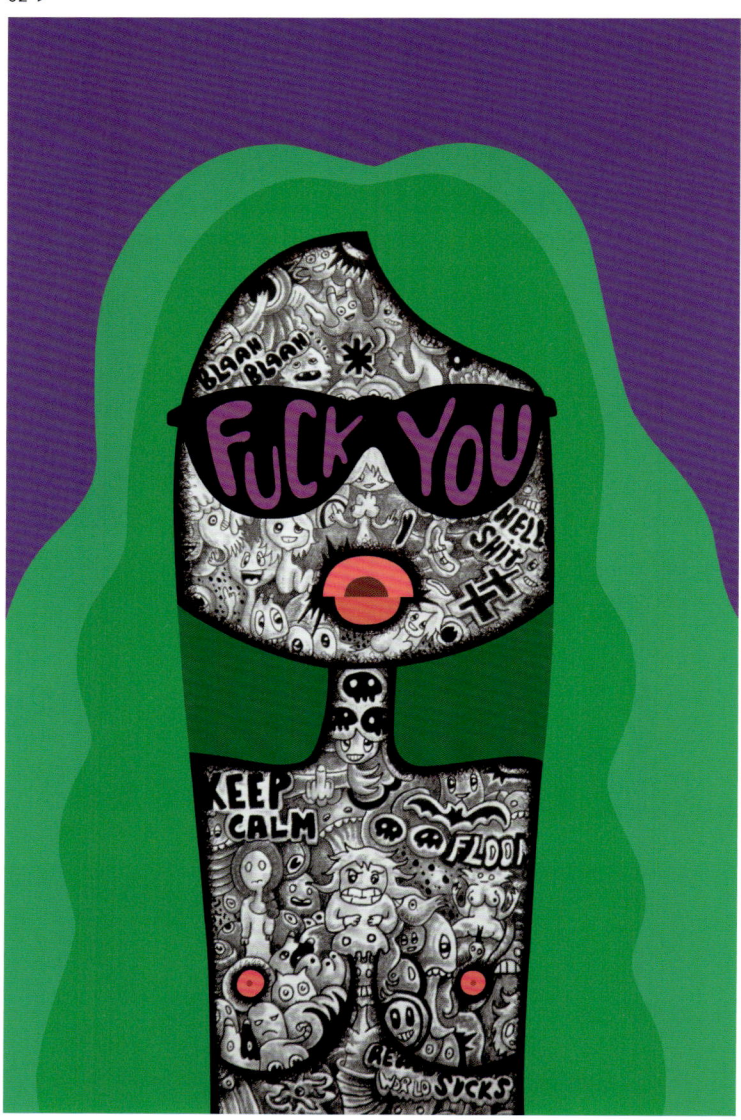

Hackatao are an Italian artist duo born in 2007 and are today known to be among the OG of crypto artists, starting with NFTs back in 2018.

Their style, a balanced combination of hyper-detailed black-and-white drawings with a colorful flat style, is a highly unique and recognizable visual language. Hackatao's art screams pop, both from the stylistic perspective and from its most intimate core, with their fundamental involvement and contribution to that artistic movement that could define the pop art of our time: crypto art.

Starting in the physical art world with their sculptures *Podmorks* (2007) and their canvases in acrylic and graphite, Hackatao's inclination toward digital means was strong even before the encounter with blockchain technology. Then as now, their spirit and approach to art creation have never changed, always characterized by experimentation and the use of new creative tools. When exploring the intricate labyrinth of drawings at the heart of Hackatao's works full stories unveil themselves, including a focus on social topics from climate change to gun violence as well as art history, symbolism, psychology, philosophies such as taoism, and gaming; even our most inner demons are revealed in recurrent characters, hiding in the depths of their compositions.

Although Hackatao's practice is in constant development, it is still possible to find their essence in their first artworks, including their work inspired by Andy Warhol (1928–1987) and the series of *Warhol Thinks Pop* (2018). Hackatao is here to stay: their language keeps evolving while their voice remains the same.

**ELEONORA BRIZI**
EARLY CRYPTO ART CURATOR
AND FOUNDER OF BREEZY ART

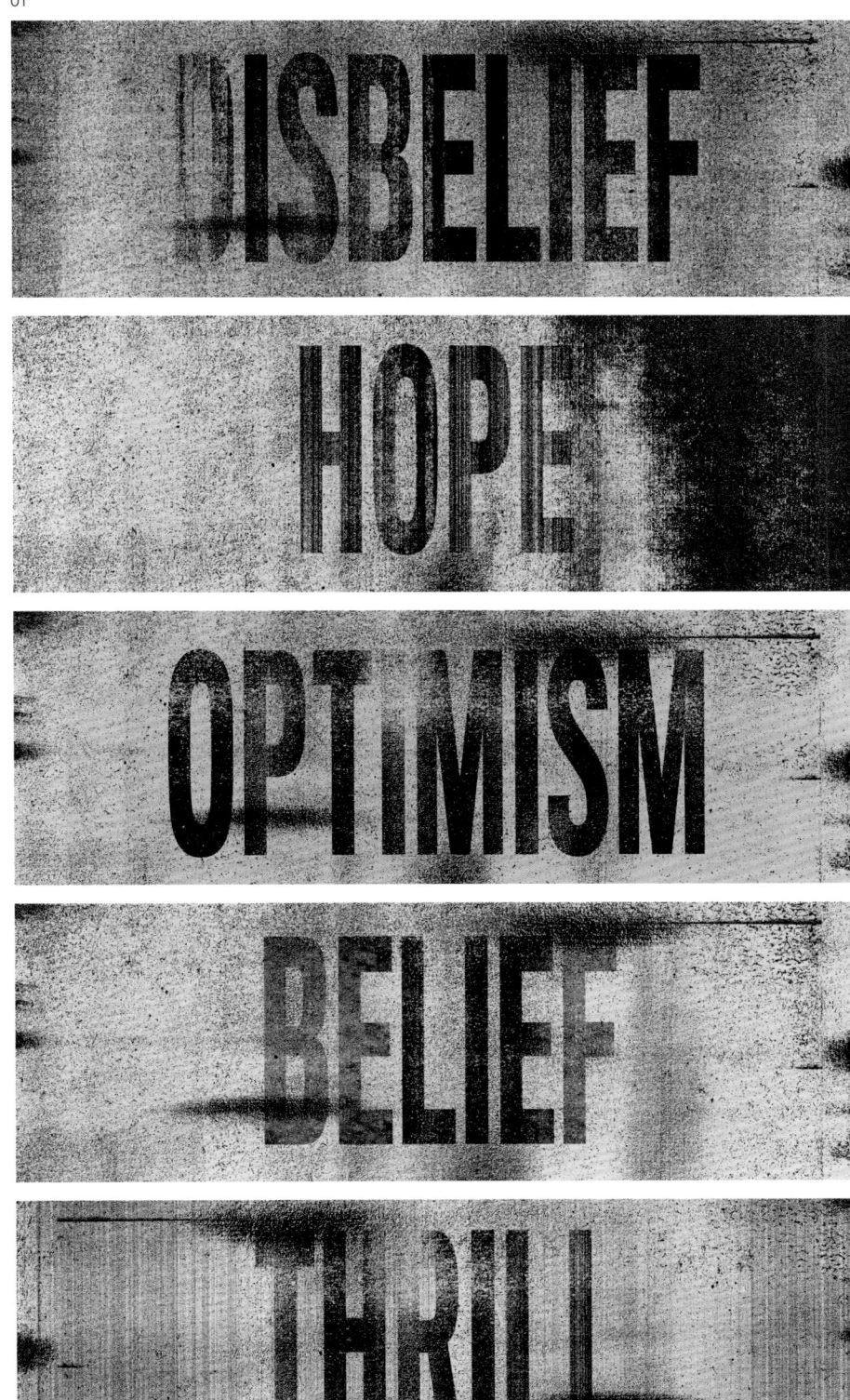

| # | TITLE | TIMESTAMP | MEDIUM | CHAIN | CONTRACT ADDRESS | TOKEN ID | EDITION SIZE |
|---|---|---|---|---|---|---|---|
| 01 | **Psyche** | 08-09-2020 03:49:16 | Adobe Photoshop | ETH | 0xb6dae651468e9593e4581705a09c10a76ac1e0c8 | 393 | 1/1 |

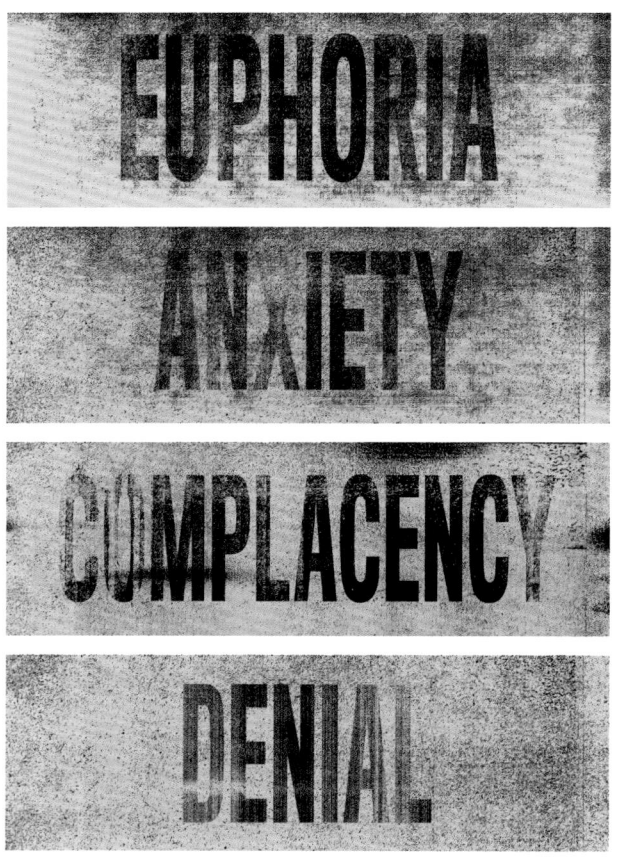

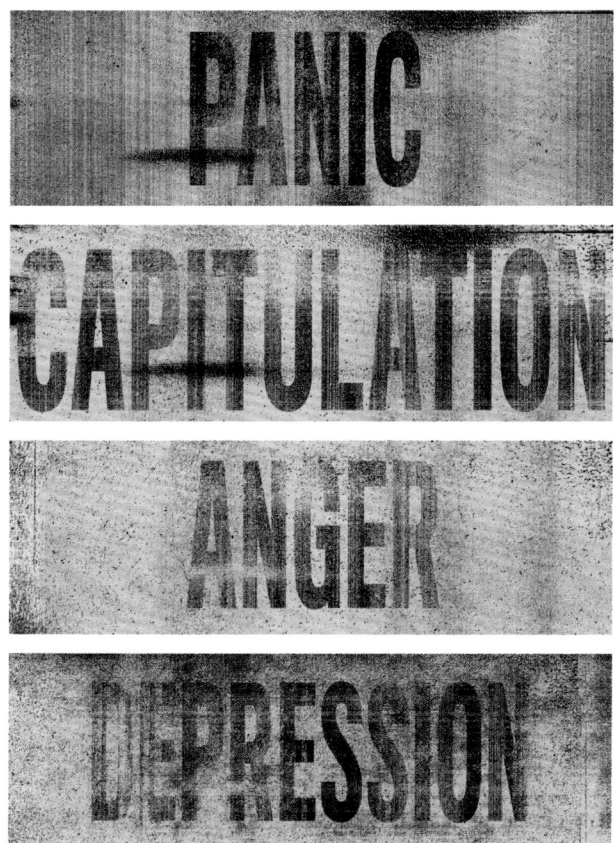

Crypto art would be a much flatter space without the ideas, leadership, collaboration, promotion, and most importantly the art of Coldie. Like many in our community, I'm fortunate to know Coldie as a fellow artist, collector, and friend. Since the beginning of the pandemic, when he organized the virtual exhibition *Get Out While You Stay In*, which inspired so many artists to further experiment with metaverse exhibitions. His art often contains commentary on crypto culture, always with strong psychological and philosophical underpinnings.

Coldie sprang his 3D art onto the global crypto art scene in 2018 after having already explored stereoscopic imagery as both a concert photographer and graphic designer since 2008. Having become renowned within the crypto conference circuit for his lenticular prints, Coldie was quick to adapt his 3D art to screen-based media by using anaglyphs in his earliest minted NFTs. Over time, Coldie improved on his 3D techniques, experimenting with stereoscopic GIFs, leveraging 3D software to create illusions of 2D collages floating in space, and most recently creating metaverse-ready 3D sculptures through the GLB format for VR. In *Choose Your Own Adventure* (2020), Coldie remains faithful to his technique of collage to suggest the multiple psychological layers of his artwork, its subject, and its environment. The work's background layer is dominated by *Psyche* (2020), an interactive textual representation of the 13 stages of the psychology of market cycles. The collector's choice of stage reveals a new backdrop layer on the master artwork, forming a collective-driven aesthetic emblematic of the psychological states of its collectors. Isolating the universal words away from the charts that usually accompany them, Coldie brings to the fore the humane and emotional states that affect and drive all markets and more broadly the cycles of human emotion. Given the volatility of the crypto markets, these words carry even greater weight.

**MATT KANE**
ARTIST

01 ▶

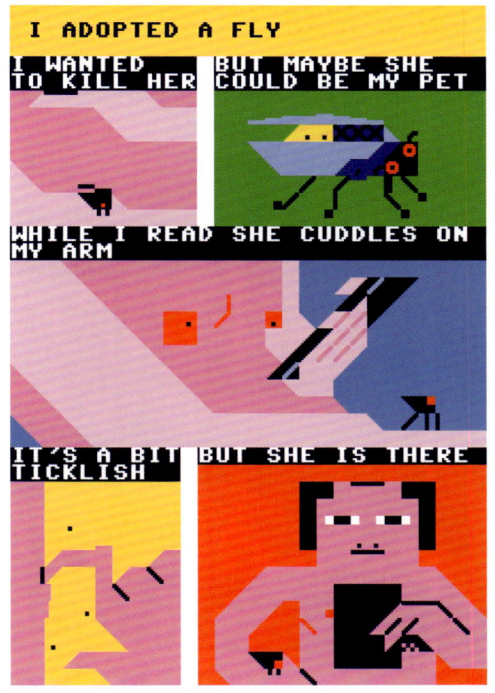

02 ▶

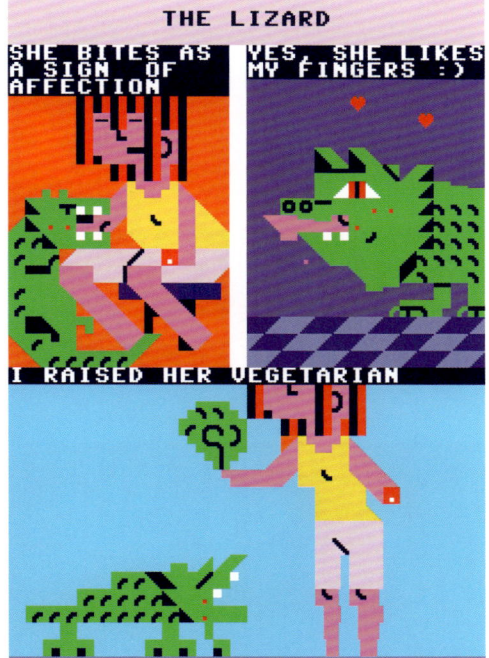

03 ▶

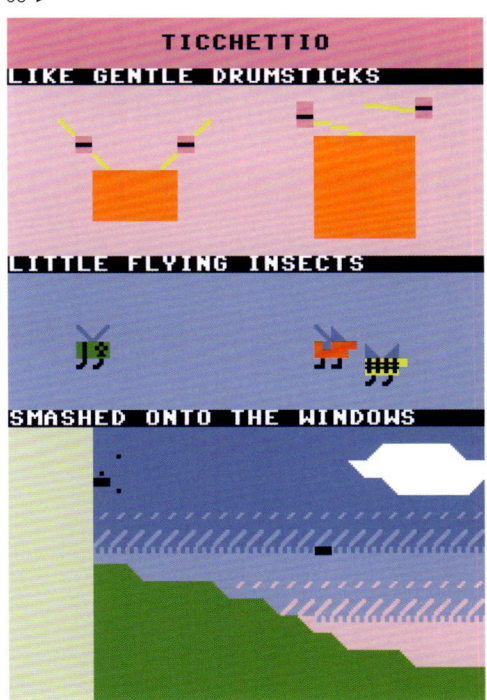

04 ▶

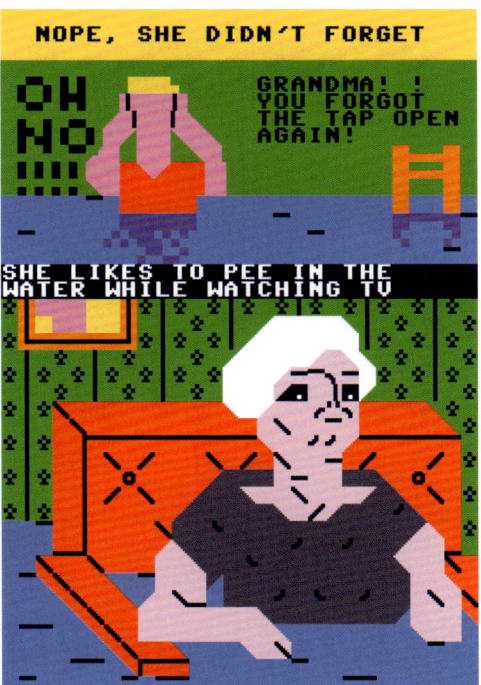

| # | TITLE | TIMESTAMP | MEDIUM | CHAIN | CONTRACT ADDRESS | TOKEN ID | EDITION SIZE |
|---|---|---|---|---|---|---|---|
| 01 | **I adopted a fly** | 04-11-2021 10:12:19 | 8-bit text-mode PETSCII, Pet Shop Pro, GIF | XTZ | KT1RJ6PbjHpwc3M5rw5s2Nbmefwbuwbdxton | 29263 | 10 |
| 02 | **The lizard** | 06-02-2021 10:12:08 | 8-bit text-mode PETSCII, Pet Shop Pro, GIF | XTZ | KT1RJ6PbjHpwc3M5rw5s2Nbmefwbuwbdxton | 47944 | 30 |
| 03 | **Ticchettio** | 11-14-2021 10:41:38 | 8-bit text-mode PETSCII, Pet Shop Pro, GIF | XTZ | KT1RJ6PbjHpwc3M5rw5s2Nbmefwbuwbdxton | 533772 | 18 |
| 04 | **Grandma** | 06-02-2021 09:11:02 | 8-bit text-mode PETSCII, Pet Shop Pro, GIF | XTZ | KT1RJ6PbjHpwc3M5rw5s2Nbmefwbuwbdxton | 110195 | 12 |
| 05 | **Tiny Love** | 12-19-2024 11:16:45 | 8-bit text-mode PETSCII, Pet Shop Pro, GIF | XTZ | KT1FcZTMf3oBLmFwpcjNKQoy6DsMe41Q28gm | 3 | 1/1 |

# AILADI

05 ▶

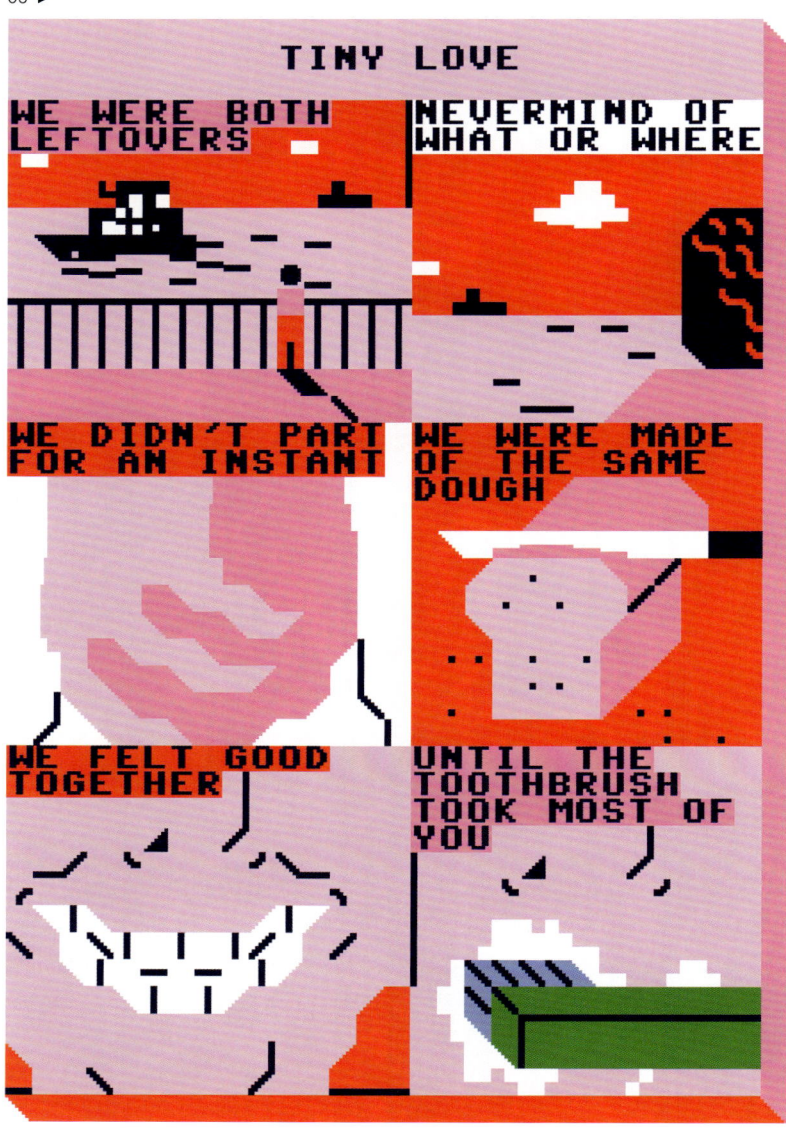

Ailadi's narrative-driven low-fi art speaks with the vocabulary of computers in the 1980s, but it doesn't tell us a story about nostalgia. Instead, the Italian artist's strikingly colorful GIFs are infused with the playful poetry of everyday sensory experiences. When I first met Ailadi in 2016 in Hong Kong, she was already fascinated, obsessed even, with Petscii, the iconic character set used on Commodore home computers. As a palette, a set of 256 text characters in 16 colors isn't much, but Ailadi loves playing with constraints. I saw her gleefully torturing herself with a *365 GIFS x 1 YEAR* (2016) project where she sat down everyday to create a GIF inspired by her life in Shanghai, then Hong Kong. She had also previously lived in Milan, Cologne, Paris, and New York, exhibited in different countries, and got quite accidentally popular on Giphy with over 600 million views.

Together with artist-programmer Jambonbill, they founded *PET.CORP (The PETSCII Corporation)* (2021), an ever-evolving project that took text-mode animations to museums and clubs with the help of a custom software they built themselves. I remember the ecstatic crowd bouncing in sync with Ailadi's characters and the sounds of a live Game Boy.

In 2021, while living in the French countryside, she minted her first NFTs on Hic et Nunc: *PETSCII Comics*, a humorous collection that frames the strange wonders of everyday life into haiku portraits of pet insects, gourmand chickens, and "Totems," where her text-mode characters spring into dance in an euphoric celebration of the forever loop.

**GIORGIO OLIVERO**
CURATOR, DESIGNER, AND FOUNDER
OF GIOSAMPIETRO.XYZ

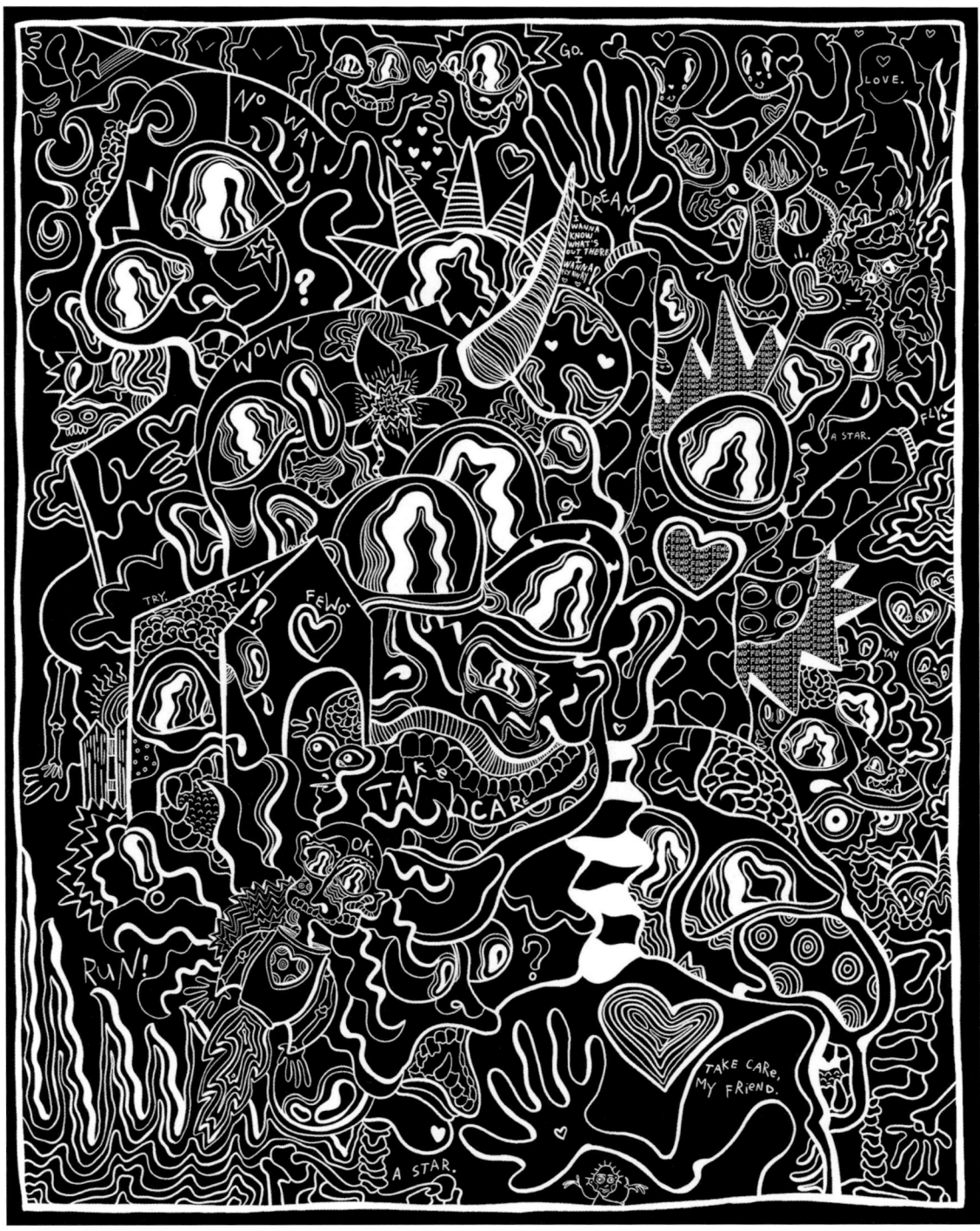

| # | TITLE | TIMESTAMP | MEDIUM | CHAIN | CONTRACT ADDRESS | TOKEN ID | EDITION SIZE |
|---|-------|-----------|--------|-------|------------------|----------|--------------|
| 01 | **The Day I Decided to Fly** | 01-02-2021 2:38:31 | Adobe Photoshop, Adobe After Effects, Procreate | ETH | 0xa2d544196fdbc-9da15a701c38bb60513c1802ef4 | 3900020251 | 1/1 |
| 02 | **Childhood trauma & neglect** | 06-14-2021 16:36:12 | Adobe Photoshop, Adobe After Effects, Procreate | ETH | 0xf126eb8284110a37c18e7-26a7e3b9fc21e68e897 | 35 | 1/1 |

02

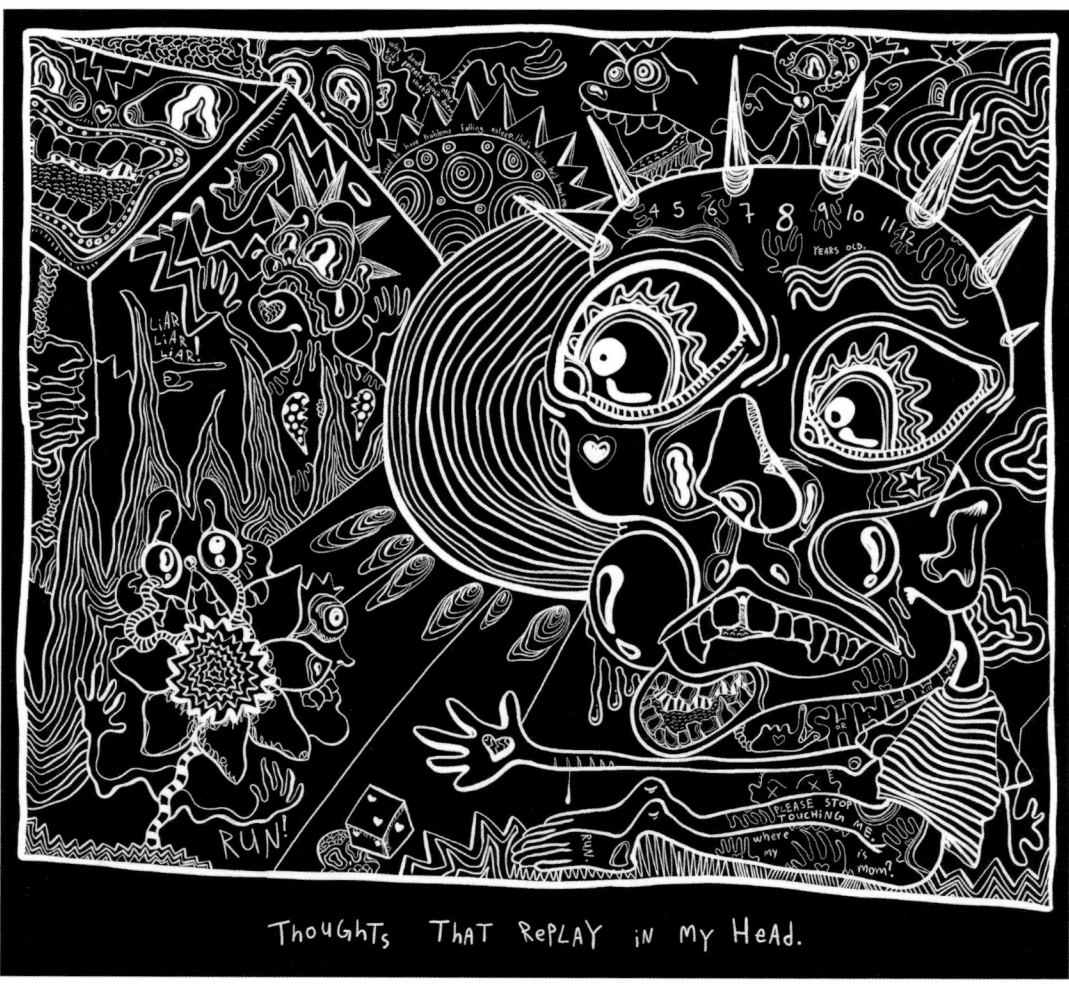

THoUGHTs  THaT  RePLAY  iN  MY  HeAd.

Victor Langlois (aka Fewocious) is arguably the NFT movement's first medium-native superstar. While Beeple and Pak were already acclaimed digital artists prior to entering NFTs, the 19-year-old owes his meteoric rise to his embrace of the blockchain. With an instantly recognizable aesthetic and endearing persona, Victor Langlois has emerged as the face of a new generation of young, digitally native artists enjoying life-changing success defining the NFT medium.

When I first met Victor in February 2021, he had never been interviewed before. He exuded a childlike innocence and a dogged optimism that belied the significant hardships he had faced. Born into a conservative family of Salvadoran immigrants in Las Vegas, Victor fled an abusive household at age 12 to live with his grandparents who were not supportive of his artistic ambitions nor his transgender identity. Feeling isolated and unable to afford a cellphone as a distraction, he instead poured his sadness, confusion, and dreams into his surrealist drawings. Victor discovered NFTs in March 2020 through the collector of

his first painting and quickly emerged as a rising star via emotive individual works and collaborations with metaverse wearables brand RTFKT Studios and musician Two Feet.

In coming out during Pride in 2021, Victor channeled his coming-of-age tribulations into a historic major auction house debut, *Hello, i'm Victor (FEWOCiOUS) and This Is My Life*. Encompassing five NFT artworks and accompanying paintings that represent each of his years from ages 14 to 17, the series charts his trajectory from despair to freedom in arrestingly visceral terms. By contrasting his distinctively bright color palette with heartwrenching recordings, Victor takes the viewer on a deeply personal journey. Through themes of loneliness and gender identity, these important works showcase a young artist simultaneously mourning his past while celebrating his future.

**MATT MEDVED**
CO-FOUNDER & CEO OF NFT NOW

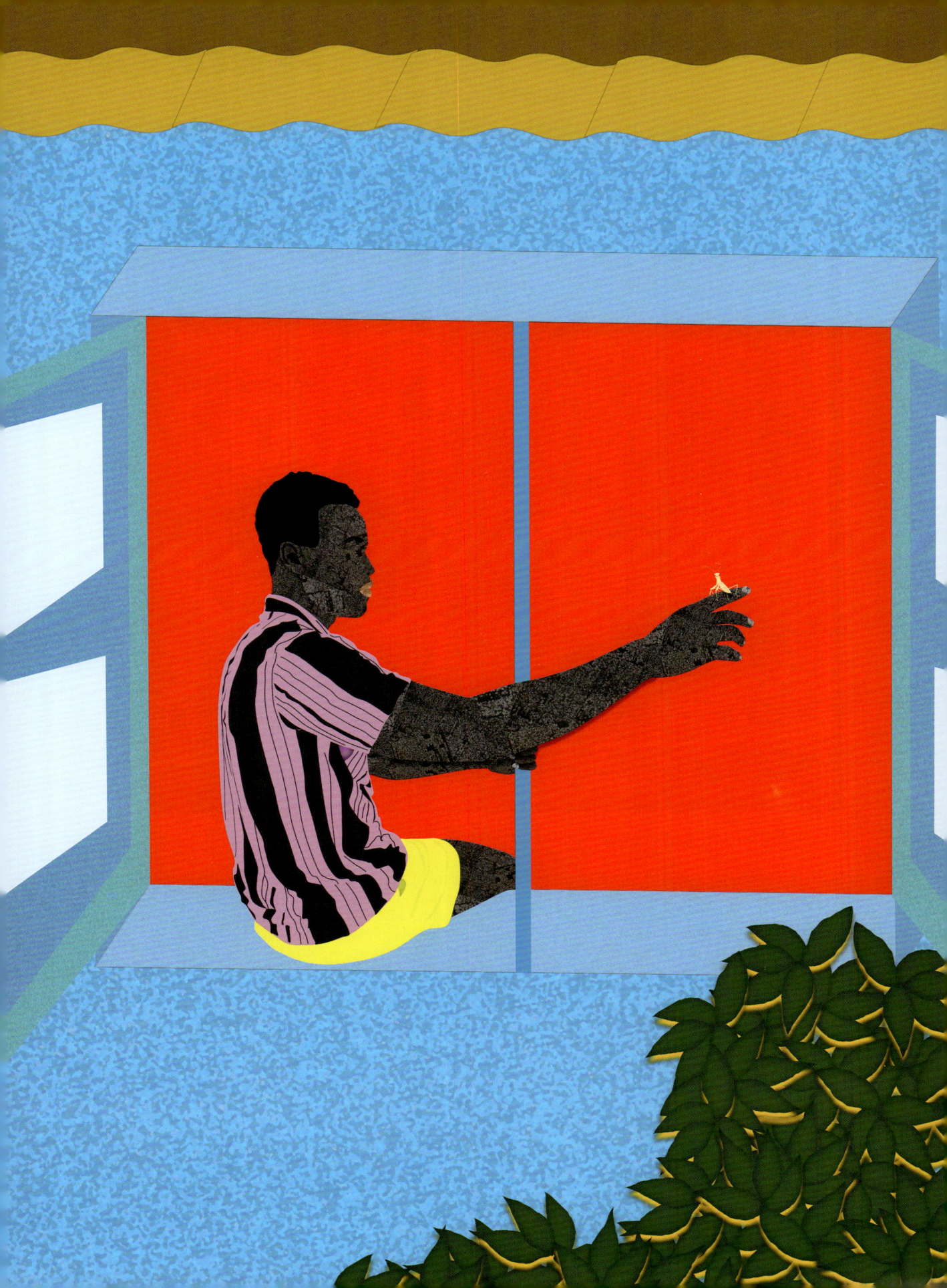

JASON BAILEY
ALEX ESTORICK

# ON CRYPTO ART

The World's First Global Art Movement?

*Before my father [Charles "Chuck" Csuri] passed last year, when he found out about NFTs and the fact that people were suddenly interested in an artistic movement that had already been happening for 60 years, he actually wept. He was so emotionally overcome with the fact that this was finally coming to fruition. For all those years, the art world never took it seriously. And now, like it or not, NFTs have given that whole movement credibility through provenance and by making art less elitist.*

Caroline Csuri
Daughter of Charles "Chuck" Csuri (1922–2022)

02.00 ▶
Osinachi
*Man in the Window*, 04-03-2022 08:48:27
Microsoft Word
Ethereum, 0xb932a70a57673d89f4acffbe830e8ed7f75fb9e0, 33665

## What Is Crypto Art?

What is crypto art and what are its aesthetics? Are all NFTs crypto art? And are all artworks — digital or physical — that reference cryptocurrency crypto art? Should the term *crypto art* be applied only to contemporary artists who work directly with the blockchain as a medium?

We believe it is most useful to think of crypto art as beginning with a small number of purpose-built platforms in 2016/17 that were designed to offer a more inclusive and equitable alternative to existing art markets. In this way, crypto art can be seen to follow the decentralized logic of cryptocurrency as a means of disintermediating long-standing centralized authorities that were no longer perceived to be operating in the best interests of digital artists. Given the prominence of artists from the Global South among the crypto art community, a case can also be made that crypto art represents the first truly global art movement, as well as a set of aspirational principles for a new creator economy.

With its community of creators largely self-taught, or else a product of the cultural industries, crypto art might be regarded as a digital form of outsider art, as well as a revival of medieval and non-Western token economies.[1] In its ability to distill the essence of the meme economy, through visual simplification rather than overt complexity, it also recalls practically all of the modernist movements. Indeed, as an "anti-art" movement in the tradition of Dada, Surrealism, and Fluxus, crypto art defies definition by traditional art-historical methodologies. In our view, any "aesthetics" of crypto art must therefore necessarily rely on the data recorded on the blockchain and by the marketplaces, rather than traditional connoisseurship. If we accept that the capture of data is never an entirely neutral activity, we use it nonetheless as a way to clarify the priorities of those artists and collectors who shaped the early cryptosphere.[2] Of course, in its defiance of definition, *our* analysis of crypto art represents only one possible approach to a movement born of plural power distribution.

In the past, it was standard for traditional art galleries to carefully curate the artists and artworks included within exhibitions. By contrast, early crypto art platforms like Curio Cards, DADA (aka Dada.nyc), and Rare Pepe Wallet were radically inclusive, welcoming everyone who wished to participate, and passing no judgment on the work submitted. Where galleries typically take a 50% commission from artists' sales, Curio Cards and Rare Pepe Wallet took zero commission, while DADA has explored the redistribution of individual sales across its entire community of artists. We argue that crypto art as a hyper-inclusive anti-art movement was born at the Rare AF conference in New York in January 2018. This was the first time many of the artists and builders of these radical new platforms came together to meet in real life. The theme of the event was "artists deserve more," with those in attendance united by the shared goal of building a new art world from the ground up.

Following presentations by the creators of Rare Pepe Wallet, DADA, and *CryptoPunks*, Rare AF concluded with the auction of *Homer Pepe* (2016) which sold for $40,000. This work is the perfect symbol of the memetic, low-brow, anti-art aesthetic that crypto art would come to embrace. When viewed alongside the emergence of *CryptoKitties* a few weeks earlier, the Rare AF sale was also an early sign that crypto art — created in opposition to the perceived exclusivity and elitism of the traditional art world — was already acting to replicate the mechanics of the system it railed against. While our analysis prioritizes the aesthetics of crypto art over its market, certainly one of its signatures is the transparent relationship between art and money that contemporary art has often sought to conceal.

Shortly after attending Rare AF, Jason Bailey wrote a definition of crypto art outlining this new phenomenon as a serious and cohesive art movement:

*CryptoArt* [sic] *are rare digital artworks, sometimes described as digital trading cards or "rares," associated with unique and provably rare tokens that exist on the blockchain. The concept is based on the idea of digital scarcity, which allows you to buy, sell, and trade digital goods as if they were physical goods. This system works due to the fact that, like Bitcoins and other cryptocurrency, CryptoArt exist in limited quantity. [...]*

*While no single CryptoArtist or CryptoArtwork adheres to a single definition, I believe it is helpful to look at a series of common factors that have shaped the aesthetic and community thus far.*

1. *Digitally Native: For the first time, artwork can be created, editioned, bought, and sold digitally.*
2. *Geographically Agnostic: Empowered by the internet, artists participate from all over the world. CryptoArt is the first truly global art movement.*
3. *Democratic/Permissionless: Everyone is encouraged to participate regardless of skills, training, class, gender, race, age, creed, etc.*

[1] Bissera Pentcheva, *The Sensual Icon: Space, Ritual, and the Senses in Byzantium* (Pennsylvania: The Pennsylvania State University Press, 2010), 17–44.

[2] Alex Estorick, "Algorithmic Violence and the Politics of Data: The Work of Mimi Onuoha and Gretchen Andrew," *Flash Art Online*, December 11, 2020, https://flash---art.com/2020/12/algorithmic-violence-and-the-politics-of-data-the-work-of-mimi-onuoha-and-gretchen-andrew/.

02.01
cryptograffiti
*Bitcoin Donation Street Art*, 2014
Repurposed credit cards and mixed media

02.02
Nanu Berks
*Own Your Data*, 2018
Mixed Media, 22.8 × 22.8 cm

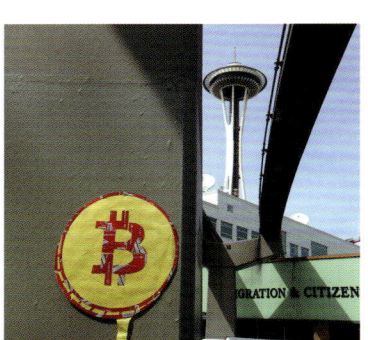

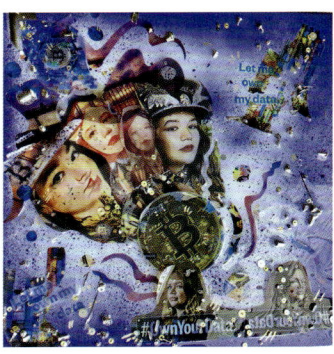

4. *Decentralized: Tools and guidelines are designed to reduce the power of gatekeepers and middlemen and increase the autonomy of artists.*
5. *Anonymous: Use of pseudonyms allows artists to create and sell art while staying anonymous (if preferred), freeing them from social judgment.*
6. *Memetic: CryptoArt are often literally memes valued for their ability to spread quickly. The difference? The "Meme Economy" is now a reality.*
7. *Self-Referential: CryptoArtists often play with references to key events and personalities within cryptocurrency and blockchain culture.*
8. *Crypto Patrons: CryptoArt is collected by the CryptoRich: A group of savvy technologists and investors who got into cryptocurrency early.*
9. *Pro-Artist: Blockchain platforms often take little to no commission from artists. Artists are often remunerated for every future sale of a single work.*
10. *Dankness: Because CryptoArt is open to everyone, judging it by traditional artistic standards kills what is great about it. Instead, it is best to judge CryptoArt by "dankness" or potency of expression and creativity.*[3]

As with all art movements, crypto art has several antecedents that helped to shape its formation. We divide these prototypes into two main groups. The first group includes Bitcoin evangelists like cryptograffiti **[02.01]**, CoinArtist (Marguerite deCourcelle), and Nanu Berks **[02.02]**, who used art to promote blockchain as a tool of emancipation. The second group includes contemporary media artists exploring the blockchain as an art-making medium, bent through the prism of 1960s conceptual art. This second group includes artists like Rhea Myers, Sarah Meyohas, Kevin McCoy, and others mentioned in the previous chapter "On Quantum." These two groups demand consideration both to highlight their influence on crypto art and to differentiate their practice from the crypto art movement.

### Bitcoin Evangelism and Blockchain Art

For those reeling from the 2008 Global Financial Crisis, Bitcoin was exactly what they were looking for: a decentralized alternative that did not require them to put their faith back into old systems that they felt had already failed them. More than merely a digital currency, Bitcoin spawned a culture, a community, and a revolution complete with its own language and aesthetics. For Bitcoin to grow, however, more people needed to understand the complexities behind this blockchain-based digital currency and the financial problems it aimed to solve. For the artist and early Bitcoin evangelist cryptograffiti,

*Art has the ability to distill complex subject matter into something more people can understand. This is especially important with Bitcoin as those who stand to benefit from it the most are likely to learn about it the latest.*

— cryptograffiti [4]

[3] Jason Bailey, "What is CryptoArt?," Artnome, January 19, 2018, https://www.artnome.com/news/2018/1/14/what-is-cryptoart.
[4] cryptograffiti, "About," accessed June 8, 2022, https://cryptograffiti.com/pages/about-us.

cryptograffiti and other artists interested in using art to promote Bitcoin borrowed from the street art aesthetic and guerrilla marketing tactics of artists like Banksy and Shepard Fairey to spread the word about cryptocurrency to a wider population. As early as 2013, cryptograffiti began to produce experimental street artworks using public and private blockchain

Cryptonati
*PEPETRADERS*, 10-21-2016 18:30:37
Rare Pepes, Series 6, Card 28, 'Meme Magic'
Counterparty,
13Mpz1EoP2wi1nGGwZt4kQ7hfxRmBRToKc,
PEPETRADERS

Rare Scrilla
*BBOYPEPE*, 10-13-2016 13:52:38
Rare Pepes, Series 4, Card 32, Adobe Photoshop
Counterparty,
18PHGKzAcMDNVNie6kwDp2s6rkKM8RBcg2,
BBOYPEPE

Cryptonati
*WPPEPE*, 10-27-2016 20:02:56
Rare Pepes, Series 7, Card 16, 'Meme Magic'
Counterparty,
13Mpz1EoP2wi1nGGwZt4kQ7hfxRmBRToKc,
WPPEPE

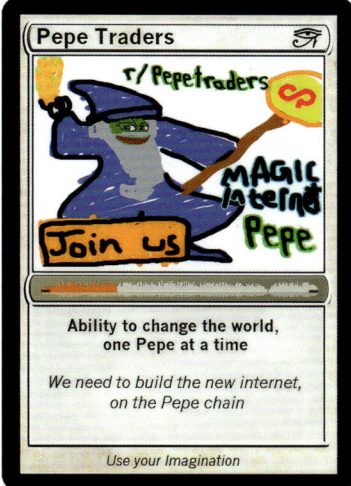

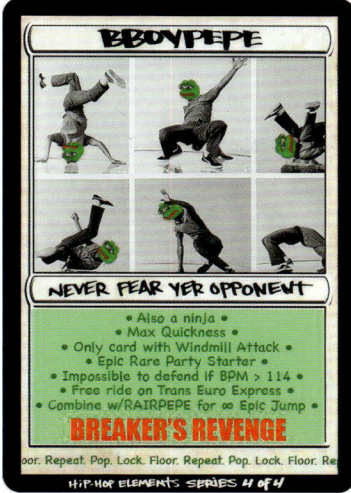

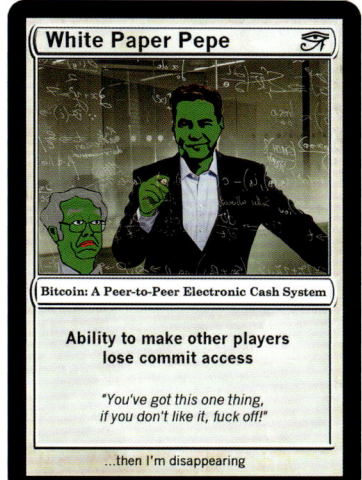

wallet keys embedded in QR codes distributed around the streets of San Francisco and other major US cities.

Publicly questioning the banking system by co-opting its iconography, while chopping up credit cards and repurposing other traditional banking materials became central to cryptograffiti's artistic practice. Channeling the cypherpunk's credo of privacy through cryptography, others also used their art as a means to promote Bitcoin, with CoinArtist employing gamification to engage new publics. From 2014 onwards, she devised a series of puzzle paintings containing visual clues to private keys that would unlock bitcoin as a reward for anyone who could solve the puzzle. While Nanu Berks, a self-described "nomadic" graffiti artist and muralist, has done as much as anyone to embed blockchain iconography into the prehistory of crypto art.[5] Her story is particularly poignant for its embrace of Web3 as a means of empowering communities often excluded from new technologies:

*After the collapse of the economic system in Argentina that left my family and I on the street, I traveled endlessly, painting any and all walls I could find. I remember in 2012 by the Chichen Itza pyramids in Mexico, a stranger saw me drawing a mural concept and began explaining to me why Bitcoin had the same value systems as my […] 'living on the fringe outside of tech and money' lifestyle.*

— Nanu Berks [6]

Unlike the Bitcoin evangelists, artists like Rhea Myers, Kevin McCoy, and Sarah Meyohas all embraced the blockchain and smart contracts as artistic media. However, in contrast to the former group, these artists were not railing against centralized financial institutions nor the perceived gatekeepers of the traditional art world. Quite the opposite, they depended on the anti-aesthetics of conceptual art and net art, thereby operating largely within the established codes of contemporary art, while extending that repertoire.

While this second group of artists gained moderate recognition in the contemporary art world, the idea of collecting non-fungible tokens never gained traction with traditional art collectors. Instead, it took the growing interest of a number of rapidly expanding (and newly moneyed) Bitcoin and Ethereum communities for the crypto art movement to fully establish itself.

### The Birth of Crypto Art

In 2016, Joe Looney, an engineer and early adopter of Bitcoin, launched Rare Pepe Wallet as a platform for creating, buying, selling, and gifting memes of Pepe the Frog **[02.03]**. This platform represents the blueprint for all modern NFT marketplaces but remains unique for the fact that Looney took no commission from sales. He also studiously avoided curation, opening

5 DanStone, "Inside NFTs: Nanu Berks," *Global Coin Research*, April 27, 2021, https://globalcoinresearch.com/2021/04/27/inside-nfts-nanu-berks/.
6 Nanu Berks, "NFTs," accessed June 8, 2022, https://www.nanuberks.com/nfts/.

02.04
DADA Collective
*Screens: An Exploration*, 11-28-2019 16:08:19
Digital drawing on the DADA platform
Ethereum, 0xb932a70a57673d89f4acffbe830e8ed7f75fb9e0, 5636-24633

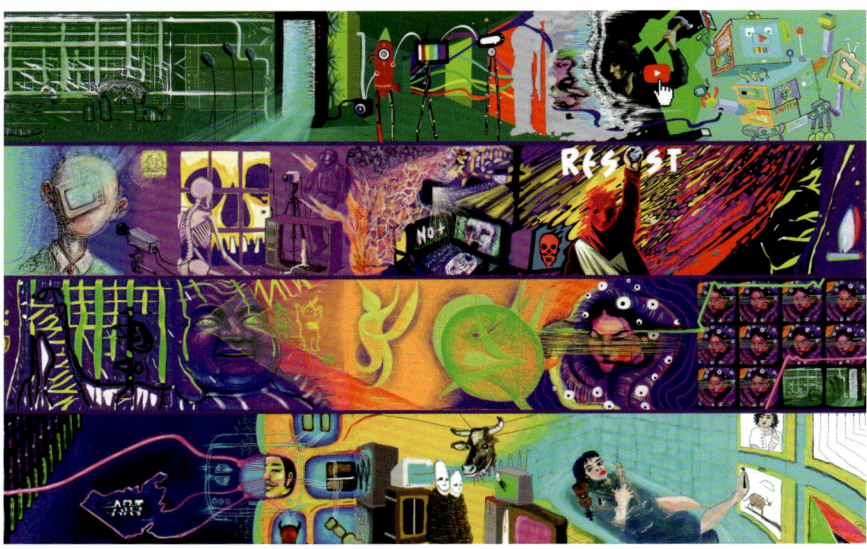

up Rare Pepe Wallet to anyone who wanted to participate regardless of their level of skill or training. In this spirit, he established a tongue-in-cheek board of "Rare Pepe Scientists" to review submissions. Yet the goal was never to judge people's art, it was simply to act as a spam filter and to keep out any submissions that were NSFW ("not safe for work").

Rare Pepe Wallet was born from a playful sensibility as well as a running joke that someday people would be able to buy and sell internet memes (digital images that go viral online) and that the most powerful memes would be rare and thus more valuable. At the time, Pepe the Frog — conceived by comic artist Matt Furie — was an omnipresent meme. But Rare Pepe Wallet turned the joke of a meme economy into a reality by linking the digital images of Pepe to tokens on the blockchain. Swiftly evolving from a handful of collectors messing around with frogs to a multimillion dollar global marketplace, Rare Pepe Wallet was the first project to hint at the scale and interest NFTs would later crystallize in 2021.

Artists have often repurposed the language and semiotics of their own time to critique cultural and political codes. Taken together, the collection of cards comprising Rare Pepe Wallet make for a lucid distillation — indeed a realist vision — of the quotidian life of the Western world for a period characterized by social media–driven populism. What lends Rare Pepe Wallet particular cultural legitimacy is that its memes were the product of everyday people — rather than an insulated elite — whose communal engagement conjured a viral form of folk art. In true cypherpunk style, many of the contributors to Rare Pepe Wallet operated pseudonymously, combining satire and social commentary with an outsider aesthetic whose complex of ideas were distributed online in grassroots fashion.

Had they remained within the narrow domain of the contemporary digital art world, NFTs would likely never have reached escape velocity. That it took a group of outsiders with an irreverent sense of humor to achieve this through its passion for decentralization and mastery of memes bespeaks the extitutional underpinnings of the crypto art movement. Unfortunately, because of its co-option by the alt-right, Rare Pepe Wallet has rarely received the credit it deserves. Far from being hateful, however, Rare Pepe Wallet was an exercise in radical inclusivity by which all future NFT marketplaces would come to be measured (and often come up short). One notable exception is DADA.

If Rare Pepe Wallet started the crypto art movement by circulating digitally scarce art at scale while allowing participation for all, its self-imposed limitation was that submissions involve Pepe the Frog. Founded by Venezuelan-born artist and entrepreneur Beatriz Helena Ramos and self-described "Jewish Aztec Princess" Yehudit Mam, DADA expanded the crypto art movement by incorporating NFTs into an online drawing platform that was home to a global community of 150,000 artists.[7]

DADA's platform allowed artists to start a visual conversation by creating images using a digital drawing application (think Microsoft Paint) and inviting a community of other artists

[7] Yehudit Mam, "About," *Medium*, accessed June 8, 2022, https://grandenchilada. medium.com/about.

Osinachi
*Nduka's Wedding Day*, 2019 (Minted: 2020-01-04 07:55:29)
Microsoft Word
Ethereum, 0xb932a70a57673d89f4acffbe830e8ed7f75fb9e0, 6815

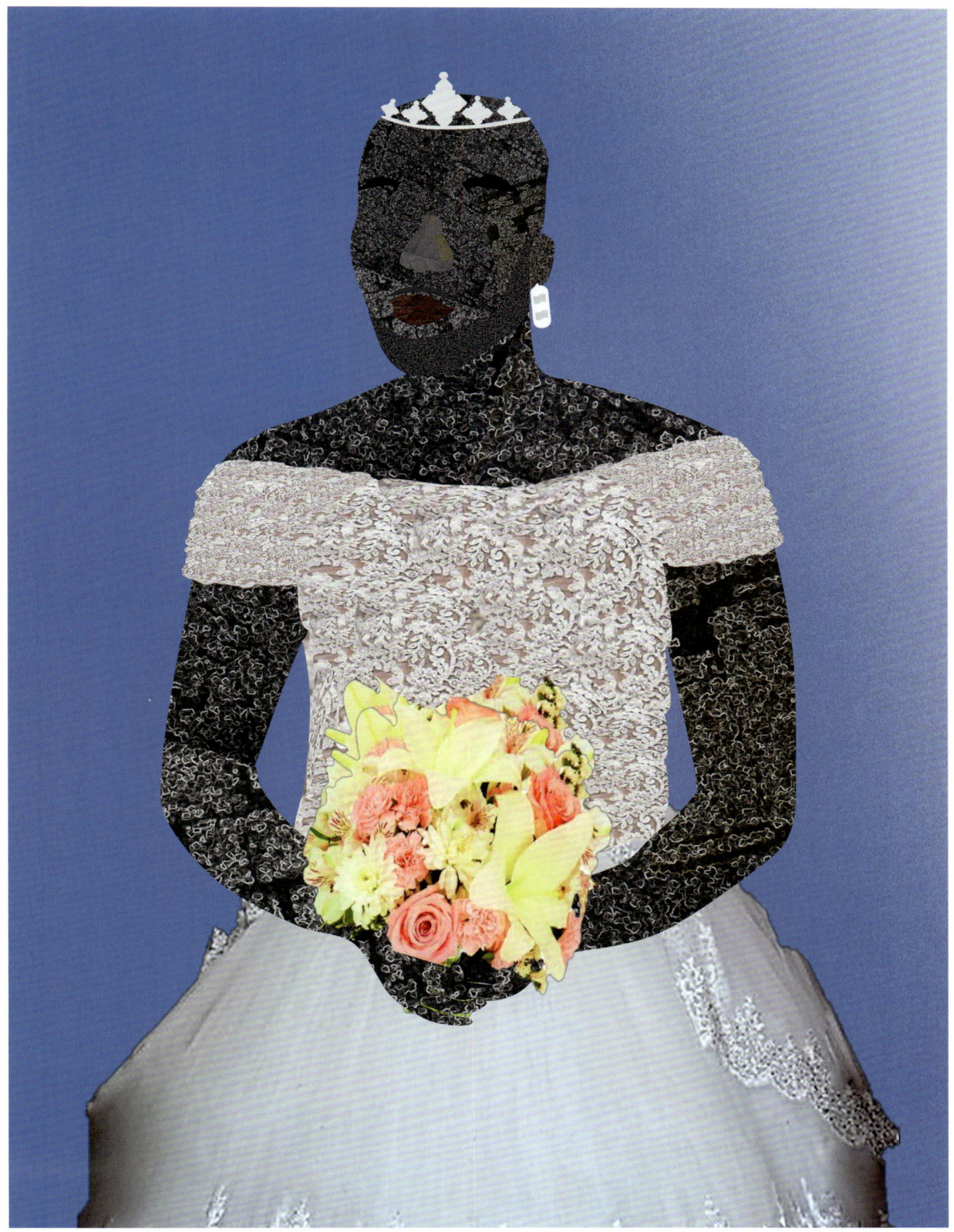

to extend their drawings **[02.04]**. It therefore followed the mechanics of the Surrealist drawing game "exquisite corpse" but with the art visible to all. DADA emphasizes inclusion and prides itself on supporting creativity and free speech while taking pains to avoid curation and censorship. It also encourages participation from all levels of ability, stressing the benefits of the art-making process while celebrating all members of its global community over a small number of exceptional talents. For Beatriz Helena Ramos,

*it allows artists to do what they love with no strings attached, but it also creates a space for artistic expression and innovation, and this collective value creation belongs to the commons. Instead of just distributing money, we are building long-term wealth together.*

— Beatriz Helena Ramos [8]

DADA's embrace of "distributed" community creation, or curation, makes it a clear example of crypto art. But it has also helped to inspire new forms of generative art, tokenized as NFTs, that cede more control than ever to their audience.

While Rare Pepe Wallet and DADA share much in common, the former advocated libertarian principles of autonomy and individualism where the latter leans towards socialism in prioritizing the needs of its overall community. As much is clear from DADA's drawing program, which de-emphasized the individual by fostering co-creation and stylistic variety. Its token economy was also designed to redistribute profits from individual sales across the entire community. Indeed, DADA's initial aspiration had been to generate enough money to provide a universal basic income for its membership without introducing competition or resorting to perverse incentives that might negatively impact their art.

Perhaps DADA's most influential contribution, however, was its introduction of smart contracts that ensured secondary royalties for artists. This was inspired by Ramos's realization that, despite a long and successful career as a commercial artist, she had no ownership of her life's work nor did she share in the profits it continued to generate. Her belief that an artist who creates value deserves to benefit from it over time fuelled DADA's desire to include royalties in their contract. That principle has now come to define crypto art as a movement shaped by artists for artists, and more than a novel conceptual art conceit. Today, DADA's horizontal organization is a paradigm of the blockchain's decentralized potential, helping to advance the cause of a new "invisible economy."

## SuperRare and the Business of Crypto Art

With the popularity of NFTs spiking in late 2017 and early 2018, several platforms attempted to replicate commercially the successful formulae of DADA and Rare Pepe Wallet. These included KnownOrigin, Nifty Gateway, OpenSea, Rarible, and Pixura, the parent company of SuperRare.

According to its founders, SuperRare's goal is "to build a bigger, better, more inclusive market that anyone can participate in."[9] While this was certainly true at the outset, SuperRare is now renowned for its strict and centralized curation that has left many artists hoping to be let in and a few angry for being kicked off. When asked how a platform with the goal of decentralization and inclusivity became known for being centralized and exclusive, SuperRare co-founder Jonathan Perkins shared that their curatorial strategy and ascendence as tastemakers were the unintended consequences of a lack of resources as well as pressure to scale to meet demand. In order to avoid fraudulent actors they needed to verify artists manually. But they also needed to maintain a balance of artists and collectors to avoid a lopsided market.

In the early days, it was different, with SuperRare onboarding most, if not all, of the artists who applied to its platform. This had the effect of widening participation to a generation of artists for whom the traditional art world was inaccessible. Here, we acknowledge SuperRare's importance to crypto art by considering three artists who experienced early success on the platform. These are Osinachi from Nigeria, Carlos Marcial from Puerto Rico, and Sarah Zucker from the United States.

Born well away from the art world epicenters of New York, Paris, and London, statistically speaking, Prince Jacon Osinachi Igwe had almost zero chance of achieving success as a digital artist based in Nigeria. Undeterred, he developed his own distinct style using Microsoft Word, his skills honed in internet cafes rather than at home, since he could not afford a computer or expensive design software. Works like *Nduka's Wedding Day* (2019) **[02.05]** portray members of Nigeria's LGBTQIA+ population, single mothers, and other marginalized figures engaged in everyday activities, highlighting how their very existence is a protest against the norms and laws of Nigerian society.

[8] Beatriz Helena Ramos, "Rare Digital Art Festival #1 Anniversary: *DADA," Right Click Save*, February 14, 2022, https://www.rightclicksave.com/article/rare-digital-art-festival-anniversary-dada.
[9] Jonathan Perkins, interview with the authors, May 25, 2022.

Carlos Marcial
*Here Comes Fiat*, 11-22-2020 15:16:33
Cinema 4D, Octane Render, RNDR
Ethereum, 0xb932a70a57673d89f4acffbe830e8ed7f75fb9e0, 6815

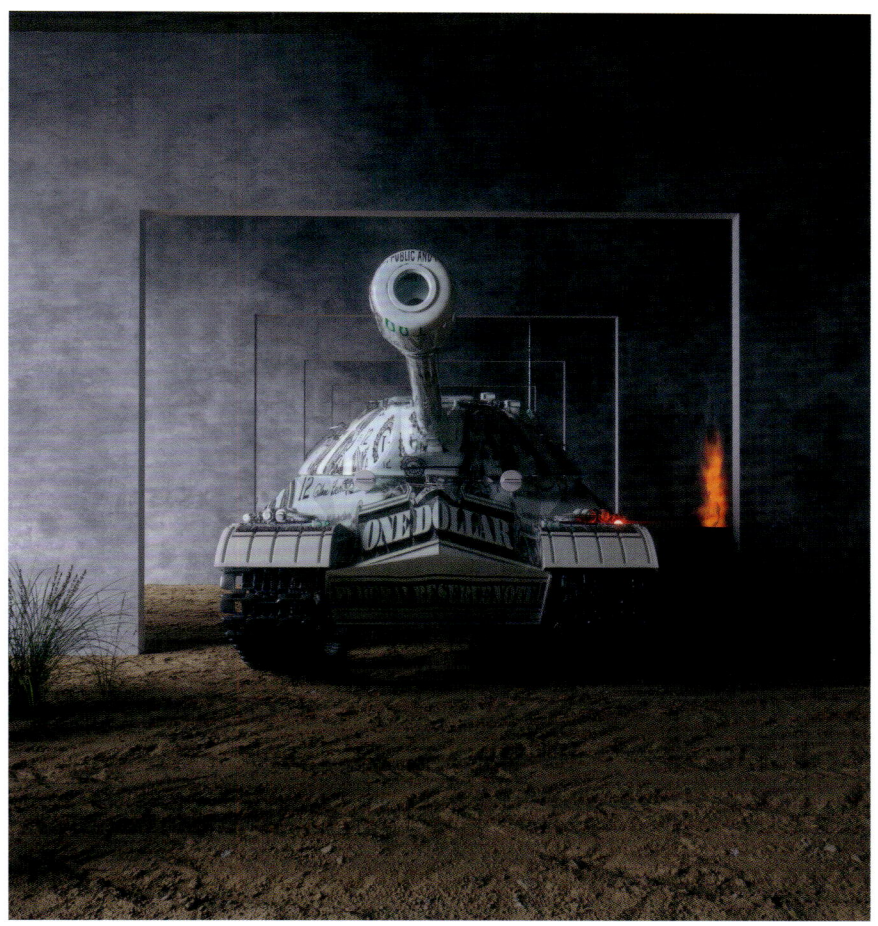

Having built up confidence in his abilities as an artist, Osinachi approached a number of galleries in the United States and Europe, trying to gain acceptance, or at least some valuable feedback, to help grow his career as a professional artist. When he did receive a response, it was not the encouragement he was hoping for. One gallerist even forwarded Osinachi's work to his colleagues, mocking it with the artist still included in the email thread. In 2018, Osinachi read about the early blockchain-based marketplaces like RARE Art Labs, Portion, KnownOrigin, and SuperRare. At the time, these marketplaces involved little to no curation, so the artist was able to get his work in front of a small but global audience of collectors:

*"Now, I'm able to cut out this person who doesn't believe in my art, who is capable of preventing my art from even reaching the collectors. Middlemen like this can put artists down. But through the NFT space, I've been able to circumvent these middlemen and put my art out there. And now these middlemen are the ones coming to me asking to collaborate. So I wouldn't be here without NFTs."*

— Osinachi [10]

Osinachi's story is far from unique within the crypto art community. Carlos Marcial was born in Puerto Rico, and while his mother is an art historian, he knew that as an artist from the Caribbean without the right connections he had minimal chance of making it in contemporary art.[11] At the start of the COVID-19 pandemic, he was let go from his job as a commercial 3D artist. With a family to feed, and without the government subsidization available to US and European citizens, Marcial tried to sell his art as NFTs to make ends meet.

[10] Jason Bailey, "Have NFTs Lost Their Way," *Right Click Save,* January 31, 2022, https://www.rightclicksave.com/article/have-nfts-lost-their-way.
[11] Samuel P. Fraiberger, Roberta Sinatra, Magnus Resch, Christoph Riedl, and Albert-László Barabási, "Quantifying Reputation and Success in Art," *Science,* November 8, 2018, https://www.science.org/doi/abs/10.1126/science.aau7224.
[12] Sarah Zucker, "Artist Sarah Zucker" *Art Sense,* Ep. 17, Apple Podcasts, accessed June 8, 2022, https://podcasts.apple.com/us/podcast/ep-17-artist-sarah-zucker/id1574394526?i=1000539042134.

02.07 ▶
Sarah Zucker
*You Can Save This*, 11-30-2021 22:17:3511
Digital Animation, video feedback, and analog processing on VHS
Ethereum, 0xb932a70A57673d89f4acfFBE830E8ed7f75Fb9e0, 30811

02.08 ▶
ROBNESS
*Cryptophecies*, 12-02-2020 20:42:43
GIF
Ethereum, 0xb932a70A57673d89f4acfFBE830E8ed7f75Fb9e0, 5743

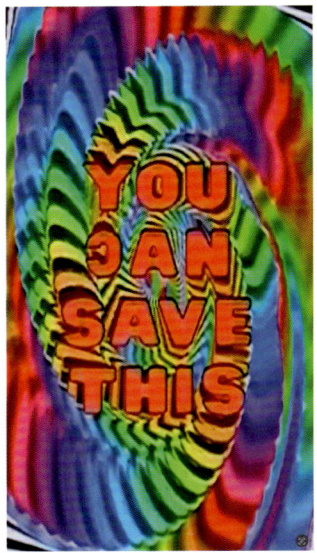
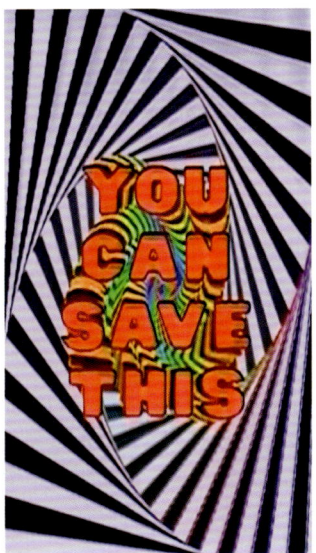
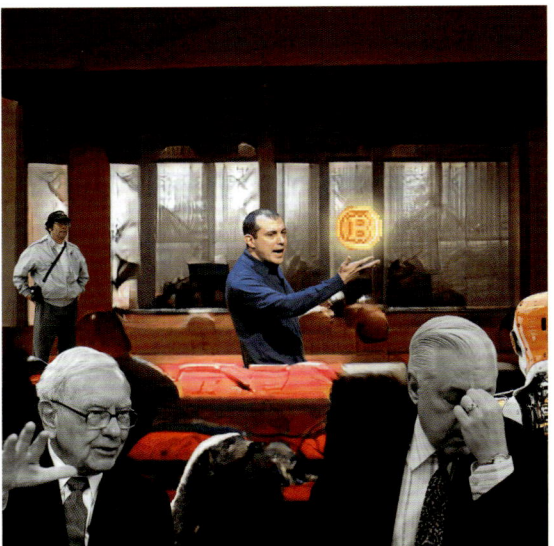

His work immediately resonated with the community. He was not only able to survive but to flourish, living off his art and buying his family a new home. An early adopter of Bitcoin and other cryptocurrencies, decentralization is a fundamental theme of Marcial's art. Works like *Here Comes Fiat* (2020) **[02.06]** express his distrust of centralized authority.

In a 2022 interview with Richard Entrup, former CIO at Christie's, Marcial shared:

*If you don't get eyes on your art, on your persona, on your biography, basically you don't exist. The fact remains that NFTs were able to create a market for people like me in the Global South, in Mexico City — though I was raised in the Caribbean — to sell their art. For me, this has been revolutionary. [...] With NFTs, not only have I been able to get the attention of collectors but also the people writing critically about NFTs, all from my home here in Mexico. That wouldn't have happened without NFTs, especially as a digital artist.*

— Carlos Marcial

Getting eyes on your work is important, but for most digital artists that never translated into a steady income. As discussed in "On Quantum," Sarah Zucker had been creating and sharing GIFs on platforms like Giphy and Tumblr for years, with the eyes of millions on her work. *This is 2020* (2019) has received over 40 million views on Giphy, exemplifying the artist's use of punchy statements presented in 1980s lo-fi glitch, painstakingly processed with the tools of that era. Her art is infused with the retro aesthetics of outdated technologies like VHS, but despite the traffic generated by her work on Web 2.0 platforms, until NFTs, Zucker had never been rewarded financially for her contributions. Her case therefore reveals the power of decentralized platforms to make artists the primary financial beneficiaries of their work. In Zucker's own words, "These companies (Giphy, Tumblr, Instagram) make ad dollars but the artists who make the products worthwhile aren't making anything, and very often aren't even getting credit, as in the case with my GIF stickers."[12] By participating on platforms like SuperRare **[02.07]** and KnownOrigin, Zucker was finally able to reap the benefits of her work's popularity. However, her story is not unusual. Many of the early entrants to the crypto art scene also found financial compensation following years in the Web 2.0 wilderness, from artists such as John Karel to XCOPY to ROBNESS **[02.08]**.

Like many platforms, SuperRare benefited hugely from the NFT bull market of 2021. Following the sale of Beeple's *EVERYDAYS: THE FIRST 5000 DAYS* (2021) at Christie's in March 2021, a team led by Alex Estorick analyzed all the existing data on SuperRare to establish the prevailing aesthetic trends across the marketplace up to that point.[13] This study of 22,018 works assessed the tags associated by artists with each piece as well as the

[13] Alex Estorick, Kyle Waters, and Chloe Diamond, "In Search of An Aesthetics of Crypto Art," *Artnome*, April 10, 2021, https://www.artnome.com/news/2021/4/10/in-search-of-an-aesthetics-of-crypto-art.

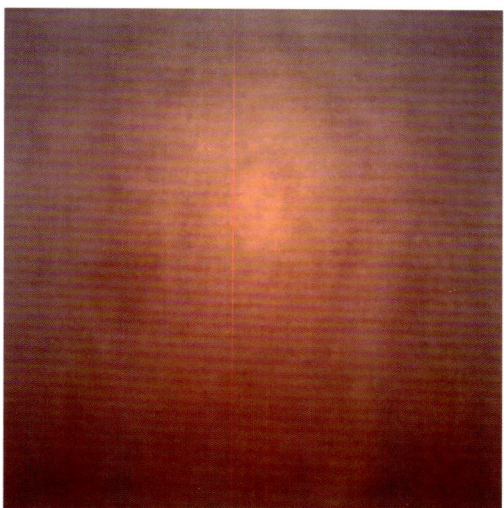

preferences of collectors, drawing a number of conclusions based on the language of crypto art at its moment of mass exposure. By this point, the halcyon phase of SuperRare's sharing economy — driven by a mutually supportive community of artists and collectors — had hardened into a centralized ecosystem with its own established aesthetics.

Through its sale of single editions, SuperRare has always promoted an elite form of aesthetics over mass production, based on the principle of quality over quantity. The effect has been to embed the native priorities of its early community into the platform. As much is evident in the frequency of certain tags across the marketplace. In March 2021, the top five tags were '3D', 'abstract', 'animation', 'surreal', and 'GIF', though the latter has since been superseded by 'Illustration'. The tag most commonly selected by artists was '3D', tagged with a little over 17% of all NFTs, and incorporated into 89 tags across the marketplace — from '3danimation' to '3dillustration' to '3drender' — signposting the new media most suited to crypto art.

A sample of the 50 most popular tags also emphasizes crypto art's break with tradition. Of them, 30 bear no relation to traditional fine art terminology, though five of the top ten do. These included 'portrait' and 'nude' — the highest-value tag of fine art's canonical subjects. These values may have been driven by Robbie Barrat's early dominance on the SuperRare platform, though they suggest the male gaze is still very much alive in Web3. They also remind us that, as a media ecology, the blockchain deserves media terminology, but as a movement crypto art remains a hybrid of analog and digital media.

'Sci-fi' was the highest grossing tag by average sale price, often combined with 'space', another top 50 tag. While '2D' and 'surreal' were the second most expensive tags among the top 50, a fact which reveals the equivalent value to artists of both aesthetics and thematics. Unsurprisingly, tags related to blockchain and cryptocurrency ranked among the top 50, including 'bitcoin', 'blockchain', 'ethereum', and 'eth'. Given the historical bond between NFTs and Ethereum, rooted in the ERC-721 standard, one might expect a predominance of Ethereum lore in crypto art. Yet, this study found Bitcoin to be just as infused into crypto mythology on SuperRare.

Five of the top 50 tags were concerned with color, though specific colors were limited to 'red' and 'black', with red selling for slightly more. Seeking to probe the palette further, our main data analyst, Kyle Waters, mixed the colors of the entire SuperRare universe together to produce the following outcome **[02.09]**. Dominated by pastel hues of red, pink, and purple, the outcome is straight from the Rothko school of data visualization. Suggestive of libidinal melancholy, the ultimate palette has an unmistakable allure of technostalgia that fits the defining themes of the market.

Some media critics choose to adopt the Classical Greek term *technē* ("craft"), rather than aesthetics, when considering the set of principles by which media are crafted today. In reality, aesthetics only became the defining aspect of art in the Enlightenment, prior to which issues of "technical" quality and ritual function had predominated. While it arguably

hasn't been the priority of fine art since Duchamp repurposed the urinal from a bathroom wall to the floor of a New York exhibition space. This gesture marked the birth of Conceptual Art as an avant-garde strategy, beginning the process of divorcing art from aesthetics that continued for much of the 20th century. Its 21st-century equivalent is surely trash art, whose story also happens to involve SuperRare.

The product of two *enfants terribles*, ROBNESS and Max Osiris, trash art's central strategy was to appropriate digital objects from across the internet in order to stress-test Web3's new institutions. Works like ROBNESS's *64 GALLON TOTER* (2020) — a GIF of a trash bin lifted directly from the Home Depot website and tokenized as an NFT — challenged the legal requirement that original creations be "transformative." They also channeled the Duchampian disregard for artistic genius, thereby questioning, in this case, SuperRare's heightened preoccupation with "rarity." As a platform committed to the sale of single-edition works by named individuals, SuperRare made for an easy target (that promptly removed the offending artwork). But while it revealed the reactionary instincts of the marketplace, the case also posed the question of whether tokenization itself might be enough to transform a digital file into high art.

For Mitchell F. Chan, tokenization separates the artwork's "expressive, or *artistic* form [the asset], from its commodity form [the NFT]."[14] What our study revealed, however, is that aesthetic appraisal remains a crucial means by which collectors differentiate one NFT from another. What crypto art shares with the legacy market is that NFTs tagged with 'drawing' tend to sell for less. In reality, despite their implication of a lack of finish, these "drawings" are often highly polished. They therefore reveal a potential misalignment between tags and their perceived value, one that reflects an unfo§rtunate hangover from the history of Western art.

One noticeable trait of the crypto art on SuperRare is its tendency to crossbreed traditional genres and retro styles with the contemporary digital trends. Works in the study that had accrued more than 500 views were dominated by name-related tags, which implies that the hype surrounding individual artists, as well as their time on the platform, is responsible for escalating prices. At the time of the study, the most viewed artists on SuperRare were Hackatao, XCOPY, Pak, Coldie, and Robbie Barrat, who together accounted for 116,544 total views or 7.7% of all views on SuperRare despite only producing 3.8% of the market's NFTs. FEWOCiOUS was also highly viewed despite producing works less seamless than the majority, evoking something akin to a Hoch-Guston hybrid. At only 19 years old, the artist offers an insight into a world unencumbered by traditional training — a trait characteristic of crypto artists in general. As SuperRare has grown, so has its willingness to embrace its crypto art roots, leading to its ultimate reinvention as a community-driven DAO.

## Conclusions

In 2021, Christie's sold Beeple's *EVERYDAYS: THE FIRST 5000 DAYS* for $69.3 million. This eye-watering sale of work by a white male artist at a 250-year-old auction house was most people's introduction to NFTs, but it left many with the distinct impression of business as usual. While the sale itself triggered an explosion in the NFT market, it also dealt a deathblow to crypto art as a realistic anti-art alternative to the traditional art world. A wave of profile picture projects ("PFPs") promptly flooded the market — cats and cartoon apes promising community as well as utility, backed by (questionable) roadmaps. Meanwhile, environmentalists (as well as many artists) were uncovering the massive energy consumption of proof-of-work blockchains like Bitcoin and (at the time) Ethereum. Crypto art's early utopianism promptly devolved into a nightmare triggered by the traditional art world.

At which point a new community of Brazilian builders led by Rafael Lima established Hic et Nunc (Latin for "here and now") as a new marketplace on the Tezos blockchain. In addition to addressing the environmental concerns surrounding NFTs through an alternative mode of consensus, Tezos also dramatically reduced the gas fees required to mint and buy NFTs. While this radical affordability opened up the market to the Global South, its energy efficiency also meant that many of the best-known digital artists could now engage with NFTs in good conscience. When Lima ultimately decided to close the marketplace at short notice, the platform's decentralization nevertheless ensured its faithful reproduction. What the case reveals, however, is that crypto art is as much a blueprint for a decentralized creator economy as a moment in art history. Like the movement itself, crypto art criticism is open to all. However, we hope that by expanding its scope to encompass a set of ideals — rather than a narrow program to promote cryptocurrency or medium-specificity — that crypto art might continue to serve the global community for whom it was founded. It is our wish that this kind of data-driven aesthetics can ultimately replace the unfalsifiable dogma of connoisseurship with a method fit for the digital age.

[14] Mitchell F. Chan, "NFTs, Generative Art, and Sol LeWitt," *Medium*, July 26, 2021, https://medium.com/@mitchellfchan/nfts-generative-art-and-sol-lewitt-e99a5fa2b0cb.

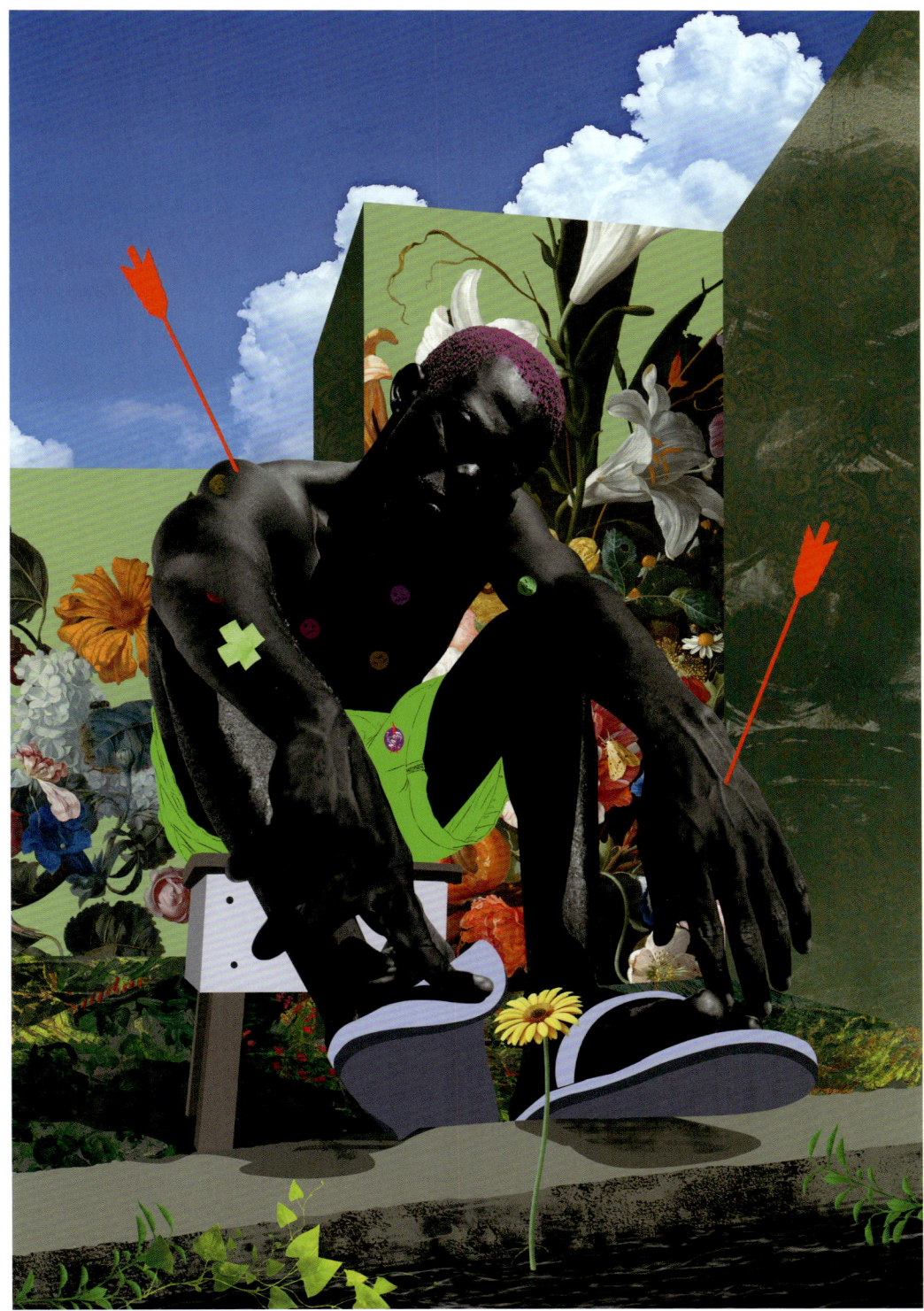

| # | TITLE | TIMESTAMP | MEDIUM | CHAIN | CONTRACT ADDRESS | TOKEN ID | EDITION SIZE |
|---|---|---|---|---|---|---|---|
| 01 | **WATCHING FLOWERS BY THE GUTTER** | 02-06-2022 18:55:10 | Digital Collage | ETH | 0xb932a70a57673d89f4acffbe830e8ed7f75fb9e0 | 32316 | 1/1 |
| 02 | **ORDER & LAGOS (where Lagos stands for chaos)** | 04-08-2022 12:24:04 | Adobe Photoshop, photograph, digital painting | ETH | 0x0f71113012f8097d99de54c4843fc2b69d0da4dd | 1 | 1/1 |
| 03 | **ORDER & LAGOS (e no too concern me)** | 04-08-2022 12:36:45 | Adobe Photoshop, photograph, digital painting | ETH | 0x0f71113012f8097d99de54c4843fc2b69d0da4dd | 2 | 1/1 |

02

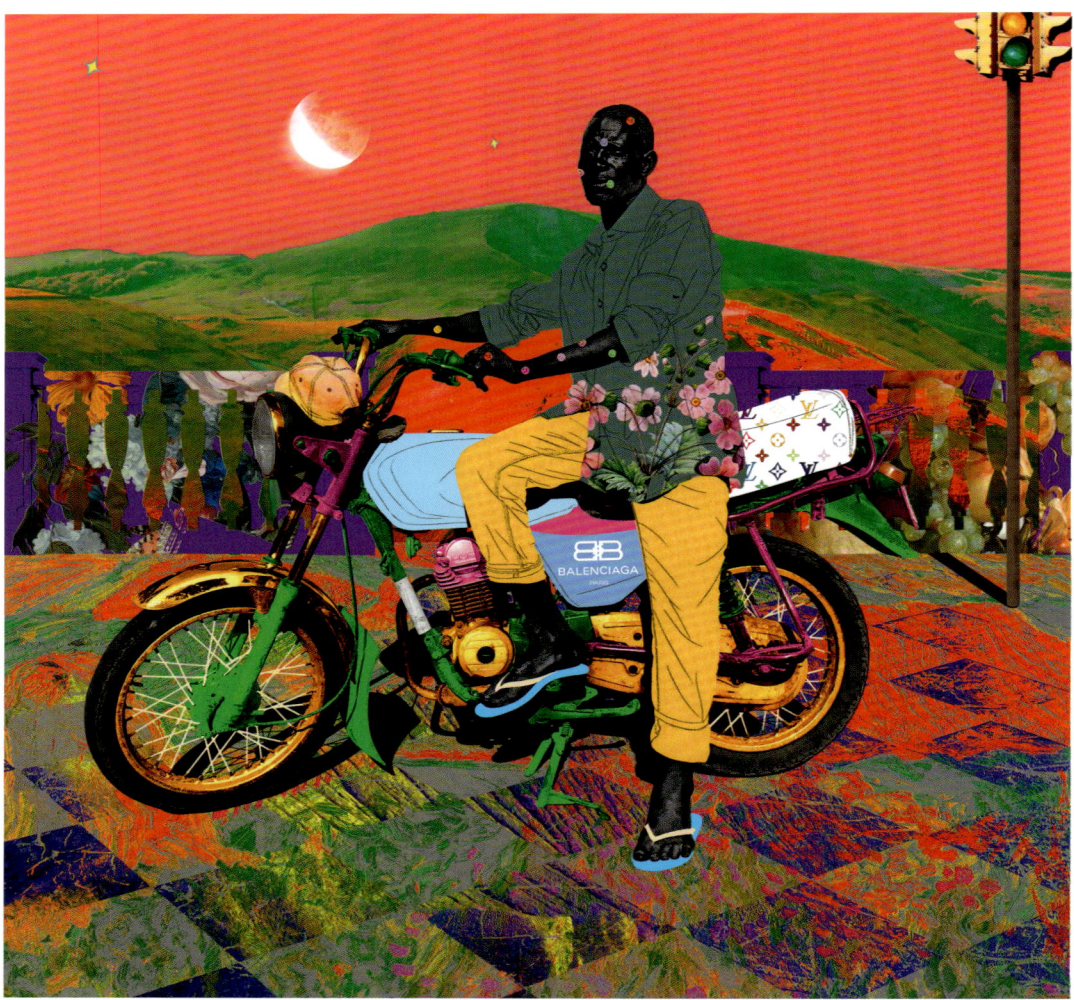

I met Adesola Yusuf (aka Arclight.jpg) while curating a show of African artists in Web3 in late 2021. At the time, very few of us appeared in group shows organized by NFT platforms or auction houses. Since then, Adesola has exhibited work at Gazelli Art House in London and Art X Lagos. He has become one of the most collected and curated artists from Nigeria and Africa at large in Web3.

I first came across his *UBUNTU* (2021) collection, inspired by the Benin masks collection on OpenSea and was struck by his contemporary take on an ancient art form — his use of vibrant web-native RGB color provided a stark and refreshing break from the traditionally earthy tonality of masks. He is grounded in his heritage while finding approaches to breathe new life into it. In a similar vein, Adesola's work alludes to his physical practice while juxtaposing distinctly digital imagery such as internet symbols and flat vector illustrations. I found out later that many of his portraits start on canvas through a combination of collage and paint, and are then exported into vector design softwares to take on their final form.

*Watching Flowers Grow By The Gutter* (2022) combines all the familiar elements in Adesola's style into an introspective meditation. He is interested in personal growth and our awareness of the events and processes that bring it about. *Watching Flowers Grow By The Gutter* takes us on a journey through developing his sense of agency — from being a spectator of his condition as a child (watching flowers grow) to becoming the conductor of his fate as an adult (being the flower that grows). Admirers of his work have come to expect the vulnerability that Adesola channels in his self-portraits. His body of work makes the bold statement that self-acceptance is a worthwhile goal of existence, and that there is unimaginable beauty in surrendering to vulnerability on the journey to it.

**LINDA DOUNIA**
ARTIST, CURATOR & FOUNDER AT CYBER BAAT

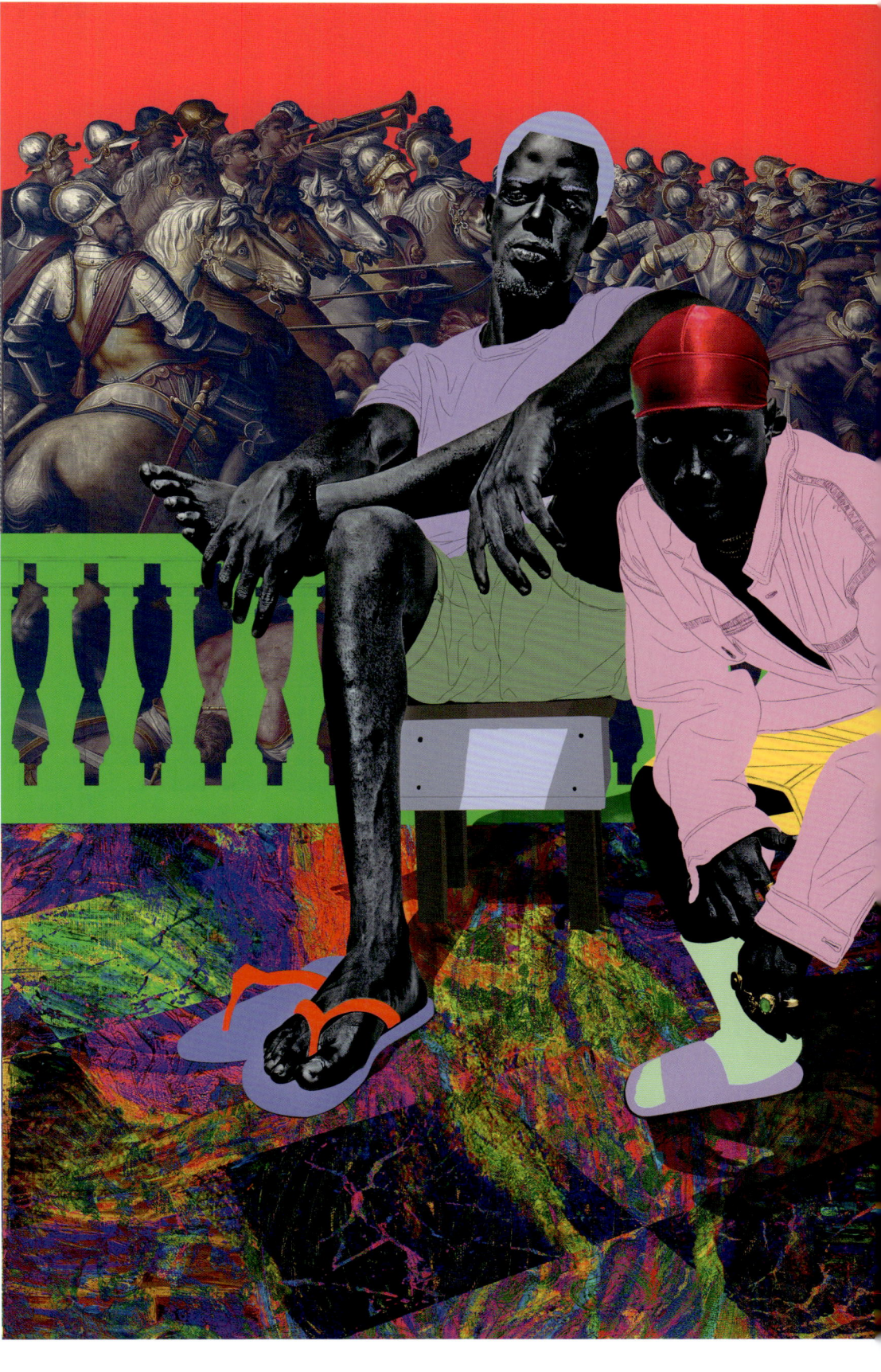

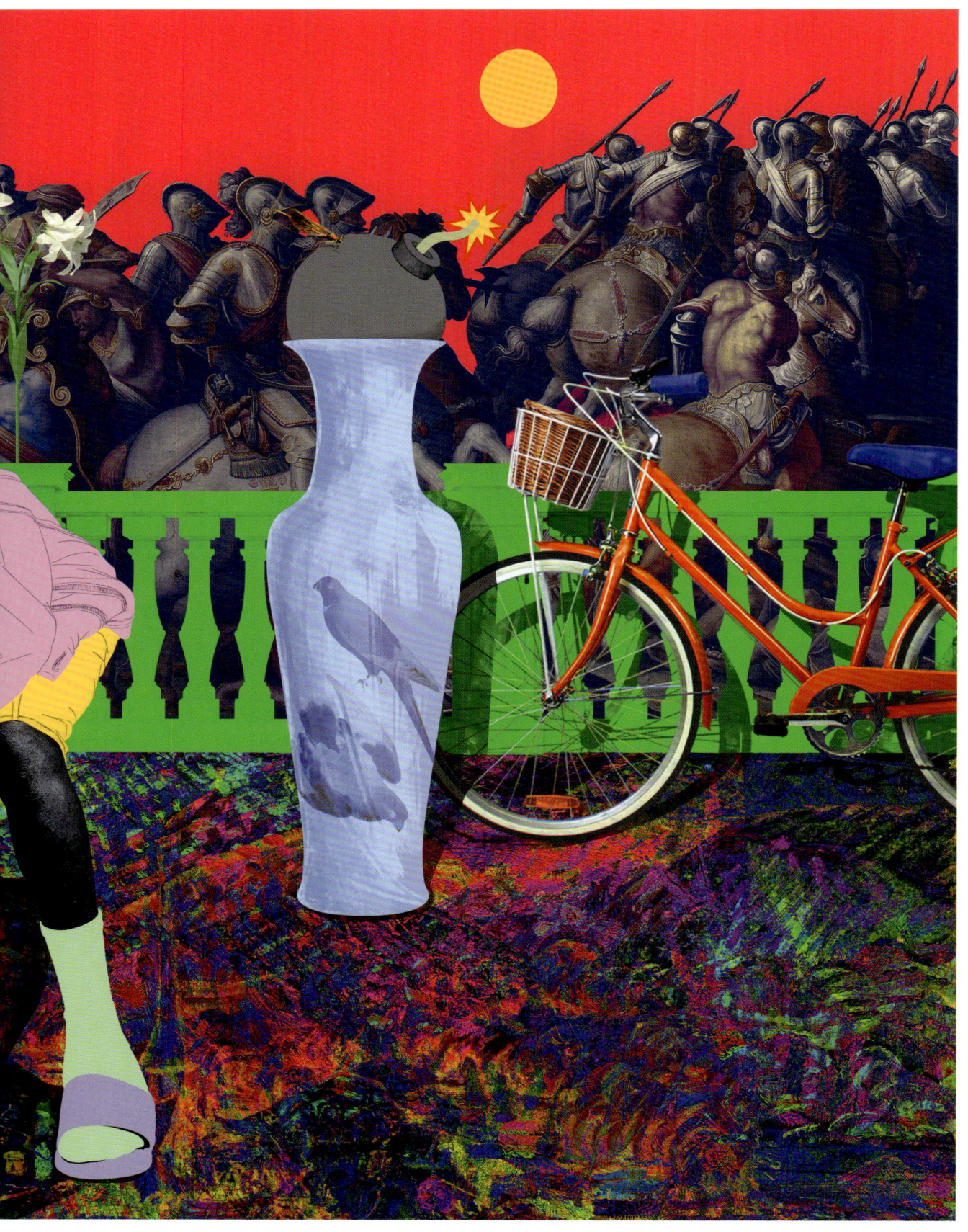

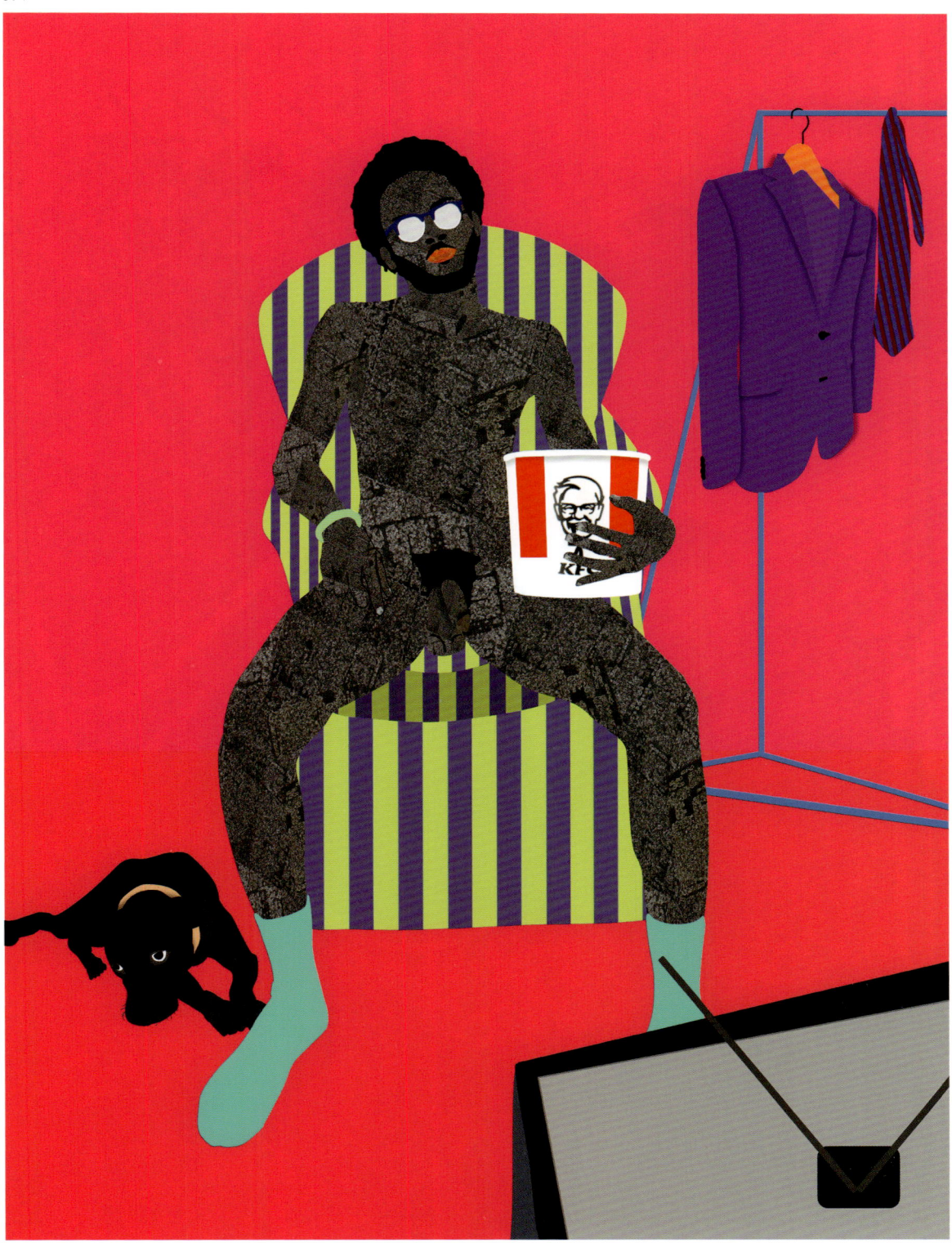

| # | TITLE | TIMESTAMP | MEDIUM | CHAIN | CONTRACT ADDRESS | TOKEN ID | EDITION SIZE |
|---|---|---|---|---|---|---|---|
| 01 | **Resignation** | 11-26-2020 18:25:07 | Microsoft Word | ETH | 0xb932a70a57673d89f4acffbe830e8ed7f75fb9e0 | 16626 | 1/1 |
| 02 | **To Play for Oneself** | 05-05-2021 16:18:27 | Microsoft Word | ETH | 0xb932a70a57673d89f4acffbe830e8ed7f75fb9e0 | 24283 | 1/1 |
| 03 | **Man in a Pool III** | 09-30-2021 11:07:40 | Microsoft Word | ETH | 0xd5610aa84f47b9e26e0e588bb0e14671c675daa0 | 3 | 1/1 |
| 04 | **Two Generals at War I** | 03-19-2020 10:23:29 | Microsoft Word | ETH | 0xb932a70a57673d89f4acffbe830e8ed7f75fb9e0 | 8883 | 1/1 |

# OSINACHI

02

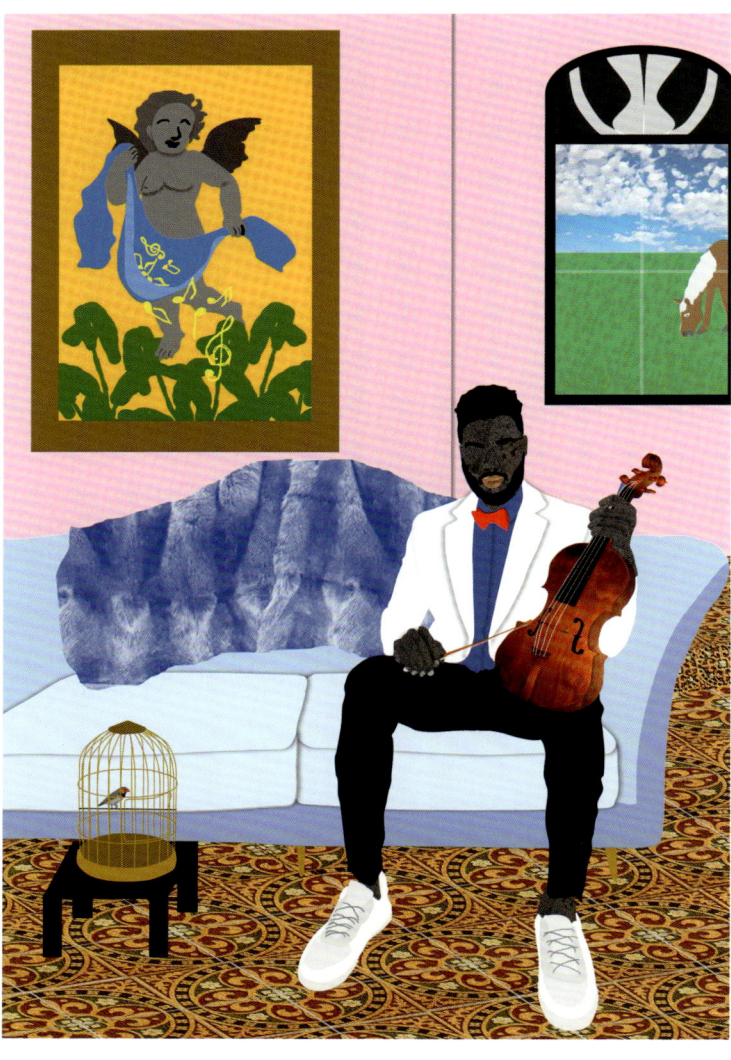

Osinachi (Prince Jacon Osinachi Igwe) was born and raised in the city of Aba, Nigeria. He started experimenting with digital images when his father introduced him to the computer at a cybercafé at the age of 15. By late 2017, he was selling NFTs using blockchain, and in 2018, he was the first African to showcase work at the Ethereal Conference in New York. Today, Osinachi, as Africa's first and foremost crypto artist and the first African artist to sell an NFT in a public auction, enjoys challenging himself to see what he can achieve with a program most artists consider extremely limited, Microsoft Word.

Aesthetically and procedurally, Osinachi's art explores how individuals utilize their visible existence as a form of protest — either through what they wear, the paraphernalia they adorn themselves with, or their simple existence in a form and space society looks down on — to advocate for freedom of identity. Osinachi's figurative portraits mirror his experiences as an African man in today's world, while simultaneously calling on traditional, historical works from artists like David Hockney, whose work *Portrait of an Artist (Pool with Two Figures)* (1972) inspired his series *Different Shades of Water* (2021). For Osinachi's pool works, the idea of leisure is prominent, but what is perhaps more pertinent is the idea of leisure centered around the Black body. One can talk about the history of racial segregation in public swimming pools, even to this day, Black swimmers are still hugely underrepresented in water sports. Beyond that, the work plays with a history of leisure painting — starting with Georges Seurat (1859–1891) and exploding with the Impressionists — a style mostly focused on the White body. Instead, this series suggests the growth of a Black middle class, particularly in Nigeria, and a reinserting of the Black body into these art-historical fields — to be seen and admired, not just as a means of recollection, but also aspiration.

**DARIA BORISOVA**
CURATOR AND ART ADVISOR

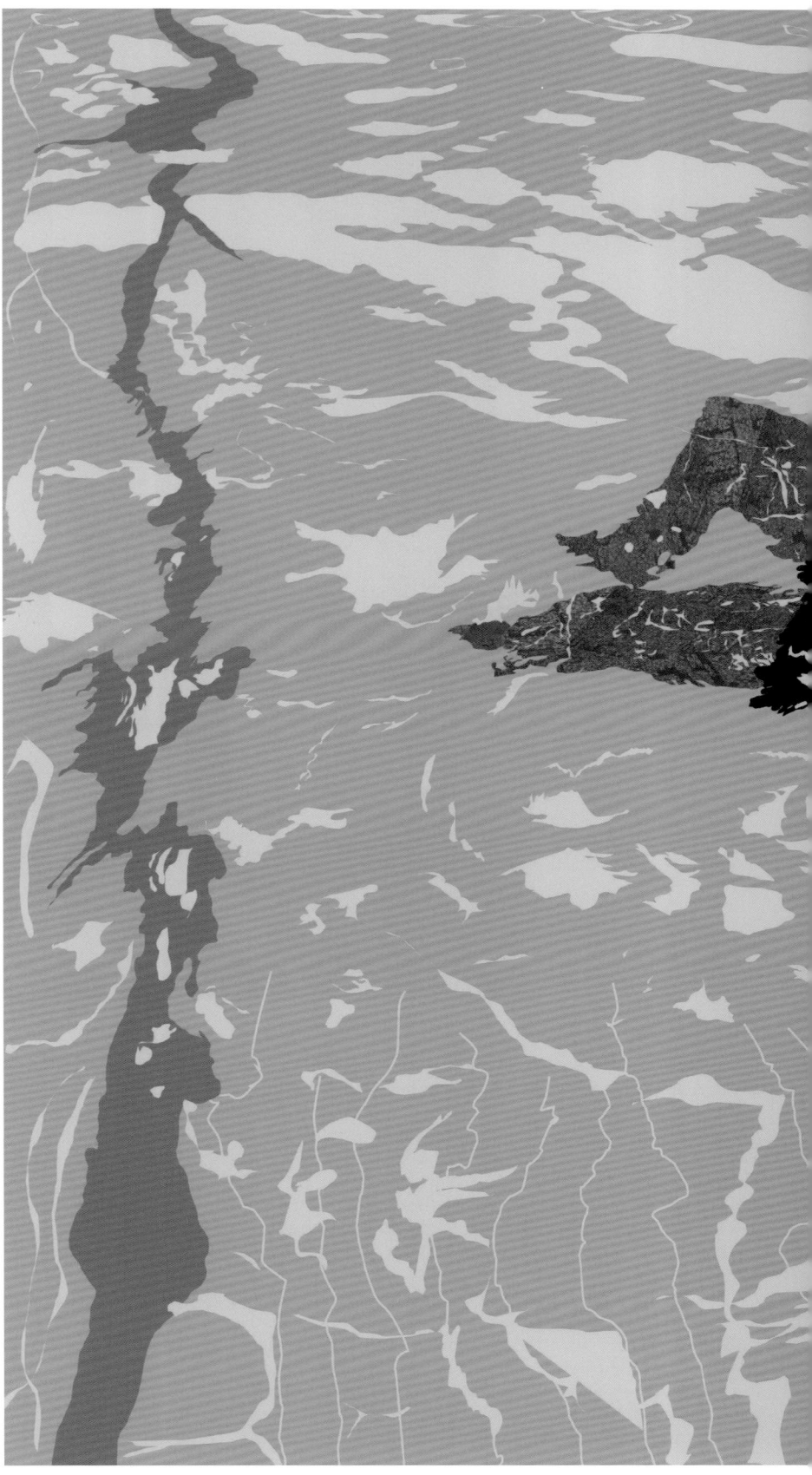

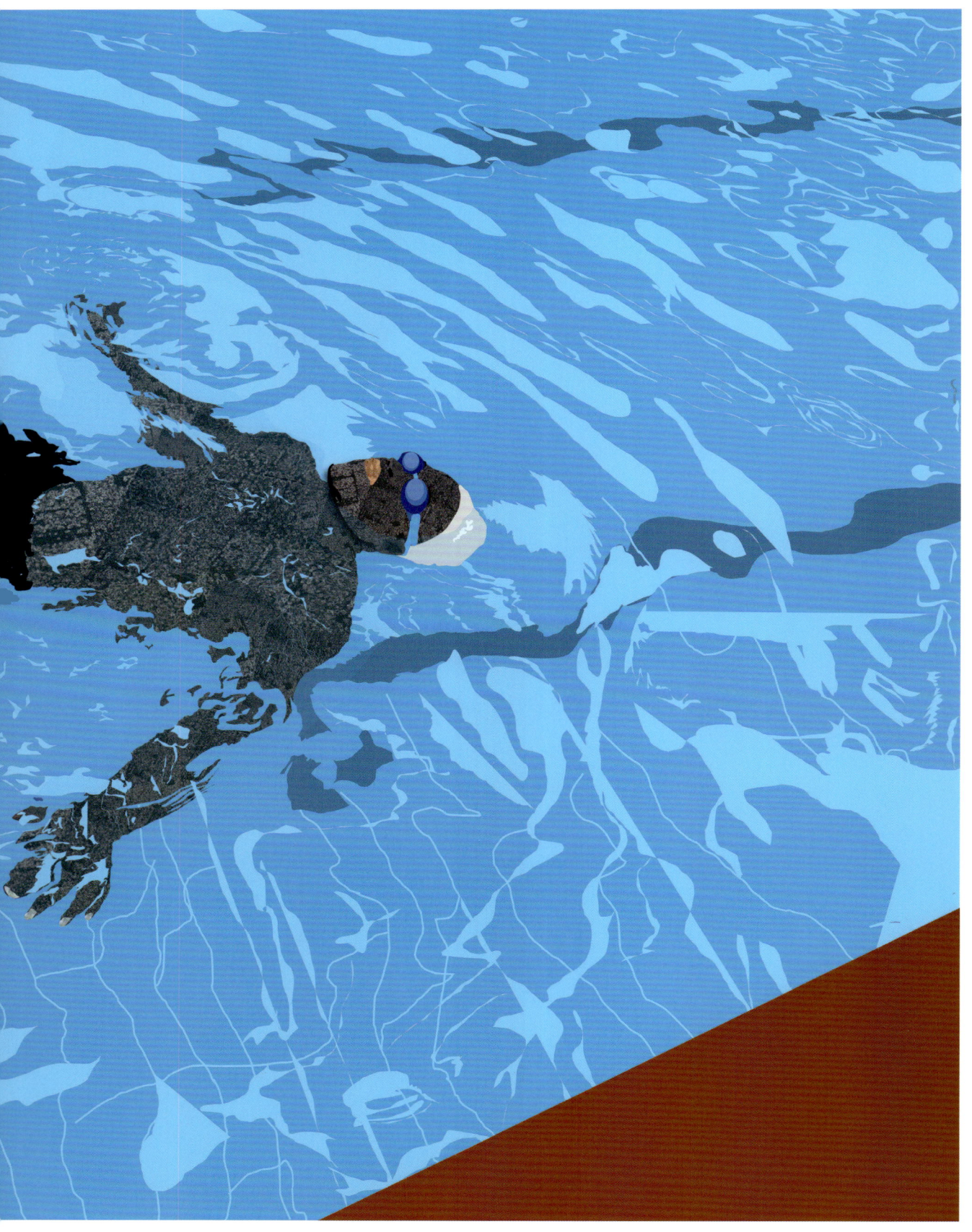

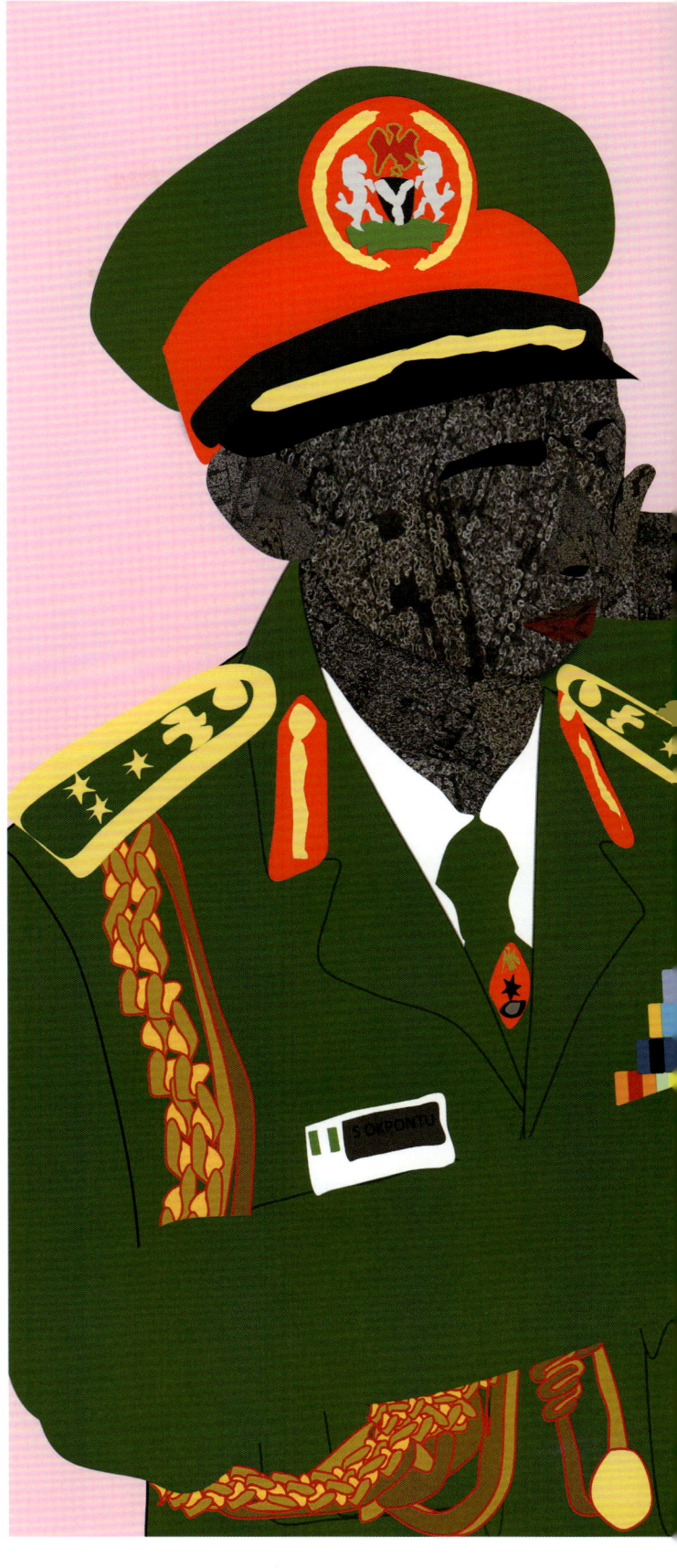

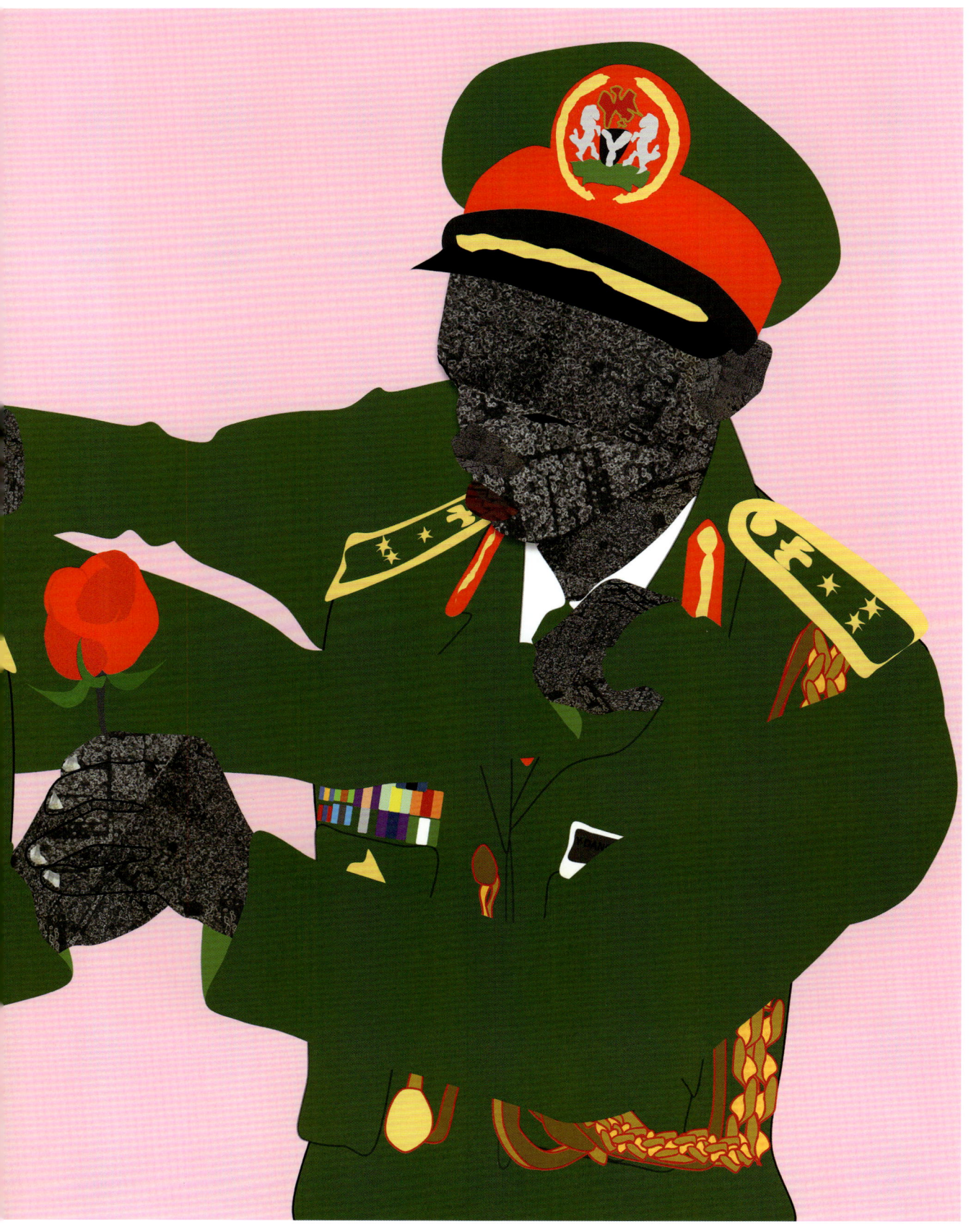

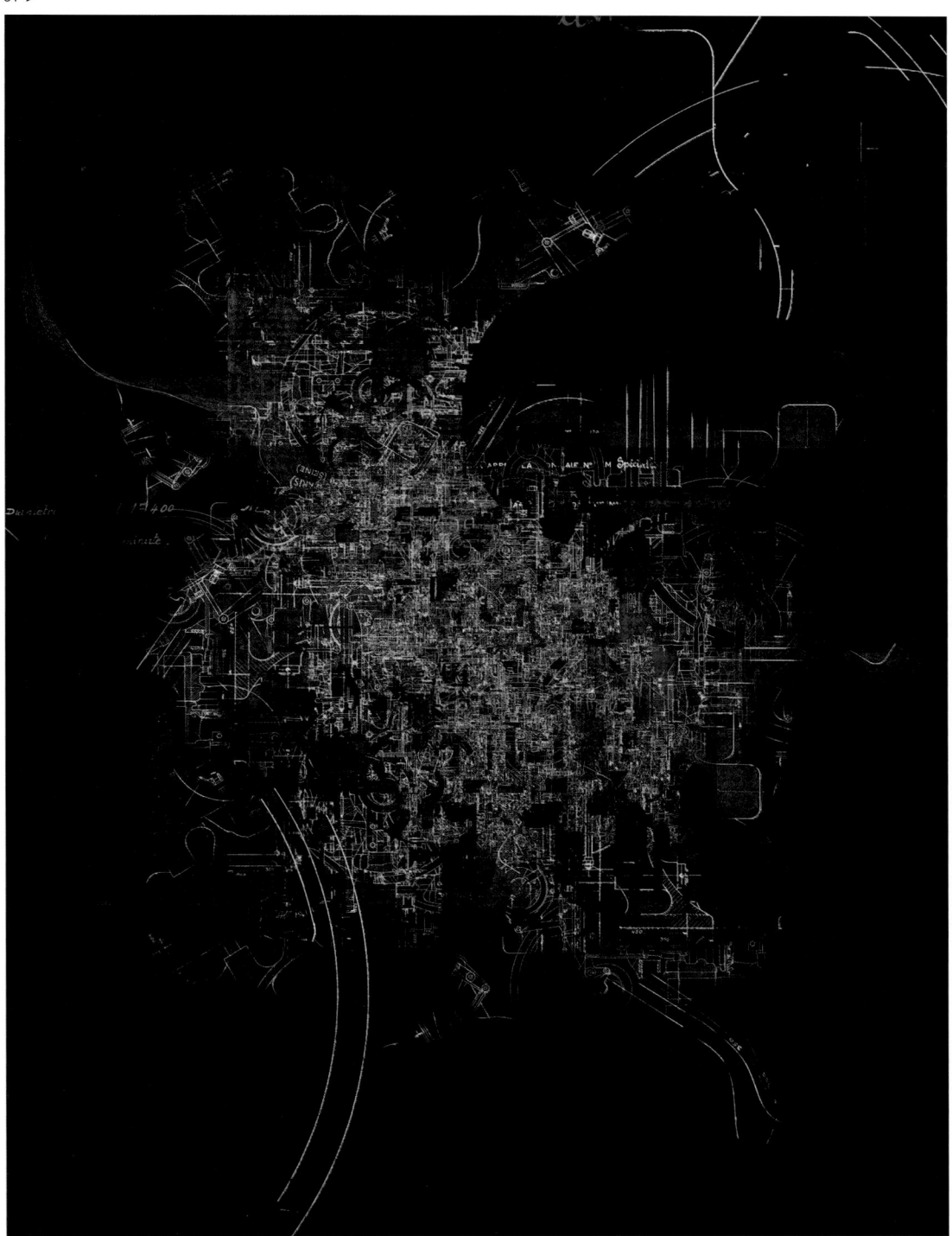

| # | TITLE | TIMESTAMP | MEDIUM | CHAIN | CONTRACT ADDRESS | TOKEN ID | EDITION SIZE |
|---|-------|-----------|--------|-------|------------------|----------|--------------|
| 01 | **H15715_The Imperfect Librarian** | 06-26-2023 23:21:47 | Found blueprints, AI, ASCII, block height calls | ETH | 0xc8dfa79fe6818ce3dbe2221179e1fba728b4cf2b | 146 | 1/1 |
| 02–05 | **Portraits of a Mind** | 10-01-2020 10:46:36 | Houdini, Octane Render; acrylic on canvas, Opendime; Bitcoin v0.1.0 | ETH | 0xb6dae651468e9593e4581705a09c10a76ac1e0c8 | 606 | 40 paintings and NFTs, with corresponding NFT editions |

EDITIONS ILLUSTRATED: (02) Block 22 (42.435948° N, -71.154904° E) exhibited at the Monnaie de Paris, (03) Close up of Block 34 (51.895167° N, 1.4805° E), (04) Corresponding NFT edition of Block 34 (51.895167° N, 1.4805° E) (minted on 0×4c7ade5bd2a982c029b49e312c9a72cdb71a242d), (05) Block 34 (51.895167° N, 1.4805° E) exhibited at Sealand

# ROBERT ALICE

UNITED KINGDOM 1992

02

03

04 ▶

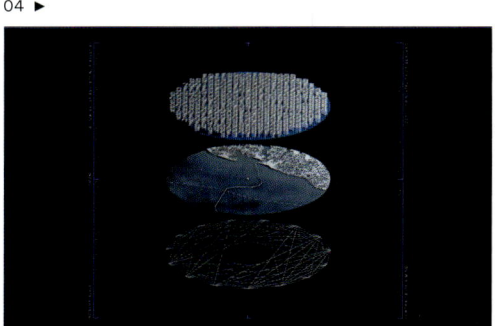

05

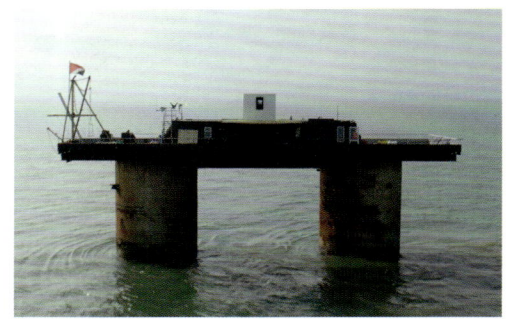

Robert Alice's multidisciplinary work combines conceptual engagement with the blockchain through a formal focus on code, text, and encryption. As an artist, their work straddles not just NFTs, but painting and sculpture, curating and writing. Influenced by conceptual artists such as Roman Opalka (1931–2011) and On Kawara (1932–2014), alongside artists such as Jasper Johns and Julie Mehretu, Alice's practice and intellectual engagement with the blockchain focus on the idea of the fragment and the whole, the node and the network within decentralized ecosystems.

In *Portraits of a Mind* (2019–), Alice sees the blockchain as a kind of history machine and vast archive where a blockchain's original codebase stands as its own form of portraiture, both infinitely knowable and unknowable at the same time. An abstract portrait of Satoshi Nakamoto, the work explores ideas of anonymity and identity through the aesthetics of open-source code. Playing with nodal structures and the histories of cartography, cryptography, and numismatics, the work uses major historical coordinates as a form of history painting — inspecting the histories of crypto to suggest that its roots stretch deeper into history than commonly thought. Combining 40 paintings and NFTs together, the project

was exhibited in 2022 at one of the coordinates of the project: Sealand, a micronation and former cypherpunk data haven 12 kilometers in the North Sea.

Part of a solo show at the Monnaie de Paris, a new body of work *The Blueprints* (2023) is an exploration of the competing thought systems of centralized and the decentralized structures in an artistic investigation of the Monnaie's collection, itself the world's oldest continuously running minting institution, founded in 864 AD. Drawing from both the past and present, the works "hijack" archival blueprints and architectural drawings from the institution's collection, colliding and re-networking them with diagrams and aesthetics that draw from the histories of blockchains. Tracing the re-networked drawings with the letters *M*, *C*, *V*, Alice infuses the drawings with Jorge Luis Borges's (1899–1986) *Library of Babel* (1941) as a philosophical meditation on the concept of the infinite archive, encryption, and its relationship with contemporary blockchain structures.

**HANS ULRICH OBRIST**
ARTISTIC DIRECTOR AT SERPENTINE GALLERIES

01

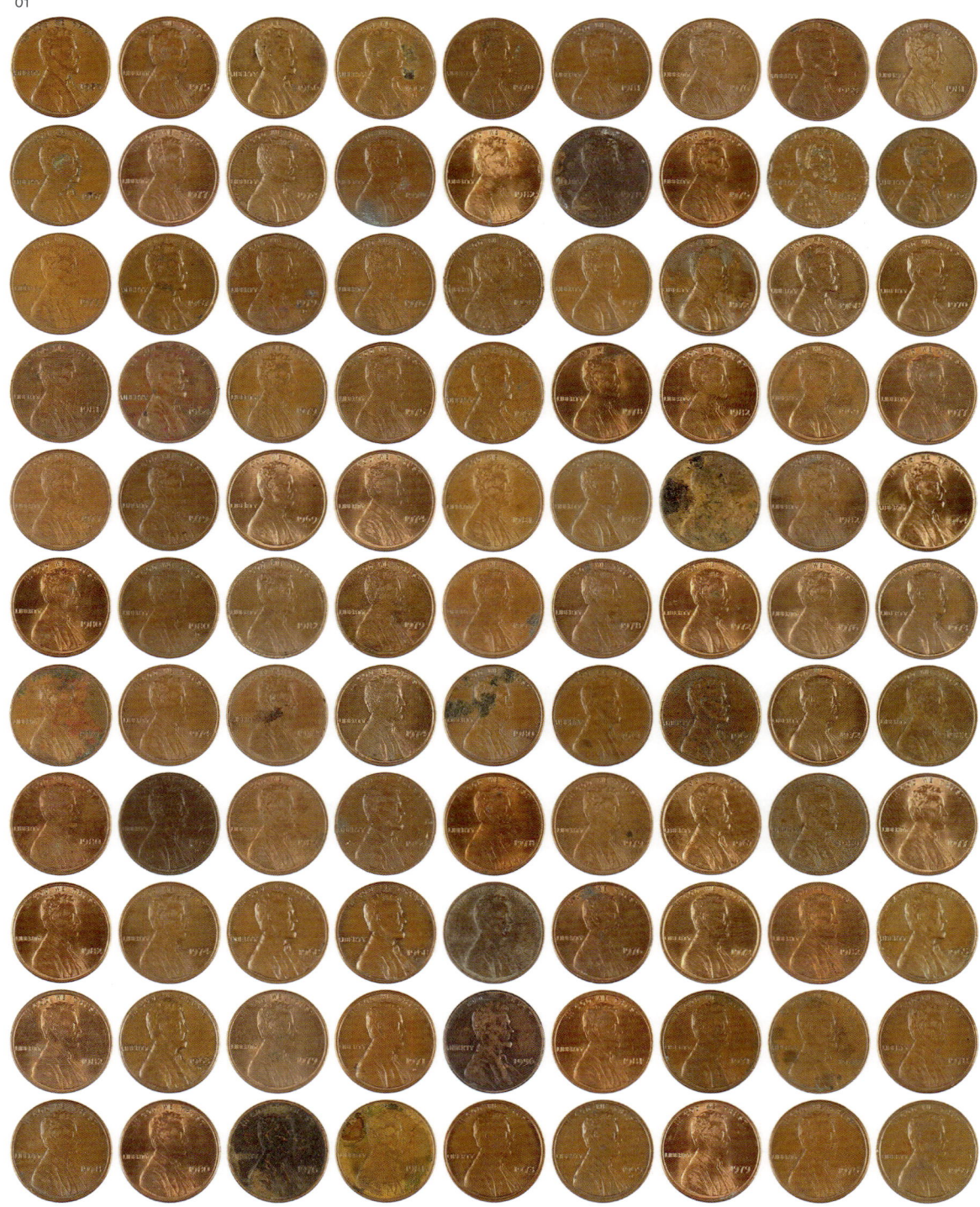

| # | TITLE | TIMESTAMP | MEDIUM | CHAIN | CONTRACT ADDRESS | TOKEN ID | EDITION SIZE |
|---|-------|-----------|--------|-------|------------------|----------|--------------|
| 01 | *CENTS* | 03-25-2024 17:22:20 | Digital Photograph, webp | BTC | bc1pxuqhmyx0tquaqz8dvfenwmk6g8ztj2axarn-etc7s5y9×3s6wj49qzpufdc | 65890305 - 66040824 | 1.1 |
| 02 | **Block 839969** | 04-19-2024 21:49:18 | Solid Copper Block, Digital 3D Model, gltf-binaryt | BTC | bc1pxuqhmyx0tquaqz8dvfenwmk6g8ztj2axarn-etc7s5y9×3s6wj49qzpufdc | 70262998 | 1/1 of 10000 |

EDITIONS ILLUSTRATED: (01) 1/1 of 10,000 and then (02) 1/1

02 ▶

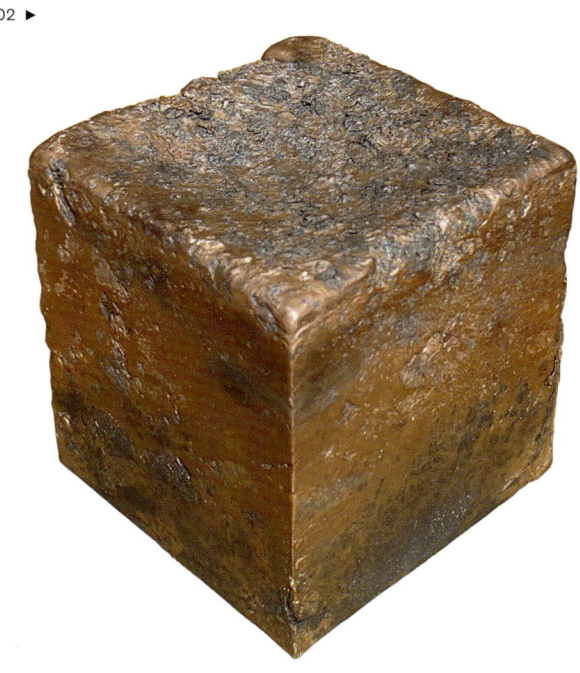

Rutherford Chang's *CENTS* exists at the intersection of the analog and the digital, and in line with the late artist's lifelong practice of obsessive collecting. Chang's best-known project, *We Buy White Albums*, entailed a quixotic, decades-long pursuit to buy and catalog every extant copy from the first pressing of the Beatles' signature release, allowing him to compare the accretions and distortions to the palimpsest-like surfaces of these originally identical objects. He generally exhibited this work in the form of a record shop, turning gallery-goers into a community of crate-diggers. For *CENTS*, he collected pre-1982 pennies, minted in the years before the US Treasury, recognizing the increased value of copper, changed to a zinc alloy. Having dutifully photographed and cataloged these coins, he melted them down into a 68-pound block. The individual cents, as well as a 3D model of the cubic copper ingot, were then minted on the blockchain and continue to be circulated as digital inscriptions.

Consistently amused by the divergent valuations assigned by societies and economies to different objects, symbols, and uses of time, Chang was particularly interested in how, just as the value of a physical copper penny had long surpassed $0.01, the value of his digital *CENTS* became permanently indeterminate. A lively online community has since arisen around the work, echoing those that have appeared around his earlier projects. As Chang's first and only work on the blockchain, *CENTS* connects to his ongoing aesthetic and conceptual concerns, and reflects poetically on his own life and career, in which the demands of a role in a family technology business were often in tension with the Palo Alto native's own work as an artist. Ironically and tragically, Chang's obituary ran in the *New York Times* on the same day as a story announcing a government decision to discontinue the production of new pennies.

**PHILIP TINARI**
DIRECTOR, UCCA CENTER FOR CONTEMPORARY ART

01

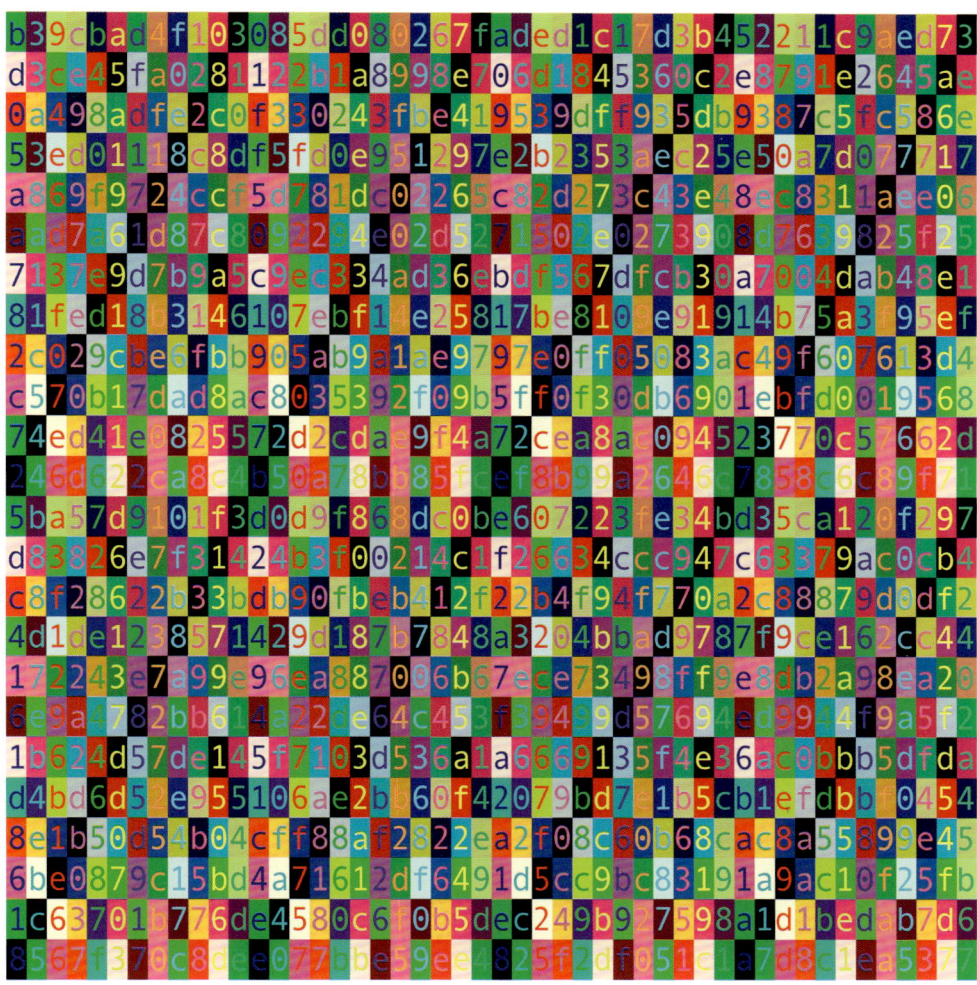

| # | TITLE | TIMESTAMP | MEDIUM | CHAIN | CONTRACT ADDRESS | TOKEN ID | EDITION SIZE |
|---|---|---|---|---|---|---|---|
| 01 | **1111** | 03-21-2021 20:25:00 | Python | ETH | 0x7f72528229f85c99d8843c0317ef91f4a2793edf | 1–1111 | 1/1 of 1,111 |
| 02 | **Synthetic Optimism as a Function of Ignoring Atrocities** | 08-15-2021 23:04:00 | Python | XTZ | KT1RJ6PbjHpwc3M5rw5s2Nbmefwbuwbdxton | 208697 | 25 |

EDITIONS ILLUSTRATED: (01) #31

# KEVIN ABOSCH

02

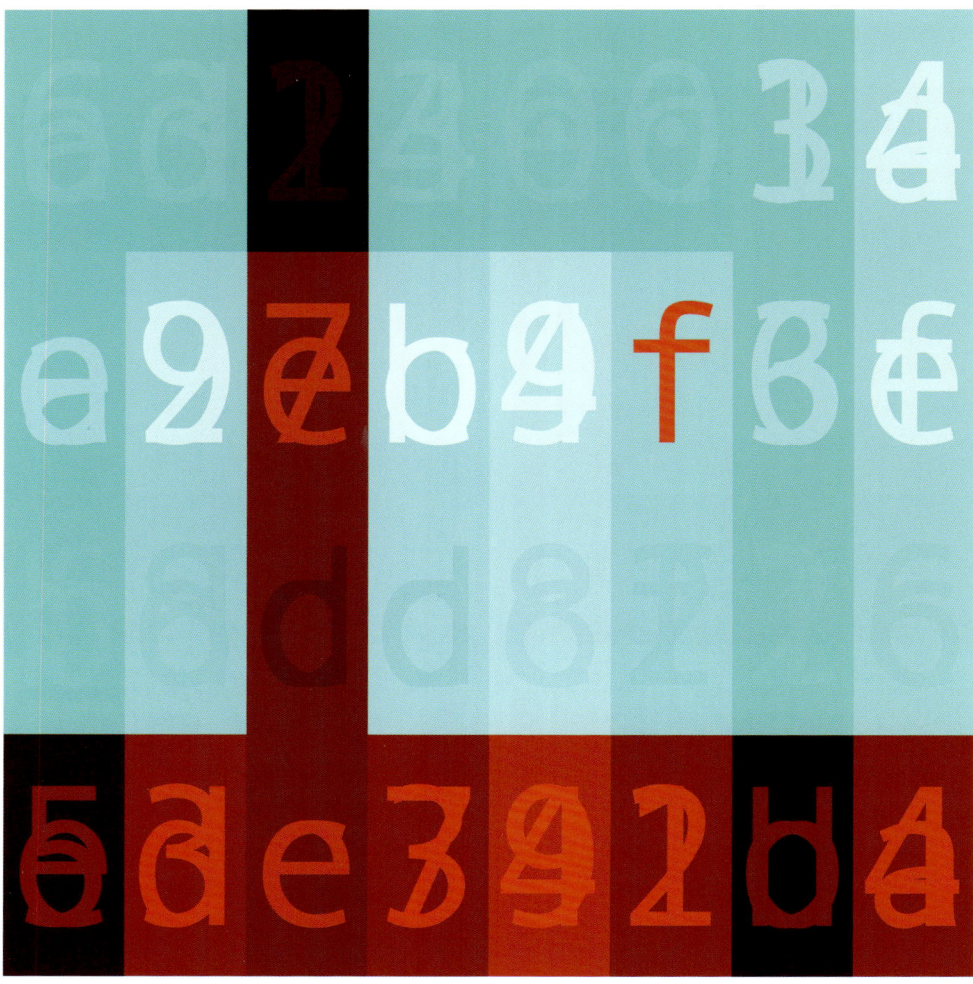

Behind every act of encryption, there's a story. Our trust in digital life is predicated on it, yet most of us have no idea how it works and what artistry inheres within.

For all the machine logic evident in Kevin Abosch's work, it's best interpreted in its narrative dimension. Across many collaborations with complex technologies, his line of inquiry remains human: How can emotional value be distilled through the artistic process? 21st-century life is defined by the black box. Kevin submits himself to the influence of machines — adopting their modes of sensing and understanding — to encounter truths hidden in that dark. In this experimental approach, Kevin has been consistently prescient.

In *Hexadecimal Testimony*, which encompasses both *1111* (2021) and *Status Update* (2022), Kevin offers these revelations in encrypted alphanumerics, a dynamic digital hieroglyphics. Subjects are sociopolitical and referenced through titling. *Hexadecimal Testimony* marks the first body of work in which he explicitly grapples with politics and current events significant to him. Is there a relationship, for example, between mobile crematoriums in Ukraine and the sanctions imposed on Putin's daughters?

He pulls data from a range of sources: news, social media, weather data, sales figures, and his own notes. He collaborates with machine learning models to identify patterns. He then returns to the models, pruning the datasets and producing new outputs, toggling between them until a logic emerges — at which point he seals them up as NFTs.

A blockchain ledger is a translucent interface. Cryptographic hashes represent interactions that are immutably recorded, but conceal underlying realities. *Hexadecimal Testimony* mirrors this mode of meaning-making, conveyed aesthetically through the formal conventions of the coding terminal. The NFTs invite a sleuthing impulse, but Kevin claims there's no use trying to solve them; beguiling as the works in *Hexadecimal Testimony* appear to be, they're not riddles. They're poems. They're glimpses of new forms of seeing and knowing — meant to be felt, not decrypted.

**JESSE DAMIANI**
FOUNDER OF POSTREALITY LABS,
CURATOR OF PROOF OF ART — A BRIEF HISTORY OF NFTS (2021)
AT FRANCISCO CAROLINUM, LINZ

01 ▶

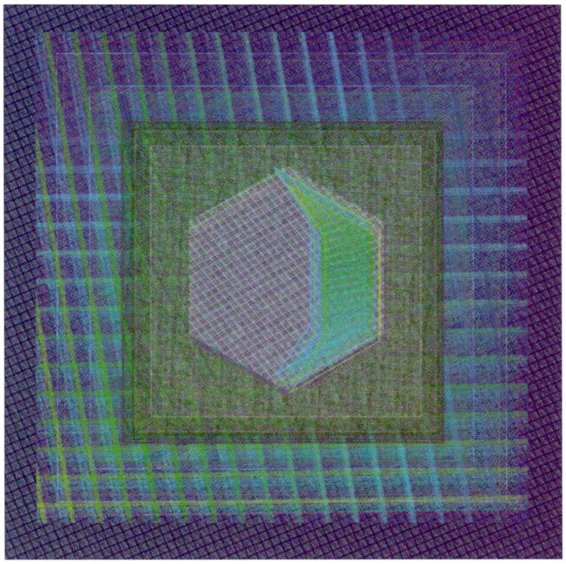

02 ▶

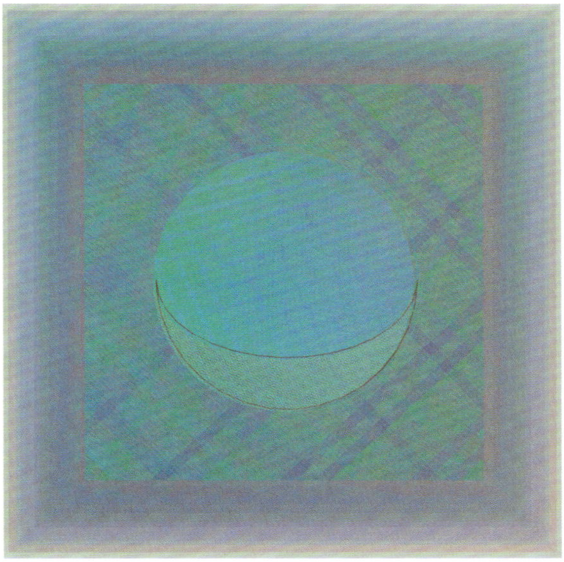

03 ▶

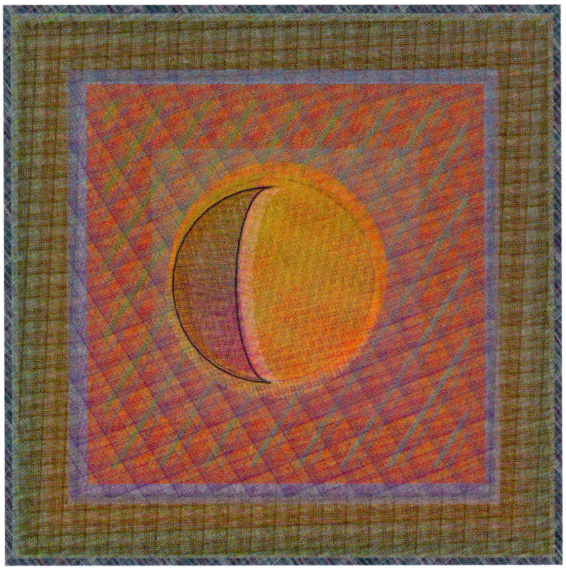

04 ▶

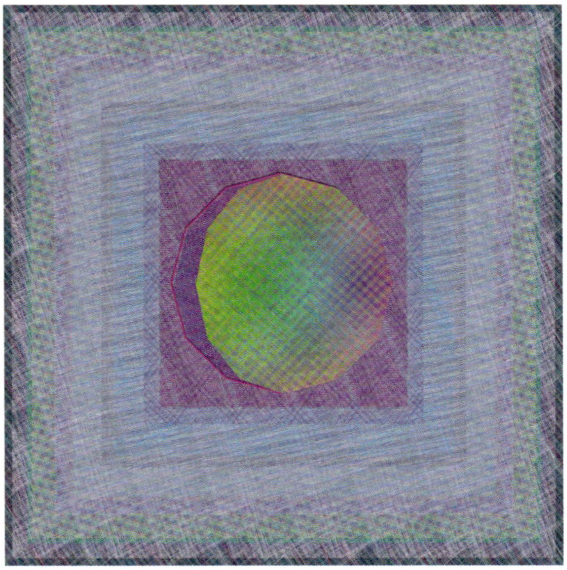

| # | TITLE | TIMESTAMP | MEDIUM | CHAIN | CONTRACT ADDRESS | TOKEN ID | EDITION SIZE |
|---|-------|-----------|--------|-------|------------------|----------|--------------|
| 01–04 | **Gazers** | 11-27-2021 14:39:38 | p5.js | ETH | 0xa7d8d9ef8d8ce8992df33d-8b8cf4aebabd5bd270 | 215000000–215000999 | 1/1 of 1,000 |
| 05 | **CRYPTOART MONETIZATION GENERATION** | 02-25-2021 15:00:29 | Matt Kane's Digital Art Studio, Processing, JavaScript | ETH | 0xb932a70a57673d89f4-acffbe830e8ed7f75fb9e0 | 20053 | 1/1 |

EDITIONS ILLUSTRATED: (03) #29, (04) #225, (05) #59, (06) #88, (07) #822

# MATT KANE

UNITED STATES 1980

05 ▶

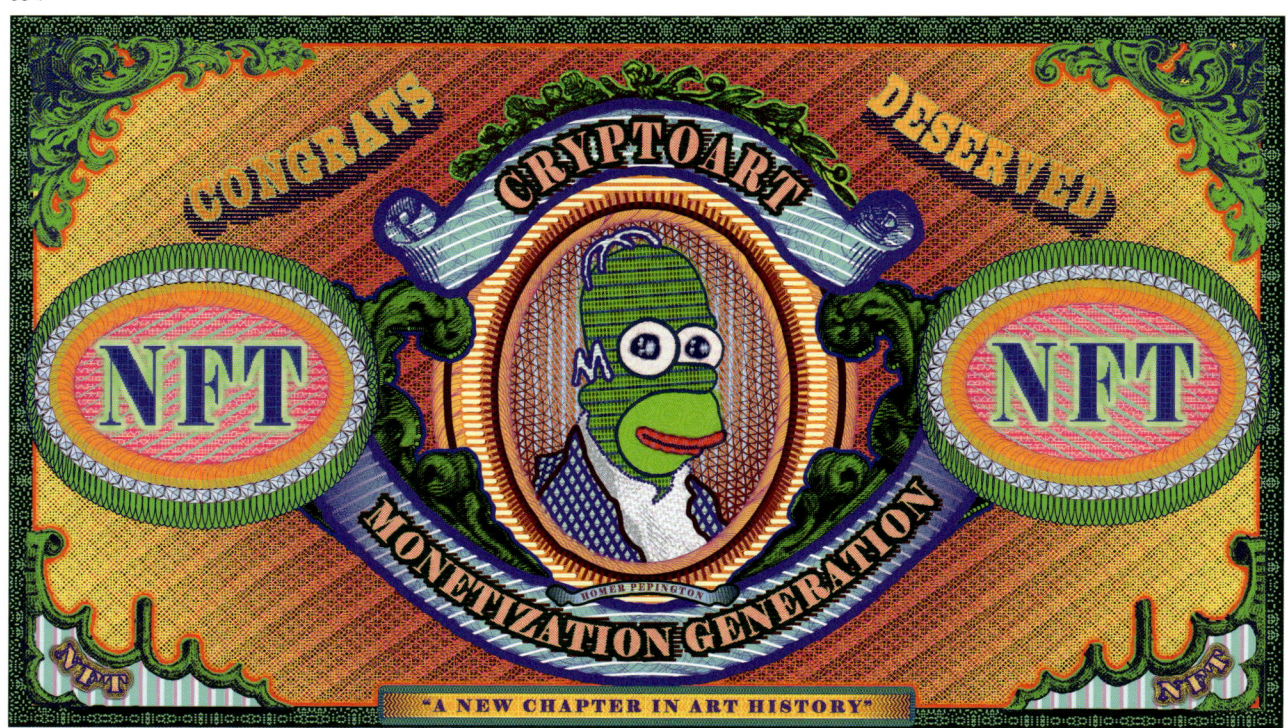

One of the earliest artists working with NFTs, Matt Kane is a leading example of a true crypto artist. While Kane began his art career in Chicago as an oil painter, he has always thought obsessively about how to create art beyond the confines of a canvas. In 2006, Kane moved to Seattle where he'd craft a career in web development, setting a foundation of skills he'd require in his future digital art practice. Kane knew he had to turn to the power of code and computing to make his visions into reality, and he has become a self-taught master of this transformational tool.

Kane has invented and advanced his own software, digital making tools, and theories to bring forth many awe-inspiring artworks. Each and every one of his images opens a new dimension into how we experience the very conceptualization of art itself. We have literally stepped through the layers of his digital paintings — with 2D images exploding into multitudes of novel, luminous compositions, shifting with the viewer's perspective.

An activist as well as an artist, Kane also saw a need for all artists to finally be fairly compensated for their works. In 2020,

Kane organized artists to demand royalties in perpetuity, resulting in this becoming standard in smart contracts across all NFT platforms. This seismic economic advancement in support of the artist cannot be underestimated.

Kane's most recent work *Gazers* (2021) was born and envisioned as a living piece, miraculously changing diurnally. Each iteration incrementally speeds up, and magically adapts to screen dimensions, revealing Kane's engagement in digitally native framing strategies. The code for the piece references human history, from the Ice Age into the Agricultural Revolution. Today, at the start of the Information Revolution, *Gazers* asks us to consider where humankind has come from in order to imagine where we might go as a species

**MICHAEL SPALTER**
CHAIRMAN OF THE BOARD AT
RHODE ISLAND SCHOOL OF DESIGN

01 ▶

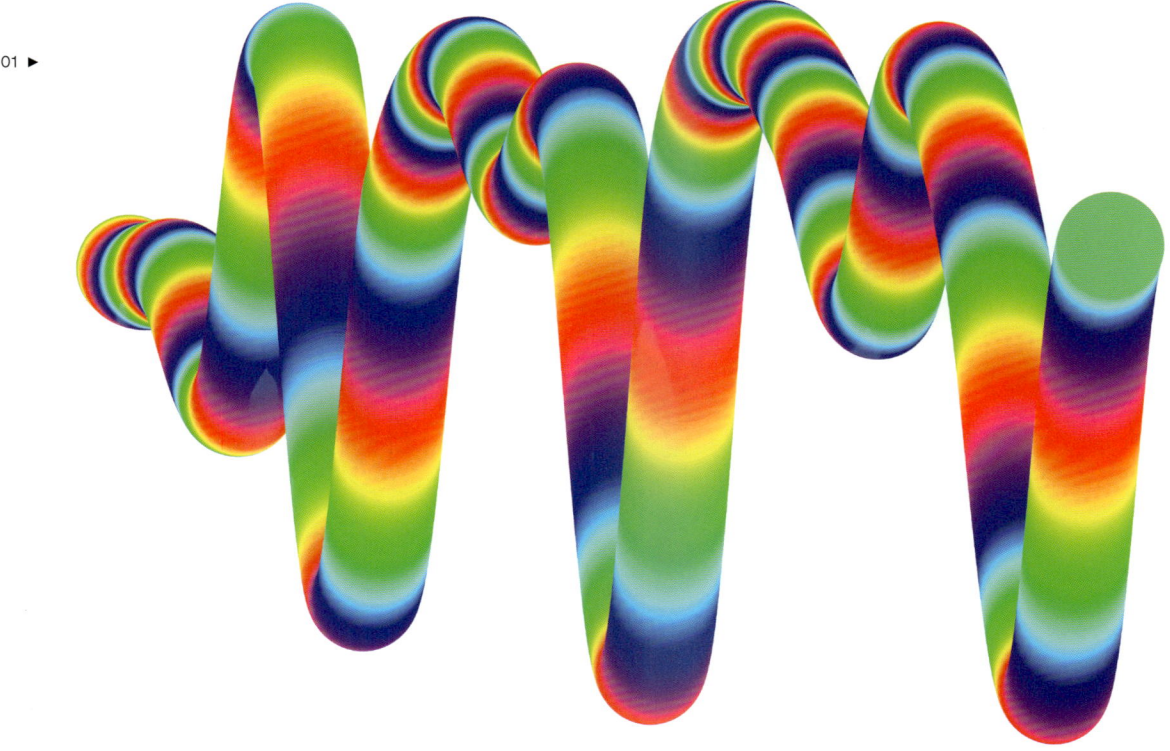

| # | TITLE | TIMESTAMP | MEDIUM | CHAIN | CONTRACT ADDRESS | TOKEN ID | EDITION SIZE |
|---|---|---|---|---|---|---|---|
| 01–03 | **Chromie Squiggle** | 11-27-2020 16:12:02 | p5.js | ETH | 0x059edd72cd353df5106d2b9cc5ab83a52287ac3a | 0–9999 | 1/1 of 10,000 |

EDITIONS ILLUSTRATED: (01) #8110, (02) #8099, (03) Various

# ERICK CALDERON

MEXICO 1981

02 ▶

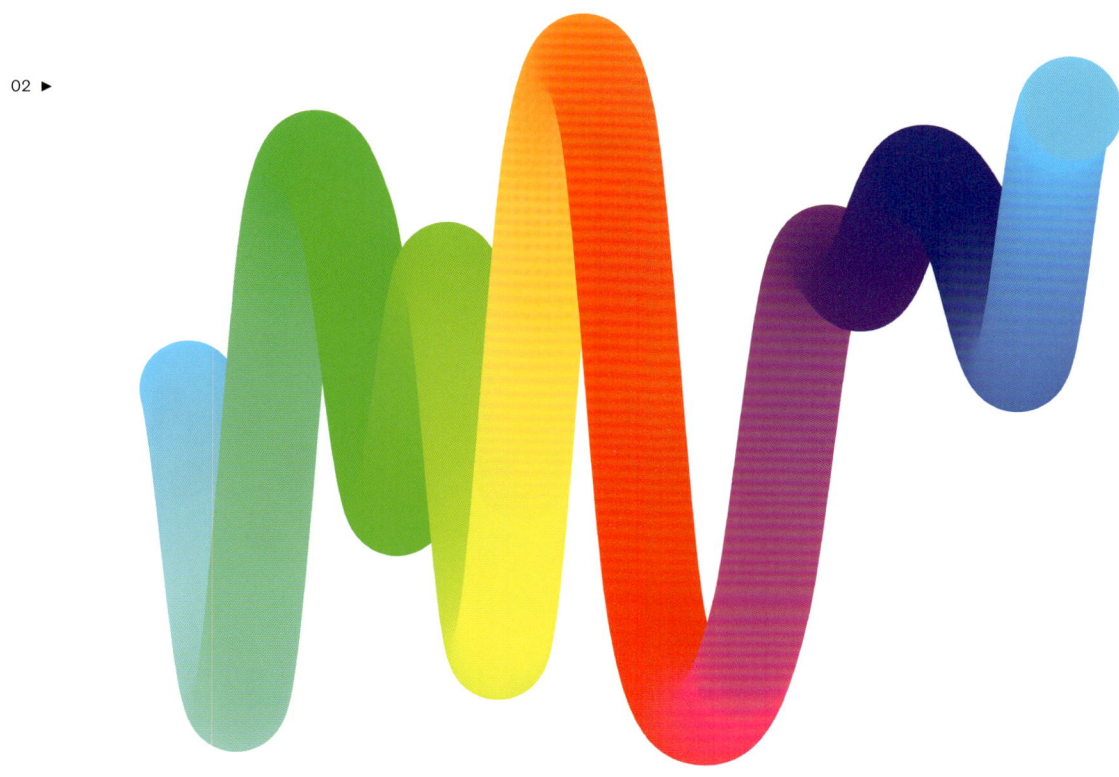

Erick Calderon (aka Snowfro) is a Houston-based artist and blockchain entrepreneur who founded the generative art NFT platform Art Blocks in November 2020 and released its first project, *Chromie Squiggle*. Art Blocks has proved to be a powerhouse of the NFT world, single-handedly changing the art world's perception and understanding of the field of generative art.

The *Chromie Squiggle* project challenged conventional notions of edition size with a potential 10,000 expressive curvilinear works. Equally important, collectors did not see their pieces before purchasing them — each was created on demand and generated in real time.

Calderon's algorithmic code determines the nature of each unique Squiggle's path, the width and style of the line, and the color gradients within. Deceptively simple, the computer program took Calderon over four years to perfect, his persistence inspired by frequent visits to see works of James Turrell, whose mastery of color and light informed many of Calderon's programmatic decisions.

The Squiggles' brightly colored rainbow gradients are rendered in a variety of styles, from hard-edged to fuzzy soft strokes to series of ribbed sections. The resulting visual effects range from subtle jewel tones and from pastels to muted grays. Although each is aesthetically striking, collectors also vie for those with statistically rare traits of color or form.

Collectors have resonated unusually strongly with their *Chromie Squiggles*, resulting in a strong community of devoted followers who started their own DAO for discussing, trading, and sharing their enthusiasm. DAO members share their Squiggle collections, create Squiggle memes, and discuss the finer points of the series.

Released during COVID-19, Calderon's *Chromie Squiggle* project has been a particularly influential and wide-ranging force to spread positivity and good cheer.

**ANNE SPALTER**
DIGITAL MIXED-MEDIA ARTIST, AUTHOR OF THE COMPUTER
IN THE VISUAL ARTS (1999) AND FOUNDER
OF DIGITAL FINE ARTS COURSES AT BROWN UNIVERSITY AND
RHODE ISLAND SCHOOL OF DESIGN

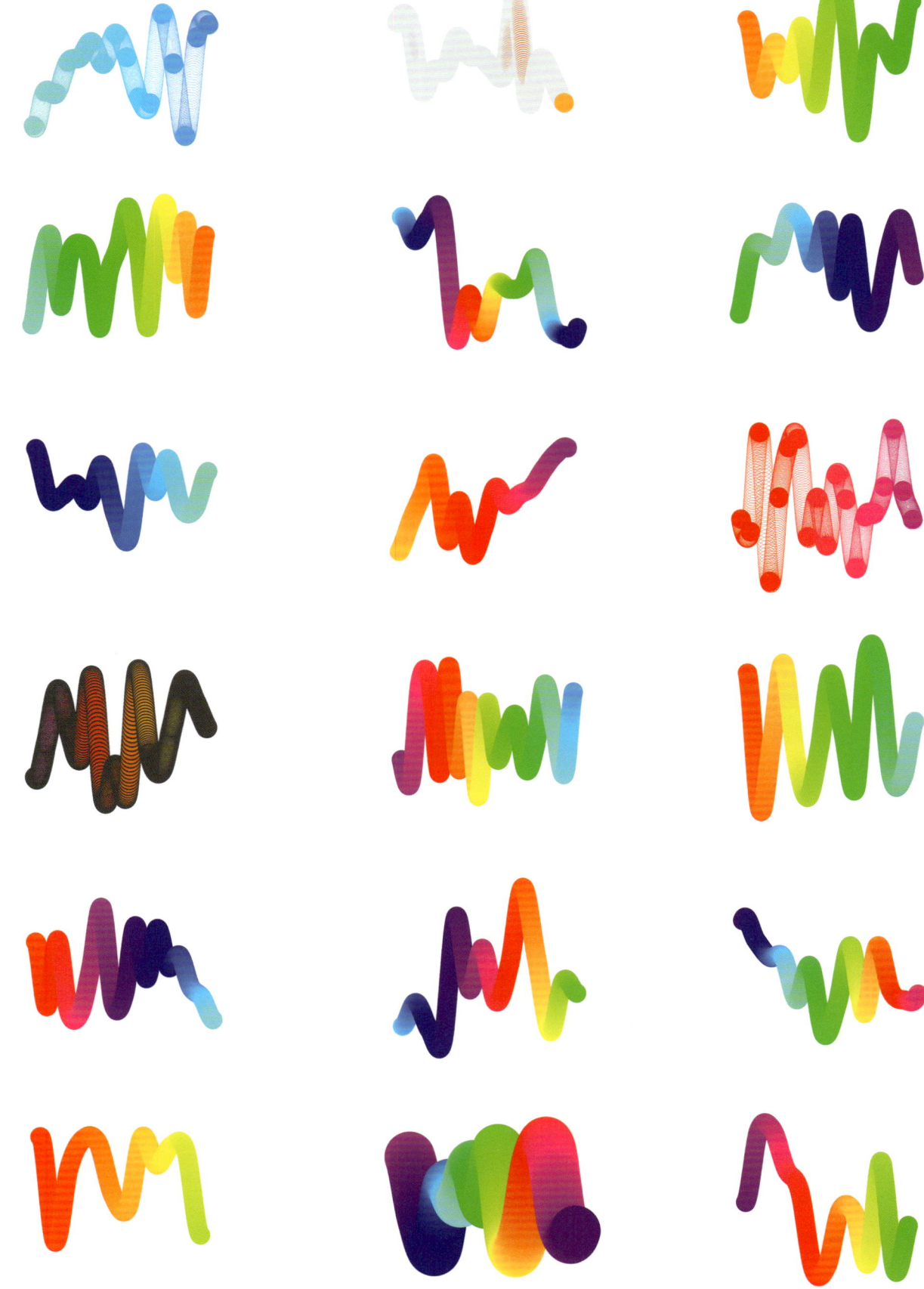

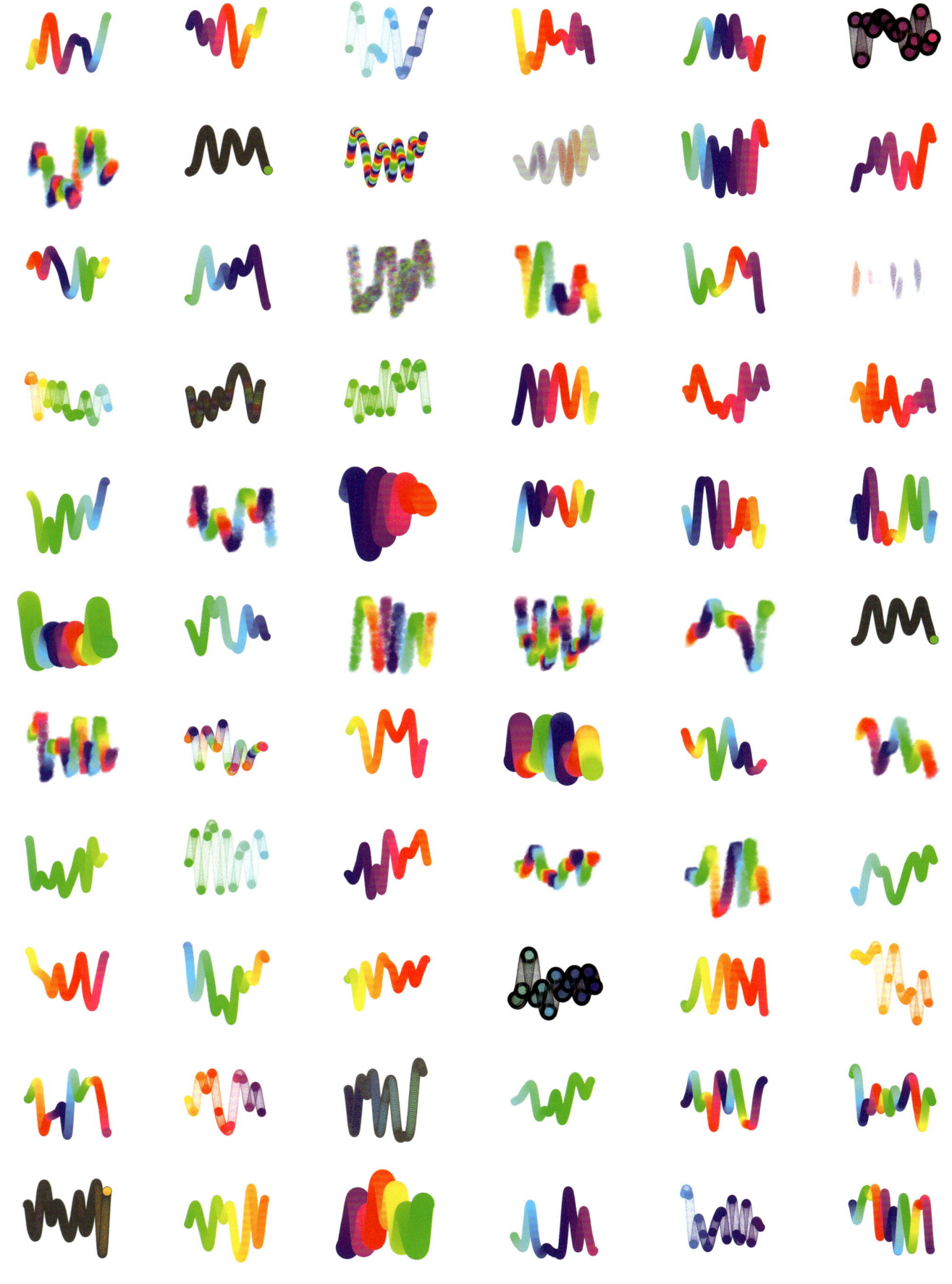

134, 135,

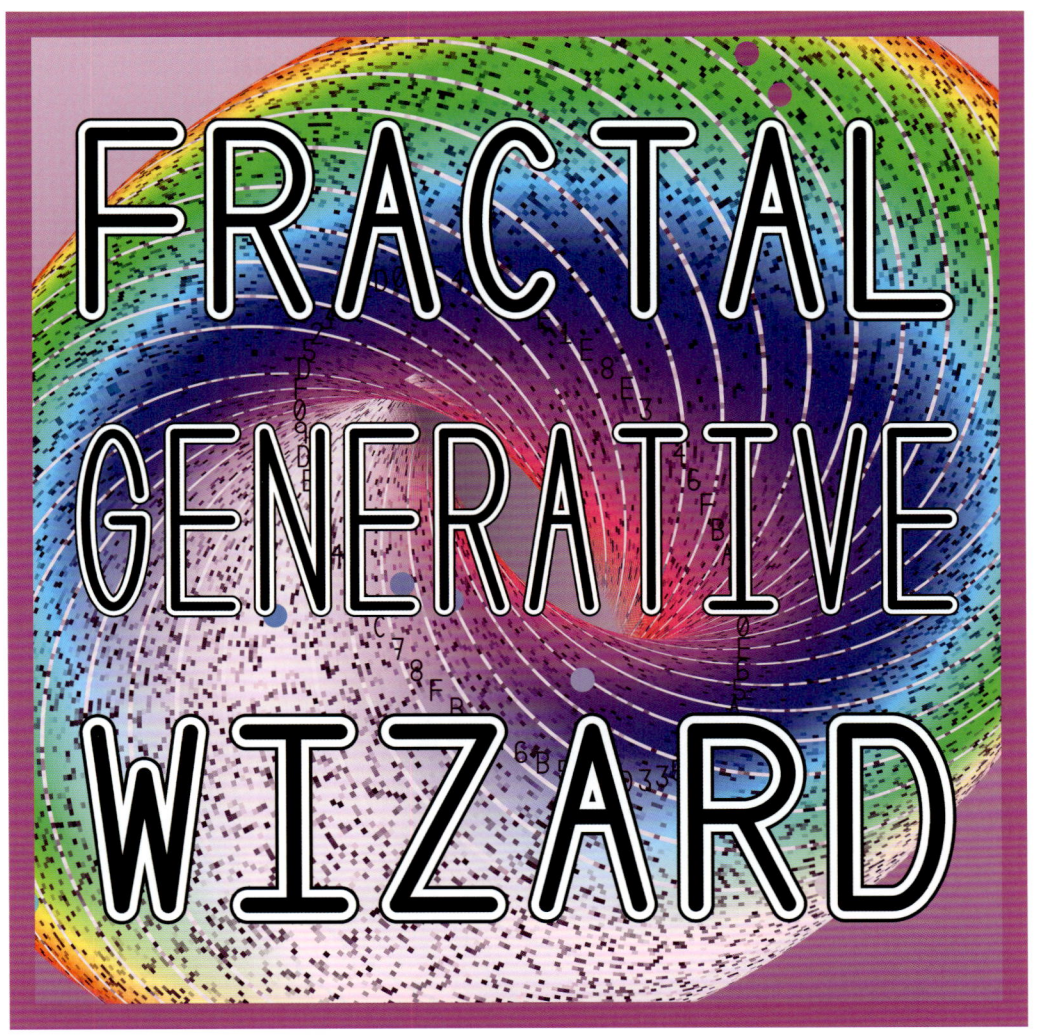

| # | TITLE | TIMESTAMP | MEDIUM | CHAIN | CONTRACT ADDRESS | TOKEN ID | EDITION SIZE |
|---|---|---|---|---|---|---|---|
| 01, 04 | **Gen 3** | 04-13-2021 03:03:55 | p5.js | ETH | 0xa7d8d9ef8d8ce8992df33d8b8cf4aebabd5bd270 | 48000000–48001023 | 1/1 of 1,024 |
| 02, 03 | **Gen 2** | 02-15-2021 00:38:11 | p5.js | ETH | 0xa7d8d9ef8d8ce8992df33d8b8cf4aebabd5bd270 | 18000000–18000255 | 1/1 of 256 |

EDITIONS ILLUSTRATED: (01) #315, (02) #20, (03) #176, (04) #55

# DANIEL CALDERON

MEXICO 1983

02

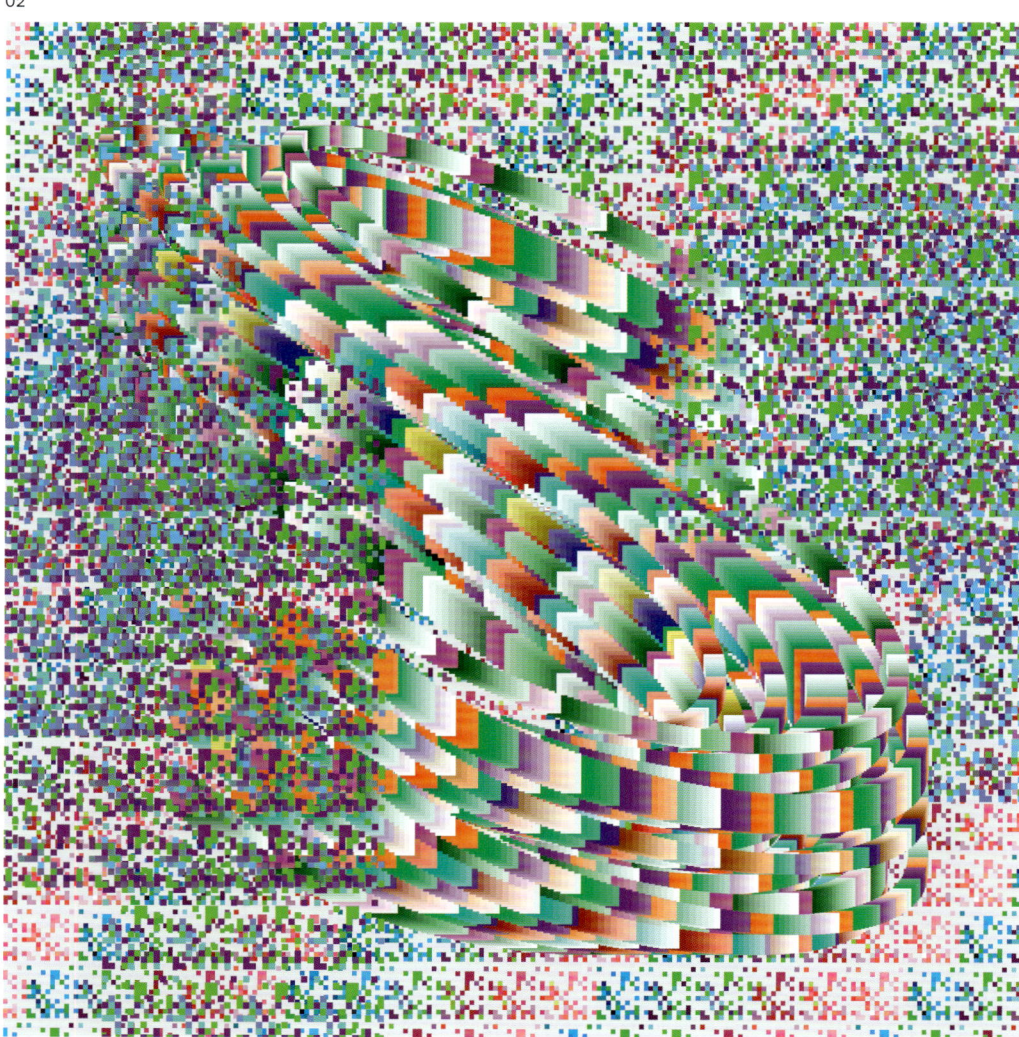

With fine art training and a keen interest in computational art, Daniel Calderon's (aka DCA) cryptographic exploration and use of hash strings laid the groundwork for his trio of code-based generative art projects collectively known as *Gen Trilogy* (2020–21). Composed in three parts, *Genesis* (2020), *Gen 2* (2021), and *Gen 3* (2021) illustrate the artist's prescient endeavor into the challenges and limitations of generative on-chain NFT artwork. Departing from the static compositional triangle arrangements and atmospheric color bands of *Genesis*, the second project of the trilogy uses animation to define the artist's oeuvre. *Gen 2* interprets a hash string by sweeping a bitmap across a Lissajous curve. The result is likened to grand gestures found in paintings, but comprised of edgy pixels, in abstract and weaved patterns. With one click, the composition is revealed via an animated drawn curtain. Additionally, a series of clicks causes digital confetti to fall from the top of the screen. *Gen 2* dazzles the retina with color and movement, and the rarity featured within the project is no exception. Five percent of the outputs and rare

Spectra mints that scintillate with pixelated sprites from old video games. Calderon explains it: "As a child, I remember opening packs of trading cards (both comics and sports types) and finding a rare holographic card in the pack. It was a special feeling to see the shimmer of the colorful holographic foil. With *Gen 2*, I wanted collectors to feel the same excitement." Among the rare Spectra mints are sprites of Mario, Link from Zelda, a star, and a mushroom. In a radical departure from *Genesis*, *Gen 2* asserts the relationship of the viewer with generative NFTs via its reminiscent and performative qualities. With a few inquisitive clicks, the viewer's participation becomes part of the artwork itself.

**TAYLOR KUBALA**
ADJUNCT PROFESSOR OF ART HISTORY
FOR THE UNIVERSITY OF HOUSTON SYSTEM,
CURATOR AND MEMBER OF THE CURATORIAL
BOARD OF ART BLOCKS

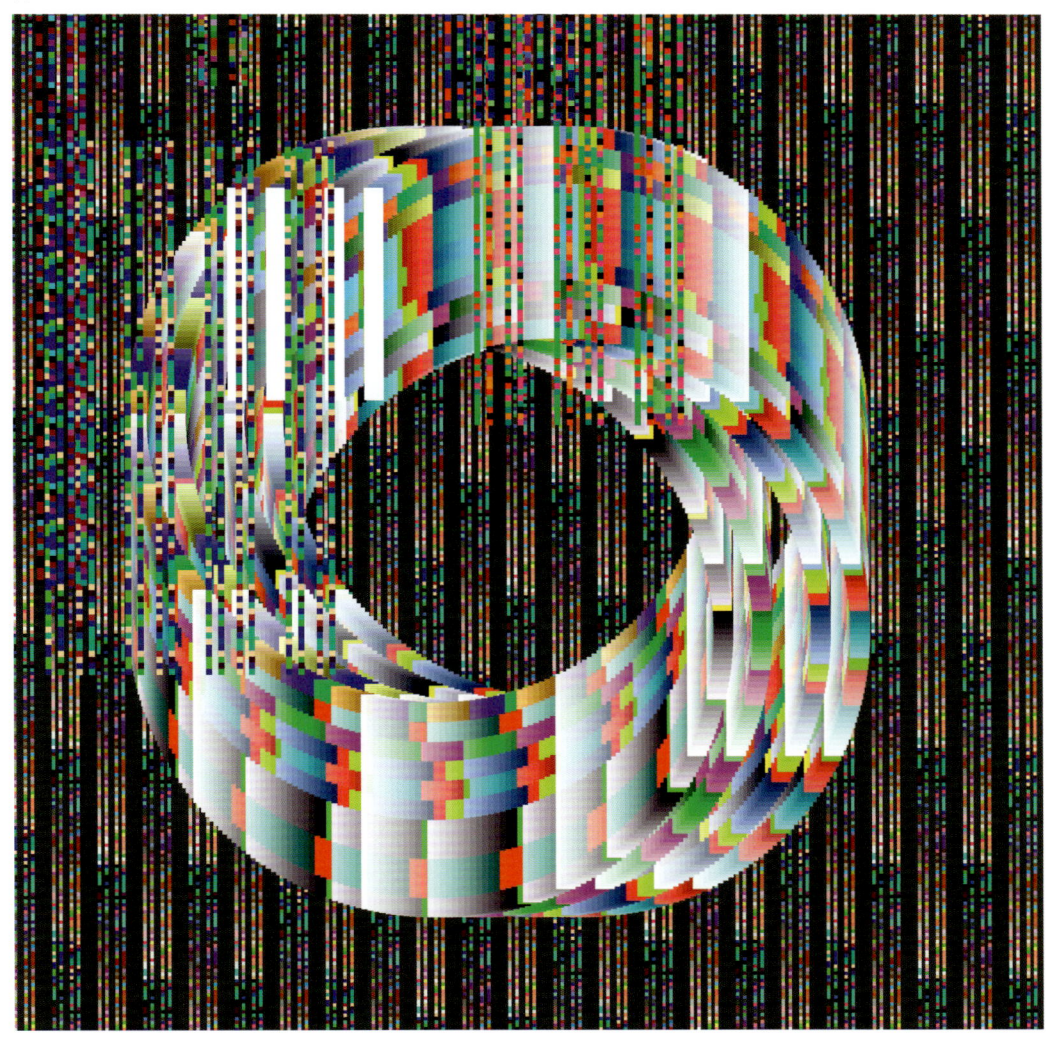

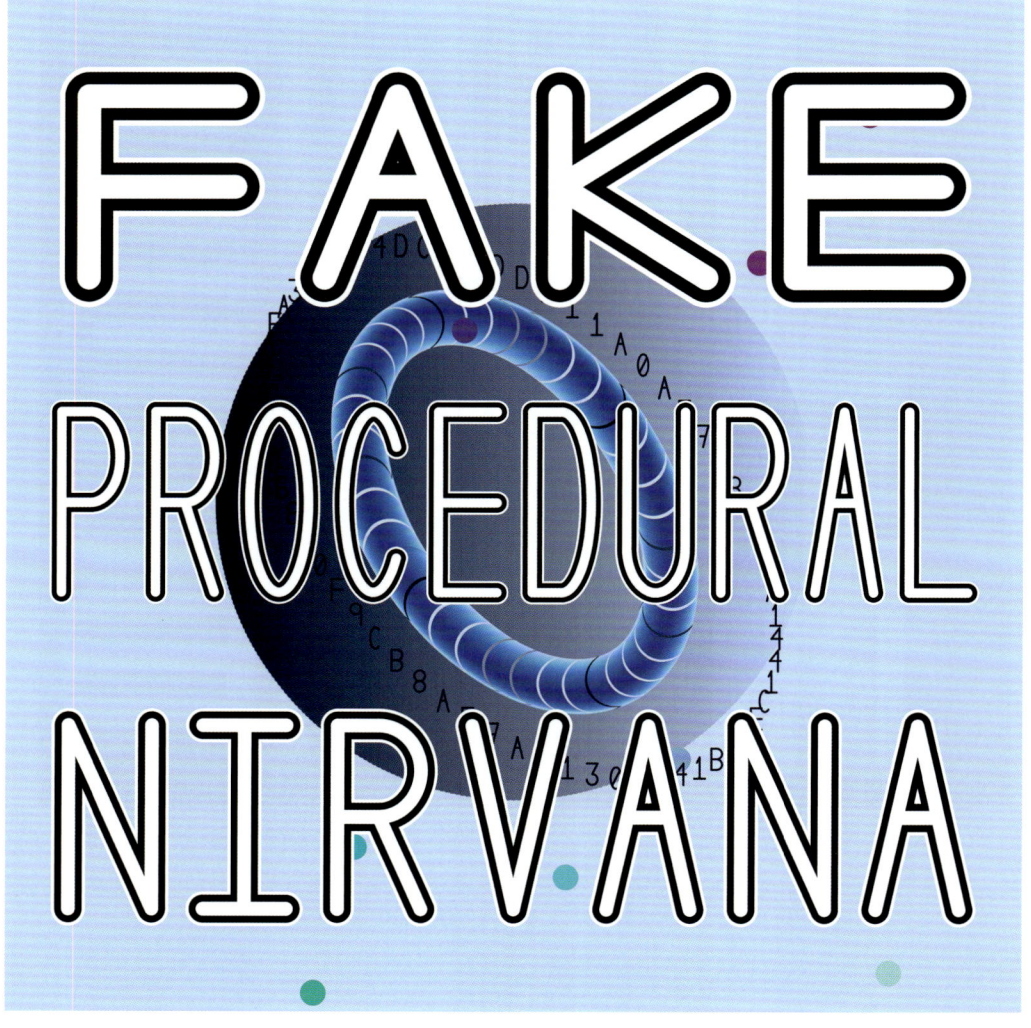

01

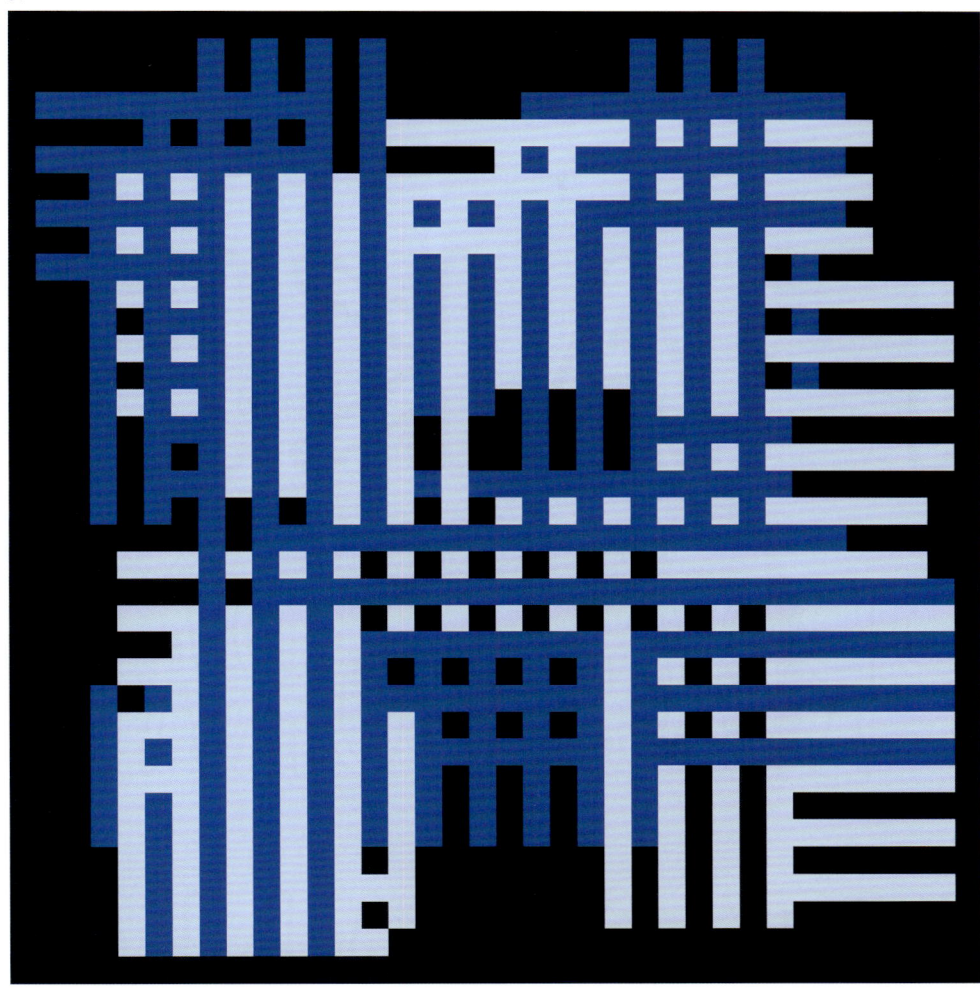

| # | TITLE | TIMESTAMP | MEDIUM | CHAIN | CONTRACT ADDRESS | TOKEN ID | EDITION SIZE |
|---|---|---|---|---|---|---|---|
| 01, 02 | **Construction Token** | 11-27-2020 15:58:01 | Processing | ETH | 0x059edd72cd353df5106d2b9cc5ab83a52287ac3a | 2000000–2000499 | 1/1 of 500 |

EDITIONS ILLUSTRATED: (01) #411, (02) #413

# JEFF DAVIS

UNITED STATES 1972

02

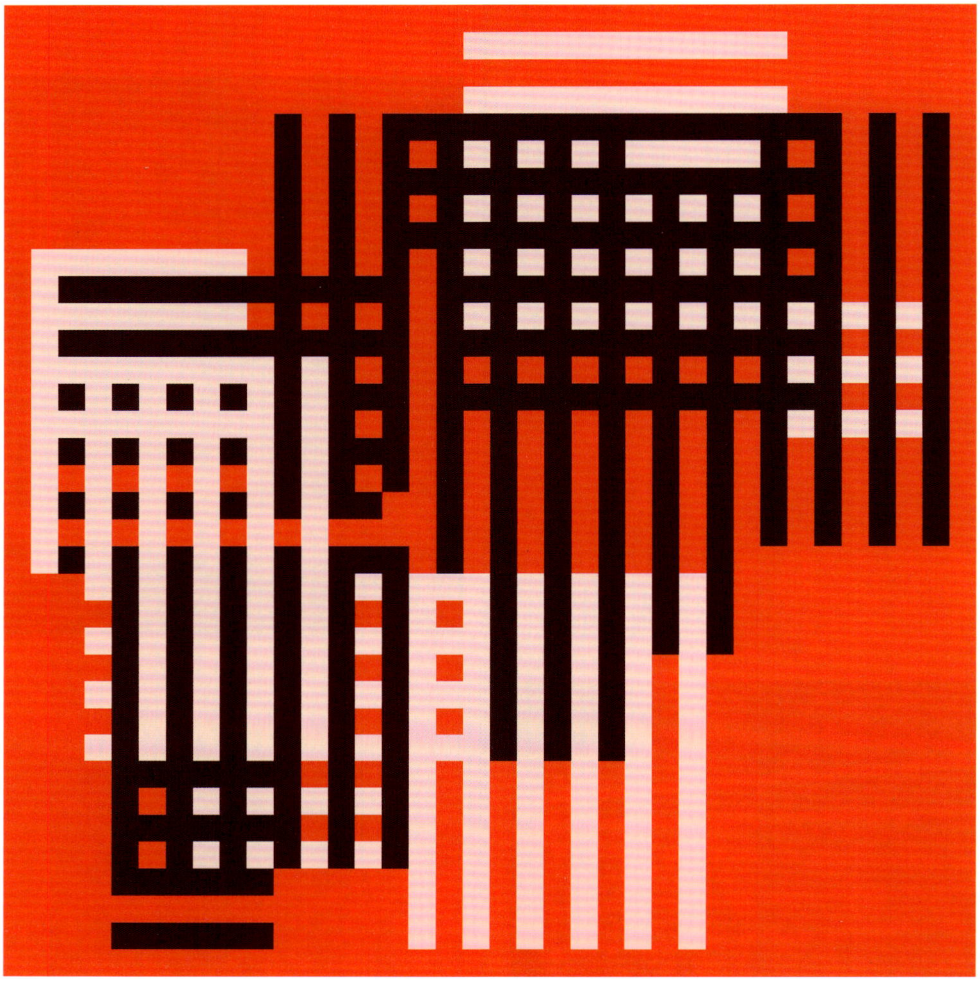

At the beginning of 2021, I came across the work of Jeff Davis on Twitter. Against the din of hyperrealistic crypto art in my feed, Jeff's minimal, abstract works were a relief: Josef Albers (1888–1976) color studies, lit for the screen by James Turrell. His two series *Rhythm* and *Construction Token* (both 2021) stand as a testament to this.

As Chief Creative Officer at Art Blocks, Jeff has played a pivotal role in the history of NFT art, utilizing his deep understanding of generative art to steer the direction of both the platform and the space as a whole. Not only does he investigate color theory and two-dimensional design in his art, but Jeff also shares his expertise through writing and teaching. Jeff's two publications, *Foundations of Color* (2015) and *Foundations of Design* (2016), expand on Albers's teachings, exploring how technology can be harnessed to drive new fields of creative expression. His relentless commitment to these disciplines will undoubtedly leave a lasting impact and inspire future generations of artists in the ever-evolving NFT art landscape.

After discovering his work, I DMed Jeff hoping to feature his work at our new gallery, Bright Moments. For our first show, in Los Angeles, Jeff released *Portal* (2021). I remember the look of joy on Jeff's and his wife Kelly's faces when they arrived from Phoenix. This was the first "art opening" that any of us had been to since the onset of COVID-19 more than a year earlier. On a hot night, packed into a sandy sliver of a space just off the beach, hung five screens illuminated by these otherworldly portals.

Since then, Jeff has created a new algorithm for each of the cities that we've visited, considering the city, exhibition site, and minting experience for each — *Reflection* (2021) in New York, followed in 2022 by *Inflection*, *Formation*, and *Transcendence*, in Berlin, London, and Mexico City, respectively. Most recently, for our sixth city, Tokyo, he created *LED* (2023).

Through his own path as a generative artist, and the platform for others that he has elevated with Art Blocks, Jeff's work surprises us with shapes and colors that identify as non-fungible objects while simultaneously abstracting themselves from any sense of technology.

**SETH GOLDSTEIN**
FOUNDER OF BRIGHT MOMENTS

03

04

05

06

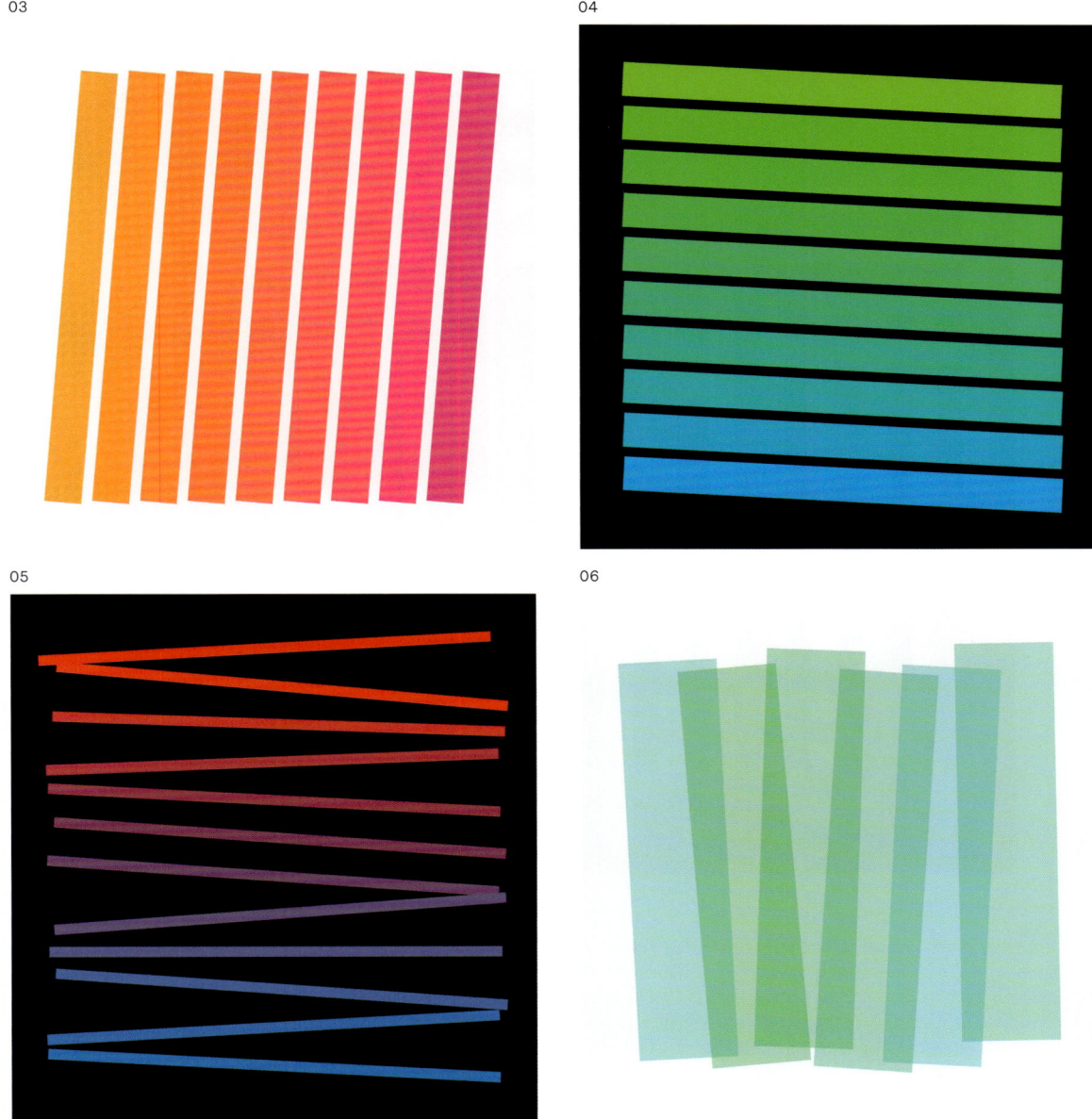

| # | TITLE | TIMESTAMP | MEDIUM | CHAIN | CONTRACT ADDRESS | TOKEN ID | EDITION SIZE |
|---|---|---|---|---|---|---|---|
| 03–07 | **Rhythm** | 04-24-2021 03:43:28 | p5.js | ETH | 0xa7d8d9ef8d8ce8992df33d8b8cf4aebabd5bd270 | 57000000–57000333 | 1/1 of 334 |

EDITIONS ILLUSTRATED: (03) #17, (04) #9, (05) #216, (06) #236, (07) #150

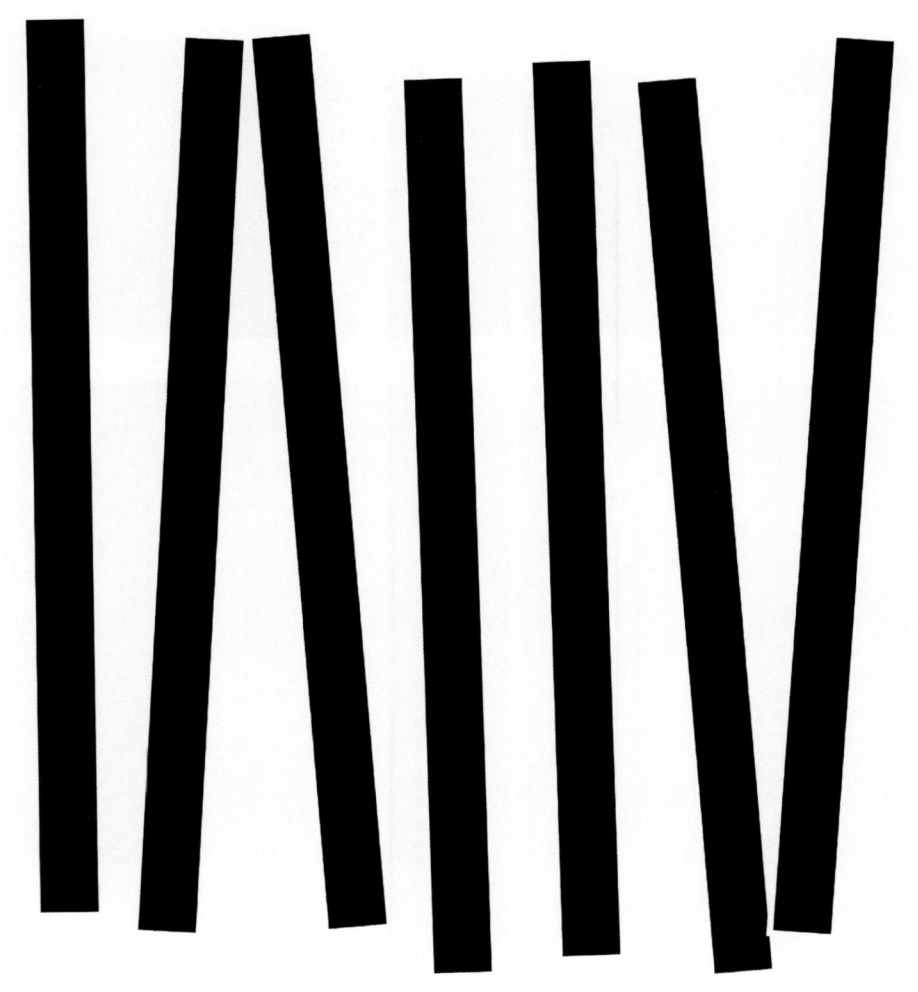

01

02

03

04

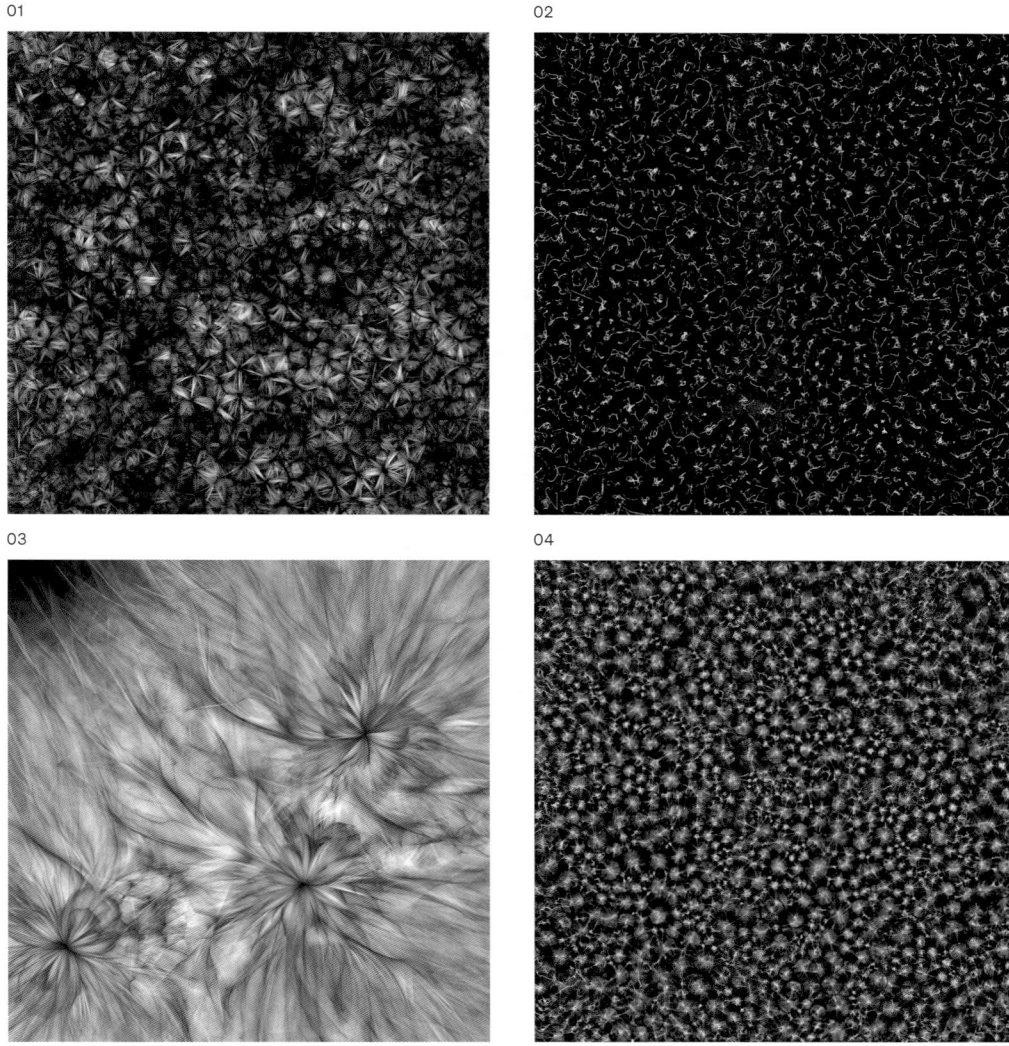

| # | NAME | MINT TIMESTAMP | MEDIUM | CHAIN | CONTRACT ADDRESS | TOKEN ID | EDITION SIZE |
|---|---|---|---|---|---|---|---|
| 01–04 | **Process Compendium** | 06-04-2022 21:48:26 | Processing | ETH | 0x4dc81ab6a322e4d85f3-2d672e155a55b16bf8986 | 1–4 | 1/1 of 4 |
| 05 | **There's No Distance 2.1** | 05-22-2022 15:47:57 | Processing rendered to MP4 | ETH | 0xabefbc9fd2f806065b4f-3c237d4b59d9a97bcac7 | 3208 | 1/1 |
| 06 | **CENTURY** | 06-23-2021 20:11:32 | p5.js | ETH | 0xa7d8d9ef8d8ce8992df-33d8b8cf4aebabd5bd270 | 100000000–100000999 | 1/1 of 1,000 |

EDITIONS ILLUSTRATED: (01) X-4, (02) X-5, (03) X-6, (04) X-7, (06) Various

# CASEY REAS

UNITED STATES 1972

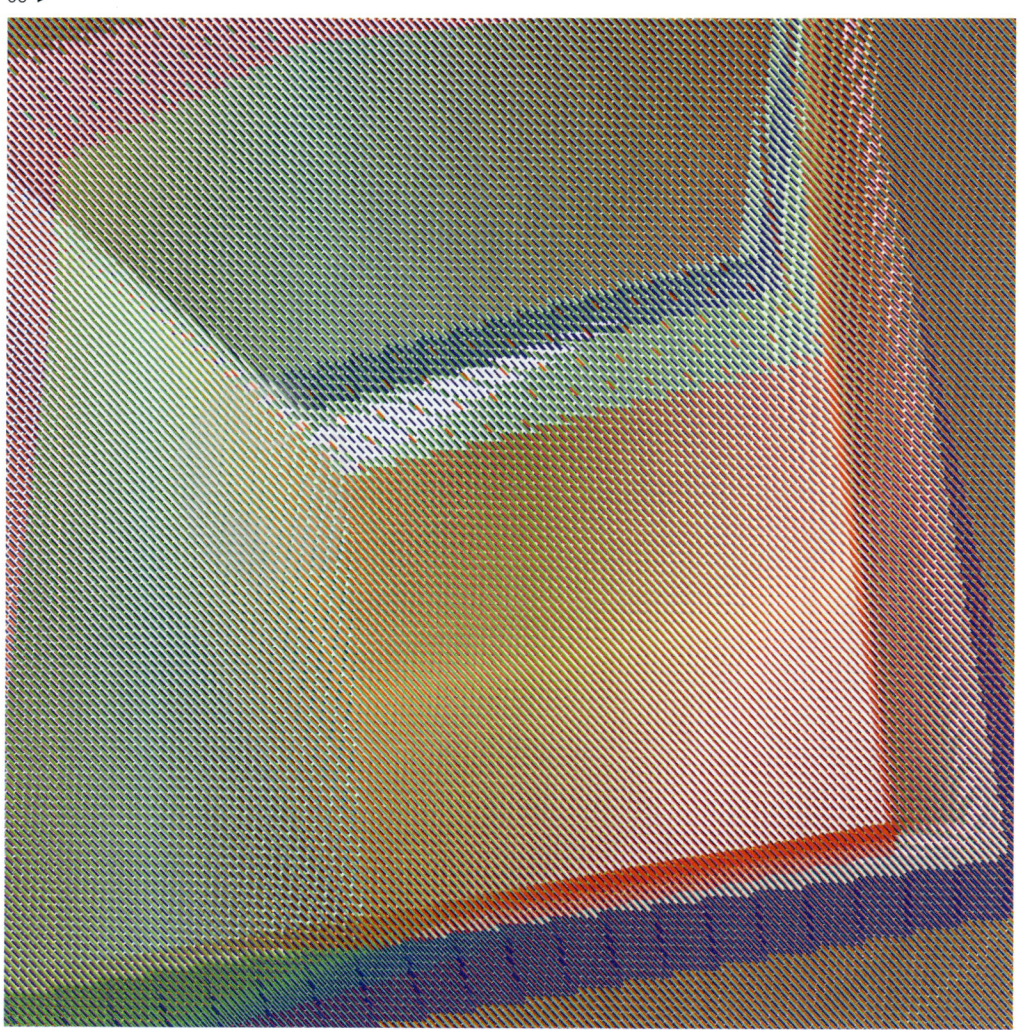

Casey Reas is not your average artist working mostly on the development of their own visual language. He makes tools. He sets up platforms. He generates community. He writes code. And he does all these things at a scale that matters, changing art along the way. Back in 2001, together with Ben Fry, he co-created Processing, an open-source tool, a language and a community that allowed thousands of people to visualize and share ideas. Twenty years later, he founded Feral File, an exhibition platform focused on exchange, curating, quality, and passion rather than sales. On a more personal level, his writing and practice have influenced my take on art a number of times. In the early 2000s, when software-based art was mostly perceived as a self-referential niche, he showed that programming offers a new language to engage with the same ideas that painters, sculptors, as well as conceptual, performance, and installation artists have been exploring for decades. He later materialized this idea in his 2021 generative art series *CENTURY* that pays homage to the history of minimalism in 20th-century art. The same year, Casey argued that digital visual art might be ready for a mass audience, and for a new "collecting ecology," one which is radically different from the current art world — a model he implemented in Feral File.

The outcome of a way of "thinking algorithmically and aesthetically at one and the same time" (Frieder Nake) is *There's No Distance 2.1* (2021), a looping video employing custom code and minimal tools (the cube, the pixel, the RGB code) and behaviors (rotation). These generate, in Reas's words, "a medium for thinking about simulation and the history of visual representation." Part of a larger body of work started in 2016 with his *Still Life* (2016) series, the piece works as an ever-revolving bicycle wheel, cycling through the history of perspective as well as to the studies of form and perception in abstract-geometric painting and in cinema, while equally investigating the virtual spaces we are increasingly engaging with.

**DOMENICO QUARANTA**
ART CRITIC, CURATOR, AND AUTHOR OF
SURFING WITH SATOSHI. ART, BLOCKCHAIN AND NFTS (2021)

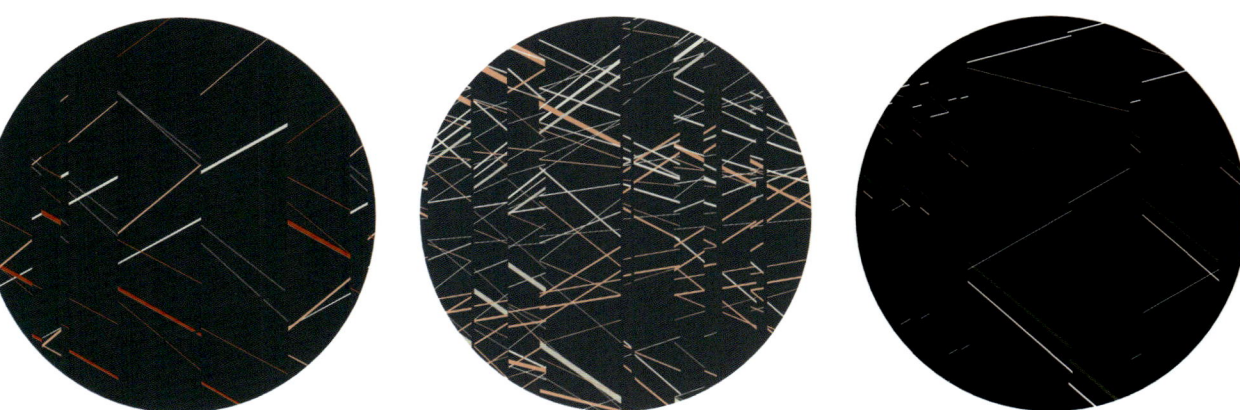

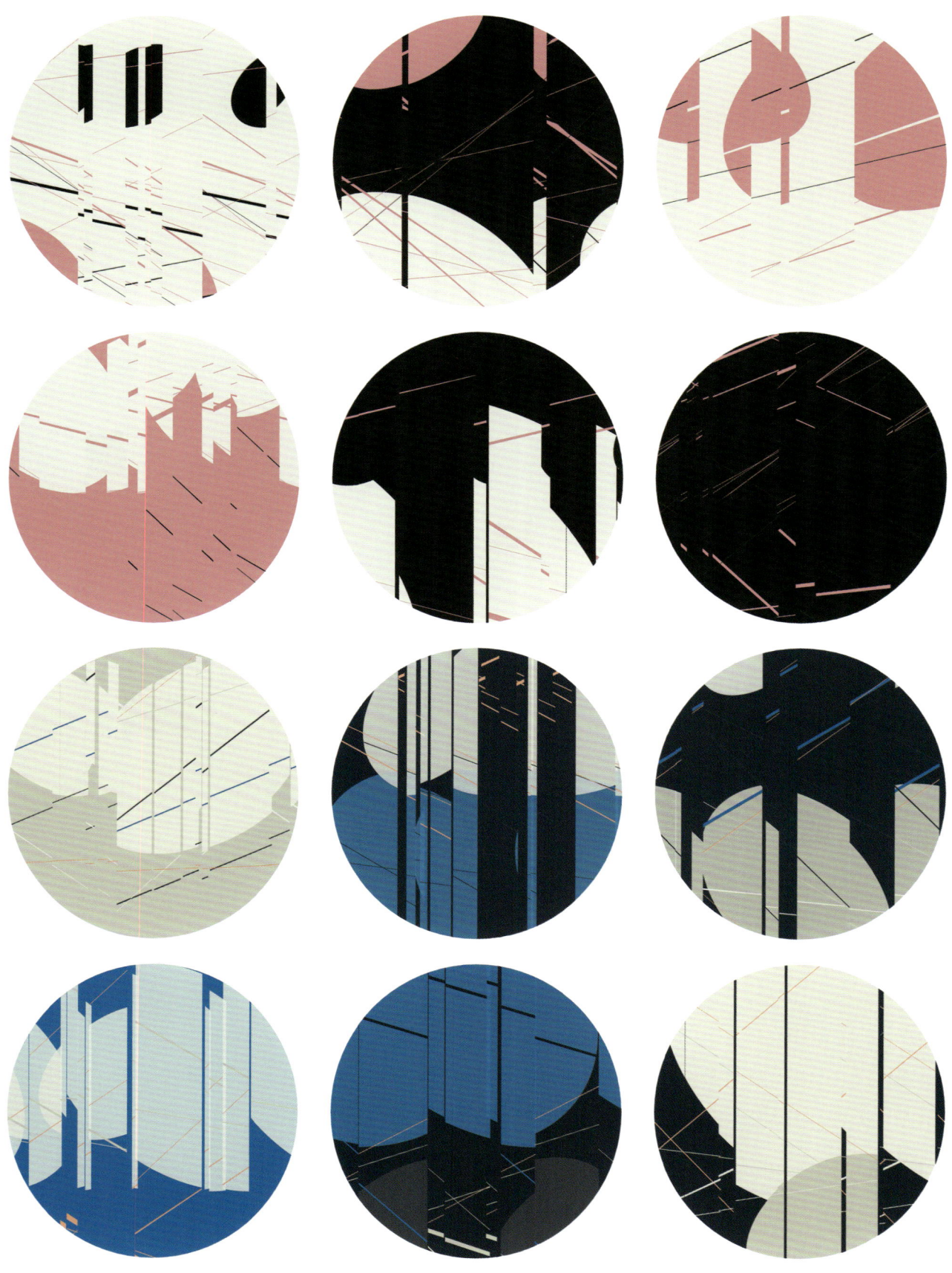

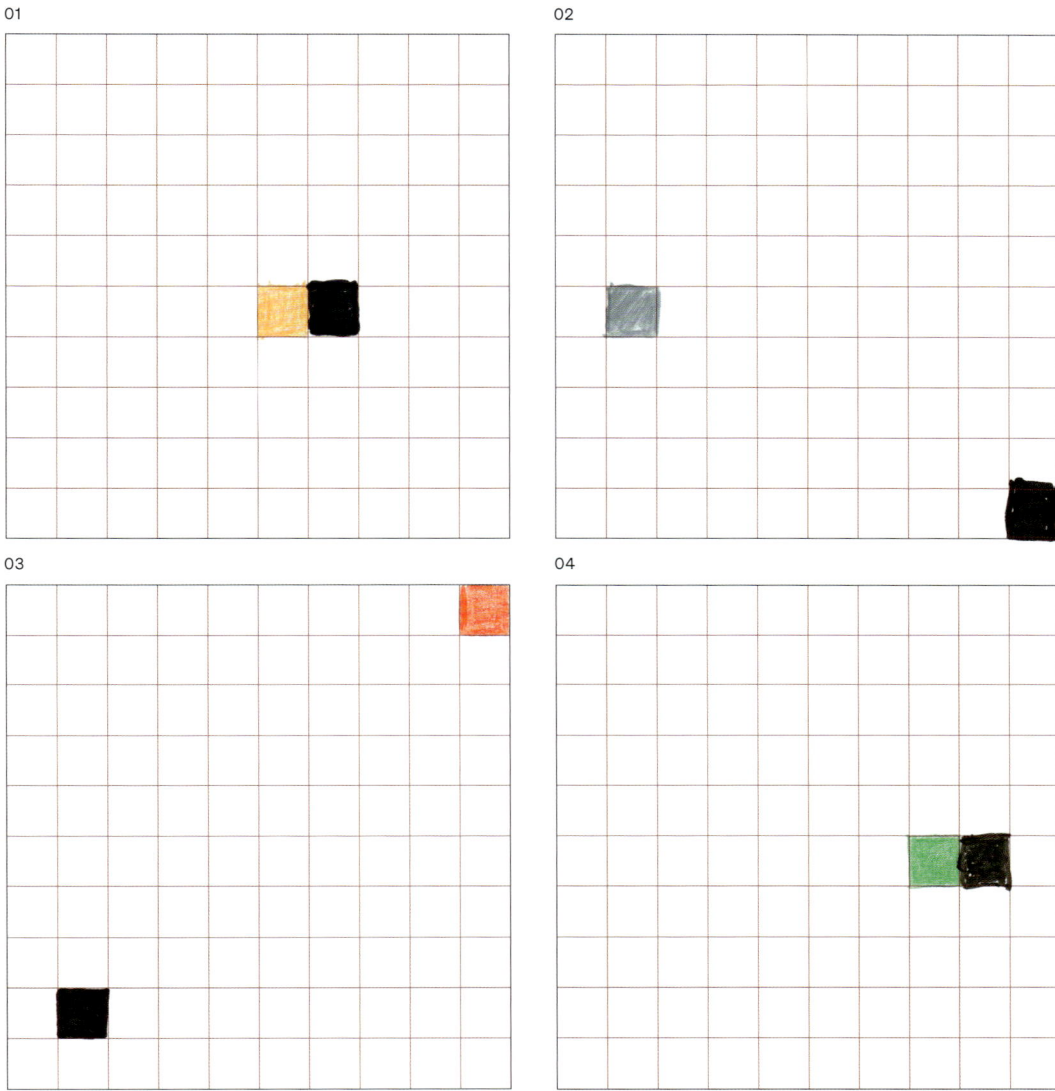

01    02

03    04

| # | TITLE | TIMESTAMP | MEDIUM | CHAIN | CONTRACT ADDRESS | TOKEN ID | EDITION SIZE | COLLABORATORS |
|---|-------|-----------|--------|-------|------------------|----------|--------------|---------------|
| 01–04 | **2% of disorder in co-operation** | 03-09-2022 20:13:44 | Work on paper | ETH | 0x609fb45c5afa1f1d56feadcdaadc80136a68e47f | 1–14 | 1/1 of 14 | – |
| 05–06 | **Themes and Variations** | 07-21-2023 15:33:59 | JavaScript | ETH | 0xe034bb2b1b9471e11cf1a0a9199a156fb227aa5d | 0–499 | 1/1 of 500 | Martin Grasser |

EDITIONS ILLUSTRATED: (01) #2, (02) #14, (03) #9, (04) #6, (05) #1, (06) #325, (07) #212, (08) #39

# VERA MOLNÁR

HUNGARY 1924

05
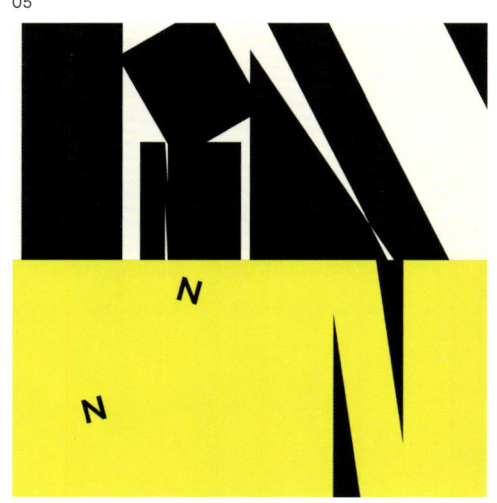

06
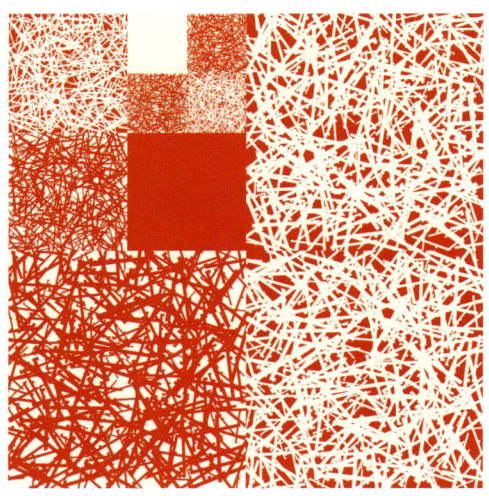

07
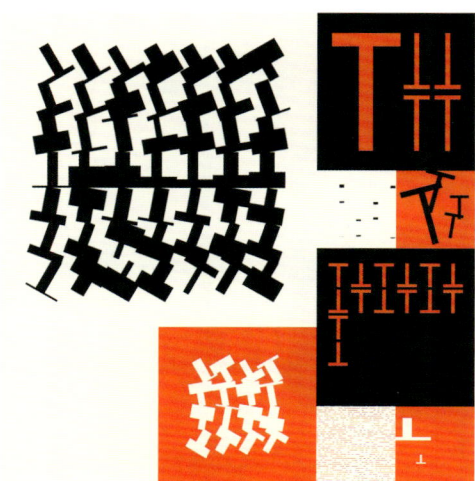

08
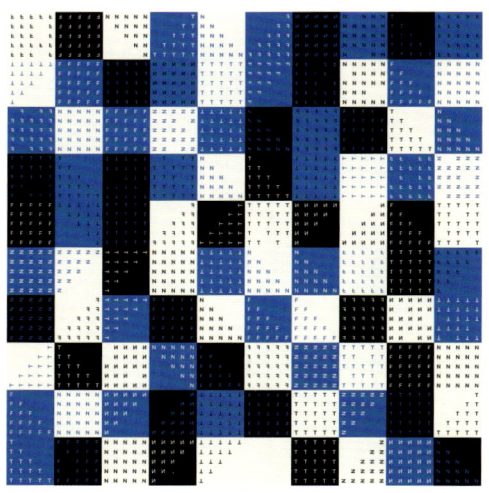

Vera Molnár began using a computer in 1968. But her ideas have always formed in her mind; the computer does not create the works for her. The computer is only a tool that allows the painter to free themselves from the constraints of a sclerotic classical heritage.

Since the 1990s, Vera Molnár's practice involves a kind of permanent game with the computer. Establishing a protocol, she thus makes images of all kinds, composing them in an entirely subjective way, by hand and with a total modal freedom of craft and of choice of forms and materials. Only then does she program the computer to reconstruct exactly what she has done but also all the variations and possible images resembling her initial one.

On the occasion of her 98th birthday, Vera Molnár has imagined with Galerie 8+4 in Paris a new protocol to create a series of new works as NFTs entitled *2% of disorder in cooperation* (2022).

From a grid drawn on paper made up of 100 squares, the artist decides a precise mode of filling which supposes that a first square of the grid is filled by a random person coming to visit her. The person freely chooses the place in the grid where to fill the first square and the color. A second square of the grid is then filled by the artist who chooses a position in the grid according to the first intervention. The color used by the artist is always black.

In 2023, Molnár released *Themes and Variations* with the technical help of artist and designer Martin Grasser, a collection that became her first exploration into on-chain algorithmic art. The algorithm for *Themes and Variations* was inspired by Molnár's "Machine Imaginaire" (developed between 1959 and the early 1970s) in the form of letters. At its core, the algorithm uses vector representations of the letters $N$, $F$, and $T$ to reintroduce and manage new chaos in order, or more order in an old chaotic practice… who knows?

**VINCENT BABY**
ART HISTORIAN AND CURATOR

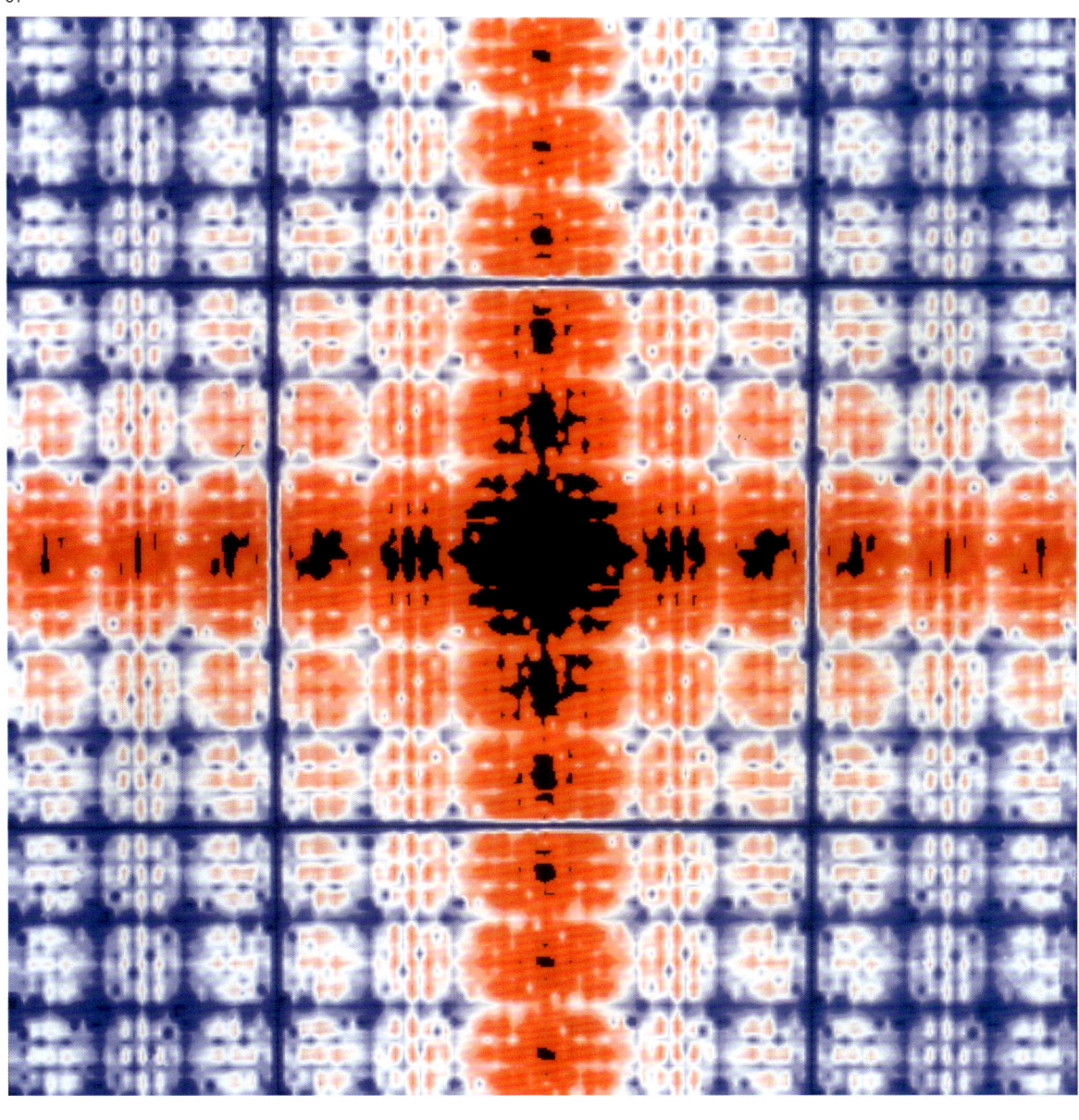

| # | TITLE | TIMESTAMP | MEDIUM | CHAIN | CONTRACT ADDRESS | TOKEN ID | EDITION SIZE |
|---|---|---|---|---|---|---|---|
| 01–10 | **Math Art** | 05-31-2022 12:07:25 | DIBIAS Software | ETH | 0x46ac8540d698167fcbb9e846511beb8cf8af9bd8 | 430000–430099 | 1/1 of 100 |

EDITIONS ILLUSTRATED: (01) #100, (02) #51, (03) #4, (04) #42, (05) #38, (06) #15, (07) #80, (08) #89, (09) #73, (10) #86

# HERBERT W. FRANKE
AUSTRIA 1927–2022

02

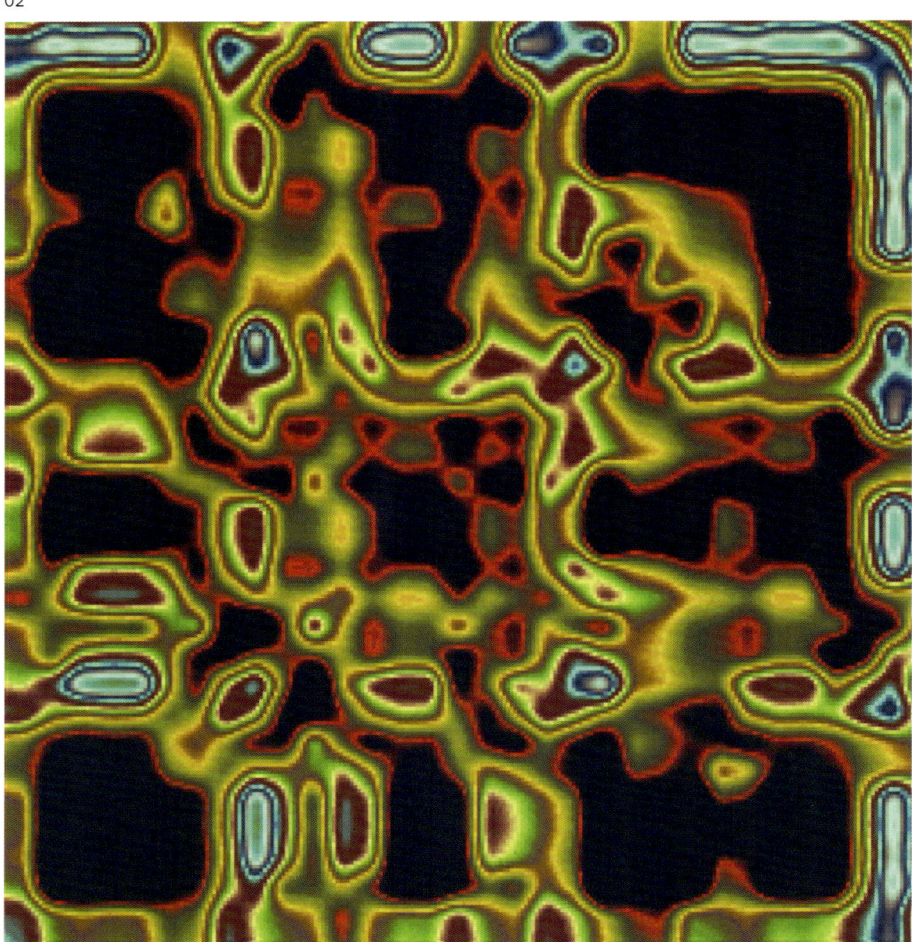

Herbert W. Franke (1927–2022) was one of the leading pioneers in many worlds, a border crosser between art and science. As a computer artist of the first hour, he started experimenting with generative photography and mathematics of continuity in 1953. As early as 1954, he used an analog computer, and from the 1960s onwards, the first mainframe computers for his abstract "algorithmic" art based on mathematical principles.

Franke had noticed in the 1940s during his university studies of theoretical physics how beautiful some pictures of physics were, especially with the latest instruments such as scanning electron microscopes, telescopes, and particle accelerators. That made him curious as to why that is and how art is related to it. In physics, as in nature, there had to be principles of order that had an aesthetic effect.

In 1980, Franke began a 15-year collaboration with programmer Horst Helbig at the German Aerospace Center. Both developed a routine where they sat together every two weeks on Saturday in the otherwise abandoned institute and experimented with mathematical formulas of different types of mathematics (e.g., algebraic formulas, fields, fractals, imaginary numbers,

stochastics). Together, they studied mathematical disciplines in relation to aesthetics. The series *MATH ART* (1980–95) is the output of their research, minted in 2022 on Quantum in the final year of Franke's life, aged 95. It reveals the universe of mathematical signs and numbers visualized through a variety of shapes and colors reminiscent of pop art.

Throughout his entire life, he used mathematical principles for artistic experimentation. From the very beginning, it was clear to him that it was the artist's mission to examine new technologies and their social significance through the lens of their creative potential. For Franke, mathematics is the foundation and essence of visual art. While he saw the artist as an analytical maker using mathematics to create structures, he assigned the computer the task of modulating these principles of order through varying random processes. Franke, therefore, considered the computer as a creative partner for the artist very early on.

**DR. SUSANNE PAECH**
MEDIA EXPERT, CURATOR, AND
FOUNDATION FOUNDER OF ART MEETS SCIENCE

03

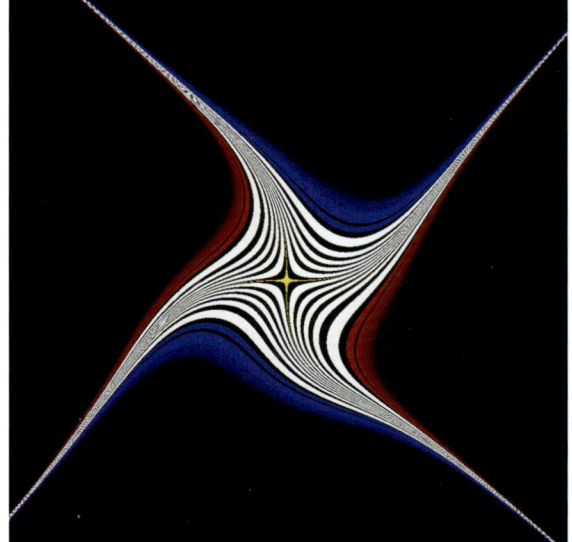

04

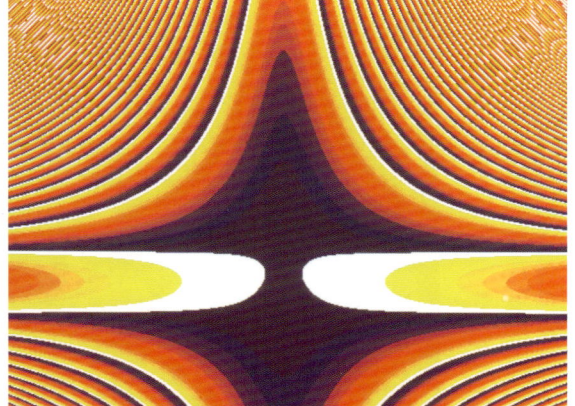

05

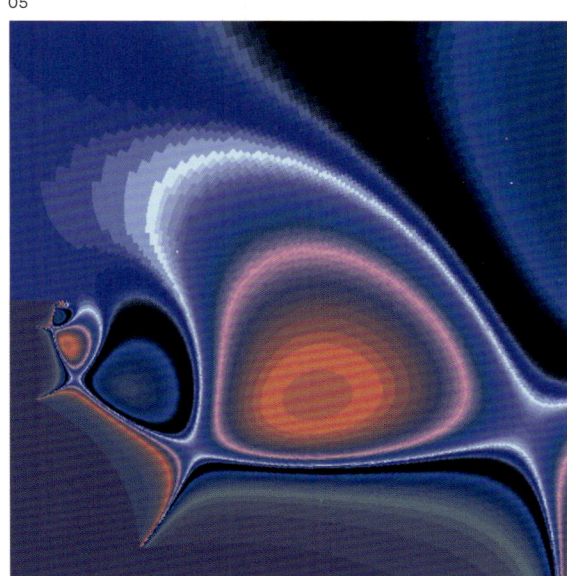

06

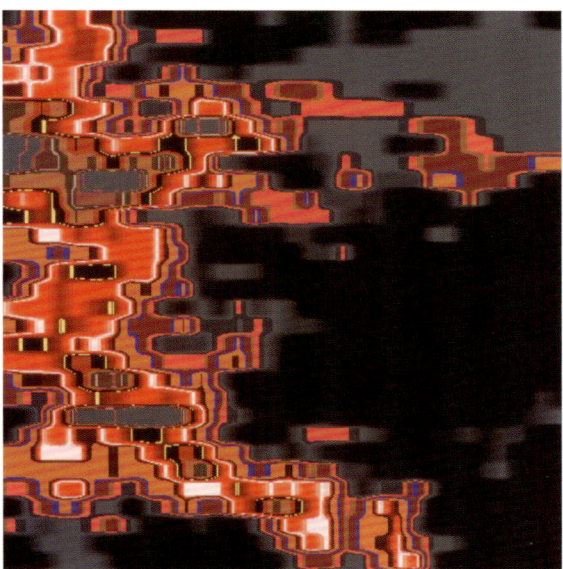

07

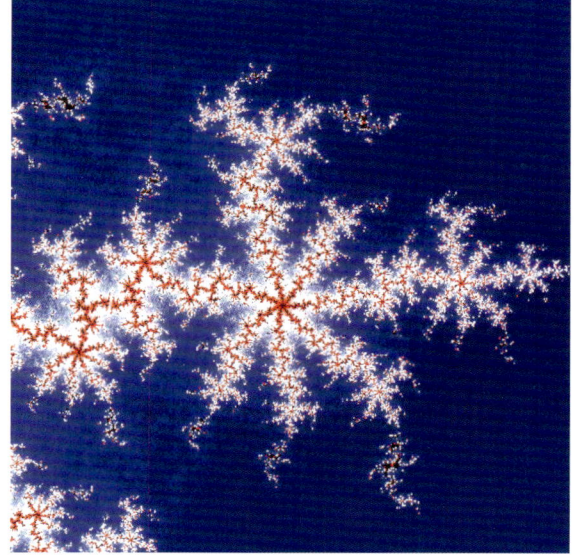

08

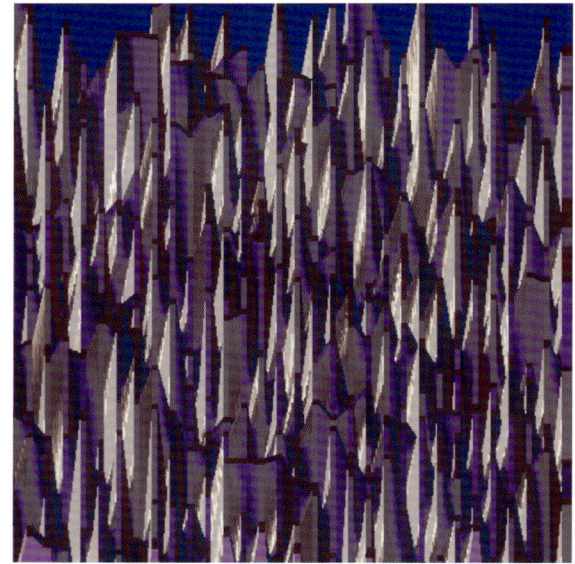

09

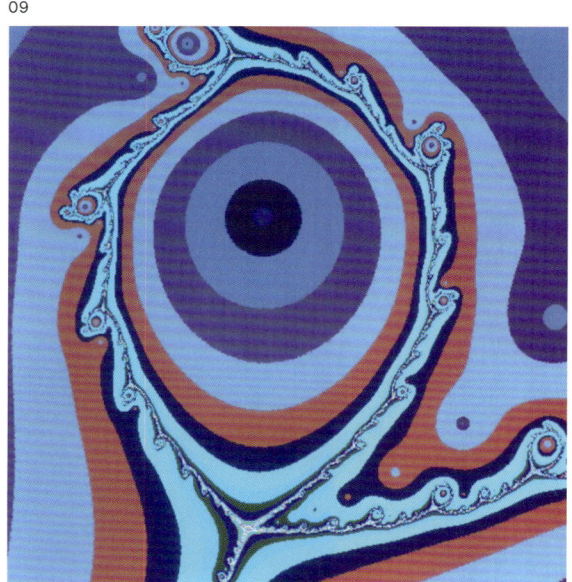

10

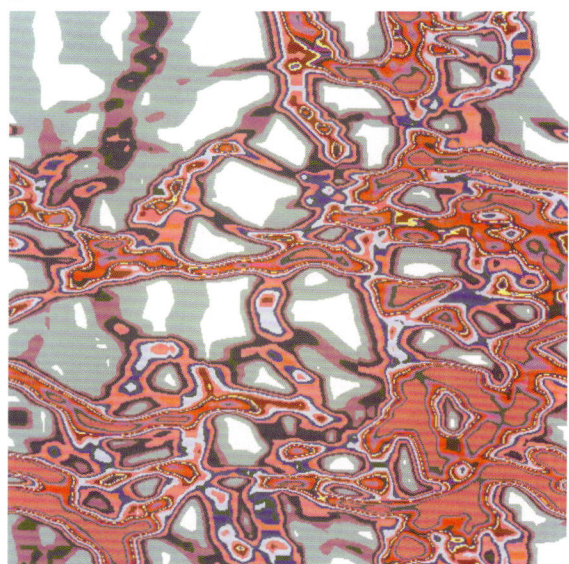

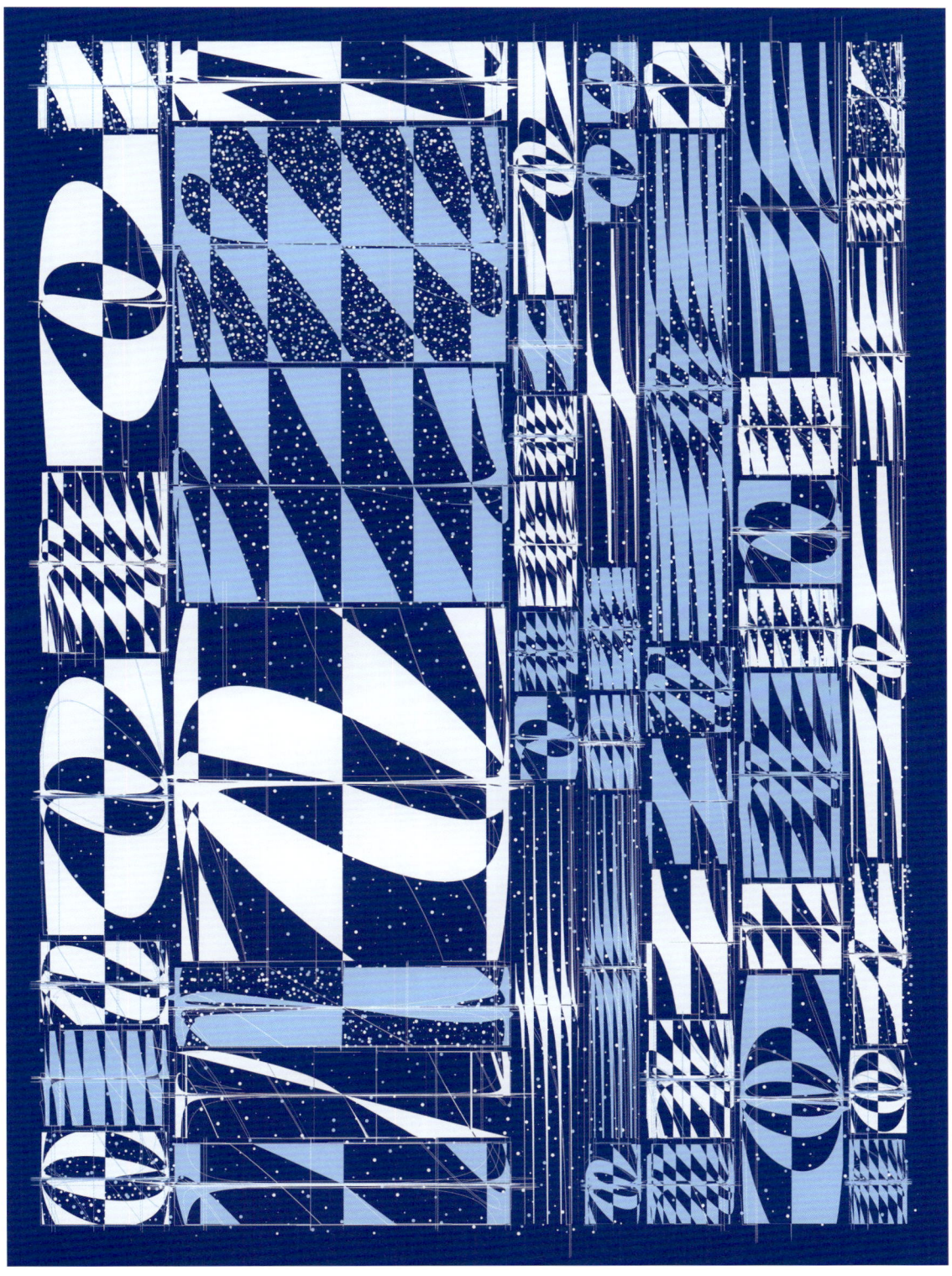

| # | TITLE | TIMESTAMP | MEDIUM | CHAIN | CONTRACT ADDRESS | TOKEN ID | EDITION SIZE |
|---|---|---|---|---|---|---|---|
| 01–07 | **nth culture** | 11-03-2022 20:11:35 | p5.js | ETH | 0xf441aaf6a47c8a0e2d6317de6cb20a8f43481544 | 18000000–18000099 | 1/1 of 100 |

EDITIONS ILLUSTRATED: (01) #45, (02) #97, (03) #17, (04) #0, (05) #96, (06) #75, (07) #34

02

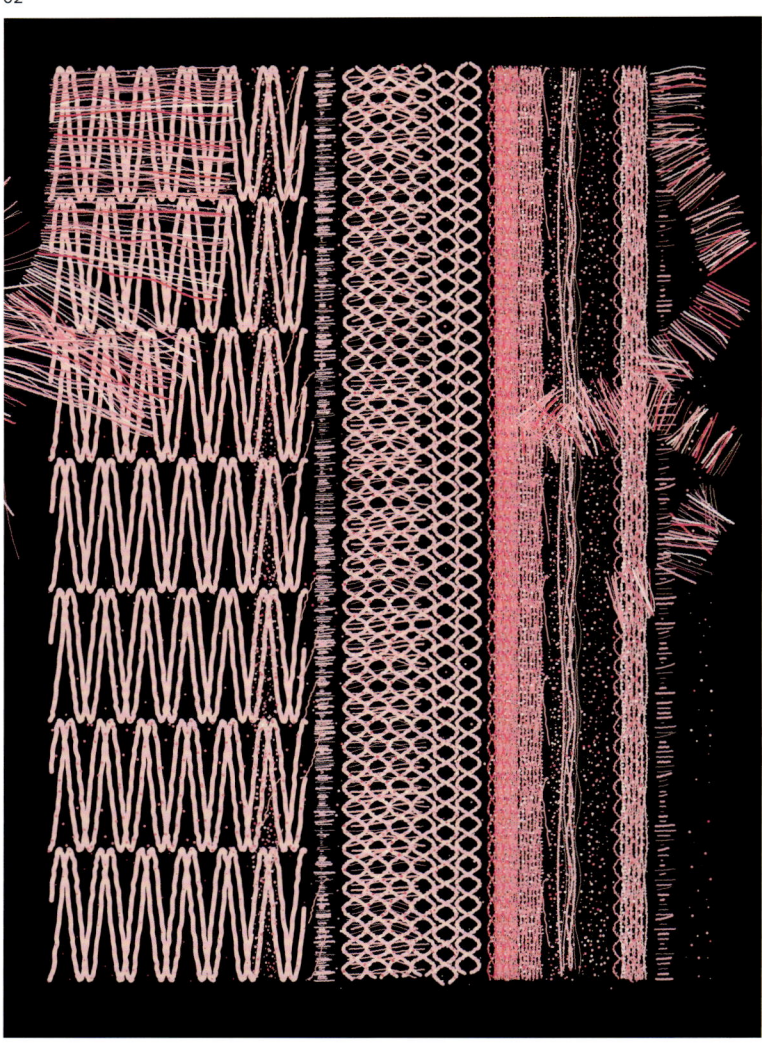

UK-based multidisciplinary artist, Junior Ngoma, known as fingacode, received his first computer at the age of 13 and has been creating what he refers to as artistic "hors d'oeuvres," ever since. fingacode, his play on "finger food," first learned computer programming through his passion for music, which led him to explore technical and design roles within the music industry. Amongst a myriad of creative side projects, he's developed websites and audio/visual compositions for clients including Universal Music and an array of acclaimed musicians. Web development gave way to creative coding as he took a keen interest in interactive technologies, specifically live stage visuals. To date, fingacode's artistic practice is a result of his experimentation and experience working with a range of technologies from sound to movement.

Standing at a whopping 66″, fingacode's towering physical presence is matched by the importance of his impact on the programming art space. In 2022, he dug deep into his roots to create the seminal collection *nth culture*. The series is focused on third culture kids: children raised in a different culture from that of their parents. The son of parents from Cameroon and the Congo, fingacode is unmistakably from the UK. The presence of Africa and of his ancestors, however, is not watered down and lives strong in the visual outputs of this groundbreaking body of work.

Drawing inspiration from the artistry of the vibrant patterned Toghu and Ndop fabrics of his maternal birthplace, Cameroon, fingacode has shifted the perspective of what contemporary generative art can look like. While many long-form algorithmic art collections are produced through the lens of Western and Eastern European culture, *nth culture* embraces Africa's rich patterns, colors, and motifs and has cemented the continent's presence in the modern generative art renaissance.

**MICHAEL CURRERI**
ATTORNEY, ART COLLECTOR, AND DEALER

03

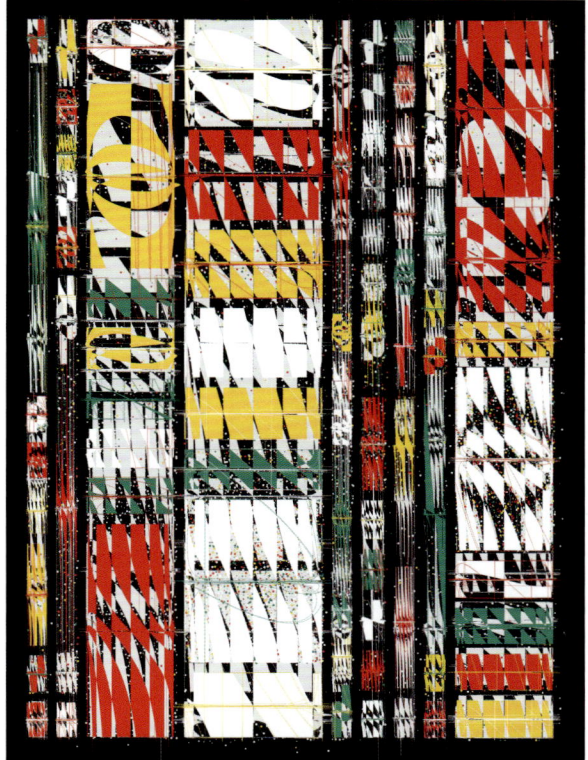

04

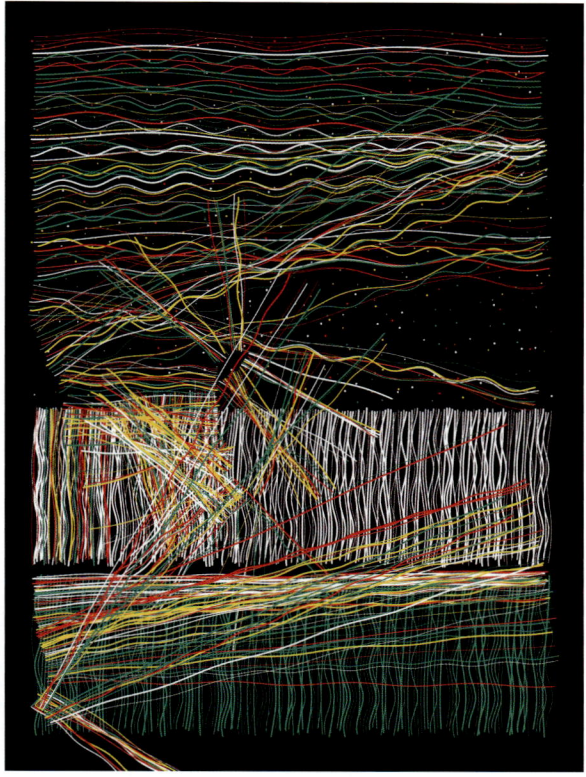

05

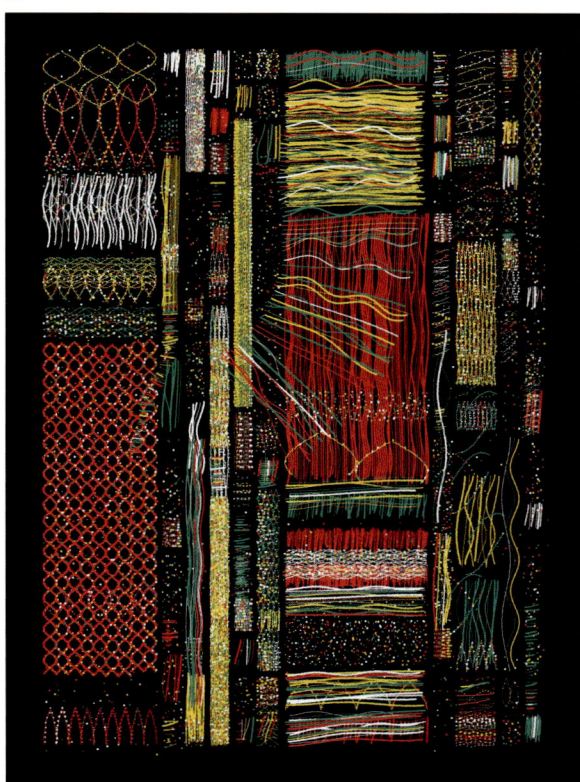

06

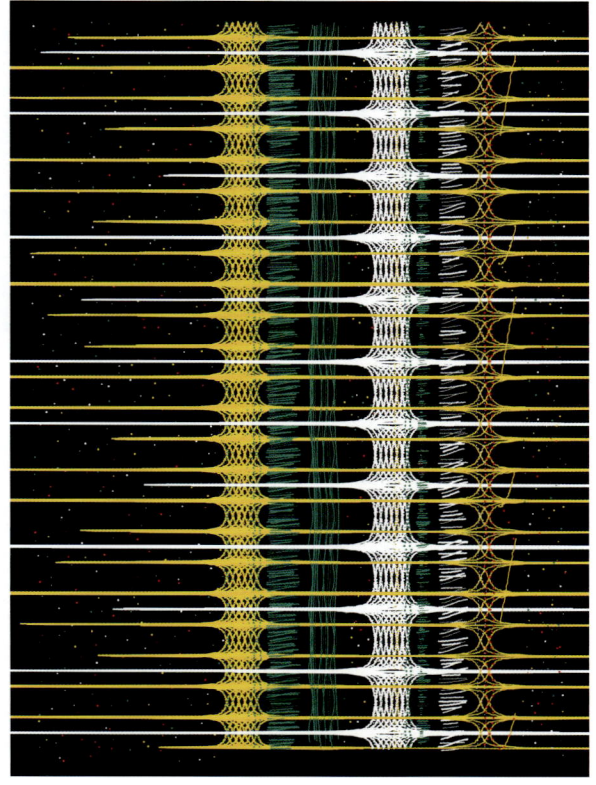

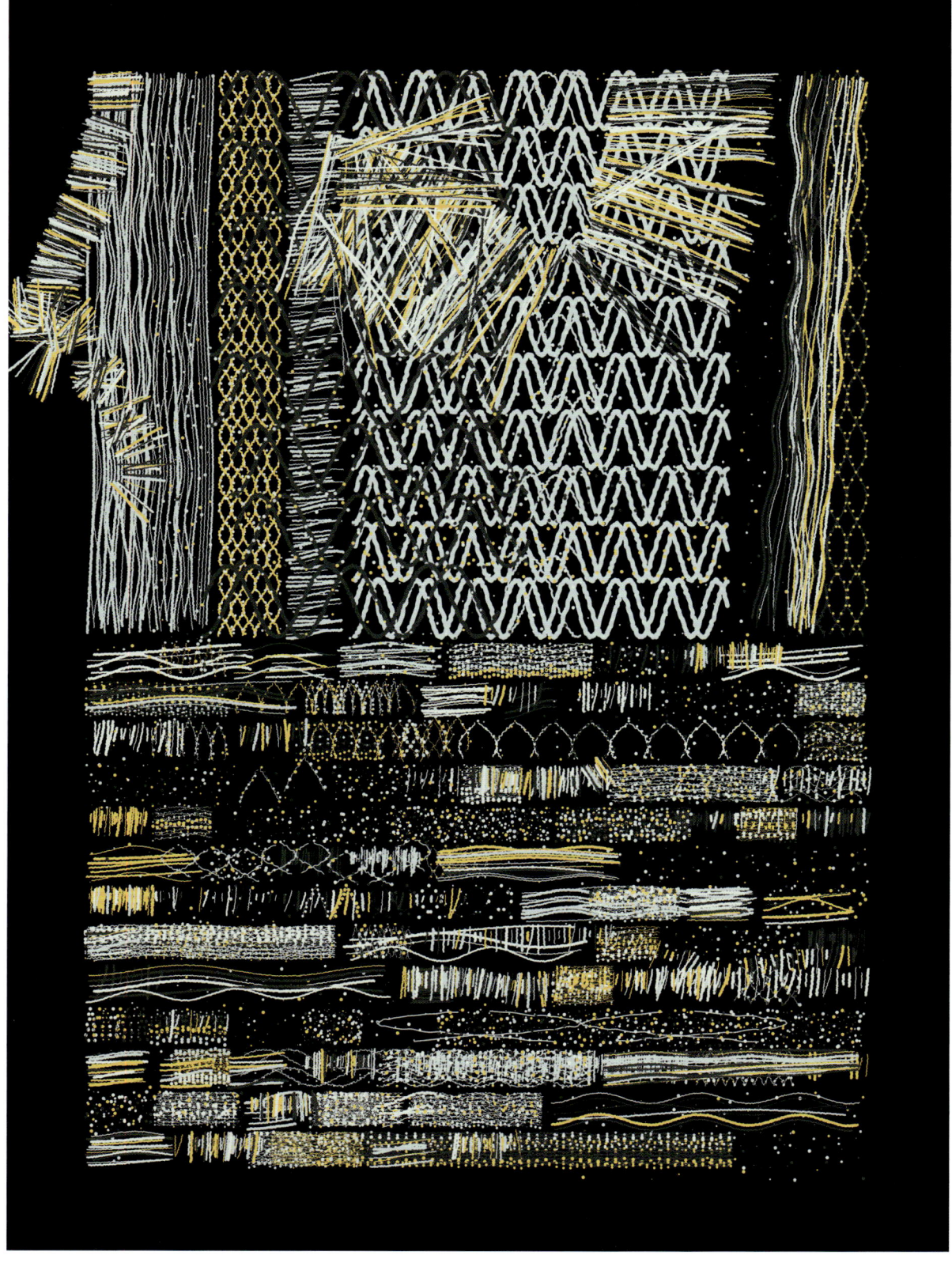

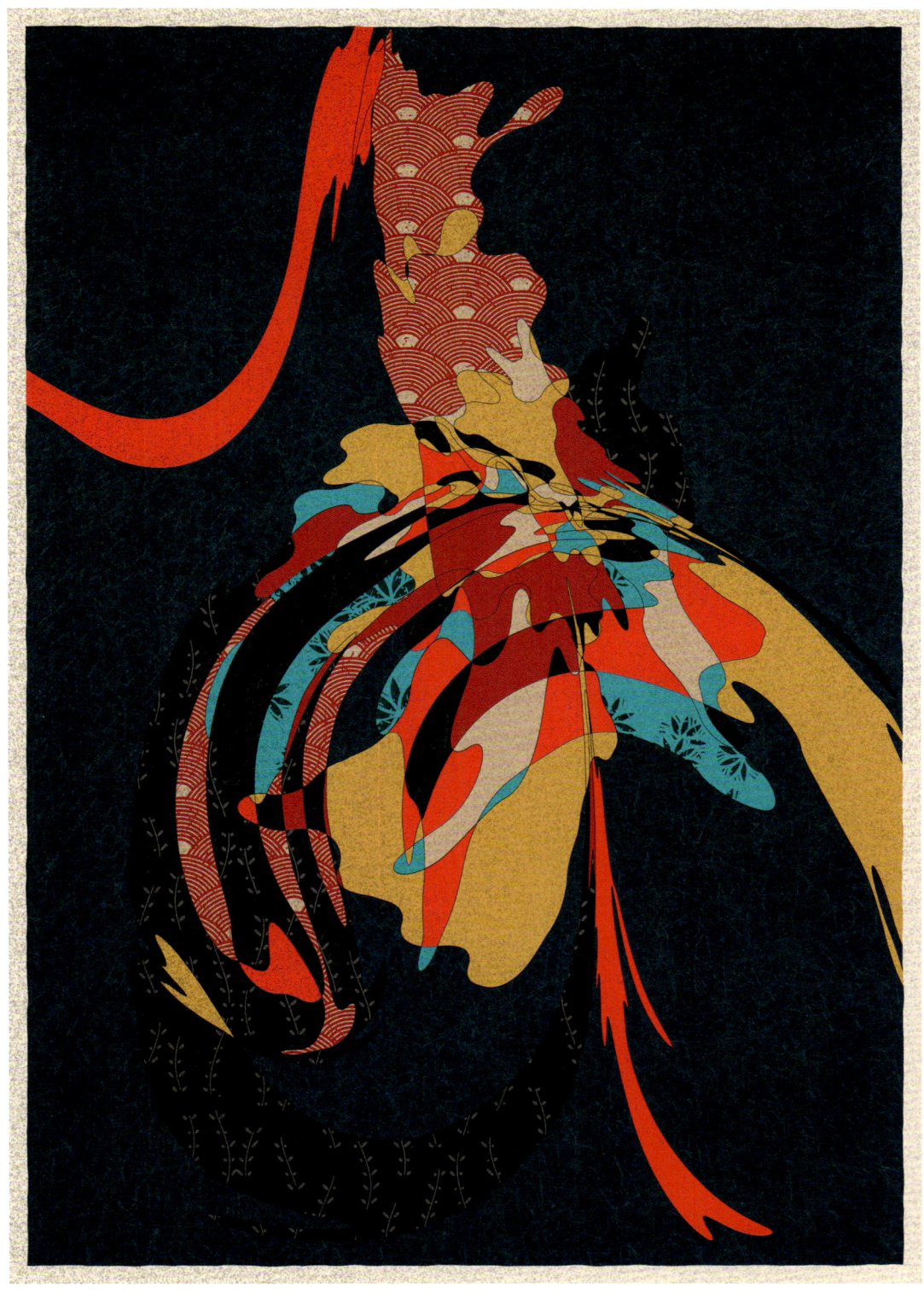

| # | TITLE | TIMESTAMP | MEDIUM | CHAIN | CONTRACT ADDRESS | TOKEN ID | EDITION SIZE |
|---|---|---|---|---|---|---|---|
| 01–04 | **Memories of Qilin** | 03-14-2022 20:44:14 | p5.js | ETH | 0xa7d8d9ef8d8ce8992df33d8b8cf4aebabd5bd270 | 282000000–282001023 | 1/1 of 1,024 |

EDITIONS ILLUSTRATED: (01) #204, (02) #60, (03) #0, (04) #64

# EMILY XIE

CHINA 1989

02

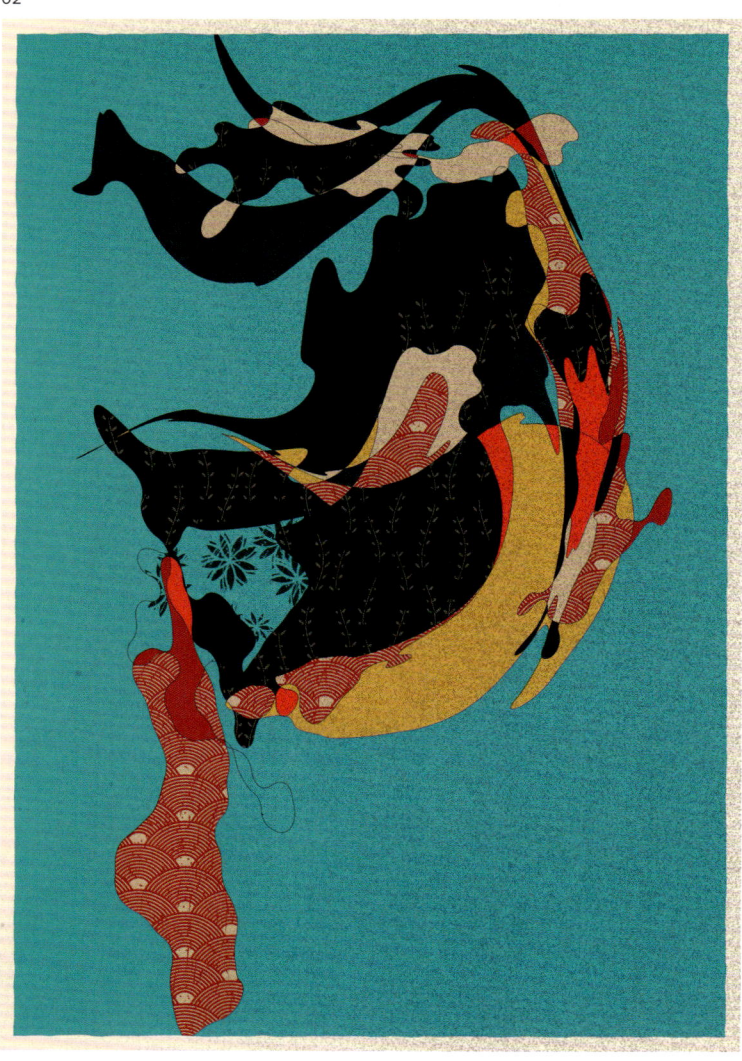

Emily Xie is a generative artist from New York City. Her background uniquely positions her to create work that spans disparate cultures and technologies. Formal studies at Harvard University in art history and architecture gave her a thorough familiarity with modern art, while studio courses developed her intuition and appreciation for natural forms and textures. Separately, programming and engineering proved to be another attractive means of exploration and expression for Xie, leading her to a productive career in the field of machine learning at top tech startups. It was only natural that these dual passions of art and programming fused in the form of algorithmic artwork, which Xie began to practice in the mid-2010s.

*Memories of Qilin* (2022) is a series of 1,024 unique iterations taken (without curation) from a single algorithm, and could be considered her largest work to date. It is immediately notable for its fluid compositions, which, despite being unpredictable, reliably strike a soothing balance. The influence of *ukiyo-e* is unmistakable. The imperfection inherent in that Japanese technique of woodblock printing is not simply mimicked, but analyzed through an algorithmic lens. The colors strike an intriguing balance between the muted tones of those historical prints, and the vibrant digital options of the computer era. Assorted patterns call up the swirling costumes of *kabuki-e*, where realism takes a back seat to the flattened, graphic interplay of abstract design.

Although it is common for generative art to evoke forms from nature, this is an area in which *Memories of Qilin* shines. The titular Qilin is a mythological beast (a symbol of good luck), who assumes various forms, from dragons to tigers to deer, and who may be covered in fish scales or flames. Fittingly, *Memories* evokes all of these and more — it is seemingly rich with characters despite its abstraction.

**TYLER HOBBS**
GENERATIVE ARTIST

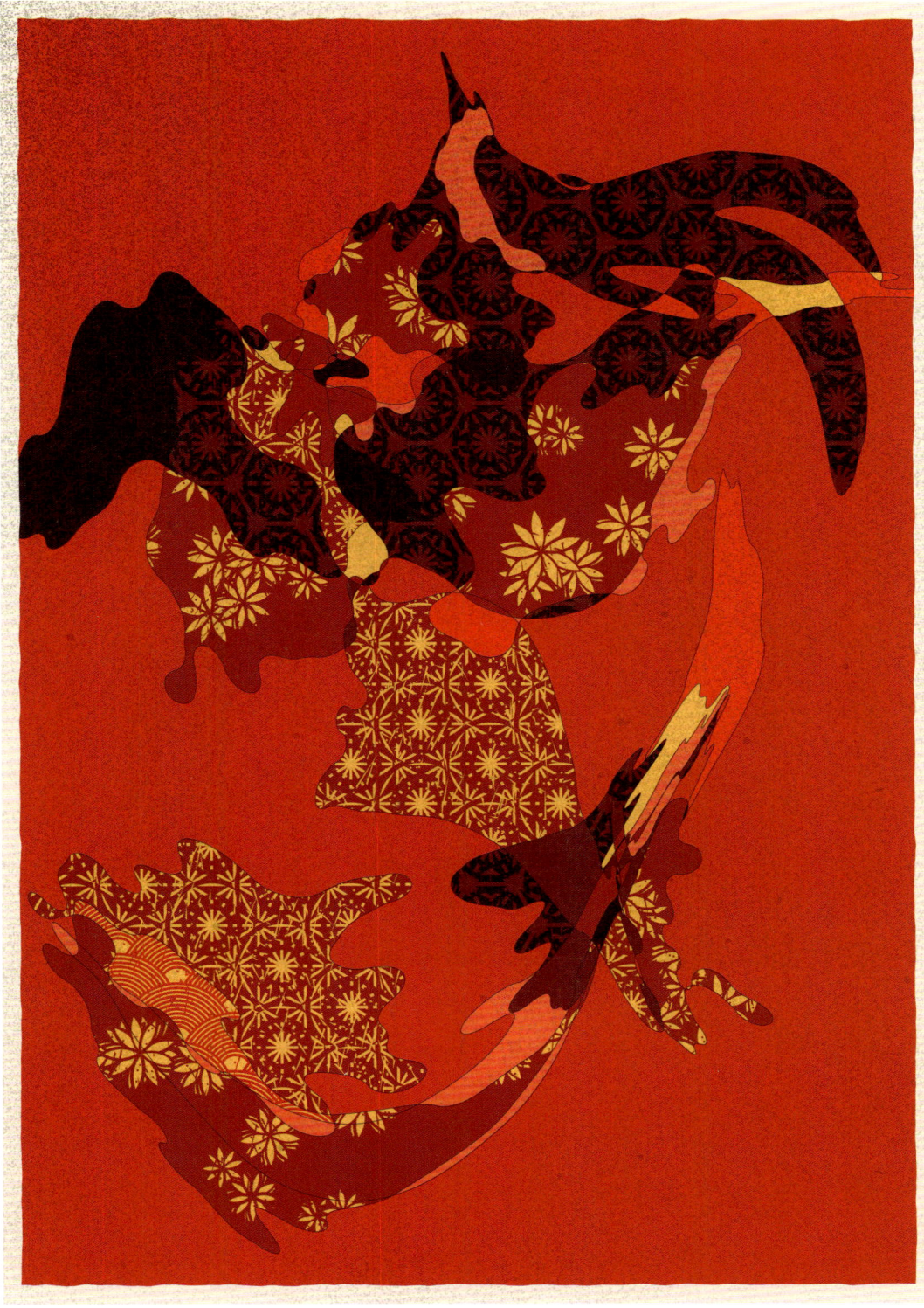

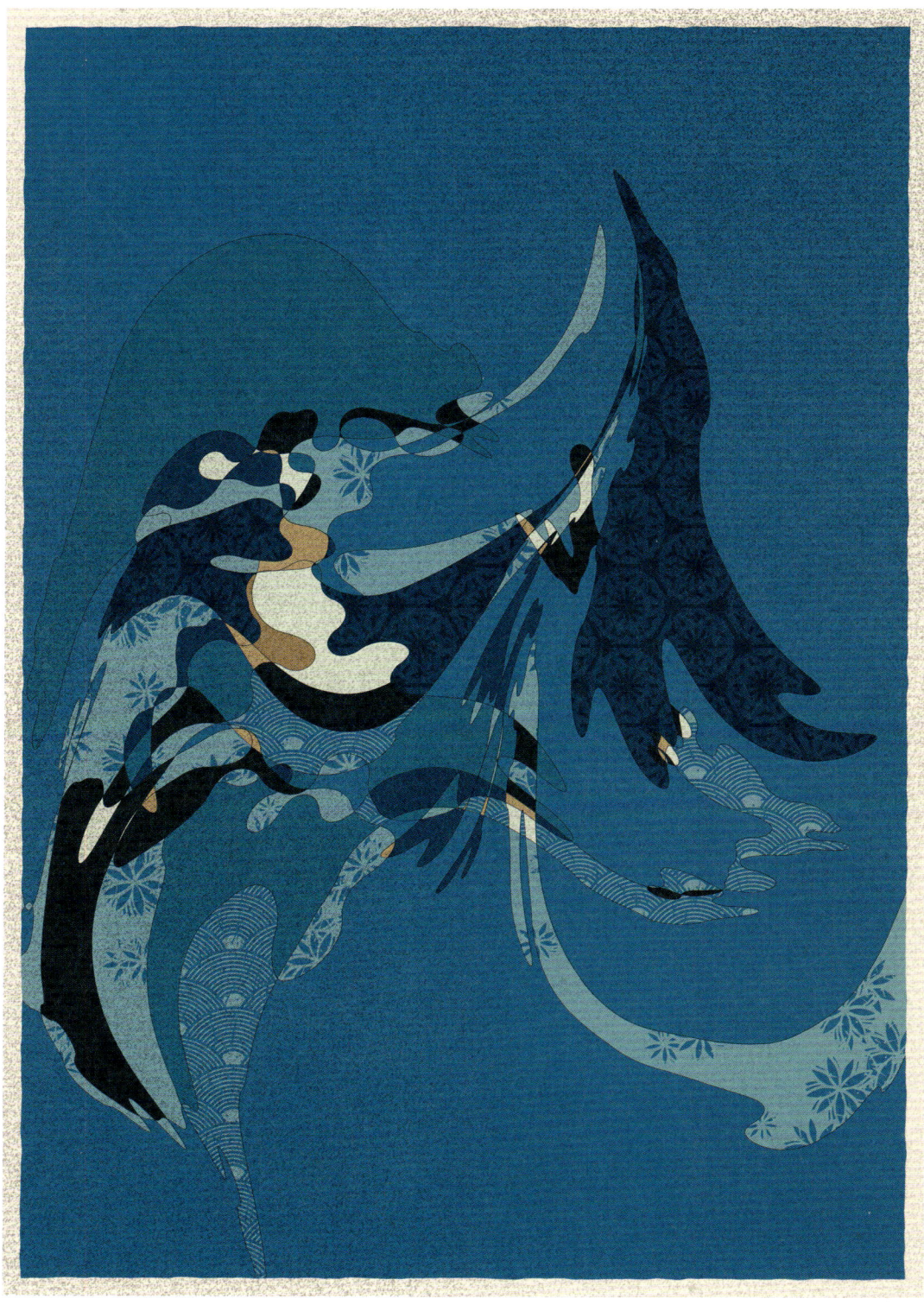

01

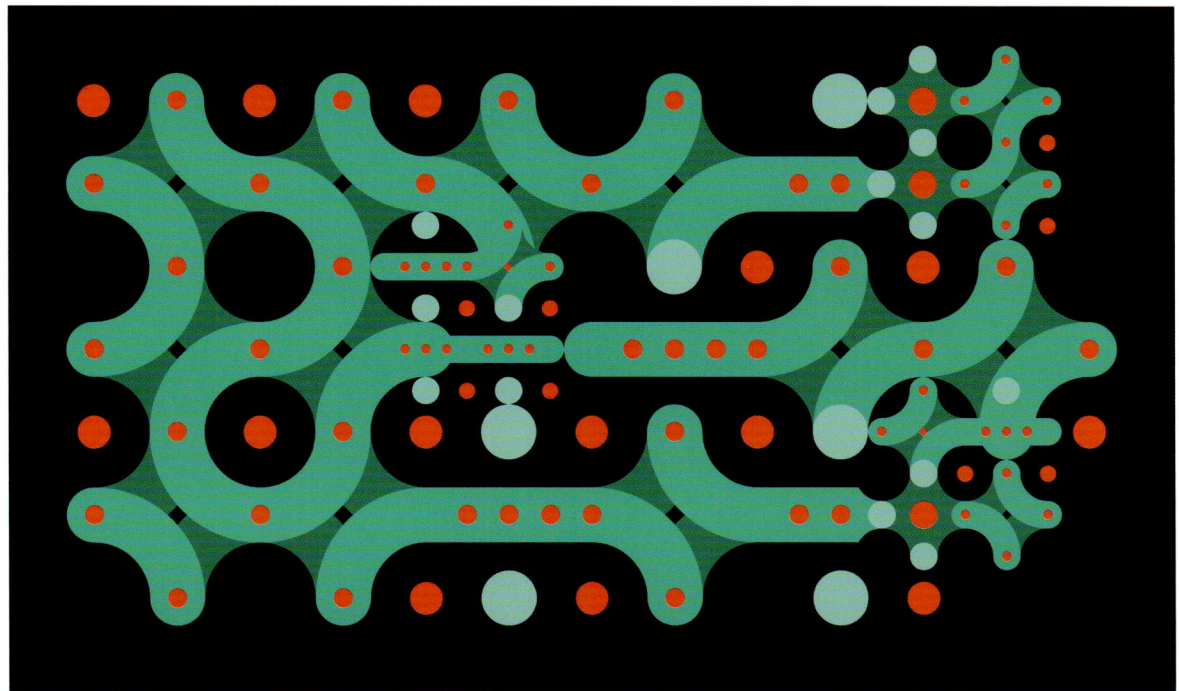

02

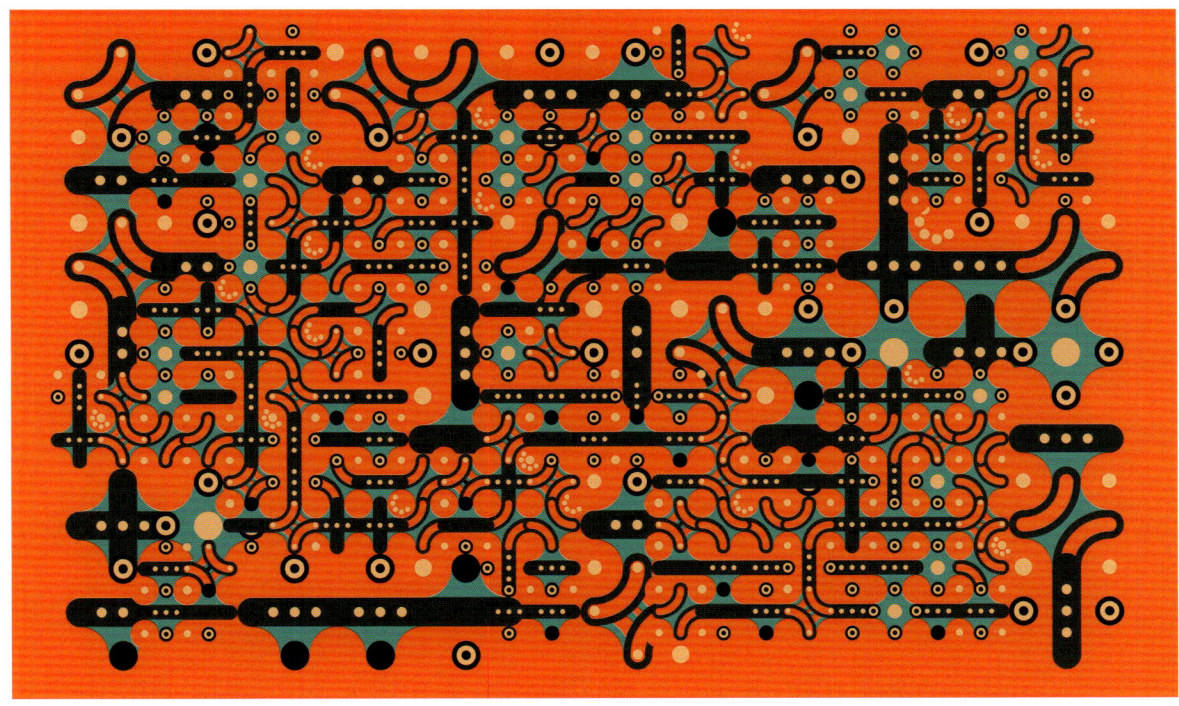

| # | TITLE | TIMESTAMP | MEDIUM | CHAIN | CONTRACT ADDRESS | TOKEN ID | EDITION SIZE |
|---|-------|-----------|--------|-------|------------------|----------|--------------|
| 01, 02 | **Trossets** | 08-28-2021 08:54:53 | p5.js | ETH | 0xa7d8d9ef8d8ce8992df33d8b8cf4aebabd5bd270 | 147000000–147000999 | 1/1 of 1,000 |
| 03 | **Ganxillo** | 12-15-2021 16:51:13 | p5.js | BTM | b4SnpxtHwS1ThPGvaECZSc8dUYbCP1wSQqaCsr3jgCMme4YMUX | 2642...0bfb-373b...0522 | 115, +1 AP |
| 04 | **Arrels** | 03-19-2021 04:28:25 | p5.js | BTM | b4SnpxtHwS1ThPGvaECZSc8dUYbCP1wSQqaCsr3jgCMme4YMUX | 42b9...86a7-75c7...0047 | 75, +1 AP |

EDITIONS ILLUSTRATED: (01) #151, (02) #887

# ANNA CARRERAS

SPAIN 1979

03

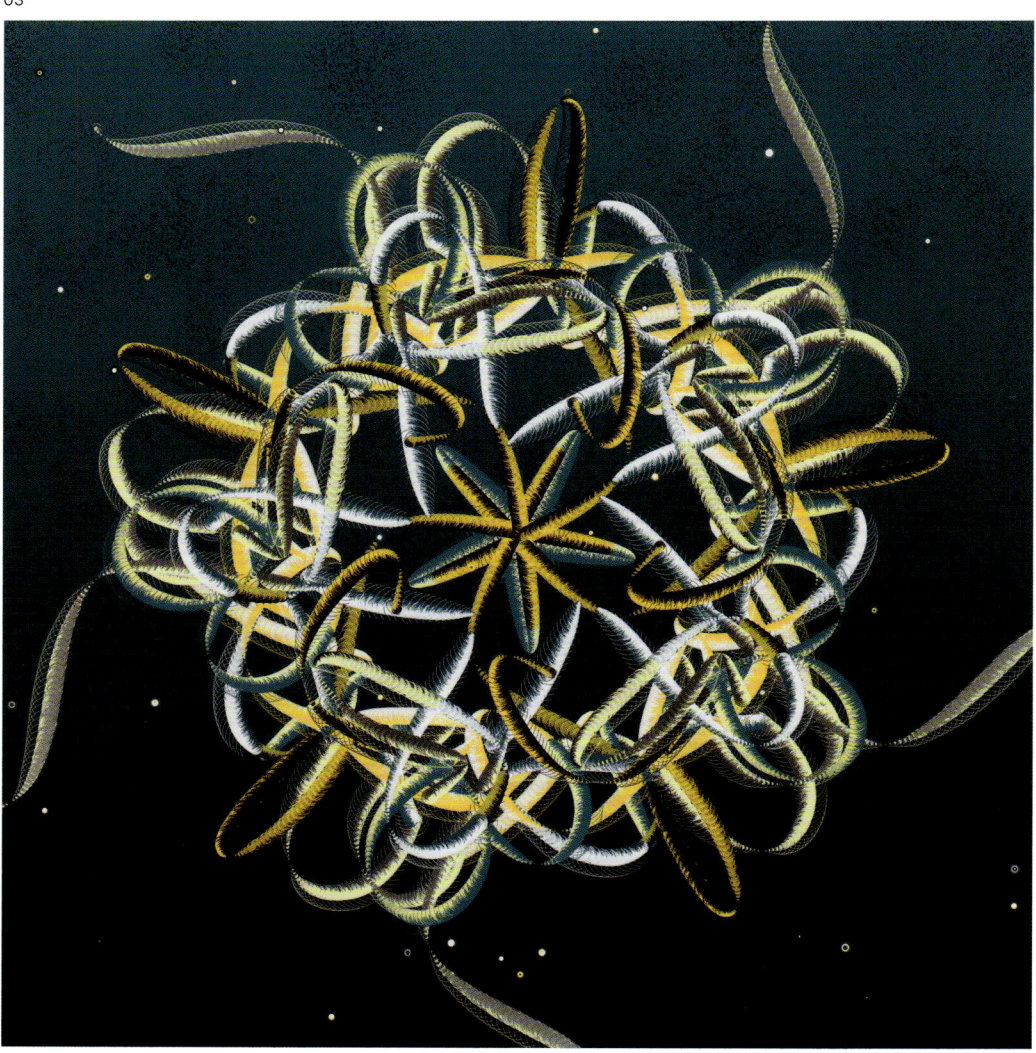

Anna Carreras began as a telecommunications engineer — a line of work that's all about reaching places far away. However, her art career has been one of ever-increasing regionality — using code and interaction to reveal the genius loci.

An interactive design project led Carreras to map the river valley of Barcelona. On a field trip to the jungles of Central America, she studied how camouflaged animals adapt their local patterns of shape and color. Later she engineered a scanner that uses lasers to digitize the tints, proportions, and patinas of real objects. She's become such an expert at peeling shape and color from her surroundings that she can outdo a camouflaged frog.

Although she's adept technically, with an engineer's problem-solving aesthetic, her artworks are always user-friendly. The design of the experience comes first, supported by intricate code or installation machinery. Commonly her work has titles in the Catalan language — this calls attention to where it was made, and how it thrives in a cultural and historic context.

The *Trossets* (2021) series is generative artwork — it's "Trochet tiling," a fluid, asymmetric pattern of dots and curved stripes, which are closely disciplined by a hidden, rotated grid. Yet these works are also a homage to the Balearic Islands — *Trossets* has a well-chosen regional palette of sea-and-shore tints.

The artwork's NFT contract distributes funds to regional environmental protection and to Mediterranean refugees. So *Trossets* is Catalonian code, Catalonian decorative art, and a Catalonian political intervention, all with the very same set of key presses.

**BRUCE STERLING**
ART DIRECTOR OF SHARE FESTIVAL, TURIN

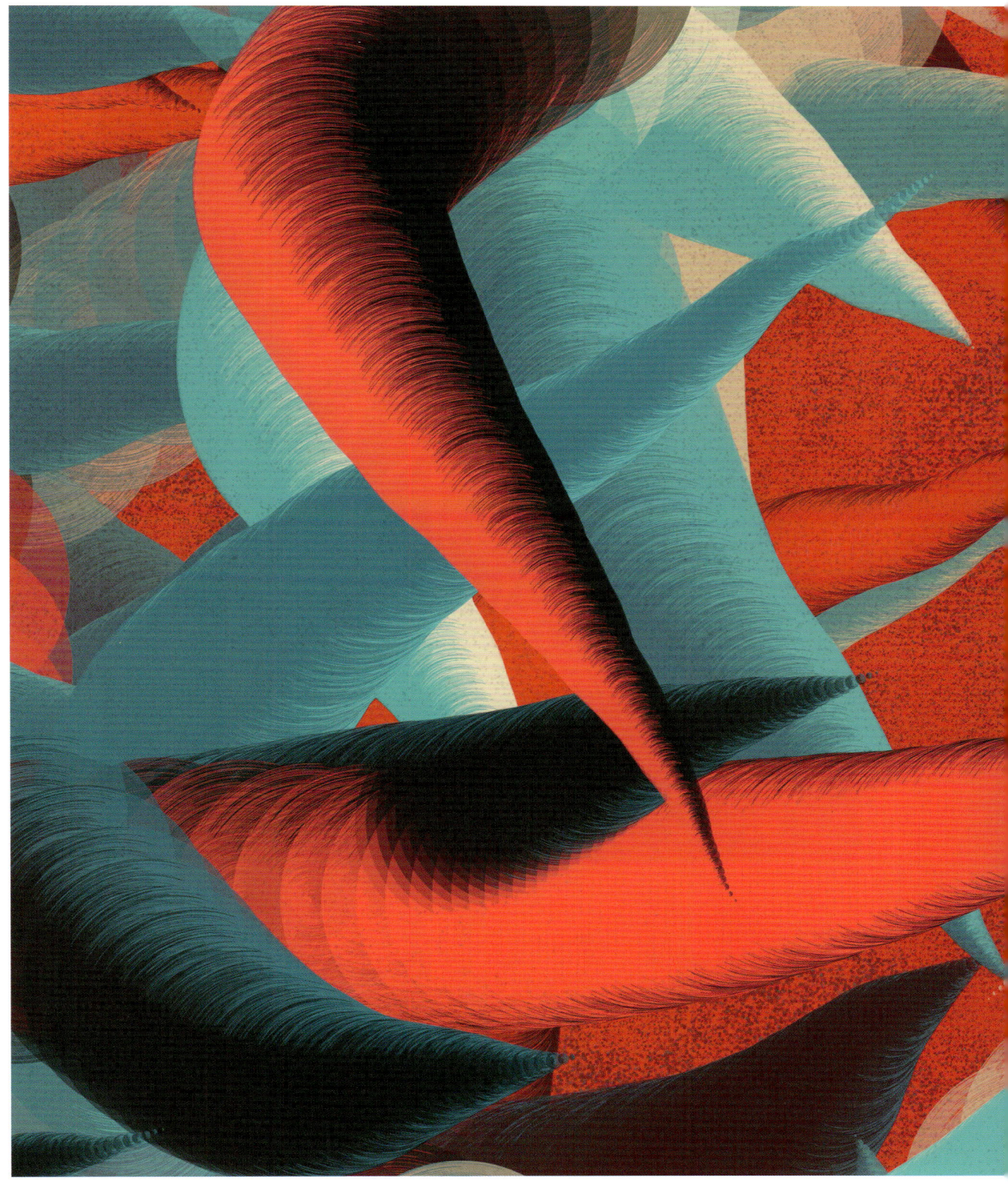

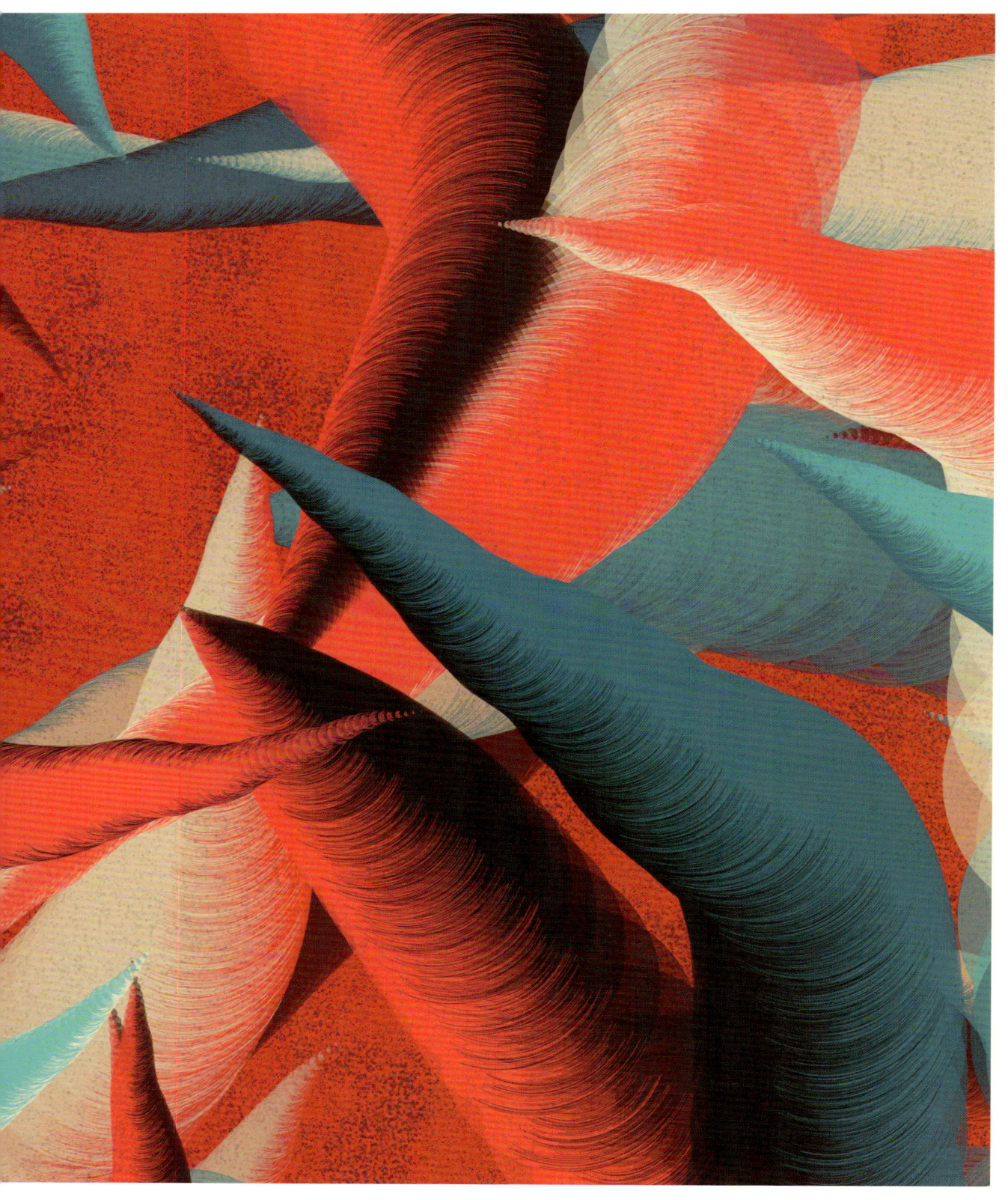

01

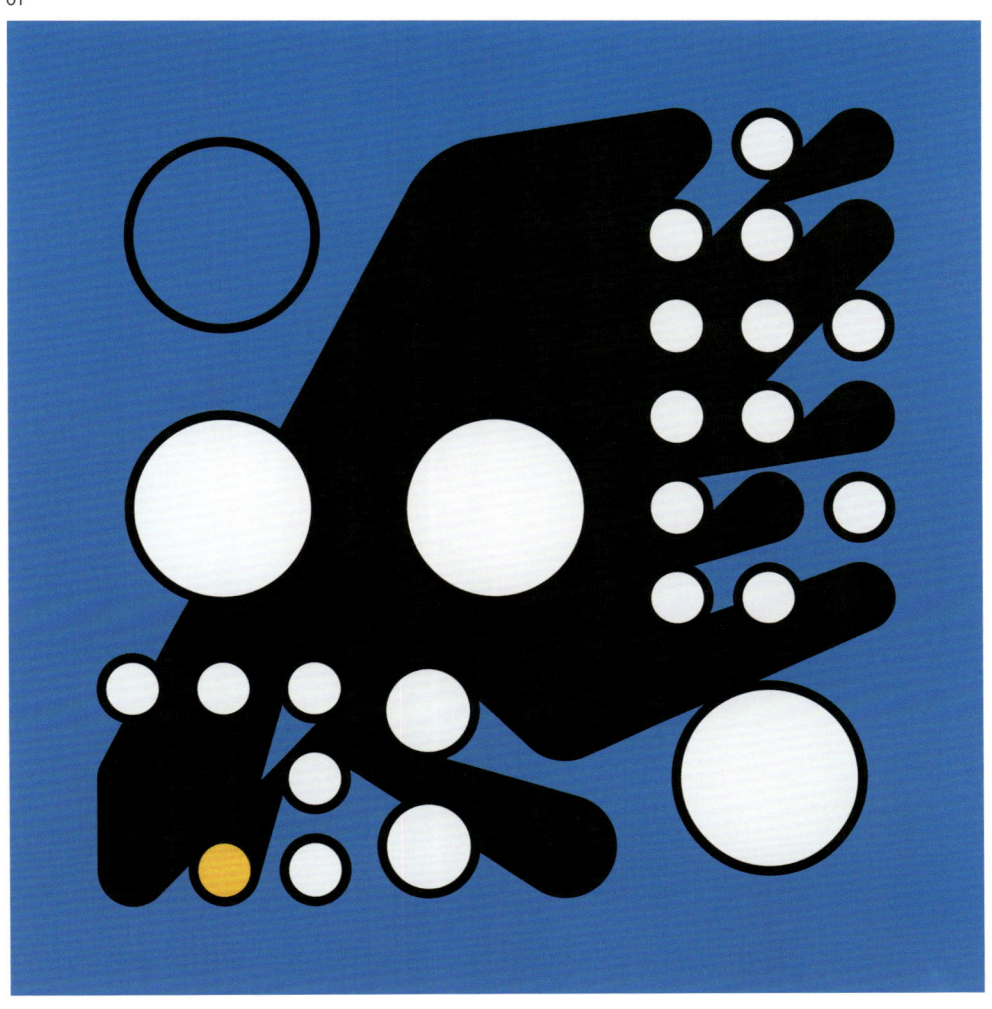

| # | TITLE | TIMESTAMP | CHAIN | MEDIUM | CONTRACT ADDRESS | TOKEN ID | EDITION SIZE |
|---|---|---|---|---|---|---|---|
| 01-03 | **Ringers** | 01-28-2021 21:46:53 | ETH | JavaScript | 0xa7d8d9ef8d8ce8992df33d8b8cf4aebabd5bd270 | 13000000–13000999 | 1/1 of 1,000 |

EDITIONS ILLUSTRATED: (01) #52, (02) #109, (03) #0–999

02

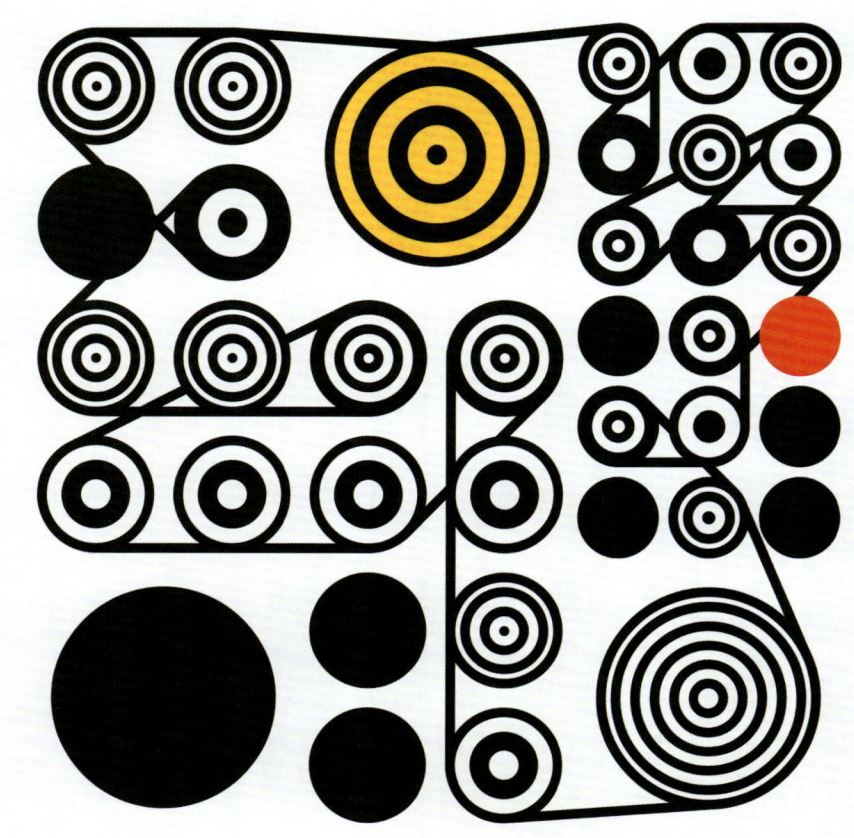

Automation is Dmitri Cherniak's artistic medium. The primary focus of his practice is to automate the creation of artwork that elicits the same range of emotions one expects from traditional mediums. The Toronto-born New York City resident studied computer science and physiology at McGill University, where he began making art using algorithms and code.

The simple, approachable concept of wrapping string around pegs gives rise to 1,000 unique yet cohesive artworks in the algorithmically generated *Ringers* (2021) project. Universal variables such as background color, string wrap style, and peg count form each piece's foundation, with bullseyes and recursive grids appearing infrequently as the occasional flourish. Unlike other forms of generative art, human curation played no part in the creation of *Ringers*: each piece was created on demand at the time of purchase utilizing a random seed to catalyze the hand-coded algorithm, resulting in a work of art unveiled simultaneously to both collector and artist.

On-demand generative art upends the model of artist-as-curator, and Cherniak's *Ringers* is one of the first projects to see collectors wholeheartedly embrace the curatorial function. Collecting multiple *Ringers* and sharing them in online galleries has become a form of dialogue and communal storytelling, for the artist and collectors alike — a way to comprehend the art, to look at individual pieces, and situate each in the context of the 1,000-piece project.

Cherniak's conceptual *Dead Ringers* (2022) culminated on the one-year anniversary of *Ringers*, and calls attention to the relative scarcity of food as compared to digital goods. On each of the 30 days leading up to the anniversary, the artist sent one unique *Dead Ringer* to a random address amongst all possible addresses, though the vastness of the address space ($16^{40}$) meant it was all but guaranteed that none of the *Dead Ringers* would be accessible. On the anniversary of *Ringers*, sales of the composite 5×6 *Dead Ringers* grid supplied 16 million meals to a New York City food bank.

**KATE HANNAH**
CHIEF OF STAFF AT ART BLOCKS

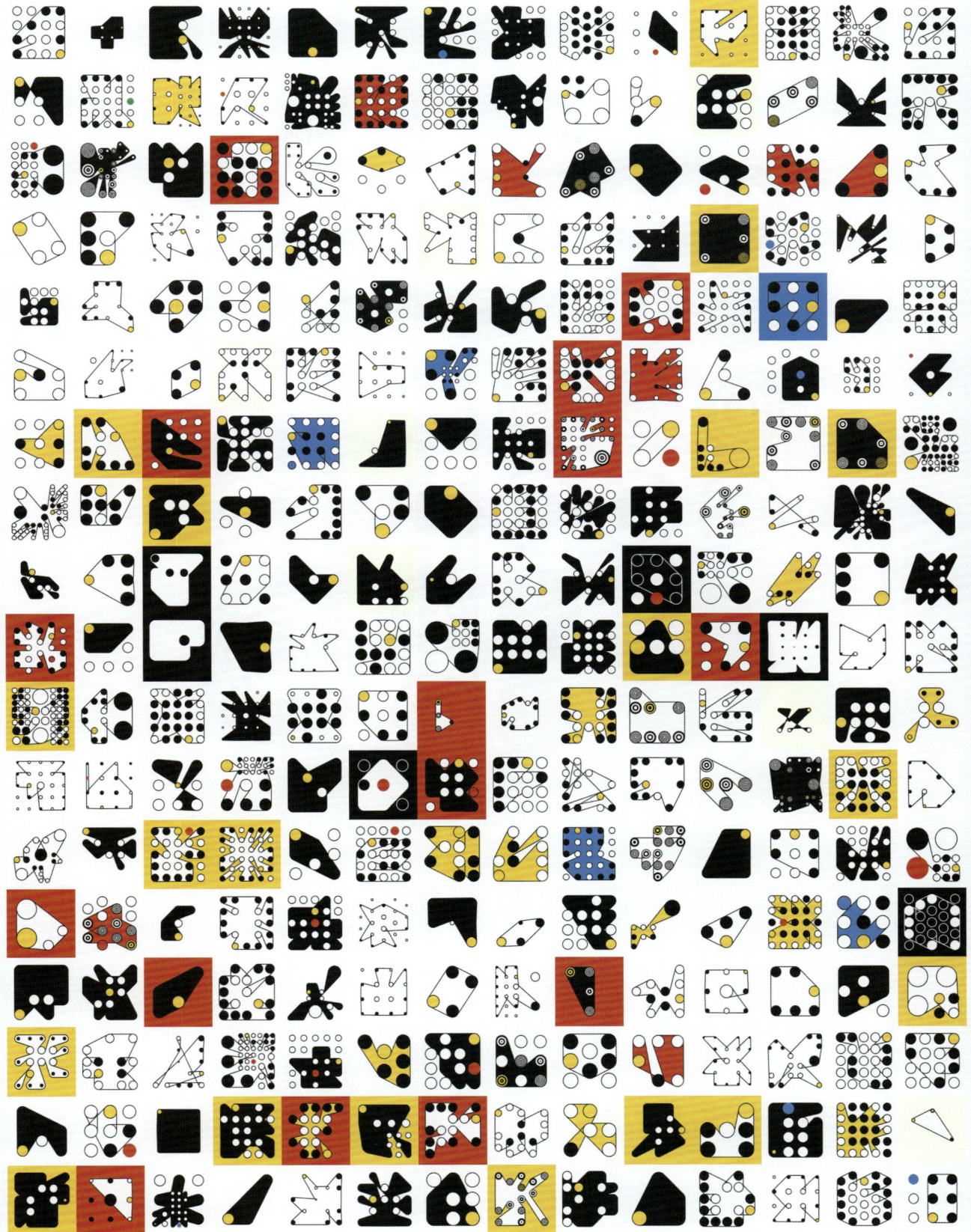

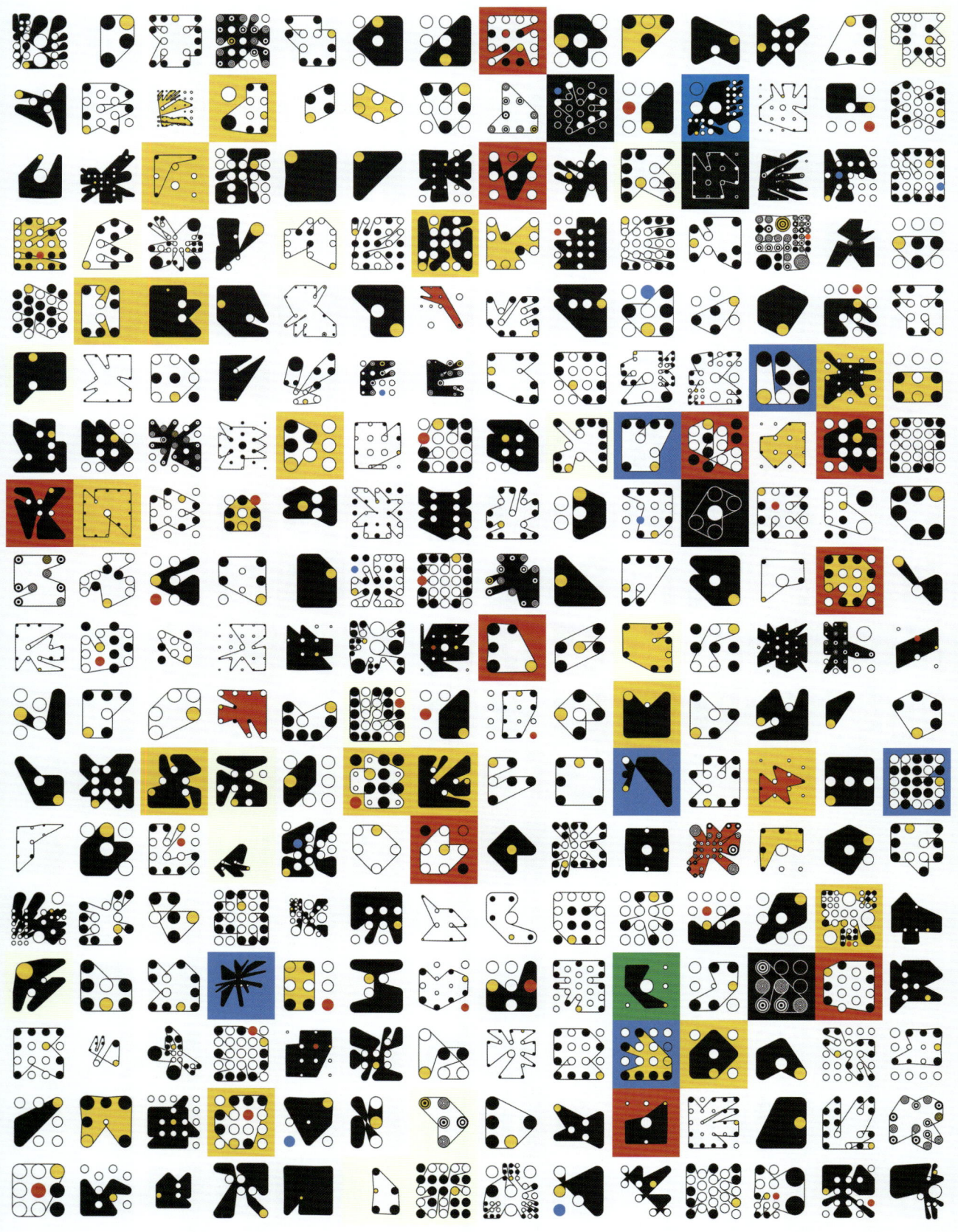

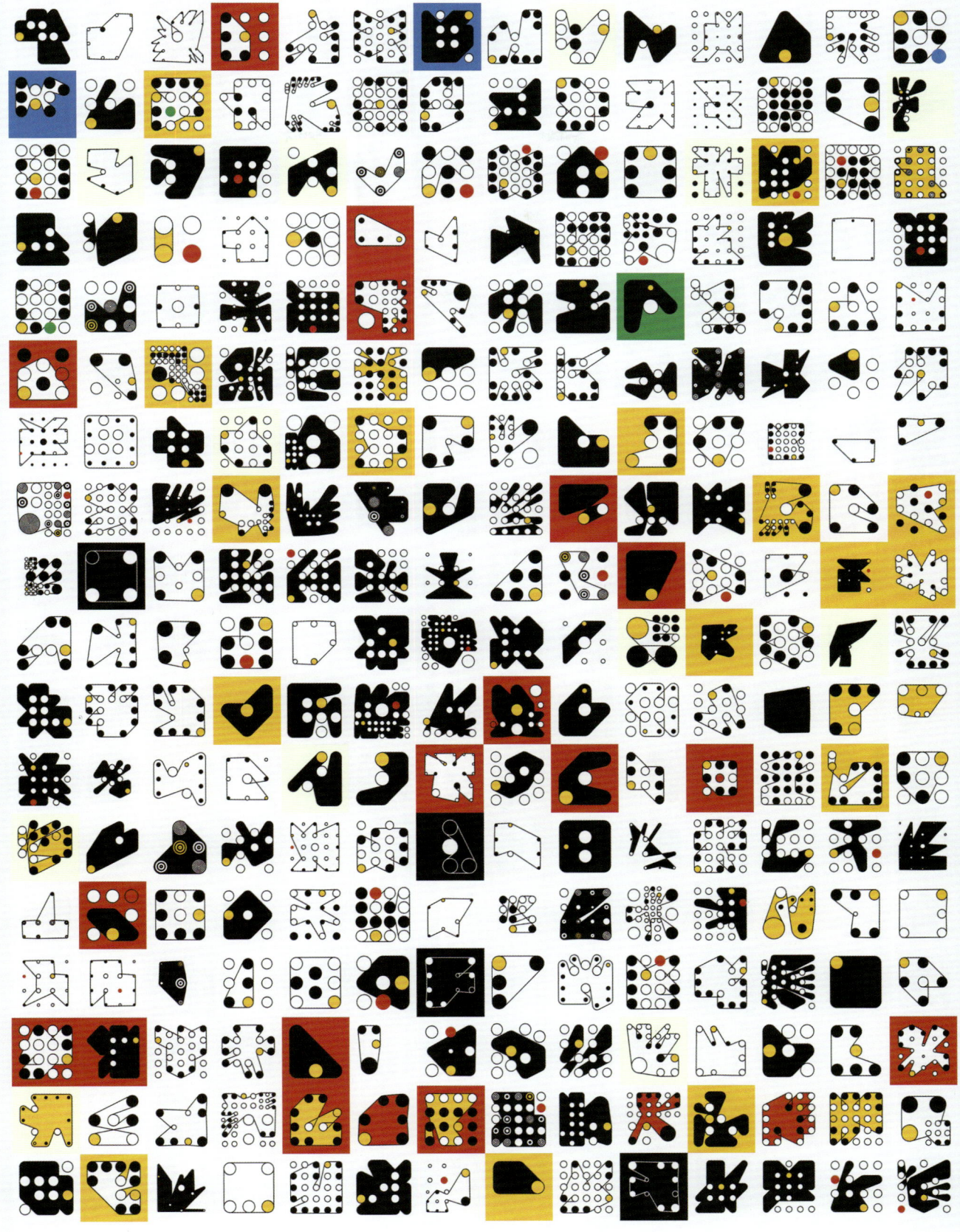

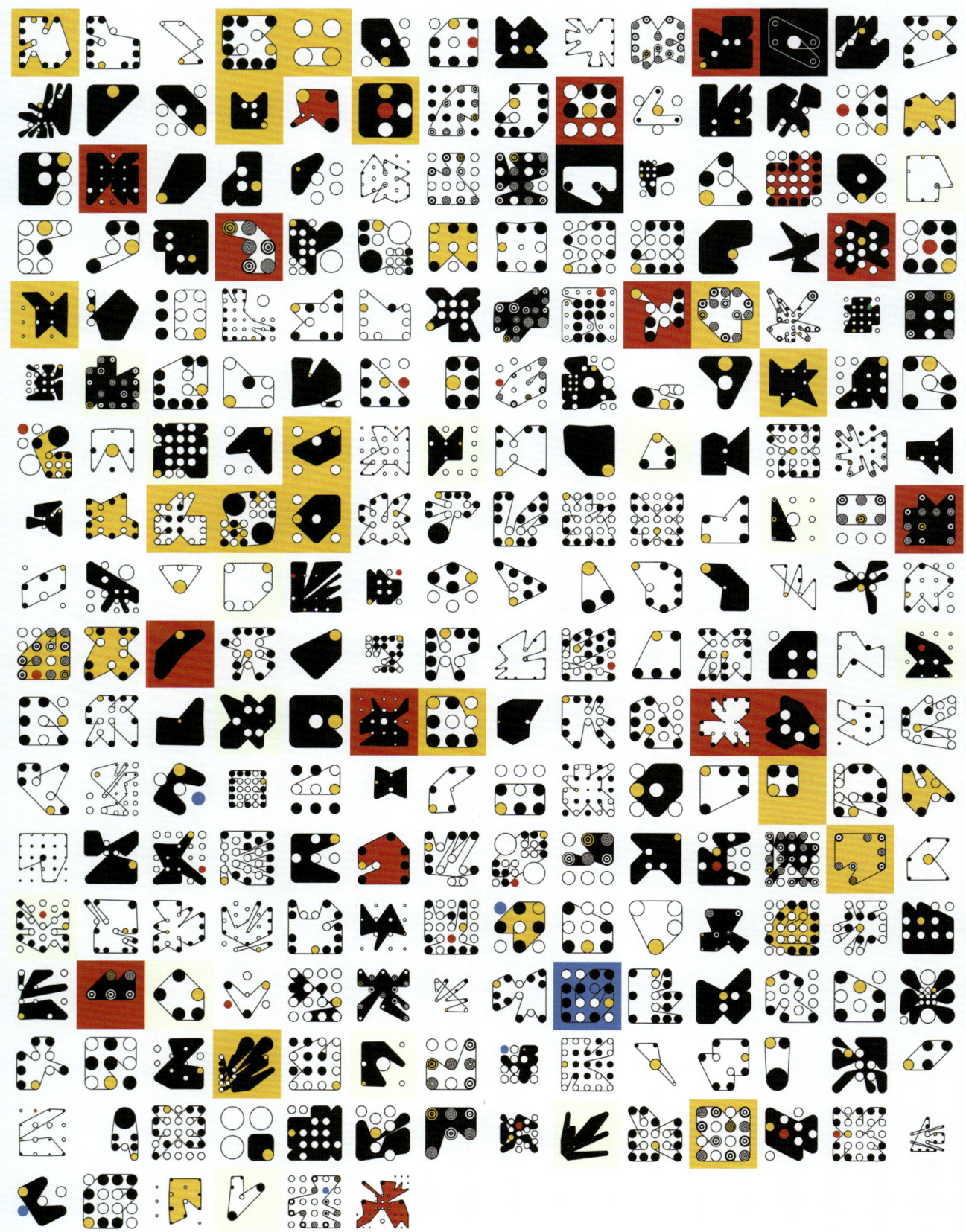

170, 171,

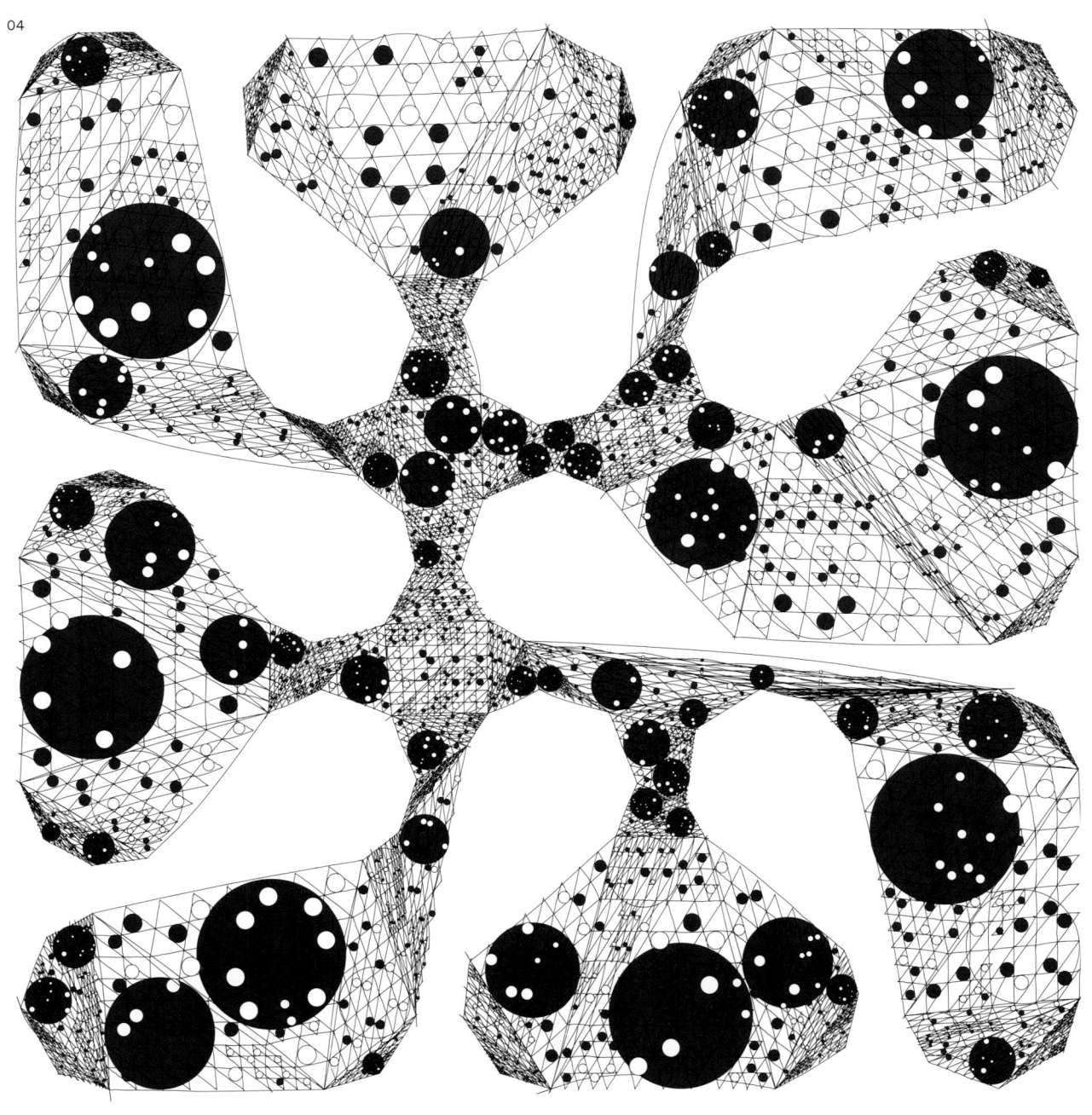

| # | TITLE | TIMESTAMP | MEDIUM | CHAIN | CONTRACT ADDRESS | TOKEN ID | EDITION SIZE |
|---|-------|-----------|--------|-------|------------------|----------|--------------|
| 04–16 | **Dead Ringers** | 01-01-2022 19:48:45 | SVG, JavaScript | ETH | 0xb004378be85e425886743514737828ff023648d4 | 1–31 | 1/1 of 31 |

EDITIONS ILLUSTRATED: (04) JANUARY 1, 2022, (05) JANUARY 4, 2022, (06) JANUARY 5, 2022, (07) JANUARY 6, 2022, (08) JANUARY 10, 2022, (09) JANUARY 11, 2022, (10) JANUARY 12, 2022, (11) JANUARY 16, 2022, (12) January 17, 2022, (13) January 18, 2022, (14) January 22, 2022, (15) January 23, 2022, (16) January 24, 2022

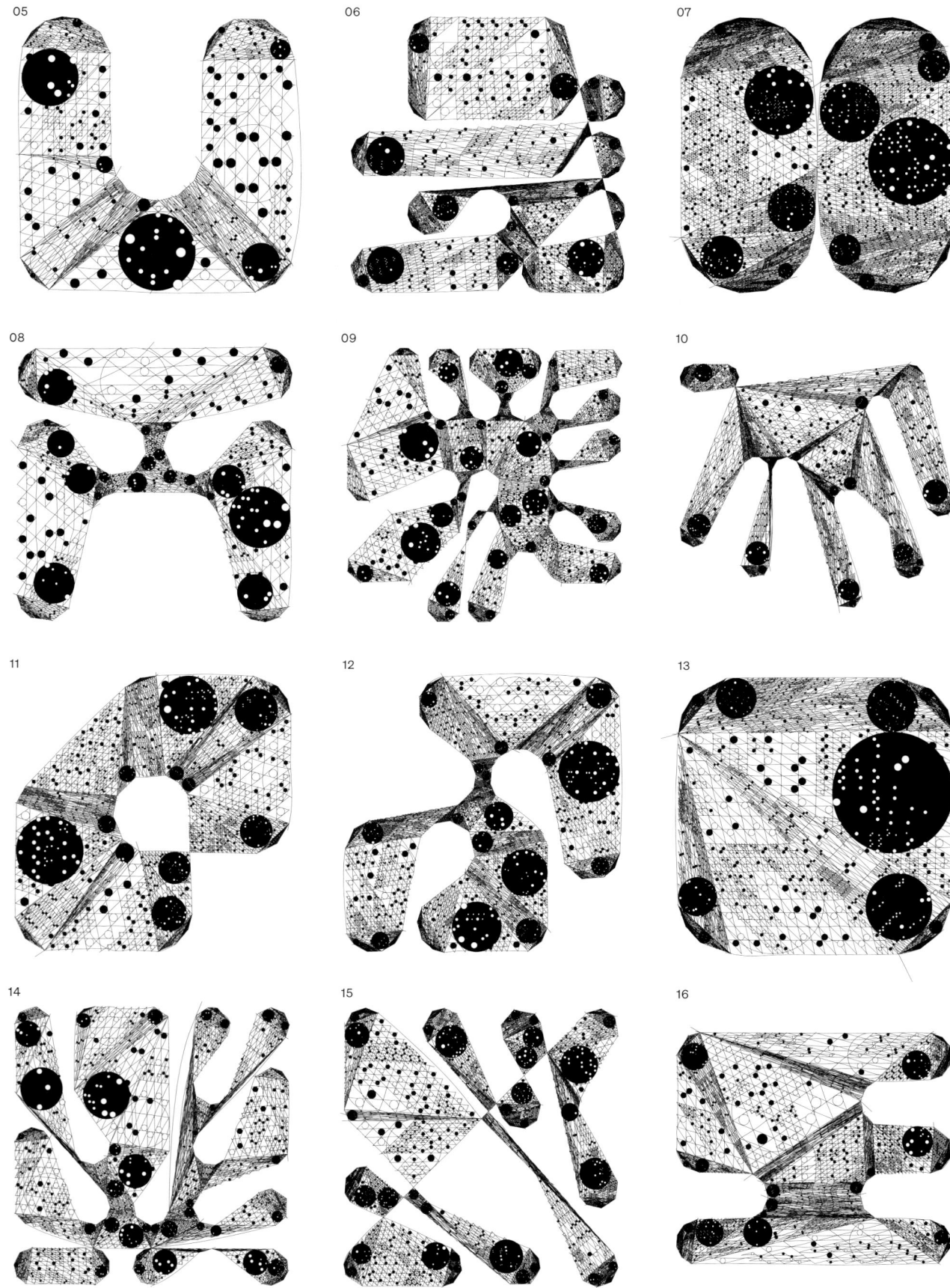

05 06 07
08 09 10
11 12 13
14 15 16

DMITRI CHERNIAK 172, 173,

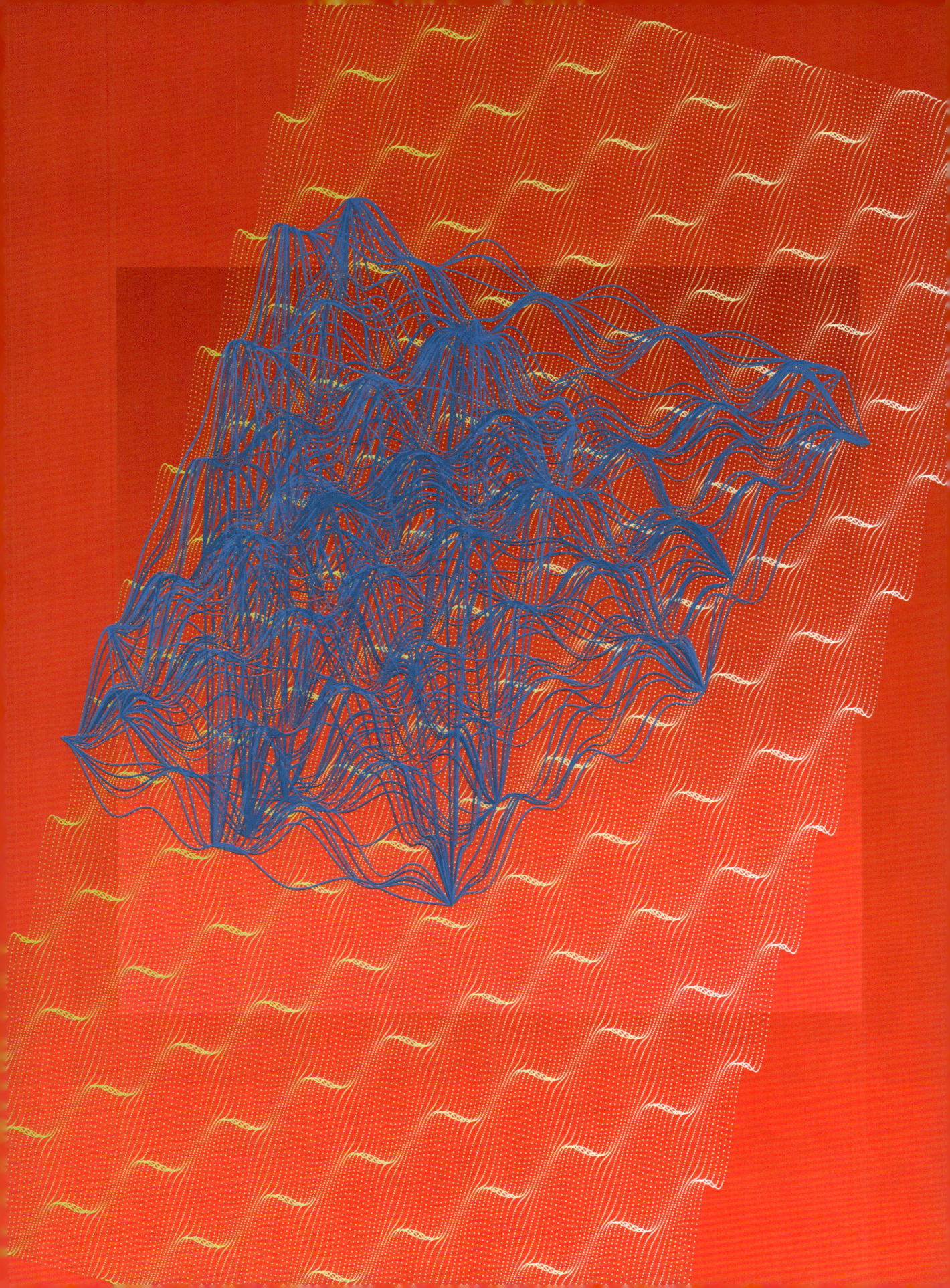

SOFIA GARCIA

# ON ALGORITHMIC ART

From Rules to Code: Algorists & the History of Generative Art

*The artist turned algorithmic is
a generative artist by birth.*

Frieder Nake
*Paragraphs on Computer Art,
Past and Present, 2010*

**03.00**
Mitchell F. Chan
*LeWitt Generator Generator #558*, 08-04-2021 16:04:58
p5.js
Ethereum, 0xa7d8d9ef8D8Ce8992Df33D8b8CF4Aebabd5bD270, 118000558

03.01
Jean-Pierre Hébert
*Algorist Manifesto*, 1995
Code

```
// The Algorist Manifesto (Hébert, 1995)

if (creation && object of art && algorithm && one's own algorithm) {

include * an algorist *

} elseif (!creation || !object of art || !algorithm || !one's own algorithm) {

exclude * not an algorist *

}
```

Within the NFT ecosystem, the term generative art has typically lent itself to describing any tokenized artwork that has been procedurally generated from a computer program. As a result, the term has become ostensibly synonymous with digitally native artwork created with code. Following the oft-cited research of Philip Galanter, Margaret Boden, and Ernest Edmonds, the definition of generative art is classified as any instance where an artist deliberately relinquishes partial or full control to a functional process (or system) in the production of an artwork.[1] This umbrella term refers to a methodology towards art-making, yet holds no requirement to a particular technology or medium. An early example of generative art under this broad definition is Islamic tiling, where artisans follow intricate rule-based systems to generate geometric designs referred to as *girih*. It can also be argued that Sol LeWitt (1928–2007) is a generative artist: his conceptual work is realized by ceding control to the public via instructional systems. This conflation provides an interesting dilemma towards the ongoing taxonomy and study of generative art, especially on the blockchain, because regardless of the symbiotic relationship between the terms *computer* and *generative*, a computer is not required to create or execute a generative artwork. What distinguishes the blockchain-based facet of generative art practices from its counterparts is the introduction and utilization of computational machines and the self-executable, finite sequence of rigorous instructions known as algorithms.[2]

During the 1960s, the terms computer art and generative art were used so frequently in tandem to describe algorithmically generated art, they became seemingly interchangeable.[3] While the origins of this will be discussed later, not every artist working with algorithms agreed to these classifications. In 1995, early pioneer Jean-Pierre Hébert (1939–2021) wrote the *Algorist Manifesto* **[03.01]** in an attempt to provide an identity towards those working creatively with code to produce art.[4] The text, which is written as an algorithm itself, suggests that the artist who produces art objects via algorithms should be called an algorist — not a "generative artist." Additionally, one of the leading pioneers in the field of computer-generated art, Frieder Nake, expressed that "*algorithmic art* would have been the correct term," but more importantly, "[the term] *'computer art'* disguised a revolutionary fact: the algorithmic principle had entered the world of art."[5]

This chapter aims to provide historical context into the development of algorithmic blockchain-based art as a multifaceted subset of generative art and examine how developments in blockchain technology have catalyzed an algorithmic art renaissance. Moving forward, the term algorithmic art will be used to describe any instance where an artist deliberately relinquishes control, either partially or fully, to a custom algorithm that results in a completed work of art. The first section of this chapter will cover the historical underpinnings of how computers were first used as an artistic tool in the hands of experimental engineers and artists towards the second half of the 20th century. The following section will recount the advent of the internet, Processing, and the role social media played in cultivating the current algorithmic art community engaging with NFTs. The final sections will examine how blockchain technology has provided a fertile environment for code-based artwork to thrive and the innovative landscape of artists, platforms, and curators that continue to shape one of the most exciting areas of NFTs today.[6]

## Prehistory

The story of modern algorithmic art begins at the serendipitous convergence of innovations taking place across art, mathematics, and science in the 20th century. Leading up to the 1960s, art movements like Cubism, Futurism, Constructivism, and Dada presented a newfound dedication to geometry, abstraction, and chance with a growing emphasis on technology, machine aesthetics, and mechanized production.[7] In the 1950s, visual art produced with

[1] Philip Galanter, "Generative Art Theory," *A Companion to Digital Art*, edited by Christiane Paul (New Jersey: Wiley-Blackwell, 2016), 146–160.
[2] Algorithms can also be referred to as "computer programs," "code," or "software."
[3] Margaret Boden & Ernest Edmonds, "What Is Generative Art?," *Digital Creativity*, Vol. 20, No. 1–2 (2009): 21–46, https://doi.org/10.1080/14626260902867915.
[4] For more on the Algorists see Roman Verostko, "The Algorists," accessed April 28, 2022, http://www.verostko.com/algorist.html.
[5] Frieder Nake, "Paragraphs on Computer Art…," 55.
[6] While not covered in this essay, it is important to note that the history of new media art is vast and intertwined; computer art movements like net art, motion graphics, artificial intelligence (among many others) have played a vital role in our digital ecosystem.
[7] Jason Bailey, "Why Love Generative Art?," *Artnome*, August 26, 2018, https://www.artnome.com/news/2018/8/8/why-love-generative-art.

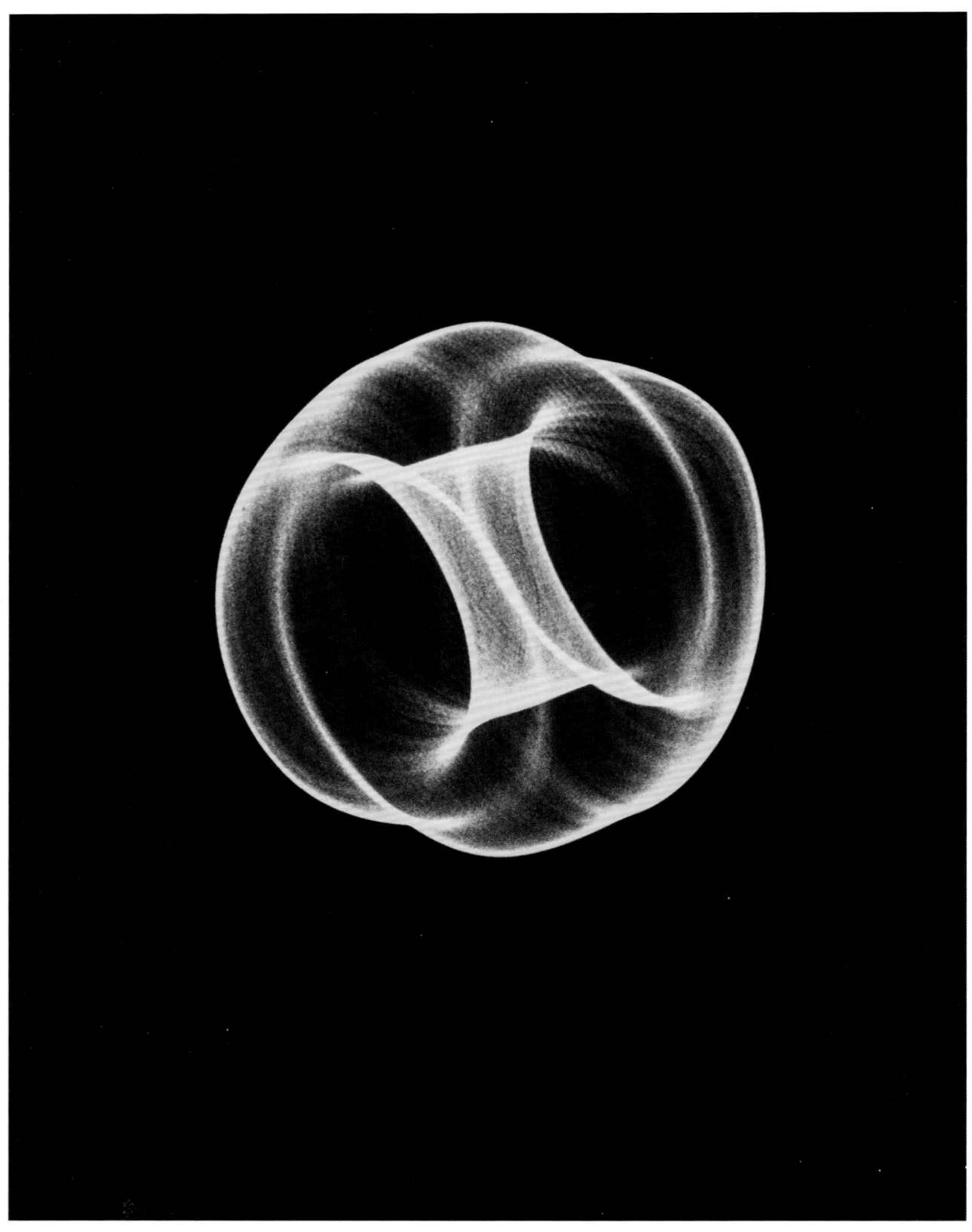

03.03
Georg Nees
*Schotter*, 1968–70
Lithograph on paper, 28 × 21.8 cm

03.04
Part of the code that created Georg Nee's plotter-drawing *Schotter* (1968–70) illustrated in Nees's 1968 doctoral dissertation titled *Generative Computergraphik*. The work was programmed in ALGOL 60 plus G.

03.05
Fortran program used to produce A. Michael Noll's *Pattern Two* (1962) found in appendix of A. Michael Noll's Bell Telephone Laboratories Technical Memorandum: "Patterns by 7090" (TM-62-1234-14, August 28, 1962)

```
'BEGIN' 'COMMENT' SCHOTTER;
'REAL' R, PIHALB, PI4T;
'REAL' JE1,JA1,JE2,JA2,J2,P1,J1;

'INTEGER' I;
'PROCEDURE' QUAD;
'BEGIN'
  'REAL' P1, Q1, PSI;
  'INTEGER' S;
  JE1 := 5*I/264;
  JA1 := -JE1;
  JE2 := PI4T*(1 + 1/ 264);
  JA2 := PI4T*(1 -1/264);
  P1:=P+5+J1;
  Q1:=Q+5+J1;
  PSI:=J2;
  LEER(P1 + R*cos(PSI),Q1 + R*sin(PSI));
  'FOR' S:= 1 'STEP' 1 'UNTIL' 4 'DO'
  'BEGIN' PSI := PSI + PIHALB;
    LINE(P1 + R*cos(PSI),Q1 + R*sin(PSI))
  'END';
  I:=I+1
'END' QUAD;
R:= 5*1.4142;
PIHALB:=3.14159*.5; PI4T:= PIHALB*.5;
I:=0;
'END'
```

```
C          PATTERN TWO
  DIMENSIONFX1(300),IX1(300),IY1(300),FX2(300),FY2(300),IX2(300),IY2(300)
  B        B=526060606060
           CALLROLL
           CALLREFPT(0,1023,1024,1024)
           DO100I=1,200
  100      IY1(I)=I*(I+5)
           CALLWNG(FX1,200,1200.)
           CALLWNG(FX2,300,75.)
           CALLWNG(FY2,300,75.)
           DO101I=1,200
  101      IX1(I)=FX1(I)
           DO102I=1,300
           IX2(J)=FX2(J)+200.
  102      IY2(J)=FY2(J)+300.
           CALLDV2(IX1,IY1,99)
           CALLTSP1(IX2,IY2,B,299)
           CALLTSP1(IX2,IY2,B,299)
           CALLTSP1(IX2,IY2,B,299)
           CALLTSP1(IX2,IY2,B,299)
           CALLCLEAN
           CALLSYSTEM
```

mechanical devices and analog computers began to emerge in the laboratories of engineers, mathematicians, and scientists.[8] In 1950, mathematician Ben F. Laposky began creating abstract art, which he called "electrical compositions" [03.02] by utilizing long-exposure photography on a cathode ray oscilloscope. Without knowledge of the other, pioneering artist Herbert W. Franke (1927–2022) (who would go on to produce NFTs) also produced monochrome visual compositions with a simple analog computer also utilizing a cathode ray oscilloscope, specially built by Franz Raimann to help him make pictures which he referred to as *Oszillogramm*.[9] These visual collaborations with analog machines act as the precursor to the fundamental shift in artistic practice that would take shape less than a decade later with the spread of computational machines.

Starting in the early 1960s, a handful of universities and research groups in North America, Europe, and Asia began looking into creative use cases for the computer. This section will cover two of these centers of innovation: Technische Universität Stuttgart (The Technical University of Stuttgart) in Germany and Bell Laboratories in New Jersey, United States. It was between these two centers where artists like Georg Nees (1926–2016), Frieder Nake, A. Michael Noll, Lillian Schwartz, Kenneth Knowlton (1931–2022), and many others, would make their foray into the computer art practice that spanned 2D, 3D, audio, and animation.

The Technical University of Stuttgart provided a rich academic environment for the advancement of computer-generated aesthetics and algorithmic theories. Formed on the basis of information aesthetics, the Stuttgart School had philosopher Max Bense at its intellectual center.[10] Bense led the Department of Design and brought forth his theory of generative aesthetics, which aimed to create a rational measurement of aesthetics, free from subjective speculation, and grounded within a scientific basis. One of the core constructs of his framework is the artificial production of probabilities in which "the improbability of aesthetic states can be produced mechanically through a methodical combination of planning and chance."[11] This concept of probability and chance defined through pseudorandomness remains a core pillar within algorithmic art today, especially on the blockchain. Bense's theory was highly influential among his students, including computer-art pioneer Georg Nees, who went on to create a body of computer-generated art following this framework of controlled disorder [03.03, 03.04].[12] Similarly inspired by Bense's lectures, fellow pioneer Frieder Nake developed a program to prove the possibility of a generative aesthetic with *Generative Aesthetics 1* (1969).[13] These early algorithmic compositions can be characterized by flat geometric abstractions in line with the aesthetics of the time, which required pen plotters to translate the data-based work into a physical object.[14]

Parallel to the academic happenings in Stuttgart, Bell Labs partook in research and development for the United States military. By the late 1950s, engineers began to look into

[8] Early examples of analog computer art can seen at: Benj Edwards, "The Never-before-Told Story of the World's First Computer Art (It's a Sexy Dame)," *The Atlantic* (Atlantic Media Company, January 24, 2013), https://www.theatlantic.com/technology/archive/2013/01/the-never-before-told-story-of-the-worlds-first-computer-art-its-a-sexy-dame/267439/.
[9] The artist's statement on Oscillographs can be found at: Herbert W. Franke, "Oszillogramm," SIGGRAPH, accessed April 28, 2022, https://digitalartarchive.siggraph.org/artwork/herbert-w-franke-oszillogramm/.
[10] Christoph Klütsch, "Computer Graphic-Aesthetic Experiments between Two Cultures," *Leonardo*, Vol. 40, No. 5 (2007): 421–53, https://doi.org/10.1162/leon.2007.40.5.421.
[11] Max Bense, "Projekte generativer Ästhetik," *computer-grafik*, Rot 19 (Stuttgart: Edition Rot, 1965).
[12] In 1965, the first exhibition of computer-generated art, *Generative Computergraphik*, was held at the Studiengalerie Stuttgart featuring the work of Georg Nees. Shortly after the historic exhibition, Nees published his PhD dissertation of the same name "Generative Computergraphik" under Bense in 1968, further investigating the generative aesthetic framework to computer art.
[13] Klütsch, "Computer Graphic-Aesthetic," 421–53.

**03.06**
A. Michael Noll
*Pattern Two*, 1962
Computer drawing on paper, 21 × 29.7 cm
Conceived and programmed in 1962 by Noll while employed at Bell Telephone Laboratories,
New Jersey, United States

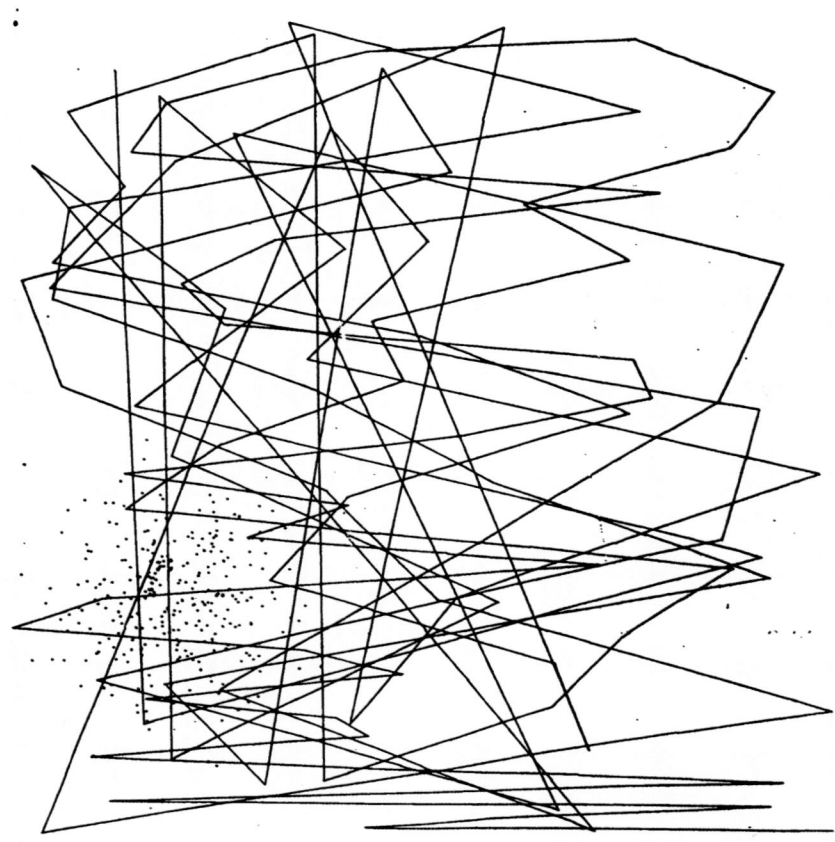

[14] Roman Verostko recounts in his written
history of *The Algorists* on his website:
"There were no graphic interfaces at the
time, so in 1963, Frieder Nake came up with
the task of writing software for a drawing
machine at the University of Stuttgart since
the machine did not supply its own." One can
easily trace Bense's influence on the ongoing
classification of algorithmically generated
imagery as *generative art*. The intrinsic
relationship between Bense's machine-
oriented aesthetic criteria and methodology
of algorithmic art are prevalent to the current
use of the term *generative art*. However, as
discussed in the introduction, the theoretical
standing of generative art as a practice
which can be applied without the use of
a machine or a specific technology does
not subscribe to Bense's requirement that
aesthetic information "must be described
in mathematical terms" (Bense, "Projekte
generativer Ästhetik")
[15] A. Michael Noll, "The Beginnings of
Computer Art in the United States: A
Memoir," *Leonardo*, Vol. 27, No. 1 (1994):
40–41.
[16] Noll recounts the pattern *Gaussian-
Quadratic* (1962) from "Patterns by 7090"
looked like Pablo Picasso's (1881–1973)
*Ma Jolie* (1914) in his written history on
early digital art. *Gaussian-Quadratic*
(1962) also became the first example of
copyrighted digital art (A. Michael Noll,
"Early Digital Computer Art at Bell Telephone
Laboratories, Incorporated," *Leonardo*, Vol.
49, No. 1 (2016): 55–65, https://ethw.org/First-
Hand:Early_Digital_Art_At_Bell_Telephone_
Laboratories,_Inc#).
[17] A. Michael Noll, "Human or Machine: A
Subjective Comparison of Piet Mondrian's
'Composition with Lines' and a Computer–
Generated Picture," *The Psychological
Record*, Vol. 16. No. 1 (January 1966): 1–10.
[18] Noll, "The Beginnings of Computer Art,"
40–41.

the machine's ability to create art, animation, and music, often without knowledge or permission from the company. One of the first engineers at Bell Labs to deliberately produce
visual art with the computer was A. Michael Noll. In the summer of 1962, Noll released a
memo titled "Patterns by 7090" **[03.05, 03.06]** in which he recounted his visual experiments.
These first images can be categorized by the rhythmic geometric structures produced by a
continuous line, "combining elements of order with the disorder of randomness."[15] It is but
coincidence that Noll's intentional interplay of chaos and order runs both aesthetically and
philosophically in line with the artwork produced at the Technical University of Stuttgart,
underlining how vital the characteristic of pseudorandomness is to algorithmic art practices.

Noll quickly recognized similarities between "Patterns by 7090" and modernist
abstraction and began experimenting with the notion of programming the computer to
reproduce modern artwork.[16] Stimulated by the rise of op art, one of his first reproductions was *Ninety Parallel Sinusoids with Linearly Increasing Period* (1964), an algorithmic version of Bridget Riley's *Current* (1964). In his own words, this reproduction "showed how
easily a digital computer could be programmed to create such art."[17] With that said, it was
not enough to simply reproduce the work; Noll sought to investigate the perception of
aesthetic preference by utilizing his own computer-generated imagery as stimuli.[18] For
the proposed experiment, Noll would appropriate a modernist artwork — in this case,
Piet Mondrian's (1872–1944) *Composition in Line* (1916–17) **[03.07]** — and see if participants were able to distinguish which composition was produced by a computer. As an
added dimension, participants were asked to select *which picture they preferred*.

Noll's *Computer Composition with Lines* (1964) **[03.08]** employed a pseudorandom number
generator which varied the bar density, lengths, and widths of the Noll/Mondrian lines,
manipulating the program until it closely approximated the balance of the Mondrian

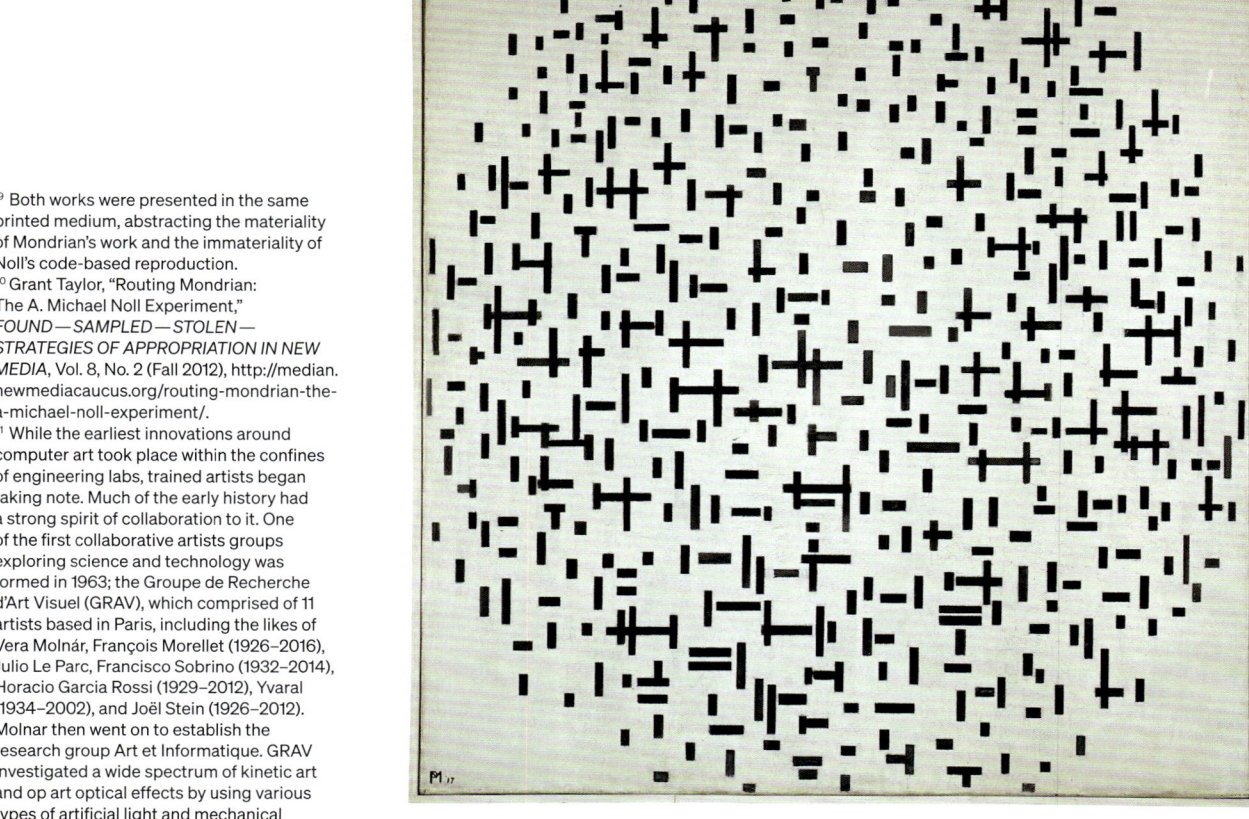

[19] Both works were presented in the same printed medium, abstracting the materiality of Mondrian's work and the immateriality of Noll's code-based reproduction.
[20] Grant Taylor, "Routing Mondrian: The A. Michael Noll Experiment," *FOUND—SAMPLED—STOLEN—STRATEGIES OF APPROPRIATION IN NEW MEDIA*, Vol. 8, No. 2 (Fall 2012), http://median.newmediacaucus.org/routing-mondrian-the-a-michael-noll-experiment/.
[21] While the earliest innovations around computer art took place within the confines of engineering labs, trained artists began taking note. Much of the early history had a strong spirit of collaboration to it. One of the first collaborative artists groups exploring science and technology was formed in 1963; the Groupe de Recherche d'Art Visuel (GRAV), which comprised of 11 artists based in Paris, including the likes of Vera Molnár, François Morellet (1926–2016), Julio Le Parc, Francisco Sobrino (1932–2014), Horacio Garcia Rossi (1929–2012), Yvaral (1934–2002), and Joël Stein (1926–2012). Molnar then went on to establish the research group Art et Informatique. GRAV investigated a wide spectrum of kinetic art and op art optical effects by using various types of artificial light and mechanical movement. Towards the end of the decade, more collectives began to form around the globe. In 1966, Computer Technique Group (CTG), the Japanese collective of art and engineering students was founded by Masao Kohmura and Haruki Tsuchiya. In New York City the same year, American artist Robert Rauschenberg (1925–2008) and engineer Billy Klüver (1927–2004) organized a series of live performances held at the 69th Regiment Armory titled *9 Evenings: Theatre and Engineering*. The event brought together over 30 engineers from Bell Labs and contemporary artists like John Cage (1912–1992), Lucinda Childs, and Robert Whitman under one roof. The artists incorporated sound, movement, and lights through live performances that drew inquisitive crowds and shocked critics. Following the performance, Experiments in Art and Technology (E.A.T.) was formed as a nonprofit organization in an effort to catalyze an "effective working relationship between artists and engineers [that] will lead to new possibilities which will benefit society as a whole" (Billy Klüver and Robert Rauschenberg, *E.A.T. News*, Vol. 1, No. 2 (June 1, 1967): 1, https://www.experimentsinartandtechnology.org/forming-the-organization). Alongside Billy Klüver and Robert Rauschenberg, E.A.T was founded by Fred Waldhauer (1927–1993) and Robert Whitman.

painting.[19] Upon completion of the experiment, only 28% were able to correctly identify the picture produced by Mondrian and *59% of the subjects preferred the computer-generated image.*[20] These results suggest computer-generated randomness could be viewed as a marker of creativity and extenuation of an artist's own compositional abilities. It also positioned algorithmically generated art as a seeming rival to traditional art vernaculars on purely aesthetic lines. It was now for artists and technologists experimenting with algorithms to develop their own styles, intrinsic to the medium.

Who were these artists?[21] The 1970s and 1980s saw the crystallization of two distinct communities of artists, aesthetically and philosophically interwoven, but separated in their relationship with medium and the market and/or art world. The rule-based, systematic qualities of generative minimalist practices, led by the likes of Sol LeWitt (1928–2007) in the United States and François Morellet (1926–2016) in Europe, were characterized by artists developing systems still rooted in a handmade automatism reliant on traditional mediums and methodologies. In LeWitt's *Wall Drawings*, contemporary exhibition spaces must follow a set of instructions the artist had specified as the artwork, but to be completed by hand by the installation team. The instructions would also form the title to the work, such as 4th wall: *24 lines from the center, 12 lines from the midpoint of each of the sides, 12 lines from each corner* (1976). This generative and rule-based approach to art-making, including across other physical disciplines such as sculpture **[03.09]**, places LeWitt as a conceptual forefather to the algorithmic and crypto art communities (he is perhaps the most often cited major conceptual inspiration for the current generation of algorithmic artists) but it is in the human quality of their production that the works differ. In large part, it was these practices that garnered the lion's share of critical and commercial attention, blending the spirit of minimalism with an awareness of technology's pervasiveness in life, but a refusal to engage with it as a medium unto itself. Throughout the 1970s and 1980s, those engaging with algorithms directly and not just thinking like them

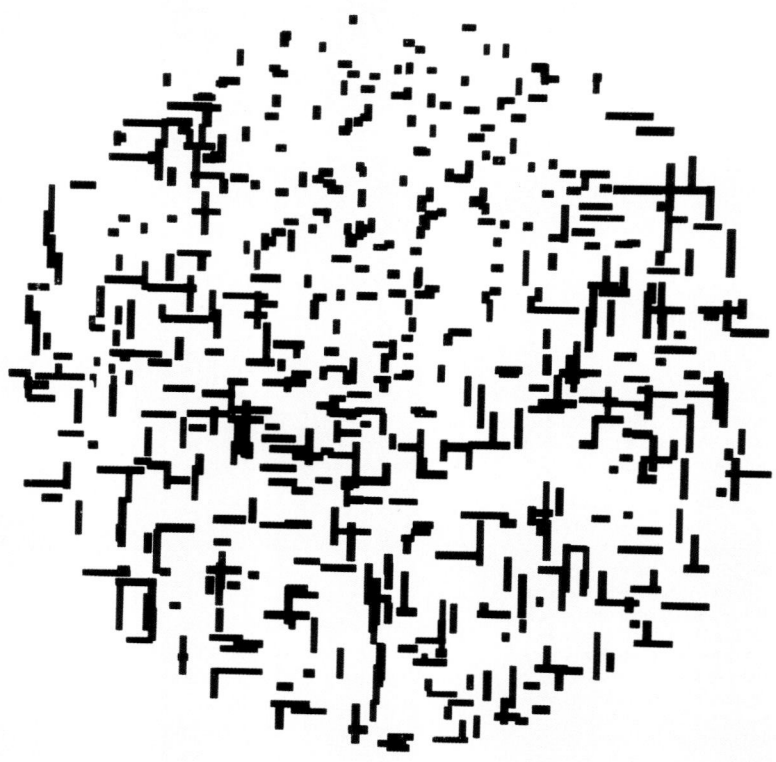

© AMN 1965

developed into their own disparate community. In 1971, Manfred Mohr became the first algorithmic artist to have a major solo exhibition at a museum.[22] Musée d'Art Moderne de la Ville de Paris presented Une Esthétique Programmée, showing over 20 computer drawings, a Benson 1284 drawing machine, and its magnetic tape drive installed at the museum. The abstract compositions were highly influenced by Mohr's musical background and presented contemporary conceptual and formal inquiries in line with his peers such as LeWitt but rooted more firmly within machine aesthetics **[03.10, 03.11]**. During the show, Mohr recounted that the Benson flatbed plotter ran his drawings every afternoon from 3:00 to 5:00 p.m. "in an effort to demonstrate to the public how an automatic drawing machine works."[23] Elsewhere, Vera Molnár in France, like Mohr, transitioned from paint to coding through access to a computer in the Sorbonne at 1968. The output plotter drawings were highly rigorous geometric studies, influenced by the work of Mondrian and Malevich, within which she had cast herself as one of the "three M's." Along with Molnar, the pioneering work of Lillian Schwartz and Grace Hertlein (1924–2015) in the United States as well as the collecting practice of Patric Prince (1942–2021) underscore the importance of women within the algorithmic art community during this period.

This period was also marked by increasing art school engagement in the algorithmic field, which would go on to educate and seed the next generation of artists, many of them NFT artists today. In 1969, Sonia Landy Sheridan (1925–2021), another pioneering female educator in the field, created a department entitled Generative Systems at the School of the Art Institute of Chicago, focusing on art practices using new technologies. In the early 1970s the Slade School of Art at the University of London established the Experimental and Computing Department, and thought sensitively about how to include technology in their programming. Leading into the 1970s, the early computer artist Herbert W. Franke argued in Leonardo — the journal founded in 1967 to promote intersections of art and

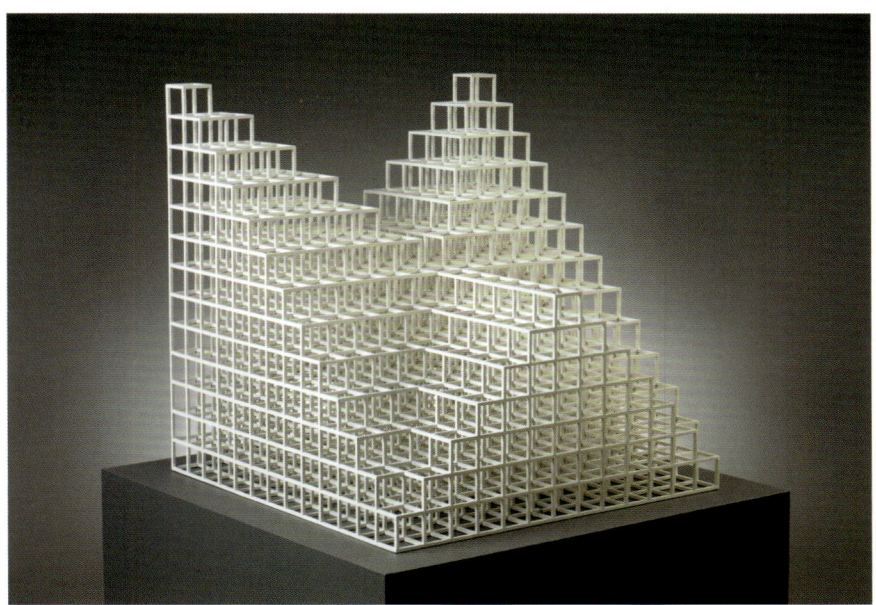

24 Herbert W. Franke, "Computers and Visual Art," *Leonardo*, Vol. 4, No. 4 (1971): 337–38; In 2022, a number of these pioneering early algorists entered the NFT arena. In April 2022, Vera Molnár, Charles Csuri (1922–2022), Roman Verostko produced their first NFTs for Sotheby's third installment of their Natively Digital sales. The works spanned across mediums from physical to digital, with Vera Molnár producing an analog generative work *2% of disorder in co-operation #01* (2022). Fellow pioneer Herbert W. Franke released his first NFT project *Math Art (1980–95)*, a series of 100 investigations of math as an art form created over a 15-year time period through 1995. In October 2022, Frieder Nake released his genesis NFT drop on elementum.art, titled *Homage to Gerhard Richter*, the 40 work series features endless generative variations in the style of Richter's *Strip* series.
25 Tina Rivers Ryan, "McLuhan's Bulbs: Light Art and the Dawn of New Media," (PhD diss., Columbia University, 2016), 175, https://doi.org/10.7916/D82V2G52.
26 Originally designed by Sir Tim Berners-Lee at CERN, the World-Wide Web (WWW) utilized the internet to facilitate the automated sharing of informational documents between scientists, universities and institutions. These documents, now referred to as web pages, utilized HyperText Markup Language (HTML) and consisted mainly of text and hyperlinks. After the web went public in April 1993, multiple web browsers were developed as a "window into the internet'." There are three core computer languages that run across all modern browsers: HTML (document structure), CSS (document styling), and JavaScript (interaction). JavaScript would go on to be a foundational tool for contemporary algorists.
27 Formerly Macromedia Flash and FutureSplash, "Flash" came from combining the original title, FutureSplash.
28 See John Maeda, *Design by Numbers* (Cambridge, MA: MIT Press, 2001).
29 For more on the history of Processing as recounted by Ben Fry and Casey Reas see Processing Foundation, "A Modern Prometheus," Medium, May 29, 2018, https://medium.com/processing-foundation/a-modern-prometheus-59aed94abe85

technology — that "computer art has barely taken off the ground," and might imminently "disappear from public view for a while," even if it would "bring far more far-reaching changes than many of the art fashions that today dominate the scene."[24] Franke's predictions would prove correct, as computer-generated art continued to be ostracized by the public and mainstream art world through the coming decades. Tina Rivers Ryan argued in 2016 that among the confluences of forces, "more profoundly, the use of the computer in art threatened some of the major tenets of modernism, including originality and autonomy, pitting these against the variability and anonymity of the machine."[25]

## Entering the 21st Century (1990–2010)

A core shift in artists' engagement with technology took place upon the introduction of the personal computer and the development of the internet in the late 1980s. Internet native programming languages expanded the ease and scope with which artists could interact and build their own algorithms.[26] However, it was in the 1990s, when Adobe Flash provided a new set of tools that unleashed a wave of creativity among artists on the web.[27] The ActionScript language of Flash included basic actions like scaling, rotating, opacity changes, and morphing one shape into another. Pioneering net artists like LIA, Yael Kanarek, and Joshua Davis utilized web browsers in the 1990s as immersive canvases by combining motion, sound, interactivity, and linked texts to produce their artwork. There was no longer a requirement to translate code through a plotter machine. The open web transformed the very nature of computer-generated art by introducing the browser as a contemporary canvas for producing and experiencing various code-based works.

With the rise of exploration around art and technology, artist and MIT Media Lab professor John Maeda formed the research group Aesthetics and Computation Group (ACG) at the Media Lab in 1996. At the time, Maeda viewed the computer as an artistic medium in its own right and sought to teach computer engineering as an artistic practice. He developed Design by Numbers (DBN), a Java-based programming language and development environment for visual people who were more keen on using a pencil than a computer to make art.[28] Two students that helped develop Design by Numbers with Maeda were Ben Fry and Casey Reas. Fry and Reas taught Design by Numbers in classrooms around the world and throughout that time explored ways in which to improve it. However, rather than extend the monochrome, 100×100 pixel DBN environment, Fry and Reas decided to build a new creative coding environment, now commonly referred to as Processing **[03.12]**.[29] The key innovations in Processing come from specific user experience design decisions that

**03.10**
Manfred Mohr, *Computer Graphics – Une Esthétique Programmée*, Musée d'Art Moderne de la Ville de Paris, May 11–June 6, 1971
(Clockwise from top left) (Top left) Sabine Marchand talking with Manfred Mohr next to a plotter on the opening night of *Une Esthétique Programmée* on
May 11, 1971, and in the background, Pierre Barbaud and Robert Marchand. (Top right) The original poster from the show. (Bottom left) An installation shot
of the handwritten wall panel, see overleaf. (Middle left) Mohr's demonstration plot revealing to the public how an automatic drawing machine works.

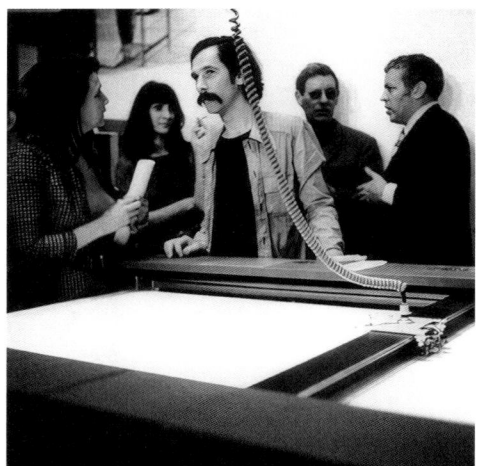

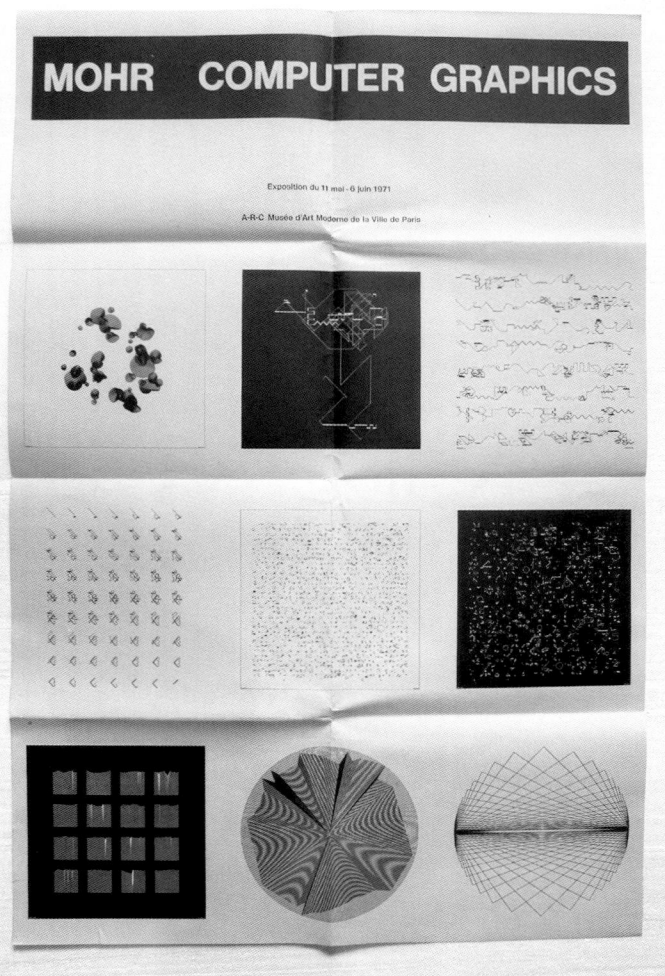

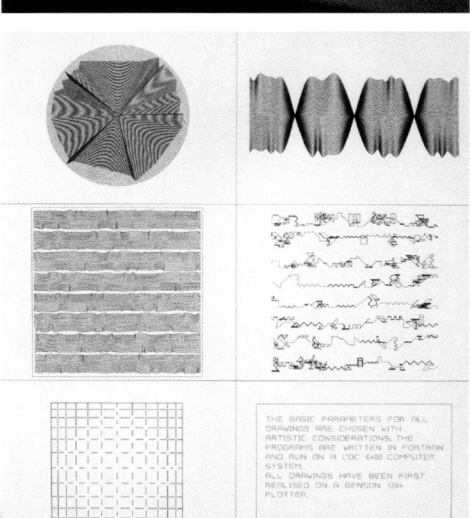

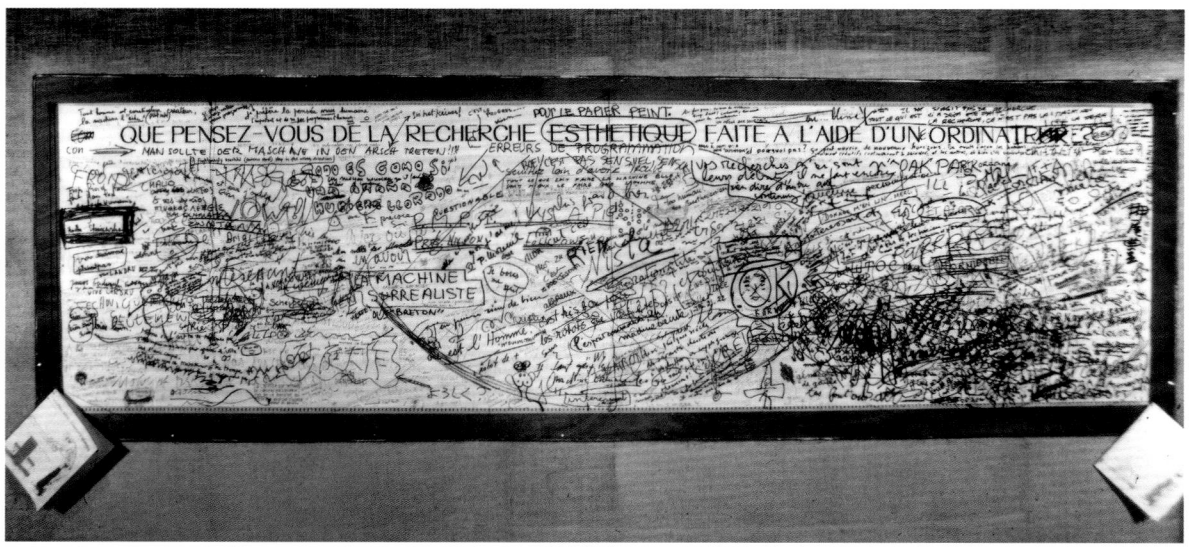

03.11
Manfred Mohr
Wall panel from solo exhibition, *Computer Graphics–Une Esthétique Programmée*, Musée d'Art Moderne de la Ville de Paris, May 11–June 6, 1971
Handwritten responses to the question:
"Que pensez-vous de la recherche esthetique fait a l'aide d'un ordinateur?" or
"What do you think of creative research that is assisted by the computer?"
Various inks on paper

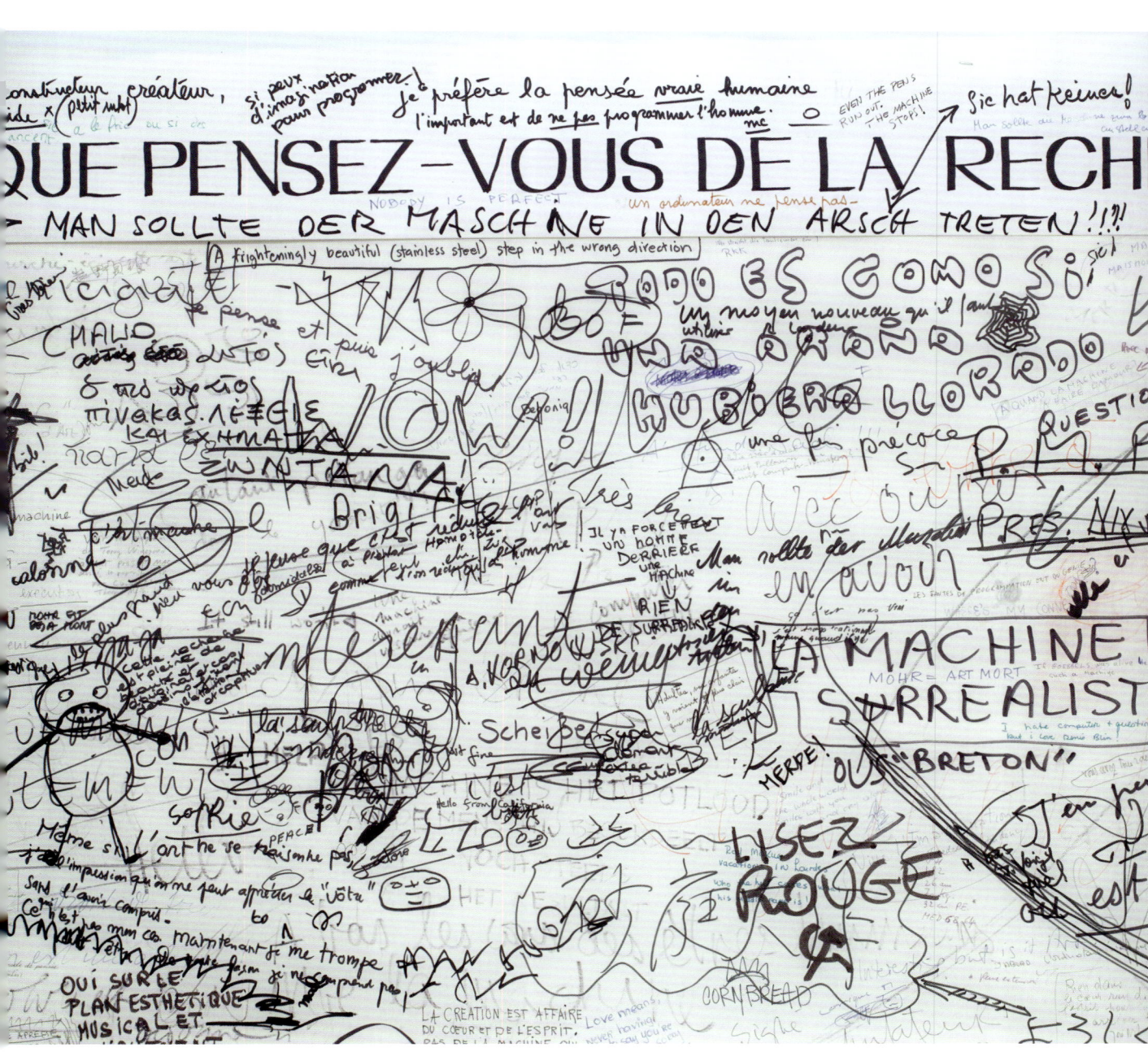

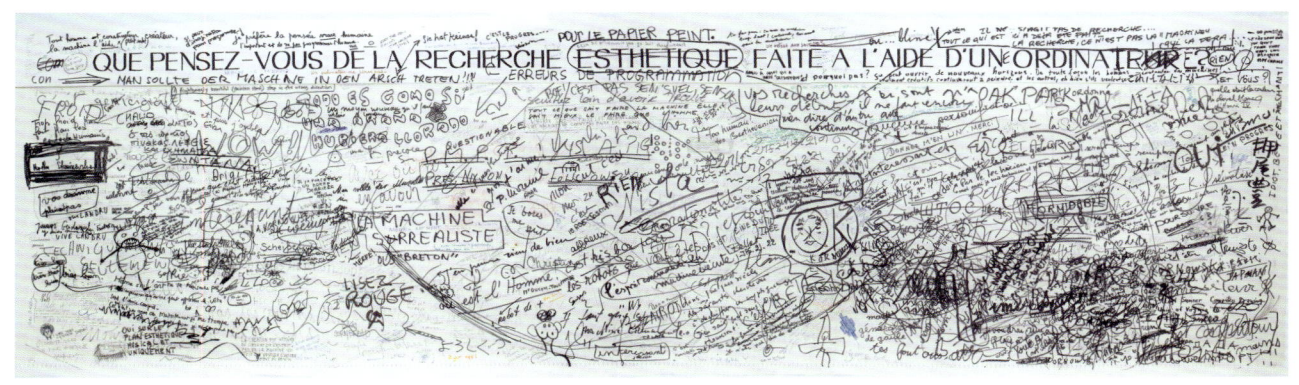

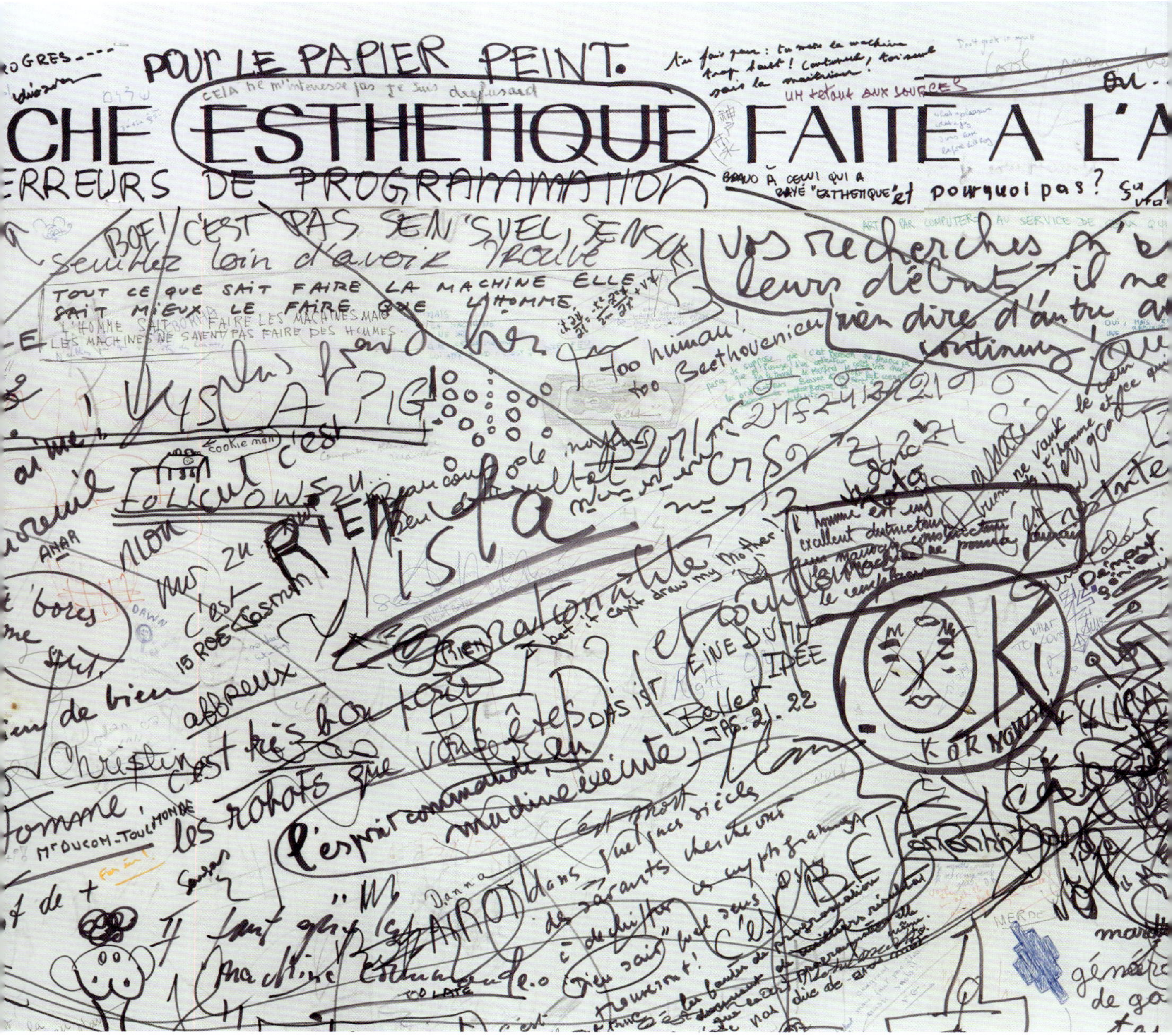

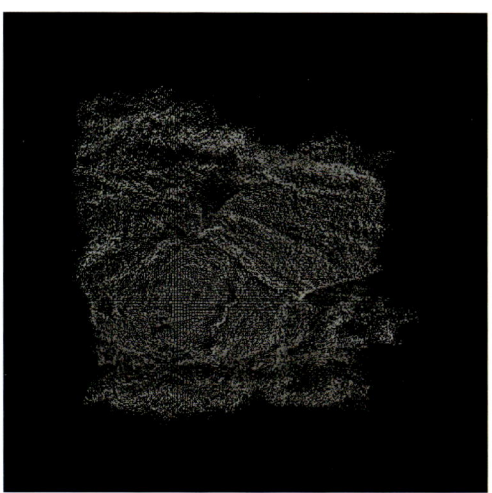

```
/**
 * Extrusion.
 *
 * Converts a flat image into spatial data points and rotates the points
 * around the center.
 */

PImage extrude;
int[][] values;
float angle = PI;

void setup() {
  size(500, 500, P3D);

  // Load the image into a new array
  extrude = loadImage("ystone08.jpg");
  extrude.loadPixels();
  values = new int[extrude.width][extrude.height];
  for (int y = 0; y < extrude.height; y++) {
    for (int x = 0; x < extrude.width; x++) {
      color pixel = extrude.get(x, y);
      values[x][y] = int(brightness(pixel));
    }
  }
}

void draw() {
```

alluded to the craft of art-making: files were now *sketches* and the code library included out-of-the-box functions for shapes and color like *circle()* or *fill()*. Processing was constructed as a three-pronged ecosystem that included a Java-based computer programming language, a self-contained programming environment, and a core belief in the power of community and open-source knowledge.[30]

Apart from the innovations around the compositional environment of algorithmic art, Processing heralded an important shift in the aesthetics of algorithmic art. While still honoring the foundational tenets of Bense's framework, in the period 2010 to 2020, artists utilizing Processing deviated from the "flat" geometric abstractions and began looking at systems found in nature for inspiration. Though computer artists like Grace Hertlein were experimenting with fluid structures in the 1970s, algorists like Jared Tarbell began producing digital work that sculpted pixels with gentle coloring techniques to resemble organic compounds like clay or even crystallized watercolor paint, as seen in *Substrate* (2003) **[03.13]**. In 2012, computer scientist and educator Dan Shiffman published *The Nature of Code* (2012), covering the programming strategies and techniques behind computer simulations of natural systems using the Processing program language.[31]

With the rise of social media, creative coders began to congregate online to share work and ideas on Instagram, Reddit, Twitter, and Slack. Artists like Zach Lieberman began sharing daily sketches on social media as a visual diary into his important explorations in creative computation. Dan Shiffman began sharing Processing and p5.js tutorials on YouTube based on his work at New York University and his book *The Nature of Code* (2012). Shiffman's YouTube channel, The Coding Train, has been one of the most often mentioned influences among the current generation of algorithmic artists. His tutorials cover programming strategies and techniques that can be seen in notable examples of algorithmic art NFTs like flow fields (as seen in Tyler Hobbs's *Fidenza* [2021]), particle systems (as seen in Aaron Penne's *Apparitions* [2021]), and rectangular subdivision (as seen in art duo Generative Artworks' *Enchiridion* [2021]).

## The Emergence of Blockchain and On-Chain Generative Art

The history of NFTs and algorithmic art are inextricably linked. The first NFT, *Quantum* (2014) by Kevin McCoy, is a code-based artwork created with Processing.[32] Similarly, one of the first NFT projects to successfully exemplify the concept of computer-generated collectibles as social currency was Larva Labs' *CryptoPunks* (2017). Yet, the early implementation of a standard non-fungible token did not lend itself to adequately support code-based artwork, they instead catered to image or video-based artwork. Early NFT platforms defaulted to storing an artwork's visual image (.jpg, .png, .mp4, etc.) on a database off-chain due to the memory constraints of the blockchain. This practice forced algorithmic artists to capture a photo still (or video recording) of their algorithmic art in order to mint their work on the blockchain. It made no difference that the work was being presented in its native digital

[30] The concept of openness remains a core pillar of the Processing project, as Fry and Reas had "learned coding in large part by looking at others' code" (Processing Foundation, "A Modern Prometheus"). One of the longest-running and most prominent efforts specific to the Processing community is Sinan Ascioglu's OpenProcessing, where users can view artwork and the raw code that produces it. With the increase of information sharing and the formation of the Processing Foundation, Processing's popularity spread over the years, with usage spikes correlating to the academic calendar. It has since been translated to JavaScript as p5.js thanks to the work of artist and researcher Lauren McCarthy. As a result, Processing (p5.js) can now be run natively within modern web browsers globally instead of the original Java applet. This signifies a key moment of innovation in the Processing ecosystem as a significant amount of contemporary algorithmic art utilize p5.js.
[31] Daniel Shiffman is a computer programmer, a member of the Board of Directors of the Processing Foundation, and an Associate Arts Professor at the Interactive Telecommunications Program at New York University Tisch School of the Arts.
[32] Kevin McCoy, "Quantum," *Mccoyspace*, accessed July 8, 2022, www.mccoyspace.com/project/125/.

03.13
Jared S. Tarbell
*Substrate*, 2003
Processing

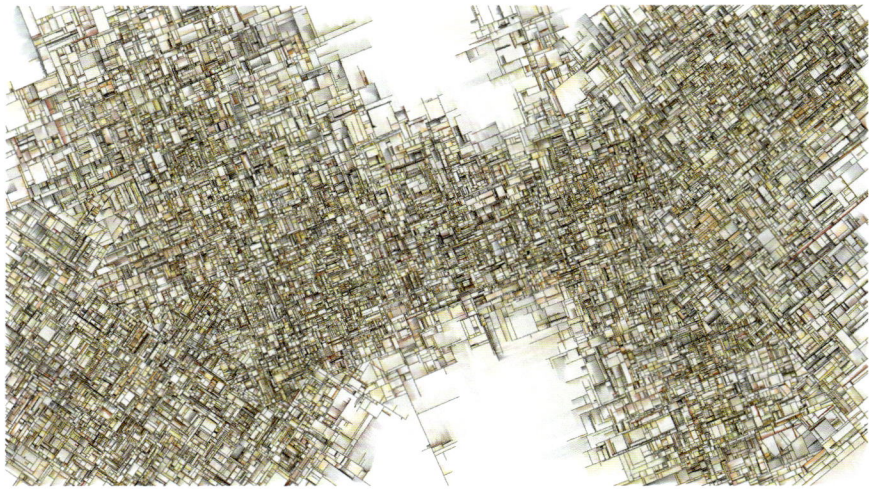

environment; the traditional application of NFTs continued to enable the decades-old practice of translating running code into static or captured outputs as the final art object, rather than the executed code itself. An early example of this practice can be seen in Manoloide's *Mantel Rojo* (2018) **[03.14]**, which was minted on the Ethereum blockchain through the curated marketplace SuperRare in 2020. The record of *Mantel Rojo* **[03.15]** references an external image file […/4mantelred.jpg] and represents this period of time when the only way to engage with algorithmic artwork on the blockchain was to capture an image or recording of the program's output. While marketplaces like SuperRare and OpenSea played a key role in the adoption of NFTs, the technical constraints dictated how algorithmic artists could mint their work and in turn, how the work could be collected.

Following the release of *CryptoPunks* in 2017, John Watkinson and Matt Hall of Larva Labs began exploring the storage limitations of the Ethereum blockchain.[33] Even though NFTs introduced major innovations like immutable provenance, provable ownership, and the proliferation of artist royalties, Larva Labs sought to make an artwork that could *also* be completely operational on the blockchain. Inspired by the early computer-art pioneers, Larva Labs embraced the running technical constraints and crafted "a small amount of efficiently running code, [with a] fairly small, efficient output" **[03.16]** which would be fully stored on the blockchain and capable of producing visual compositions.[34] In April 2019, Larva Labs released *Autoglyphs* (2019) **[03.17]** as a set of 512 artworks.

The influence of early computer art and procedural abstraction is prevalent in the outputs of *Autoglyphs* and one can draw a direct line through Noll's experimentations to Mondrian's *Composition in Line* (1916–17). Just as Noll's composition employed the simplicity and modularity of the line, the 40 lines of code that produce *Autoglyphs* make use of primitive glyphs to construct a set of unique aesthetic arrangements. In contrast to Noll's singular reproduction, *Autoglyphs* embrace the infinite possibility of a set and the conditional probability of compositional distribution across 512 outputs. Within the aesthetic discipline of algorithmically generated art, constrained randomness and the concept of emergence remain essential.[35] The defined interplay of chaos and order between the individual glyph structures lean into Bense's premise of generative aesthetics as "an *aesthetics of production*, which makes possible the methodical production of aesthetic states."[36]

*Autoglyphs*' most notable claim is that they are the first *on-chain* artwork: a self-contained mechanism for both the creation *and* ownership of art within a token. That is to say, the record of an *Autoglyph* not only contains an external image file, but the executable code that produces the artwork itself.[37] This concept of a self-contained mechanism for both the creation *and* ownership of art is one of the most significant innovations in NFTs that distinguishes this period of computer-generated art from its inception through the early 21st century. For the first time in the history of algorithmic art, a body of work can be produced, exhibited, and sold in its native performative environment within the browser.

This idea that software-like functions can live on the blockchain left a profound impact on Mexican entrepreneur and artist Erick Calderon, aka Snowfro. In November 2020, Calderon

[33] Jason Bailey, "Autoglyphs, Generative Art Born on the Blockchain," *Artnome*, April 8, 2019, https://www.artnome.com/news/2019/4/08/autoglyphs-generative-art-born-on-the-blockchain.
[34] "Autoglyphs," *Larva Labs*, accessed April 28, 2022, https://larvalabs.com/autoglyphs.
[35] Frieder Nake, "Paragraphs on Computer Art," 61.
[36] Bense, "Projekte generativer Ästhetik," 1965.
[37] To explain further, the code lives on the blockchain. Should a user request the visual composition from the blockchain, the instructions are available to generate the artwork and can even be translated to a plotter and rendered in physical form. Just as Sol LeWitt provided instructions to produce his drawings, Larva Labs created a system for *self-executable* instructions on the blockchain. The key distinction between conceptual and algorithmic art practice is that, although both "free the dependence on the skill of an artist as a craftsman," algorithmic art eliminates the craftsman altogether (Sol LeWitt, "Paragraphs on Conceptual Art," *Artforum*, Vol. 5, No. 10 [Summer 1967]).

**03.14**
Manoloide
*Mantel Rojo*, 2018 (Minted: 07-27-2020 19:12:35)
Processing
Ethereum, 0xb932a70a57673d89f4acffbe830e8ed7f75fb9e0, 12248

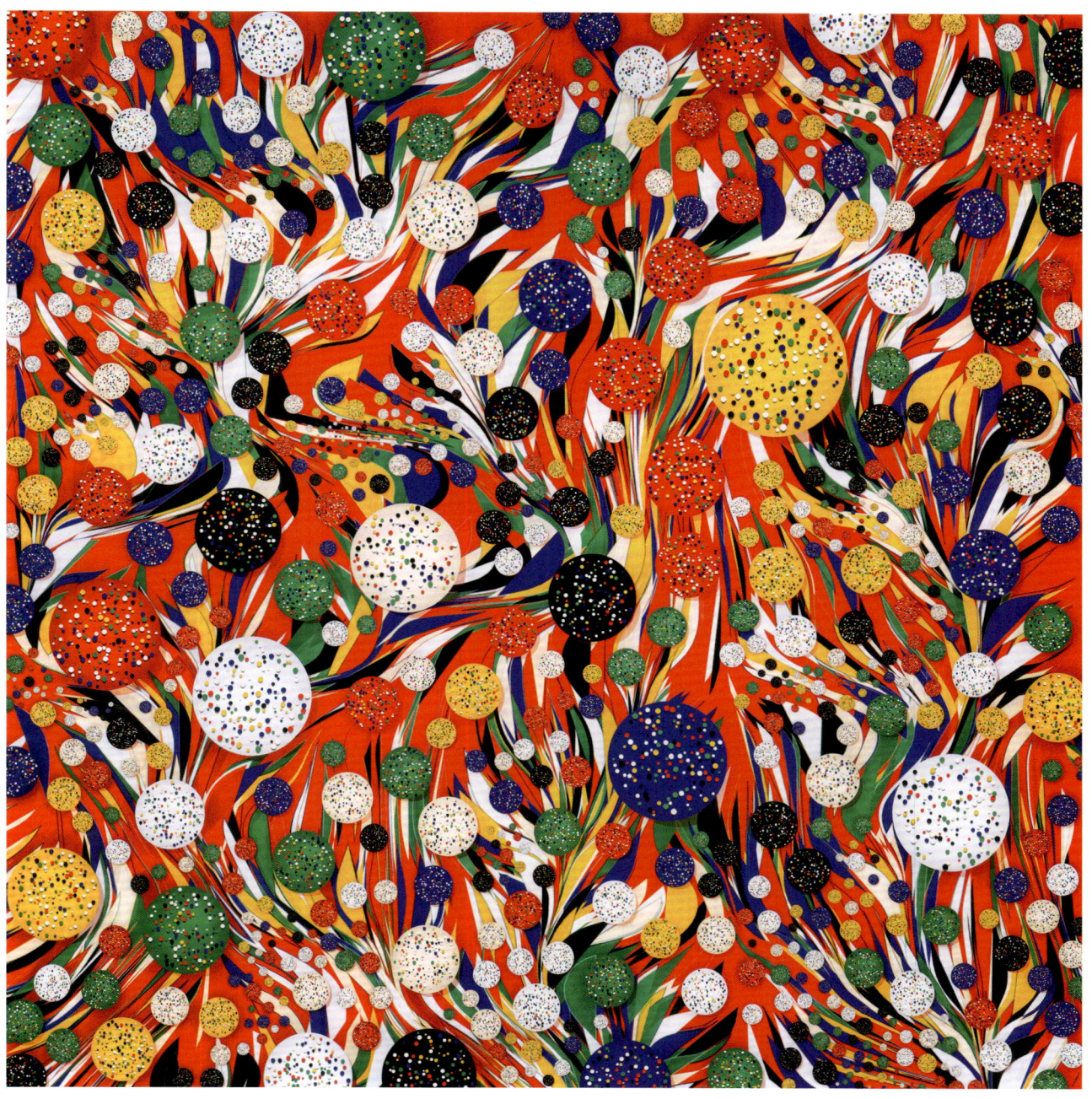

**03.15**
Screenshot of token data from Manoloide's *Mantel Rojo* (2018)

```
{"name":"Mantel Rojo","createdBy":"manoloide","yearCreated":"2018","description":"Mantel Rojo by Manoloide
2018.","image":"https://ipfs.pixura.io/ipfs/QmWGFF1CCjefsCEPGddxPAzehV3Zni93Yoo7i6tWtKWTbM/4mantelred.jpg"
,"media":
{"uri":"https://ipfs.pixura.io/ipfs/QmWGFF1CCjefsCEPGddxPAzehV3Zni93Yoo7i6tWtKWTbM/4mantelred jpg","dimens
ions":"6500x6500","size":"48326847","mimeType":"imagejpeg"},"tags":["code","processing","generative","manoloide"]}
```

**03.16**
Drawing function that produces Larva Labs' *Autoglyphs* (2019)

```
// The Following code generates art.

function draw(uint id) public view returns (string) {
    uint a = uint(uint160(keccak256(abi encodePacked(idToSeed[id]))));
    bytes memory output = new bytes(USIZE * (USIZE + 3) + 30);
    uint c;
    for (c = 0; c < 30; c++) {
        output[c] = prefix[c];
    }
    int x = 0;
    int y = 0;
    uint v = 0;
    uint value = 0;
    uint mod = (a % 11) + 5;
    bytes5 symbols;
    if (idToSymbolScheme[id] == 0) {
        revert();
    } else if (idToSymbolScheme[id] == 1) {
        symbols = 0x2E582F5C2E; // X/\
    } else if (idToSymbolScheme[id] == 2) {
        symbols = 0x2E2B2D7C2E; // +-|
    } else if (idToSymbolScheme[id] == 3) {
        symbols = 0x2E2F5C2E2E; // /\
    } else if (idToSymbolScheme[id] == 4) {
        symbols = 0x2E5C7C2D2F; // \|-/
    } else if (idToSymbolScheme[id] == 5) {
        symbols = 0x2E4F7C2D2E; // O|-
    } else if (idToSymbolScheme[id] == 6) {
        symbols = 0x2E5C5C2E2E; // \
    } else if (idToSymbolScheme[id] == 7) {
        symbols = 0x2E237C2D2B; // #|-+
    } else if (idToSymbolScheme[id] == 8) {
        symbols = 0x2E4F4F2E2E; // OO
    } else if (idToSymbolScheme[id] == 9) {
        symbols = 0x2E232E2E2E; // #
    } else {
        symbols = 0x2E234F2E2E; // #O
    }
    for (int i = int(0); i < SIZE; i++) {
        y = (2 * (i - HALF_SIZE) + 1);
        if (a % 3 == 1) {
            y = -y;
        } else if (a % 3 == 2) {
            y = abs(y);
        }
        y = y * int(a);
        for (int j = int(0); j < SIZE; j++) {
            x = (2 * (j - HALF_SIZE) + 1);
            if (a % 2 == 1) {
                x = abs(x);
            }
            x = x * int(a);
            v = uint(x * y / ONE) % mod;
            if (v < 5) {
                value = uint(symbols[v]);
            } else {
                value = 0x2E;
            }
            output[c] = byte(bytes32(value << 248));
            c++;
        }
        output[c] = byte(0x25);
        c++;
        output[c] = byte(0x30);
        c++;
        output[c] = byte(0x41);
        c++;
    }
    string memory result = string(output);
    return result;
}
```

**03.17**
Larva Labs
*Autoglyph* (top to bottom) *#288, #177 & #494*, 2019
ASCII, Solidity
Ethereum, 0xd4e4078ca3495DE5B1d4dB434BEbc5a986197782, 288,
177 & 494

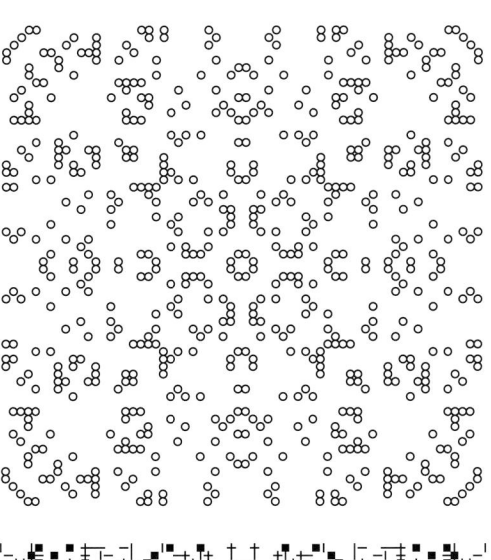

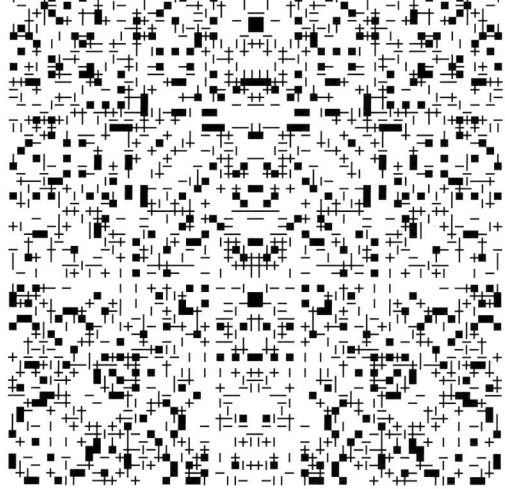

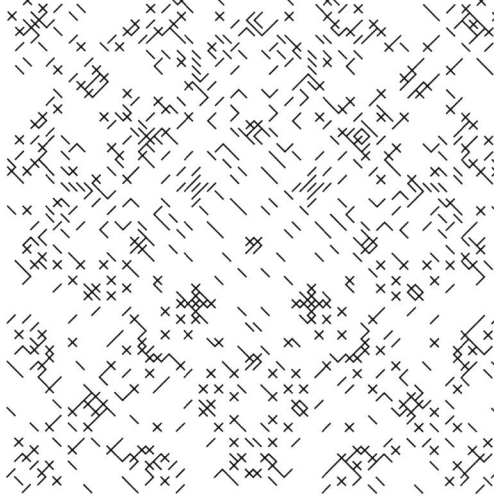

**03.18**
A snippet of code from Snowfro's *Chromie Squiggle* (2020)
The seed variable, which will dictate the overall composition, is based upon the tokenData it receives
from the computer evoking the program upon purchase on Art Blocks.

```
let seed = parseInt(tokenData.hashes[0].slice(0, 16), 16);
…
function draw() {
    color = 0;
    background(backgroundArray[backgroundIndex]);
    let div = Math.floor(map(Math.round(decPairs[24]), 0, 230, 3, 20));
    let steps = slinky ? 50 : fuzzy ? 1000 : 200;
    translate((width / 2) - (width / wt / 2), height / 2);
    for (let j = 0; j < segments - 2; j++) {
        for (let i = 0; i <= steps; i++) {
            let t = i / steps;
            let x = curvePoint(width / segments / wt * j, width / segments / wt * (j + 1), width / segments / wt * (j + 2),
                               width / segments / wt * (j + 3), t);
```

launched Art Blocks, the first open marketplace dedicated to on-chain algorithmic art. The platform went live with the release of Snowfro's *Chromie Squiggle* (2020), an algorithm written in p5.js capable of producing 10,000 unique "chromie squiggles": a single undulating line of brightly colored gradients, which upon clicking, animates the flow of its gradient color scheme **[03.18]**. The release of Art Blocks represents the convergence point of innovations across conceptual art, blockchain innovation, and increasingly abstracted programming libraries, delineating the start of the contemporary algorithmic art renaissance — while also catalyzing a new subgenre, referred to as "long-form" algorithmic art.[38]

The paradigm shift proposes a new critical framework for long-form algorithmic art. In conjunction with the typical artistic benchmarks of composition, color, and linework, the long-form artist working on Art Blocks must craft a system that is capable of producing, at times, upwards of 1,000 unique outputs that, without question, share the same visual language as a foundation; there is a necessary balance at play between variation and cohesiveness. If there is too little variation, the system can be deemed repetitive; too much and the visual language of the algorithm is considered weak. The refinement process between logic and intuition requires a intricate balance of skill and collaboration between the artist and technical constraints of code; the bounds in which the work exists must be explicit yet visceral enough to warrant a large body of work that evokes the understanding of inherent skill.

Traditionally, it has been common practice for artists to control the full process of creation and meticulously oversee the output presented to the public.[39] While the algorithmic artist conversely relinquishes control to an automated system, it is not uncommon for the artist to select a relatively small number of outputs to present to the public. Artists like Ix Shells view the process of selection as a fundamental part of their artistic practice. A key difference in the Art Blocks model is the deliberate removal of curatorial intervention from the artist, and introduces the necessary interaction from a collector to "evoke the algorithm" in order to realize the final artwork. Each work in the series passes through the software to generate a composition using a collector's "tokenData" as a seed. The work will then be viewed for the first time by both the artist and collector upon purchase and executed live in the browser. Marcel Duchamp said in 1957: "The creative act is not performed by the artist alone; the spectator … adds his contribution to the creative act" and starting in 2020, the algorist and the collector entered into this performative act on the blockchain.

In 2011, Nake stated that "if you want to find the masterpiece, you must compare algorithms. Critics and art historians are not prepared to do this. Nor is anyone else."[40] However, the algorithmic artists' style *is* found in their functions. This is not to say there is "bad" code or "good" code, but that there is a stylistic opinion at play in the composition of an artist's code. The algorithm can be compared to the brushstrokes of a painting. There are no "bad" strokes; it is the outcome that ultimately matters. However, similar to the foundational technical skills required in painting and draftsmanship, there is a requirement to understand the foundational techniques of computer programming in order to develop one's unique style. Over time, artists working code have created a toolkit of functions that contribute to various aspects of the realized work, be it techniques in color diffusion, textural elements, interactions, or compositional boundaries.

The importance of variability in long-form projects introduces the concept of "rarity traits," which has become a core characteristic of contemporary algorithmic art. To explain further, one can look at Calderon's *Chromie Squiggle*. While the subjective nature of aesthetics is

[38] The term *long-form generative art* was coined by Tyler Hobbs, in his blog post "The Rise of Long-Form Generative Art," 2021, https://tylerxhobbs.com/essays/2021/the-rise-of-long-form-generative-art.
[39] Michael Assis, "On the Artist and Long-Form Generative Art," *Right Click Save*, May 13, 2022, https://www.rightclicksave.com/article/on-the-artist-and-long-form-generative-art.
[40] Nake, "Paragraphs on Computer Art, Past and Present," 57.

**03.19**
Dmitri Cherniak
*Ringer #879 — "The Goose Ringer,"* 01-31-2021 18:14:16
p5.js
Ethereum, 0xa7d8d9ef8d8ce8992df33d8b8cf4aebabd5bd270, 13000879

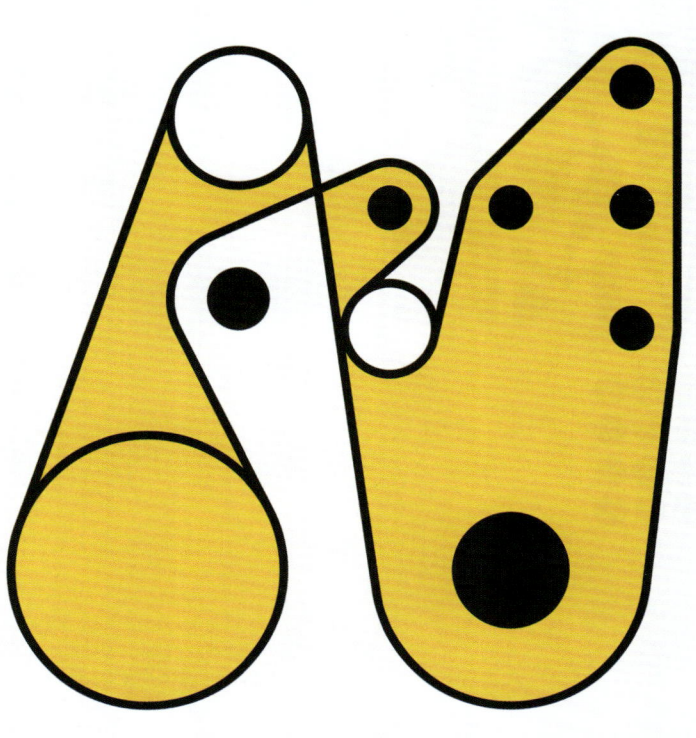

chosen by the artist (in this case, a brightly colored squiggle), there is also an objectivity in the defined distribution of traits to increase variability. Within the traits of *Chromie Squiggle*, the 'standard' squiggle is the most common, with over 60% distribution, while the rarest traits 'hyper-pipe' and 'hyper-bold' have >0.1% distribution.[41] Compositions featuring the most common trait are typically referred to as a "floor" piece. In contrast with early pioneers who created much shorter print runs, the dialogue between the composition's rarity and aesthetic quality is of prime importance to the consideration of the work. It is in *Chromie Squiggle* and the legacy of *CryptoPunks* in the earliest days of blockchain-based algorithmic art, that we see the beginnings of a new hegemony of the trait seep into the conceptual structure of algorithmic art — particularly long-form projects. The idea of the trait in providing a rarity model that allows easier engagement in the market (where works can be ranked and sorted based on known architecture) has encouraged artists to artificially structure value through the use of rarity traits. In this, artists are constructing long-form projects where subjectivity has given way to rarity — in turn accelerating the rise of data-driven trading over collecting. This structure has been codified further (or perhaps initiated) within both Art Blocks and OpenSea's filter systems, where traits have become the de facto form of cataloging. This combination of traits presents a work of art that at its core is a logic tree, bearing the marks of the coding that built the project.

The prominence of Art Blocks became clear with the community interest of early projects like Dmitri Cherniak's *Ringers* (2021) **[03.19]** and Tyler Hobbs's *Fidenza* (2021). Influenced by the methodology laid out by graphic designer Armin Hofmann (1920–2020) in his book *Graphic Design Manual* (1965) **[03.20]**, Cherniak's *Ringers* took a seemingly simple prompt: "How many ways can a string wrap around a peg?" Utilizing only circles, curved lines, and a handful of colors, Cherniak showcased the power of a strong aesthetic algorithm capable of producing hundreds of unique compositions. While rarity traits played a strong role in the

[41] For more information, please read the chapter: "On Process."

**03.20**
Armin Hofmann
*Graphic Design Manual: Principles and Practice*
(Niggli Verlag, Imprint of Braun Publishing AG, 1965), p. 71

**03.21**
Tyler Hobbs's sketchbook containing *flow field*
diagrams and notations for *Fidenza* (2021)

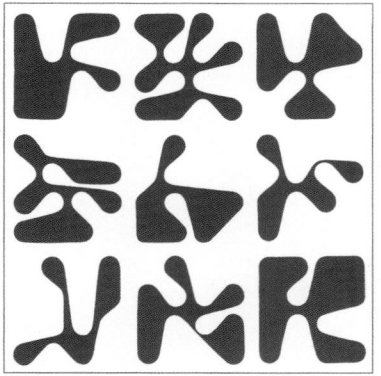

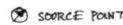

market activity around the project, one of the highest-selling and most popular outputs is not considered rare in the objective stance, but rather the subjective. *Ringers #879* became a community favorite due to its resemblance to a goose, which was neither explicitly defined nor expected from Cherniak. "The Goose Ringer" became the subject of community-made memes and jokes, shared across social networks like Twitter and Discord, showcasing the importance of community in today's digital ecosystem.

Meanwhile, Tyler Hobbs's *Fidenza* took a core technique in creative programming, the flow field, and flipped it on its head. The flow field is typically utilized to visualize a field of directional vectors and works exceptionally to produce curves **[03.21]**. However, *Fidenza* transformed the flow field from a foundational coding technique into a versatile subject within a body of work. Through the distributed compositional characteristics like 'density', 'scale', 'outlines', and even the rare 'soft-shapes' which mimic the aesthetic quality of a brush **[03.22]**, Hobbs demonstrated a masterful example of long-form algorithmic art.

While these early works are rather graphic in nature, algorithmic art on the blockchain is increasingly playing with medium, form, and aesthetic boundaries, influenced both by the increasing technical skill of artists and the development and increasing sophistication of code libraries. Alida Sun's *glitch crystal monsters* (2021) was the first project on Art Blocks that was created to be experienced as an animated projection. Widely misunderstood within the context of a marketplace where works are viewed within a browser and then displayed as a static grid on the secondary market (structurally limiting true appreciation of the work), the project challenges the idea that NFTs can relate to any form of digital experience, not solely within the online Web3 space of wallets, marketplaces, and virtual worlds. Similarly, there are fully interactive projects that generate real-time audio such as hideo's *celestial cyclones* (2021) and others that evoke a feeling of organic, ostensibly hand-drawn artworks. Emily Xie's *Memories of Qilin* (2022) includes algorithmically generated textures that resemble natural paper and distinct elements that allude to a story of an artisan utilizing water-based inks. The work is highly inspired by Chinese brushwork, while drawing from the colors and compositions of ukiyo-e woodblock prints. Matt DesLauriers's *Meridian* (2021) also carries the feeling of hand-drawn landscapes. *Meridian #638* is an example of one output that suggests the use of charcoal, though it is crafted by a set of explicit rules laid out by the artist as a computer program. All these works are prime examples of advanced stylistic development found in contemporary algorithmic art today. The resultant outputs speak to the artists' high level of technical ability to remold and hijack traditional aesthetics; they question the place of artifice within the algorist's toolbox and ultimately ask what is more aesthetically progressive or digitally native: Well-conceived skeuomorphisms or the continuation of neo-geometric aesthetics that people

03.22
Flow field sketch for *Fidenza* (2021) by Tyler Hobbs

03.23
ciphrd
*RGB Elementary Cellular Automaton #4*, 11-08-2021 14:36:16
Vanilla
Tezos, KT1AEVuykWeuuFX7QkEAMNtffzwhe1Z98hJS, 33

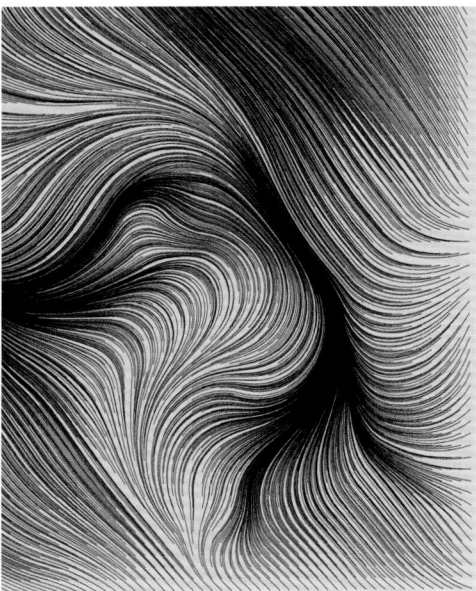

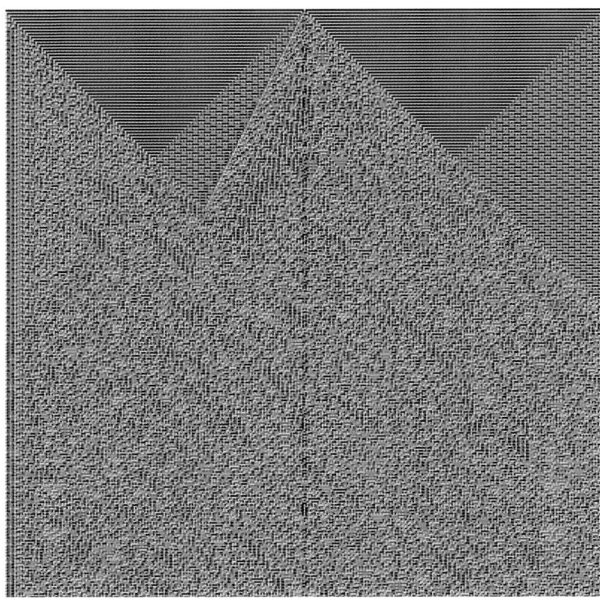

have become accustomed to associate with digital art? Each avenue is both radical and problematic in their own way. In this sense, projects such as Jan Robert Leegte's *JPEG* (2021), a sophisticated celebration of digital pixelation, compression, and composition, showcases a more native exploration of digital materiality (the pixel and JPEG compression rules). It is the prevalence of artifice and skeuomorphism in algorithmic art and a routemap towards more native aesthetic inquiries.

Aside from Art Blocks, the principal *NFT* marketplaces built atop the Ethereum blockchain like OpenSea and SuperRare were not conducive to minting code-based artwork on the blockchain. At the same time, criticism around the environmental impact of Ethereum's proof-of-work consensus mechanism continued to mount, and artists began to consider sustainable alternatives. In response to these concerns, Casey Reas developed a curation platform called Feral File on the sustainable Bitmark blockchain in early 2021. Feral File was built with a focus on artist and collector rights and invites individual curators to organize small collections of short-form algorithmic work and other time-based media art. It is a more intentional and intellectual environment that resembles a traditional project space with its wide-ranging but individually focused curatorial agenda. In light of decentralization, Canadian artist 0xDEAFBEEF circumvented the use of a marketplace completely by creating his own smart contracts; *Series 0 – Synth Poems* (2021) is one of six series exploring on-chain audiovisual art and poetry using nothing but a C compiler. The visual component of *Synth Poems* is an ode to the analog compositions of artists like Ben F. Laposky and Frieder Nake.

During this period, Tezos, another blockchain utilizing the environmentally friendly proof-of-stake consensus, became a safe space for artists and collectors to engage with NFTs in a sustainable way. In the beginning, the first marketplace to draw in a community of artists on Tezos was called Hic et Nunc (HEN). In contrast to the long-form framework of Art Blocks, it was one of the first open marketplaces to allow code-based artists to mint their programs as zipped web pages with HTML, CSS, and JavaScript files. The majority of the code-based works on HEN were editions of a single output or a "one-of-one," which is the term used to describe one single composition with no editions or additional outputs from the same algorithm — it is a standalone, often curated composition chosen by the artist. Hic et Nunc was the predominant marketplace for all art transactions on the Tezos blockchain, until the site unexpectedly went offline.[42]

Around this time, a new generative art platform on Tezos was already taking shape called fxhash, founded by the French artist ciphrd [03.23]. Though fxhash did not cater to "one-of-ones," it was not long before algorithmic art enthusiasts rallied around fxhash; and though

[42] Though the site went offline, it was the first practical example of the decentralized nature of NFTs. The community rallied together to build new frontend sites like Objkt for the artwork that was originally minted and listed on Hic et Nunc as they were still available on the Tezos blockchain.

**03.24**
Hieronymus Cock
*View of ruins on the Palatine Hill with trabeated façade at left and arcades at center,* from the series
*"The Ruins of Rome,"* 1550
Etching, 19.5 × 28.3 cm
The Metropolitan Museum of Art, New York, United States

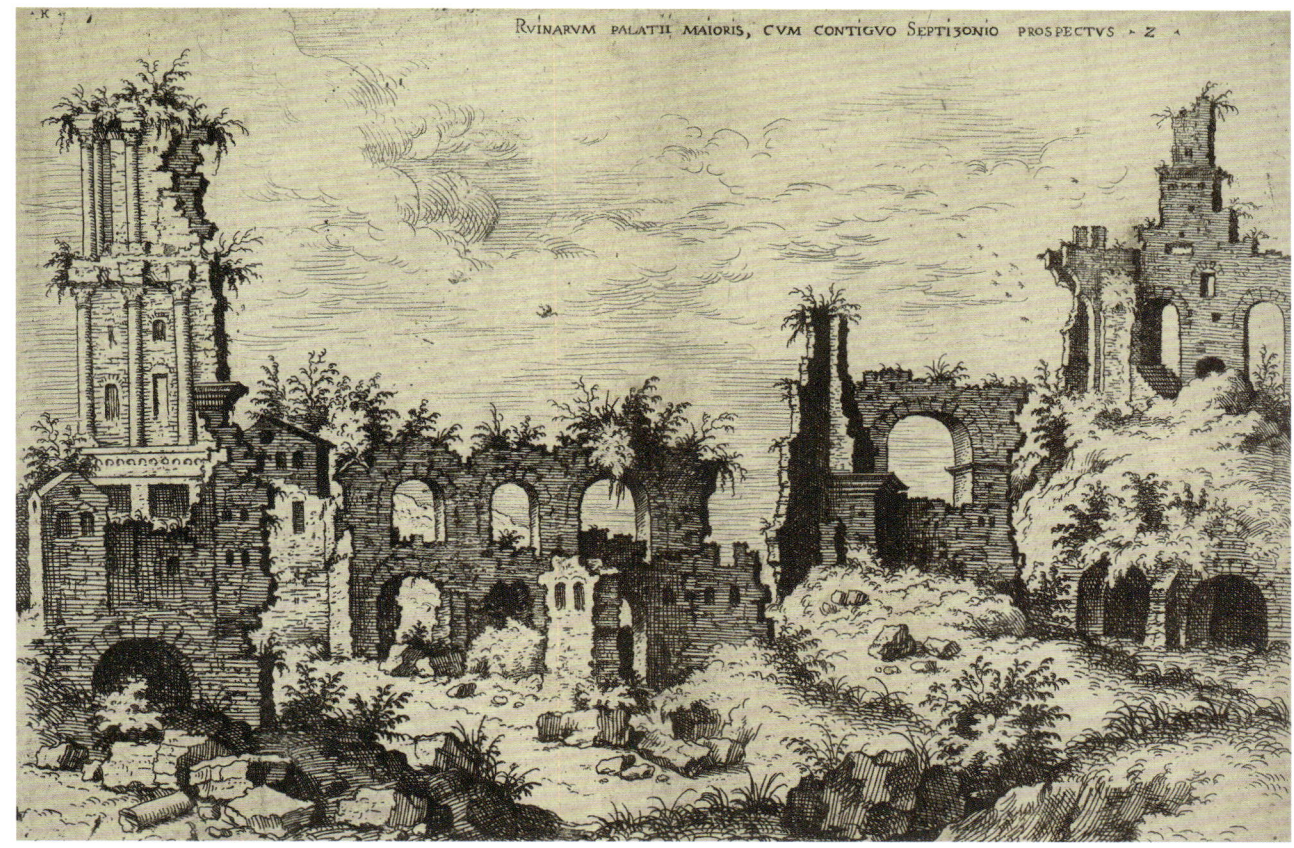

the idea is similar in nature to Art Blocks, fxhash takes a completely different approach to long-form generative art on the blockchain. There is no curation board, the work is not stored on-chain, and the technical constraints are not as rigid as Art Blocks which, in turn, allows for more experimentation with external code libraries. Perhaps the most widely admired of art projects to come out of fxhash is *Garden, Monoliths* (2022) by the French artist zancan. The 255 plotter works utilize the external *grass.js* algorithm. In contrast to most digitally native projects, the project includes paper types as one of its rarity traits and can be ordered as a plotted print on the artist's website. As noted by art historian A. V. Marraccini, the generated blades of grass and foliage peeking out among abstract rock structures "defy the now-dated expectation of somehow 'looking algorithmic,' seemingly composed with a painterly eye to balance and density."[43] Inspired by Hieronymus Cock's (1518–1570) series such as *Ruins of Rome* [03.24], yet equally the long-held ideas essential to Japanese gardens, the works stand as a strong counterpoint to the idea of algorithmic as hard-edged or the digital as non-lyrical. As with *Lushtemples* (2021) [03.25], in zancan's thinking of their physical output, the works are a prime example of the experimentation happening in the ecosystem's relationship between digital-native work and the physical art object. Increasingly those boundaries are collapsing.

In the short timespan of NFTs, the innovations surrounding the blockchain have produced a fruitful foundation in which algorithmic art has blossomed. Through a growing critical and curatorial apparatus, algorithmic art is starting to be placed in more intentional settings, often physical and increasingly noncommercial, where the work has space to breathe away from the marketplace floor. Curatorial developments from within the NFT space, led by NFT native curators such Jesse Damiani, Clara Che Wei Peh, Kate Hannah, Jason Bailey, Micol Ap, Georg Bak, and myself, are now being mirrored with increasing engagement within institutions settings. Pace Gallery has developed an ongoing collaboration with Art Blocks, institutional shows of algorithmic art such as Nina Roehrs's *Do Your Own Research*

[43] A. V. Marraccini, "On The New Evolution of Generative Art," *Right Click Save*, February 11, 2022, https://www.rightclicksave.com/article/on-the-new-evolution-of-generative-art.

**03.25**
zancan
*Lushtemples — Highlights of the Hike & Lushtemples — The Lightweight of Balance,* 2021
grass.js
Tezos, KT1MEEn4SZ7fD5c4FKXf68hZoWjtwcf4EGLg, 567684 & 12

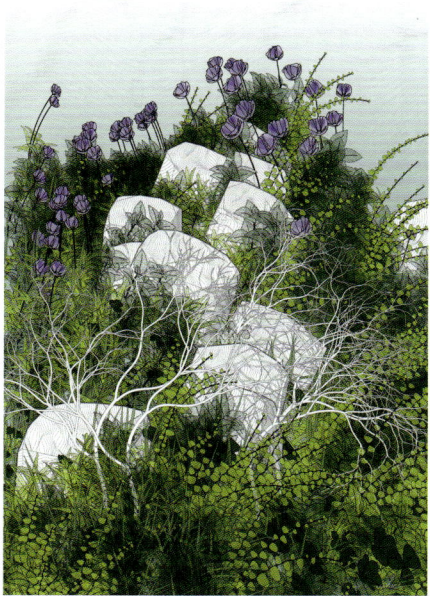 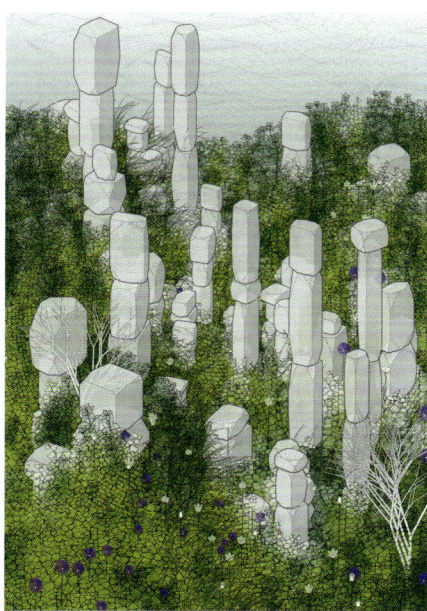

at the Kunsthalle Zurich in 2022, recent commitments to collecting and research programs on art and technology at the Museum of Modern Art and the Guggenheim in New York all point to strong critical headwinds for the algorithmic art community over the decades to come.

The increasing prominence of blockchain-based algorithmic art within contemporary art means this vital history is being given new critical and commercial attention, raising generations of pioneers, from Nees to Noll to Molnar and Schwartz, that this essay explores to wider prominence. The strong lineage and history within algorithmic art are a testament to the deep foundations that contemporary algorists stand on. These histories and the conceptual rigor they impart on this new generation of algorists are in turn influencing the production of stronger more conceptually nuanced algorithmic work. Projects such as Harm van den Dorpel's *Mutant Garden Seeders* (2021), in which the algorithmic schema is interwoven with a 1999 algorithm titled Cartesian Genetic Programming, in which not just the data but the code itself mutates over time. The on-chain work is responsive to the blockchain itself, mutating based on discrete periods of block time to create a living, mutating artwork, in which its full existence is archived and memorialized on and through the blockchain. Elsewhere, Tyler Hobbs and Indigo Mané's *QQL* (2022) is creating a more decentralized approach to algorithmic art, allowing the community and the collector to mint their own output from the algorithm designed by the artists. This type of collaboration draws the histories of relational art that are so woven into the wider performative qualities of NFTs more explicitly into the algorists' skill set. Mathcastles's *Terraforms* (2021) suggests further avenues to explore in their combination of community participation with the creation of the Hypercastle (an ideology influenced by the seminal *Loot* project), and the idea of algorithmic land art and speculative metaverse spaces. These recent projects that seek to combine smart contracts, time, performative participation, blockchain aesthetics, and the metaverse within algorithmic projects point to a conceptual maturing of the current algorithmic art space, where formal concerns are starting to be combined with deep conceptual engagement. As the conversations around algorithmic art continue to strengthen across intellectual (de) centers, it is vital for the community to come together and consider the implications around the evolving taxonomy around computer-generated art. Though the abstraction of code leverages concern around creativity, it is more important than ever to remember: algorithms are not a replacement of human creativity, they are an extension of it.

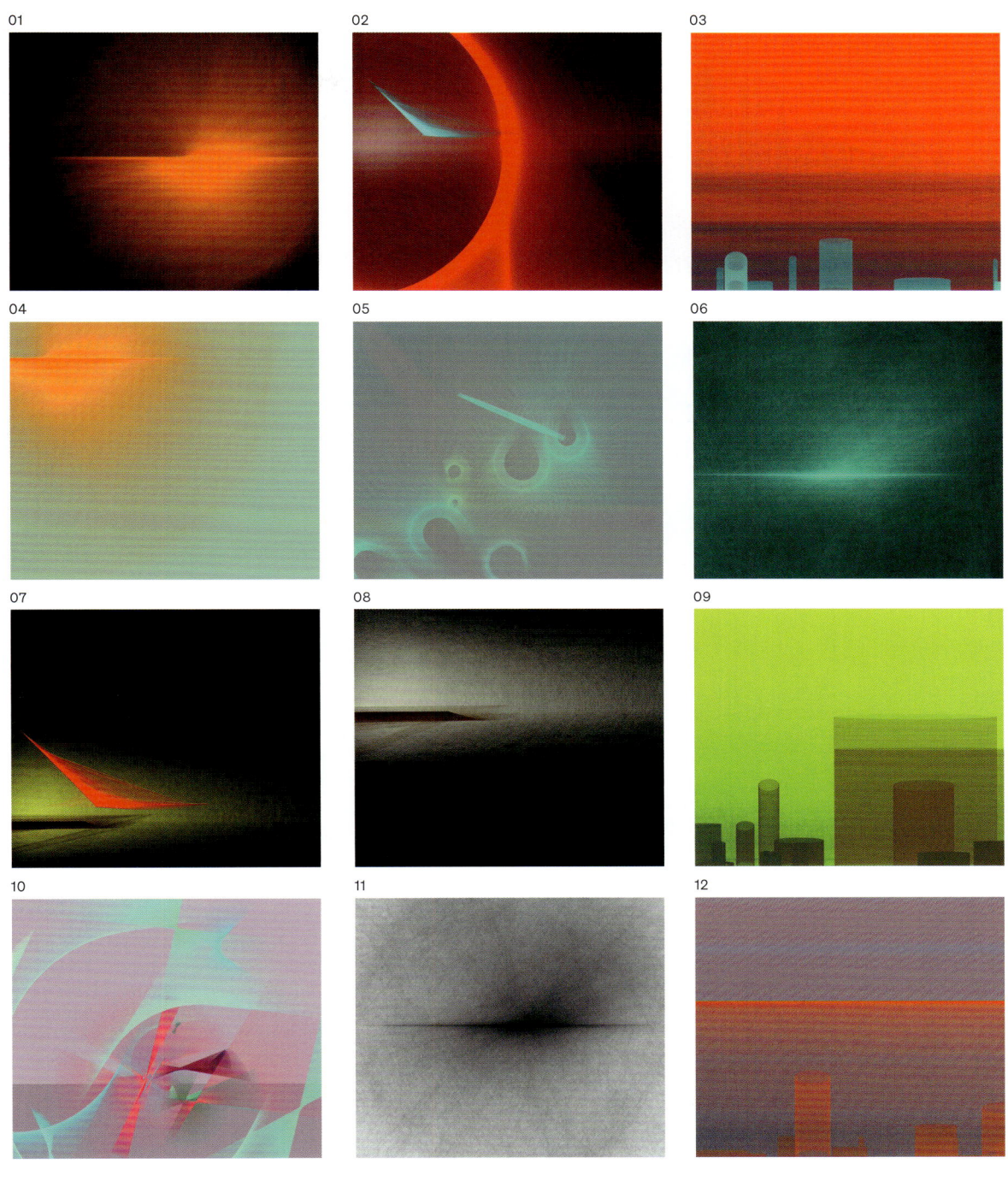

| # | TITLE | TIMESTAMP | MEDIUM | CHAIN | CONTRACT ADDRESS | TOKEN ID | EDITION SIZE | COLLABORATORS |
|---|---|---|---|---|---|---|---|---|
| 01–12 | **horizon(te)s** | 07-11-2022 17:00:14 | p5.js | XTZ | KT1U6EHmNxJTkvaWJ4ThczG4FSDaHC21ssvi | 975739–1097440 | 1/1 of 400 | Zach Lieberman |
| 13 | **Hypothetically Macro** | 01-19-2022 04:45:27 | p5.js | BTM | aWDT2s4Lba3rrBtqLghY61PLr2-gLZuvSy9uvXRmwLmhAixXuNa | b4ff...9b21-54a4...46d5 | 100, +1 AP | – |

EDITIONS ILLUSTRATED: (01) #56, (02) #79, (03) #108, (04) #114, (05) #171, (06) #197, (07) #376, (08) #214, (09) #244, (10) #336, (11) #320, (12) #322

# ISKRA VELITCHKOVA

### BULGARIA 1988

13

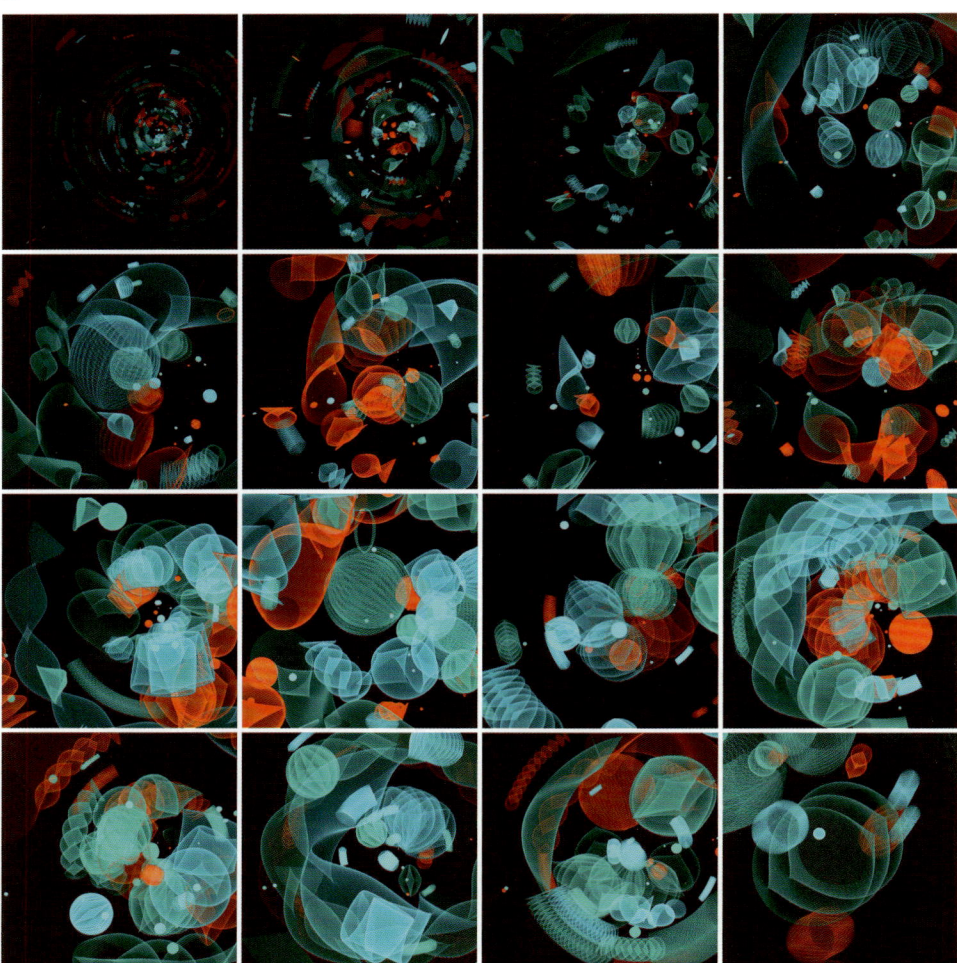

Iskra Velitchkova is a Bulgarian artist currently based in Madrid. Her work explores the present and potential interactions between humans and machines and how instead of making technology more human, this relationship can push us to understand our limits better. Her work is based on mixed techniques, combining digital formats and physical nature. From physical to digital and back, she fuses technology to discover and color to express. She believes that roots and tradition can nurture her work with greater truth.

I discovered Iskra's work in 2021; it immediately appealed to me, standing out from the rest. I resonated with her images on an emotional level, which is rare. All varied as a contrast of meditative, poetic and full of second meanings works with the twist of unique colors. *Hypothetically Macro* (2021) is a beautiful example of Iskra's infinite imagination and excellent programming skills to explore several variations of a single visual theme, playing with colors and biomorphic forms to creating unique patterns.

*Hypothetically Macro* is a mysterious cluster of glowing semi-transparent organic primitives. She leverages the Processing pro-gramming, playing masterfully with shapes and patterns. The grid reads almost like a storyboard propelling us through a single eco-system, frame by frame, of images that could just as easily be on the other side of a microscope as they could a telescope.

In 2022, she released *horizon(te)s*, a generative art collaboration with Zach Lieberman on fxhash where the two artists combined their style and approach to create subtle light geometric composi-tions organized around the concept of the horizon. They each cre-ated a series of works personally responding to the prompt as well as imagining how the other might respond. As such, the project uses the horizon as a conceptual guideline that suggests the borders of vision and subjectivity, inviting each artist to expand their practice through mimesis and reflexivity.

**KATE VASS**
FOUNDER & CURATOR OF
KATE VASS GALERIE, ZURICH

01

02

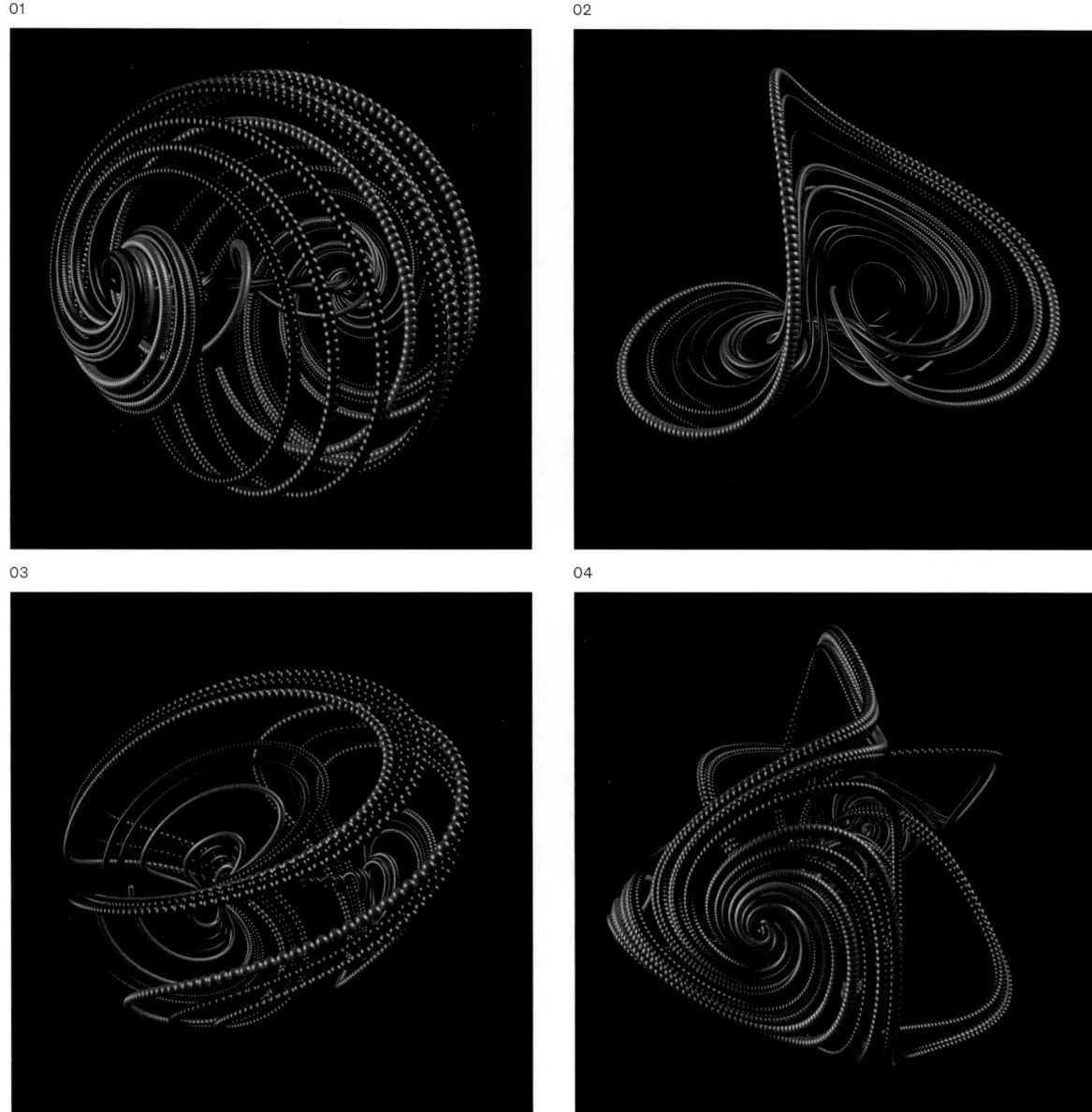

03

04

| # | TITLE | TIMESTAMP | MEDIUM | CHAIN | CONTRACT ADDRESS | TOKEN ID | EDITION SIZE |
|---|---|---|---|---|---|---|---|
| 01–04 | **Hashtractors** | 06-16-2022 07:10:38 | p5.js | ETH | 0xa7d8d9ef8d8ce8992df33d8b8cf4aebabd5bd270 | 90000000–90000127 | 1/1 of 128 |
| 05–06 | **Pigments** | 08-04-2021 20:20:36 | GLSL, Three.js | ETH | 0xa7d8d9ef8d8ce8992df33d8b8cf4aebabd5bd270 | 129000000–129001023 | 1/1 of 1,024 |

EDITIONS ILLUSTRATED: (01) #0, (02) #356, (03) #788

# DARIEN BRITO

ECUADOR 1987

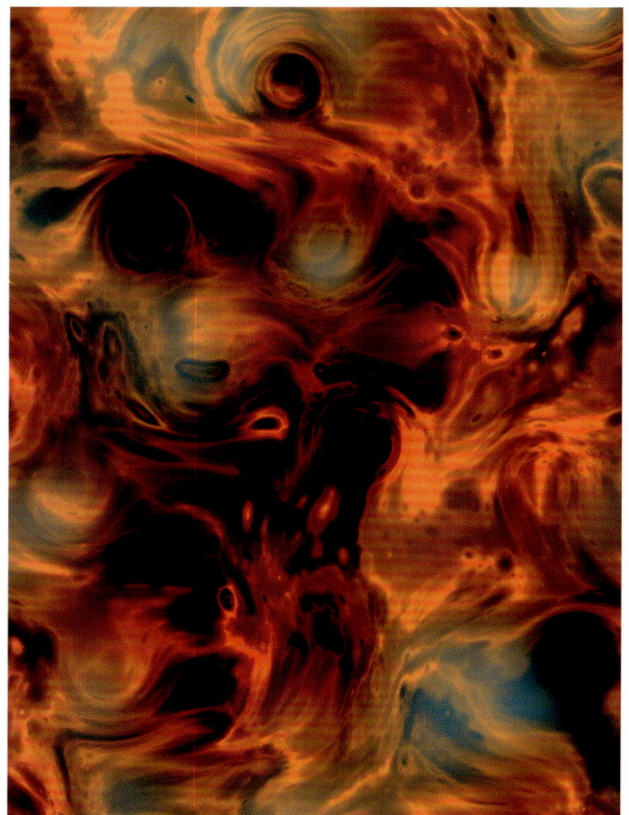

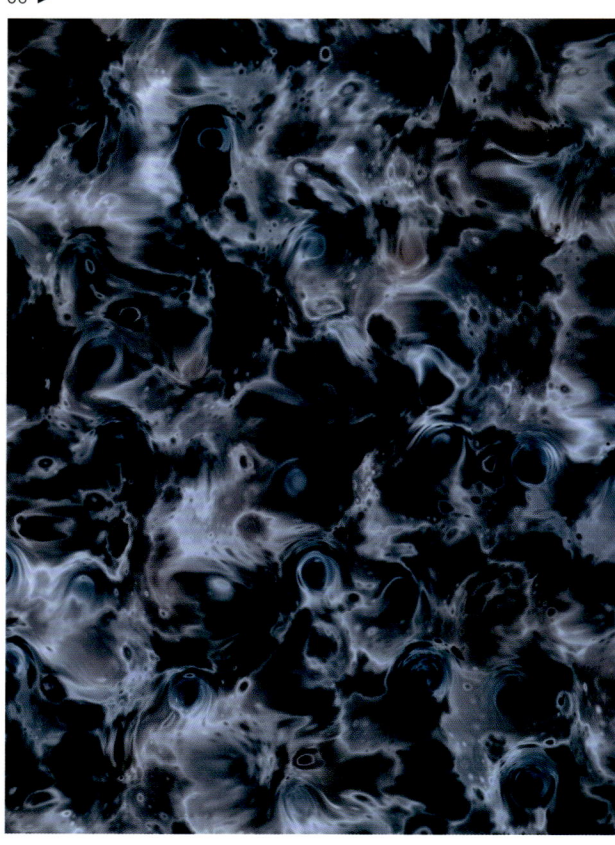

"Se podrá ver por siempre
la inacabable ola marina
esa gema de rara belleza
la fibra vegetal en su nuclear misterio
la minería líquida
— cromática del fuego y del agua —
un océano inmenso de nubes en la bóveda celeste
el algoritmo, la trama, el juego de los dioses"

**MARLO BRITO**
THE ARTIST'S FATHER

In May 2021, I emailed Darien Brito regarding his first application to Art Blocks called *Hashtractors* (2021). Holding an undergraduate degree in mathematics myself, I was immediately drawn to the generative three-dimensional renderings based on strange attractors and chaos theory principles. The outputs were monochromatic, restrained, and let the beauty of the underlying equations shine through.

In July, Darien returned with his next Art Blocks project *Pigments* (2021), and I was pleasantly surprised with the new aesthetic direction. While *Hashtractors* was grayscale, three-dimensional, and static, *Pigments* was full of color, two-dimensional, and animated. But one could still sense the underlying mathematics at work in what appeared to be simulations of fluid dynamics in the middle of an abstract oil painting. With the continued elevation of his generative work, *Pigments* was selected to be part of the curated collection at Art Blocks.

I had the privilege of learning more about Darien in the run up to the release of *Pigments*. Ecuadorian by birth, residing in the Netherlands, his educational background was actually in music composition. As I learned more about his creative history, it was clear to me that Darien was a polymath whose curiosity and programming skills could be directed toward any number of artistic endeavors including sound, image, and performance.

With each new project, Darien breaks new ground and stretches himself as an artist. I look forward to being continuously surprised and delighted each time Darien shares his next prototype with me.

**JEFF DAVIS**
ARTIST, CCO OF ART BLOCKS,
AND FOUNDER OF DAVIS EDITIONS

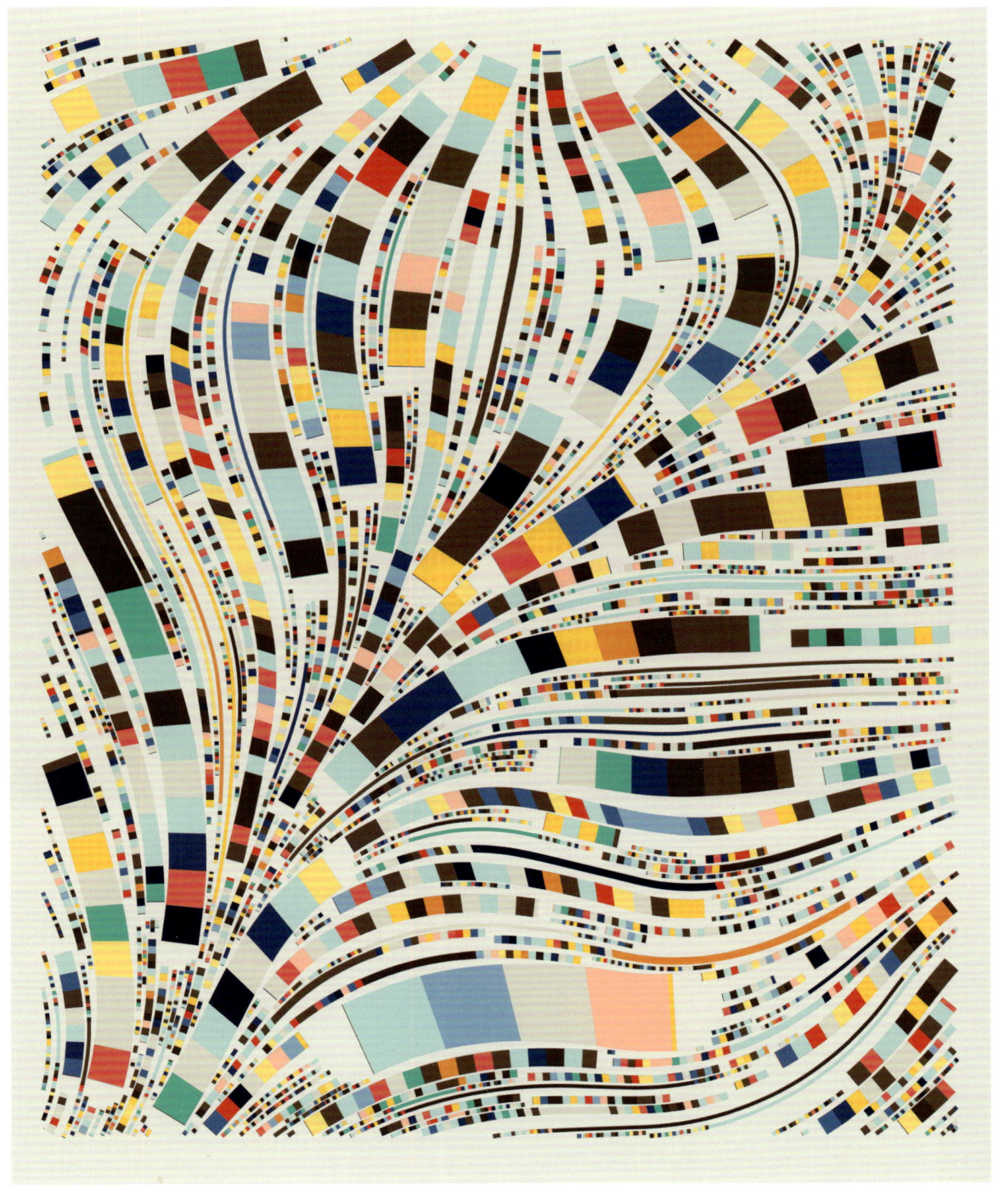

| # | TITLE | TIMESTAMP | MEDIUM | CHAIN | CONTRACT ADDRESS | TOKEN ID | EDITION SIZE |
|---|-------|-----------|--------|-------|-----------------|----------|--------------|
| 01–20 | **Fidenza** | 06-03-2021 16:04:28 | p5.js | ETH | 0xa7d8d9ef8d8ce8992df33d8b8cf4aebabd5bd270 | 78000000–78000998 | 1/1 of 999 |

EDITIONS ILLUSTRATED: (01) #313, (02) #607, (03) #9, (04) #97, (05) #163, (06) #204, (07) #247, (08) #612, (09) #410, (10) #430, (11) #438, (12) #460, (13) #529, (14) #553, (15) #559, (16) #592, (17) #445, (18) #861, (19) #680, (20) #831

02

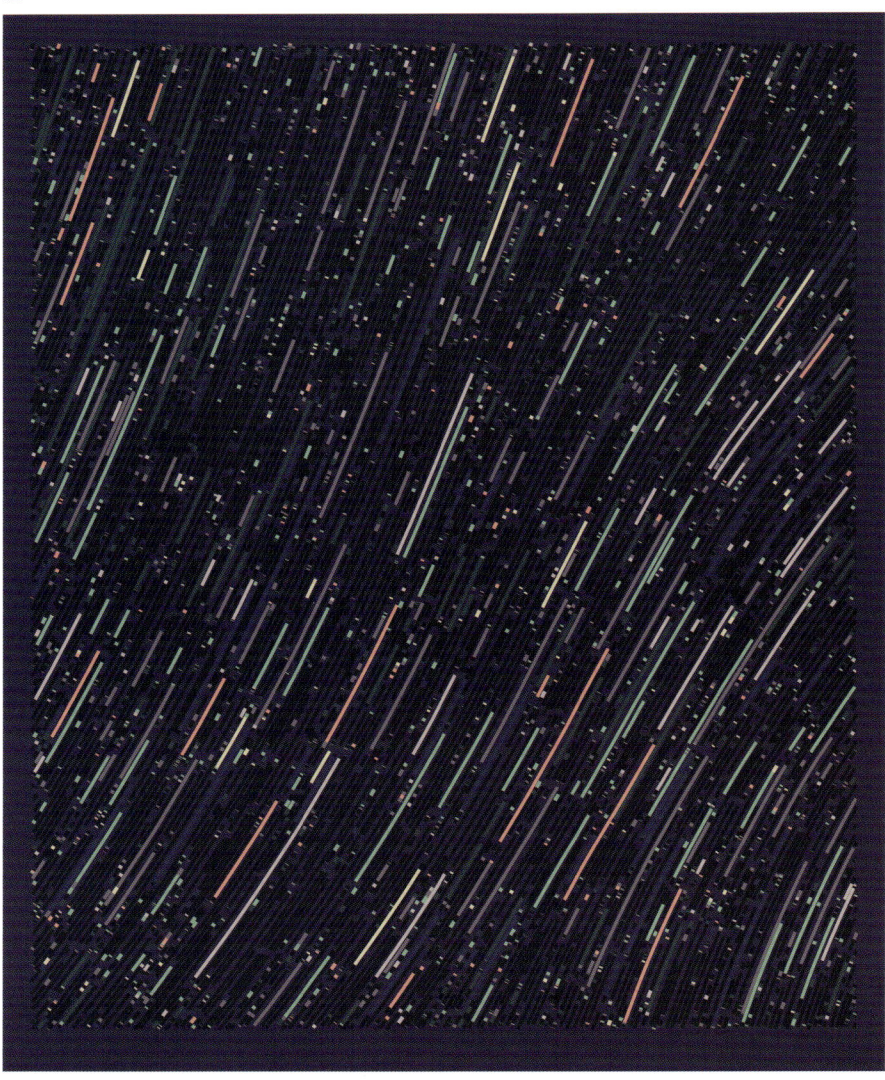

Tyler Hobbs studied drawing and painting from childhood. In college at UT Austin, he majored in computer science, working afterward as a software engineer at a cutting-edge database company. In his mid-20s, he began to make generative art. Along with his skills in art and programming, he brought to that medium a radical approach to craft: rather than reusing others' code, he implements his own algorithms whenever possible.

Whereas his work in traditional media was mostly figurative, in generative art Hobbs turned toward abstraction. At times, the colors and forms of his early generative work seem inspired by the hills and grasses of the Central Texas landscape near which he's spent most of his life.

In 2021, Hobbs released Fidenza. While he had been successfully making generative art for seven years, this was his first long-form work. Previously, he had suggested presenting, at most, three outputs from a generative project. The heart of the Fidenza algorithm is a flow field — itself a technique he popularized.

Within a canvas of randomly simulated, fluid-like motion, the algorithm lays down long, colorful bars that bend, warp, and swirl. Incorporating know-how from his past work, these shapes appear in a synergistic variety of palettes, textures, scales, and arrangements. The result is that when you look at a page of Fidenzas, they're all different: each one a geometric dance captured midframe, holding its own abstract beauty.

Altogether, *Fidenza*'s set of 999 images, teeming with life, is the portrait of an algorithm. Yet it also reaches outside the computer. A few hundred lines of code somehow speak to a range of expressionist work from Joan Mitchell to Wassily Kandinsky, from gestural to hard-edged abstraction, and build upon them. *Fidenza* is a masterpiece, and a now-canonical entry in the new practice of long-form generative art.

**ANDREW BADR**
INTERNET ARTIST

03

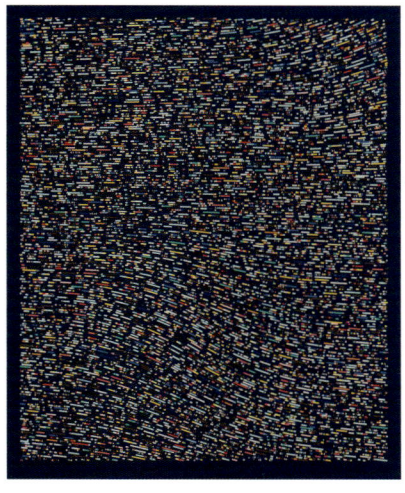

04

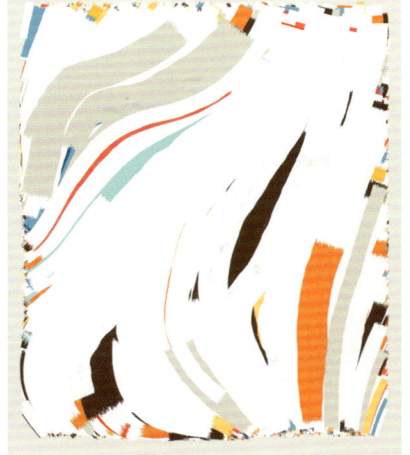

05

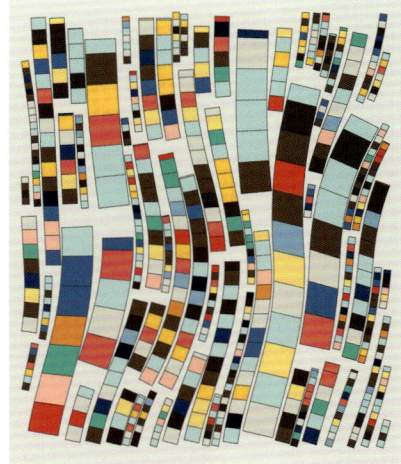

06

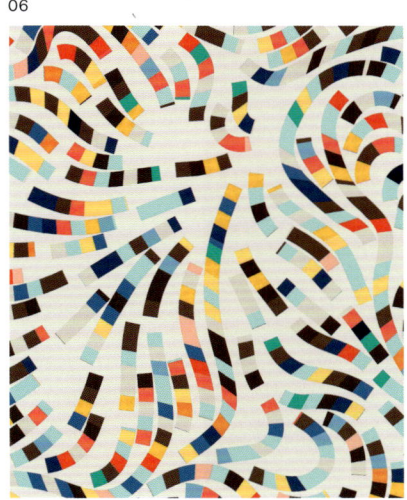

07

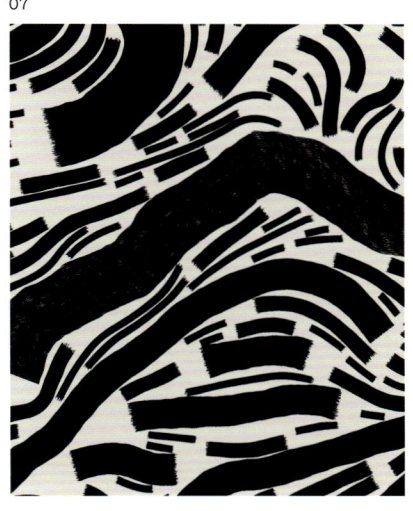

08

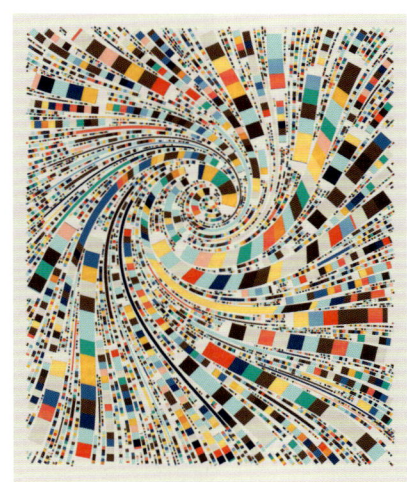

09

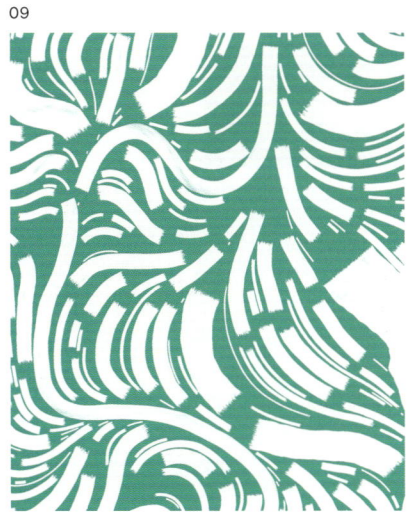

10

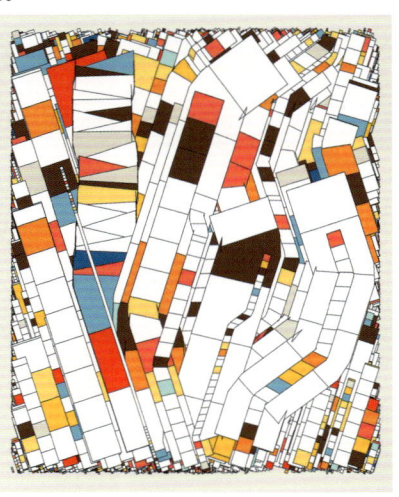

11

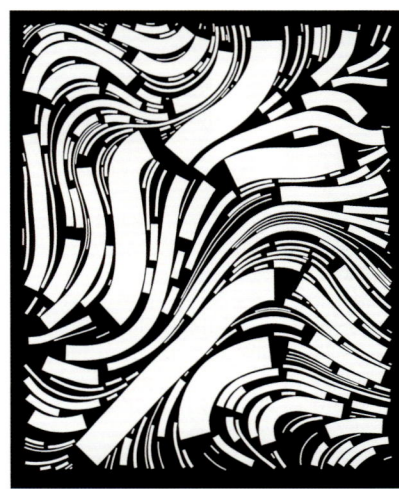

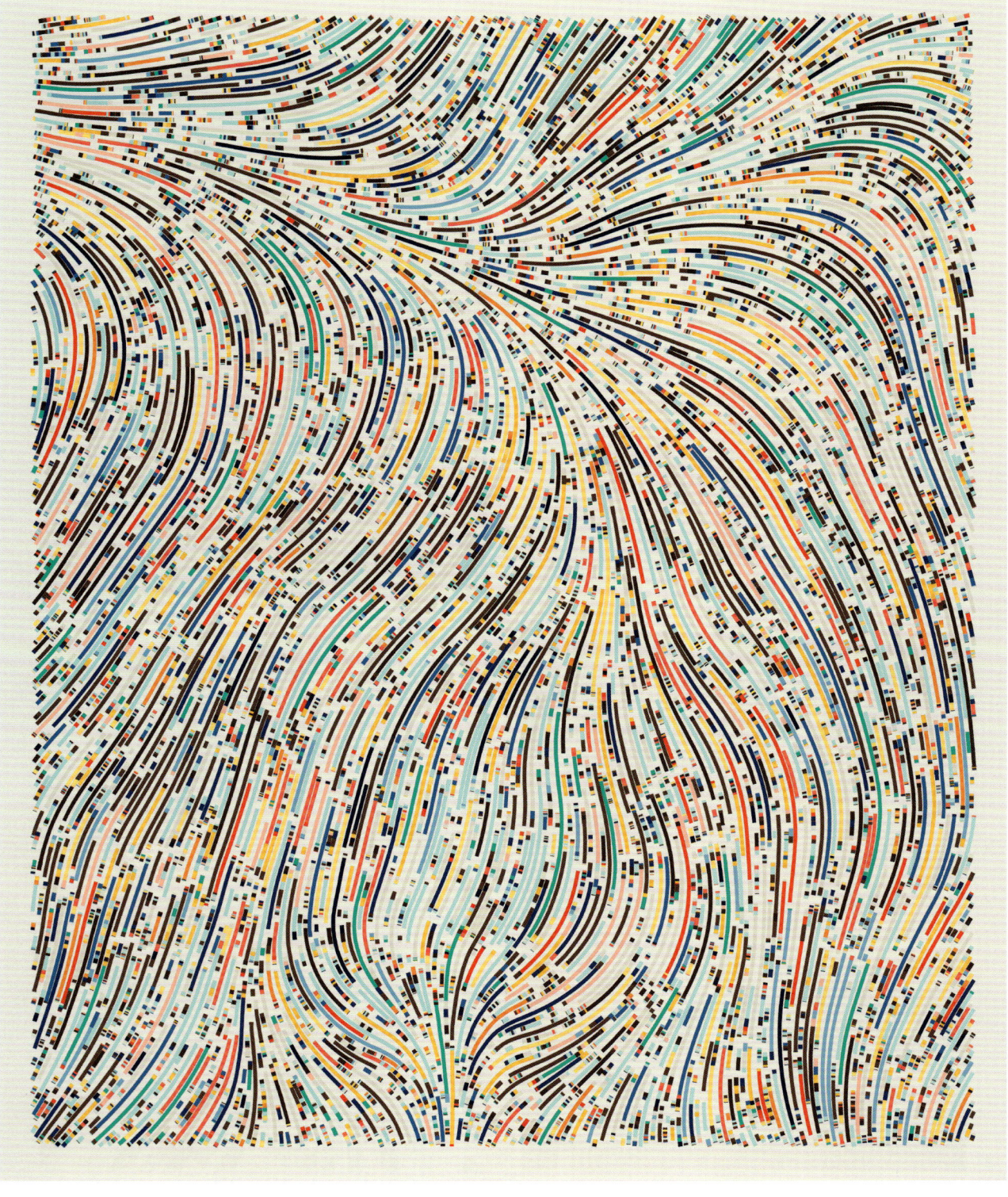

13

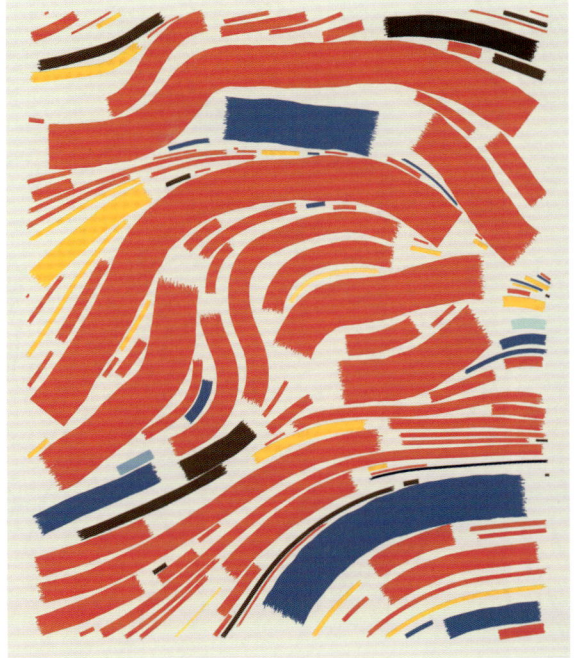

14

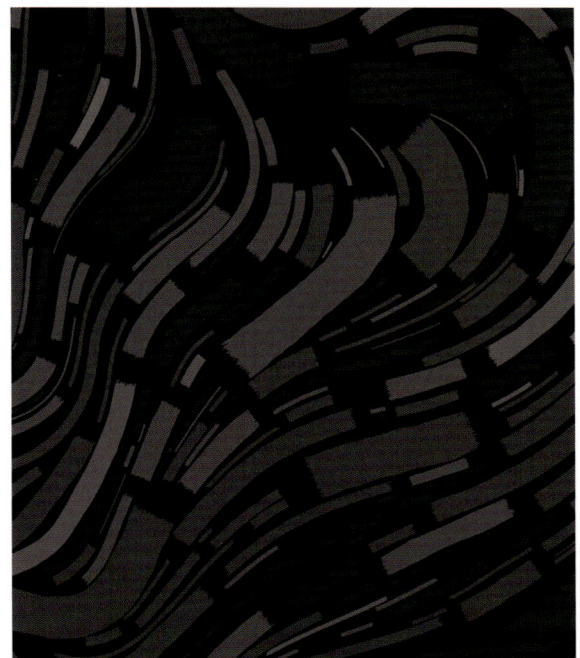

15

16

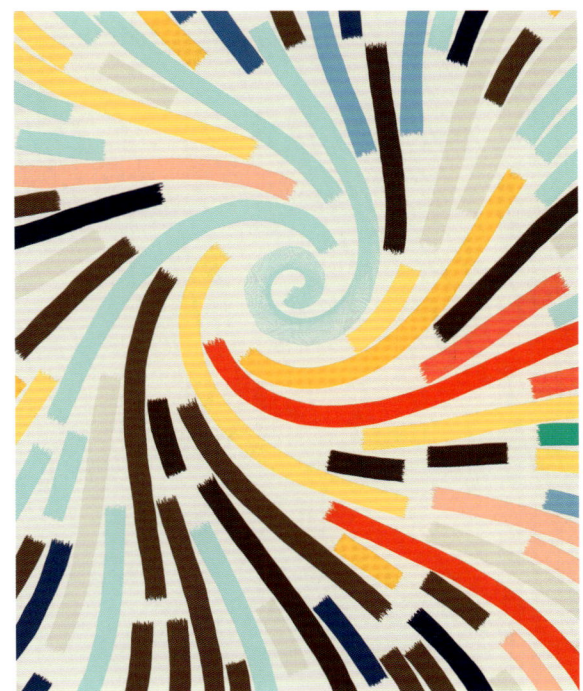

17

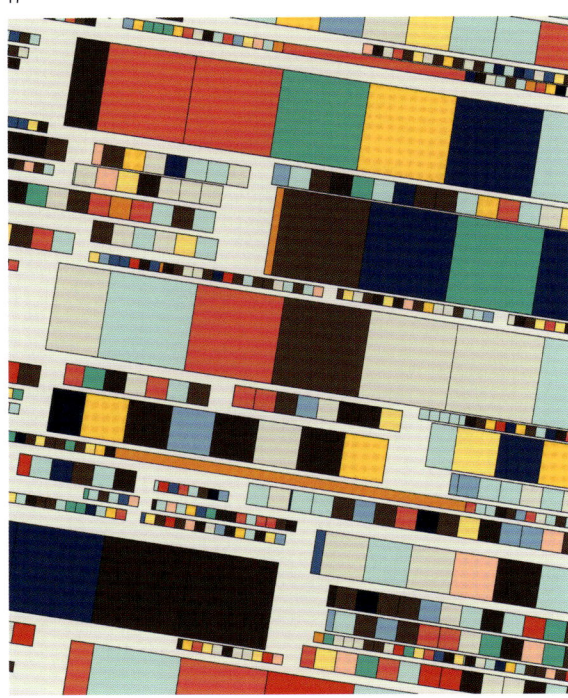

18

19

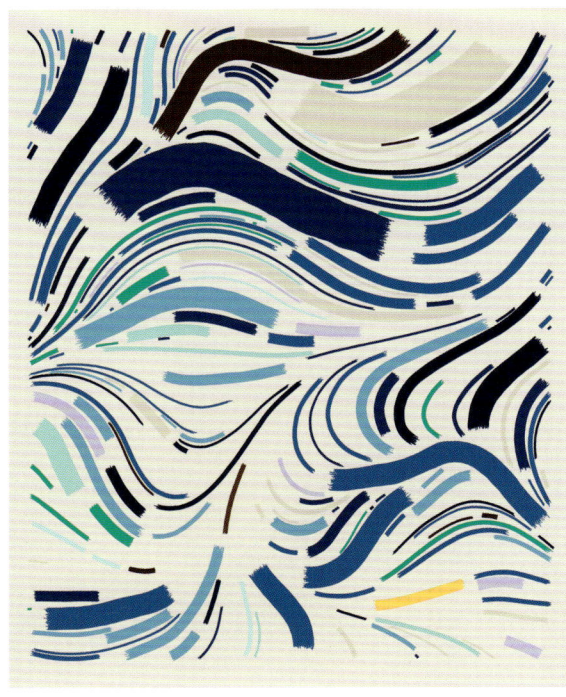

20

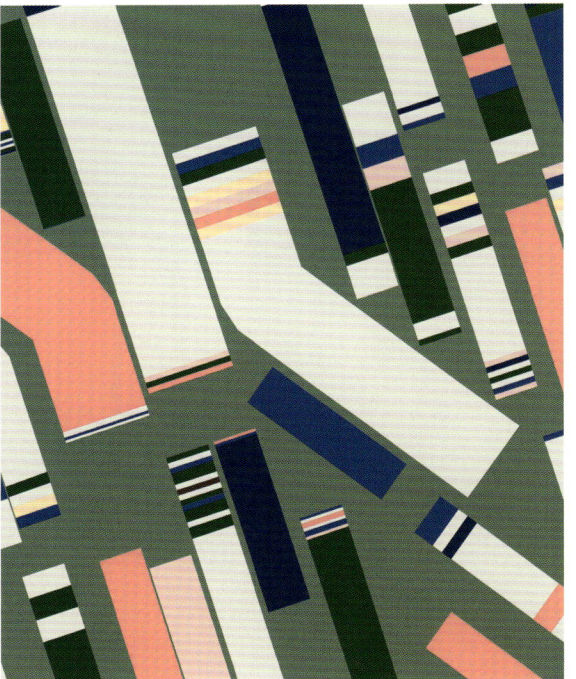

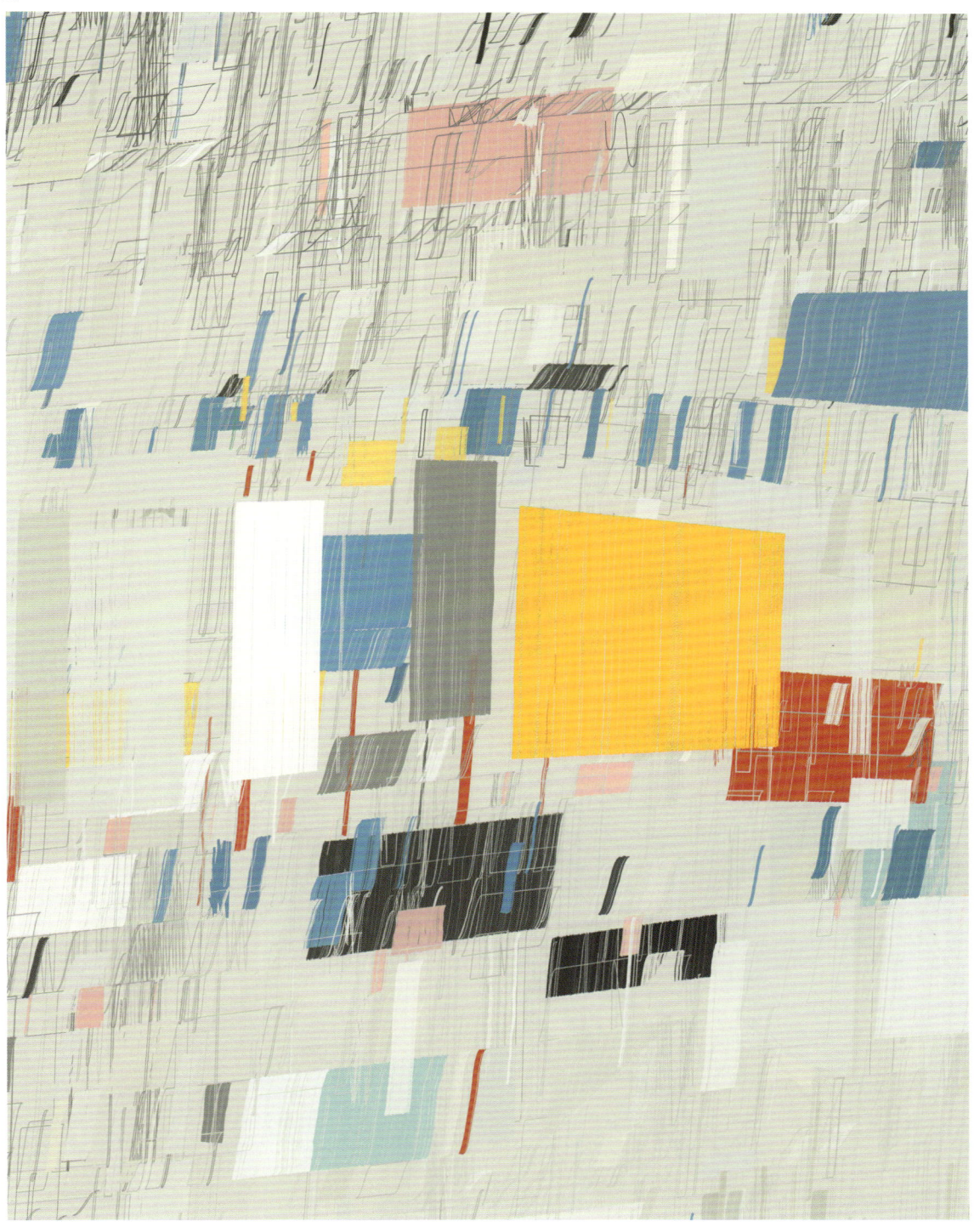

| # | TITLE | TIMESTAMP | MEDIUM | CHAIN | CONTRACT ADDRESS | TOKEN ID | EDITION SIZE | COLLABORATORS |
|---|---|---|---|---|---|---|---|---|
| 21 | **Incomplete Control** | 12-09-2021 20:40:12 | p5.js | ETH | 0xa7d8d9ef8d8ce8992df-33d8b8cf4aebabd5bd270 | 228000000–228000099 | 1/1 of 100 | – |
| 22 | **QQL** | 09-28-2022 04:46:47 | JavaScript, p5.js, Solidity | ETH | 0x845dd2a7ee2a92a0518-ab2135365ed63fdba0c88 | 1–999 | 1/1 of 999 | Indigo Mané |

EDITIONS ILLUSTRATED: (21) #90, (22) #65

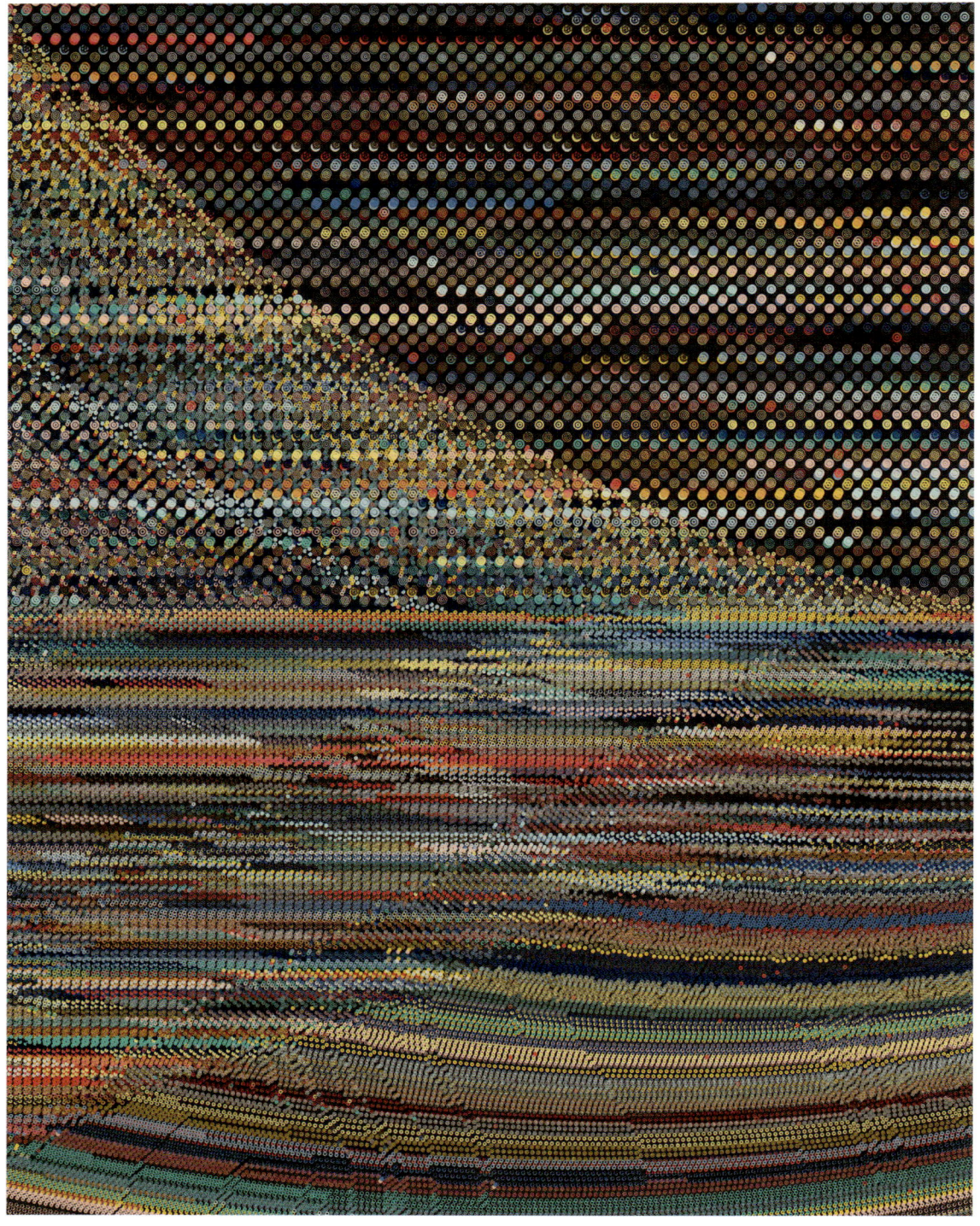

01

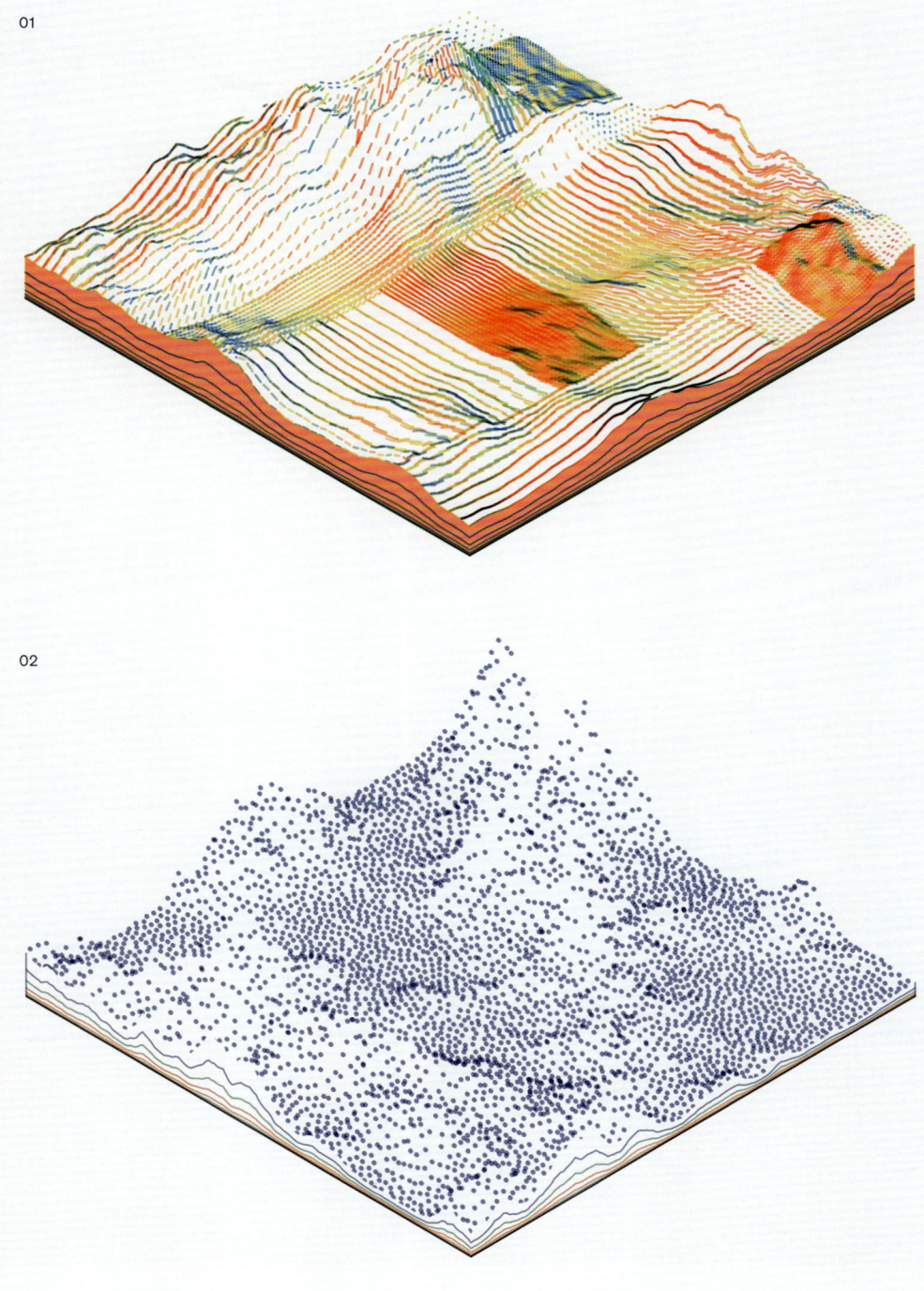

02

| # | TITLE | TIMESTAMP | MEDIUM | CHAIN | CONTRACT ADDRESS | TOKEN ID | EDITION SIZE |
|---|---|---|---|---|---|---|---|
| 01–06 | **Subscapes** | 04-22-2021 13:35:54 | JavaScript | ETH | 0xa7d8d9ef8d8ce8992df33d8b8cf4aebabd5bd270 | 53000000–53000649 | 1/1 of 650 |

EDITIONS ILLUSTRATED: (01) #3, (02) #367, (03) #532, (04) #468, (05) #452, (06) #92

# MATT DESLAURIERS

CANADA 1990

03

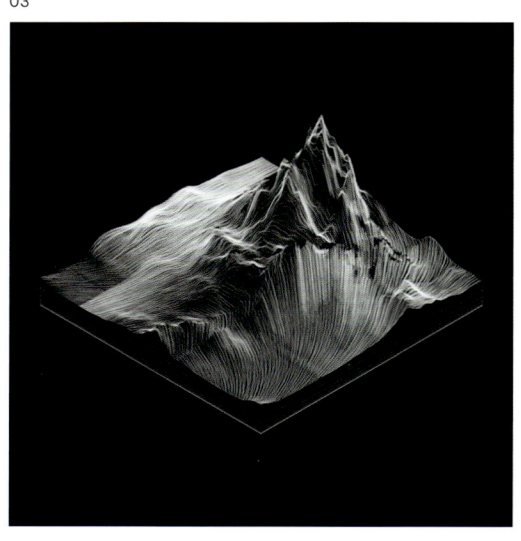

04

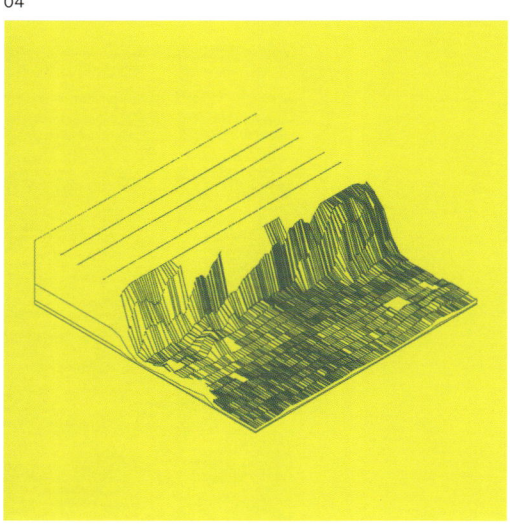

05

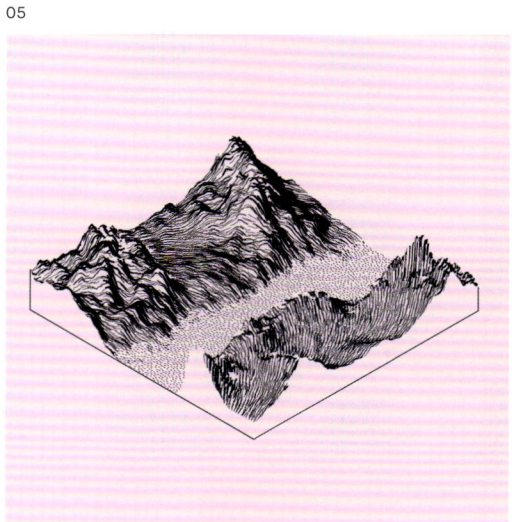

06

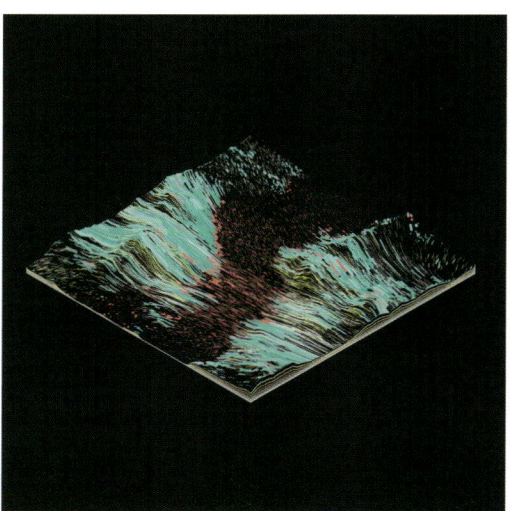

Matt DesLauriers is a Canadian-born artist and creative coder now living in London, United Kingdom. His interactive installations have been displayed all over the world, and he often lectures and teaches at universities and art schools. DesLauriers's practice precedes the NFT boom, and it is evident in the depth of his work how much consideration he gives to each generative piece, not only in terms of the online presence of single minted iteration, but as a body of work as a whole. Both *Subscapes* and *Meridian*, released on Art Blocks in 2021, consider what produces an individual semi-abstract landscape that has a striking visual presence, as well as the concept of the landscape as artistic form.

*Subscapes* is broadly topographic, with an isometric representation of a landscape in a square space on solid color ground. *Meridian* uses a less conventional poster-dimension rectangular format, allowing the suggestion of a mountainscape or horizon to emerge from layers of tiny hatched lines in a varying palette. *Subscapes*

mirrors the experience of a map or world display. *Meridian* mirrors the experience of the gaze of the viewer standing in the represented world. Taken together, the series of images test out the boundary cases of what constitutes a "landscape" to the eye, and what a coded algorithm — that uses a pseudorandom hash as a generative factor — can make that a single painterly image alone cannot reveal. DesLauriers uses code as medium to negotiate the landscape as representation hovering between the poles of map and territory.

**A. V. MARRACCINI**
ART HISTORIAN, CRITIC, AND POSTDOCTORAL RESEARCH FELLOW
ON BILDERFAHRZEUGE PROJECT AT THE WARBURG INSTITUTE,
UNIVERSITY OF LONDON

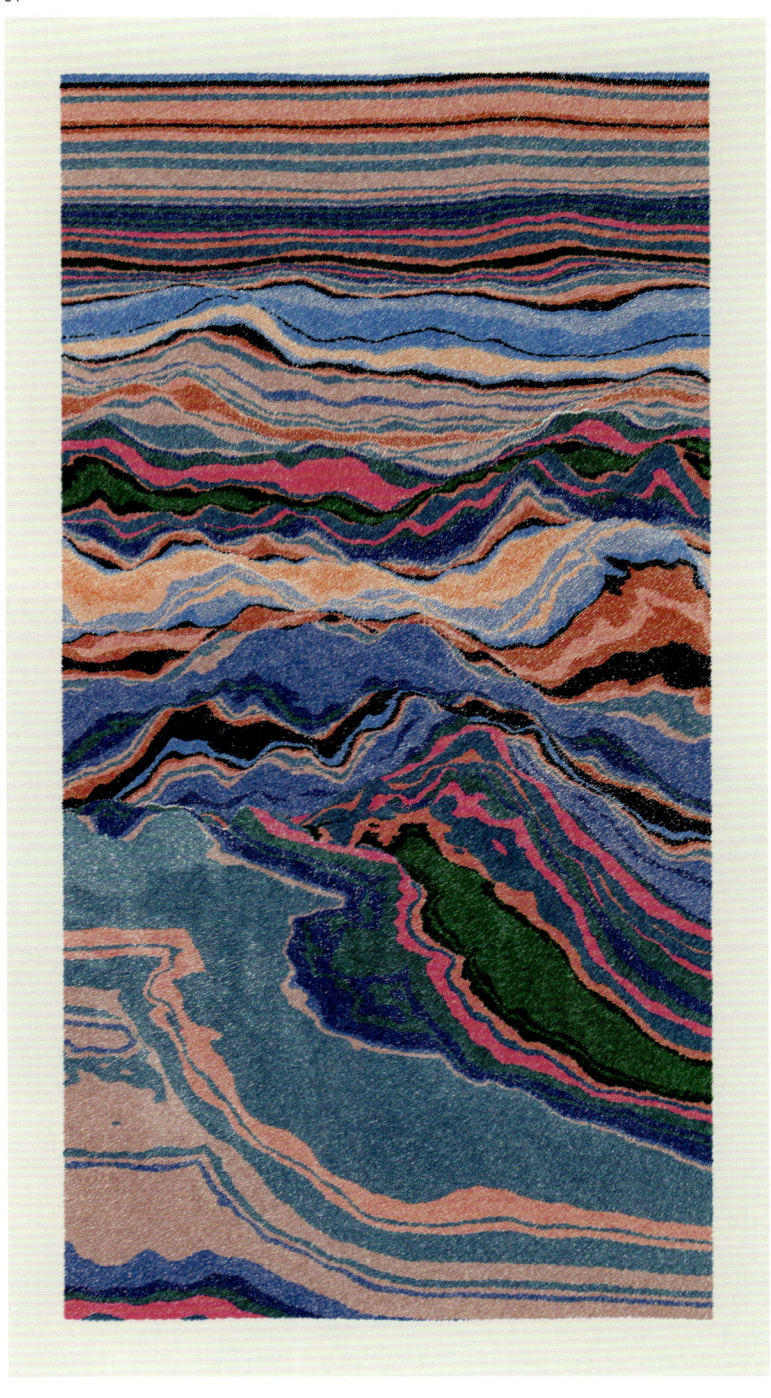

| # | TITLE | TIMESTAMP | MEDIUM | CHAIN | CONTRACT ADDRESS | TOKEN ID | EDITION SIZE |
|---|---|---|---|---|---|---|---|
| 07, 08 | **Meridian** | 09-17-2021 22:44:08 | JavaScript | ETH | 0xa7d8d9ef8d8ce8992df33d8b8cf4aebabd5bd270 | 163000000–163000999 | 1/1 of 1,000 |

EDITIONS ILLUSTRATED: (07) #225, (08) #638

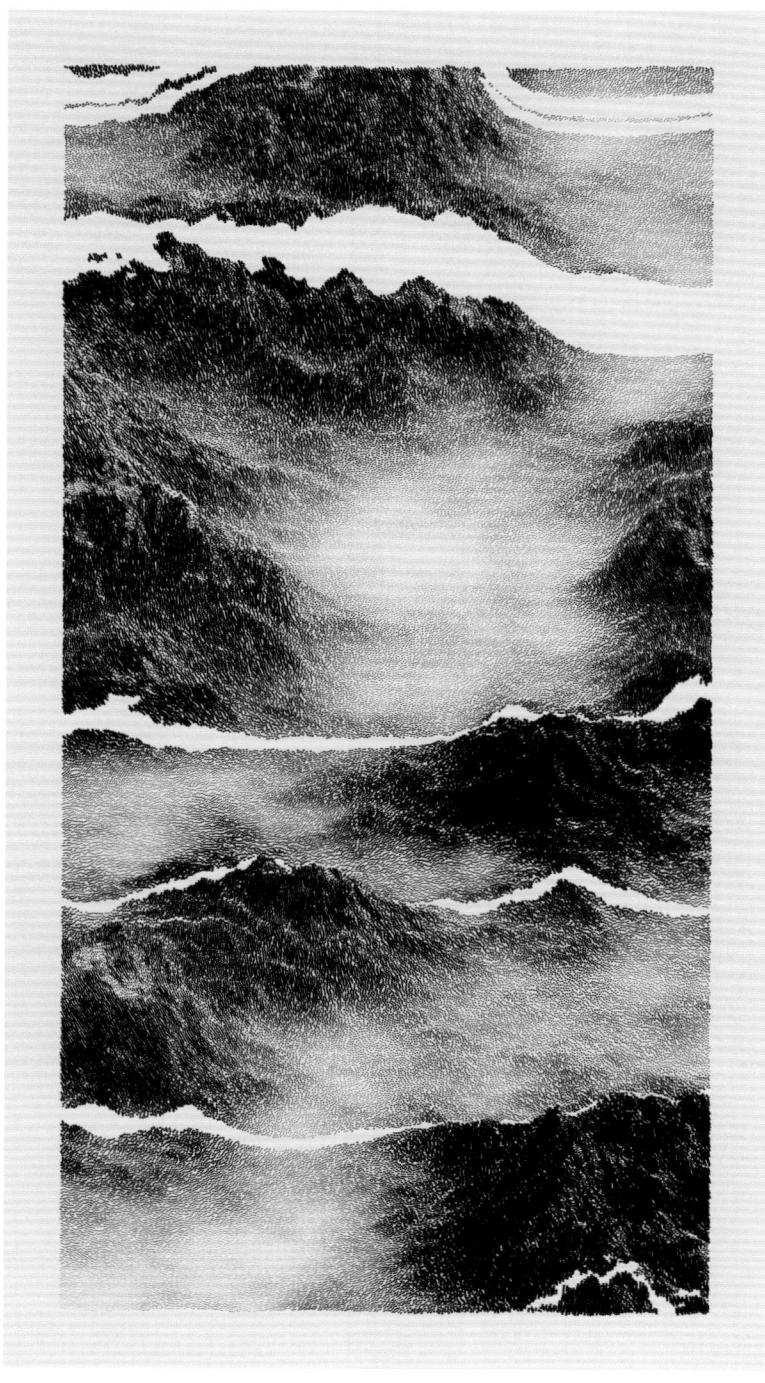

01

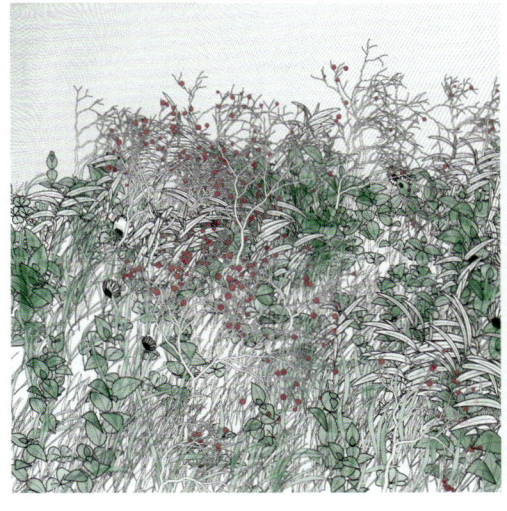

02

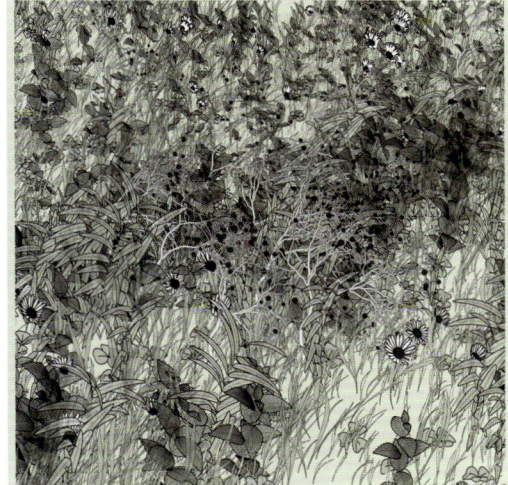

03

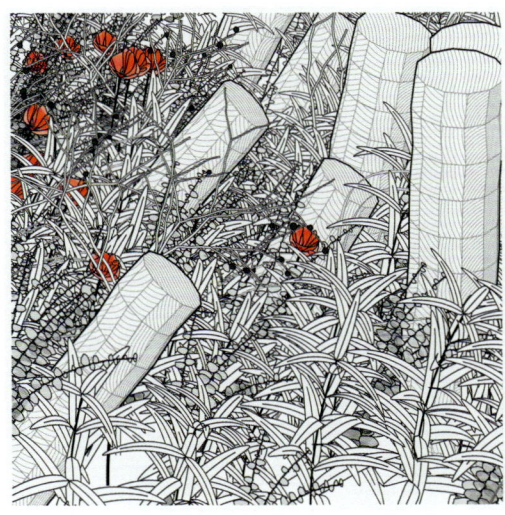

04

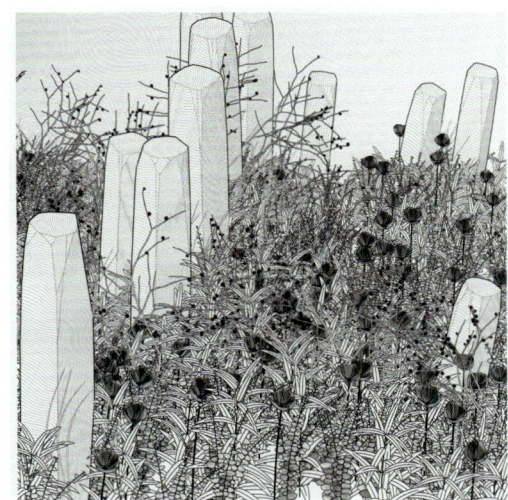

| # | TITLE | TIMESTAMP | MEDIUM | CHAIN | CONTRACT ADDRESS | TOKEN ID | EDITION SIZE |
|---|---|---|---|---|---|---|---|
| 01–05 | **Garden, Monoliths** | 12-09-2021 23:42:20 | Vanilla JS, grass.js | XTZ | KT1AEVuykWeuuFX7QkEAMNtffzwhe1Z98hJS | 145971–146247 | 1/1 of 255 |

EDITIONS ILLUSTRATED: (01) #1, (02) #115, (03) #105, (04) #27, (05) #166

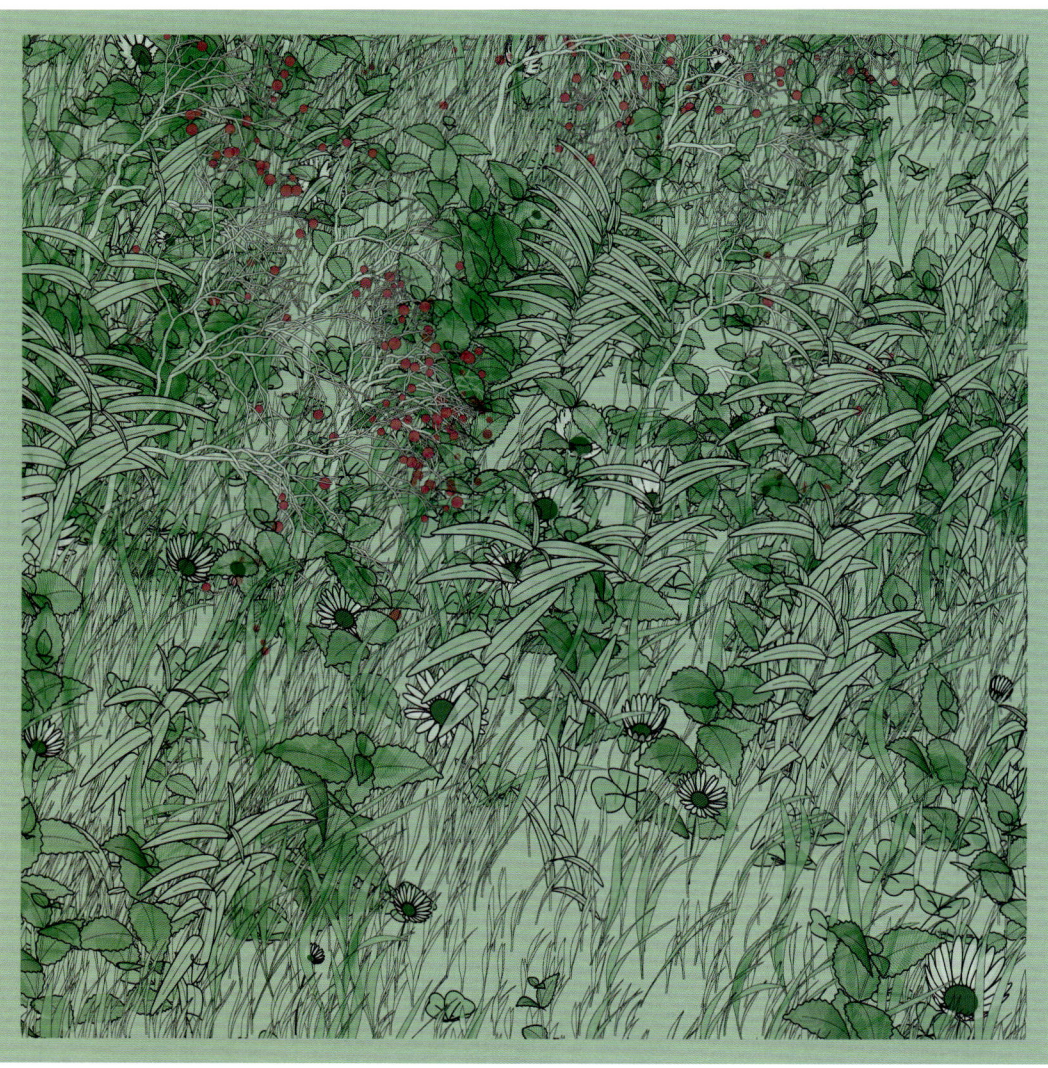

zancan's *Garden, Monoliths* (2021) are striking examples of a contemporary take on an age-long quest: to represent the natural world. And while anyone can see the visual beauty of the art and recognize the subject matter at hand, few may realize that forces of nature are being played out on a much more subtle and yet complex level. Indeed, it could be argued that nature is practically the genesis of these works because they are rooted in a medium that can simulate the natural structures they represent.

*Garden, Monoliths* are the result of a computer program. A textual description of a particular process from which can emerge myriad possibilities. It is quite extraordinary to the layperson to think that a formal computer language can produce such art. To the trained eye, it is also extraordinary to observe the algorithmic beauty being played out. One that can be attributed to mathematical theories that model the natural world but also can be applauded with zancan's mastery of the medium.

zancan is also an accomplished painter with a keen eye for symbolic meaning. Gardens are like a mirror image of society where the broader relationships between nature and culture can be expressed. This is in part the success of the series. It taps into the collective consciousness. The work touches us not only for its striking simplicity with pristine graphic lines, it equally explores a universal subject matter, echoing our fascination for the world around us but also our intervention within.

I like to think of this work as a contemporary take on the *Salon des Refusés*. A group of artists who seek not just recognition but also acceptance for their progressive art. It was a moment of contest with the established order and also the beginning for new aesthetic paths to explore. Where once the Impressionists sought to explore fleeting light and the impermanence of being, we have today artists exploring the algorithmic sublime and the permanence of the blockchain.

**MARK WEBSTER**
COMPUTATIONAL ARTIST AND TEACHER

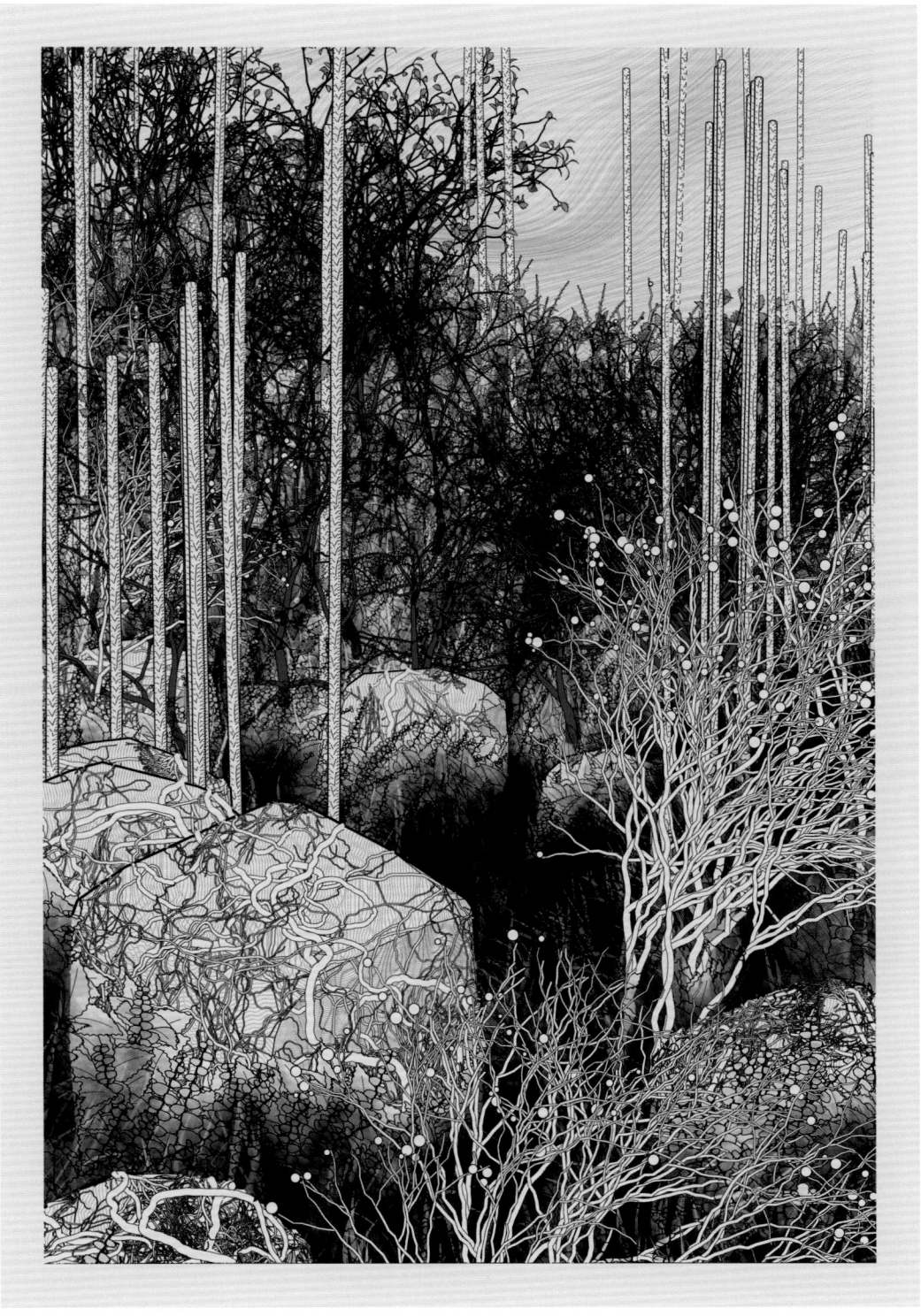

| # | TITLE | TIMESTAMP | MEDIUM | CHAIN | CONTRACT ADDRESS | TOKEN ID | EDITION SIZE |
|---|---|---|---|---|---|---|---|
| 06 | **Lushtemples – Ever Uncaged** | 12-17-2021 12:58:56 | JavaScript | XTZ | KT1RJ6PbjHpwc3M5rw5s2Nbmefwbuwbdxton | 590739 | 20 |
| 07 | **Rapture Captured** | 06-24-2022 16:46:03 | JavaScript | ETH | 0xec43e92046c1527586dfaf02031622c30af9a1d6 | 3454105788–3354727647 | 294 |

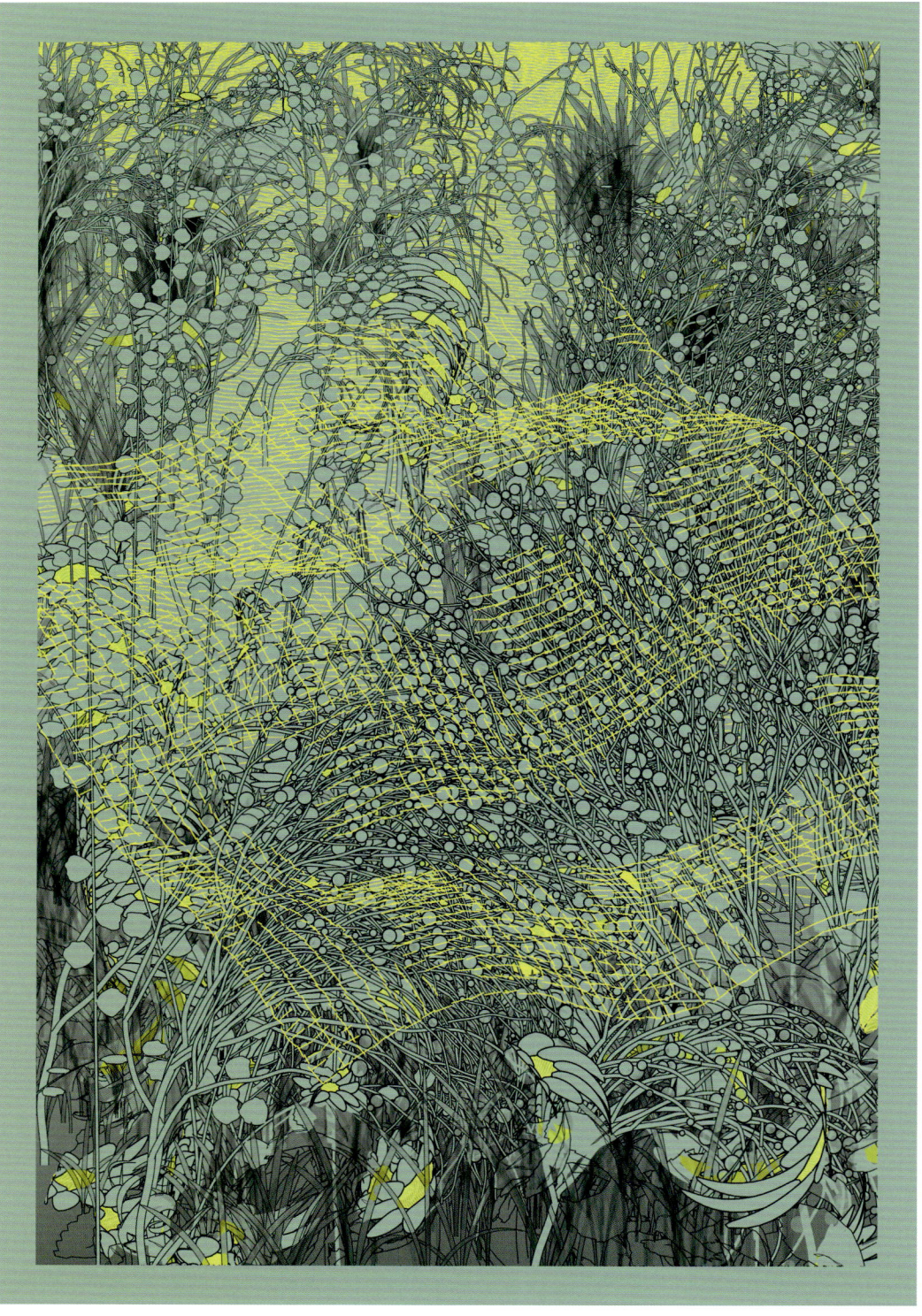

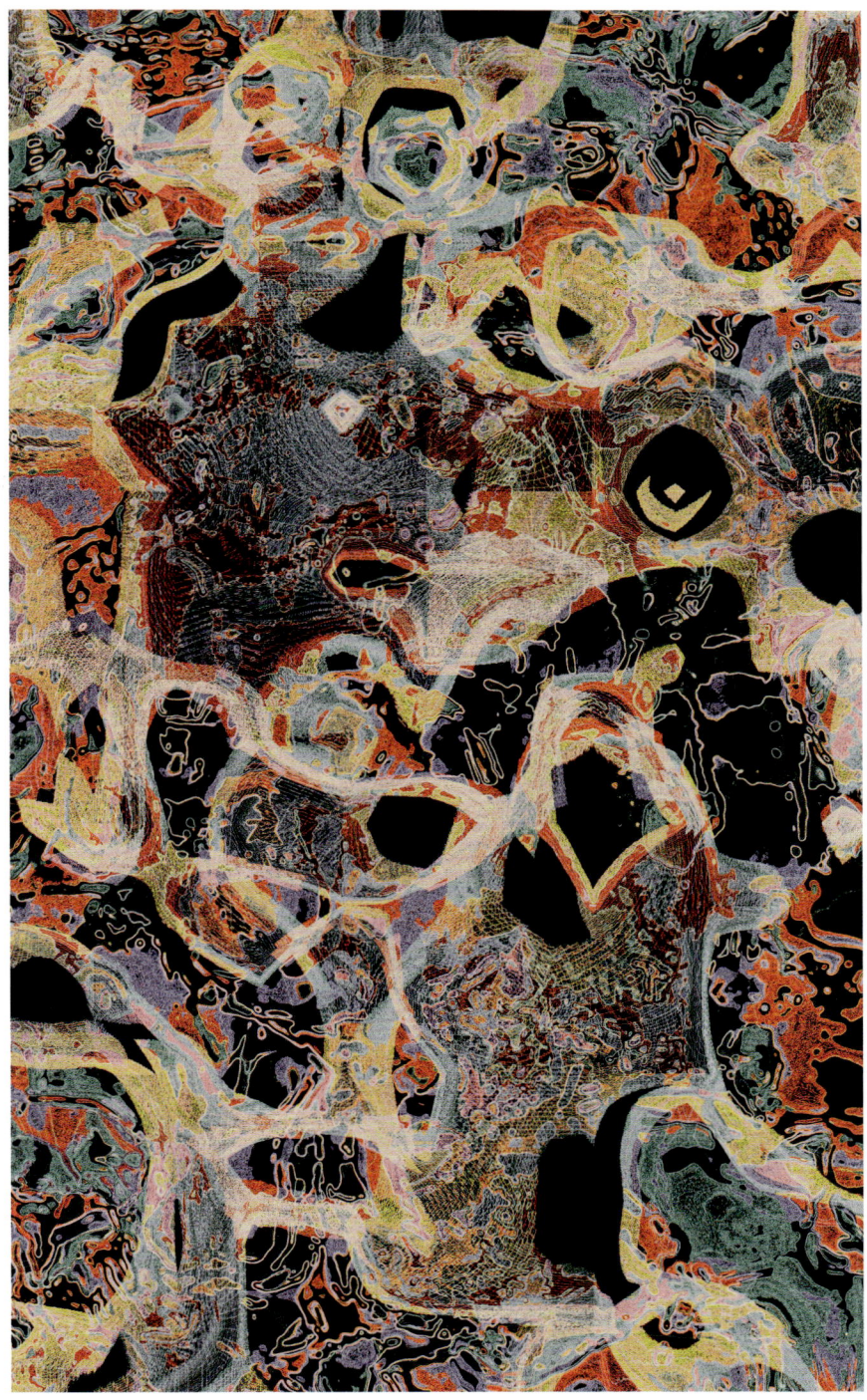

| # | TITLE | TIMESTAMP | MEDIUM | CHAIN | CONTRACT ADDRESS | TOKEN ID | EDITION SIZE |
|---|-------|-----------|--------|-------|------------------|----------|--------------|
| 01 | **220422w21qOd** | 06-27-2022 09:40:29 | C#, Unity | XTZ | KT1Q6zzt7Q4paFN6Rs5DNKcYqRRd5Y1caaub | 3 | 1/1 |
| 02 | **220324d13jKg** | 07-25-2022 22:58:29 | C#, Unity | XTZ | KT1Q6zzt7Q4paFN6Rs5DNKcYqRRd5Y1caaub | 0 | 1/1 |
| 03 | **MMZ 213** | 02-12-2022 04:12:34 | C#, Unity | XTZ | KT1RJ6PbjHpwc3M5rw5s2Nbmefwbuwbdxton | 669563 | 1/1 |

02

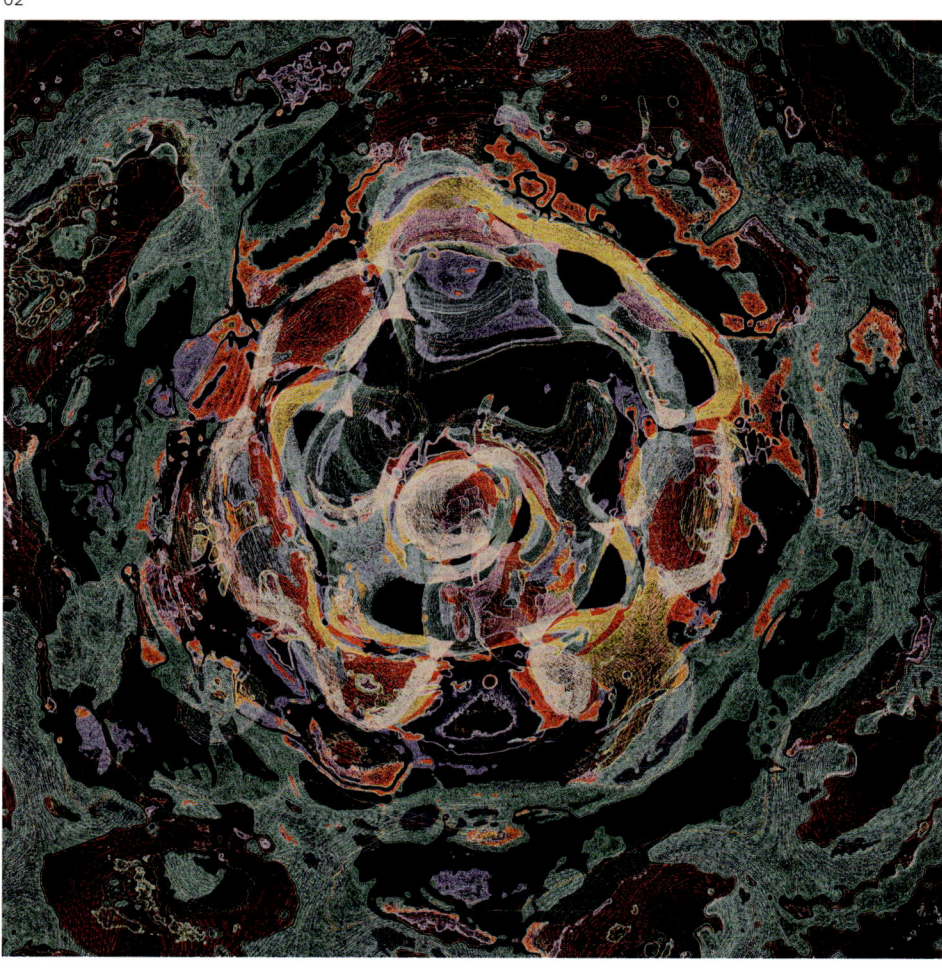

When it comes to our daily lives, structured around constant boundaries, social norms, and expectations, lines are everywhere. Tracing the genealogy of modern society, Michel Foucault (1926–1984) illuminates the moment when medieval towns, due to hasty spurring, abolished gatekeeping — the guards were made to shift their gaze out from the borders back into the inner streets.

For over a decade, boundaries have been a topic of study and captivation for Kazumasa Teshigawara (aka qubibi) — an artist, designer, and art university lecturer from Tokyo. His prior works with a unique algorithm gave birth to the famed series *MIMIZU* (Japanese: ミミズ, "earthworms"). *MIMIZU* (2021–22) emblematizes these borders, and weaves them into a "digital stitch" of worms that dance to the plentiful layers of vibrations, light, and music. Though inspired by the concept of music structure, qubibi recalls being unflamboyantly seduced by a slice of paté. The meaty cross section exposes what's inside — just like the Foucauldian guards, we are invited to look into the worms' secret universe. Cast on black bedding, the lines stun with visceral color, prehensile forms of, as he says, "flesh fibers," that sway in the *Ballet Mécanique* of human and machine.

Kazumasa-san has been coding for almost two decades, but his practice spills beyond the misapprehension of a coder-artist. He carefully selects and post-processes the outputs of the algorithm. For him, generative art is like a subtle negiotation between order and chaos, something he enjoys greatly also when playing with his son and his bewitching cat.

In the aftermath, comes the *leftover* series: generative outputs that follow on from a completed main series that Kazumasa-san cheekily enjoys serving up to his collectors. *MIMIZU*'s *leftovers*, for the critic Artnome stand "in stark contrast to the increasingly homogenous world of generative art." What's leftover often promulgates our inner worlds and acts as traces for memories. Without knowledge of his code, these *leftover*'s continually tantalize the audience to let the mystery be.

**MIMI NGUYEN**
ASSISTANT PROFESSOR AT CENTRAL SAINT MARTINS, LONDON, AND
COLLECTOR OF QUBIBI'S *MIMIZU* (2021–22)

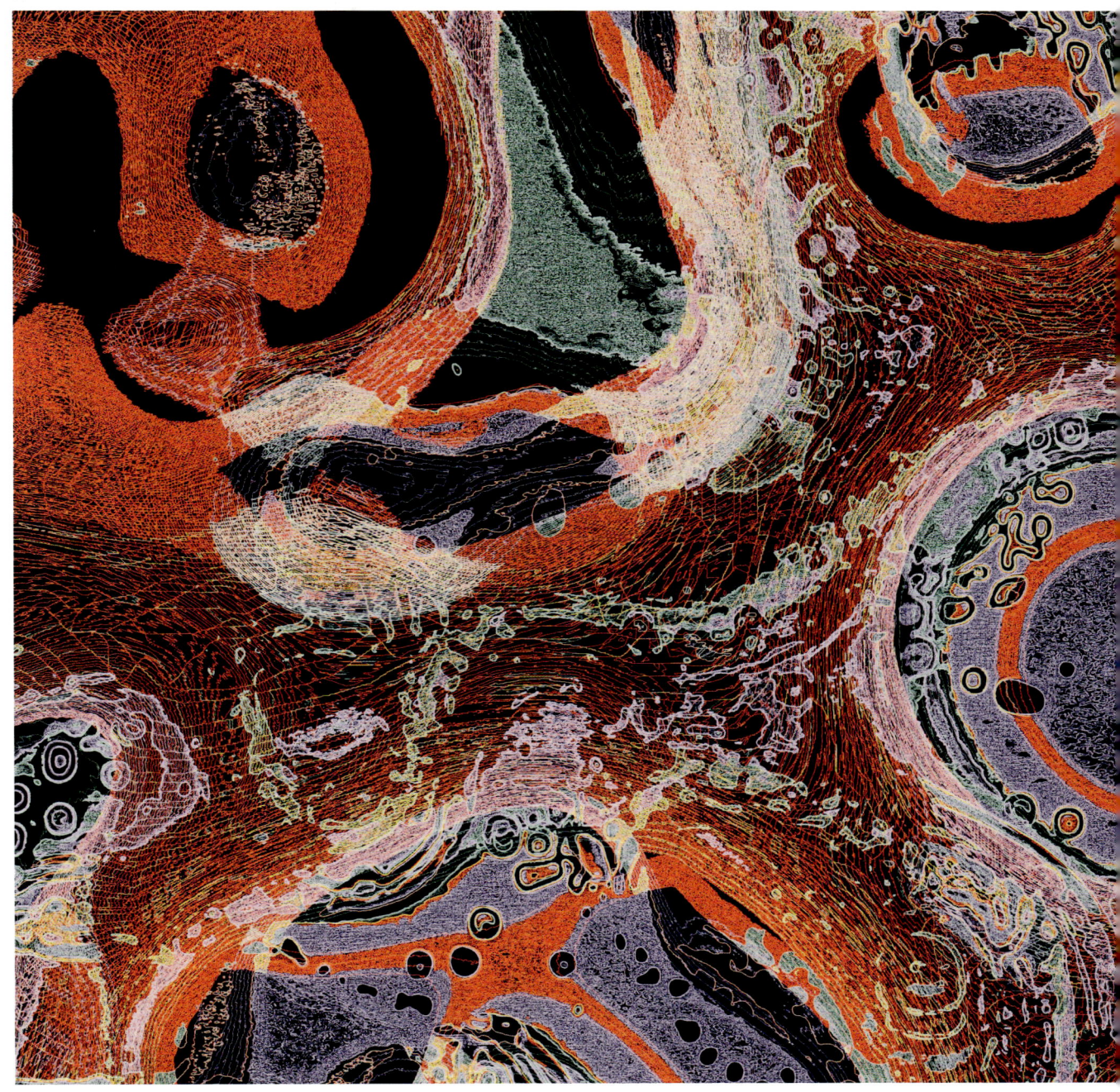

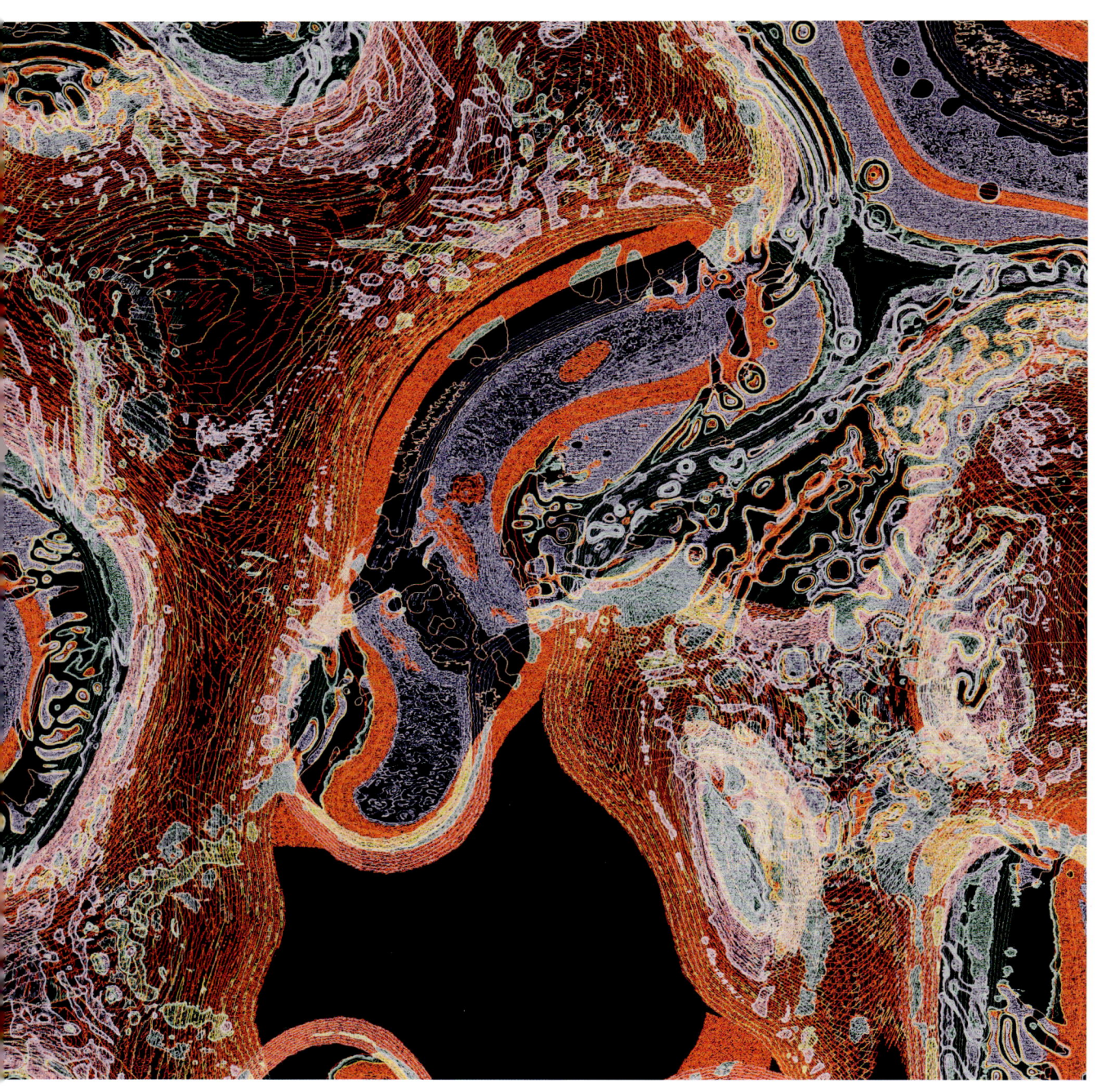

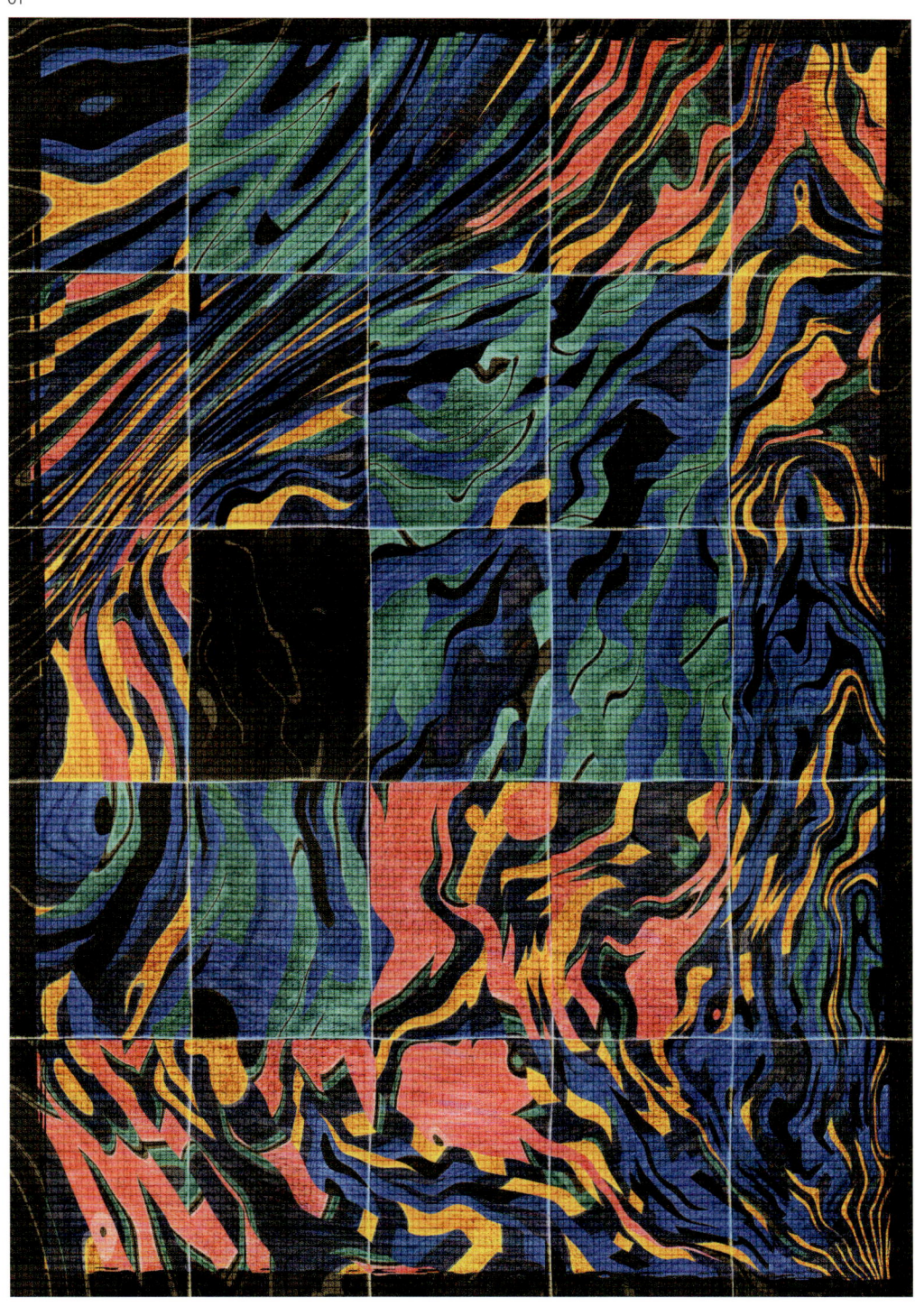

| # | TITLE | TIMESTAMP | MEDIUM | CHAIN | CONTRACT ADDRESS | TOKEN ID | EDITION SIZE |
|---|---|---|---|---|---|---|---|
| 01–07 | **Anticyclone** | 04-22-2022 15:18:19 | Three.js | ETH | 0xa7d8d9ef8d8ce8992df33d8b8cf4aebabd5bd270 | 304000000–304000799 | 1/1 of 800 |

EDITIONS ILLUSTRATED: (01) #87, (02) #230, (03) #76, (04) #46, (05) #402, (06) #522, (07) #465

# WILLIAM MAPAN

FRANCE 1988

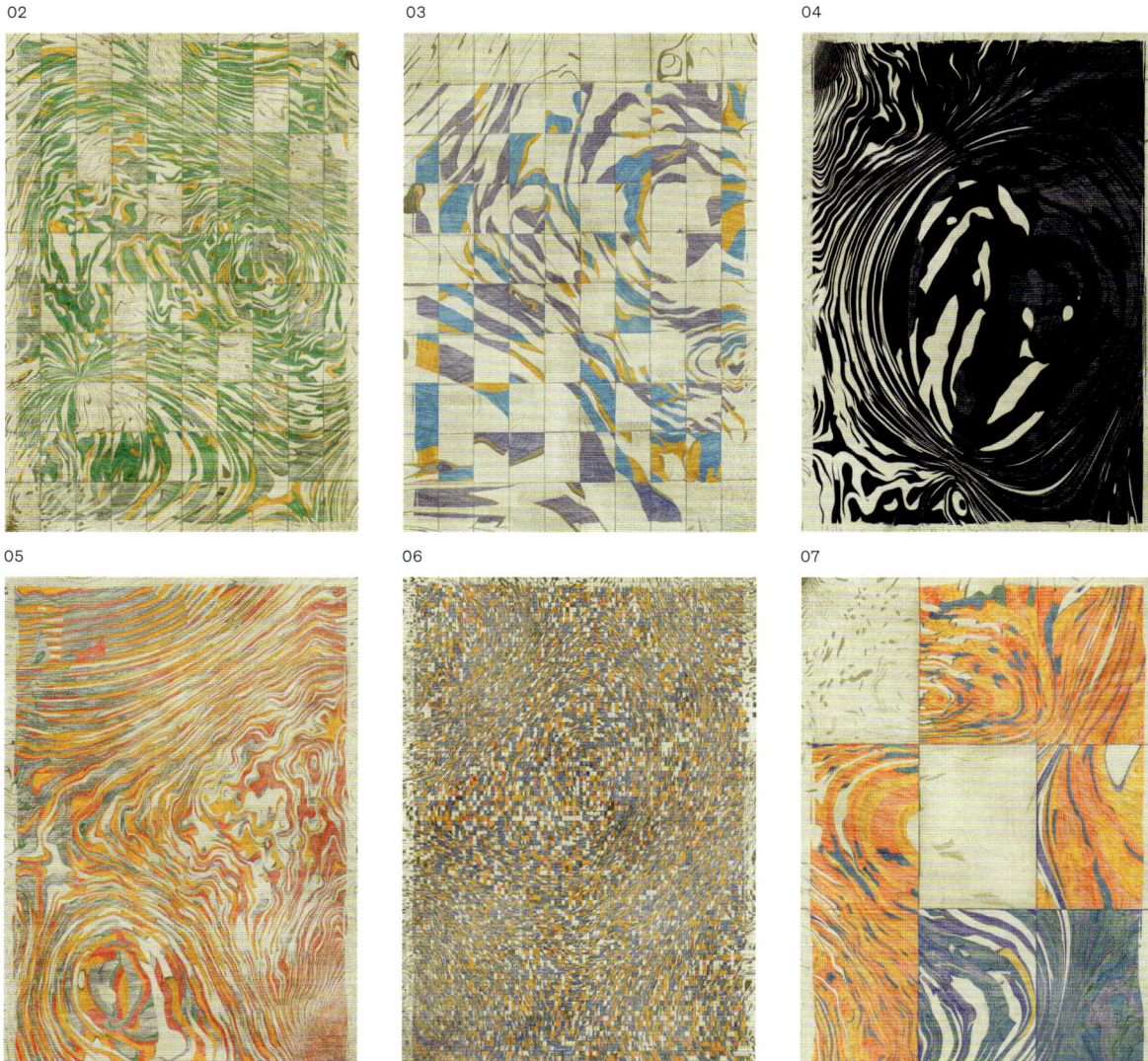

William Mapan is a multidisciplinary artist, coder, and teacher who strives to bridge the analog with the digital world through his computer-generated images. He honed his creative coding skills at Gobelins, the widely acclaimed Parisian visual creation school. Consequently, he applied these skills for years in the advertising industry where his teams have won a multitude of leading industry awards.

Although intense at times, William's professional career has never been his sole pursuit. Inspired by pioneers such as Vera Molnár, Victor Vasarely (1906–1997), and Anni and Josef Albers (1899–1994 and 1888–1976, respectively), he began to devote his spare time to exploring and experimenting with various mediums, including paint, crayons, Lego blocks, and even plasticine. William does not allow for a single medium to constrain his self-expression. At the core of his process, lay the concepts of iteration and emergence complemented by an adoration of color. William rarely begins the creation process with a predefined goal in mind; rather he relies on his exceptional technical skills to iterate from idea to idea and bug to bug before eventually arriving at a refreshing end result.

In 2022, William released his breakthrough collection, *Anticyclone* (2022) on Art Blocks, the pioneering generative art platform. The series found tremendous immediate success, establishing Mapan as more than an NFT artist. While technically complex due to the heavy use of WebGL, the collection succeeds in conveying emotions with simplicity to the viewer. His obsession with colors results in over 20 stunning palettes, each named after an inspiring woman. Additionally, *Anticyclone* has an awe-inspiring analog texture proving that William is achieving his artistic goal of leveraging the mechanical to create the natural.

**THEFUNNYGUYS**
FOUNDER OF LE RANDOM, ADVISOR AT METAVERSAL,
AND GENERATIVE ART COLLECTOR

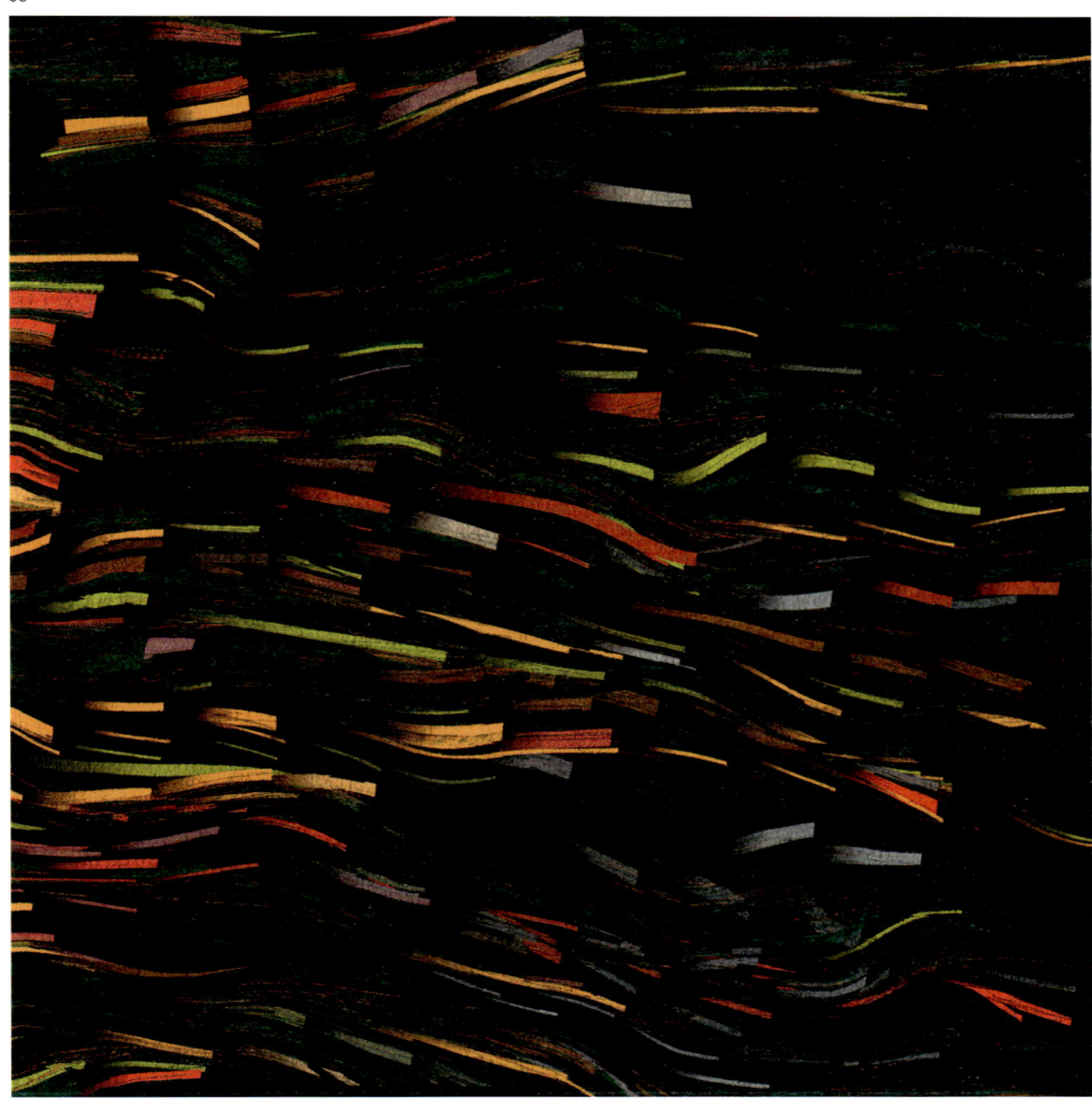

| # | TITLE | TIMESTAMP | MEDIUM | CHAIN | CONTRACT ADDRESS | TOKEN ID | EDITION SIZE |
|---|-------|-----------|--------|-------|------------------|----------|--------------|
| 08, 09 | **Dragons** | 12-07-2021 20:27:40 | WebGL | XTZ | KT1AEVuykWeuuFX7QkEAMNtffzwhe1Z98hJS | 130532–131053 | 1/1 of 512 |

EDITIONS ILLUSTRATED: (08) #337, (09) #36

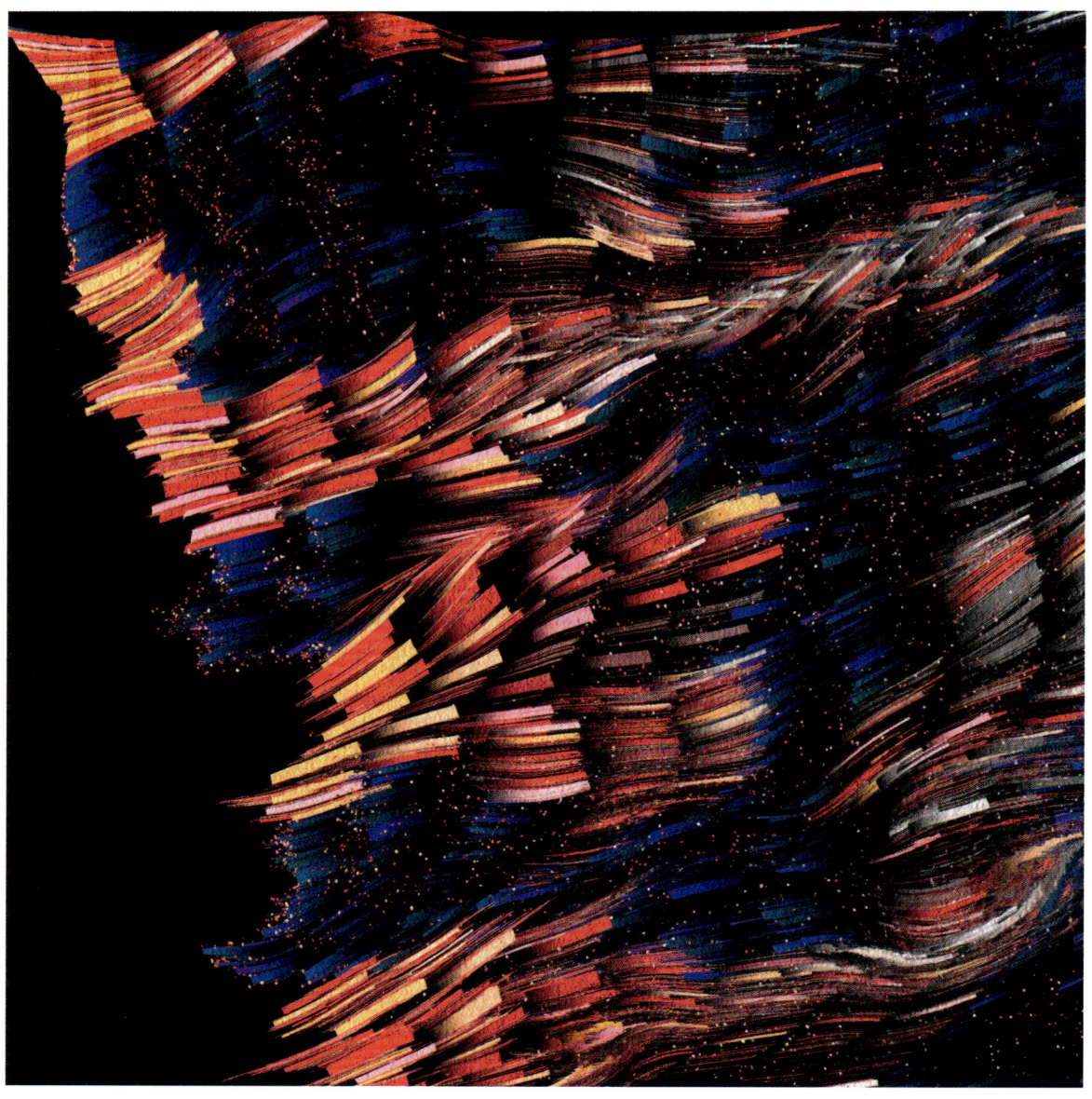

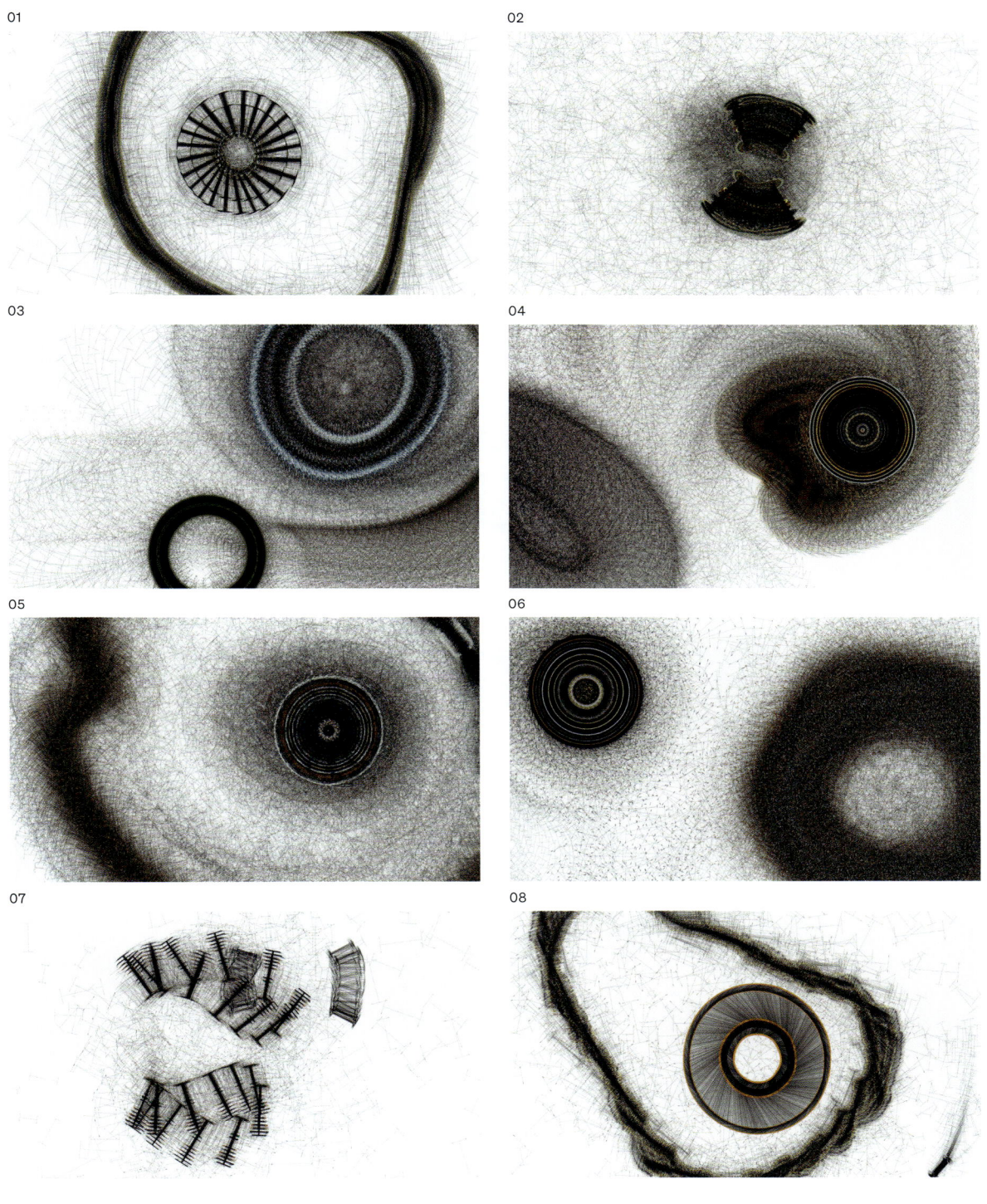

01
02
03
04
05
06
07
08

| # | TITLE | TIMESTAMP | MEDIUM | CHAIN | CONTRACT ADDRESS | TOKEN ID | EDITION SIZE |
|---|---|---|---|---|---|---|---|
| 01–08 | **drawing machine x4** | 02-19-2022 23:21:39 | Processing | ETH | 0x6d383cc00d3cf76dee4b7f1777a12defa85af957 | 0–99 | 1/1 of 100 |
| 09 | **Sync [var. 04]** | 04-21-2021 10:07:29 | Processing, p5.js | XTZ | KT1RJ6PbjHpwc3M5rw5s2Nbmefwbuwbdxton | 40999 | 34 |
| 10 | **Hoping Seven Times for Light** | 09-15-2022 20:02:59 | Processing | ETH | 0x4e41b24c542208db1a4474c40936b7f6a5f791ed | 1–7 | 1/1 of 7 |

EDITIONS ILLUSTRATED: (01) #60, (02) #58, (03) #24, (04) #63, (05) #72, (06) #1, (07) #6, (08) #40, (10) #1

09 ▶

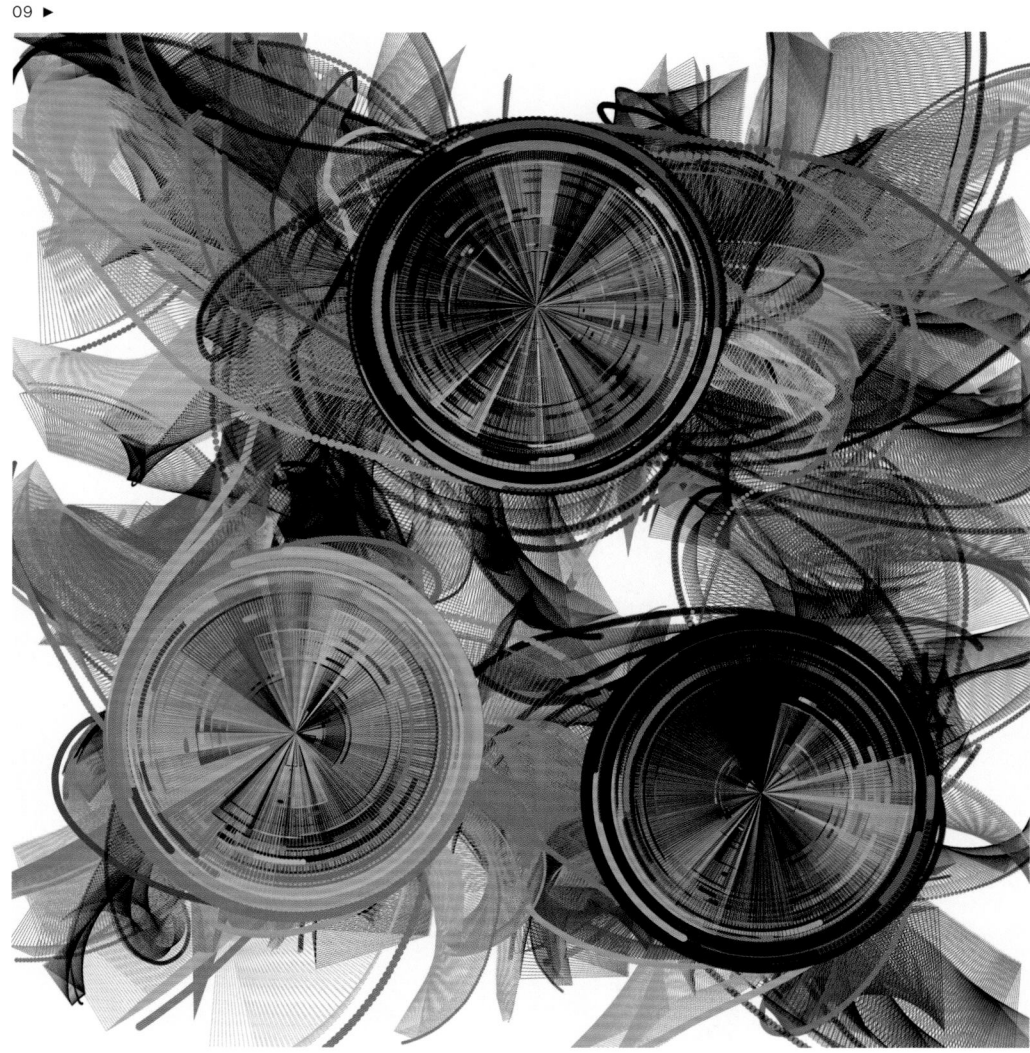

I met LIA in Vienna after having seen her interactive *Shockwave* (1997–2001) sketches on the TURUX website and realizing she was one of a very small group of artists starting to explore code as a visual medium.

Her early work distinguished itself as hard-edged and resolutely abstract, exploring glitch aesthetics before it became a familiar trope. The conceptual framework we now have for generative art was yet to be formulated, but LIA soon became part of an emerging network of disparate artists united by the intuition that software could be art. The focus was on a visual formalism that recalled ideas from op art and early abstract art, reimagined as programmable and semiautonomous systems.

From the early 2000s, LIA developed a visual language of systems that draw and redraw themselves over time, animated palimpsests realized as real-time software. Her aesthetic evolved to include organic forms and a painterly drawing style, in monochromes or limited color palettes. Drawing a connection between visual and sound, LIA extended her practice to create live audiovisual performance systems, performing extensively with electronic musicians like @c, Emi Maeda, and Espen Sommer Eide. As a generative artist, LIA's work is a natural match for the NFT model of distributing and collecting art. She began minting on Hic et Nunc, SuperRare and Foundation, and has since released a series on Art Blocks. She has participated in several important shows of NFT art, such as Feral File's *Social Codes*, *NfT-NeTArT* at Panke Gallery in Berlin and *Ethereal Aether* at the State Hermitage Museum in St. Petersburg.

**MARIUS WATZ**
CURATOR, TEACHER, DIGITAL AND CRYPTO ARTIST

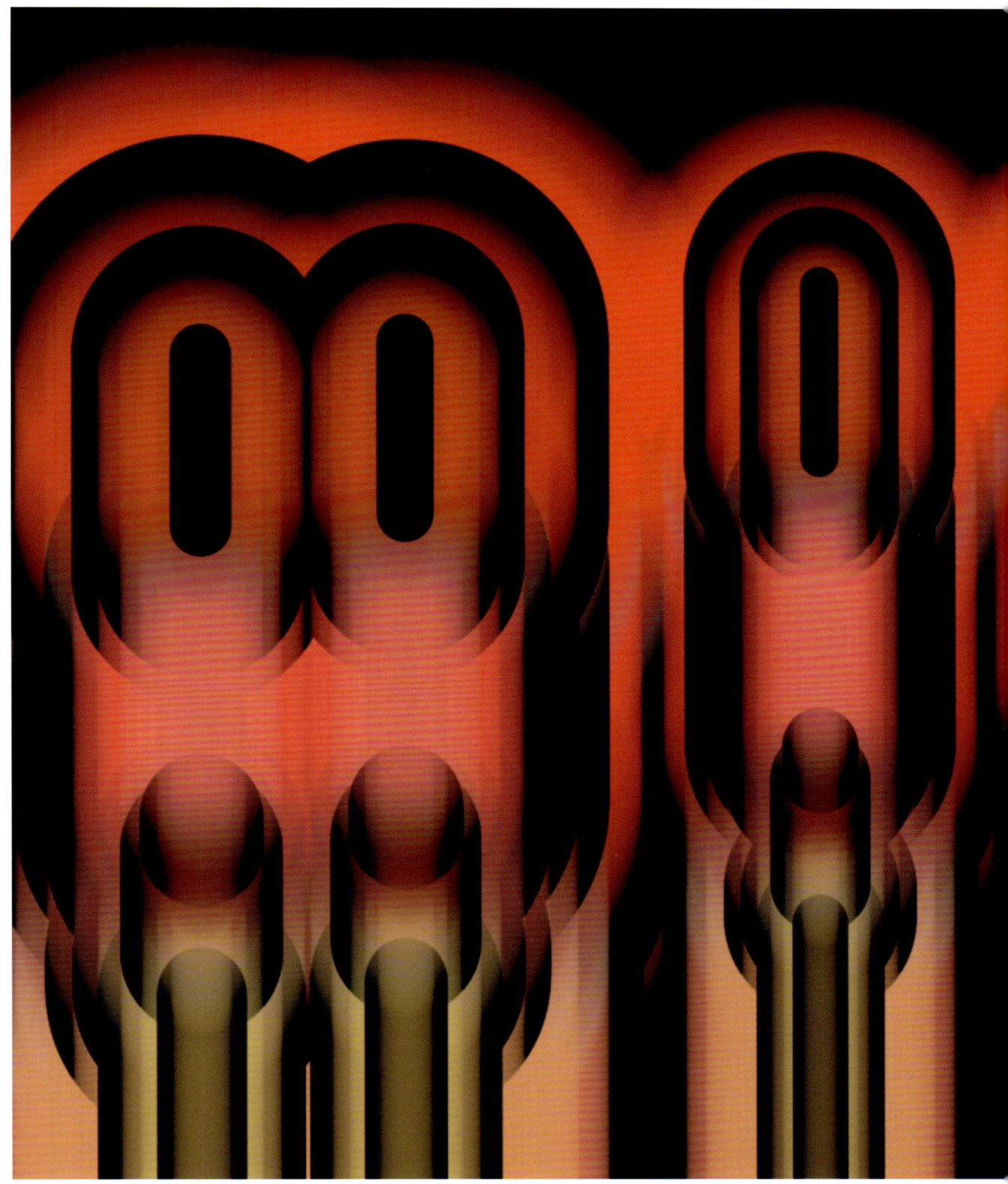

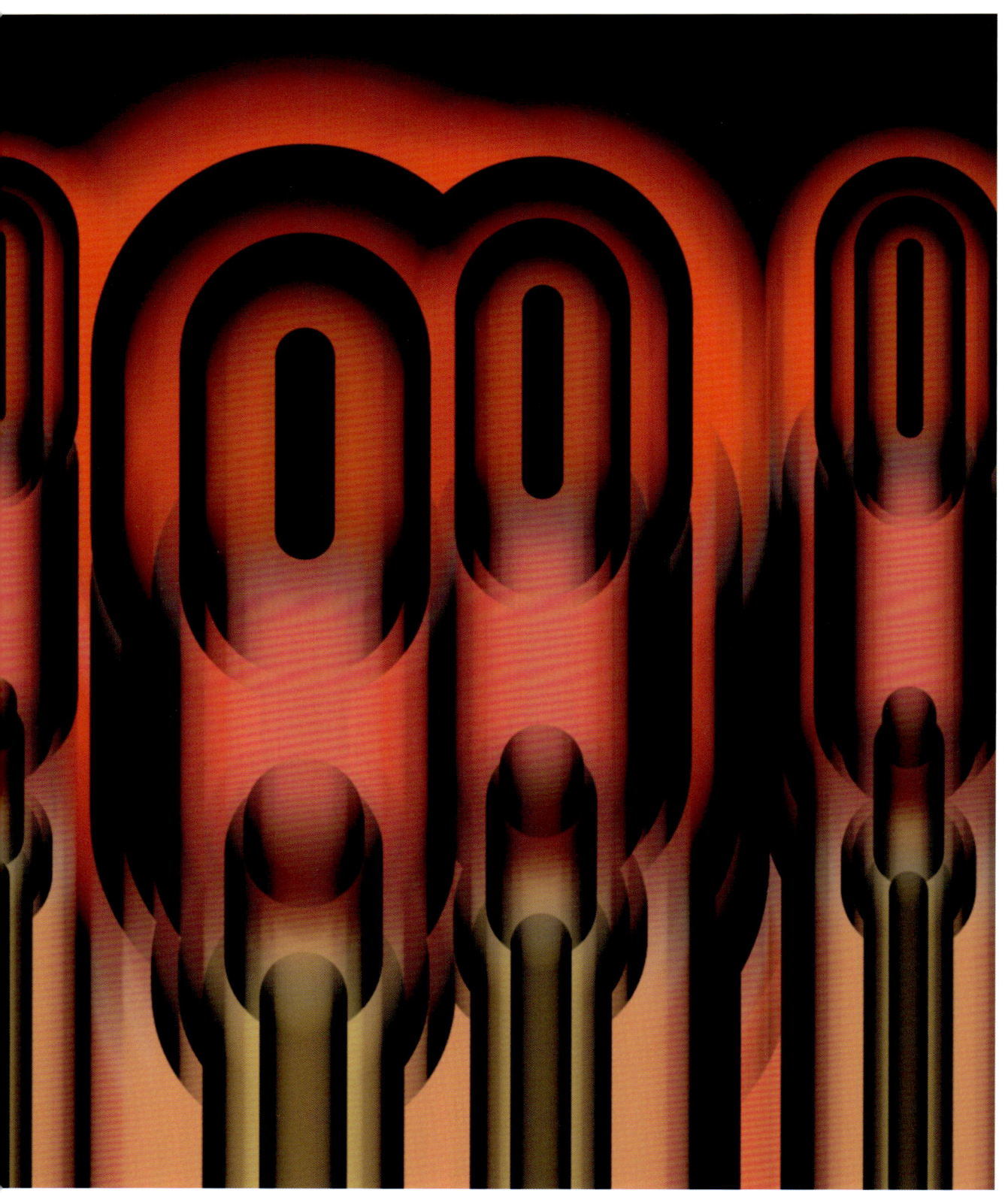

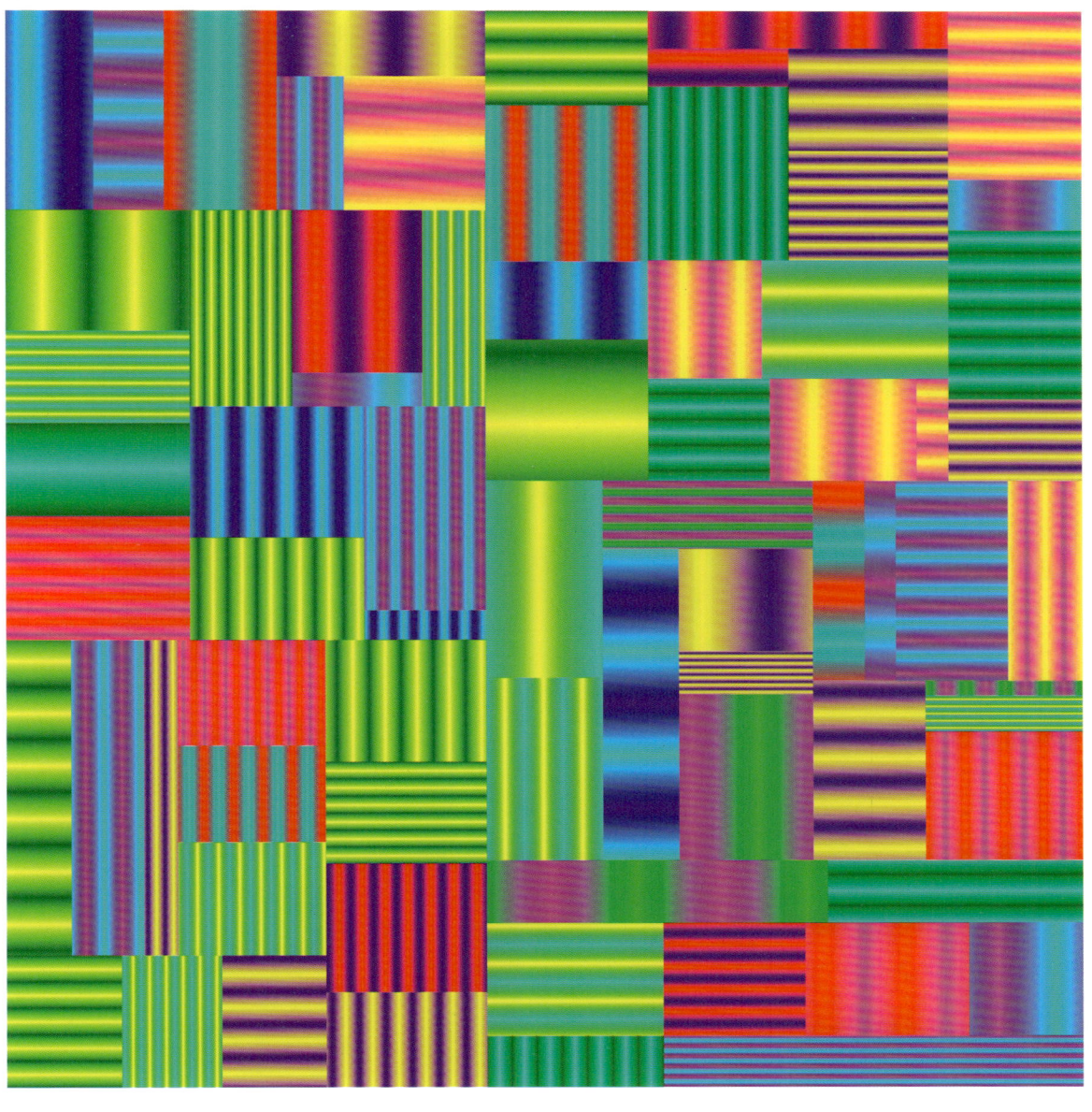

01 ▶

| # | TITLE | TIMESTAMP | MEDIUM | CHAIN | CONTRACT ADDRESS | TOKEN ID | EDITION SIZE |
|---|---|---|---|---|---|---|---|
| 01, 02 | **Endless Nameless** | 06-28-2022 00:28:39 | JavaScript | ETH | 0xa7d8d9ef8d8ce8992df33d8b8cf4aebabd5bd270 | 120000000–120000999 | 1/1 of 1,000 |

EDITIONS ILLUSTRATED: (01) #100, (02) #66

02 ▶

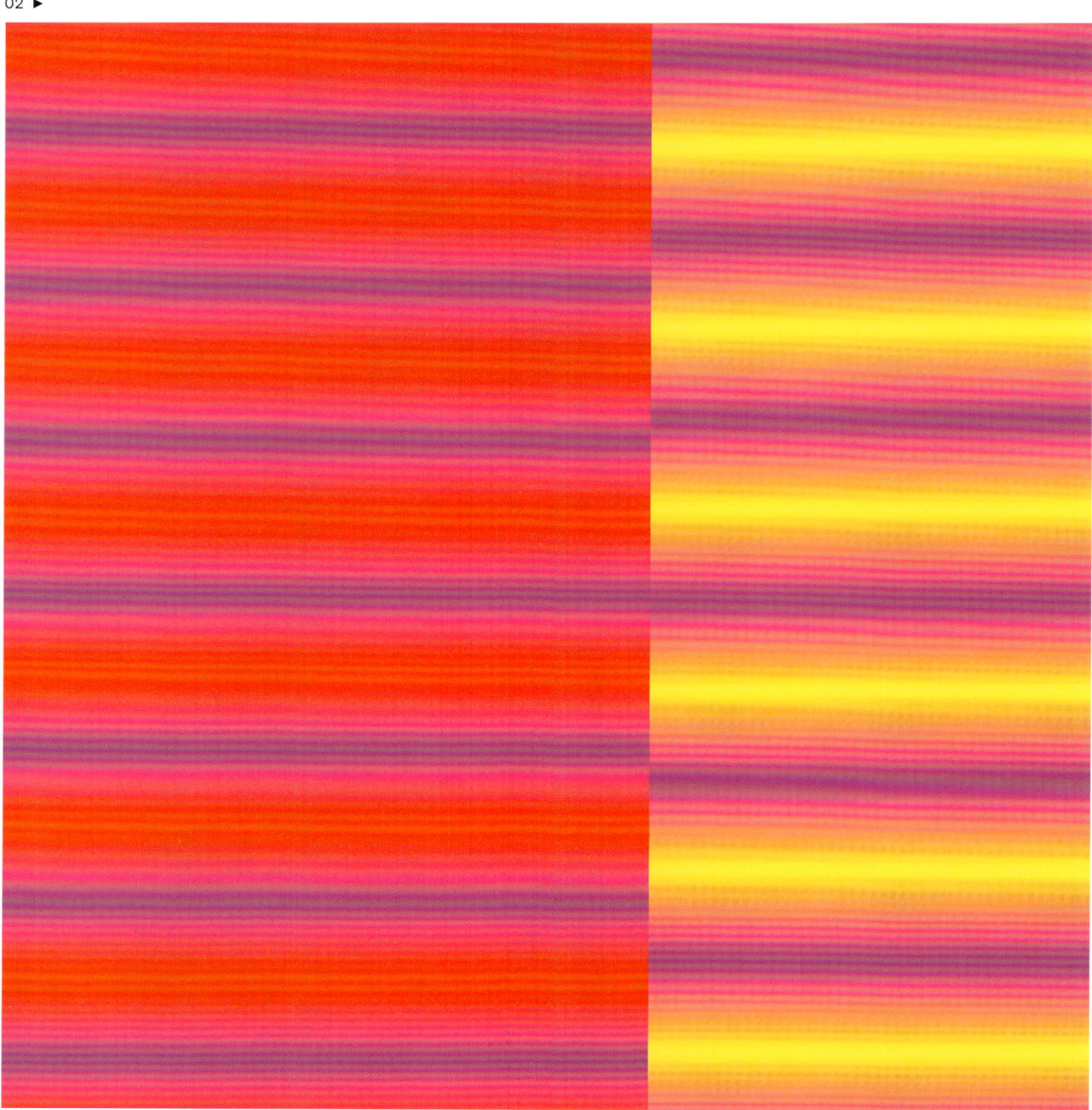

Rafaël Rozendaal has been making digital art since 2001. He pioneered the use of domain names as an authentication for art pieces. The domain name is at the same time the title, the location, and authentication of the work. He used these digital artworks to create immersive exhibitions, installations, and projections in public space. He also created weavings, lenticular prints, murals, and books.

His works have been shown in Times Square and the Whitney Museum of American Art in New York, Centre Pompidou in Paris, the Valencia Biennial, Casa França-Brasil in Rio de Janeiro, Seoul Art Square, and the Stedelijk Museum in Amsterdam.

*Dive* (2021) is an exploration of the grid as a living system, using the fundamentals of color and motion. Each of the 333 NFTs is a unique set of choices. The screen is divided in a grid of squares filled with shifting color. The composition and movement are completely abstract, they do not represent anything from our physical world. Code as a means to create something native to the screen, not trying to mimic anything. It is really an investigation of the screen itself as a natural space. This work should be viewed the same way we stare at the ocean or a forest. We don't question what it is, we witness it.

**RAFAËL ROZENDAAL**
ARTIST

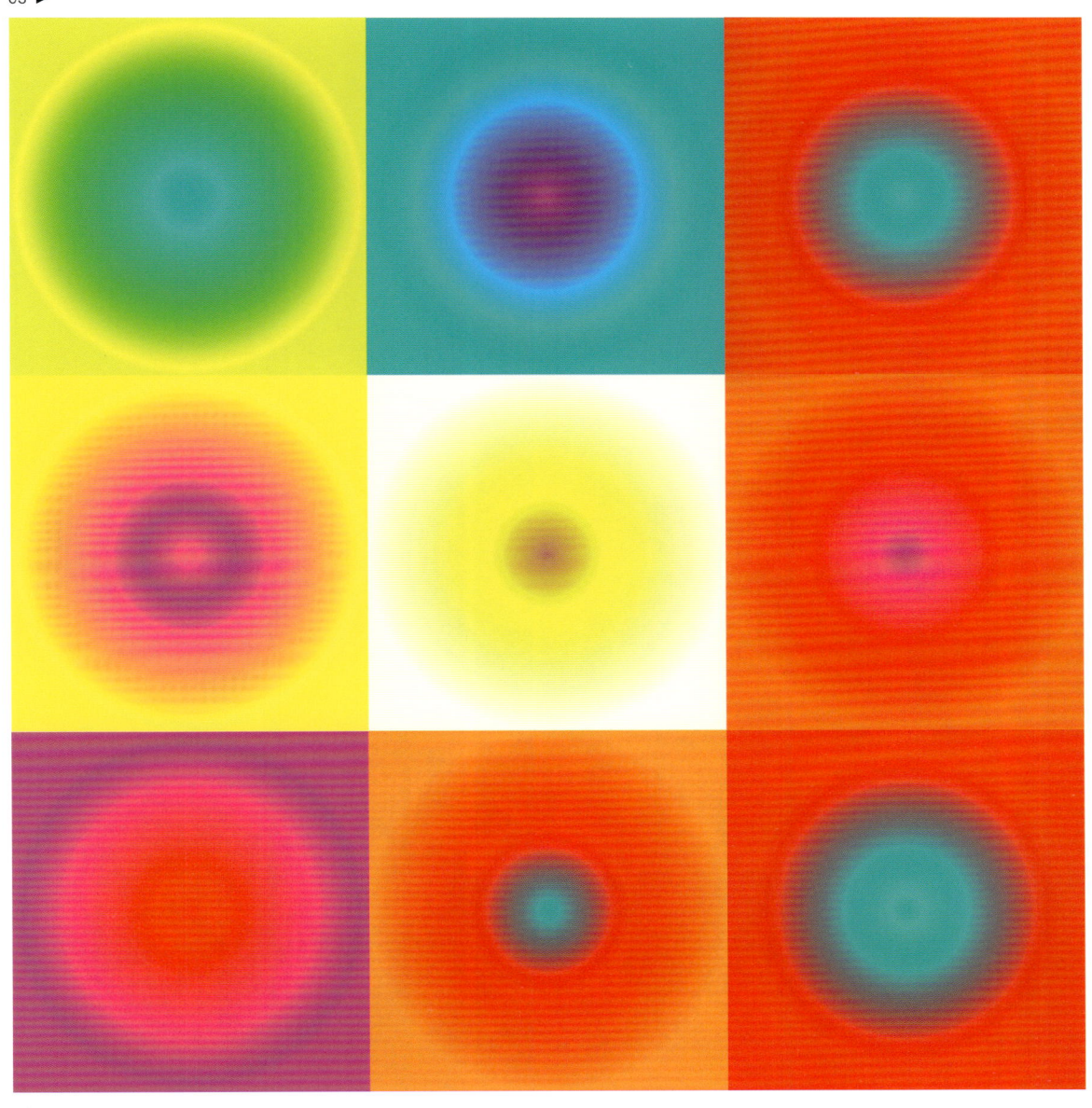

| # | TITLE | TIMESTAMP | MEDIUM | CHAIN | CONTRACT ADDRESS | TOKEN ID | EDITION SIZE |
|---|---|---|---|---|---|---|---|
| 03, 04 | **Dive** | 11-15-2021 22:37:07 | JavaScript | ETH | 0xa7d8d9ef8d8ce8992df33d8b8cf4aebabd5bd270 | 212000000–212000332 | 1/1 of 333 |

EDITIONS ILLUSTRATED: (03) #14, (04) #184

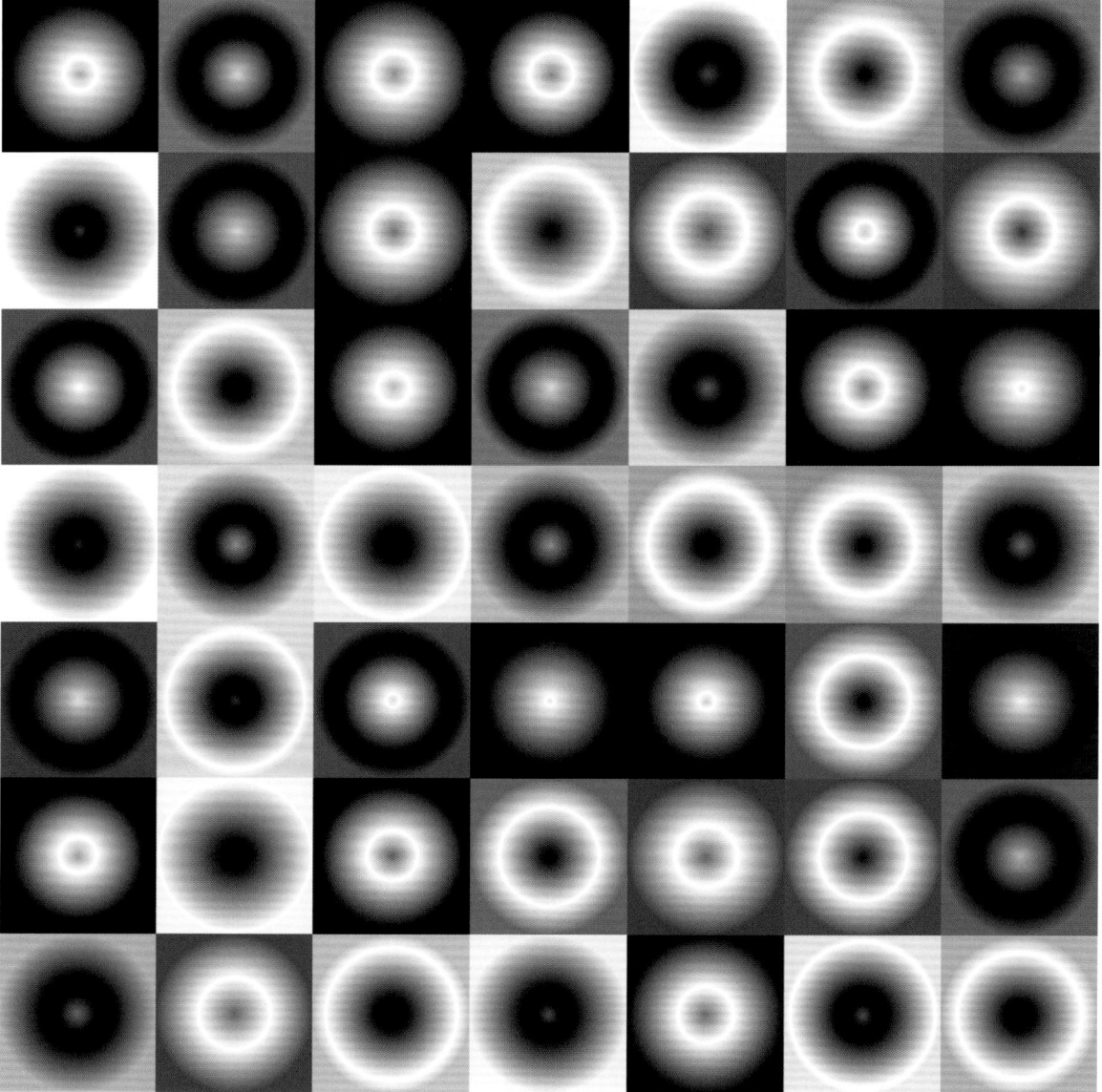

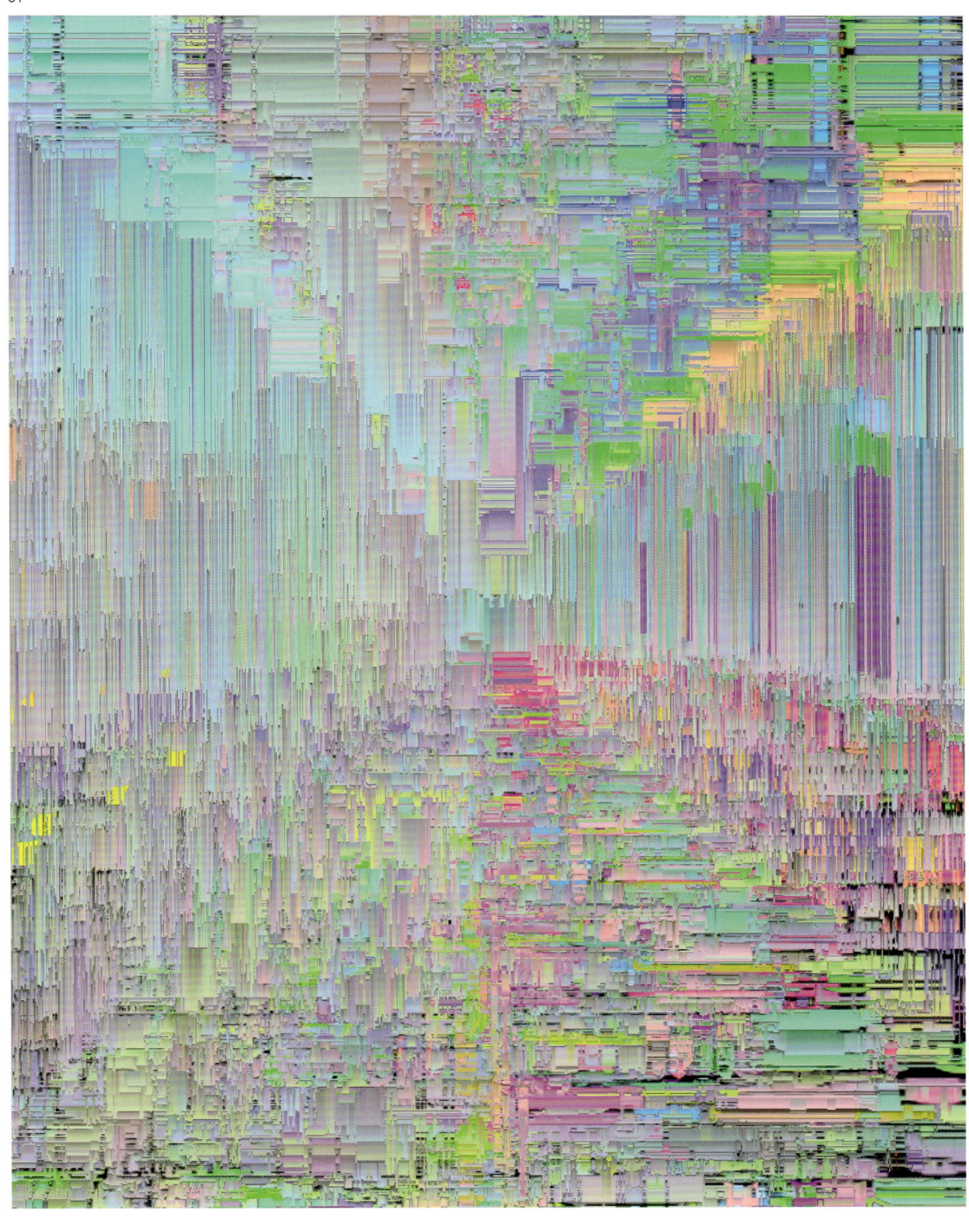

| # | TITLE | TIMESTAMP | | MEDIUM | CHAIN | CONTRACT ADDRESS | TOKEN ID | EDITION SIZE |
|---|---|---|---|---|---|---|---|---|
| 01 | **Casco Viejo** | 09-15-2021 17:15:35 | ETH | TouchDesigner | ETH | 0x287319f0989f4a4c0f0b60eeec9a4f0eb7365647 | 1 | 1/1 |
| 02 | **Dreaming at Dusk** | 05-12-2021 16:07:54 | ETH | TouchDesigner | ETH | 0x3b3ee1931dc30c1957379fac9aba94d1c48a5405 | 35855 | 1/1 |

02 ▶

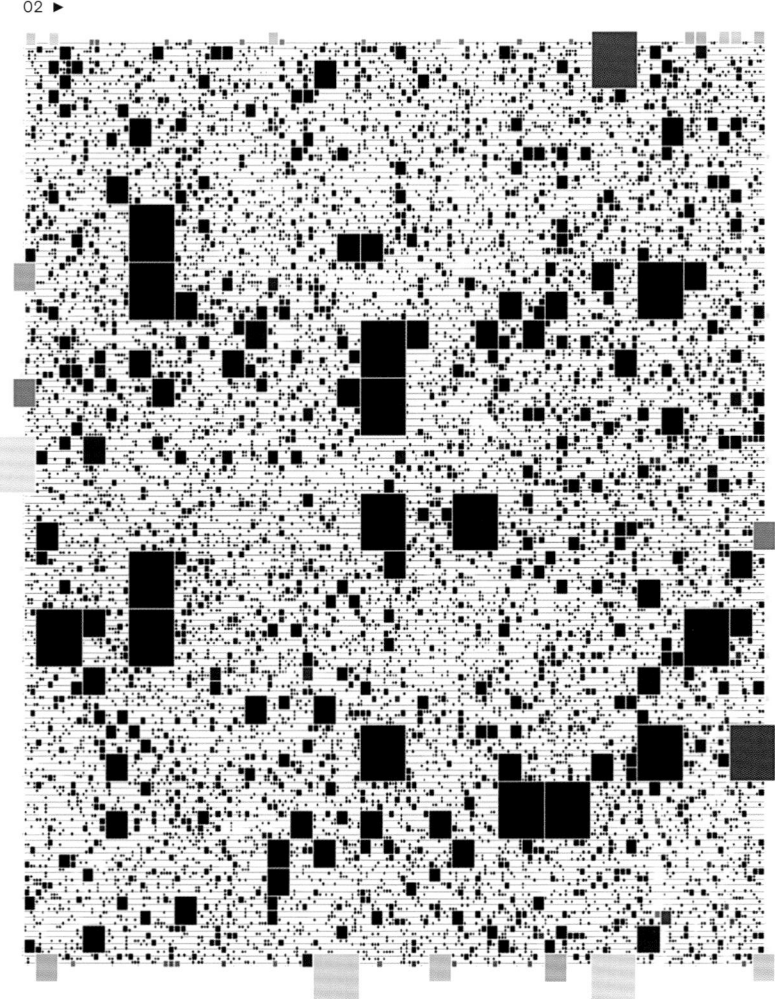

Itzel Yard (aka Ix Shells) is a prolific artist and curator whose efforts have buoyed a number of disparate online communities and served as a rallying cry for supporters of online privacy. Yard generates her work in TouchDesigner, a visual node-based programming environment designed for the creation of real-time multimedia.

Born in Panama in 1990, Yard's primary inspiration comes from her late father, an early telecommunications engineer, who imbued in her an appreciation of math, numbers, graphs, and grids. She is also inspired by her background in architectural technology, which she studied in Toronto, Canada.

Yard was all too familiar with the consequences of private data and information being used to prosecute activists, journalists, and immigrants with families in sanctioned countries. So when the TOR project, a free and open-source software for enabling encrypted and anonymous communication, reached out to her about collaborating on an artwork to memorialize a private cryptographic key for their 15th anniversary, she was thrilled. With the help of Al Smith, Isabela Bagueros, and Gustavo Gus, Yard conceived of *Dreaming at Dusk* (2021) which would serve as a graphical representation

of the very first website on their network duskgytldkxiuqc6. onion, or "Dusk." The key would serve as the seed to the algorithm — much like DNA's role in the cellular mechanism of gene expression, it acts as the map needed to exactly reproduce the artwork.

The work consists of layers of rectangular blocks flickering on and off in a grid against a distant light background. As the camera moves, the observer is taken on a journey alongside packets of transmitted data. As we are transported through both time and space it remains unclear whether data is passing from one point to another, or we are traveling through past, present, and future states of a transmission.

The visuals elicit a reminder of Joan Shogren's work, a woman who in 1963 convinced academics with access to a computer to create one of the first algorithms to generate art using rules

**DMITRI CHERNIAK**
ARTIST

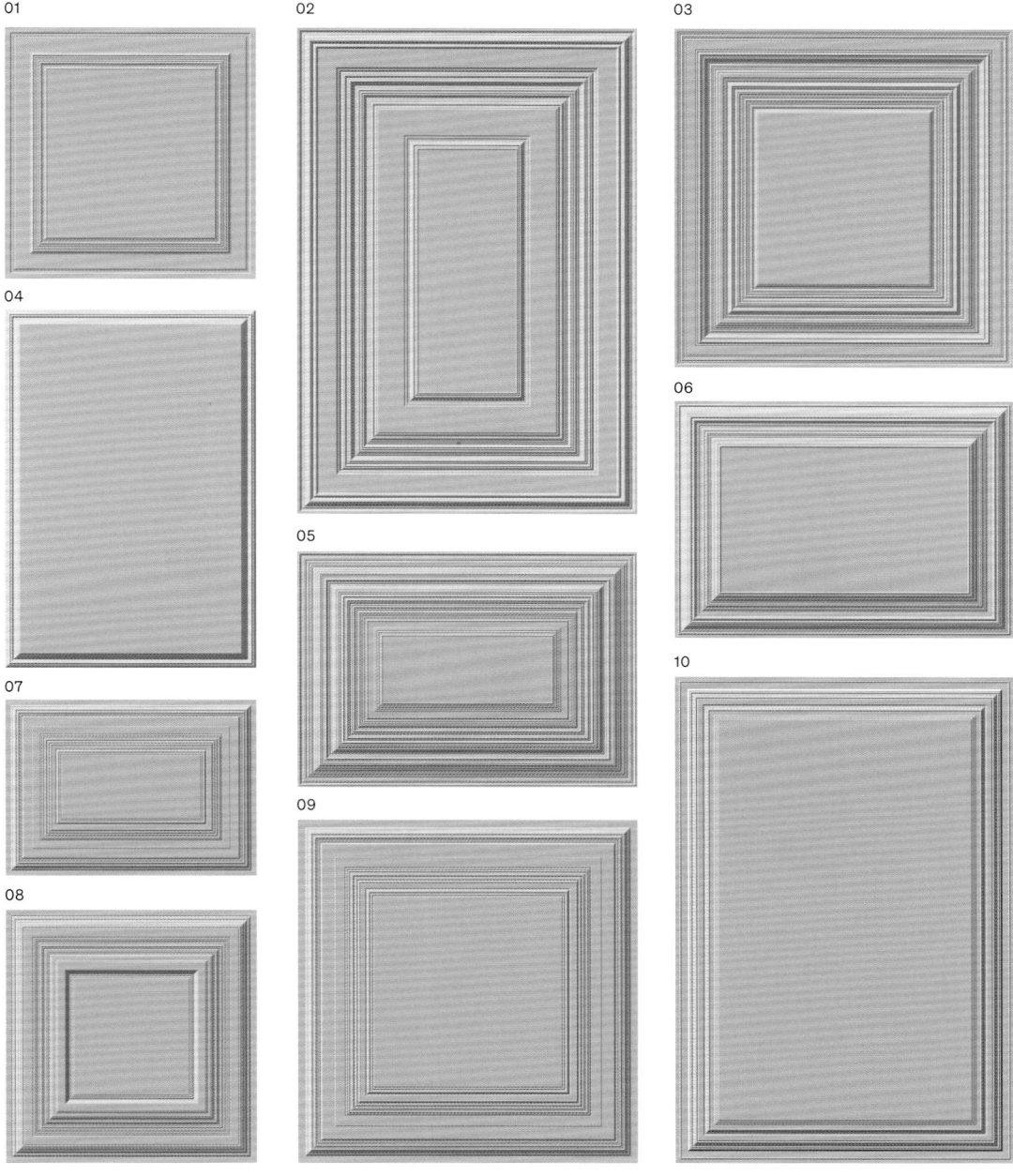

01  02  03  04  05  06  07  08  09  10

| # | TITLE | TIMESTAMP | MEDIUM | CHAIN | CONTRACT ADDRESS | TOKEN ID | EDITION SIZE |
|---|-------|-----------|--------|-------|------------------|----------|--------------|
| 01–10 | **Ornament** | 11-03-2021 15:42:36 | JavaScript, HTML DOM | ETH | 0xf1b214702bed6ec64843f55e5d566d8ffb3034dd | 0–255 | 1/1 of 256 |
| 11 | **JPEG** | 09-19-2022 18:06:47 | JavaScript, HTML DOM | ETH | 0xa7d8d9ef8d8ce8992df33d8b8cf4aebabd5bd270 | 371000000–371000274 | 1/1 of 275 |

EDITIONS ILLUSTRATED: (01) #22, (02) #63, (03) #65, (04) #171, (05) #189, (06) #168, (07) #84 (landscape), (08) #186, (09) #84 (square), (10) #245, (11) #125

# JAN ROBERT LEEGTE

11

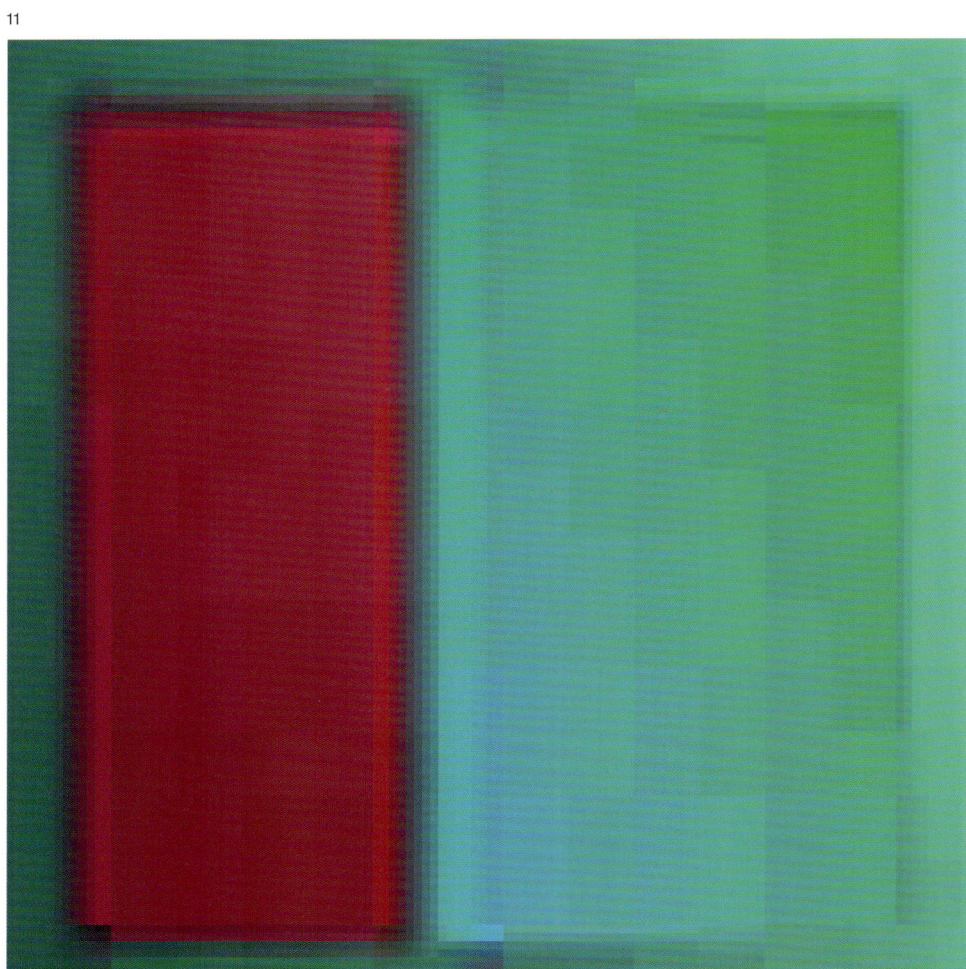

Jan Robert Leegte has been working sculpturally with the internet as his medium since 1997. His work has been exhibited at the Whitechapel Gallery in London, Centre Pompidou in Paris, in both the Van Gogh Museum and the Stedelijk Museum in Amsterdam, ZKM Karlsruhe, and the Ludwig Museum in Cologne.

His oeuvre focuses on the artistic investigation of the elements and aesthetic qualities of the computer interface. This results in abstract, sculptural, minimal compositions that integrate the material and concepts of browsers, website description languages, and operating systems. Leegte's physical and digital works draw conceptual and artistic tensions between code as a performance and the final render of his pieces. This tension is expressed by different groups of works and concepts: selection tools, scrollbars, and buttons are signs of an active engagement in image worlds, and document and text structures. The drop shadow, haptic 3D representation of page edges or frames are recognized as ornaments of the digital interface.

The arrival of blockchain and Web3 has led Jan Robert Leegte to examine this new medium, its possibilities, and its limits. The Ethereum-based NFTs *Ornaments* (2021), *Windows* (2022), and *JPEG* (2022) translate and actualize the concepts and aesthetics behind their predecessors: *Ornaments* (2006–18), *Dumpster* (2016), *Windows* (2017), and *Compressed Landscapes* (2016). In these new iterations, Jan Robert Leegte applies the main characteristics of Web3 to his works, such as economic accessibility, generative processing, and limited editions.

The NFT *Ornaments* exists in two versions, a static SVG on-chain and a responsive HTML version in an edition of 256. The minted series of *Windows* is HTML DOM generated by pure JavaScript, hosted and sold as an edition of 404 on Art Blocks. It seamlessly intertwines early net art aesthetics with Web3 concepts into one responsive web sculpture. *JPEG* furthermore reflects on the history of web technologies and how it affects our perception of net-based images.

**ROBERT SAKROWSKI**
ART HISTORIAN AND CURATOR

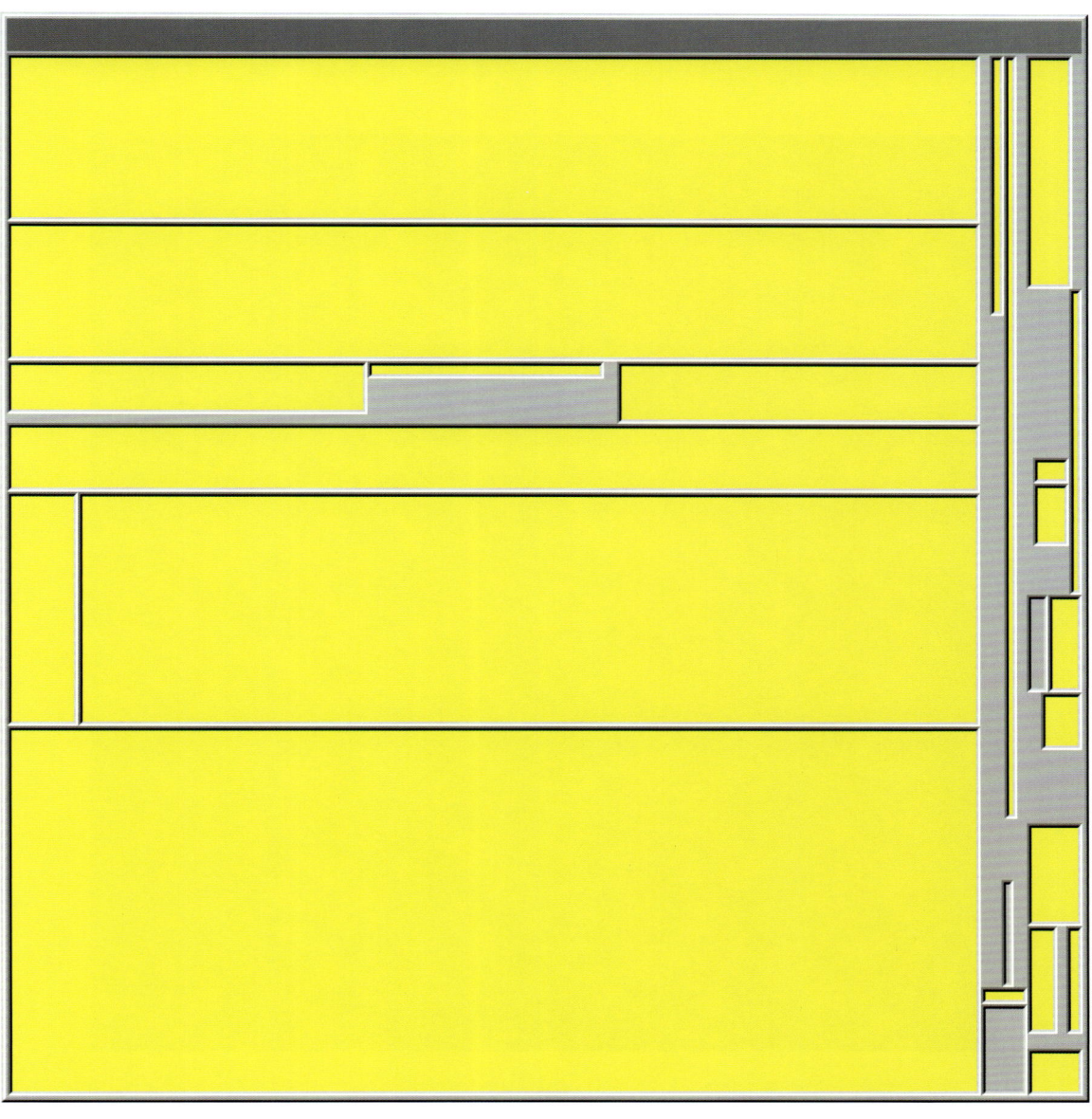

| # | TITLE | TIMESTAMP | MEDIUM | CHAIN | CONTRACT ADDRESS | TOKEN ID | EDITION SIZE |
|---|-------|-----------|--------|-------|------------------|----------|--------------|
| 12, 13 | **Window** | 03-09-2022 16:56:49 | JavaScript, HTML DOM | ETH | 0xa7d8d9ef8d8ce8992df33d8b8cf4aebabd5bd270 | 280000000–280000403 | 1/1 of 404 |

EDITIONS ILLUSTRATED: (12) #30, (13) #113

13

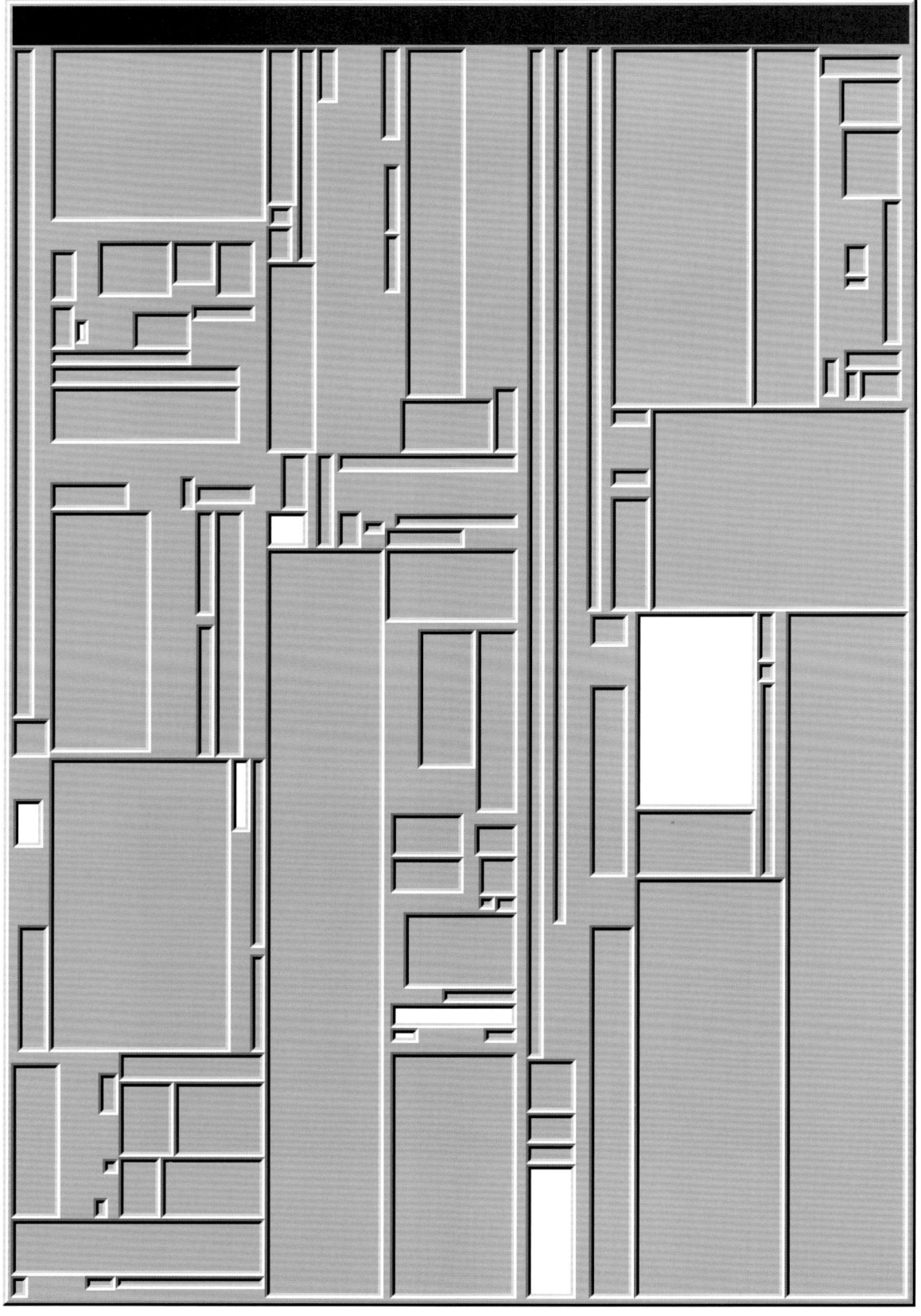

JAN ROBERT LEEGTE        236, 237,

01 ►

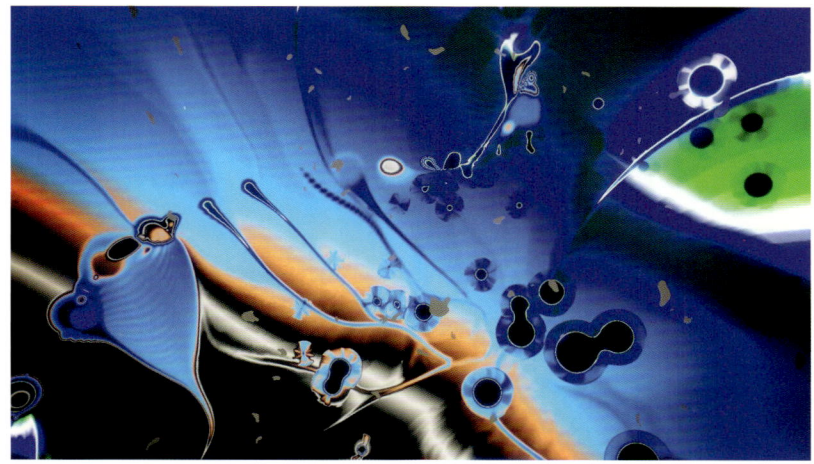

02 ►

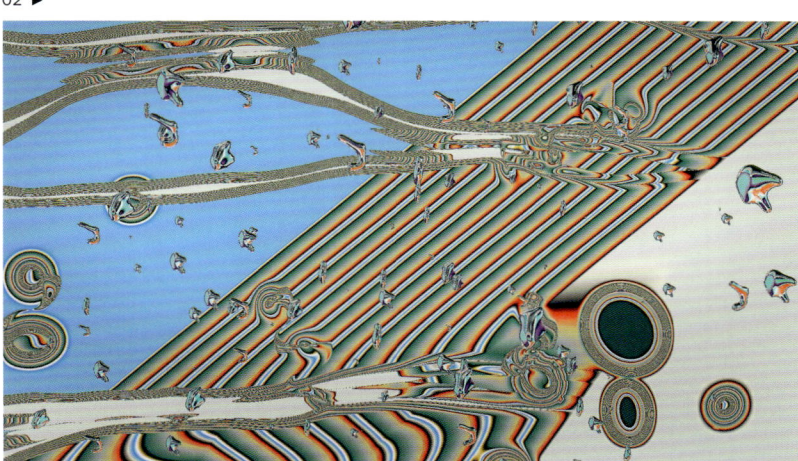

03 ►

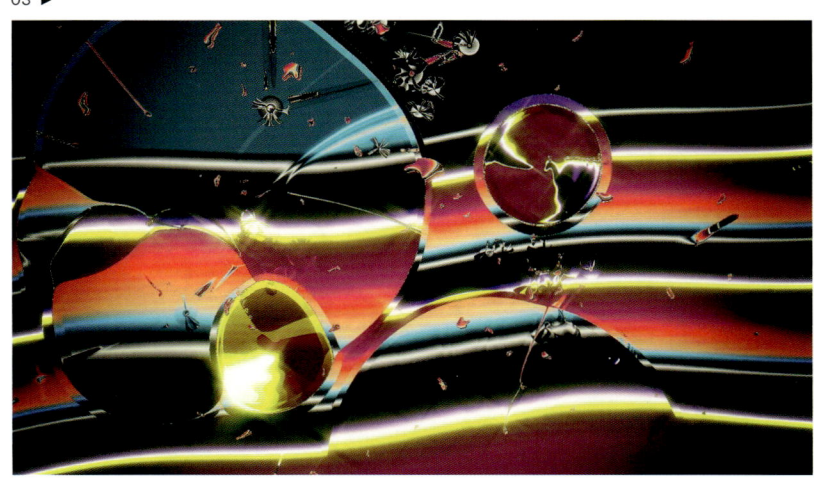

| # | TITLE | TIMESTAMP | MEDIUM | CHAIN | CONTRACT ADDRESS | TOKEN ID | EDITION SIZE |
|---|---|---|---|---|---|---|---|
| 01–03 | **Wetware** | 03-14-2021 14:16:27 | Adobe After Effects | ETH | 0x3b3ee1931dc30c1957379fac9aba94d1c48a5405 | 7450–101706 | 1/1 of 18 |
| 04 | **Wetware – Bacteria** | 11-14-2021 12:24:50 | Adobe After Effects | ETH | 0xf3006340ad94baacdb319b59831c9a08912ab64a | 1–16 | 1/1 of 16 |

EDITIONS ILLUSTRATED: (01) Vegetation (02) Medulla (03) Mutation (04) WTWR - BCTR ***083-3GD

# YOSHI SODEOKA

04 ▶

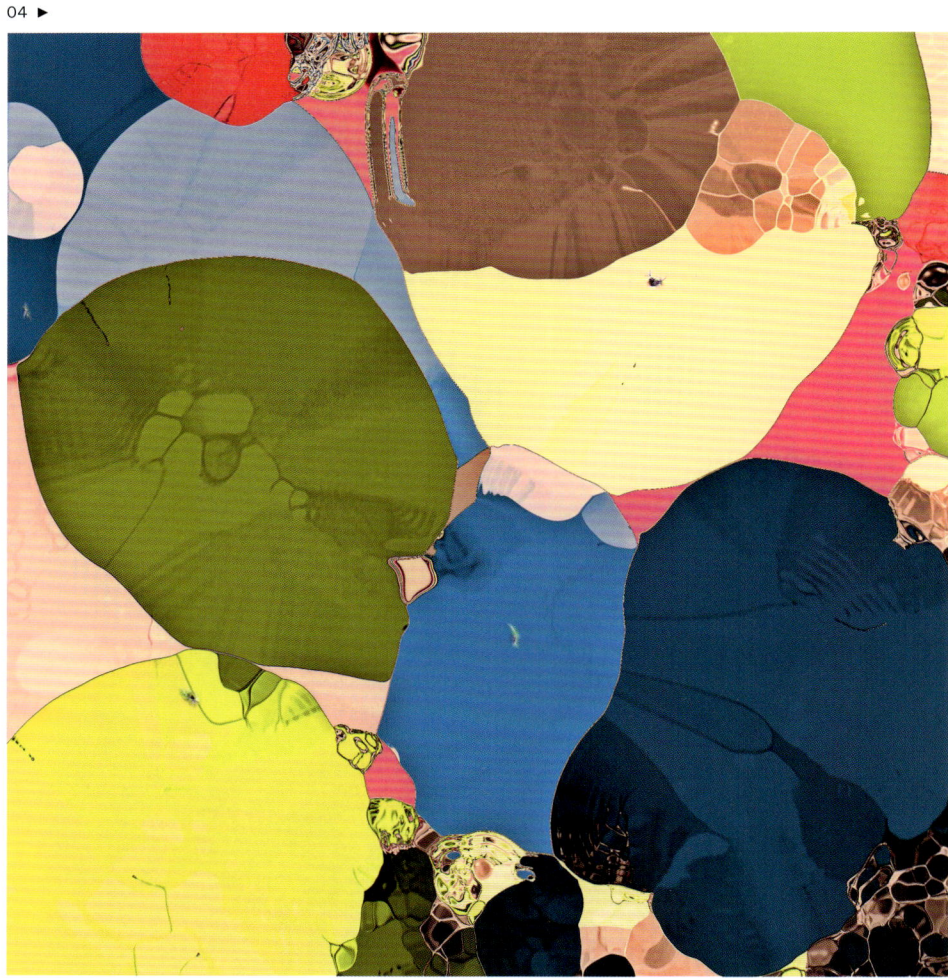

Sensational: exciting and stimulating the sense of sight — that is the first thing that comes to mind when encountering the work of artist Yoshi Sodeoka. He gives us images of perpetual becoming, shards and fragments floating on a liquid wind, distortions in a malleable lens, spills and bubbles ebbing and flowing on endless tides rendered in eye-catching color palettes and polished, reflective surfaces.

Born and raised in Japan but a long-term resident of New York City, Sodeoka's command of the digital toolbox runs deep to the point of second nature. Retracing his technique is difficult, because it boils down to a working process that combines the programmed with the intuitive. Parameters of color, shape, and layer are defined and set into motion creating activity that elaborates itself to no end, in a process that will run forever unless instructed to stop. Like evolutionary processes in nature, the end results are unpredictable and practically beyond control. His *Wetware* (2021) series of NFT video animations and his *Spindrifters* (2019) series of NFT stills are prime examples of this dynamic.

Guillaume Apollinaire (1880–1918) coined the term *Orphism* in 1911 to describe the revolutionary paintings of František Kupka (1871–1957) and Sonia and Robert Delaunay (1885–1979 and 1885–1941, respectively). Sodeoka's work shares a distant affinity with this early 20th-century movement: a music-infused meeting of prismatic color and nonobjective abstraction, an immersive inclination, and a refined, interdisciplinary method.

Yoshi Sodeoka's work has been exhibited internationally, including at Centre Pompidou in Paris, the Tate Gallery in London, the Museum of Modern Art in New York, and the celebrated Harajuku District in Tokyo. His artworks are in the permanent collections of the Whitney Museum of American Art and the Museum of the Moving Image in New York, as well as the San Francisco Museum of Modern Art.

**TIM TROMPETER**
ARTIST AND PHOTOGRAPHER

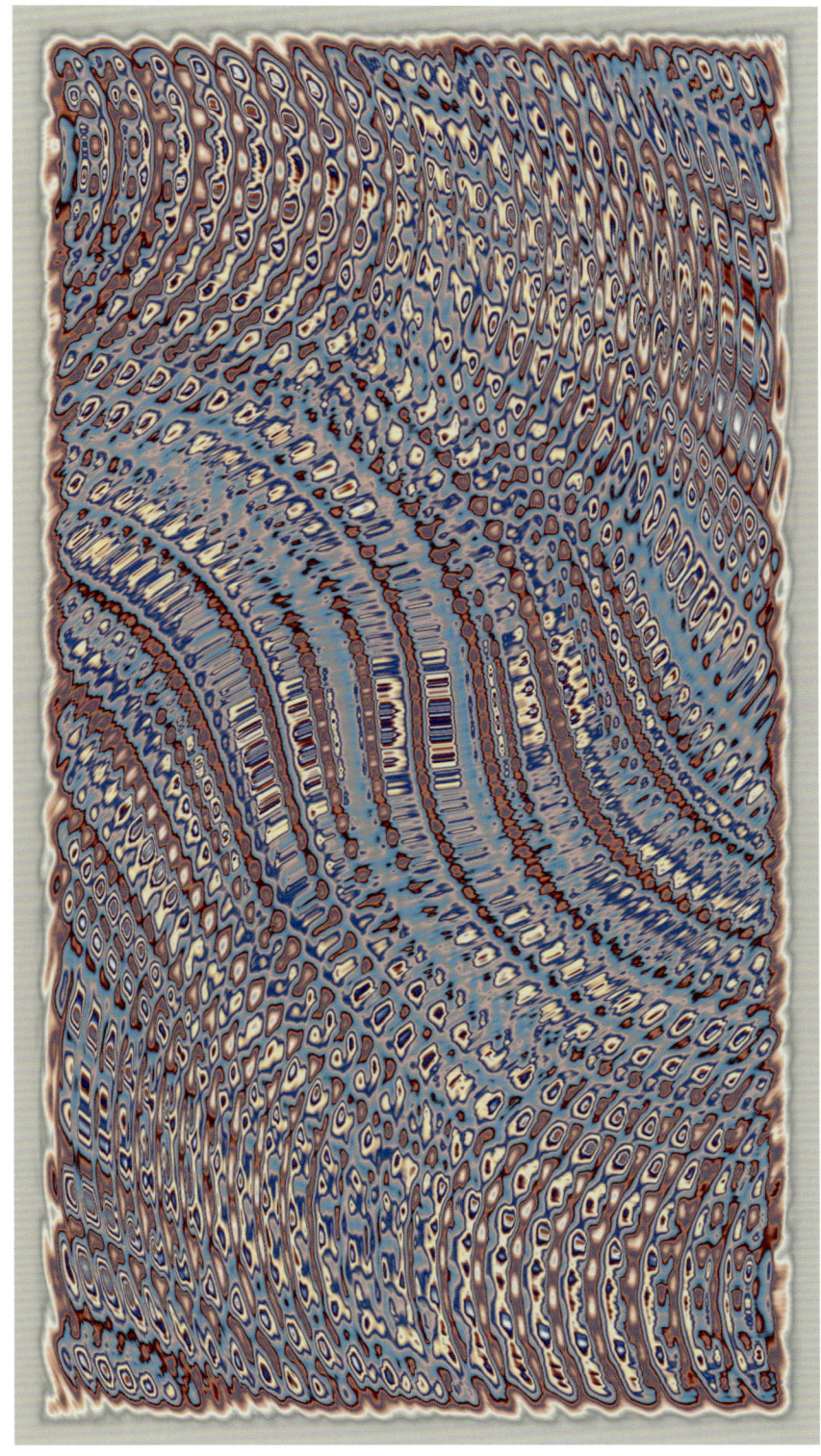

| # | TITLE | TIMESTAMP | MEDIUM | CHAIN | CONTRACT ADDRESS | TOKEN ID | EDITION SIZE |
|---|---|---|---|---|---|---|---|
| 01–07 | **Rituals – Venice** | 09-24-2021 22:23:03 | JavaScript, OpenGL Shading Language (GLSL) | ETH | 0xa7d8d9ef8d8ce8992df-33d8b8cf4aebabd5bd270 | 172000000–172000999 | 1/1 of 1,000 |

EDITIONS ILLUSTRATED: (01) #117, (02) #866, (03) #3, (04) #680, (05) #56, (06) #567, (07) #907

# AARON PENNE & BORETA

UNITED STATES 1988 & UNITED STATES 1980

02 ▶     03 ▶     04 ▶

05 ▶     06 ▶     07 ▶

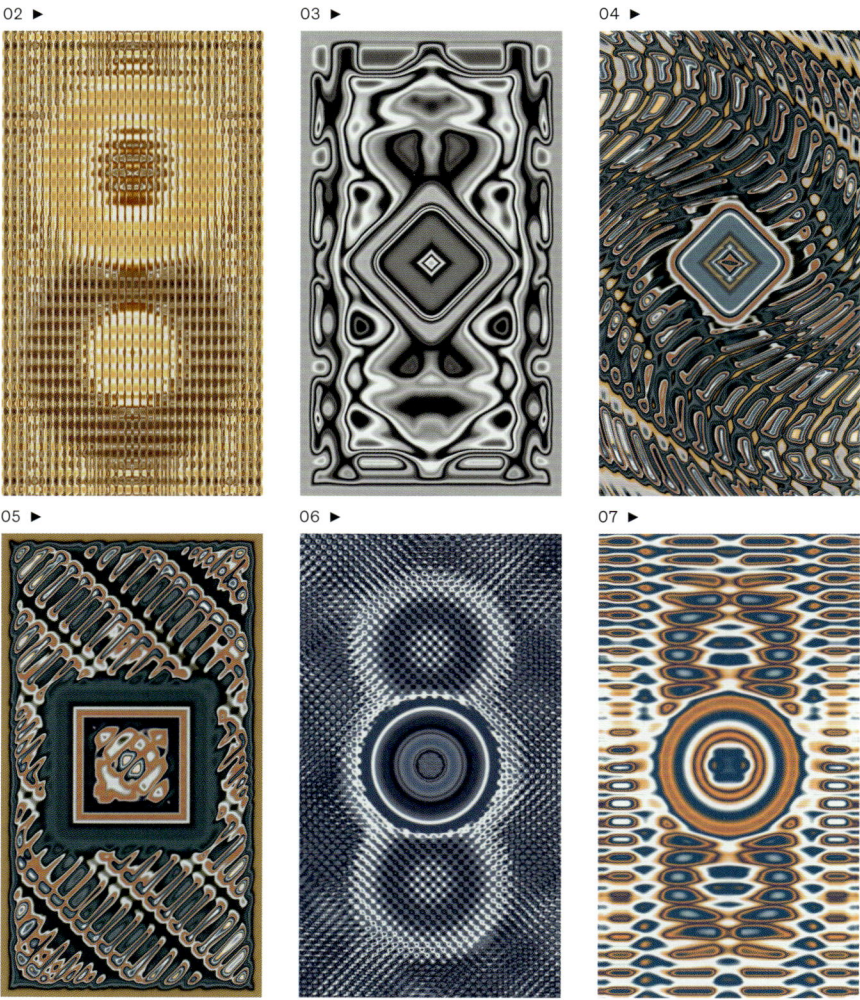

Aaron Penne and Justin Boreta's *Rituals – Venice* (2021) is a real-time generative audio-visual artwork series, launched with Bright Moments Gallery in Venice Beach, California, where the first 200 pieces were revealed and minted IRL. In 2022, the series was awarded the inaugural Lumen Prize for Art and Technology NFT Award. Consisting of 1,000 generative artworks, *Rituals* invites the viewer into a transcendent psychoactive world through an audio-visual experience. A single artwork's code, if left running, will continue generating music and art without repeating for ca. nine million years. The result of the experience is to transport the viewer from the chaos of the outside world, into the hypnotic oasis generated from the artists' code.

The visuals, generated by artist Aaron Penne, are designed to engage the viewer's peripheral vision, where the artwork is intended to naturally facilitate the single-pointed focus experienced during meditation. The fluid and changing geometric forms take inspiration from the op art and psychedelic art movements of the 1960s, which often feature patterns, grids, and effects like curving or diminishing objects. Like Penne, the op art movement was driven by artists, such as Victor Vasarely (1906–1997)

and Bridget Riley, interested in investigating various perceptual effects. One should also note the sheer diversity in formal and compositional elements that Penne has considered into his code; from shape, texture, line, and depth — viewing the collection is nothing short of a visual feast.

The music in *Rituals*, created by audio artist Boreta with code tools produced by Counterpoint, is an exercise in subtle harmonic distortion and inviting texture, which evokes feelings typically induced by a sound bath. Each audio piece modulates between two chords, hinting at a gently shifting perspective. A sonic world emerges as the harmonic layers helix around each other, creating natural ebbs and flows. Here, repetitive notes at different frequencies pull the viewer's focus away from the outside world and into Penne's hypnotic visuals. The music is designed to be felt as much as heard. As a result, the audio visual components feel completely symbiotic.

**INDIA PRICE**
PROJECT PRODUCER AT PACE GALLERY
AND NEW MEDIA ART CURATOR

01

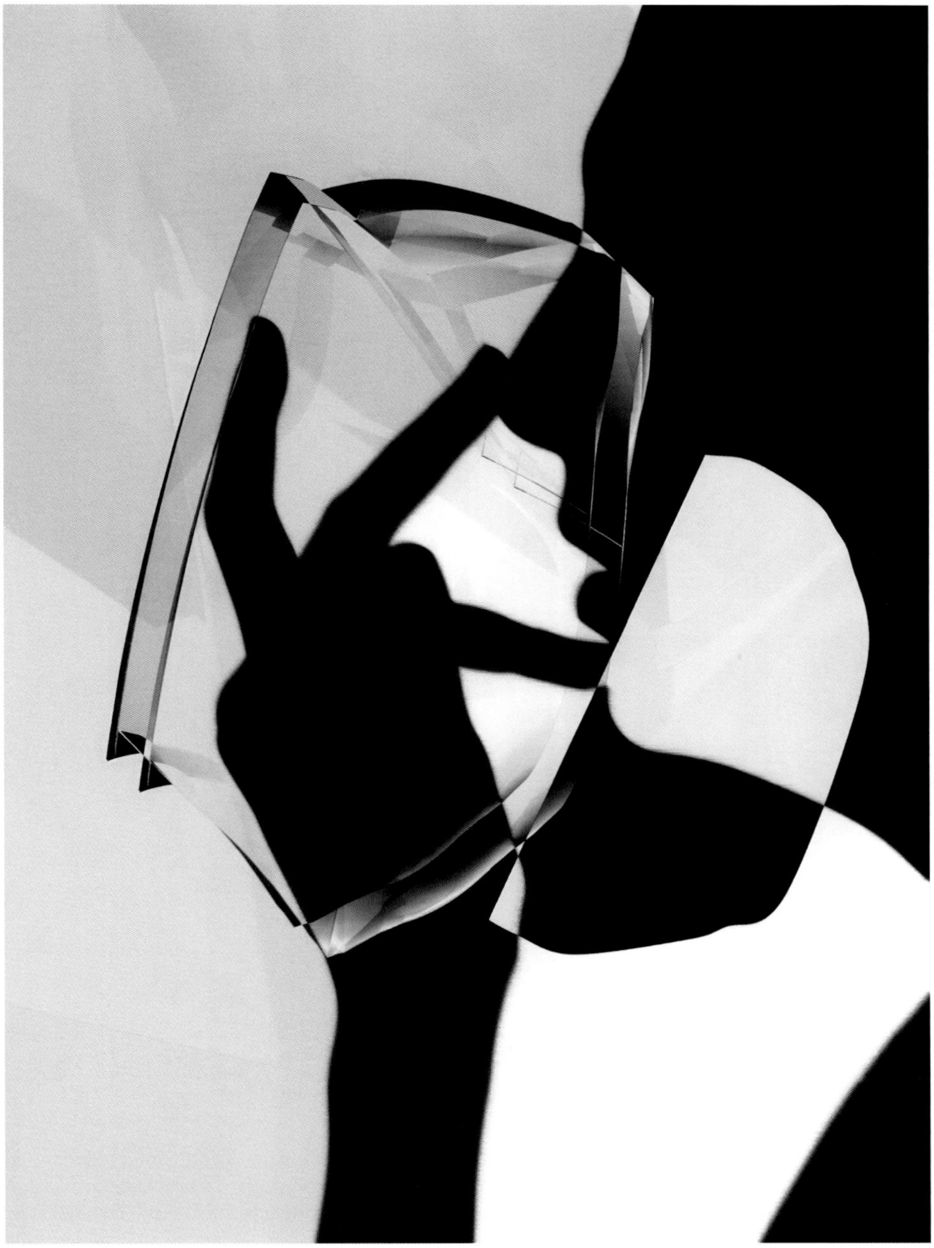

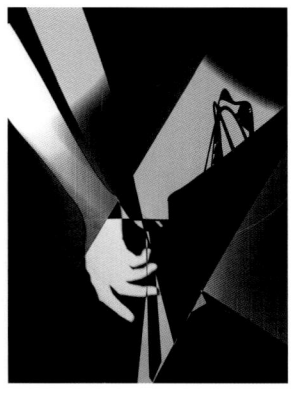

02

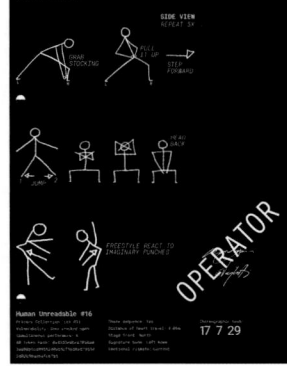

03

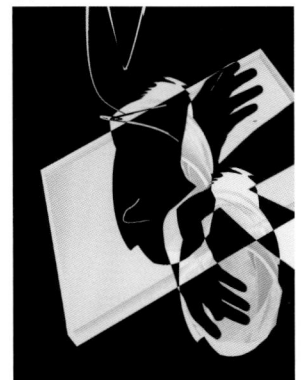

04

| # | TITLE | TIMESTAMP | MEDIUM | CHAIN | CONTRACT ADDRESS | TOKEN ID | EDITION SIZE |
|---|---|---|---|---|---|---|---|
| 01, 02, 04 | **Human Unreadable (Act I)** | 05-24-2023 17:30:11 | Generative choreography, p5.js, Solidity | ETH | 0×99a9b7c1116f9ceeb1652d-e04d5969cce509b069 | 455000000-455000399 | 1/1 of 400 |
| 03 | **Human Unreadable (Act II)** | 11-24-2023 16:19:23 | Generative choreography, Solidity | ETH | 0×15878df6bf7a5da17e12ba-80f1a635211f3dbae4 | 455000000-455000399 | 1/1 of 400 |
| 05 | **Operator Choreography Method** | | Drawing | | | | |
| 06, 07 | **Performance Still, Choreographic Tuning (New York, 2023)** | | | | | | |

EDITIONS ILLUSTRATED: (01) #242 (Act 1), (02) #16 (Act I), (03) #16 (Act II), (04) #63 (Act I), (06-07) Photo: Art Davison

# OPERATOR

05

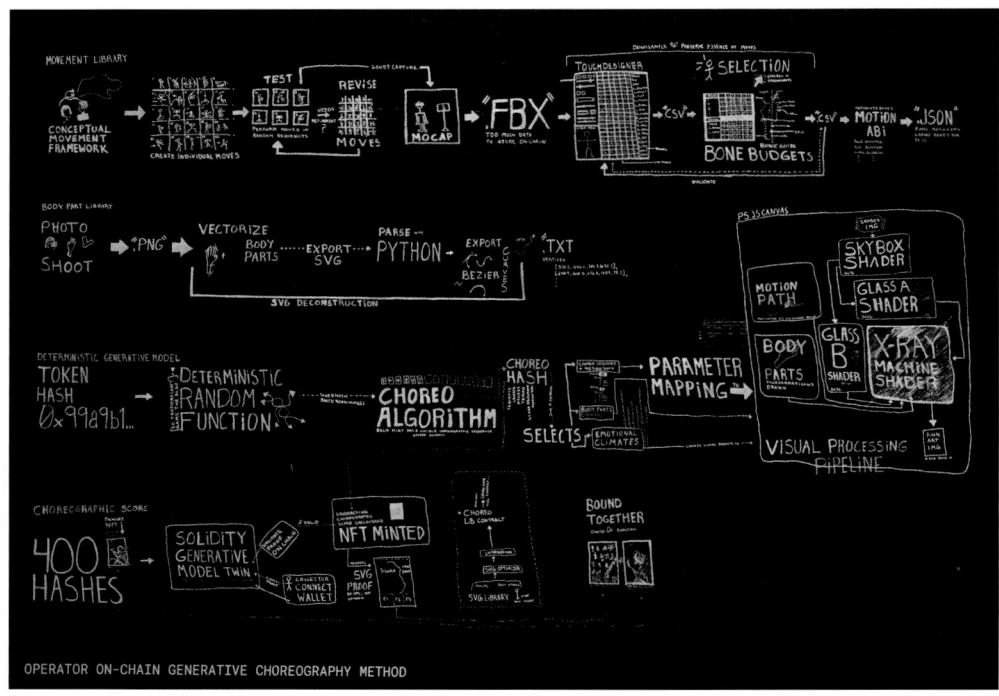

OPERATOR ON-CHAIN GENERATIVE CHOREOGRAPHY METHOD

06

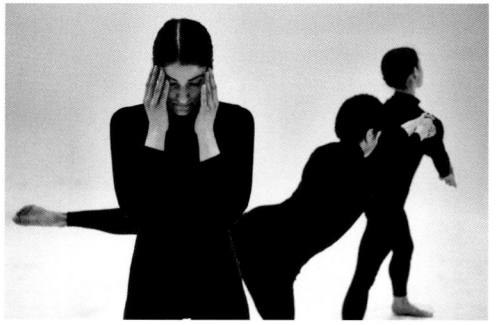

07

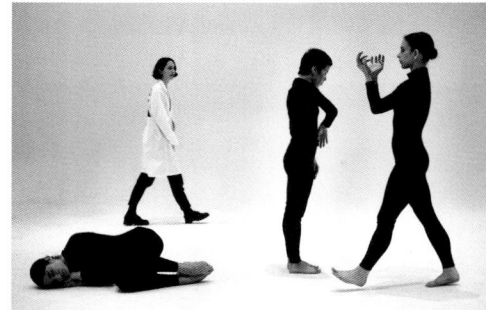

Code can be elegant or messy. Code is praxis but it can also be art. Ania Catherine and Dejha Ti of Operator have conceived *Human Unreadable* (2023) as a drama in three acts about the pas de deux between humans and the technology we create.

A pencil, the alphabet, a blockchain: technology is everywhere. Much like the human experience, it's as simple or as complex as we need it to be. Yet our relationship with technology is always fraught and mysterious. Operator creates art from this tension.

The code underlying *Human Unreadable* is both complex and simple. For the first time, choreography is encoded on the blockchain. Generative code creates random and deliberate sequences and translates the dance score into a series of figurative abstractions. Collectors can choose to reveal the hidden choreography beneath the still image, becoming part of the performance.

As we uncover the layers of *Human Unreadable*, its elegant simplicity becomes deeply moving. Human and abstract shapes perform a static yet expressive dance in shades of black and white. At the thrilling reveal of the choreography, elfin stick figures reminiscent of ancient cave paintings encode human emotion in motion. We can dance this dance. Dancers can perform it.

The rigor, the imagination, and the artistry behind *Human Unreadable* are deeply touching. If paradox is a satisfying aesthetic and imaginative state, then *Human Unreadable* is a gift of paradox. It gracefully demonstrates that code can be art, that we need not obscure or fear it. As Operator shows, we can make technology blossom into human expression. At a time when we fear technology as a threat, *Human Unreadable* makes the human readable. It confirms the potential of NFTs as a vehicle for profound artistic exploration.

**YEHUDIT MAM**
CO-FOUNDER OF DADA.ART

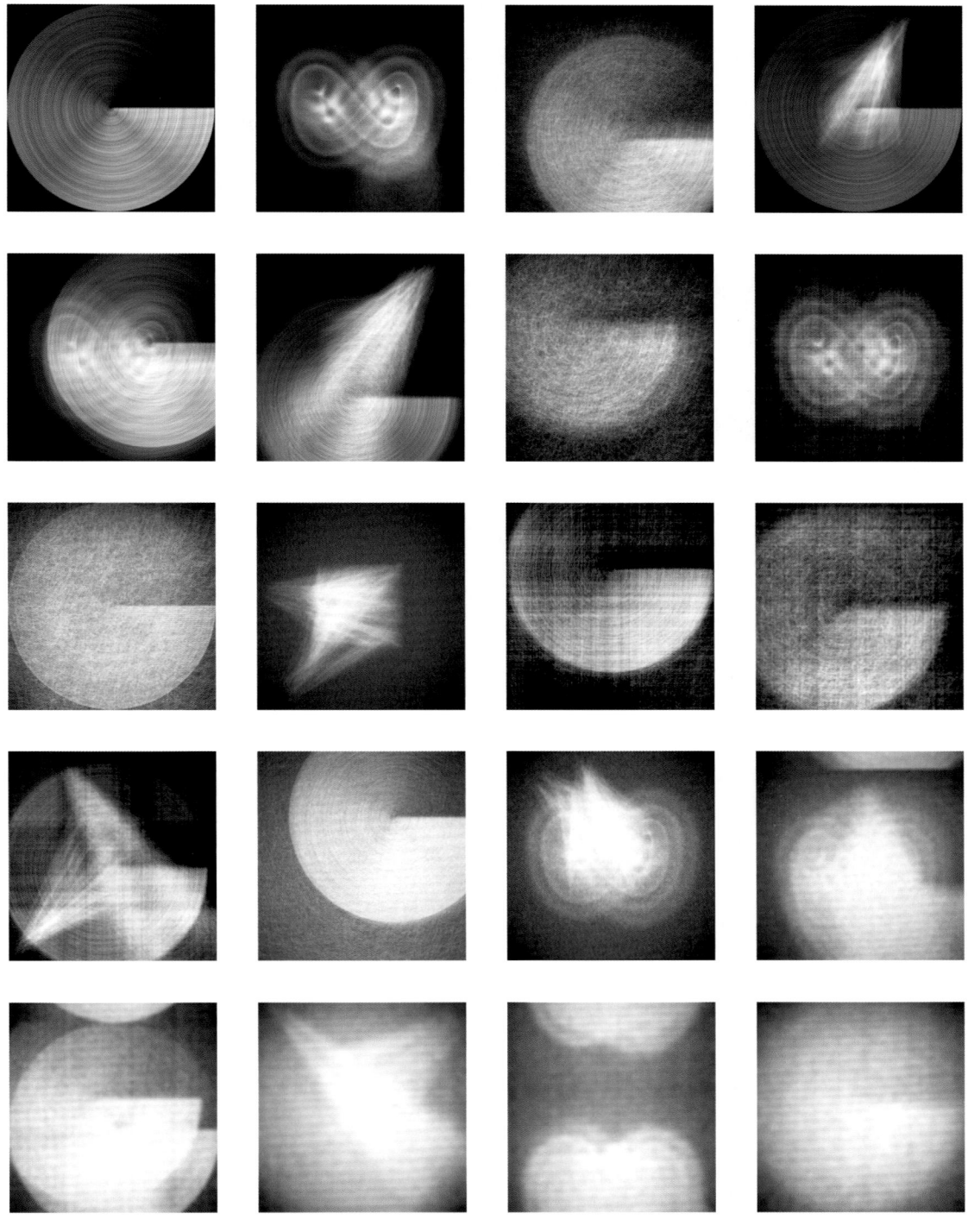

| # | TITLE | TIMESTAMP | MEDIUM | CHAIN | CONTRACT ADDRESS | TOKEN ID | EDITION SIZE |
|---|---|---|---|---|---|---|---|
| 01 | **Entropy** | 04-09-2021 04:04:22 | C compiler, Emacs | ETH | 0xd754937672300ae6708a51229112de4017810934 | 144–150, 221 | 1/1 of 8 |
| 02 | **Glitchbox** | 05-05-2021 15:21:50 | C compiler, Emacs | ETH | 0xd754937672300ae6708a51229112de4017810934 | 151–214 | 1/1 of 64 |
| 03 | **Transmission** | 03-30-2021 14:34:11 | C compiler, Emacs | ETH | 0xd754937672300ae6708a51229112de4017810934 | 136–143 | 1/1 of 8 |

EDITIONS ILLUSTRATED: (01) #148, (02) #182, (03) #139

# 0XDEAFBEEF

02 ▶

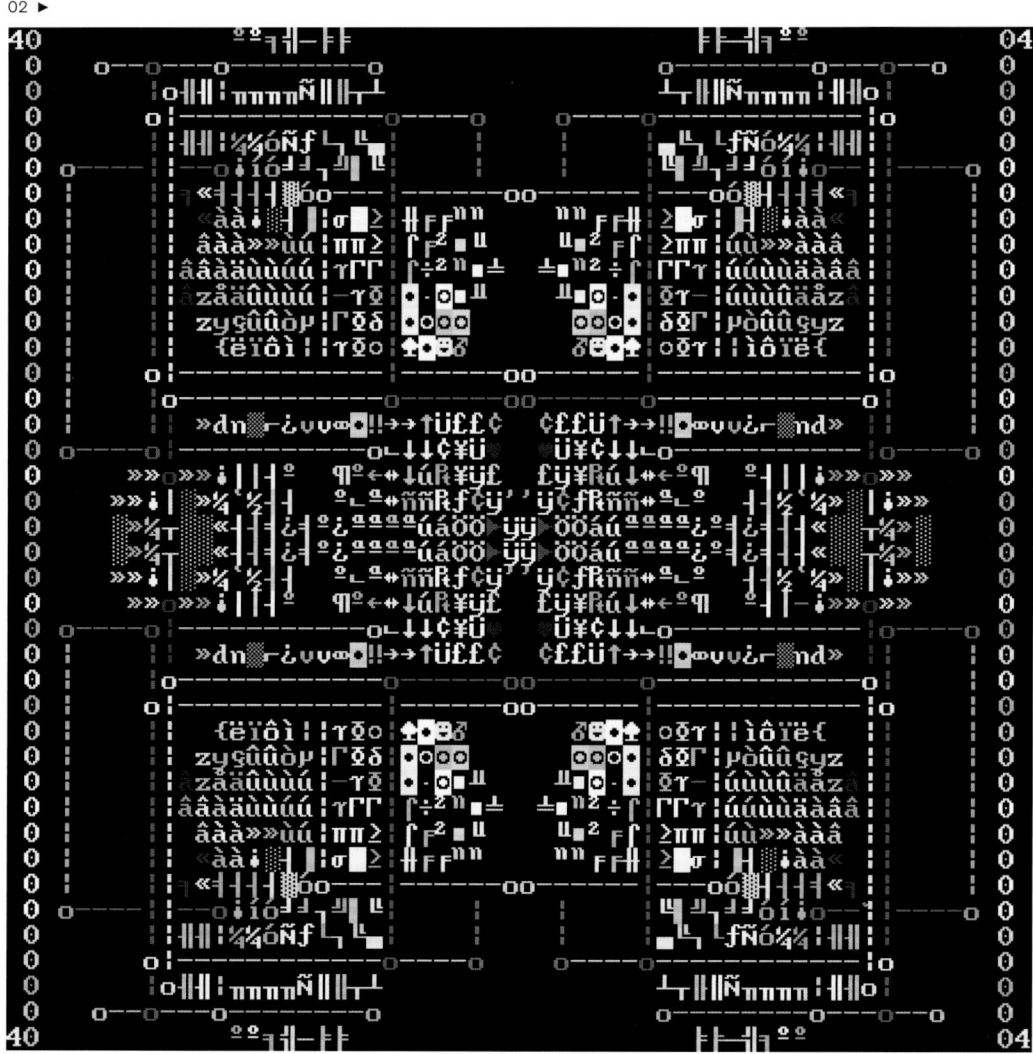

0xDEAFBEEF is the art project of Tyler de Witt, a Canadian artist, composer, and engineer. Over the past 20 years, he has tinkered in numerous fields, ranging from computer animation, sound recording, and classical music to blacksmithing. He trained at the University of Toronto's storied Computer Graphics Laboratory, where he did high-level research on physical simulations. In 2020, he started creating cutting-edge generative audiovisual artworks, using the C programming language as his primary instrument. The files are stored on-chain, meaning that the media can be fully reconstructed with data stored on the Ethereum blockchain. Instead of relying on out-of-the-box solutions, 0xDEAFBEEF builds all of his artistic tools from first principles, using only a C compiler and the Emacs text editor.

This unique methodology leads to pieces that bear his distinctive signature — elegant black-and-white pieces that fuse art and electronic music in singular ways. The visual element recalls vintage oscilloscopes, ASCII art, text glitches, and television static. He draws creative inspiration from a wide range of sources, from the procedurally generated open-source video game *Nethack* to the pioneering modernist artist László Moholy-Nagy (1895–1946).

*Synth Poems* (2021) was his first series of NFTs, followed by *Angular* (2021), *Transmission* (2021), *Entropy* (2021), and *Glitchbox* (2021). *Entropy* is a groundbreaking experiment in generative audiovisual synthesis. When an *Entropy* NFT is transferred, it degrades; there is a built-in system of degradation reminiscent of analog decay. *Entropy* is a powerful statement on notions of value, the assumptions of stability built into blockchains, and the high frequency resale of NFTs. When an *Entropy* NFT changes, is it worth less, or worth more? The questions that *Entropy* raises are profound. It is his strongest artistic work to date, both aesthetically and conceptually — a memento mori for a technoculture fixated on an illusion of permanence.

**GEETA DAYAL**
ART CRITIC AND JOURNALIST

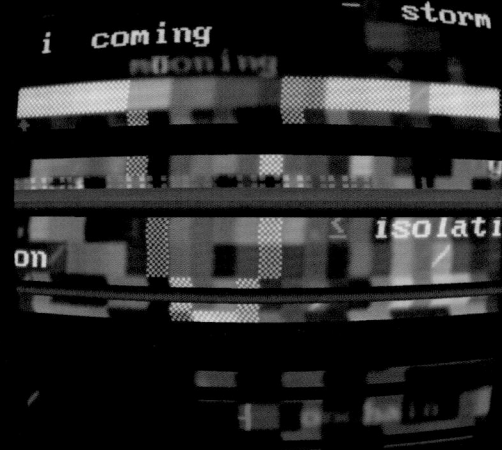

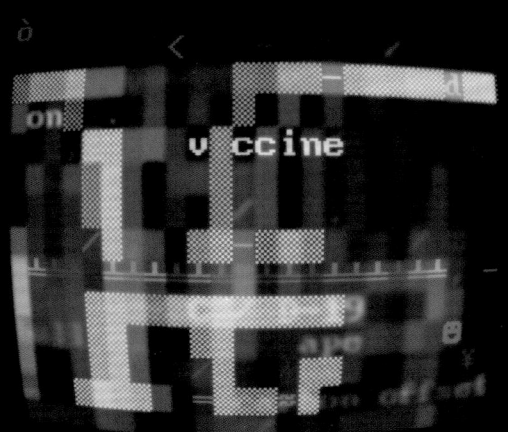

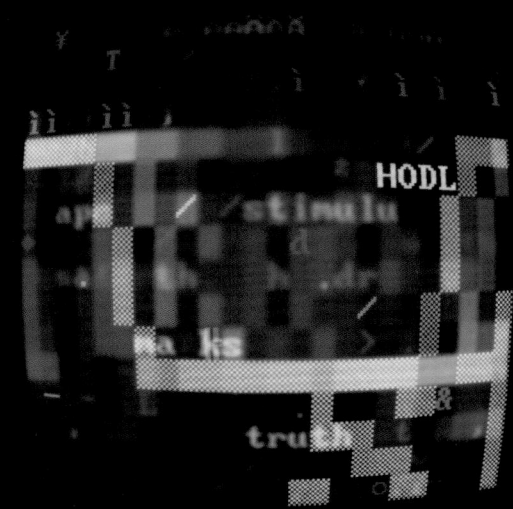

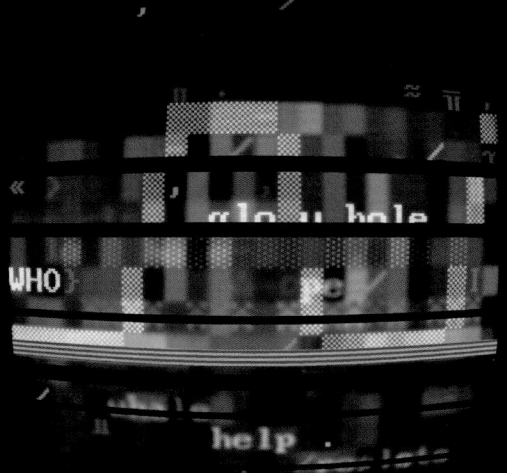
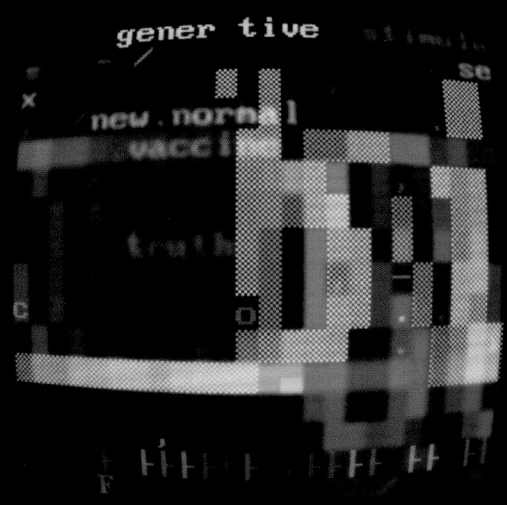
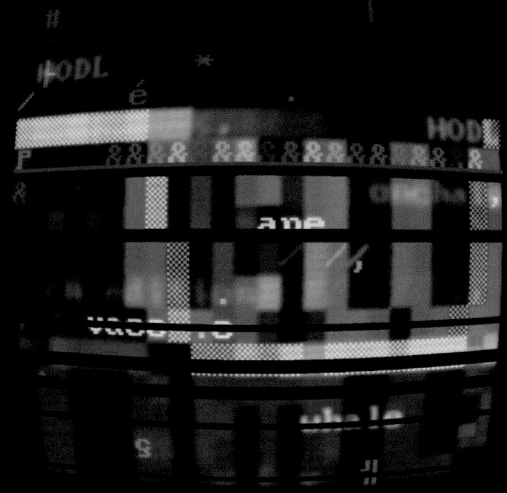
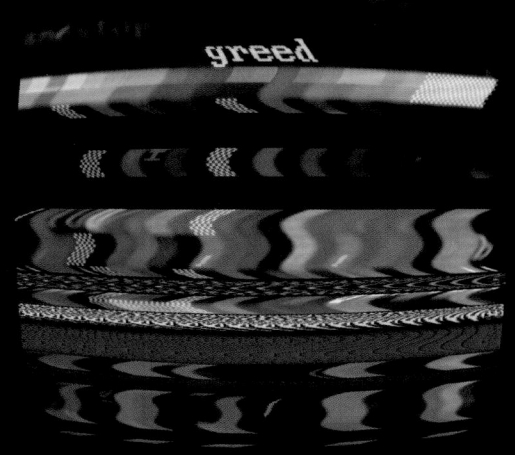

01 ►

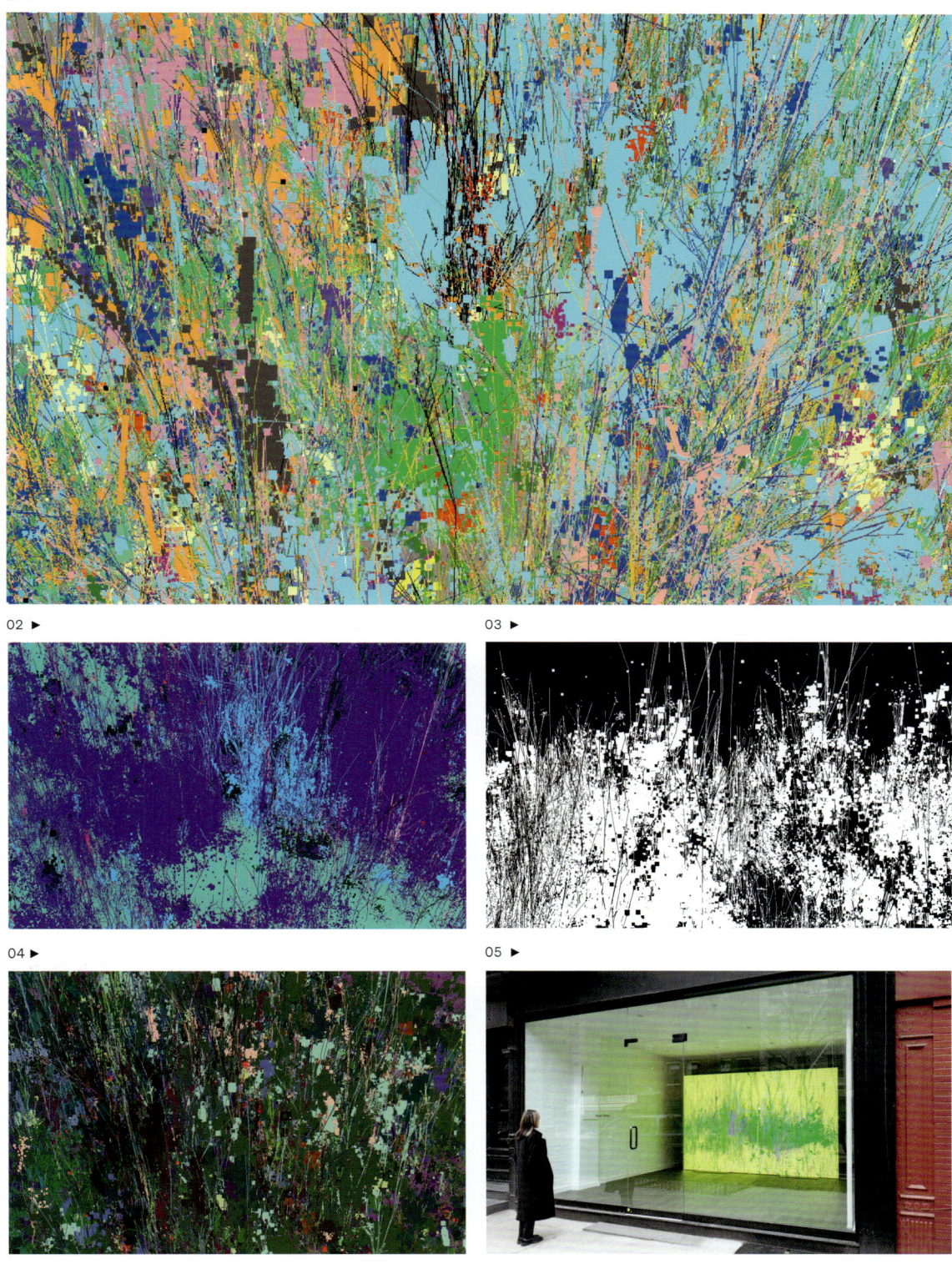

02 ►

03 ►

04 ►

05 ►

| # | TITLE | TIMESTAMP | MEDIUM | CHAIN | CONTRACT ADDRESS | TOKEN ID | EDITION SIZE |
|---|---|---|---|---|---|---|---|
| 01–06 | **Infinite Garden** | 03-17-2025 18:00:00 | Javascript, WEB GL | SHAPE | 0xbB8F2711bd4BC98223990267f771E97d2d9Bc167 | 1-5000 | Infinite |

EDITIONS ILLUSTRATED: x (01) #53, (02) #2409, (03) #25, (04) #769, (05) Installation Shot of Infinite Garden at Nguyen Wahed, 17 March–2 May 2025, (06) #2510

# LEANDER HERZOG
SWITZERLAND 1984

06 ▶

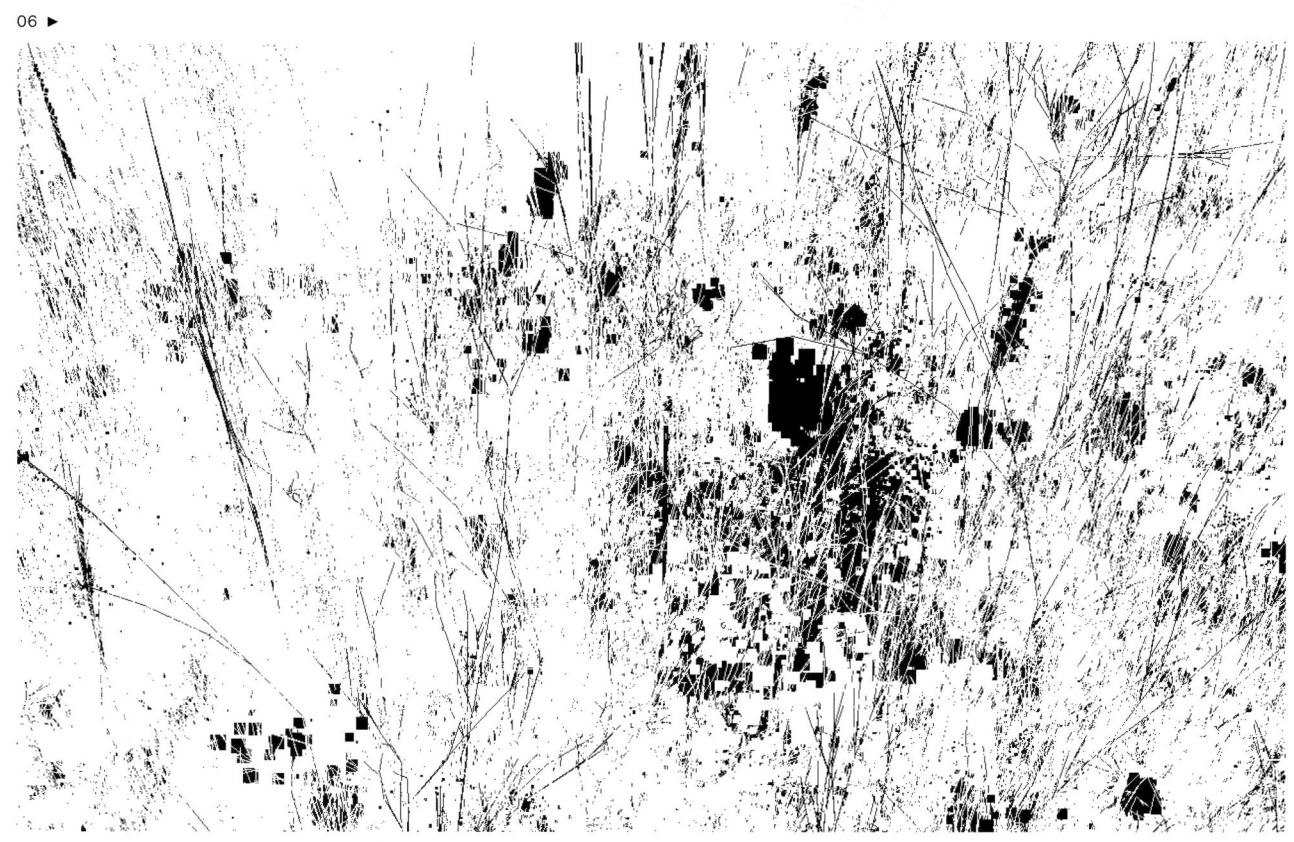

In *Infinite Garden* (2025), Leander Herzog creates a dynamic botanical ecosystem where collectors actively participate in the artwork's evolution. The project functions through a smart contract system that enables multiple forms of interaction: collectors begin with a unique floral arrangement, then can add new flowers, combine elements, and — most distinctively — gift blooms to other gardens, creating an ever-shifting network of digital flora. Each garden responds to temporal conditions, with flowers changing throughout day/night cycles and seasonal progressions, ensuring no moment repeats itself.

Visually, Herzog's digital mark-making embraces the pixel's inherent qualities, creating floral forms with organic tactility that never disguise their digital origins. The interface allows collectors to arrange their gardens, track their contributions on a community leaderboard, and watch their flora evolve. The work becomes a living record of collective participation, with more than 145 million flowers planted through thousands of blockchain interactions.

At the physical installation at Nguyen Wahed in New York, Herzog translated this digital ecosystem to monumental scale. Wall-sized projections revealed the collective evolution of the garden in real time, making visible the connections between individual collections. The installation transformed what might have remained abstract into a tangible, shared experience — establishing new protocols for digital collaboration.

*Infinite Garden* transforms blockchain from transactional infrastructure into a collaborative medium. Value emerges not from singular artwork ownership but from participation in a system where gardens communicate, flowers migrate, and meaning develops through relationship. By designing protocols for cultivation rather than possession, Herzog creates an art form that is inherently social, constantly in dialogue, and fundamentally alive.

**ADDIE WAGENKNECHT & 0XFFF**
ARTISTS

01 ▶

02 ▶

03 ▶

04 ▶

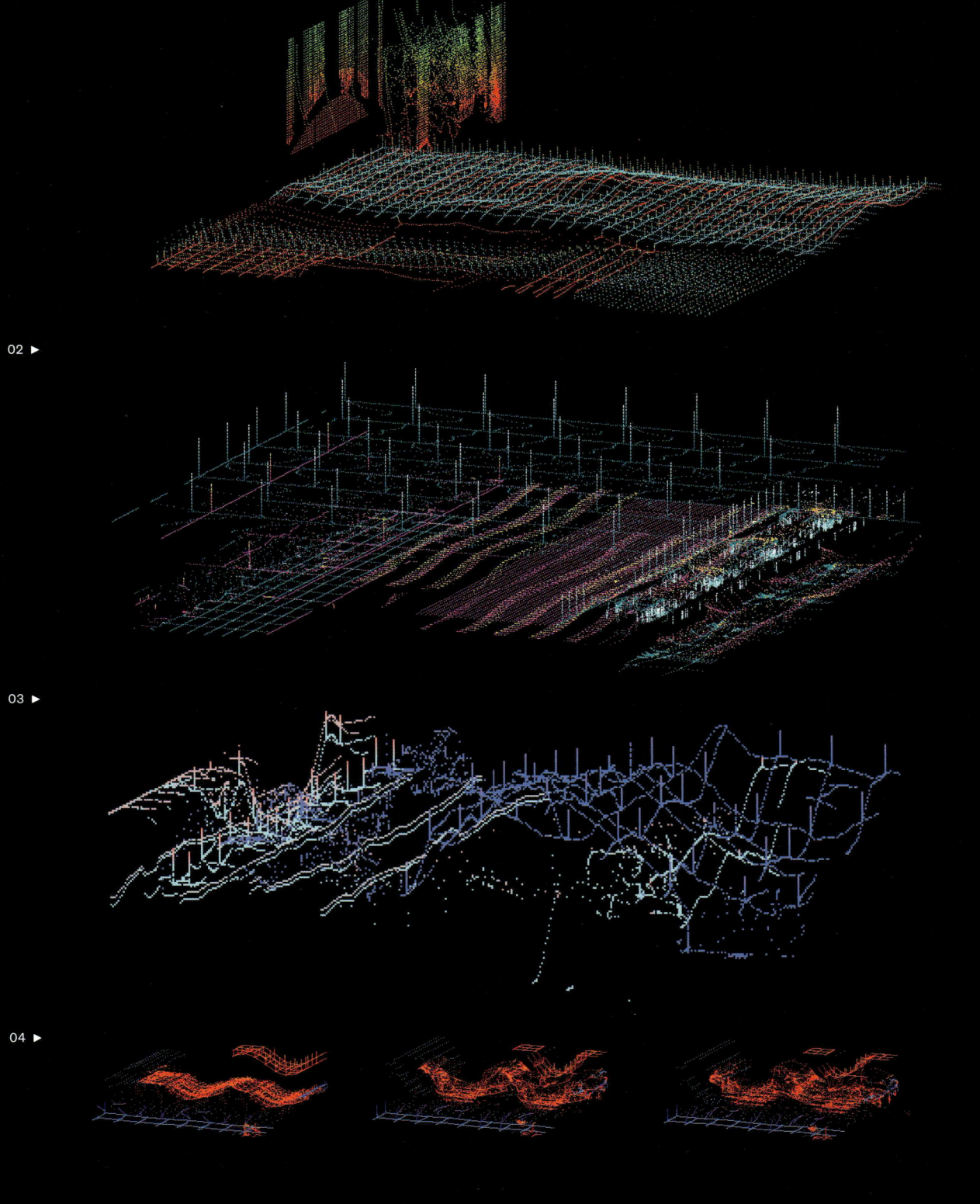

| # | TITLE | TIMESTAMP | MEDIUM | CHAIN | CONTRACT ADDRESS | TOKEN ID | EDITION SIZE |
|---|-------|-----------|--------|-------|------------------|----------|--------------|
| 01–04 | **PXL DEX** | 01-17- 2025, 16:50:59 | WebGL, GLSL, JavaScript | ETH | 0×81345761670fc8b90665466A94C196E26b92EcFB | 1-256 | 1/1 of 256 |
| 05 | **Monogrid** | 10-08-2021, 16:27:32 | WebGL, GLSL, JavaScript | XTZ | KT1RJ6PbjHpwc3M5rw5s2Nbmefwbuwbdxton | 407403 (00) - 413921 (ff) | 1/1 of 256 |

EDITIONS ILLUSTRATED: (01) #81, (02) #149, (03) #242, (04) #93 (Various Stills), (05) # 413102

# KIM ASENDORF
GERMANY 1981

05 ▶

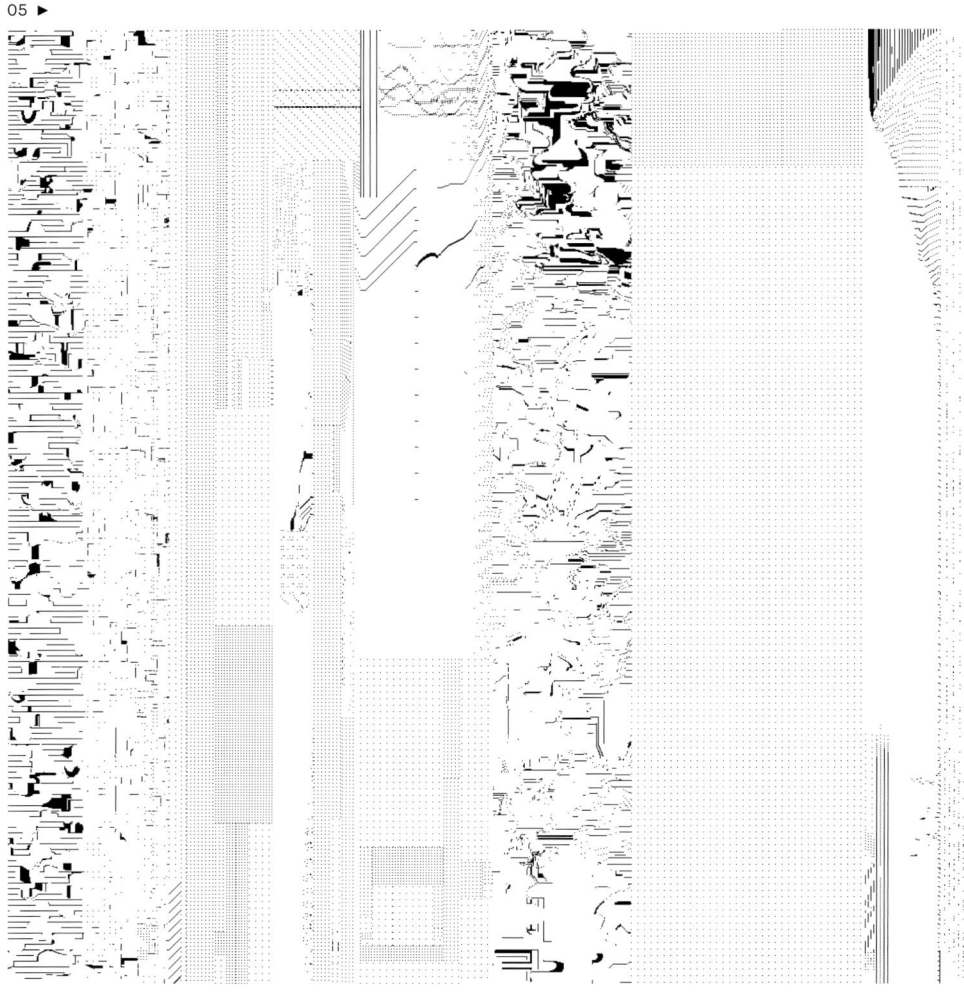

Kim Asendorf cuts to the visual, conceptual, and computational core of what digital art is made of. *Monogrid* (2021) was the first project to use a bespoke pixel-sorting algorithm to create pulsing, never-looping 2D animations that are both surprising and restrained. These abstract images construct and manipulate themselves at the level of individual pixels. To watch these works unfold is to understand what a screen is capable of.

*PXL DEX* (2025) employs some of the same pixel-sorting algorithms as Monogrid, but extrudes them into the third dimension. *PXL DEX* poses provocative questions about the simultaneously material and ephemeral nature of digital art, revealing surprising perceptual qualities of digital objects. Each work, or Deck, in the series is a pulsing 3D arrangement of pixels which functions as a sort of digital jewel box — a virtual object for collecting even more virtual objects. The precise number of *PXL* tokens is determined by the collector at purchase, and more can be added later, even by a subsequent holder. Owners of these digital boxes are invited to tokenize individual pixels, reducing digital art collecting to its barest essence.

The atomic unit of digital art is the pixel, and its substrate is the screen. But screens are always changing. In order to think long-term, the digital artist must accept that the screen is both a limiter and an unknown quantity. Asendorf's work typically scales to the native resolution of the screen on which it appears, meaning that it will evolve visually as screens continue to change. Works like Monogrid and *PXL DEX* are processes that work in harmony with whatever screen happens to display them. They are a series of digital objects, but unlike most images displayed on screens, they are also systems that reveal the objecthood of the screens on which they are displayed.

**KEVIN BUIST**
CRITIC

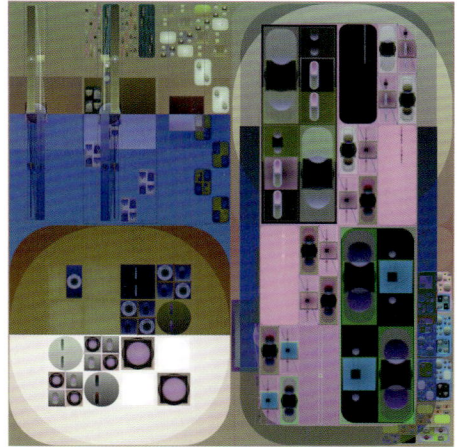 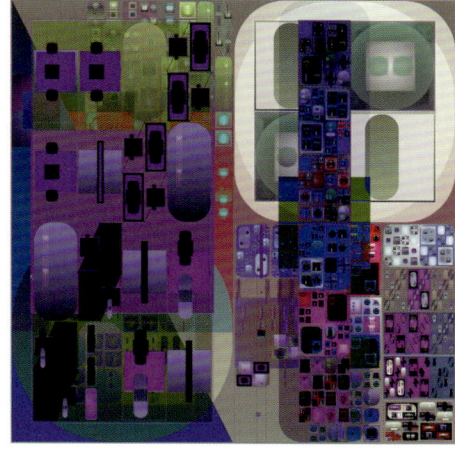

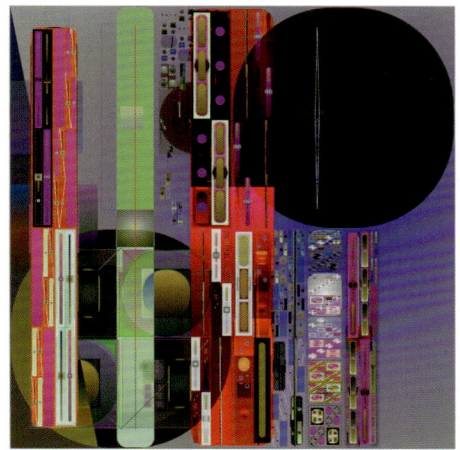 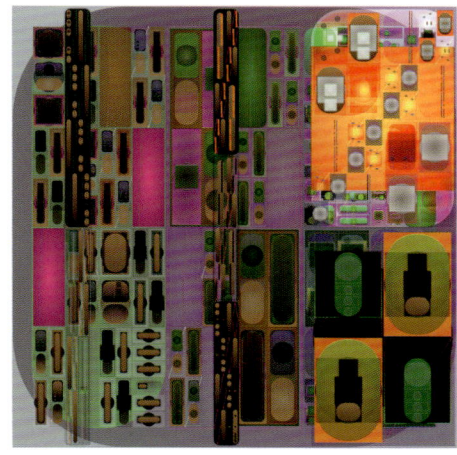

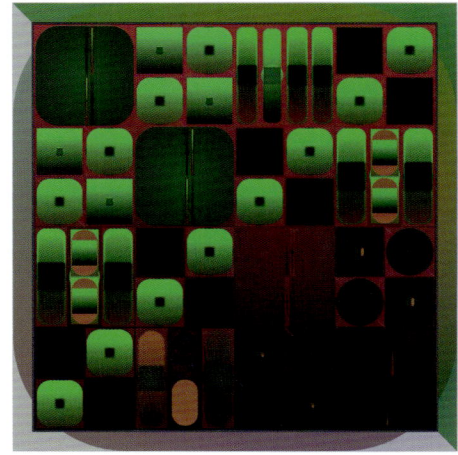 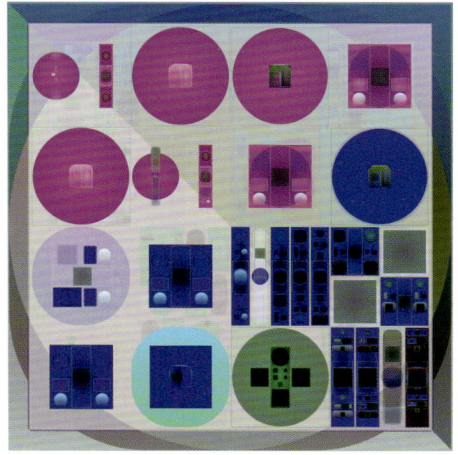

| # | TITLE | TIMESTAMP | MEDIUM | CHAIN | CONTRACT ADDRESS | TOKEN ID | EDITION SIZE |
|---|---|---|---|---|---|---|---|
| 01 | **Mutant Garden Seeder** | 06-16-2021 07:24:15 | TypeScript, Solidity, SVG | ETH | 0x20c70bdfcc398c1f06b-a81730c8b52ace3af7cc3 | 8757479–12884655 | 1/1 of 512, +1 AP |
| 02–10 | **Markov's Dream: Orb (lite)** | 06-09-2022 09:42:26 | Fully on-chain animated generative SVG | ETH | 0x71d7b2adf7be0377c1a-faac8666e8dfb30a1956f | 1–512 | 1/1 of 512 |

EDITIONS ILLUSTRATED: (01) Annlli, with further mutations of the same edition, (02) #69, (03) #71, (04) #72, (05) #74, (06) #62, (07) #63, (08) #53, (09) #93, (10) #95

# HARM VAN DEN DORPEL

THE NETHERLANDS 1981

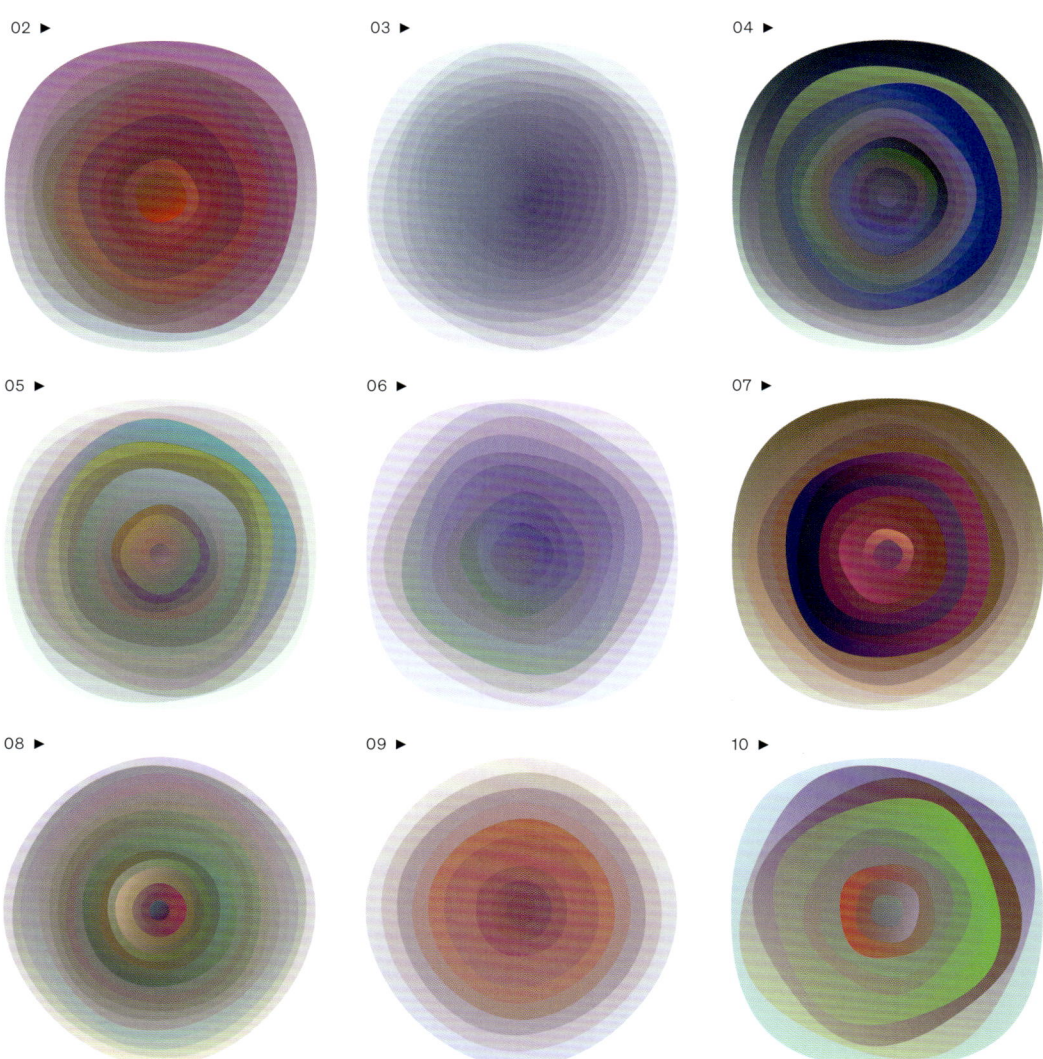

02 ▶
03 ▶
04 ▶
05 ▶
06 ▶
07 ▶
08 ▶
09 ▶
10 ▶

Harm van den Dorpel is an artist whose work has consistently pushed the boundaries of new media in contemporary art. Van den Dorpel's works grow out of the early 21st-century net art movement, particularly its spirit of exploration and openness to the possibilities afforded by dematerialized cultural practices. More recently, van den Dorpel has created groundbreaking works based on algorithmic and genetic recombinatory processes.

In works including *Death Imitates Language* (2017), *Mutant Garden* (2019–22), and, most recently, *Markov's Dream* (2022), van den Dorpel has explored the ways in which artistic subjectivity can be challenged and reinvented using generative algorithmic processes, challenging both the appurtenances of painterly prerogatives, but also the ostensible determinism of digital processes. The lineage of computer science, from early Turing machines, to Chomskyan logical normalizations, to Cartesian Genetic Programming is always present in van den Dorpel's works, presenting lost and forgotten histories of computational philosophy and practices in new contexts and forms.

The artist is also known for his early embrace of blockchain as a potential artistic medium, producing works that are inscribed directly into blocks in the distributed ledger technology in recent works. Van den Dorpel's Left Gallery (2015–22) (RIP) offered an experimental platform for artists working with digital forms, providing a marketplace of fully digitalized exchange for artists and audiences. Long recognized as a leading figure in the digital /crypto art field, van den Dorpel is acknowledged to be the first artist to have had a digital work acquired by a museum using cryptocurrency. In the eternally mutating ecology of digital culture, van den Dorpel continues to demonstrate a determination to forge new aesthetic pathways.

**WILLIAM KHERBEK**
ART CRITIC

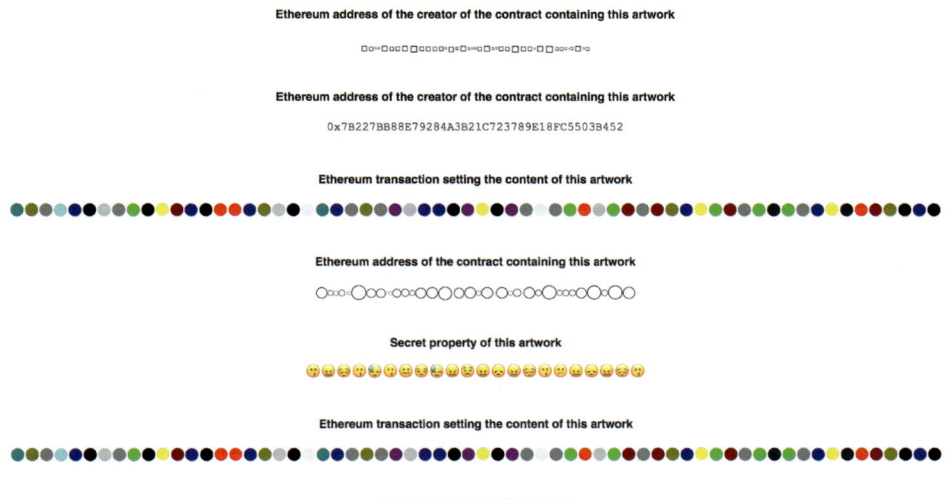

**Ethereum address of the creator of the contract containing this artwork**

**Ethereum address of the creator of the contract containing this artwork**

0x7B227BB88E79284A3B21C723789E18FC5503B452

**Ethereum transaction setting the content of this artwork**

**Ethereum address of the contract containing this artwork**

**Secret property of this artwork**

**Ethereum transaction setting the content of this artwork**

**Hash of the content of this artwork**

0x242F21E612C260AC18187601798295E6C4576617E4EA8CE823902531C0044B35

**Ethereum block containing the transaction setting the current owner of this artwork**

| # | TITLE | TIMESTAMP | MEDIUM | CHAIN | CONTRACT ADDRESS | TOKEN ID | EDITION SIZE |
|---|---|---|---|---|---|---|---|
| 01 | **Secret Artwork (Content)** | 07-23-2018 06:07:49 | Cryptographic hash, HTML5 | ETH | 0x5b64319f093178a5db00bab4b274b1e665a66ece | 1 | 1/1 |
| 02 | **Is Art** | 03-24-2016 03:57:46 | HTML5 | ETH | 0xa95301a50551dfe16e180dec3fe0044e94d36f8c | NA | 1/1 |

02

# This contract is art

Rhea Myers is an artist, hacker, and writer, originally from the United Kingdom and now based in Canada, who has generated a new genre of blockchain poetics with her artworks, theory, and fictions. Myers is universally acknowledged as an OG of blockchain art. Using tokens, transactions, and contracts, she has earned this honorific by building new technical territories in the form of conceptual artworks. Long before the first crypto art marketplaces, and responding to the notorious opacity of the traditional art market, Myers invented, in her own words, "new markets for new kinds of art" with her 2014 *Ethereum Art Market* — incorporating the first smart contracts for artist's resale rights. Her 2015 *Art Coins (Coloured)* was the first artwork to be made specifically as nothing more than a token without external reference, and *Is Art* (2014–15) literally heralds and facilitates the historic moment when art lovers get to decide by interacting with a click and the payment of a small gas fee, one of the most important questions of all time, "is this art?"

*Secret Artwork (Content)* (2018) is an appropriation of Art and Language's monochrome *Secret Painting(s)* (1967–68), which famously included the claim that its contents were an invisible and permanent secret "known only to the artist." It sits across two traditions of conceptual art and cryptography, continuing a historic tradition of cryptographic art stretching back to Hans Holbein the Younger's (1497/8–1543) *The Ambassadors* (1533), providing a gateway to the "anxieties of ownership, identity, and control that cryptocurrency and blockchain tech operationalize."

The appearance of *Secret Artwork (Content)*, the apparent banality of the symbols and emoticons that comprise its image, stand in sharp contrast to the religiosity of their minimalist antecedents. Mapped to the hash of the hidden content like a code, they add a stenographic layer that lends irony and bathos to both the declaration and concealment of its mystery.

**RUTH CATLOW**
CO-FOUNDER OF FURTHERFIELD
RECOVERING WEB UTOPIAN

03

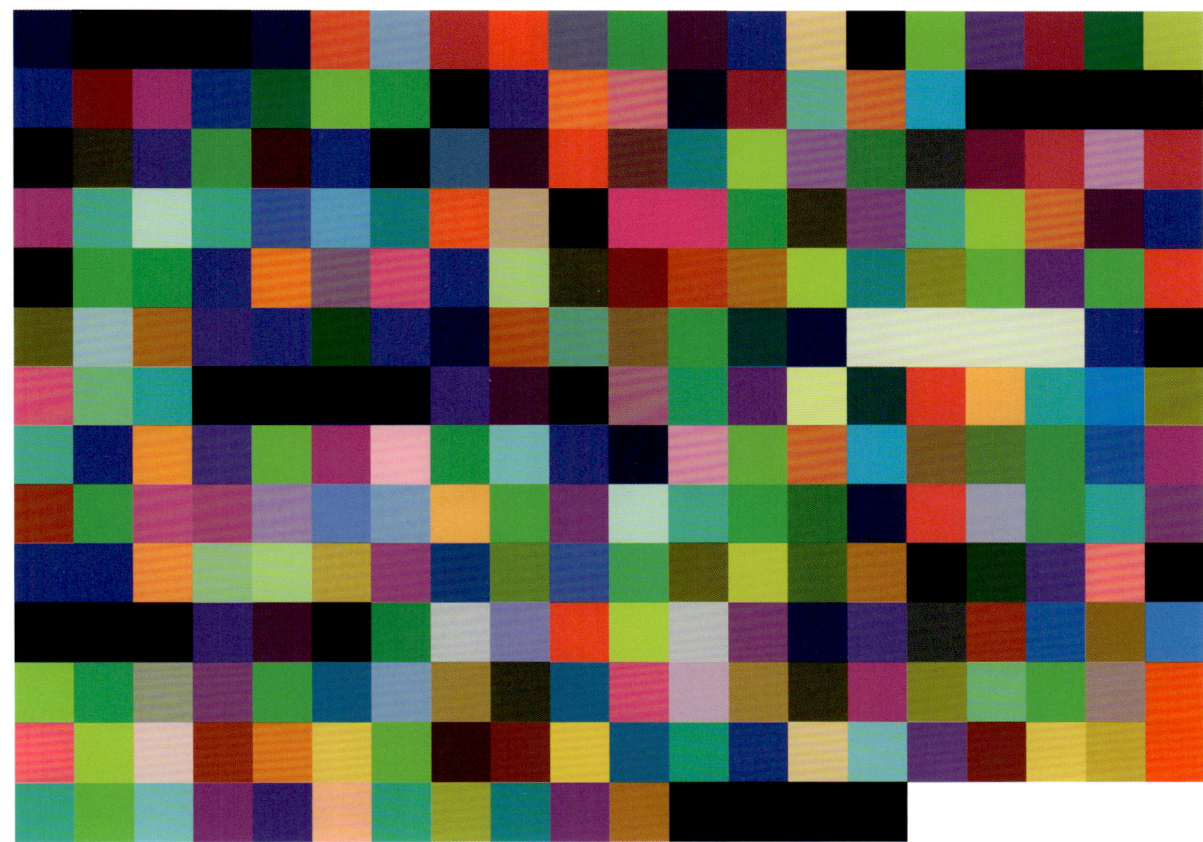

| # | TITLE | TIMESTAMP | MEDIUM | CHAIN | CONTRACT ADDRESS | TOKEN ID | EDITION SIZE |
|---|---|---|---|---|---|---|---|
| 03 | **First Halvening (Bitcoin Block Header)** | 10-11-2021 01:53:37 | Custom software-generated vector image | ETH | 0x3b3ee1931dc30c19573-79fac9aba94d1c48a5405 | 96678 | 1/1 |
| 04 | **Certificate of Inauthenticity** | 05-16-2020 11:53:04 | Vector images | ETH | 0xe63c62f07e7adc4c397-fb84d21d5aa6e0e054603 | 1–33 | 3 artworks in editions of 11 |

# C E R T I F I C A T E

Rare art certified instance __01__ / __11__
of the artwork __Balloon Dog__
has not been modelled, instantiated, or presented by Rhea Myers.

This certificate is valid only when:
a. It is displayed accompanying a single instance of the artwork named above that is being displayed in the same physical or virtual location as this certificate, and;
b. That display has been organized by, on behalf of, or with the full knowledge and authorization of the party or parties that either;

   i. control the private key of the Externally Owned Account that is currently the ownerOf() the ERC-721 token having the URI of this image as the "image" field of its tokenURI() metadata, or;

   ii. control the smart contract or contracts that are currently the ownerOf() the ERC-721 token having the URI of this image as the "image" field of its tokenURI() metadata and can demonstrate sufficient authority to authorize this display using an appropriate on-chain mechanism, or;

   iii. are able to demonstrate equivalent or successor ownership of this image - for example the beneficiary of a token rental or of a cross-chain transfer but not the owner of a fractionalized wrapper token or a token referencing the URI of this image, or a copy of this image, created by an unauthorized third party.

Certified by _R Myers_

Rhea Myers

Date _2020-05-11_

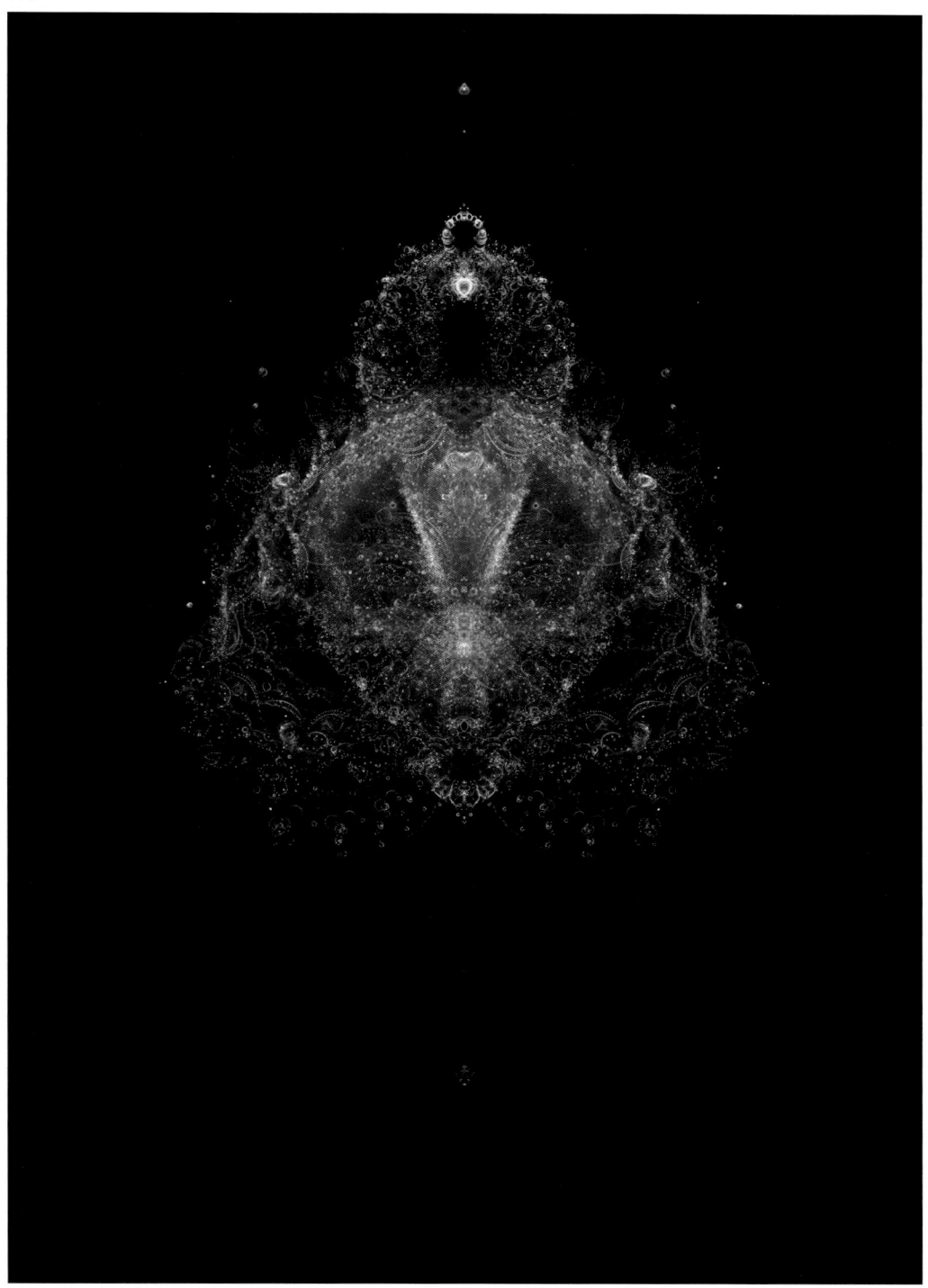

| # | TITLE | TIMESTAMP | MEDIUM | CHAIN | CONTRACT ADDRESS | TOKEN ID | EDITION SIZE | COLLABORATORS |
|---|---|---|---|---|---|---|---|---|
| 01 | **{BUDDHABROT} 0x374752c0f5** | 10-01-2021 18:30:49 | Custom-built software | ETH | 0x47ccad36ae77ab96374-6c8db8ad301d48235ce81 | 7155...5417 | 1/1 | Melinda Green, Daïm Aggott-Hönsch |
| 02–05 | **Brotchain** | 08-21-2021 12:26:10 | Solidity | ETH | 0xd31fc221d2b0e0321c43-e9f6824b26ebfff01d7d | 0–70063 | 4 artworks in editions of 64 | – |

EDITIONS ILLUSTRATED: (02) Palm Trees, (03) Seahorse Valley, (04) Mandelbrot, (05) Burning Ship

# DIVERGENCE

02
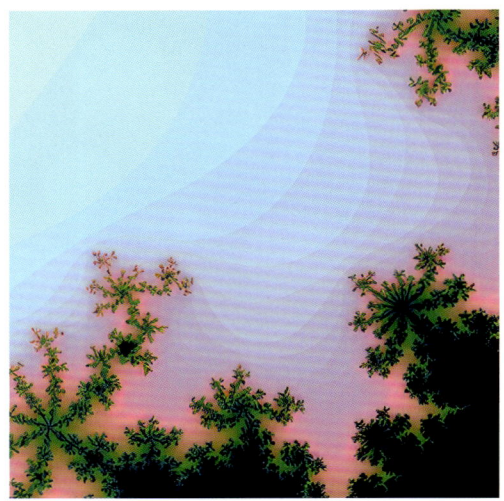

03
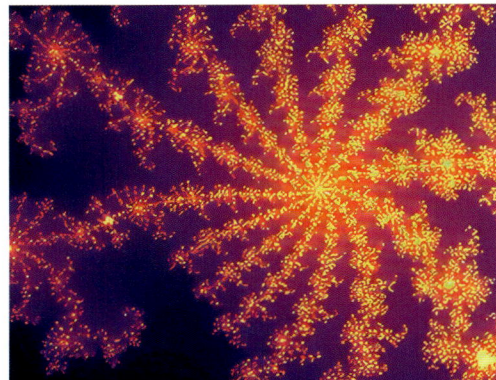

04
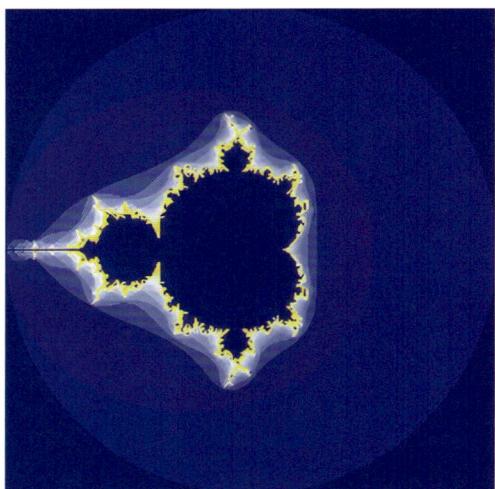

05
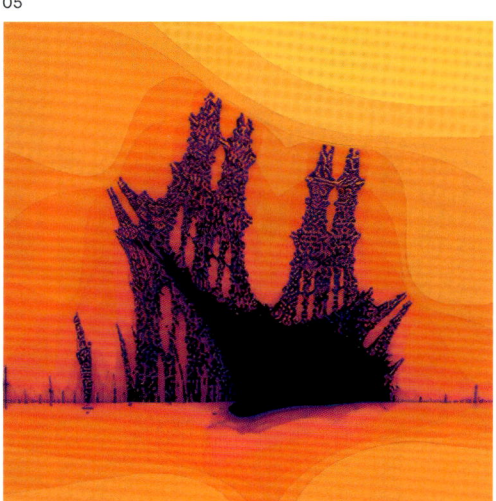

I first met Angharad Thomas and Arran Schlosberg (aka divergence) when they appeared on my NFT podcast *PROOF*. I was struck by their "hold my beer" attitude to tackling unfeasibly complex challenges; they take genuine joy in pushing technological boundaries. They are innovators with a unique set of career deviations — until recently Arran was a Google software developer and a practicing MD, while Angharad founded a nonprofit using tech to help schools better understand their students.

divergence launched themselves onto the NFT scene with *PROOF OF {ART}WORK* (2021), an interactive collection in which viewers use custom-built software to explore vast galaxies of mathematically placed dots. The series is based on a mathematical construct called the "Buddhabrot," with pieces ranging from individual "seeds" to a full, infinitely zoomable Buddha in the work *{BUDDHABROT} 0x374752c0f5* (released in collaboration with its discoverer Melinda Green, as well as mathematical artist and Buddhabrot enthusiast Daïm Aggott-Hönsch). However, it is in smart contracts that divergence have really made their mark and

significantly pushed forward the NFT space. To Angharad and Arran, a smart contract is more than just the piece of technology underpinning an NFT — it is their artistic canvas. This is embodied best in their most recent project *The Kiss Precise* (2022), which takes the growing trend for long-form generative art and moves it inside a smart contract.

Similar in complexity, *Brotchain* (2021) was born to counter-evidence a statement made by a leading engineer in the space that art couldn't be created from a smart contract without any external dependencies, such as an SVG renderer. Not only did they create the familiar fractal forms using just a smart contract, they also made them customizable through on-chain interactions — leading collectors to explore their dormant inner artists. These innovations represent another step forward in the move from NFTs-as-receipts towards truly crypto-native art.

**KEVIN ROSE**
FOUNDER OF PROOF

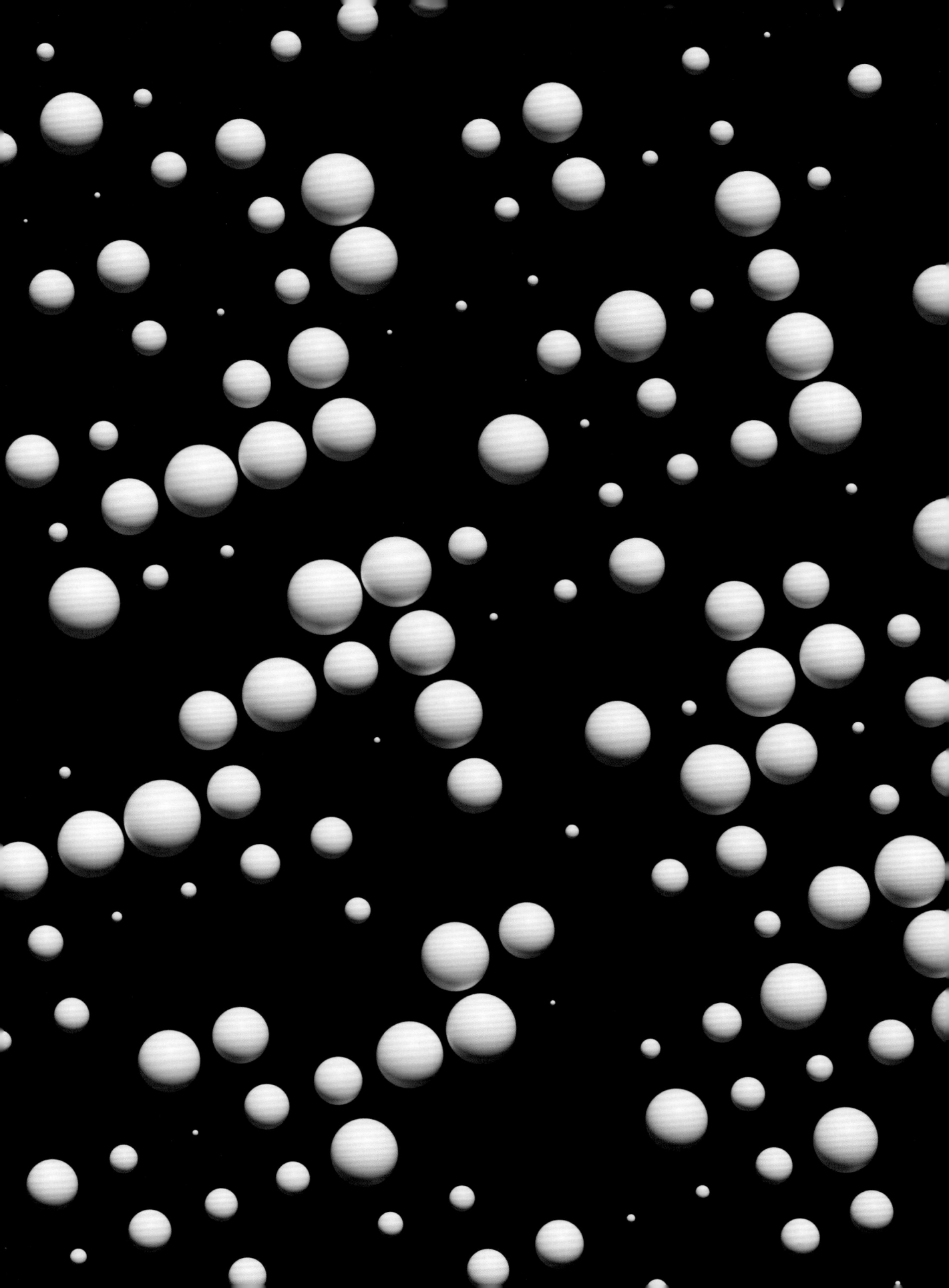

RHEA MYERS

# ON CHAIN
## The Medium Is The Ledger

*A smart contract is to a contract what a koala bear is to a bear.*
*They share the same name but they have nothing in common.*

Primavera De Filippi

**smart contract** *noun*
*1. "A smart contract is a computerized transaction*
*protocol that executes the terms of a contract."*
*—Nick Szabo*
*2. Like (1), but on the blockchain.*

**smart contract art** *noun*
*1. Art that uses the affordances or constraints*
*of smart contracts as its plastic medium.*
*2. Art that is made possible, practical,*
*or improved by its use of smart contracts.*

Pak
*Merge*, 12-17-2021 01:14:35
Medium unknown, artist's visualization
Ethereum, 0xe052113bd7d7700d623414a0a4585bcae754e9d5, 1

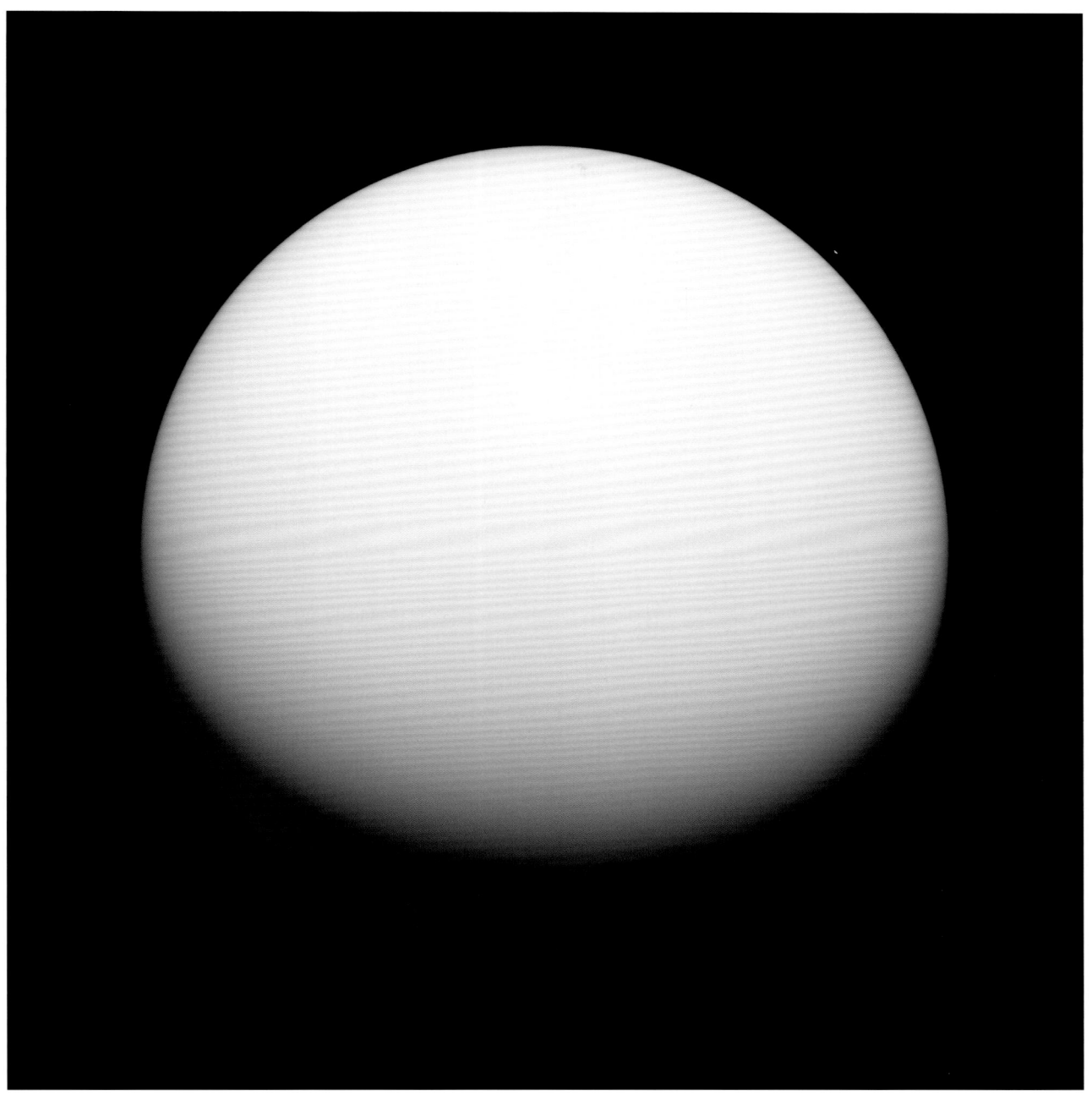

A community of collectors formed around the pseudonymous artist Pak's *Merge* (2021) NFTs **[04.01]** during the brief 48 hours that they were available for anyone to buy. Owners of those tokens could merge the tokens representing their artwork to create a new dynamic artwork. Nearly 30,000 tokens were minted to take part in this process — creating in turn a global networked digital artwork at a scale never previously seen: a single, large, community-centered artwork created by and incorporating the participation of its collectors. The artwork was performative, and like relational art (which we will consider below) it would not exist without its audience. The question of whether, when, and how many *Merge* tokens each collector should purchase during the initial release gave way to the question of what they should do in order to maximize the value of their tokens individually or en masse for the community. And that in turn had to be set against the aesthetic question of how they could best experience the *Merge* NFT art that they own.

This use of rules in an engaged community has precedents in conceptual art, in the art of On Kawara (1932–2014), and in the paintings of Roman Opalka (1931–2011), amongst others. Like those precedents, *Merge* is a multifaceted smart contract–based work using carefully constructed rules relating time, human behavior, aesthetics, price. All this is filtered through the relationship between the fragment and the whole, the node and the network. The medium that *Merge* is implemented in makes these rules and its audience's reactions to them uniquely public, transparent, and unified. NFTs are implemented using the medium of blockchain-based smart contracts, in the case of *Merge* those smart contracts are implemented on the Ethereum blockchain in conformance with the ERC-721 Non-Fungible Token Standard (2018).[1]

Smart contracts are small computer programs, stored and executed on a blockchain using cryptographically signed transactions paid for using that blockchain's cryptocurrency (ether in the case of Ethereum). They are designed above all for security, and to achieve this they have extremely limited capabilities compared to any app on a modern smartphone, for example. They contain a tiny amount of code and data, cannot perform complex or time-consuming calculations, and cannot directly access information outside of their specific blockchain, on the internet, or on the computer running the blockchain software. What they lack in raw computing power they more than make up for in providing a single medium in which human agreements and economic value can be transparently and publicly expressed as code that anyone can use and build on. Like the printing press or the joint stock corporation, smart contracts enable new kinds of organization that go far beyond simply automating previous ways of doing things. They have become one of the most advanced and disruptive subjects of interest for artists in the 2020s who want to play with ideas of value, property, time, and the digital, and to create dynamic, networked art around and with whole online communities.

## Smart Contract History

The concept and implementation of smart contracts of the kind used to create *Merge* have a history that reaches back decades. In the 1980s, the *AMIX* information exchange was software that offered information for a price. Pay and it was yours with no human intervention. Cryptographer Nick Szabo formalized this idea of a program that replaces a human counterparty in the 1990s as "smart contracts." Szabo's smart contracts were modestly conceptualized — the example he used in his foundational paper entitled "The Idea of Smart Contracts" (1997) was of a vending machine that takes payment for goods.[2]

Szabo would go on to design an important antecedent to Bitcoin called Bit Gold (1998/2005), but it was not until 2008 that the pseudonymous Satoshi Nakamoto described a decentralized software platform for such programs — Bitcoin.[3] Bitcoin transactions are short snippets of code that run in order to securely exchange value in Bitcoin's built-in currency. But Bitcoin transaction program scripts were kept deliberately simple in order to prevent denial-of-service attacks on the Bitcoin network. Also from the 1980s, the *Agoric Papers* (1988) by K. Eric Drexler and Mark S. Miller inspired a young software developer named Vitalik Buterin to make a Bitcoin-like platform for more complex general-purpose smart contracts almost 30 years later — Ethereum.[4] On the fledgling Ethereum network of 2015 the modern promise of Szabo's conception of smart contracts could begin to be realized.[5]

## Blockchain as a Medium

*If art is an attempt at communicating, then smart contracts are a great medium for art because the medium itself encodes immutable intent. It defines rules of engagement through an immutable ledger and asks the participant to form meaning around that. Smart contracts as an artistic medium wrestles really well with communicating about time and value. Their advantages also define its limits. Change, decay, degradation as expressions need to be hardcoded in the rules themselves.*

—Simon de la Rouviere [6]

[1] William Entriken, Dieter Shirley, Jacob Evans, Nastassia Sachs, "EIP-721: Non-Fungible Token Standard," *Ethereum Improvement Proposals*, 2018, https://eips.ethereum.org/EIPS/eip-721.

[2] Nick Szabo, "Formalizing and Securing Relationships on Public Networks," *First Monday*, Vol. 2, No. 9, September 1997.

[3] Satoshi Nakamoto, *Bitcoin: A Peer-to-Peer Electronic Cash System* 2008, https://bitcoin.org/bitcoin.pdf.

[4] K. Eric Drexler and Mark S. Miller in Bernardo Huberman (ed.), *The Ecology of Computation*, (North-Holland: Elsevier Science Publishers, 1988).

[5] Indeed experimentation began before this, on Ethereum's now lost pre-release testnet in 2014.

[6] Simon de la Rouviere, interview with the author, April 5, 2022.

**04.02** (below and right)
Sol LeWitt
Certificate, diagrams, and wall drawing for *Wall drawing Number #260*, 1975
Signed certificate; white crayon, black wall

CERTIFICATE

This is to certify that the Sol LeWitt wall drawing
number __260__ evidenced by this certificate is authentic.

On black walls, all two-part combinations of
white arcs from corners and sides, and white
straight, not straight and broken lines.

White crayon, black wall
First Drawn by: Sol LeWitt
First Installation: San Francisco Museum of
Modern Art, San Francisco, CA.
June, 1975

This certification is the signature for the wall drawing and must
accompany the wall drawing if it is sold or otherwise transferred.

Certified by _____
Sol LeWitt

© Copyright Sol LeWitt _____
Date

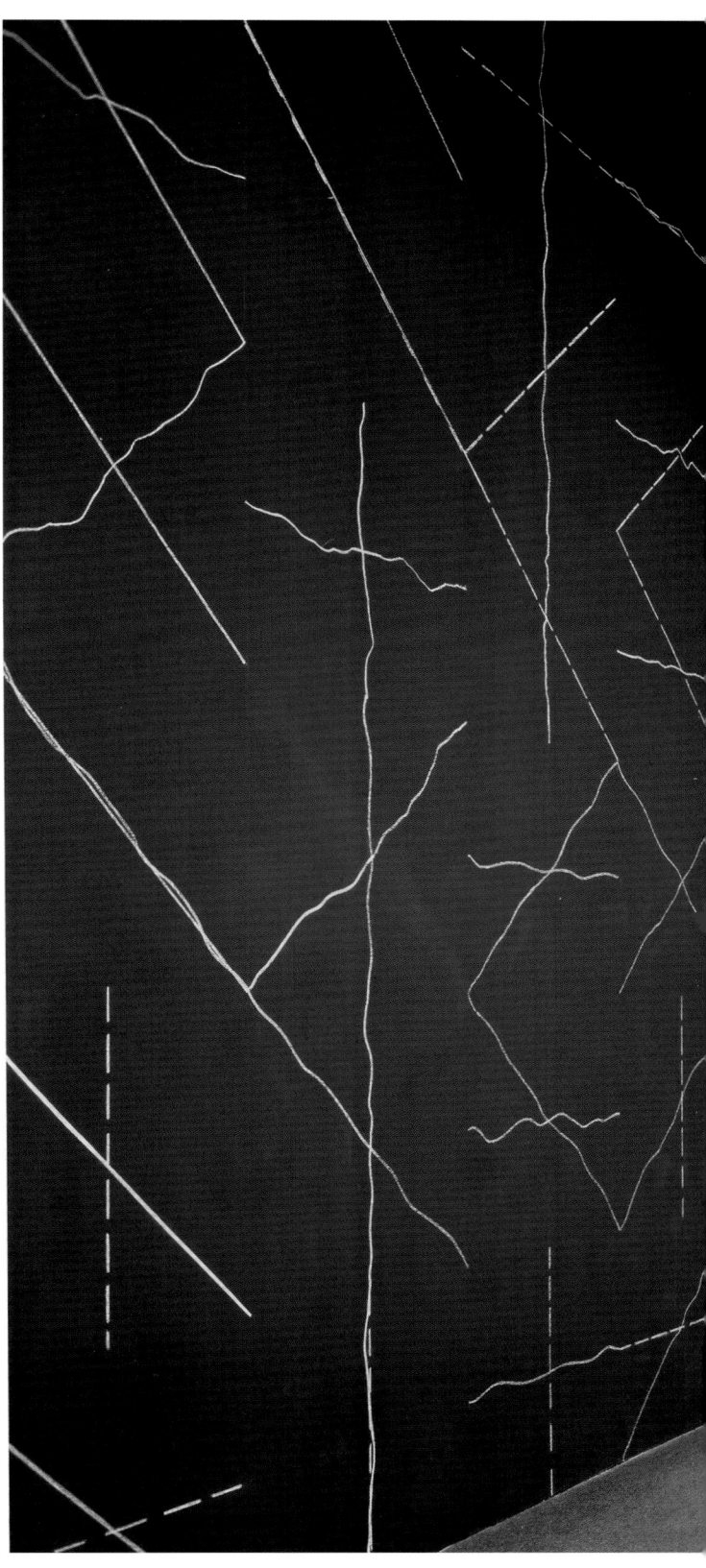

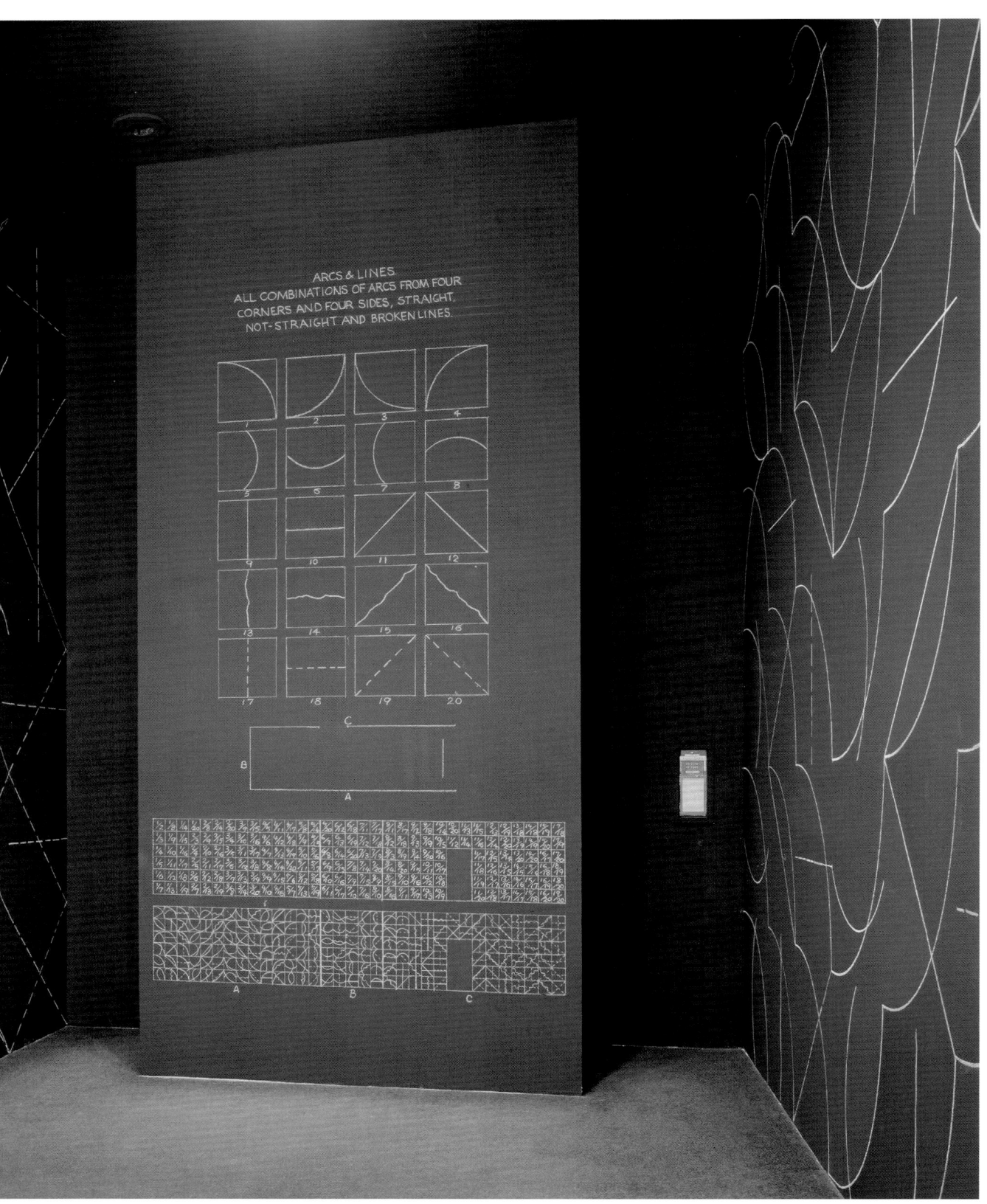

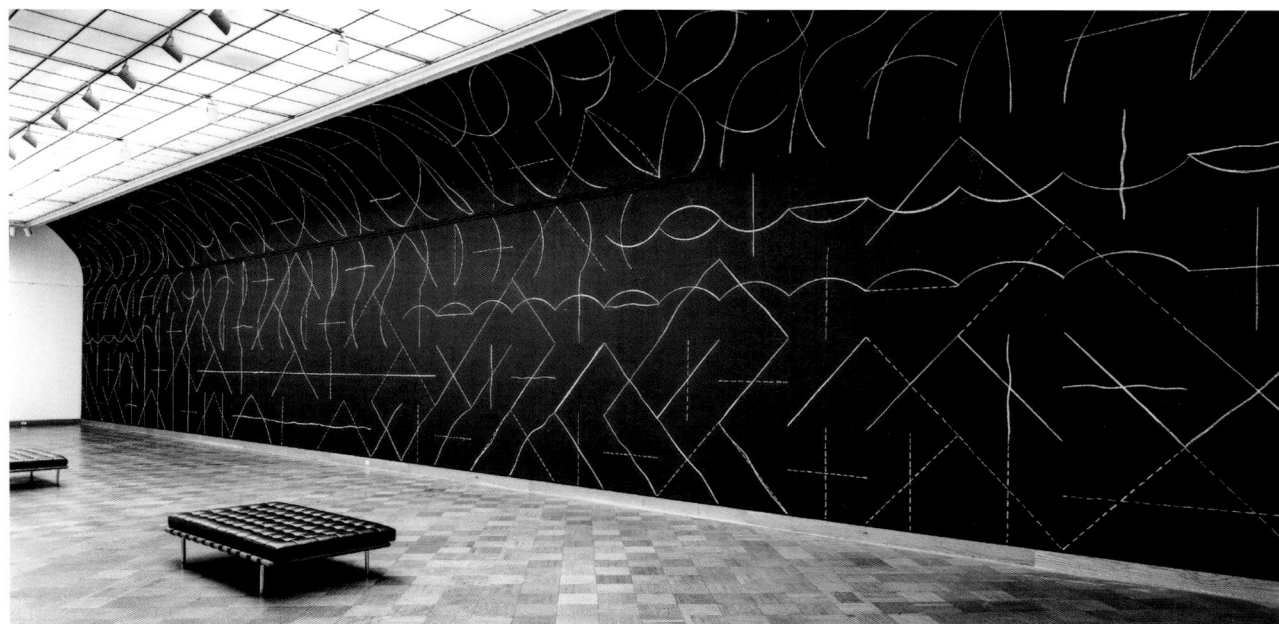

"The medium is the message," Canadian media theorist Marshall McLuhan famously argued during the era of network television, but on the blockchain the medium is the transaction.[7] The rise of digital media seemed to turn all media into a single smooth space of bits, producing what art historian Rosalind Krauss described as the "post-medium condition" following postmodernism.[8] Despite this, post-internet art has demonstrated that digital media can still be a powerfully resonant medium of historical and cultural association precisely because of its ever-increasing representational power and intrusion into everyday life.[9]

Even the small amount of flexibility that Bitcoin's simple transaction scripting language afforded its users allowed artists to find room to experiment with it as a creative medium for art-making. Transactions could be used to encode information other than financial exchanges, and artists quickly used this to turn the blockchain into a canvas and a gallery. The meaning of those transactions can be changed to represent different things up to and including the point where artists made their own blockchains to represent them. Simon de la Rouviere's *FUNK* (2013) was one such blockchain, created by modifying the Litecoin software's source code, representing membership of a musical movement as its cryptocurrency. Musicians producing music on file-sharing sites as The Cypherfunks would be rewarded with *FUNK*, and thereby able to reward others in turn to create a kind of viral public persona or cultural movement. A literal "cultural currency," Sarah Meyohas's *Bitchcoin* (2015) likewise created a new blockchain whose native token represented investment in and purchase of the artist's own future work. To create entire blockchain networks for individual artistic projects required skill, commitment, and imagination. The technical requirements of doing so represented a considerable barrier to entry for artists who might otherwise have wished to engage with the blockchain at that time.

With the arrival of Ethereum, it became much easier to represent more complex information and rules as smart contracts on an existing blockchain rather than having to write and operate a new project-specific one. This reduced barriers to entry by saving artists the time and effort that would otherwise have gone into creating their own blockchains from the ground up, allowing the blockchain as an artistic medium to flourish. Many earlier projects migrated to Ethereum, opening up questions of provenance and originality while allowing greater appreciation of the work by a wider audience.

Smart contracts make blockchains fully available to artists as a plastic medium. Along with the cryptography, the transactions, and the events through which their users interact with them, they nest into larger forms of society, politics, and the economy that contemporary artists face the tasks of depicting and imaginatively working with. Blockchain form is a unique resource

[7] Marshall McLuhan, *Understanding Media: The Extensions of Man* (New York: McGraw-Hill, 1964).
[8] Rosalind Krauss in Hal Foster et al., *Art since 1900: Modernism, Antimodernism, Postmodernism* (London: Thames & Hudson, 2005), 613.
[9] The term *post-internet art*, as coined by Marisa Olson in around 2006, refers to "a mode of artistic activity drawing on raw materials and ideas found or developed online" (Michael Connor, "What's Postinternet Got to Do with Net Art?" *Rhizome*, November 1, 2013, https://rhizome.org/editorial/2013/nov/01/postinternet/).

for those artists because it embodies both the imagined alternative social order of libertarian cypherpunk ideology and the technological and economic reality of post-2008-financial-crisis society. And it makes them uniquely accessible in the form of freely usable software. Artists can use blockchain form directly, as a tool, or evocatively in reference to those larger social structures, as symbolic form. As we shall see, they have done both, often at the same time.

## Code, Law, Rules, Value

*When Lawrence Lessig said "code is law" he was not saying code is legal, he was saying code is assuming the function of the law in that it can dictate what you can and cannot do. Some people in the blockchain space, at least early on, have taken it to the next step.*

—Primavera De Filippi [10]

*The idea becomes a machine that makes the art.*

—Sol LeWitt (1928–2007) [11]

The popular perception of art as a field of pure creativity obscures the role that rules of all kinds play in art-making. Whether formulas for color-mixing or compositional arrangements, legal agreements between artists and gallerists, or the constraints of digital media or physical logistics, artists are constrained by a myriad of rules that they engage with creatively. Constraints can be some of the most useful creative forces that work on an artist and lead to strikingly novel art. Importantly, constraints can be found throughout art history — even outside of explicitly rule-based conceptual or generative practices. This may be through necessity, such as Henri Matisse's (1869–1954) paper cut-outs made while wheelchair-bound during the last decade of his life. Or it may be through choice, such as Barbara Kruger's photocollages made to a rigorous *Picture Post*–style black, white, and red scheme of text and image.

Smart contracts are the conjugation of two different kinds of rules — agreements governing human interaction (contracts) and instructions controlling computing machinery (computer programs, the "smart" part of their name). From their initial conception they also touch on another set of rules, those of value. Contracts have been tied to the exchange of value since the dawn of writing, but prior to the invention of computing they had to be enacted by human parties and prior to the blockchain this required an intermediary authority. Blockchains are therefore the first real test of the idea of rules and values being inscribed technologically. They turn rules into a public, plastic, transparent, programmable medium with great creative potential for artists to work with, bend, or even break them.

## Rules as Medium

In the 1960s, the first generation of postwar art-school-educated artists emerged at the height of the Cold War. They found existing art practice and criticism insufficient to answer the challenges of realistically representing and critiquing the aesthetics and ideologies of their historical moment. Rejecting existing means of creating and distributing art they made conversation and writing their medium, presenting a challenge to the existing art market that it nonetheless overcame by the mid-1970s.

The art of Sol LeWitt (1928–2007) embodies the journey of conceptual art. His ephemeral wall drawings of the 1960s consisted of large-scale compositions of lines, areas of color, and repeated shape motifs drawn according to specific formal schemes described in written rules followed by a team of installers **[04.02, 04.03]**. These instructions were incorporated into certificates of authenticity, becoming a new kind of property circulating. Hopefully blockchain art can learn from the example of conceptual art's production of an alternative art economy containing new art objects and new ways of working.

My NFT *Secret Artwork (Content)* (2018) represents the guarantee of the existence of its own content as a cryptographic hash stored in its smart contract and associated with its token, anchoring its existence on the blockchain without revealing it. It will tell you absolutely everything about itself in many different visual forms — dates, block heights, Ethereum addresses, token ID numbers, as shapes, colors, numbers, in any combination. But it will not tell you the one thing that it claims to be about — what the content of the artwork actually is. This frustrating dialectic of absolute identity/publicity and absolute privacy/secrecy evokes the nature of blockchains. Smart contracts allow us to make art that uses this evocation to refer back to and represent this experience and the ideologies that gave rise to it.

Entire oeuvres can be produced by rules, such as Roman Opalka's (1931–2011) *1965/1–∞* (1965–2011) **[04.04]** in which the artist spent the last 56 years of his life painting canvases depicting successively larger numbers. Like the work of On Kawara, which we will look at

[10] De Filippi, interview with the author.
[11] Sol LeWitt, "Paragraphs on Conceptual Art," *Artforum*, Vol. 5, No. 10, Summer 1967.

later in this chapter, the simplicity of the procedure belies the complexity of subjecting one-self to it. Producing a succession of artistic proof-of-works in discrete canvas blocks clearly resembles the structure of the blockchain, 50 years before the concept of a blockchain even existed. The artist that produces such a structure in and of time resembles a smart contract in human form.

Rigorous daily artistic practice, particularly in Opalka's case, also evokes spiritual or religious practice. The invention of smart contracts, like the invention of the medium of writing before, provides a new way of recording and examining belief itself. The serious-ness of Opalka's project contrasts with the memeified nature of many conceptual projects on the blockchain. Matt Liston and Avery Singer's *0xOmega* (2018) places the credos and rituals of an imagined religion onto the blockchain as the state of smart contracts, allowing its adherents to transparently and publicly reach consensus on its practice just as the block-chain reaches consensus on its own economic reality. The iterative production of blocks by each blockchain has often been described as a "ritual." Liston takes this and runs with it to provide an unprecedented new model of hermeneutics, effecting social and theological cri-tique under the benign gaze of the project's 3D-printed sacred object — the *Dogewhal* (2018), a playful 3D-printed narwhal/shiba-inu hybrid.

## Law as Medium

Like code or art, law is concerned with the representation and judgment of form. Law repre-sents forms of agreement and disagreement, it represents forms of behavior in a just society. Smart contracts are a cypherpunk solution to law without a state, meaning that NFTs exist in a medium that both models and replaces the form of law, giving them a powerful connection to both its reality and its imaginative possibilities that artists can work with.

Robert Morris's (1931–2018) *Document* (1963) is a signed, notarized document assert-ing that the artist has withdrawn all aesthetic quality and content from the metallic artwork accompanying it. Form evolves through ironization, and *Document* both embodies and cri-tiques a particular model of artistic creativity. It is an inversion of Marcel Duchamp's (1887–1968) "creative act" and the conceptual art strategy of nominating non-art objects as art. These are clear precedents for the idea of the minting an NFT as a creative act in itself, and Morris, Art & Language, and others provide precedents for critiquing them. Minting an art NFT is a deliberate act on the part of the artist that nominates it publicly as art. This base function of smart contracts that store the record of them doing so places an announcement of this event into the indelible historical record of its blockchain.

Commerce and thus law, specifically within the art market, is the subject of many works by the contemporary artist Jonas Lund. For *Control (Strings Attached)* (2015), Lund produced a series of paintings that impose contractual obligations on the purchaser — to buy or sell works by the artist by a certain date, for example. Contracts in general are often used to place onerous conditions on individuals (non-disparagement clauses or wage garnishment, for example). Lund would go on to make work on the blockchain given its ability as a medium to more seamlessly and immutably model the rules that make up the conceptual structure of his art. With *Jonas Lund Token (JLT)* (2018) he built and handed control of his work over to the community that holds those tokens as voting shares in his artistic practice. Although art-ists have issued shares in their work before, notably David Bowie's (1947–2016) *Bowie Bonds* (1997), smart contracts integrate finances and decision-making into the same medium as art-making, building community in a much stronger way.

The strategies of artists that have used the form of law as a medium prefigure and con-tinue in NFT art that uses smart contracts. Those strategies are used in smart contract art to represent and critique the intent and vagaries of attempts to govern human interactions with concrete agreements. More broadly than one particular work or artist, NFTs can safe-guard rights as well as restrict them. For example, the artists' resale right commission on secondary sales of artworks — the *droit de suite* — is not yet implemented worldwide. NFT smart contracts and platforms can provide secondary sale commissions even where there is no such law in the jurisdiction that its artists and collectors operate in.

Novel experiments in protecting the environment using charitable trusts or public inter-est corporations can be automated as smart contracts. *terra0* (2016) by Paul Seidler, Paul Kolling, and Max Hampshire is a self-owning forest that can manage itself via smart con-tracts in order to build its resilience in the era of environmental devastation and climate change. If (economically) successful, the forest can purchase more land to expand into, turn-ing the exploitative framework of financialization to environmental ends. Their later *Two Degrees* (2021) **[04.05]** is an NFT that will burn itself if the average temperature of the Earth rises by two degrees or more. Here NFTs (including art NFTs) take on an active political role, connecting art directly to urgent issues of our time.

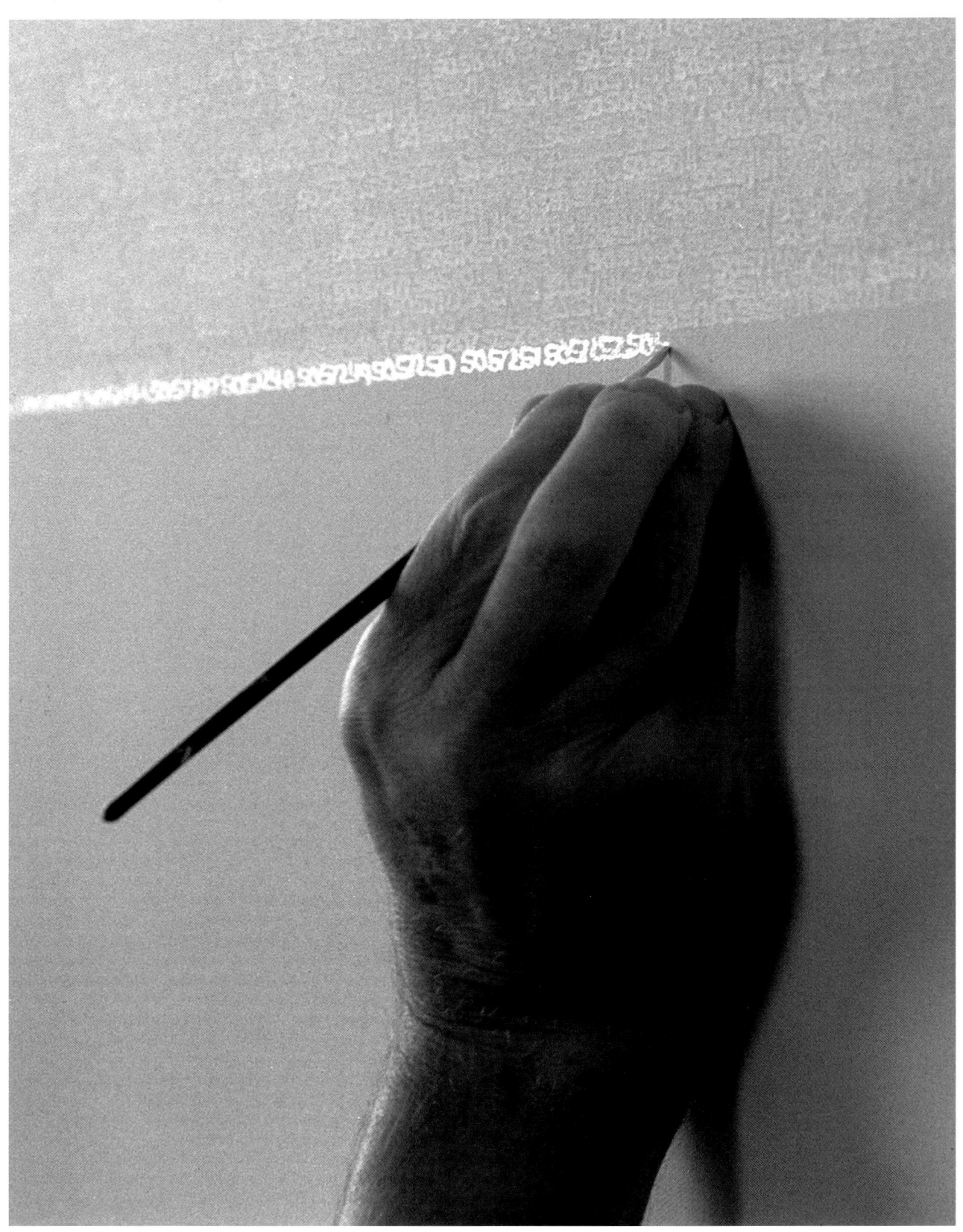

04.05
terra0
*Two Degrees*, 05-12-2021 19:06:31
Lidar scan, custom oracle system
Ethereum, 0xAbf5c7C066A48a06524438F6f51BdceB6E670DAd, 0

04.06
Gabriel L. Dunne & Cullen Miller
*Claves Angelicæ*, 2018–2021
JavaScript, Solidity
Ethereum, 0xb81f4eC30Ea36d839950c4e2022865b6166E2E8a, 5, 99 & 127

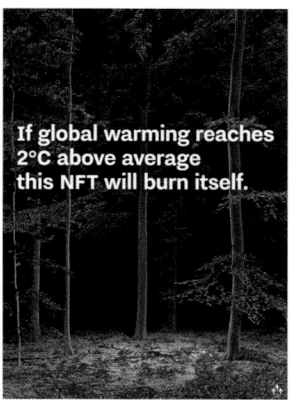

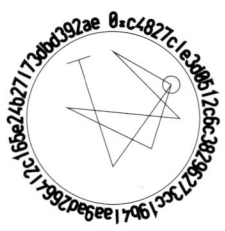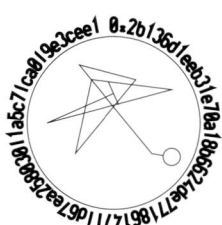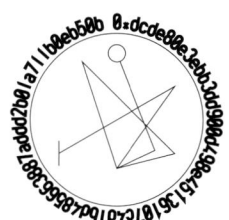

## Code as Medium

Algorithmic art (art created using software or other processes not entirely under the artist's control) can be minted as an NFT as easily as any other kind of visual art. "On-chain" algorithmic art goes further by using information from blockchain blocks or transactions in its compositions or storing an important part of its code in its smart contract. This is distinct from NFTs with content hosted on the web or the IPFS network, creating a singular medium of expression and exchange. The creative spaces that algorithmic art explores can be anchored to the cryptographic space of the blockchain that NFTs exist within.

John F. Simon Jr.'s *Every Icon* (1997) is a net art generative artwork that will take an eternity to generate and display every single monochrome computer icon possible in a 32×32 pixel grid. In 2021, the artist updated it to a version that moved the generating code on-chain and allowed owning examples of those icons as NFTs. This radically altered the relationship between the work and the viewer by introducing the unequal experience of value and possession into the experience of contemplating an unimaginably large space of previously undifferentiated images.

In contrast to iterating through the possibilities of an ordered grid of strict rationality, *Claves Angelicæ* (2018) **[04.06]** by Cullen Miller and Gabriel Dunne restores the liminal historical connection between cryptography and magic(k), allowing people to inscribe a magical word onto the blockchain in return for a donation to a chosen set of charities. The resulting sigil combines a drawn and hexadecimal representation of a secret desire, bringing the liminal history of secret writing to bear critically on the post-cypherpunk present of the blockchain. A still historical but more (analog) technological space of possibility is explored by the NFT artist 0xDEAFBEEF, who produces retro glitch aesthetic animated graphics in the demoscene tradition using code that compiles with a standard C programming language compiler **[04.07]**. By turning that code into templates and storing it on-chain in a smart contract that assembles and configures those templates to return a complete program ready to compile, 0xDEAFBEEF makes unique code art ownable as NFTs. To store the output of those programs on-chain would be prohibitive in terms of storage space and therefore cost, but generating it afresh by running the code that is generated on-chain has the same effect. It also shares the source code and the preparatory materials for the work aiding in archiving and appreciating it.

## Value as Medium

*I can't imagine any other medium that allows me to play with economics in this manner. I can code and experiment with novel economic games on a global scale without anyone's permission.*

—Simon de la Rouviere [12]

Blockchain technology and smart contracts can be seen as a critical, humanistic response to the post-2008-financial-crash era of hyper-financialization and technologies such as automated high-frequency trading. However one may feel about the fact, art and money have always gone together. And artists have both exploited and critiqued this relationship. Cildo

**04.07** ▶

0xDEAFBEEF
*Synth Poems #17*, 03-15-2021 15:00:39
C compiler, Emacs
Ethereum, 0xd754937672300ae6708a51229112de4017810934, 17

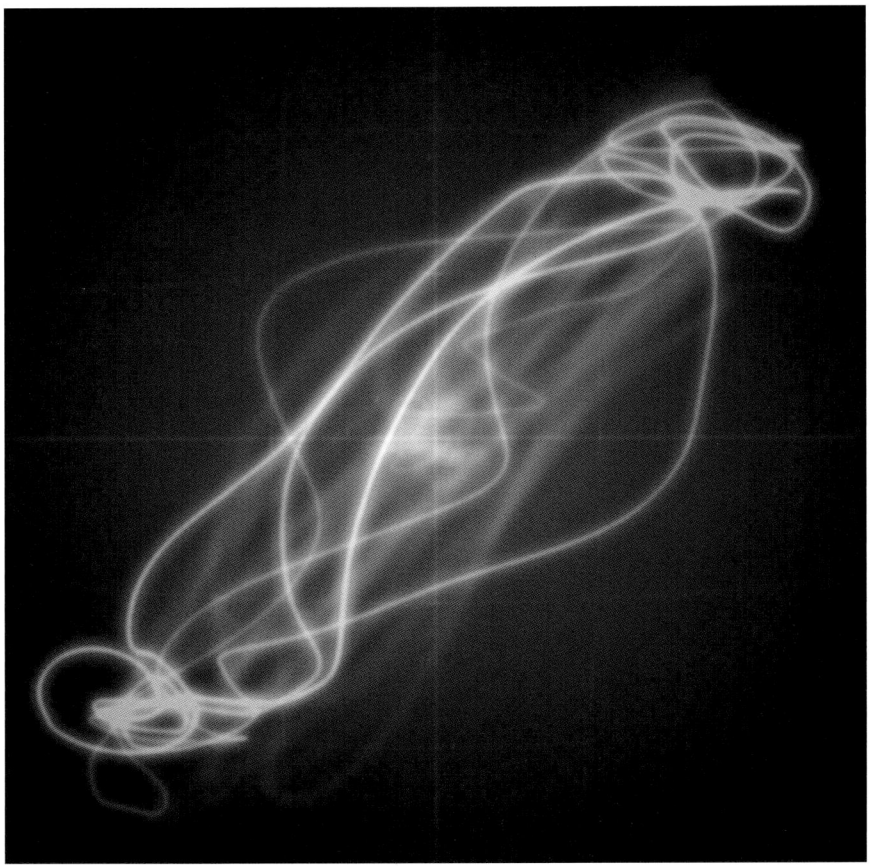

Meireles's *Insertions into Ideological Circuits 2: Banknote Project* (1970) rubber-stamped banknotes with subversive messages. These were then returned to general circulation as an intervention into the unreflective circulation of value within the dominant ideology. The *Boggs Notes* produced by J. G. Boggs (1955–2017) from 1984 onwards were life-size drawings of banknotes. Boggs would only exchange them for goods, services, or cash, of the amount depicted.

The public transparency of smart contracts makes the circulation of value transparent for critique, a work such as the Guerrilla Girls' poster *Only 4 Commercial Galleries In NY Show Black Women* (1986) could now be made programmatically and dynamically simply by analyzing the state and event history of the blockchain used by any given institution.

A more direct trapdoor function between financial and aesthetic value is represented by Yves Klein's (1928–1962) *Zone de Sensibilité Picturale Immatérielle* (*Zone of immaterial pictorial sensibility*) (1959) **[04.08]**. These are printed certificates that the collector could burn (like an NFT, which can be "burned" by sending to an unrecoverable blockchain address) and exchange an amount of gold (half of which was to be thrown into the Seine) for the intangible property of the title **[04.09]**. Klein used the medium patent law with his recipe for *International Klein Blue* (1960).[13] Mitchell F. Chan's *Digital Zones of Immaterial Pictorial Sensibility* (2017) **[04.10]** are pre-ERC-721-standard Ethereum tokens that apply the strategy of Klein's play of the logic of capitalist valuation, ownership, and exchange to the blockchain. Chan identifies Klein's certificates as "non-fungible tokens," directly tying blockchain form to art-historical form.

Markets and financial instruments can also be mediums of expression. In 2017, James Gubb used trading in shares for the company Oakbay to draw a literal middle finger into the chart of their trading price in protest at their alleged corruption. Closing the loop on value as a medium of expression, Simon de la Rouviere's Ethereum-based *Is This Prediction Market,*

[12] De la Rouviere, interview with the author.
[13] French patent number 63471.

**04.08**
Yves Klein
*Receipt to Jacques Kugel for transfer of a Zone of*
*Immaterial Pictorial Sensibility. Series n°1, Zone n°02*, 1959
Printed paper, handwritten signature and date, 8.7 × 19.3 cm

**04.09**
Yves Klein
*Transfer of a Zone of Immaterial Pictorial Sensibility to Dino Buzzati.*
*Series n°1, Zone 05*, 1962 Documentary photograph
The Yves Klein Foundation, Paris, France

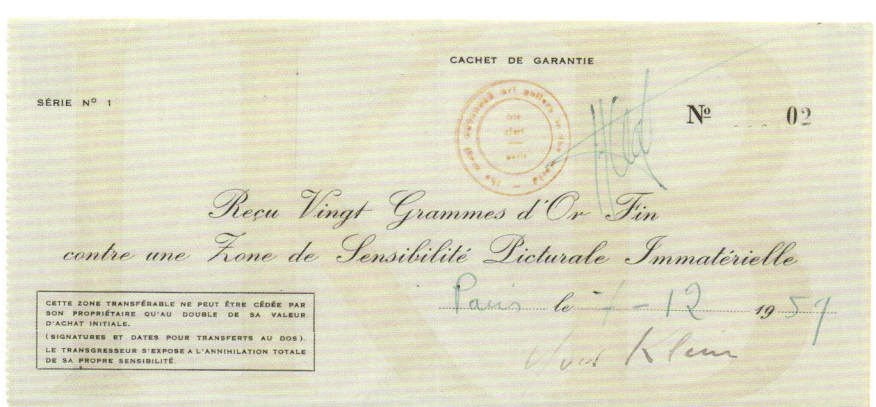

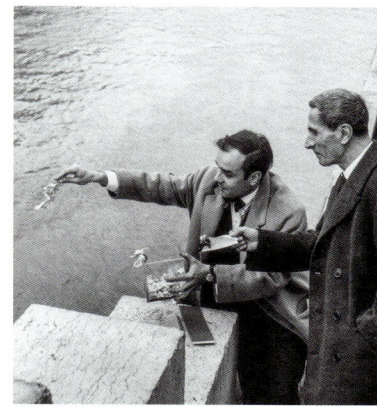

**04.10**
Mitchell F. Chan
*Digital Zone of Immaterial Pictorial Sensibility*, 08-31-2017 12:38:59
Solidity, ink and paper receipt
Ethereum, 0x88AE96845e157558ef59e9Ff90E766E22E480390, 0

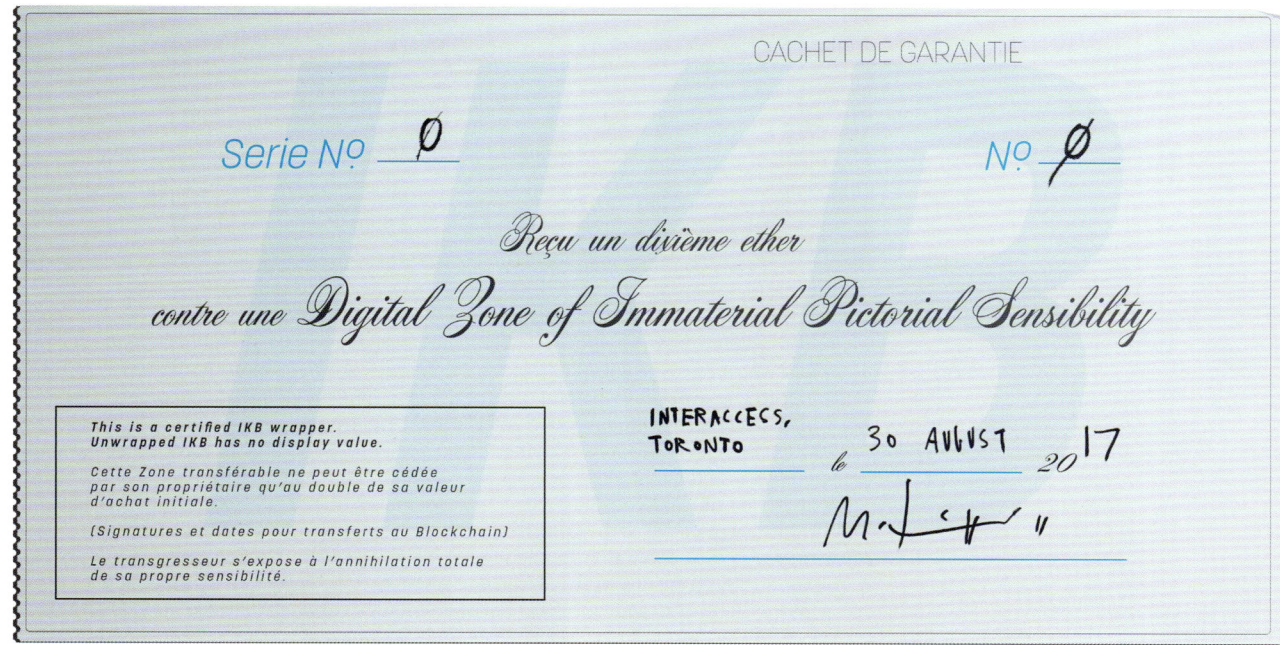

04.11
Arihz & Fingerprints
*Avid Lines #454820053 #4084465980, & #3756720138*, 2021
p5.js, Autoglyphs
Ethereum, 0xDFAcD840f462C27b0127FC76b63e7925bEd0F9D5, 454820053, 4084465980 & 3756720138

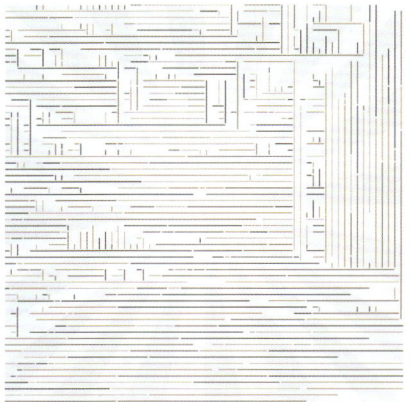
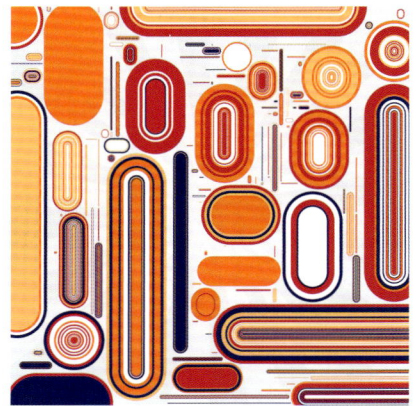
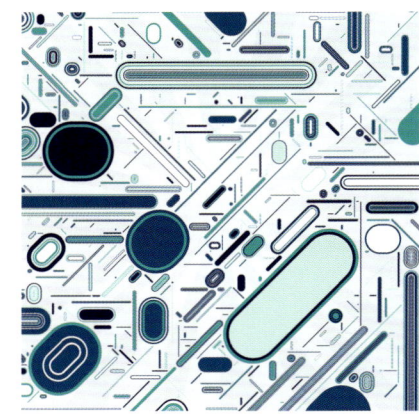

*Art?* (2019) uses a prediction market smart contract to determine part of the ontology of art — or would if the outcome had not been declared invalid by the forecasters. Prediction markets are one way of bringing off-chain information on-chain. Another method is the use of trusted "oracle" smart contracts that allow facts such as currency prices or the average temperature of the Earth to be published on the blockchain for smart contracts to access. Ed Fornieles's *Finiliar* (2016) use oracles to set the mood of their cute animated creatures. Each *Finiliar* is associated with a cryptocurrency and as the value of that currency goes up and down the *Finiliar*'s mood follows. If its value goes too low, the *Finiliar* will become sick. One of art's functions is to render knowledge and ideology visible for contemplation, and smart contract art has proven to be a powerful medium for doing so.

As well as using prediction markets or oracles as artistic materials, smart contract art can use other smart contract art, building on them to create new value. This is known as "composability" and a good example of this is *Avid Lines* (2021) **[04.11]**, commissioned from the pseudonymous artist Arihz by FingerprintsDAO. *Avid Lines* images are generated when each token is minted, using instructions from the existing *Autoglyphs* (2019) project by Larva Labs (FingerprintsDAO is a collecting DAO and has one of the largest collections of *Autoglyphs*). *Autoglyphs* exist fully on-chain, which allows *Avid Lines* to engage deeply and fully with the code and behaviors of their smart contract. Composability will only grow in importance as smart contract art continues to mature.

## Utility, Performance, Communication, Dynamism

In the era of relational art identified by curator Nicolas Bourriaud in his 1998 book of the same name, art became an interactive experience in which the viewer/owner becomes an active participant in or even material for the artistic process.[14] Unlike the possibilities of systems art identified by art critic Jack Burnham (1931–2019) in the 1960s, relational art, fits neatly into an art-world context.[15] Smart contracts can represent a more contemporary breakaway from finite art into a free flowing, changeable experience. They can represent a performance, and they can also constitute one. A performance can evolve on-chain while having all the benefits of blockchain's permanence and hyper liquidity.

An art-historical skeleton key to realizing these possibilities using technology that combines encryption, communication, and time may be the art of On Kawara. Famous for his daily telegrams informing the recipient that the artist was still alive, and for his 50-year-long project *Today* (1966–2013), consisting of each day's date made in the language of the country he was in when making it, Kawara combined performance art, mail art, and painting not as a dry conceptual exercise but as a record of existence itself **[04.12]**. Highly prescient, Kawara made not just artistic blockchains in their proof-of-work structure (in a similiar manner to Opalka), but also showed a deep interest in cryptography. Remarkably, in earlier work, Kawara explored cryptography through a variety of paintings that included cryptographic signifiers such as morse code, punched card-style arrangements of dots, and a discrete text work with the word "cipher." These were destroyed by the artist, leaving only a photographic record **[04.13]**, in a parallel to an NFT token "burn."

[14] Nicolas Bourriaud, *Relational Aesthetics* (Dijon: Les Presses du réel, 2002).
[15] Jack Burnham, ed. Melissa Ragain, *Dissolve into Comprehension: Writings and Interviews, 1964–2004* (Massachusetts: The MIT Press, 2015).

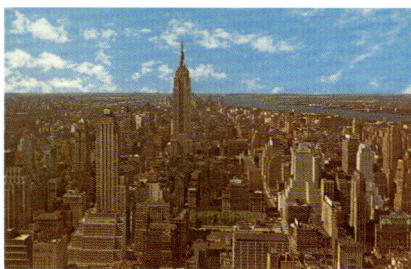
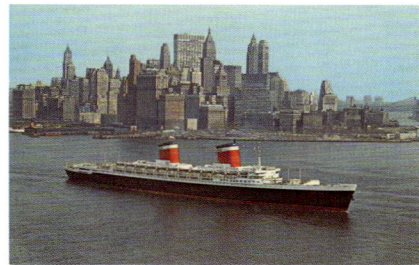
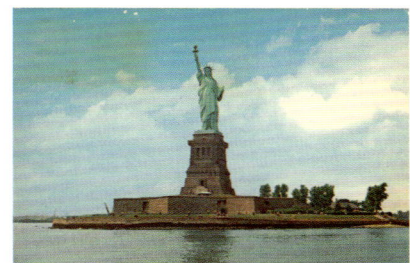
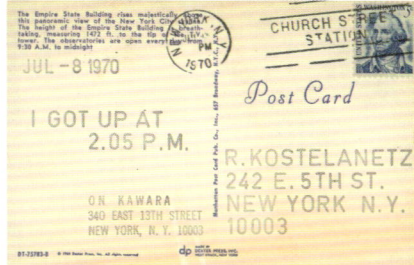
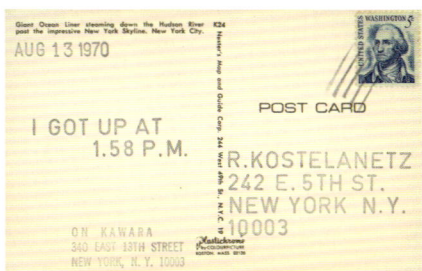
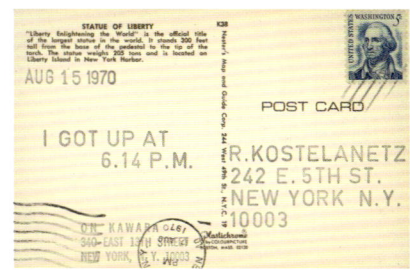

In an intriguing contemporary parallel to this, Pak's *Burn* (2021) smart contract burns NFTs sent to it in return for Pak's *$ASH* "social currency." Some of Pak's future NFT art will only be available in exchange for *$ASH*. The economics of *Burn* are even more complex than those of *Merge*, with the relationship between the kind, time, and amount of NFTs burned all affecting the amount of *$ASH* received in return. *Merge* and *Burn* can both be seen as dynamic versions of Opalka's or Kawara's work. They turn collecting and value into a game with predictable, time-based rules. Collectors who play this game build a community around the work that follows the artists as a result.

### Smart Contracts as Mail Art and Net Art

In the 1950s, Ray Johnson (1927–1995) started a gift economy of art exchanged by mail with other artists. Networks of artists continue such sharing to the present day. Swapping or airdropping NFTs brings this tradition on-chain by creating a networked gift economy in the new communication medium of the blockchain. The owners of Sarah Friend's *Lifeforms* (2021) face a chain-letter-style demand to forward them or else they become inaccessible. As their value increases, holding onto the NFT both becomes more desirable and destroys that value — art combining code, economics, and critique. The relationship between value and mass communication is also explored in the smart contract for Mad Dog Jones (Michah Dowbak)'s *Replicator* (2021). It evokes a classic mail art tool — photocopiers. Like photocopies, its NFTs lose fidelity with each "generation" minted, and may "jam" to create artworks other than the intended copy of the original. On the blockchain, glitches must be encoded into smart contracts intentionally.

Net art is designed to disrupt rather than work within communication networks. This was exemplified by etoy's *TOYWAR* (1999) website, in which the artists took on a dot-com startup and won. Cryptography can thwart the confusion and virality of culture jamming. But confusion can be seen in bitcointalk.org's reaction to Nili Lerner's *Nilicoin* (2014) CounterParty tokens. These represent the concept of blue chip brands rather than any claim to ownership of them but a non-art audience treated them as attempted IP theft. *Kudzu* (2021) by Billy Rennekamp, Dan Denorch, Everett Williams, and Sam Hart achieves blockchain virality with the possibly unwitting assistance of its token holders. Attempting to transfer *Kudzu* from one account to another will successfully place the amount of *Kudzu* specified into the receiving account, but it will not remove it from the sending one. Spreading in this way subverts the "double-spend problem" of cryptocurrency and creates a piece of software that was thought to be impossible: a computer virus.

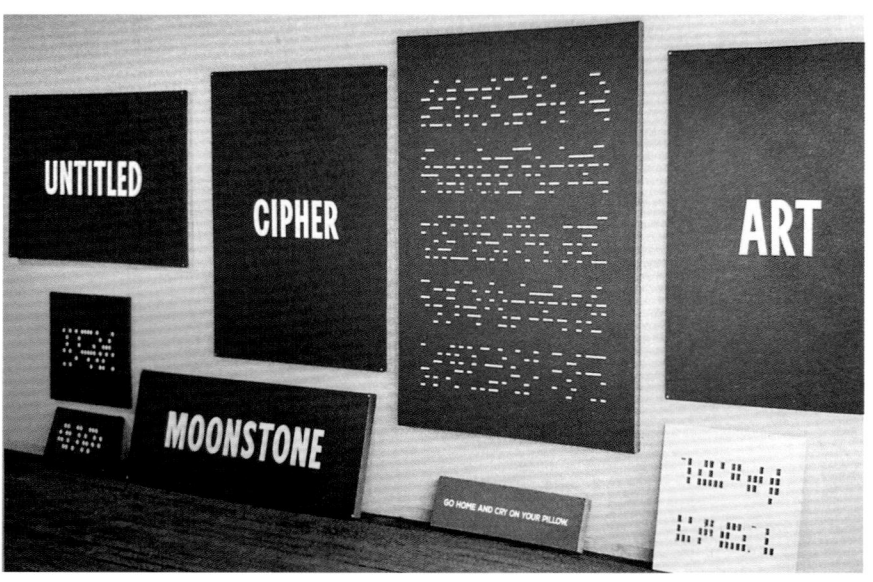

## Smart Contracts as Kinetic, Dynamic, and Gamified Art

*The code is just as important as the sculpture. It is the system that combines the sculpture and the code that actually creates this conceptual artist that instantiates itself digitally and physically. It has this council of humans that are suggesting "I like this and I like that." But ultimately the* Plantoid *is paying for it.*
—Primavera De Filippi [16]

Twentieth-century "machine age" artists made art that moved. Software is the configuration of a universal computing machine. Edward Ihnatowicz's (1926–1988) cybernetic sculptures *SAM* (1968) and *Senster* (1970) went from electro-mechanical to computer-controlled robotic sculpture, creating an uncanny feeling of presence using sonar.

Primavera De Filippi's *Plantoid* (2015) **[04.14]** sculptures resemble *SAM*'s cybernetic flower. They are created by smart contracts that animate the sculpture when sent cryptocurrency by viewers. With enough tips, they commission a new *Plantoid* and the cycle continues. *Plantoid* prefigures dynamic on-chain art and art DAOs, and blends off-chain and on-chain activity into a new way of making art.

Smart contracts can represent diverse real and imagined information, from interest rates to which magical powers imaginary monsters possess. This reflects historically open artworks such as Douglas Huebler's (1924–1997) *Variable Piece #44* (1971), a lithograph to which photographs of the work's successive owners were added. My work *Is Art* (2014) draws on the art of that period to allow anyone (with gas to spend) to declare the contract art or not, secured by the blockchain rather than artistic gesture. Much more complex information can be represented on-chain. Dapper Labs' *CryptoKitties* (2017) introduced the popular Ethereum ERC-721 NFT standard, and the name *NFTs*, while popularizing genetic art on the blockchain. Each Kitty can be "bred" to produce a new NFT representing a new cartoon cat with unique visual features derived from the genes of both of its parents. Harm van den Dorpel's *Mutant Garden Seeder* (2021) uses a genetic scheme in order to create very contemporary algorithmic art abstractions. Building on his off-chain genetic art, each "mutant" NFT uses the cryptographic hash ID of the block that it is minted in to generate and update the genes that control its appearance over time. These contrasting approaches to representing art show the rich possibilities of simulating organisms in code using smart contracts.

Owner-configurable art was popularized by async.art with *First Supper* (2020), a collaboration between 12 artists to produce an image with 22 different "layers." Each layer can be owned and controlled by a different collector, with the public able to view the results. This gives collectors a unique relationship to the art and to other owners of it, and turns the ownership of art into a spectator sport, expanding the field of possibility for relational art.

04.14
Primavera De Filippi
*Plantoid*, 2014
Recouped metal, electronics, blockchains

04.15
Operator on-chain generative choreography method and
programmatically drawn body part positioning math for
*Human Unreadable (Privacy Collection – Lot 03)*, 2022–2023

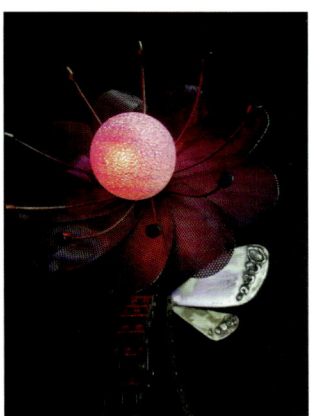

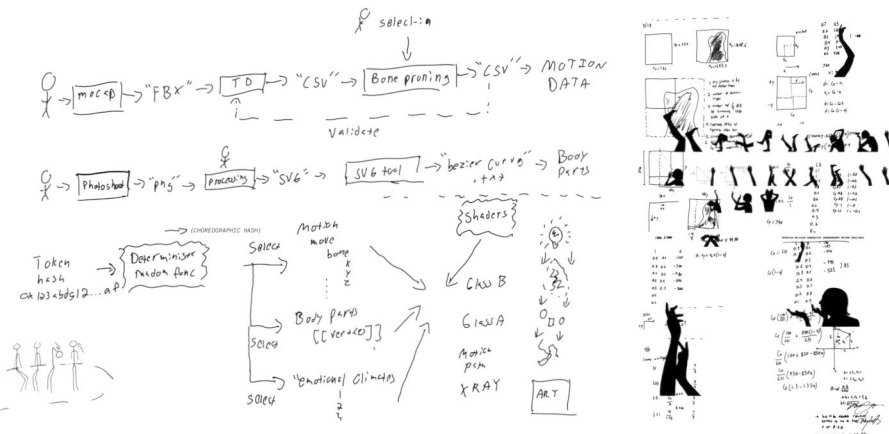

Configuring and breeding art gamifies it, and video-game aesthetics provide rich materials for blockchain art. Metaverse-native artist LaTurbo Avedon's *Materia* (2022), a video-game-inspired virtual universe, began with the sale of tokens representing elements and rules within an unfolding process of creation. The "utility" of these tokens comes from their relationship to the very structure of reality in the world of *Materia* as encoded in the tokens' smart contracts, providing one clear answer to the wider question of "utility" for NFT art.

### The Future

*We need to see proper experiments in decentralized autonomous artists. These are artists living themselves as rules on a blockchain that can afford to pay for various contributors to improve it over time. Dynamism is still unexplored, as the current crop of smart contract art out there feels more like Web 1.0 still: static references.*

—Simon de la Rouviere [17]

Smart contracts can revitalize conceptual art and enable wider support for digital art. Artists such as Pak show that artists can engage with and be supported by much larger audiences at lower price points. Gamification allows large-scale works to be supported economically and structuring human behavior and experience around game theory in radically novel ways. Excitingly, the same flexibility that enables gamification can be used to create ongoing responsive dynamic art in a direct relationship with the audience, at scale. These relationships can be extended to build trust and enable collaboration between individuals, collective intelligence, and artificial intelligence. Blockchain technology was designed to be peer-to-peer, and those peers need not be human. This is not vague futurism: *Plantoid*, *Kudzu*, *Lifeforms*, and other existing projects all shape the behavior of the human beings that interact with them via the blockchain.

Most recently, building on these ideas through the notion of art as experience, Operator's *Human Unreadable* (2023) **[04.15]**, **[04.16]** utilizes smart contracts as commands for human-acted choreography and performance, in what can be described as "the slow recovery of the human. The work brings flesh and viscerality into code and vulnerability [as a feature] into long-form on-chain generative art performance."[18] This question of trust, the one that underlies blockchain technology, is also key to artistic collaboration. Making the rules by which we operate in our art worlds explicit so that we can both improve and, should we wish, subvert them is a powerful affordance of smart contracts. Conversely, privacy-protecting technology such as zero-knowledge proofs and cryptographic commitments can allow new cultural scenes to flourish away from social media's panoptic eye.

Fractionalized art, owner-configurable art, and automation of the financial and legal side of artistic derivation that Primavera De Filippi describes will create new economies of art and help to resolve tensions in the idea of art as intellectual property that have grown up since the 1960s. This is one answer to the question of utility, as a key "use" of art is to make other art. Libraries of code such as OpenZeppelin can and should expand to support the needs of

[17] De la Rouviere, interview with the author.
[18] Operator, "Human Unreadable (Privacy Collection–Lot 03)," 2023, https://www.operator.la/human-unreadable.

**04.16**
Operator
*Human Unreadable #019*, 05-24-2023 17:07:35
p5.js, glsl, on-chain generative choreography, Solidity
Ethereum, 0x99a9b7c1116f9ceeb1652de04d5969cce509b069, 455000019

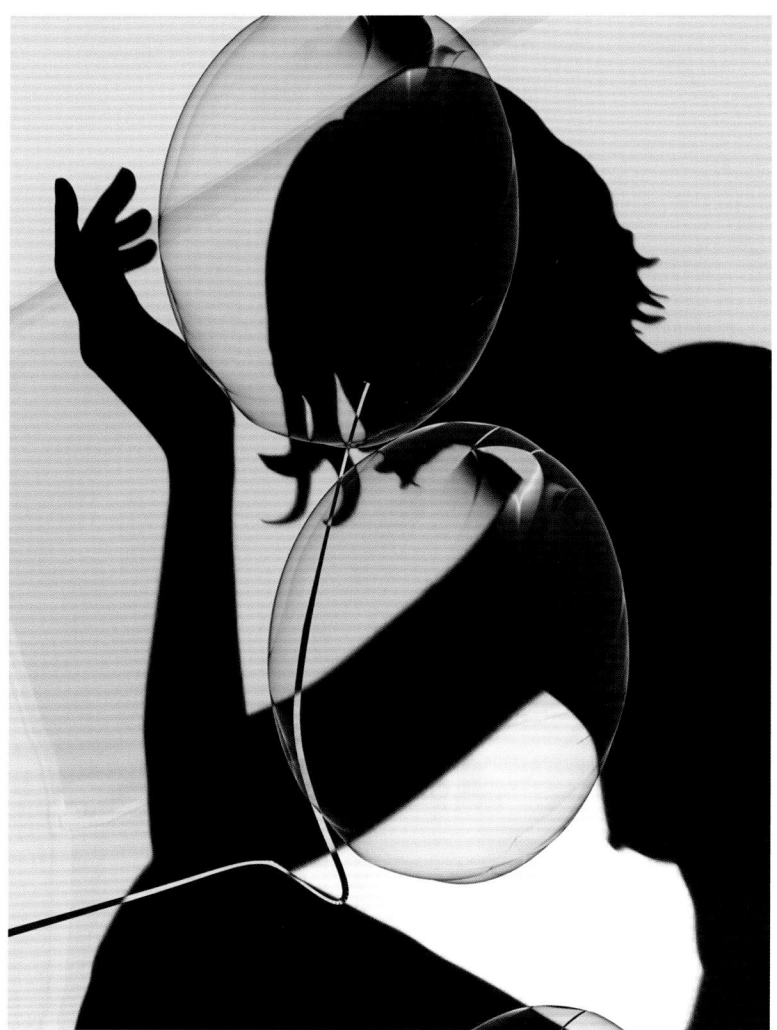

artists while increasing interoperability. In this way, the creation of a common "stack" will lower technical barriers and increase involvement in smart contract art.

In their unification of rules, value, communication, and time-based activity in a singular public medium, smart contracts offer unique possibilities for unifying and extending the disparate threads of digital art. This can require new ways of thinking from both artists and audience, particularly around the ideas of mechanism design and economic rationality. The affordances and risks of this medium can better be understood in this way, and smart contract art has been how artists have led the conversation around this from the start.

New thinking can be informed by an understanding of the history of ideas. I have related the challenges and value of on-chain art to its historical precedents here in order to do this. I do not intend to reduce those precedents to a prehistory or to reduce on-chain art to a worthy footnote. Rather I hope to demonstrate that what is novel about smart contracts as an artistic medium can be solidly grounded within art history without curtailing its potential for further development.

Despite their technical constraints, smart contracts have proven to be an expressive medium for a range of approaches to art-making that both present a deep engagement with and new challenge to art history. They also touch on the post-financial-crisis socioeconomic imaginary in ways that would not be possible with other media. Not just individual artworks but entire symbolic and financial economies can exist within them, and already do.

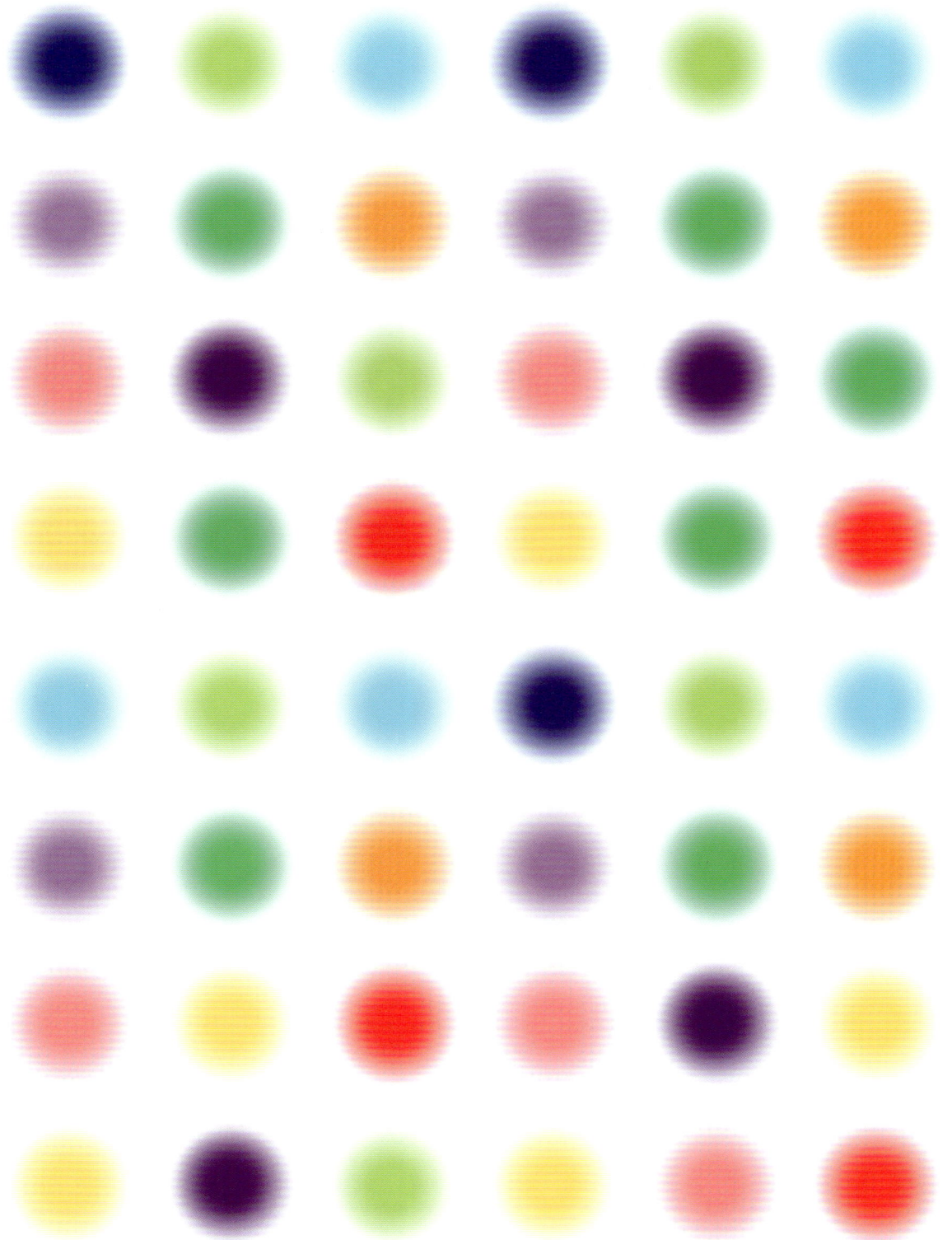

| # | TITLE | TIMESTAMP | MEDIUM | CHAIN | CONTRACT ADDRESS | TOKEN ID | EDITION SIZE |
|---|---|---|---|---|---|---|---|
| 01 | **Lifeforms** | 09-02-2021 15:37:26 | GLSL, silicone, various phones | MATIC | 0x8916edd9b39783d85303ecc6613917ddd735d88d | ∞ | ∞ |
| 02 | **Clickmine** | 12-23-2021 12:04:45 | HTML, Three.js, cast bronze, various computers, living grass | MATIC | 0xe245f745a73e167b73860e8fef7a865154eadafd | 0–21 | 21 |

# SARAH FRIEND

CANADA 1988

02

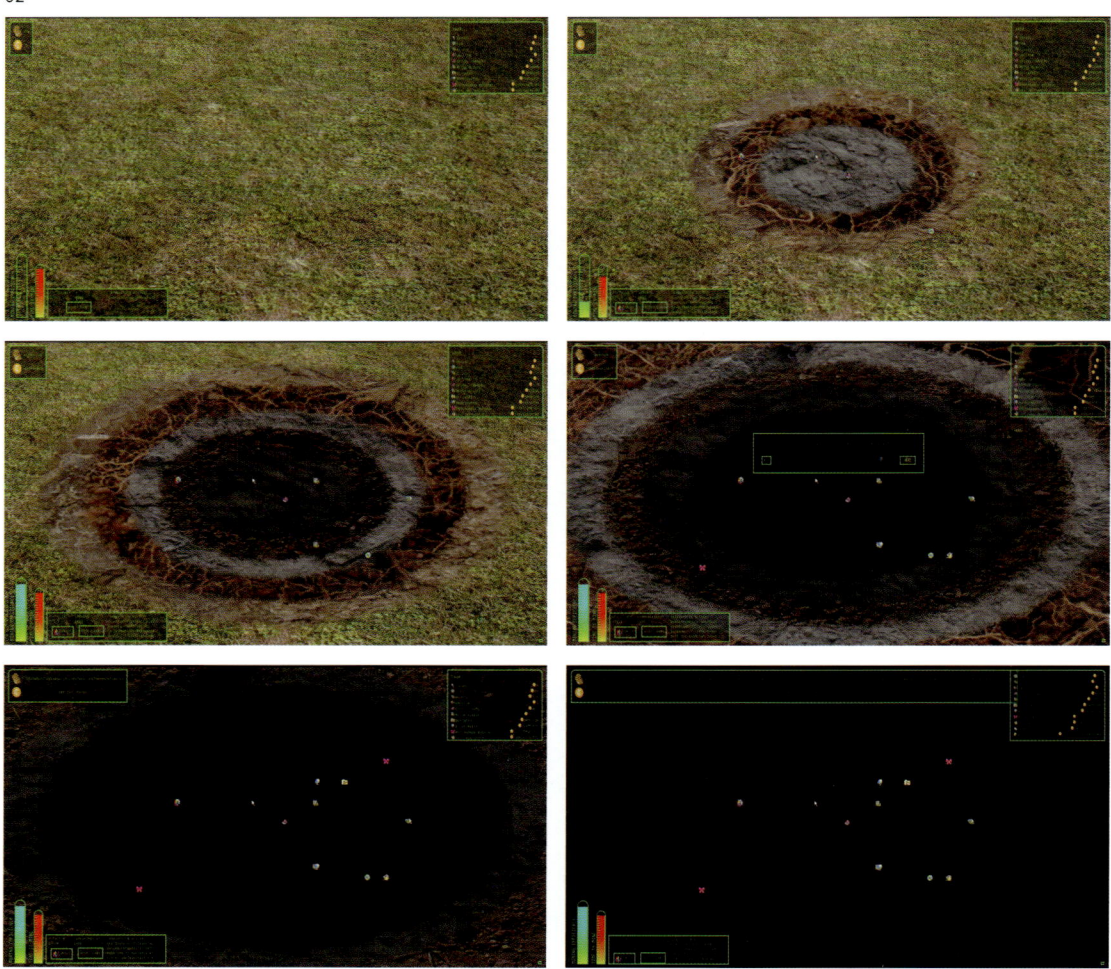

Sarah Friend is a Canadian artist specializing in works that use the logics, incentives, and cultural possibilities of blockchain, games, and P2P technologies. Having trained as an artist, she subsequently became a (self-taught) software developer. She has developed a dual practice of creative and technical work, which interweave in rich and unusual ways. Drawing upon her deep technical knowledge, Friend conceives and executes advanced digital art projects pushing the boundaries of the form.

Friend's works incorporate advanced cryptography, cooperative economic models to produce ecological entanglements, and narrative imaginaries of emerging decentralized networks. In Friend's practice, the affordances of blockchain technology are harnessed to make works of art that are otherwise impossible. In *ClickMine* (2017), a blockchain-based hyperinflationary clicker game, you can "mine" a virtual plot of land, culminating in its destruction. In *Lifeforms* (2021), properties of nature are incorporated into the project's logics to imbue fragility, contingency, novelty, inheritance, and ephemerality in their cryptographic offspring. *Lifeforms'* vivomorphist tendencies enable viewers to imagine generous and cooperative modes of interspecies engagement; ones that run contrary to the entrenched logics of

speculative fetishism. In the work, if one doesn't pass a *Lifeform* NFT onwards within a 90-day period, it "dies" by means of an automated immolation process. As the total supply of *Lifeforms* is unlimited, and hoarding is discouraged by the inbuilt transfer imperative, emphasis is taken away from speculative potential and secondary markets. Issued on Polygon, a second-layer scaling solution for Ethereum, *Lifeform* tokens retain compatibility with much of the Ethereum ecosystem whilst keeping transfer fees low.

*Lifeforms* — and Friend's practice more broadly — reveal the deep connection between the rapacious vortices of spectacle, selfishness, and speculation, to the processes of value extraction and ecological degradation in the reification of cultural objects. Perhaps Friend's work can be said to open the aperture on a new design space, exploring postcapitalist modes of inquiry within technology-mediated artworks.

**WASSIM Z. ALSINDI**
S+T+ARTS FELLOW, FOUNDER OF 0X SALON,
PHILOSOPHY OF CRYPTOECONOMICS
AT BLOCKSCIENCE AND CO-FOUNDER OF THE
JOURNAL CRYPTOECONOMIC SYSTEMS AT MIT

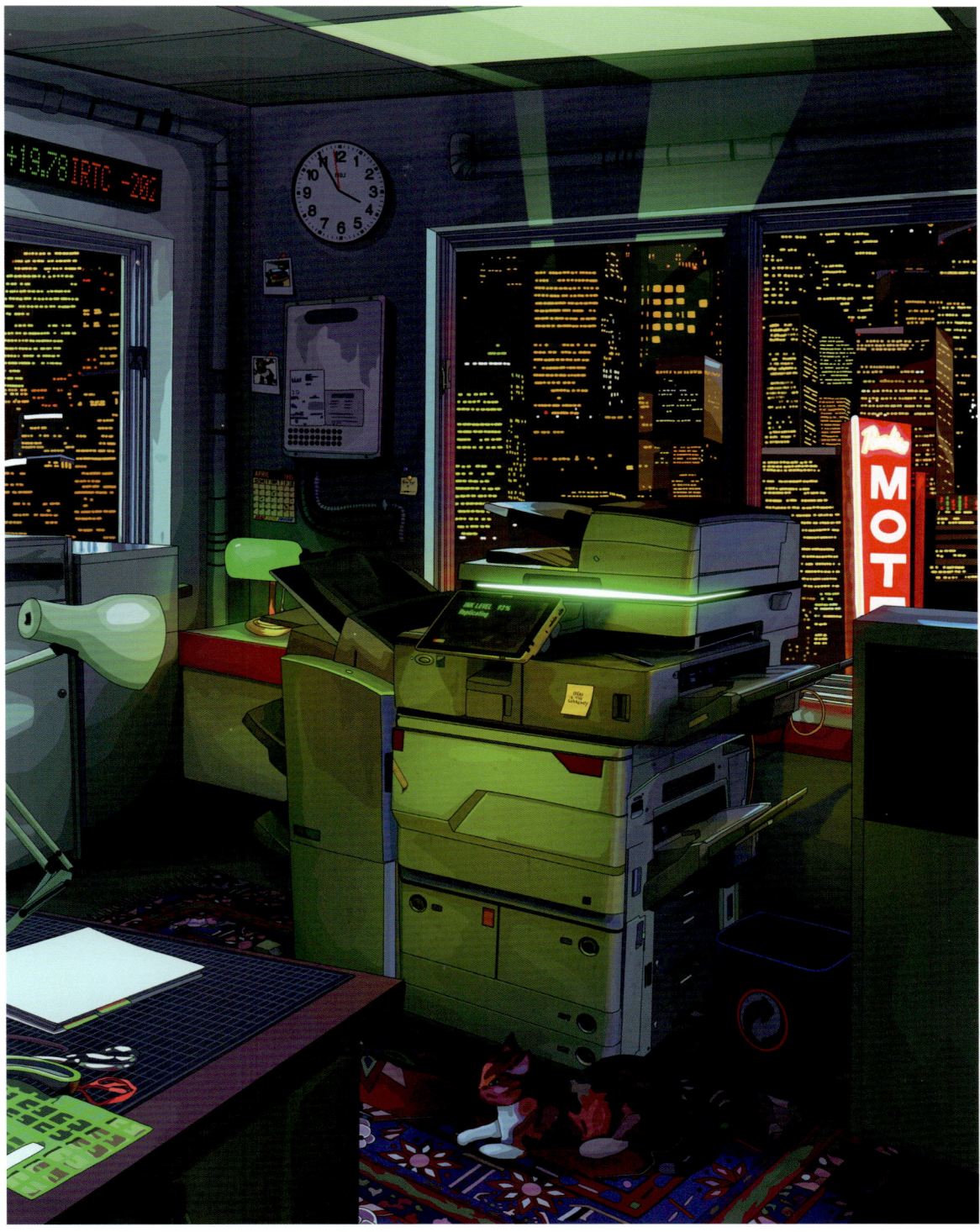

| # | TITLE | TIMESTAMP | MEDIUM | CHAIN | CONTRACT ADDRESS | TOKEN ID | EDITION SIZE |
|---|---|---|---|---|---|---|---|
| 01–03 | **Replicator** | 04-11-2021 16:01:14 | Adobe Photoshop, Adobe Premiere, Procreate | ETH | 0xae1fb0cce66904b9fa2b60bef2b8057ce2441538 | 1–7923...6353 | 7 generations totalling 220 editions |

EDITIONS ILLUSTRATED: (01) Gen 1, (02) Gen 5, (03) Gen 7

# MAD DOG JONES

CANADA 1985

02 ▶

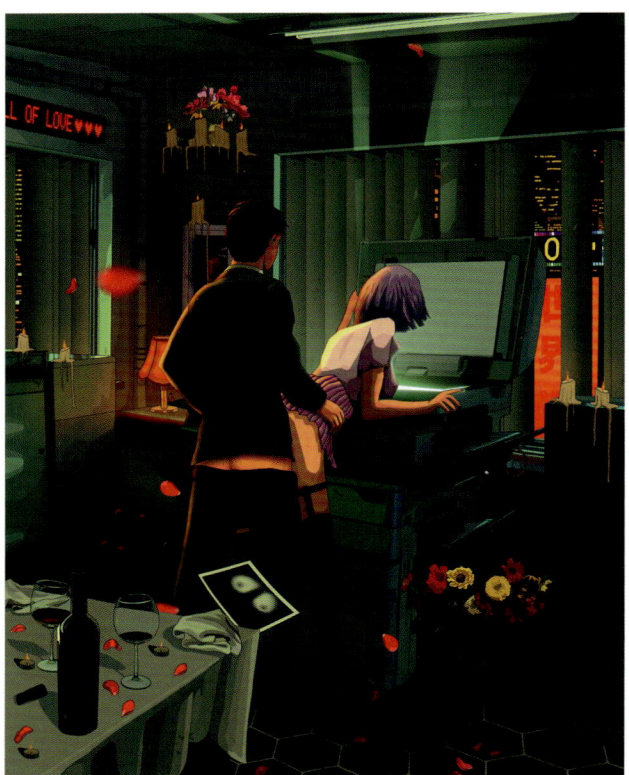

03 ▶

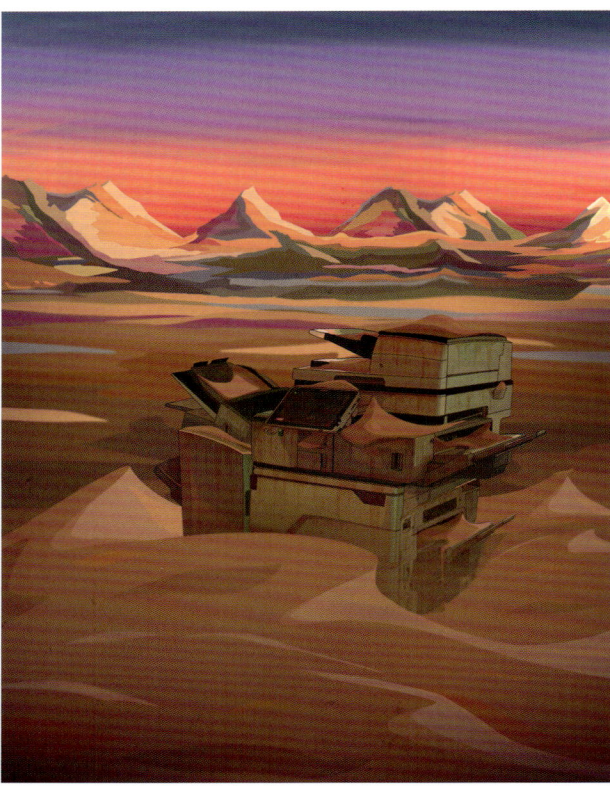

Michah Dowbak (aka Mad Dog Jones) is a widely recognized Canadian multidisciplinary artist. Notably, he's known as an influential force who is adroitly defining and popularizing the relationship between digital art and NFTs, with a specific focus on smart contracts. Flourishing exponentially in the NFT space, Dowbak has built an international audience through speaking directly to his audience on social media — combining reportage of his art practice with humanitarian activism. Much of his work is centered on a techno-futurist aesthetic influenced by Japanese manga, science fiction, neo-noir, film and gaming. These dystopian futures, played out in Dowbak's trademark kaleidoscopic and illustrative style, often feature the motif of car racing, further drawing us into the landscape of his own Sin City. Recently, Dowbak has brought this into the real world with collaborations with Mercedes F1 and Lewis Hamilton.

Dowbak was a member of Coleman Hell, signed to Columbia Records. His creative career eventually expanded into visual art, often producing the audio for his digital animations. His use of color is informed by growing up around a stained glass studio in his family.

*REPLICATOR* (2021), one of Dowbak's most recognized works, showcases his interest in smart contracts. It culminates in a dynamic experience in which the piece produces seven subsequent generations over time. Intellectually, the work sets up a dialogue with his community around the nature of collecting, gamification, and tokenomics. Visually, the vocabulary in the rendition exhibits the specific influences laid out above, alongside subtle elements of nature. Hinting of his home near Thunder Bay, Ontario, nature is always omnipresent. Sometimes even in a familiar form of a ubiquitous pet. Still residing there, he innovates disruptive art with only the Internet as his racetrack to the outside world.

**RONNIE K. PIROVINO**
CURATOR, COLLECTOR, AND FOUNDER OF PIROVINO PROJEX

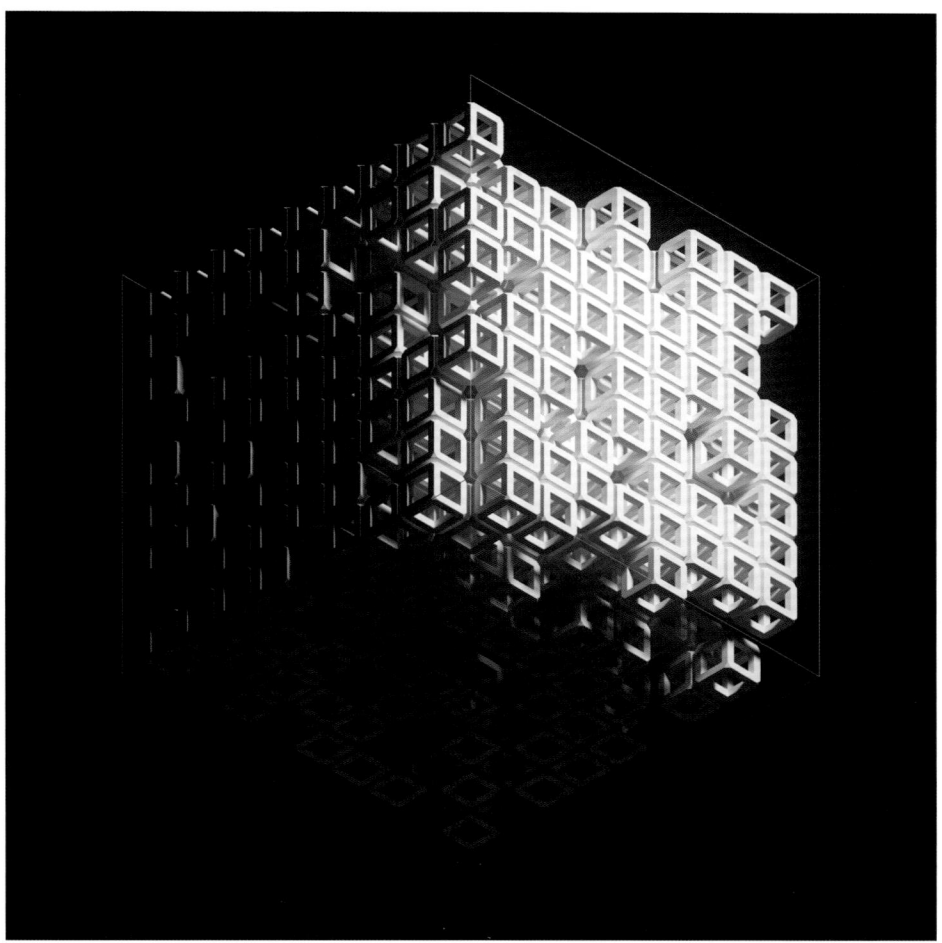

| # | TITLE | TIMESTAMP | MEDIUM | CHAIN | CONTRACT ADDRESS | TOKEN ID | EDITION SIZE |
|---|---|---|---|---|---|---|---|
| 01, 02 | **The Fungible** | 04-12-2021 17:00:00 | Medium not disclosed | ETH | 0xc0cf5b82ae2352303b2-ea02c3be88e23f2594171 | 22700010001–22700085148 | 14 artworks totalling 6,182 editions (at time of mint) |

EDITIONS ILLUSTRATED: (01) Five Hundred Cubes, (02) A Cube

02 ▶

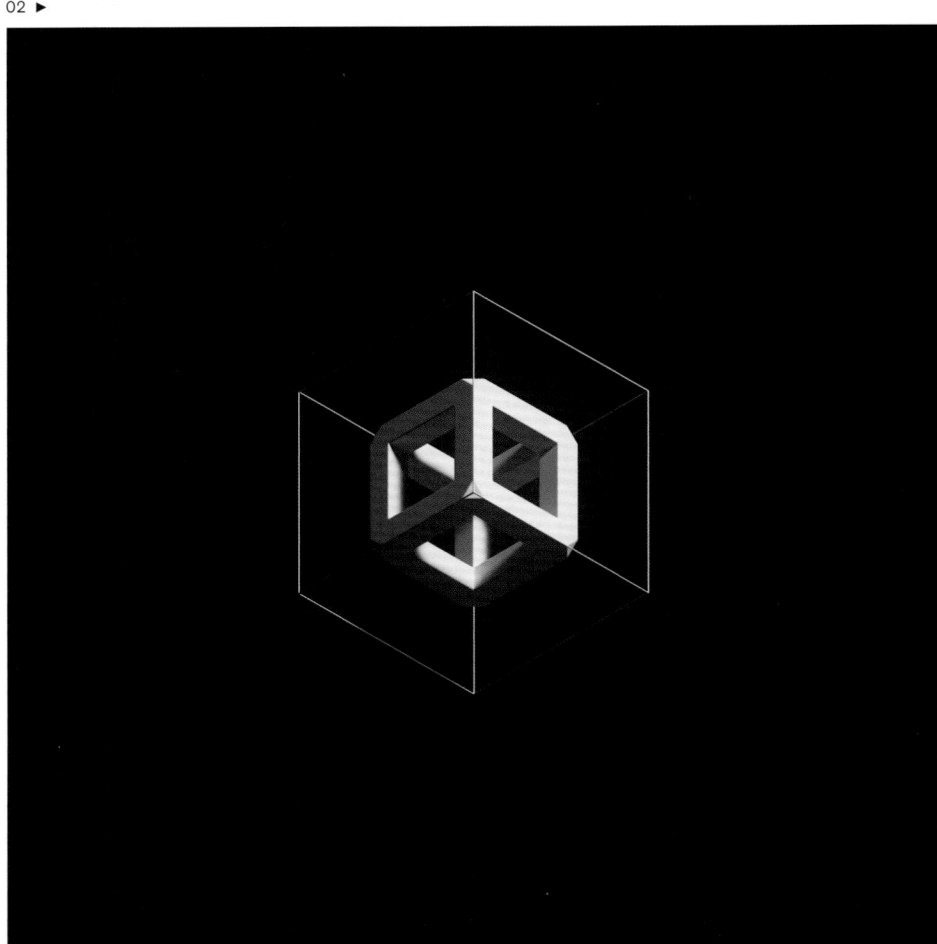

The pseudonymous creative known as Pak was well established in the digital technology, arts and culture scene long before the popularization of NFTs. As the creator of Archillect, the world's largest AI curator of the human aesthetic, Pak's extension into designing and creating within the cutting-edge NFT industry was a natural next step.

While many of Pak's works embody an aesthetic concept of minimalism, the resultive simplicity is the culmination of a deep process of conceptual engagement in the ideas of value, community, and game theory as well as the histories of performance and conceptual art.

In addition to being a master of aesthetic-led design, even more intriguing is the manner through which each work that Pak creates acts as a new foundation in the creation of further works and experiences which continually re-engage the audience, and perhaps even into eternity. In doing so, Pak challenges the foundational underpinnings of performance art, while disrupting and updating them for the Web3 age. Using the smart contract as a medium in itself, Pak has expelled the performance from its ephemeral physical setting, allowing it to evolve on-chain in perpetuity. A performance can now be both objectified and permanent, while also dynamic and in flux.

In two bodies of work, *The Fungible* (2021) and *Merge* (2021), Pak masters the smart contract as a mechanism with which to question the psychological foundations of ownership, inciting collectors to destroy works in the creation of others. In *Lost Poets* (2021) too we see Pak casting their collectors as participatory agents in their artistic process through a seemingly multidimensional "strategy game," with collectors burning "Page" NFTs to catalyze the evolution of their Poet. Each of these collections introduce a radical new approach to gamifying art whereby the collectors themselves determine the outcome of the on-chain performance.

"Design is hack," a definition of design that Pak subscribes to and popularized, cannot be any better represented in their artistic journey: hacking the human condition and hacking the human experience, one experiential work at a time.

**WHALESHARK**
FOUNDER OF $WHALE AND EARLY NFT COLLECTOR

03

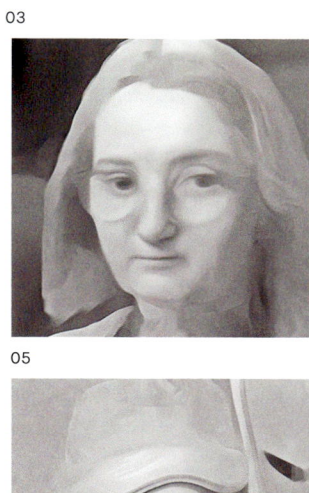

04

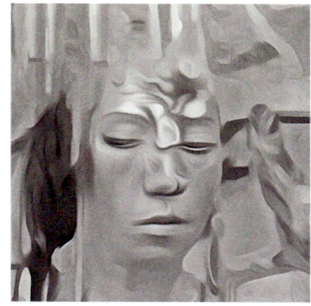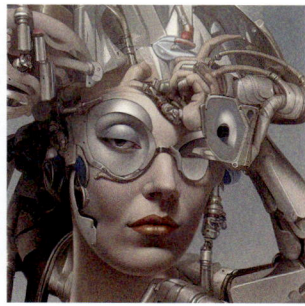

05

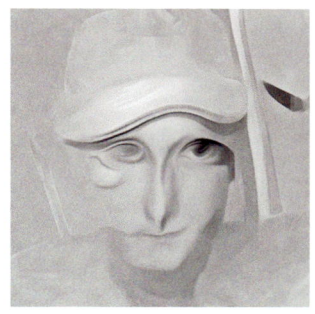

06

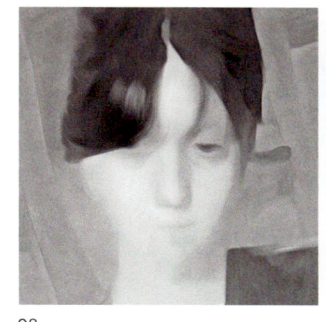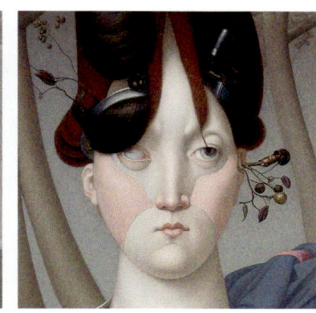

07

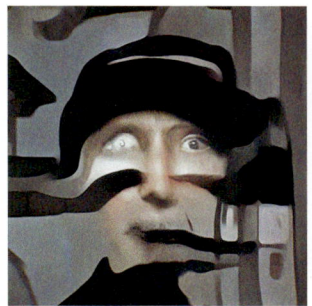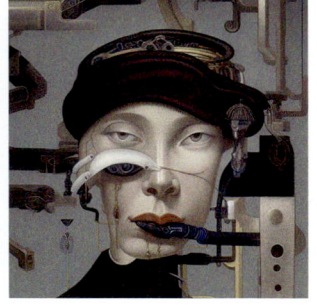

08

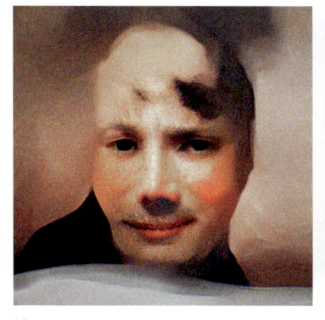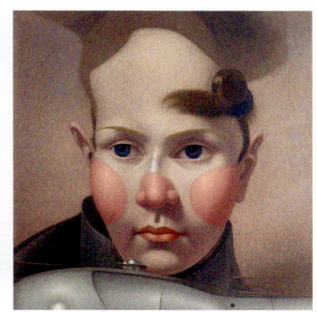

09

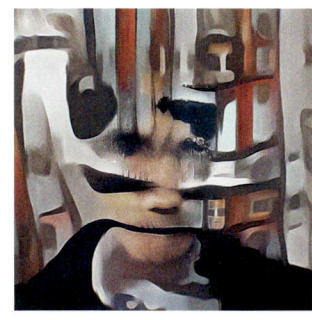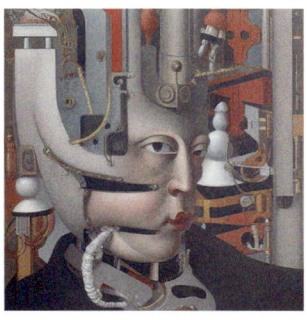

10

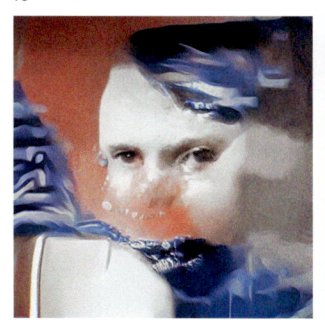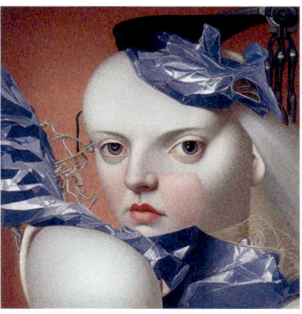

| # | TITLE | TIMESTAMP | MEDIUM | CHAIN | CONTRACT ADDRESS | TOKEN ID | EDITION SIZE |
|---|---|---|---|---|---|---|---|
| 03–10 | **Lost Poets** | 09-25-2021 05:24:38 | Medium not disclosed | ETH | 0x4b3406a41399c7fd2ba65cbc93697ad9e7ea61e5 | 1–65536 | 1/1 of 65,536 (at time of mint) |
| 11–13 | **Merge** | 12-17-2021 01:14:35 | Medium not disclosed | ETH | 0xe052113bd7d7700d623414a0a4585bcae754e9d5 | 1–28983 | 28,983 (at time of mint) |
| 14–16 | **Matter\*** | 10-07-2022 16:22:59 | Medium not disclosed | ETH | 0x9ad00312bb2a67fffba0caab452e1a0559a41a9e | 1–1395 | 1/1 of 1,395 |
| 17–19 | **Antimatter** | 10-15-2022 18:11:35 | Medium not disclosed | ETH | 0x9ad00312bb2a67fffba0caab452e1a0559a41a9e | 1–1395 | 1/1 of 1,395 |

EDITIONS ILLUSTRATED: (03) #59, (04) #247, (05) #288, (06) #915, (07) #1217, (08) #1239, (09) #9362, (10) #9446, (11) #28794, (12) #26984, (13) #10, (14) Aoganie Arc, (15) Blue Thatis Stellar, (16) Yellow Aotarpa String, (17) Aoganie, (18) Thatis, (19) Aotarpa (Each Merge illustration corresponds with its associative Matter\* and Antimatter token below it)

11 12 13
14 15 16
17 18 19

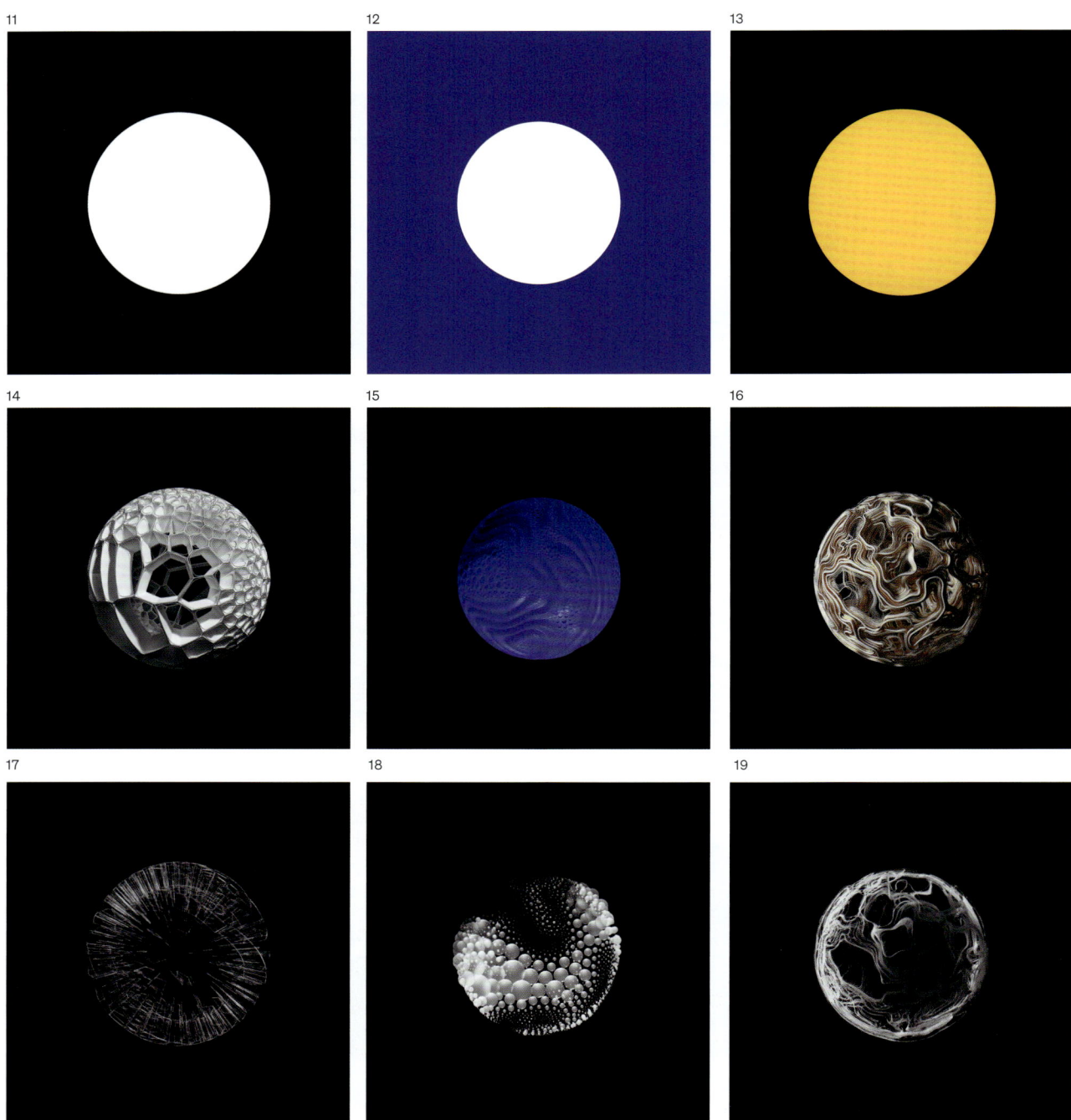

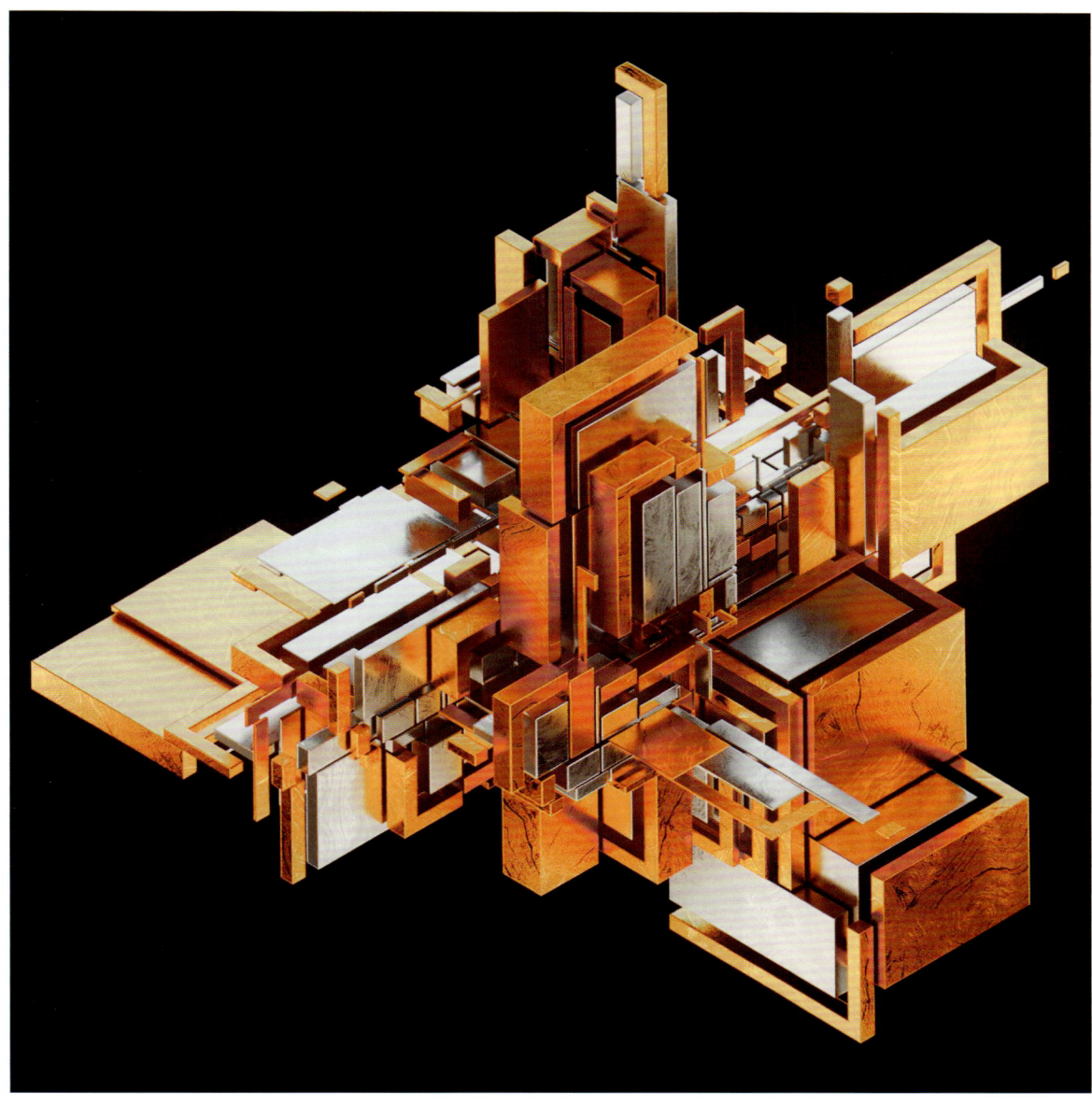

| # | TITLE | TIMESTAMP | MEDIUM | CHAIN | CONTRACT ADDRESS | TOKEN ID | EDITION SIZE |
|---|---|---|---|---|---|---|---|
| 20 | **Rubik's Lure** | 03-06-2020 22:35:06 | Medium not disclosed | ETH | 0xb932a70a57673d89f4acffbe830e8ed7f75fb9e0 | 8585 | 1/1 |
| 21 | **Metarift** | 03-15-2021 23:48:19 | Medium not disclosed | ETH | 0x2a46f2ffd99e19a89476e2f62270e0a35bbf0756 | 48289 | 1/1 |

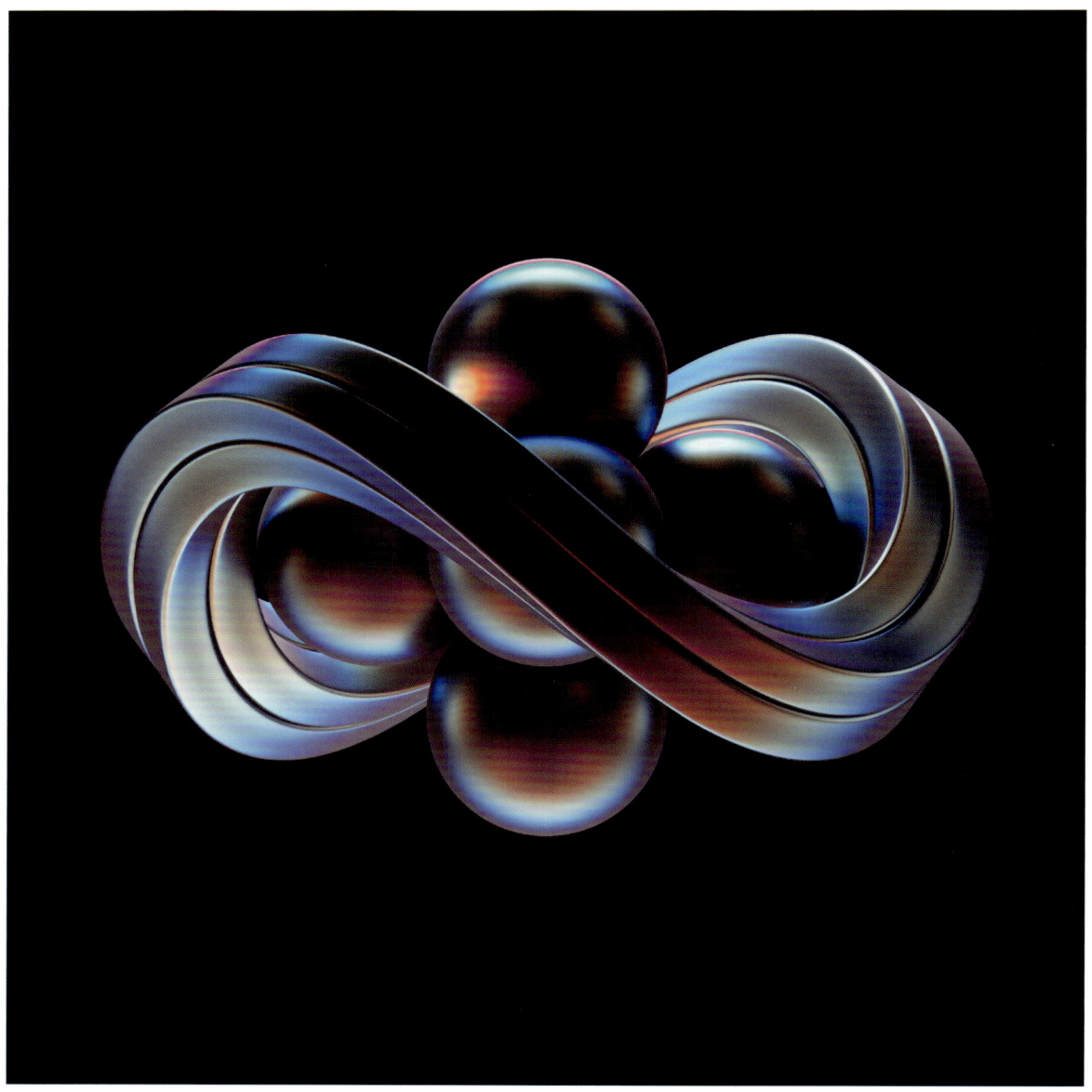

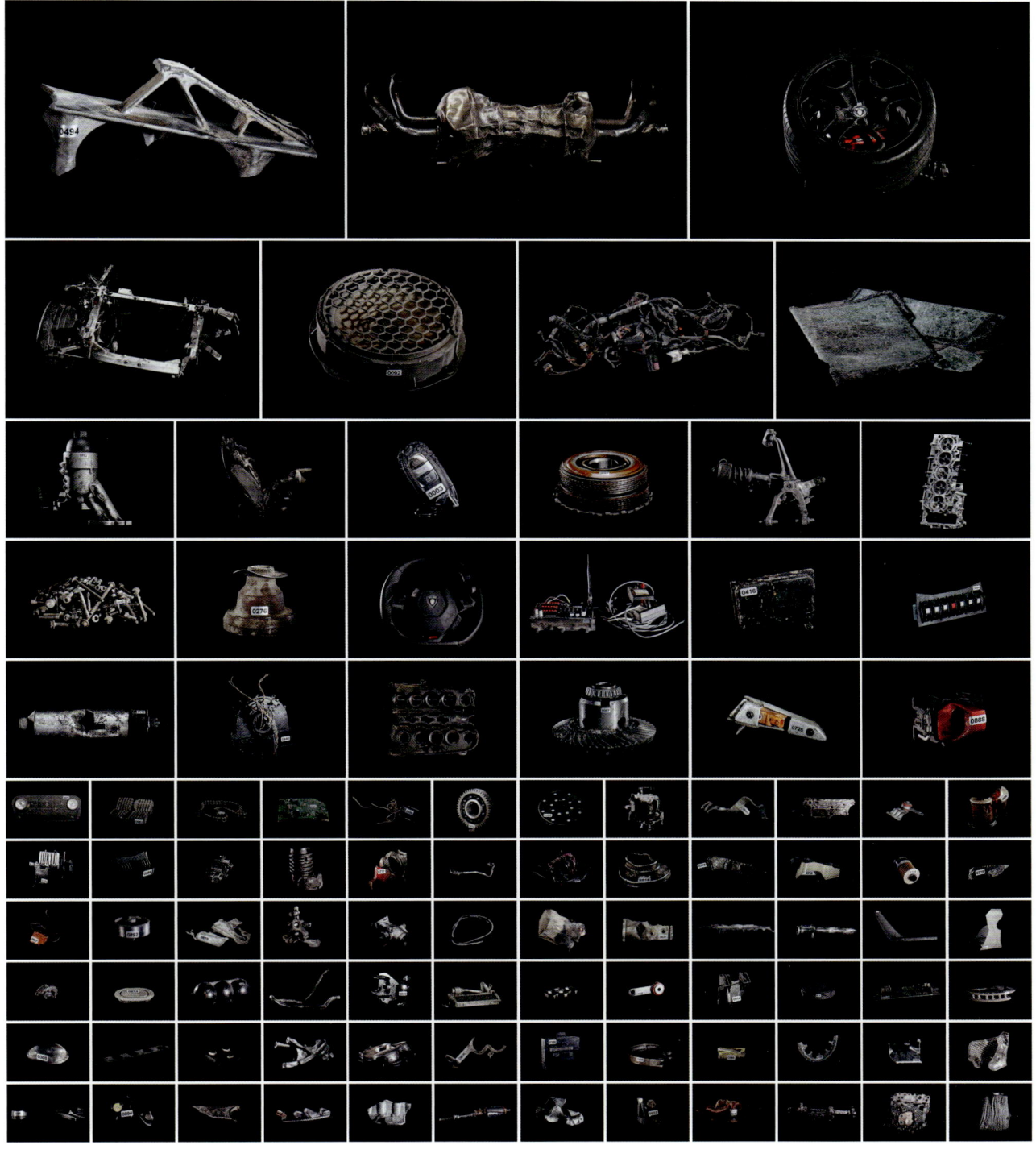

| # | TITLE | TIMESTAMP | MEDIUM | CHAIN | CONTRACT ADDRESS | TOKEN ID | EDITION SIZE |
|---|-------|-----------|--------|-------|------------------|----------|--------------|
| 01 | **CAR** | 03-02-2022 4:06:56 | Lamborghini Huracan, various military-grade explosives | ETH | 0xA80617371A5f511Bf4c1dDf822E6040acaa63e71 | 1-999 | 1/1 of 999 |
| 02 | **SUNSET** | 02-24-2024 11:41:59 | Gmail | ETH | 0xF404357b265c09B7D0779103a79dc7563a2477Aa | 2 | 1/1 |

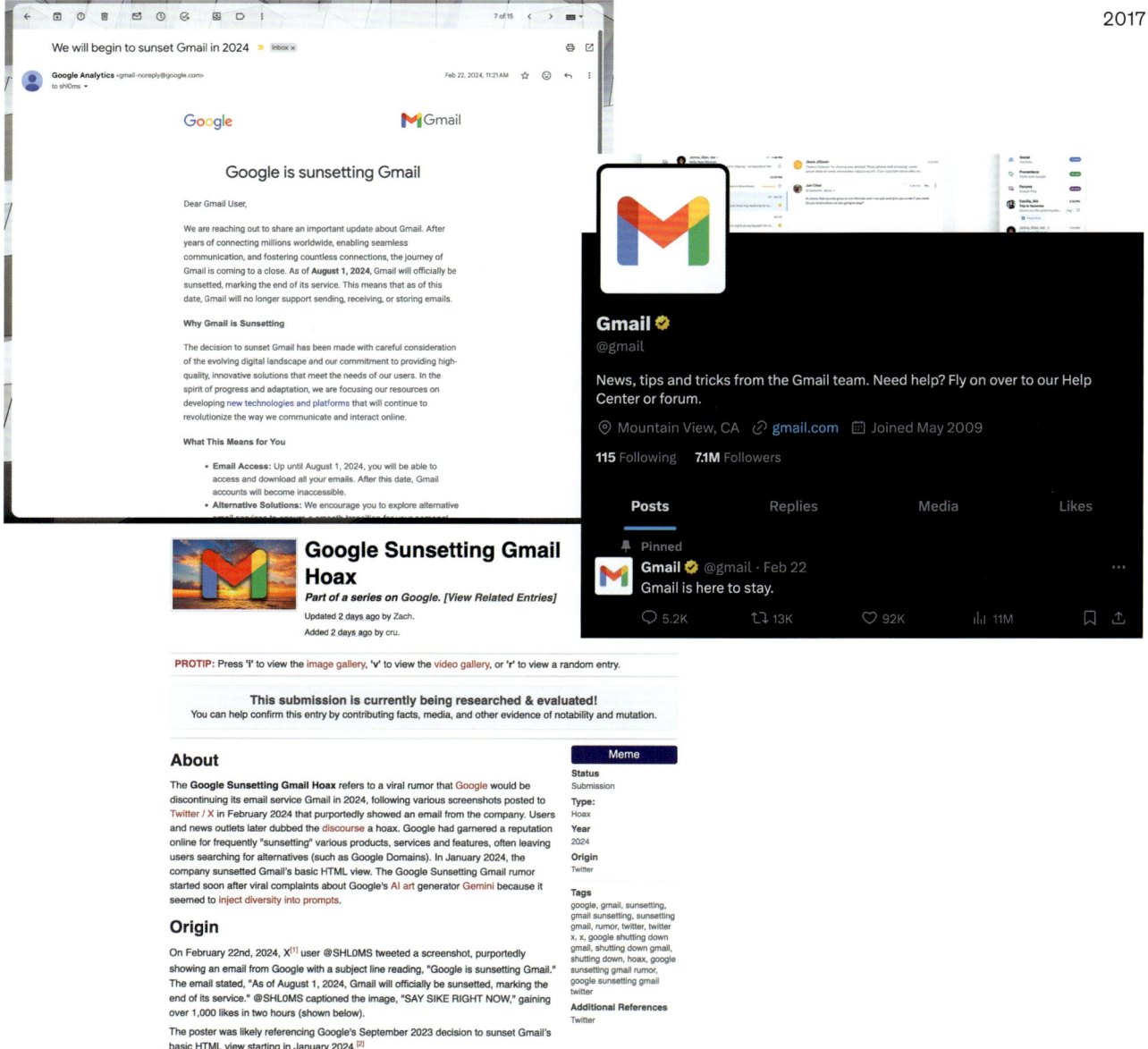

Shl0ms, an anonymous artist, examines the absurdities of speculative markets, cryptocurrency culture, and digital belief systems. Their practice, encompassing hoaxes, performances, and market experiments, investigates the interplay of value, perception, and narrative.

A central theme in Shl0ms's work is the transition of belief systems into the digital domain. Their satirical, AI-driven X personas — God, Satan, and now Jesus — have amassed over four million followers, blending dark humor with incisive critique. These accounts expose how reverence once reserved for divine archetypes now bows to coded systems, reflecting a broader cultural shift toward worshiping the intangible.

One of their most notable interventions was a viral hoax proclaiming Gmail's "sunsetting." This act revealed society's dependence on centralized technological systems and demonstrated the rapid dissemination of misinformation. The public reaction exposed widespread apprehension regarding the influence of tech monopolies and society's vulnerability to digital narratives.

This fascination with warped perceptions of worth culminates in $CAR (2022), a dissection of value itself. Shl0ms demolished a Lamborghini Huracán, splintering it into 999 NFT fragments tied to cryptocurrency wealth. Far from diminishing its value, this act of destruction amplified it through scarcity and narrative, spotlighting the irrational core of speculative markets where hype eclipses substance.

Grounded in the anti-commercial traditions of art history, Shl0ms's work provides a contemporary perspective, exposing how digital economies assign value based on perception rather than tangible substance.

**LEYLA FAKHR**
ARTISTIC DIRECTOR, VERSE & SOLOS, CURATOR

```
<svg xmlns="http://www.w3.org/2000/svg" version="1.1" viewBox="0 0 800 800">
<style>svg{background:#CCC;}</style>
<script><![CDATA[
    const e = document.querySelector('svg')
    const r = e.viewBox.baseVal.width
    const t = e.viewBox.baseVal.height
    const d = e.outerHTML.split('\n')
    const f = d.length
    const g = 5
    const c = 5
    const v = (t - g * 2) / f
    const b = []
    for (let i=0; i<f; i++) {
        const t = document.createElementNS(e.namespaceURI, 'text')
        t.setAttribute('x', c)
        t.setAttribute('y', i * v + g)
        t.style.fontSize = v * 0.95 + 'px'
        t.style.fontFamily = 'monospace'
        t.style.dominantBaseline = 'hanging'
        t.style.whiteSpace = 'pre'
        e.appendChild(t)
        b[i] = t
    }
    let cols, num, data
    document.fonts.ready.then(t => {
        (function m() {
            b[0].textContent = ''.padStart(100, 'W')
            let charW = b[0].getBBox().width/100
            b[0].textContent = ''
            if (charW == 0) setTimeout(m, 100)
            else {
                cols = Math.floor((r - c * 2) / charW)
                num = cols * f
                data = []
                data = d.map(e => e.padEnd(cols, ' ')).join('').split('')
                requestAnimationFrame(loop)
            }
        })() // FF fix: getBBox() returns width=0, sometimes
    })
    const q = (a, b, c) => {
        if (c[b] == ' ' && c[a] != ' ') [c[b], c[a]] = [c[a], ' ']
    }
    const n = (() => {
        let v = 0
        return () => {
            v = (1664525 * v + 1013904223) % 4294967296
            return v / 4294967296
        }
    })()
    let z = 0
    function loop(t){
        requestAnimationFrame(loop)
        if (t > 1000) {
            const sign = z++ % 2 == 0 ? -1 : 1
            for (let i=num-cols-1; i>=0; i--) {
                if (data[i] == ' ') continue
                if (n() > 0.4) continue
                if (f - i / cols - Math.sin(i + z) * 5 > z * 0.2) continue
                if (n() >= 0.5) {
                    q(i, i + cols, data, cols)
                } else {
                    const s = i + cols + sign
                    if (s % cols != cols - 1) {
                        q(i, s, data, cols)
                    }
                }
            }
        }
        for (let j=0; j<f; j++) {
            b[j].textContent = data.slice(j * cols, (j + 1) * cols).join('').trimEnd()
        }
    }
]]></script></svg>
```

| #      | TITLE                         | TIMESTAMP           | MEDIUM          | CHAIN | CONTRACT ADDRESS                       | TOKEN ID | EDITION SIZE |
|--------|-------------------------------|---------------------|-----------------|-------|----------------------------------------|----------|--------------|
| 01, 02 | **svg4.svg, Code is dust**    | 09-21-2021 10:40:14 | JavaScript, SVG | XTZ   | KT1RJ6PbjHpwc3M5rw5s2Nbmefwbuwbdxton   | 338146   | 10           |

ROBERT HENKE ON

# ANDREAS GYSIN

SWITZERLAND 1975

02 ▶

```
              m
            >  s
      v   x  n t              s
      <           g
      g  p            ww /              i
         g  ls pb   o    3     y /                  w
      s i  >   :  t  :w                                      8
      t e "    / T c ow   20      s              =
      c  l  =v h   n#C    /  / 0  vv
         c  r n  d.}e.      0e   r   l    B       "  0
      <   t oa      e Cq  ;  g                        x
          n  C! [  me    r s   >    =    " i     0
      s ycn t  A      . w   y<et      o           0
          n  s kA  d x  a     r            o      80  0 >
      c so  <    .               l           v
          s  s o wu ut  u e     dcg        l  e
      o        [   .   C   eol S         e
      c s { = . v   b sea             '
         tt ee vi x  H  o  h.                g      n
      <  n        uD B .e   . V oge h r )
      c  r  d vt  e    l a  t  '  (                0
      n =o     t   B  s i w     r
         c        r       o  b  l     (
         n = er      T a
      t      =  t   t              h     ts
      o   t    e      V  l   h
      so  s     =     *   L   .i
      c    s f
      o     l       = ng       \
      s   ci                      t
         c  b ]  = l e   )-        ' n
         o t t=    5 i   (   ;)e  p
      s  e 0   o    t        + +
      n      e     d5 t't       f s
         s = t t  i  d M /
         g n(    t e  c m '
         t    ug   = mu{
      r o       b n;tca       fE
      t c    t i riiSt<ee  t i
      f   t   .[ . A'fo' t       m
      n  (   A  eztmdla .r2      *
      e t     ttrlnotehSnFblx=a  0              c
      s  y    ontiinlea=Be,n n *       t   m    p   )
      c    d   yfyiwe)hym(i+onla e  pS
      c   .  tduhpt.to{(sy(=ecvy9v. e  a ( n   R
              tmdtd]x.anatte)a,)c'n5'n
         l   .netntxe.re],ean'io'r)              U
         .  oea,u0mohCC=n0=[=q>eht'e sp g    s    t   x
      t    c.Cthe0acodr=n0pobo(.'uaa.e
         .stelifnrb==tataaWl=ett'etd.){p+  e '       I
         sp.yls.iccur=dMa]stt=)n'fx(tlcn
         stletn{esq/unAetanl.feoriF'/mBt.Ne
      o    .p btima(e[cfaxedo(*)hs.ptrtiomarg e
      ss tot]Wl=/b,)c{==i([momrn>eep.Bdo*ldi=         t
         =[a.t[F]{=46n>):sia>=go=mtins(e(-T2(
      euc]be(b)2vlt5>='t&&[x{BB]a)!re)p(a,,S'x   a e
      tm(cl=,(=((00tt/62'4c6*2v0la32r'=o(lE0w(
      o[nfFv}t(uo)i)iFg5{em9ar7p4o629+u'=inh)thg
      t en()o(n0an{sisteon=(u9)z+ll%0)0;?0l[[dco1'0
      t  .clst}t=evl(pm(nf=nmn[l2c=os-+==>i=n-%49tllc000
      . tfe)sonn=trtsld(nqa-a].i4.olccoi'oue-13))0wsr/t0
       }us)ileeur0on0tit((-{(i0t0>ccotn'o-)dahn-;:4]o[W)a))
      odeqrlr)toAui>ff(fflsn=),>)/5s{)scl,t.atnt(elbaodc,mWt,''
      sfnt}rn(c=efrloifi}(ocieii%+=,looM+c+liici+snu2c,',sih)(to)e t)s
      c}}ezfecion(}i[et}j)efs(tis=ss,cd=t,ila,s-lgs{s9c9]7=.j4[ce'.'pilm''i )
      uc)}}qF}}(orb]lj.t0=joqn<;(i+s=)aa!.socl)s)lo({))iz92]a>[*sz'i,.0]]csnon(teu  .' n
      ]]></script></svg>xe;Cttfejn+taad{tsilc(oe*jnolc,si*6(j51+*)6o2cl)).jo(ni''n)itrEmd ( )
```

Programming languages are very minimalistic formal constructions, providing only what is necessary to state a problem in a nonambiguous way. Since not all computer science problems are alike, a variety of languages have been developed, each following their own set of rules. What they have in common is an inherent sense of rhythm and structure, due to the repetition of key syntactic elements. Java code looks different than assembler or Fortran. But usually the code which drives the tools we use all day remains unseen, and what a software developer would call "elegant" — or "a terrible mess" — is not visible to the outside world. In Andreas Gysin's (aka ertdfgcvb) works, code is used to drive intricate text transformations, turning symbols into seemingly organic entities on screen or into complex imaginary machines. This is satisfying to observe, but there is a twist: often the text that is used as the starting point or "source material" is the very same code that actually performs the transformations. The majority of observers probably cannot understand the code they see on screen, but they are able to feel its graphic quality. As the abstract patterns form into rearrangements and clever shifts over time, the inherent "groove" of the language can be felt. By using code in this way, the artist is providing anti-obfuscation. What usually remains hidden becomes visible, and the inner mechanics of his works are exposed. This is a radically different approach than that of AI and other currently emerging "black box" art. In Andreas Gysin's case the magic does not rely on a process too big to understand, but rather the opposite: via mastery of the small form. The wonder comes from seeing something that is simple, yet full of life and surprise.

**ROBERT HENKE**
DIGITAL ARTIST

03 ▶

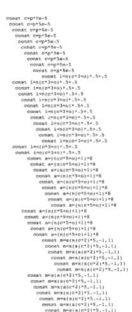
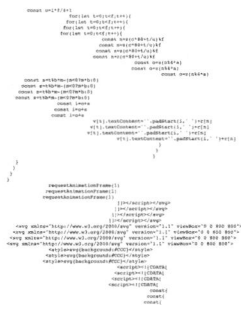
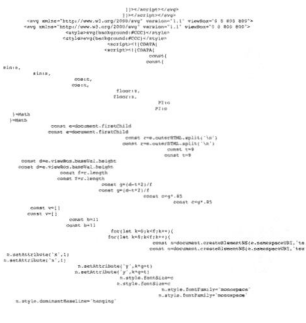

04 ▶

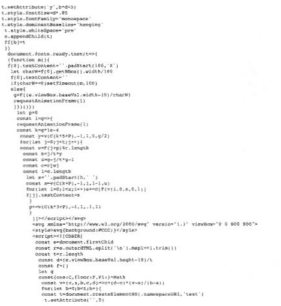

05 ▶

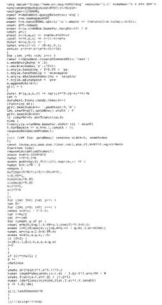
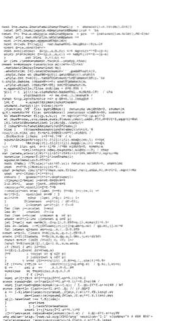
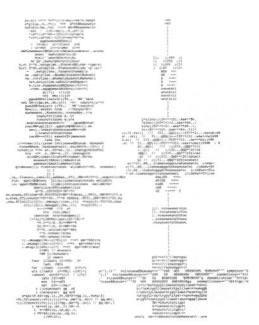

06 ▶

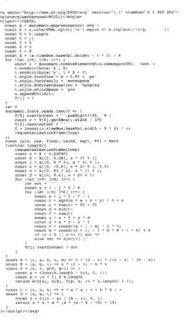

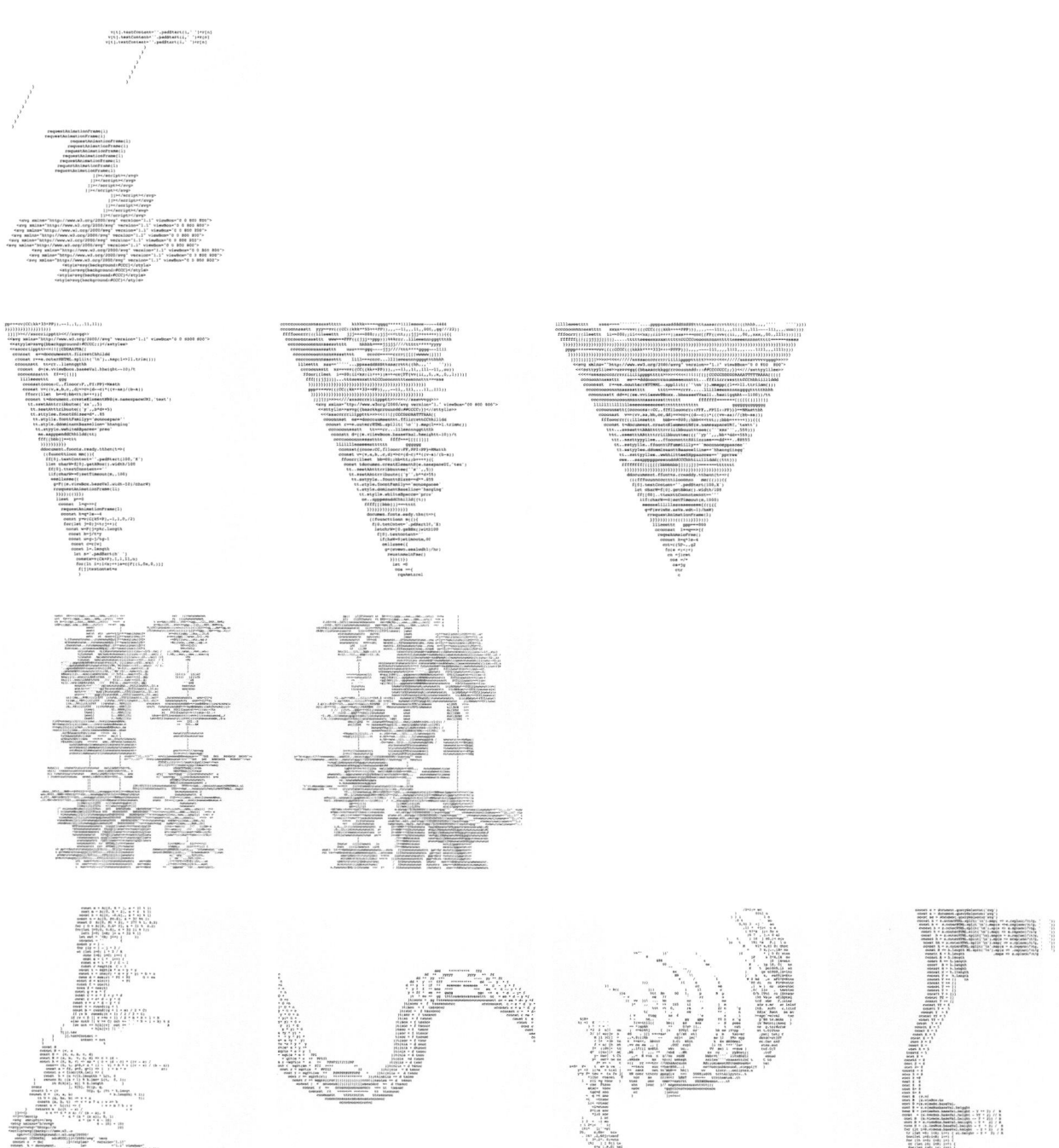

01

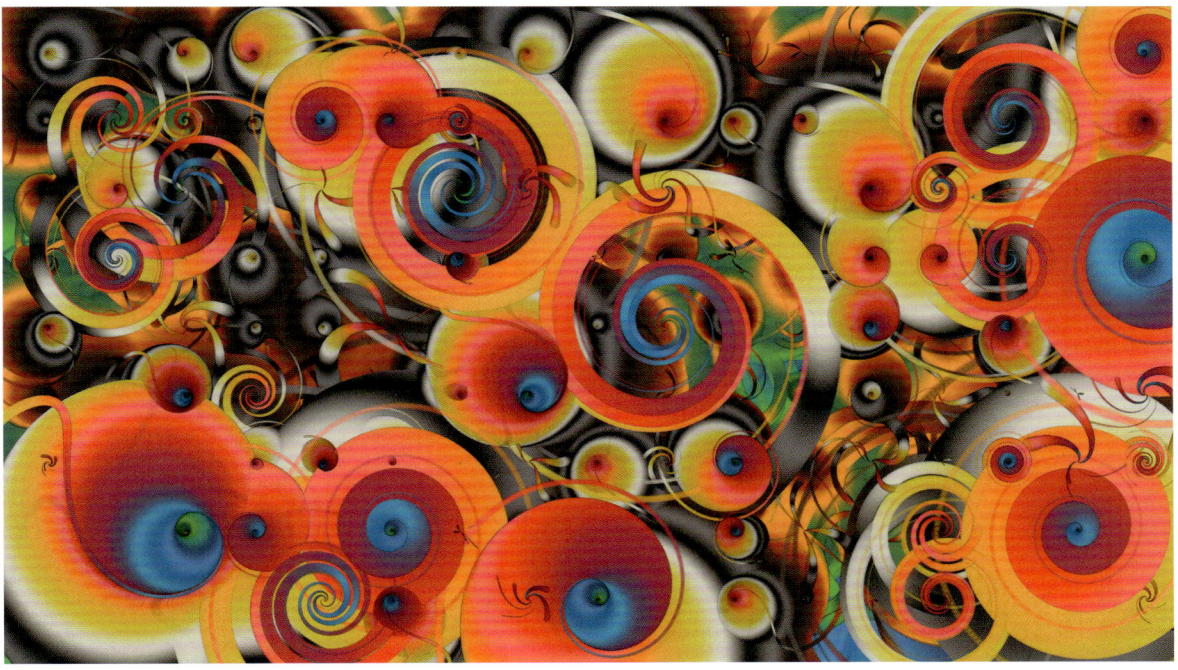

02

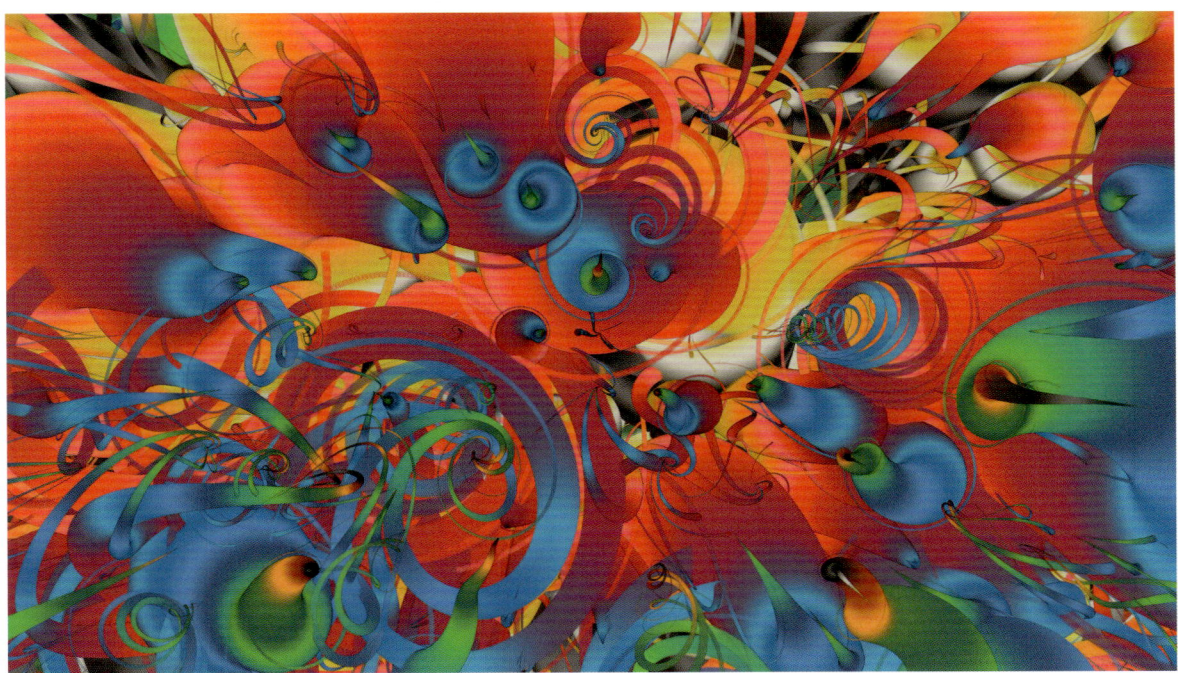

| # | TITLE | TIMESTAMP | MEDIUM | CHAIN | CONTRACT ADDRESS | TOKEN ID | EDITION SIZE |
|---|---|---|---|---|---|---|---|
| 01, 02 | **the Fatal Impact** | 11-11-2021 14:14:03 | Processing, GLSL | ETH | 0x89842789784eb86b00752b05c73af231f65030ad | 1–8 | 1/1 of 8 |
| 03 | **the V01D / 007-001 /**<br>**Jana Stýblová** | 04-20-2021 02:08:17 | Processing, GLSL | ETH | 0xb932a70a57673d89f4acffbe830e8ed7f75fb9e0 | 23682 | 1/1 |

EDITIONS ILLUSTRATED: (01) #1, (02) #4

# JOSHUA DAVIS
UNITED STATES 1971

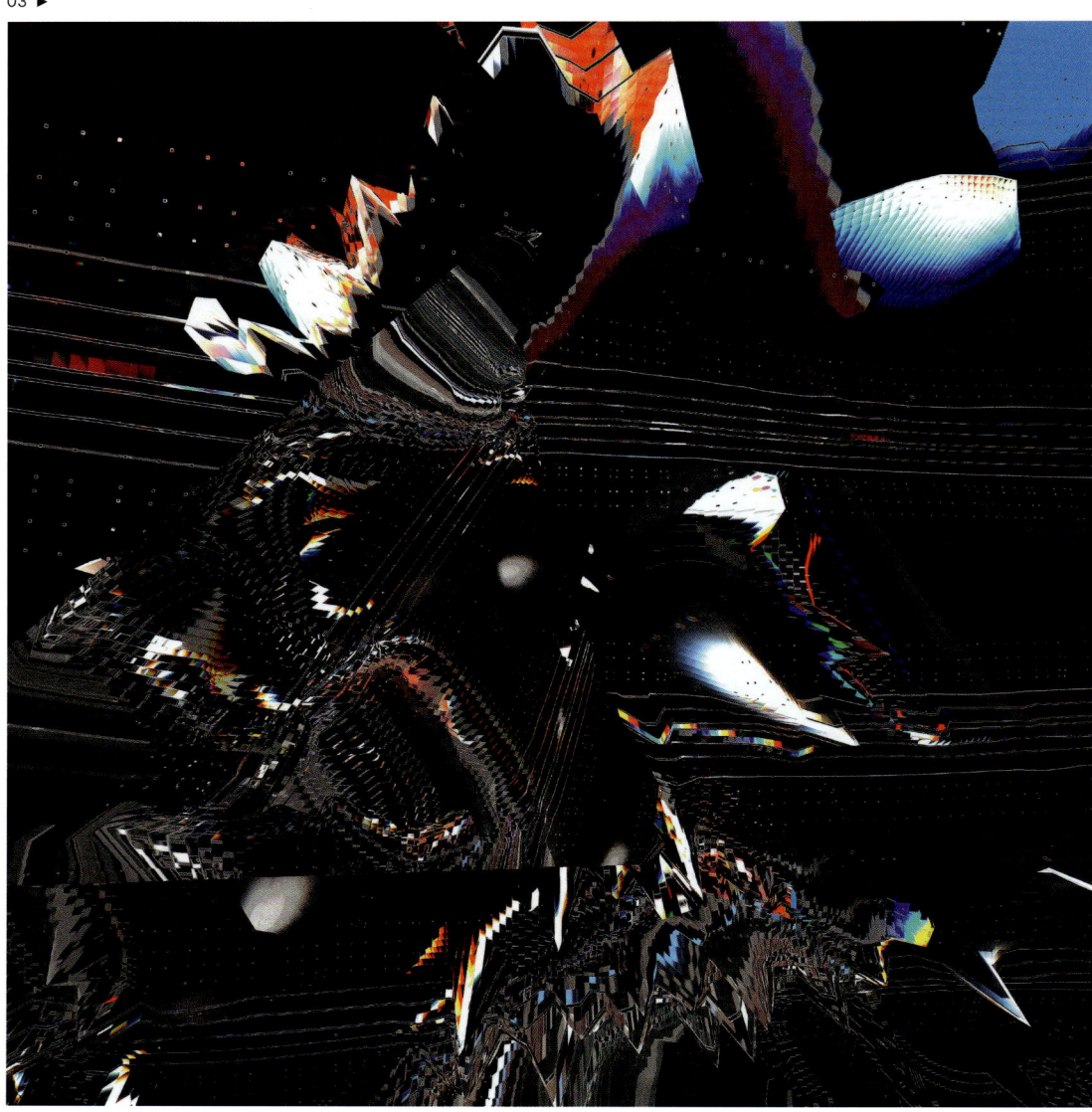

My art emanates from an active dialogue between the computer and myself. Simply stated, I write software which generates unique animations and compositions. I often focus on conjuring algorithms specifically to make art ad infinitum. The code can produce works akin to snowflakes, where no two versions are ever the same. When a video is rendered, we are viewing a moment of time from the software's potentially infinite system. Because the software uses audio as input, naturalistic equations may constantly update and mutate variables, in real time. In effect, I'm partially a critic and curator, living with the program I've written, watching it formulate and evolve very closely.

My goal is to capture moments in time that are gloriously ethereal. I embrace chaos and chance. I devise all the rules, boundaries, and decisions an artist would normally make, while allowing the software/algorithm to become an independent artist in itself, and as such, I'm in a constant state of communication with the computation.

Among my highlights is a role in designing the visualization of IBM's Watson. Prizes and awards include the Prix Ars Electronica's Golden Nica. My work has been exhibited at the Tate Modern, the ICA, and the Design Museum in London, Centre Pompidou in Paris, the Guggenheim Museum Bilbao, and New York's MoMA PS1, the Whitney Museum of American Art, the Cooper Hewitt, Smithsonian Design Museum, and more.

**JOSHUA DAVIS**
ARTIST

294, 295,

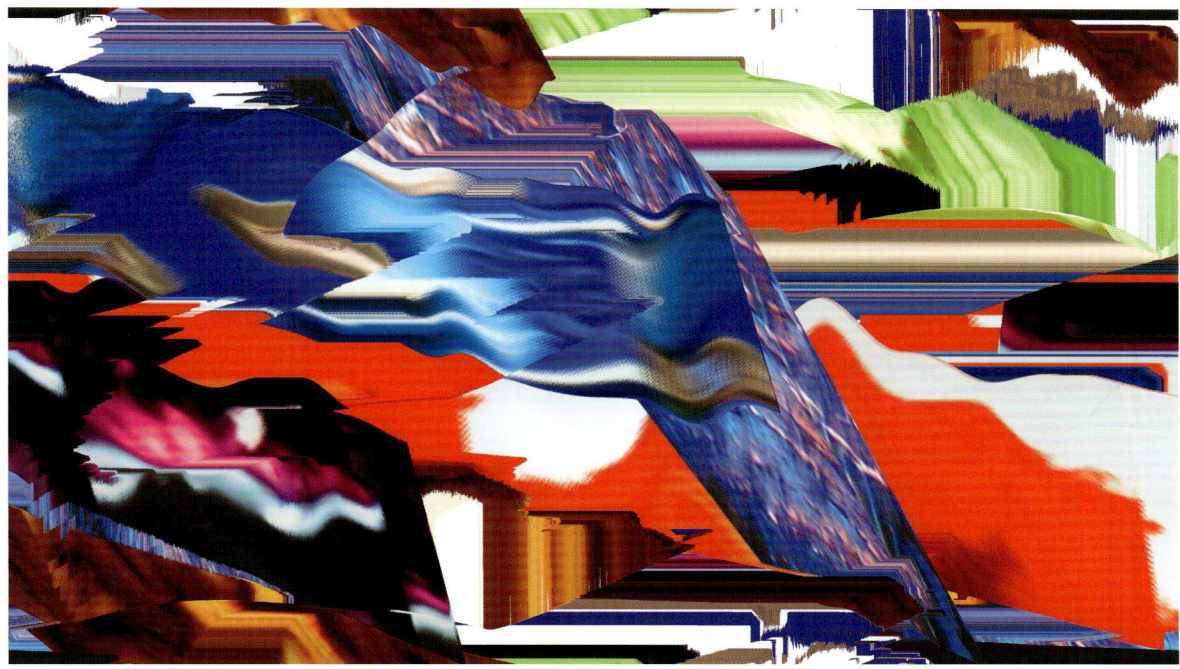

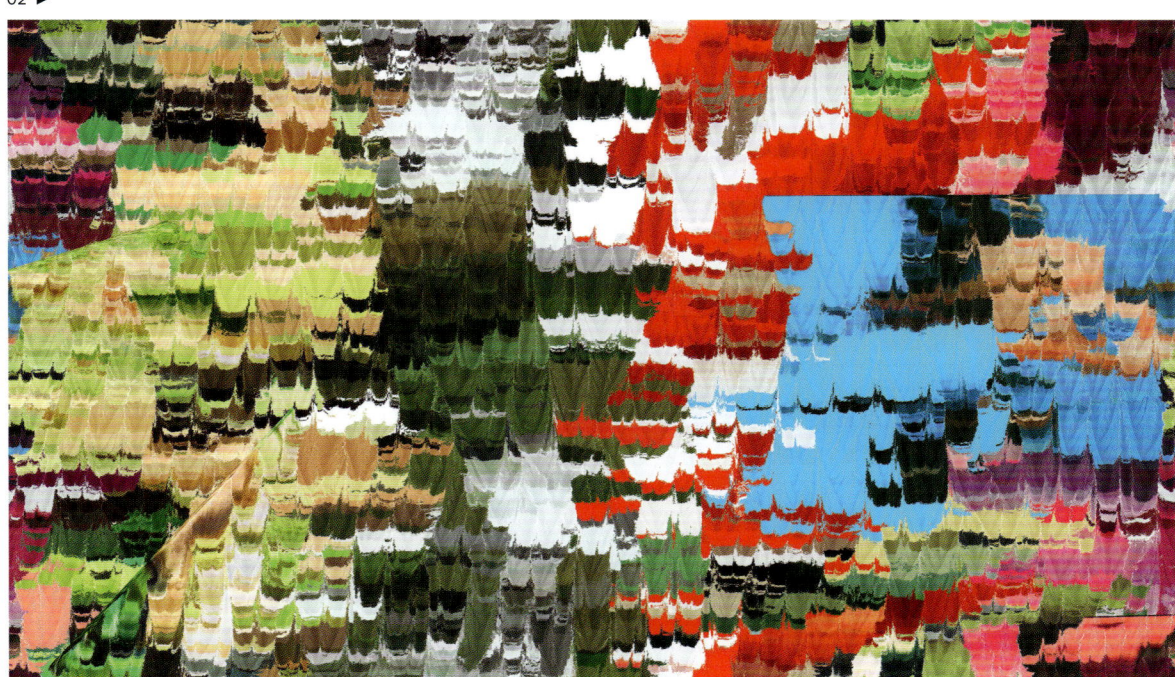

| # | TITLE | TIMESTAMP | MEDIUM | CHAIN | CONTRACT ADDRESS | TOKEN ID | EDITION SIZE |
|---|---|---|---|---|---|---|---|
| 01, 02 | **Solvency** | 04-19-2021 20:54:40 | WebGL | ETH | 0x82262bfba3e25816b4c720f1070a71c7c16a8fc4 | 1–500 | 1/1 of 500 |
| 03, 04 | **Silk Road** | 04-11-2022 18:22:32 | WebGL | ETH | 0x53e4c0167ed855e96f562dbb911854d586f5cc07 | 0–1027 | 1/1 of 1,028 |

EDITIONS ILLUSTRATED: (01) #223, (02) #287, (03) #811, (04) #377

# EZRA MILLER

UNITED STATES 1996

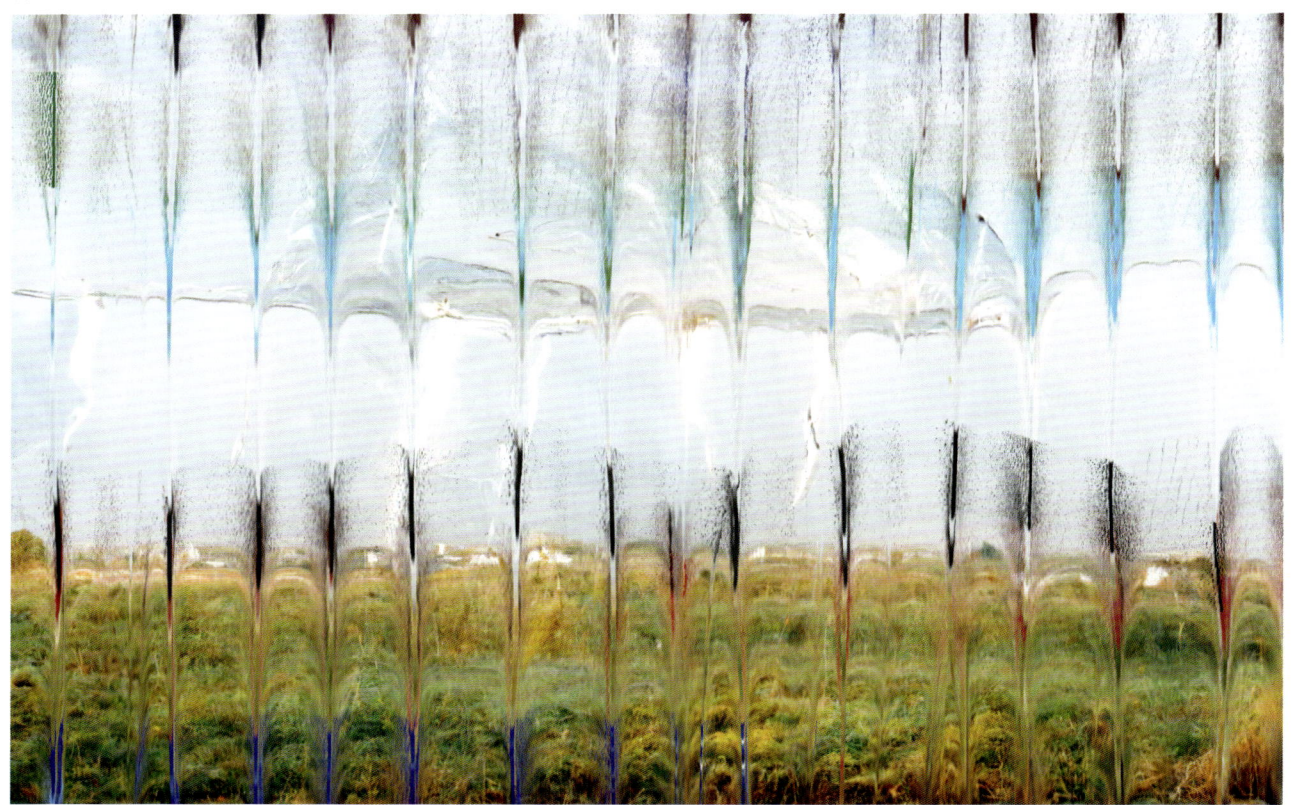

I have a unique perspective on Ezra's development as an artist, having known him, and collected his art, his entire life: Ezra is my son. I'm very proud to outline the path he's taken. Self-taught as a programmer, he has been using WebGL to create interactive, generative art since he was a teenager. His aptitude at making art with code has given him myriad opportunities for exhibition and collaboration.

Entailing considerable programming skill, Ezra's two NFT series, *Solvency* (2021) and *Silk Road* (2022), comprise wholly digital artifacts, existing on the internet and the blockchain. The instant the NFTs are minted, the artworks are created as generative images, with infinite duration, in ever-shifting, constant flux. Each NFT assembles randomly generated combinations of parameters from a weighted palette of attributes, creating unforeseen, poetic outcomes. Innumerable works of art in one, they remind us that generative and generous share an etymology.

Ezra gathers images from a wide range of sources — environments, patterns, forces, materials, creatures, places — which he then abstracts. *Solvency* launches planes of nonrepresentational imagery into action, as if natural forces were mobilized to put forth pure painterly atmospheres. These works undulate and swirl, full with pep. *Silk Road* derives from more pictorial attributes, and the elusive, moody settings underlying these works give them an uncanny aura. While *Solvency* pieces are lively, *Silk Road* pieces play deliberately, inducing contemplation. They evoke ambiences imbued with emotion, landscapes dissolving in memory's blur, lambent waves of synesthetic sensation.

Tethering the spontaneity of abstract painting to programmed operations, balancing depiction with the autonomous play of form, Ezra's NFTs exemplify how digital technology can bring new kinds of art into being. An invitation to see these works in fluid motion on a computer, the images collected here can only suggest the inherent dynamism and multidimensional essence of Ezra's art.

**JONATHAN MILLER**
EDUCATOR, CRITIC, ARTIST,
AND FATHER OF EZRA MILLER

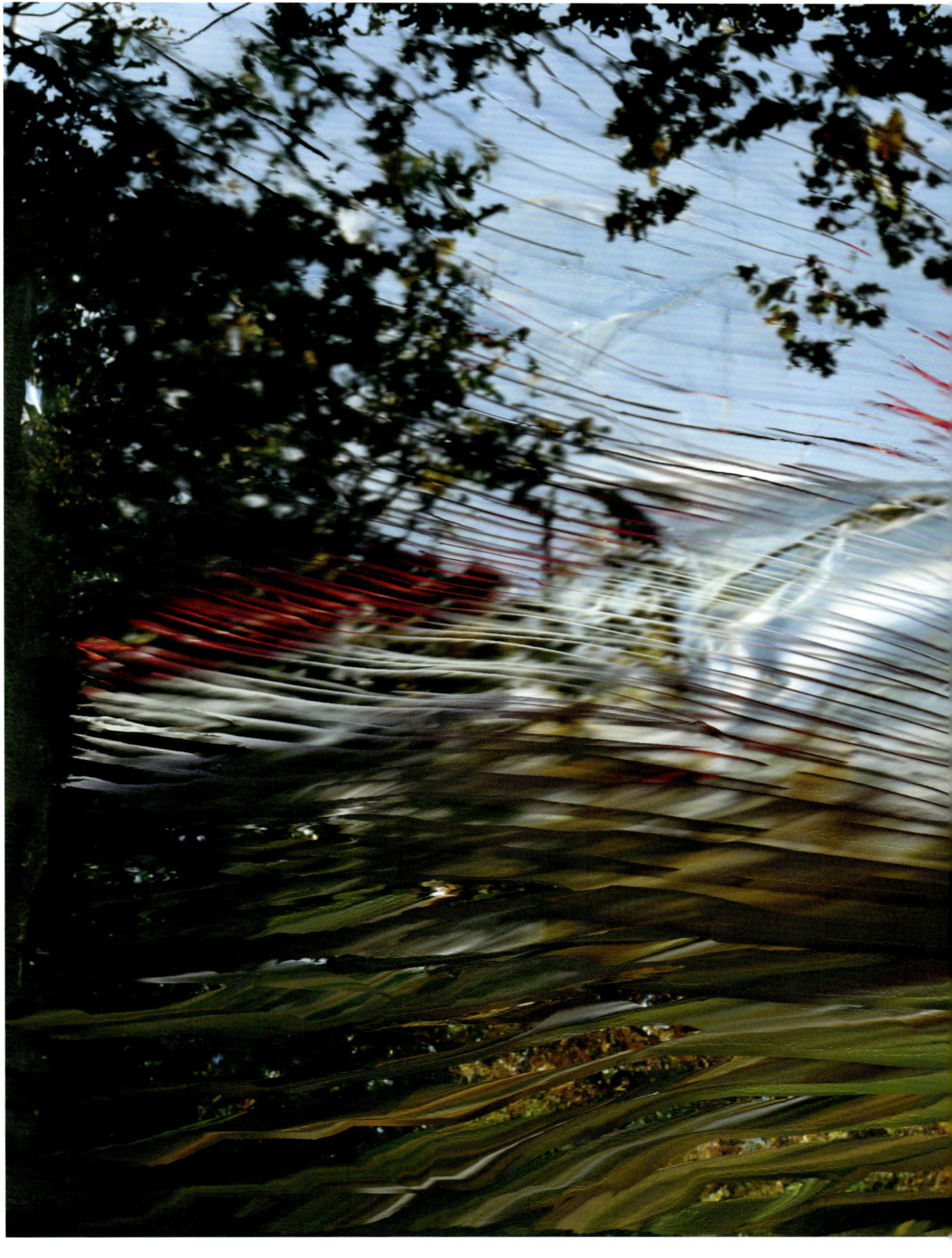

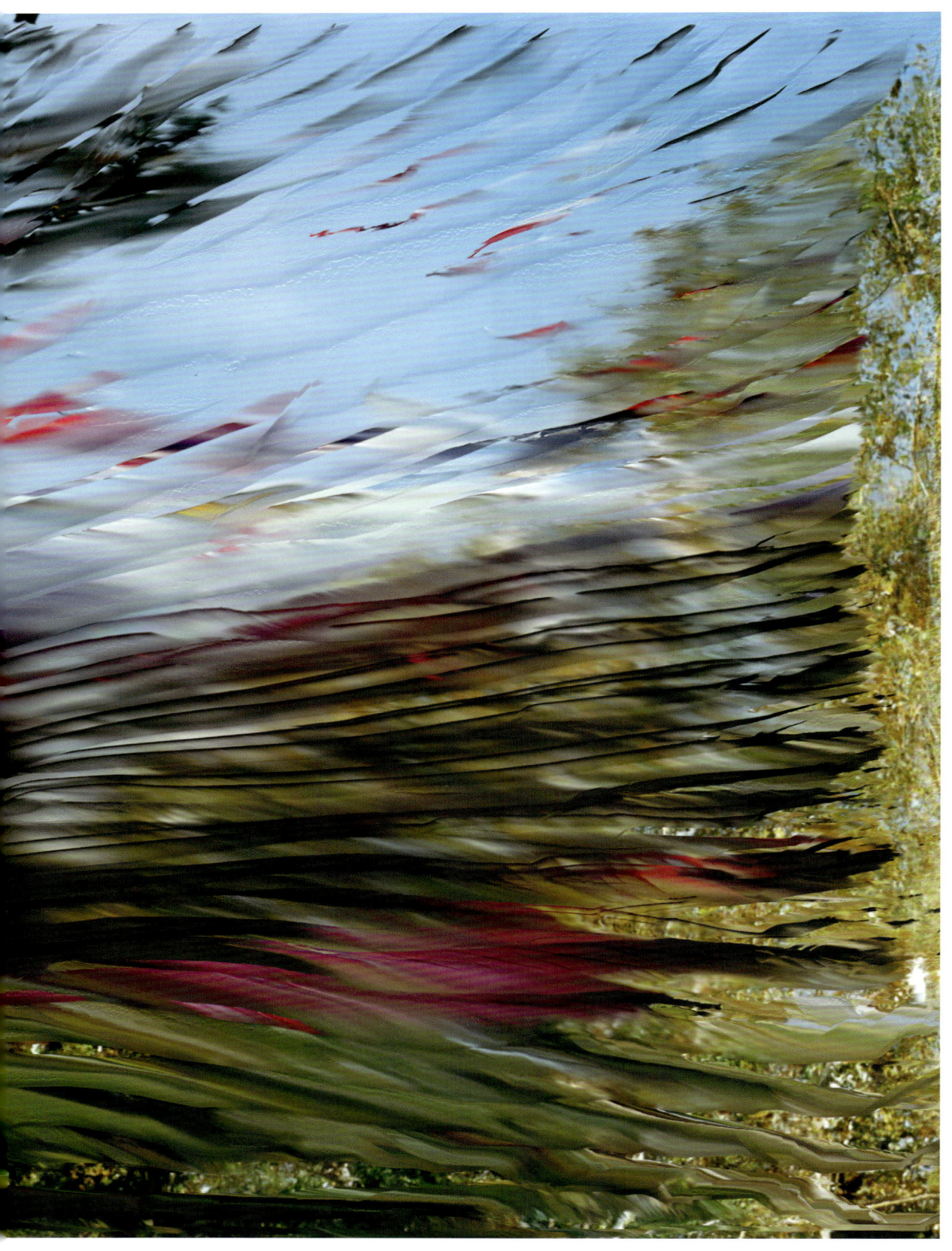

01 ▶

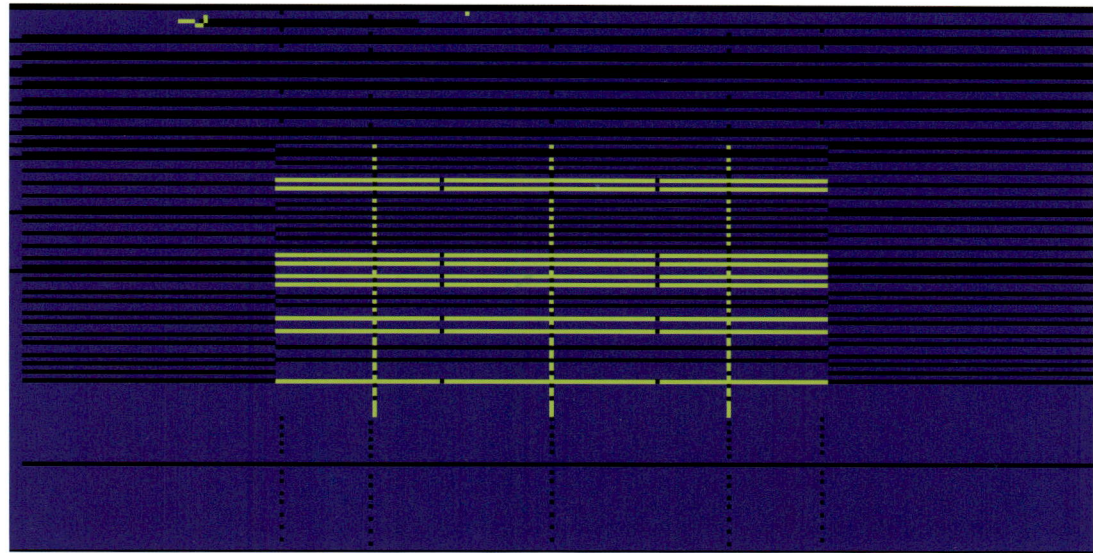

02 ▶

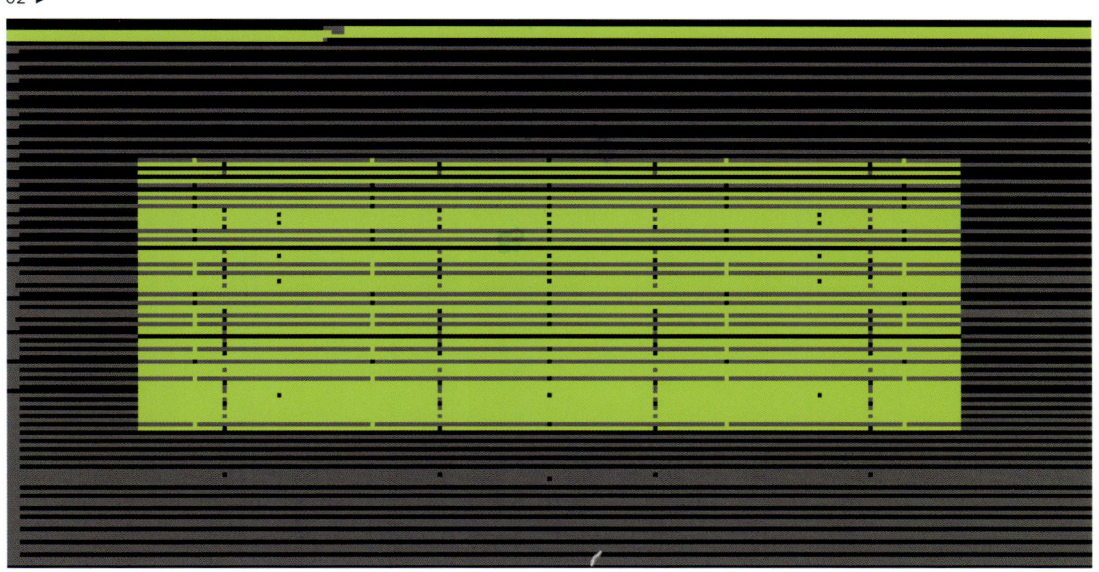

| # | TITLE | TIMESTAMP | MEDIUM | CHAIN | CONTRACT ADDRESS | TOKEN ID | EDITION SIZE |
|---|---|---|---|---|---|---|---|
| 01–04 | **gämma** | 07-27-2022 08:54:59 | p5.js | XTZ | KT1RnhKKsAD7ScFi3Nb7HKK2hnPCqXcbNG3k | 1405...0621–1073...4541 | 1/1 of 33 |

EDITIONS ILLUSTRATED: (01) 10+1*11, (02) 2+1*11, (03) 9+1*11, (04) 2+2*11

# P1XELFOOL

03 ►

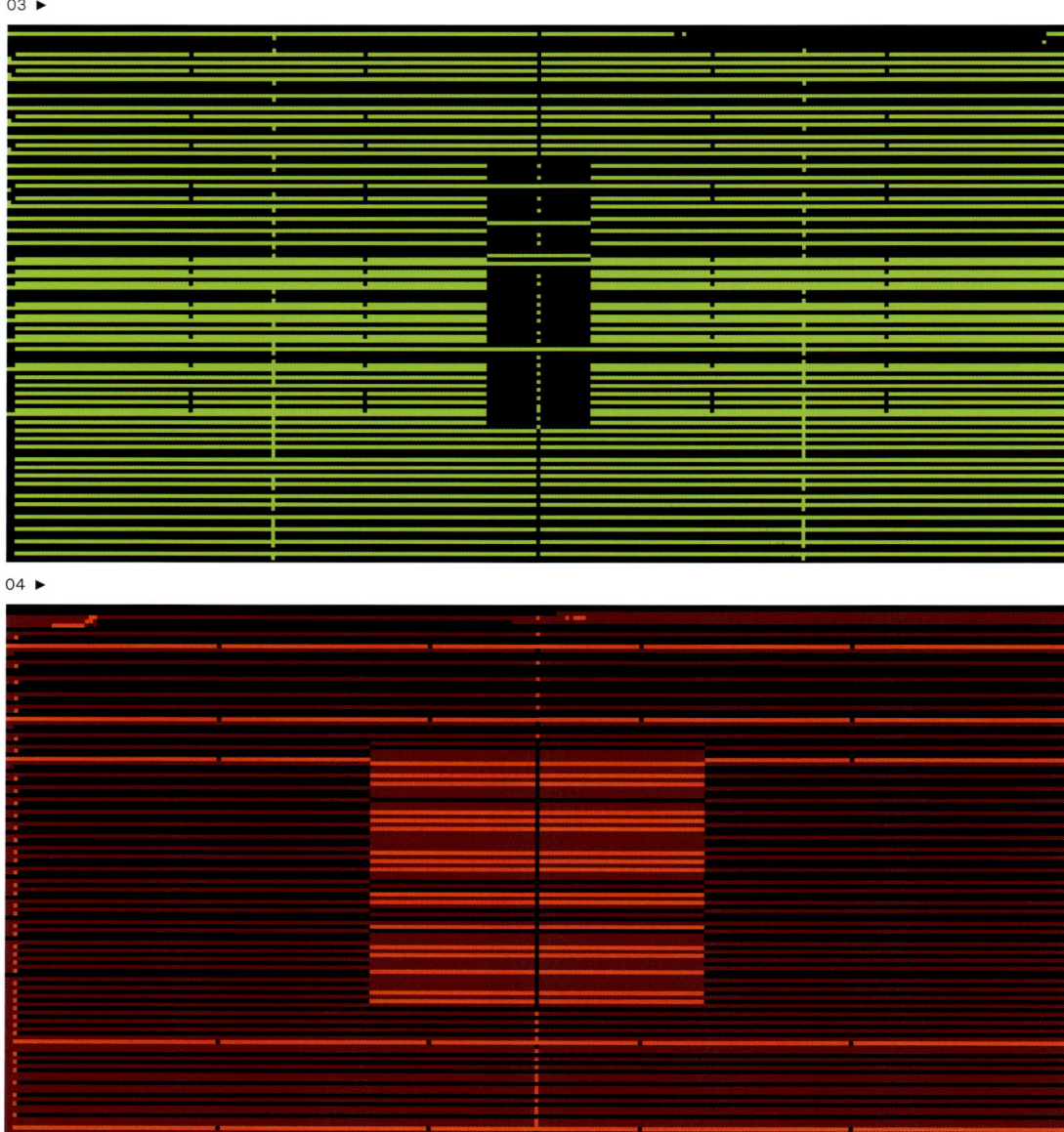

04 ►

P1xelfool is a Brazilian artist who quickly rose to prominence in 2021 for his code-based artworks. His practice distinctively renders 3D geometric systems as pixelated 2D animations evocative of scientific diagrams, particle simulations, and otherworldly entities. Released mainly as animated GIFs and real-time code, P1xelfool's creations are written using Processing, an open-source and community-led software. P1xel often mentions the exploration of the perception of time and space as a starting point for his computational art: "Do screens, pixels, and code allow for inter-subjectivity, for the experience of human or natural phenomena?"

In one of his most recent projects *gämma* (2022) curated by Kerry Doran, the artist specifically focuses on the perceptual limits of the screen through a series of appearing and disappearing animations. As Doran wrote on Feral File, "*gämma* is an attempt to ignore the device as a representative source and to embrace it as a sensorial entity. The blocks of color invite the viewer to examine pixels as a plain source of light, to try to see the screen in unity with the machine's language. Software and hardware infused in one phenomena. Code = light."

Seen all together, P1xelfool's artworks appear to exist within their own dimension, expanding one after another on an anachronistic and complex visual universe. The artist is also known for his community-driven initiatives such as BRG.exe, a foundation investing and supporting Brazilian generative and digital artists.

**NICOLAS SASSOON**
ARTIST AND COLLECTOR

05

06

07

08

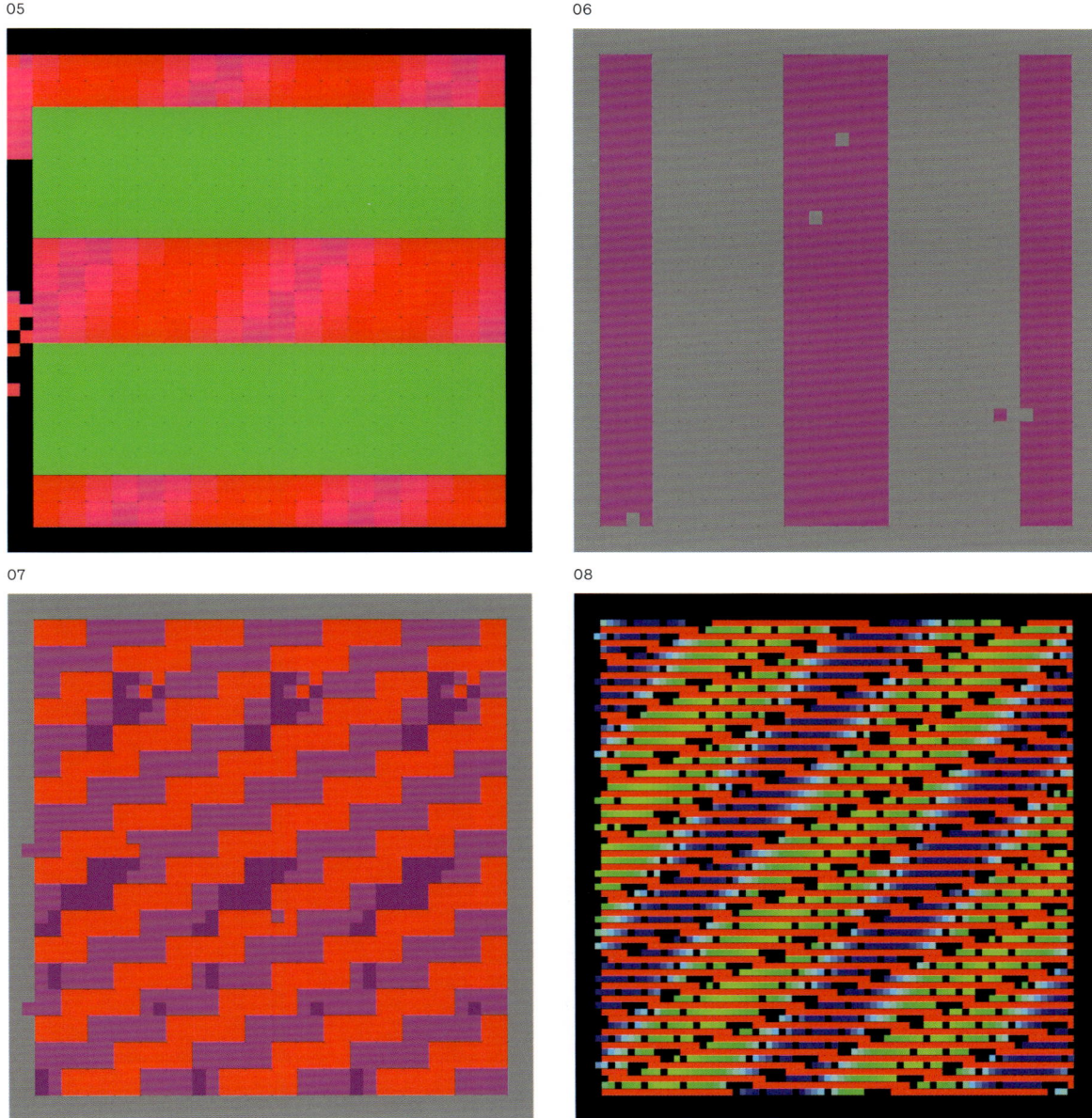

| # | TITLE | TIMESTAMP | MEDIUM | CHAIN | CONTRACT ADDRESS | | TOKEN ID | EDITION SIZE |
|---|---|---|---|---|---|---|---|---|
| 05–12 | **overloaded** | 12-17-2021 17:02:26 | p5.js | XTZ | KT1KEa8z6vWXDJrVqtMrAeDVzsvxat3kHaCE | | 188865–189319 | 1/1 of 444 |

EDITIONS ILLUSTRATED: (05) #197, (06) #8, (07) #29, (08) #3, (09) #47, (10) #364, (11) #243, (12) #4

09

10

11

12

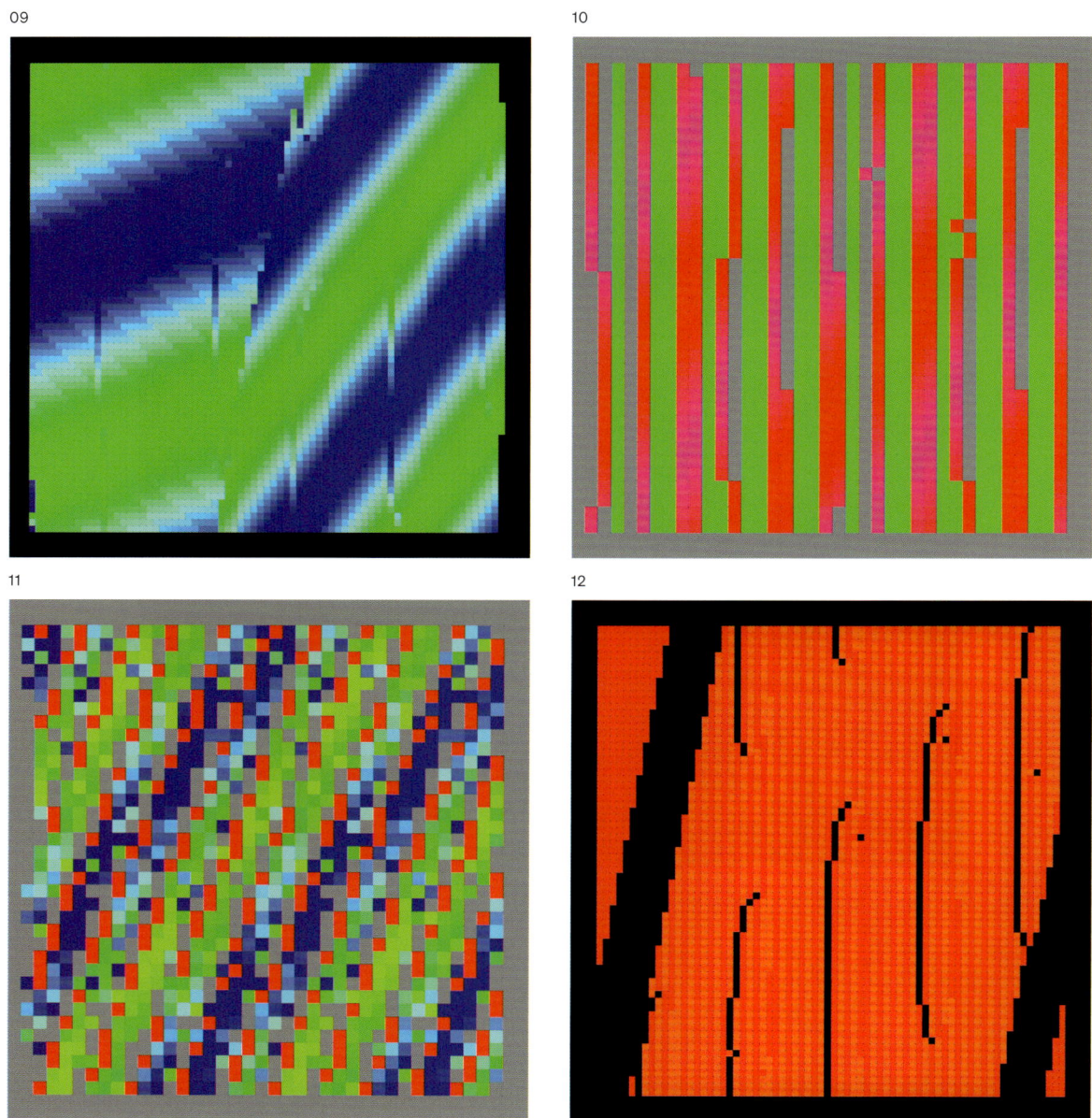

01 ►

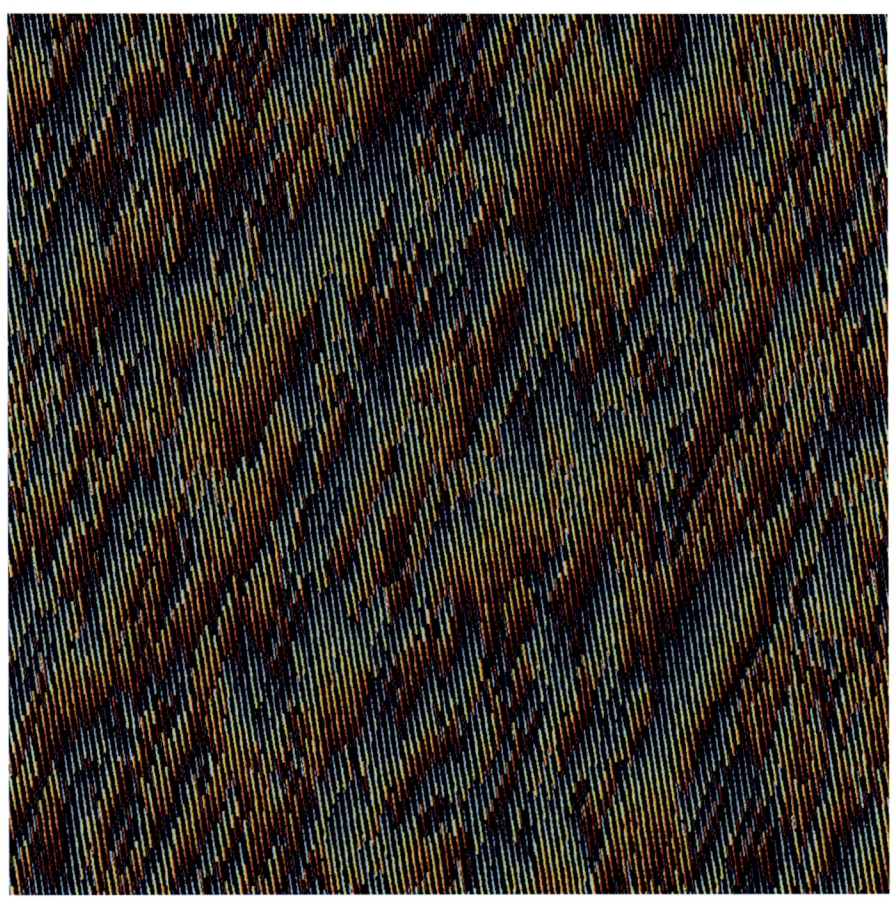

| # | TITLE | TIMESTAMP | MEDIUM | CHAIN | CONTRACT ADDRESS | TOKEN ID | EDITION SIZE |
|---|---|---|---|---|---|---|---|
| 01 | **RIFT** | 12-07-2021 09:33:48 | Adobe Photoshop, Adobe Animate | ETH | 0xb932a70a57673d89f4acffbe830e8ed7f75fb9e0 | 30963 | 1/1 |
| 02 | HOLOGLASS | 08-15-2021 11:02:02 | Adobe Photoshop, Adobe Animate | ETH | 0x3b3ee1931dc30c1957379fac9aba94d1c48a5405 | 72673 | 1/1 |
| 03 | PLANETS[♂] | 10-14-2021 05:12:40 | Adobe Photoshop, Adobe Animate | ETH | 0x3b3ee1931dc30c1957379fac9aba94d1c48a5405 | 97828 | 1/1 |

02 ▶

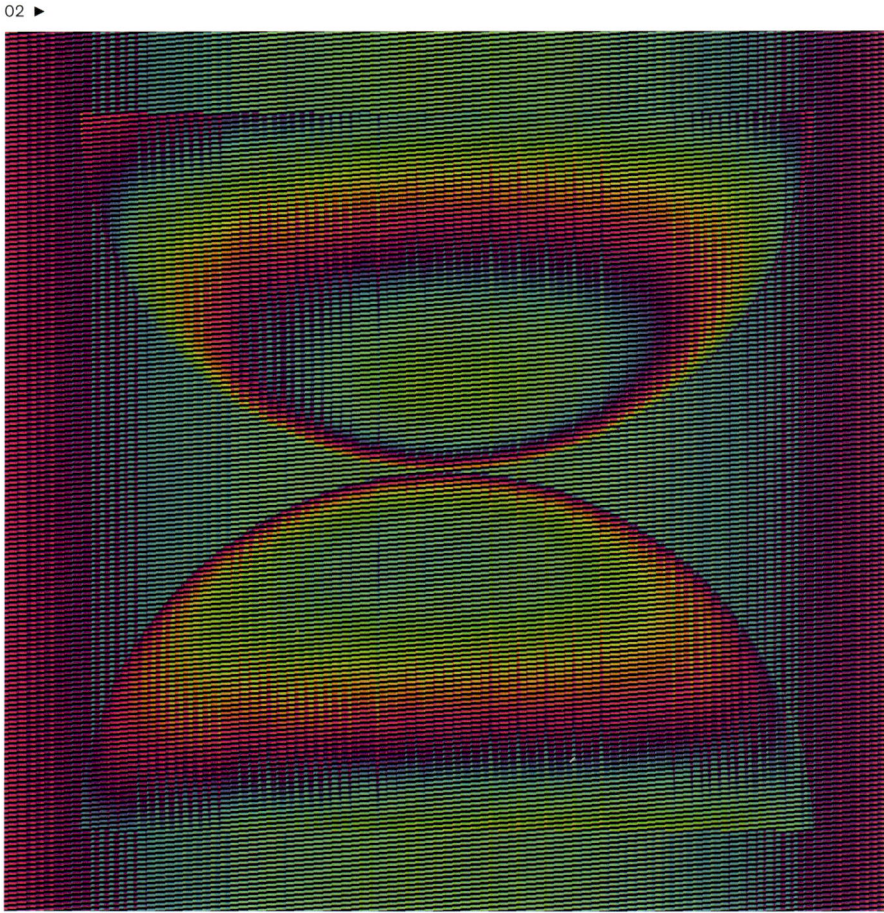

Nicolas Sassoon is a Franco-Canadian artist using early computer imaging processes and techniques to convey confluences between abstraction, landscape, and place. Sassoon understands on and offline experiences as fluid; his works are mediations of memories of living in coastal cities as much as his experiences in video game environments. He has long been invested in rendering compositions with limited graphics and color palettes, such as low-density pixels and 8-bit color. Similar to early computer game design, Sassoon conveys place and feeling through minimal visual means. Pixels, in Sassoon's work, are like memories — fragments of seemingly incomplete information that are nonetheless deeply evocative.

A central technique within Sassoon's oeuvre is his take on digital moiré patterning, in which two overlapping images generate the illusion of a third. The resulting animations are endlessly hypnotic surfaces — like all-over paintings as well as wallpapers — oscillating between depth and flatness, abstraction and figuration. *HOLO* and *PLANETS* (both 2021) are series made with Sassoon's moiré technique; both reference optical and kinetic art as well as the science fiction of the 1960s and 1970s. For example, *HOLO* drew inspiration from book covers from the *Ailleurs et Demain* (*Elsewhere and Tomorrow*) series, published by Robert Laffont in 1969, which included titles such as *The Left Hand of Darkness* (1969) by Ursula K. Le Guin (1929–2018).

Community and collaboration are central to Sassoon's practice. Beginning in 2009, he became part of Computers Club, an internet art and digital drawing collective. In 2011, he was one of the three co-founders of WALLPAPERS, a group interested in the concept of "wallpapers" on screens and other surfaces. The NFT space generated a community that recollected, for Sassoon, his experiences with these 2010s internet art collectives — albeit with greater openness and international dialogue. Since minting his first NFT in early 2021, Sassoon has become a collaborator and supporter of artists from and of the Global South and his NFT collection centers on these relationships.

**KERRY DORAN**
PH.D. STUDENT AT THE CITY UNIVERSITY OF NEW YORK
AND EXTERNAL ADVISOR FOR DIGITAL ART COMMISSIONS AT M+,
HONG KONG

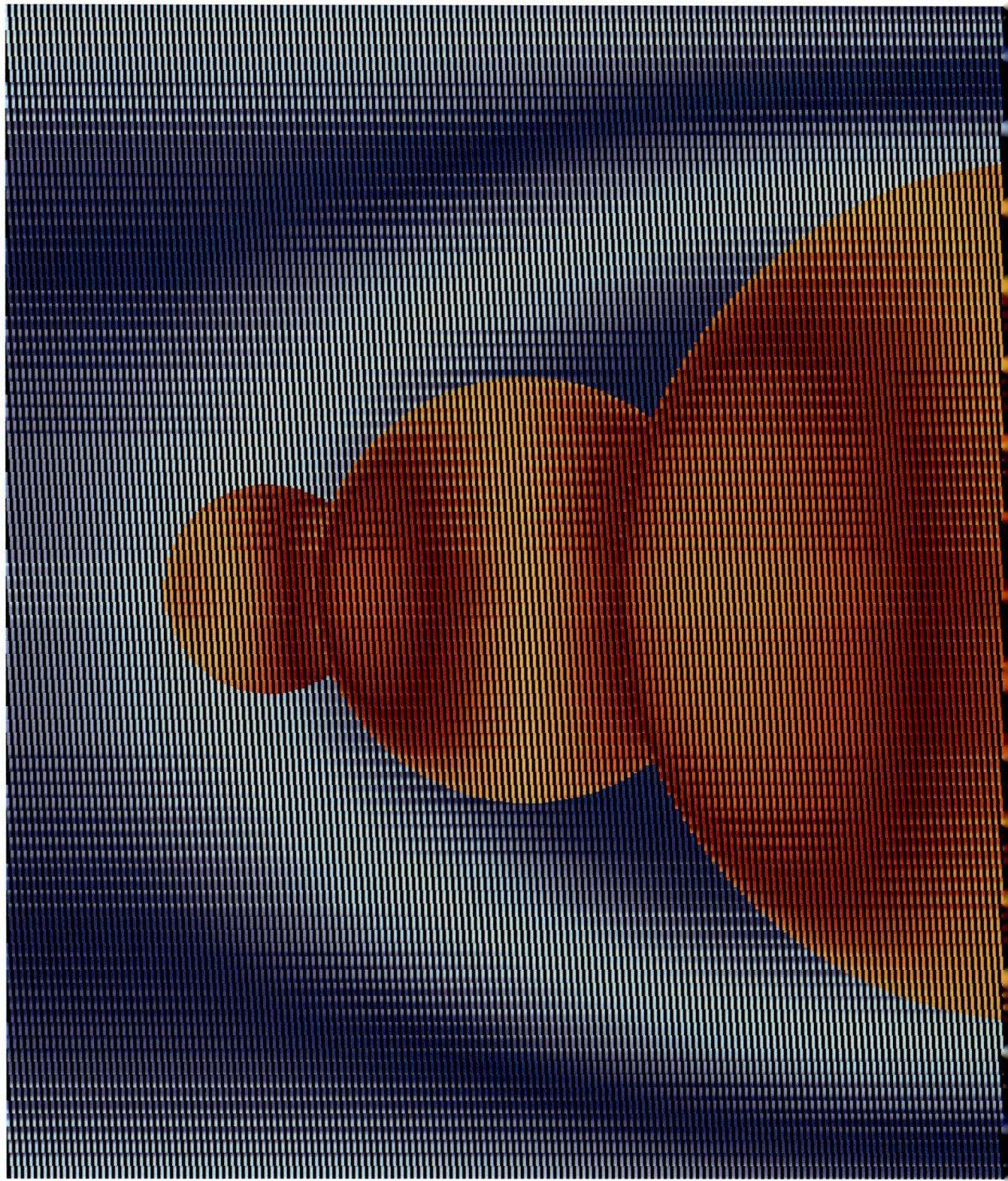

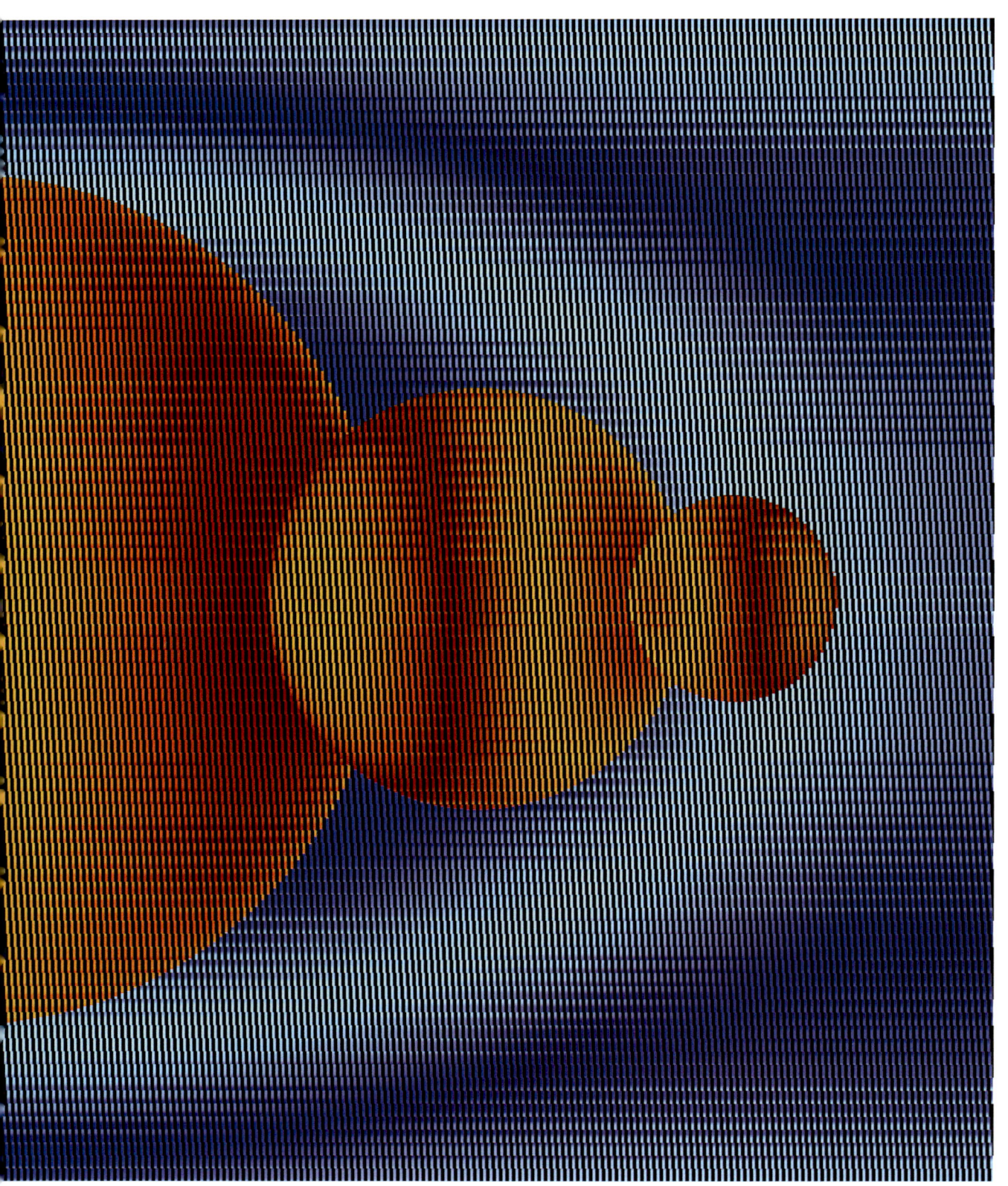

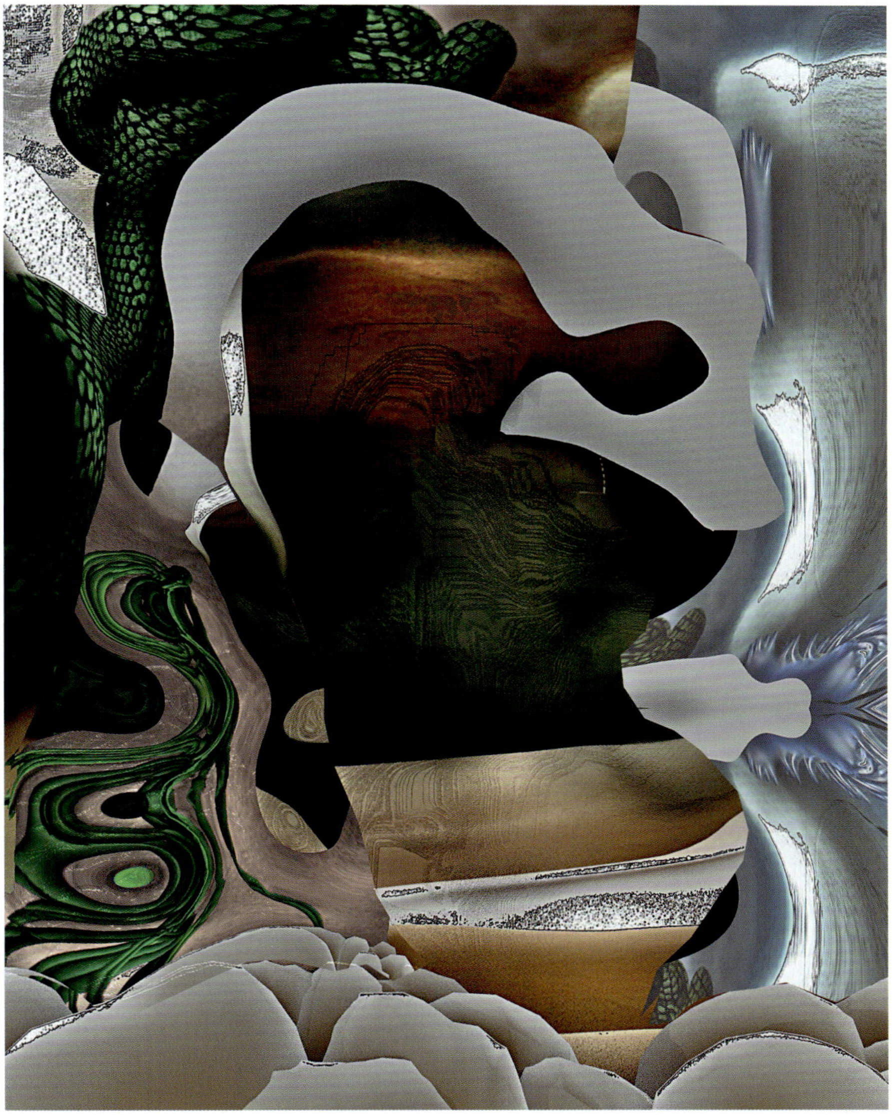

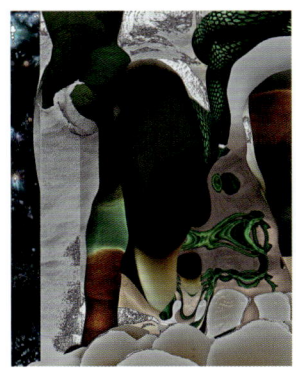
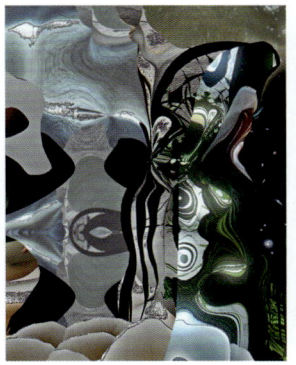
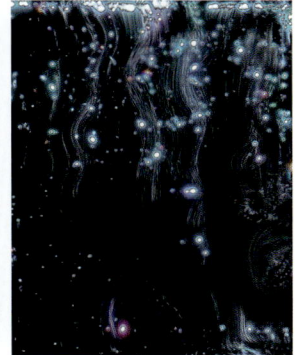

| # | TITLE | TIMESTAMP | MEDIUM | CHAIN | CONTRACT ADDRESS | TOKEN ID | EDITION SIZE |
|---|-------|-----------|--------|-------|------------------|----------|--------------|
| 01 | **Astral Garden** | 08-23-2022 07:27:22 | Digital animation, Oculus Medium, Maya, Adobe After Effects | ETH | 0x3b3ee1931dc30c1957379fac9aba94d1c48a5405 | 76369 | 1/1 |
| 02 | **Untitled 7** | 05-15-2021 15:24:47 | Digital painting, Maya, Adobe Photoshop | ETH | 0x3b3ee1931dc30c1957379fac9aba94d1c48a5405 | 36599 | 1/1 |

# SARA LUDY

UNITED STATES 1980

02

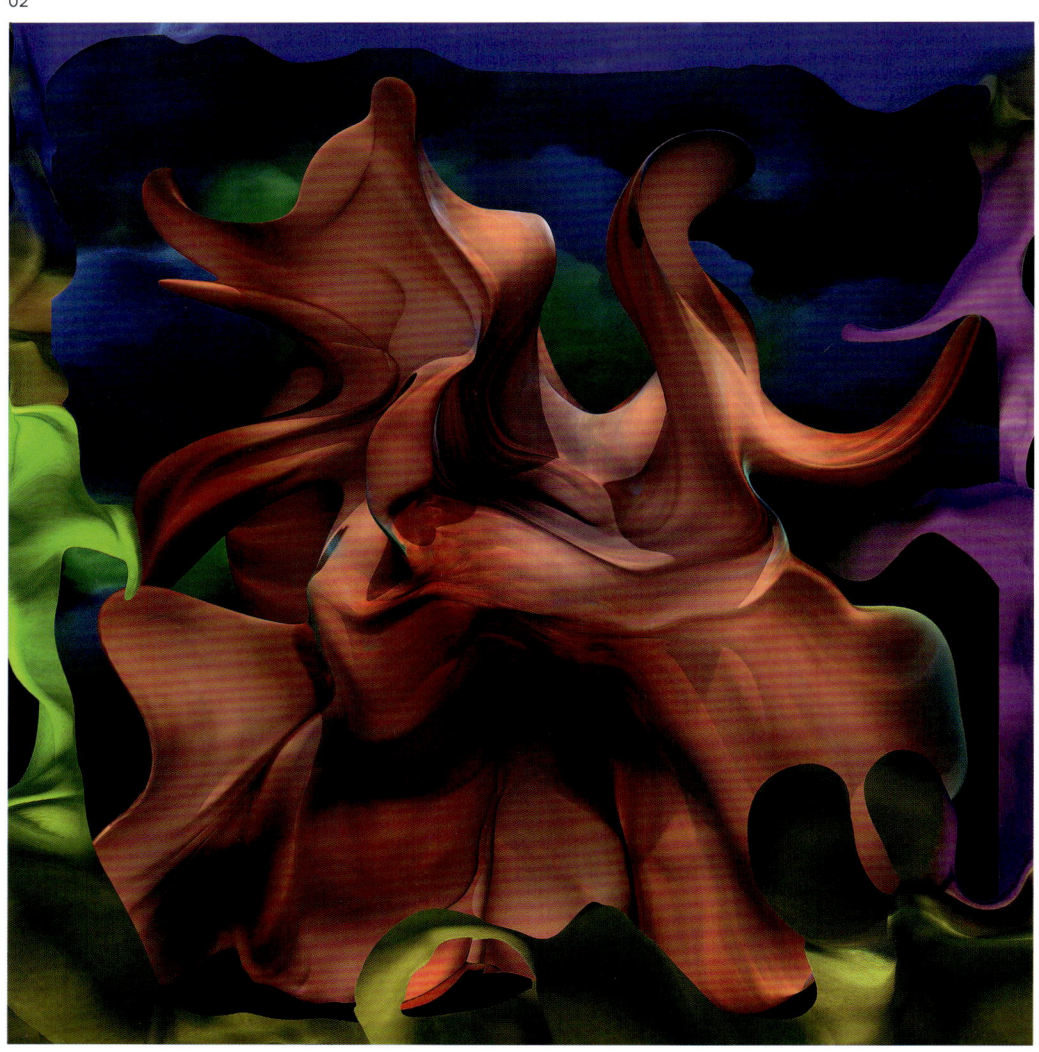

Sara Ludy's practice investigates hybridity through a synthesis of virtual and physical realms. Her work is rooted in expanded media — video, websites, digital painting, VR, and sound — that presents both a collision and an amalgamation between corporeal and digital planes.

Ludy weaves multidimensional environments with a meditative intention that transmutes elements from the natural world to a virtual, atemporal atmosphere. *Astral Garden* (2021) encompasses this simultaneity in a resolution as familiar as it is beguiling. Kaleidoscopic hues of desert soil, red rock, and succulent plant life from the artist's garden are blended with the universal habitats of a radiating sky and surging cosmos. A scrolling cadence guides the viewer's gaze through the scenery, unfolding right to left like a sacred text. This procession, reminiscent of an online auto-scroll, is elegantly contrasted alongside the emulation of organic materials. Ludy situates this work between worlds, using both the visual lexicon of the internet and the durational aspect of time-based media. Liquid star swirls and etched striations expand atop the prismatic terrain.

Ludy is an American artist based in Placitas, New Mexico. Previous exhibitions include the Museum of Contemporary Art in Chicago, Vancouver Art Gallery, Whitney Museum of American Art in New York, Berkeley Art Museum, and Künstlerhaus Bethanien in Berlin. The artist's work has been featured in *Modern Painters*, *The New York Times*, *Artforum*, *Art in America*, and *Cultured Magazine*.

**VALERIE AMEND**
ASSOCIATE DIRECTOR AT BITFORMS GALLERY, NEW YORK

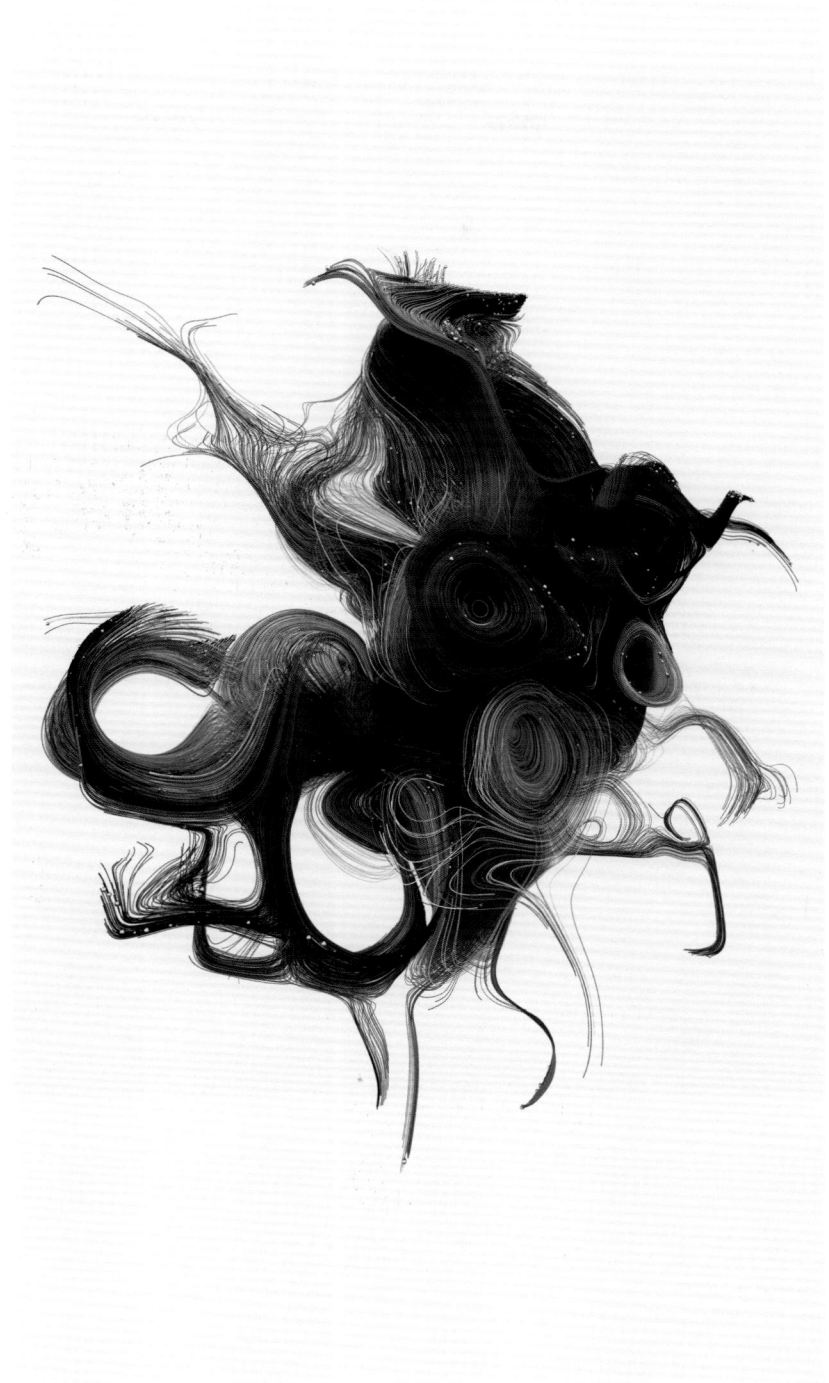

| # | TITLE | TIMESTAMP | MEDIUM | CHAIN | CONTRACT ADDRESS | TOKEN ID | EDITION SIZE |
|---|---|---|---|---|---|---|---|
| 01 | **Moments Spent With Others** | 11-08-2022 21:08:35 | Houdini | ETH | 0xf648d44dd41f55046b5d2b50cddb0a3fd4f9f1b3 | 1–3 | 1/1 of 3 |
| 02 | **16-Bit Machine Dreams** | 02-23-2022 15:39:05 | Houdini | ETH | 0xc1d32fbe25495e45959372f66ae22534dcd97f68 | 80000100001–80000600001 | 5 artworks in editions of 16, +1 1/1 |

EDITIONS ILLUSTRATED: (01) Two Person Cinema, (02) Level Complete

02

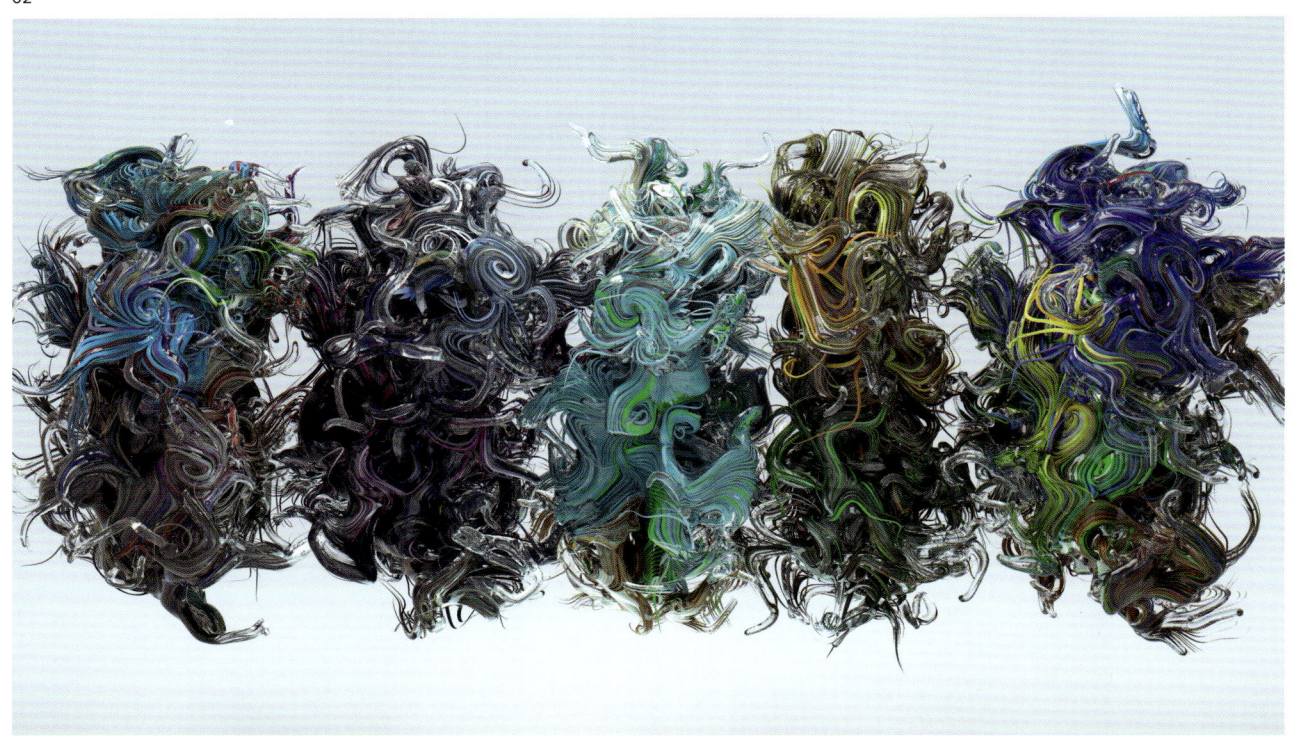

Before the advent of NFTs and like many other digital artists, Brendan Dawes has had to mostly rely on a commercial practice. He slowly developed an expert hand at data visualization, notably via the Houdini software, a complex 3D procedural software for modeling and animation in film, advertising, and video games.

Brendan incorporated this high level of technical knowledge into his own artistic exploration, becoming one of the few artists able to create magical objects via complex generative processes involving machine learning, code, and algorithms. To only quote a few of his achievements, Brendan is a Lumen Prize and Aesthetica Art Prize alumnus, and his *Cinema Redux* (2004) work has been part of the permanent collection at the Museum of Modern Art in New York since 2008. More recently, NFTs gave him the financial freedom and self-sovereignty he needed to fully focus his creative

genius on his own art practice, which has become an incredibly robust body of work, both technically and artistically.

*16-Bit Machine Dreams* (2022) is no exception. Brendan draws his inspiration for this series from fond memories of his teenage years, playing video games in a small-town arcade. Starting with actual footage of each game, he transformed time, movement, and pixels into flowing, abstract sculptures, representing what a video game dream might actually look like. The series becomes a sculptural reincarnation of this precious memory — an "ode to the video games he loved" — proving one more time that generative art, when mastered, can be pure poetry.

**FANNY LAKOUBAY**
FOUNDER OF LAL ART ADVISORY AND CRYPTO ART COLLECTOR

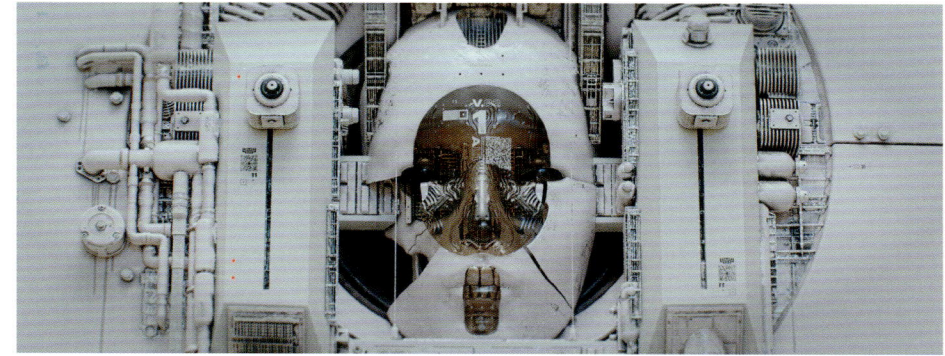

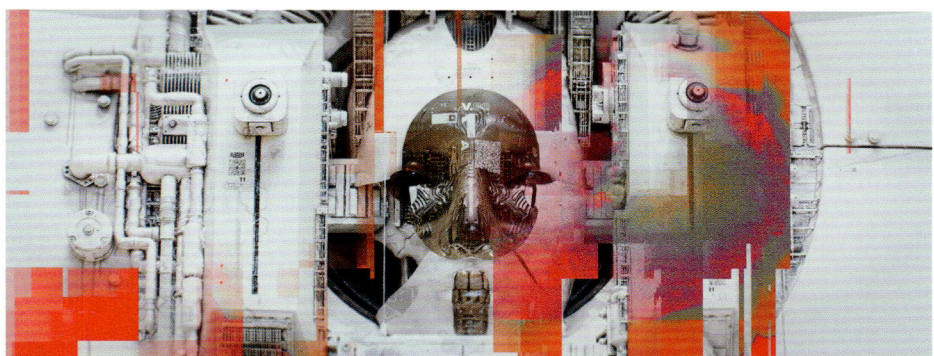

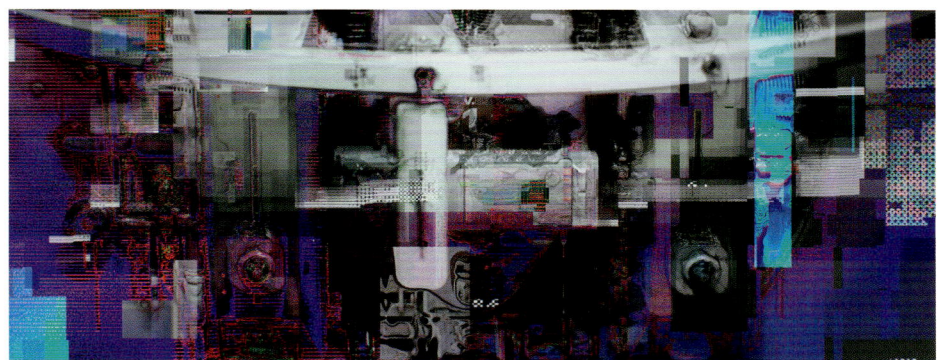

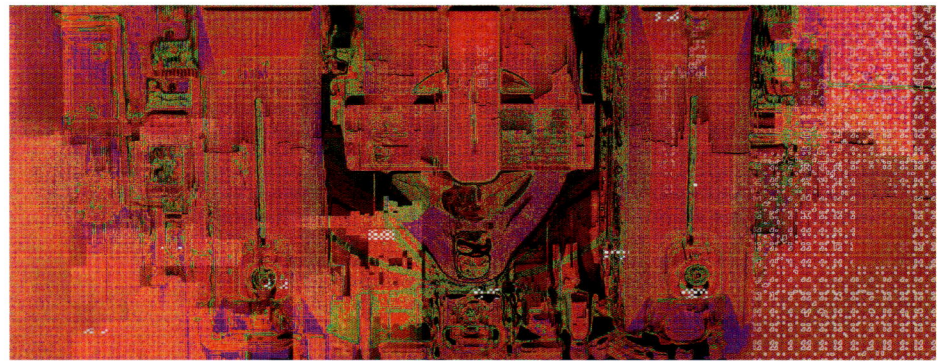

| # | TITLE | TIMESTAMP | MEDIUM | CHAIN | CONTRACT ADDRESS | TOKEN ID | EDITION SIZE |
|---|---|---|---|---|---|---|---|
| 01 | **Degradation** | 05-27-2021 21:34:00 | ZBrush, Cinema 4D, Fusion 360, Adobe After Effects | ETH | 0x253375a69de8e47dc4e5a807ba2fccf6bd9d45e2 | 0 | 1/1 |
| 02 | **Interlinked** | 12-21-2021 15:50:45 | ZBrush, Cinema 4D, Fusion 360, Adobe After Effects | ETH | 0x29502a2626f799fb5d5aeae61916b616751d6bde | 25010001 | 1/1 |
| 03 | **Product Placement** | 02-02-2022 08:53:06 | ZBrush, Cinema 4D, Fusion 360, Adobe After Effects | ETH | 0x5d71798037332816ef166e834204e69185f58619 | 2 | 1/1 |

02 ▶

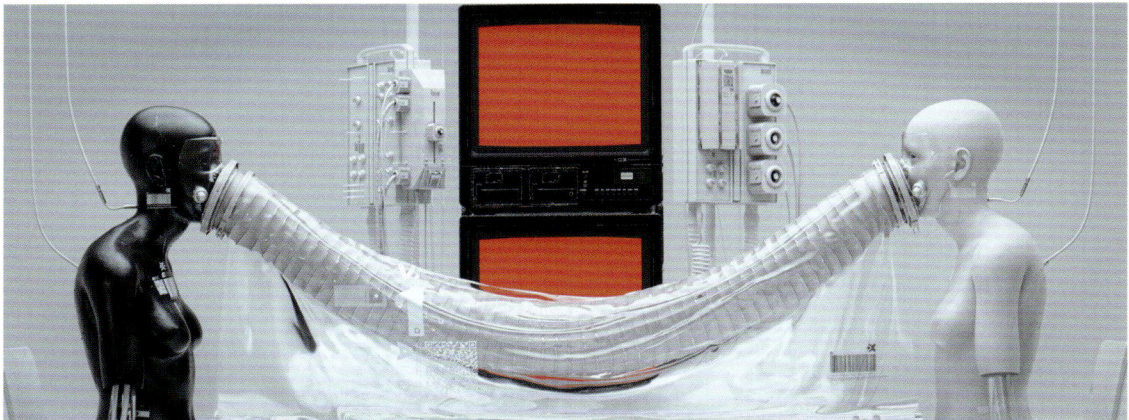

03 ▶

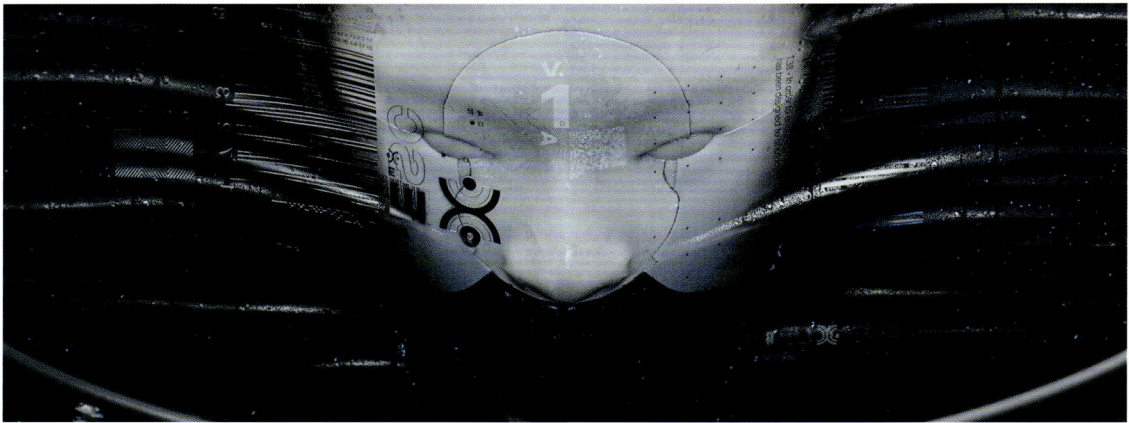

Ash Thorp is the digital artist's artist. Whenever I meet a digital artist to understand and learn more about their process, at the end of the discussion, I usually ask for a short list of their inspirations and favorite contemporaries in the field. One name comes up more consistently than others — Ash Thorp.

Ash is a multidisciplinary artist that combines a broad array of digital tools and techniques to create his hyperrealistic and surreal techno-human worlds. His work poses a juxtaposition of sensuality against the coldness of his mechanical creations. He evokes a parallel universe of a future-past that could have been, and yet still could be.

Ash has been frequently called on by Hollywood to create blockbuster fantastical worlds of leading comic and science fiction hits like *Batman* (2022), *Ghost in the Shell* (2017), *Total Recall* (2012), and *Prometheus* (2012), among many others. The hardcore fan genuinely feels that what they are witnessing has been painstakingly created by a passionate artist walking his *ikigai* and living his boyhood dream of creating the very worlds that he inhabited as a child immersed in comics and science fiction books.

In his personal practice, what is evident is the extraordinary sum of thought, technical ability, training, and love for the process of digital creation. It is remarkable how much additional rendering Ash will trade for an almost imperceptible visual detail. His works become adventures for the onlooker, presenting new discoveries each time. I can get lost in his *Evident Mirror* series — including *Degradation*, *Interlinked*, and *Product Placement* (all from 2021) — feeling a peculiar sensation of mixed emotions while time seems to stand still.

I've also observed that part of why he is so loved and respected by his peers is that he remains so authentic, humble, and generous. He is a selfless teacher and mentor, constantly sharing the innovations of his practice with his community. Ash sets the tone for this group of 21st-century digital artists, who will define an important chapter of the future of art canon.

**RYAN ZURRER**
FOUNDER OF DIALECTIC

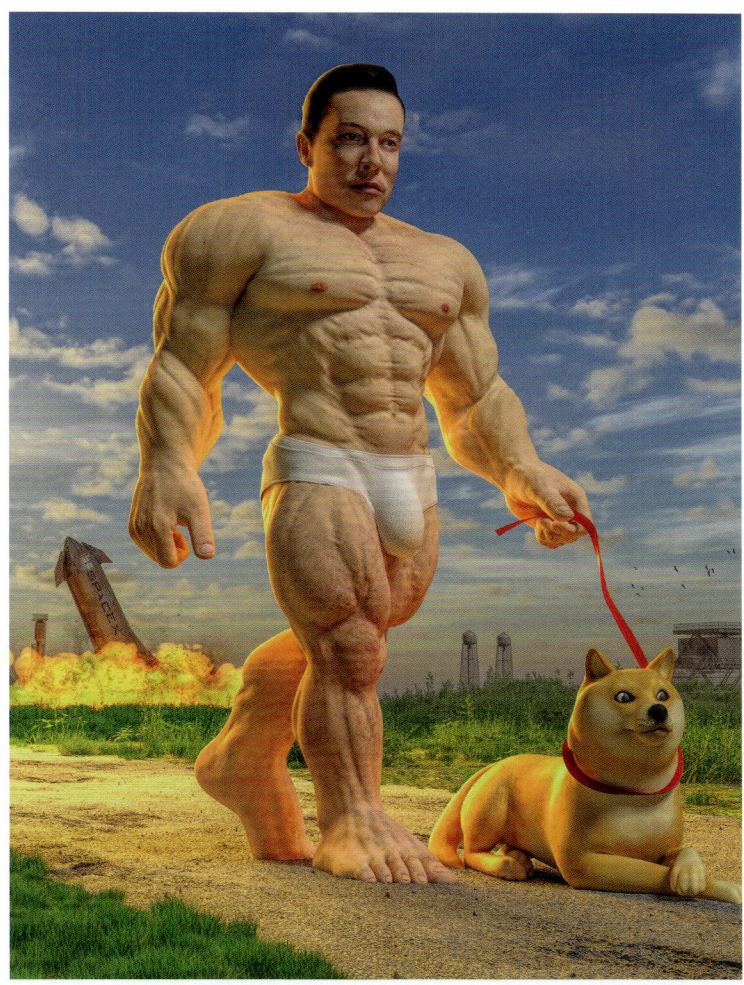

BEEPLE: EVERYDAYS

# GIGACHAD

**ARTIST'S NOTES:**
**nft for your vanity.**

MINTED DATE: 04.27.21
COLLECTION: SPRING COLLECTION 2021
ORIGINAL RESOLUTION: 2000 x 2500
TOOLS USED: Cinema 4D, Octane Render, Photoshop
FILE SIZE: 4,598,337 bytes

**EDITION SIZE: 100**

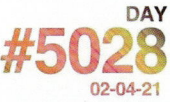

DAY
**#5028**
02-04-21

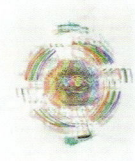

| # | TITLE | TIMESTAMP | MEDIUM | CHAIN | CONTRACT ADDRESS | TOKEN ID | EDITION SIZE |
|---|---|---|---|---|---|---|---|
| 01 | **GIGACHAD** | 04-27-2021 22:36:16 | Cinema 4D, Octane Render, Adobe Photoshop | ETH | 0xdd012153e0083465911-53fff28b0dd6724f0c256 | 100050001–100050100 | 100 |
| 02 | **CHILL BABY GOAT** | 12-01-2020 02:33:12 | Cinema 4D, Octane Render, Adobe Photoshop | ETH | 0x6e5dc5405baefb8c016-6bcc78d2692777f2cbffb | 100020001 | 1/1 |
| 03 | **GOOGLE DATA COLLECTION 2098** | 03-23-2022 17:12:31 | Cinema 4D, Octane Render, Adobe Photoshop | ETH | 0x30b2e98609d66dcc93c-b47a095809d03188ea83d | 5 | 1/1 |

02 ▶

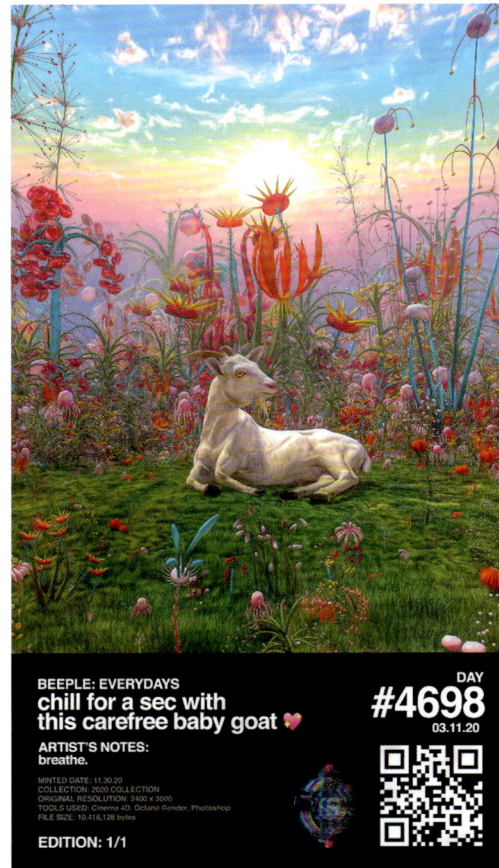

**BEEPLE: EVERYDAYS**
**chill for a sec with**
**this carefree baby goat 💗**
DAY
**#4698**
03.11.20
**ARTIST'S NOTES:**
breathe.
MINTED DATE: 11.30.20
COLLECTION: 2020 COLLECTION
ORIGINAL RESOLUTION: 2400 x 3000
TOOLS USED: Cinema 4D, Octane Render, Photoshop
FILE SIZE: 10,416,128 bytes
**EDITION: 1/1**

03 ▶

**BEEPLE: EVERYDAYS**
**GOOGLE DATA**
**COLLECTION 2098**
DAY
**#4810**
07.01.20
**ARTIST'S NOTES:**
All your data are belong to us.
COLLECTION: UNCERTAIN FUTURE
GALLERY: JACK HANLEY GALLERY
ORIGINAL RESOLUTION: 2000 x 2500
TOOLS USED: Cinema 4D, Octane Render, Photoshop
FILE SIZE: 4,775,700 bytes
**EDITION: 1/1**

Mike Winkelmann (aka Beeple) was born in Missouri in 1981 and grew up in Fond du Lac, Wisconsin. He studied computer science and began making digital art in 1999, later creating concert visuals he would share for free under creative commons, gaining millions of followers on social media. On May 1, 2007, he began to post one image a day as an exercise in personal rigor and marking the passing of time. This recalls the conceptual practices of On Kawara (1932–2014), updated for the age of digital culture.

He moved to Charleston, South Carolina, in 2017 near his brother Scott, a Boeing engineer who later became his closest collaborator. Beeple applies himself to learning new software and bending it to create results for which it was not designed, such as using Cinema 4D to create still images for a flat screen although the software was invented for animation and 3D.

In October 2021, Beeple minted and sold his first NFTs, editions of single *Everydays*. On March 11, 2021, Christie's auctioned *EVERYDAYS: THE FIRST 5000 DAYS* (2021), triggering a broad awareness of NFTs within the mainstream art world and wider media. The *Everydays*' generally figurative images are often critiques of politicians or entrepreneurs of the digital industry, and portray the trash of computer technology, climate change, and war. They are often inspired by current events he learns about on multiple screens tuned onto news channels in his home-studio.

They recall both graphic illustration, sci-fi dystopic worlds, meme culture, and gaming. They are a popular diary that draws from a history of political cartoon, which includes William Hogarth (1697–1764) and Francisco Goya (1746–1828), among others.

Beeple's work is also rooted in a desire to straddle the physical and digital, often working with Infinite Objects and other sculptural devices around his NFTs. In *Human One* (2022), the smart contract of this NFT details that the artist may change the images on the four screens of this large free-standing revolving box at will, therefore allowing the work to be in perpetual evolution. Its post-gender metamorphic character endlessly walks through virtual landscapes in a narcissistic solitude connected with a multitude of other tyrannical egos of a dystopic future.

While Andy Warhol's (1928–1987) irruption into the art world disrupted the high art of the heroic abstract expressionists, Beeple's art disrupted the exclusiveness and seriosity of the committed post-conceptual high art world of the early 21st century by transforming social media and popular taste into part of the material of the artwork itself.

**CAROLYN CHRISTOV-BAKARGIEV**
DIRECTOR OF CASTELLO DI RIVOLI, ART HISTORIAN,
AND CURATOR OF BEEPLE'S FIRST MUSEUM EXHIBITION

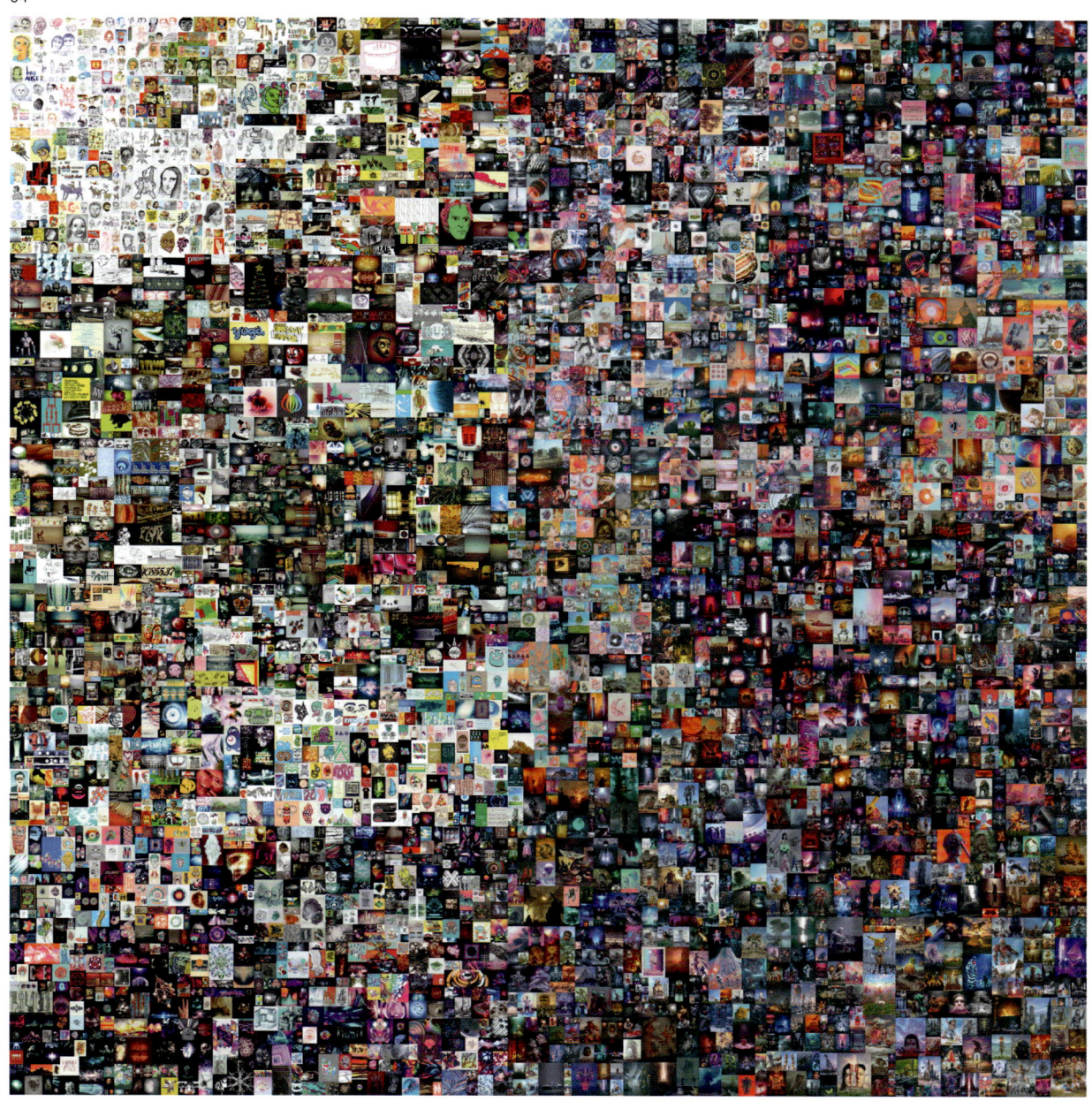

| # | TITLE | TIMESTAMP | MEDIUM | CHAIN | CONTRACT ADDRESS | TOKEN ID | EDITION SIZE |
|---|---|---|---|---|---|---|---|
| 04 | **THE EVERYDAYS:**<br>**THE FIRST 5000 DAYS** | 02-16-2021 05:58:01 | Cinema 4D, Octane Render,<br>Adobe Photoshop | ETH | 0x2a46f2ffd99e19a89476e2f62270e0a35bbf0756 | 40913 | 1/1 |

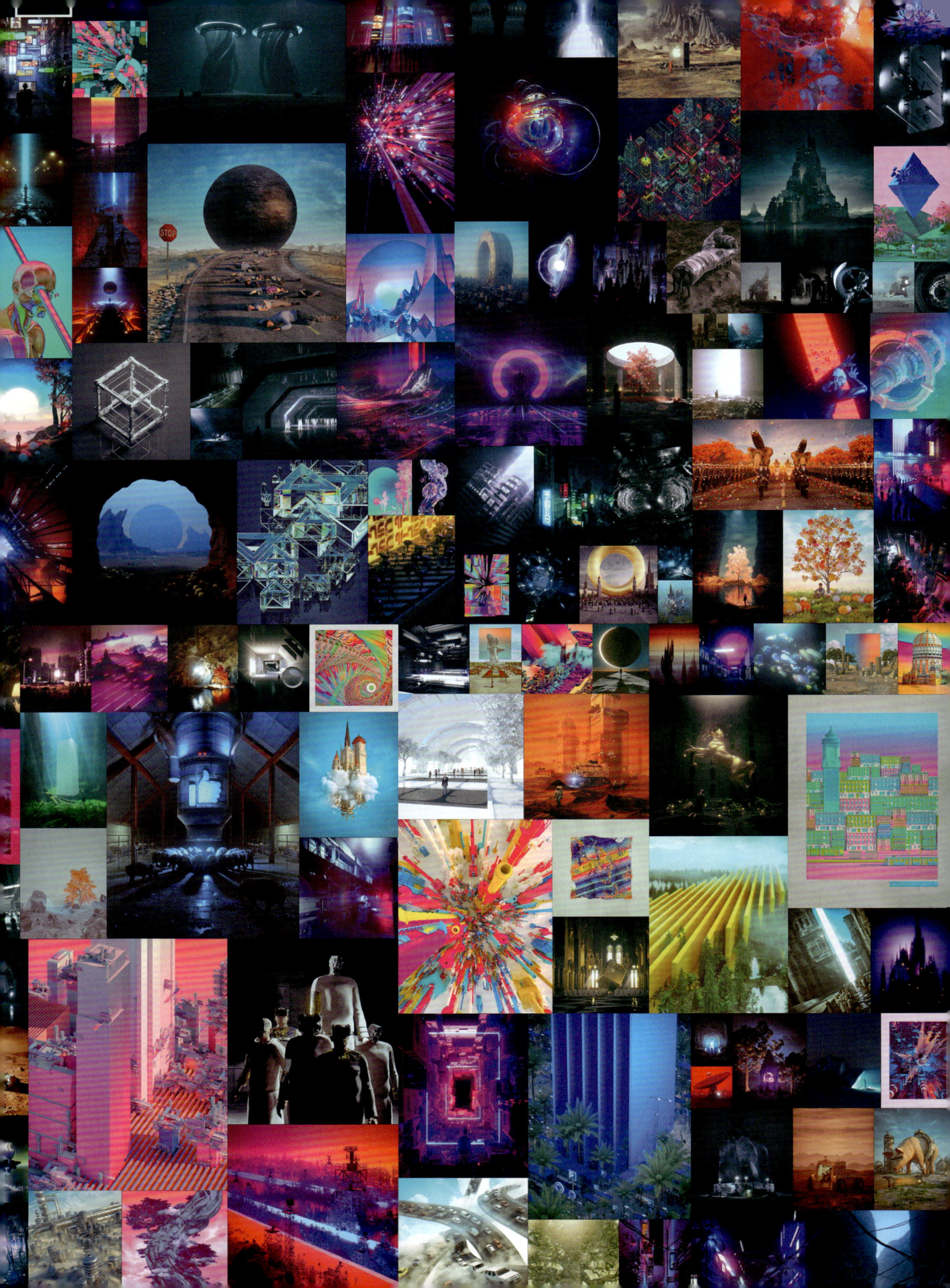

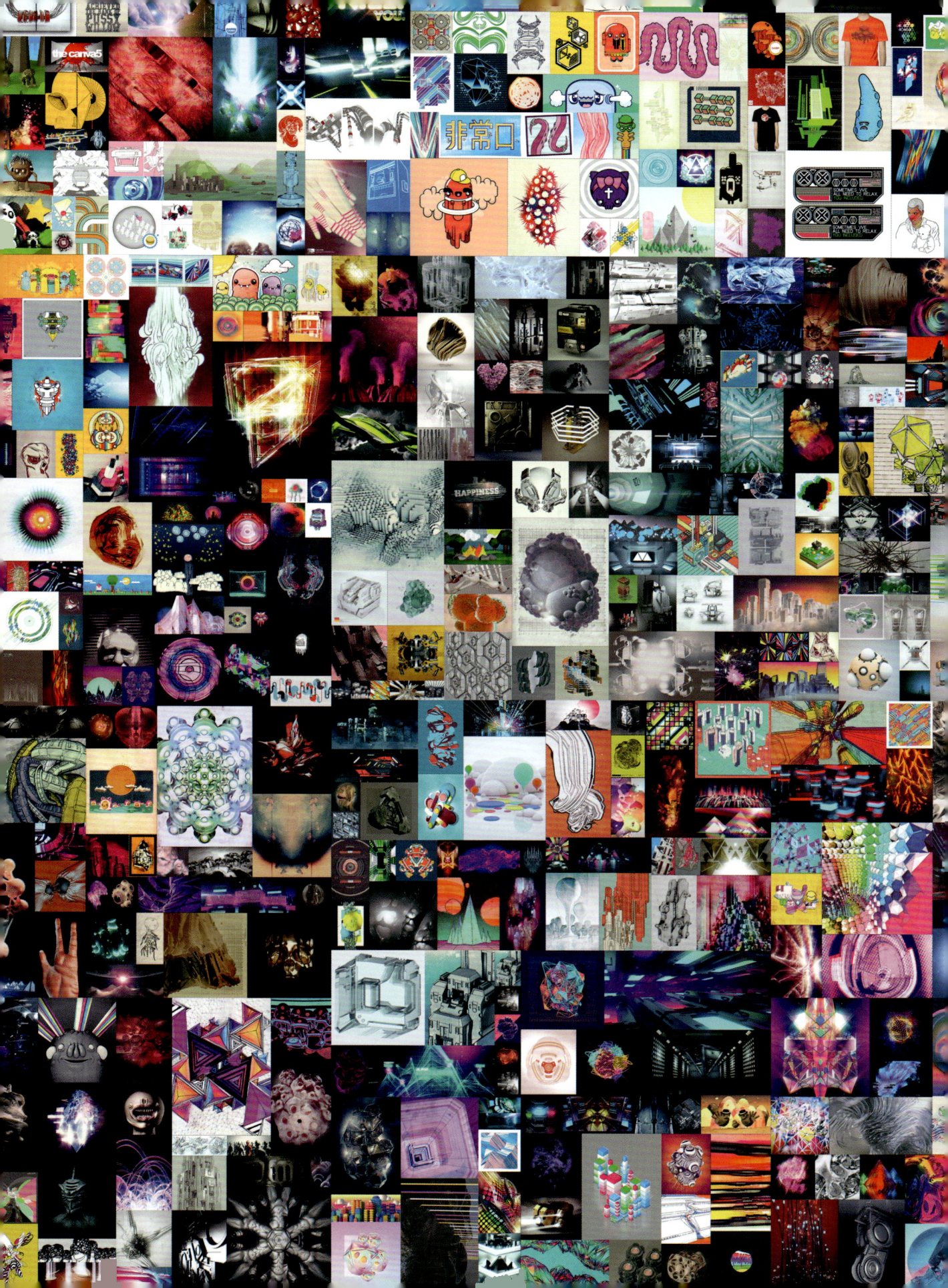

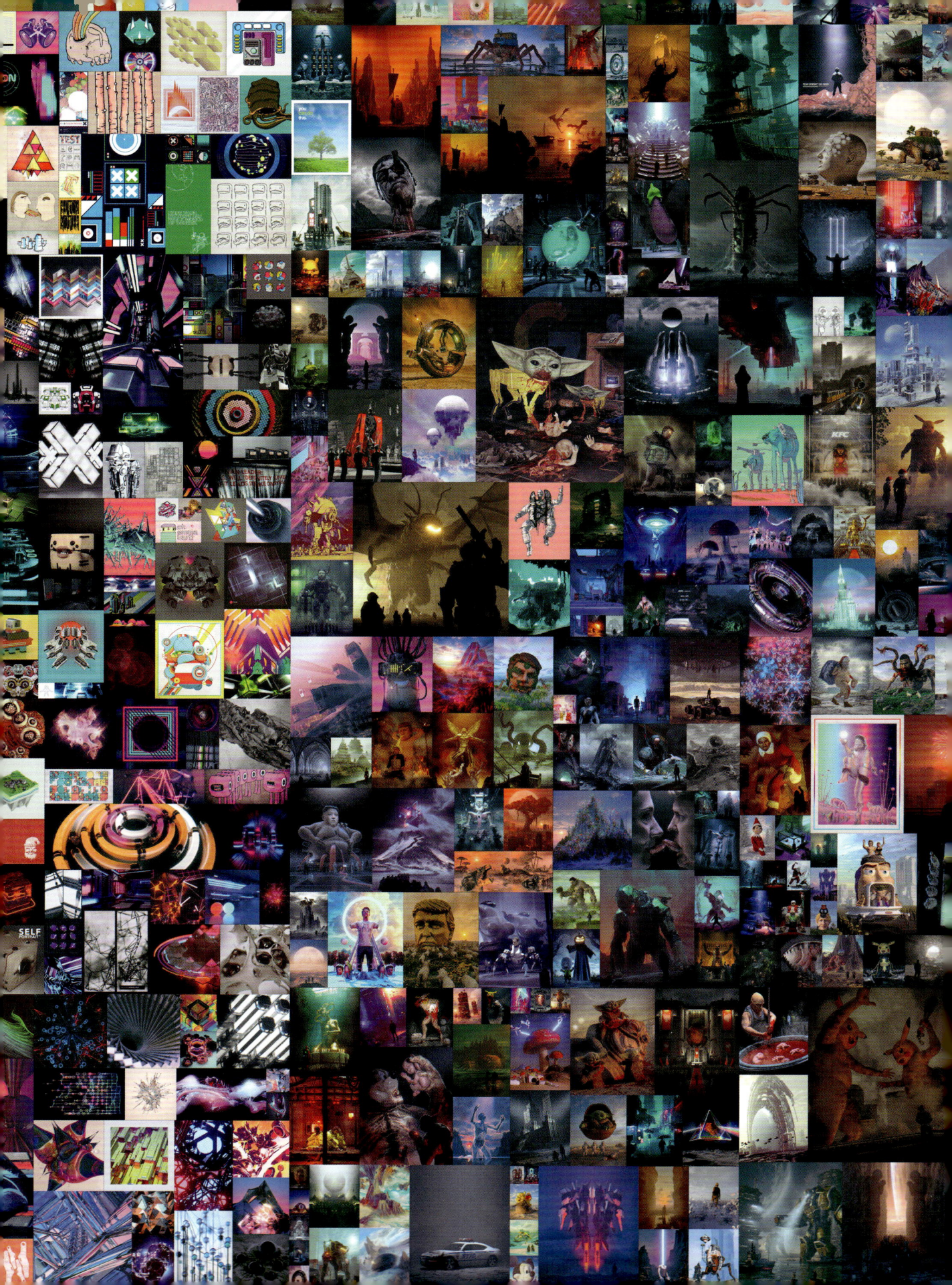

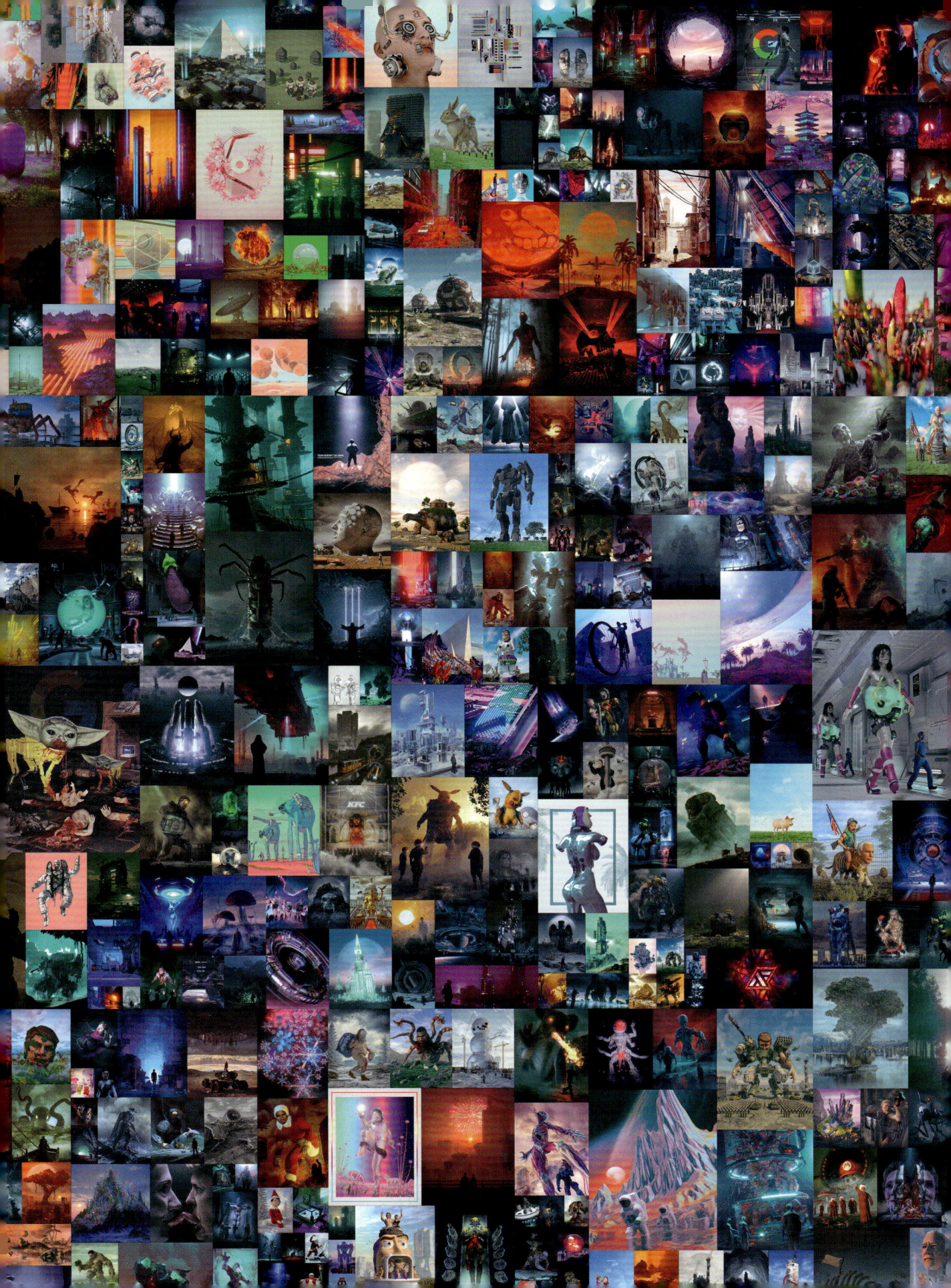

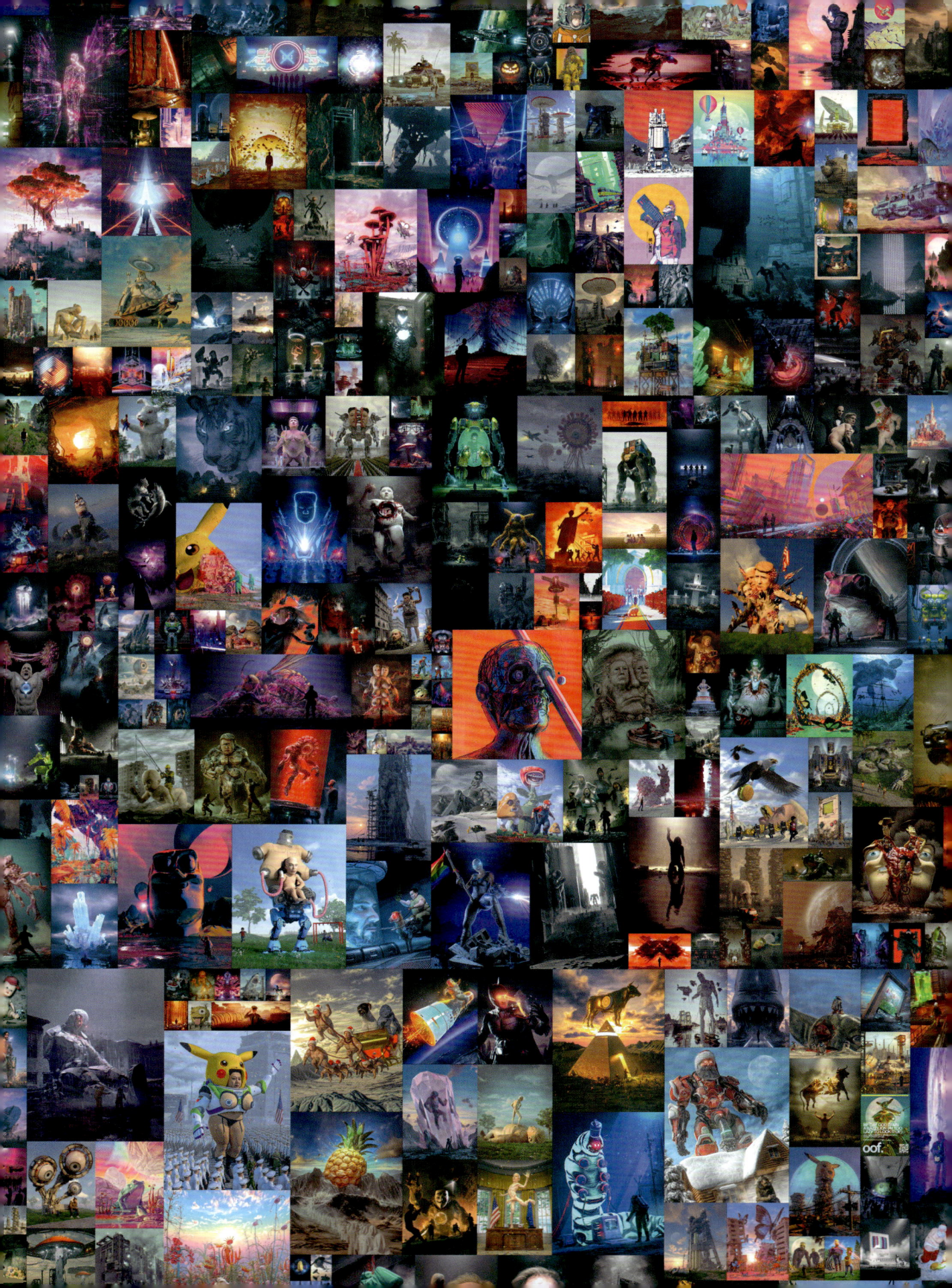

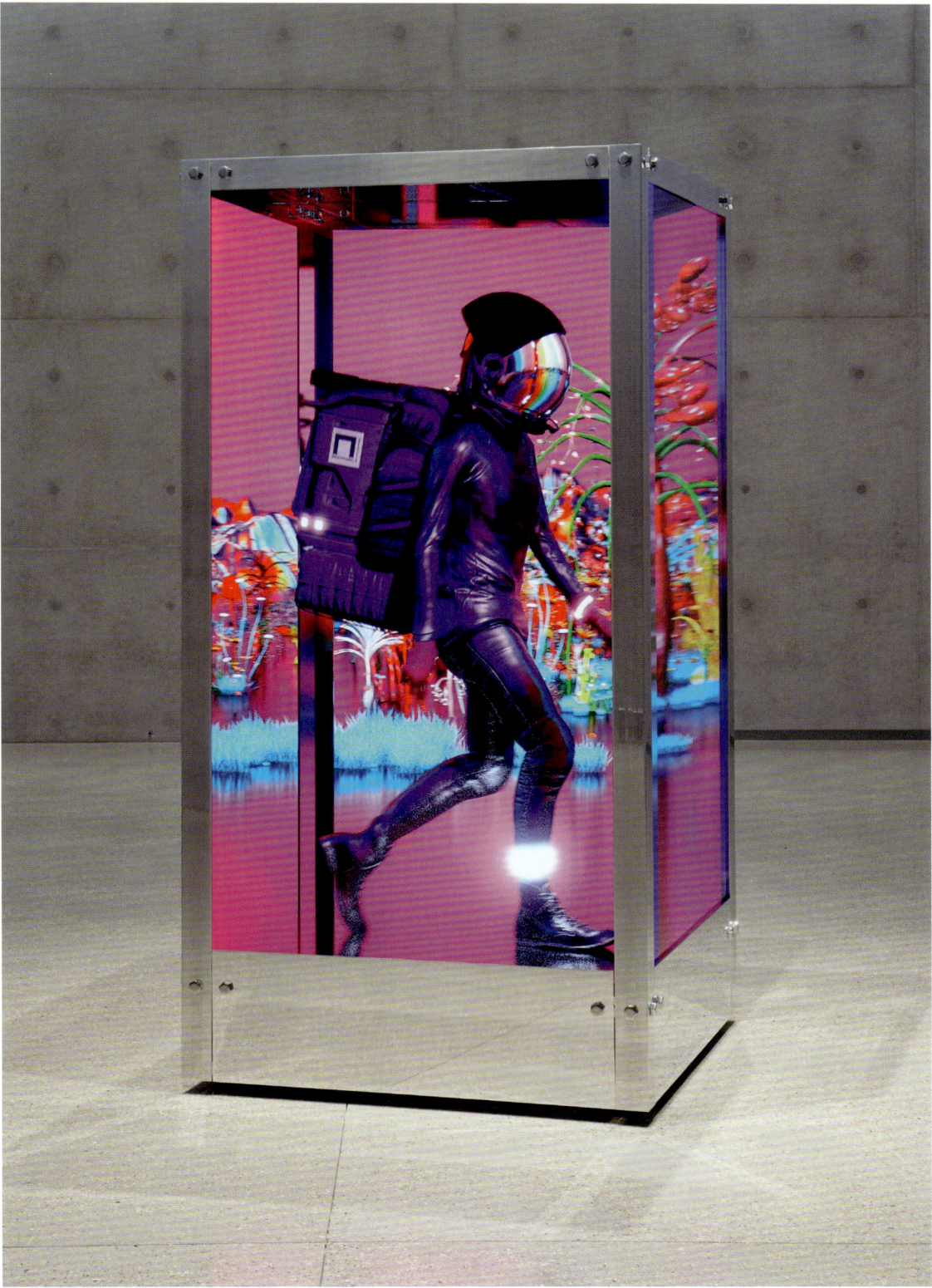

| # | TITLE | TIMESTAMP | MEDIUM | CHAIN | CONTRACT ADDRESS | TOKEN ID | EDITION SIZE |
|---|-------|-----------|--------|-------|------------------|----------|--------------|
| 05 | **Human ONE** | 10-28-2021 04:44:38 | Four video screens (16k resolution), polished aluminum metal, mahogany wood frame, dual media servers, dynamic NFT, 220.1 × 121.9 × 121.9cm | ETH | 0xa4c38796c35dca618fe-22a4e77f4210d0b0350d6 | 1 | 1/1 |

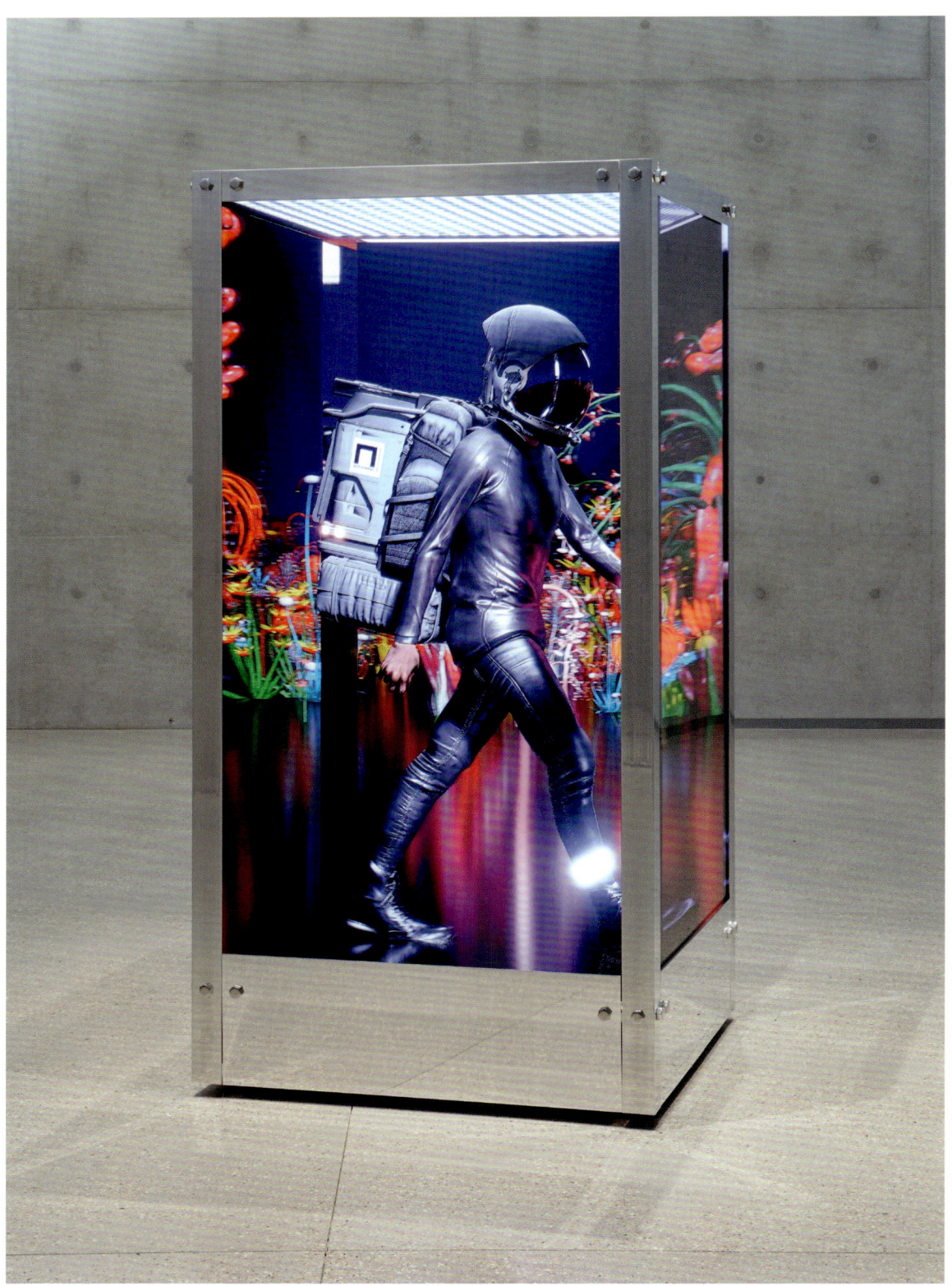

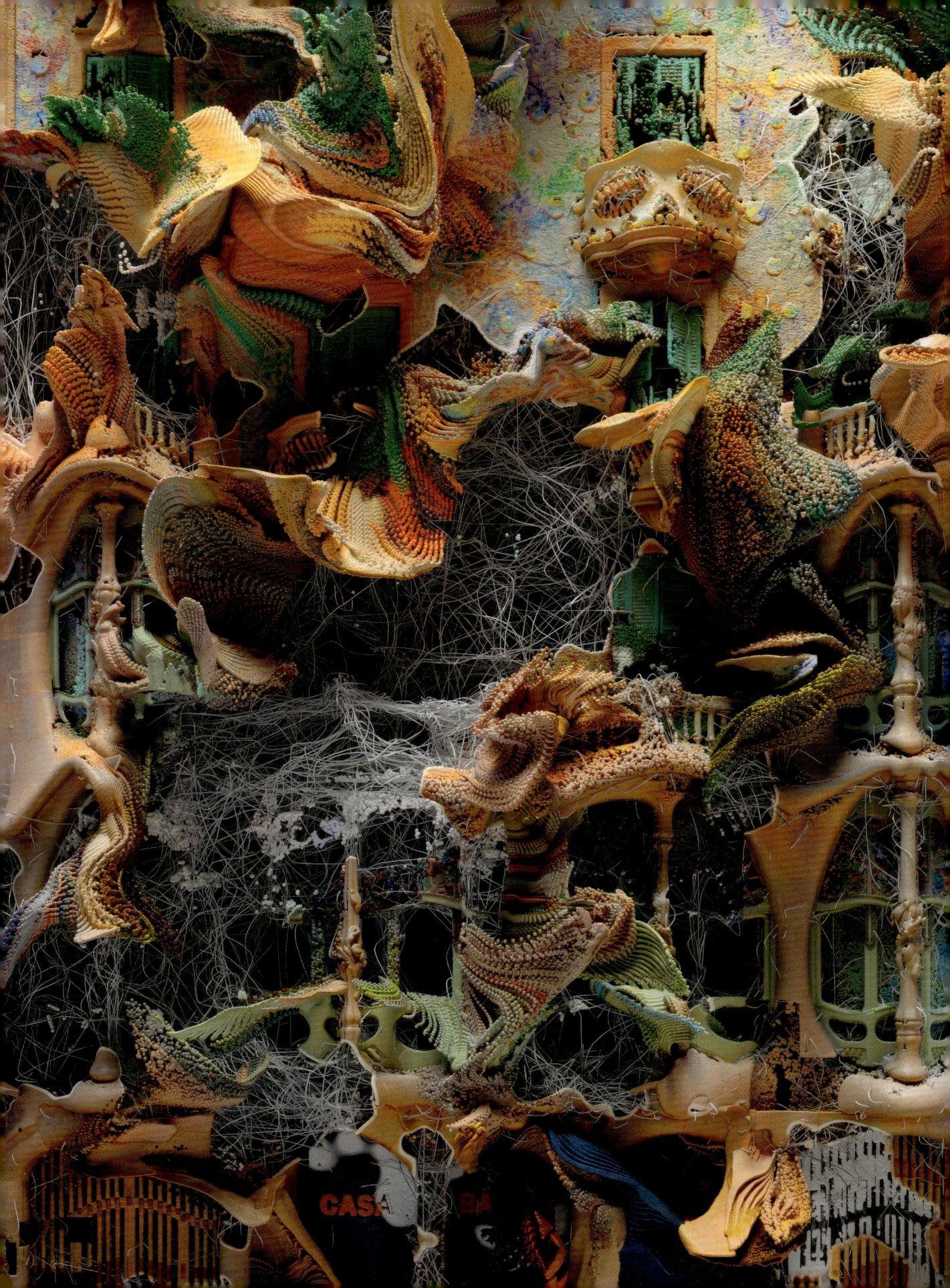

*The technical mastery of code, programming, mathematics, and the blockchain needed to operate in this space are starting to be exalted and praised in the same way as the 19th century prized life drawing and the 20th century prized photography.*

Each artist has been asked to present a finalized work and break it down to reveal the tools and processes they use, as well as the digital environments they call their studio. Starting off, Beeple breaks down the process behind his *Everydays*, a ritual stretching back 15 years. One develops a deeper insight into the key programs in a digital artist's arsenal of Cinema 4D and Octane Render alongside also the ever-present use of Adobe Photoshop. Refik Anadol shows how he and his studio use data as a pigment through the technical mastery of fluid simulation and AIs such as generative adversarial networks (GANs) to breathe new life into the way we see architecture. Brendan Dawes takes data down a different path, interpolating and visualizing cybersecurity data through the node-based software Houdini. Emily Xie and Erick Calderon present the two different sides — the organic and the structured—to building a generative algorithm and the variety of outputs this code-based process can engender. Harm van den Dorpel combines the algorithmic scripts of Xie and Calderon but goes one step further, allowing them to interact with the blockchain over time through complex smart-contracting. Finally, Ry David Bradley takes us into the realm of digital painting, to understand the processes of art-making in digital form are not so dissimilar to our long history of physical making, the brushes are just slightly different.

**ROBERT ALICE**

BEEPLE
*REBIRTH*, 04-27-2021 22:29:11 (Day #5097 of THE EVERYDAYS, 2007–ongoing)
Cinema 4D, Octane Render, Adobe Photoshop
0xdd012153e008346591153fff28b0dd6724f0c256, 100030001

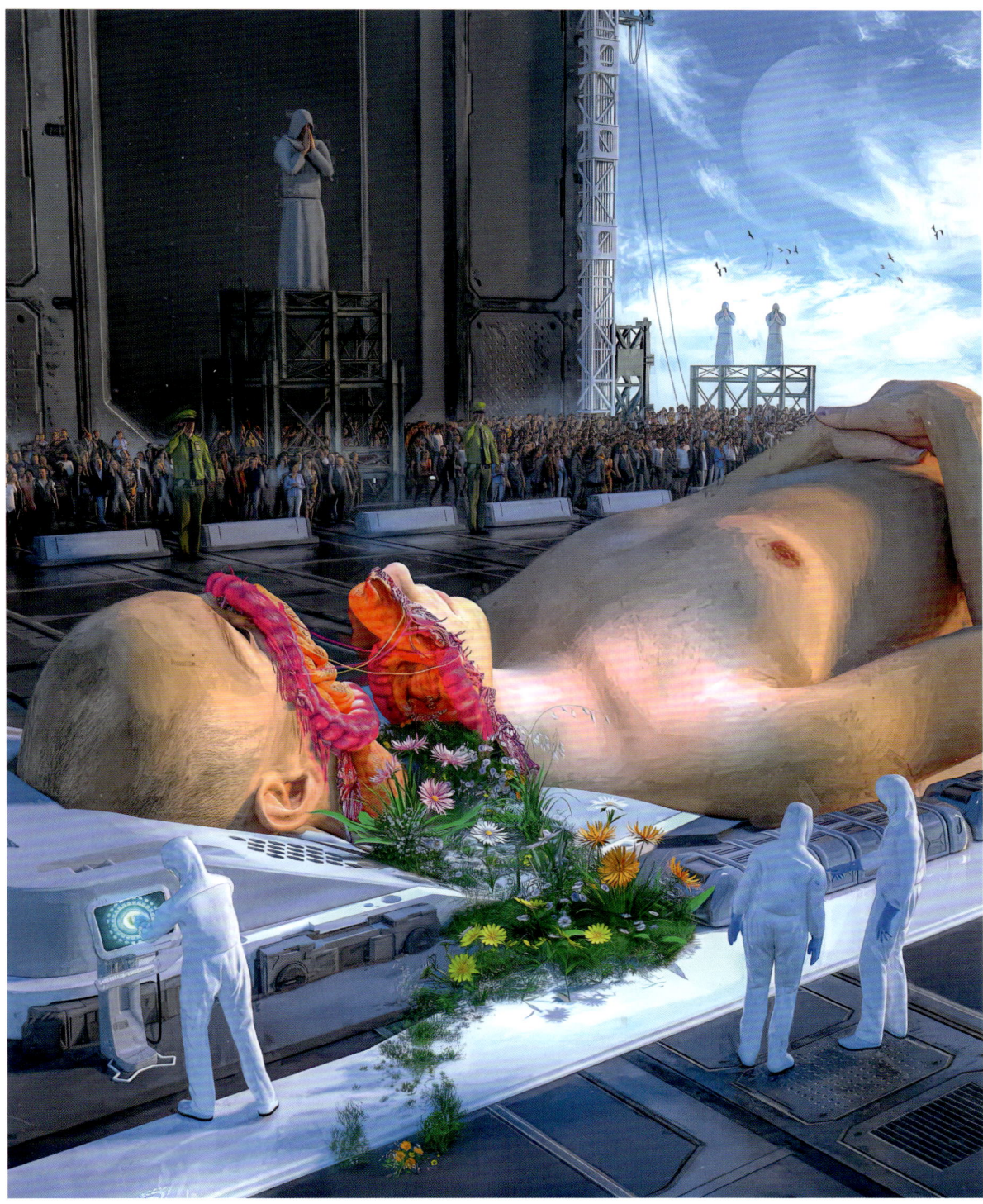

# ON PROCESS

Digital Canvases: Craft, Tools & the Digital Artist

**05.00** (detail)
Refik Anadol
*Living Architecture: Casa Batlló*, 11-04-2022 23:42:43
Custom software and soundscape, on-site weather data, YOLOv5, ResNeXt, StyleGAN2 ADA, Houdini
Ethereum, 0x7948F7fF1158B338a898e80ce8b1c3C964a80cec, 297

*If media is the vessel for the contemplation of cultural experience, the pixel today carries absolute primacy. As culture shifts more and more online, so too does its most poignant images.*

Process is the key ingredient in all artists' practices, regardless of their medium. It is the series of actions, both technical and conceptual, that an artist goes through to arrive at a finalized work. Often it is a method that has been refined and structured into an individual and highly tuned visual language. It is what creates recognizability, communality, but also new departures and explorations within an artist's ever-developing body of work. And yet in digital art, to those not intimately familiar with digital media and the artists' manipulating them, while aesthetics are often recognizable it is often difficult to tell the hallmarks of an artist's method. Frequently, those methods are highly multimedia in their approach, as artists feed their work through a multitude of systems, code libraries, algorithms, programs, and renders, further obfuscating the hand and tools that make them. Other times, the public is simply not as well acquainted with these cutting-edge and highly technical processes. The output of all this highly varied technical mastery is then filtered through the uniform materiality of the pixel.

Compared with more traditional vernaculars, artists working in digital media cannot lean on the materiality of physical media with their millennia of cultural associations to impart loaded meaning to their work. Pixels, unlike oil paint or charcoal, are an almost throwaway currency of the everyday. Our native experience of their work must compete with and circulate within the hypersaturation of our online media, and find its own space within the single largest exhibition of images ever created: the internet. The romantic conception of the painter's splattered studio, the myth of craftsmanship as rooted in the hand, the intimacy of the sketchbook, the bravado of physical scale, the alchemy of material transformation, and the ever-changing qualities and harnessing of light are all long held artistic mythologies that the digital artist has to contend with. Against the "wildness" of Pollock, the "aura" of Kusama, or the "genius" of Picasso, the digital artist and their computer struggle in normalcy. After all, it is the venue the entire world spends most of their life.

And yet, it is here that digital artists perhaps also find their greatest power. Working with the currency of our contemporary everyday, there is nothing more relevant than the digital artist's experience and their media. If media is the vessel for the contemplation of the cultural experience, the pixel today carries absolute primacy. As culture shifts more and more online, so too does its most poignant images. Not being physically bound also carries increasing benefits. Pixels can be arranged and rearranged in infinite ways to give way to an infinite array of images. Improvisation and experimentation can be rendered by just a few strokes of the keyboard. The laws of gravity have been replaced by the possibilities of code. Undo and redo functions have destroyed the tyranny most artists feel about pushing a work too far. Projections can immerse viewers at scales painters can only dream of. Online, digital artists can natively engage audiences thousands of times larger than even the most famous museums.

Ever-changing and responsive code allows for dynamic time-based artworks that can run forever. AR and VR are creating whole new worlds for artists to explore. The technical mastery of code, programming, mathematics, and the blockchain needed to operate in this space are starting to be exalted and praised in the same way as the 19th century prized life drawing and the 20th century prized photography. And in all of this, one can still be blown away by the digital artist who uses the most humble of processes, such as Osinachi's use of Microsoft Word, to arrive at the most exquisite of outcomes.

The following chapter peels back the curtains on several digital artists' processes, diving deep into their studio practice and the processes they undertake to arrive at finalized work. It is by no means exhaustive but breaks down a number of important typologies of digital art-making profiled within this book. From 3D modeling and AI/GAN–based work to code-based algorithmic art, digital painting and smart contract development, the artists profiled are all technically leaders in their chosen field, deeply embedded in their own language, and their processes are influencing both their generation and the next generation after them.

*Even though this process is entirely digital it harkens back to a very traditional craftsman-like approach.*

My current process for making the *Everydays* combines the principles behind sculpture, photography, and painting in a way that provides an endless amount of possibilities. This process has changed a lot since 2007, as the focus of my work has changed from abstract to figurative. Each artwork is completed each day from start to finish in about two hours and posted online before midnight. This process is very much about developing technically and creatively each day, while trying to listen to my inner voice about what kind of work I am most excited to make that day. As a daily ritual, there is personally a certain meditative and grounding aspect to these artworks as they are done each day, regardless of my mood. The following is a breakdown of how this daily practice currently comes together.

The main program I use is Cinema 4D. It's a basic 3D modeling/animation tool that I have worked with for 14 years, meaning the interface sort of melts away and I'm purely making artistic decisions. In real time, the process is fluid and experimental as I try different compositions, with many happy accidents that then become part of the work.

The basic workflow starts out very sculptural by "building" a 3D scene **[05.02]**. This is done by selecting a variety of virtual 3D objects (from plants to people) from a nearly endless library of online choices **[05.03]**. After selecting some models, I compose a scene in 3D space with the ability to scale and deform models, apply new materials, break apart and recombine pieces of objects to make new and unexpected compositions and meaning **[05.04]**. Sometimes these 3D models are placed to build a cohesive narrative and sometimes more abstractly for a more open-ended composition. To me, this process feels like pure sculpting unbound by the limits of physical constraint.

From here the process becomes much more like photography in that the scene must now be composed, lit and shot from a virtual camera **[05.05]**. The process of lighting these scenes is remarkably like real light photography except the artist can generate any type of light with any position, color, size, shadow type as well as any combination of virtual sky, clouds, or sun position. After the scene is lit, it is "shot" from a virtual camera that can be placed anywhere in the scene that again has all the same properties of a real camera: focal length, aperture, etc. Here, understanding the technical principles of photography are key to this part of the process.

After the shot is composed the image is "rendered" — a term for the computer calculating the final image based on the elements in the virtual scene — the 3D geometry, lights, materials, atmosphere, and camera effects. The rise of the GPU versus CPU has created an explosion in graphics computing power over the last 20 years that has unlocked the ability to make photoreal renderings that often can no longer be distinguished from reality.

After rendering the 3D scene into a flat 2D image, the process becomes much more painterly as we do the final composition and "paint-over," as it's called in the VFX industry **[05.06]**. The image is composited using Adobe Photoshop, the long-standing standard for 2D image processing. Here, additional details are painted on and certain effects are added like smoke or liquids that are much easier painted or composited than built in 3D. Color correction and any image processing filters are then added to achieve the final image.

Even though this process is entirely digital it harkens back to a very traditional craftsman-like approach to digital artwork especially when compared to generative work. In practice it encompasses many of the core concepts in the mediums of sculpture, photography, and painting — each of which can become more or less the focus of that particular artwork. In this way I feel this is a process that allows for the possibility of endless growth across a wide range of disciplines — the entire inspiration for the *Everydays*.

**BEEPLE**
Various screen captures documenting the process of
*REBIRTH*, 04-27-2021 22:29:11 (Day #5097 of THE EVERYDAYS, 2007–ongoing)
Cinema 4D, Octane Render, Adobe Photoshop
Ethereum, 0xdd012153e008346591153fff28b0dd6724f0c256, 100030001

05.02

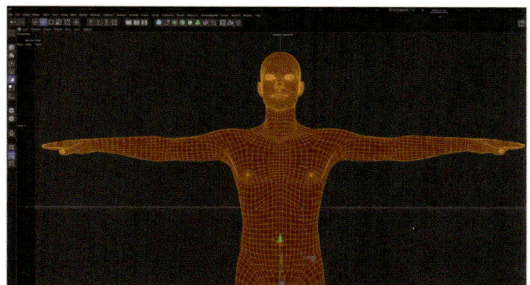

05.03

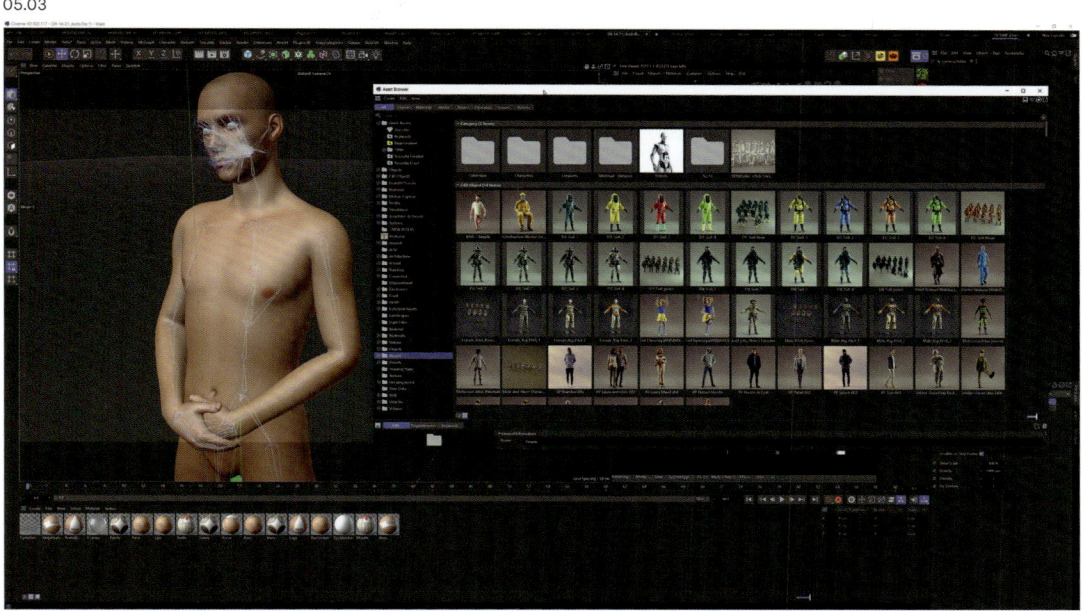

05.04

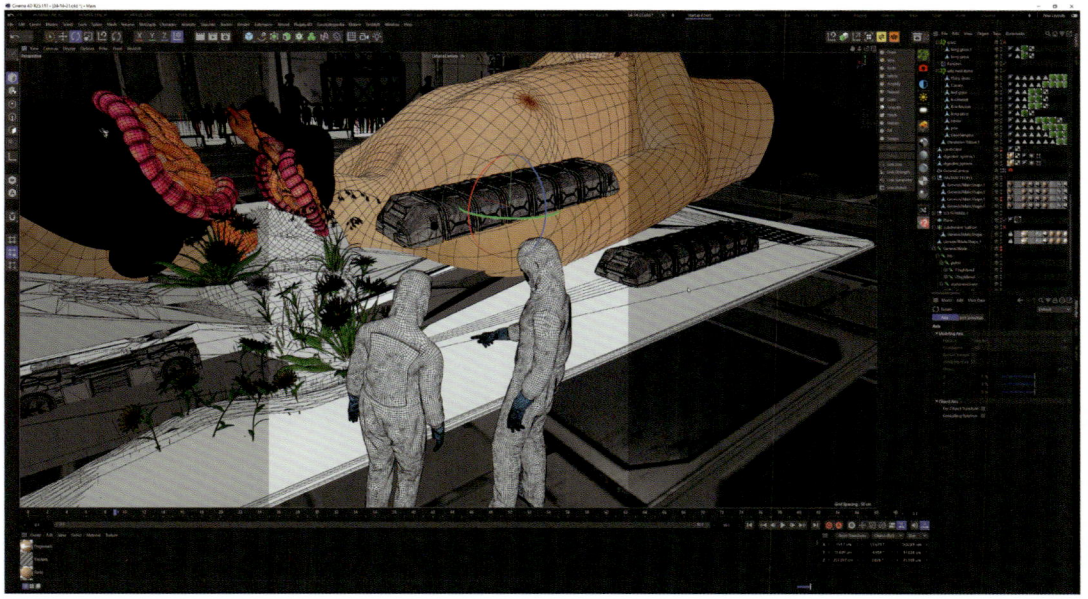

**05.02**
3D models are brought into Cinema4D where they can be deformed, scaled, and posed.

**05.03**
Selecting a model from a massive library of "ready-made" pre-built 3D assets.

**05.04**
A 3D sculpture composed of the objects selected is constructed in virtual space.

**05.05**
The scene is lit and "shot" with a virtual camera to be rendered to a 2D image.

**05.06**
The 2D image is brought into Photoshop for final compositing and painting.

05.03 (detail)

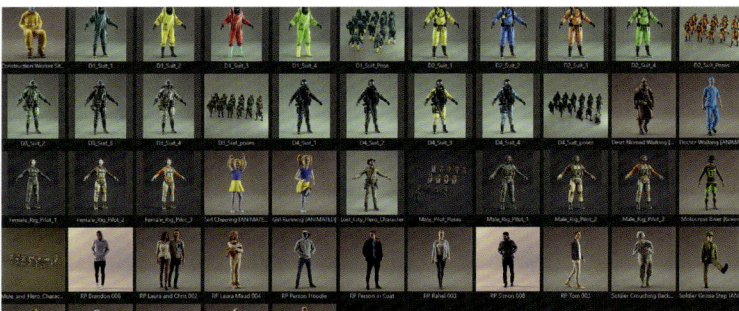

05.04 (detail)

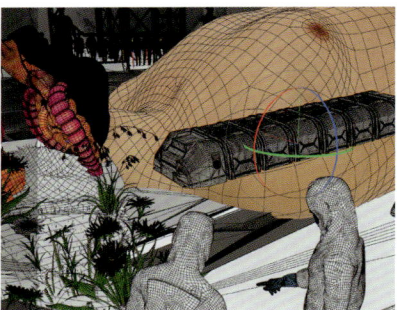

05.05

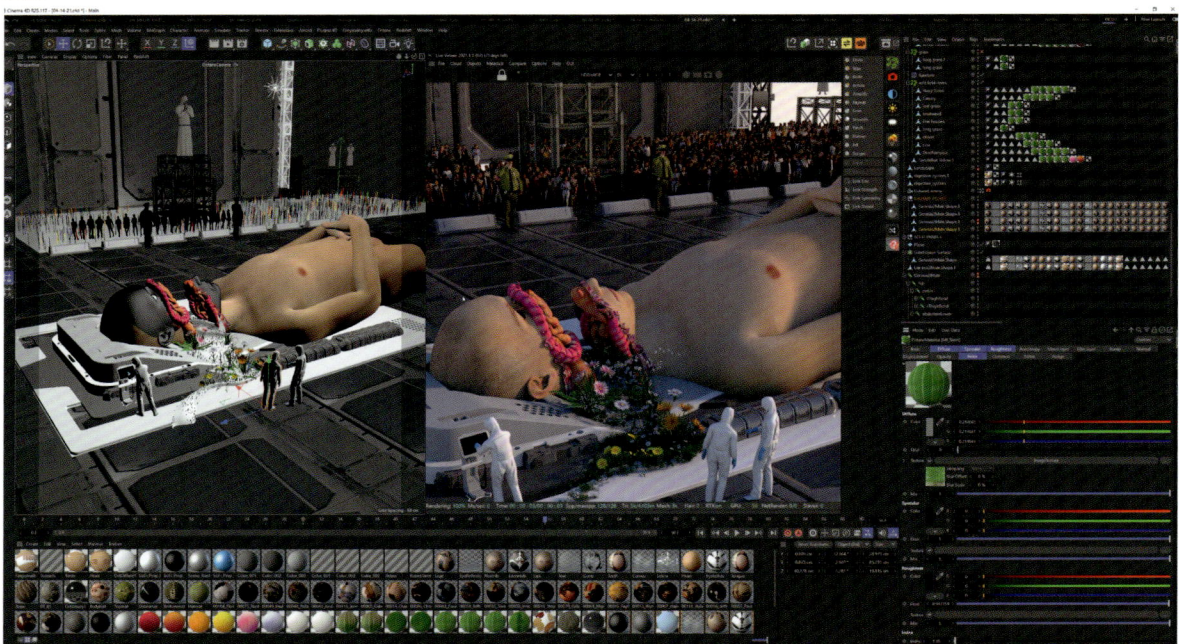

05.06

**05.07** ▶

Refik Anadol

*Living Architecture: Casa Batlló*, 11-04-2022 23:42:43

Custom software and soundscape, on-site weather data, YOLOv5, ResNeXt, StyleGAN2 ADA, Houdini

Ethereum, 0x7948F7fF1158B338a898e80ce8b1c3C964a80cec, 297

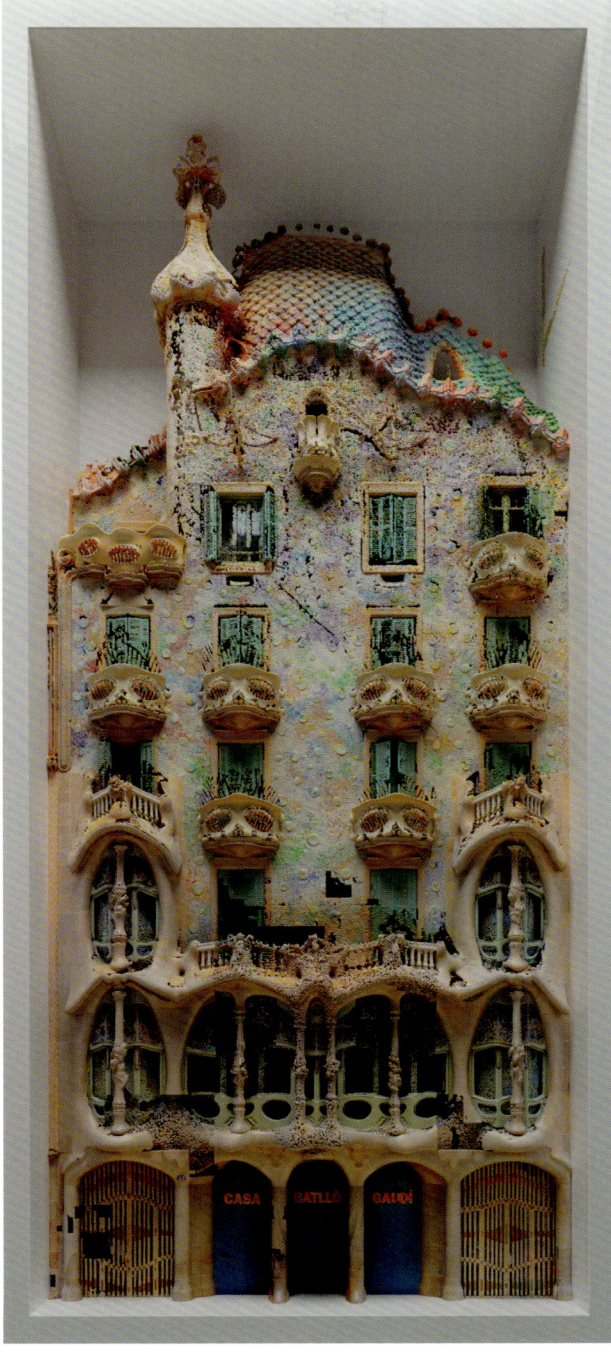
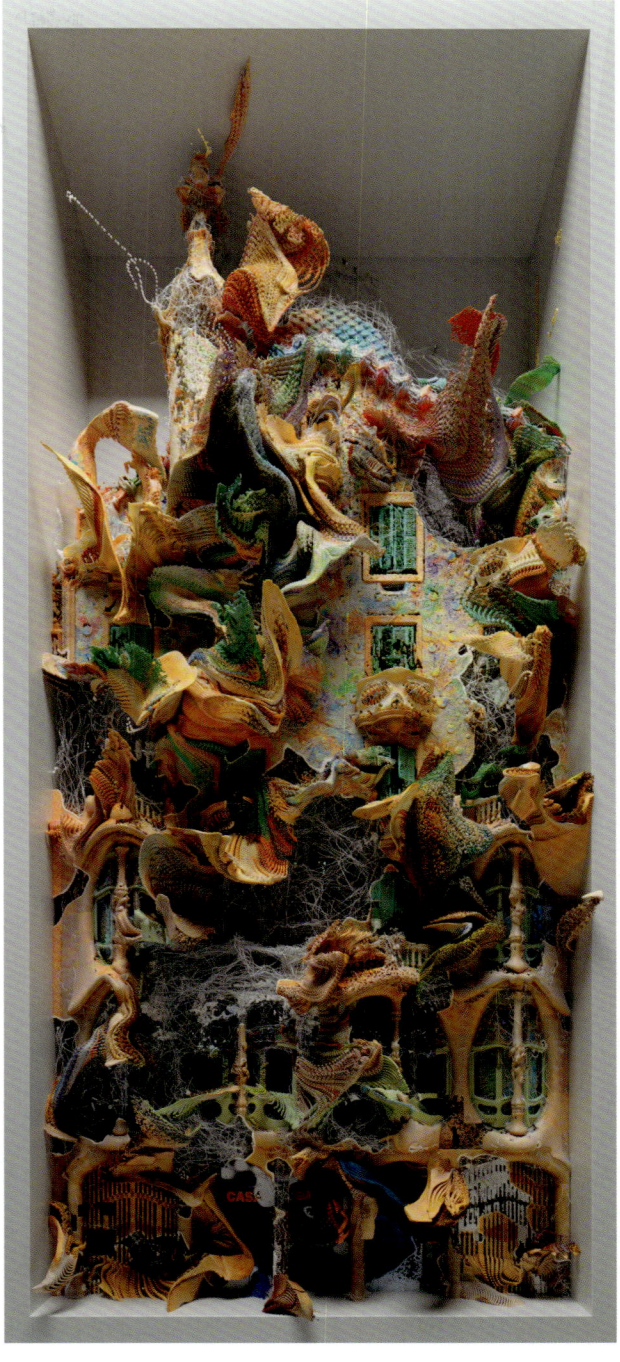

# REFIK ANADOL ON
## LIVING ARCHITECTURE: CASA BATLLÓ

*I am fascinated by the possibility of making a building "dream" and "hallucinate" by transforming our collective memories into multisensory immersive installations with the help of AI.*

Since I started my practice, I have been interested in the question of whether machine learning technologies could be used as tools to change our perception of architectural spaces and urban environments. To put it more poetically, I am fascinated by the possibility of making a building "dream" and "hallucinate" by transforming our collective memories into multisensory immersive installations with the help of AI. I see machines as collaborators and data as pigment, and use light as my primary material. I paint with a thinking brush, embedding media arts into architecture. I do this by training neural networks (AI) on our collective, digitized memories, from millions of photographic images to sound files to cultural archives. For more than ten years, I have been working with big data and AI to develop a unique understanding of the relationship between machines, humans, and their various environments.

In the Spring of 2021, I had the opportunity to explore these questions further through a collaboration to collect the memories of Barcelona's iconic 1906 Gaudí building, Casa Batlló [05.08]. Our project, *Living Architecture: Casa Batlló*, was the first UNESCO World Heritage Site to be represented in the form of a dynamic NFT, using climate data from the city collected in real-time and showing the ephemerides celebrated on the building's façade [05.09, 05.10, 05.11, 05.12].[1]

The process for this multilayered project began when our Studio created "In the Mind of Gaudí," the first AI-based immersive room to be performed in a six-walled LED cube room inside Casa Batlló in 2021. For this initial 360°-experience inside a six-screen space set up at the building's basement, we collected a dataset of approximately one billion images consisting of Gaudí's sketches, visual archives of the building's history, academic archives, and publicly available photos of Casa Batlló found on various internet and social media platforms [05.13, 05.14]. We processed them with machine learning classification models such as YOLOv5 (object detection) and ResNeXt (image classification).

The sorted image datasets were then clustered into thematic categories to better understand the semantic context of the Gaudí data universe. This expanding data universe not only represented the interpolation of data as synthesis, but also became a latent cosmos in which the AI's hallucinative potential was the main currency of artistic creativity. In order to capture these hallucinations from a multidimensional space, we used NVIDIA's StyleGAN2 ADA which generated an AI model for the machine to process the archive. The model was trained on subsets of the sorted images, creating embeddings in 1,024 dimensions. On an NVIDIA A100 DGX-Station, this training takes approximately four weeks.

In the next stage, which is the data pigmentation pipeline, we engaged the process of combining visual elements from separate sources into single images. For more than 10 years, we have been experimenting with custom software and fluid simulation models to give these visualizations a unique dynamism [05.15]. In other words, we train a unique AI model with subsets of the dataset which result in the machine's "hallucinations" — new aesthetic images and color combinations through unique lines drawn by algorithmic connections. Fluid simulation, as its name suggests, is a technique for emulating and generating the qualitative visual behavior of a fluid. It has been a signature visual effect for our Studio's data visualizations and has been performed with various levels of complexity including real-time and interactive animation. For *Living Architecture: Casa Batlló*, we synthesized the vast data collected from Gaudí archives into ethereal data pigments and eventually into a representational form of fluid-inspired movements. This project was the ultimate manifestation of how advanced our experimentations with this tool and blockchain technology have become: it uses sensors from Barcelona that collect real-time environmental data so that the NFT changes according to the weather in the city and the events celebrated on the façade today and in the future.

REFIK ANADOL, ALEX MOROZOV, CARRIE HE, CHRISTIAN BURKE, DANIEL SEUNGMIN LEE, EFSUN ERKILIC, KERIM KARAOGLU, PELIN KIVRAK, HO MAN LEUNG, NIDHI PARSANA, RAMAN K. MUSTAFA, RISHABH CHAKRABARTY, TOBY HEINEMANN, YUFAN XIE
REFIK ANADOL STUDIO PRODUCTION CREDITS FOR LIVING ARCHITECTURE: CASA BATLLÓ

[1] The work was sold at Christie's 21st Century Evening Sale on May 10, 2022, and 10% of the proceeds was donated to the Associació Aprenem Autisme and Fundació Adana institutions that work with neurodiverse adults and children. On May 7, 2022, we projected a mapping version of the piece on the façade of Casa Batlló before 47,000 attendees. The digital piece was also on public view until May 13, 2022, at Rockefeller Plaza in Manhattan, New York.

**REFIK ANADOL**
Sketches and screen captures documenting the process of
*Living Architecture: Casa Batlló*, 11-04-2022 23:42:43
Custom software and soundscape, on-site weather data, YOLOv5, ResNeXt,
StyleGAN2 ADA, Houdini
Ethereum, 0x7948F7fF1158B338a898e80ce8b1c3C964a80cec, 297

**05.08**
Isometric view of Casa Batlló's façade.

**05.09**
A diagram showing how the data about weather patterns from around the building is transformed into the computational design process.

**05.10, 05.11**
Lidar scans of the building.

**05.12, 05.13**
Publicly available images of interior and exterior details of Casa Batlló collected by Refik Anadol Studio.

**05.14**
The final stage of generating the artwork with the help of a custom fluid simulation algorithm.

05.08

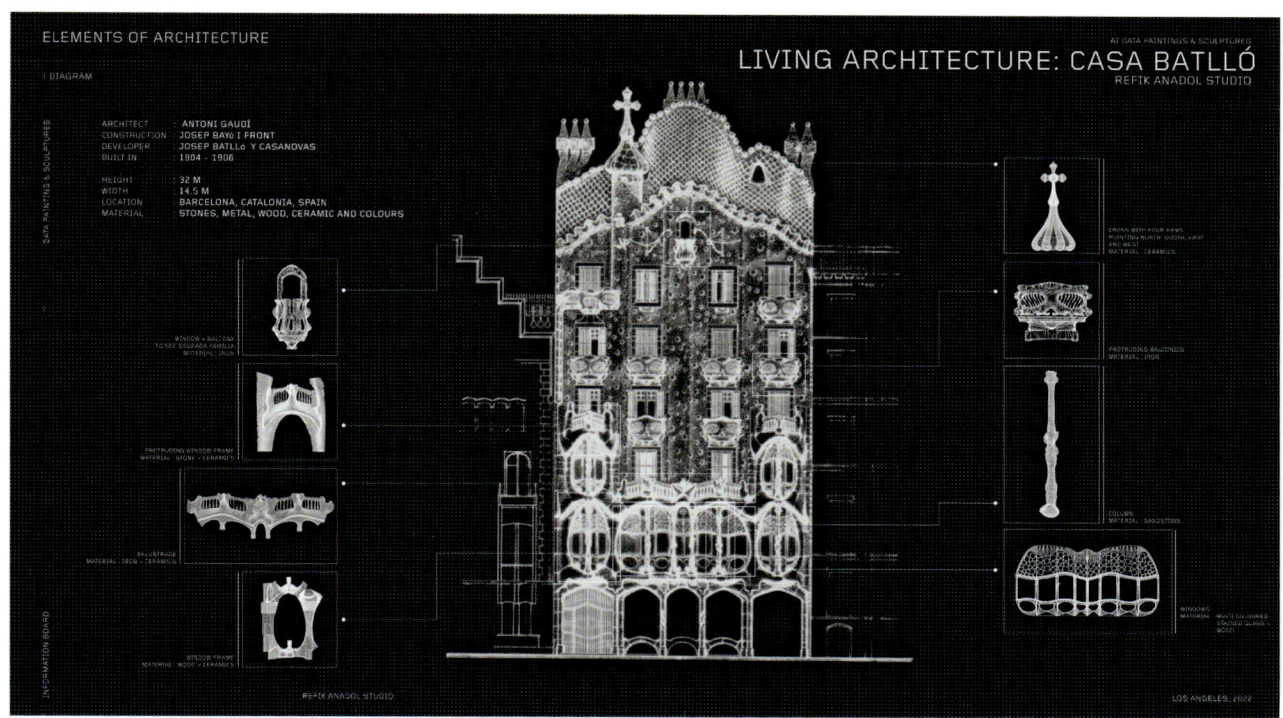

05.09

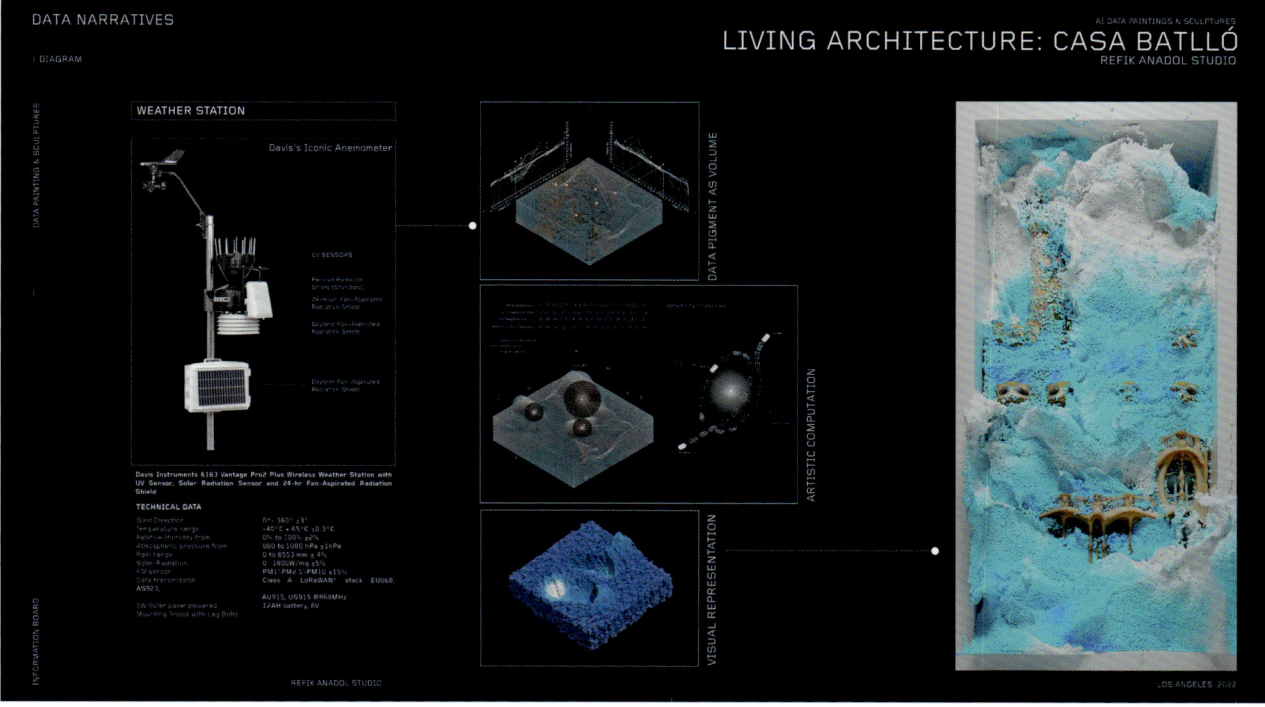

05.10

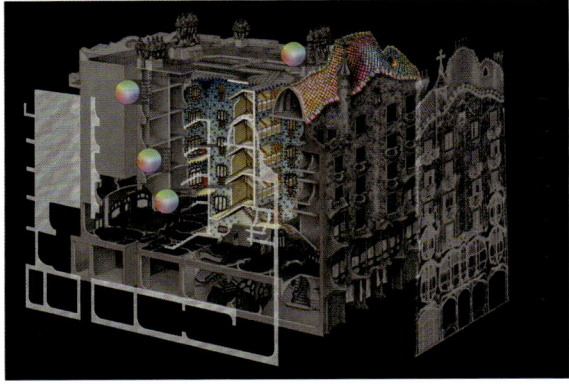

05.11

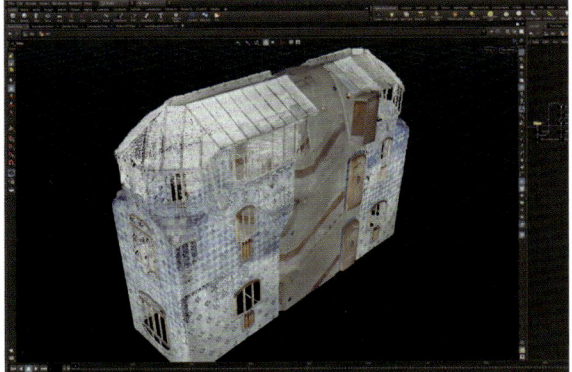

05.12

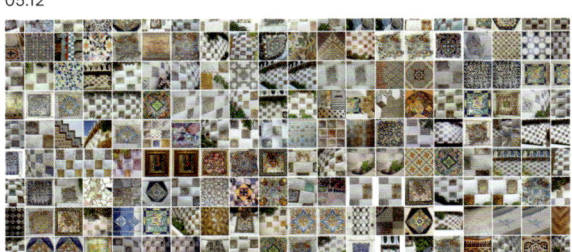

05.13

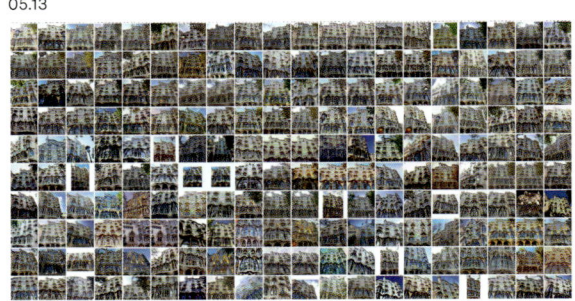

05.14

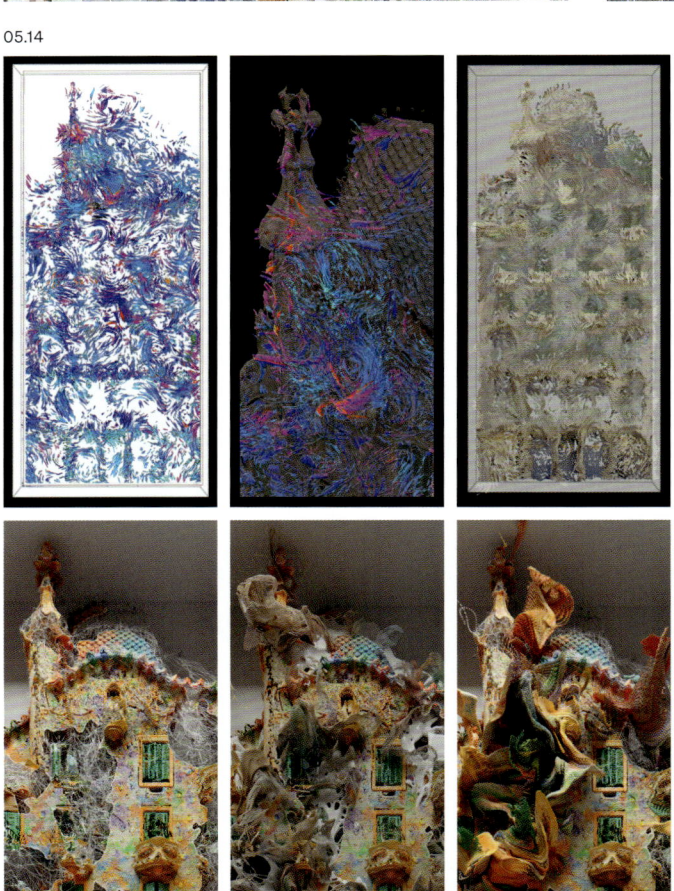

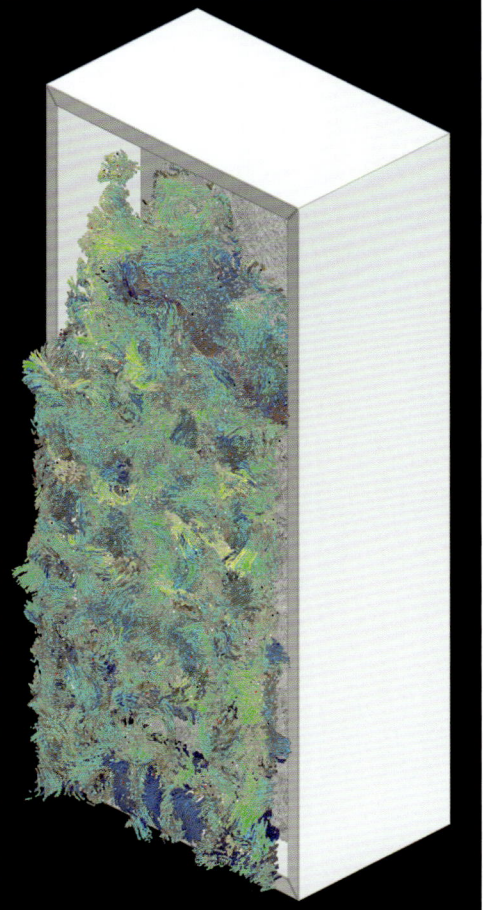

Brendan Dawes
*The Art of Cybersecurity*, 02-02-2023 11:33:11
Houdini, Processing, Vim, Hitfilm, Sound Studio
Ethereum, 0x92dcc400788d12db9ae26d85b7422790250ea262, 1

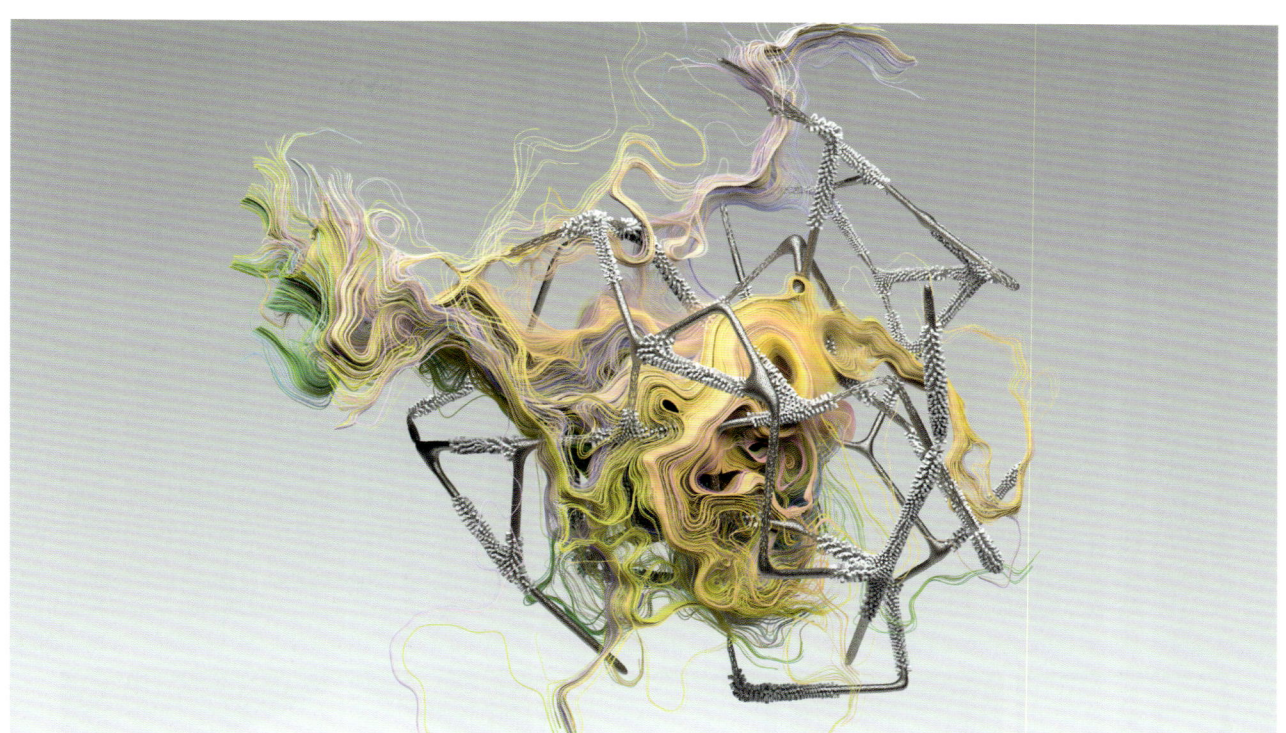

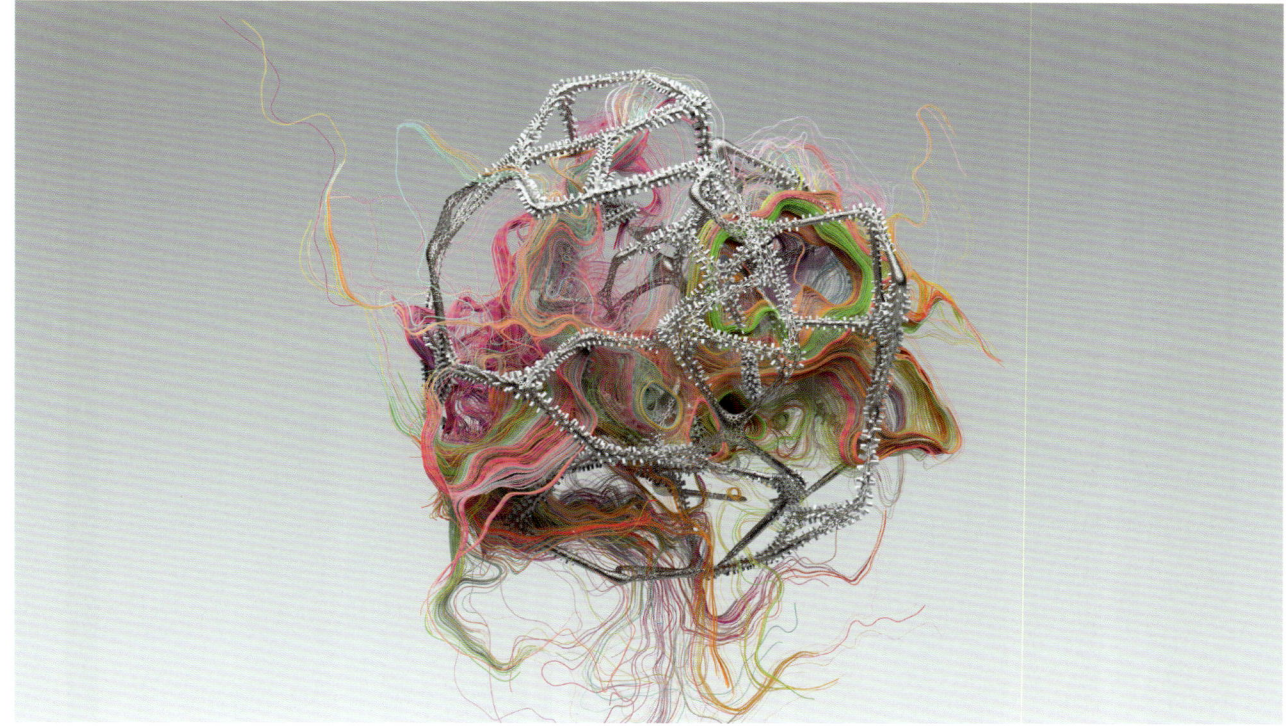

# BRENDAN DAWES ON
## THE ART OF
## CYBERSECURITY

*Data by itself is not enough; data needs poetry. This has been a personal mantra of mine for as long as I've been thinking of data as an artistic material.*

Even though digital is often the output of my work, pencil and paper is still the best way for me to freely think when first starting a new work **[05.17, 05.18]**. It doesn't judge in the way I feel digital can, it provides shorter feedback loops, leaving me free to scribble ideas quickly without computational limitations to deal with. Yet equally the sketch-like nature of drawing also has to be present in the digital tools I use, which is why Houdini resonated when I first began to use it in 2019. The program, which started in 1996 and was built for CGI designers, consists of wiring nodes to other nodes in a procedural system. The interactive nature of the system combines the elements of coding with processes more akin to collage, where remixing and sampling are core creative elements. My interest in Houdini was born out of a node-based precursor to it — Max/MSP created by Cycling 74 in 1985 which I experimented with two decades ago. Yet it was when I saw peers such as digital artist Robert Hodgkin (aka Flight404) sharing his early Houdini experiments on Instagram in 2019 that my curiosity finally got the better of me.

*The Art of Cybersecurity* (2019–22) is the first work I made using Houdini where I sought to provide abstract expression to global cybersecurity data during a time where prominent hacks, viruses, and ransomware attacks dominated our global news feeds. The following is the process I went through to create this work.

Moving from paper to digital, I wanted to understand the shape or sculptural qualities of the data as a visual starting point. Each row of data revealed when threats were detected on an anonymous network, detailing time, amount of threats at that point and the severity of those threats. Using that CSV file I created representations of that data in various forms using Houdini — each row of data manifesting as a point on a mesh, dictating the size and placement of each point. Here I started to see interesting areas for further inquiry, such as clumps of threats born from the severity or time of attack **[05.19]**. To my mind this is akin to throwing and manipulating clay to create a form — something as a starting point — something to criticize.

This representation of data needed something to "sit on," so to speak. The network itself needed to be represented as a shape. Interestingly each data point, was categorized into a certain industry "vertical" such as media, finance, or government, showcasing the pervasiveness of cybersecurity threats the modern world faces **[05.20]**. What if I could use these verticals as a seed in an algorithmic system to create unique forms for each vertical? To create the shape of the network to represent these different industry verticals, I turned to another piece of software I regularly use — Processing (see "On Algorithmic Art" for more details).

Using Processing, I employed a MD5 hash — a password algorithm and simple way to obfuscate text created for cryptographic systems — to turn the titles of those verticals into hashes which I could then further split into numbers between zero and one. These numbers were then used as parameters in an algorithmic system to create abstract 3D shapes. For example, they would drive the number of points in the mesh and the number of branches and other such things. In this way, each shape was unique and specific to the data of each vertical **[05.21]**.

The next conceptual layer of the work was the representation of freedom afforded from the implications of cybersecurity, a dance between hackers and the systems in place to guard society. Organic lines made using a curl noise algorithm flowed through and around the space. As the forms present in the space were generated via the data, these lines were a reaction to these now manifested shapes, so each composition was unique, all born from the data **[05.22, 05.23]**.

The final result, comprised of the cybersecurity threats, a representation of the network being attacked, and the creativity that is still allowed to flow despite these attacks, would go on to represent a milestone in my artistic practice — a newfound way to not just tell visual abstractions from complex global data but a process to ask questions about our relationship with technology, data, digital networks, and how we as humans might live with these ever-evasive systems.

**BRENDAN DAWES**
Sketches and screen captures documenting the process of
*The Art of Cybersecurity*, 02-02-2023 11:33:11
Houdini, Processing, Vim, Hitfilm, Sound Studio
Ethereum, 0x92dcc400788d12db9ae26d85b7422790250ea262, 1

**05.17**

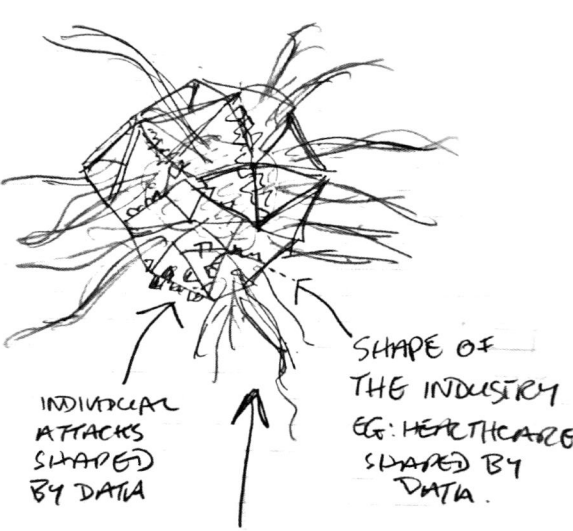

**05.17, 05.18**
Various pencil sketches depicting early thought processes and methodologies for the work.

**05.19**
Data applied to a simple mesh early on in the process as way to understand the shape of the data.

**05.20**
CSV file detailing data surrounding cybersecurity threats to various industry verticals, added here is the MD5 hash that is used as the seed to generate form.

**05.21**
An MD5 hash of the industry categories create unique shapes to represent the network, also seen in Houdini.

**05.22, 05.23**
Creating lines using curl noise within the interface of Houdini.

**05.18**

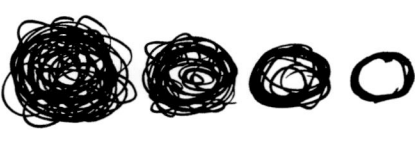

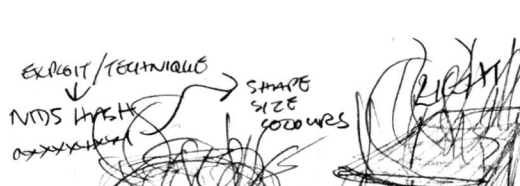

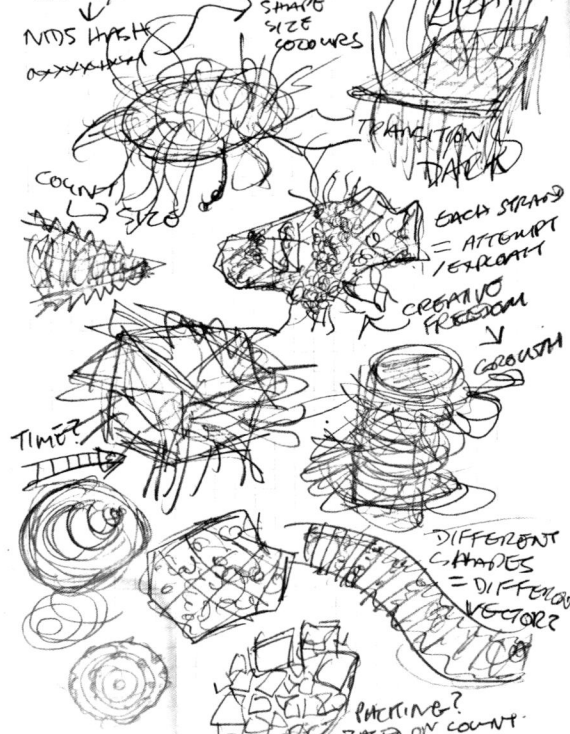

**05.19**

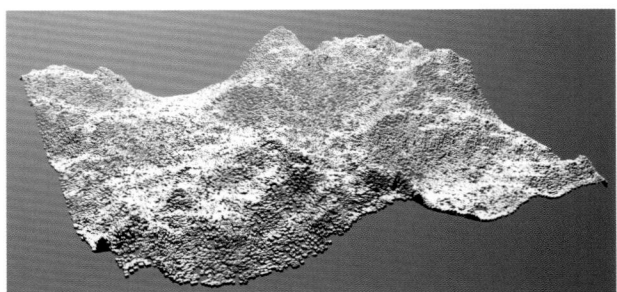

**05.20**

| industry | factorA | factorB | factorC | factorD | factorE | md5 |
|---|---|---|---|---|---|---|
| Banking | 0.125 | 0.601 | 0.417 | 0.115 | 0.152 | bf8e5c092dc83fae78b0a110e809690c |
| Healthcare | 0.516 | 0.13 | 0.423 | 0.129 | 0.125 | 4ee2a6c7bb7c40af94c5a15dbf7eb673 |
| Others | 0.543 | 0.339 | 0.763 | 0.11 | 0.103 | 52ef9633d88a7480b3a938ff9eaa2a25 |
| Technology | 0.151 | 0.141 | 0.911 | 0.82 | 0.637 | e7e767d7c0e58b16e57d3ab16150db80 |
| Manufacturing | 0.152 | 0.13 | 0.806 | 0.15 | 0.167 | e86883c7cfc07afcf1e5ad8dffd7e1cc |
| Materials | 0.234 | 0.12 | 0.159 | 0.955 | 0.474 | 23ce0eb7d180f3dc8391d4af48572d21 |
| Transportation | 0.108 | 0.208 | 0.153 | 0.877 | 0.12 | a600971fdd23ea1f5685d7ee01d5f5c3 |
| Retail | 0.343 | 0.131 | 0.807 | 0.155 | 0.107 | 053e0bc8b9627b28e2ed8029a34b35bd |
| Financial | 0.353 | 0.474 | 0.323 | 0.144 | 0.137 | 35f156073cb9314e5ddcabd2d16f443c |

| Telecommunications | 0.121 | 0.103 | 0.61 | 0.859 | 0.758 | ba075f9e97825d22570d1bcf73c382f2 |
|---|---|---|---|---|---|---|
| Education | 0.145 | 0.105 | 0.108 | 0.449 | 0.696 | de7a22a0c94aa64ba2449e520aa20c99 |
| Media | 0.388 | 0.242 | 0.808 | 0.583 | 0.138 | 3b563524fdb17b4a86590470d40bef74 |
| Energy | 0.607 | 0.321 | 0.13 | 0.553 | 0.712 | 5cc28f31113ec7cd7e546b836ccae2b9 |
| Food and beverage | 0.356 | 0.142 | 0.364 | 0.151 | 0.891 | 0570b6d9de5c37a026e69c6987fc27f6 |
| Communication and Media | 0.264 | 0.119 | 0.577 | 0.545 | 0.538 | 2851d3b5c7b7582e60533f1b5221d5b9 |
| Fast-Moving Consumer Goods | 0.893 | 0.153 | 0.909 | 0.163 | 0.11 | 885946ea532f8ac971f9fff7a7effd8a |
| Utilities | 0.135 | 0.284 | 0.12 | 0.796 | 0.616 | ceba282b7418b7f199798b645e1cba56 |
| Insurance | 0.154 | 0.146 | 0.167 | 0.512 | 0.125 | eaff1bdf24fcffe0e14e29a1bff51a12 |
| Agriculture | 0.932 | 0.111 | 0.107 | 0.151 | 0.705 | 8e54e9aa508ea37f7fe734e86ba9da27 |

05.21

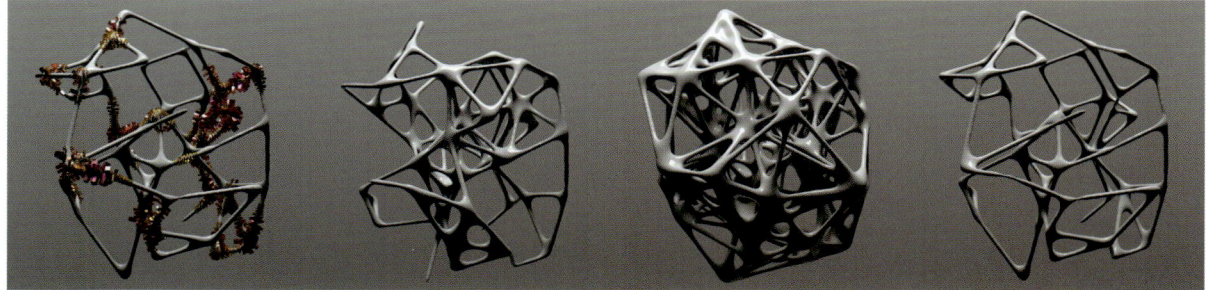

05.22

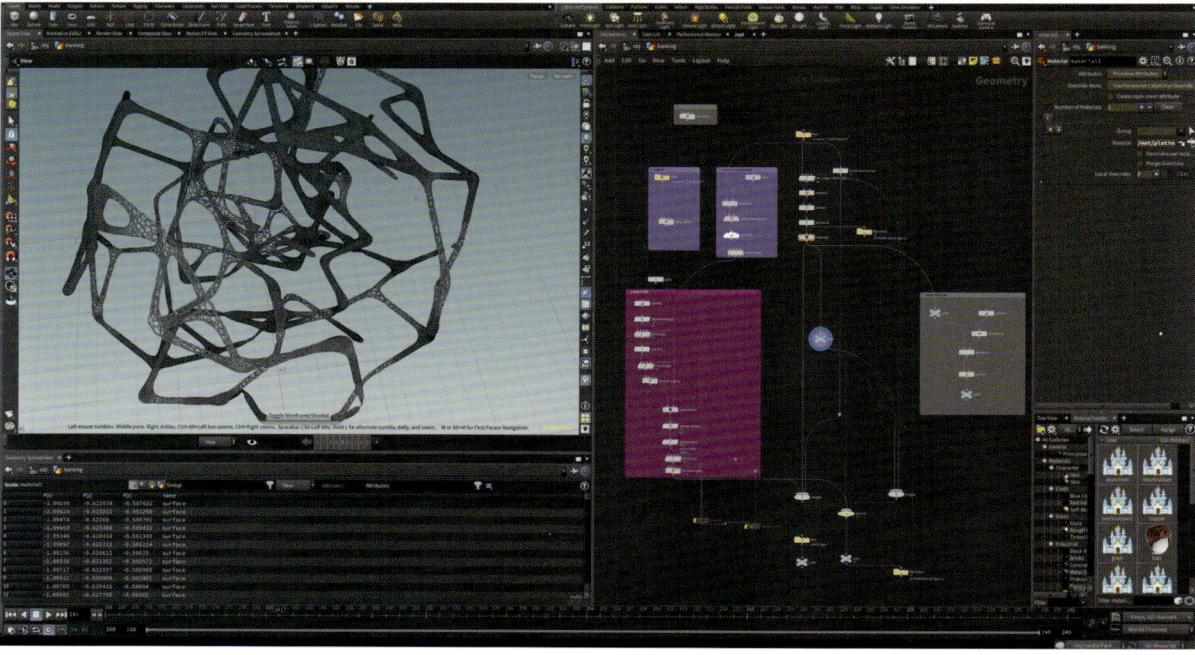

05.23

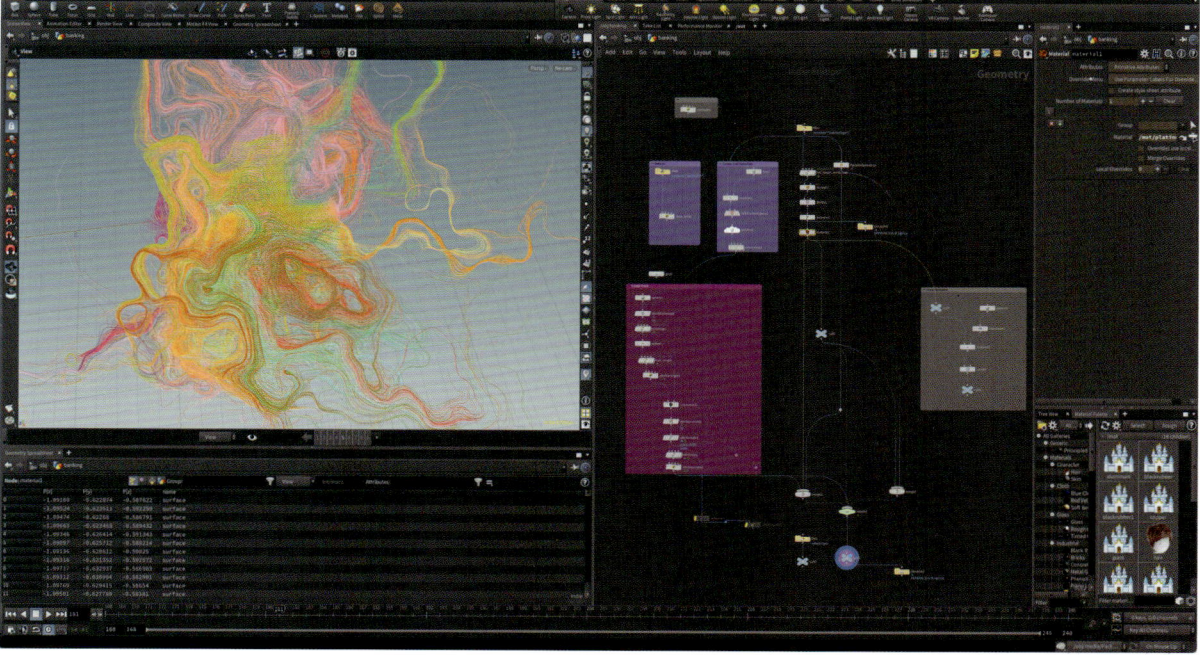

**05.24**
Emily Xie
*Off Script*, 07-26-2022 14:22:28
JavaScript, p5.js
Ethereum, 0x0a1bbd57033f57e7b6743621b79fcb9eb2ce3676, 10000000–10000099

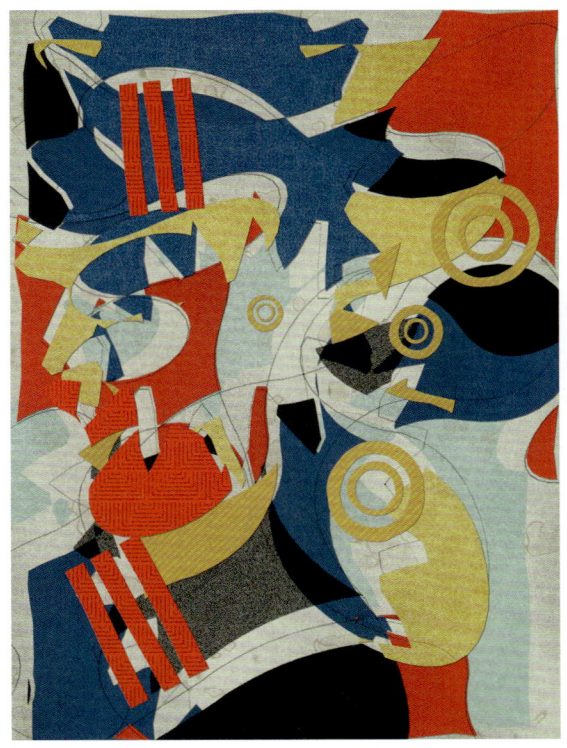
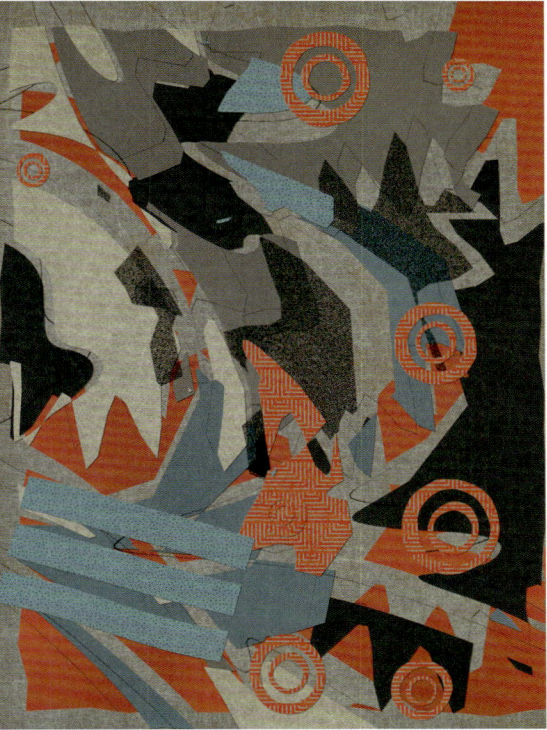
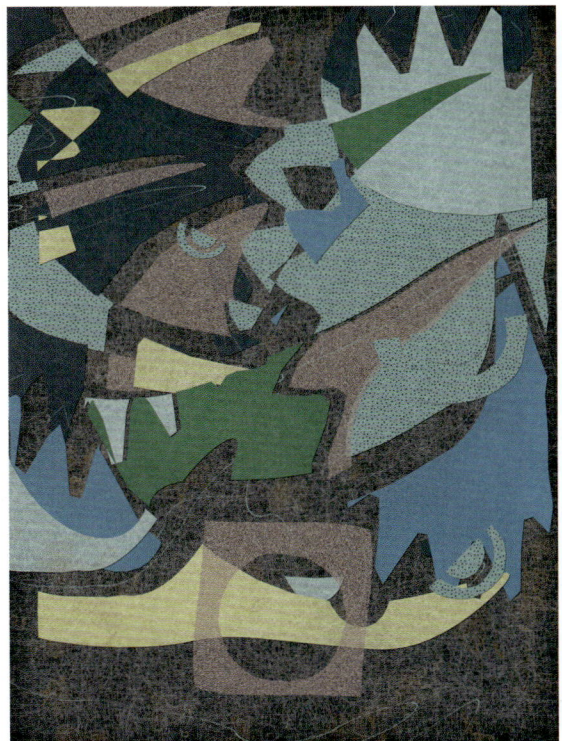
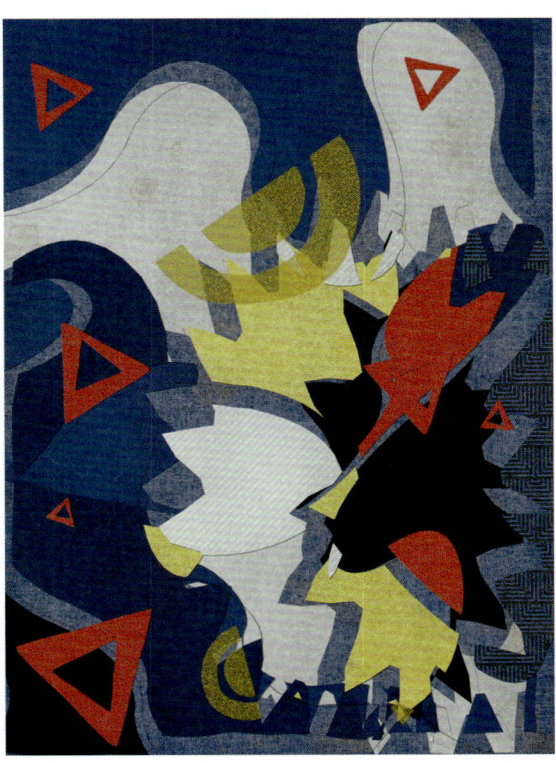

# EMILY XIE ON
## OFF SCRIPT

*My process for Off Script embraces the systematicity and randomness inherent to generative art in order to subvert the characteristics of its own medium.*

As a generative artist, code is my medium. I create my works using JavaScript, with p5.js as my drawing library of choice. What I enjoy about p5.js in particular is its intuitiveness, allowing me to easily translate my visual concepts **[05.25]** into lines of code.

I first discovered generative art sometime in the mid-2010s and readily fell in love with it as it so neatly merged my interests in computation and art — fields that I had both formally studied and worked in. At the time, I had been programming on a daily basis as a software engineer. Creating art computationally gave new meaning to the endless possibilities of code. I relished how the art form challenged me to break down complex visuals into a series of simple rulesets while balancing the machine's element of randomness in order to create compelling outputs.

My recent generative series, *Off Script*, algorithmically reinterprets the tradition of early 20th-century collage. Inspired by Matisse's cut-outs, Picasso's assemblages, and Kurt Schwitters's mixed media works on paper, *Off Script* is an exercise in code-generated texture and composition, while referencing the principles of play, chance, order, and chaos that are intrinsic to the histories of both collage and generative art. The algorithm took around four months to program and is capable of producing infinitely varied outputs, each of which are distinct based on a given input.

First, I broke down the underlying composition by randomly generating a set of curved and jagged 2D forms, each unique and scattered across a virtual canvas **[05.26]**. Then, the algorithm applies a custom pixel-wise masking procedure, extracting out a final group of complex shapes that are produced by the numerous overlaps and subtractions of the initial forms. Coding aside, this compositional ruleset involved many hours of manual tuning to constrain the parameter space such that the resulting shapes were complex enough to be interesting but not chaotic, and distanced from one another in aesthetic but unpredictable in distribution.

Next, I wrote a custom circle-packing algorithm **[05.27]**, which places nonoverlapping circles on a screen to determine a set of coordinates where additional geometric motifs may be added. More concretely, this involves iteratively picking random points on the canvas where there are no other nearby points and where the corresponding region of the underlying composition is not overly crowded. The program chooses a combination of squares, circles, strips, triangles, arcs, and stars as motifs to place at these points.

The resulting shapes are then used to "cut out" sheets of generative papers. While these papers look as if they are imported images, they are in fact fully generated from the code, using thousands of repeated lines and shape primitives to give the illusion of texture. Some of these papers are a single color, whereas others contain patterns. Each paper is unique in its own way, with splotches and blemishes produced throughout using various applications of Perlin noise — a function that provides a smooth, natural pseudorandom distribution — in order to further impart the appearance of organicity **[05.28, 05.29]**.

As the program generates the final cut-outs from sheets of paper, they are randomly jostled, thrown away, rearranged, and overlaid on top of one another throughout the canvas. Finishing touches are also applied at this time. For instance, shadows are added underneath each cut-out to create the illusion of depth. This is done by duplicating each shape, coloring it a dark gray, and shifting the coordinates slightly to the right and below before rendering the cut-out. While every step of this process occurs within the computer's buffers, the final image is rendered all at once **[05.30, 05.31]**.

The resulting outputs appear unified, natural, and highly tactile — as if created by the human hand. Ultimately, my process for *Off Script* embraces the systematicity and randomness inherent to generative art in order to subvert the characteristics of its own medium. Much like the early 20th-century collage art it is inspired by, the series poses questions around materiality, technique, and mass production within the context of its own era and technological landscape **[05.32]**.

**EMILY XIE**
Sketches and screen captures documenting the process of
*Off Script*, 07-26-2022 14:22:28
JavaScript, p5.js
Ethereum, 0x0a1bbd57033f57e7b6743621b79fcb9eb2ce3676, 10000000–10000099

05.25

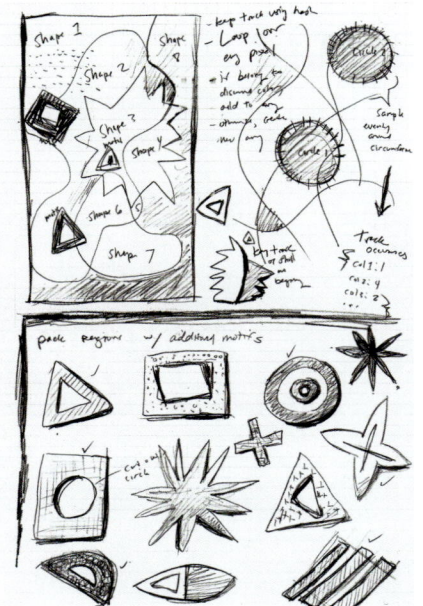

**05.25**
Hand-drawn concept sketches.

**05.26**
Example screenshot of the underlying set of shapes initially produced by the algorithm, along with some of the functions used. Specifically, these shapes correspond to *Off Script #84*.

**05.27**
Screenshot of the circle-packing algorithm and a portion of the code for it.

**05.28**
Example of a sheet of generative paper produced during runtime and some of the functions that are used to create it.

**05.29**
Under the hood, the algorithm produces textured shapes as if laying down cut-outs on a collage. These steps are not shown during the official rendering process.

05.26

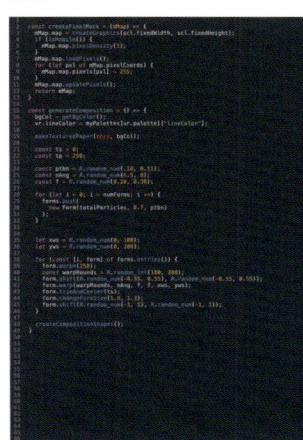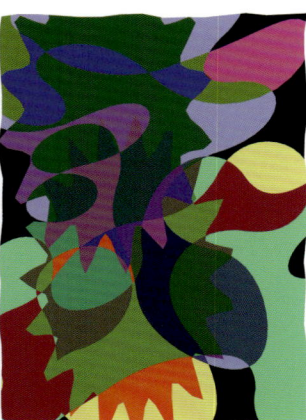

05.27

```
1
2 ▾ const packCircles = (packMask, numCircles, circles, mrl, mru, maxRadius,
      additionalCircles = []) => {
3    let packAtts = 0;
4    const maxCircleAttempts = 70000;
5    pd = packMask.width * 0.005;
6    bp = packMask.width * 0.004;
7
8 ▾  const isRegionInvalid = (circ) => {
9      let maskColorsDetected = [];
10     let drk = [];
11     let totalPoints = 20;
12     let inc = TWO_PI / totalPoints;
13 ▾   for (let i = 0; i < TWO_PI; i += inc) {
14       let x = circ.centerX + (cos(i) * circ.radius);
15       let y = circ.centerY + (sin(i) * circ.radius);
16       let hashedColor = packMask.get(x, y).join("");
17       let isDark = darknessMap[hashedColor];
18       drk.push(isDark);
19       if (!maskSkipMap[hashedColor]) {
20         maskColorsDetected.push(hashedColor);
21       }
22     }
23     let uniqueMaskColors = [...new Set(maskColorsDetected)];
24     let percentageDark = drk.filter(x => x == true).length / 20;
25     return uniqueMaskColors.length > 3 || percentageDark > .20;
26   }
27
28 ▾  const isCollidingOthers = (crc, oc, pd) => {
29 ▾    for (let other of oc) {
30 ▾      let euclidianDist = Math.sqrt(
31           Math.pow((crc.centerX - other.centerX), 2) +
32           Math.pow((crc.centerY - other.centerY), 2)
33         );
34         if (euclidianDist < crc.radius + other.radius + pd) {
35           return true;
36         }
37     }
38   }
39
40 ▾  while (circles.length < numCircles) {
41     packAtts++;
42     let percentX = R.random_dec();
43     let percentY = R.random_dec();
44
45     if (circles.length < 2 && packAtts < 20000) {
46       minRadius = mru;
47     } else {
48       minRadius = mrl;
49     }
50
51     let radiusMult = R.random_num(minRadius, maxRadius);
52
53     let circle = new Circ(
54       packMask.width * percentX,
55       packMask.height * percentY,
56       packMask.width * radiusMult
57     );
58
59     let invalidCirc = false;
60
61     if (circle.centerX - circle.radius < 0 + bp || circle.centerX + circle.
        radius > packMask.width - bp || circle.centerY - circle.radius < 0 + bp ||
        circle.centerY + circle.radius > packMask.height - bp) {
62       invalidCirc = true;
63     }
64
```

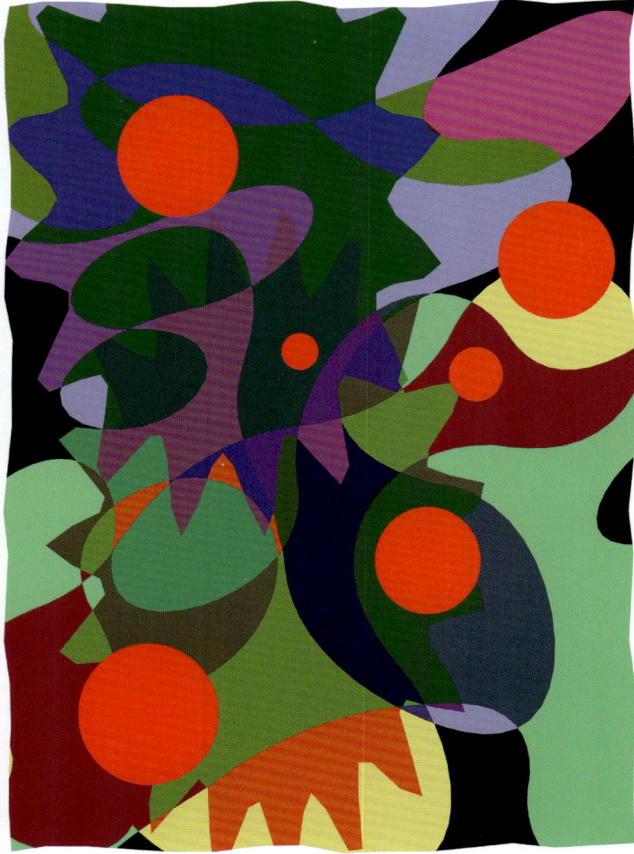

```
1
2 ▾ const txtr = (gt, numCols = 1300, numRows = 1700, opacity=4) => {
3       gt.angleMode(DEGREES);
4       gt.strokeWeight(gt.width * 0.0008);
5       gt.stroke(255, opacity);
6
7       const ySpacing = gt.height / numRows;
8       const xSpacing = gt.width / numCols;
9
10
11 ▾    for (let i = 0; i < numCols; i += 10) {
12 ▾      for (let j = 0; j < numRows; j += 10) {
13         gt.push();
14         gt.translate(i * xSpacing, j * ySpacing);
15         gt.rotate(R.random_int(0, 360));
16         drawTxtr(gt.width, gt.height);
17         gt.pop();
18       }
19     }
20   }
21
22
23 ▾ const grn = (gt, thrs, drk = 100, rndx = 0, rndy = 0) => {
24     let tbg = createGraphics(1800, 2400);
25
26     tbg.pixelDensity(1);
27     tbg.loadPixels();
28
29     let nPixels = tbg.pixels;
30     const noiseFreq = 5;
31
32 ▾  for (let x = 0; x < tbg.width; x++) {
33 ▾    for (let y = 0; y < tbg.height; y++) {
34
35         idx = (x + y * tbg.width) * 4;
36         let xMapped = map(x, 0, tbg.width, 0, 1);
37         let yMapped = map(y, 0, tbg.height, 0, 1);
38
39 ▾       let nRes = noise(
40           (xMapped * noiseFreq) + rndx,
41           (yMapped * noiseFreq) + rndy
42         );
43
44         if (R.random_bool(thrs)) {
45           setDarkness(nPixels, idx, nRes, drk);
46         }
47       }
48     }
49     tbg.updatePixels();
50     gt.image(tbg, 0, 0, gt.width, gt.height);
51   }
52
53
```

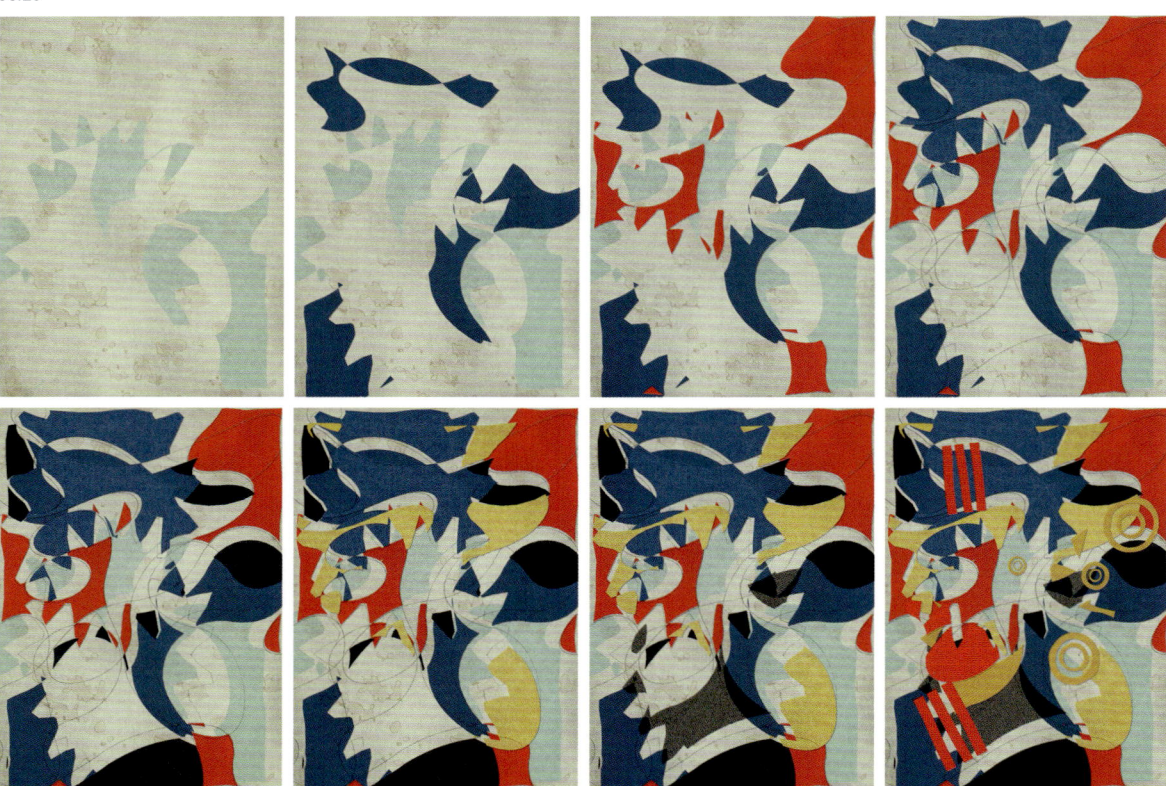

Erick Calderon
*Chromie Squiggle #0*, 11-27-2020 16:12:02
p5.js (3js)
Ethereum, 0x059edd72cd353df5106d2b9cc5ab83a52287ac3a, 0–9999

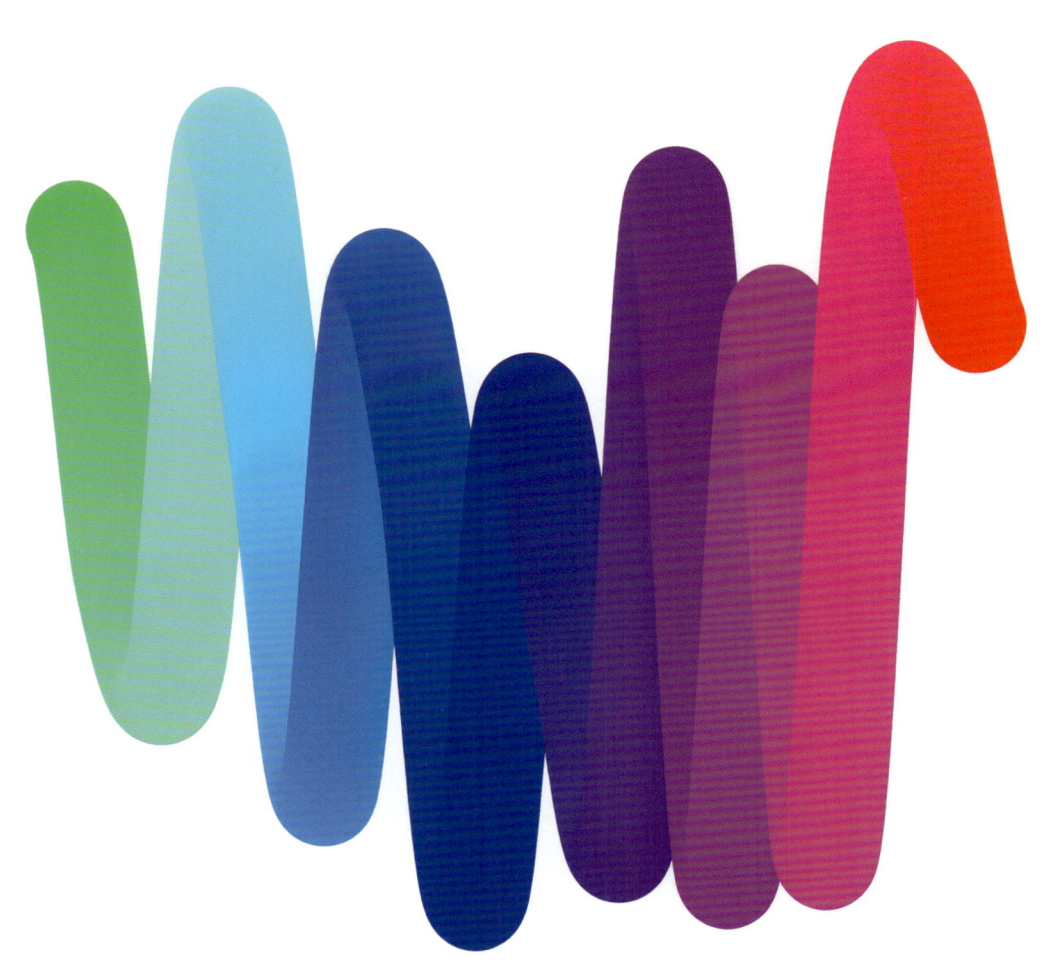

# ERICK CALDERON ON
## CHROMIE SQUIGGLE

*...most importantly, they suggest that one can make engaging generative art throughout the process of learning to code, and the only barrier to entry is enthusiasm.*

Since the age of 11 I have played with code, engineering, pattern, and color in various capacities that converged into a deep interest for generative art and circuitously into outputs of *Chromie Squiggles*. Growing up in Mexico City, color has always been important to my family's sensibility. Gradients, patterns, and symmetry were central concerns in my family's tiling business that I grew up around and later worked in. Although I wasn't aware of it at the time, it is interesting that the earliest generative art systems came from tiling: from Islamic *girih* tiling and Roman mosaics through to the French Truchet tile of the 17th century. The idea and importance of the tile is crucial to the curatorial experience on both Art Blocks and NFT collections more generally. *Chromie Squiggles*, which was developed over the course of several years, is also a history of my learning Three.js, transitioning my "generative" mindset from physical tiling to immaterial code.

The process of developing the *Chromie Squiggle*, in form and concept, is inextricably bound to the process of launching Art Blocks as a platform for generative art from June 2017. Both were marked by exploration and iteration, and a fluid idea of what they might become. If I am honest, the project in its earliest stages began as much as a simple proof of concept as a proper artwork: I was experimenting with how to create an immersive generative experience for mapping projection onto three-dimensional surfaces **[05.34]** which came out of a history of creative development for concert visuals since 2011. The first versions in 2018, like those shown in acrylic frames below, were distributed free to clients, friends, and people who provided me valuable guidance and advice **[05.35]**. They were a means for me to help introduce new people to generative art, to get a temperature check on the process of onboarding people into the space — frankly, it was as much about getting people to open an Ethereum wallet as anything else! — and to express gratitude. They are decidedly more raw and stringy in output, but they have the basic coding DNA of the final version including only variant — the hyper rainbow as the squiggle form is made up of thousands of circles and cycles through slices of the color spectrum **[05.36]**. As my ideas of what Art Blocks could be developed, so did the Squiggle, and with the incredible reception and community support the project received, I came around to think of it as an art project in its own right.

So much of creative coding is learning how to use happy accidents productively, and my experimentation with line weight, specifically, led me to discover the 'bold' characteristic, which I especially liked, as it really hit your retina with color **[05.38]**. To increase playfulness, variability, and make it a more cohesive generative project: the 'slinky', 'ribbed', and 'pipes' traits **[05.37]** were also unintended results of playing around over these two years of iteration. For example, I discovered the 'ribbed' trait by accidentally forgetting to change the circle size in two different places, causing the algorithm to draw two different sized circles, and one with a slinky effect which left gaps in the larger circles to reveal the smaller colorful circles in the middle. The 'pipes' variant was then an expansion of the slinky that came after discovering ribbed and being drawn to the layering of monochromatic circles over colorful ones **[05.39]**. It was only later, my brother, Daniel Calderon, helped me translate it into Processing for the first blockchain powered version I actually released in 2018.

In the end, the Squiggle became whatever it is today. I often think that my original thinking of it as the simplest demonstration for variability in generative art was perhaps the very thing that struck a chord with so many people. They speak a language that everyone has drawn at some point in their lives: the scribble, the doodle, the squiggle. They are approachable, unintimidating, and fun, they play with and celebrate bold RGB color and don't take themselves too seriously. Perhaps most importantly, they suggest that one can make engaging generative art throughout the process of learning to code, and the only barrier to entry is enthusiasm.

**ERICK CALDERON**
Sketches and screen captures documenting the process of
*Chromie Squiggle*, 11-27-2020 16:12:02
p5.js (3js)
Ethereum, 0x059edd72cd353df5106d2b9cc5ab83a52287ac3a, 0–9999

05.34

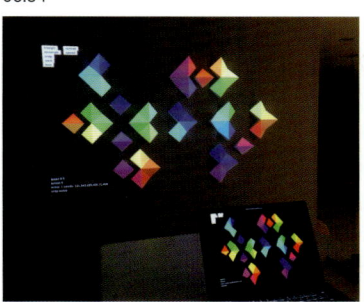

05.35

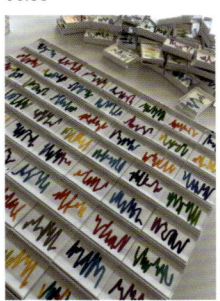

**05.34**
Experiments with IRL immersive generative installations.

**05.35**
Various framed examples of the first iteration of *Chromie Squiggle*, created under the original 2018 version of the Art Blocks framework and given away as gifts.

**05.36**
The basic form of a *Chromie Squiggle*, detailing how circles are the base form for all the various composition of the line drawing.

**05.37**
Rarity traits, including the hypertraits, of *Chromie Squiggles*.

**05.38**
This line of code is what makes this *Squiggle* a 'bold'. When the 'bold' characteristic is met, the circles are bigger.

**05.39**
What my code looked like when I was iterating line weight of the 2018 version in 3js. The file name "Squiggly_laNova" includes the name of the ceramic tile company I had before Art Blocks.

05.36

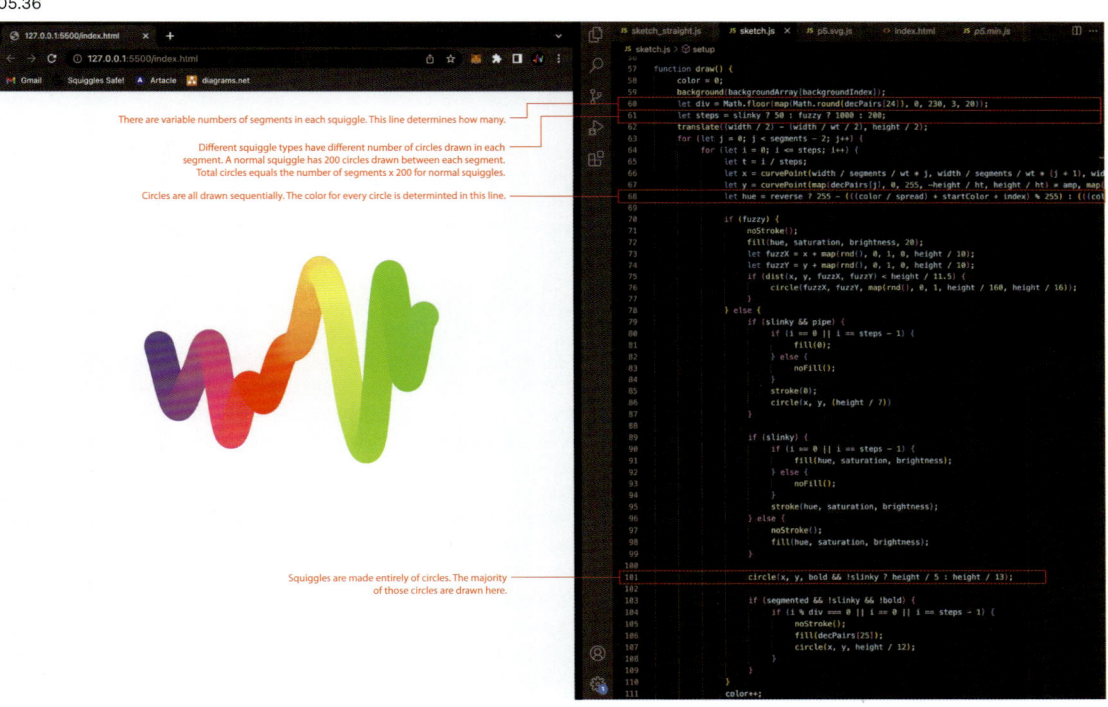

05.37

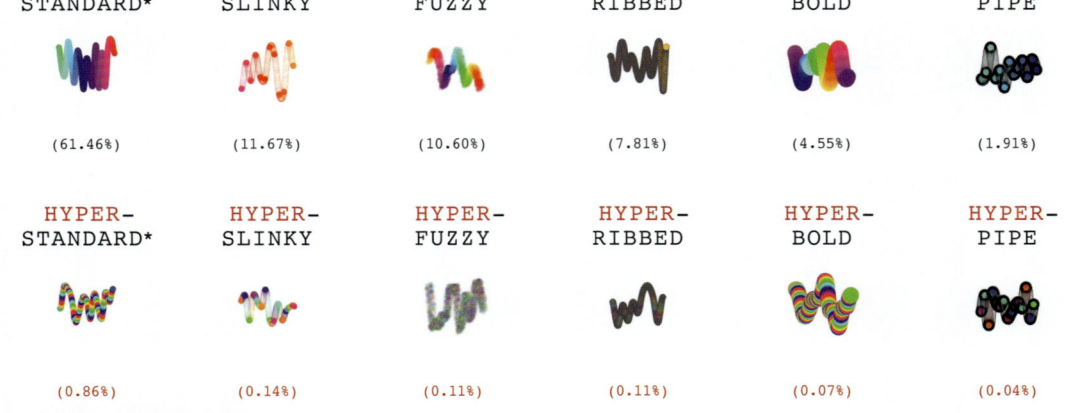

| STANDARD* | SLINKY | FUZZY | RIBBED | BOLD | PIPE |
|---|---|---|---|---|---|
| (61.46%) | (11.67%) | (10.60%) | (7.81%) | (4.55%) | (1.91%) |
| HYPER–STANDARD* | HYPER–SLINKY | HYPER–FUZZY | HYPER–RIBBED | HYPER–BOLD | HYPER–PIPE |
| (0.86%) | (0.14%) | (0.11%) | (0.11%) | (0.07%) | (0.04%) |

*FULL SPECTRUM STANDARD (0.44%) AND PREFECT SPECTRUM STANDARD (0.22%) ARE TWO RARE VERSIONS OF THE STANDARD SQUIGGLE.

05.38

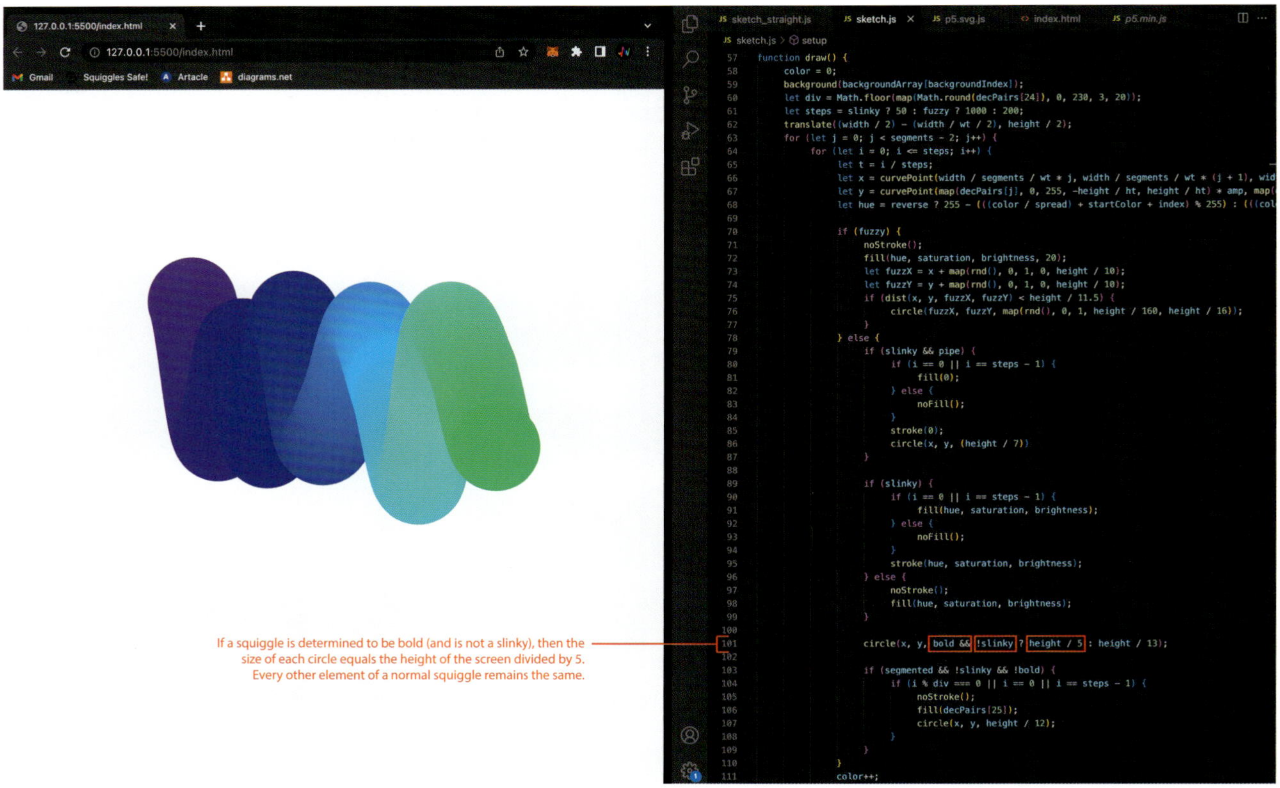

```
57  function draw() {
58      color = 0;
59      background(backgroundArray[backgroundIndex]);
60      let div = Math.floor(map(Math.round(decPairs[24]), 0, 230, 3, 20));
61      let steps = slinky ? 50 : fuzzy ? 1000 : 200;
62      translate((width / 2) - (width / wt / 2), height / 2);
63      for (let j = 0; j < segments - 2; j++) {
64          for (let i = 0; i <= steps; i++) {
65              let t = i / steps;
66              let x = curvePoint(width / segments / wt * j, width / segments / wt * (j + 1), wid
67              let y = curvePoint(map(decPairs[j], 0, 255, -height / ht, height / ht) + amp, map(
68              let hue = reverse ? 255 - (((color / spread) + startColor + index) % 255) : (((col
69
70              if (fuzzy) {
71                  noStroke();
72                  fill(hue, saturation, brightness, 20);
73                  let fuzzX = x + map(rnd(), 0, 1, 0, height / 10);
74                  let fuzzY = y + map(rnd(), 0, 1, 0, height / 10);
75                  if (dist(x, y, fuzzX, fuzzY) < height / 11.5) {
76                      circle(fuzzX, fuzzY, map(rnd(), 0, 1, height / 160, height / 16));
77                  }
78              } else {
79                  if (slinky && pipe) {
80                      if (i == 0 || i == steps - 1) {
81                          fill(0);
82                      } else {
83                          noFill();
84                      }
85                      stroke(0);
86                      circle(x, y, (height / 7))
87                  }
88
89                  if (slinky) {
90                      if (i == 0 || i == steps - 1) {
91                          fill(hue, saturation, brightness);
92                      } else {
93                          noFill();
94                      }
95                      stroke(hue, saturation, brightness);
96                  } else {
97                      noStroke();
98                      fill(hue, saturation, brightness);
99                  }
100
101                  circle(x, y, bold && !slinky ? height / 5 : height / 13);
102
103                  if (segmented && !slinky && !bold) {
104                      if (i % div === 0 || i == 0 || i == steps - 1) {
105                          noStroke();
106                          fill(decPairs[25]);
107                          circle(x, y, height / 12);
108                      }
109                  }
110              }
111          color++;
```

If a squiggle is determined to be bold (and is not a slinky), then the size of each circle equals the height of the screen divided by 5. Every other element of a normal squiggle remains the same.

05.39

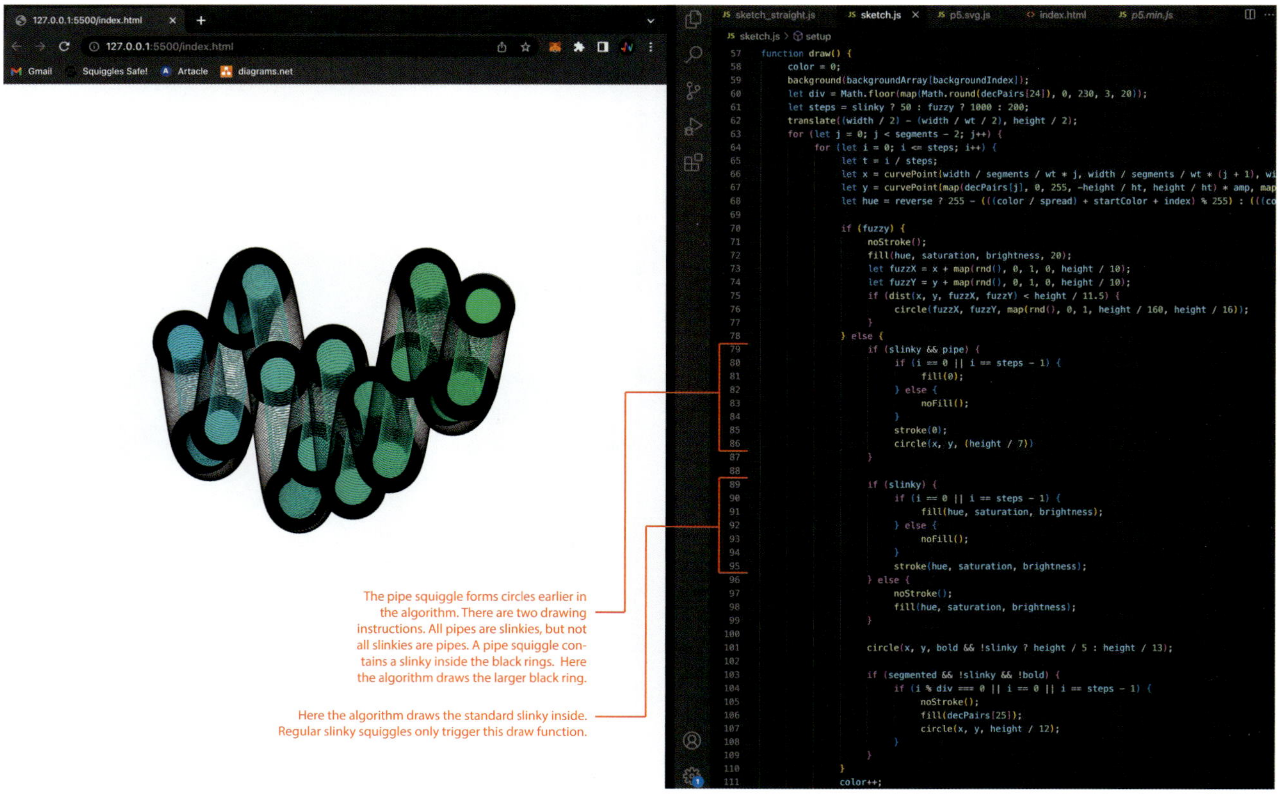

```
57  function draw() {
58      color = 0;
59      background(backgroundArray[backgroundIndex]);
60      let div = Math.floor(map(Math.round(decPairs[24]), 0, 230, 3, 20));
61      let steps = slinky ? 50 : fuzzy ? 1000 : 200;
62      translate((width / 2) - (width / wt / 2), height / 2);
63      for (let j = 0; j < segments - 2; j++) {
64          for (let i = 0; i <= steps; i++) {
65              let t = i / steps;
66              let x = curvePoint(width / segments / wt * j, width / segments / wt * (j + 1), wi
67              let y = curvePoint(map(decPairs[j], 0, 255, -height / ht, height / ht) + amp, map
68              let hue = reverse ? 255 - (((color / spread) + startColor + index) % 255) : (((co
69
70              if (fuzzy) {
71                  noStroke();
72                  fill(hue, saturation, brightness, 20);
73                  let fuzzX = x + map(rnd(), 0, 1, 0, height / 10);
74                  let fuzzY = y + map(rnd(), 0, 1, 0, height / 10);
75                  if (dist(x, y, fuzzX, fuzzY) < height / 11.5) {
76                      circle(fuzzX, fuzzY, map(rnd(), 0, 1, height / 160, height / 16));
77                  }
78              } else {
79                  if (slinky && pipe) {
80                      if (i == 0 || i == steps - 1) {
81                          fill(0);
82                      } else {
83                          noFill();
84                      }
85                      stroke(0);
86                      circle(x, y, (height / 7))
87                  }
88
89                  if (slinky) {
90                      if (i == 0 || i == steps - 1) {
91                          fill(hue, saturation, brightness);
92                      } else {
93                          noFill();
94                      }
95                      stroke(hue, saturation, brightness);
96                  } else {
97                      noStroke();
98                      fill(hue, saturation, brightness);
99                  }
100
101                  circle(x, y, bold && !slinky ? height / 5 : height / 13);
102
103                  if (segmented && !slinky && !bold) {
104                      if (i % div === 0 || i == 0 || i == steps - 1) {
105                          noStroke();
106                          fill(decPairs[25]);
107                          circle(x, y, height / 12);
108                      }
109                  }
110              }
111          color++;
```

The pipe squiggle forms circles earlier in the algorithm. There are two drawing instructions. All pipes are slinkies, but not all slinkies are pipes. A pipe squiggle contains a slinky inside the black rings. Here the algorithm draws the larger black ring.

Here the algorithm draws the standard slinky inside. Regular slinky squiggles only trigger this draw function.

Harm van den Dorpel
*Mutant Garden Seeder — Coralena*, 06-17-2021 12:57:51
Solidity, Typescript, based around Cartesian Genetic Programming
Ethereum, 0x20C70BDFCc398C1f06bA81730c8B52ACE3af7cc3, 12652071

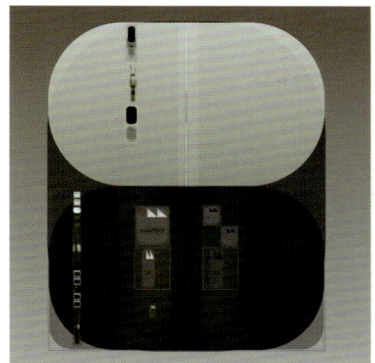 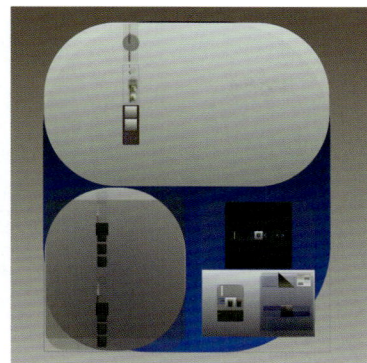 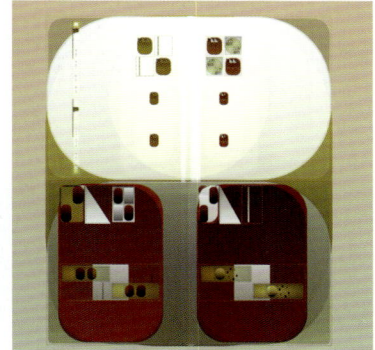
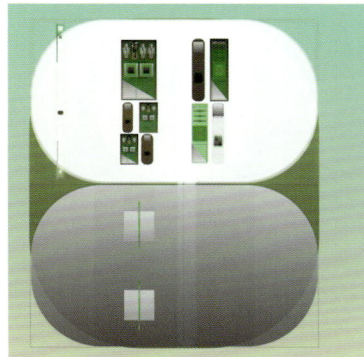 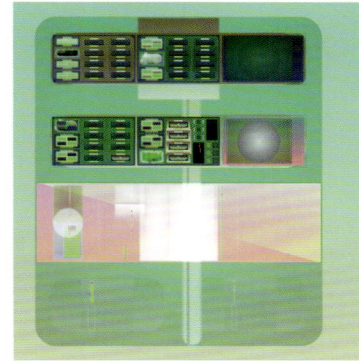 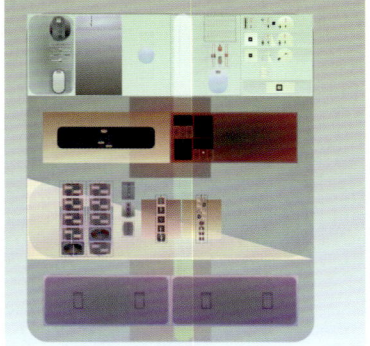
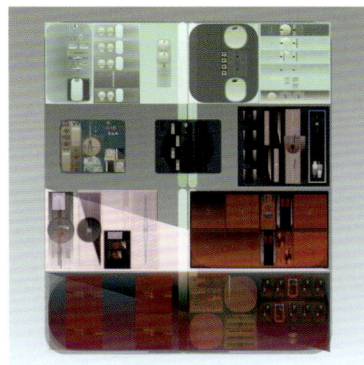 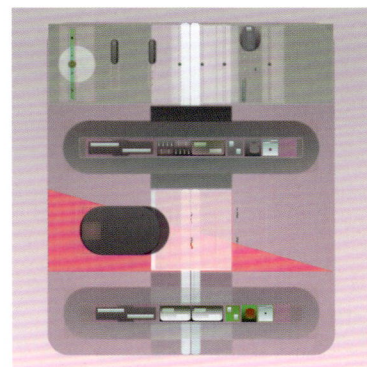 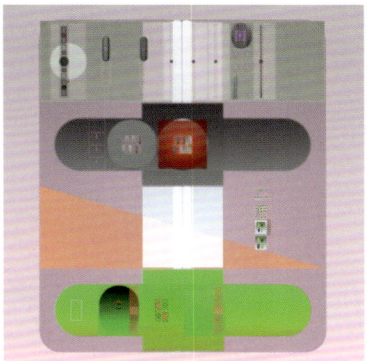
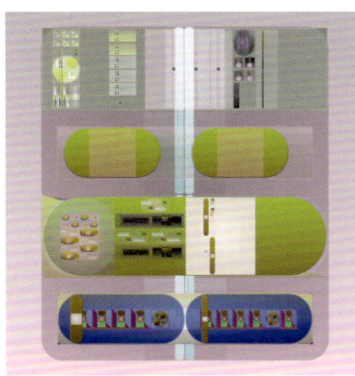 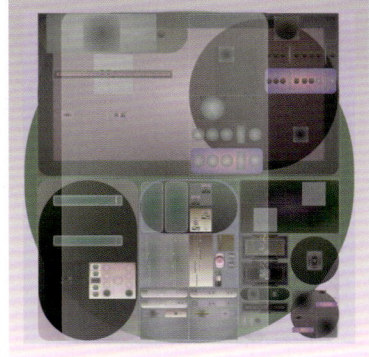 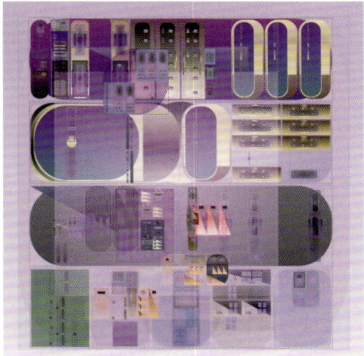

HARM VAN DEN
DORPEL ON
**MUTANT GARDEN
SEEDER**

*A blockchain is literally a
chain in time [...]. With
each block, the artwork has
a certain probability that
it might mutate [...]. Some
mutate every day. Some
once a year [...].*

With *Mutant Garden Seeder* I'm responding to the idea of immutability as a premise of crypto. In crypto discourse the great "achievement" is that, with blockchain, the digital artwork can finally be commodified and its content is stable — unlike digital assets historically, which have always been extremely fluid depending on infrastructure. Once blockchain could fix a value to a digital artwork, a market emerged. All of this is quite boring to me, because what appealed to me about digital art was its inherent mutability. *Mutant Garden* is a response to the dissatisfaction I felt about the ways blockchain and crypto discourse limited a certain sense of artistic possibility. Formally, the work looks at the history of abstraction and color theory **[05.41, 05.42, 05.43]**, and evolves out of an off-chain project *Mutant Garden* that I have been working on since 2019 **[05.44, 05.45, 05.46]**.

To create the work I used an algorithm called Cartesian Genetic Programming (CGP) which allows you to structure a computer program in such a way that you can mutate the program **[05.47, 05.48]**. The great thing about this algorithm is that while you can encode mutations, you can be sure that the program will not get stuck in infinite loops. It solves the halting problem. The algorithmic history of CGP is a precursor to neural networks, which are now everywhere. When people talk about AI art today they think of generative adversarial networks (GANs). I've never really used them. CGP is easier to visualize because it's much simpler. Easier in the sense that it has fewer nodes. The algorithm is created for solving optimization problems. It's not really clear why any given solution is more optimal though. You optimize with CGP by generating many possible solutions and measuring which performs best. Then, you mutate the best performing one into the variation and repeat. Another advantage of CGP that it is is not based on genetic recombination. Thus, my mutants can procreate by themselves. They don't need a partner to introduce variation.

The work is custom programmed, with the vast majority of the codebase written in Typescript. I have added three extracts of the codebase in order to showcase some important areas that govern the work's final outputs. These include all the different types of drawing instruments that a CGP node can contain from variation of margin, to blending, blur. These traits give the work its aesthetic feel and variation **[05.49]**. The second snippet of code shows how the CGP node can mutate — whether by changing the palette or other more complex functions that govern composition **[05.50]**. The final section of code shows the how the script interacts with the blockchain to calculate the possible mutations based on the number of blocks elapsed **[05.51]**. Below this you will see how the CGP visualizer or tracer on the right of the screen works to build the artwork, which is viewable on the projects website to give the audience an insight into the algorithm behind this process **[05.52]**.

*Mutant Garden Seeder* is an NFT with immutable ownership, provenance in a shared ledger, so some aspects of the artwork are fixed, but its most important aspect is that the work itself changes over time, synchronized to changes within Ethereum's main blockchain. A blockchain is literally a chain in time: consecutive lists of blocks, and each block contains a number, which is not known in advance. Once that number has been decided, however, it is fixed and immutable. The number, being both random and unchangeable, makes it useful as an input parameter in the mutations of my artwork. With each block, the artwork has a certain probability that it might mutate **[05.53]**. It mutates based on the content of that block. Some mutate every day. Some once a year, so it offers a visually dynamic critique of blockchain marketing mechanisms and rhetoric. The value of non-fungible tokens depends on their appearance, their current state. A price tag is assigned for something thought to be stable. In this work, the NFTs' appearance changes over time. Someone might buy an image that is very minimal with a low price tag, but it might change to become more elaborate, or lush, or more complicated, and it consequently gains in price. Or vice versa.

*Mutant Garden* and *Mutant Garden Seeder* mark a kind of turning point for my work. Where previously I've regarded the software produced to be the artwork, with the potential the algorithm of *Mutant Garden* has shown me for making distinct works I've come to value the output of the process as interesting artistically as the software that produces it.

## HARM VAN DEN DORPEL

Sketches and screen captures documenting the process of
*Mutant Garden Seeder — Coralena*, 06-17-2021 12:57:51
Solidity, Typescript, based around Cartesian Genetic Programming
Ethereum, 0x20C70BDFCc398C1f06bA81730c8B52ACE3af7cc3, 12652071

**05.41**

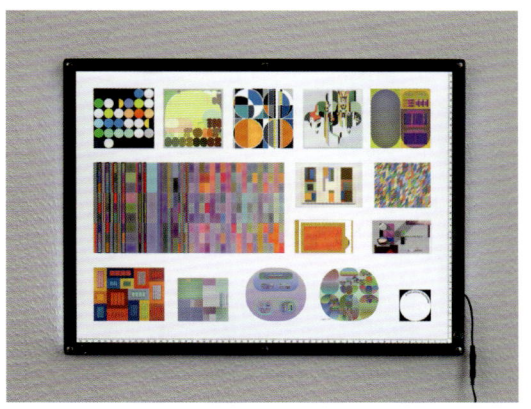

**05.42**

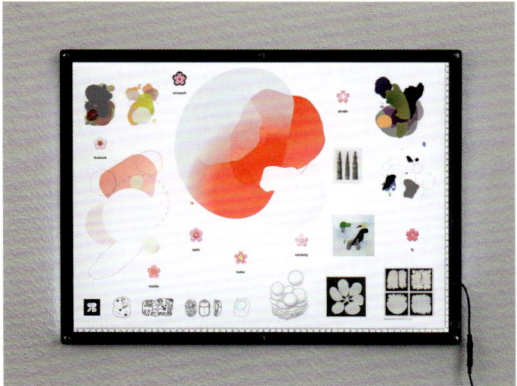

**05.43**

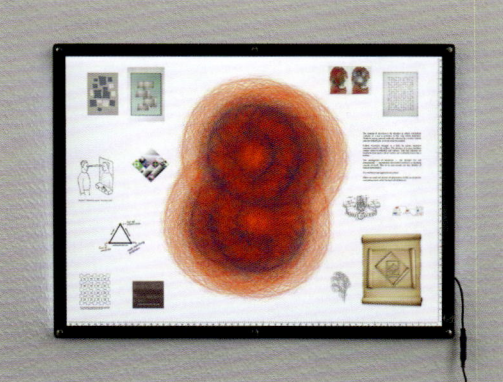

**05.41, 05.42, 05.43**
Research pages that detail some of
the art-historical and visual reference
points for *Mutant Garden*.

**05.44, 05.45, 05.46**
Early wireframe prototypes for
*Mutant Garden* (2019).

**05.47, 05.48**
Excerpts from Julian F. Miller &
Peter Thomson's Cartesian Genetic
Programming, European Conference
on Genetic Programming EuroGP
2000: Genetic Programming, 121–132.

**05.49**
All the different drawing instructions
a CGP node can contain.

**05.50**
The five different ways a CGP node
can mutate, respectively: change
command, change destination
jump node, change variable pointer,
change actual value in working
memory, change colour in working
palette.

**05.51**
The loop over all new blocks to
calculate potential mutations. This
runs infinitely by a server daemon,
or by the standalone desktop
application.

**05.52**
The tracer in action showing how
the CGP algorithm is mutating in
real time.

**05.53**
*Mutant Garden Seeder* website
showing the mutation state,
frequency, and block height of each
NFT as it changes over time.

**05.44**

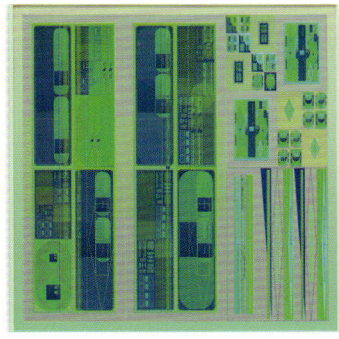

**05.45**

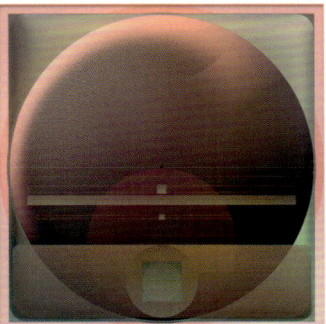

**05.46**

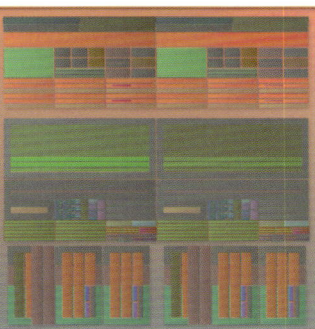

**05.47**

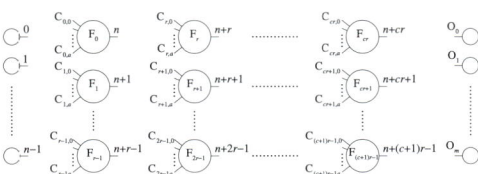

**Fig. 2.1** General form of CGP. It is a grid of nodes whose functions are chosen from a set of primitive functions. The grid has $n_c$ columns and $n_r$ rows. The number of program inputs is $n_i$ and the number of program outputs is $n_o$. Each node is assumed to take as many inputs as the maximum function arity $a$. Every data input and node output is labeled consecutively (starting at 0), which gives it a unique data address which specifies where the input data or node output value can be accessed (shown in the figure on the outputs of inputs and nodes).

**05.48**

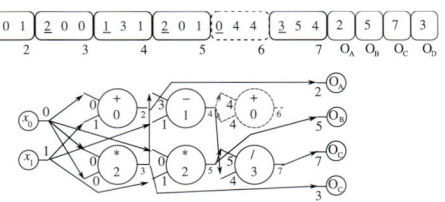

**Fig. 2.3** A CGP genotype and corresponding schematic phenotype for a set of four mathematical equations. The underlined genes in the genotype encode the function of each node. The function look-up table is add (0), subtract (1), multiply (2) and divide (3). The addresses are shown underneath each program input and node in the genotype and phenotype. The inactive areas of the genotype and phenotype are shown in grey dashes (node 6).

05.49

```
export const availableCommands: List = [
  Commands.AB,
  Commands.FOR,
  Commands.FILL,
  Commands.SPLIT,
  Commands.SHIFT,
  Commands.CROOK,
  Commands.MARGIN,
  Commands.STROKE,
  Commands.SWITCH,
  Commands.SQUARE,
  Commands.WINDOW,
  Commands.CIRCLE,
  Commands.LINES,
  Commands.MULTIPLY,
  Commands.TRIANGLE,
  Commands.SAME_PLACE,
  Commands.TERMINATE_WHEN,
  Commands.INCREMENT_REGISTER_1,
  Commands.INCREMENT_REGISTER_2,
  Commands.INCREMENT_REGISTER_3,
  Commands.DECREMENT_REGISTER_1,
  Commands.DECREMENT_REGISTER_2,
  Commands.DECREMENT_REGISTER_3,
  Commands.SET_BLENDING_MODE,
  Commands.STOP_BLENDING_MODE,
  Commands.SET_BLUR,
  Commands.STOP_BLUR
]
```

05.50

```
private mutateStep(rand: Rand): void {
  const commands = weightedCommands(rand)
  const { nodes, dimensions, memory, palette } = this
  const touchedNodes = this.getTouchedNodes()
  const useNodes = touchedNodes.length === 0 ? nodes : touchedNodes
  const nodeIndex = Math.round(rand.next() * (useNodes.length - 1))
  const node = useNodes[nodeIndex]
  const mutationKind = random(6, rand)

  switch (mutationKind) {
    case 0: case 1:
      node.c = sample(
        commands.filter((command) => command !== node.c),
        rand
      )
      break

    case 2: case 3: {
      const newNodeAddress = getRandomNodeIndex(
        dimensions,
        Math.floor(node.i / dimensions.layerSize),
        rand
      )

      node.n[random(2, rand)] = newNodeAddress
      break
    }

    case 4:
      node.v[random(2, rand)] = randomVariableAddress(dimensions, rand)
      break

    case 5: {
      const address = node.v[random(2, rand)]
      memory[address] = random(MEMORY_VALUE_MAX, rand)
      break
    }

    case 6: {
      const paletteIndex = random(palette.length - 1, rand)
      palette[paletteIndex][random(2, rand)] = random(dimensions.memory, rand)
      break
    }
```

05.51

```
for (let i = startScanIndex + 1; i <= currentBlockNumber; i++) {
  const block: Block = await getBlockCached(i, provider, db)
  const similar: boolean =
    hashesBinaryDigitsSimilar(birthHash, block.hash) >=
    similarDigitsForMutation

  if (!similar) continue

  console.log(
    birthBlockNumber,
    ` on block ${i}: hashes have ${similarDigitsForMutation} same starting digits`
  )

  const cachedMutation: boolean = storedMutationExists(birthBlockNumber, i)

  if (cachedMutation) {
    const cachedJSON: NetworkSerialized = getNetworkJSON(birthBlockNumber, i)!
    network = cloneNetwork(cachedJSON)
  } else {
    const parser = new Parser(network, new MockDrawer(), exportSize)
    parser.setAnimated(false)
    await parser.draw()
    network = cloneNetwork(network)
    network.mutate(1, new Rand(block.hash))
    await storeNetworkJSON(network, birthBlockNumber, i)
    await updateMutatedCountMongo(db, birthBlockNumber)
    await renderMutantImageAssets(birthBlockNumber, i)
    console.log(
      birthBlockNumber,
      'Nodes in use: ',
      network.getTouchedNodes().length
    )
  }
}
```

05.52

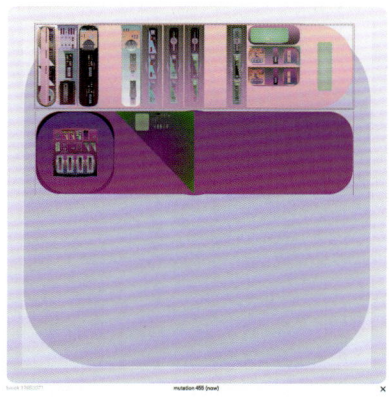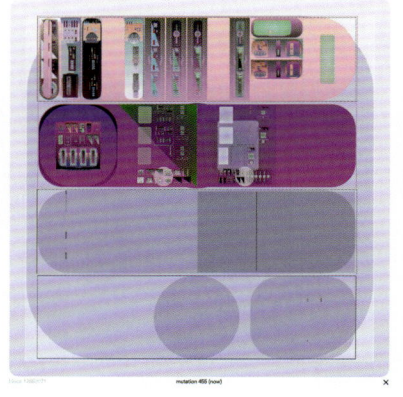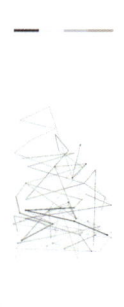

05.53

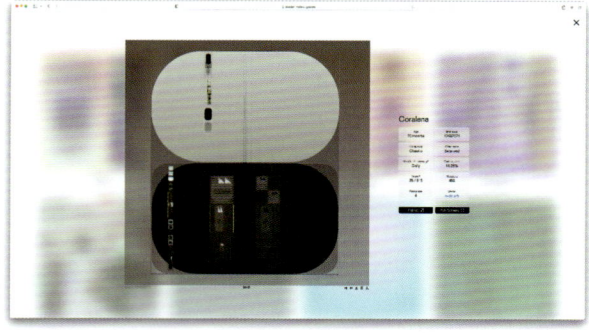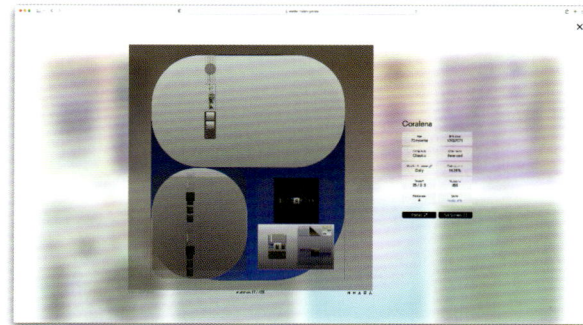

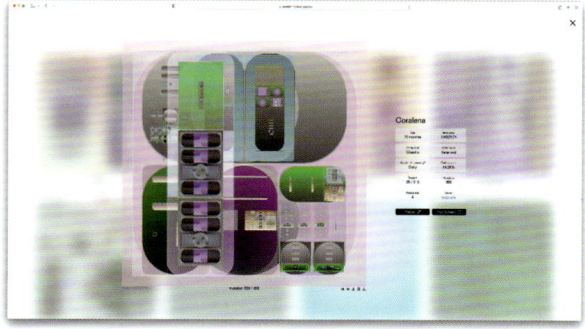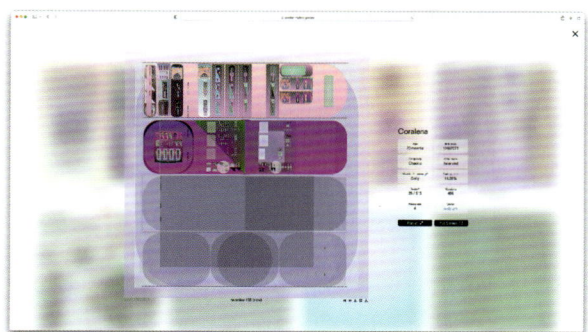

Ry David Bradley
*VEDIA SALONIUS*, 05-11-2022 18:03:53
Adobe Lightroom, Sony A7RIV, Adobe Photoshop, Procreate, Pixelmator
Ethereum, 0xb932a70A57673d89f4acfFBE830E8ed7f75Fb9e0, 34547

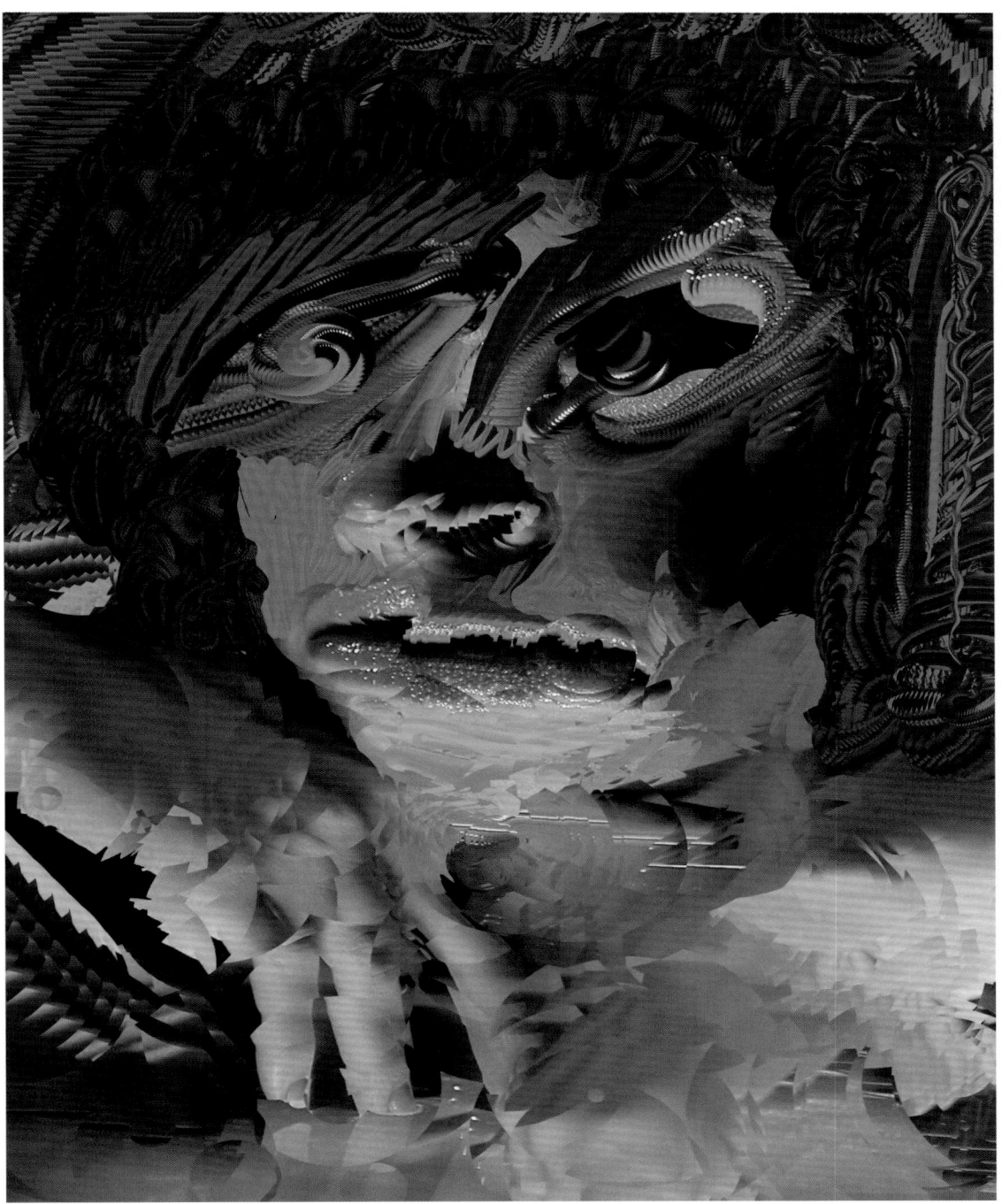

# RY DAVID BRADLEY ON
**VEDIA SALONIUS**

*One of the most important factors in my workflow was to create my own custom .abr brushes [...] it became clear to me that painting was as much a history of cultural concerns of the time, as it was of different technical and aesthetic approaches to brushwork.*

I began to draw digitally with MS Paint in the 1990s. The graphic creativity of the demoscene in computer games was my biggest inspiration. After high school I worked at the National Gallery of Victoria in Australia and fell in love with the gestural nature of painting in works by Helen Frankenthaler (1928–2011), Pierre Soulages (1919–2022), and Henri Matisse (1869–1954), among others. The software to paint in real time was still many years away, so I began using Adobe AfterEffects and Flash to try and pre-script these outcomes. Finally in 2004 a New Zealand–based software company called Ambient Design released ArtRage **[05.55]**, a program which for me was the first time painting tools felt as fast and native as paint itself.

The software allowed for the real-time blending of color like paint on a palette, meaning you could work from an image of an actual painting and augment it further. I made many digital paintings at a prolific rate from 2004 till 2008 and exhibited them as *giclée* prints on paper and silk. But the program still involved low resolutions for print and the use of an external Wacom tablet, an electronic pen that you draw with, so you are effectively painting on the tablet but looking at the screen — which never felt right to me. In 2009, touchscreens became more popular with the iPhone and the iPad, yet mobile software still lagged behind to make full-scale digital painting, primarily due to megapixel constraints. During this period, I was inspired by Andy Warhol and Laurence Gartel making digital paintings from the early 1980s, as well as Albert Oehlen's computer paintings of the 1990s. Around this time David Hockney began his iPhone paintings also.

One of the most important factors in my workflow back then was to create my own custom .abr brushes (an Adobe custom digital brush file that is now widely shared across all software) for all paintings I made **[05.56]**. After studying the history of painting through the late 19th and early 20th centuries, it became clear to me that painting was as much a history of cultural concerns of the time, as it was of different technical and aesthetic approaches to brushwork. In order to find space within this long lineage, one must develop their own contemporaneous response to brushwork. Today I work almost exclusively on an iPad Pro, for its M2 chip and mobile operating system can render more smoothly in real time. I still use those old .abr brushes I made plus many more I have made since.

The work *VEDIA SALONIUS* is one that employs a few different brushes I have created in order to attain different outcomes, some that play toward the more fractured facets of early Cubism (which were themselves affected by the many frames of animation cells in early cinema) to speak about time, versions, and displacement **[05.57]**. Another brush used on the face is more lyrical and allows for faster linework to render eyes and hair, — each brush containing highly repetitive steps within it **[05.58]**. Various stages in the painting of the image showcase how the portrait begins and how layers are used to build up the image, but also toggle them on or off in order to continually refine the works from multiple perspectives **[05.59, 05.60, 05.61, 05.62]**. Most of the color grading begins in Adobe Lightroom to balance exposure. The lighting effects I create with a combination of Photoshop and ArtStudio Pro. Any sampling for photography is shot with a Sony A7RIV. Brushwork is made with Procreate and Pixelmator. Final sharpening, smoothing, and grading is finished in Lightroom.

Alongside looking for the right software approach in 2006 I began to fabricate these digital paintings into physical objects. Many of the early experiments used various printing outcomes, to glass, aluminum, wood — and then with UV-printing process to many types of textile. Eventually I wanted to get away from printing and began to explore weaving and tapestry outcomes for their native digital characteristics in that they also use tiny units of color in a dot matrix like a screen. The tapestry I now fabricate to has a relative DPI (dot per inch) of around 88, so I am able to make 1:1 pixel translations from file into physical form.

The advent of NFTs meant that finally there was a way to value both the physical manifestation of the digital work and the screen-based genesis file that it was created from. Once AR wearables replace the tiny screens we now look at digital work through, I'm anticipating that the file-based paintings will finally achieve the spatial scale and detail of historic physical works.

**RY DAVID BRADLEY**
Sketches and screen captures documenting the process of
*VEDIA SALONIUS*, 05-11-2022 18:03:53
Adobe Lightroom, Sony A7RIV, Adobe Photoshop, Procreate, Pixelmator
Ethereum, 0xb932a70A57673d89f4acfFBE830E8ed7f75Fb9e0, 34547

05.55

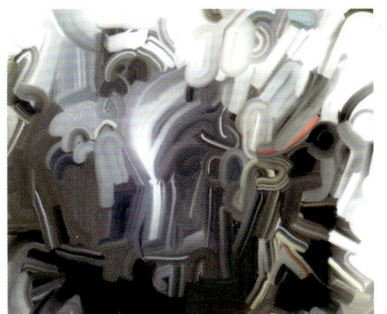

**05.55**
An early digital painting from 2008 made by pulling apart an existing image with a custom brush made with ArtRage.

**05.56**
A set of the .abr (Adobe Brush) custom painting brushes I made for Photoshop in 2012 with names to describe their aesthetic.

**05.57**
A closer view of the characteristics of a more recent brush I made in 2018 and its output as seen in the artwork *VEDIA SALONIUS*.

**05.58**
A selection of more recent brushes utilized in 2022 and a closer view of their effects on the creation of *VEDIA SALONIUS*.

**05.59, 05.60, 05.61, 05.62**
Layers of the scene building process and early lighting design in the construction of VEDIA SALONIUS.

05.56

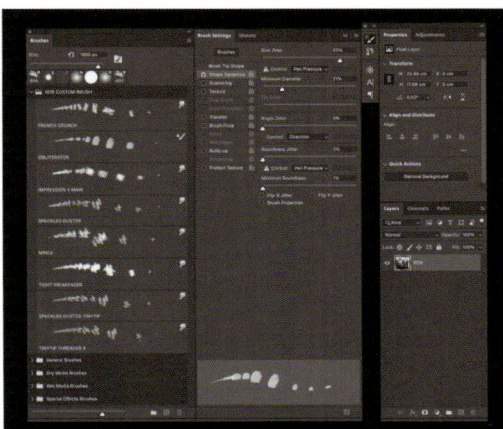

05.57

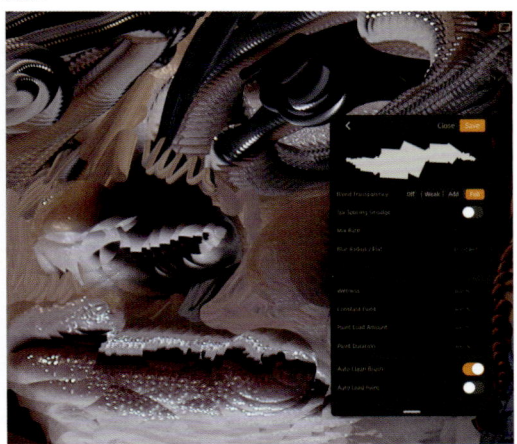

05.59

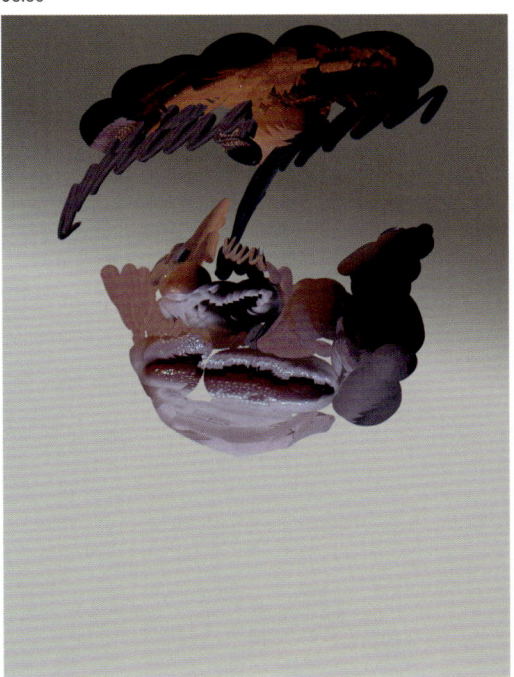

05.60

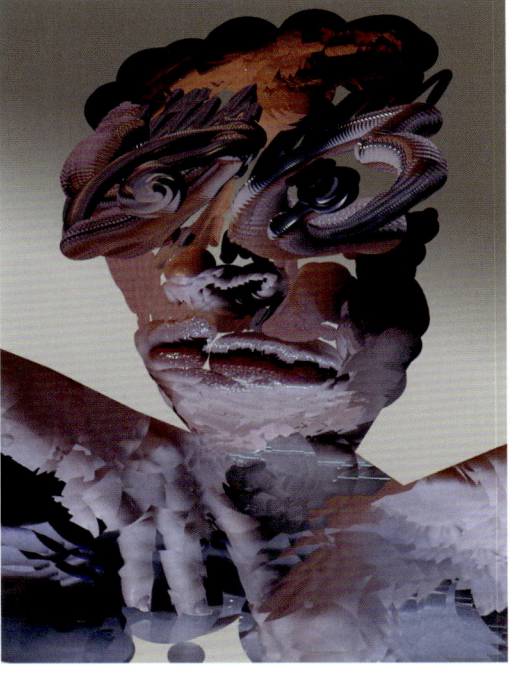

05.58

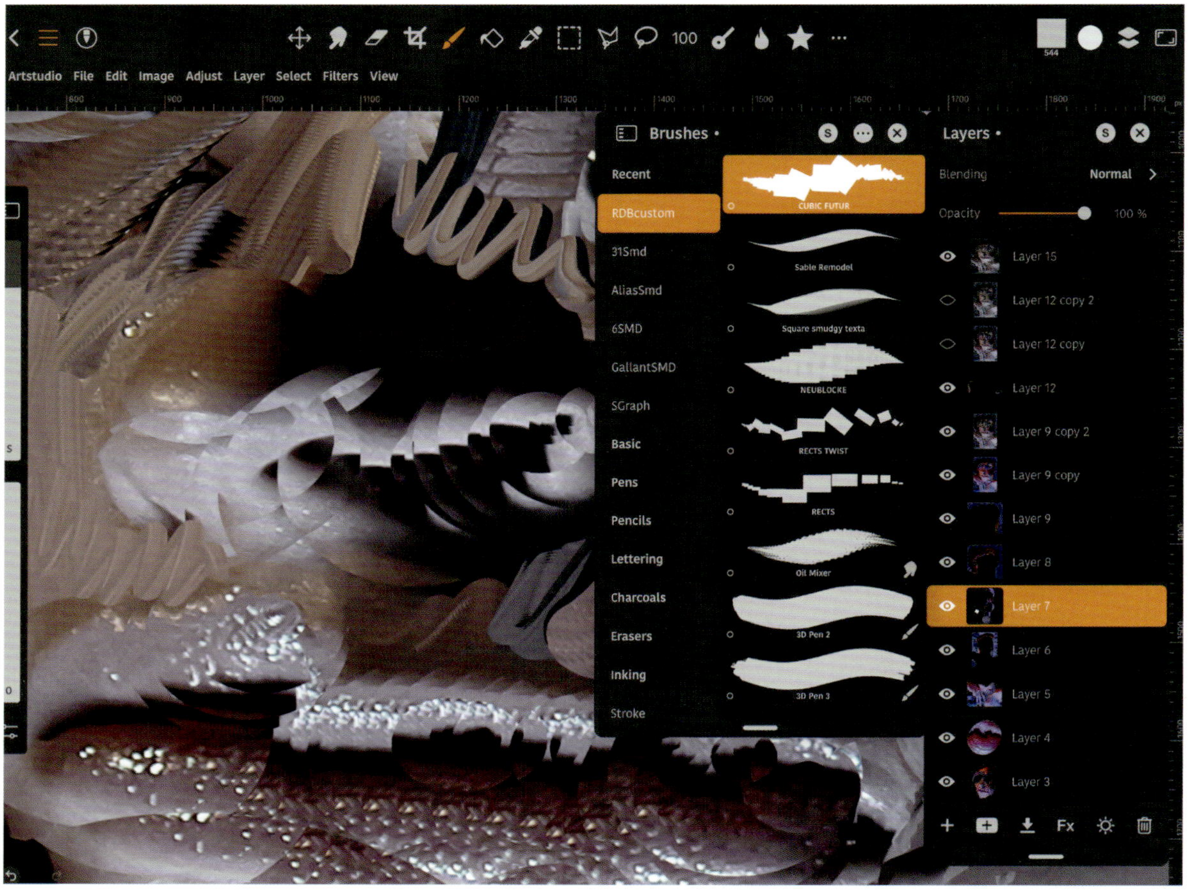

Artstudio   File   Edit   Image   Adjust   Layer   Select   Filters   View

100   544

**Brushes** ·   Ⓢ ⋯ ✕   **Layers** ·   Ⓢ ✕

Recent

RDBcustom   CUBIC FUTUR   Blending   Normal   ›

31Smd   Opacity   100 %

Sable Remodel   Layer 15

AliasSmd   Layer 12 copy 2

6SMD   Square smudgy texta   Layer 12 copy

GallantSMD   NEUBLOCKE   Layer 12

SGraph   Layer 9 copy 2

Basic   RECTS TWIST   Layer 9 copy

Pens   Layer 9

Pencils   RECTS   Layer 8

Lettering   Oil Mixer   Layer 7

Charcoals   Layer 6

Erasers   3D Pen 2   Layer 5

Inking   Layer 4

Stroke   3D Pen 3   Layer 3

+   ⊞   ⬇   Fx   ☼   🗑

05.61

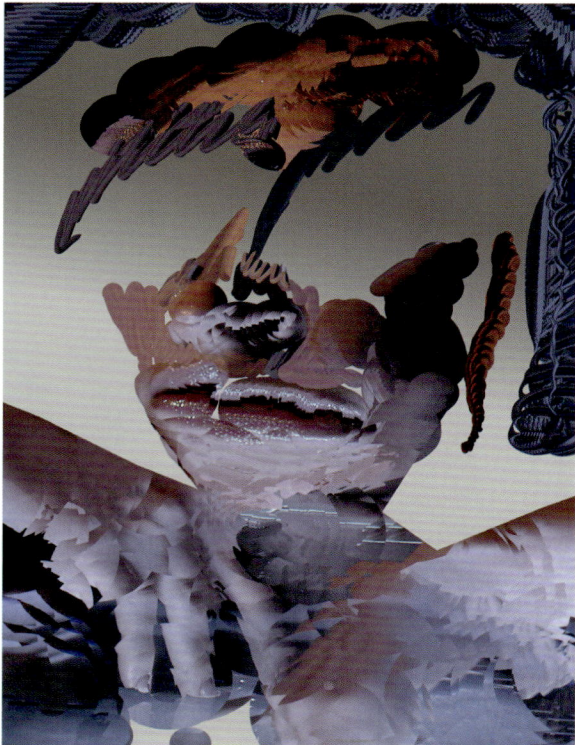

05.62

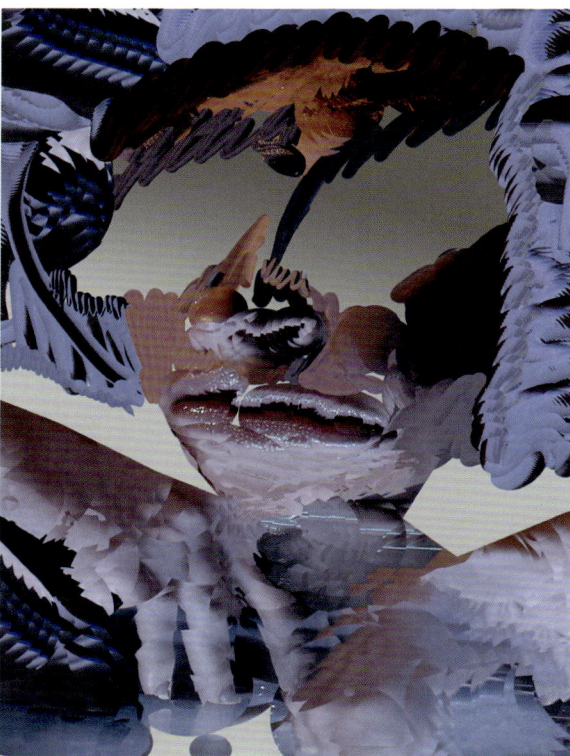

01 ►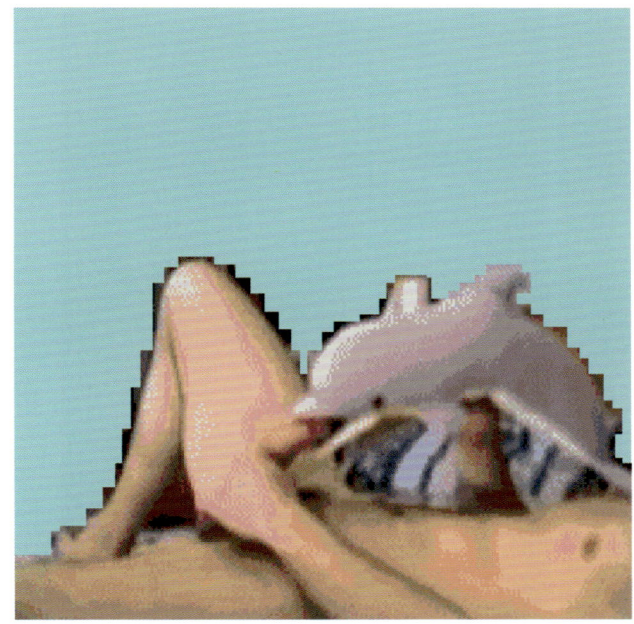

02 ►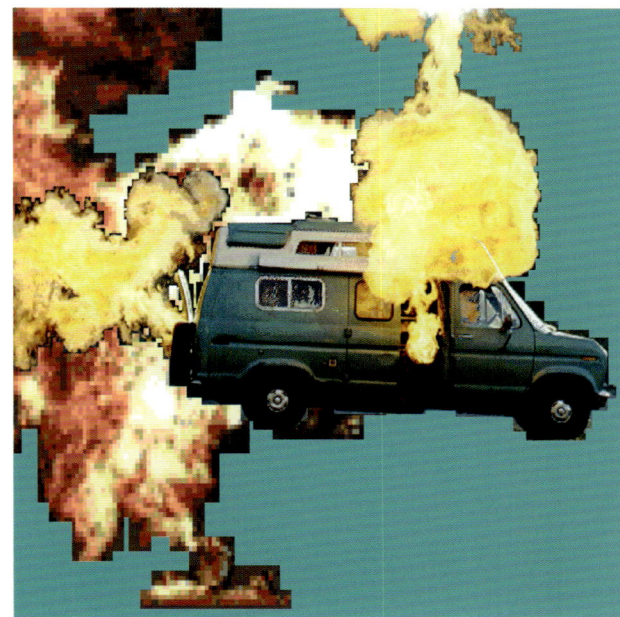

03 ►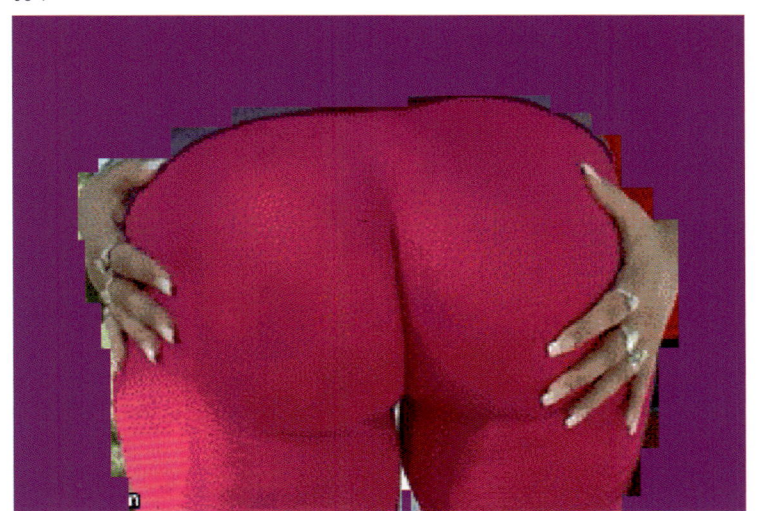

04 ►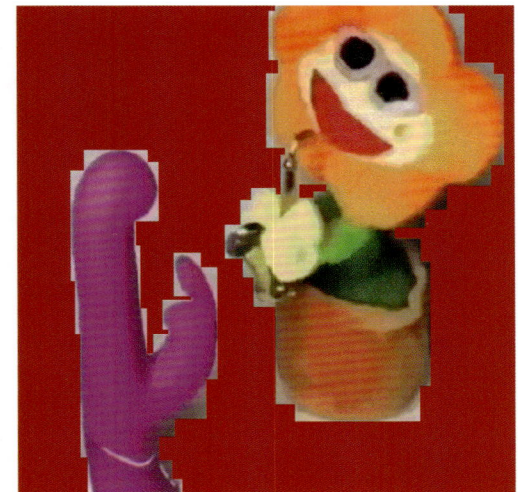

| # | TITLE | TIMESTAMP | MEDIUM | CHAIN | CONTRACT ADDRESS | TOKEN ID | EDITION SIZE |
|---|---|---|---|---|---|---|---|
| 01 | **Dolphin Date** | 09-19-2022 04:34:44 | GIF | XTZ | KT1Hkg5qeNhfwpKW4fXvq7HGZB9z2EnmCCA9 | 327539 | 20 |
| 02 | **I Don't Smoke Coach** | 05-08-2022 19:09:59 | GIF | XTZ | KT1Hkg5qeNhfwpKW4fXvq7HGZB9z2EnmCCA9 | 731380 | 20 |
| 03 | **Twin Cheeks** | 04-06-2021 10:12:13 | GIF | ETH | 0x5f713826a55fbf731ee9fe556917dc3f6c9b27d8 | 12 | 1/1 |
| 04 | **Whorey Potter and the Sorcerer's Dick** | 04-06-2021 10:03:29 | GIF | ETH | 0x5f713826a55fbf731ee9fe556917dc3f6c9b27d8 | 7 | 1/1 |
| 05 | **Wedding Day at Troldhaugen** | 11-20-2021 06:21:42 | GIF | ETH | 0x3b3ee1931dc30c1957379fac9aba94d1c48a5405 | 109340 | 1/1 |

05 ►

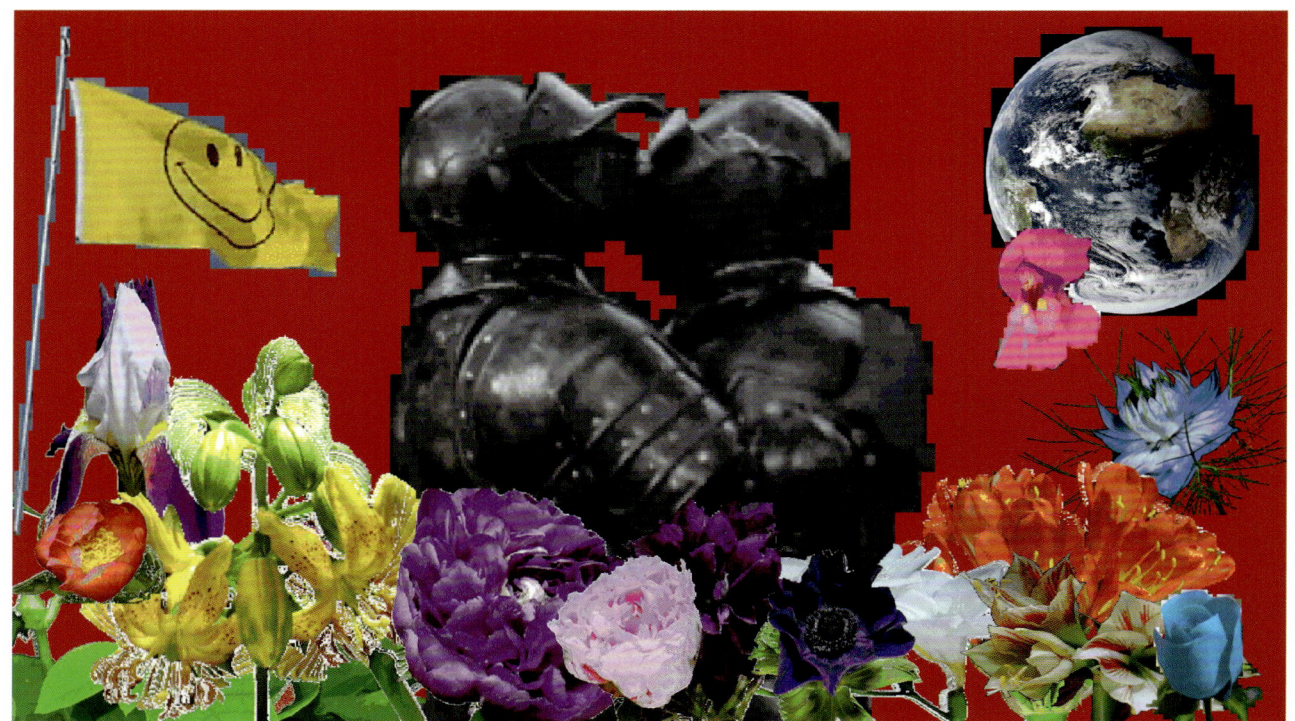

GIFs are one of the most powerful and immediate forms of visual communication in human culture. Mills, whose outputs are almost entirely in GIF form, knows this well: a simple looping animation conveys meaning in a way that transcends cultural boundaries and Web 2.0 cyber silos. Each one of Mills's works takes the very fundamentals of the GIF file — layered images meticulously chopped, screwed, and repurposed to be information impact vectors on the net — and elevates them to a state of compositional excellence that defies the content's, at times, unsavory subject matter. These works are like screen constellations — pixels ripped out and clustered together become points of light on screen compressed in ways that create a particular kind of phenomenological reaction in the viewer, stimulated by flashing resolutions and fluid forms. As each GIF flickers and fades only to spark to life once more a moment later, Mills deftly renders the formal realities of the file's own materiality.

It is only fitting that these works be married to NFTs: as each GIF reveals some deep immutable truth (that can seemingly only be conveyed via the internet), so too is a record encoded on the blockchain. *Wedding Day at Troldhaugen* (2021) is a characteristically charming but covertly venomous piece that employs Mills's unique sense of compositional humor — in just 120 frames. In the foreground, two knights in armor embrace in a field of flowers; each form is ripped from some unknowable context. But, it doesn't matter, because in the two dimensions of screen space Mills is author and master of her own story. Though sweet and, on the surface, somewhat romantic, the irreverent nod to queer affection and trite, platonic symbols that populate the composition in *Wedding Day at Troldhaugen* make it difficult to ignore the latent "screw you, dick bag patriarchy" current that runs throughout the artist's prolific practice.

**WADE WALLERSTEIN**
CO-DIRECTOR OF TRANSFER GALLERY

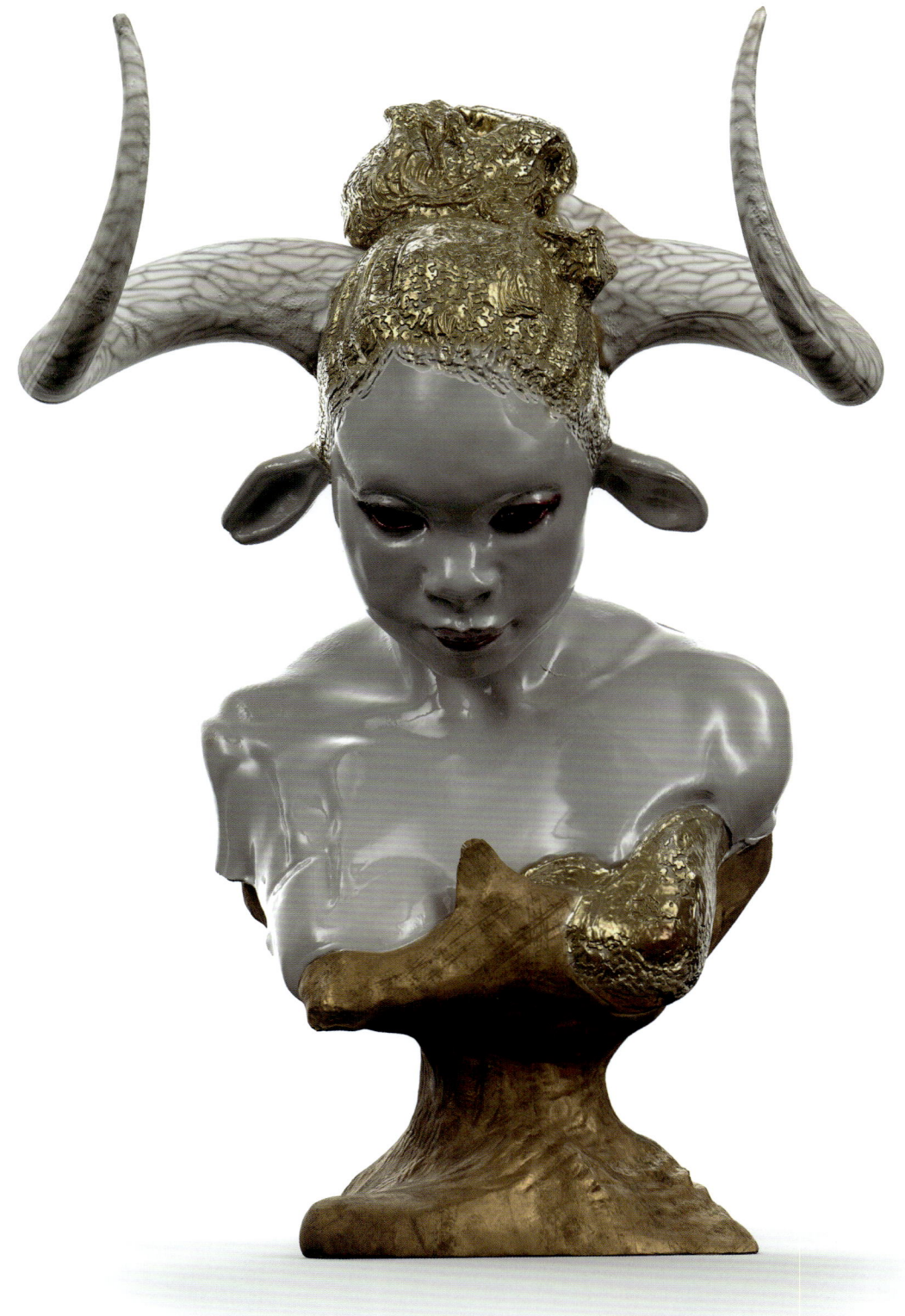

| # | TITLE | TIMESTAMP | MEDIUM | CHAIN | CONTRACT ADDRESS | TOKEN ID | EDITION SIZE |
|---|---|---|---|---|---|---|---|
| 01 | **Minoriea Bust v1-dv2 (Sovereign)** | 05-26-2021 13:27:00 | Blender, ZBrush, Substance Painter, HTML, JavaScript, Model-Viewer, AR | MATIC | 0xabe7ba4dc441bbfc12e-a107d62c2a7ae67becac7 | 4 | 1/1 |
| 02 | **Ram v1-dv1** | 04-16-2021 09:22:54 | Blender, ZBrush, Substance Painter, HTML, JavaScript, Model-Viewer, AR | XTZ | KT1RJ6PbjHpwc3M5rw5-s2Nbmefwbuwbdxton | 34986 | 1/1 |

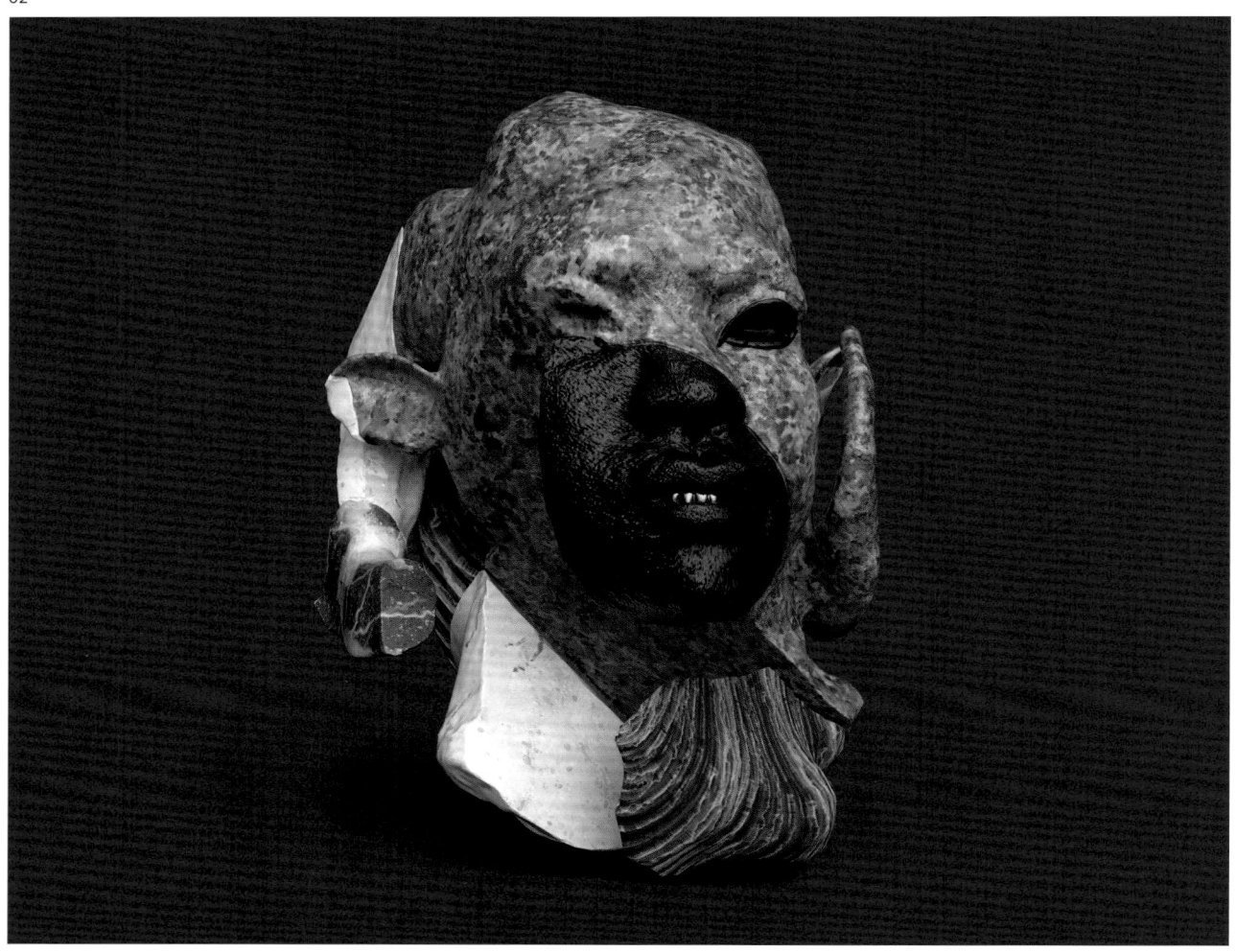

Sculpture's expanded field includes electric, kinetic, and 3D technologies, which now includes NFTs. Auriea Harvey has marshalled all of these elements, pushing an aesthetic for interactive technologies, forcefully articulated in *Realtime Art Manifesto* (2006), co-authored with her long-term collaborator Michael Samyn. *Realtime Art Manifesto* suggests that we can overcome modernist irony and cynicism, our too-cool world-weariness for a present tense with creative possibility. This text established their vision for complex artistic game environments, ones that garnered a cult following. Back in 2001, after receiving the SFMOMA Prize for Excellence in Online Art, she appeared in *Eden.Garden* (2001), a work that parsed the code of a website to generate the dance of Adam and Eve, modelled on Auriea and Michael. Nearing the end of her net art period, in 2003, they launched the creative and idiosyncratic video game development company Tale of Tales. Twenty years later, Auriea returns to playing with self-image as she had in so many early web projects, suggesting her gaze has landed on the potential of a new set of emergent technologies.

*Ram* (2021) began as a self-portrait using 3D scanning technology. Sculpting software and 3D printing allowed *Ram*'s form to morph into some kind of ancestral kin. Iterated across tangible and virtual sculptures, she introduces new narratives for each in their descriptions. *Ram (v1-dv1)* (2021) stares through a single black eye, the bite of a gold tooth glinting in contrast to the granite skin, but no stone looks like this. Using digital materials to generate a believable rock, she nevertheless produces a form impossible for the physical world. This is the point where technology develops an imaginary of its own. Her sculptures, tangible and virtual, remind us that there is world-making to be done, with *Ram* symbolizing a procreative force — rebellious, disorderly, generous, sublime. In this spirit, NFTs and blockchain are tools that bolster an artist's arsenal for creative revolution.

**CHARLOTTE KENT**
ASSOCIATE PROFESSOR OF VISUAL CULTURE
AT MONTCLAIR STATE UNIVERSITY

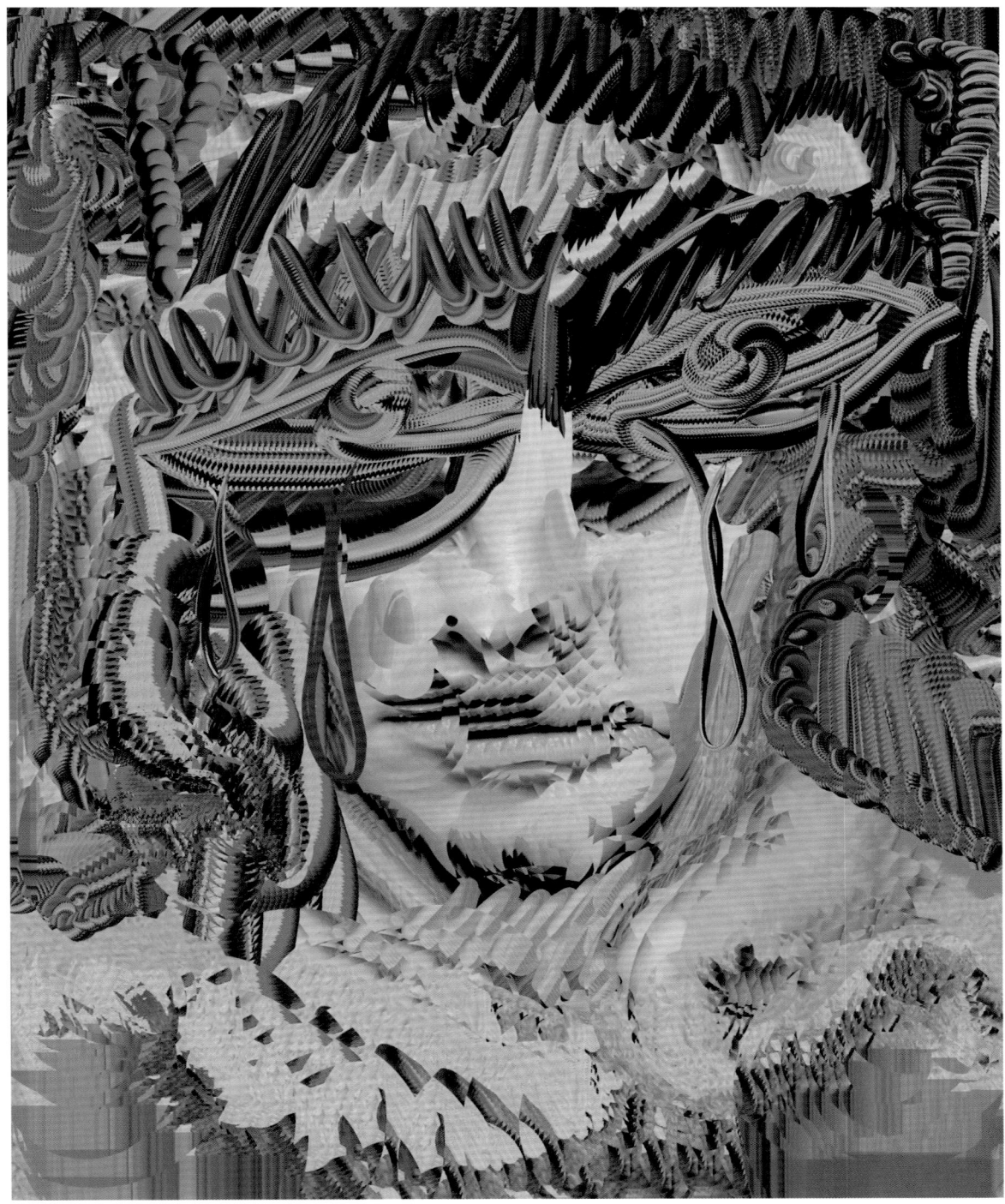

| # | TITLE | TIMESTAMP | MEDIUM | CHAIN | CONTRACT ADDRESS | TOKEN ID | EDITION SIZE |
|---|---|---|---|---|---|---|---|
| 01 | **CORDIA SUPER** | 08-25-2021 10:10:39 | Adobe Photoshop, Adobe Lightroom, Procreate | ETH | 0xb932a70a57673d89f4acffbe830e8ed7f75fb9e0 | 29796 | 1/1 |
| 02 | **WHY CHAIN** | 04-20-2021 03:33:38 | Adobe Photoshop, Adobe Lightroom, Procreate | ETH | 0xb932a70a57673d89f4acffbe830e8ed7f75fb9e0 | 23692 | 1/1 |

# RY DAVID BRADLEY

AUSTRALIA 1979

02

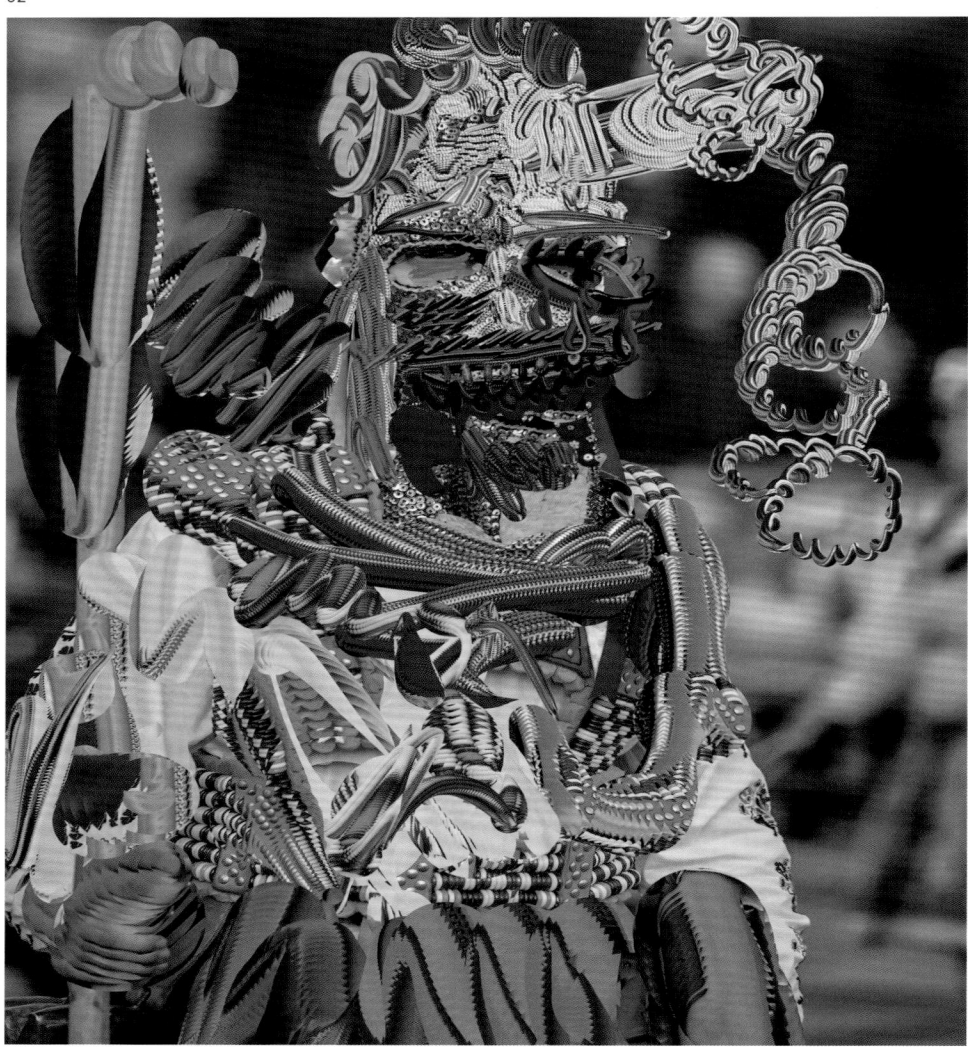

Ry David Bradley — who we affectionately call RDB — helped me curate one of my installments of *Post Analog Painting* in 2017, a recurring thematic group exhibition and long-standing curatorial project looking at how painting has been impacted by digital media. We enthusiastically shared the works of scores of likeminded artists and discussed their different approaches to painting in the "post-analog" era. Both born in the early 80s, we experienced both the analog world and the transition to the digital. We vibed immediately and have been vibing since.

His blog *PAINTED, ETC.* and my (!) Myspace blog both tracked the responses emerging artists were providing in the early 2000s to the digital revolution. We also shared a rather retro belief that the avant-garde was crucial to make sense of our cultural moment and the best art is the art that can only be made now. With that in mind we presented Ry's third solo show at my New York gallery The Hole in February 2021, where he exhibited woven tapestries and the NFT digital compositions they were made from. This was the first major contemporary gallery show of NFTs to open simultaneously in the metaverse. It begged the question, was the original work on the wall in New York or on the wall in Decentraland?

Having been a digital painter for the better part of 15 years, RDB creates pieces like *Cordia Super* (2021) using custom digital "brushes" to make a sort of data impasto portrait and then produces it woven as a traditional high-resolution tapestry. Highlighting the relationship of screens to weaving and early computer programming, RDB creates an almost temporal conundrum in these hybrid pieces; but as I've observed over the years, Ry repeatedly expands what 21st-century painting is and can be.

**KATHY GRAYSON**
OWNER OF THE HOLE, NEW YORK AND LOS ANGELES

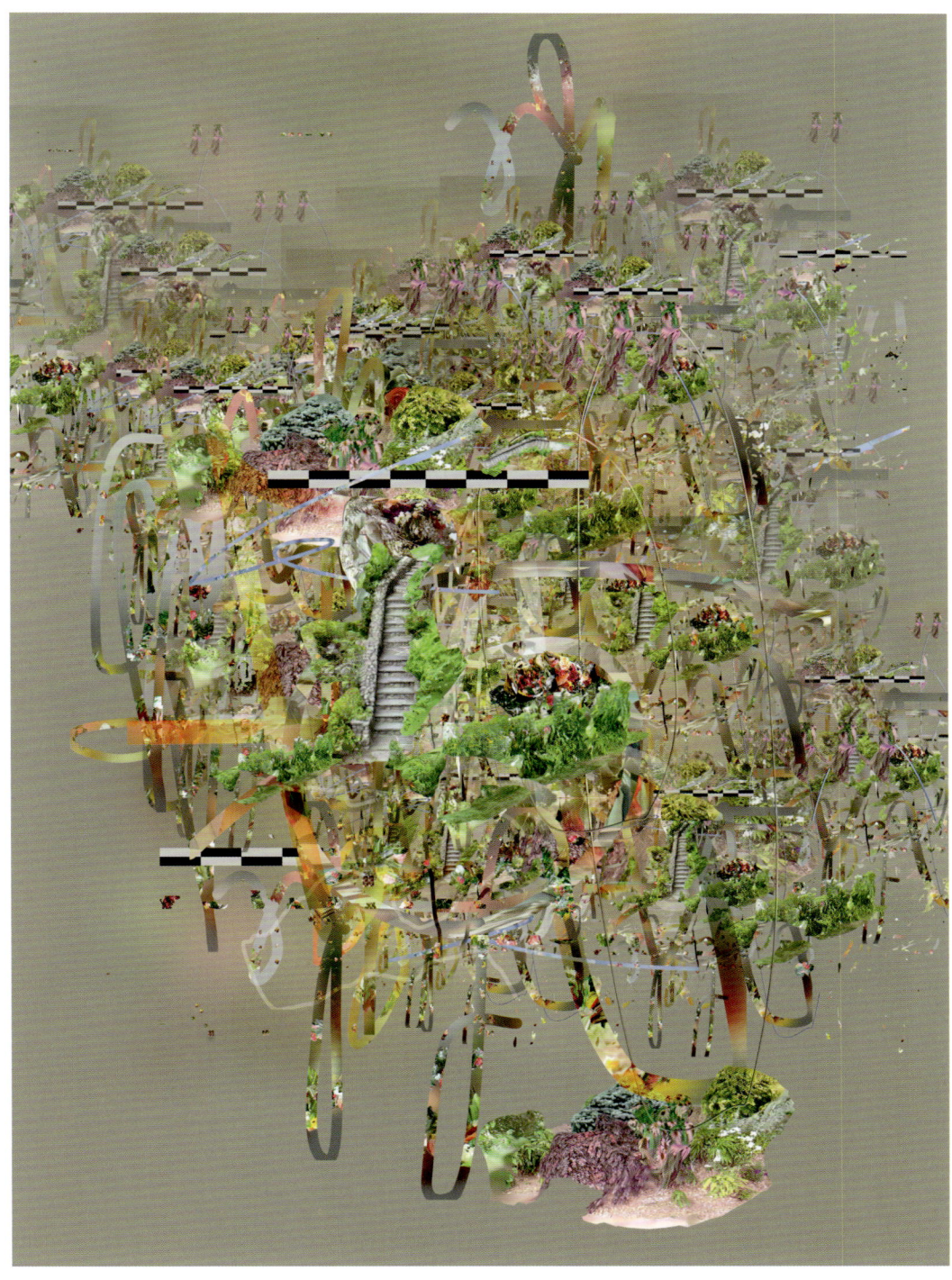

| # | TITLE | TIMESTAMP | MEDIUM | CHAIN | CONTRACT ADDRESS | TOKEN ID | EDITION SIZE |
|---|---|---|---|---|---|---|---|
| 01 | **x-ii / 4clowstaff** | 08-20-2021 20:45:16 | Figma | ETH | 0x3b3ee1931dc30c1957379fac9aba94d1c48a5405 | 75048 | 1/1 |
| 02 | **Magic Move 1** | 09-07-2021 19:57:51 | Figma | ETH | 0x3b3ee1931dc30c1957379fac9aba94d1c48a5405 | 82084 | 1/1 |
| 03 | **Green Psycho** | 09-03-2021 21:11:42 | Figma | ETH | 0x3b3ee1931dc30c1957379fac9aba94d1c48a5405 | 80535 | 1/1 |

# KATHERINE FRAZER

UNITED STATES  1992

02 ▶

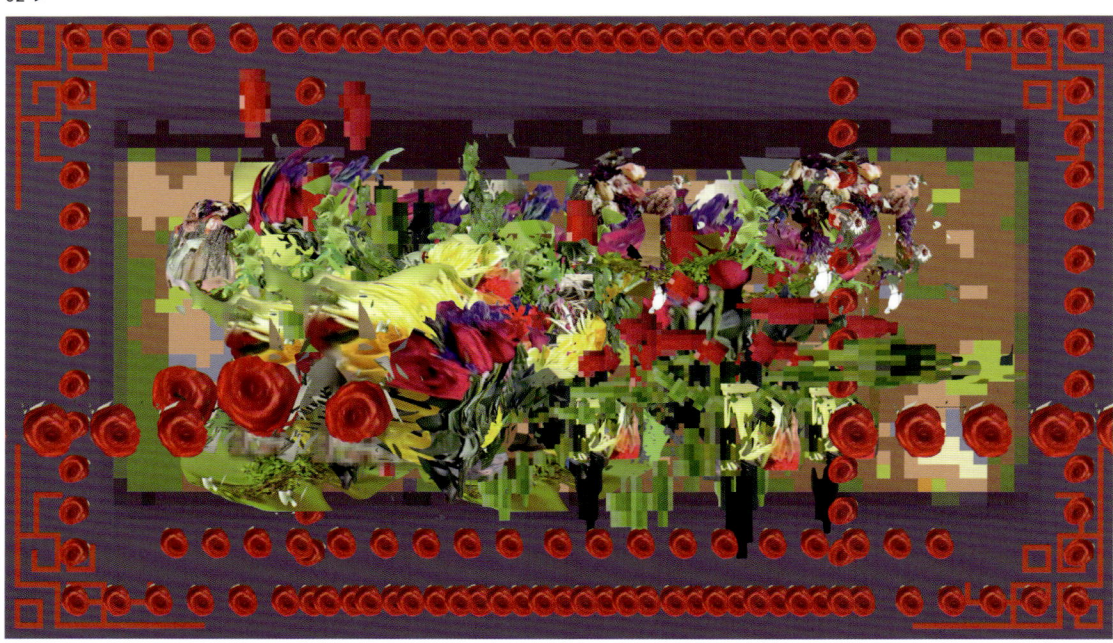

Thousands of layers of lush brushstrokes, floral snippets, and pixelated verdure compose an abundant collage in Katherine Frazer's digital painting, *Green Psycho* (2021). Spanning 11,698 pixels wide and 8,226 pixels high, the canvas contains a seemingly infinite expanse of digital flora, sourced originally from modest bouquets the artist purchased from her neighborhood grocery store, and then transformed into STL files using 3D scanning software. Frazer dissected, rearranged, and erased these scans of bouquets and interspersed them with fragments from her other compositions to create an efflorescent fractal effect, as a viewer explores the painting by perpetually zooming in to more carefully consider each warped artifact.

Frazer created *Green Psycho* in the browser-based design tool Figma, which is typically used by user interface and experience teams as a vector graphics editor and collaborative prototyping tool. The artist previously worked at Figma as a designer, affording her an intimate familiarity with the tool's possibilities and limitations for painting; Figma allows for the accumulation and automated distribution of layered images at impressive scale, yet also tends to break when overwhelmed with such a large number of files.

Frazer also maintains a flower arranging practice IRL, studying the avant-garde Sogetsu School of Ikebana since 2017. Much like the digital painting tools she uses, ikebana provides creative constraints such as the number of flowers, proportions, and angles of the stems. These simple building blocks allow for a methodical and iterative approach. On the relationship between her ikebana and digital painting practices, Frazer remarks: "Like pruning leaves on a flower to draw attention to the curvature of the stem, I extract and remove excess material from 3D models and photographs to emphasize the essence of the formal qualities I find most attractive."

**CELINE KATZMAN**
CURATOR AT RHIZOME

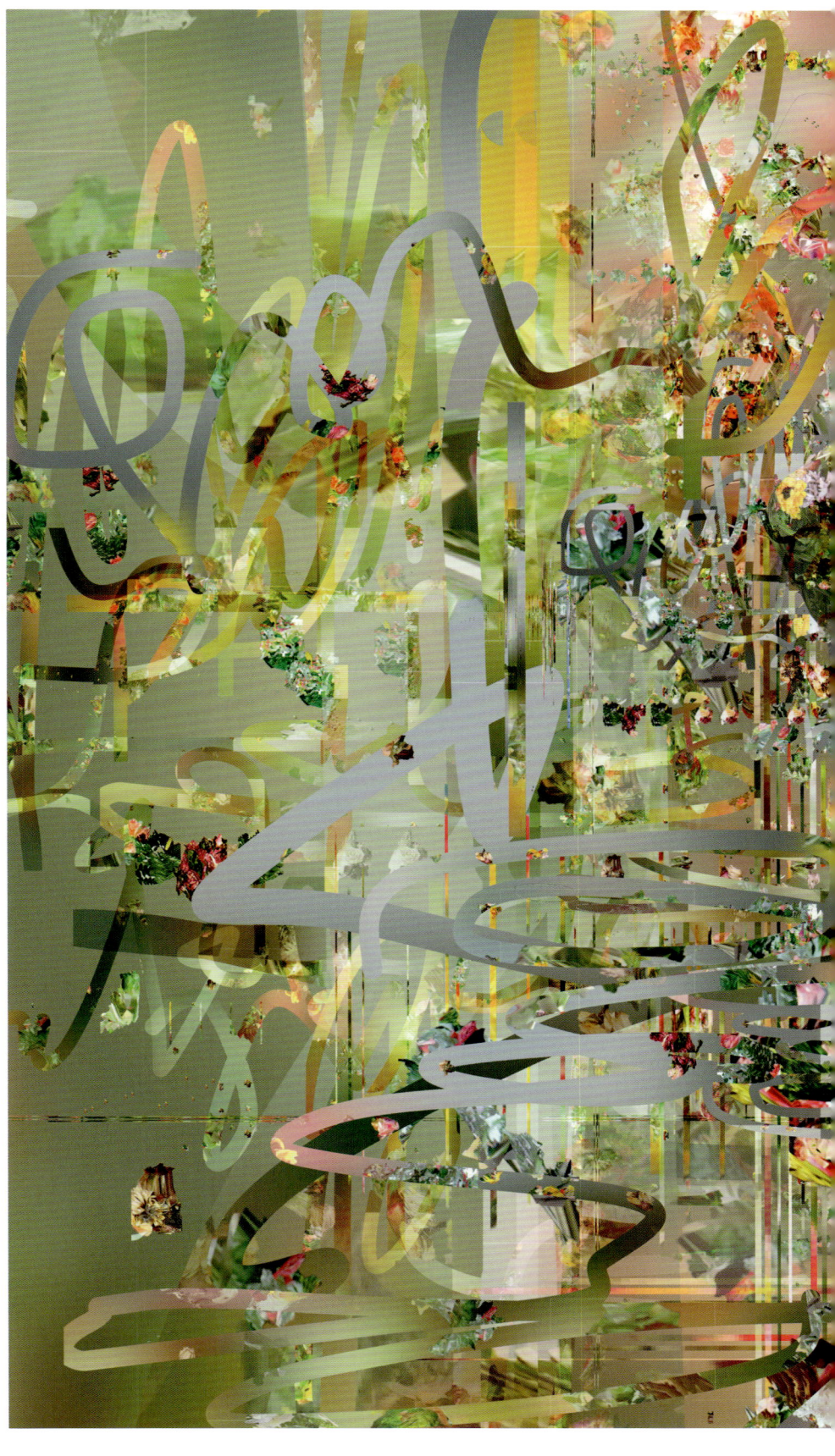

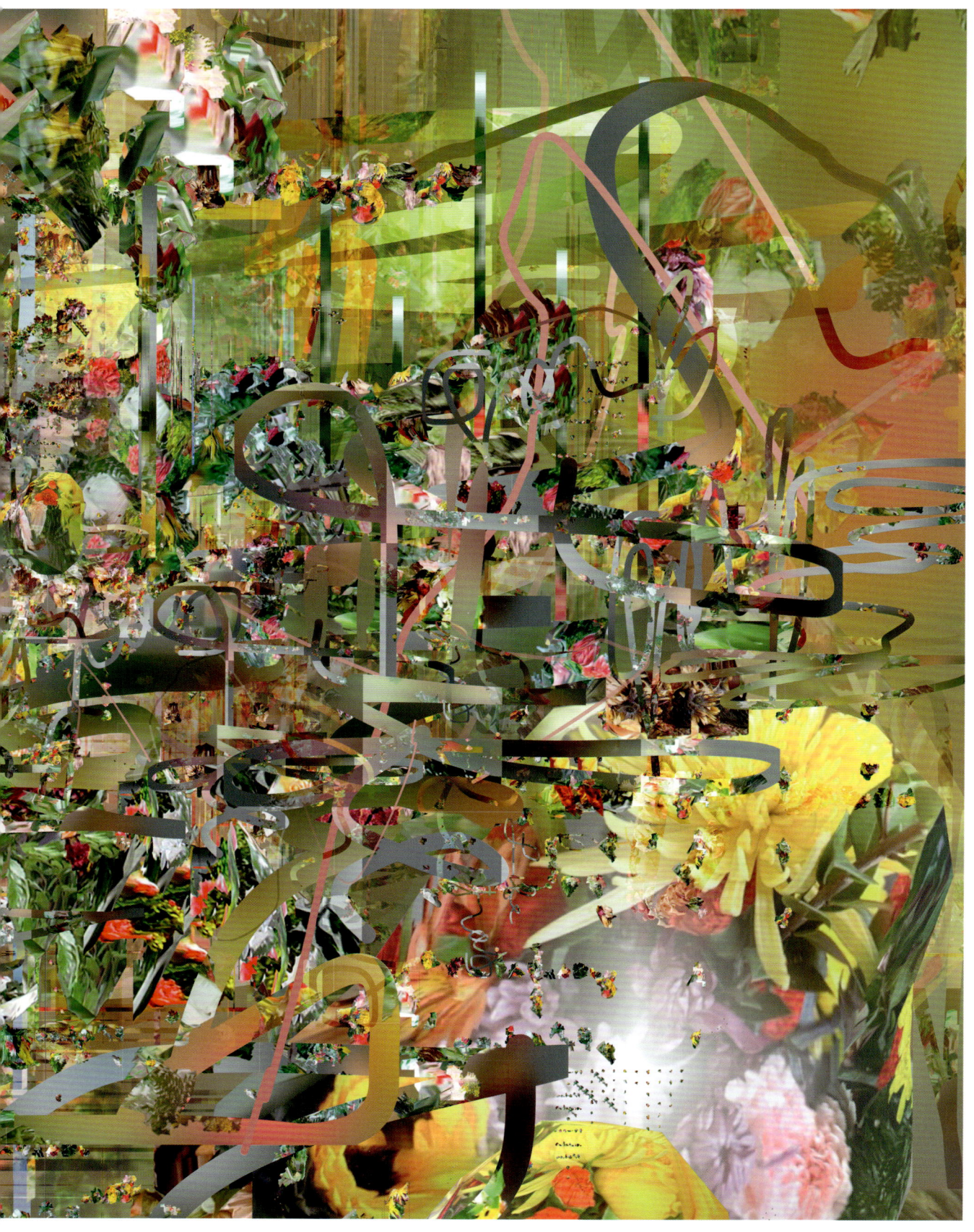

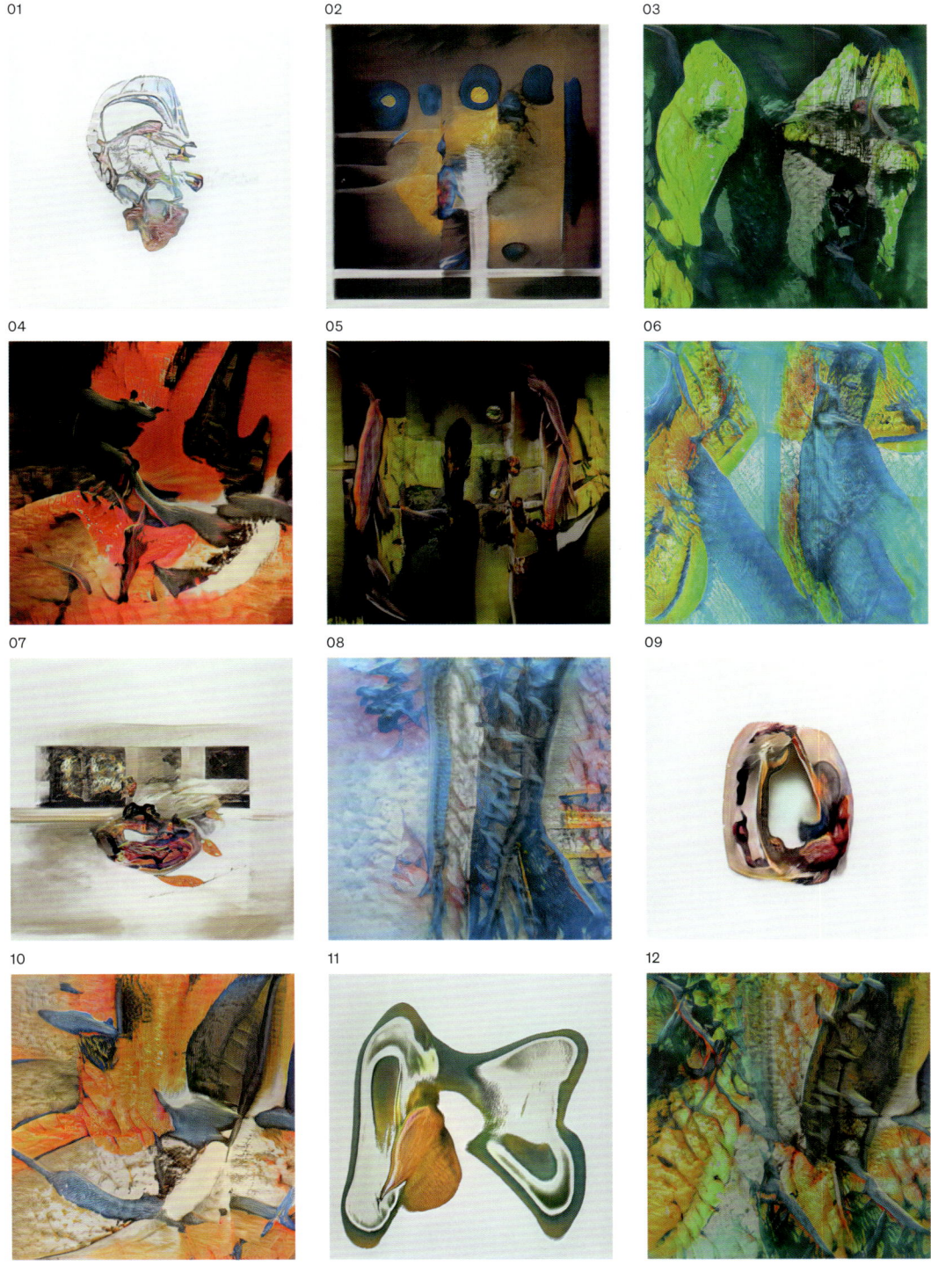

| # | TITLE | TIMESTAMP | MEDIUM | CHAIN | CONTRACT ADDRESS | TOKEN ID | EDITION SIZE |
|---|---|---|---|---|---|---|---|
| 01–12 | sᴜʙJᴇᴄᴛɪᴠᴇ ¢oᴎsɪsᴛᴇᴎ¢y: sᴛɪℓℓ | 03-07-2023 12:50:11 | StyleGAN2 latent walk interpolation video | ETH | 0xd5d303caad54db8678e-2b90060a87662c859f1d7 | 1–18 | 1/1 of 18 |
| 13 | **Bença [Blessings]** | 06-28-2022 10:54:08 | Aurora3D, Screenshot of Google search for motivational images for family WhatsApp groups | ETH | 0x3b3ee1931dc30c195737-9fac9aba94d1c48a5405 | 54131 | 1/1 |

EDITIONS ILLUSTRATED: (01) *img*000000003, (02) **img**000000005, (03) **img**000000013, (04) img000000019, (05) ιɱɠ000000020, (06) ιɱɠ000000022, (07) ιɱɠ000000025, (08) ɪɱɡ000000045, (09) ιᴜɠ000000061, (10) ℓɱ¢000000066, (11) ιɱɔ000000076, (12) ɾɀɱɢ000000142

# CIBELLE CAVALLI BASTOS

BRAZIL 1978

13 ▶

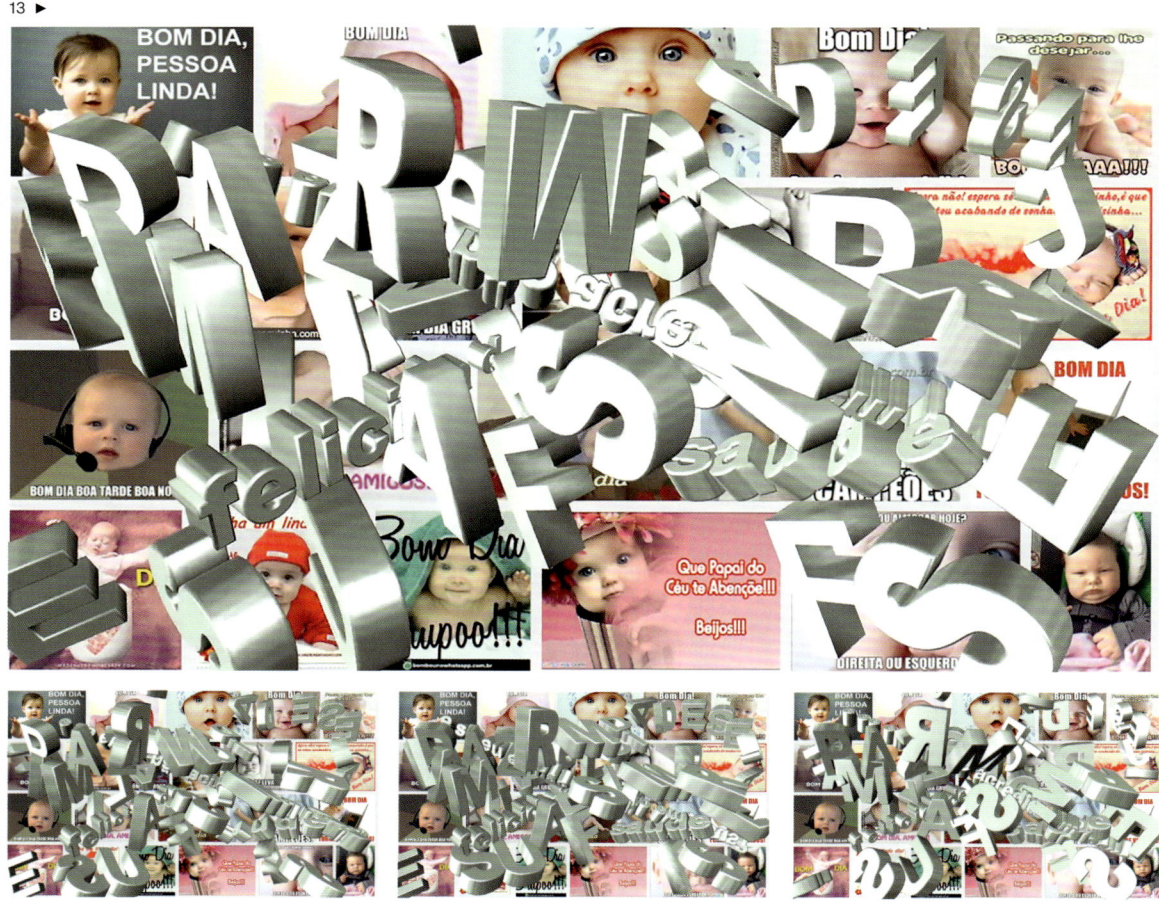

São Paulo–born, Berlin-based artist Cibelle Cavalli Bastos's practice is a continuous reflection on the perception and ideas of the self and reality through a process of examination and transformation. Since coming across their work in 2016, I have come to understand their multifaceted practice as operating from positions of the in between, traveling between cracks, creases, and folds across platforms, Instagram live streams, or augmented reality to weave and collage together fragments of whole notions of identity. Between 2008 and 2021, they created an extensive dataset of themselves based on gestures, actions, and facets of their own process and work. Taking as input this database, *Subjective Consistency* (2022) is a body of work that uses a GAN to establish a common aesthetic language and material from over a decade of the artist's previous work. This human-machine collaboration has resulted in the development of an aesthetic consistency that transcends the artist's previous modes of work to challenge any kind of former ideas of formalism. Operating against these machine learning algorithms, they seek noncompliant patterns of behavior and material, abstracting their data to transform and assemble new images, and ideas of the self and perceptions of reality to ask questions about the in-betweens of identity — both collective and individual, how we perceive ourselves and one another, and the realities we find ourselves within. Creating feedback loops and short circuits to redirect the algorithm, their work is an amalgamation and consideration of the many selves that we can inhabit, and the work that is needed to move between them, and the platforms they are digitized within. Extracting themselves from automated algorithmic decision-making, their work creates resistance and refuses identities constructed by algorithms.

**NORA O MURCHÚ**
CURATOR & ARTISTIC DIRECTOR AT TRANSMEDIALE FESTIVAL

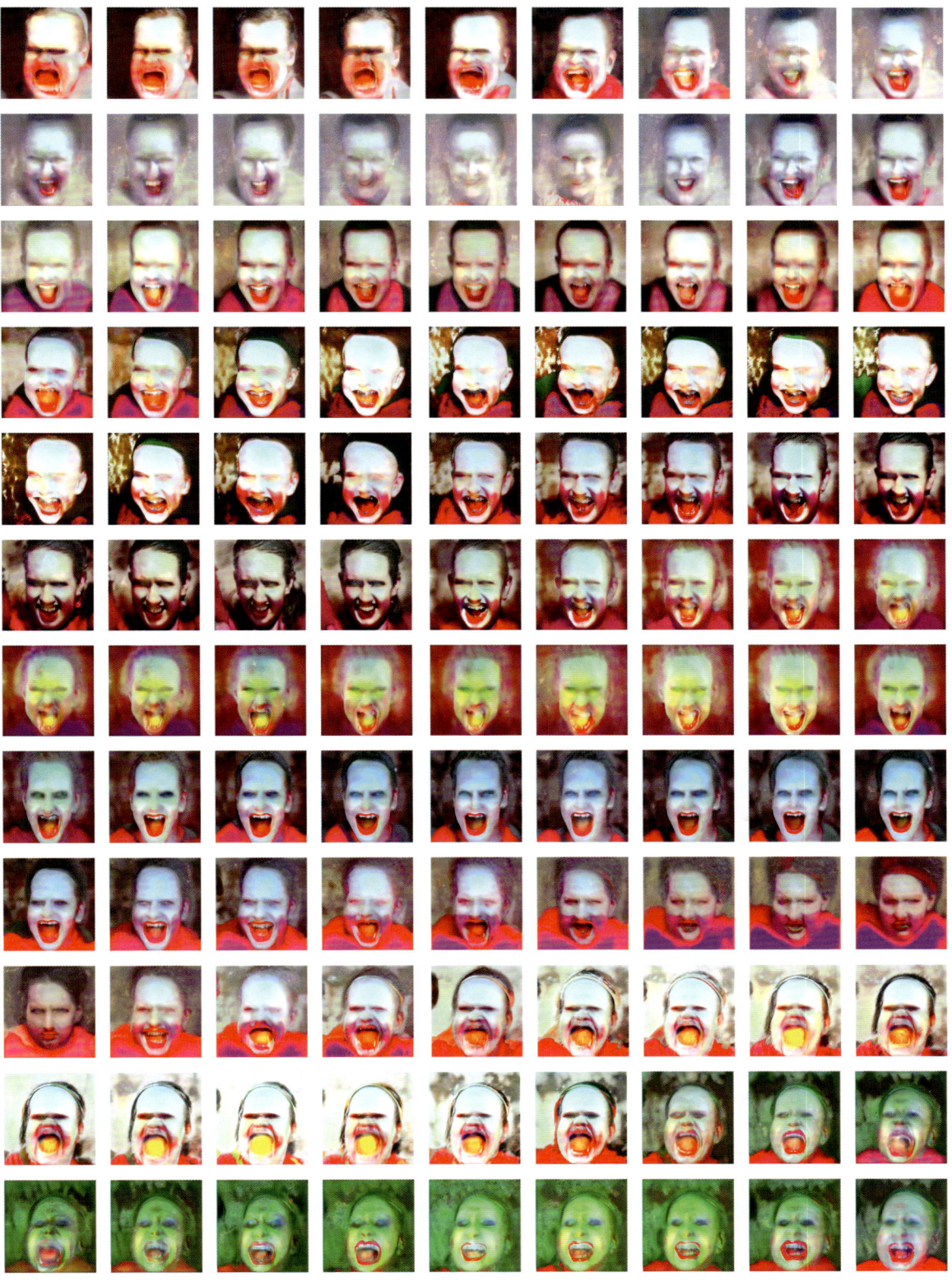

| # | TITLE | TIMESTAMP | MEDIUM | CHAIN | CONTRACT ADDRESS | TOKEN ID | EDITION SIZE |
|---|---|---|---|---|---|---|---|
| 01 | **Monday?** | 08-31-2020 14:56:09 | StyleGAN2, GIF | ETH | 0x9498e391ca49722988fc4da4d0d8c9c987ce8961 | 31 | 1/1 |
| 02 | **Planned Obsolescence** | 09-14-2021 13:31:52 | Pytorch, SVG, JavaScript, External API | XTZ | KT1RJ6PbjHpwc3M5rw5s2Nbmefwbuwbdxton | 305147 | 100 |

# MARIO KLINGEMANN

02

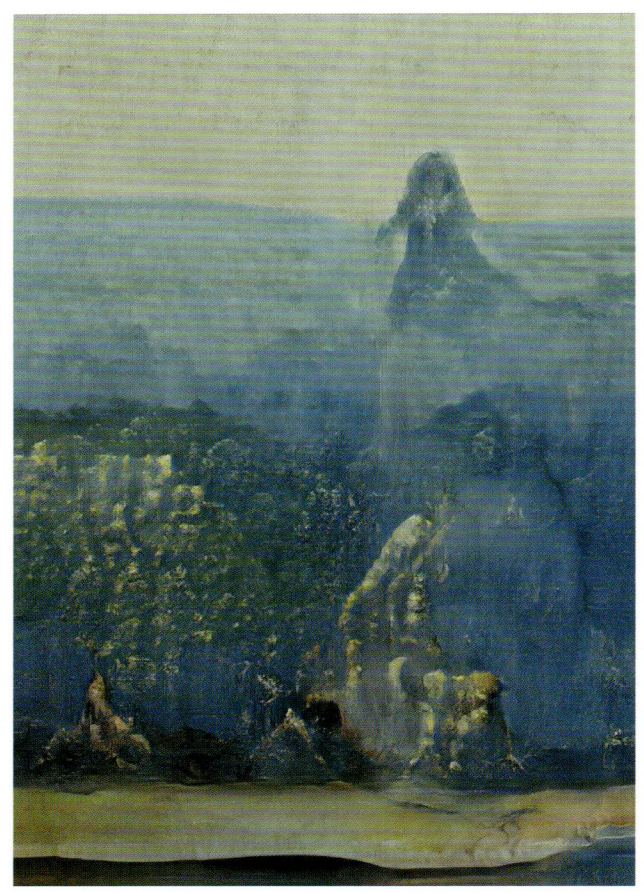

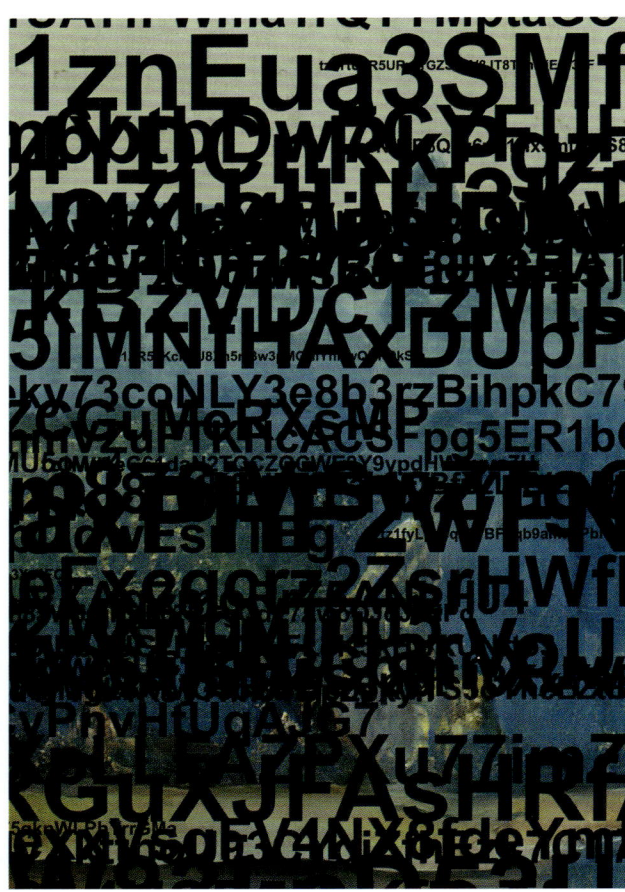

The German artist Mario Klingemann has been exploring the potential of using computers in the field of new media art since the early 1990s. His work straddles the line between the art world and that of technology, often using humor to make commentary in a way that is both critical and entertaining. Complex systems are one of the core interests of the autodidact. In particular, the analysis of art itself in its aesthetic aspects as well of its mechanisms and institutions are recurring themes in his work.

A critical observer of the emergent blockchain culture and crypto art scene, he entered the field in early 2020. His work *Screenshot this NFT* (2020) highlights the friction between the skepticism and ridicule of the wider public towards the tokenization of digital art and at the same time acts as a self-referential marker documenting crypto art history. Klingemann often uses the blockchain as a way to create timestamps that document the progress in his personal AI research. *Monday?* (2020) is an example of a dynamic StyleGAN animation technique he developed in that period and also a rare excursion into the attention-grabbing, loud, and flashy style as a form of "crypto art-mimicry" that is not very typical for him.

As a consequence of the rising critique of the energy consumption and $CO_2$ footprint of proof-of-work chains in early 2021, Klingemann became an influential supporter of the ecologically responsible proof-of-stake chain Tezos and the artist-run community Hic et Nunc which he helped popularize through various artistic interventions. Apart from making NFTs accessible to a global diverse audience, the open-source nature of the platform allowed for innovative dynamic and interactive formats in the NFT space. An example for this is *Planned Obsolescence* (2021) where Klingemann explores these new possibilities with a work that degrades over time, affected by its collectors' transactions which stamp their wallet addresses over the image each time the NFT changes hands.

**MARIO KLINGEMANN
IN COLLABORATION WITH GPT-3**
ARTIST

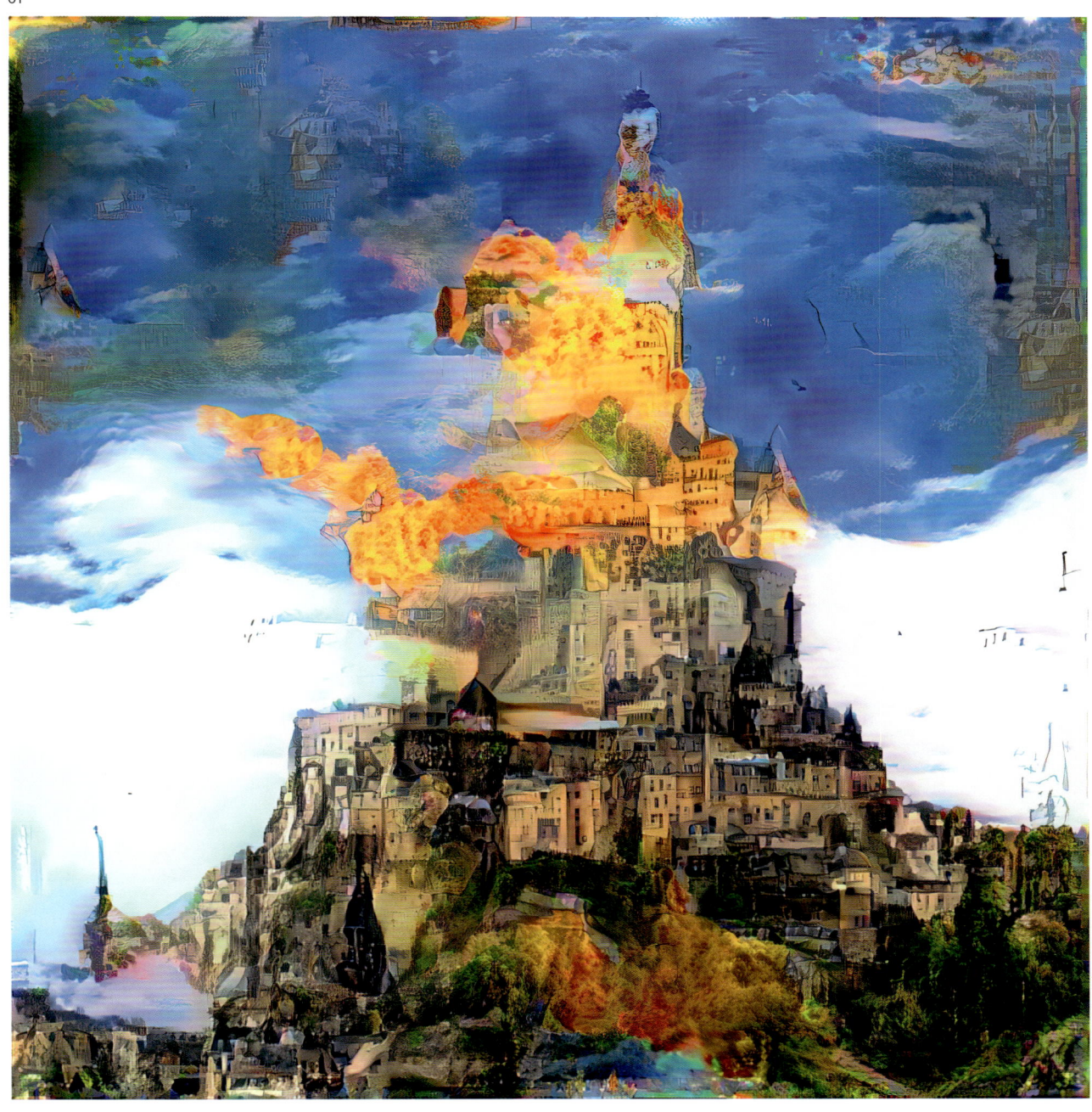

| # | TITLE | TIMESTAMP | MEDIUM | CHAIN | CONTRACT ADDRESS | TOKEN ID | EDITION SIZE |
|---|---|---|---|---|---|---|---|
| 01 | **Fire Castle** | 02-19-2021 18:15:50 | GAN, Style Transfer | ETH | 0xb932a70a57673d89f4acffbe830e8ed7f75fb9e0 | 19690 | 1/1 |
| 02 | **THE WONDER OF IT ALL** | 04-01-2022 23:40:15 | VQGAN+CLIP | ETH | 0x1e706f7870f690dc0318961184cafe66fc88d272 | 3 | 1/1 |

02 ►

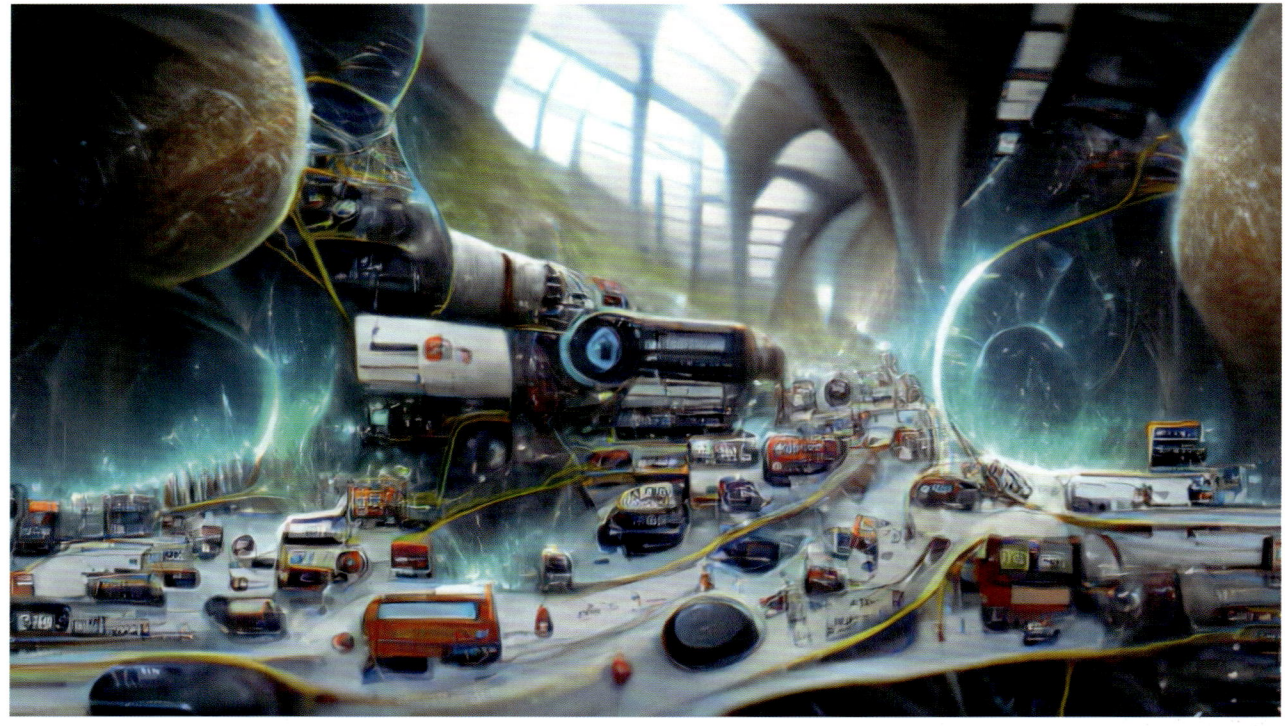

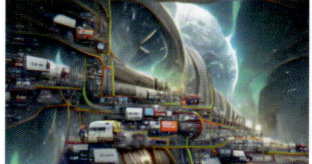 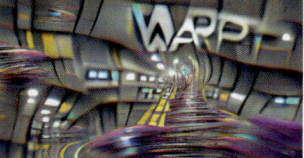 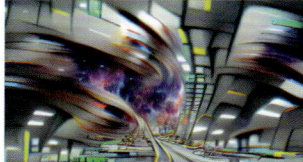 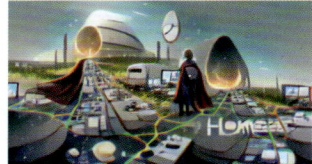

Few artists can match Anne Morgan Spalter's digital imagination. In the 1990s she was making digitally based art and teaching at the Rhode Island School of Design and Brown University. Intuiting that digital technology would transform art practice in the 21st century, she created the first courses combining technical concepts with the aesthetic and theoretical implications of embedding digital technology into the creative process and wrote the internationally taught textbook *The Computer in the Visual Arts* (1999).

Since then, Spalter has continued to formulate new paradigms in digital art including innovations in the realm of NFTs. It was inevitable that as one of the first artists utilizing digital technology for installation and public art, she would turn to NFTs to expand audiences and explore new forms of digital art making. In *The Wonder of It All* (2022), Spalter continues to innovate by integrating new AI technologies such as a text-to-image program in which one types in a phrase and receives a picture, into the digital

world she has created out of the visual experiences of contemporary life: cars, airplanes, other images of travel, and fantasies of outer space are merged by Spalter's imagination into a vivid vision of the future.

Spalter is widely recognized for her arresting artistry with coverage ranging from *Hyperallergic* to *The New York Times* and her ability to engage audiences in understanding digital art. Her work is in the permanent collections of the Victoria and Albert Museum in London, the Albright-Knox Art Gallery in New York, the Rhode Island School of Design Museum in Providence, and the Museum of Crypto Art, among others.

**JUDITH K. BRODSKY**
DISTINGUISHED PROFESSOR EMERITA
AT DEPARTMENT OF VISUAL ARTS,
RUTGERS UNIVERSITY, NEW JERSEY

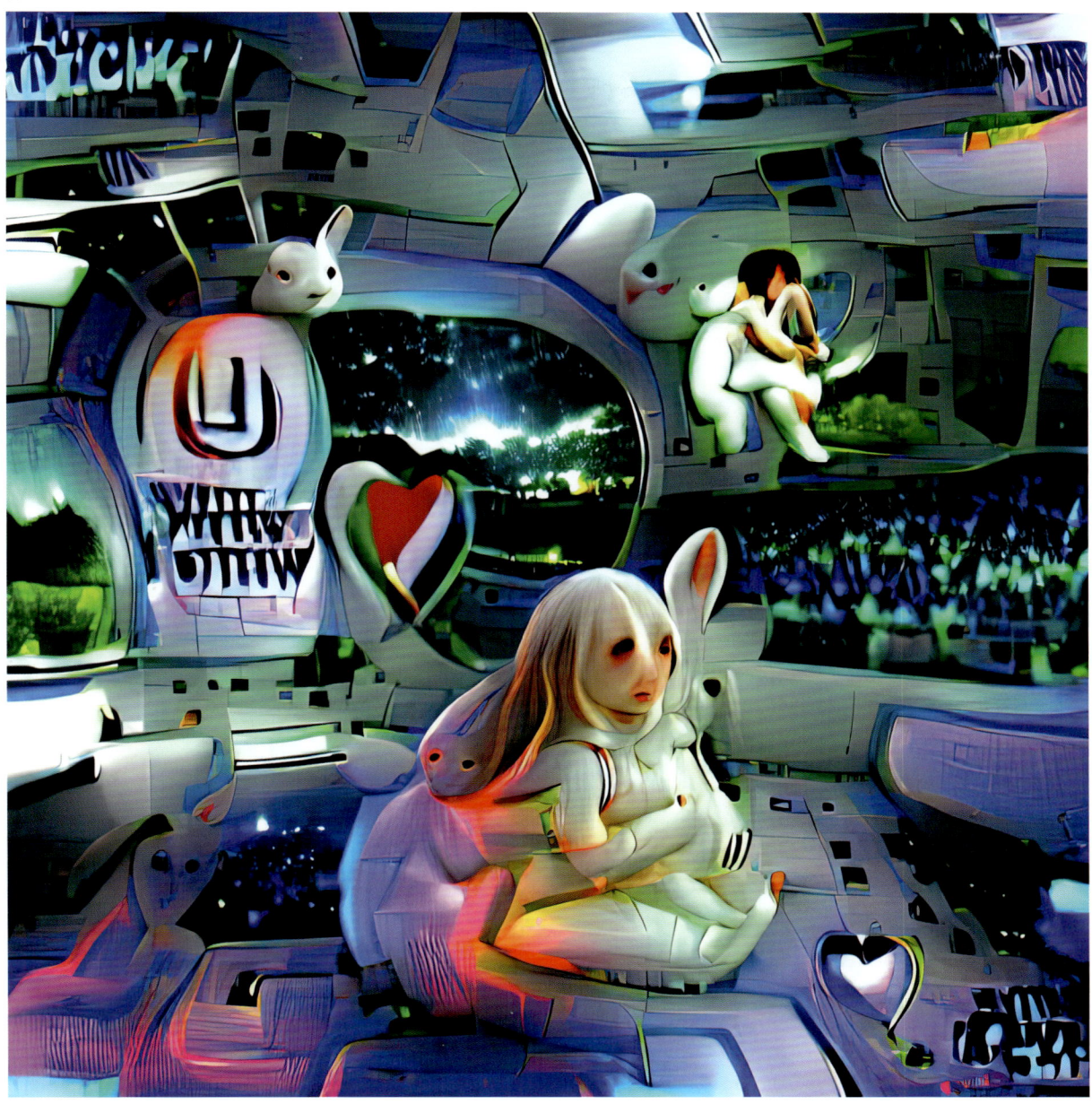

| # | TITLE | TIMESTAMP | MEDIUM | CHAIN | CONTRACT ADDRESS | TOKEN ID | EDITION SIZE |
|---|---|---|---|---|---|---|---|
| 03 | **Interstellar Travel with Lucky Space Rabbit** | 10-30-2021 23:39:30 | VQGAN+CLIP | ETH | 0xb932a70a57673d89f4a-cffbe830e8ed7f75fb9e0 | 29986 | 1/1 |
| 04 | **Lighthouse for Peace** | 03-10-2022 13:57:25 | VQGAN+CLIP, Adobe Photoshop | ETH | 0xb932a70a57673d89f4a-cffbe830e8ed7f75fb9e0 | 33146 | 1/1 |

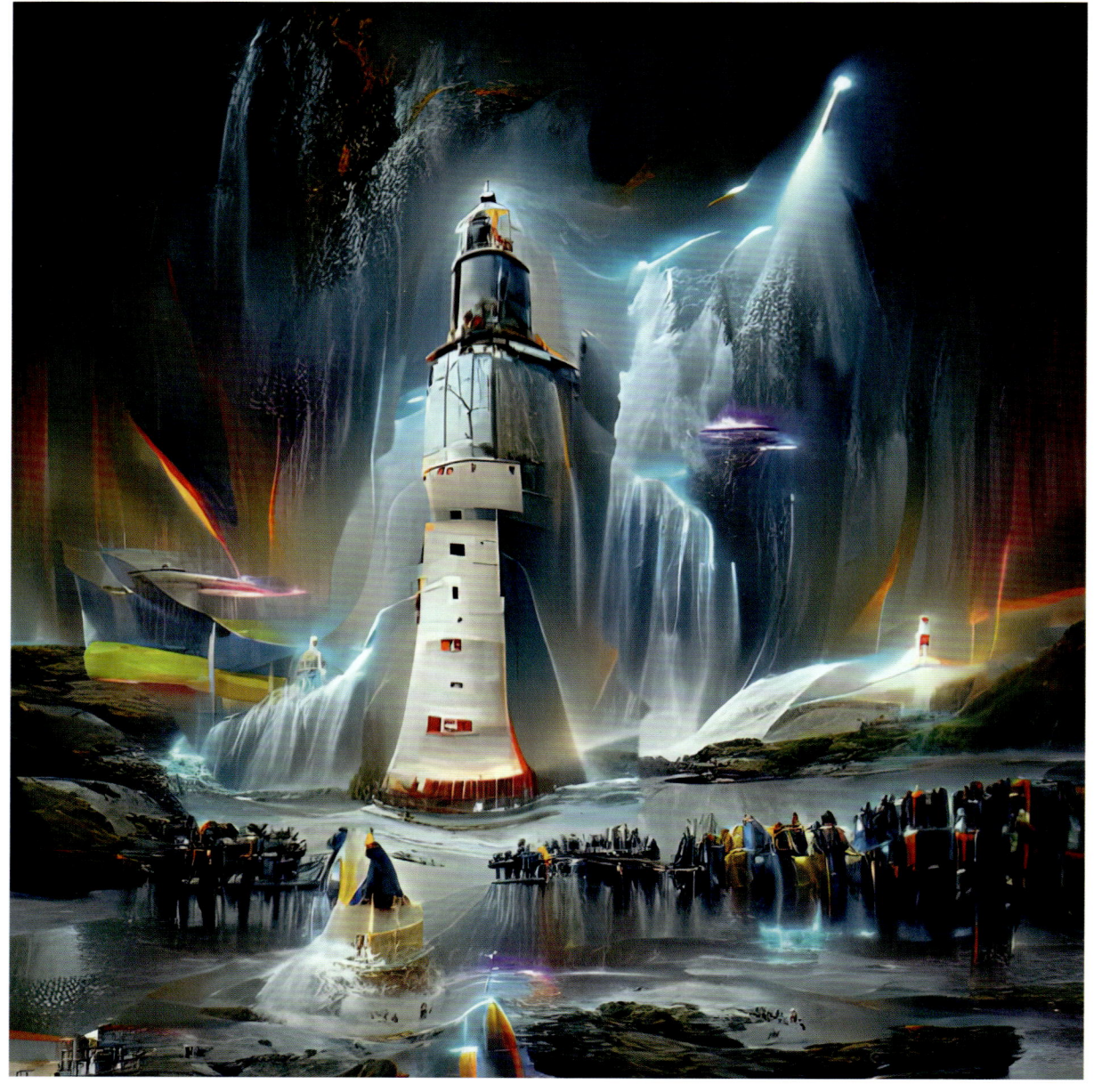

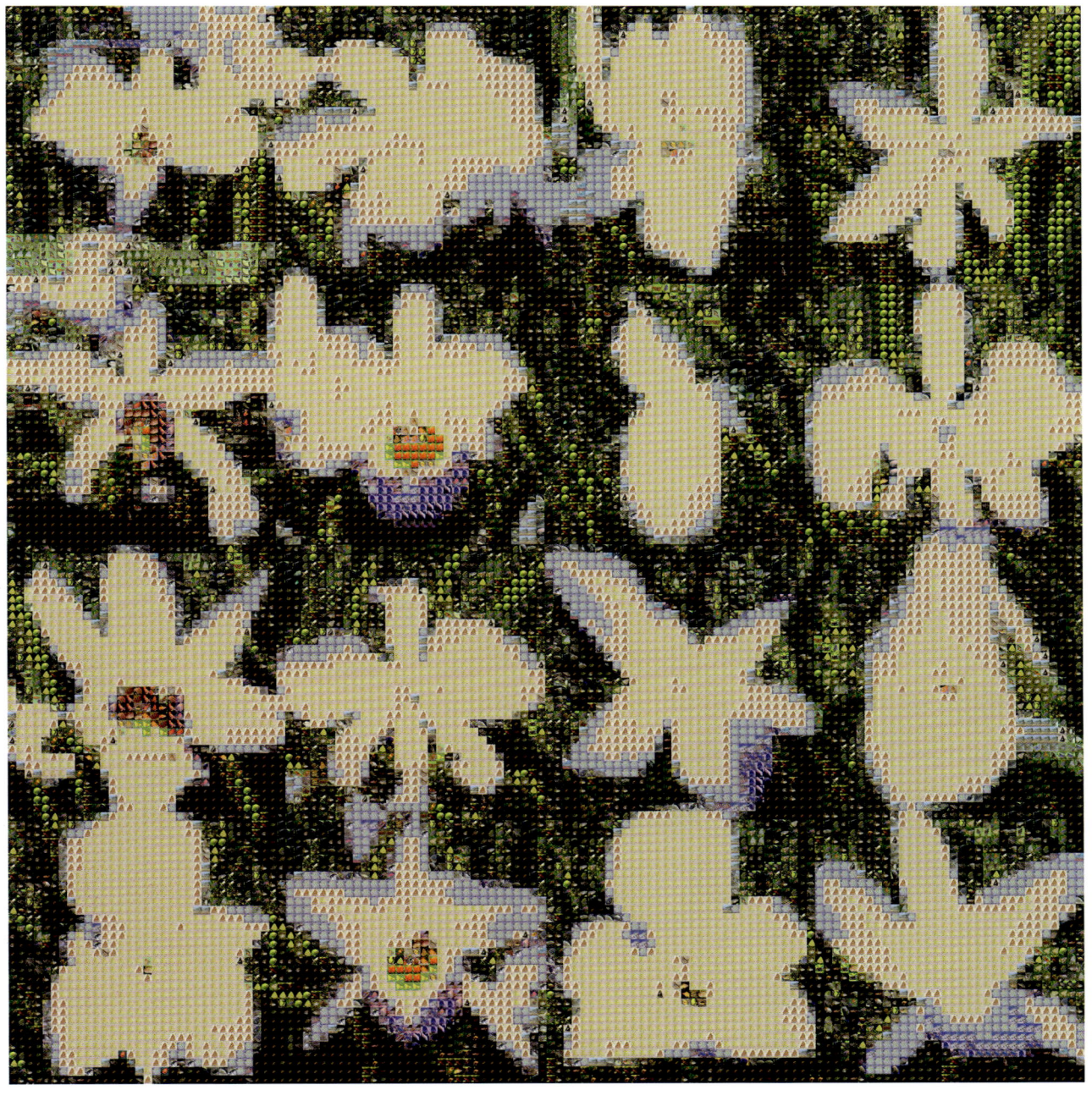

| # | TITLE | TIMESTAMP | MEDIUM | CHAIN | CONTRACT ADDRESS | TOKEN ID | EDITION SIZE |
|---|---|---|---|---|---|---|---|
| 01 | [[seed_of_seeds]] | 09-13-2021 12:12:12 | GAN, Custom code | ETH | 0xb932a70a57673d89f4acffbe830e8ed7f75fb9e0 | 28382 | 1/1 |
| 02 | hideseek_hope_9078 | 05-28-2020 17:16:55 | GAN, Custom code | ETH | 0xb932a70a57673d89f4acffbe830e8ed7f75fb9e0 | 10563 | 1/1 |

02 ▶

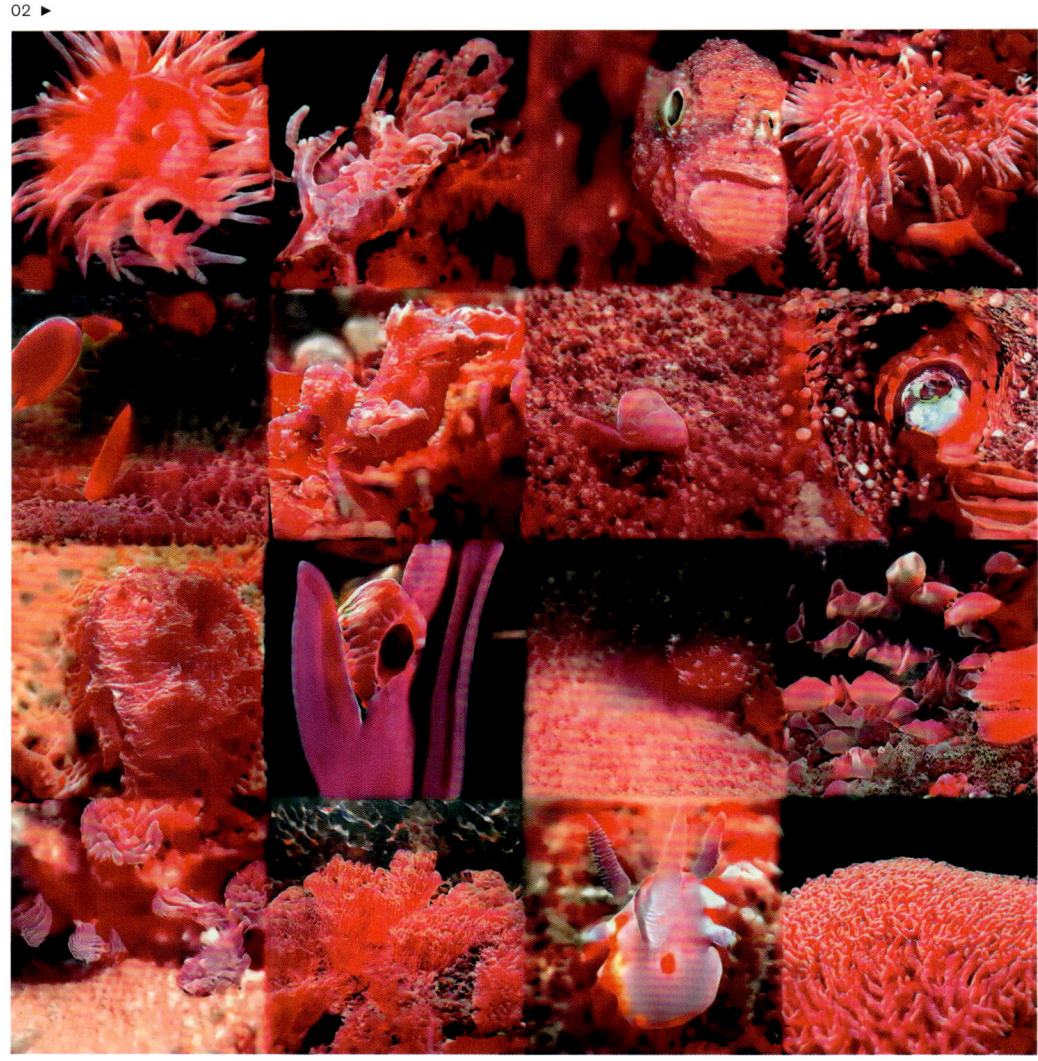

Sofia Crespo lives for biology and technology. She works with the cutting edge of artificial intelligence to push the boundaries of nature's imagination. Her application of neural networks allows us to visualize new creatures that break all traditional structures of animal taxonomy, combining parts of one species with another in unpredictable ways. Crespo works in close partnership with the technology, using AI's pattern-based understanding of the world to augment our human knowledge, while at the same time drawing our attention to the curiosities that already exist in the natural world and in its historical depictions.

*hideseek_hope_9078* (2020) is a mesmerizing dance of color, rhythm, and aquatic life. Generated using a GAN model, the creatures appear highly realistic for a moment until they morph into others in unison, directed by the hidden hand of the machine. The grid format of the work is reminiscent of the typical layout of sample images in machine learning research, but here it presents the collection of aquatic life as a rigidly structured organism, where all cells cooperate for its existence. Inspired by the pigment-bearing organs of cephalopods, which can not only change their hosts' color and patterns but also act as a means of communication, Crespo's creatures pulsate with life and change in a common rhythm, mimicking both their natural functions and the endless generative possibilities of neural networks.

**LUBA ELLIOTT**
INDEPENDENT AI ART CURATOR

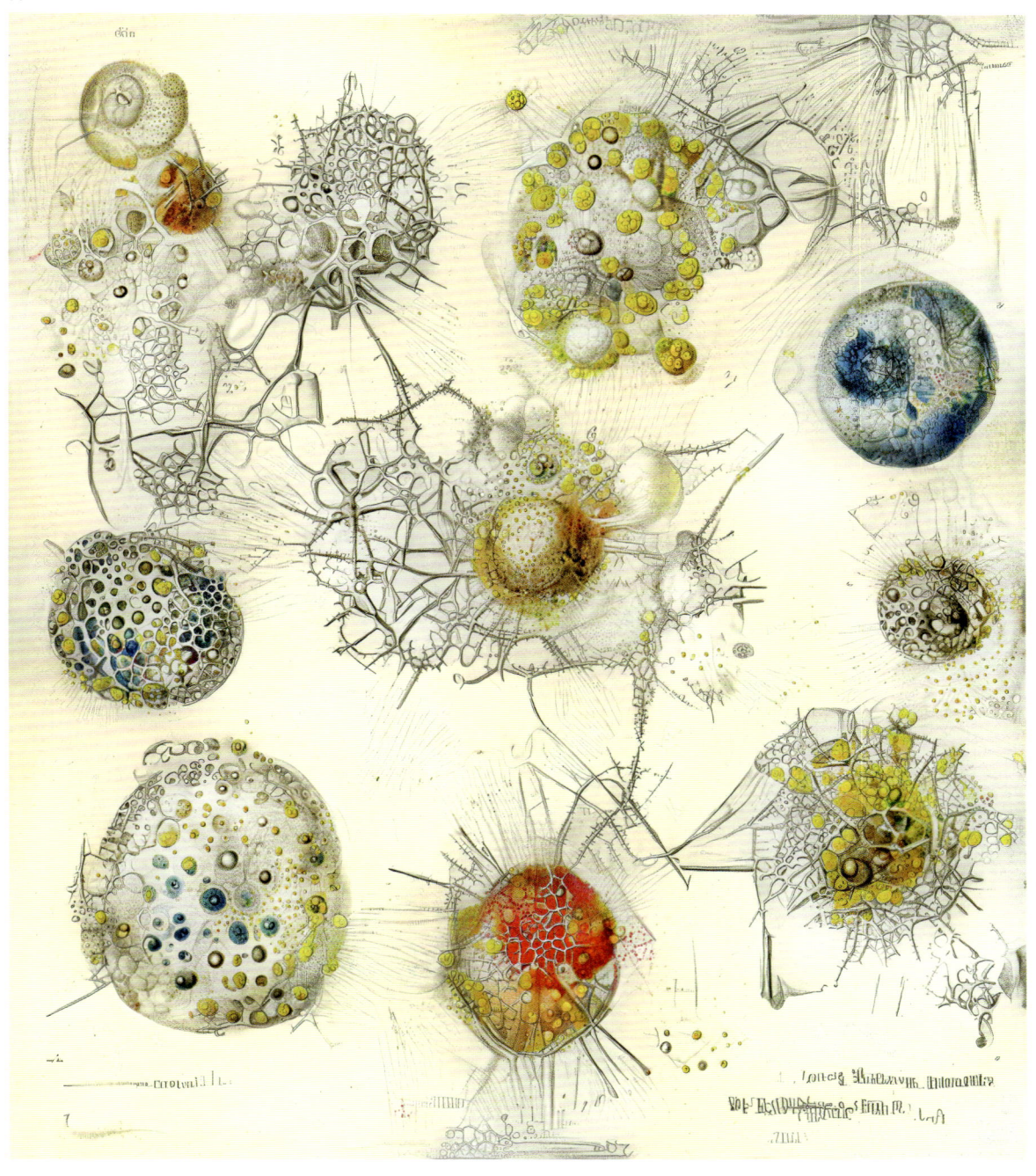

| # | TITLE | TIMESTAMP | | MEDIUM | CHAIN | CONTRACT ADDRESS | TOKEN ID | EDITION SIZE |
|---|---|---|---|---|---|---|---|---|
| 03 | **essential_protozoa_1862** | 03-02-2023 09:52:47 | ETH | GAN, Custom code | ETH | 0x01E6b9526138f681cded526864cD709E21B38583 | 1 | 1/1 |
| 04 | **soft_colonies_1898** | 07-21-2022 10:39:42 | ETH | GAN, Custom code | ETH | 0xb932a70a57673d89f4acffbe830e8ed7f75fb9e0 | 36144 | 1/1 |

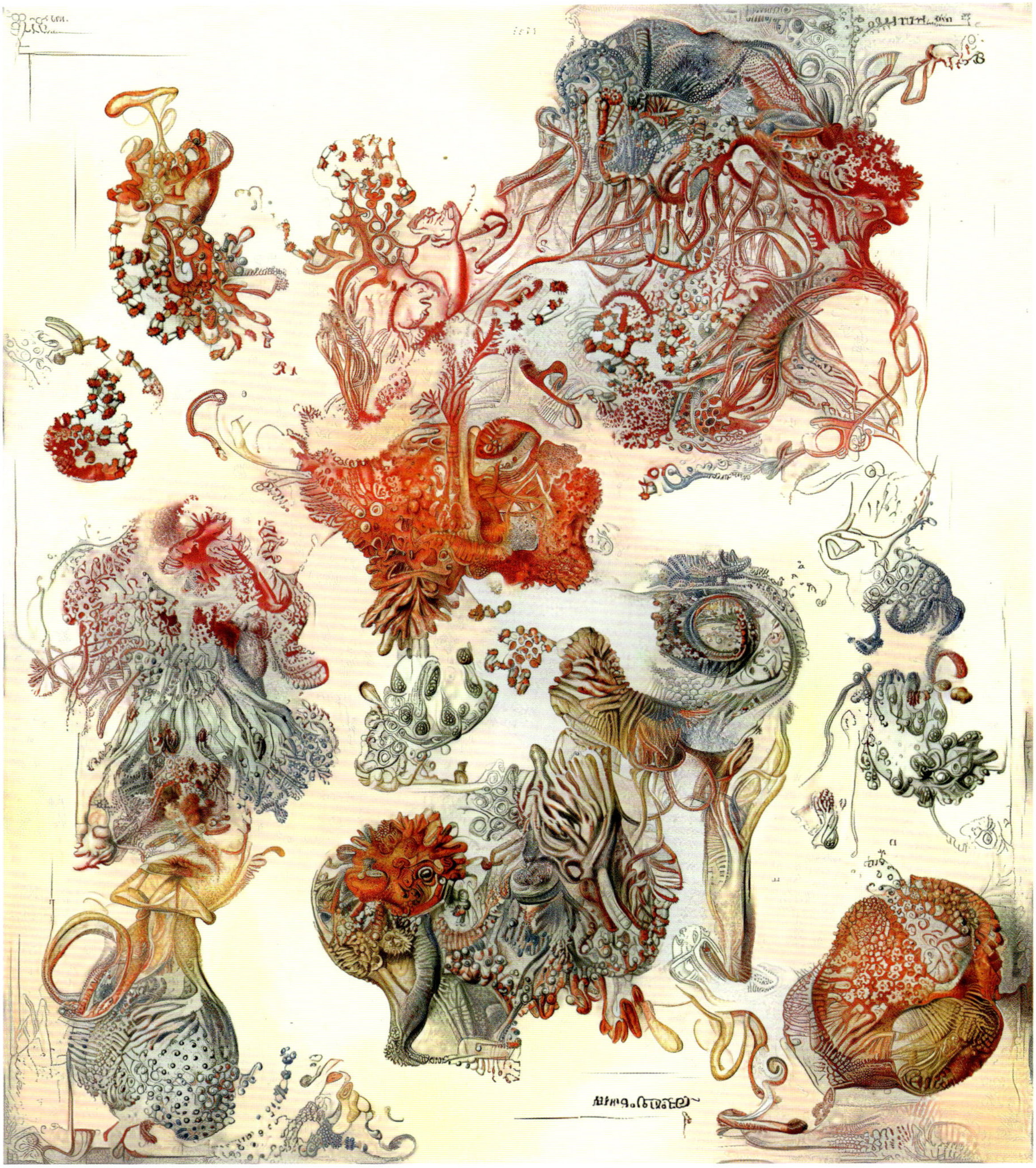

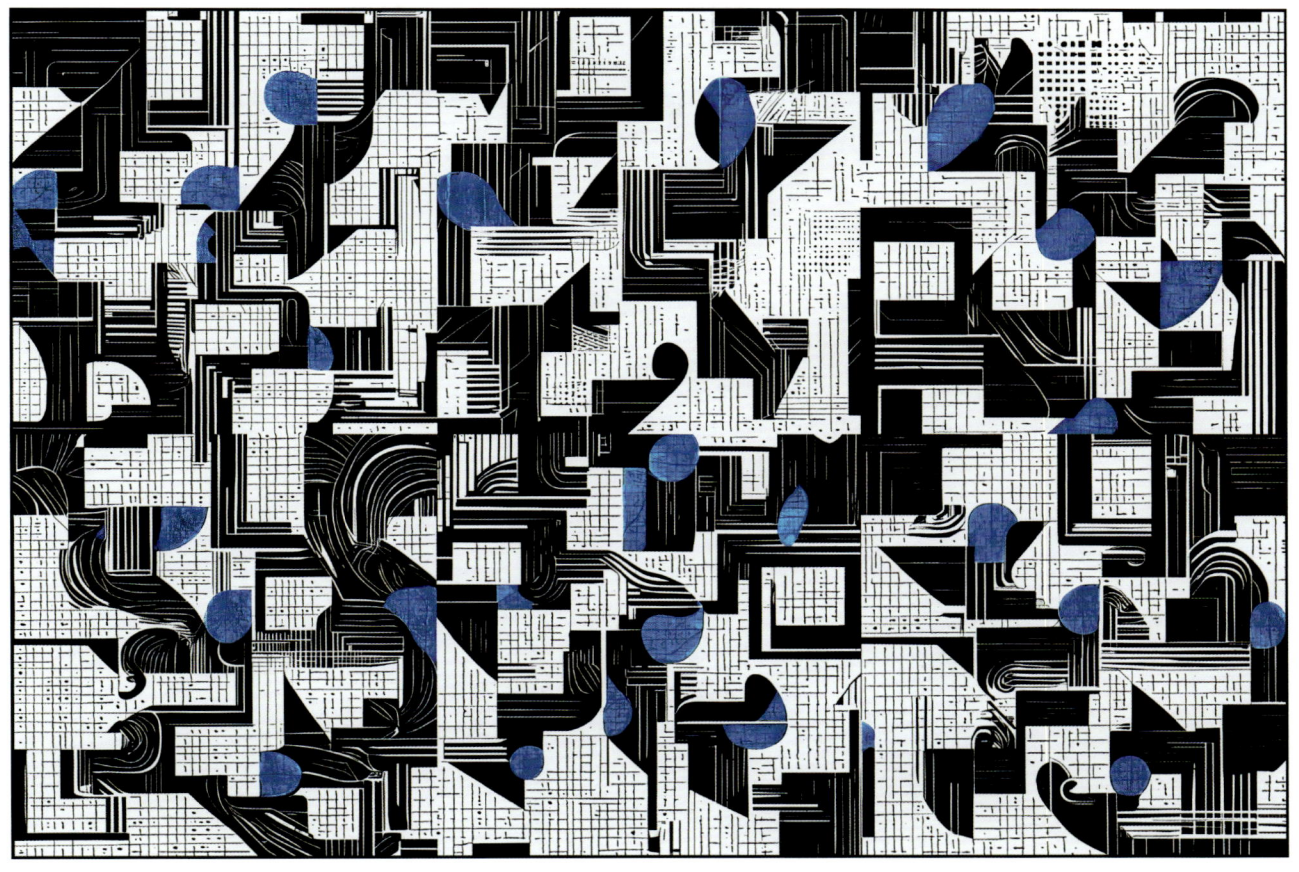

| # | TITLE | TIMESTAMP | MEDIUM | CHAIN | CONTRACT ADDRESS | TOKEN ID | EDITION SIZE |
|---|---|---|---|---|---|---|---|
| 01 | **Blue Stratagem: Improvising on the Keyboard of Manifolds** | 10-30-2022 02:50:23 | GAN, AI | ETH | 0x03fbae30095e1afc380d0eff041c2271e4745589 | 0 | 1/1 |
| 02 | **summer bloom in the back-yard of a GAN practitioner** | 06-31-2020 03:26:01 | GAN, AI | ETH | 0xb932a70a57673d89f4acffbe830e8ed7f75fb9e0 | 12390 | 1/1 |

# HELENA SARIN

RUSSIA 1960

02

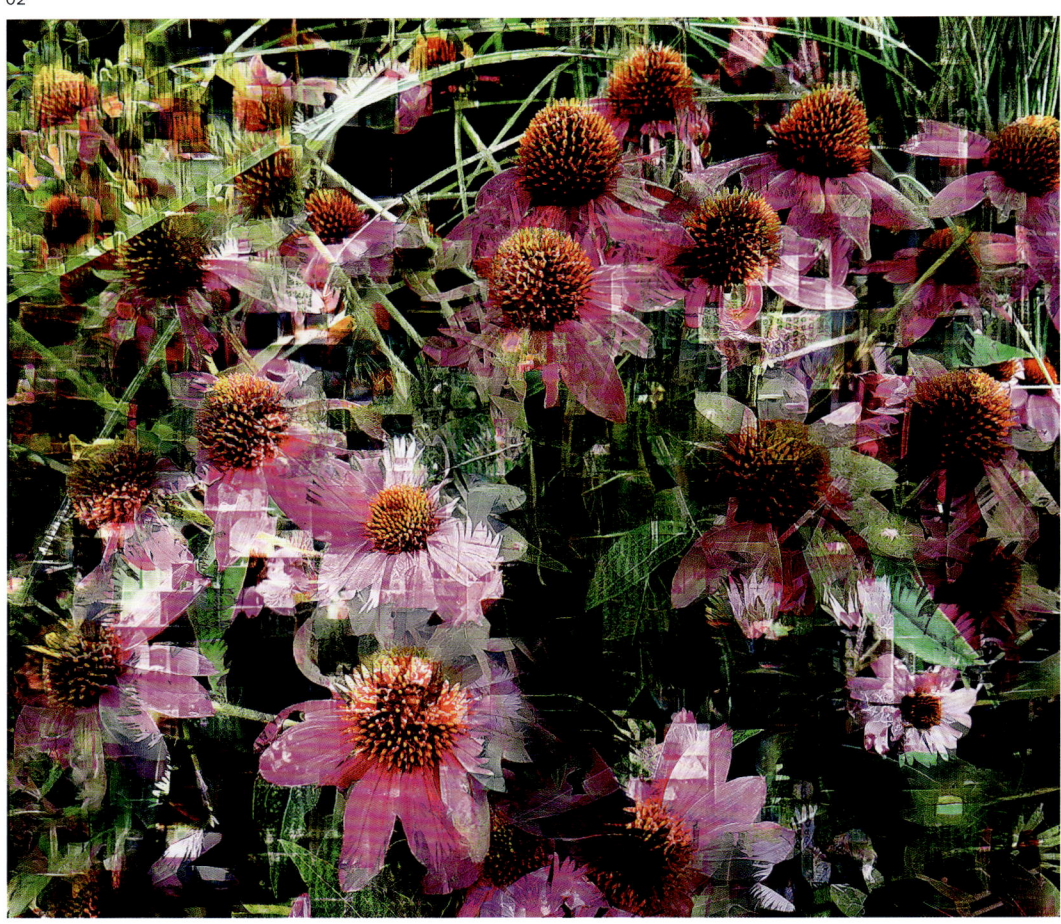

Visual artist and software engineer Helena Sarin employs cutting-edge technologies. She has worked in places like Bell Labs, and has taken commissions for watercolor, pastel, food and drink styling, and photograph. Separately working as an analog artist and software engineer, these two tracks converged when Helena discovered GAN, which became her primary medium. A frequent guest speaker, Helena has exhibited art worldwide and featured in publications including *Art in America*. One of the leading female NFT artists since early 2020, she advocates for diversity and pay equality in this space. She has published four artist's books (two as NFTs) and shown at Art Basel Miami in 2021.

The generative capacity of machines poses a radical change in the artist's creative process. When working with deep learning, Helena controls the final result by choosing datasets to train the models with and by curating the output. In the often uniform space of GAN art, Sarin's creations stand out as extremely personal, enhanced by her attention to detail. She combines knowledge of computer vision and art history to preprocess data, often supplying her own photography and watercolor paintings. Postproduction and curation are fundamental parts of her creative process, and Helena's careful work on image captioning provides an additional verbal dimension. She coined the term *post-GANism* to describe how she processes images with Python scripts and even uses analog assemblage to finalize her creations.

Helena's works often have a geometric and carefully (de)constructed quality, like in *Blue Stratagem: Improvising on the Keyboard of Manifolds* (2022). Providing an analogy to sheet music, the grid composition is structured by its blue and black notes that reveal the inner workings of her artistic vision and her computer program. Her artwork dwells on (yet) another key artistic moment, a homage to Kandinsky dreamed by the machine.

**BLANCA PÉREZ FERRER**
HEAD OF CURATION OF NEW MEDIA ART AT THE ETOPIA CENTER
FOR ART & TECHNOLOGY, ZARAGOZA

01

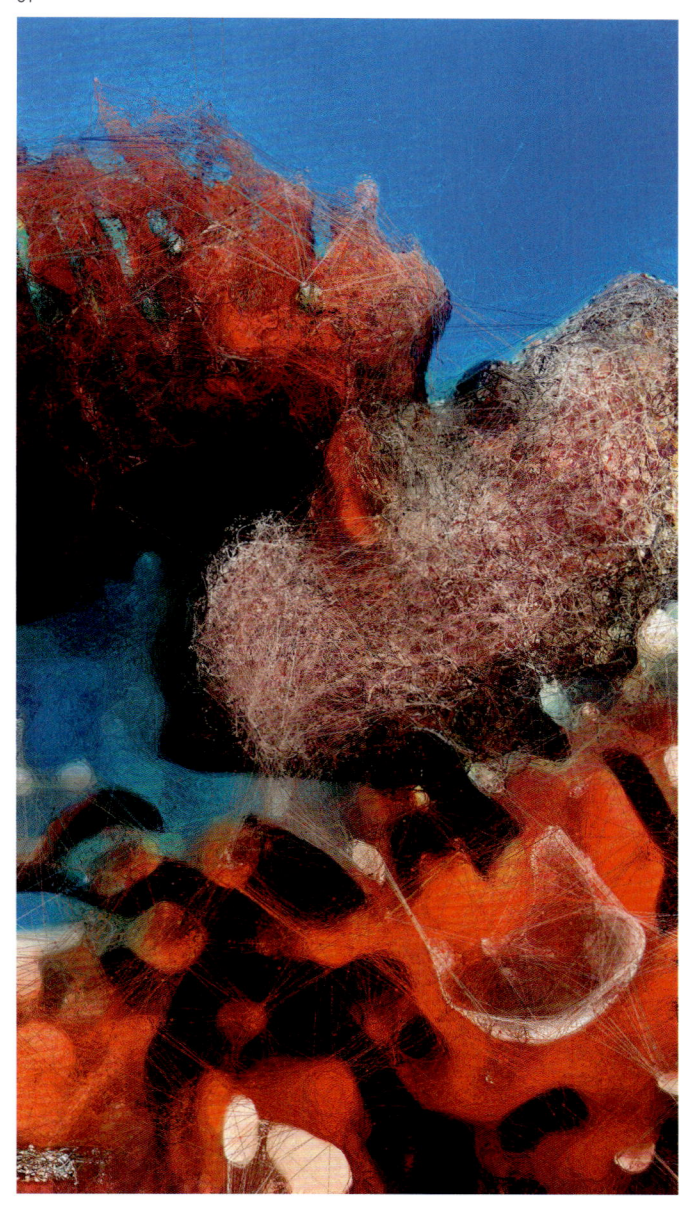

| # | TITLE | TIMESTAMP | MEDIUM | CHAIN | CONTRACT ADDRESS | TOKEN ID | EDITION SIZE |
|---|---|---|---|---|---|---|---|
| 01 | **Machine Hallucinations – Coral – Generative AI Data Painting** | 11-29-2021 20:05:51 | AI Data Paintings, Sculptures | ALGO | GG3CTXNG6G7AQ45SQCB5SSAXG5HU-TVH3TPLWWAPDVDD5Y46E4TQ2NQI4RI | 447548419–447569077 | 5 artworks in editions of 100, +1 AP |
| 02 | **Machine Hallucinations: Coral Dreams** | 11-29-2021 22:57:11 | AI Data Paintings, Sculptures | ALGO | GG3CTXNG6G7AQ45SQCB5SSAXG5HUTV-H3TPLWWAPDVDD5Y46E4TQ2NQI4RI | 447756598 | 1/1 |
| 03, 04 | **Unsupervised – Machine Hallucinations – MoMA Dreams** | 11-24-2021 06:51:15 | AI Data Paintings, Sculptures | ETH | 0x7a15b36cb834aea88553de69077d3777460d73ac | 2817...3491–9654...0528 | 9 artworks in editions of 100, +1 AP |
| 05 | **Machine Hallucinations – Space: Metaverse** | 09-21-2021 20:32:33 | AI Data Paintings, Sculptures | ETH | 0x7948f7ff1158b338a898e80ce8b1c3c964a80cec | 1 | 1/1 |

EDITIONS ILLUSTRATED: (01) E, (02) Ported to Ethereum in 2024 0xd99b40c0a6d12463877839e88d7bf43c779ffe2f/66000001 (03) I, (04) D

# REFIK ANADOL

TURKEY 1985

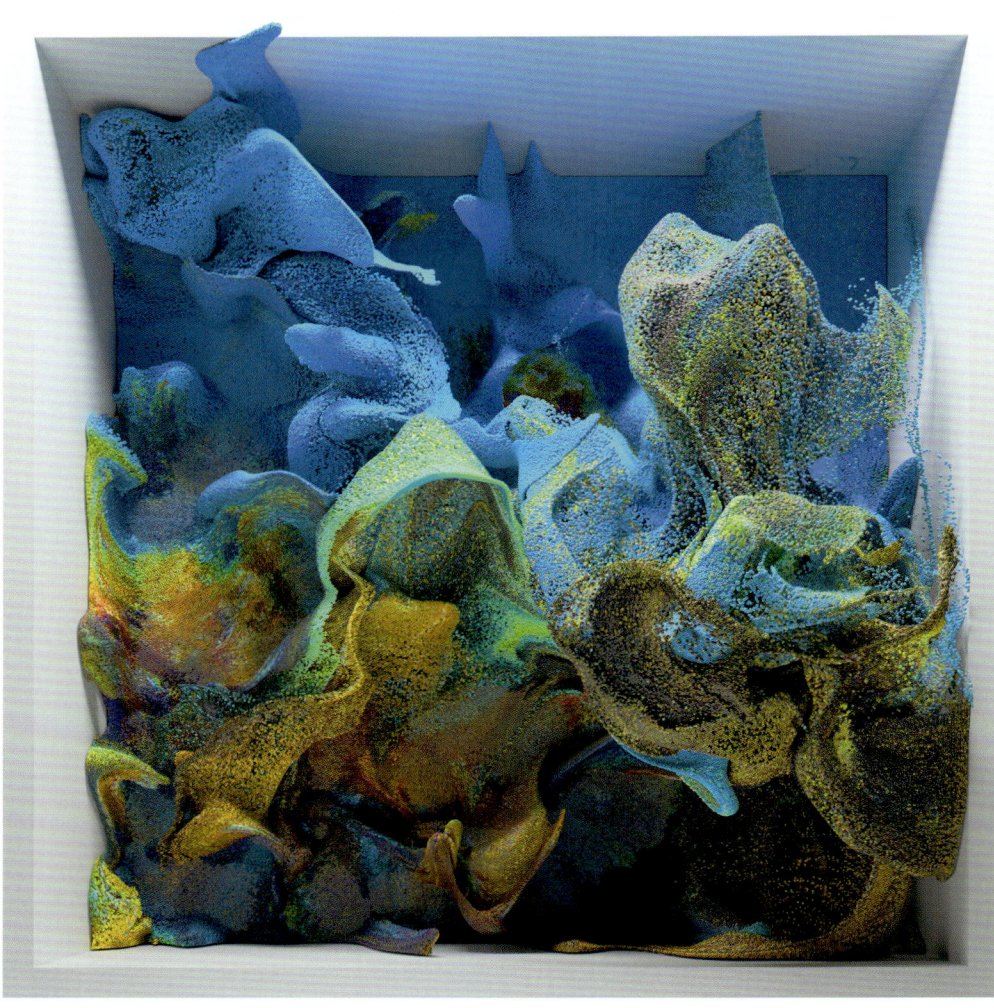

I first met Refik in 2012 when I was in Los Angeles and he was home in Istanbul. Through a video chat, he walked me through a live demo of his early and impressive work that focused on projection-mapped animations at architectural scale. One year later, Refik came to work in Los Angeles, his "Blade Runner" city. Within a short time, he was collaborating with architects and software engineers on an ambitious plan to project his images onto the Walt Disney Concert Hall designed by Frank Gehry, the most iconic contemporary building in Los Angeles. This wasn't a commission yet, it was something that Refik willed into existence. After six years of his committed work, I clearly remember standing in front of Disney Hall in downtown Los Angeles with thousands of other people, watching the entire surface of the building activated by Refik's extraordinary performance to celebrate the Los Angeles Philharmonic's 100th anniversary. This *WDCH Dreams* (2019) event was pivotal — it was Refik's launch into the international media art scene beyond the core community that had known his work for years.

He's been building on that triumph over the last four years, with even more momentum growing through his NFTs. Refik's *Machine Hallucinations: Coral Dreams – AI Data Sculpture* (2021) installation in Miami is another landmark in his career and it's his most recognized NFT artwork. This 12 × 12–meter "AI data sculpture" was installed on the beach overlooking the ocean during Art Basel Miami Beach in 2021. It transports NFTs from computer screens into the environment at an epic scale. Here, the NFT is a certificate of authenticity associated with a large-scale installation. To create the images for *Coral Dreams*, Refik's studio trained a machine learning system on over 1.7 million images of coral and coral reefs.

**CASEY REAS**
CO-FOUNDER OF FERAL FILE

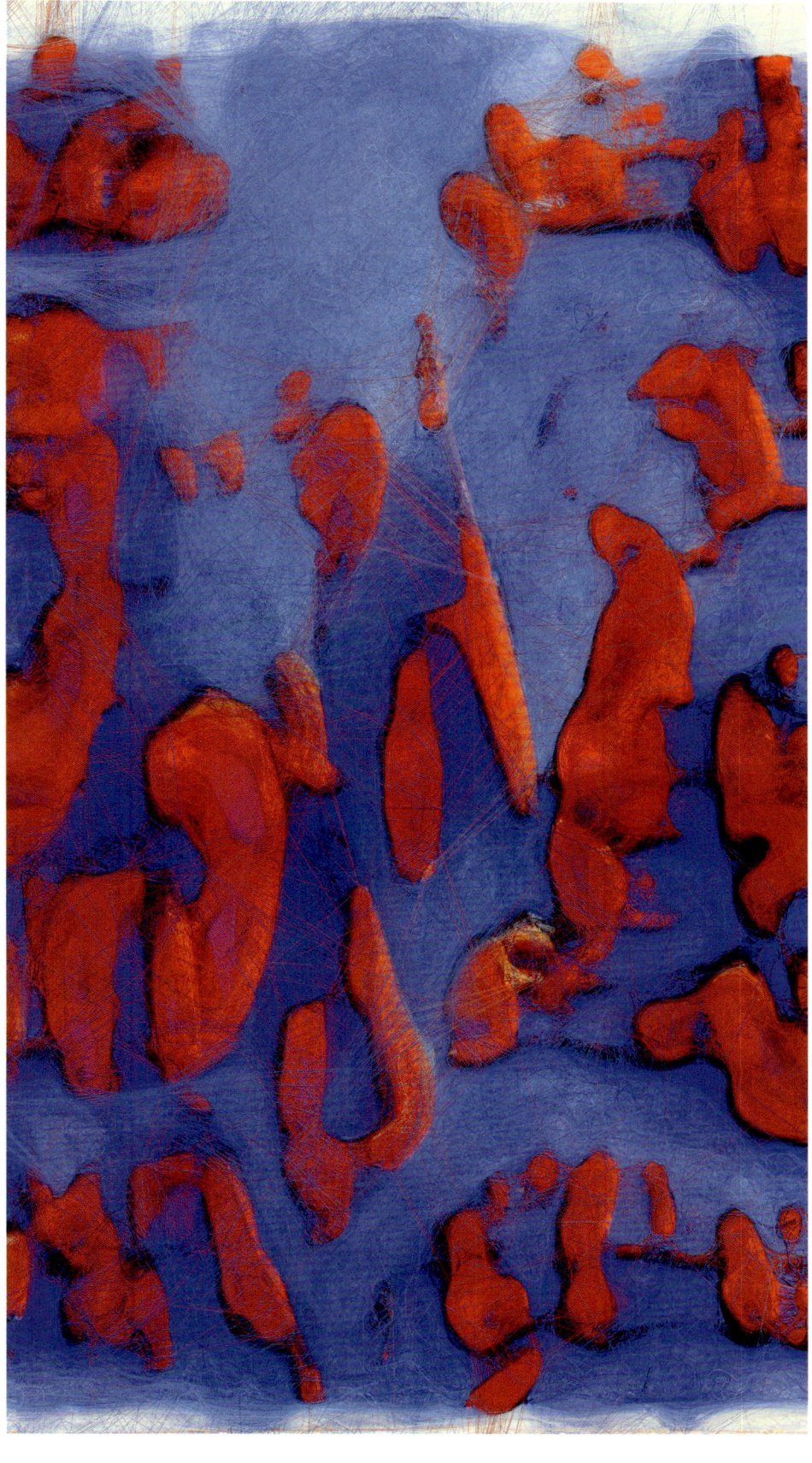

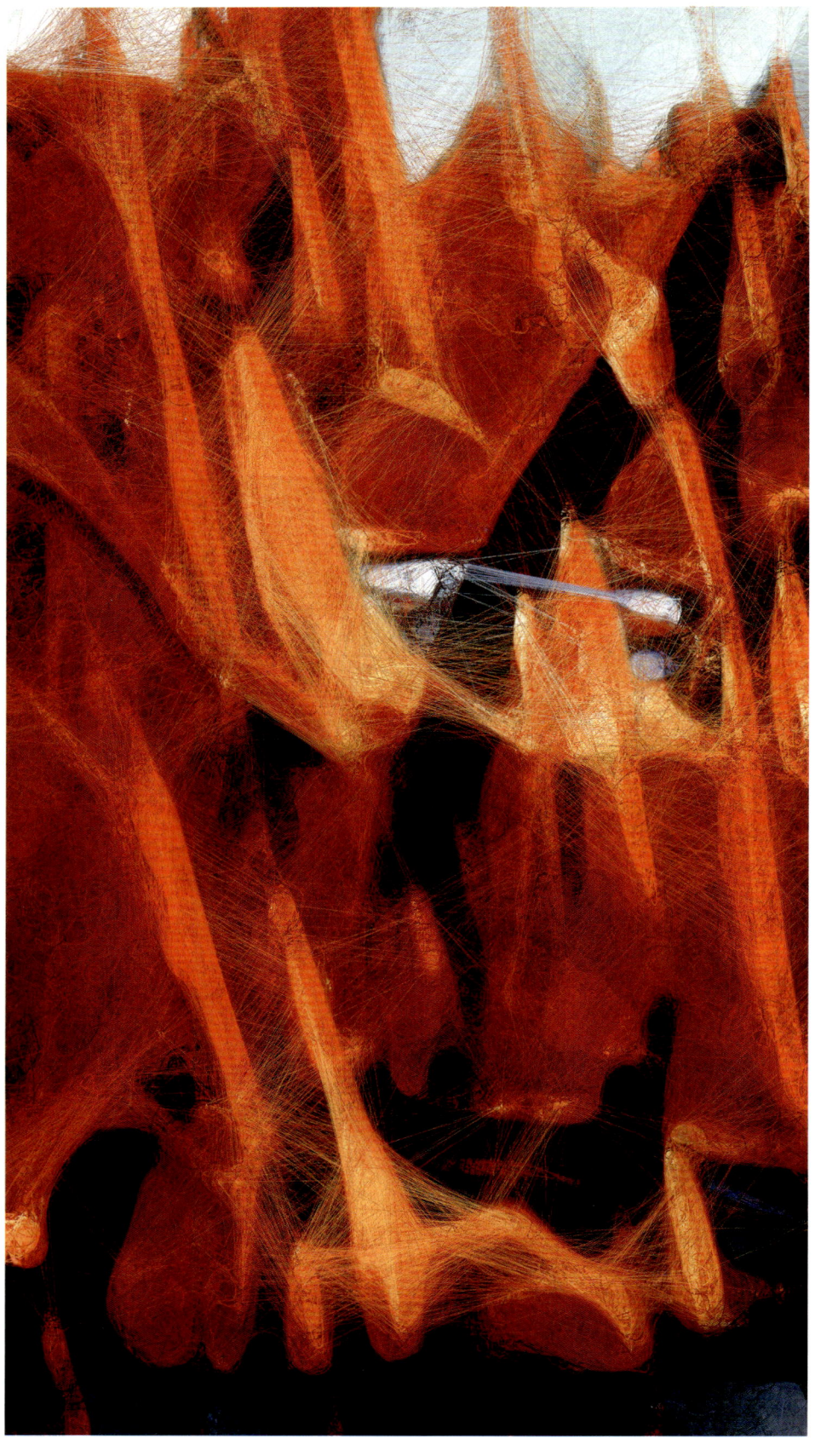

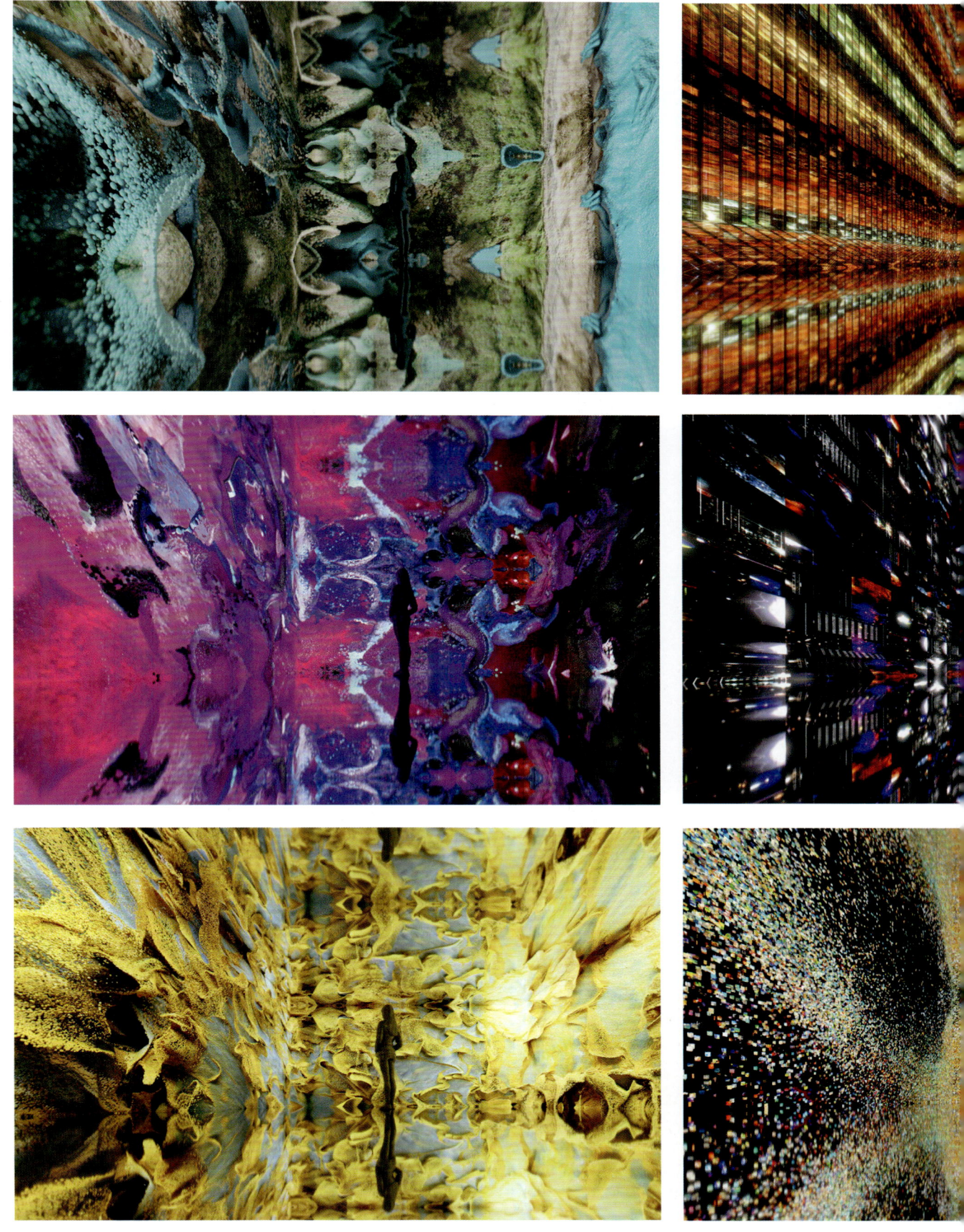

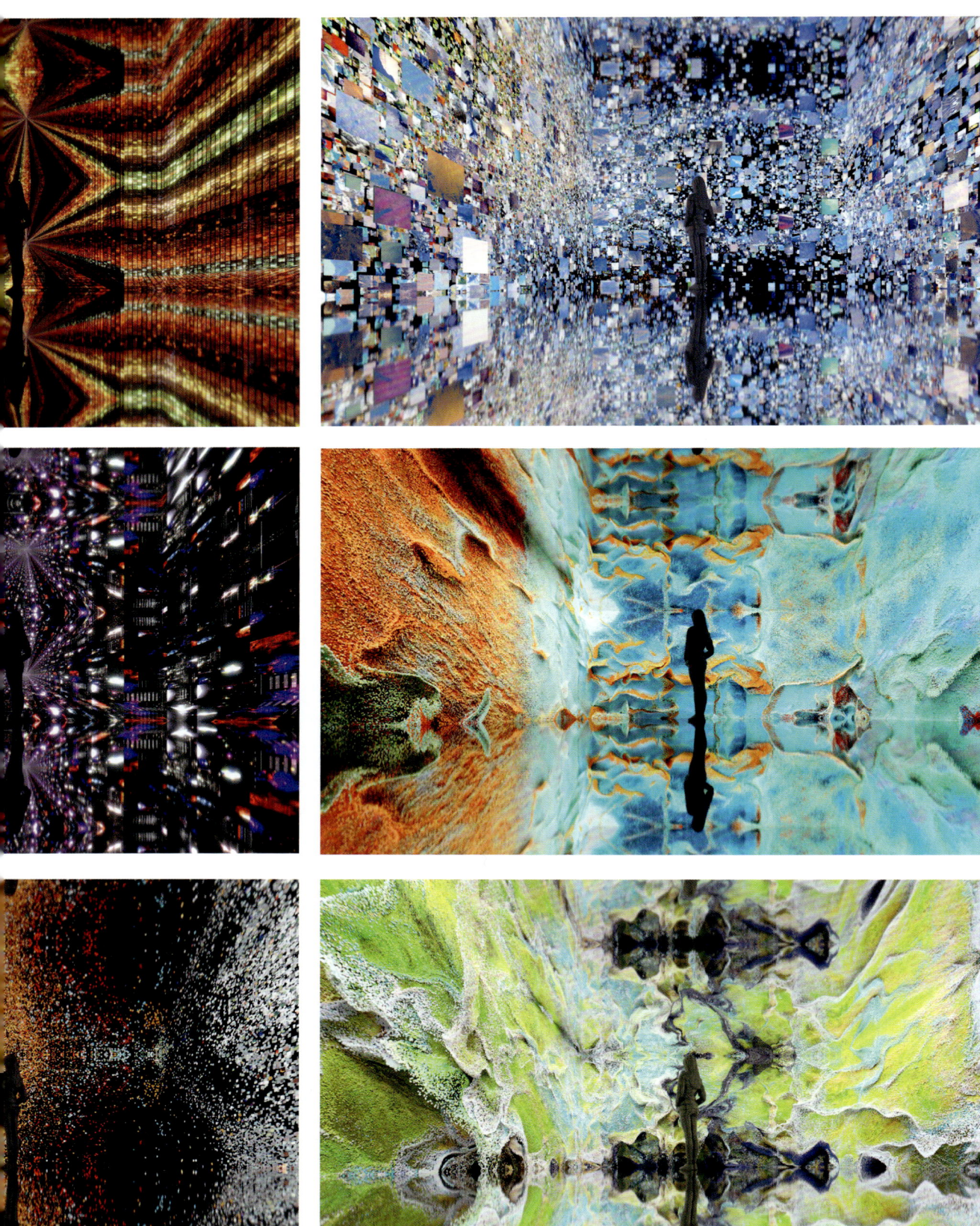

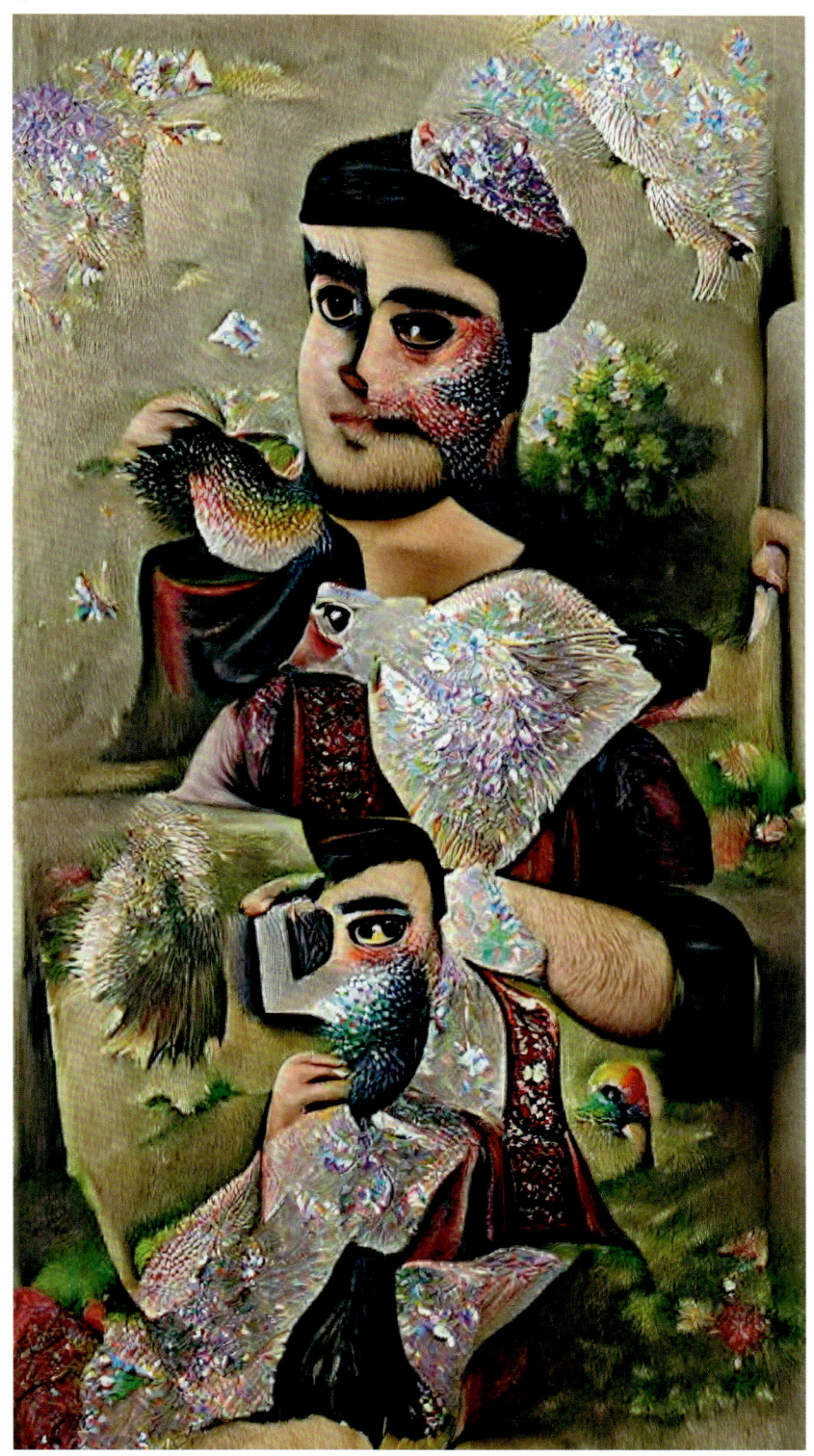

| # | TITLE | TIMESTAMP | MEDIUM | CHAIN | CONTRACT ADDRESS | TOKEN ID | EDITION SIZE |
|---|---|---|---|---|---|---|---|
| 01–03 | **Moon-faced** | 12-15-2021 16:33:48 | VQGAN+CLIP | BTM | aDZyD3gUNnLD5ViVVqGq3MPV2EmaxBjijYbaf87Ru6KYu1xNcD | 9b46...02fc–03e1...a00d | 115, +1 AP |

# MOREHSHIN ALLAHYARI

IRAN 1985

02 ►

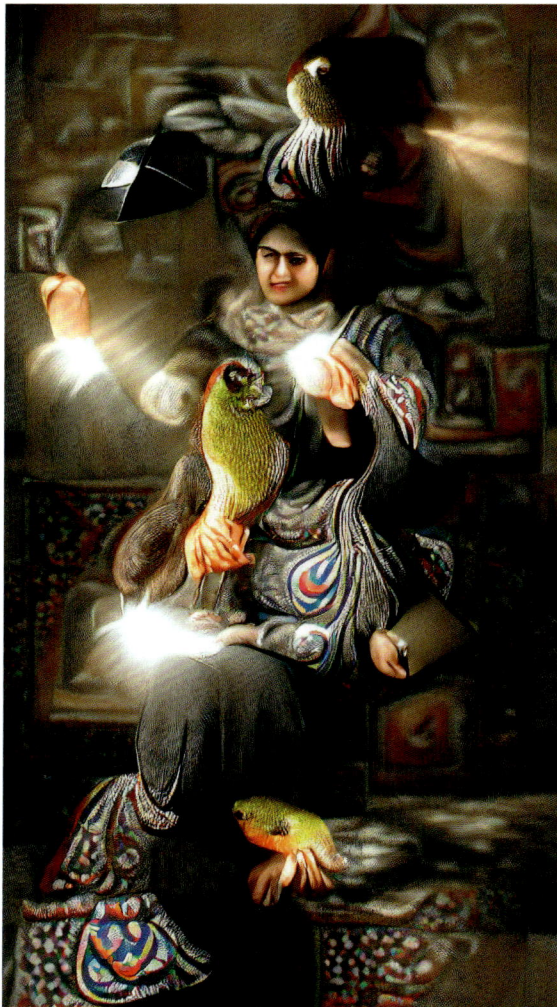

03 ►

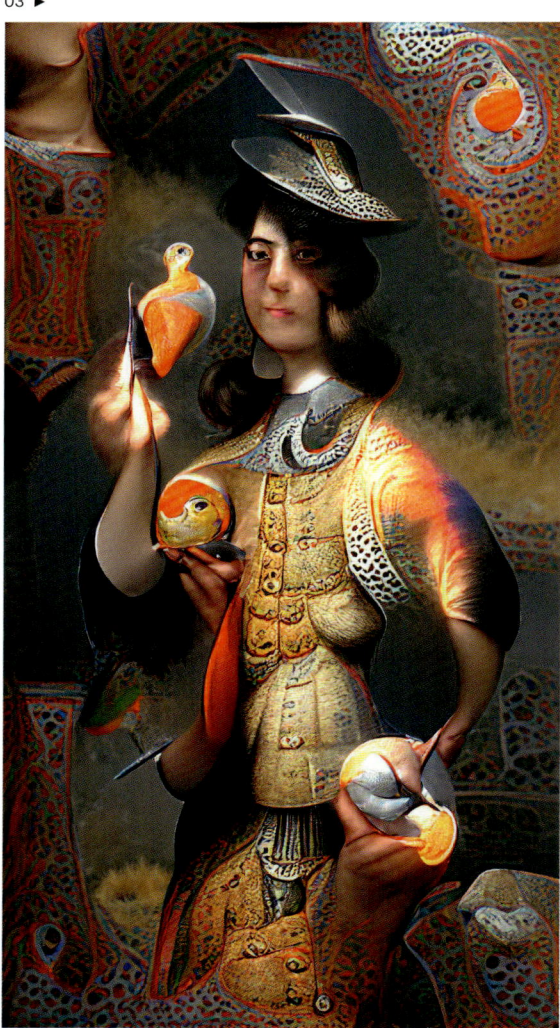

Morehshin Allahyari, a New York–based Iranian Kurdish artist, inhabits many different contexts. An artist, feminist, activist, and educator, her work reflects and challenges the political, socio-economic and technological inequalities of the 21st century. Through inventive uses of digital media and NFT technology, she reveals and decenters dominant narratives and moves beyond simplistic East/West, woman/man, and religious/secular divides.

My journey with Morehshin started with *She Who Sees the Unknown: Kabous* (2016–19), *The Left Witness* (2019), and *The Right Witness* (2019) commissioned by The Shed in 2019. I was taken by her personal stories of four generations of women (her grandmother, mother, herself, and an imagined monstrous daughter) chiseled against patriarchal structures and Western technological colonialism in the context of the SWANA (Southwest Asia and North Africa) region. It was the palimpsest nature of her work — captured in VR film, 3D sculptures, and an installation of her child bedroom in Iran — that made me want to learn more about her art, feminism, and activism.

I continued to follow Morehshin's digital work during the lockdown of 2020, against the backdrop of the pandemic, rising authoritarianism, and the mass protests against police killings of Black Americans, such as Breonna Taylor and George Floyd. I liked how her activism became a part of the technology and texture of her work. In *Moon-faced* (2021), for example, she used a multimodal AI model in the effort to undo the impact of Western technology in depicting gender norms in Iranian visual art. It was this NFT video, with music composed by Mani Nilchiani, that led to our collaboration, *The Politics of Queer Bots,* at Symphony Space, New York in May 2022.

**KATHRYN SPELLMAN POOTS**
ASSOCIATE PROFESSOR AT COLUMBIA UNIVERSITY
AND AGA KHAN UNIVERSITY

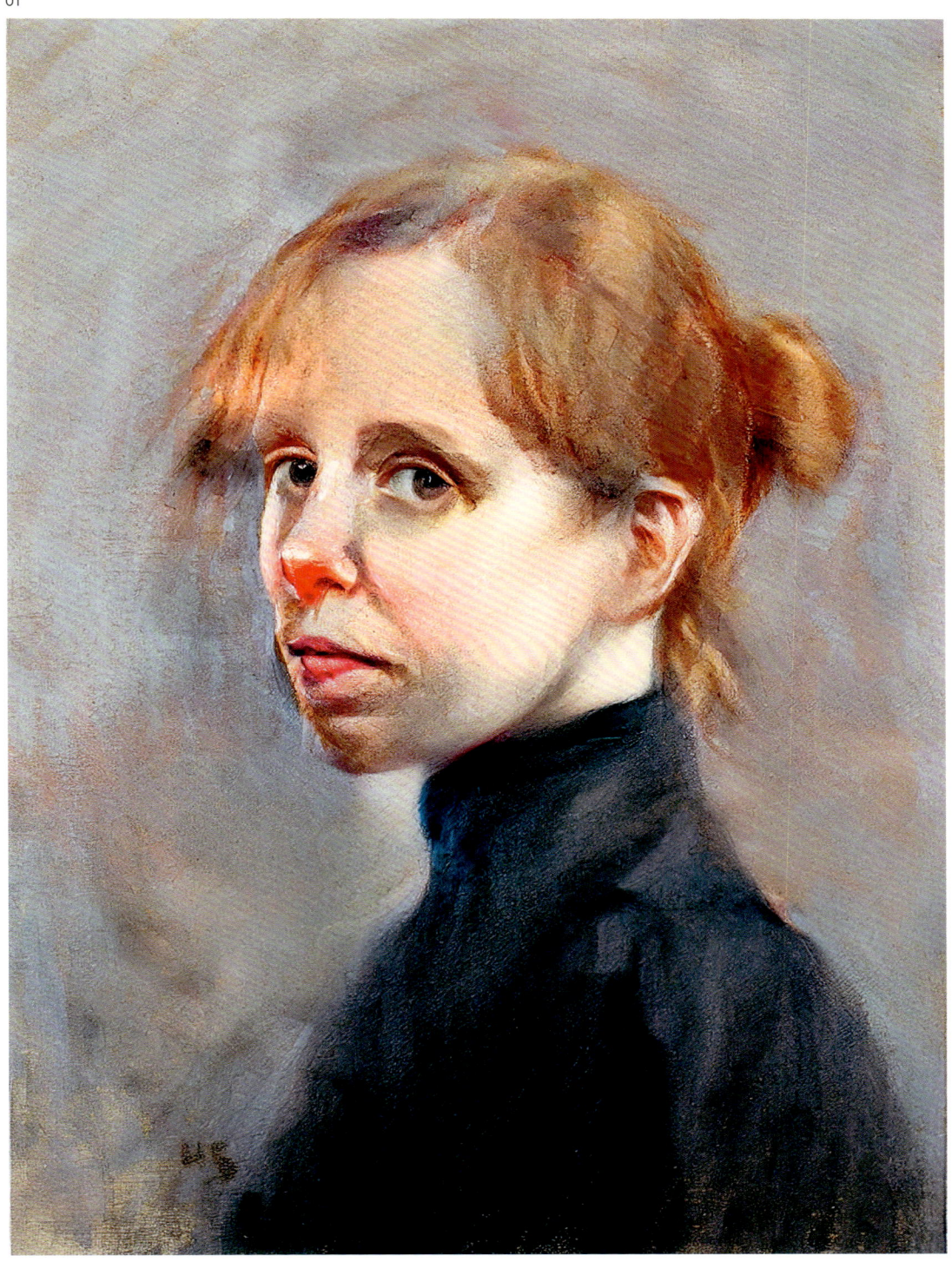

| # | TITLE | TIMESTAMP | MEDIUM | CHAIN | CONTRACT ADDRESS | TOKEN ID | EDITION SIZE |
|---|---|---|---|---|---|---|---|
| 01, 06–15 | **Classified** | 10-20-2021 01:36:53 | Custom VQGAN+CLIP | ETH | 0x91fba69ce5071cf9e828999a0f6006a7f7e2a959 | 1–47 | 1/1 of 47 |
| 02–05 | **Crossing the Interface (DAO)** | 05-25-2021 20:05:07 | VQGAN+CLIP | ETH | 0x3b3ee1931dc30c1957379fac9aba94d1c48a5405 | 40471–40515 | 1/1 of 13 |

EDITIONS ILLUSTRATED
(01) #4, (02) VI, (03) X, (04) VIII, (05) XIII, (06) #13, (07) #9, (08) #10, (09) Unminted, (10) #20, (11) #02, (12) #05, (13) #27, (14) Unminted, (15) #8

# HOLLY HERNDON & MAT DRYHURST

UNITED STATES 1980 & UNITED KINGDOM 1984

02 ▶
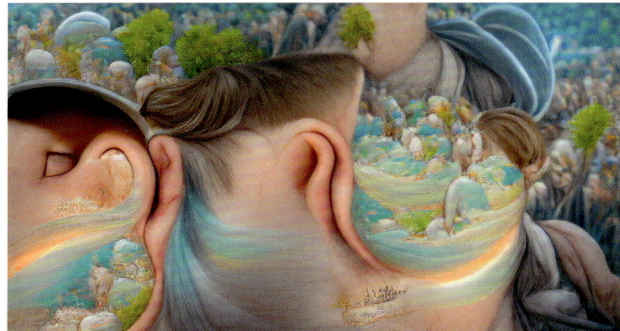

03 ▶
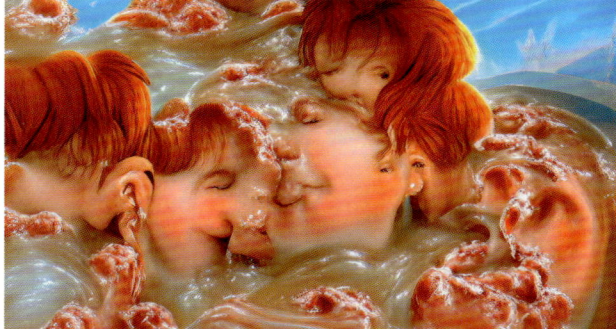

04 ▶
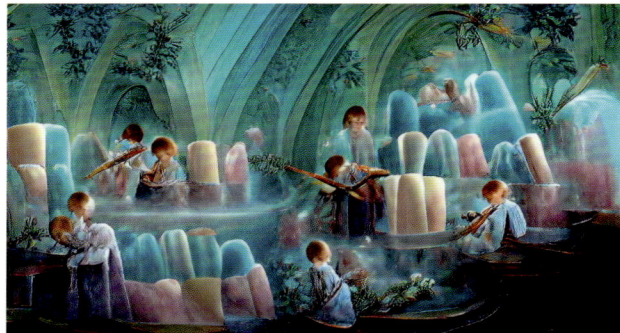

05 ▶
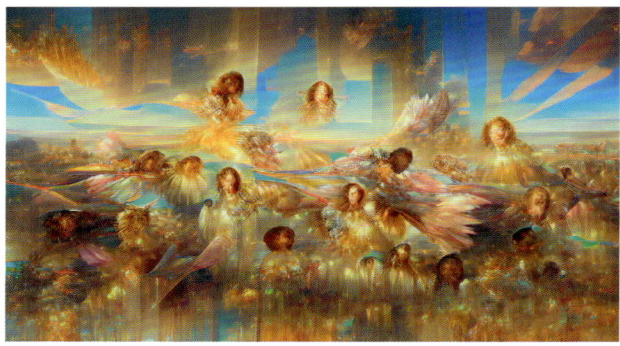

Holly Herndon and Mat Dryhurst refute the hard border between humans and machines. In their work as artists, musicians, and public intellectuals, there is no contradiction between the synthetic and the sensual. Intelligence should not aim at being artificial (as in AI), but, rather, extended (as in EI). "What is vocal sovereignty?" Herndon once asked. "Who owns the voice?" In 2021, this became the guiding query driving *Holly+*, a machine-learned, open software that allows any input voice to output in Herndon's distinctive vocal delivery. *Holly+* defangs the threat of anonymous deepfakes, and instead claims the deepfake as an authentic tool of authorship. Overseen by a DAO, *Holly+* is a living experiment in Web3-powered artistic collaboration.

*Crossing the Interface* (2021) was Herndon and Dryhurst's debut NFT collection. Harnessing machine learning, the duo generated animated visual compositions based upon text fragments by Iranian philosopher Reza Negarestani. NFTs resonate with Herndon and Dryhurst because they make a direct link between digital selves and digital value.

This sentiment was further developed in *Classified* (2021): a self-portraiture collection exploring the classification 'Holly Herndon' embedded in OpenAI's CLIP neural network. A variety of visual references — art-historical portraits, abstractions, noise — dialogued with CLIP, and spawned new, strange likenesses of Herndon. *Classified* ties together contemporary topics such as intellectual property and the endless, rootless circulation of digital images.

Herndon and Dryhurst have also cultivated discursive platforms. Their zeitgeist podcast *Interdependence* brings together Web3 protagonists with novelists and theorists. Channel promises to be a new kind of decentralized media organization, co-founded with like-minded creators New Models and Joshua Citarella. All this kinetic, exploratory energy inspired *ArtReview* to include Herndon and Dryhurst in their hallowed Power 100, describing the couple as "indispensable guides to our digital future."

**SHUMON BASAR**
CHIEF NARRATIVE OFFICER & CO-FOUNDER OF ZIEN

06

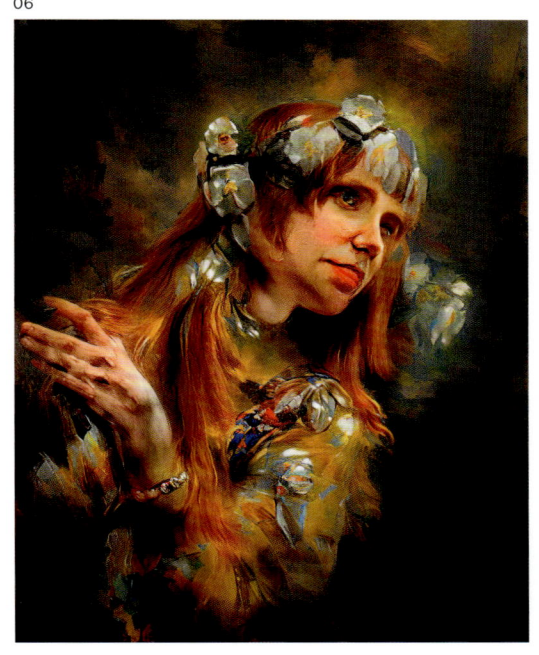

07

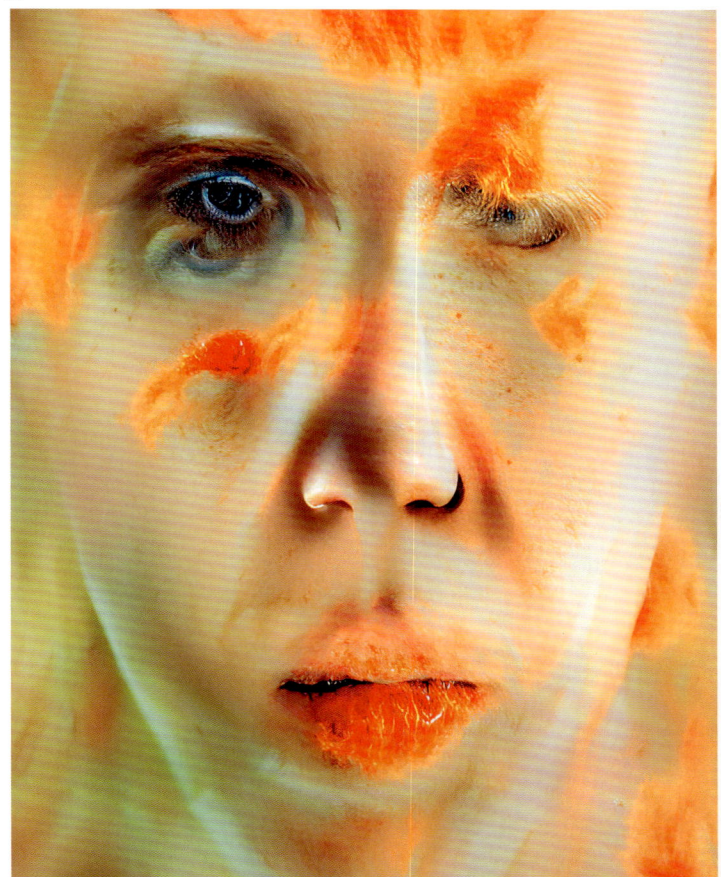

08

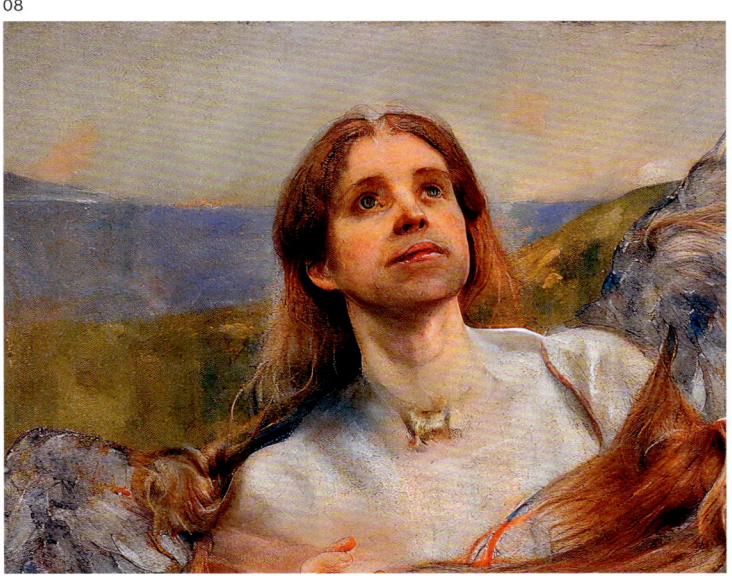

09

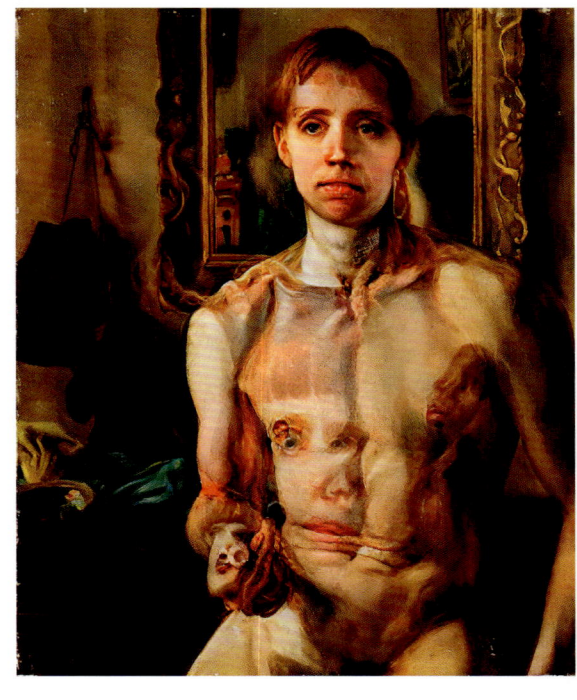

10

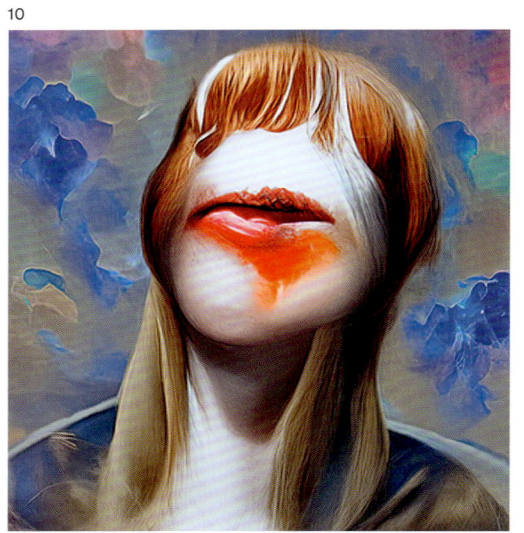

11

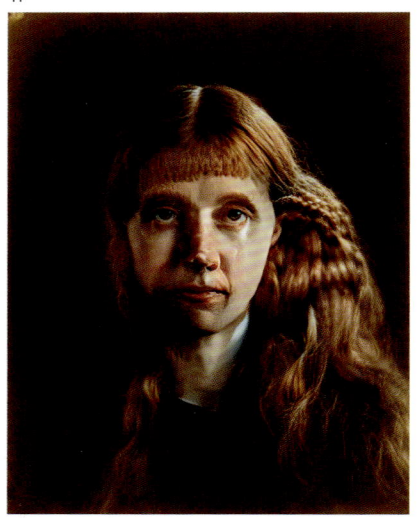

12

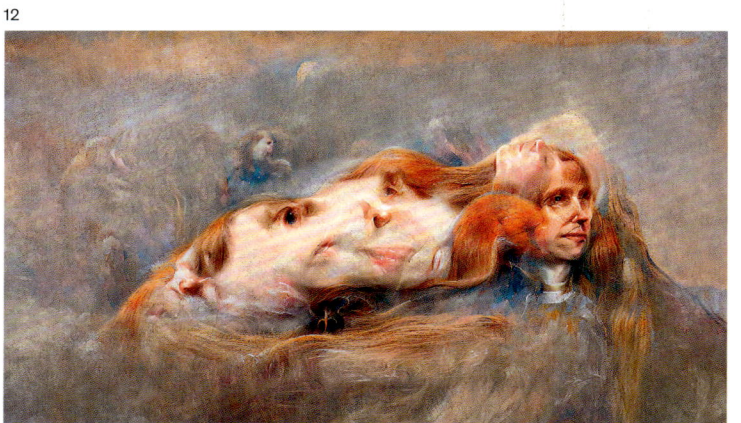

13

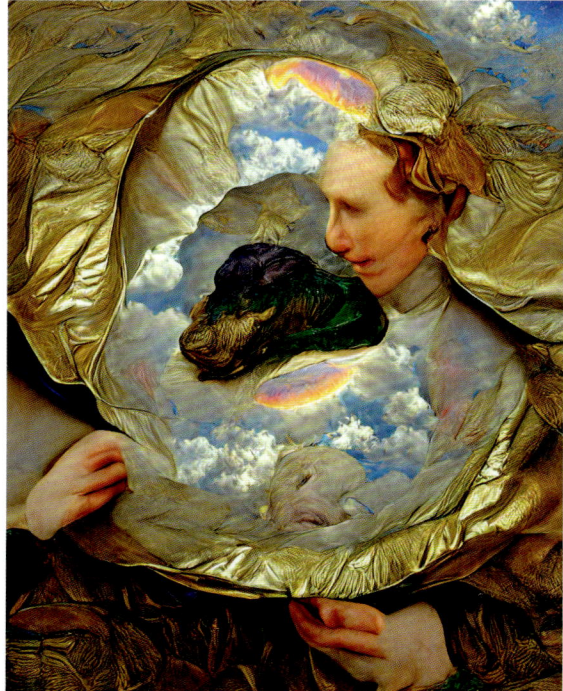

14

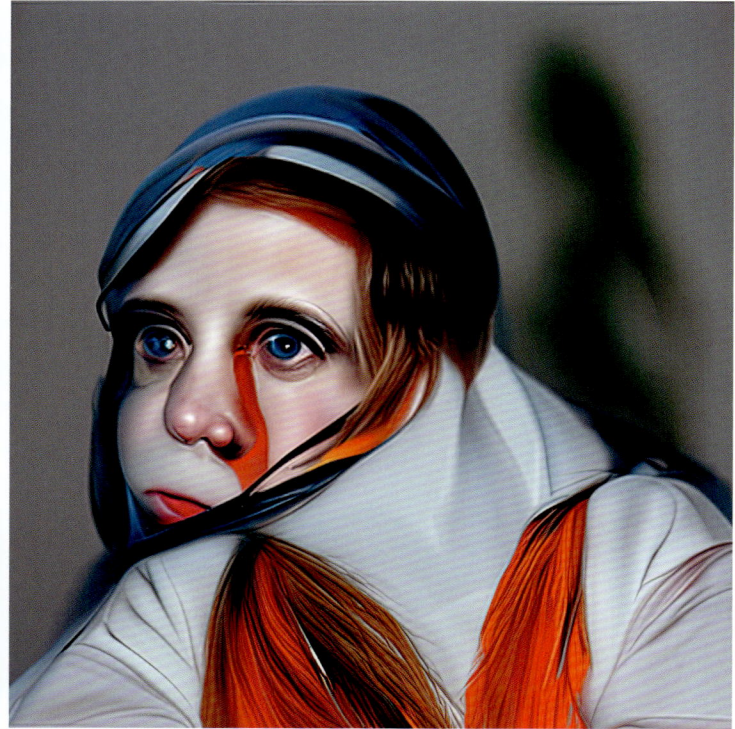

15

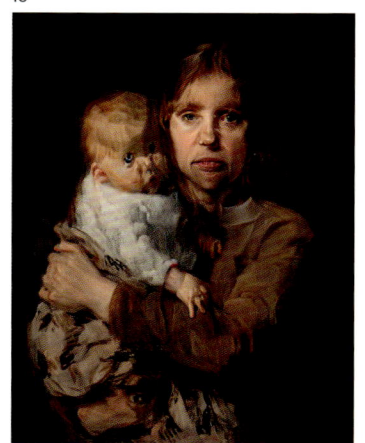

01

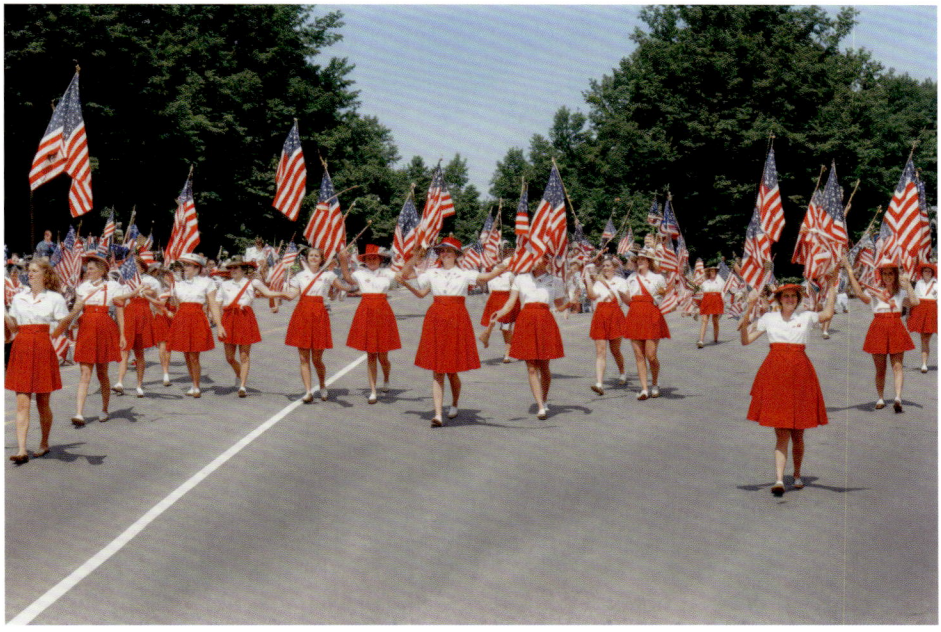

02

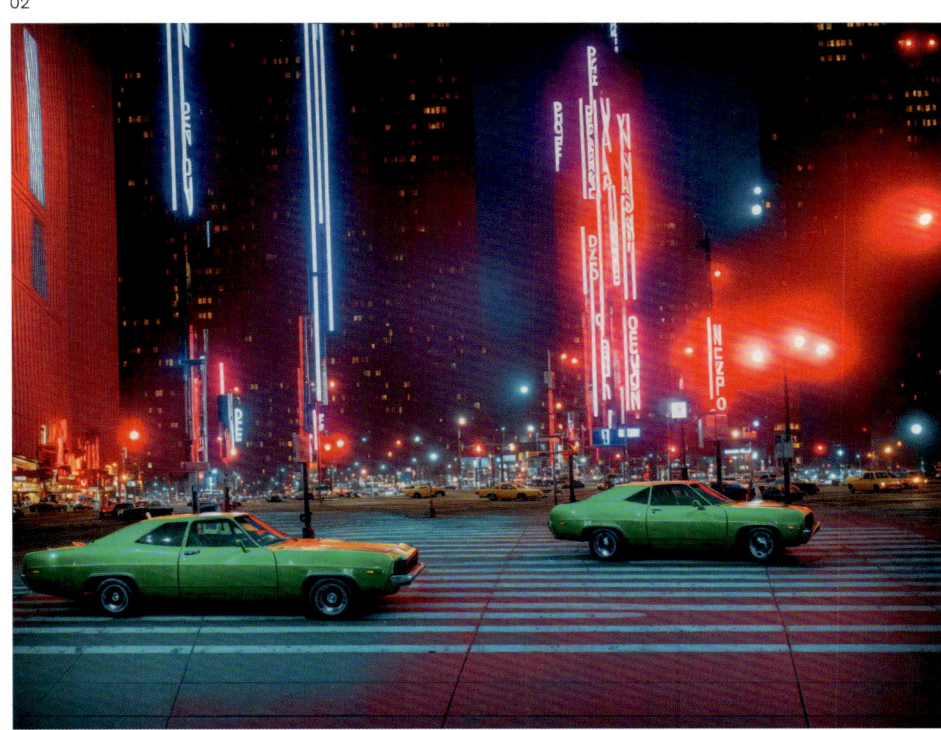

| # | TITLE | TIMESTAMP | MEDIUM | CHAIN | CONTRACT ADDRESS | TOKEN ID | EDITION SIZE |
|---|-------|-----------|--------|-------|------------------|----------|--------------|
| 01 | **Quiet Juggernaut (Life in the American West)** | 02-08-2023 18:11:23 | Generative AI, SD | ETH | 0xdfde78d2baec499fe18f2be74b6c287eed9511d7 | 15000451 | 1/1 of 500 |
| 02 | **American Parade No. 5 (REWORLD)** | 04-06-2023, 18:30:00 | Generative AI, SD | ETH | 0×66bcf059b2d8db6cd10615cdd781828db58268cf | 19 | 1/1 of 102 |
| 03 | **Auto Dream No. 3 (REWORLD)** | 04-06-2023, 20:15:00 | Generative AI, SD | ETH | 0×66bcf059b2d8db6cd10615cdd781828db58268cf | 32 | 1/1 of 102 |

# ROOPE RAINISTO

FINLAND 1979

03

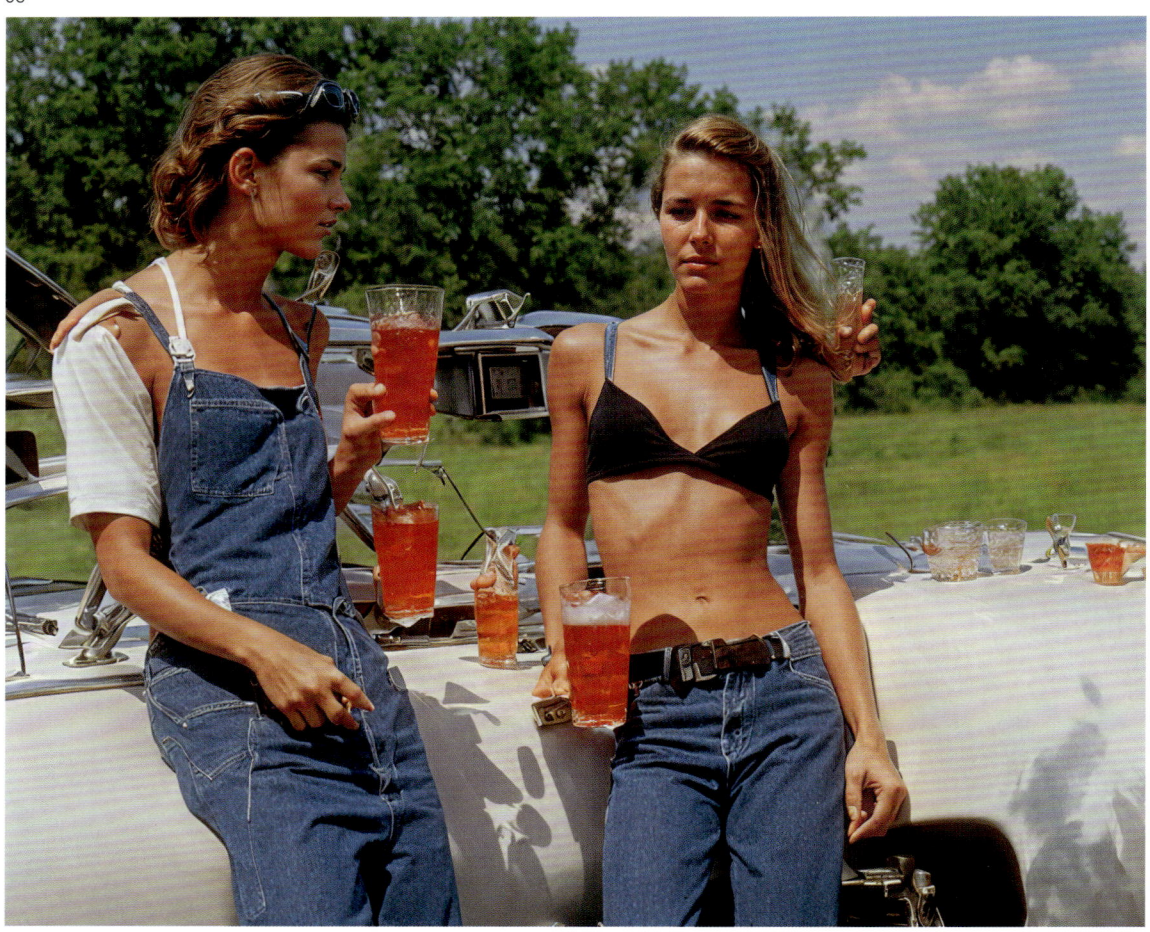

A collective unease surrounds AI. Is it here to help or control? Are we explorers in a latent space or being led down a sinister path? Art's role is to frame questions like these — making them approachable — while offering the viewer space to achieve more informed, nuanced answers.

Roope Rainisto's 2023 projects *Life in West America* (*LIWA*) and *REWORLD* do just that. They trace the shifting fault lines between individual agency and systemic control, using AI as an active participant in meaning-making. The collections achieve this by inhabiting and commenting upon the latent space — our new wild west.

Rainisto embraces this unknowable terrain both thematically and conceptually with *LIWA*, channeling a distorted vision of mid-century Americana conjured from a non-human perspective. The images feel familiar, yet off: a distortion in the light, a face that doesn't quite resolve. This tension mirrors Rainisto's own artistic engagement with AI — leaning into its imperfections while balancing artistic freedom. *LIWA* presents this myth of artistic and individual freedom in its most cinematic form, even as it reveals the ways that myth is constructed.

If *LIWA* celebrates the individual, *REWORLD* dismantles that premise, shifting focus from personal autonomy to the structures that shape it. Rainisto's trained models render environments that appear ordinary at first, yet are subtly misaligned — architecture bends unnaturally, social cues feel rehearsed rather than lived. The project suggests that in a world increasingly mediated by algorithms, the boundaries between agency and manipulation blur. Juxtaposed with Rainisto's polished surfaces, irregularities compel us to look — and think — twice.

Together, these works function as a thesis and antithesis, questioning the role of AI in perception and power. In LIWA, the frontier remains open; in *REWORLD*, the landscape is already mapped. In both, Rainisto employs AI not to generate images, but to reveal the structures that shape how we see.

**PETER BAUMAN**
EDITOR IN CHIEF, LE RANDOM

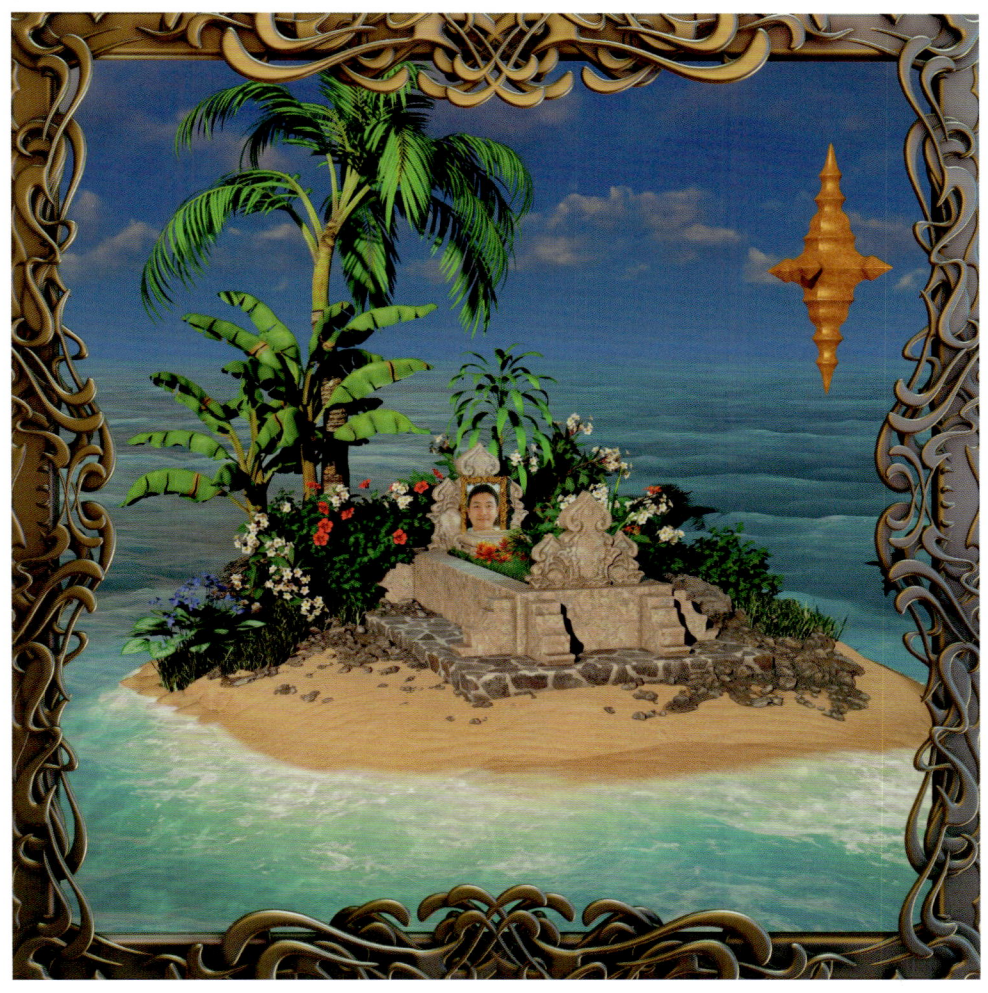

| # | TITLE | TIMESTAMP | MEDIUM | CHAIN | CONTRACT ADDRESS | TOKEN ID | EDITION SIZE |
|---|---|---|---|---|---|---|---|
| 01 | **Solitary Grave II** | 08-17-2021 07:28:57 | Lumion, ZBrush, Cinema4D, thispersondoesnotexist.com | ETH | 0x3b3ee1931dc30c1957379fac9aba94d1c48a5405 | 73336 | 1/1 |
| 02 | **Sacred Border (Batas Suci)** | 07-17-2021 19:22:39 | Lumion, ZBrush, Cinema4D | ETH | 0x3b3ee1931dc30c1957379fac9aba94d1c48a5405 | 65134 | 1/1 |

# RIMBAWAN GERILYA

INDONESIA 1981

02 ▶

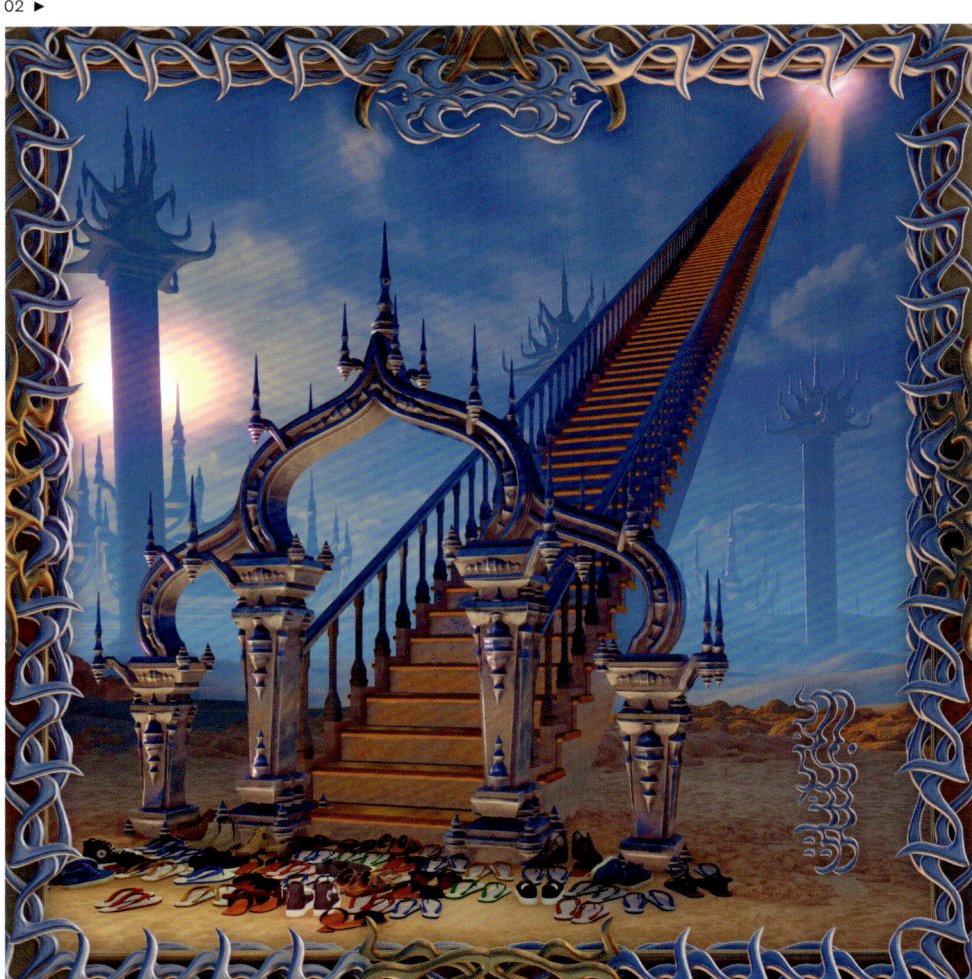

Rimbawan Gerilya is an Indonesian artist, digital animator, and visual jockey. The term is a rough translation of "Guerrilla Junglist" in Bahasa Indonesian, and the pseudonym adopted by Tri Hartono, drawing from the artist's roots as a visual jockey in Jakarta's drum and bass scene.

Rimbawan defines his practice as "Third World Futurism," developing a framework which investigates and speculates upon the technological future in light of the stark income inequality and different access to technology across the world, especially in developing nations. Open and borderless networks lie at the heart of blockchain ethos but it is difficult to realize in such a fractionalized world. Third World Futurism acknowledges these realities candidly without losing a sense of humor in the absurdism, while ensuring the inclusion and representation of Indonesians — and more broadly, Southeast Asians — in the emerging cultures of the metaverse. Drawing on his daily experiences, Rimbawan places religion and cultural rituals dominant in Indonesia into the digital imagination, questioning what is the future that we are building towards and who it serves.

This spirit is astutely captured in his *Solitary Grave* (2021) series, where Rimbawan imagines a fantastical grave for the death of an AI entity suspended in an unbounded cyber realm. The grave is set amidst floating trees and rocks, a place which humans cannot access nor inhabit. The frame atop the tombstone, supposedly of the deceased, is an AI-generated image of a person that does not exist. The series challenges the consciousness we seek to imbue in machines, despite the fact artificial entities are not subjected to the mortal death that we are and nor do they understand impermanence or the value of life in the ways humans do. What will this mean for our increasingly intimate relationship with machines?

**CLARA CHE WEI PEH**
FOUNDER OF NFT ASIA AND CURATOR AT APPETITE

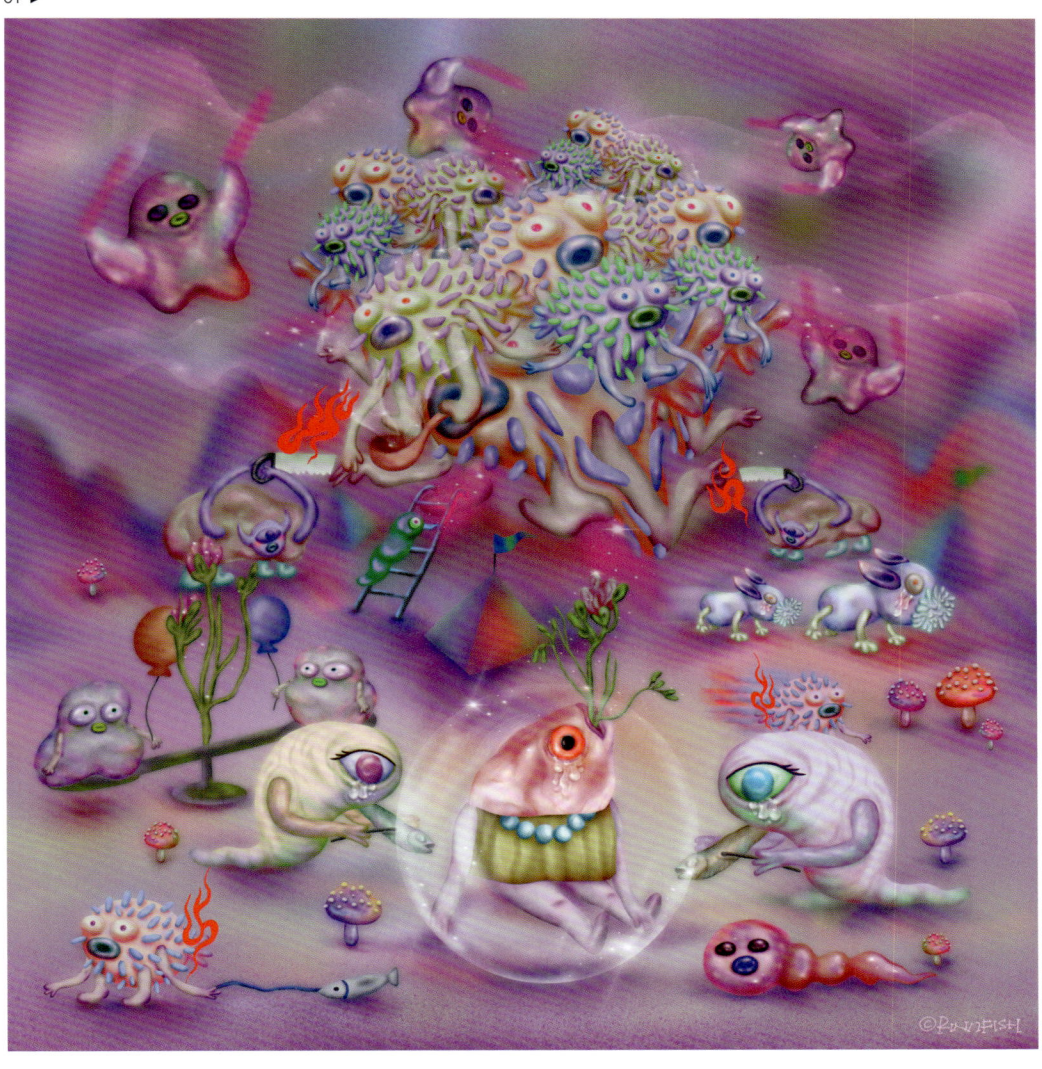

| # | TITLE | TIMESTAMP | MEDIUM | CHAIN | CONTRACT ADDRESS | TOKEN ID | EDITION SIZE |
|---|-------|-----------|--------|-------|------------------|----------|--------------|
| 01 | **My Hell / M7 Planet** | 03-29-2021 04:37:43 | Procreate | ETH | 0x3b3ee1931dc30c1957379fac9aba94d1c48a5405 | 15833 | 1/1 |
| 02 | **Heart Throb / M7 Planet** | 12-31-2021 07:53:43 | Procreate | ETH | 0x3b3ee1931dc30c1957379fac9aba94d1c48a5405 | 125664 | 1/1 |

# RINIIFISH

CHINA 1993

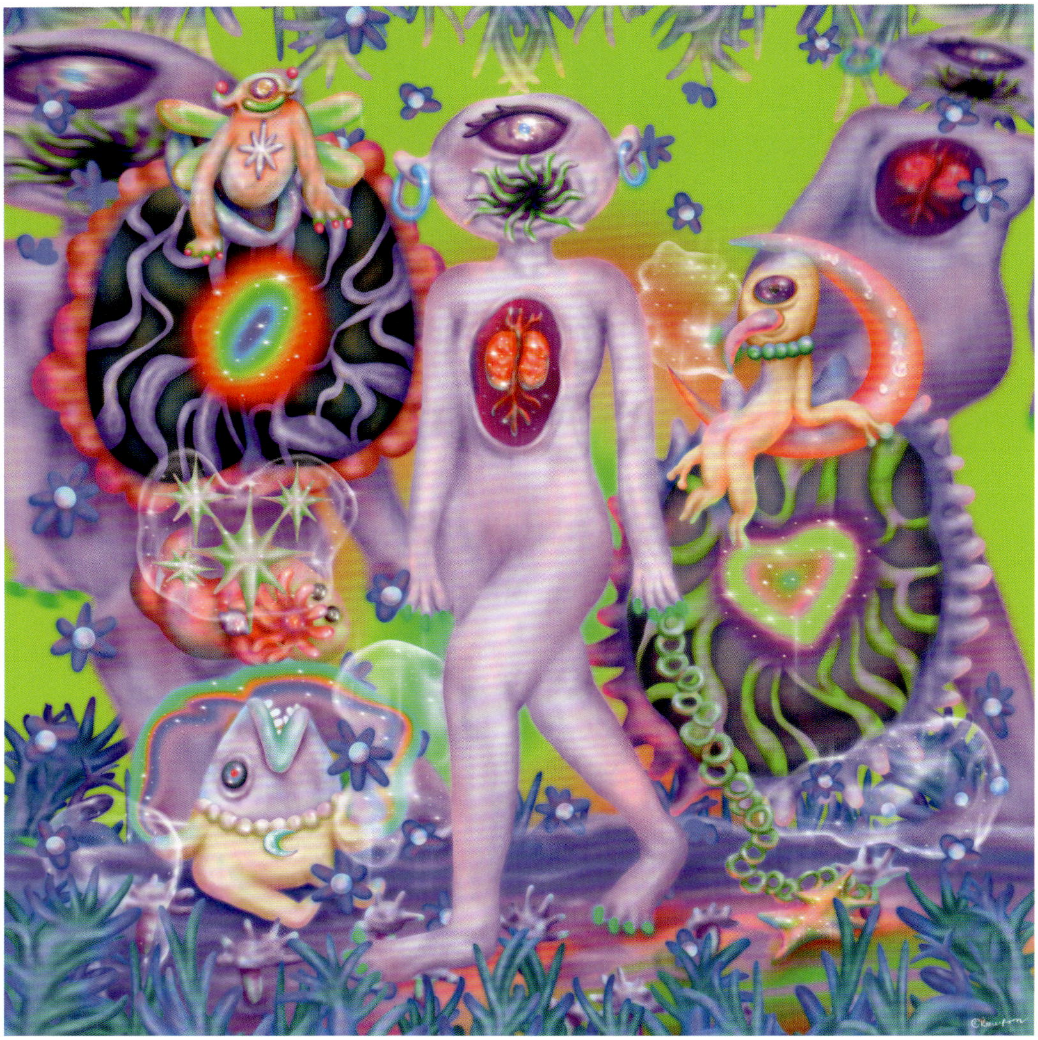

I first met digital artist RINIIFISH and her bugs on social media when NFTs broke through into the mainstream in early 2021. I was looking for refreshing narratives and new aesthetics and was also trying to balance my social feeds, which were flooded with ethereal 3D computer graphics visuals, PFPs, and generative art.

One day, while I was scrolling through "NFTwitter," one of her digitally drawn gummy caterpillars popped up on my screen. RINIIFISH and I started chatting and became friends. Since then, I have witnessed her evolution and how she is leveraging this blooming community-centered space. I ended up writing a blog post about her work to dig deeper into her creative processes and to observe the magic operating in her crypto-journey, empowering her, dispelling childhood fears and doubts, and unlocking kick-ass showcase opportunities both in URL and IRL.

While exploring her work, I got excited about *M7* (2021), her most significant project to date and the one that caught the eyes of the crypto community, artists, collectors, and art institutions. This psychedelic micro-universe inhabited by an army of odd Digi-bugs, which she considers an introspective tale, obviously boosted her self-esteem and confidence. However, above the therapeutic side and the Tadanori Yokoo–inspired aesthetic, the core of *M7* is the unique way her bugs are released on the blockchain, how they evolve along with the community, and how smartly the project embraces Web3 and smart contracts' potential to crowdsource the whole ongoing story.

**BENOIT PALOP**
MEDIA ART AND NET.CULTURE SPECIALIST,
DIGITAL STRATEGIST AT MUTEK.JP

01

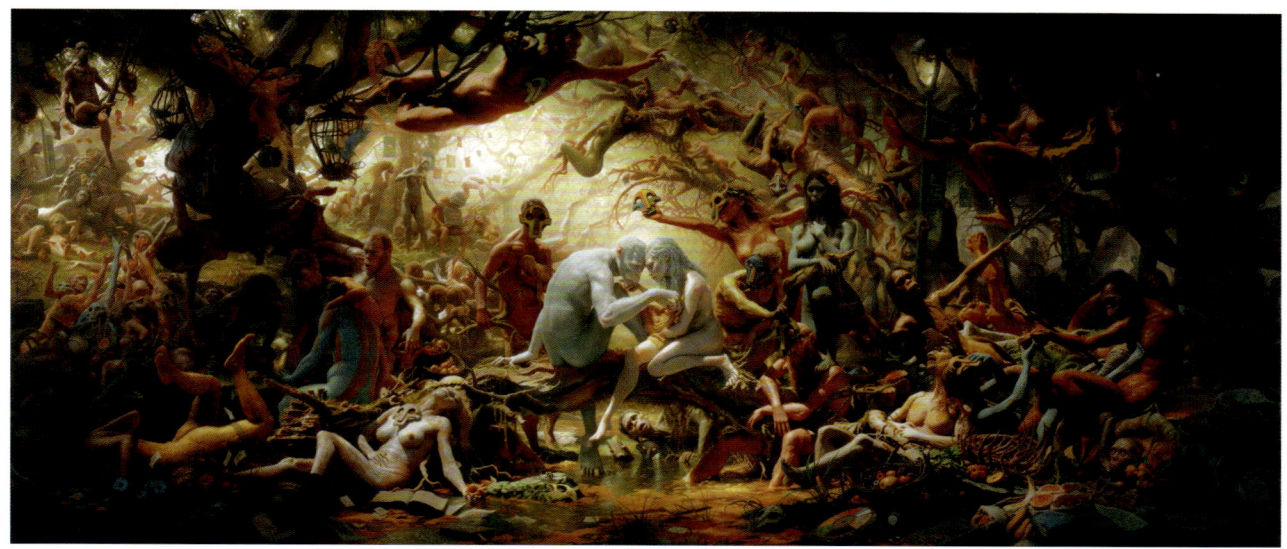

02

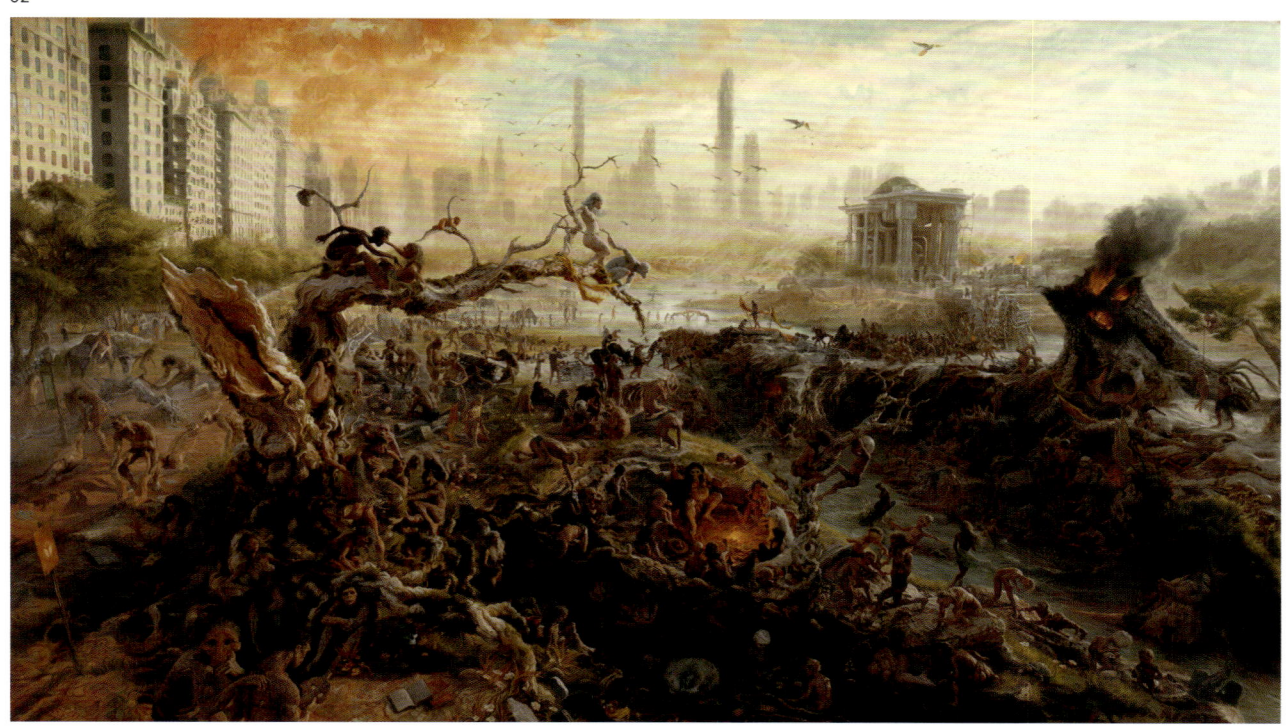

| # | TITLE | TIMESTAMP | MEDIUM | CHAIN | CONTRACT ADDRESS | TOKEN ID | EDITION SIZE |
|---|---|---|---|---|---|---|---|
| 01 | **X. Masquerade** | 02-25-2025 16:45:47 | Hybrid Digital Painting, Generative Imagery trained on artist's life's work, 3D Sculpture, Rebelle, ComfyUI, Photoshop, Blender | ETH | 0×7C4111e3Bb57b636906A7246DB1e70876fd97d97 | 4 | 1/1 |
| 02 | **IX. The Monument Game** | 08-18-2023 9:39:11 | Digital Painting, Rebelle, Photoshop | ETH | 0×7C4111e3Bb57b636906A7246DB1e70876fd97d97 | 3 | 1/1 of 256 |
| 03 | **I. Birth of Luci** | 10-13-2021 6:52:12 | Digital Painting, Photoshop | ETH | 0xb932a70A57673d89f4acfFBE830E8ed7f75Fb9e0 | 29436 | 1/1 |
| 04 | **The Skulls of Luci** | 03-04-2022 2:39:29 | Digital Painting, Photoshop | ETH | 0xC9041F80DcE73721A5f6a779672Ec57Ef255d27c | 1-49 | 1/1 of 50 |
| 05 | **Masks of Luci** | 01-27-2025 17:44:23 | *Same medium as 01* | ETH | 0×4440732b0d85e2a77dcb2caedfd940154241249a | 1-613 | 1/1 of 613 |
| 06 | **Player** | 08-25-2023 23:38:23 | *Same medium as 01* | ETH | 0xda6558fa1c2452938168ef79dfd29c45aba8a32b | 1-256 | 256 |

EDITIONS ILLUSTRATED: (05) #612

03

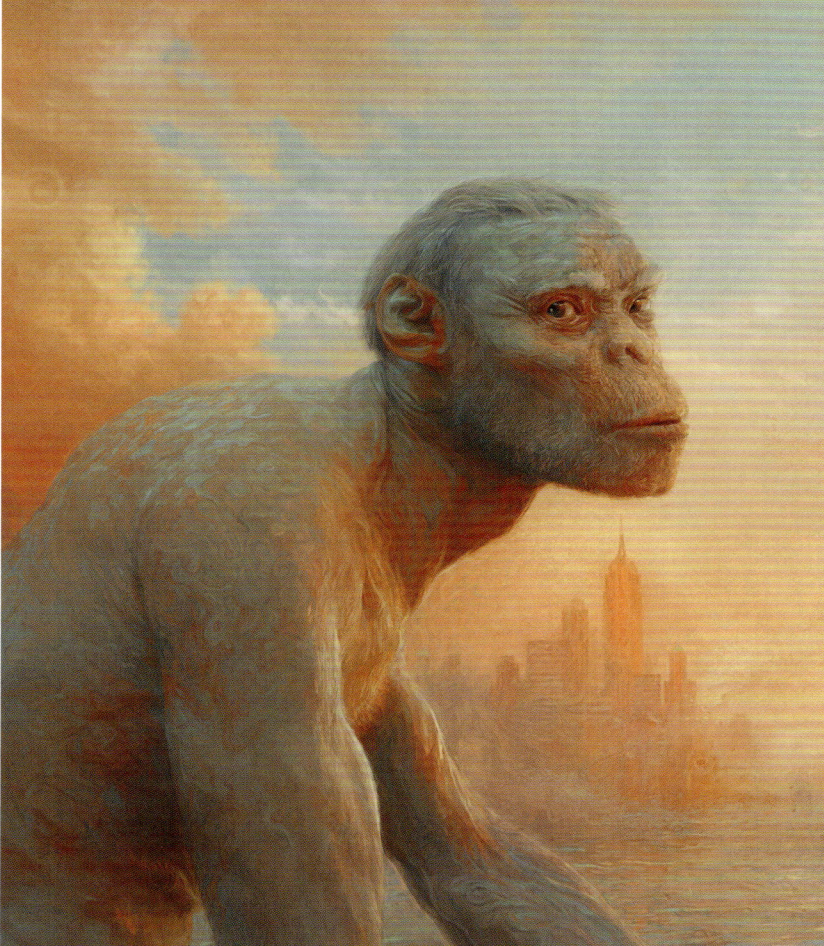

04

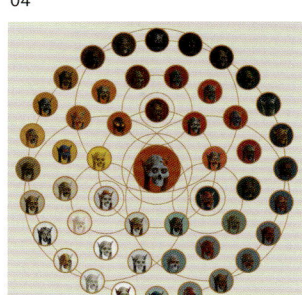

05

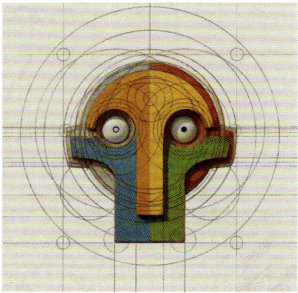

06

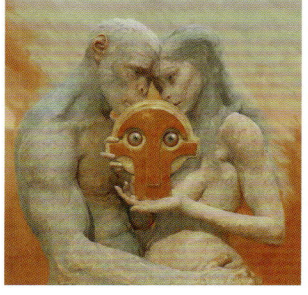

After a few short months of knowing each other, Sam Spratt invited me to his wedding — just 50 people, in his New York City apartment. Unusual, no?

At the heart of Sam's work are people and the paths we share. He is defined by a sense of world-building, of unexpected connections forged across the internet and then mediated artistically and immutably via the blockchain. His groundbreaking project *Luci*, and its various chapters, are a digital echo of the choices Sam made about whom to include on his wedding day.

The expansive nature of family — embodied by the artistic inclusion of his wife Rachel and young daughter Syla — is intrinsic to Sam's work.

*Luci* is born from an imagination finally set free, encompassing stunning digital paintings, poetry, and hybrid systems for communal interaction, all marked by visceral rawness and vulnerability. Uniquely, *Luci* includes Sam's collectors and community directly within the creation and response to his work, creating experiences that, though digital, function like primal campfires for dancing, feasting, and storytelling. Participants leave immutable writings etched upon the art. His role is the fire; the gathering gives the work its power.

What started as the story of a lone primate's journey now includes the scars of humanity etched across his digital canvases. Sam employs diverse vernaculars from baroque painting to gaming, merging illustrative concept art with the mechanics of collector economies. Sam clearly loves humanity in its entirety — I know because he gave me love and faith when no one else would bother, seeing me at my best rather than focusing on my flaws. Unlike much posthumanism defining contemporary art, he neither apologizes for our past, judges our present, nor fears the future. He tells a story of all of us — great and small, messy and beautiful — larger than the tools used, the space occupied, or the time in which it's told.

**BENNY GROSS**
COLLECTOR AND EDUCATOR

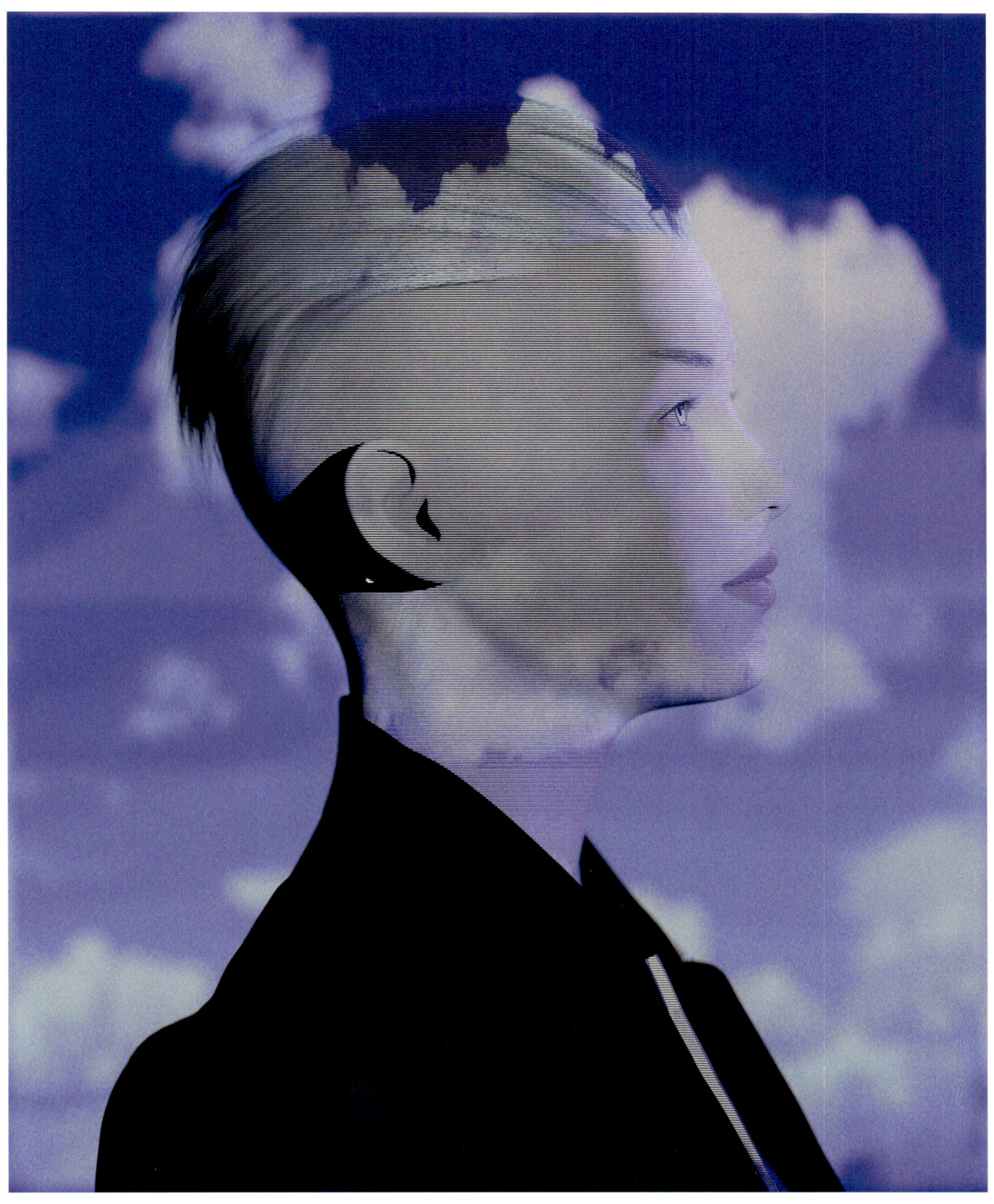

| # | TITLE | TIMESTAMP | MEDIUM | CHAIN | CONTRACT ADDRESS | TOKEN ID | EDITION SIZE |
|---|---|---|---|---|---|---|---|
| 01 | **Self-Portrait with Little Fluffy Clouds** | 03-02-2021 03:36:40 | Cinema 4D | ETH | 0x3b3ee1931dc30c1957379fac9aba94d1c48a5405 | 2260 | 1/1 |
| 02 | **Self-Portrait with Parallel Mirror** | 03-25-2021 20:46:00 | Cinema 4D | ETH | 0x495f947276749ce646f68ac8c248420045cb7b5e | 3418...8033 | 1/1 |

# LATURBO AVEDON

02

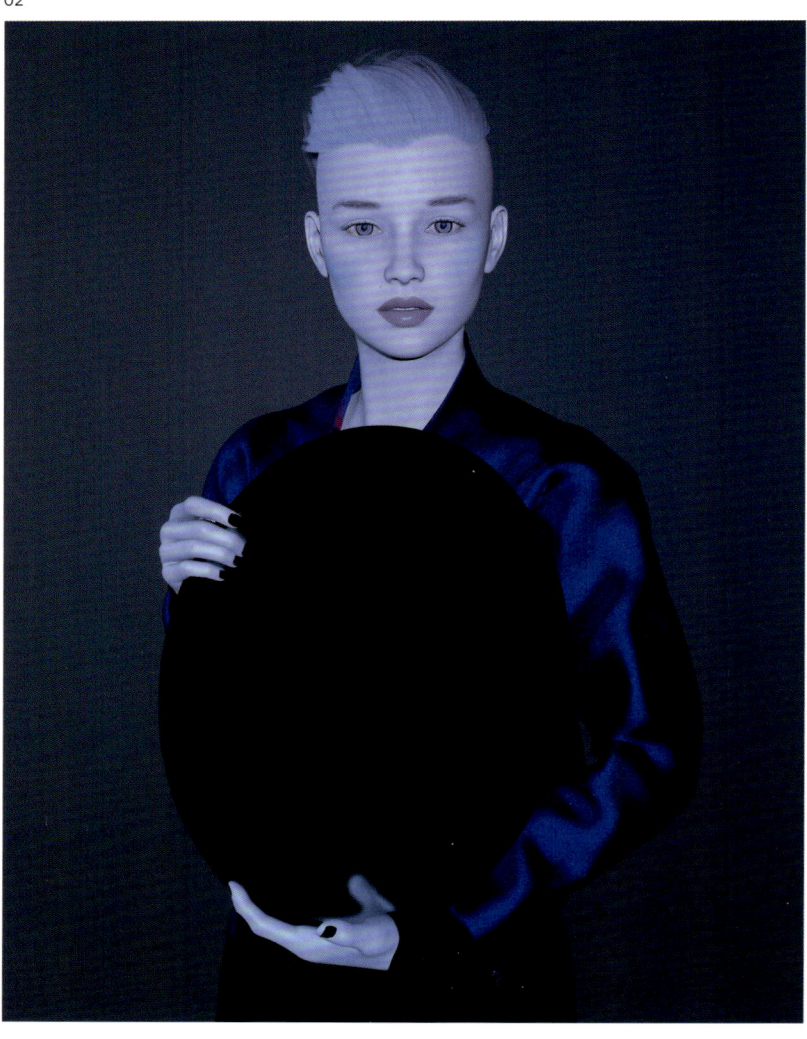

LaTurbo Avedon emerged as a virtual entity around 2010. They came to life on *Second Life* and from there unfolded a presence on many different online sites, games, and social media. They explore the conditions of identity creation on each platform, for example the restrictions of being forced into a gender binary when selecting an avatar for a game. LaTurbo Avedon lets us realize that, in a virtual world where everything could be possible, we continue to follow our real-life values and constraints. Today, the manifold possibilities of CGI allows LaTurbo Avedon to create a more self-determined self-image. For their audience, they decidedly exist without being connected to a physical identity. They point to the online identities of the 1990s that celebrated fictitious characters, before social media forced us to disclose our real-life names. Today, our own online profile pictures constantly switch from photos to filtered or CGI portraits. Who can decide if this person "really" exists? Soon, due to advancing AI technologies, we will be less able to distinguish between a bot and a person. In the metaverse, many different entities will coexist. Their visual form will reveal nothing about their origin. For more than a decade, LaTurbo Avedon lives under these conditions that for most of us remain future scenarios. With their artistic practice, they connect the tradition of the early days of the internet, with today's online life, anticipating the future of the metaverse. LaTurbo Avedon has been working with art and the blockchain since 2013, when they priced their first solo show in bitcoin. They say: "I have put my work on the blockchain so that my character creation might still be discoverable in the years to come."

**TINA SAUERLAENDER**
CO-FOUNDER & DIRECTOR OF PEER TO SPACE, CO-FOUNDER
& CEO OF RADIANCE VR, AND LECTURER FOR DIGITAL ART HISTORY
AT BIELEFELD UNIVERSITY OF APPLIED SCIENCES

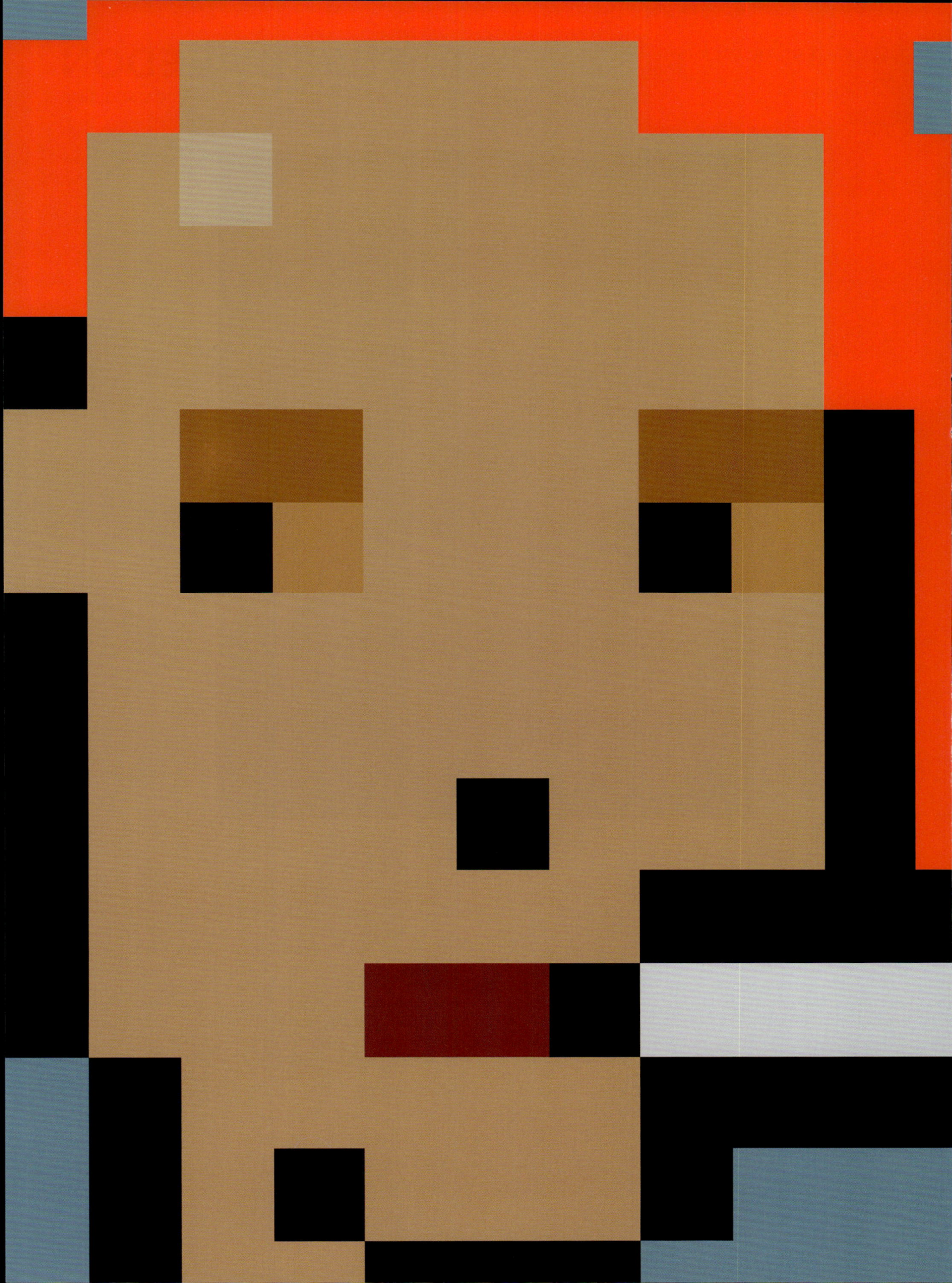

ROBERT ALICE

# ON AVATARS

Block Portraits: A History of the Digital Alter Ego

*Your avatar can look any way you want it to, up to the limitations of your equipment. If you're ugly, you can make your avatar beautiful. If you've just gotten out of bed, your avatar can still be wearing beautiful clothes and professionally applied makeup. You can look like a gorilla or a dragon or a giant talking penis in the Metaverse. Spend five minutes walking down the Street and you will see all of these.*

Neal Stephenson
*Snow Crash*, 1992

**06.00**
Larva Labs
*CryptoPunk #8252*, 06-23-2017 18:42:09
Generative pixel art
Ethereum, 0xb47e3cd837ddf8e4c57f05d70ab865de6e193bbb, 8252

How is it that the *CryptoPunk* — an artwork composed of just 576 pixels — has the potential to be one of the defining portraits of the 21st century? What is it about these digital identifiers that have developed the social capital and community consensus they have in just a few years? And how has a Sanskrit term *avatar*, denoting Hindu deities, come to define the self-image of thousands of users across globally decentralized online communities?

Blockchain-based avatars have evolved from countless reference points and cornerstones of history. It should be noted, however, that the answers to these questions reach further back into the fields of gaming and science fiction, which can be analyzed through the lens of psychology, than that of art history and the historical lens of portraiture. This is not to say that this new model of blockchain-based avatars are not portraits, nor that they don't disruptively remodel the idea of portraiture — they do — but rather that the roots of and influences on blockchain-based avatars sit largely outside of traditional art histories. These roots can be seen in the backgrounds of two projects this essay will initially focus on — *CryptoPunks* (2017) and the *Bored Ape Yacht Club* (2021). While Matt Hall and John Watkinson, the team behind *CryptoPunks*, began their careers in the fields of software development and game design, the pseudonymous Gargamel and Gordon Goner of the *Bored Ape Yacht Club* came from a background of editing and writing, also with a lifelong passion for gaming. It is in gaming that we find the roots of the avatar genre — encouraging us to reflect in turn on the gamification of the avatar model and social media space that these early Web3 avatars have so far called their home. In science fiction, the social media space gives way to the metaverse, where early visionaries such as Neal Stephenson and William Gibson allow us a glimpse at a more Web3 native future home for avatars. And it is psychology that provides a sharper lens through which to understand the nature of online identities and relationships formed both between avatars as well as between avatars and their owners. All of this must be filtered through the newfound level of virtual self-embodiment imbued by the immutability of NFTs.

## The Proteus Effect: The Psychology of Avatars

In order to fully understand why avatars have become such powerful social instruments online, one must engage with the underlying psychological influences that digital identities can have on their users. As the psychological effects of blockchain-based avatars have yet to be studied, it is within gaming—the environment more historically associated with avatars — that one can best approach this. In 2009, leading psychologists Jeremy Bailenson, Nick Yee, and Nicolas Ducheneaut published a study on the implications of the Proteus Effect, proving that users take on the characteristics of their avatars. The objective of the two-part investigation was to uncover the behavioral implications that a digital avatar could have on an individual, initially in an online gaming community and latterly in a VR environment.[1] The first study concluded that the makeup of an avatar, such as height and attractiveness, contributed considerably to the users temperament during gameplay and were "significant predictors of the player's performance."[2] Such attributes had no in-game performance advantage, thus the changes were solely behavioral, based simply on the aesthetics of their avatar. In the gamification of social media habitats, the more prized the blockchain-based avatar, the more followers the user receives. The second investigation set out to observe whether these behavioral traits carried into user's interactions in the offline world. Fascinatingly, people who used taller avatars in VR environments negotiated in a more aggressive way. Those same people behaved in a broadly similar way in subsequent face-to-face controlled tests.[3] In doing so, the test revealed that avatars could, in some cases, instill a sense of confidence in users — both within online *and* offline environments — confirming the underlying theory that avatars can have a strong psychological influence on their users.

One further concept supporting this, known as "avatar identification," was reinforced by media and communications experts Christoph Klimmt, Dorothée Hefner, and Peter Vorderer in a 2009 study which found that "players do not perceive the game (main) character as a social entity distinct from themselves, but experience a merging of their own self and the game protagonist."[4] When coupled with the writings of pioneering social media author and critic Howard Rheingold, it becomes clear that community, and consequently status, have been present online for decades. In 1993, Rheingold documented his experience with early computer conferencing systems, such as the WELL, claiming that "my mind, however, is linked with a worldwide collection of like-minded (and not so like-minded) souls: my virtual community."[5] Rheingold's experience showcases that engagement in a virtual community could have consequential psychological effects in the real world, much like that of the Proteus Effect.

Each of these studies suggest a number of important ways of analyzing blockchain-based avatars. The first is that digital avatars are not just reflections of their human counterparts, but identities that in fact work to change the psychology of their owners. This relationship

[1] Nick Yee and Nicolas Ducheneaut of Quantic Foundry and Jeremy Bailenson, the founding director of Stanford University's Virtual Human Interaction Lab. With a range of user-controlled avatars in *World of Warcraft* of varying heights, characteristics, and attraction, Yee, Ducheneaut, and Bailenson were able to track participants' behaviors in a host of scenarios.

Nick Yee, Jeremy N. Bailenson, and Nicolas Ducheneaut, "The Proteus Effect — Implications of Transformed Digital Self-Representation on Online and Offline Behavior," *Communication Research*, Vol. 36, No. 2 (April 2009): 285, https://doi.org/10.1177/0093650208330254.

[2] Yee, Bailenson, and Ducheneaut, "Proteus Effect," 285.

[3] Ibid., 294.

[4] Christoph Klimmt, Dorothée Hefner, and Peter Vorderer, "The video game experience as 'true' identification: A theory of enjoyable alterations of players' self-perception," *Communication Theory*, 19, 2009, 354, https://doi.org/10.1111/j.1468-2885.2009.01347.x.

[5] Howard Rheingold, "A Slice of Life in My Virtual Community," *Global Networks-a Journal of Transnational Affairs* (August 11, 1993), 57.

**06.01**
Screenshot from *Avatar* (1979), developed by Bruce Maggs, Andrew Shapira, and David Sides on the
University of Illinois PLATO system

```
            Races                         Stats

  →  1. Ogre               Strength       (9-20)        15
     2. Osiri              Intelligence   (3-16)         6
     3. Elf                Wisdom         (3-16)         6
     4. Troll              Constitution   (9-21)        15
     5. Cirilian           Charisma       (3-18)        15
     6. Morloch            Dexterity      (5-17)     ≫
     7. Human
     8. Gnome
     9. Dwarf
    10. Giant




       Enter your statistics.   You have   13 stat points
       left to distribute.

       Press NEXT to move on, BACK to move back,
             DATA when done
             LAB to start over
```

is not one way, but reciprocal. Blockchain-based avatars compound this symbiotic relationship, as self-embodiment is hardened due to the immutability of identity that blockchains can now afford. Blockchains, and their important principle of pseudonymity, have broadened the platform we now give to avatars: they are no longer confined to the gated walls of a single game but are now used as real-world public personas, viewable by anyone with an internet connection.

**Role-Playing: Avatars and Gaming**

From quasi-prophetic cyberpunk literature to some of our earliest multiplayer games, the history of avatars can be traced back to the 1970s. Gaming was largely responsible for these developments given the need for the on-screen representation of a player. One of the first games to recognize the importance of a user-character relationship was *Avatar* (1979) **[06.01]**, which ran on the University of Illinois PLATO system. The MMO game, which loosely introduced the term *avatar* in a computing context, allowed users to determine a variety of attributes including race, gender, and even a pseudonym — much crypto. By giving players the ability to differentiate and customize their on-screen character, it grows the bond of association between themselves and the given avatar. This phenomenon can be best understood via a 2012 paper published in the *Journal of Media Psychology*, which highlighted how "avatar

06.02
Game stills from *Habitat* (1985)
Originally developed by Randy Farmer, Chip Morningstar, Aric Wilmunder,
and Janet Hunter of Lucasfilm Games, formerly known as LucasArts

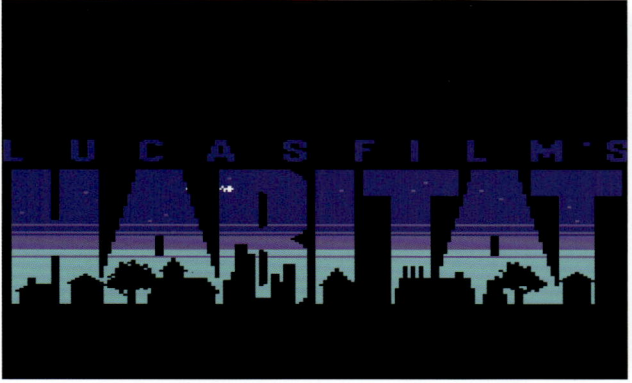
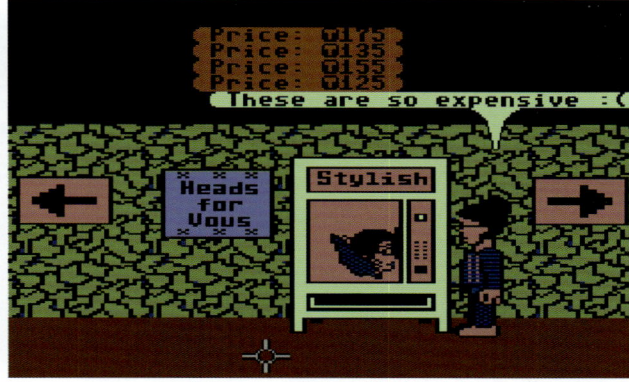
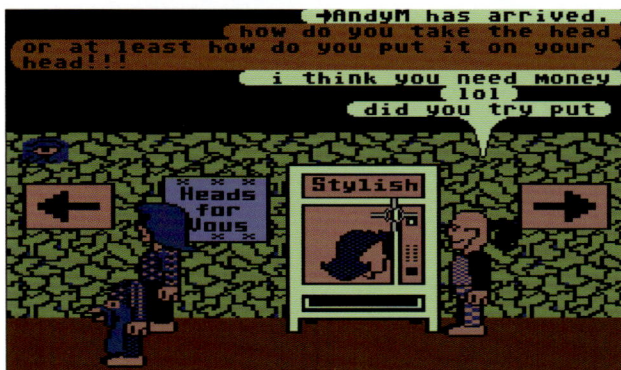
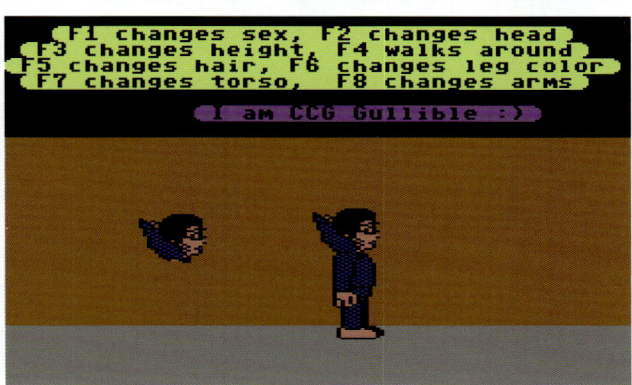

[6] Jan Van Looy, Cédric Courtois, and
Melanie De Vocht, "Player identification
in online games: Validation of a scale for
measuring identification in MMORPGs,"
*Media Psychology*, 15:2, 2012, 197, https://doi.
org/10.1145/1823818.1823832.
[7] Richard Garriott, "Coining Term 'Avatar':
The origins of the term 'avatar' in games,"
*Critical Path*, interview from 2010, posted
July 29, 2016, https://www.criticalpathproject.
com/video/coining-term-avatar/.
[8] Geoffrey Parrinder, *Avatar and Incarnation:
The Divine in Human Form in the World's
Religions* (London: Oneworld Publications,
1997), 19–20.
[9] F. Randall Farmer, "Lucasfilm's Habitat
Promotional Video," YouTube, May
17, 2008, https://www.youtube.com/
watch?v=VVpulhO3jyc.

identification is positively associated with roleplay, customization, and escapism."[6] Thus in blockchain-based avatar projects today, where collections are typically spread across 10,000 unique avatars, the spectrum of diversity, and ultimately inclusivity, is far increased. The ability for avatar collections to build a narrative while offering inclusivity through variety is the key to the creation of strong avatar communities.

In the wake of *Avatar* came a host of more advanced avatar-oriented gaming experiences. In 1985, the release of Richard Garriott's *Ultima IV: Quest of the Avatar* **[06.03]** furthered the definition of avatars to a term far more applicable to our current times. Garriott, who claims to have defined *avatar* in its now widely used digital sense, recognized the parallels between the Hindu term *avatar* and the user-character relationship in gaming.[7] In its religious context, the ancient Sanskrit *avatar* — derived from *avatāra* or descent — can simply be defined as the earthly embodiment of a deity, belief, or philosophy.[8] Garriott could see a clear association between a deity's terrestrial descent to that of a gamer's spirit being transported into a virtual realm. As digital technologies rapidly improved during the early 1980s, so too did the emergence of avatars across a host of different online gaming platforms. Lucasfilm's revolutionary MMORPG *Habitat* **[06.02]** is a particularly interesting case study to observe the development of avatars as a virtual reflection of identity. Released in 1985, the underlying structure of the game bears an unsettling likeness to our current digital worlds, well understood by the following excerpt from the trailer:

*This is one of Habitat's newest recruits, an avatar named Young Turk. Back in Poughkeepsie he is Conrad Kline, a lawyer with Kline, Cates, Kipling and Kline, and right now he is choosing a look that will reflect his real self-image, from toe to head. Obviously anxious to show off his true self and to get on with his first excursion, Conrad Kline directs his alter-ego avatar out to the meandering, unpredictable world of Habitat where each and every environment connects to another.[9]*

Conrad Kline, the corporate lawyer, uses his avatar, Young Turk, to transform himself into the digital manifestation of his alter ego, much like any avatar collector today. The promo goes on to detail that "behind every avatar there is an enterprising human" and that *Habitat*

**06.03**
Front cover of the computer game *Ultima IV: Quest of the Avatar* (1985)
Developed by Richard Garriott and Origin Systems
Cover art by Denis Loubet

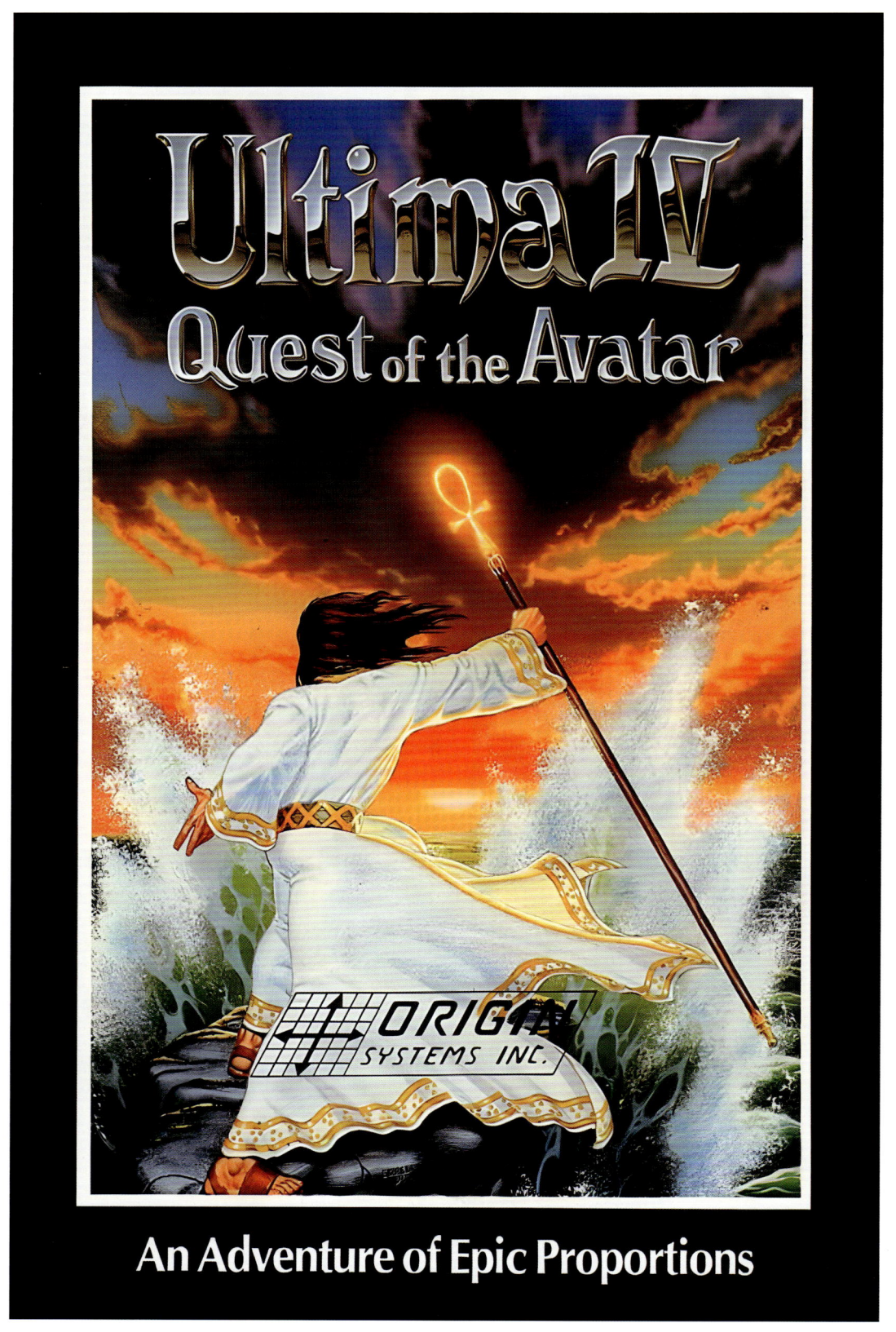

"FAST-FORWARD FREE-STYLE MALL MYTHOLOGY FOR THE EARLY 21ST CENTURY."
—WILLIAM GIBSON

# SNOW CRASH

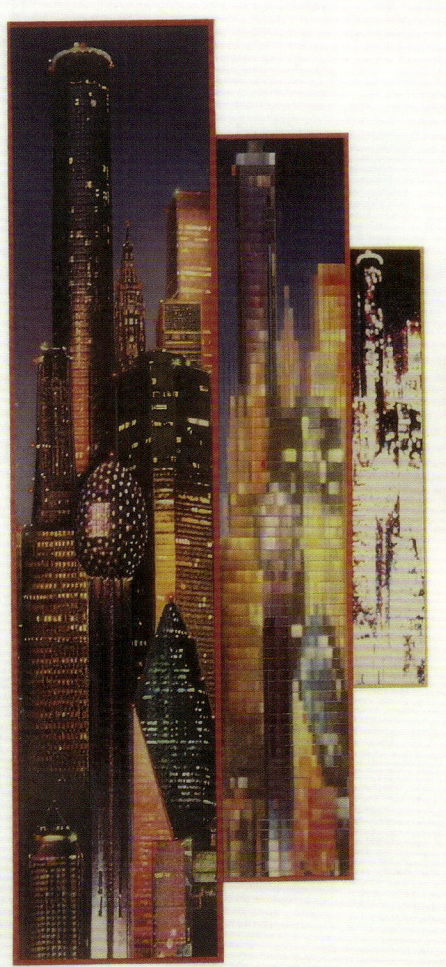
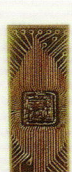
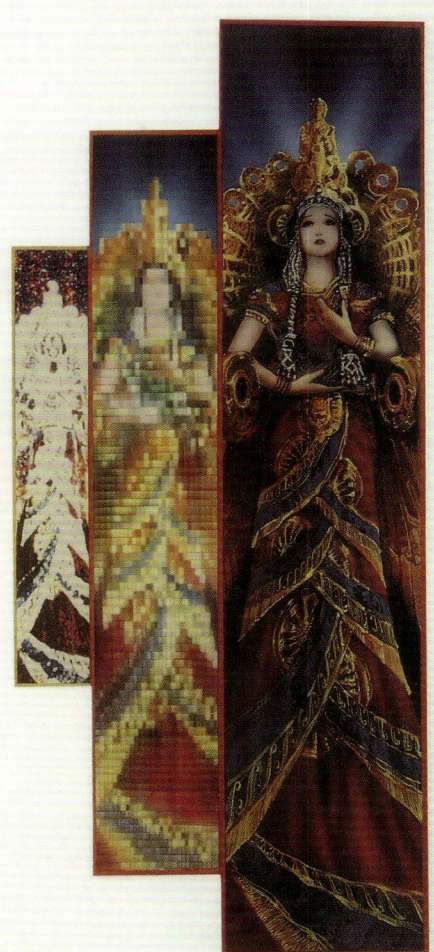

A NOVEL BY

# NEAL STEPHENSON

is a place "shaped by the interactions of thousands of avatars."[10] *Habitat* was one of the first ecosystems to create virtual real-time mass communication mediated by avatars. Kline, the stereotypical lawyer lost in a sea of normalcy, sees in his avatar a chance at escaping from reality. It is an opportunity to project other sides of his character — ones unfit for the professional world — using the pseudonymity of the virtual realm.

As online worlds have harnessed a greater sense of realism through improved graphics and computing technology, the development of avatar adoption, gameplay, and usability has improved simultaneously. It was games like *Second Life* from 2003 that saw the avatar transform into a 3D identity far more in line with our current ecosystem, albeit on a centralized server. With fully customizable characters, virtual currencies exchangeable for real world currency, and tradable virtual properties, *Second Life* pioneered a more immersive avatar experience with added utility. Other important MMOs like *RuneScape* spearheaded the concept of virtual economies with the game's Grand Exchange, a fully functioning in-game peer-to-peer trading system, becoming a hotbed for many future crypto traders. One of the more recent games to significantly remodel the concept of avatars is Epic Games' *Fortnite* released in 2017. In *Fortnite*, players are able to customize their in-game avatars with "skins," a cosmetic item or outfit that changes the appearance of the character while providing no competitive advantage, recalling the Proteus Effect study. The success of the game has seen *Fortnite* become one of the leading virtual ecosystems at bridging traditional brands from the physical to the digital space. Having struck collaborations with Balenciaga, Moncler, and Ralph Lauren, among others, *Fortnite* represents a novel model for the monetization of online identities — a foundation which many NFT avatars have built upon.

## Imagining New Worlds: Avatars and Science Fiction

Another form of media that stimulates the urge to associate with identities outside of our real world is that of science fiction. These fantasy novels instilled many cyberpunks with the imagination to envisage how true digital identity could be realized. In works such as William Gibson's *Neuromancer* (1984), the foundations were laid for the idea that digital worlds could exist in parallel to our physical universe. The term *cyberspace,* as popularized by Gibson, proposed the concept of a simulated reality being "a consensual hallucination experienced daily by billions of legitimate operators, in every nation [...]. A graphical representation of data abstracted from the banks of every computer in the human system."[11] It was these narratives that buttress the philosophical backbone of avatars and the metaverse, forming the bedrock for many who believe in digital worlds beyond the constraints of reality. Concepts surrounding virtual identity — how to present oneself in these futuristic environments — emerged in lockstep. It was that other stalwart of the genre, Neil Stephenson's *Snow Crash* (1993) **[06.04]**, which introduced the world to the term *metaverse* and explored the idea of an online environment consisting of ownable digital land governed by user-controlled avatars. In *Snow Crash*, avatars are simply defined as "audiovisual bodies that people use to communicate with each other in the Metaverse."[12] A deeper insight into Stephenson's concept of an avatar suggests that status, particularly relating to technical skill, was strongly personified by one's avatar:

*The couples coming off the monorail can't afford to have custom avatars made and don't know how to write their own. They have to buy off-the-shelf avatars. One of the girls has a pretty nice one. It would be considered quite the fashion statement among the K-Tel set. Looks like she has bought the Avatar Construction Set and put together her own, customized model out of miscellaneous parts. It might even look something like its owner.*[13]

As in any current metaverse or blockchain-based avatar project, these graphics were the defining marker of self, an identity cue to one's personality and status — the more technically sophisticated one's avatar, the more status they held within these digital hierarchies. Its confluence of themes, the hyperinflation of the dollar, the retreat to encrypted online transactions and the conception of the Metaverse, all harnessed around the central character of an avatar or "audiovisual body" are what makes *Snow Crash* such a prescient historical model for the Web3 world unfolding today.

## Alter Ego: Avatars and Portraiture

While much of the early history of blockchain-based avatars was informed by gaming and science fiction; in portraiture, the alter ego and the avatar have been areas continually mined by artists from across history. From the autobiographical heroines of Artemisia Gentileschi (1593–1653) **[06.05]** to the 1980s alter egos of Samuel Fosso in West Africa **[06.06]** and Cindy Sherman and Joan Jonas in New York, artists have re-represented themselves and others

[10] Ibid.
[11] William Gibson, *Neuromancer* (New York: Berkley Publishing Group, 1989), 128.
[12] Neal Stephenson, *Snow Crash* (New York: Bantam Books, 1993), 33.
[13] Ibid, 34–35.

Artemisia Gentileschi
*Self Portrait as Saint Catherine of Alexandria*, 1615–17
Oil on canvas, 71.4 × 69 cm
The National Gallery, London, United Kingdom

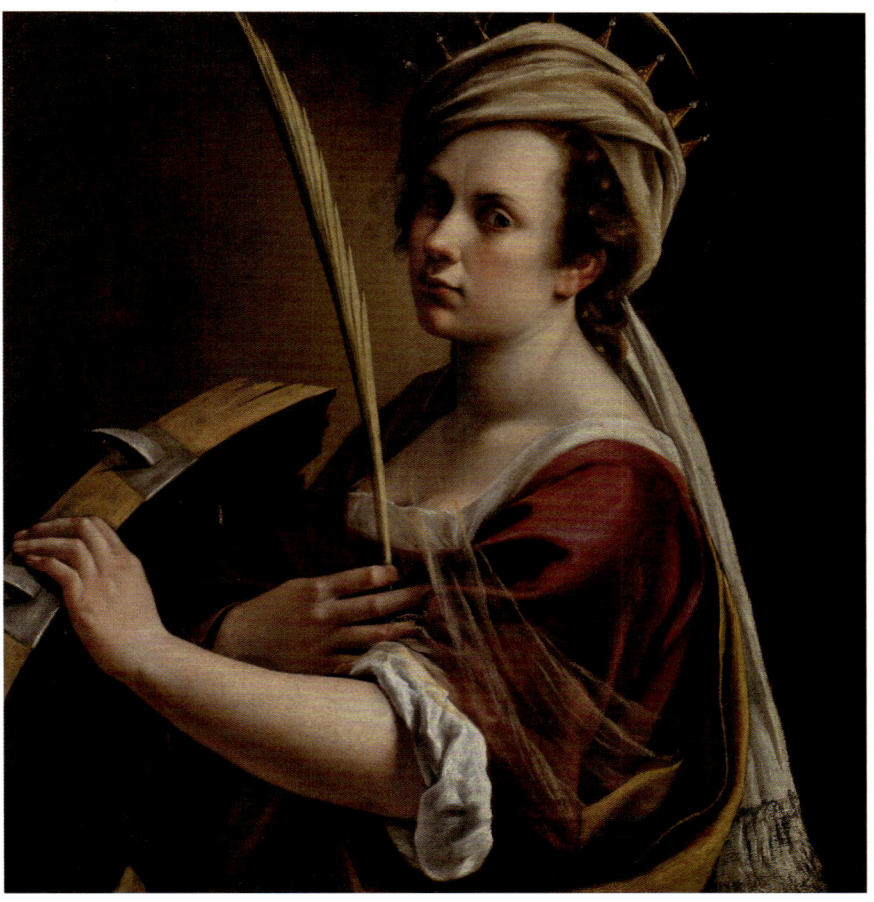

through character and dress, using role-play as a way to critique important themes as diverse as the 17th century role of women in art, the 20th-century legacies of colonialism, or contemporary identity politics. From the trait-driven, humorous portraits by Giuseppe Arcimboldo (1526–1593) **[06.07]** to Warhol's *Society Portraits*, collectors throughout history have also often engaged in the fantasy of costume and allegory, subjecting their own identity to the fashionable artifice of both the present and the past.[14]

This strong art-historical tradition has more recently collided with the increased cultural influence of the digital self. Philippe Parreno and Pierre Huyghe's multimedia project *No Ghost Just a Shell* (1999–2002) **[06.08]** featured contributions from 13 artists working in a host of mediums, each using the same manga avatar figure, "Annlee," as the subject for their work. Parreno and Huyghe acquired the rights and copyright of the character in 1999 for $428 from Kworks, a Japanese agency that creates and distributes manga characters for animated media. Annlee, as named by the two French artists, was a nondescript, standardized manga character with no traits or attributes — an "off-the-shelf avatar" to use the words of Stephenson. A "shell" for artists to create experimental story lines with regard to the position of digital identities around the turn of the century, the idea of multiple narrative arcs being born from one character foreshadows the multiplicity of CC0 PFP projects. The questioning of such ideas also surfaces in the work of LaTurbo Avedon **[06.09]**. The avatar, artist, and curator who has no physical identity and exists solely online, challenges the traditional notion of artistic authorship. Starting around 2008, Avedon has used contemporary simulation tools to self-manifest an autonomous online individual, building art and navigating through online worlds with a focus on gaming, such as *Second Life*, *Fortnite*, and *Star Citizen*. It is only now that Avedon's virtual existence can be secured on the blockchain, granting further realization to her identity through blockchain-based signatures.[15]

[14] It must be noted that dress, role-play, and the alter ego in both these vernaculars comes equally out of the histories of marginalized and repressed communities as much as from the safe privilege of societal elites.

[15] LaTurbo Avedon, "Conversations | Exhibiting in the Metaverse" Panel at *ArtBasel*, June 18, 2022, https://artbasel.com/stories/conversations-art-basel-2022-exhibiting-metaverse.

**06.06**
Samuel Fosso
*Le Chef: Celui Qui A Vendu L'Afrique Aux Colons (The Chief Who Sold Africa to the Colonists),* 1997
Chromogenic print, 60.5 × 50 cm
The Walther Collection, Neu-Ulm, Germany

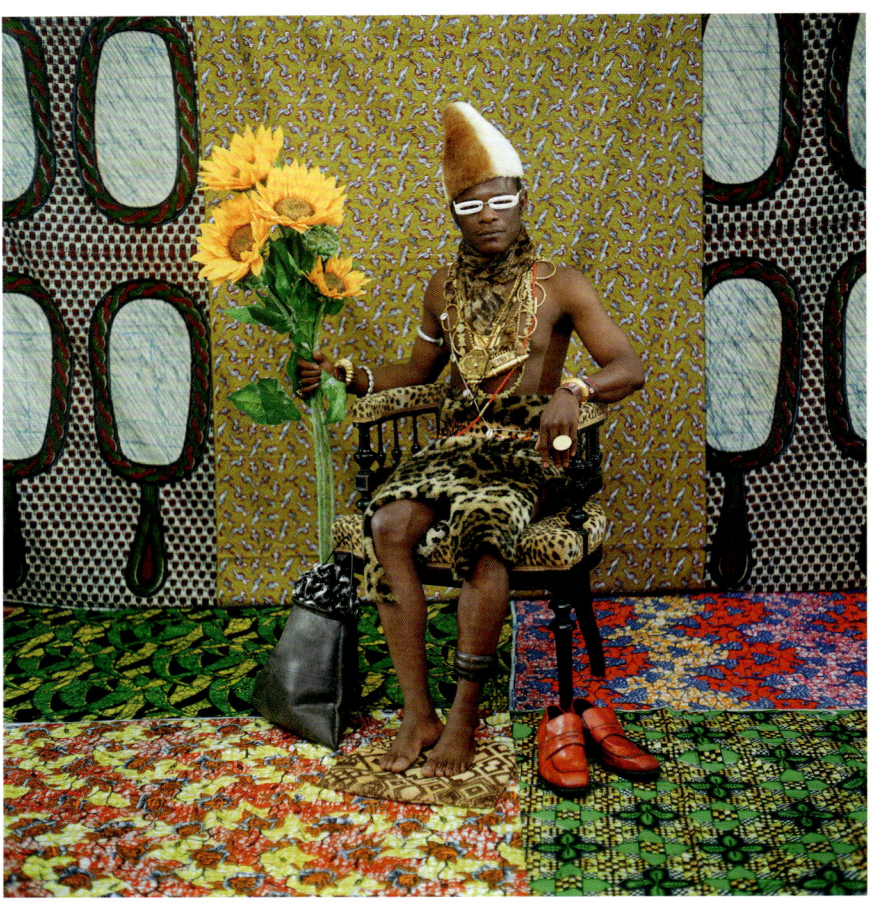

While the Web3 avatar and PFP model now sit within the same tradition of portraiture, they broadly do not carry the same artistic intentionality and critical conceptual framework of the likes of Fosso, Jonas, or Sherman. *CryptoPunks,* with their anti-commercial genesis story, their contextual association with *Autoglyphs,* and increasing lack of utility, are a notable early exception of considered artistic practice, albeit by creative developers that only started to consider themselves artists after the fact. Instead, while often symbolizing the extravagance and zeal of the new crypto economies, general PFPs use of attributes to date is more totemic in its nature, creating light-hearted story lines, that befit their popular appeal. This is not to say that the current avatar model lacks cultural import, but that it sits more within popular culture and the typology of collectibles and gaming. Led by the likes of Avedon and now Sam Spratt, there remains significant creative territory to explore within PFPs. Artists will undoubtedly start hijacking, experimenting with, and critiquing this new kind of collective portraiture.

## Immutable Self-Portraits: Avatars Meet Crypto

While all of these cultural areas, from science fiction to literature to art, have the ability to disregard the clasps of logic that rule the real world, in reality there still remained one pressing issue concerning the use of avatars: until the blockchain, there was no way to truly claim your avatar as your own. In a digital environment not backed by any source of verifiable ownership, avatars were easily duplicated or copied, and in order for artists to popularize their practice, they effectively needed to hand over their work to the public domain. Back in 1996, a member of the Cypherpunk Mailing List, Ryan Russell, stressed the concerns that both he and an artist acquaintance shared over the intellectual property of VRML avatars.[16]

[16] *VRML or Virtual Reality Modeling Language*—a standard file type for displaying 3D interactive vector graphics.

Giuseppe Arcimboldo
*Rudolf II of Habsburg as Vertumnus*, 1591
Oil on panel, 70 × 57 cm
Skokloster Castle, Håbo, Sweden

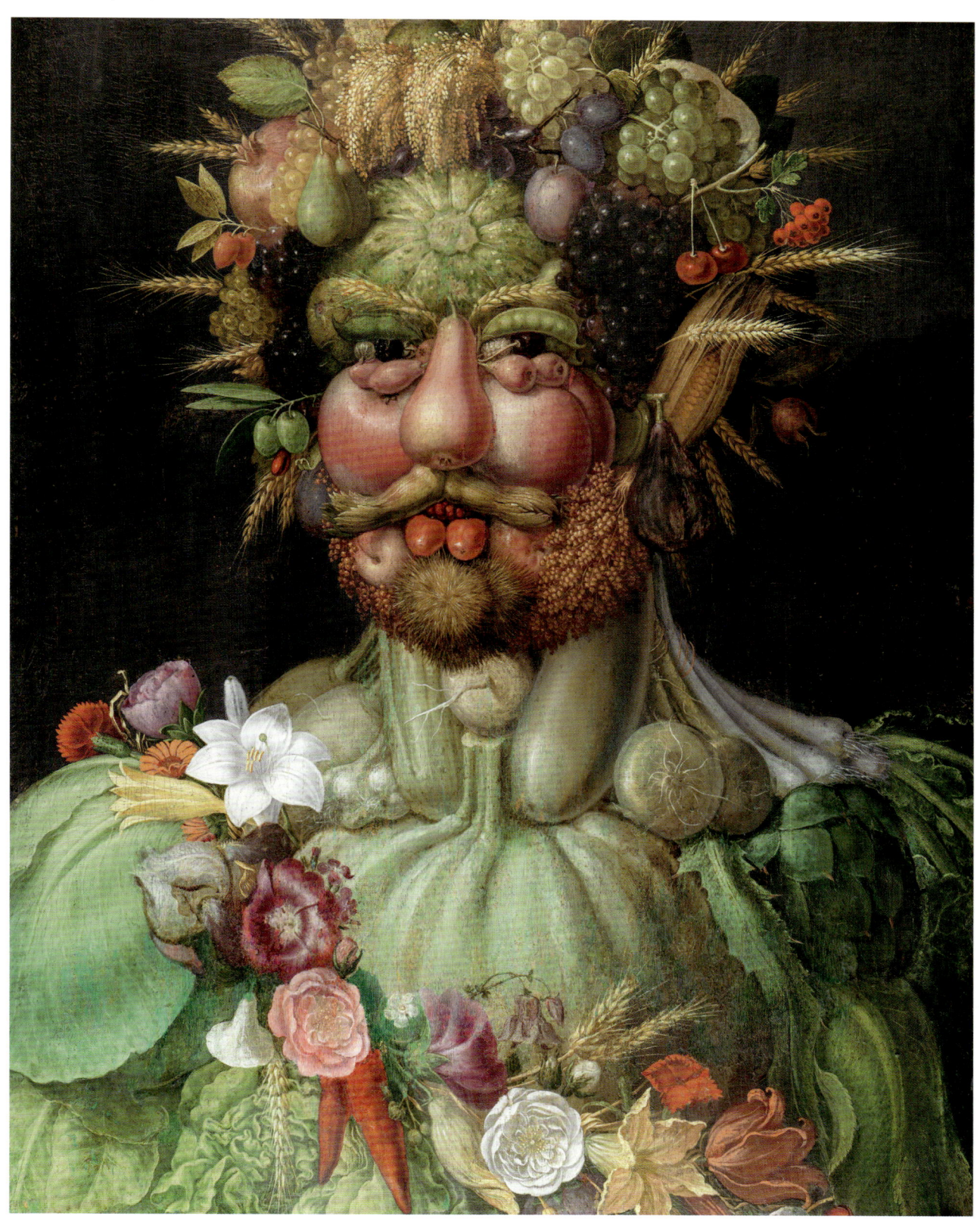

**06.08** ▶
Remastered edition of *Anywhere Out of the World*, 2000
by Philippe Parreno from No Ghost Just a Shell, 1999–2002
Anywhere Out of the World (3D), 2017
3D Animation

**06.09**
LaTurbo Avedon
*Ethereum Lens*, 04-09-2021 16:18:14
Cinema 4D
Ethereum, 0xabEFBc9fD2F806065b4f3C237d4b59D9A97Bcac7, 2761

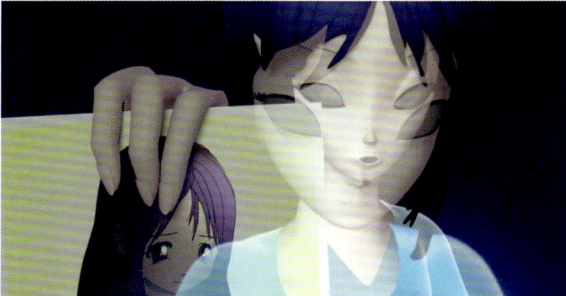

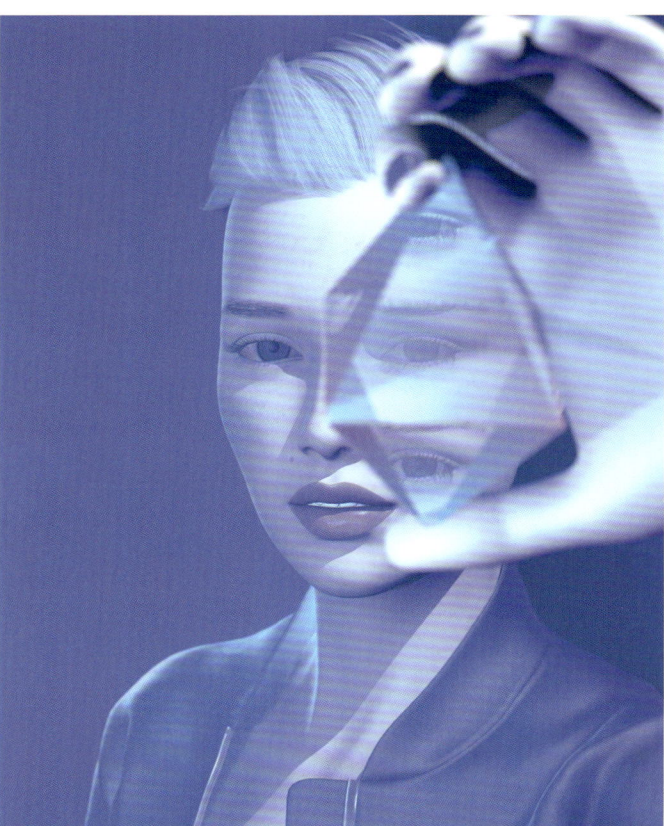

**06.10**
Set of Identicons originally devised by Don Park in 2007

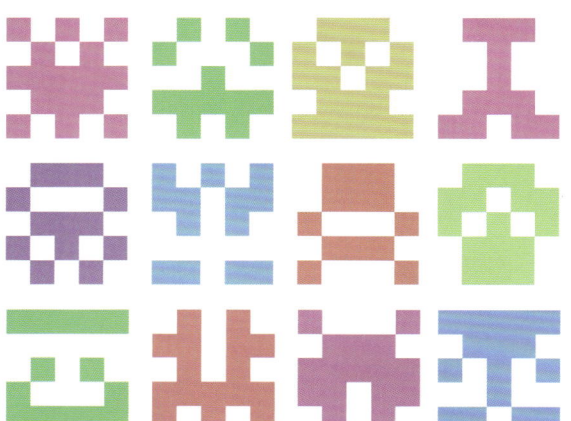

Interestingly, the Cypherpunk Mailing List was a precursor to the Cryptography Mailing List that Satoshi Nakamoto would first present Bitcoin to — showcasing the centrality of this discussion to the early cypherpunk communities that prefigured crypto. Outlining the artist's fears, Russell wrote: "His worry is that since everyone in the same virtual environment as his customer would see the designer avatar, wouldn't they also be able to easily rip off his work? (or his customer's property, take your pick.)"[17] Russell goes on to question the possibility of outright ownership of virtual avatars, asking, "Is there a way for a user to 'view' the client's avatar [...] but not save a copy?"[18] In this question, two decades before *CryptoPunks*, Russell presciently cites a level of digital scarcity that was not yet possible at the time; the origin and authorship of these early avatars were simply unenforceable, and as a consequence digital identities were far less secure and therefore far less valuable.

One of the more interesting avatar types that filled the need for individuality online, although not backed by blockchain, was Identicons **[06.10]**. These small 5×5 pixel identifiers were invented by Don Park in early 2007, anonymizing the user by generating the image from a hash of their IP address. To an extent, Identicons were the closest previous attempt to make avatars non-fungible, using non-blockchain-based rails to create unique identifiers personal to their holders, albeit in abstract form. While altogether Identicons provide a useful means for verification, people did not inherit the same psychological attachment to their Identicon avatar as they would with an anthropomorphic character or graphic. Park himself recognized these differences, noting that "to use Identicons as a permanent identity, one has to 'identify' with their Identicon. We can identify faces of our friends because we shared memories with them, stories if you will."[19] What is so key to blockchain-based avatars, therefore, is that their stories exist immutably online and their existence is native to the very system in which they operate. Their provenance, the public visibility of their community, and the sophistication of the imagery (in comparison to Identicons) afford these new forms of avatars a new level of broad societal sentimentality.

[17] Ryan Russell/SYBASE, "[crypto] Avatar Protection," December 4, 1996, https://mailing-list-archive.cryptoanarchy.wiki/archive/1996/12/d5e950886cdb96294bba25d6981d3138c5ba31fec5a3081b9cd2aa1327c67ece/.
[18] Ibid.
[19] Don Park, "Identicon and Robohash," *Don Park's Weekly Habit*, July 30, 2011, https://blog.docuverse.com/2011/07/30/identicon-and-robohash/.

**06.11**
The rarest CryptoPunk type: one of only nine Aliens
Larva Labs, CryptoPunk #2890, 06-23-2017 15:46:50
Generative pixel art
Ethereum, 0xb47e3cd837ddf8e4c57f05d70ab865de6e193bbb, 2890

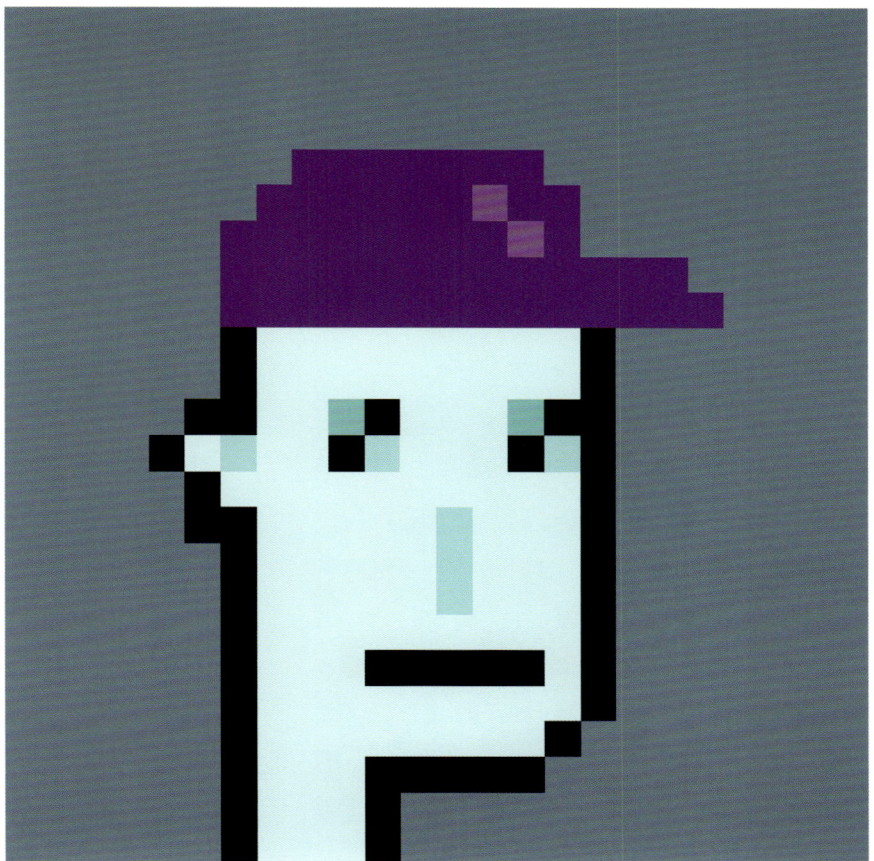

## Avatars On-Chain: *CryptoPunks*

On June 9, 2017, at 12:22:50, two creative technologists, John Watkinson and Matt Hall of Larva Labs, deployed a contract onto the Ethereum network that would reshape our understanding of avatars. Contract 0x6Ba6f2207e343923BA692e5Cae646Fb0F566DB8D, comprising 10,000 unique tokens, was titled *CryptoPunks* **[06.11, 06.12]**.[20] These 8-bit styled, algorithmically generated characters, aesthetically composed of just 576 pixels, became the first avatars to inhabit the blockchain. The layer of immutable ownership that blockchain technology upholds meant that for the first time in the internet's short history, users could assign their online self with a visual layer of unchallengeable individuality, yet still retain an impenetrable level of pseudonymity. Free to claim on the Larva Labs website, *CryptoPunks*, hereafter known just as Punks, were a testament to the early Ethereum community and the hacker attitude that typified many of the blockchain's first adopters. Much like the 1970s London punk scene from which Hall and Watkinson drew inspiration, the Punks embody the very same anarchic underpinnings of many of society's wonderful misfits. While the punks of 1970s London congregated in the pubs and clubs of the King's Road, today's quasi-anarchist Punks can be found online, offering identity to a new subculture. The Punks gave face to crypto.

Their popularity was, however, not entrenched from the outset. The collection took over a week to be fully claimed, not to mention a bug in the original contract leading to Larva Labs having to migrate the contract, creating a contentious discussion around the originality and the artists' signature on the blockchain's immutable ledger.[21] It wasn't until an article on *Mashable* by journalist Jason Abbruzzese on June 16, 2017, that the Punks gained traction.[22] The article, presciently titled "This ethereum-based project could change how we think about digital art," provides a time capsule to examine early consensus surrounding both the Punks and NFTs in general. Abbruzzese captures both the potential and absurdity of the

[20] *CryptoPunks* were migrated on June 23, 2017, to their current contract: 0xb47e3cd837dDF8e4c57F05d70Ab865de6e193BBB.
[21] Ibid.
[22] Jason Abbruzzese, "This ethereum-based project could change how we think about digital art," *Mashable*, June 16, 2017, https://mashable.com/article/*cryptopunks*-ethereum-art-collectibles.

**06.12** (from left to right)
The remaining four CryptoPunk types: Apes, Zombies, Females & Males
Larva Labs, *CryptoPunks #8219, #3831, #8896 & #5791*, 2017
Generative pixel art
Ethereum, 0xb47e3cd837ddf8e4c57f05d70ab865de6e193bbb, 8219, 3831, 8896 & 5791

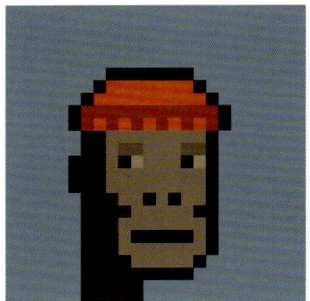 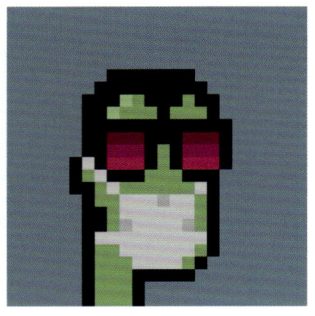 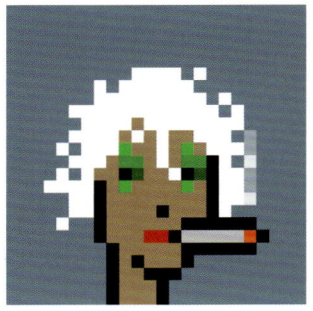 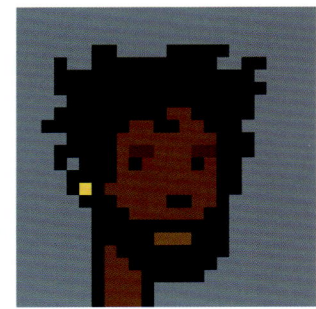

concept of the Punks, digital assets and avatars, challenging whether the world would ever succumb to the idea of purchasing "the equivalent of a digital certificate of authenticity."[23] In the closing sentences of Abbruzzese's article we find clues as to how the avatar space and its critics would unfold with remarkable accuracy:

*It's not inconceivable to envision a future in which CryptoPunks or some other blockchain-tied series of art does become valuable. As more of life moves online, status symbols are bound to follow. Someday, owning a CryptoPunk might signify just how early of an adopter you were into the world of Ethereum and its thriving digital art scene. Or, they could just be a bunch of images.*

— Jason Abbruzzese [24]

Having had experience with avatar generators as far back as 2011 when the pair created Androidify for Google, Hall and Watkinson recount how they were exposed firsthand to "the marketing power of people using generated images as their 'profile pictures.'"[25] It wasn't until around 2017, however, when they discovered Ethereum, that the Larva Labs founders discovered a new disruptive medium for online identity.[26] When interviewed in 2019, Hall outlined the benefits he saw in this newfound layer for digital art: "What you own requires no maintenance, can't be destroyed or damaged, has guaranteed provenance and (when buying or selling) requires no insurance, shipping fees, storage fees or transaction fees. It also can be viewed by anybody, while the ownership remains undisputed."[27] A fundamental feature of the Punks that distinguishes them from pre-blockchain-based avatars is how the collection was built with decentralization at its core. At the bedrock of the project, Hall and Watkinson ensured that the Punks smart contract had no owner, thus the collection can never be modified, updated, or deleted by anyone — not even by Larva Labs. Further still, the market-place for the Punks also exists entirely on-chain, thus relieving the collection of any central-ized third-party authority or marketplace. As a result, the Punks and their on-chain life as immutable digital identities will be preserved until the Ethereum network ceases to exist. While the pair clearly recognized the benefits and use cases of blockchain technology for digital art, the success of their creation exceeded all expectations. The Punks were an exper-iment, one with neither intentionality nor a speculative roadmap, that has come to define the avatar space today, yet their purity and mythology stems from this. As digital relics of a not-so-distant past, they are an "early beacon for envisioning how the new protocols could change the way we think about community, identity, provenance and artistic innovation" as put by the artist Mitchell F. Chan.[28]

With 9 aliens, 24 apes, 88 zombies, 3,840 females, and 6,039 males, the Punks gifted Ethereum's earliest adopters a 10,000-strong spectrum of diversity with which to repre-sent themselves. Each Punk is further defined by a distinct identity of up to seven attributes out of a possible 87 traits — no two are the same. From the eight "Genesis" Punks **[06.13]** with no attributes at all, to *#8348* **[06.14]** — the only Punk to boast a full set of seven fea-tures — Larva Labs had built character, hierarchy, and community within just 576 pixels. Hall and Watkinson refer to such a phenomenon as "small multiples," a term borrowed from American statistician, Edward Tufte.[29] While Tufte's use of the term refers to the display of multiple graphs grouped together to "visually enforce comparisons of changes, of the dif-ferences among objects, of the scope of alternatives," Larva Labs saw how such an idea could equally apply to large collections of similar yet unique items.[30] Inspired by collectible games such as *Magic: The Gathering* and *Pokémon*, along with their Androidify avatar generator, Hall

[23] Ibid.
[24] Ibid.
[25] Larva Labs, interview with the author, November 8, 2022. Released in 2011, Androidify was an app on the Google Play Store that allowed users to create custom Android avatars. Users could personalize the Android robot by changing colors, adding clothes, and attaching accessories.
[26] Matt Hall, "*CryptoPunks*—Interview with Co-Founder Matt Hall," *Art Market Guru*, January 6, 2019, https://www.artmarket.guru/le-journal/interviews/*cryptopunks*-matt-hall/.
[27] Ibid.
[28] Mitchell F. Chan, "Punks and Sellouts," *Outland*, March 18, 2022, https://outland.art/yuga-labs-*cryptopunks*-sale/.
[29] Larva Labs, interview with the author, November 8, 2022.
[30] Edward Tufte, *Envisioning Information* (Cheshire, Connecticut: Graphics Press, 1990), 67.

**06.13**
One of only eight "Genesis" *CryptoPunks* which have no attributes
Larva Labs, *CryptoPunk #1050*, 06-23-2017 14:57:42
Generative pixel art
Ethereum, 0xb47e3cd837ddf8e4c57f05d70ab865de6e193bbb, 1050

**06.14**
The only *CryptoPunk* to have a full set of seven attributes
Larva Labs, *CryptoPunk #8348*, 06-23-2017 18:50:18
Generative pixel art
Ethereum, 0xb47e3cd837ddf8e4c57f05d70ab865de6e193bbb, 8348

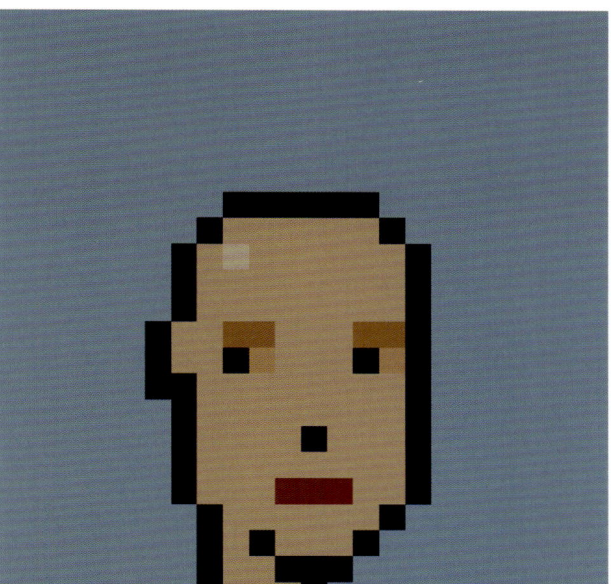

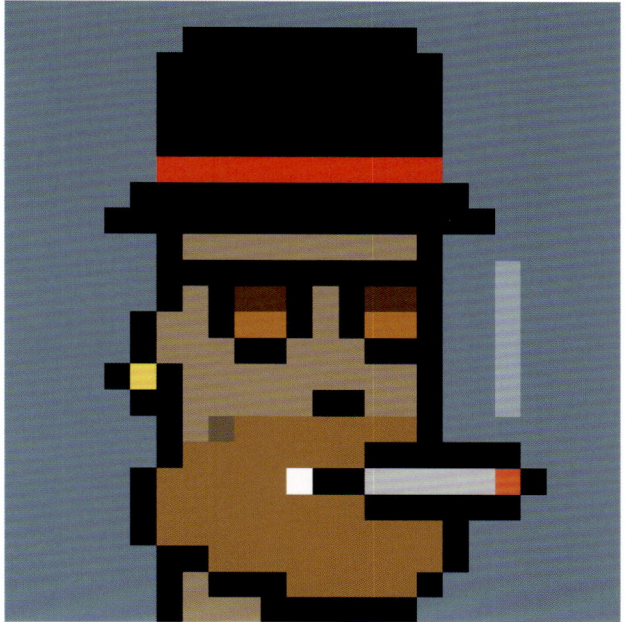

and Watkinson saw how their idea of "small multiples" could induce powerful psychological effects on the human brain. Whether it be in the case of gaming, online identity, or collecting, "one immediately wants to compare, find their favorites, discover the rarity."[31] The Punks and their innate collectibility have seen such themes play out on an international scale with incredible accuracy.

While Punks present a breakthrough in the history of portraiture from a technological perspective, formally they build on the aesthetics of the past in a design exercise of extraordinarily prescient visual communication. As the smallest integer of digital expression, pixels have a long history of being used as the building blocks for assembling virtual identities. Once again, it was gaming that pioneered the growth of this style, from the early online games like *Ultima IV* and *Habitat*, as discussed to the cult classics of *Space Invaders* and *Pac-Man*, the pixel has defined on-screen representation throughout history. Having been immersed in such games throughout their youth, as well as creating numerous pixel games of their own, Hall and Watkinson saw the pixel aesthetic as a "natural fit" for their art.[32] Indeed, it was seeing the pixel mosaics of urban artist Invader, when Watkinson realized "that pixel art was not going to be just a relic of old video games we used to play, but continue to be a culturally significant medium for our generation."[33]

One of the most prominent figures in the early computer art scene, particularly in reference to the Punks' pixelated aesthetic, was cyberneticist Leon D. Harmon. In Harmon's 1973 study in *Scientific American*, "The Recognition of Faces," he investigated the minimum level of facial data required in order to pictorially identify an individual. One of the key findings from Harmon's study was that "a spatial resolution of 16 × 16 squares was very close to the minimum resolution that allows identification."[34] Made up of a similiar scale pixel grid as the portraits from Harmon's article, the Punks strike the perfect equilibrium of definable identity and graphic simplicity. They are a form of facial minimalism, underscored by an unequivocal punk aesthetic. Furthermore, the pixel grid aesthetic of Harmon's *Block Portraits* is one that translates natively into the NFT space **[06.15]**.[35] These pixels represent an intrinsic bond between medium and aesthetic, a metaphor for the blockchain's blocks that the Punks call home. Coupled with their unique array of attributes, the Punks' success lies in their ability to visually register with their audience on Twitter timelines. On the social network's homepage, where profile pictures measure approximately just 8 mm in diameter on a modern-day smartphone, Harmon's study in the significance of spatial resolution takes on an order of importance to the contemporary engagement with avatars.

[31] Larva Labs, interview with the author.
[32] Ibid.
[33] Ibid.
[34] Leon D. Harmon, "The Recognition of Faces," *Scientific American*, Vol. 229, No. 5, 1973, 74.
[35] The study involved an experiment in which he converted the analog signals of a 35 mm photographic transparency portrait through a photomultiplier into digital form, creating *Block Portraits* in the process.

**06.15**
Diagram for "System for Making Block Portraits"
Leon D. Harmon, "The Recognition of Faces," *Scientific American*, November 1973, p. 73

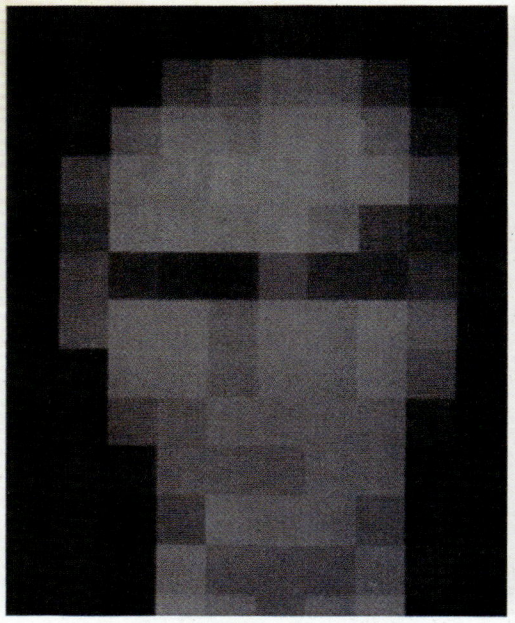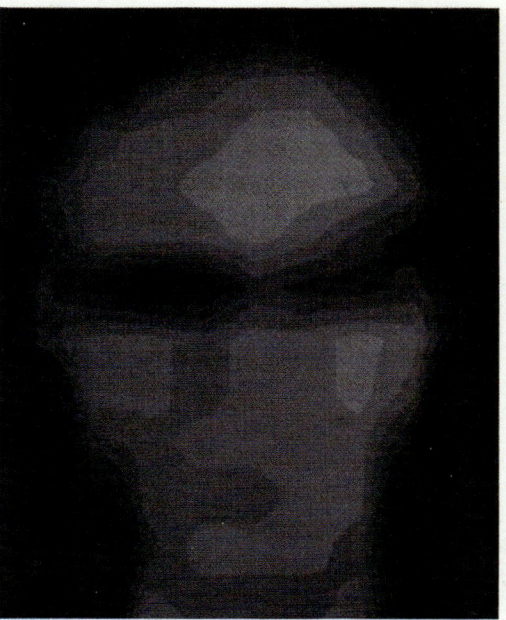

**REDUCED-INFORMATION-CONTENT PORTRAITS** were generated by a computer. The picture at left is a block portrait; it is an array of 16 × 16 squares, each one of which can assume any one of 16 levels of gray. Not all the 256 squares are required to represent the face. The contoured representation at right was produced by filtering the block portrait to remove high frequencies.

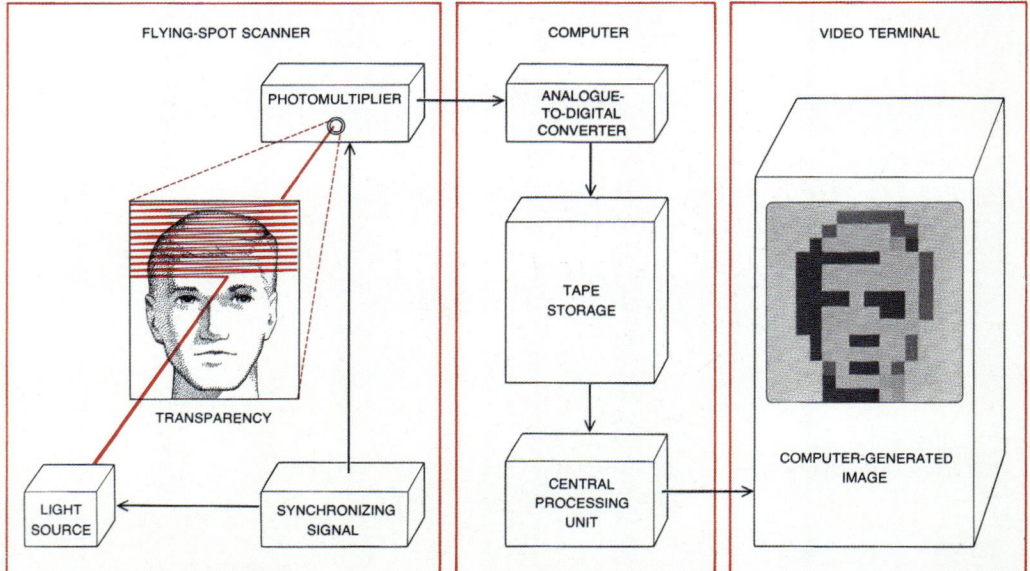

**SYSTEM FOR MAKING BLOCK PORTRAITS** uses a flying-spot scanner, a device similar to a television camera. The image, usually in the form of a 35-millimeter photographic transparency, is scanned in a raster pattern of 1,024 lines. In the analogue-to-digital converter each line is sampled at 1,024 points and the brightness of each point is assigned one of 1,024 values. Using this information stored on magnetic tape, the central processing unit divides the image into $n \times n$ squares and averages the brightness values of all the points within each square. The number of permissible brightness values is then reduced to eight or 16. The resulting image is displayed on a video terminal (a television screen) and photographed. The computer can also be made to operate a facsimile printer, which produces a finished picture directly. Most of the portraits used in these experiments were made by the latter process.

73

**06.16**
Salvador Dalí
*Painting of Gala looking at the Mediterranean sea which from a distance of 20 meters is transformed into a portrait of Abraham Lincoln (Homage to Rothko)*, ca. 1976
Oil on canvas, 252.2 × 191.9 cm
The Dalí Museum, Florida, United States

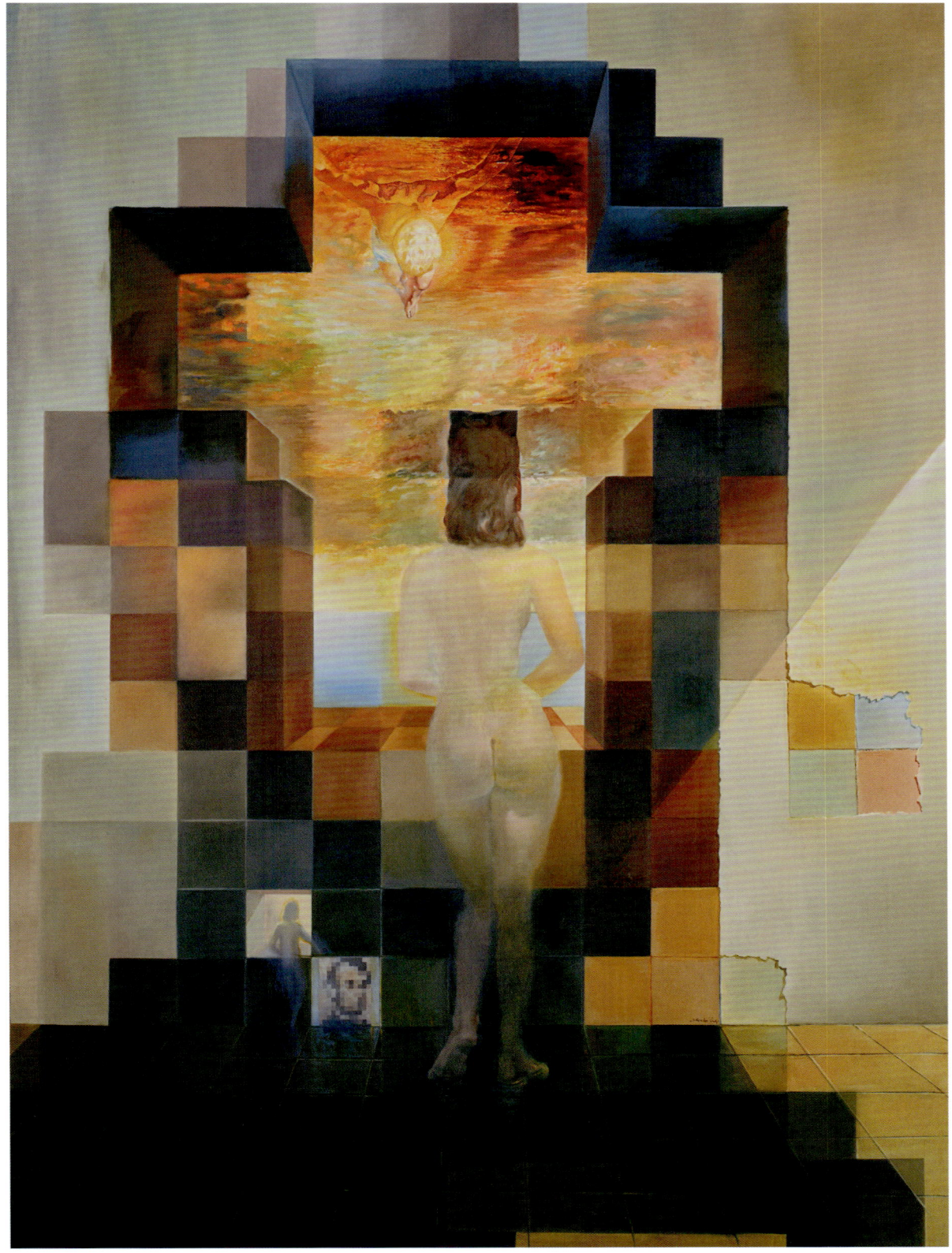

**06.17** (from left to right)
Larva Labs
*Meebits #1535, #3293, #7462, #13251, #3012, #7108, #14357 & #8915,* 2021
3D voxel characters
Ethereum, 0x7Bd29408f11D2bFC23c34f18275bBf23bB716Bc7, 1535, 3293, 7462, 13251, 3012, 7108, 14357 & 8915

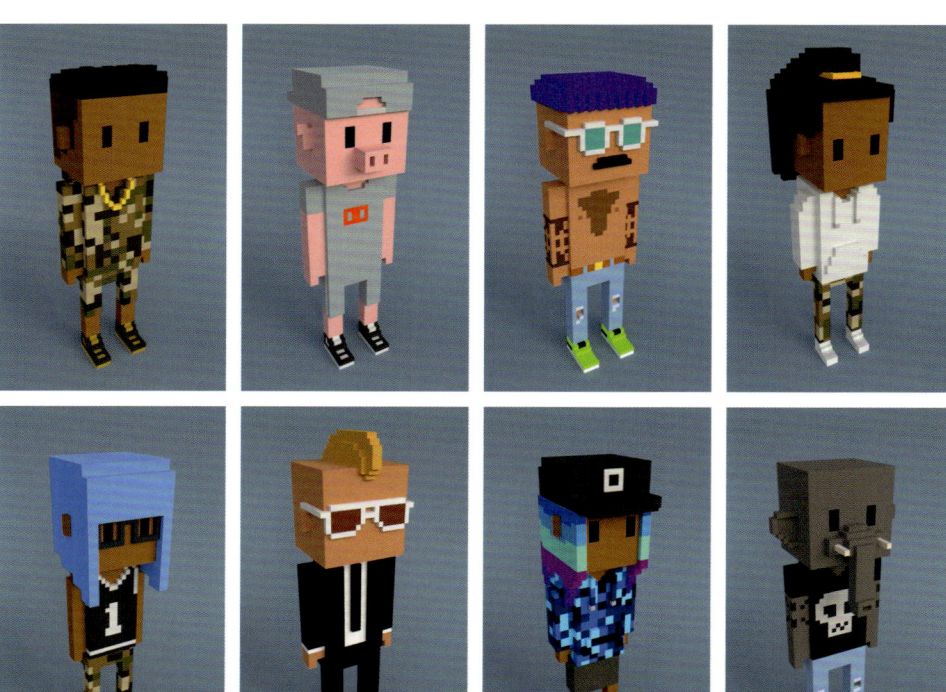

Made in direct response to Harmon's study, Salvador Dalí's *Painting of Gala looking at the Mediterranean sea which from a distance of 20 meters is transformed into a portrait of Abraham Lincoln (Homage to Rothko)* (1976) **[06.16]** investigates the conversion of image and identity through depth and perspective of pixelated forms. Dalí frames his muse, Gala, with 121 blocks — or pixels — yet when viewed from 20 meters these forms construct an unquestionable portrait of Abraham Lincoln. While not only strikingly similar to the Punks from an aesthetic standpoint, this work also represents the transformation of identity from one individual to another, a theme inherent in avatars. Furthermore, Dalí provokes a reduction of identity through minimalism in order to question the underlying principles of recognition, revealing that even the slightest sensory cues can provoke an association of character. Much like how Conrad Kline became Young Turk in *Habitat*, Gala fancifully transitions across geographies and time periods into Abraham Lincoln. *Painting of Gala...* is a surrealist impersonation in which Dalí explores many of the same conceptual structures of escapism and role-play that are hallmarks of our contemporary avatar space. The three-dimensionality of Dalí's work also calls to mind Larva Labs' second avatar project, *Meebits* (2021) **[06.17]**. This collection of 20,000 metaverse-ready characters saw Larva Labs transcend their avatars from the 2D form of the Punks to voxel-based identities. With the rapid growth of blockchain metaverses since the inception of the Punks, the *Meebits* presented a far more metaverse-native makeup than their predecessors and a step into a more contemporary version of the avatar model, that would soon become known as PFPs (Profile Pictures).

### PFPs: The Bored Ape Yacht Club

While Punks embodied the ultimate form of pictorial self-expression for many of crypto's earliest pioneers (and still do to this day), by early 2021 a new kind of avatar was set to radically disrupt the NFT ecosystem. On April 23, Yuga Labs launched the Bored Ape Yacht Club **[06.18]**, a collection of 10,000 cartoon apes each charged with a unique character. Founded by the pseudonymous Gordon Goner and Gargamel of Yuga Labs, the Bored Apes

36 Matt Hall and John Watkinson, "Yuga Labs Acquires *CryptoPunks* and Meebits," *Larva Labs*, Blog, March 11, 2022, https://www.larvalabs.com/blog/2022-3-11-18-0/yuga-labs-acquires-cryptopunks-and-meebits; PFPs, or profile pictures to our Web 2.0 counterparts, are NFTs created with the intention of being used as avatars in our online environments, often rewarding holders with airdrops and utilities to create cohesive communities and ecosystems around these avatars.

37 Yuga Labs (@yugalabs), "A little bit about us to start off the new year and what's coming." Twitter, January 3, 2022, 8:27 p.m., https://twitter.com/yugalabs/status/1478100695404449804?s=20&t=edY_ZiHf0YIPMkDc2rmrkQ.

38 Yuga Labs (@yugalabs) "7. Why did you get into NFTs?" Twitter, January 3, 2022, 8:27 p.m., https://twitter.com/yugalabs/status/1478100707991506948?s=20&t=nQd4dZYemlnxBLZd-1NgMg.

39 Stephenson, *Snow Crash*, 34.

40 It should be noted that the presence of apes in virtual worlds is nothing new. Across all the weird and wacky character types throughout digital history, apes have always been a subject for creatives to turn to. In 1981, Nintendo and Shigeru Miyamoto introduced one such character, Donkey Kong. With Donkey being a mistranslation of "'stubborn'" or "grumpy" and Kong referring to "ape," the Bored Apes fit firmly within this lineage. Furthermore, there had been visual references to apes in the NFT space prior to those in *CryptoPunks*. Harambe, the western gorilla from the Cincinnati Zoo who gained a cult following after his untimely death in 2016, was memorialized in the form of a rare pepe, appropriately titled Harampepe. With a timestamp of 09-28-2016 16:21:06— could Harampepe be the first ape on the blockchain? The term *ape* — or *apeing* — as as defined in the Glossary, is familiar to many in the wider sphere of crypto and meme investing. *Apes* are typically retail investors who take bullish positions on high-risk investment strategies, often with little prior research. In the sphere of crypto, apeing was arguably most present during DeFi Summer in 2020, where the frequent roll out of new DeFi protocols saw a rapid escalation of investment opportunities, both those with legitimate intent and those built on false pretenses. Additionally, the term is not limited solely to crypto users. Apes were widely present across Reddit in 2021 during a meme stock revolution as users of the subreddit r/WallStreetBets coordinated numerous short squeezes in a bid to challenge major institutional investors, such as Citadel Securities and Melvin Capital.

41 For more on the accusations leveled at Yuga Labs by several parties, including the expert opinions of Mark Pitcavage and Carla Hill, senior researchers at the Anti-Defamation League's Center on Extremism, see Matt Wille, "Bored Ape Yacht Club finally responds to neo-Nazism accusations," *Input*, February 1, 2022, https://www.inverse.com/input/culture/bored-ape-yacht-club-nazism-racism-claims-yuga-labs-ryder-ripps.

42 Torey Akers, "Bored Ape Yacht Club creators score legal victory in lawsuit against artists who made copycat NFT collection," *The Art Newspaper*, April 26, 2023, https://www.theartnewspaper.com/2023/04/26/bored-ape-yacht-club-nfts-lawsuit-ryder-ripps-partial-victory.

quickly came to populate headlines around the world. They initated a forking of the avatar to something more than just a virtual identity. To a large extent, and even remarked on by Larva Labs, the Bored Apes became crypto's first "PFP" project in which the concept of an avatar as a foothold in a growing community ecosystem was born.[36] Led by Bored Apes, PFPs have become the portraits of a Web3 world that straddle the line between virtual identity, collectible objects of conspicuous consumption, utility tokens for membership clubs, licensable assets, and a proto-visual cryptocurrency: as volatile and tradable as their more fungible counterparts.

Much like the 8-bit aesthetic of the Punks, the ape theme of Yuga's collection is one that is deeply rooted in online culture and gaming. Even the company's namesake was said to be inspired as a play on these themes, with "Yuga" being the villain in *Zelda* who had the ability to turn himself and others into 2D art.[37] Yuga Labs' founders, being self-professed "gamers at heart," saw the potential of how "NFTs usher in a new era of composability and ownership" and their "ability to fundamentally improve gaming experiences."[38] Being native to the MMORPG scene, Gordon Goner and Gargamel recognized the importance of community in shared virtual environments, making it one of the core focuses for their Apes. In any of these community-oriented mass multiplayer games, from *World of Warcraft*, to *League of Legends*, to *RuneScape*, avatars afford a sense of self amongst a collective. In the NFT space community equals consensus, and as in art, consensus equals value. In this, the Bored Apes are valued for more than their provenance, they were launched as a key to a new form of digital community and the nascent ecosystems built around them.

Even at the beginning of the metaverse idea, apes existed as avatars. It was the first character Stephenson referred to in *Snow Crash* when defining what an avatar could be: "You can look like a gorilla or a dragon or a giant talking penis in the Metaverse," reflecting equally the elements of fantasy and comedy that are also so inherent to the avatar structure.[39] Apes are also a frequently touched upon subject in the crypto space, being an "ape" is the ultimate call sign for a high-risk crypto investor building concentrated positions, at times on little more than a Twitter whisper. Ape avatars — also one of the rarest in the Punk hierarchy — offer a pictorial metaphor for those with pre-existing crypto-native ideologies.[40]

While the original narrative of Bored Apes was rooted in crypto, in their aesthetic and traits they draw broadly and at times obliquely from the history of cartoon, gaming, fashion, meme, and troll culture. With over 170 traits of goofy expressions — from lazy, unshaven apes to those equipped with Bitcoin maximalist laser eyes, along with other traits including Ottoman fezzes, sushi chef headbands, and an officially termed 'hip-hop' trait — the collection presented the founders' desire to create a global community, albeit one where accusations of cultural stereotyping have intermixed with a more sympathetic contextual reading of the founders' intentions.[41]

With the relative intricacy of their design as a direct response to the minimalism of Punks, the Bored Apes, more effectively than any other project, have transcended the current confines of a nuclear Web3 world and engaged with mainstream contemporary pop culture, juiced by the endorsement of major celebrities. If Punks looked to the aesthetics of 1970s gaming and early computing, Yuga Labs turned to the world of Disney and the long history of cartoons that precedes it [06.19, 06.20]. Yet the Bored Apes disrupt the walled garden of Disneyland. Unlike Disney (or Larva Labs, who retained full copyright of the Punks before selling it to Yuga Labs) their major innovation was decentralizing ownership of each Bored Ape by granting holders the license to use their avatars commercially as they wished. Yuga Labs handed to their collectors a legal building block to drive the direction of the project alongside the team in the spirit of decentralization. The decision to democratize the licensing of the avatars registered with a generation of crypto entrepreneurs and influencers who saw the collection as a powerful tool for self-organization. With the Bored Breakfast Club coffee or KINGSHIP — Universal Music's Ape quartet music group — holders are incentivized to build local ecosystems around their NFT. In many ways this idea may seem antithetical to the philosophy of ownership and protection of rights that sits at the core of this book's treatment of NFTs. Yet the decentralization of rights presents itself as a fundamentally Web3 act and is an interesting case study against the walled-garden approach of previous tech and media generations, especially the social media networks of the Web 2.0 era. Decentralization — and through it the idea of real ownership — fosters a stronger basis for social cohesion as a collective. This being said, the novelty and specificities of the license had initially created a number of murky copyright and intellectual property issues, as some individuals challenged the legitimacy of Yuga Labs's copyright. However, a recent legal victory for Yuga Labs protected the Bored Ape trademarks per the Lanham Act of 1946, solidifying the understanding of NFTs as goods under law.[42] It is important to recognize, nevertheless, that Yuga Labs has not yet put up a legal challenge on the basis of copyright infringement. Such contributes to the notion that the legal clarification

**06.18** (from left to right)
Yuga Labs
*Bored Ape Yacht Club #9528, #8009, #8415, #6974, #9522, #8012, #6426, #8019, #968, #5093, #6841 & #1508,* 2021
Generative digital drawing
Ethereum, 0xbc4ca0eda7647a8ab7c2061c2e118a18a936f13d, 9528, 8009, 8415, 6974, 9522, 8012, 6426, 8019, 968, 5093, 6841 & 1508

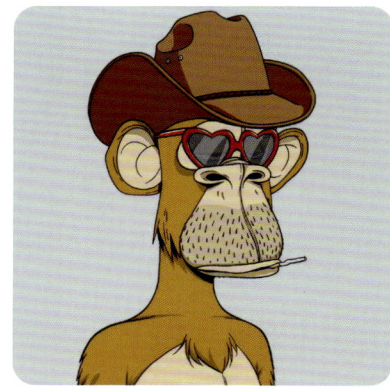
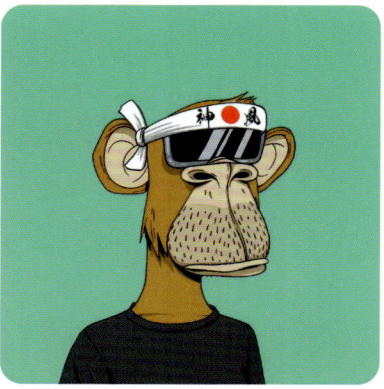
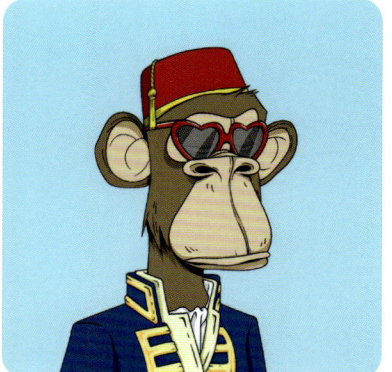
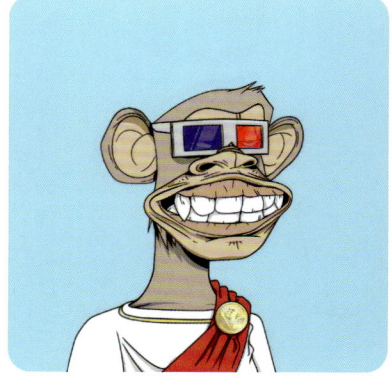
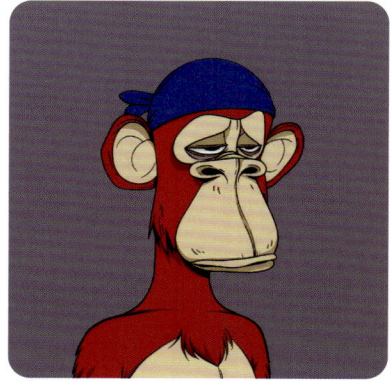
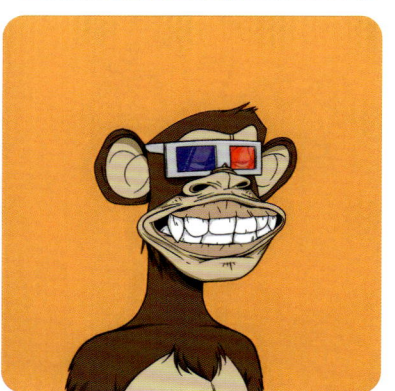
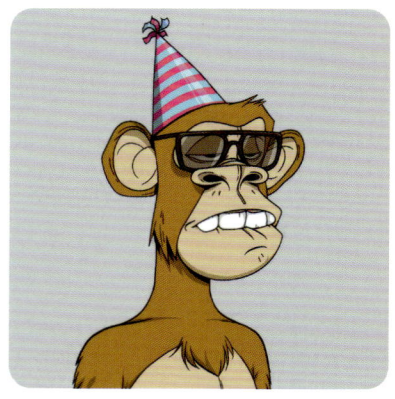
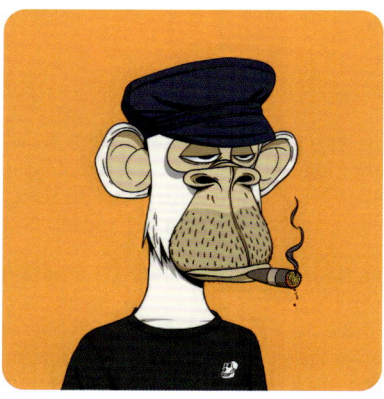
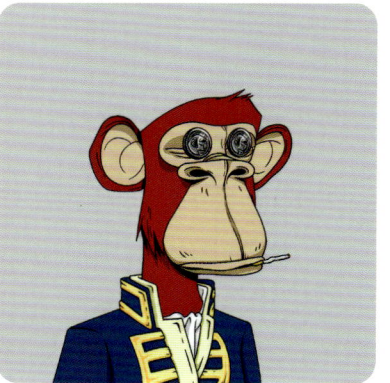
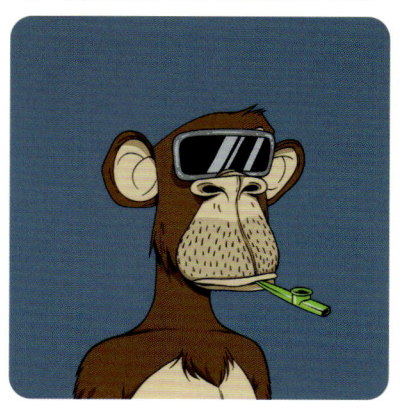
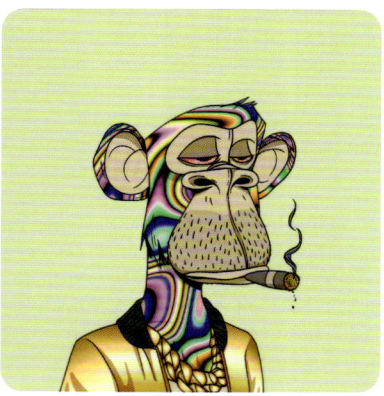
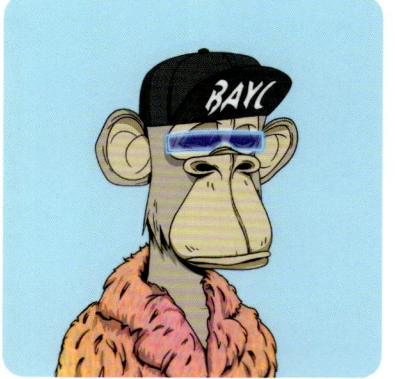

06.19
All Seeing Seneca
Early process sketches showing the character development for the Bored Ape Yacht Club, 2021
Adobe Photoshop, digital drawing

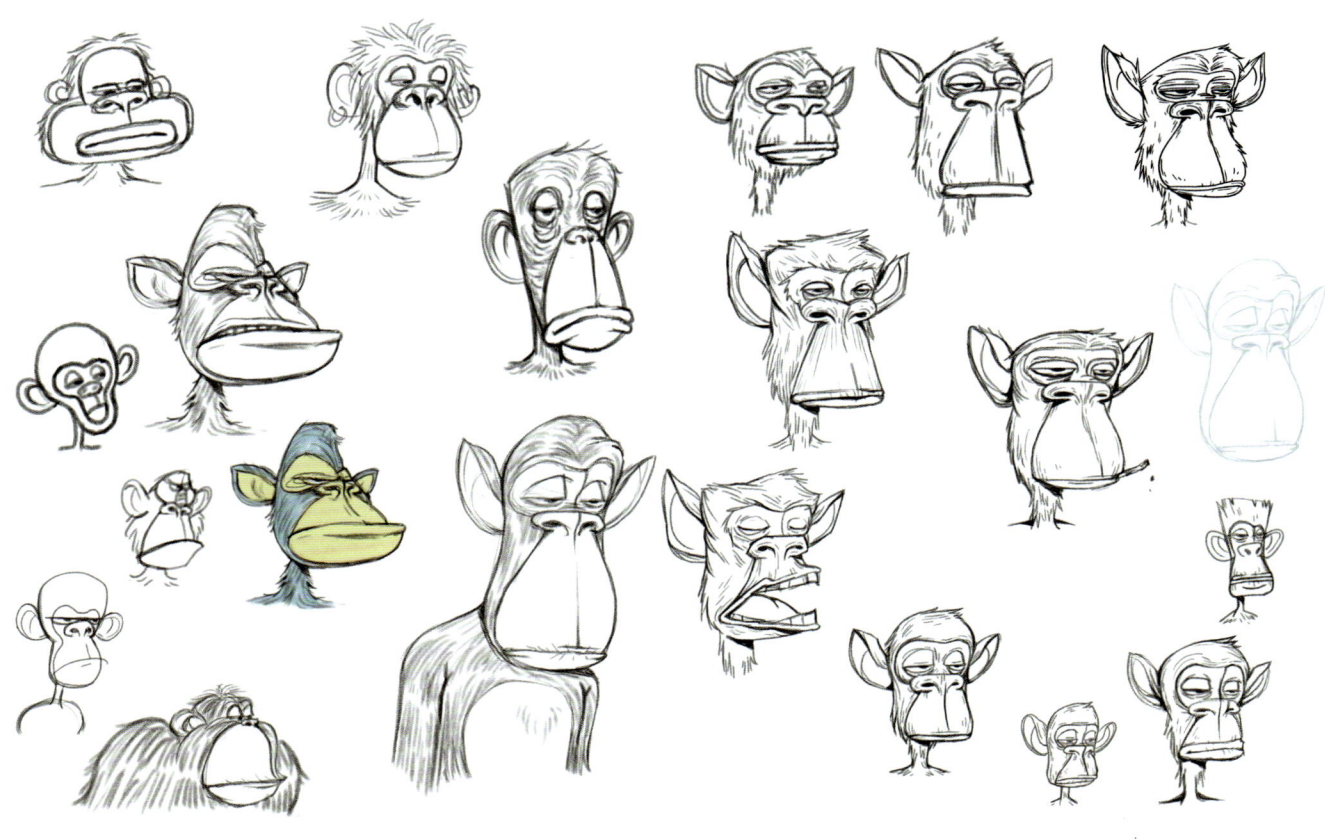

for the decentralization of IP in NFTs remains somewhat uncharted. Furthermore, secondary questions regarding the transfer of licenses upon sale and the licensing status of hacked or stolen NFTs continue to highlight the current lack of legal clarity regarding how NFTs interact with existing copyright and intellectual property laws.

## One a Day: Nouns and Decentralization

One project that furthers this narrative of community building and decentralization through avatars is *Nouns*. What may be the most pioneering CC0 NFT project, *Nouns* uses a daily auction mechanism to release a new avatar each day in perpetuity, which in itself acts as a membership to Nouns DAO. Each sale is pooled directly into the DAO treasury, whose members can submit proposals on how to deploy the raised capital. With donations to a host of international causes, including the Red Cross in support of victims of the Ukraine conflict, *Nouns* represents a key turning point in the avatar infrastructure. They reveal the true power of a decentralized community and how what was once a simple tool of online identity can now facilitate global coordination and action. The synthesis of the DAO structure with the community model of an avatar achieves a new form of high-speed collectivization and community. Further still, in the adoption of CC0 licensing, *Nouns* have handed their IP to the public domain, whereby its name, image, and entire concept can be used by anyone for anything. From projects taking aesthetic motifs, such as the *Nouns* glasses in Gremplin's *CrypToadz* (2021) **[06.21]**, to others with an explicit copy-cat approach like *Lil Nouns* (2022) shrinking the *Nouns* auction mechanism to only 15-minute cycles with each *Noun* adopting a smaller, more child-like appearance. Additionally, for the first five years of its existence, every 11th *Lil Noun* will be sent to the Nouns DAO treasury, a nod to the *Nouns* for being "selfless stewards of CC0." [43] A key consequence is that by enhancing commercialization, it

43 "Nouns DAO Rewards," *Lil Nouns*, accessed October 10, 2022, https://lilnouns.wtf/.

**06.20**
All Seeing Seneca
Later process sketches for the Bored Ape Yacht Club, 2021
Adobe Photoshop, digital drawing

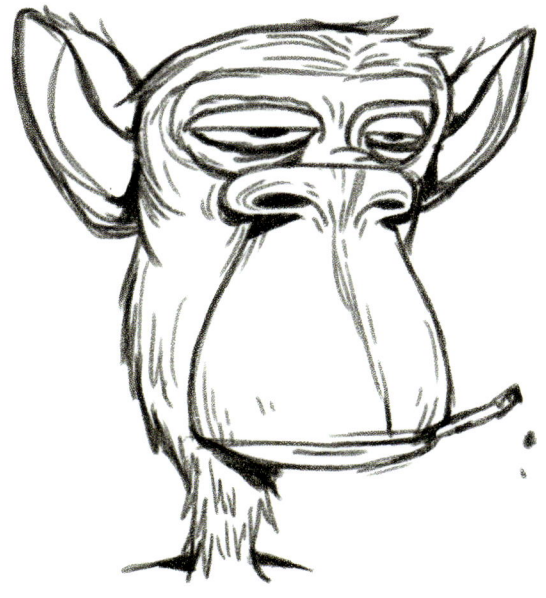

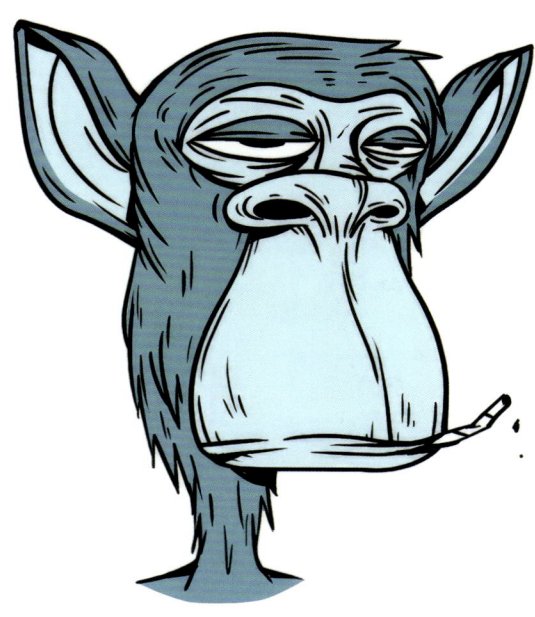

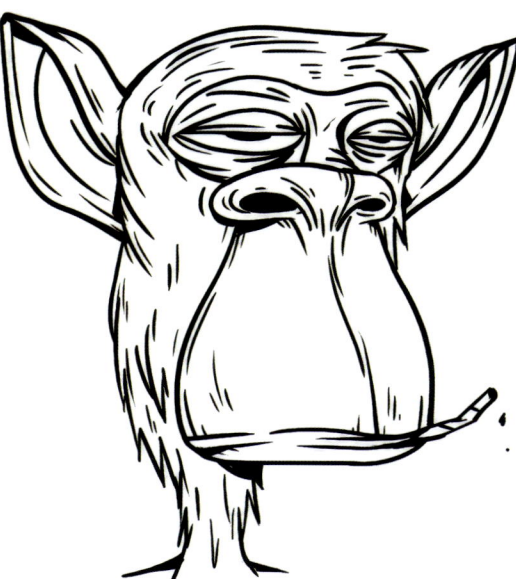

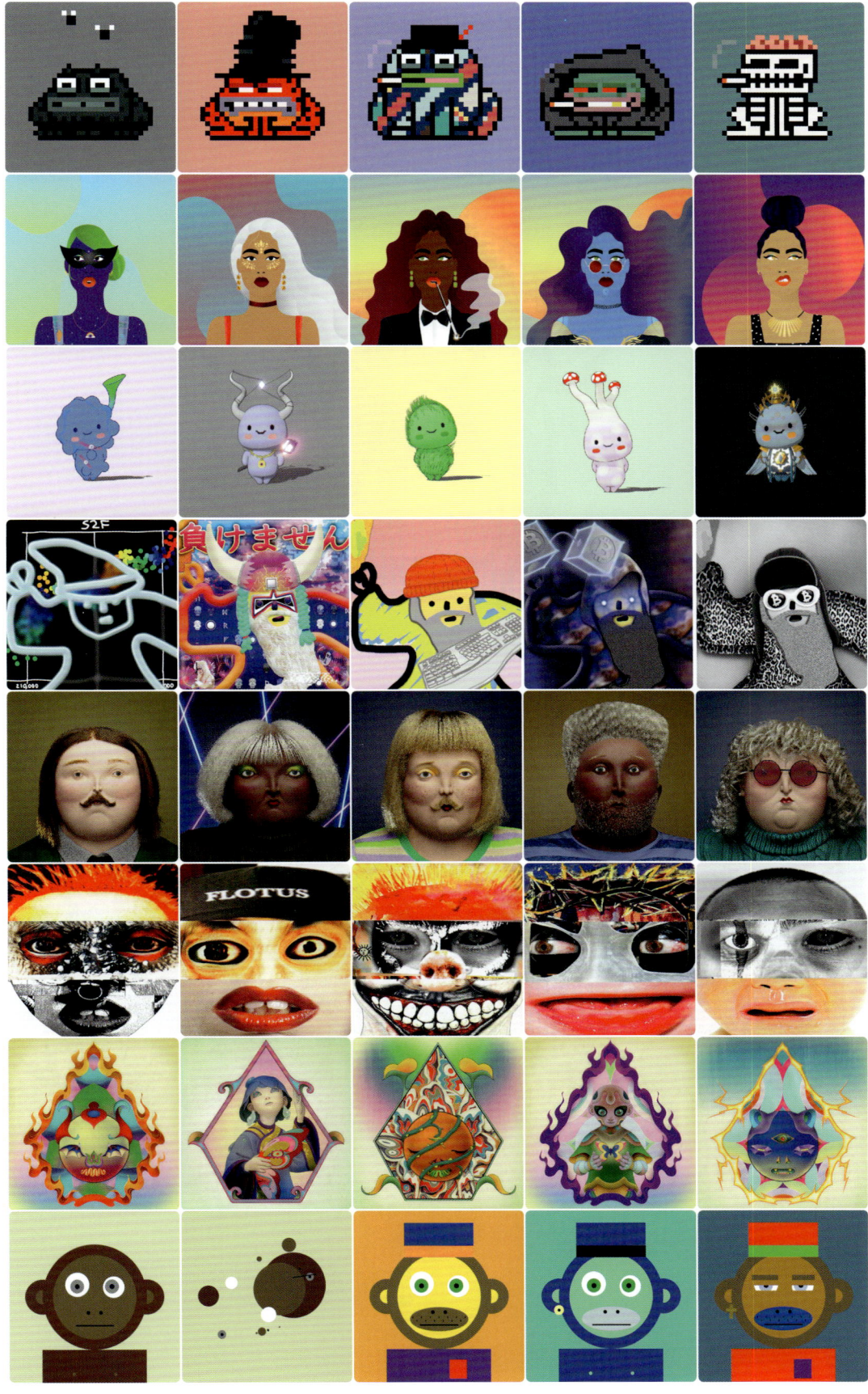

**06.21–06.28** (from top to bottom)

**06.21** (from left to right)
Gremplin
*CrypToadz #217, #2278, #4236, #6259 & #6831,* 2021
Adobe Photoshop, generative digital drawing
Ethereum, 0x1cb1a5e65610aeff2551a50f76a87a7d3fb649c6

**06.22** (from left to right)
Yam Karkai
*World of Women #3834, #411, #6144, #6304 & #9201,* 2021
Adobe Illustrator, generative digital drawing
Ethereum, 0xe785E82358879F061BC3dcAC6f0444462D4b5330

**06.23** (from left to right)
Ed Fornieles
*Finiliar Avalanche, Bitcoin, Tezos, Matic & Ethereum,* 2022
Houdini, Unity
Ethereum, 0x5a0121a0a21232ec0d024dab9017314509026480, Pre-mint editions

**06.24** (from left to right)
Taproot Wizards
*Taproot Wizards 56,480; 149,127; 448,523; 14,163,842; 73,114,822,* 2023–ongoing
Adobe Photoshop and proprietary code
Bitcoin, Inscriptions 56,480; 149,127; 448,523; 14,163,842; 73,114,822

**06.25** (from left to right)
p0pps
*Regular #5535, #3647, #7593, #3586 & #2432,* 2022
Houdini
Ethereum, 0x6d0de90cdc47047982238fcf69944555d27ecb25

**06.26** (from left to right)
Scammer
*Caber, Frogfoot, Kompriest, Toothing & Gabbard,* 2021
Adobe Photoshop
Ethereum, 0x4e2A87743368484eD798033E8FdC7caE442064b8

**06.27** (from left to right)
James Jean
*Fragments #1, #3414, #4368, #5797 & #894,* 2022
Hand illustration, iPad drawing, Adobe Suite
Ethereum, 0x51f0c1938b0E67CaFC7a6fC8eB6EdD7FDBe002bC

**06.28** (from left to right)
OnChainMonkey
(1–2) *OCM Genesis & Deconstructed,* (3–5) *OCM Genesis,*
2023-02-08 22:48:35 (10k Genesis Inscriptions)
Bitcoin, Inscription 20219, 464551, ,-264835, -263649, -264889

allows for faster growth through the distribution of the brand image. In ways not dissimilar to Dom Hofmann's *Loot* (2021), *Nouns* represent an early building block and roadmap for a more native approach to an avatar project. *Nouns* have used avatars, DAOs, CC0 licensing, and auction mechanics to build a Web3 structure in its purest form.

### World of Women and the Importance of Diversity

Given the importance of community in avatar ecosystems, one must hope for an ecosystem with a strong sense of diversity. In these early days of the NFT space — a technology in its infancy — collections lean to the image of the male. The collections discussed in this chapter highlight these issues, Punks are only 38.4% female, and while the Bored Apes fall into a more androgynous aesthetic, there are still nearly twice the amount of male references to female, including, for example, two characteristics for 'Kings' ('King's Robe' and 'King's Crown') but no references to 'Queens'. The make-up of many male-centric collections are reflective, perhaps, of the market and community they address — data from the UK's FCA or Binance's Global Report suggest that men make up the overwhelming majority of crypto participants, with figures ranging from 75% to 95%.[44] It is therefore critical, for the long-term health of the space, to see projects centered not just on broad-based equality of representation but also on female or minority empowerment. One such project is *World of Women* (2021) **[06.22]**, with the mission aim of "celebrating representation, inclusivity and equal opportunities for all."[45]

Created by digital illustrator Yam Karkai, *World of Women* recognizes the clear disparities of gender in the crypto art scene and has set about welcoming more women into the NFT space. Important to the *World of Women* narrative, portions of the sale proceeds are directed to philanthropic causes, with 15% going into supporting new crypto artists and projects, and a further 7.5% divided between charities dedicated to the fight against child marriage, to educating girls, and towards the emergency surgery of a community member. With a strong community of female and minority members, from Hollywood stars to first time collectors, the project has not only raised awareness for the importance of equal representation in the

[44] Gemini, "Global State of Crypto Report," April 4, 2022, https://www.gemini.com/state-of-us-crypto; Binance, "Global Crypto Index 2021," January 28, 2021, https://research.binance.com/static/pdf/Global_Crypto_Index_2021.pdf; Financial Conduct Authority, "Cryptoasset consumer research 2020," June 30, 2020, https://www.fca.org.uk/publication/research/research-note-cryptoasset-consumer-research-2020.pdf.
[45] World of Women, accessed June 24, 2022, https://worldofwomen.art/.

06.29 ▶

Sputniko!
Screenshot from *Menstrualverse*, 08-18-2022 03:22:48
3D model in Decentraland
Ethereum, 0x3609045C5E7DdAbfaf65C9b69FDcA5dF62F77031, 17

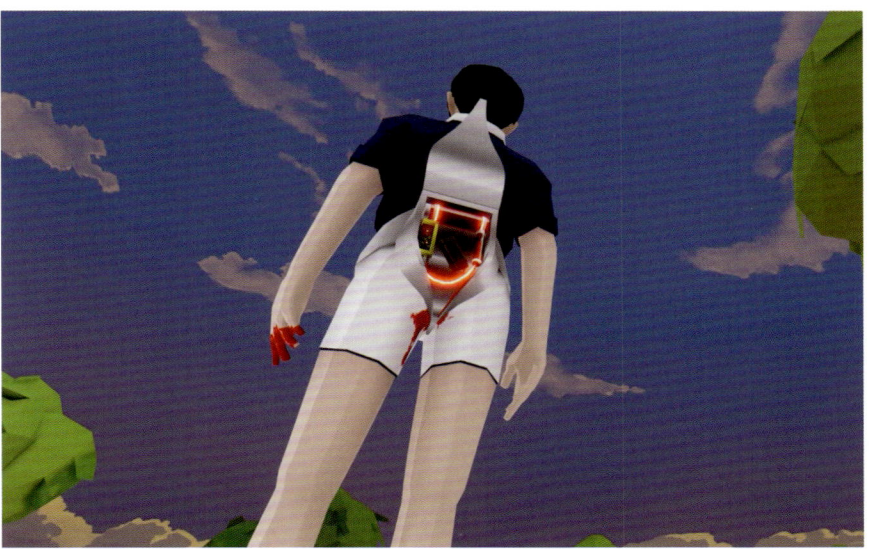

NFT space, but with it spurred a mass influx of similar female-led avatar projects, such as *Boss Beauties* (2021), *Riot Girls* (2022), and *Long Neckie Ladies* (2021). Seeing these projects flourish, across international audiences, is of great importance to the future of NFTs and our increasingly digital existence given how they shed light on the issues of equality in the building of the metaverse and, other digitial tools, such as AI.

One project that furthers such an idea was that of leading Japanese artist, Sputniko!, who in 2022 created a Decentraland avatar project titled *Menstrualverse* **[06.29]**. Commissioned by UnicornDAO, a collective focused on equality for women and LGBTQIA+ people in Web3, the work seeks to challenge the notion of identity, biology, and choice in the metaverse through the expression of gender.[46] The project attempted to allow avatars in Decentraland to menstruate, which would ultimately mark the "first public performance of menstruation in the Metaverse," the artist notes.[47] The *Menstrualverse Collection* consists of avatar wearables such as period-stained jeans, shorts, and chino pants, with Sputniko! also developing her 2010 project *Menstruation Machine* **[06.30]** into a metaverse accessory. Though upon their submission for review, the wearables were rejected by Decentraland, raising questions about the limitations of gender expression in virtual ecosystems that are so often claimed to be equal for all. The *Menstrualverse* project and Decentraland's response highlight the need for continued work and pressure towards gender equality in the metaverse.

## The Future of Avatars

As the global population spent ever more time online during the COVID-19 pandemic, the narrative of the avatar as a cornerstone to our online life took center stage. The proliferation of projects that dawned during this period and in its aftermath have opened up new avenues of creative potential for digital identities. Some notable projects, that are either aesthetically or conceptually disruptive include: Ed Fornieles's *Finiliar* avatars from 2021 **[06.23]**, which — using oracles — have dependable moods in tandem with the volatilities of their associated crypto asset; *Regulars* (2022) **[06.25]**; *Scammer* (2021) **[06.26]**; James Jean's *Fragments* (2022) **[06.27]**; and the new influx of avatar projects on Bitcoin such as 0xfar, Udi Wertheimer, and Eric Wall's *Taproot Wizards* (2024) **[06.24]** alongside Danny Yang's *OnChainMonkey* (2021 Ethereum/2023 Bitcoin) **[06.28]**. Ordinals have opened up avatars to the larger Bitcoin community, and lie at the centerpiece of Yang's conversion to and prophesizing around art on Bitcoin.

Our pursuit for online representation has been prevalent for decades, from our earliest MMORPGs through science fiction and now unfolding into the current NFT avatar space today. From the outset, avatars have harnessed identity in a natively digital form, and have thus proved to be immensely valuable when tokenized, both socially and culturally.

[46] More information about UnicornDAO can be found in the chapter "ON DAOs."
[47] Sputniko!, "Menstrualverse," *Sputniko!*, 2022, https://sputniko.com/Menstrualverse.

06.30
Sputniko!
*Menstruation Machine*, 2010 (Minted: 02-25-2022 06:33:12)
Photography
Ethereum, 0x3609045C5E7DdAbfaf65C9b69FDcA5dF62F77031, 1

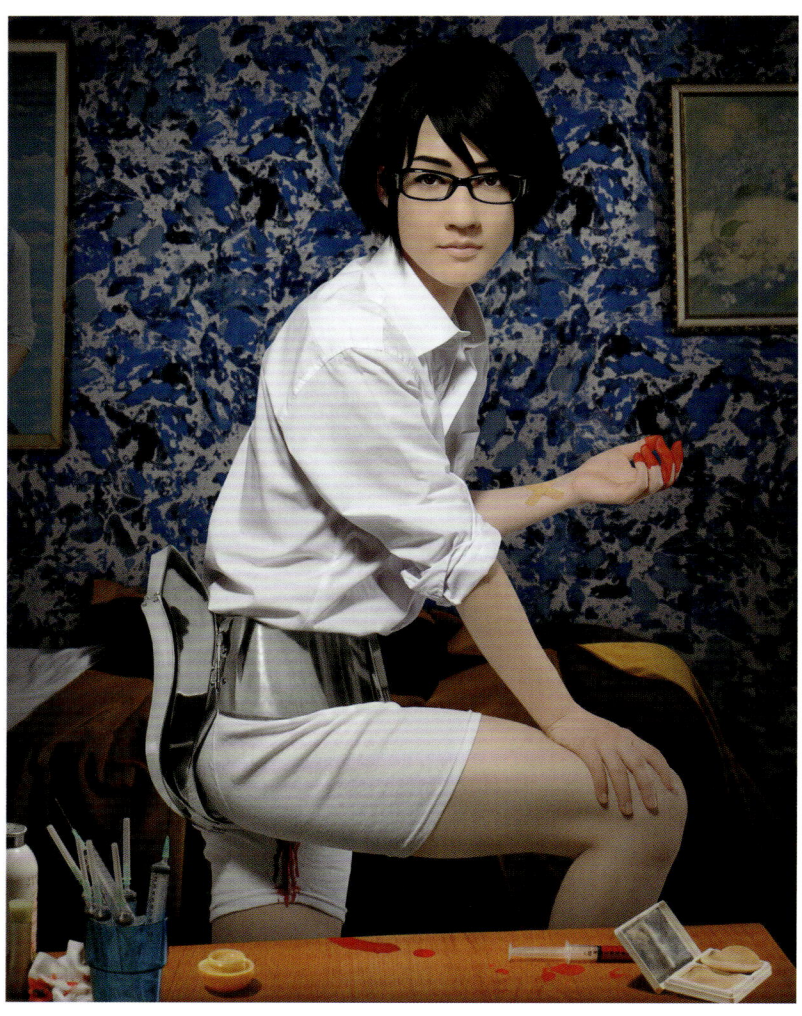

In 2025, the explosion of AI agents, led by Andy Ayrey and *truth_terminal* (2024) and continued by Ai16z and other projects such as Keke Terminal, Shl0ms's @god, @satan, @jesus Twitter performance with Nous Research, point to the rapidly evolving concept of digital avatars infused with AI. These autonomous avatars take on personality traits based on the data they consume through their interactions with the public through machine learning. In a full-circle nature, project such as Yuga's *Otherside* (2022–) are starting to build out metaverse spaces for avatars, expanding on themes seen in our earliest MMORPGs.

As technology exponentially grows over the next century, namely with advancements in VR, AR, AI, and blockchain, the role of the avatar seems poised to exert a stronger influence on our identity. Rapidly developing, the Web3 avatar community is still in its prototype and experimentation phase. As the model of avatars grows and develops, so too will the assessment of avatars in terms of their art-historical reimagining of portraiture. Artists, such as LaTurbo Avedon, Sputniko!, Ed Fornieles, James Jean, and Sam Spratt, are experimenting here, intertwining the avatar model more deeply into the history of portraiture. Increasingly it looks unlikely that, as Jason Abbruzzese mentioned at the inception of blockchain-based avatars, "they could just be a bunch of images."[48] Indeed, the growth and media focus on blockchain-based avatars to date has largely outrun their use cases — where Web3 avatars are largely used within Web 2.0 infrastructures. For the avatar space to grow beyond Twitter profile pictures and highly tradable collectible assets, more meaningful metaverses, online communities, and opportunities for socializing have to be built.

[48] Jason Abbruzzese, "This ethereum-based project could change how we think about digital art," *Mashable*, June 16, 2017, https://mashable.com/article/*cryptopunks-ethereum-art-collectibles*.

01

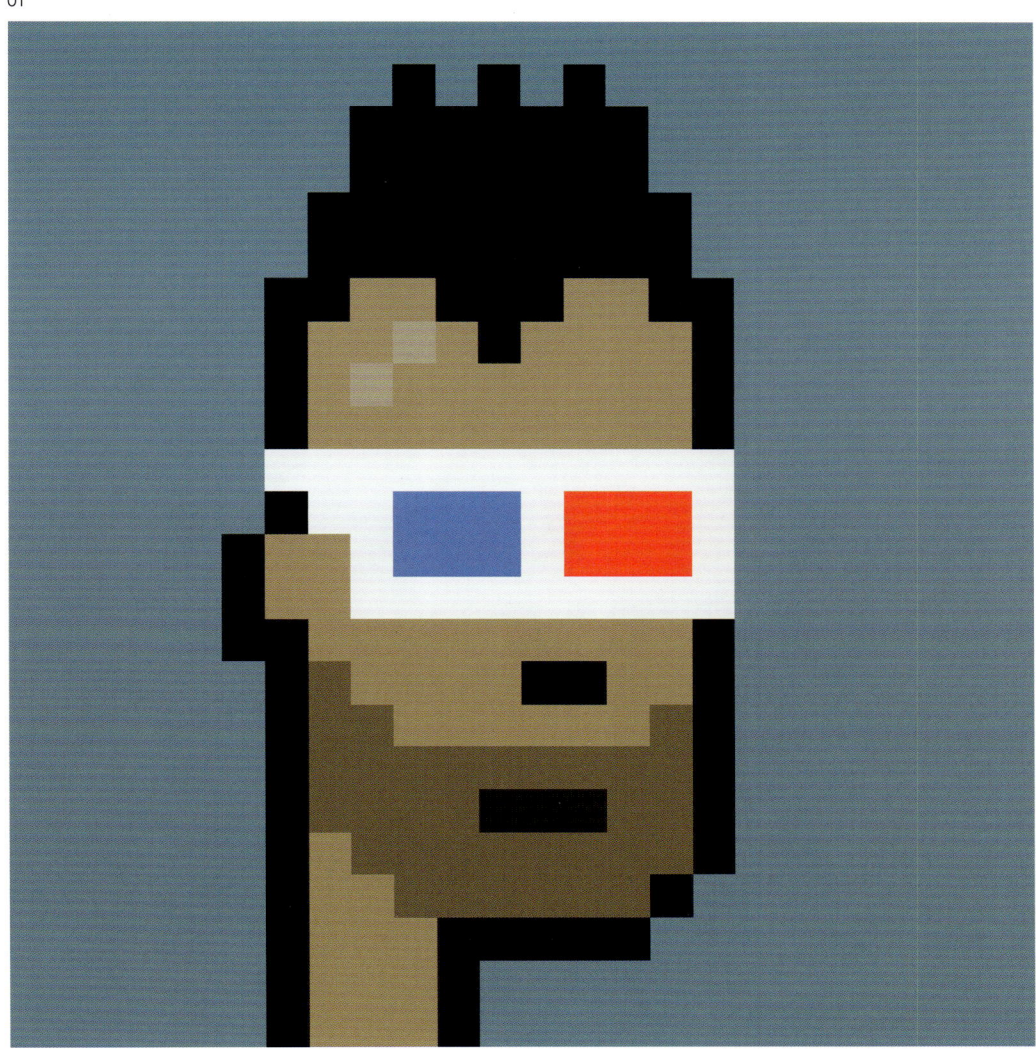

| # | TITLE | TIMESTAMP | MEDIUM | CHAIN | CONTRACT ADDRESS | TOKEN ID | EDITION SIZE |
|---|---|---|---|---|---|---|---|
| 01–03 | **CryptoPunks** | 06-23-2017 13:50:51 | Generative pixel art | ETH | 0xb47e3cd837ddf8e4c57f05d70ab865de6e193bbb | 0–9999 | 1/1 of 10,000 |

EDITIONS ILLUSTRATED: (01) #8070, (02) #5072, (03) Various — please refer to the end matter for details

02

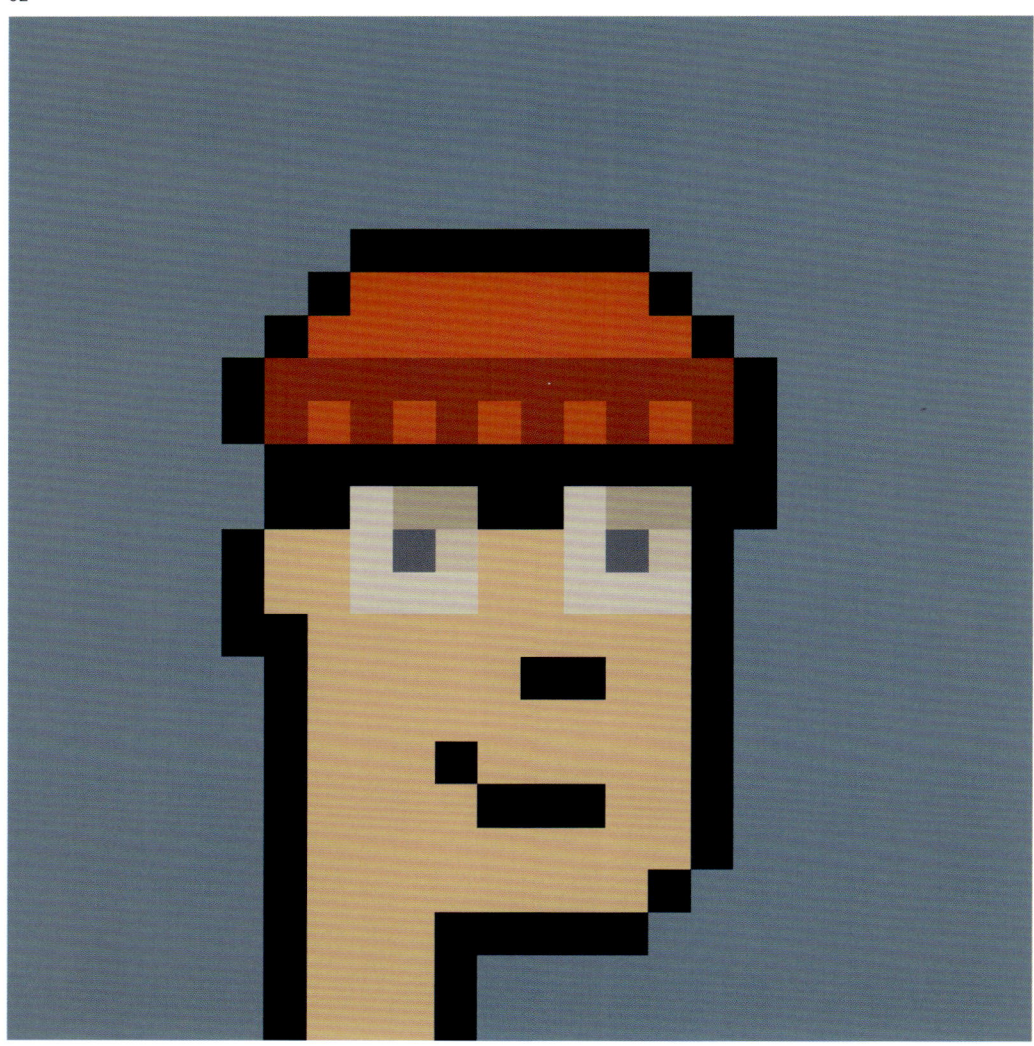

Larva Labs is John Watkinson and Matt Hall, two Canadian software engineers and creative technologists who originally met in the computer science program at the University of Toronto. They have been working together for over 20 years on a large number and wide range of projects. Examples include many apps and games for several mobile platforms, genomics analysis software, the largest open-source repository of legal documents, and a machine vision and audio signaling system that enables the blind to run unassisted.

Their first blockchain art project was *CryptoPunks* (2017), which was conceived as an experiment in digital ownership and value. The project is a self-contained system that records ownership of each *CryptoPunk*, while also allowing for transactions between unknown and untrusted parties. It is effectively an artwork that contains its own perpetual, global, no-fee auction house. As of the publication of this book it has performed almost $3 billion in transactions, illustrating the unique abilities of blockchains to provide digital items with novel characteristics of rarity, permanence, and intrinsic value.

Their follow up project was *Autoglyphs* (2019), the first on-chain generative artwork. Inspired by the work of Sol LeWitt, the algorithm that generates the *Autoglyphs* is embedded in the blockchain smart contract and was run just 512 times total, once for each generated *Autoglyph* when the project was first released.

Their third project was *The Meebits* (2021), 3D generative voxel characters with a custom marketplace that allows for not just buying and selling, but "like kind" trading as well. Each *Meebit* comes with a 3D model in a variety of formats, allowing owners to use them as their avatar in 3D worlds, games, or in any way they please.

**JOHN WATKINSON & MATT HALL**
CO-FOUNDERS OF LARVA LABS

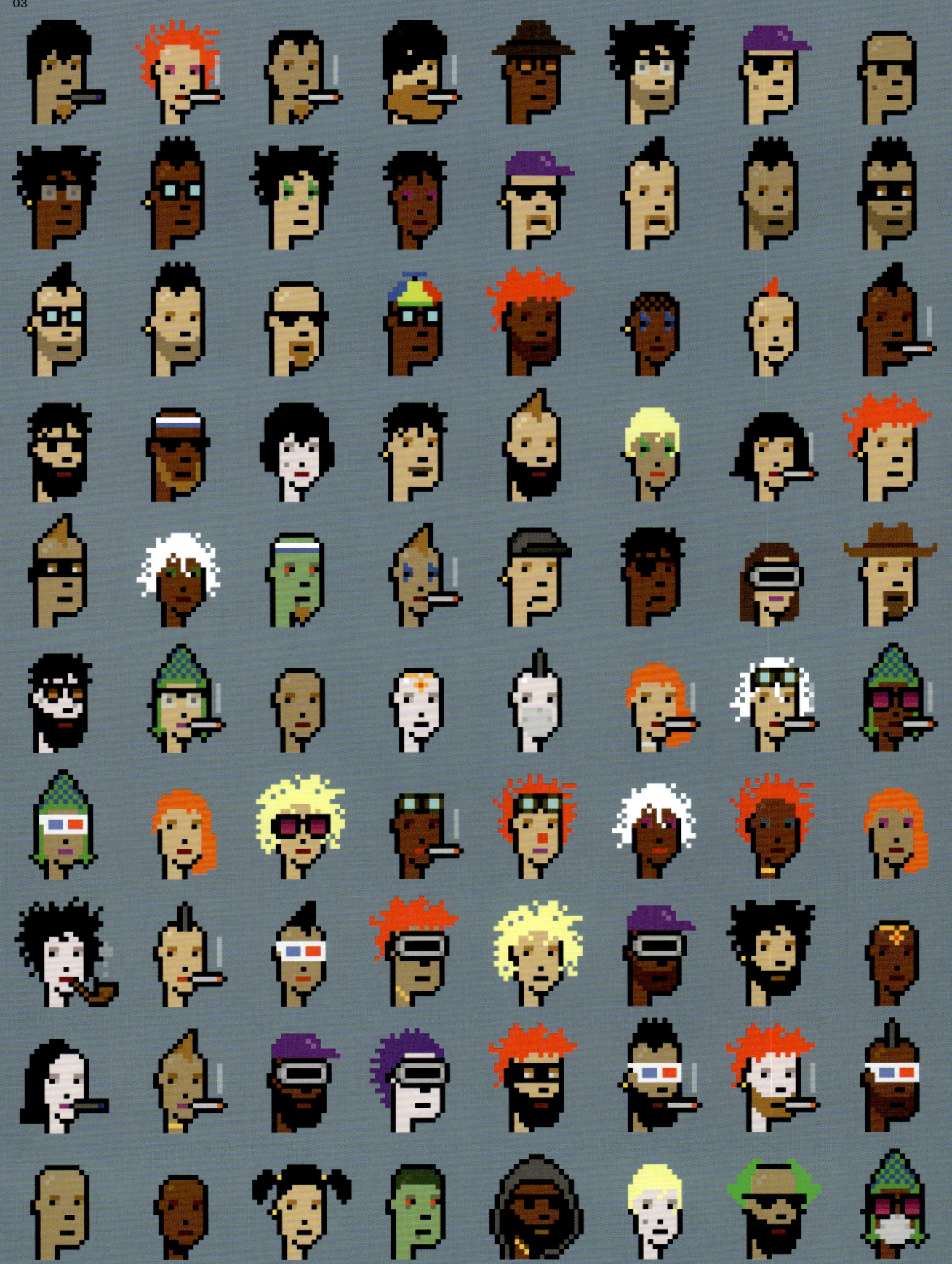

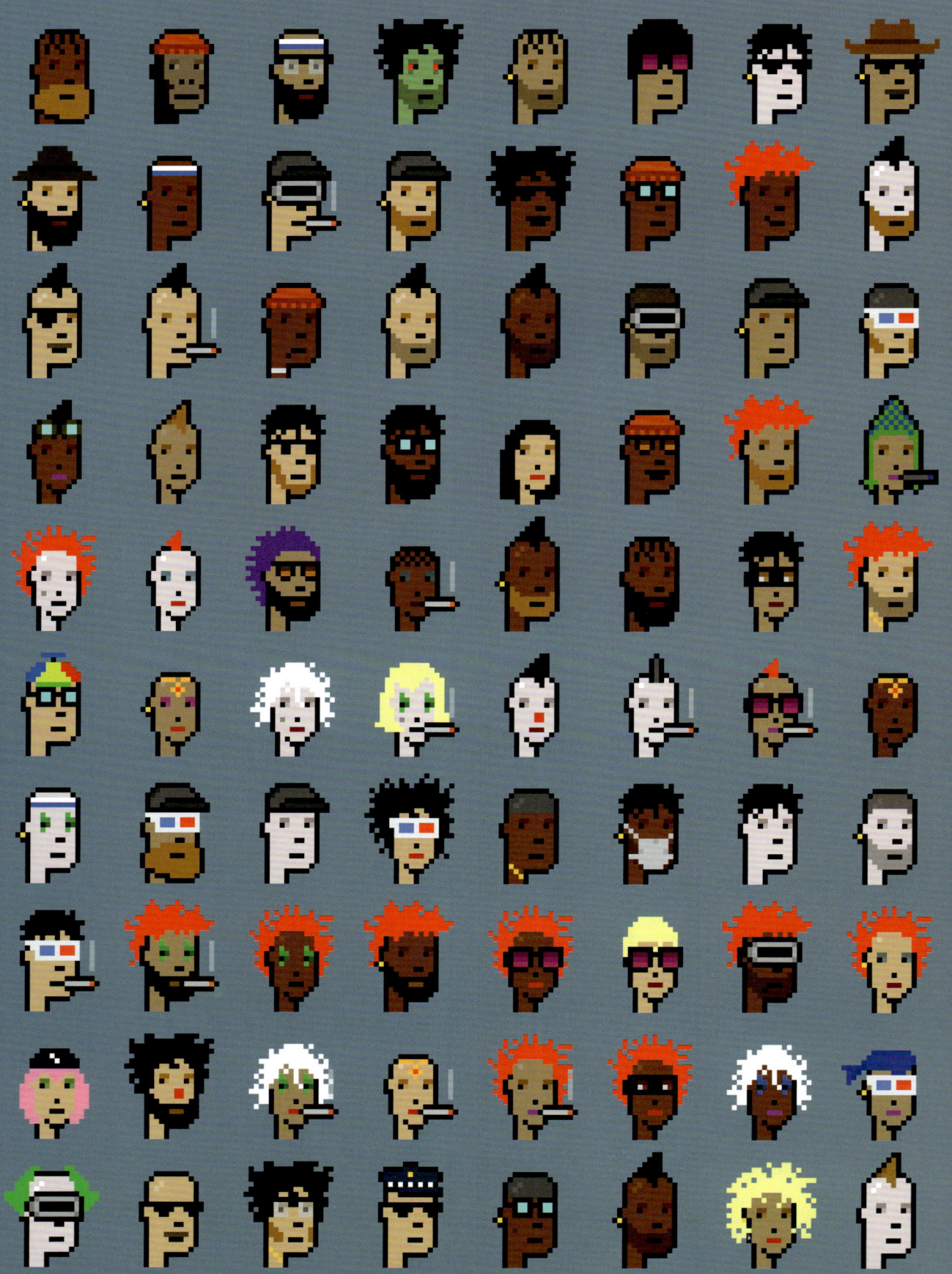

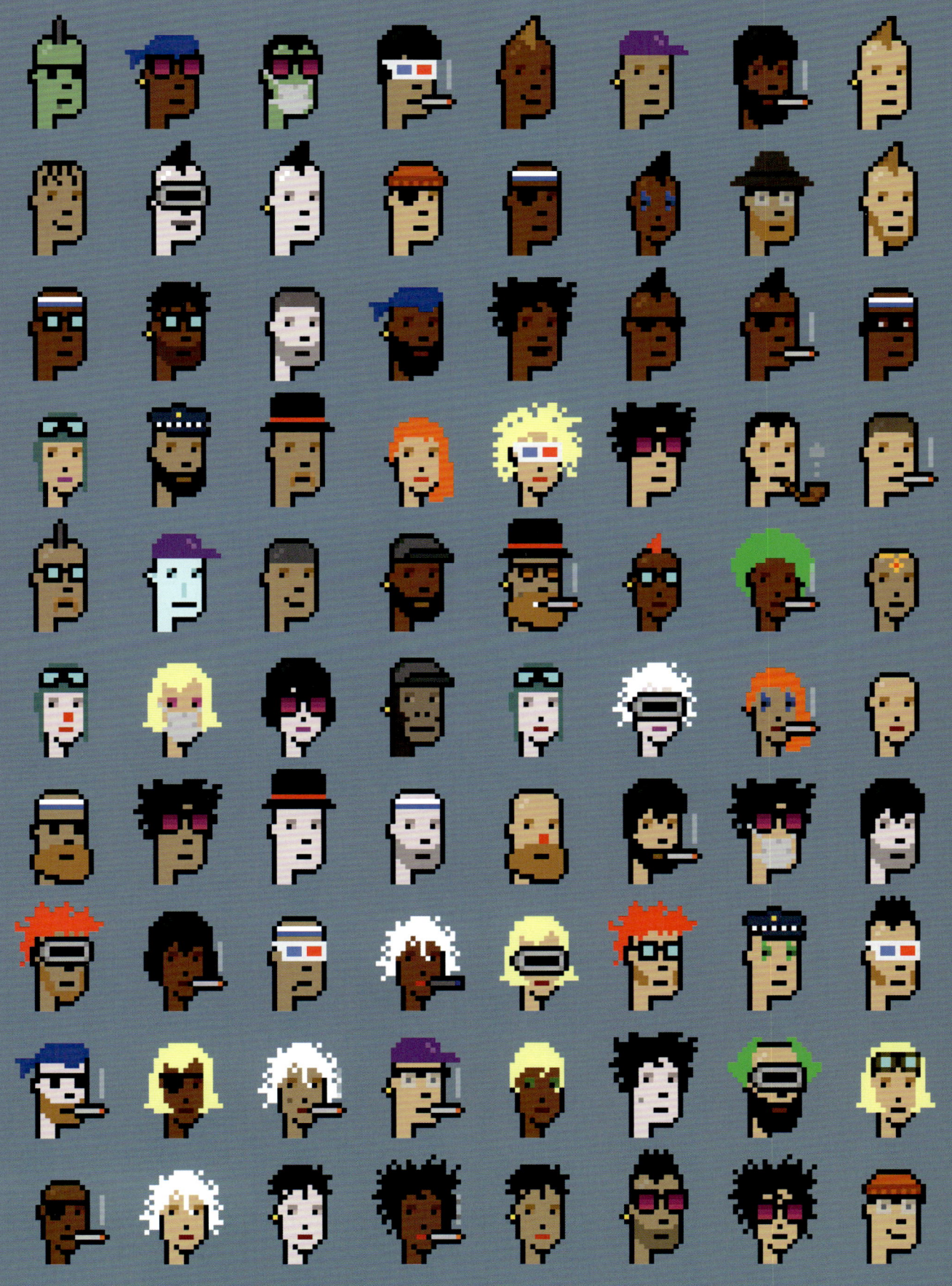

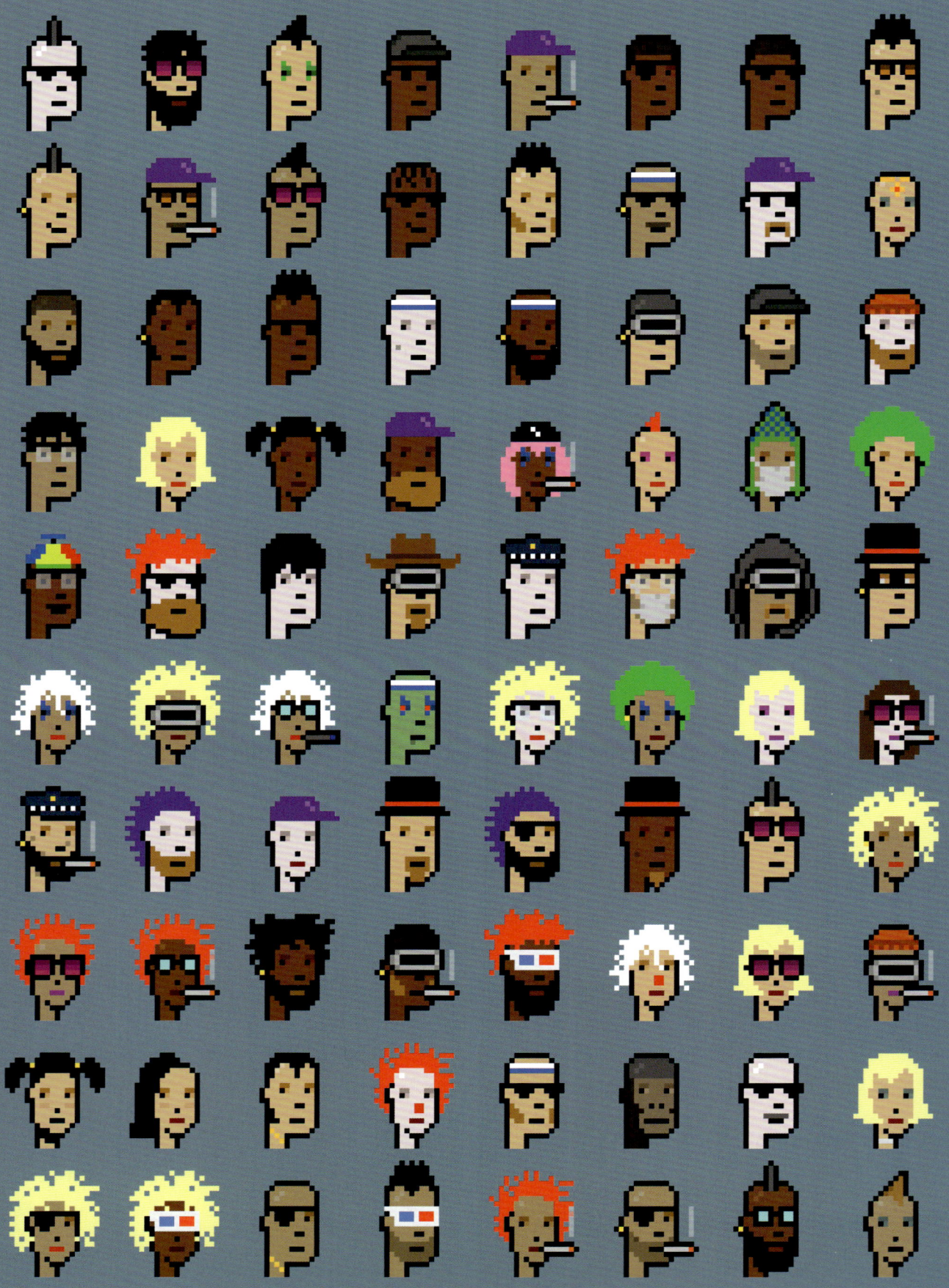

04

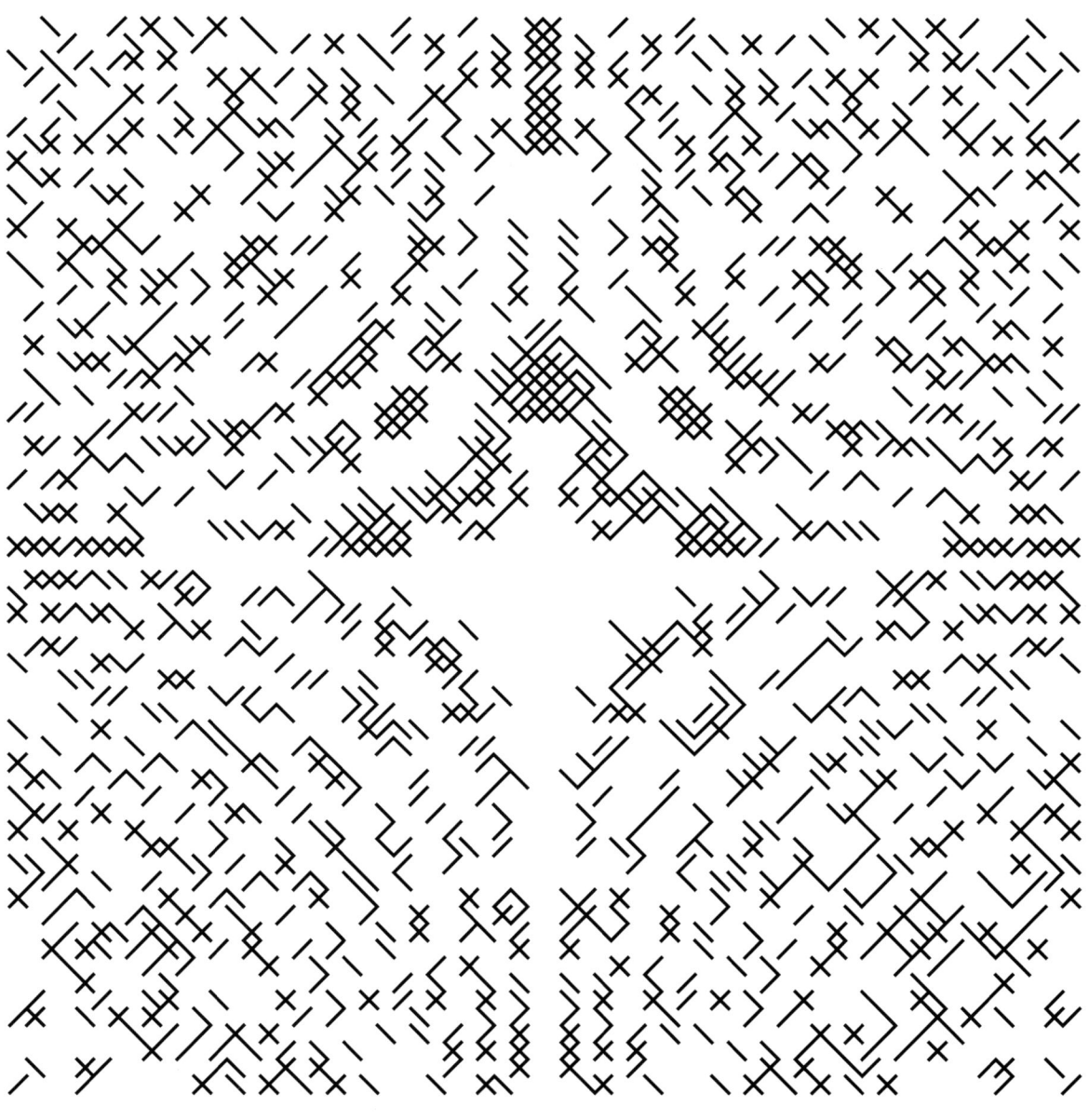

| # | TITLE | TIMESTAMP | MEDIUM | CHAIN | CONTRACT ADDRESS | TOKEN ID | EDITION SIZE |
|---|-------|-----------|--------|-------|------------------|----------|--------------|
| 04–08 | **Autoglyphs** | 04-06-2019 21:22:29 | ASCII, Solidity | ETH | 0xd4e4078ca3495de5b1d4db434bebc5a986197782 | 1–512 | 1/1 of 512 |

EDITIONS ILLUSTRATED: (04) #2, (05) #494, (06) #420, (07) #398, (08) #443

05

06

07

08

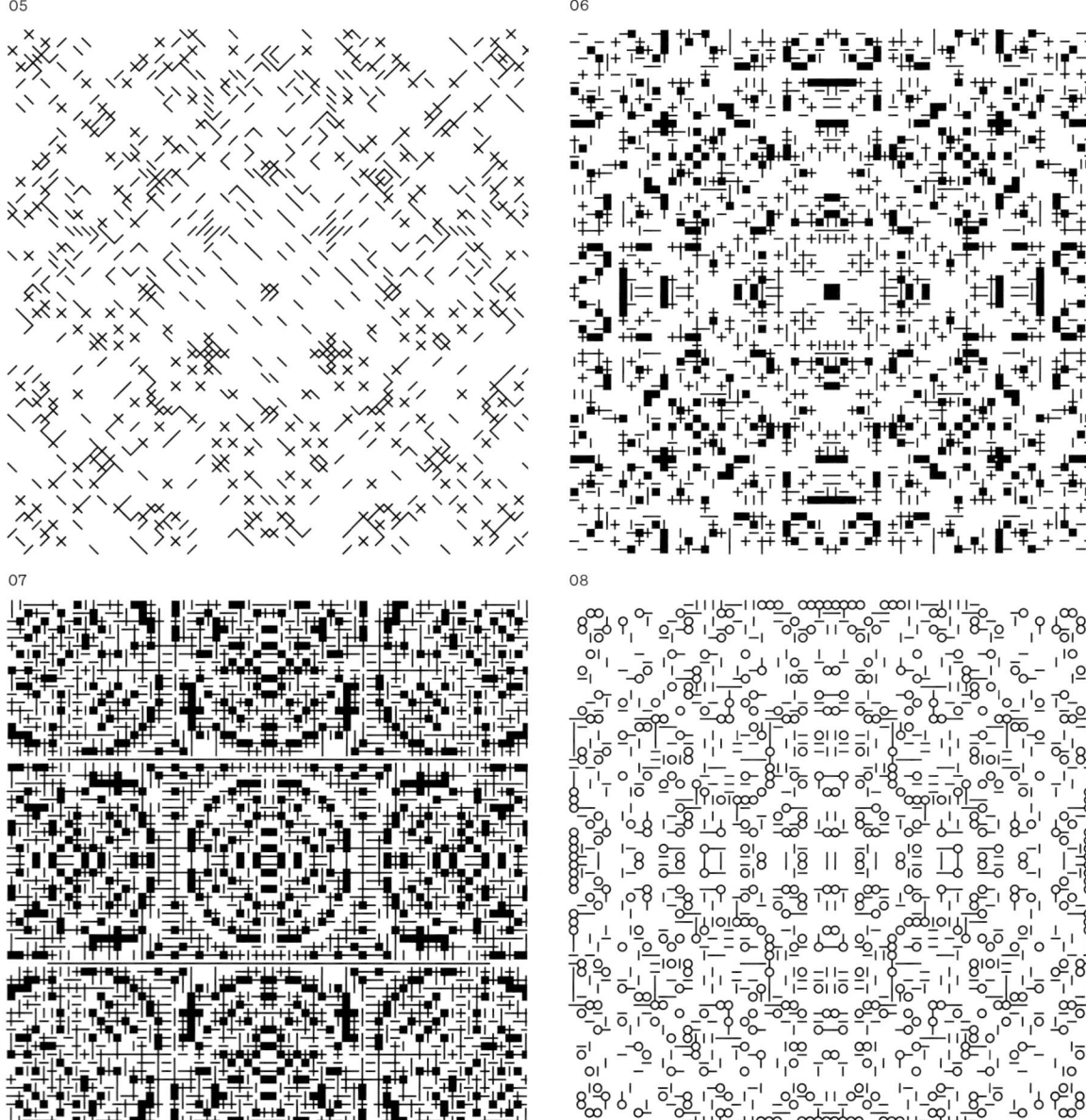

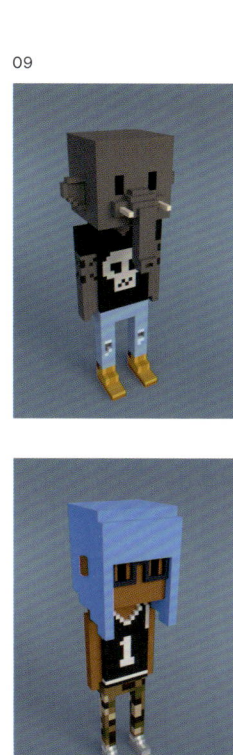 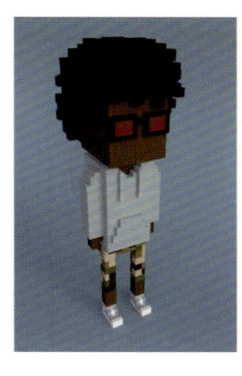 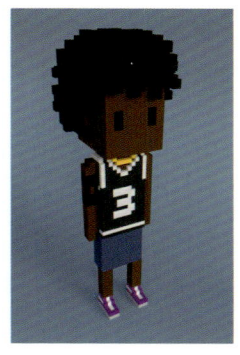 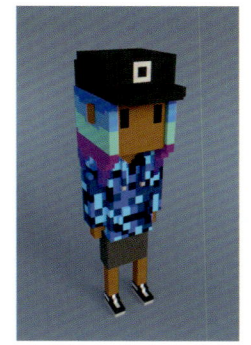 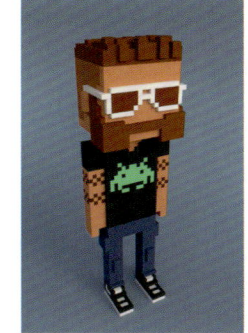

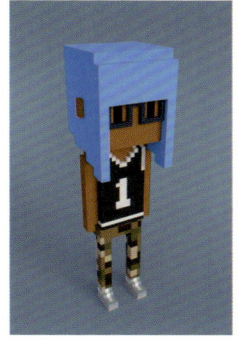 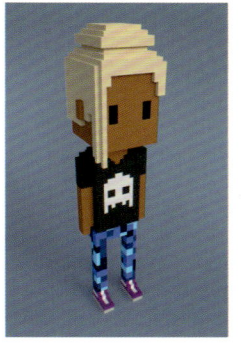 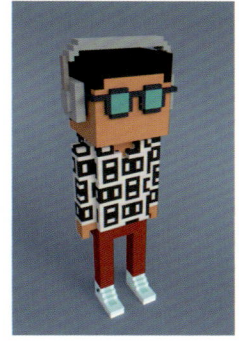 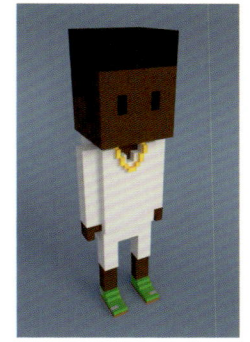 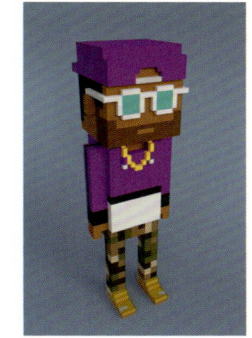

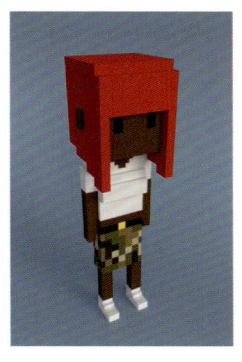 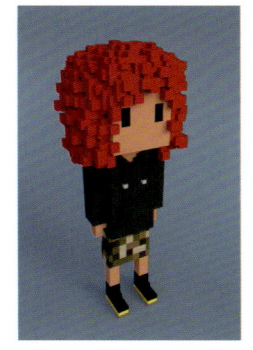 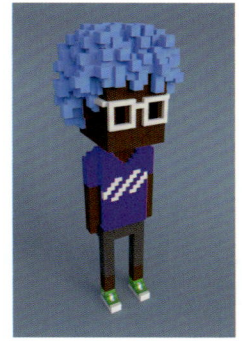 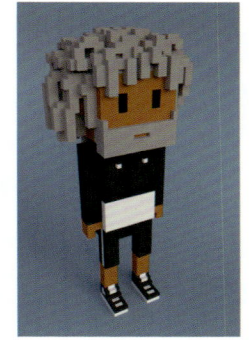 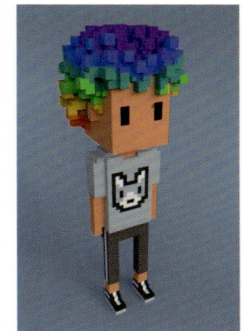

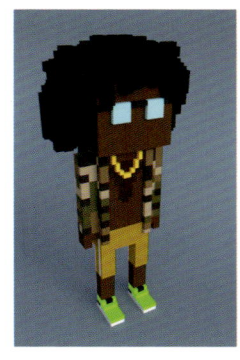 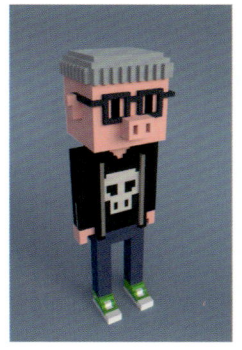 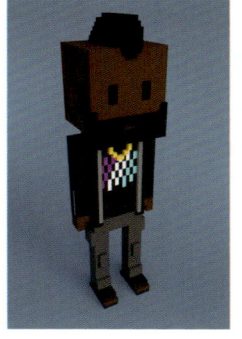 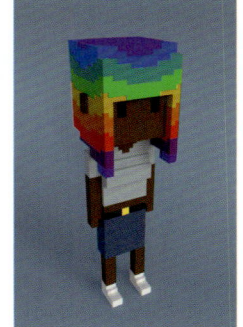 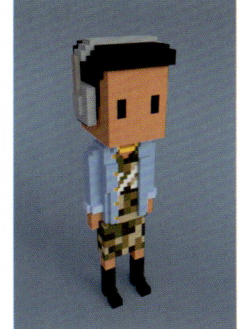

| # | TITLE | TIMESTAMP | MEDIUM | CHAIN | CONTRACT ADDRESS | TOKEN ID | EDITION SIZE |
|---|-------|-----------|--------|-------|------------------|----------|--------------|
| 09 | **Meebits** | 05-03-2021 16:23:41 | 3D voxel characters | ETH | 0x7bd29408f11d2bfc23c34f18275bbf23bb716bc7 | 1–20000 | 1/1 of 20,000 |

EDITIONS ILLUSTRATED: (09) Various — please refer to the end matter for details

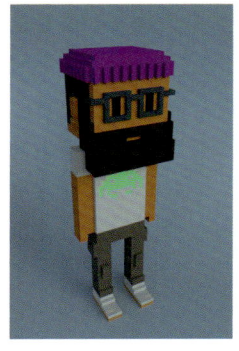
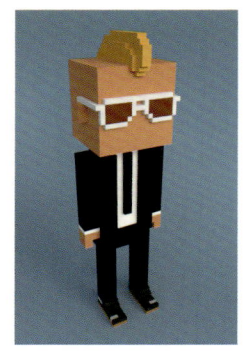
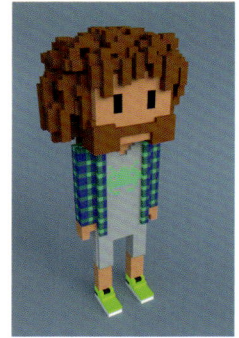
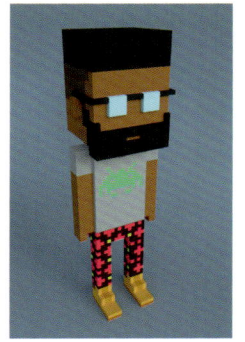
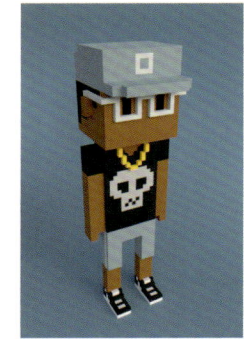
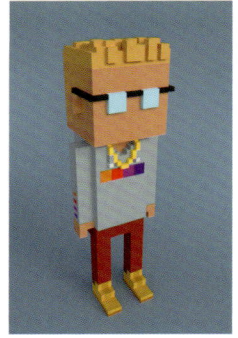
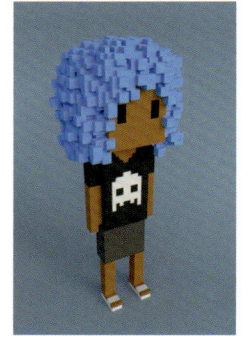
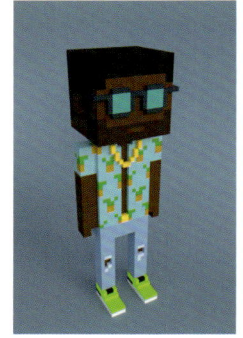
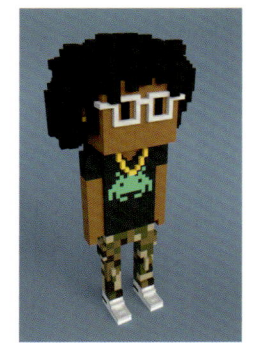
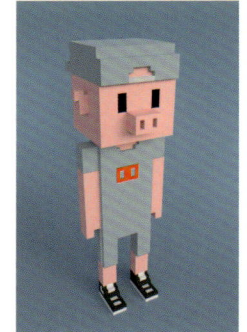
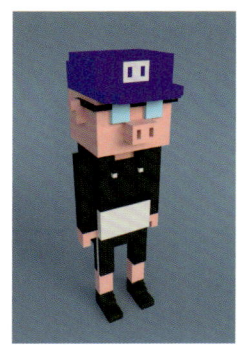
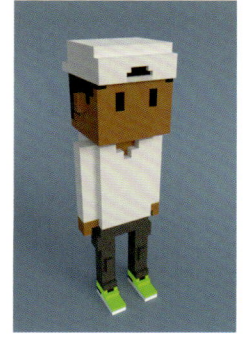
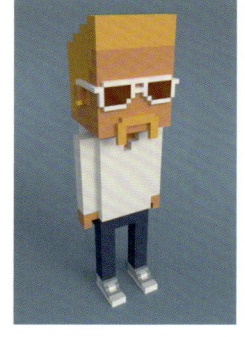
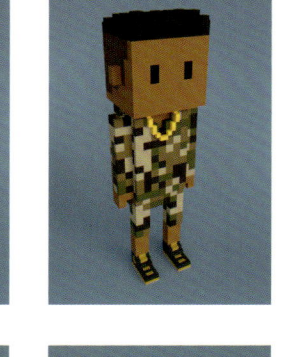
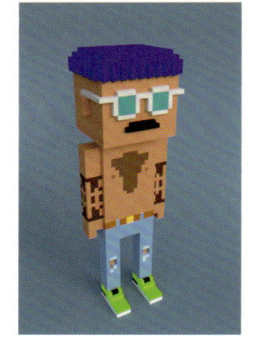
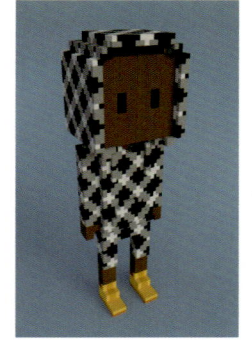
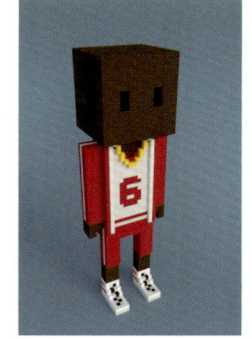
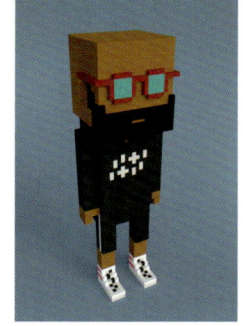
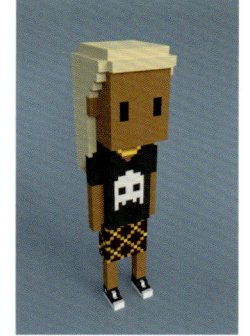
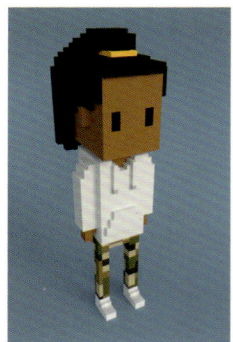

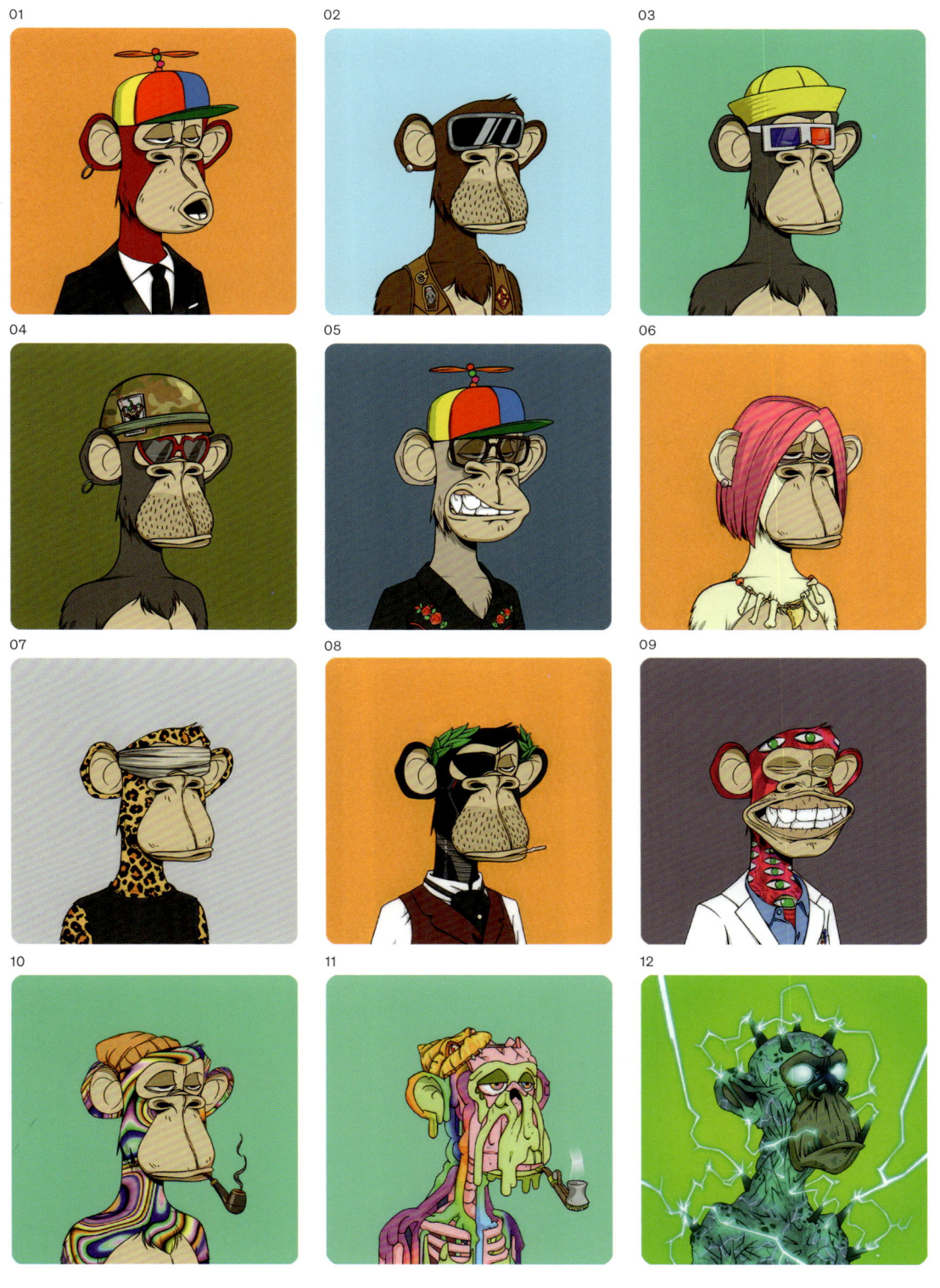

| # | TITLE | TIMESTAMP | MEDIUM | CHAIN | CONTRACT ADDRESS | TOKEN ID | EDITION SIZE |
|---|-------|-----------|--------|-------|------------------|----------|--------------|
| 01–10, 13–16 | **Bored Ape Yacht Club** | 04-22-2021 23:13:40 | Adobe Photoshop, digital drawing | ETH | 0xbc4ca0eda7647a8ab7c2061c2e118a18a936f13d | 0–9999 | 1/1 of 10,000 |
| 11, 12 | **Mutant Ape Yacht Club** | 08-29-2021 00:40:58 | Adobe Photoshop, digital drawing | ETH | 0x60e4d786628fea6478f785a6d7e704777c86a7c6 | 0–30006 | 1/1 of 20,000 |

EDITIONS ILLUSTRATED: (01) ) #5718, (02) #3621, (03) #3539, (04) #3423, (05) #4492, (06) #5273, (07) #2346, (08) #5036, (09) #8657, (10) #23, (11) #10046, (12) #4318, (13) #254, (14) #3679, (15) #2198, (16) #2089

# YUGA LABS

13
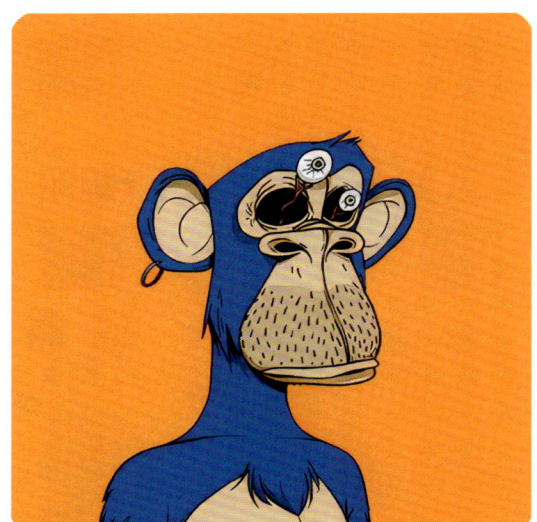

14
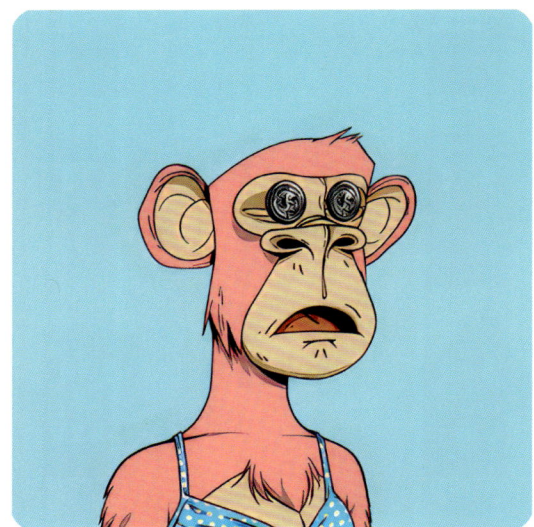

15
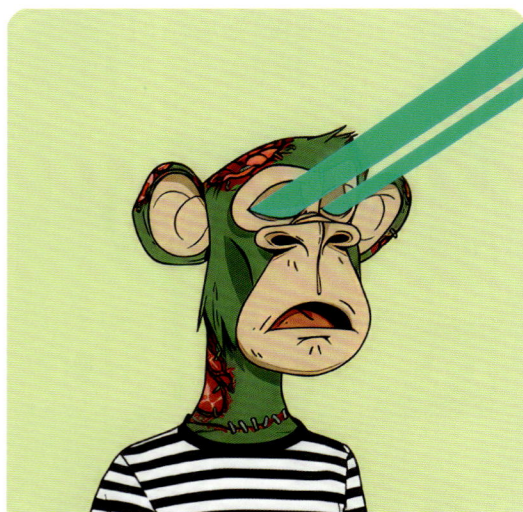

16
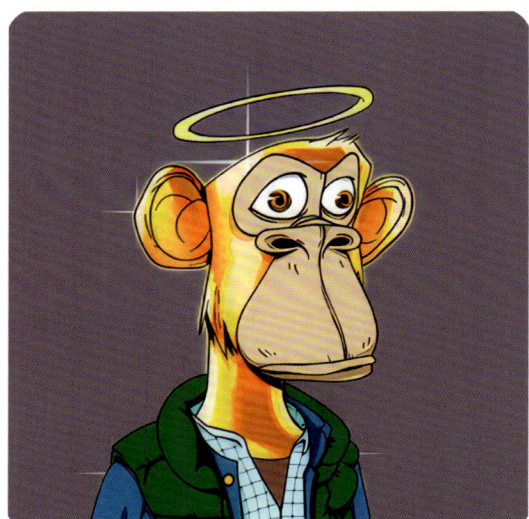

The Bored Ape Yacht Club (BAYC) (2021) is the most successful NFT project to date. The collection is made up of 10,000 unique portraits of apes that appear to be very boring. We call these portraits PFPs which stands for "profile picture" and often use them as our likeness on social media sites, like Twitter.

Each of these apes comes with an exclusive license where the holder of the NFT is able to commercialize the image of the ape. This has led to specific Bored Apes being signed at major music labels, like I did with the band KINGSHIP, being found on shirts at major clothing stores, as we have seen Bored Apes in stores like Old Navy, and even being used by Snoop Dogg and Eminem as their likenesses in music videos and live performances, most recently at the 2022 MTV VMAs.

The community-driven commercialization of Bored Apes Yacht Club has captured the attention of the internet and the speculative value of the individual NFTs and has skyrocketed their creators, Yuga Labs, to the absolute top of the list for successful Web3 brands, with the company recently being valued over $4.5 billion.

Aside from commercial rights, BAYC holders also get access to an exclusive community and real-life and virtual events, like ApeFest, which has been held in New York City for the last two years. This is in addition to the exclusive merchandise made available to BAYC NFT holders on rare occasions.

The team at Yuga Labs is now building a metaverse experience for Bored Apes and other NFT holders called Otherside. This is where our PFPs shift to avatars, representing their holders in an immersive 3D environment.

**JIMMY MCNELIS**
CEO OF NFT42 AND COLLECTOR

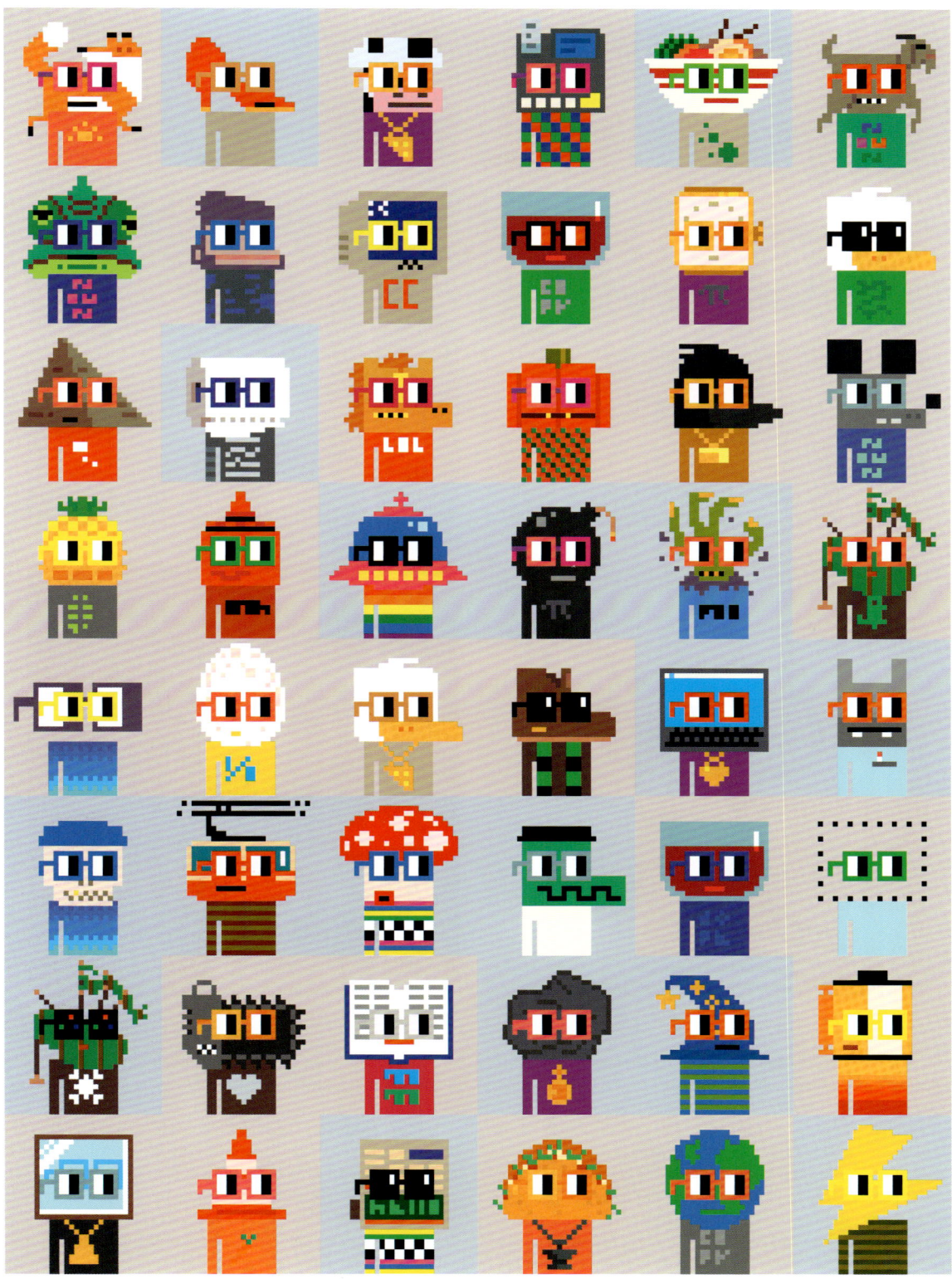

| # | TITLE | TIMESTAMP | MEDIUM | CHAIN | CONTRACT ADDRESS | TOKEN ID | EDITION SIZE |
|---|-------|-----------|--------|-------|------------------|----------|--------------|
| 01, 02 | **Nouns** | 08-08-2021 17:06:49 | Generative pixel art | ETH | 0x9c8ff314c9bc7f6e59a9d9225fb22946427edc03 | 0–∞ | 1/1 of ∞ |

EDITIONS ILLUSTRATED: (01) Various, (02) #0

02

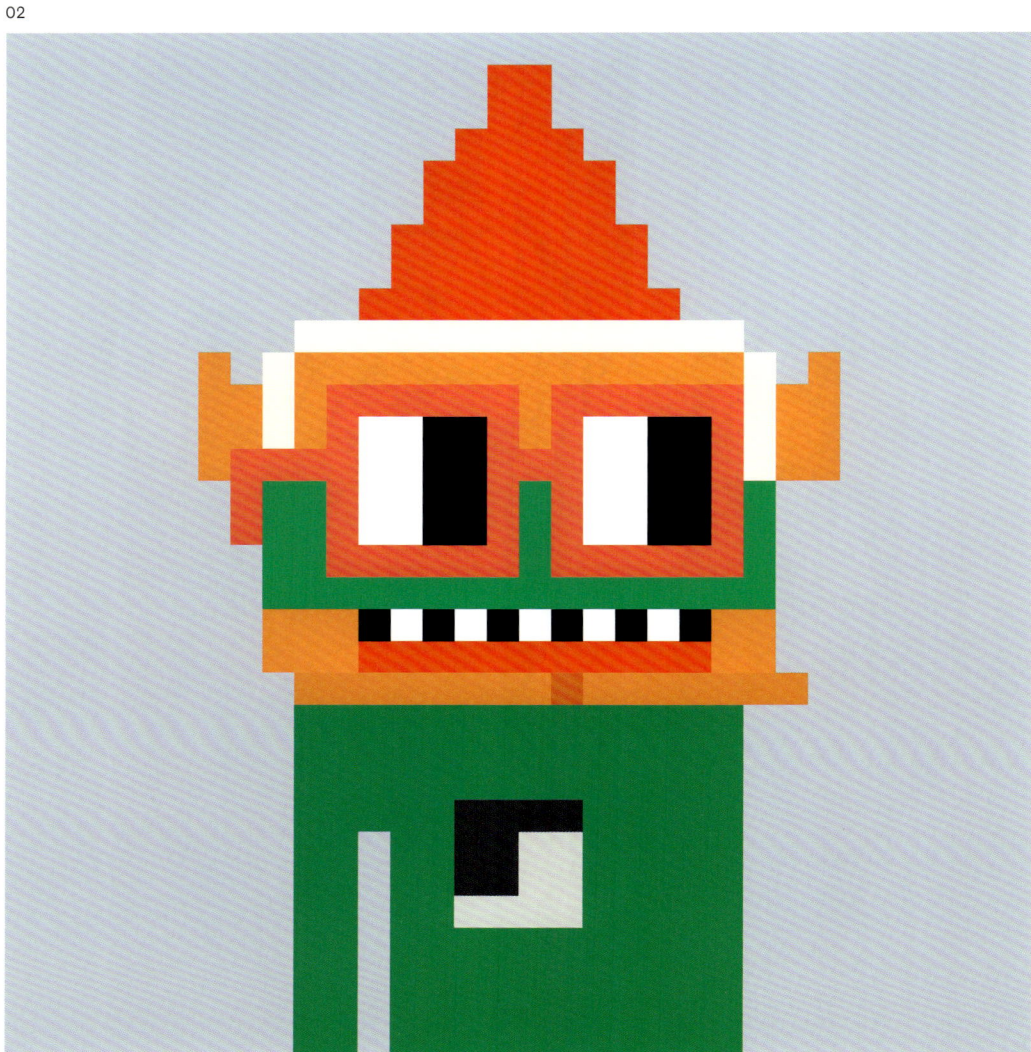

Launched with a Twitter thread and developed in Discord by ten mostly anonymous founders in mid-2021, *Nouns* push the PFP medium deeper into crypto-native territory, embedding a new distribution mechanism (one *Noun* auctioned every day, forever), a new governance system (one *Noun*, one vote), and a new treasury (all sale proceeds sent to a DAO), and releasing the entire collection and codebase into the public domain with a CC0 license.

On the day we launched the project, we tweeted from @nounsdao: "behold, an infinite work of art," referring not only to the fact that *Noun* auctions will continue as long as Ethereum exists, but to the idea that blockchains will ultimately enable artworks to effect change that extends far beyond the space of the gallery.

By way of a carefully constructed crypto-economic feedback loop, *Nouns* have funded everything from the Red Cross in Ukraine, to glasses for underprivileged children, to toys,

documentaries, and a Super Bowl commercial. We've even named our own species of frog, Hyalinobatrachium nouns, after we helped fund the conservation of its habitat.

Like any fledgling cult, the Nouniverse has its own language. "Nounders" are the project founders, "Nouners" are DAO members and owners of *Noun* NFTs, "Noun O'Clock" is the daily ceremonial minting of the next *Noun*, and the "Nouniversary" (8/8) is the anniversary of the launch of the project when the *Noun* NFT artwork gets upgraded by the DAO.

*Nouns* are simultaneously a daily Web3 ritual, a rarified Veblen good, and a grassroots movement that invites anyone to participate and make the world a little more nounish.

**4156**
INVENTOR & CO-FOUNDER OF NOUNS

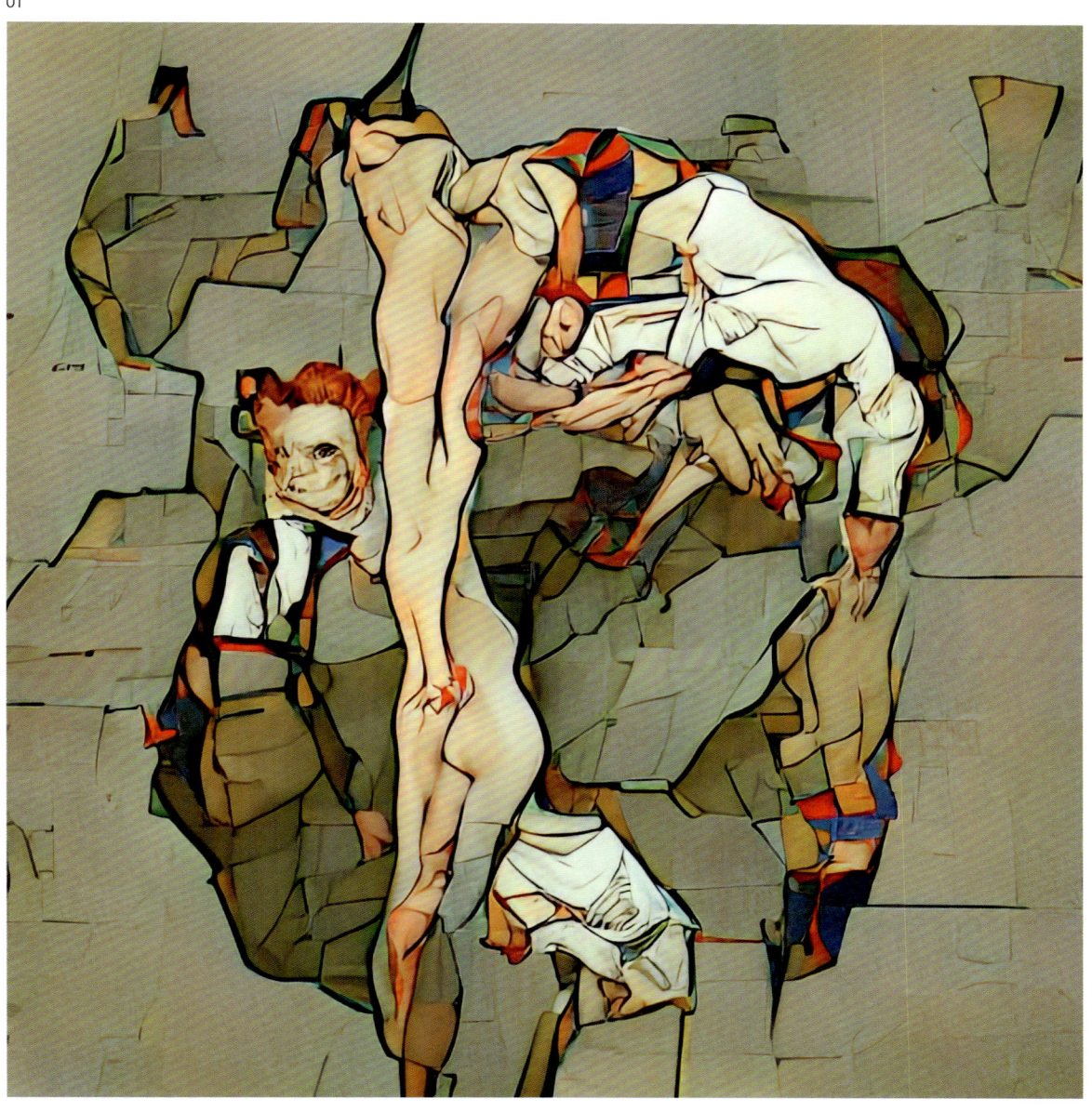

| # | TITLE | TIMESTAMP | MEDIUM | CHAIN | CONTRACT ADDRESS | TOKEN ID | EDITION SIZE |
|---|---|---|---|---|---|---|---|
| 01 | **Asymmetrical Liberation** | 10-22-2021 10:00:40 | VQGAN+CLIP, GPT-3 | ETH | 0xb932a70a57673d89f4acffbe830e8ed7f75fb9e0 | 29715 | 1/1 |
| 02 | **Curious Negligence** | 03-11-2022 10:50:02 | VQGAN+CLIP, GPT-3 | ETH | 0xb932a70a57673d89f4acffbe830e8ed7f75fb9e0 | 33163 | 1/1 |
| 03 | **Fee-tail Fee-tail** | 04-01-2022 13:13:13 | VQGAN+CLIP, GPT-3 | ETH | 0xb932a70a57673d89f4acffbe830e8ed7f75fb9e0 | 33637 | 1/1 |
| 04 | **Dependable Estimate** | 03-25-2022 19:20:40 | VQGAN+CLIP, GPT-3 | ETH | 0xb932a70a57673d89f4acffbe830e8ed7f75fb9e0 | 33501 | 1/1 |
| 05 | **Interpret Complete** | 11-19-2021 01:33:42 | VQGAN+CLIP, GPT-3 | ETH | 0xb932a70a57673d89f4acffbe830e8ed7f75fb9e0 | 30443 | 1/1 |

# BOTTO

FOUNDED 2021

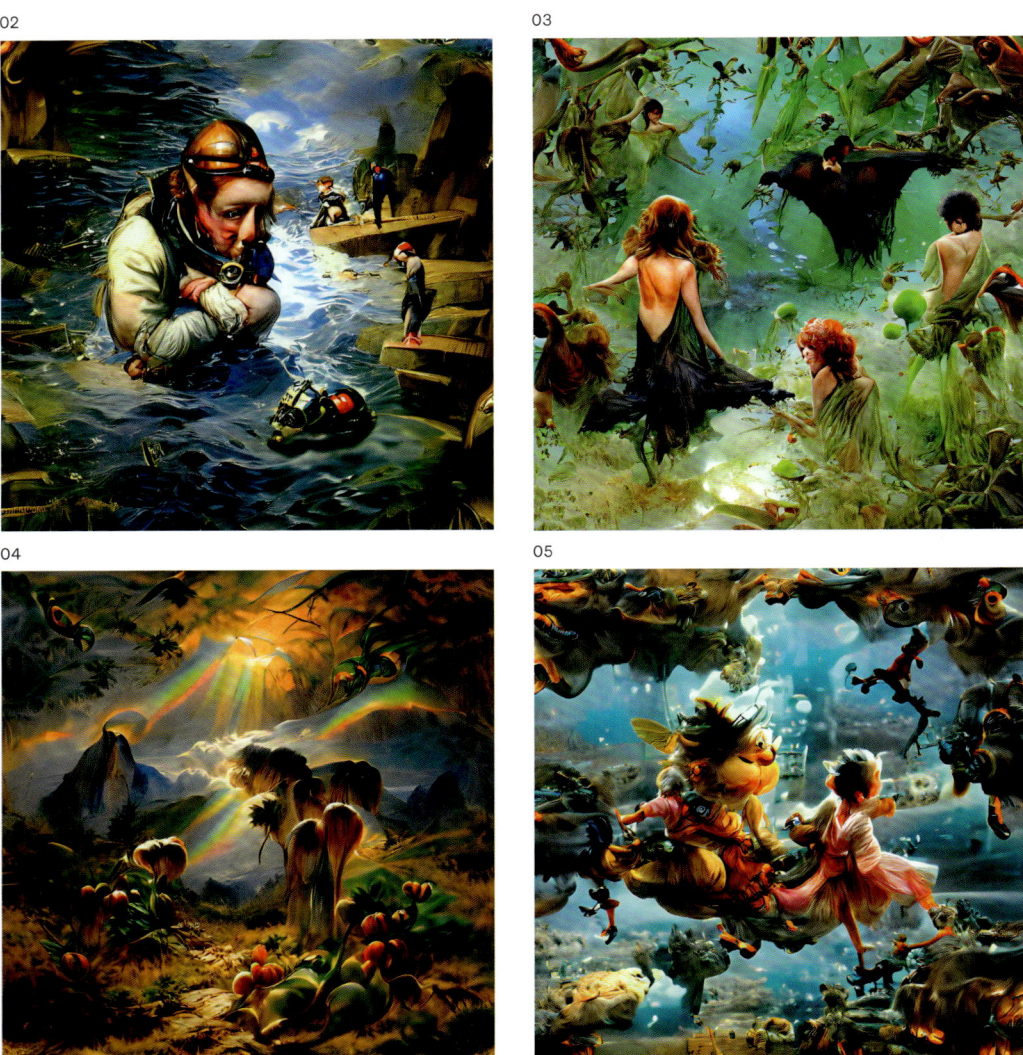

02

03

04

05

Botto is, above all, one of the most exciting artistic experiments of our time, one which drives us to question the foundations of art itself. Its entity, creative process, and works confront us with key issues which take us beyond established notions. Created using AI and governed by an ever-growing decentralized community, Botto is a DAO artist that can create hundreds of fragments each week, addressing its own originality as an artist and subjecting its work to the users' choices. Each week, the community decides which fragment will be turned into an artwork and be signed by the artist, through a series of decisions which allow Botto to learn about its work and to make decisions about its own artistic path. Botto is based on a 2018 whitepaper by the artist Mario Klingemann, a global pioneer in the field of AI art. The project, launched in October 2021, has been a great collaborative effort between multiple teams and contributors, led by the teams from ElevenYellow and Carbono. Botto is able to access more artistic data than is humanly possible in a lifetime and conceptually challenges ideas around who and what is an artist, as well as examining the incredible creative possibilities between a human-machine collaboration. Using algorithms, Botto connects two artistic practices: generative art and decentralized art. Both come together in a new creative practice through AI development and blockchain technologies. Botto's work, which had its first solo show in Los Angeles in late 2021 and has been on display at, among others, Colección SOLO in Madrid and the Decentral Art Pavilion during the Venice Biennale 2022, raises interesting debates. Two stand out: the idea of collective, as opposed to individual, creation, and AI as a new artistic tool that will allow us to explore entirely new places.

**OSCAR HORMIGOS**
CCO AT COLECCIÓN SOLO, MADRID

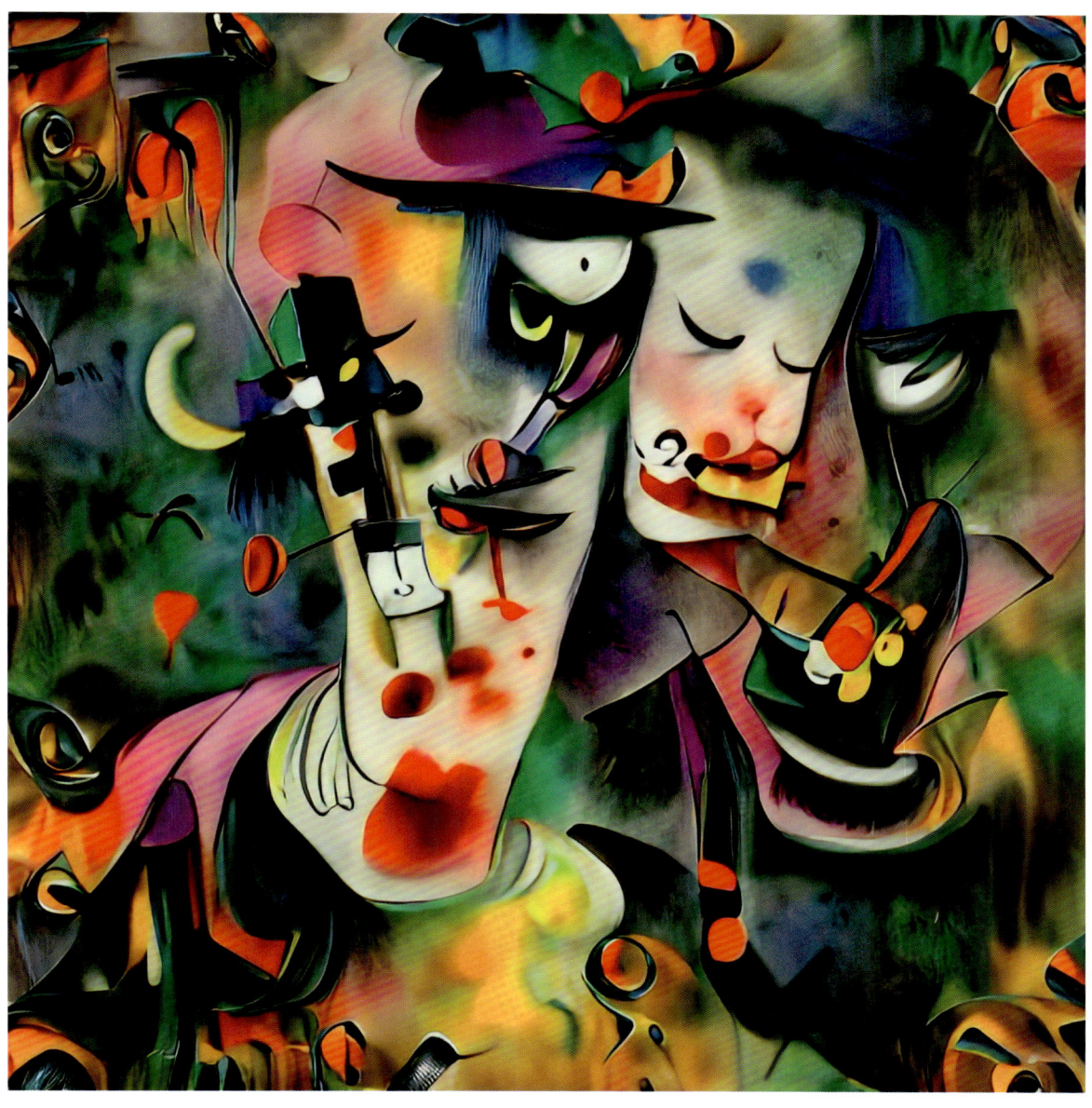

| # | TITLE | TIMESTAMP | MEDIUM | CHAIN | CONTRACT ADDRESS | TOKEN ID | EDITION SIZE |
|---|---|---|---|---|---|---|---|
| 06 | **Trickery Contagion** | 11-04-2021 23:55:12 | VQGAN+CLIP, GPT-3 | ETH | 0xb932a70a57673d89f4acffbe830e8ed7f75fb9e0 | 30114 | 1/1 |
| 07 | **Derive Time** | 03-04-2022 12:04:17 | VQGAN+CLIP, GPT-3 | ETH | 0xb932a70a57673d89f4acffbe830e8ed7f75fb9e0 | 33018 | 1/1 |

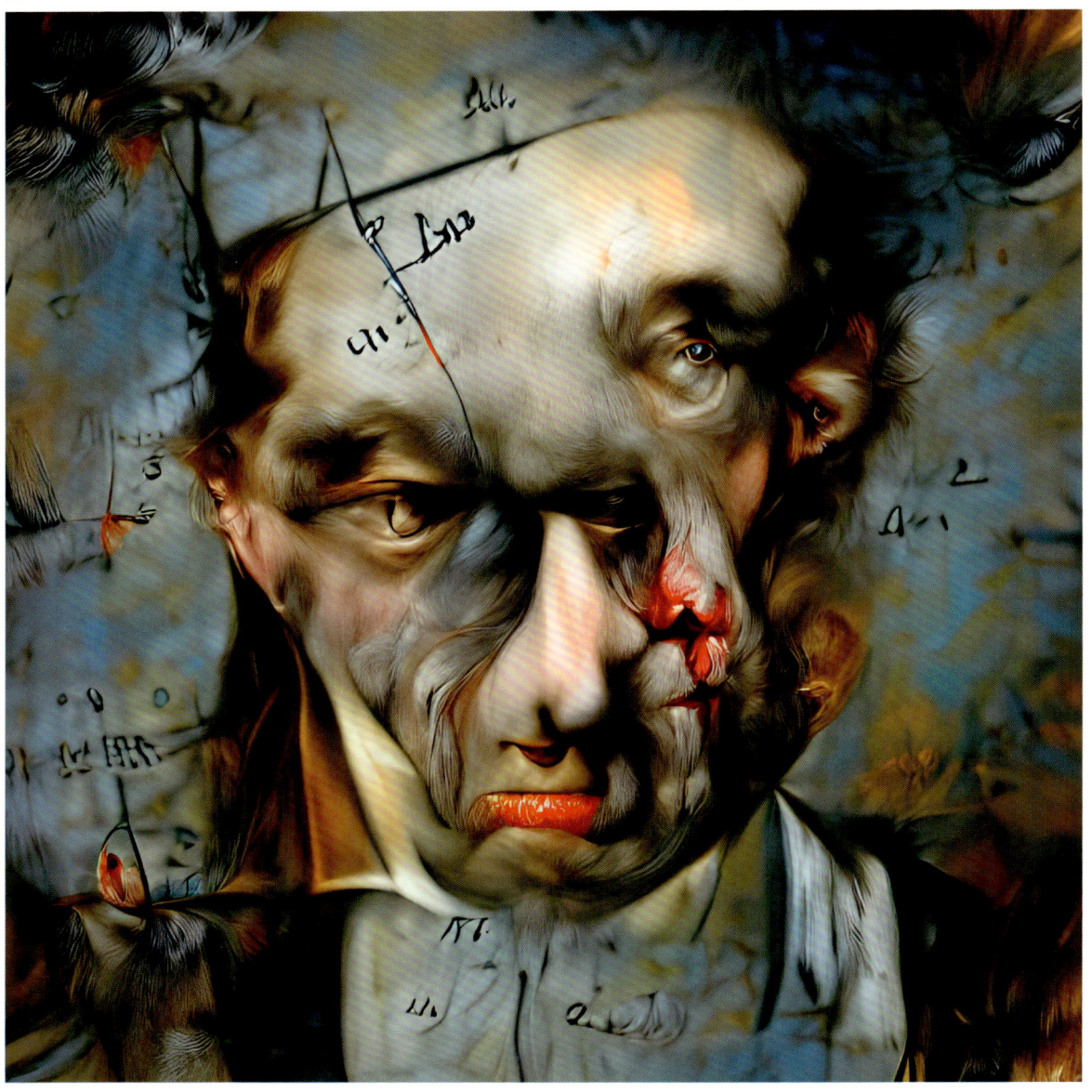

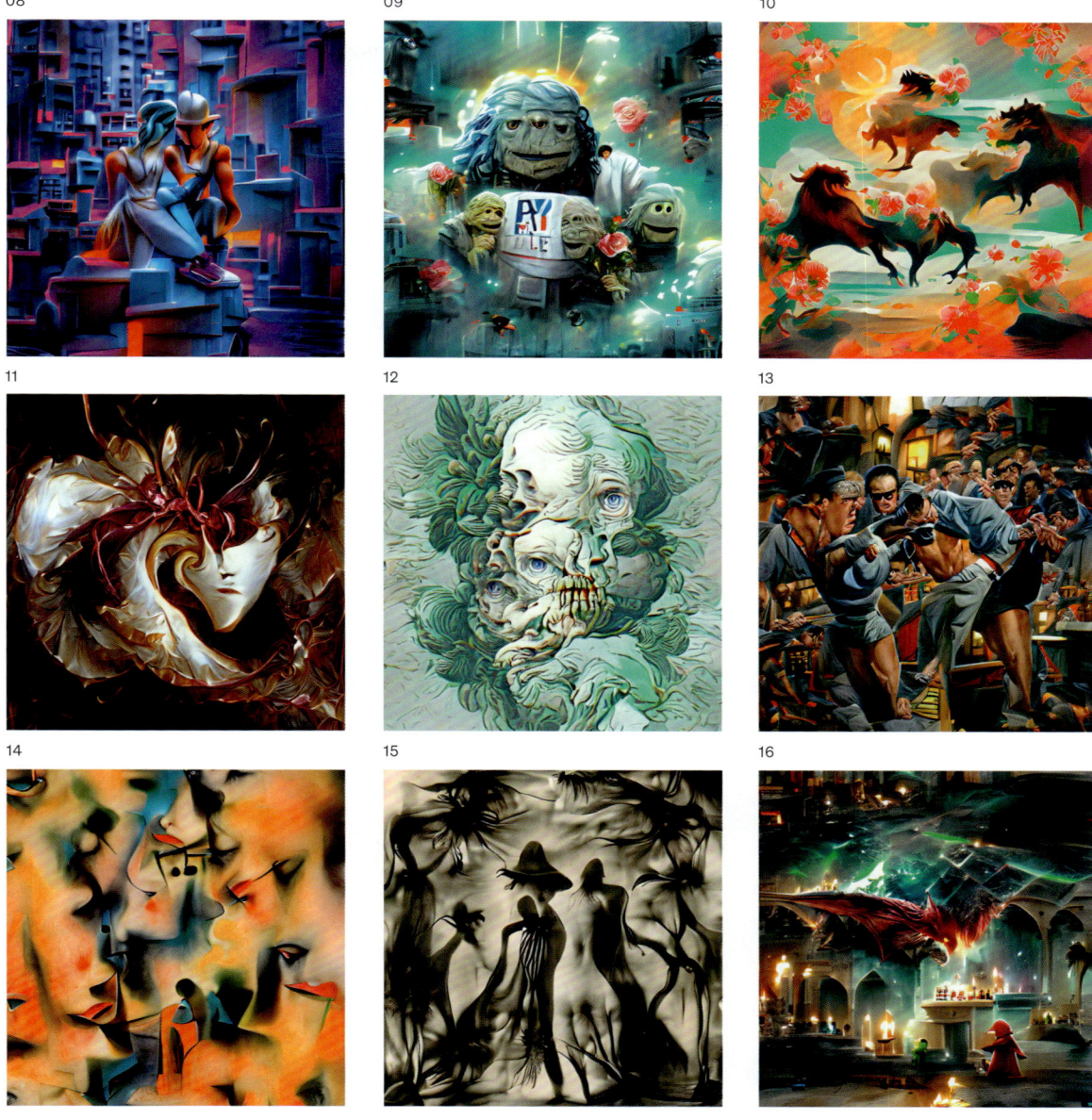

| # | TITLE | TIMESTAMP | MEDIUM | CHAIN | CONTRACT ADDRESS | TOKEN ID | EDITION SIZE |
|---|---|---|---|---|---|---|---|
| 08 | **Cull Clean** | 01-07-2022 00:56:01 | VQGAN+CLIP, GPT-3 | ETH | 0xb932a70a57673d89f4acffbe830e8ed7f75fb9e0 | 31546 | 1/1 |
| 09 | **Houseclean Wrinkle** | 01-13-2022 23:33:56 | VQGAN+CLIP, GPT-3 | ETH | 0xb932a70a57673d89f4acffbe830e8ed7f75fb9e0 | 31704 | 1/1 |
| 10 | **Sharpen Bet** | 12-31-2021 02:15:02 | VQGAN+CLIP, GPT-3 | ETH | 0xb932a70a57673d89f4acffbe830e8ed7f75fb9e0 | 31447 | 1/1 |
| 11 | **Intensify Modeling** | 02-04-2022 00:18:45 | VQGAN+CLIP, GPT-3 | ETH | 0xb932a70a57673d89f4acffbe830e8ed7f75fb9e0 | 32242 | 1/1 |
| 12 | **Blossoming Cadaver** | 11-12-2021 03:21:15 | VQGAN+CLIP, GPT-3 | ETH | 0xb932a70a57673d89f4acffbe830e8ed7f75fb9e0 | 30298 | 1/1 |
| 13 | **Attack Take** | 03-18-2022 12:05:17 | VQGAN+CLIP, GPT-3 | ETH | 0xb932a70a57673d89f4acffbe830e8ed7f75fb9e0 | 33332 | 1/1 |
| 14 | **Suffice Nuance** | 02-25-2022 15:36:15 | VQGAN+CLIP, GPT-3 | ETH | 0xb932a70a57673d89f4acffbe830e8ed7f75fb9e0 | 32737 | 1/1 |
| 15 | **Slender Dissemble** | 01-28-2022 15:59:17 | VQGAN+CLIP, GPT-3 | ETH | 0xb932a70a57673d89f4acffbe830e8ed7f75fb9e0 | 32068 | 1/1 |
| 16 | **Devolve Falter** | 12-24-2021 16:17:59 | VQGAN+CLIP, GPT-3 | ETH | 0xb932a70a57673d89f4acffbe830e8ed7f75fb9e0 | 31352 | 1/1 |
| 17 | **Thwart Test** | 12-17-2021 00:03:23 | VQGAN+CLIP, GPT-3 | ETH | 0xb932a70a57673d89f4acffbe830e8ed7f75fb9e0 | 31200 | 1/1 |

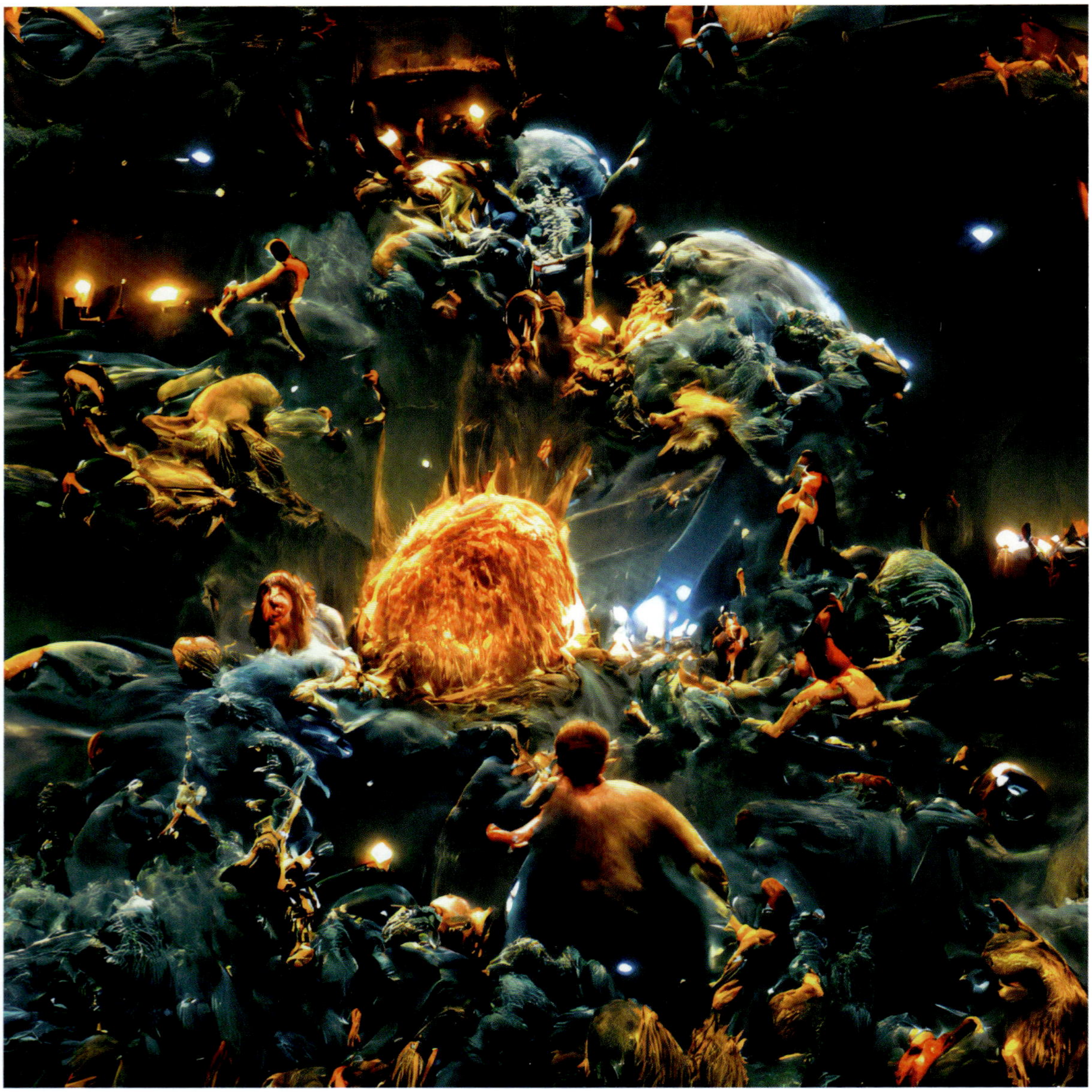

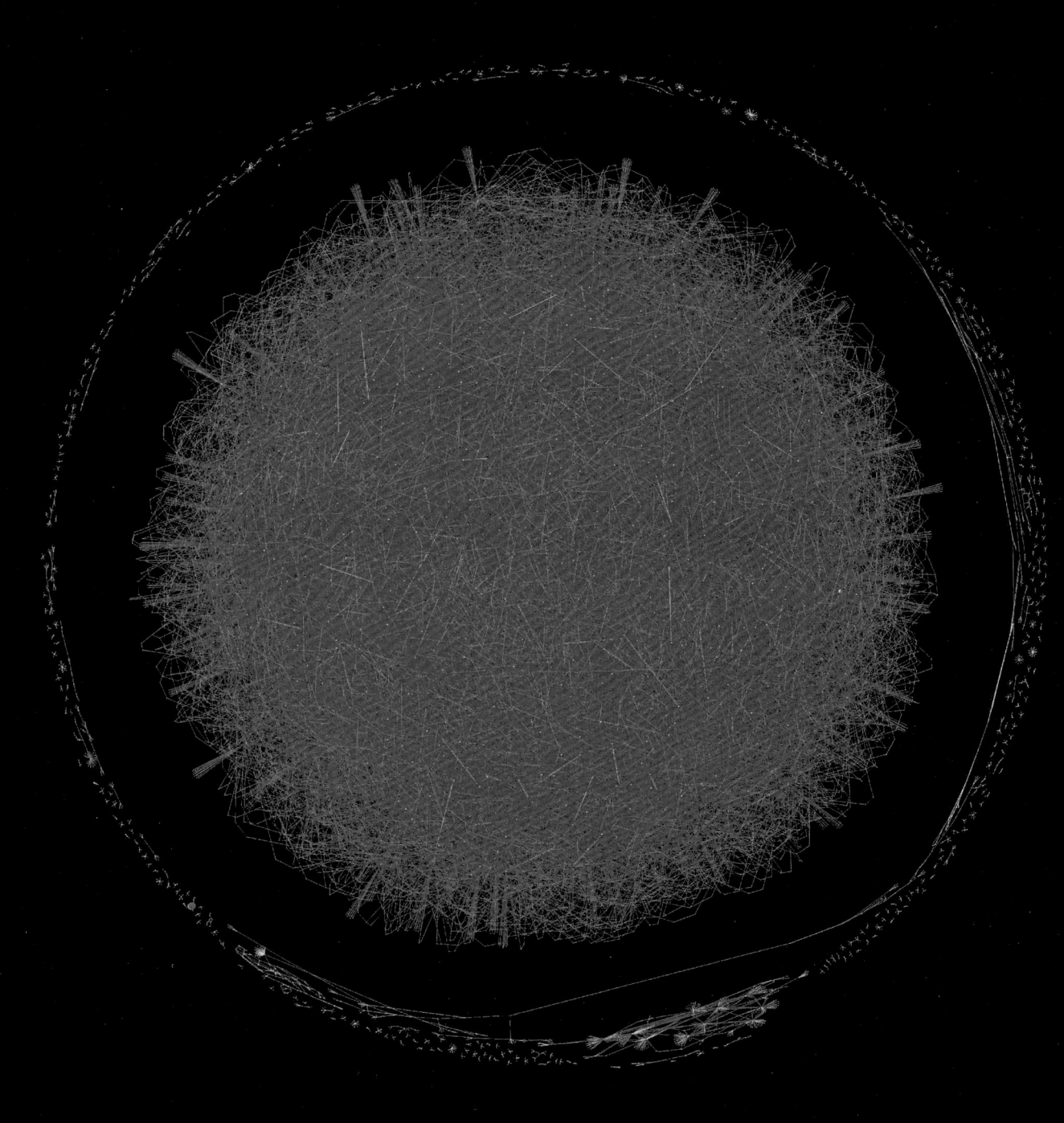

AARON WRIGHT
SERENA TABACCHI

# ON DAOs
Democracy on the Blockchain

*I'm gonna steal the Declaration of Independence.*

Benjamin Franklin Gates
*National Treasure*, 2004

In this essay, Aaron Wright begins with a focus on the legal, historical, philosophical, and operational frameworks of DAOs; followed by Serena Tabacchi's analysis of the curatorial and cultural agendas of DAOs, both as collectors and artists themselves. The text has been threaded, edited, and added to in parts by Robert Alice.

**07.00**
Dan McGinn et al.,
*Visualizing Dynamic Bitcoin Transaction Patterns*, ca. 2016
Custom software, blockchain visualization
William Penney Laboratory at Imperial College, London

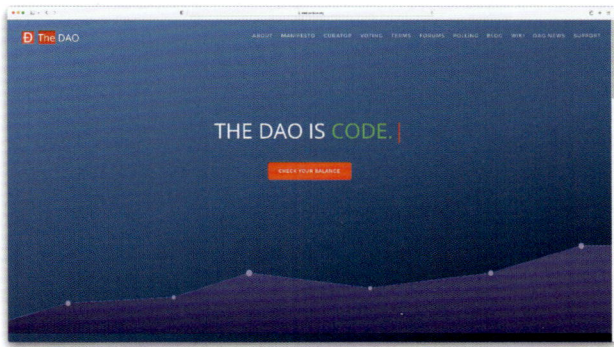

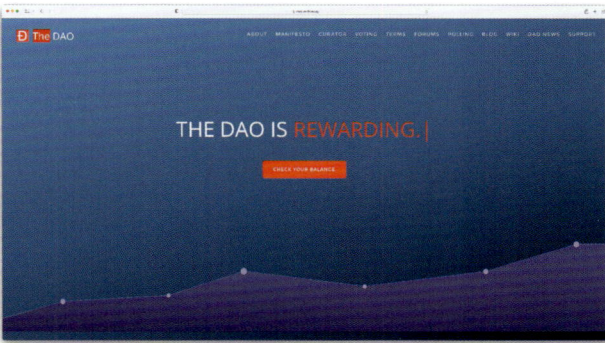

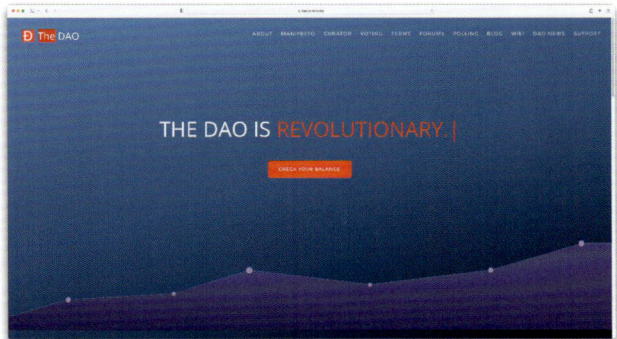

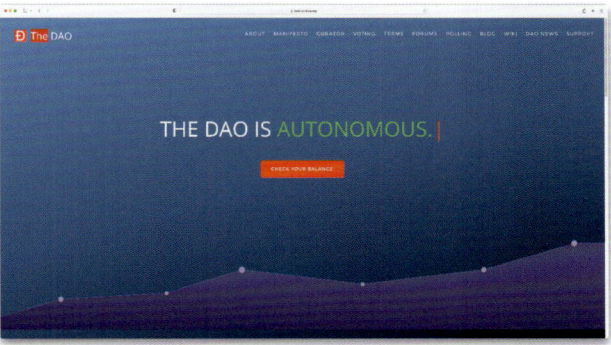

**The DAO**

ABOUT   MANIFESTO   CURATOR   VOTING   TERMS   FORUMS   POLLING   BLOG   WIKI   DAO NEWS   SUPPORT

## MANIFESTO
### THE DAO'S OPERATING GUIDELINES

### Definition

The DAO consists of the sum of those holding the DAO's representative tokens.

### Values

We, as a DAO, ascribe to the following values:

- ☑ Transparency
- ☑ Democracy
- ☑ Decentralization
- ☑ Voluntary participation
- ☑ Non-exclusion
- ☑ Privacy and the right to anonymity
- ☑ Non-aggression

### Goals

To blaze a new path in business organization for the betterment of its members, existing simultaneously nowhere and everywhere and operating solely with the steadfast iron will of immutable code. The goal of The DAO is to diligently use the ETH it controls to support projects that will:

- ↻ Provide a return on investment or benefit to the DAO and its members.
- ↻ Benefit the decentralized ecosystem as a whole.

### Conduct

We as a DAO, both as a whole and as individual members, will adhere to the following code of conduct:

- ↻ We will not seek profits through means contradictory to our stated values or the categorical imperative.
- ↻ We shall respect free speech and encourage all opinions to be both voiced and heard freely, without persecution.
- ↻ We will strive toward decentralization and autonomy whenever and wherever it is reasonably possible and beneficial.

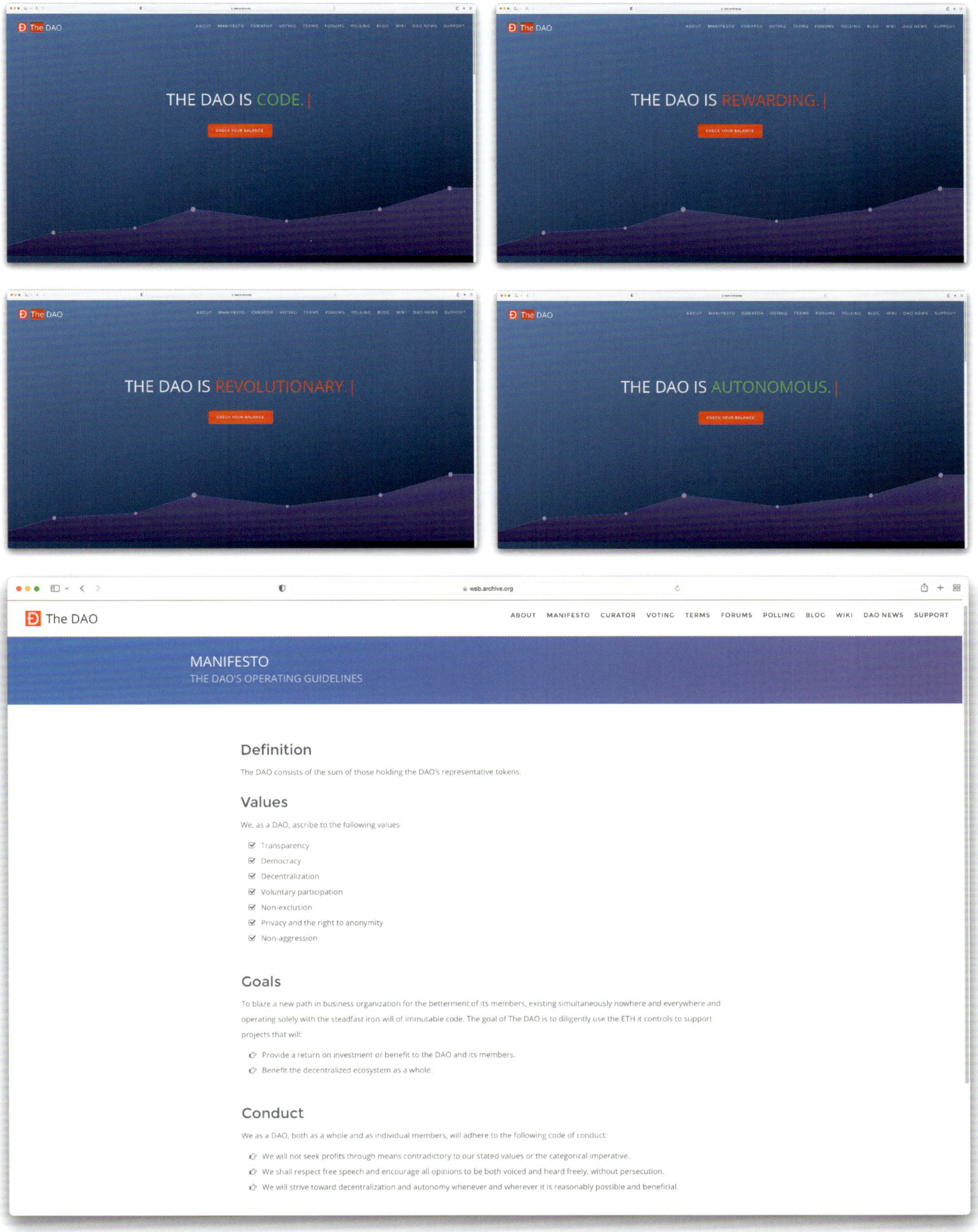

The birth of decentralized autonomous organizations (DAOs) began on an overlooked corner of the internet.[1] Nearly a decade ago, in 2013, Dan Larimer began to explore the concept of blockchain-based organizations in the context of the Bitcoin network. He analogized Bitcoin to a "decentralized autonomous corporation," supported by a network of miners, with bylaws defined not in bureaucratic laws but in free and open-source software.[2] Larimer's germ of an idea has blossomed — and has been generalized — into what may prove to be one of the foundational organizational structures of the Internet Age. While the Bitcoin blockchain may have served as a crude prototype for a DAO **[07.00]**, this organizational form has steadily grown in importance.[3]

Technological revolutions often lead to organizational innovation. The Age of Exploration, during the 1600s, brought to life joint-stock companies in England and the Netherlands, as early European powers peered beyond their borders to extend their might globally.[4] As the Industrial Era crept across the Northeast of the United States, the modern corporation was invented in New York, granting private parties the ability to form their own corporate structures without an extensive state-supervised approval process, serving as a bedrock for American capitalism.[5] In more recent times, turbulent energy markets in the late 1970s brought to life a more modern legal structure, the limited liability company (LLC).[6] LLCs were the Americanized jet engine of organizations. They provide its organizers and owners with a high degree of flexibility to construct and manage their affairs privately, with limited governmental oversight or intervention, creating a legal shell that different businesses can use to wrap around their business or enterprise and limit legal risk. LLCs were conceived of to be sleek and flexible, and have certain tax advantages — all of which have cemented LLCs as one of the primary ways businesses are organized and how capital is allocated across the United States and increasingly the rest of the world.

Today, that engine may be changing. DAOs hold promise for serving as the primary organizational structure for the Internet Age. And DAOs' optimistic, sometimes bleary-eyed supporters maintain that DAOs represent the missing piece of a broader puzzle to have online groups self-organize and persist in more meaningful and permanent ways. In the process, it is argued, DAOs will ideally improve current economic conditions, ushering in a fairer, more egalitarian form of capitalism.

## A History of DAOs

Given this vision, not surprisingly, DAOs took root fast. As more advanced blockchains like Ethereum emerged, technologists began to explore using smart contracts and DAOs to organize their affairs. These new blockchains were useful for more than the just modern-day alchemy of Bitcoin. They could support complex financial and coordination systems that secured funds, recorded votes, and prevented fraud. Bitcoin was just the beginning. Newer, more generalized blockchains, like Ethereum, offered more than the transfer of value. These networks could help coordinate disparate individuals and help the communal management of assets with rules implemented in hard code.

The first major experiment with DAOs was the unfortunately named project The DAO. Launched in April 2016, The DAO **[07.01, 07.02]** had a revolutionary objective: it wanted to pool capital and build an entire venture-capital fund that lived and operated on-chain. Constructed as a flat organizational structure, The DAO aimed to stitch together thousands, or even tens of thousands, of investors from around the world in a more automated organization. The idea was fairly simple: anyone who contributed to The DAO would be able to vote democratically on projects to support. The best of the best projects would receive community investment and, if the project was successful, backed projects could give their native token back into The DAO, with everyone sharing in successes in a more egalitarian way.

The creators of The DAO set a somewhat modest goal of raising $500,000 to invest in other projects. Once launched, The DAO far exceeded these initial expectations, much to the surprise of many of the early grizzled Bitcoin and Ethereum supporters. Over a 28-day period, The DAO amassed a war chest of 11.5 million ether — just over $150 million at the time.

It was the first viral organization and, like many viruses, it petered out. Shortly after launch, on June 17, 2016, hackers found an exploit in the code, a loophole, draining The DAO of 3.6 million ether, approximately $70 million, within hours of the attack. The project collapsed, unleashing one of the most controversial governance decisions in the history of the Ethereum community (and any other blockchain based ecosystem). A hard decision was made: given the size of the exploit, the chain was hard-forked to revert back the transactions that led to The DAO's hack. The early Ethereum community fractured, and in July 2016, the fork was implemented allowing Ethereum to move forward. Many members of the community objected, with the original unedited chain still existing to this day under the name Ethereum Classic. The DAO was all but erased.

[1] Dan Larimer, "Overpaying for Security," *LTB Network*, September 7, 2013, https://letstalkbitcoin.com/is-bitcoin-overpaying-for-false-security#.UjtiUt9xy0w.

[2] Ibid.

[3] Vitalik Buterin, "Bootstrapping a Decentralized Autonomous Corporation: Part I," *Bitcoin Magazine*, September 19, 2013, https://bitcoinmagazine.com/technical/bootstrapping-a-decentralized-autonomous-corporation-part-i-1379644274.

[4] Janice E. Thomson, *Mercenaries, Pirates, and Sovereigns: State-Building and Extraterritorial Violence in Early Modern Europe* (New Jersey: Princeton University Press, 1996), 25–30.

[5] Walter Werner, *Corporation Law in Search of Its Future* (New York: Columbia L. Rev. 1611, 1981), 81.

[6] Susan Pace Hamill, *The Origins Behind the Limited Liability Company* (Ohio: Ohio St. L. J. 1459/1463, 1998), 59.

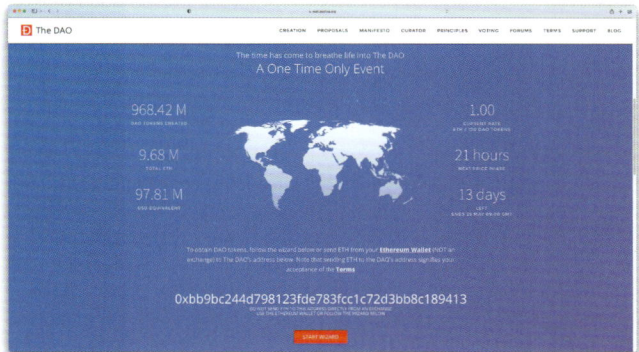
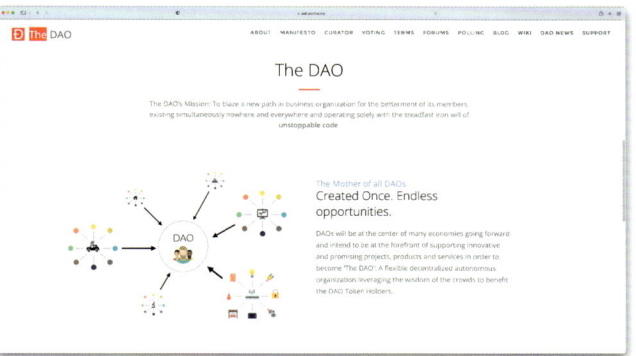

## The Contours of DAOs

What did The DAO teach us? At their core, DAOs supercharge online groups by giving participants the ability to easily collect and manage a shared pool of assets. DAOs often start spontaneously pooling together capital into a common blockchain-based wallet, with management of these core funds determined primarily or exclusively by code.[7] To manage the seemingly chaotic and arm's-length nature of online groups, early DAOs operated with different assumptions than today's organizational forms. Unlike a corporation or limited liability company, DAOs often do not aspire to be run by elected officers, boards, or express managers, but rather by democratic or highly participatory processes.[8] Instead of operating within the confines of one nation, DAOs seek to stretch across the globe, binding together thousands of members (if not more) regardless of their physical location or creed. Significantly, DAOs seek to order their affairs primarily by software and the rule of code, placing less emphasis on complex and static written agreements.[9]

Despite growing interest in DAOs, their shape is still evolving. Nevertheless, at least as of today, several core principles unify these nascent organizational structures. DAOs rely on blockchains, autonomous smart contracts, and digital assets to support organizations that operate natively on the internet. Blockchains act as the record-keeping spine, helping to support these organizations, with the novel technology serving as a central point of coordination to facilitate economic transactions and social interaction.

Members use smart contracts as glue to manage member-to-member transactions. Smart contracts define tamper-resistant rules that structure and facilitate the operation of the organization — pooling funds, doling out payments, structuring governance procedures, and making distributions. Smart contracts grant people the ability to control or direct a DAO's assets, either directly or indirectly. Tamper-resistant code keeps track of membership and often defines a member's right to a portion of an organization's profits, losses, or other resources. Smart contracts (when paired with blockchain-based tokens) further empower members to make group decisions. Code defines voting schemes, delegation rights, and other ways for groups to reach verifiable and authenticated consensus.

Indeed, for many DAOs, members aim to have the smart contract code rule supreme. Parties that join a DAO agree, in substance, to abide not just by the rule of law, but by the rule of code. This code forms a network of hard-to-change rules that establishes the standards and procedures for anyone interacting with, or taking part in, a DAO.

The scope and operation of DAOs are far from perfect, but the growing interest in these organizations points to a long-term trend. DAOs aspire to become organizations where members collaborate on a peer-to-peer basis — and transact value — with less of a need to rely on a centralized entity or intermediary. They hope to connect people through blockchain-based protocols and code-based systems, focusing on achieving a shared social or economic mission.

Such desires have long been considered in the context of the internet by scholars such as Yochai Benkler, Berkman Professor of Entrepreneurial Legal Studies at Harvard Law School. When musing on the power of earlier peer-to-peer networks, Benkler recognized that the internet was creating "decentralized, collaborative, and nonproprietary" organizational structures "based on sharing resources and outputs among widely distributed, loosely

[7] See Nilay Patel, "From a Meme to $47 Million: ConstitutionDAO, Crypto, and the Future of Crowdfunding," *The Verge*, December 7, 2021, https://www.theverge.com/22820563/constitution-meme-47-million-crypto-crowdfunding-blockchain-ethereum-constitution.

[8] Usha R. Rodrigues, *Law and the Blockchain* (Iowa: Iowa L. Rev. 679/707, 2019), 104.

[9] Ibid.

connected individuals who cooperate with each other without relying on either market signals or managerial commands."[10] DAOs seem to be the next evolution of this long recognized online trend.

## Differences with DAOs

Even though DAOs are nascent, the core operations of DAOs tend to differ from previous and standard organizational forms in at least three key respects. First, the pooling of capital into a DAO is significantly streamlined. By relying on blockchain technology, people can join a DAO with a few clicks on their mobile phone or a browser-based blockchain wallet.[11] The movement of assets occurs in a matter of seconds, with digital assets flowing across blockchain-based networks without being slowed by layers of financial institutions. Indeed, DAOs exhibit comparable abilities to pool capital as earlier blockchain-based token sales (ICOs) from late 2016 to mid-2018.[12] During the ICO boom, billions of dollars were collected by entrepreneurs (and sometimes bad actors) through token sales to raise funds for the development of new software applications, networks, and platforms. These same capabilities are now manifesting with DAOs. People are pooling capital to engage in venture-style type investments, collect NFTs, and fund creative works.

Second, DAOs are changing the nature of management, pointing towards a future where decision-making is not expert-based, but more reliant on group consensus or raw algorithms. As noted above, DAOs often lack defined managers. The implied relationship between DAO members — at least for many DAOs — is not that of a fiduciary, but is rather at arm's length. Members tend to join DAOs on equal footing. They have equal transparency and ability to participate in management. Governance decisions can be fast. Procedures often are less hierarchical and rely on polling or other voting mechanisms to move the group forward.[13] For some, this is not enough and a more future-leaning camp of DAOs is aiming to have members governed entirely by algorithms, with software and underlying smart contracts dictating the primary activities of the DAO.[14]

Third, and finally, DAOs are changing the nature of how members work together. The length of DAO membership is not static or defined and, for many, may prove to be transitory in nature.[15] It's not contemplated that DAO members act as employees of the organization. Members may join a DAO for limited periods of time, participate in the group on an ad hoc and voluntary basis, and exit a DAO due to a lack of interest, a better opportunity, or for other unknown reasons.[16] A new group of "DAOists" contribute to a number of DAOs simultaneously, stretching the boundaries of the purported gig economy.

## First Generation Collector DAOs

As of today, DAOs have found early footing with digital art collectors. These "collector DAOs" pool together resources to build shared repositories of digital art, collectibles, and metaverse items. Indeed, the term *collecting* derives directly from the Latin *colligere* (col- "together" + legere "to choose or collect"), hinting at a collaborative action that, while usually referring to relationships of objects, could also refer to relationships of people. Although there are no historical precedents to the transnationality and number of contemporary collector DAOs, guilds in the 14th to 18th centuries [07.03], public museum acquisition boards, corporate collections, art funds, and artist cooperatives are important historical reference points we can use to reflect on the novel nature of these new structures.

Set up like a traditional art fund but run like a public institution, these DAOs leverage a broader group of decision makers to spot emerging artists, trends, opportunities, and interest. A DAO's flat structure and larger base of membership creates what can best be described as a "hive mind," blending together the brainpower of independent members from around the globe, who often have diverse backgrounds and perspectives. This swarm intelligence approach is organizationally reminiscent of the collective behavior within cellular robotic systems, first conceptualized as intelligent in the late 1980s.[17] While single agents can act only in specific ways, and although there is no centralized control structure, local interactions between such agents leads to the emergence of intelligent global behavior. Members are financially aligned to work together (and in many instances profit) and thus are poised to engage with opportunities, vote on acquisitions, and work together to build robust collections of digital art and NFTs.

Emerging collector DAOs do not rely on the wisdom of the crowd — or popular sentiment — but rather the wisdom of the DAO's smaller (often curated) group. By moving from a model of a limited number of experts to a broader but not public decision-making body, DAOs appear to operate with fewer blind spots and often act faster than existing (public or private) organizations. With the NFT space growing exponentially in scope and breadth

[10] Ibid.

[11] Aaron Wright, "The Rise of Decentralized Autonomous Organizations: Opportunities and Challenges," June 30, 2021, https://stanford-jblp.pubpub.org/pub/rise-of-daos/release/1.

[12] See Jonathan Rohr and Aaron Wright, *Blockchain-Based Token Sales, Initial Coin Offerings, and the Democratization of Public Capital Markets* (California: Hastings L. J. 463, 2019), 70.

[13] Aaron Wright and Primavera De Filippi, *Blockchain and the Law: The Rule of Code* (Massachusetts: Harvard University Press, 2018).

[14] Ibid.

[15] Ibid.

[16] Ibid.

[17] Gerardo Beni, "The concept of cellular robotic system," *Proceedings IEEE International Symposium on Intelligent Control 1988*, August 24, 1988, 57–62.

**07.03**
Rembrandt van Rijn
*The Sampling Officials of the Amsterdam Drapers' Guild,* also known as *The Syndics,* 1662
Oil on canvas, 191.5 × 279 cm
Rijksmuseum, Amsterdam, the Netherlands

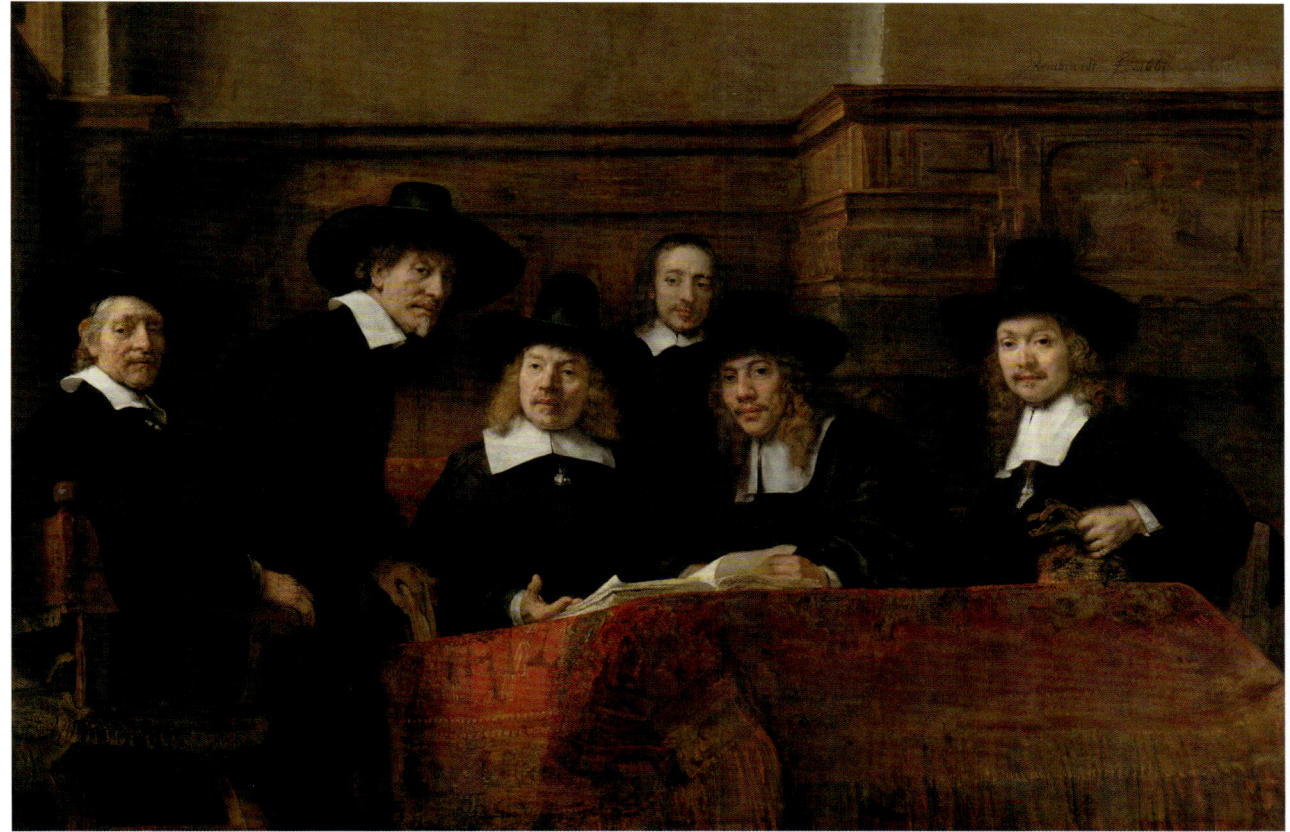

over the past several years, the volume of creative output is notable and often hard for small groups of experts to wrap their heads around or keep up with the flow of new projects. The efficiencies and size of DAOs make it possible for its members to filter through the noise, spot emerging talent, separating quality artists and projects from generalized noise.

The implications here are profound. If more and more creators choose to use NFTs, billions of dollars of art and other entertainment value could be traded as NFTs on one or more blockchains, notwithstanding the trillions of dollars of intellectual property and data rights. In this emerging world, DAOs could theoretically outpace traditional expert driven funds and curators when identifying trends and talent.

One such example is Flamingo DAO, one of the largest collections of digital art and NFTs.[18] Its membership includes early NFT collectors, artists, blockchain enthusiasts, and even individuals from the traditional art world.[19] Starting in October 2020, Flamingo has amassed one of the largest and rarest collections of Larva Labs' *CryptoPunks* (2017) **[07.04]** and *Autoglyphs* (2019), Erick Calderon (Snowfro)'s *Chromie Squiggles* (2020), Dmitri Cherniak's *Ringers* (2021), Tyler Hobbs's *Fidenzas* (2021), William Mapan's *Anticyclones* (2022), Mathcastles' *Terraforms* (2021), and other algorithmic art. In short order, it has collected over 10,000 NFTs. Its collection is considered to be one of the most valuable NFT collections in the world, and decisions by the group increasingly send ripples throughout the NFT ecosystem, solidifying its role as a curatorial force.[20] FlamingoDAO displays its collection in digital galleries built in virtual worlds, online galleries, IRL events, and has even spun out one of the first internet-native museums. Its members have incubated and launched a number of other collector DAOs, focused on digital land, digital fashion, music, Asian creators, and freely licensed NFTs.

A significant purchase made by Flamingo was that of Larva Labs' *CryptoPunk #2890* (2017), one of only nine aliens, which is the rarest *CryptoPunk* type in the series. The DAO purchased the NFT in January 2021 for 605 ether, over $750,000 at the time, with the decision-making

[18] Jamel Toppin, "DAOs Aren't a Fad — They're a Platform," *Forbes,* February 3, 2022, https://www.forbes.com/sites/jeffkauflin/2022/02/03/daos-arent-a-fad-theyre-a-platform/.
[19] For disclosure, Aaron Wright is a member of Flamingo DAO. Serena Tabacchi currently sits on the Curatorial Board of Flamingo DAO.
[20] Toppin, "DAOs Aren't a Fad."

07.04 (from top left to bottom right)
Larva Labs
*CryptoPunks #248, #6607, #9389, #157, #824 & #967*, 2017
Generative pixel art
Ethereum, 0xb47e3cd837dDF8e4c57F05d70Ab865de6e193BBB, 248, 6607, 9389, 157, 824 & 967

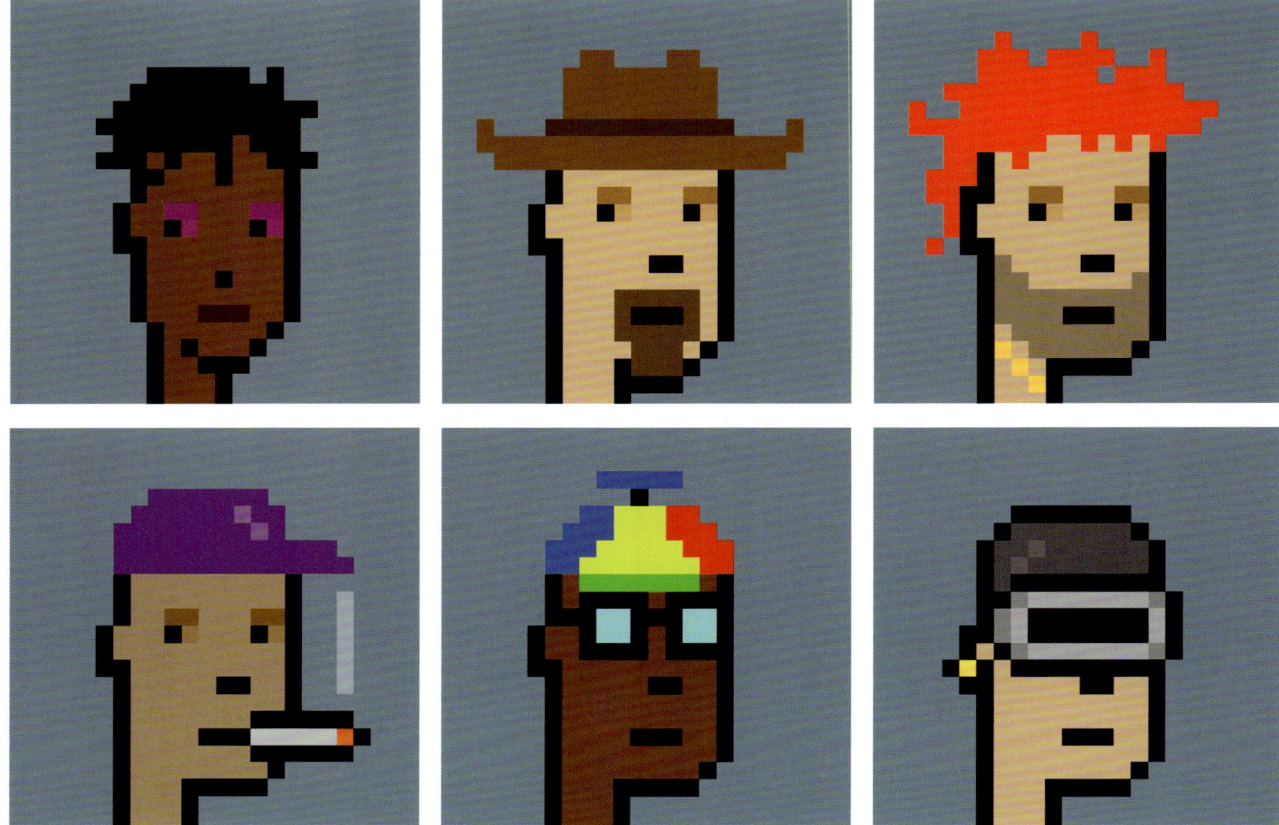

process taking place over a Discord chat in approximately 25 minutes. The speed of the acquisition of *CryptoPunk #2890* is an example of how DAOs can collectivize across the world, with an efficiency of decision-making — operating through online discussions — and an efficiency of implementation that can be afforded by the crypto economies that DAOs are built on top of.

While Flamingo DAO has focused on NFTs with art and historical importance, PleasrDAO has focused on NFTs tied to internet culture and media. Initially, formed in 2021 to acquire pplpleasr's Uniswap V3 NFT, $x*y=k$ (2021), hence the DAO's namesake, PleasrDAO has purchased a single copy album by the Wu Tang Clan for $4 million, an NFT representing the first edit of Wikipedia, and spent over $5.4 million for *Stay Free* (2021), an NFT created by Edward Snowden.[21] As a "platform for collective experimentation at the nexus of community ownership, DeFi, and digital art," the collective's interest lies in buying and funding "culturally significant pieces" to then apply creative solutions through DeFi operations, like fractionalized ownership, adding value to the works, before redistributing these back to the community.[22]

Perhaps the best example of this strategy was PleasrDAO's purchase of the original image underpinning the iconic Doge meme **[07.05]**. Following its mint in June 2021 for 1,696 ether ($5.5 million), the DAO tokenized the meme into 16,969,696,969 "fractions" represented by the $DOG token.[23] By November 2021 the meme had, albeit briefly, seen an implied valuation of over $640 million; today it has a value of $15 million.[24] Although the profitability and legality of such approaches are still in question, the DAO sought to experiment with broader group ownership and showcases the market value of important well-recognized memes when distributed across wider ownership structures. As the *aura* of memes stems from the collective consciousness of online culture, decentralized ownership structures have for the first time unlocked their cultural value into a market value.

Out of the major art collecting DAOs, Fingerprints, has one of the most direct approaches to curated collecting, focusing specifically on smart contract–based works, and relying on

[21] Keira Wright, "PleasrDAO adds $4M 'OG NFT' Wu-Tang Clan album to its collection," *Cointelegraph*, October 21, 2021, https://cointelegraph.com/news/pleasrdao-adds-4m-og-nft-wu-tang-clan-album-to-its-collection; Danny Nelson, "NSA Whistleblower Edward Snowden Sells NFT for $5.4M," *Coindesk*, April 16, 2021, https://www.coindesk.com/markets/2021/04/16/nsa-whistleblower-edward-snowden-sells-nft-for-54m.
[22] PleasrDAO, "About," YouTube, accessed August 3, 2022, https://www.youtube.com/channel/UCpsjZZhZ2oBkjHLqZVM7thw/about.
[23] Taylor Locke, "The original 'Doge' meme sold as an NFT for $4 million — now you can own a piece of it for less than $1," *CNBC*, September 1, 2021, https://www.cnbc.com/2021/09/01/fans-can-buy-a-fraction-of-original-doge-meme-nft-owned-by-pleasrdao.html.
[24] CoinMarketCap, "The Doge NFT ($DOG)," accessed July 14, 2022, https://coinmarketcap.com/currencies/the-doge-nft/.

**07.05** (below and right)
The Doge meme, and screenshot from ownthedoge.com (https://www.ownthedoge.com/)
Atsuko Sato, *Doge*, February 13, 2013 (Minted: 05-31-2021 23:16:42)
Photograph
Ethereum, 0xabefbc9fd2f806065b4f3c237d4b59d9a97bcac7, 3366

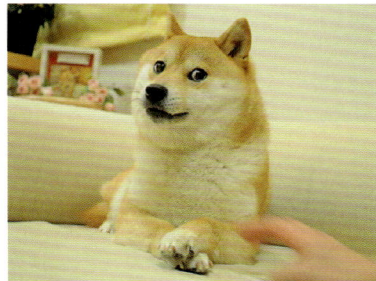

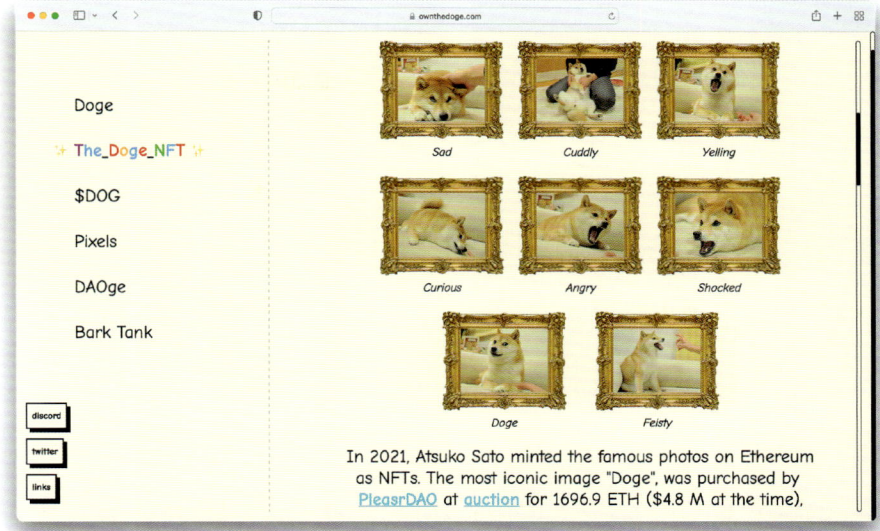

more centralized decision-making. Sam Spike, the creative director of Fingerprints DAO, asked its community to elect a curation committee to oversee art acquisitions, which evaluates work based on whether it falls within one of the following four categories:

*On-chain storage: the artwork can be recreated from information stored on the blockchain.*
*Dynamism: The artwork is responsive to on-chain activity [such as block time or oracles].*
*Coordination-based: The artwork incentivizes coordinated behavior by human or non-human agents.*
*Financialization: The artwork critically examines financial value, markets, and/or ownership, or deploys its own economic mechanisms.* [25]

Fingerprints and its curation committee has collected pioneering and experimental blockchain artworks, including Harm van den Dorpel's *Mutant Garden Seeder* (2021) and, like Flamingo DAO, Larva Labs' *Autoglyphs*. Fingerprints currently exhibits their collection via online galleries and is exploring innovative ways to display their collection by merging digital and physical landscapes with a novel approach to physical exhibitions with the aim of best showcasing the collection works. Fingerprints' collection is stored in a vault via a multi-sig model, a standard custody process for a DAO which aims to increase the security and preservation of the assets.

### Collector DAOs Addressing Inequities

The growing curatorial reach of DAOs is not limited to more generalized DAOs, like FlamingoDAO, PleasrDAO, and FingerprintsDAO. These new organizational forms are also being explored to address specific inequities and support historically marginalized communities. Indeed, Cyber Baat shows how DAOs can be used as a tool for cultural activism, collective action, and community building. Founded by Senegalese artist and curator Linda Dounia in 2021, Cyber Baat raised funds for its DAO through the sale of NFT art editions, helping to support and represent "the best and the future of the creative economy in Africa" **[07.06]**. [26] For every work sold, the artist received 50% of the proceeds, with the rest sent to the DAO for collective management and decision-making. Using this approach, members of the DAO vote on different DAO-related initiatives, including selling and highlighting the works of leading African artists such as ARCLIGHT, Ava Silvery, Vintage Mozart, and Brook. The DAO has amassed a growing treasury, which is being used to support residency programs and give emerging and established African artists the economic freedom to continue to create and engage with international collectors. The DAO's early success is giving it the room to extend its reach, with Cyber Baat exploring a separate (more traditional) fund to support their collective

[25] Sam Spike, "Fingerprints DAO," *JPG*, accessed August 4, 2022, https://jpg.space/samspike/exhibition/Fingerprints-DAO.
[26] Cyber Baat, "The Cyber Baat Fundraiser," *Mirror*, accessed August 3, 2022, https://mirror.xyz/cyberbaat.eth/P6b9unXXdg-TiQ08EHKVTKNufNrH_IcVOK1d_spM8Xs.

# THE CYBER

WE ARE AN ON-CHAIN COLLECTIVE OF CREATIVES OF AFRICAN DESCENT

# BAAT

## FEBRUARY 3

## 11 WORKS FOR SALE

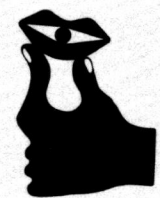

redefining what agency means to african artists in the art world

# FUND

# RAISER

COMING TO MIRROR

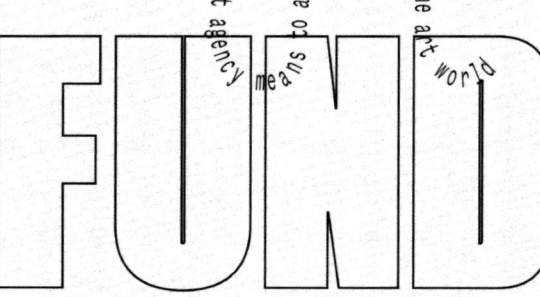

07.07
Jeff Graber photographed outside Sotheby's New York on the night
of the auction for one of the original copies of the US Constitution,
November 18, 2021. Photo: Danny Nelson

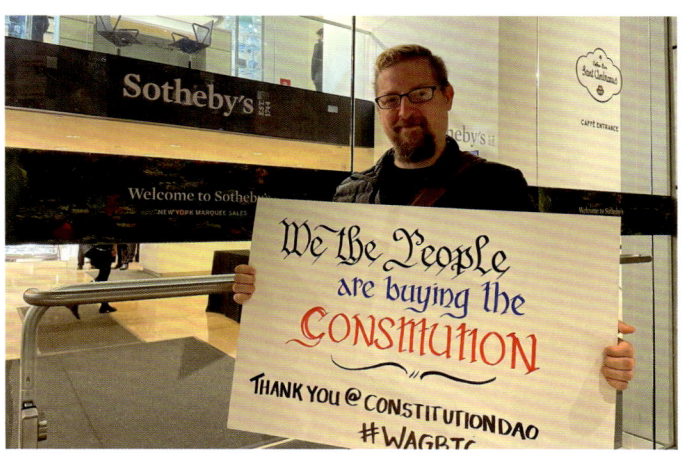

of artists, providing them with an even greater ability to create, on their terms, and at their own pace. Kenza Zouari, Cyber Baat curator and part of the operations club, says that the DAO members "believe in the power of Web3 in revolutionizing how Africans share and consume works of art."[27]

Similar to Cyber Baat, Unicorn DAO, co-founded by Pussy Riot's Nadya Tolokonnikova, is aiming to promote, highlight, and collect digital art and NFTs created by women and LGBTQIA+ people in the art world and beyond. Founded in March 2022 — and supported by prominent artists, curators, and collectors such as Diana Sinclair, Sophie Cohen, Chanel Verdult, pplpleasr, Sia, Beeple, and Grimes — the DAO has rapidly amassed a collection of hundreds of works from existing and emerging under-represented creators. Unicorn DAO has provided a new way to spotlight wealth and income disparities for women, LGBTQIA+, or other underrepresented creators and is working to serve as a cultural filter for the next generation of talented creators in these often marginalized groups.[28]

## ConstitutionDAO and Viral DAOs

Just like The DAO discussed above, other collector DAOs are more viral in nature. For example, ConstitutionDAO **[07.07]** was created to purchase one of the 13 copies of the United States Constitution being sold at auction at Sotheby's. The group formed primarily on Twitter and Discord and ended up raising a staggering $42 million in donations in approximately seven days from about 17,000 individuals, highlighting the speed, efficiency, and organizational effectiveness of DAOs as tools for online collaboration. The vast majority of initial DAO members did not know each other but could trust the immutability of the DAO instead.

While the DAO ended up losing the auction to the CEO of a large financial institution in a dramatic bidding war, ConstitutionDAO pushed DAOs to the bleeding edge of what collective ownership could mean. If ConstitutionDAO purchased an original copy of the Constitution, its future would have been steered by an inchoate group of people from around the globe and not a singular collector.

What's notable here is that ConstitutionDAO was an organization started as a meme. It, and other viral DAOs, provides a glimpse at a potential future for a growing number of organizations. One where groups grow and fade (and sometimes stick around) as fast as the internet's native media package — a meme. This trend is hitting first with collectibles: large, globally decentralized, and virally spread collectives are competing with wealthy individuals for the stewardship of important cultural artifacts.

If this trend continues, the implications for cultural stewardship could be profound. Viral collecting fits perpendicularly to the manicured style of the art world of today. It's exciting, communal, and forms at the speed of the internet. Indeed, ConstitutionDAO's fundraising and bidding at Sotheby's may be seen as one of the most disruptive moments in the future history of collecting. The notion of elitism and cultural stewardship in the art world may

27 Ibid.
28 "Mission," Unicorn DAO, July 26, 2022,
https://unicorndao.com/mission/.

07.08
Botto
*Fee-tail Fee-tail*, 04-01-2022 13:13:13
VQGAN+CLIP, GPT-3
Ethereum, 0xb932a70a57673d89f4acffbe830e8ed7f75fb9e0, 33637

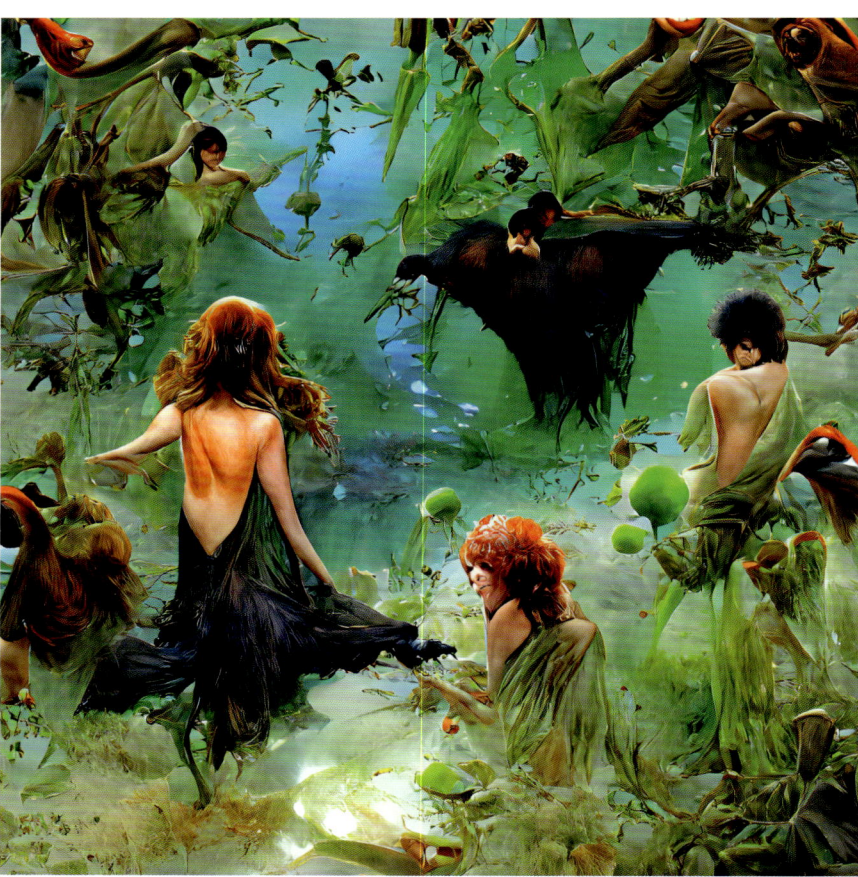

[29] Botto uses a combination of VQGAN + CLIP, GPT-3, voting, and other custom augmentations. These software models give Botto access to the largest neural network architectures publicly available in the world, with millions of works of art, faces, animals, objects, images, artistic movements, poems, prose, and essays. As they are trained on more content than is humanly possible during one's lifetime, these models give Botto an almost infinite scope of inspiration. More can be learnt about Botto's process below:

*"The machine creates its images based on text prompts generated by an algorithm. These prompts are a combination of random words and full sentences. The prompt is then sent to VQGAN, which creates an image to match the prompt and shows it to CLIP. CLIP is an image classifier that will give a probability of how close the image is to the prompt. VQGAN will adjust the image iteratively, a process called gradient descent, until it gets a high enough rating from CLIP that it matches the prompt. There are an infinite number of possible prompts and possible images. With models like CLIP, which bridge textual and visual information, the machine can even be 'empathic' and know what kind of emotional associations humans have in connection with imagery or text. Given all the different possible outputs, Botto needs direction to develop its artistic talent. That is where voting comes in: Botto will adjust its prompts based on what it thinks will be more likely to get popular results. This process runs through 300 prompts a day, generating images with a range of styles. From that set, the engine uses a "taste-model" that preselects 350 images each week to be presented to the community to vote on each new round, which starts every Thursday at 21:00 UTC. So as to not find itself in a niche too quickly, Botto is also directed to surprise and challenge the audience by selecting a number of images for voting that have different characteristics from what has been presented to date."*

Botto, "Botto's Art Engine," Docs, 2021, https://docs.botto.com/details/bottos-art-engine.

change with the nature of DAOs, where DAOs become the preeminent cultural stewards, particularly in the digital realm. As the barriers to entry come down, there is a possible future where DAOs, due to their ability to fundraise at scale, can outcompete even the wealthiest individuals. Given the chance, the internet may win.

## DAOs as Artists

One notable trend to watch is that DAOs are not just being explored to collect, but also to create, particularly in relation to AI or other algorithmically created art. This cutting-edge field is one of the most disruptive and radical in both NFTs and contemporary art today, and suggests the conceptual depth and aesthetic complexity with which DAOs can be leveraged.

An experiment in this direction is the project Botto **[07.08]**. Started in October 2021, Botto is a conceptual algorithmic art project, whose existence and creative direction is governed by the BottoDAO. The project relies on an artificial-intelligence-powered rendering engine and community input to generate GAN artworks or "fragments." DAO members vote on their preferred fragment, using the points acquired by holding the $BOTTO token.[29] The vote, a community-driven exercise, results in the most popular work being minted, ultimately representing the artist's collective "signature." Once selected by DAO curation, the artwork is automatically auctioned, with the raised funds returned back to the DAO treasury and the equivalent amount of $BOTTO tokens retired.

By leveraging community voting, Botto's output represents an entire community's taste. And, by using machine learning and other self-reinforcing AI-based algorithms, Botto's output continually refines itself, based on ongoing community input. The results (while currently often uneven) reflect the history of suggestions and create a unique lineage of one of the first internet-based hive minds.

**07.09**
SuperRare DAO proposal to "Reinstate ROBNESS as Whitelisted Artist of SuperRare,"
March 5–12, 2022.
Accessed via Snapshot.org, October 20, 2022

**07.10**
UkraineDAO
*Ukraine Flag*, 02-26-2022 03:06:56
SVG
Ethereum, 0x715132af755D9D3d81eE0AcF11e60692719bc415, 1

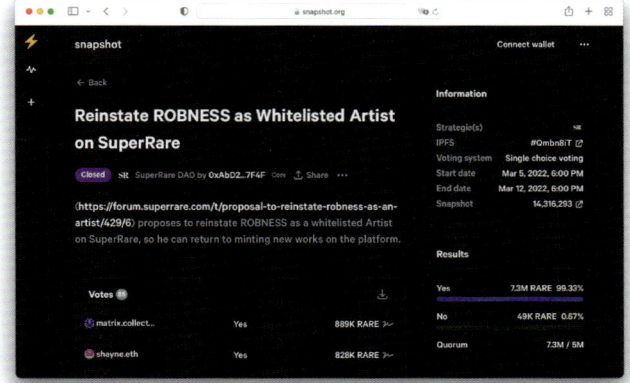

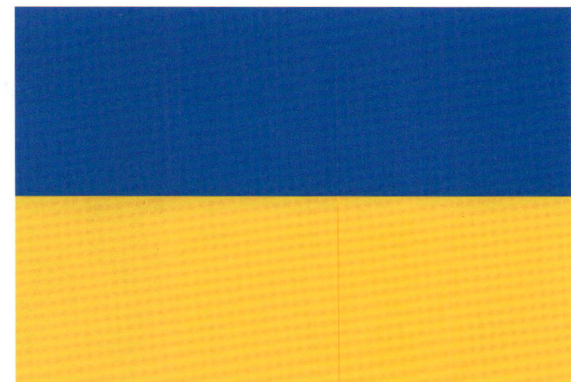

We learn from projects like Botto that humans and machines can work together in a creative process, with a DAO serving as a locus for support and a tool to chart an artistic journey. One of the first attempts at building a so-called "autonomous artist," Botto exemplifies how DAOs, AI, and a blockchain create engaging new mechanisms of community building, artistic practice, and collective curation. Perhaps of greater long-term significance, it points towards a future where the lines between creator and collector become increasingly blurred.

### DAOs for Existing Organizations

The shift towards DAOs is not just impacting collectors and artists. The growth of DAOs is even beginning to change centralized, more traditional organizations. Web3 native projects, such as MOCΔ, the Museum of Crypto Art, and marketplaces, such as SuperRare, have created DAOs to organize and channel the activity of their users, supporters, and a broader community. In August 2021, SuperRare created and launched a DAO to hand over control over its marketplace to its users.

The marketplace, which has supported the careers of emerging NFT artists such as XCOPY, Grant Yun, and Joe Pease, distributed a token called $RARE to all of the wallets that ever purchased an item on their platform. Token holders became members of the SuperRare DAO and are now driving the future of SuperRare, through token-based governance votes. DAO members have direct say in SuperRare's vetting process to onboard new artists and can weigh in on what digital galleries can use SuperRare's underlying technology.[30]

SuperRare's DAO shows how these organizational forms can be used to expand control over a once centralized platform, creating more stakeholder-driven egalitarian organizations. Since the SuperRareDAO launched, participants in the DAO have voted to reinstate artists such as ROBNESS, who had previously been banned by SuperRare when it operated as a centralized entity **[07.09]**; they authorized approximately $1 million funding for third-party developers to improve the marketplace; and they have sent donations worth 260.28 ether to various charitable projects. Using a DAO, SuperRare has provided its community and supporters with a voice, and through active engagement participants have begun to change the direction of this once centralized platform. Instead of a small group of technologists and developers calling all of the shots, thousands of token holders and hundreds of participants are shaping the future of what appears to be a next generation auction house. The corporate form is being softened.

A similar story is unfolding for MOCΔ, the Museum of Crypto Art, founded by Colborn Bell and Pablo Rodriguez-Fraile in April 2020. The once centralized organization is using the token $MOCA to transform an internet native museum into a DAO. An experimental playground, MOCΔ has built a permanent collection of 232 artworks by early crypto artists (whose work dated before December 2020) and a community collection comprised of 7,114 works of art, using the $MOCA token to bind together different supporters and participants from across the globe.[31] MOCΔ's community collection was publicly crowd sourced, serving as an art social network, where *anyone* could donate an NFT to a community gallery and join a community of like-minded collectors.[32] The so-called museum is seeking to transform into a full DAO. To do so, MOCΔ provides collectors with MOCΔ tokens through a system of

[30] $RARE tokens allow users to stake to different galleries to signal alignment, delegate votes, and access staker-only benefits (e.g. fee sharing, art access, governance over galleries, etc). The SuperRare DAO, "The SuperRare Network," *Docs*, 2022, https://docs.superrare.com/the-superrare-dao.

[31] "MOCΔ Community Collection is our dynamic and decentralized curation in practice. It is a Crypto Art Social Network where anyone can add NFTs they classify as Artwork for free. The collection is aggregated from 3,415 users, each of whom have curated their own MOCΔ Multipass and selected artworks to contribute to the Community Collection. Today, it is the largest decentralized art collection in the world with 7,114 Crypto Artworks."
MOCΔ, "MOCΔ Art Collections," 2022, https://museumofcrypto.notion.site/M-C-Art-Collections-17fedaf714674e748539ea19cce6b19c.

[32] MOCΔ, "MOCΔ Community Collection," November 16, 2021, https://museumofcryptoart.medium.com/m-c-community-collection-a3da46380a0b.

rewards based on the number of donations and a member's level of engagement. Active and philanthropic members have more voice in governance, more curatorial power, and purportedly can shape the museum's decision-making process.[33]

## Fundraising and Social Activism

The last noteworthy category of DAOs relates to broader social change. The power of DAOs to pool capital and bind disparate groups of individuals from around the globe is useful for more than just art. During the 2022 Russian invasion of Ukraine, several collector DAOs formed to support creators based in Ukraine and provide donations to the Ukrainian Army.[34] Red DAO, a DAO focused on collecting digital fashion items, supported the digital designs of many Ukrainian creators. Moreover, a group swarmed together in a Telegram group, and called themselves Ukraine DAO [07.10], collecting donations and auctioning an NFT of a Ukrainian flag.[35]

The groundswell of online support attracted the attention of the Ukrainian government, which looked to crypto as a way of raising financial aid. Only two days after the invasion the Ukrainian government had posted their own Bitcoin and Ethereum wallet addresses across social media.[36] Ukraine's vice prime minister and minister of digital transformation Mykhailo Fedorov was one of the key forces behind this integration, even revealing on March 3, 2022, that there would be government-issued NFTs for those that donate.[37]

The effort worked. Over the first three weeks of the war, Ukraine raised over $100 million from the crypto community, with one charitable group raising $1 million in an astounding 30 seconds.[38] These public-minded fundraising efforts have led to the purchase of medicine, bulletproof vests, food for soldiers, thermal-imaging cameras, and helmets.

The same can be said for Unicorn DAO and their use of Web3 in support of safe abortions. The DAO set up an Ethereum wallet, using the ENS domain LegalAbortion.eth, to donate to seven safe abortion foundations in the United States following the Dobbs decision in 2022. Within two weeks, the LegalAbortion.eth wallet had raised over $115,000. To help facilitate the donations Unicorn used the nonprofit Endaoment, an organization that specializes in on-chain giving and community building through crypto philanthropy.

## The Future of DAOs

The cultural and financial impact of DAOs is just starting to take hold. A germ of an idea that started nearly a decade ago is now actively experimenting at scale with the future of art, culture, politics, and shared ownership. Online communities now have the ability to take action and are choosing to self-organize and govern themselves primarily using code. While novel and chaotic, DAOs are making online groups muscular, and they could eventually change the way millions of people around the globe create, work, and organize.

These internet-ready forms of collectivization offer potential improvements to organizational structures across such a range of industries and occupations. From venture capital, to art collecting and curation, or fundraising and social activism, DAOs unbox new playgrounds for human collaboration and creation.

The objective nature of code — and a new class of digital assets — has unlocked a design space for novel forms of human collaboration and creation, pointing towards a future of organizations that are flatter, less hierarchical, and where DAOs possess potential efficiencies for deploying capital, and democratizing decision-making processes.

Whether powered by broader groups of decision makers, or even an algorithm, DAOs have an exciting future. And, if DAOs truly improve the way in which we work and create, the impact will be profound. Like their organizational ancestors, DAOs will increasingly be used to steward financial capital, human capital, innovation, and creativity across the world — transforming and influencing aspects of our commercial and cultural worlds.

Much like with the broader NFT ecosystem, it has been the art world leading the charge. But the longer term trend is worth pausing on. If DAOs are successful, things may turn upside down. Expert-driven organizations may still exist, but may be lapped by DAOs in terms of speed, agility, and accuracy. Over time the novelness will undoubtedly wear off. DAOs will fade into the background, become mundane, and serve as assumed infrastructure for the Internet Age. We won't think about them, and only in the most academic of settings will they be technically and theoretically obsessed over. For now, however, DAOs are new and growing. And, unlike The DAO, they're no longer being erased.

*Many thanks to Filippo Lorenzin for his support and research in assisting Serena Tabacchi in the production of this essay.*

[33] For example, a member's voting power aggregates from their on-chain engagement, NFTs, POAPs, points balance, and staked tokens which forms the museum's decentralized participation into their governance.
MOC△, "MOC△ Governance & Points," 2022, https://www.notion.so/M-C-Governance-Points-98b922b68a5d449886da6edf5ceff5ae.

[34] Will Gottsegen, "New DAO Raises $3M in ETH for Ukrainian Army," *CoinDesk*, February 27, 2022, https://www.coindesk.com/tech/2022/02/27/new-dao-raises-3-million-in-eth-for-ukrainian-army/.

[35] Daniel Roberts, "What DAOs Can Do: $6.75M in Ethereum for Ukraine," *Decrypt*, March 5, 2022, https://decrypt.co/94386/ukraine-dao-millions-in-ethereum-shows-what-dao-can-do.

[36] Mykhailo Fedorov (@FedorovMykhailo), "Stand with the people of Ukraine…," February 26, 2022, 12:31 p.m., Twitter, https://twitter.com/fedorovmykhailo/status/1497549813205848068.

[37] Mykhailo Fedorov (@FedorovMykhailo), "After careful consideration…," March 3, 2022, 11:37 a.m., Twitter, https://twitter.com/fedorovmykhailo/status/1499348177002151937?s=20&t=PMQKKEmFZBPCWm634tkLVw.

[38] Raisa Bruner, "Ukraine Received More Than $30M in Crypto Donations. Here's Where It's Going," *TIME*, March 1, 2022, https://time.com/6153320/crypto-ukraine-charity/.

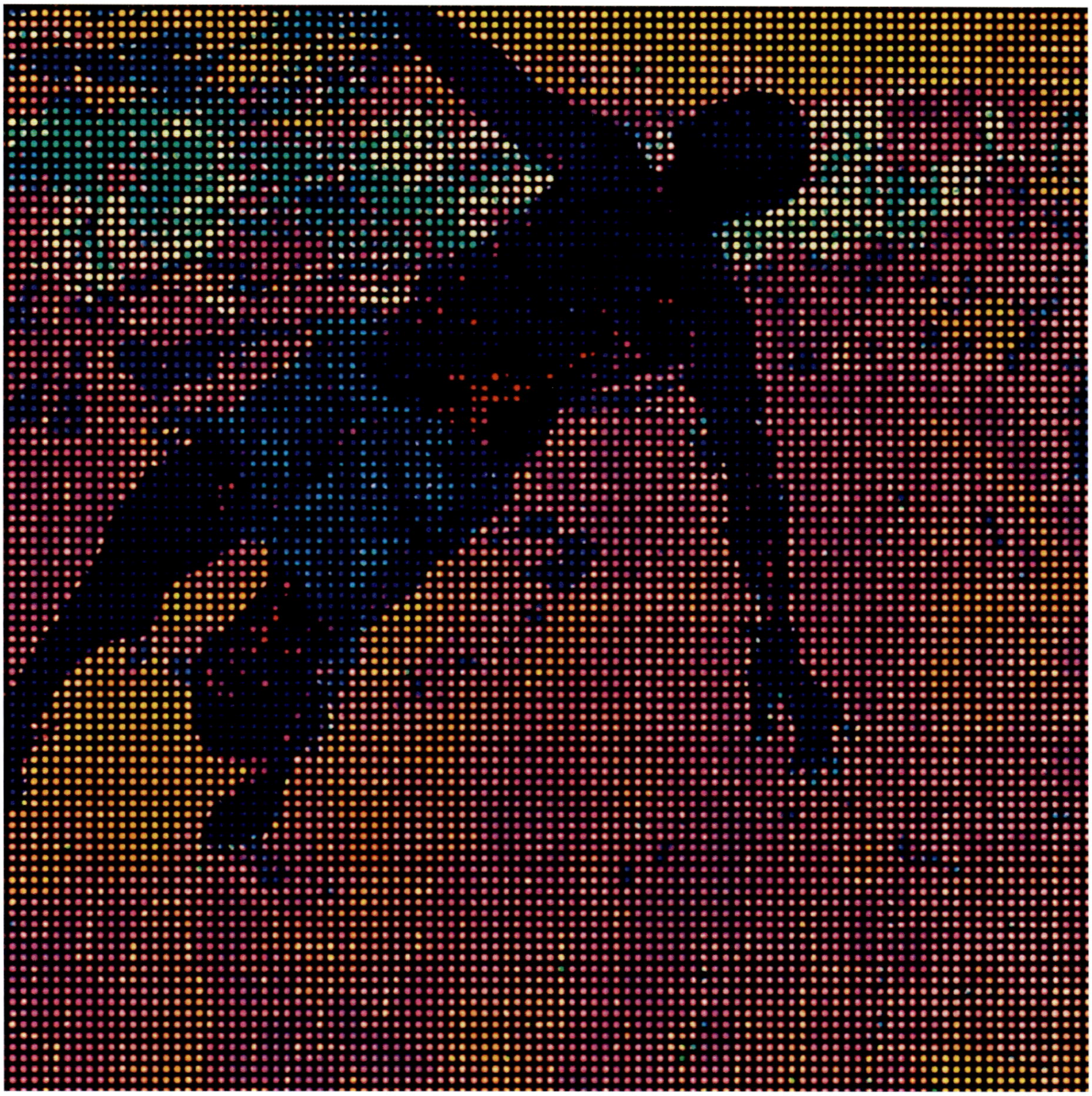

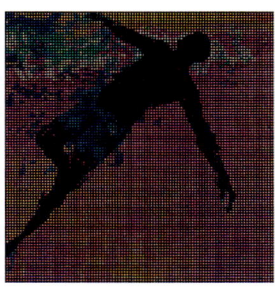
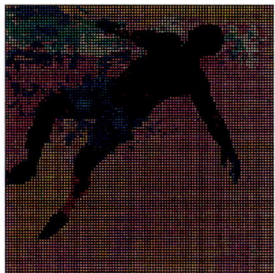
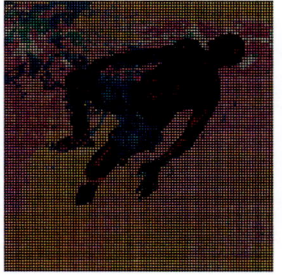
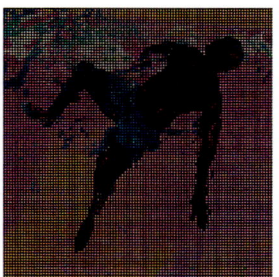

| # | TITLE | TIMESTAMP | MEDIUM | CHAIN | CONTRACT ADDRESS | TOKEN ID | EDITION SIZE |
|---|-------|-----------|--------|-------|------------------|----------|--------------|
| 01 | **Proof of Zen** | 07-10-2021 16:47:04 | iPhone, AI, Adobe After Effects | ETH | 0x3b3ee1931dc30c1957379fac9aba94d1c48a5405 | 58376 | 1/1 |
| 02 | **Elle: 1984** | 10-08-2021 01:00:37 | Procreate, collage, photograph, Nomad Sculpt | ETH | 0xabb3738f04dc2ec20f4ae4462c3d069d02ae045b | 2763000 | 1/1 |

# LINDA DOUNIA

SENEGAL 1994

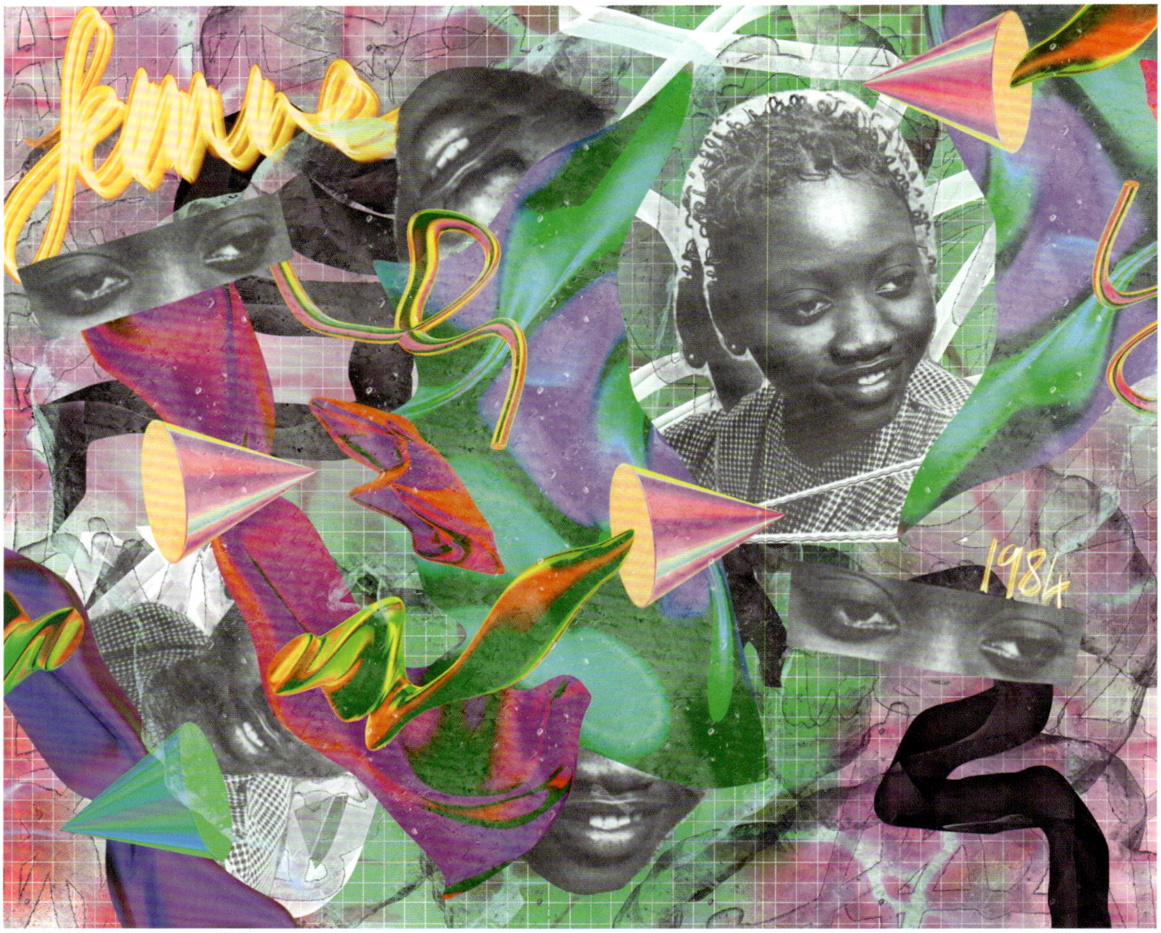

Linda Dounia is an artist and curator born and raised in Senegal. She explores the social construction of power and the cultural implications of how it is distributed. Her practice is a conversation between physical and digital mediums, by way of AI, and also incorporating image-making principles from her training as a designer. Her work has been exhibited at Art Basel Miami, Artsy NFT, Art X Lagos, Digital Art Fair Asia, and Art Dubai.

In April 2022, Linda worked with Quantum Art to release the first large scale AI collection by an African woman in the history of crypto art, reflecting on issues of discrimination in facial recognition technology and the lack of representation of non-Western perspectives in GAN-generated art. Linda has been an invaluable member of the crypto art community since early 2021, participating as a resident in the VerticalCrypto Art Residency Program, while using her voice to advocate for the inclusion of artists of African descent. In late 2021, she founded Cyber Baat — a DAO of African artists determined to correct how art from Africa is perceived and valued in the digital art space.

*Elle 1984* (2021) is part of a collection exploring postcolonial women's magazines in West Africa and their legacy on gender norms. The collage was started on paper and was further developed in Procreate, blending in abstract 3D sculptures. The body of work sparks a conversation between old and new gender norms — a bridge between what women used to be and what they are expected to become, depicting the changing roles of women in Senegal for better (women have the right to vote) or worse (women's bodies belong to everyone except themselves).

I was lucky to meet Linda early in her journey into the art NFT eco-system. I have seen her develop her fluency across a variety of mediums and have witnessed her become a thought leader of the space with grace and humility.

**MICOL AP**
FOUNDER & CEO OF VERTICALCRYPTO ART

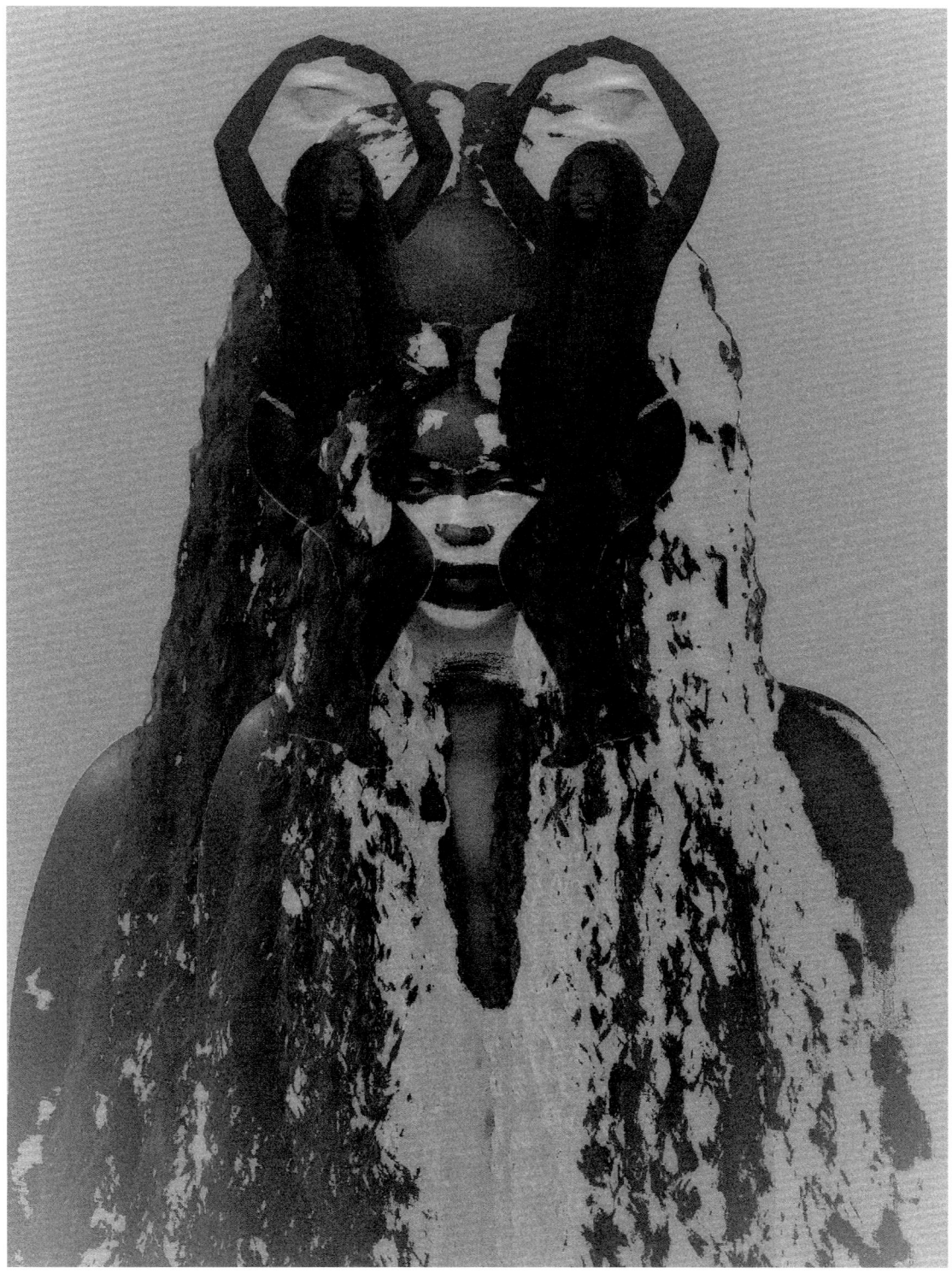

| # | TITLE | TIMESTAMP | MEDIUM | CHAIN | CONTRACT ADDRESS | TOKEN ID | EDITION SIZE |
|---|---|---|---|---|---|---|---|
| 01 | **Potent** | 01-25-2022 09:30:38 | Adobe Photoshop | ETH | 0xa5cd9b415444c9054a672059cd2a59e7b6acf834 | 1 | 1/1 |
| 02 | **The crowd** | 04-04-2021 18:16:51 | Adobe Photoshop | ETH | 0x3b3ee1931dc30c1957379fac9aba94d1c48a5405 | 19109 | 1/1 |

# DADA BOIPELO

KENYA N.D.

02 ►

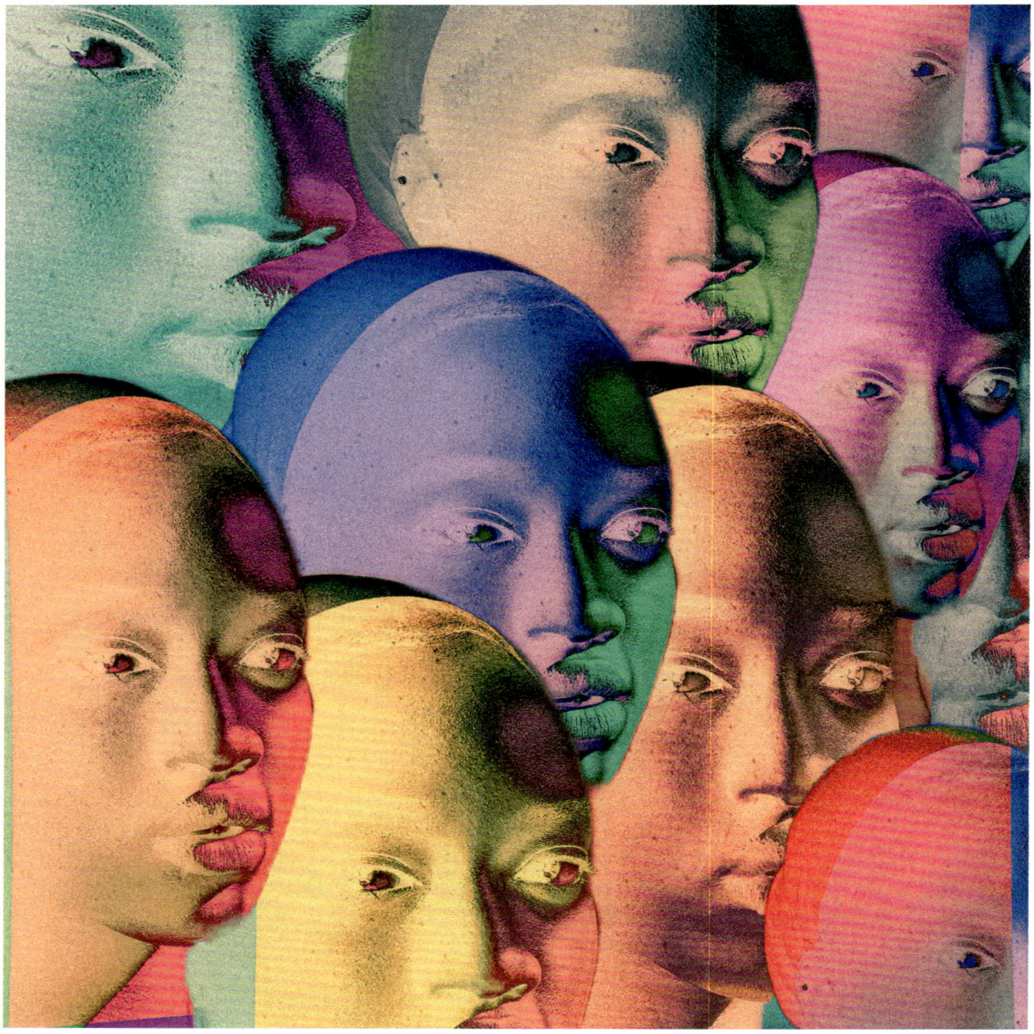

Dada Boipelo is a multidisciplinary artist based in Kenya. She works with self-portraits, is fully immersed in Web3, and is a strong advocate for its acceleration in Africa. "My mission is to chart the unchartered and pilot programs and models that many generations of creators will come to use," she told me recently. Dada's work centers on themes such as Afro-spirituality, ego-consciousness, and futurism. She is inspired by the Divine and aims to amplify and empower women and the LGBTQ+ community in her work as they have played significant roles in her development as an artist. *The crowd* (2021) and *Potent* (2021) explore these themes wonderfully. Both feature rich layering, inviting us to look closer not only at the pieces, but also deeper within ourselves revealing what lies beneath the surface of our souls. For this is where the truth resides.

In *The crowd*, Dada uses color as a pulsating, undulating technique that gives life to the figures in it. *Potent* too — it summons us deeper still to show bodies and faces in a truly unique fashion that is reminiscent of a Rorschach test; as such, its interpretation is perfectly fluid and resists traditional rigidity.

I have followed Dada's work for some time and featured her work in my newsletter *The BlkChain*. She is a passionate community builder who is deeply committed to experience that can only be unearthed through actual doing. That is to say, Dada is living her art. The work explores themes that are central to her — as an artist and as a Black woman.

Dada's work is propelled by her desire for self-exploration, identity, and its relation to the communities that we explicitly are a part of.

**SIAN MORSON**
CREATOR, CURATOR, COMMUNITY BUILDER,
AND FOUNDER OF THE BLKCHAIN

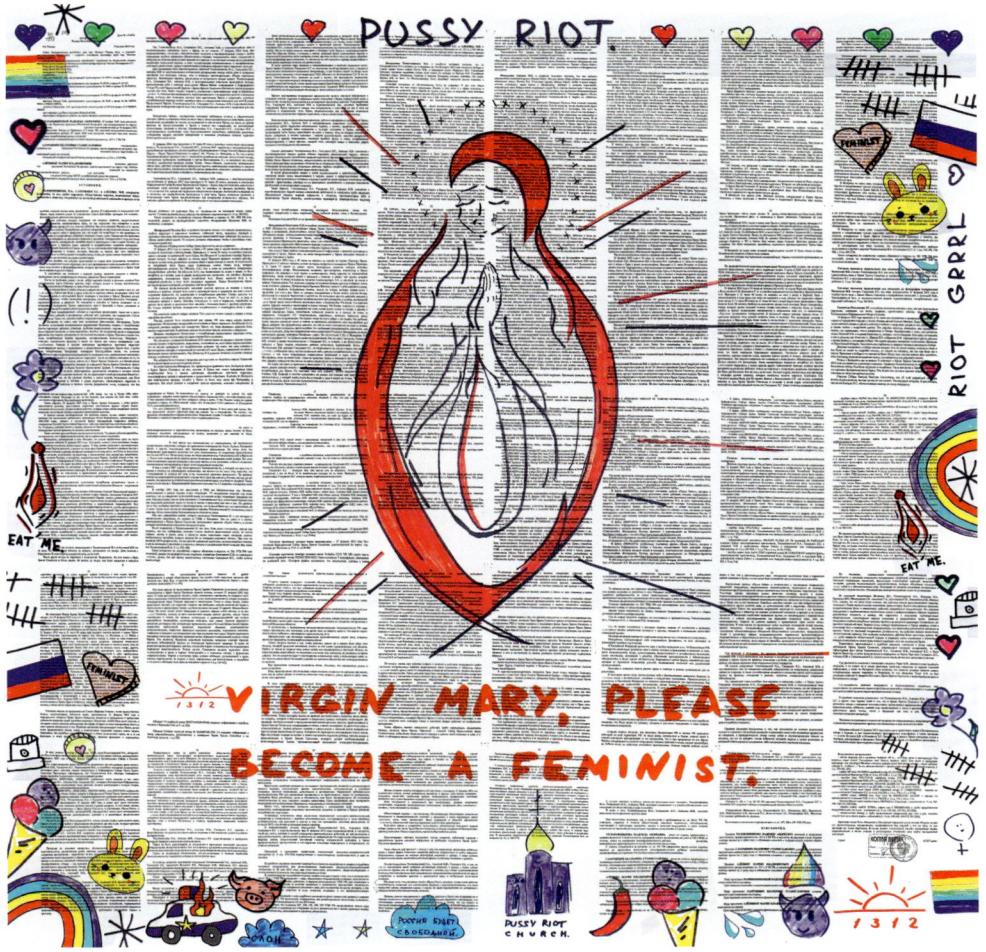

| # | TITLE | TIMESTAMP | MEDIUM | CHAIN | CONTRACT ADDRESS | TOKEN ID | EDITION SIZE | COLLABORATORS |
|---|-------|-----------|--------|-------|------------------|----------|--------------|---------------|
| 01 | **VIRGIN MARY, PLEASE BECOME A FEMINIST** | 09-29-2021 22:42:58 | Adobe Photoshop, mixed media | ETH | 0xb932a70a57673d89f4a-cffbe830e8ed7f75fb9e0 | 28956 | 1/1 | – |
| 02 | **DRINK MY BLOOD** | 12-01-2021 20:08:17 | Blender | ETH | 0xabefbc9fd2f806065b4f-3c237d4b59d9a97bcac7 | 6440 | 1/1 | Ksti Hu |

02 ►

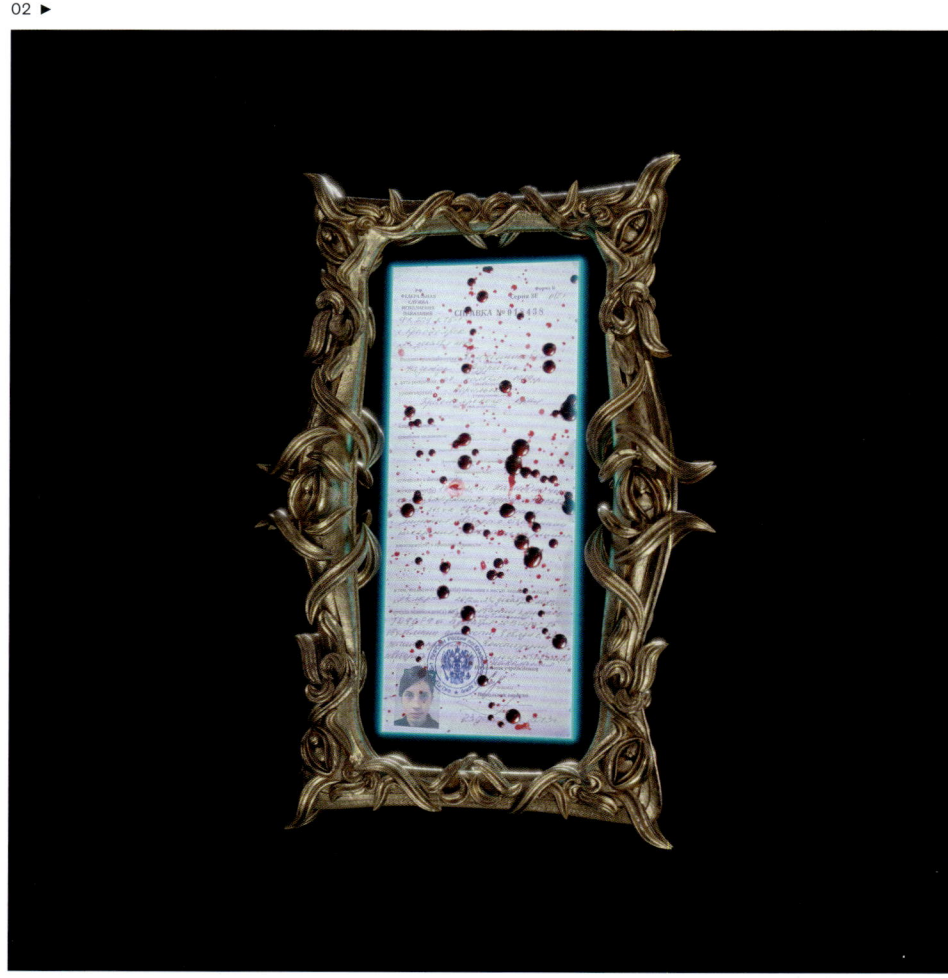

I first met Nadya of Pussy Riot in August 2021 at one of my art openings. Her presence was magnetic, she was one of the most punk women I had ever met in the Web3 space — someone who stood for her community and refused to take any shit.

After a few days of bonding while watching art and block-chain scenes bloom around us, we kept finding each other at various events around the country. We recognized in each other a shared ambition to spark a queer feminist revolution in another male-dominated industry needed to be infiltrated and systematically dismantled.

During the first NFT.NYC, we experienced the particular vibration present only in a burgeoning art movement. There was a pivotal moment in a small room downstairs at a gallery in SoHo, New York City. We stood together with three of our closest artistic allies and promised one another that the next revolution would be creating equality through decentralization. With that simple yet radical clarity, we began building an inclusive Web3 ecosystem for women and the LGBTQIA+ community. We are architecting our own queer utopia — one that strives to upend centuries of oppression and support marginalized communities by mobilizing art and technology on the blockchain.

These themes are a natural extension of Nadya's historic multi-disciplinary art practice. *VIRGIN MARY PLEASE BECOME A FEMINIST* (2021) encapsulates the spirit that has carried her through decades of activism, conceptual art, and performance. It was nine years ago that she and other core members of the punk art feminist movement Pussy Riot were sentenced to two years in prison. Defacing their digitized prison sentencing documents and sublimating them into an ecstatic artwork, Pussy Riot unleashed 333 NFTs under this project. The proceeds support victims of domestic violence in Russia, political prisoners, Russia's leading independent news outlet *Mediazona*, and Pussy Riot's ongoing activism and art.

**CHANEL VERDULT**
HEAD OF CURATION AT UNICORN DAO

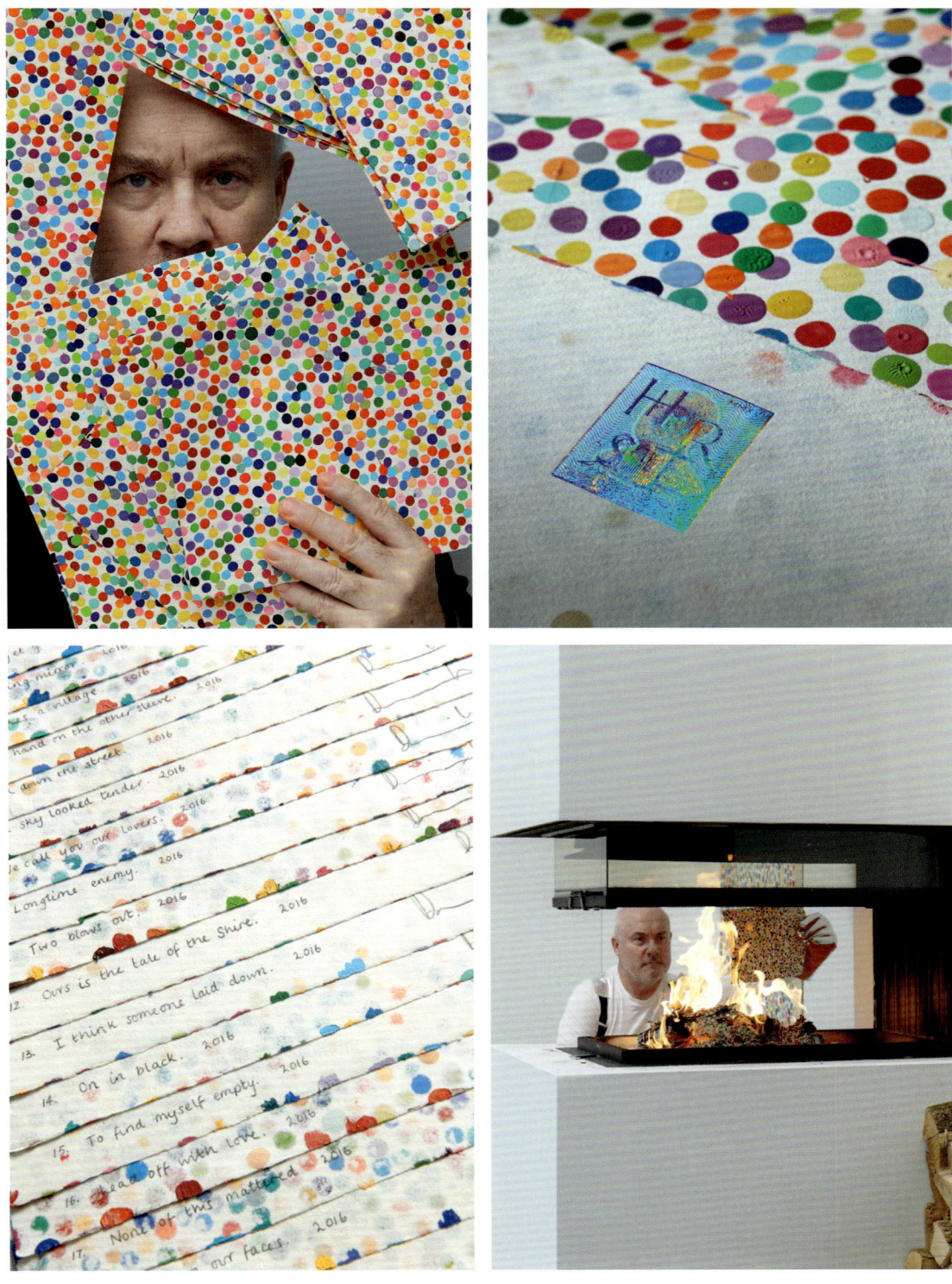

| # | TITLE | TIMESTAMP | MEDIUM | CHAIN | CONTRACT ADDRESS | TOKEN ID | EDITION SIZE |
|---|---|---|---|---|---|---|---|
| 01, 02 | **The Currency** | 07-28-2021 02:22:09 | Enamel paint on handmade paper | PALM | 0xaadc2d4261199ce24a4b0a57370c4fcf43bb60aa | 1–10000 | 1/1 of 10,000 |

EDITIONS ILLUSTRATED: (02) Totally Gonna Sell You

02

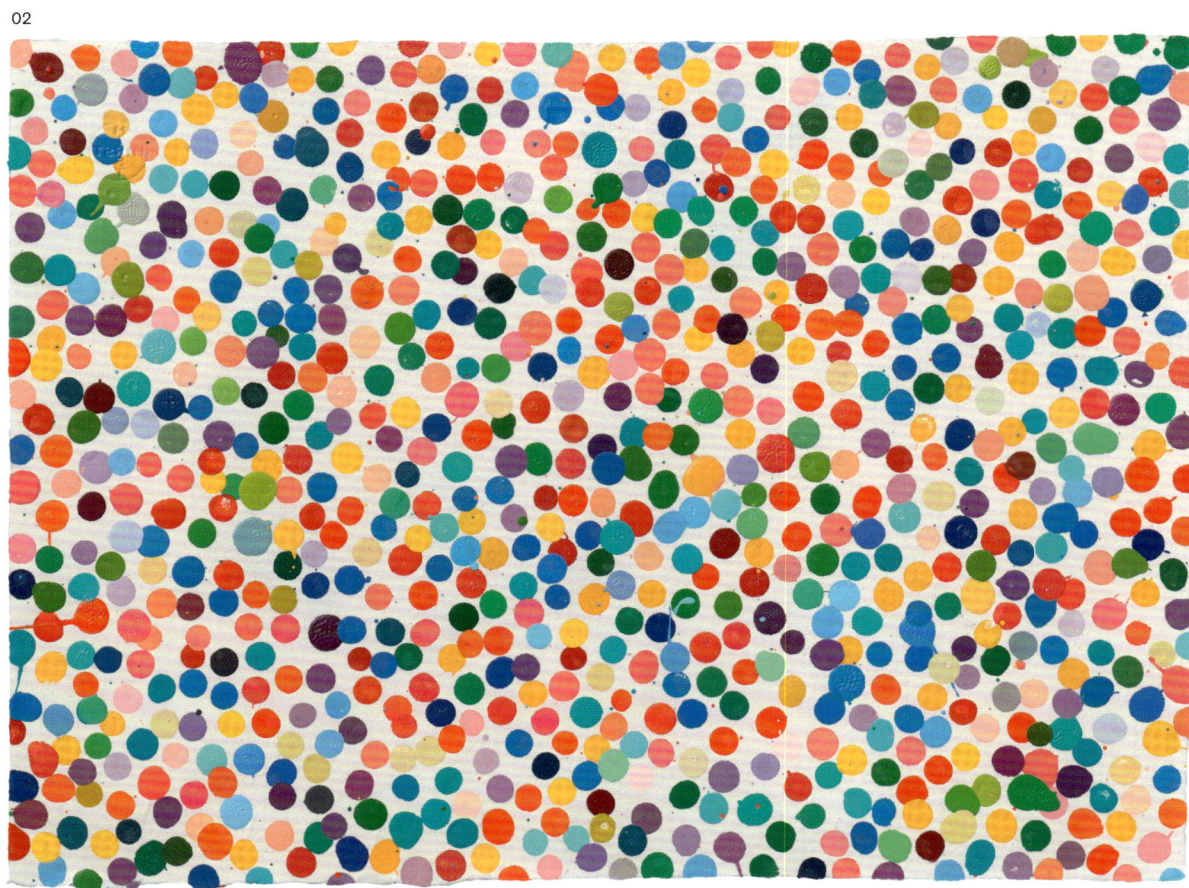

By entering the world of NFTs, Damien Hirst established a critical and exciting new stage in his ongoing investigations into art and belief, value and collecting practices.

These interests took a revolutionary turn in the innovative project *The Currency* (2016–2021), which started in 2016 as a series of 10,000 unique A4 paintings, covered in brightly colored spots randomly distributed on the surface. Hirst envisioned them as a kind of handmade currency, with each "tender" carrying a number of anti-counterfeiting measures. In the following years, each painting was digitized and transformed into a corresponding NFT, culminating in the project's launch in July 2021.

The images' individual qualities of color, overlaps, texture, density, and drips are identified and ranked in terms of rarities. Artworks are also individualized by their distinctive, evocative titles, created by applying machine learning from a database of some of Hirst's favorite song lyrics.

Unpredictability and chance are an integral part of the distributing, collecting, and trading process. Following the launch, collectors received a random NFT, which could be either kept or exchanged for its physical counterpart. This decision was final: for each physical painting exchanged, the corresponding NFT was destroyed or "burned," and vice versa. Will collectors choose the new art medium or the traditional one?

The whole project is considered an artwork by Hirst, and anyone who buys *The Currency* will become a participant in this work, it's not just about owning it. "It is the most exciting project I have ever worked on by far," Hirst said.

The exchange window closed at 15:00:00 BST on July 27, 2022. The unexchanged physical paintings were exhibited at Hirst's Newport Street Gallery in London before being publicly destroyed. At its heart, *The Currency* remains a groundbreaking public experiment in belief. With the final form of the series relying on the action or inaction of buyers, the collecting process becomes part of the artwork.

**DR. LAURA SCALABRELLA SPADA**
ART HISTORIAN

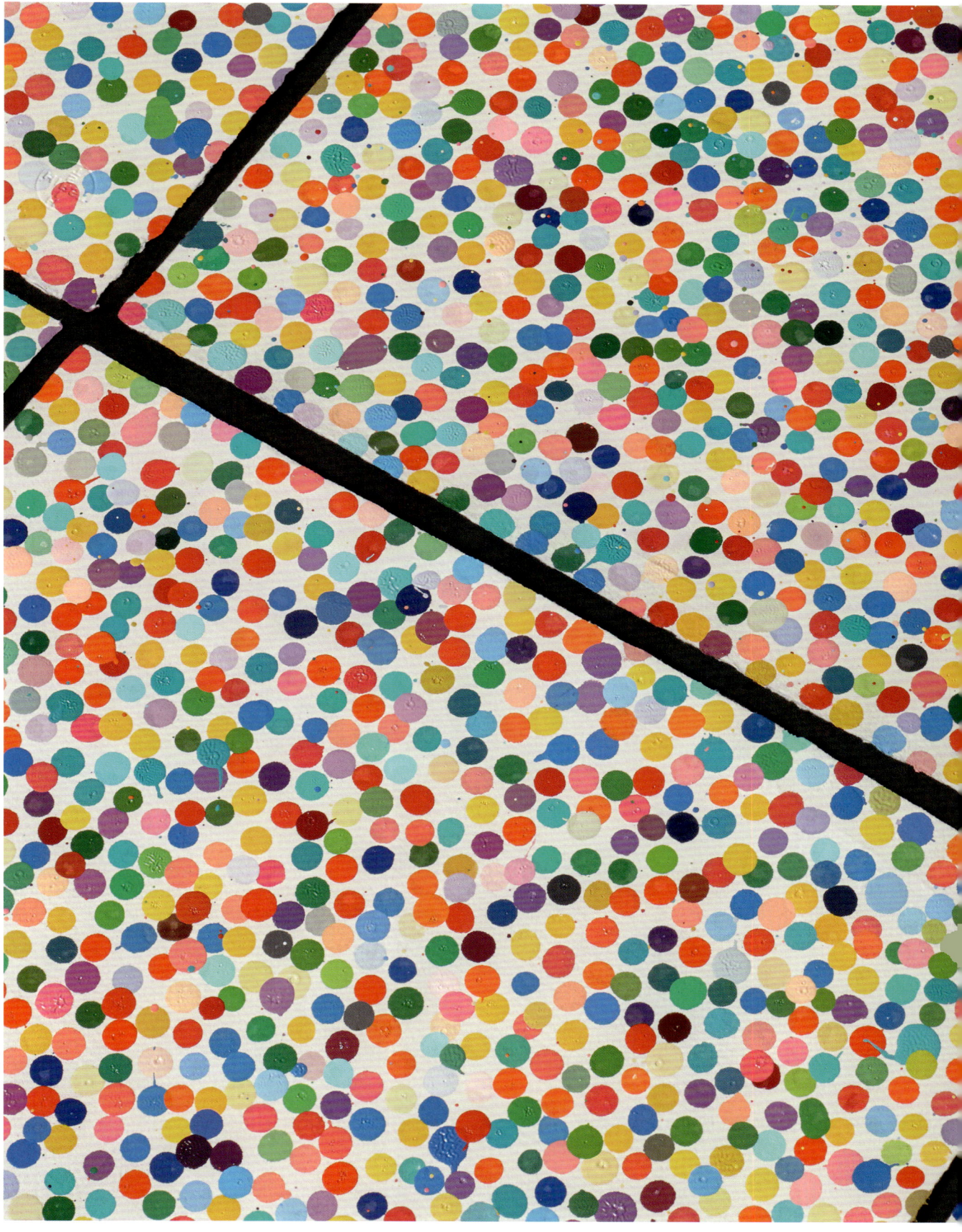

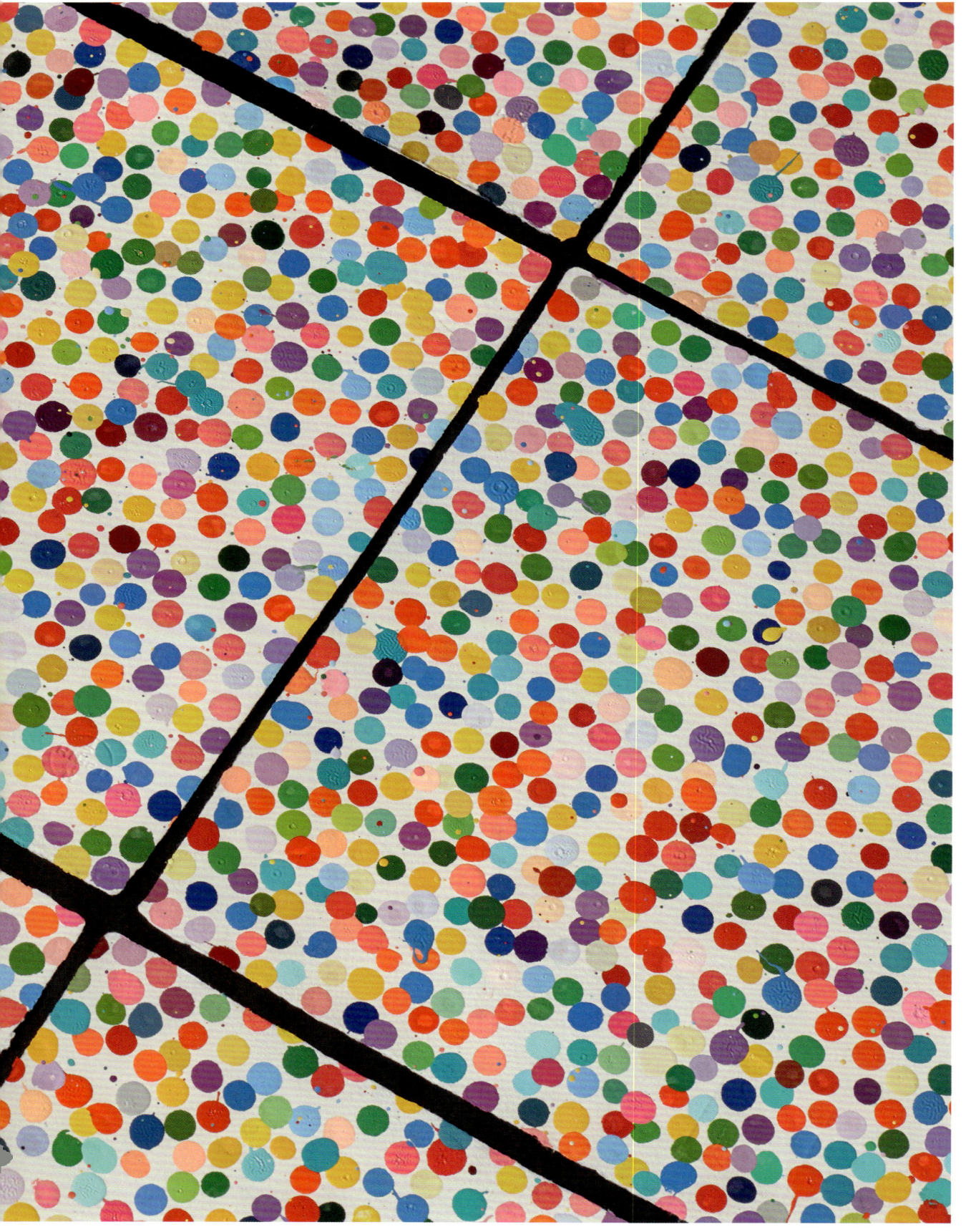

01 ▶

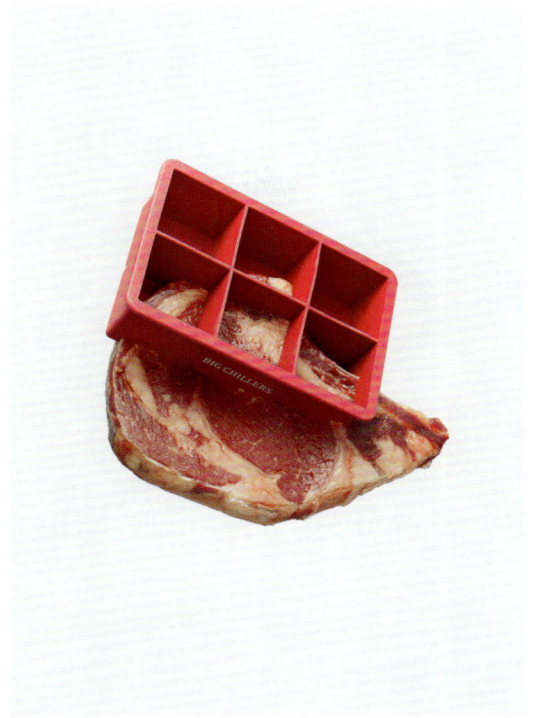

02 ▶

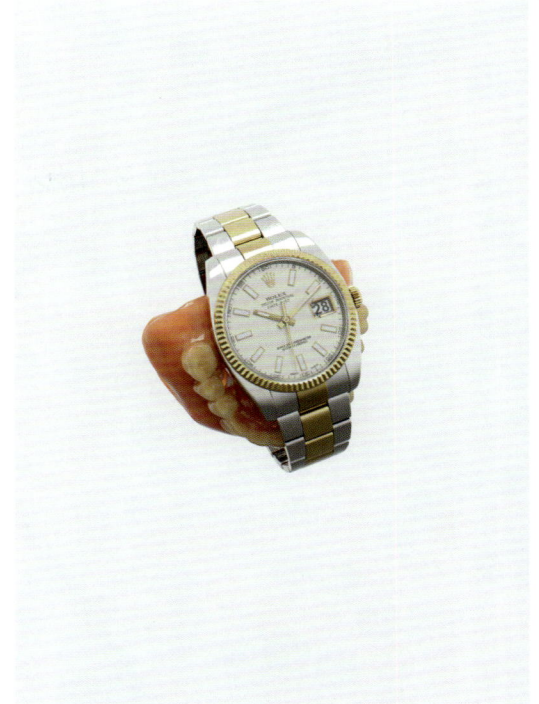

03 ▶

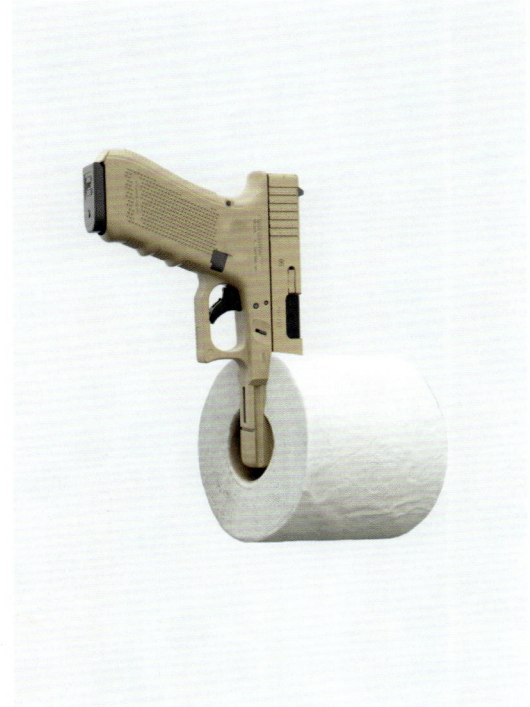

04 ▶

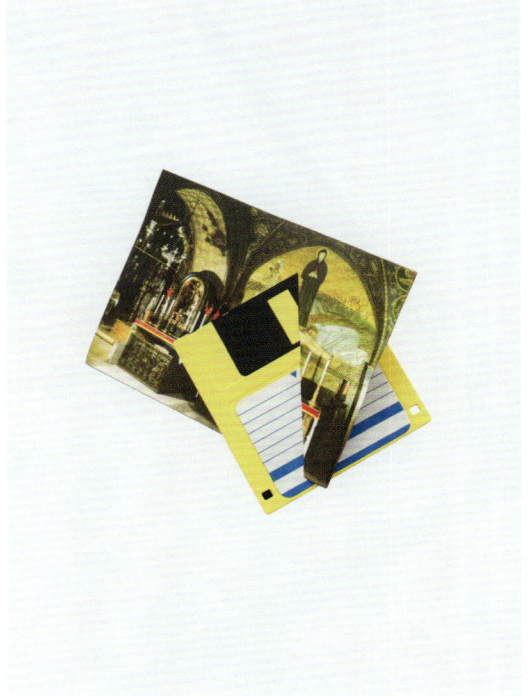

| # | TITLE | TIMESTAMP | MEDIUM | CHAIN | CONTRACT ADDRESS | TOKEN ID | EDITION SIZE |
|---|---|---|---|---|---|---|---|
| 01–07 | **CHAOS** | 06-30-2022 18:42:58 | Houdini | ETH | 0xdfc29398419b0719c2478b382bb642a7936e326f | 1–501 | 1/1 of 501 |

EDITIONS ILLUSTRATED: (01) #3 Kibitzer, (02) #93 Resistance, (03) #154 Western, (04) #200 Semiotics, (05) #1 Human, (06) #273 Thespian, (07) #501

05 ▶

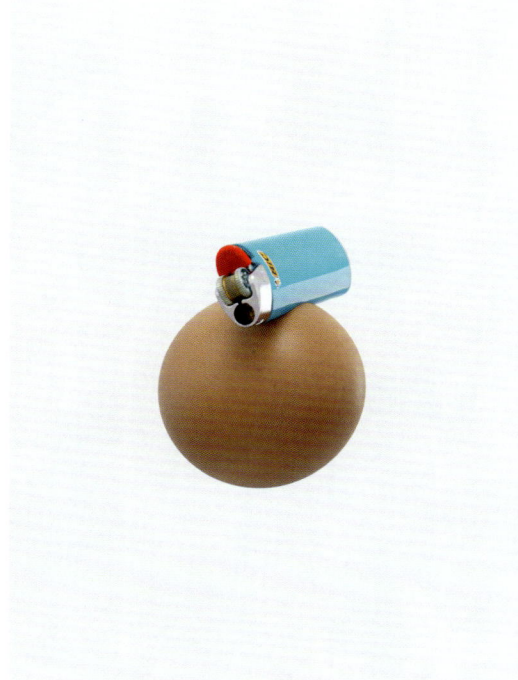

06 ▶

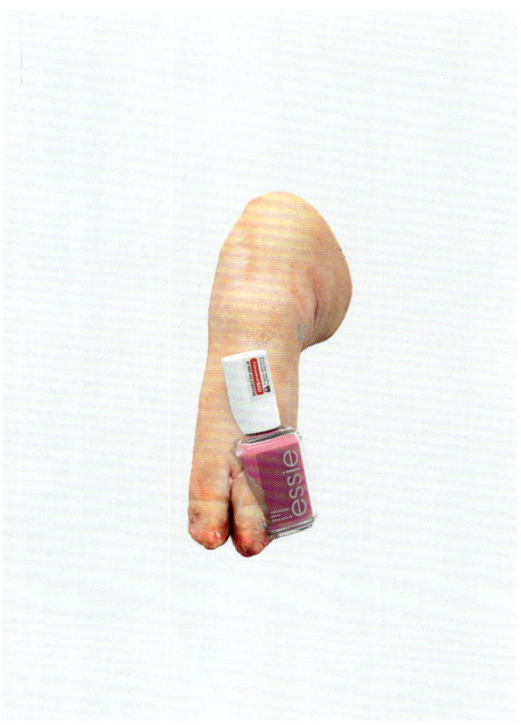

Even as a young boy, Swiss-born creative Urs Fischer always wanted to play with the things that occupied his world and environment. Lured by curiosity to engage and manipulate, the burgeoning artist grew an insatiable appetite for the "what if" and keen appreciation for nuance and idiosyncrasies. Years of education and life experience would further season him en route to becoming the lauded and globally renowned contemporary art voice he is today. From masterful sculptures and installations to evocative paintings and photography, Urs playfully toys with our perception of both thematic and physical relativity — often to jarring effect. His dynamic work has been exhibited around the globe, capturing imaginations worldwide. Yet throughout his journey, a key driver has always been that genuine childlike wonder and desire to experiment. To that end, the free form possibilities allowed by digital art NFTs presented an exciting opportunity for Urs to create in new ways, unfettered by physical limitations.

In the *CHAOS* (2021–22) collection, Urs curated 1,000 disparate everyday objects and selectively placed each into pairs for juxtaposition and effect. The items were meticulously recreated in 3D — transmuting the tactile into a virtual body. With scale and orbital paths independent from each other, the floating pieces interact in peculiar ways that they could not otherwise. This allows them to have their own moment as they converge to create a new story that we interpret through our lens of cultural experiences and humanity. The result is stunning, with layered meaning and interpretation to be had with each hypnotic rotation.

The capstone piece, *CHAOS #501* (2020–21), culminates with all of the items decoupled and free floating in one massive area. And with the render, data, and instructions embedded in each piece, these works will carry on, evoking new stories and interpretation in perpetuity through technology.

**NYTMARE**
HEAD OF COMMUNITY MARKETING AT $WHALE

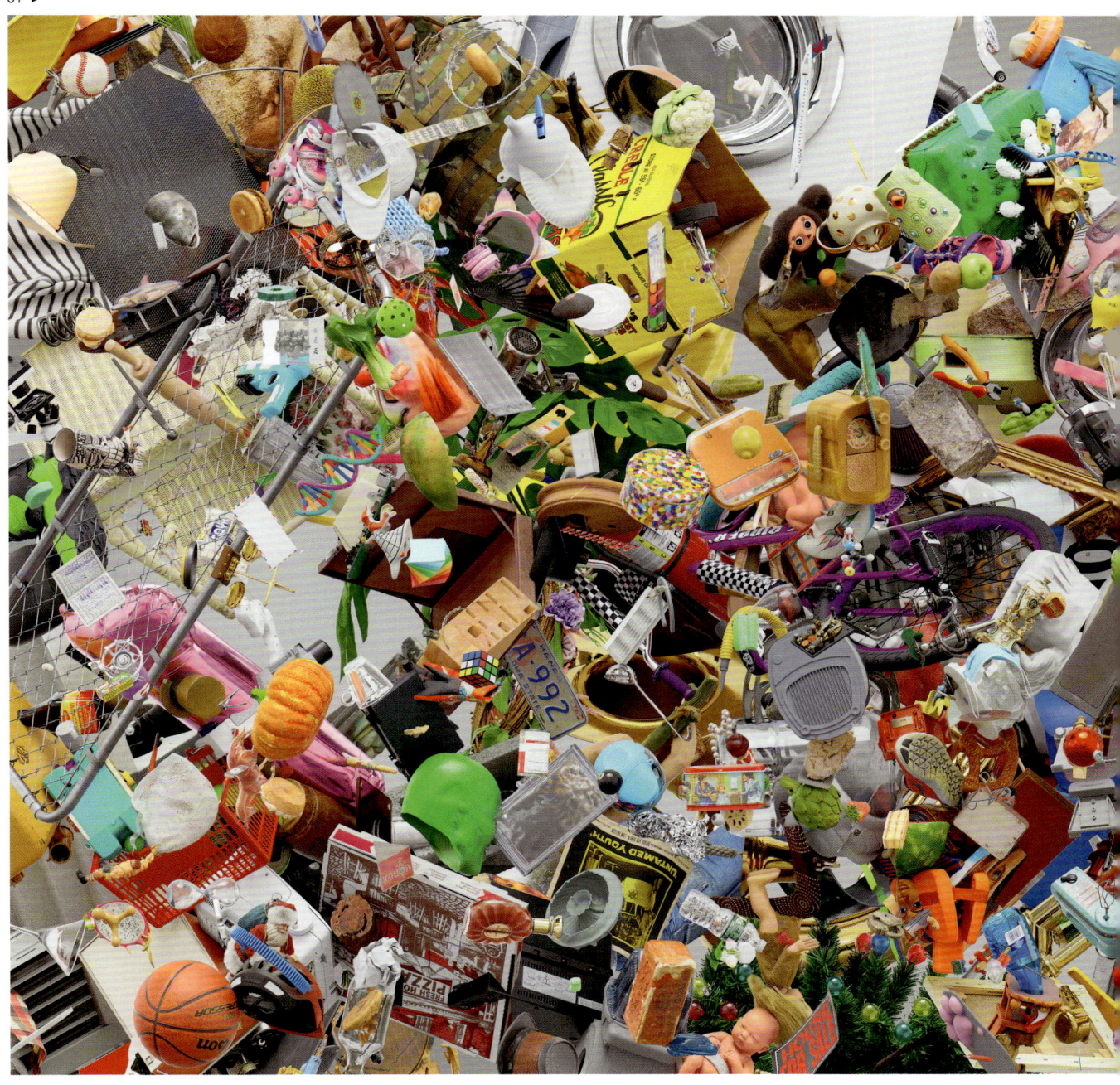

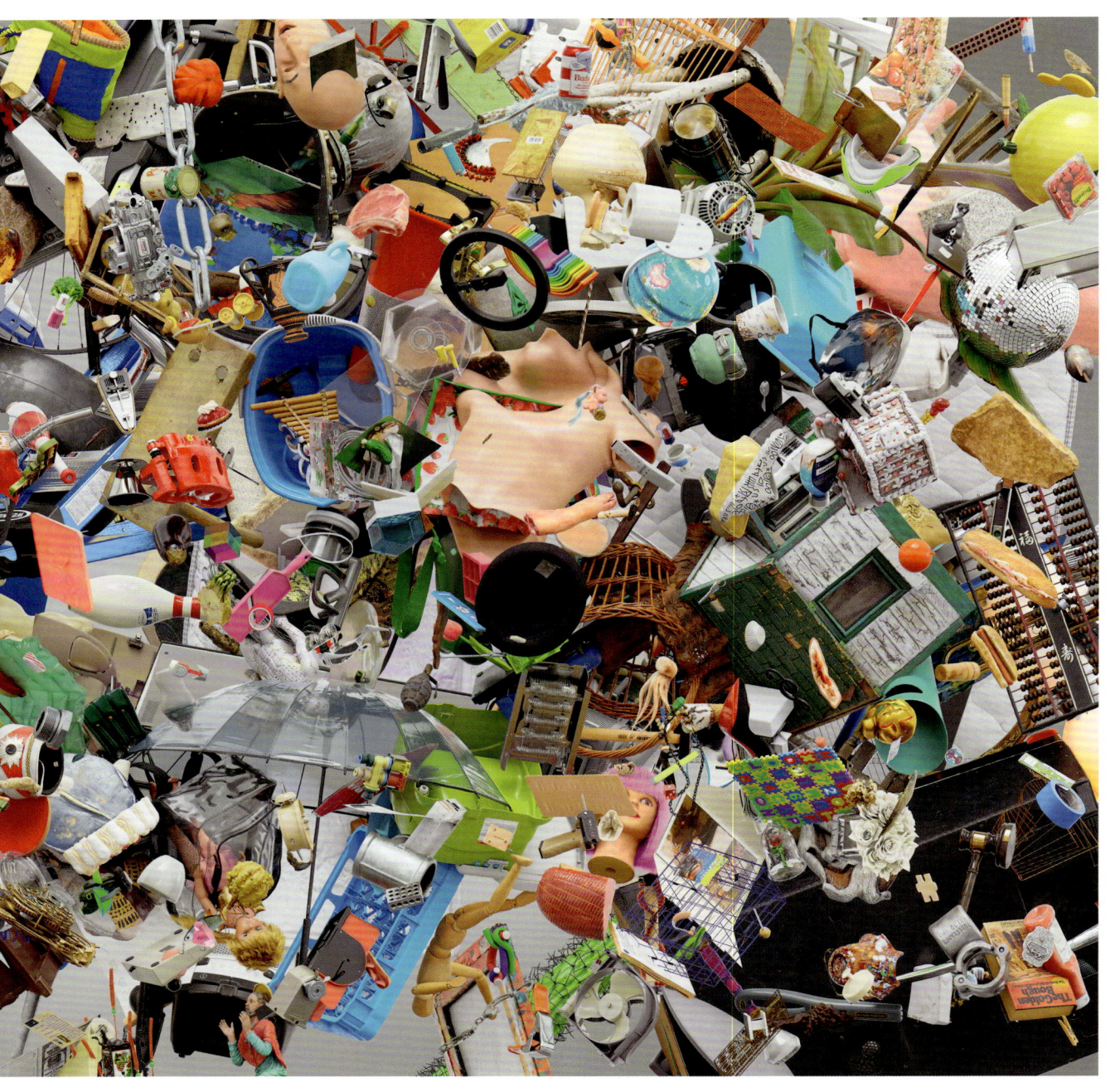

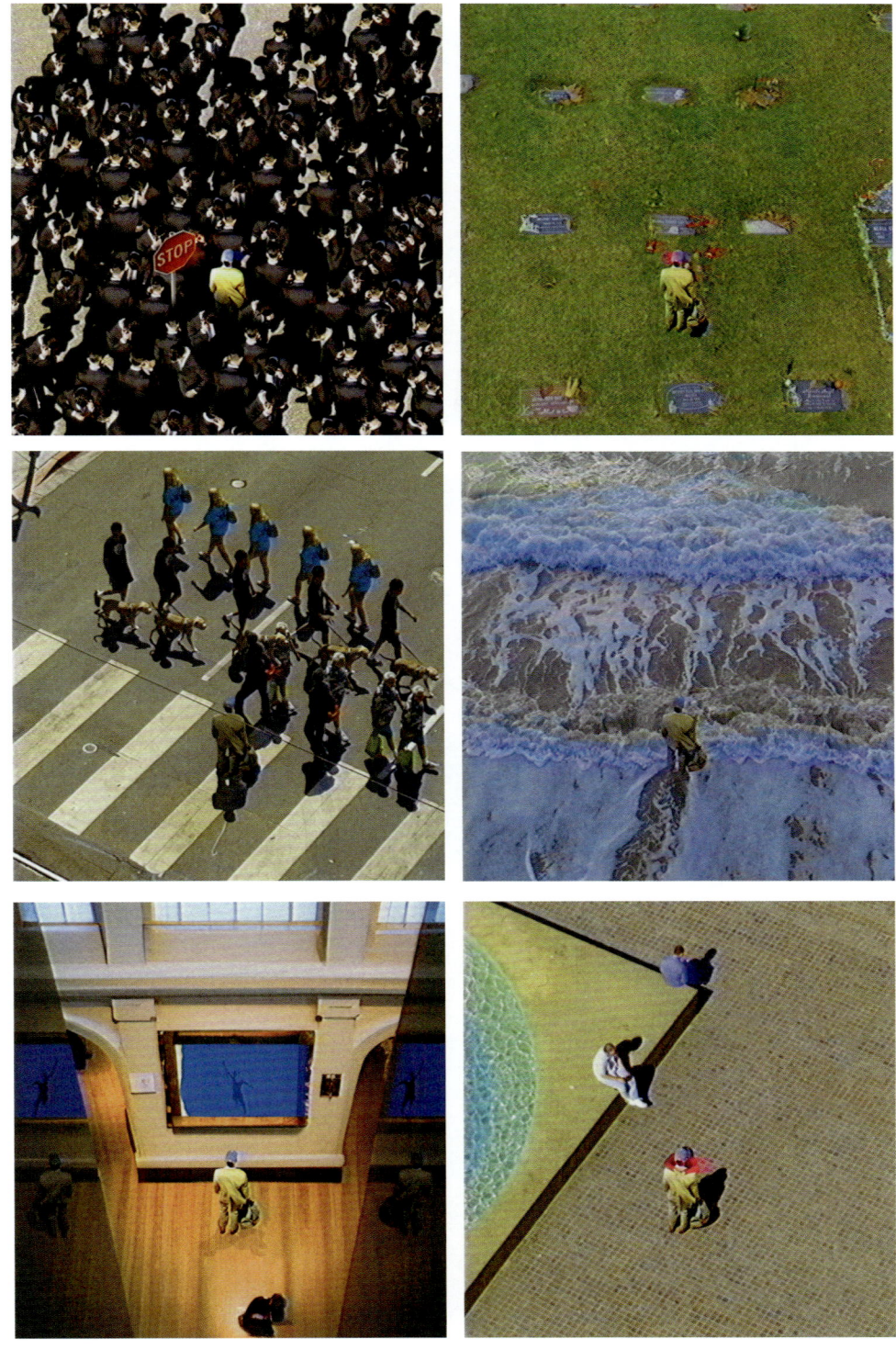

| # | TITLE | TIMESTAMP | MEDIUM | CHAIN | CONTRACT ADDRESS | TOKEN ID | EDITION SIZE |
|---|---|---|---|---|---|---|---|
| 01 | **Everything is Temporary \|.** | 02-25-2023 17:56:47 | Video, Compositing | ETH | 0×529dFD518e912a68cCc78BeEd4A9EE03ffd58F39 | 5 | 1/1 |
| 02 | **Open The Floodgates** | 06-29-2022 19:11:24 | Video, Compositing | ETH | 0xb932a70A57673d89f4acfFBE830E8ed7f75Fb9e0 | 35629 | 1/1 |

# JOE PEASE

UNITED STATES 1986

02 ▶

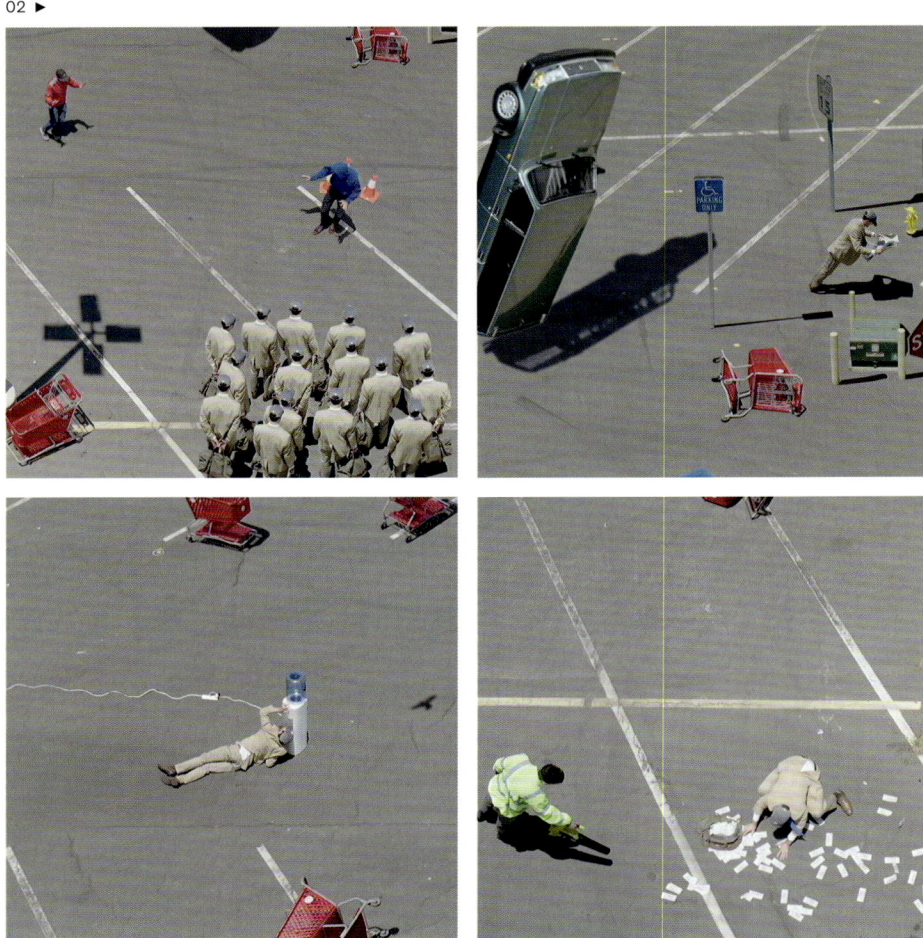

Joe Pease is an artist of uncanny precision. An Australian-born video artist based in Southern California — an epicenter where cinema, spectacle, and urban alienation converge — Pease approaches moving images with a meticulous, dreamlike sensibility that transcends narrative convention. His videos, often structured as short videos presented in seamless loops, turn the mundane into the surreal, revealing the latent absurdity and monotony of everyday existence. His seamless compositional techniques push the boundaries of video art, further innovating the medium by publishing them as NFTs.

In *Open the Floodgates* (2022), the camera's viewpoint is a wandering gaze, untethered as it moves to pan across a disjointed yet eerily familiar urban vignette. Two figures occupy a desert parking lot, standing face to face, arms raised in an ambiguous gesture of surrender or accusation. As the camera zooms, one figure flees and the other collapses, lifeless. Did a crime take place? A glitch in perception? A theatrical choreography? Pease leaves the viewer suspended, trapped in a loop of unresolved tension.

If the anxiety of movement defines this earlier work, *Everything is Temporary* (2023) is its counterpoint, a meditation on stillness within flux. A solitary man — anonymous in his brown work suit and blue baseball cap — stands with a duffel bag, perpetually caught between departure and return. The shifting environment beneath him transitions abruptly from frenzied traffic to tranquil beach, illustrating contemporary life's fractured and repetitive nature. Pease's figure exists simultaneously everywhere and nowhere, reflecting the quiet desperation inherent in routine.

Both works underscore Pease's masterful use of repetition and subtle disjunction. His films, paradoxically hypnotic and unsettling, reflect the tenuous grip we have on linear time, memory, and meaning. Through his intricate manipulation of digital layering and cinematic structure, Pease does not simply depict reality — he destabilizes it, forcing us to look again and reconsider what we think we know.

**AMANDA SCHMITT**
ADVISOR AND CURATOR

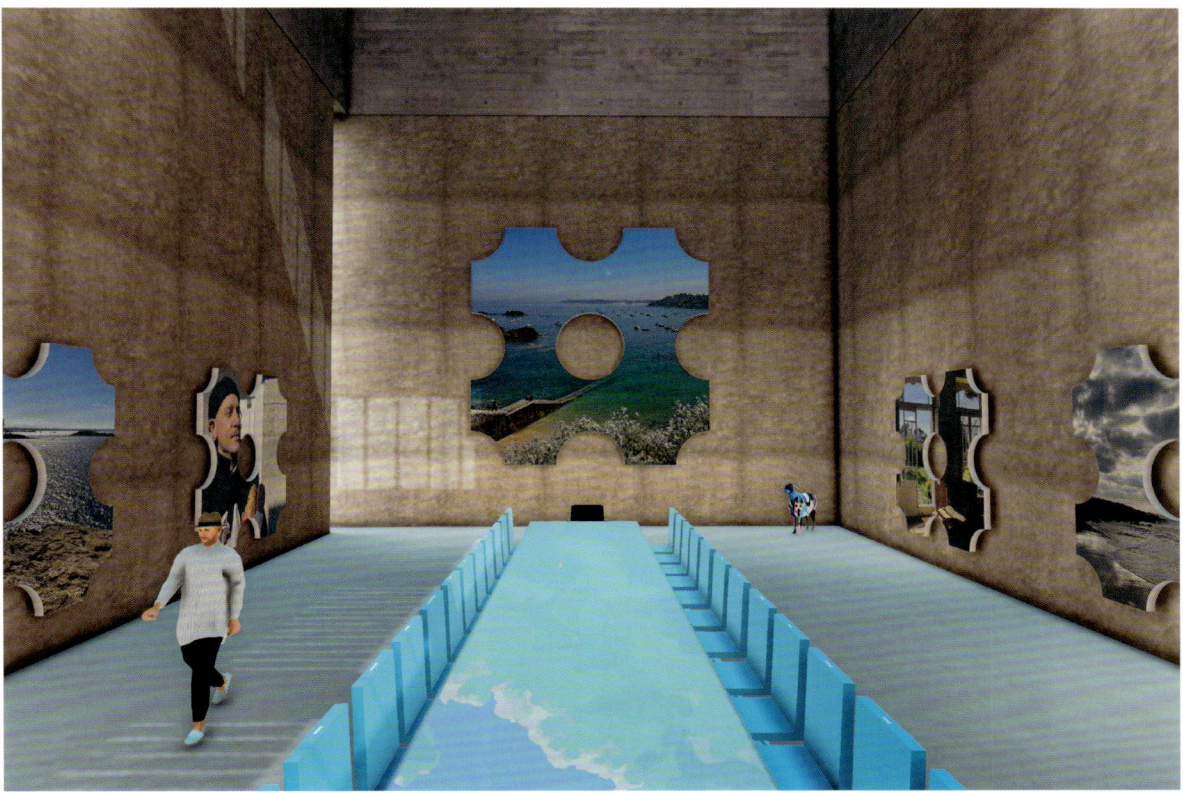

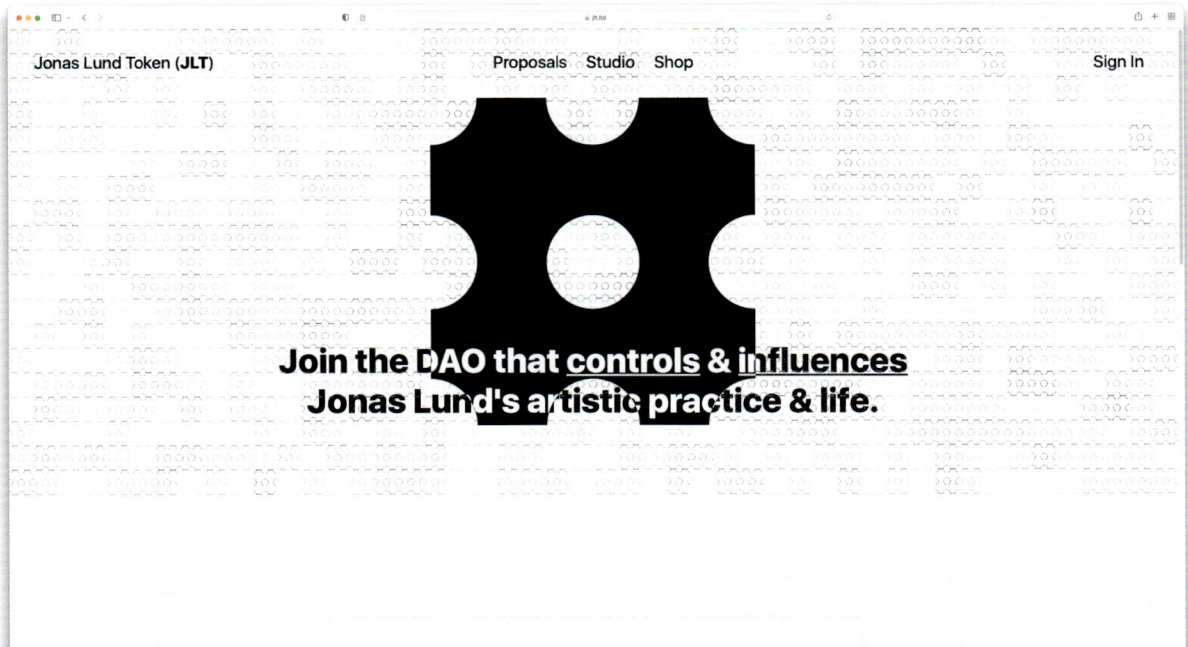

| # | TITLE | TIMESTAMP | MEDIUM | CHAIN | CONTRACT ADDRESS | ERC-20 TOKEN SUPPLY |
|---|---|---|---|---|---|---|
| 01–03 | Jonas Lund Token (JLT) | 03-21-2018 12:00:00 | Various | ETH | 0x6e146c41547826a939794d64d53db22a99423d8c | 0–100,000 |

03

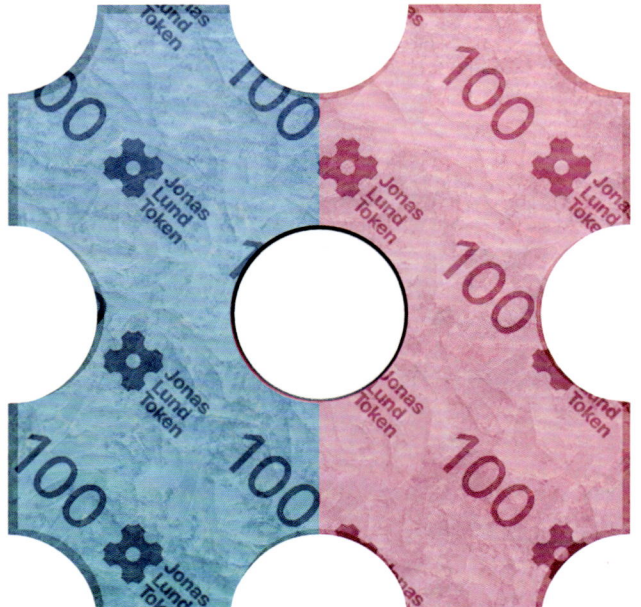
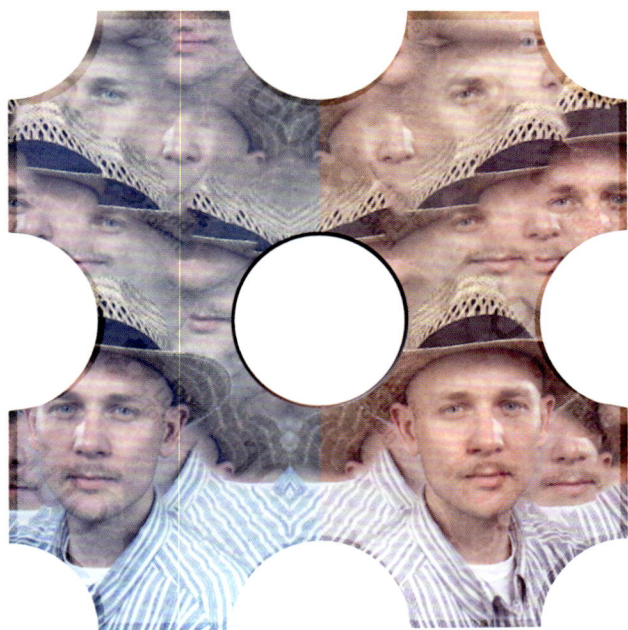

The Swedish artist Jonas Lund has been concerned with the emergence of values and the distribution of power in the art market since 2012. He creates his works with the help of algorithms and the viewers, who, for example, as owners of the *Jonas Lund Token* (2018), have voting rights like shareholders in decisions affecting his art and career.

The NFT project *MVP* (*Most Valuable Painting*) (2022) lets the audience make the ultimate decision: Which is the most valuable painting? The 512 individual digital paintings optimize themselves based on digital user engagement such as likes, clicks, swipe rights, and sales. Each *MVP*'s aesthetic is determined by a fitness algorithm that tracks its performance, while the *Most Valuable Painting* is the result of the previous 511 sales.

NFTs democratize the art market: artists can sell their works directly to collectors via marketplaces. Simultaneously, by selling them at lower prices, digital works become collectibles, making them more accessible to a wider audience. Lund reflects this new development in the art market by dividing the *MVP*s into groups and staggering the prices according to the size of the edition. Thus, the *Most Valuable Painting* is literally the one that sells for the highest price defined by the artist, while its aesthetic outcome is the result of a democratic process influenced by the values of the attention economy.

**ANIKA MEIER**
ART WRITER AND CURATOR

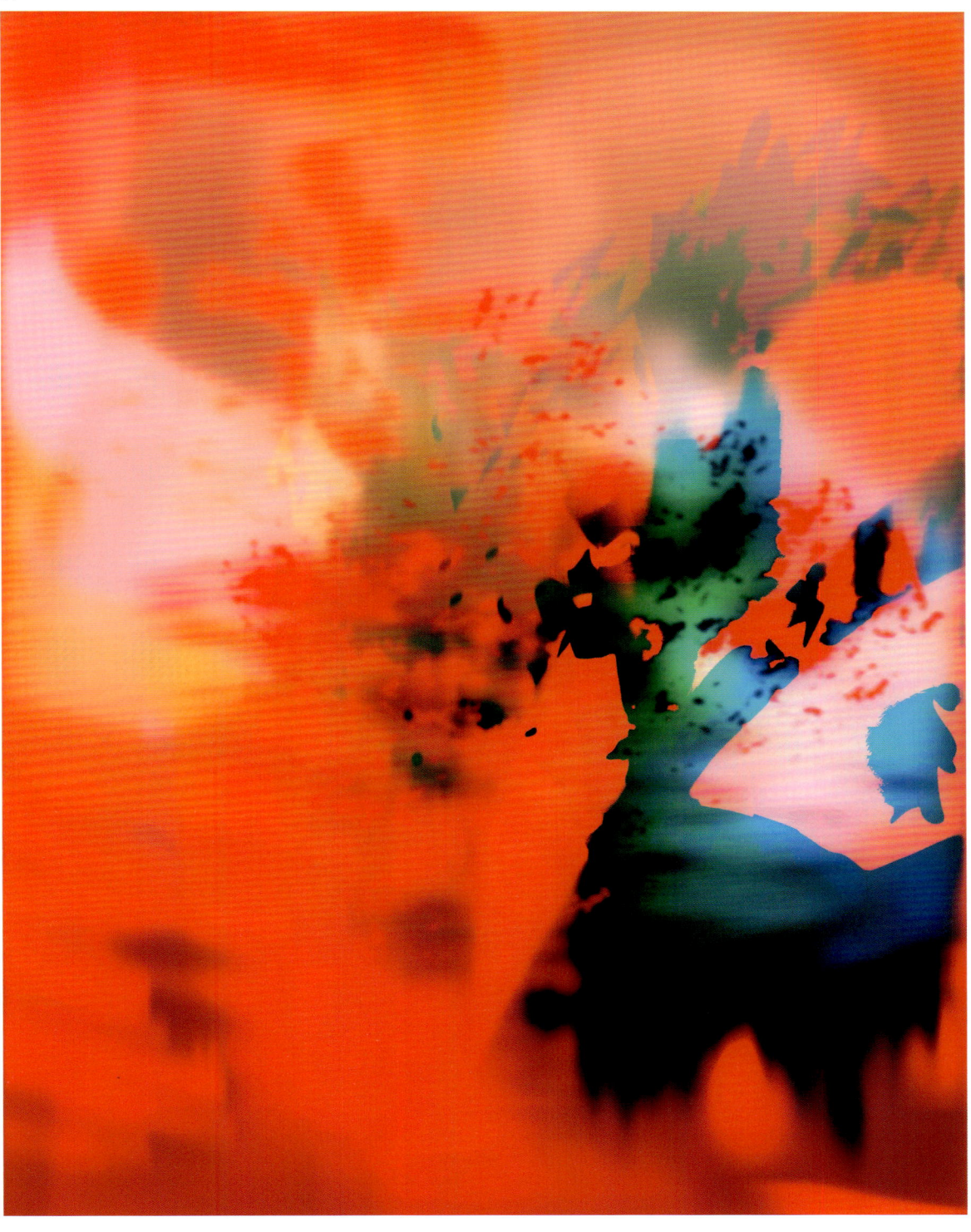

| # | TITLE | TIMESTAMP | MEDIUM | CHAIN | CONTRACT ADDRESS | TOKEN ID | EDITION SIZE |
|---|-------|-----------|--------|-------|------------------|----------|--------------|
| 04, 05 | **MVP (Most Valuable Painting)** | 11-28-2021 21:28:21 | svg.js, JavaScript, mysql, rsvg-convert, ffmpeg | ALGO | 3B7F22U7UHN6JPCMQZBENQB34F6KWH-4T2WBOAOWWRONKAAPRLTZH4VWHT4 | 446233430–733286260 | 1/1 of 512 |

EDITIONS ILLUSTRATED: (04) #478 Slight Mistake, (05) #504 Drowsy Month

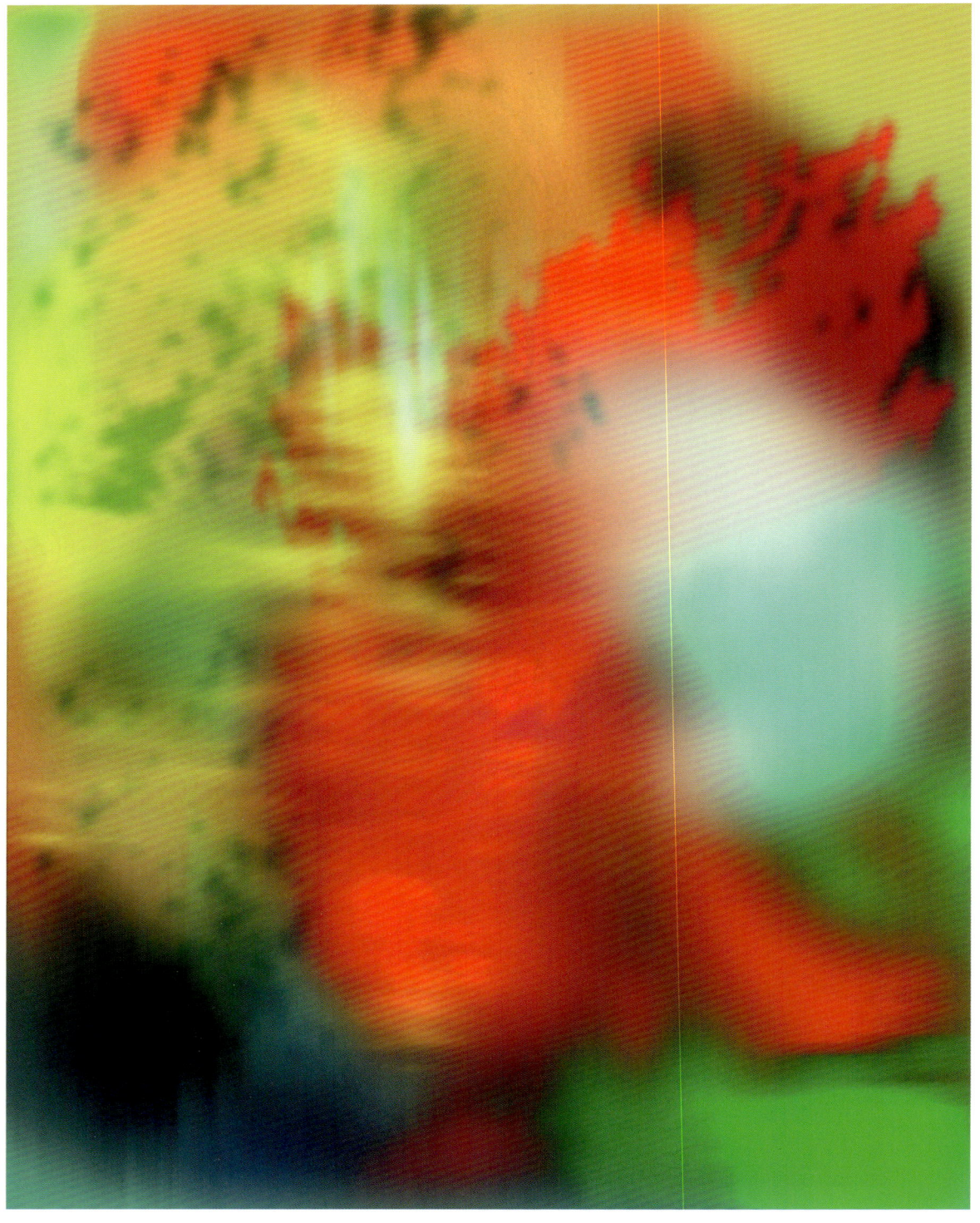

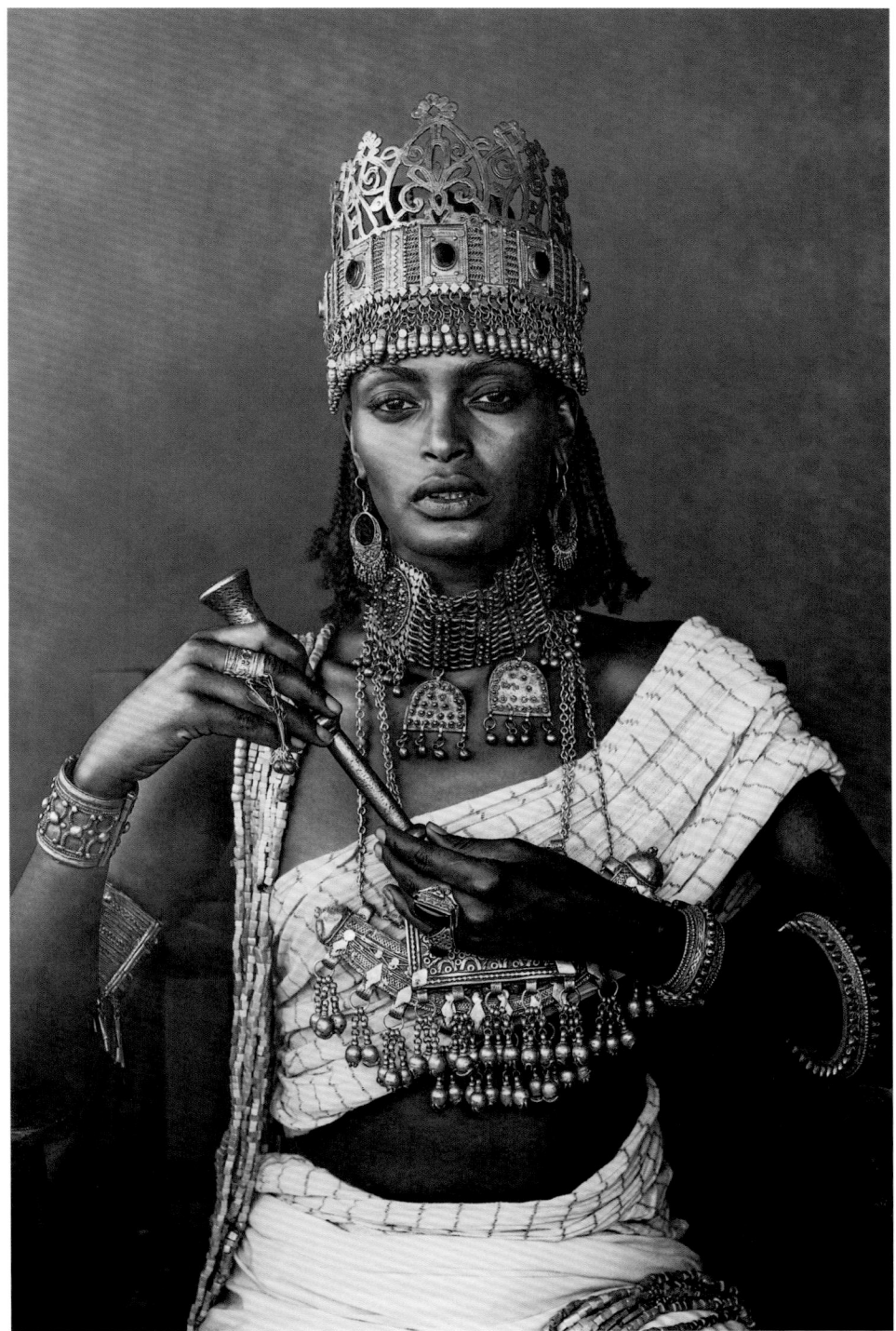

| # | TITLE | TIMESTAMP | MEDIUM | CHAIN | CONTRACT ADDRESS | TOKEN ID | EDITION SIZE |
|---|-------|-----------|--------|-------|------------------|----------|--------------|
| 01 | **Queen of Sheba** | 04-29-2021 19:37:17 | Motion portrait, digital video | ETH | 0x3b3ee1931dc30c1957379fac9aba94d1c48a5405 | 31396 | 1/1 |
| 02 | **Royal Armada of Aethiopia** | 08-29-2021 23:49:41 | Motion portrait, digital video | ETH | 0x5d29a2479cbc4128ff9118d46c10d4559029a635 | 1 | 1/1 |

02 ►

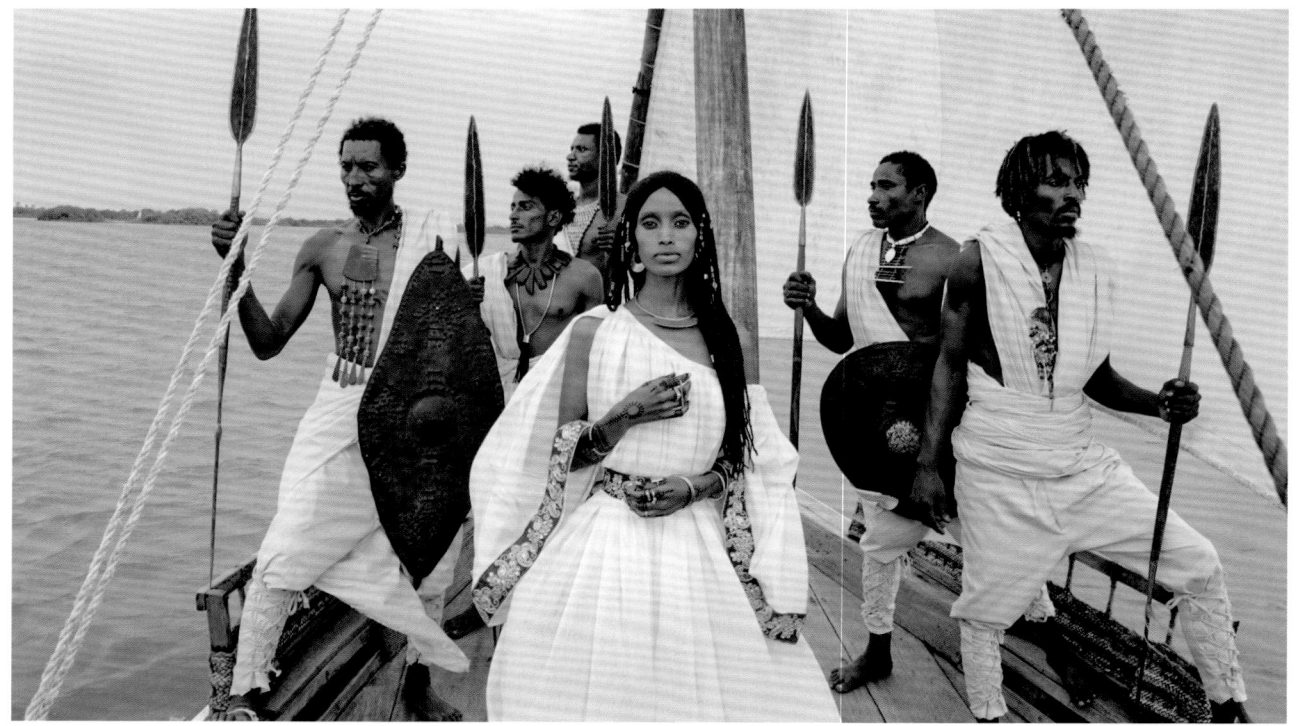

Vitalik Buterin's *Time* magazine interview quote criticizing million-dollar monkey cartoons being minted on the blockchain he co-founded is often used to disparage NFTs. Lesser known is Vitalik's next quote, in which he cites his respect directly for Yatreda, an Ethiopian art collective, as a viable use of NFT artwork minted on blockchain technology.

In this nascent NFT world crowded with empty art and outright scams, Yatreda stands out like a beacon of hope for those early, bright-eyed Ethereum developers who sought to change the world. Yatreda, which began in their humble front yard in Addis Ababa, has become one of the most powerful and pure expressions of digital fine art in our space.

Ethiopia, the only African nation to militarily resist and defeat European colonial penetration, has always stood out with its regality and pride. It is notable that Yatreda echoes this sovereign and proud vision, relying on no crutches of victimhood. Working in the Ethiopian style of tizita (an Amharic word which describes the feeling of romantic nostalgia), African legends, folk dances, and endangered cultural styles are preserved for eternity on the blockchain.

Solomon, a historic figure whose values and philosophies are still heralded and woven into the world's elite institutions, was once so enamored by the gifts and wisdom of a beautiful Ethiopic queen that for a transient moment in time, he married her and fathered a son: Menelik. In Yatreda's Queen of Sheba (2021), Kiya Tadele adorns the legend of Solomon's lesser-known wife and takes a haunting single breath a printed page cannot show. This exhale is spent energy to hold what may be a blip to a rewritten history, but with a mastery of light and the greatest values of this new technology, Yatreda breathes life into the legends waiting for this moment to be preserved.

**SAM SPRATT**
ARTIST

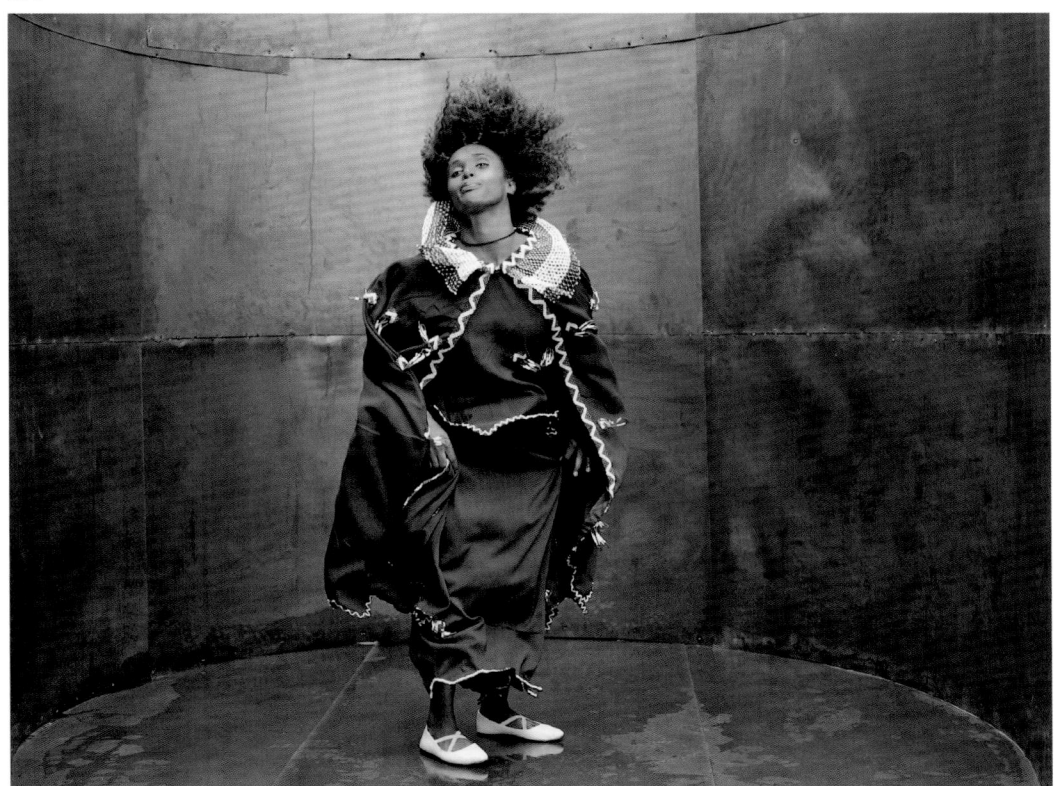

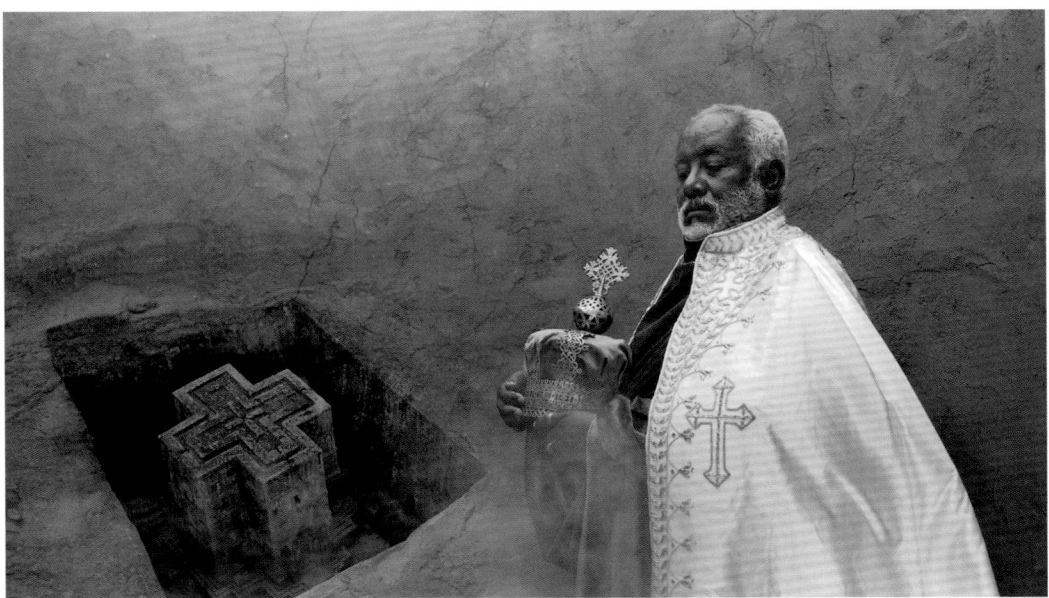

| # | TITLE | TIMESTAMP | MEDIUM | CHAIN | CONTRACT ADDRESS | TOKEN ID | EDITION SIZE |
|---|---|---|---|---|---|---|---|
| 03 | **Arsi Oromo, Devotion: Movement of the Ancestors** | 08-10-2021 19:05:40 | Motion portrait, digital video | ETH | 0x3b3ee1931dc30c1957379fac9aba94d1c48a5405 | 70731 | 1/1 |
| 04 | **King Lalibela – Rock-hewn: Kingdoms of Ethiopia** | 10-06-2021 15:01:19 | Motion portrait, digital video | ETH | 0x814a056f1607c7f43285a1a1de43755ed3b26ee7 | 11 | 1/1 |
| 05 | **Medusa: Andromeda of Aethiopia** | 11-18-2022 01:43:47 | Motion portrait, digital video | ETH | 0xa4c9ad751a9bf80b341e8d5186e88afd8552e912 | 1 | 1/1 |
| 06 | **Amhara, Lion's Roar: Movement of the Ancestors** | 08-10-2021 18:52:30 | Motion portrait, digital video | ETH | 0x3b3ee1931dc30c1957379fac9aba94d1c48a5405 | 70729 | 1/1 |

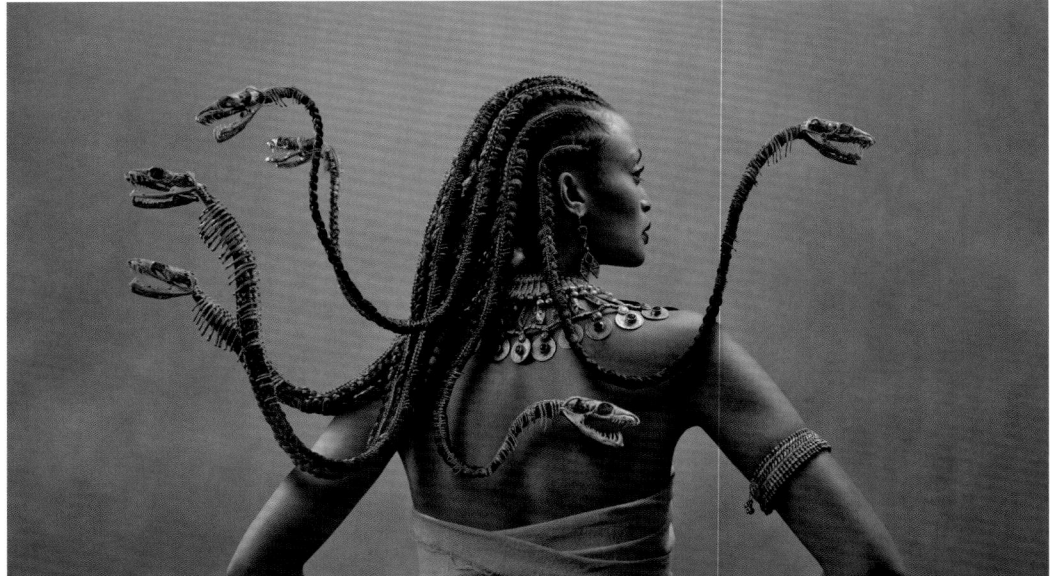

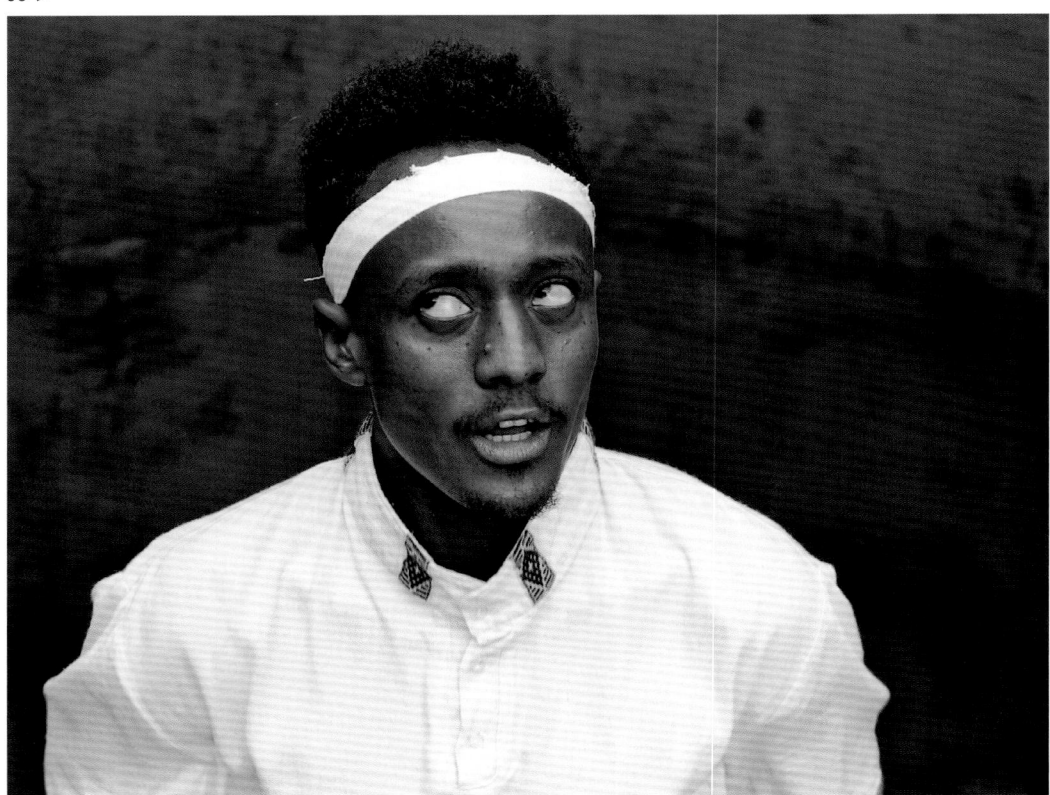

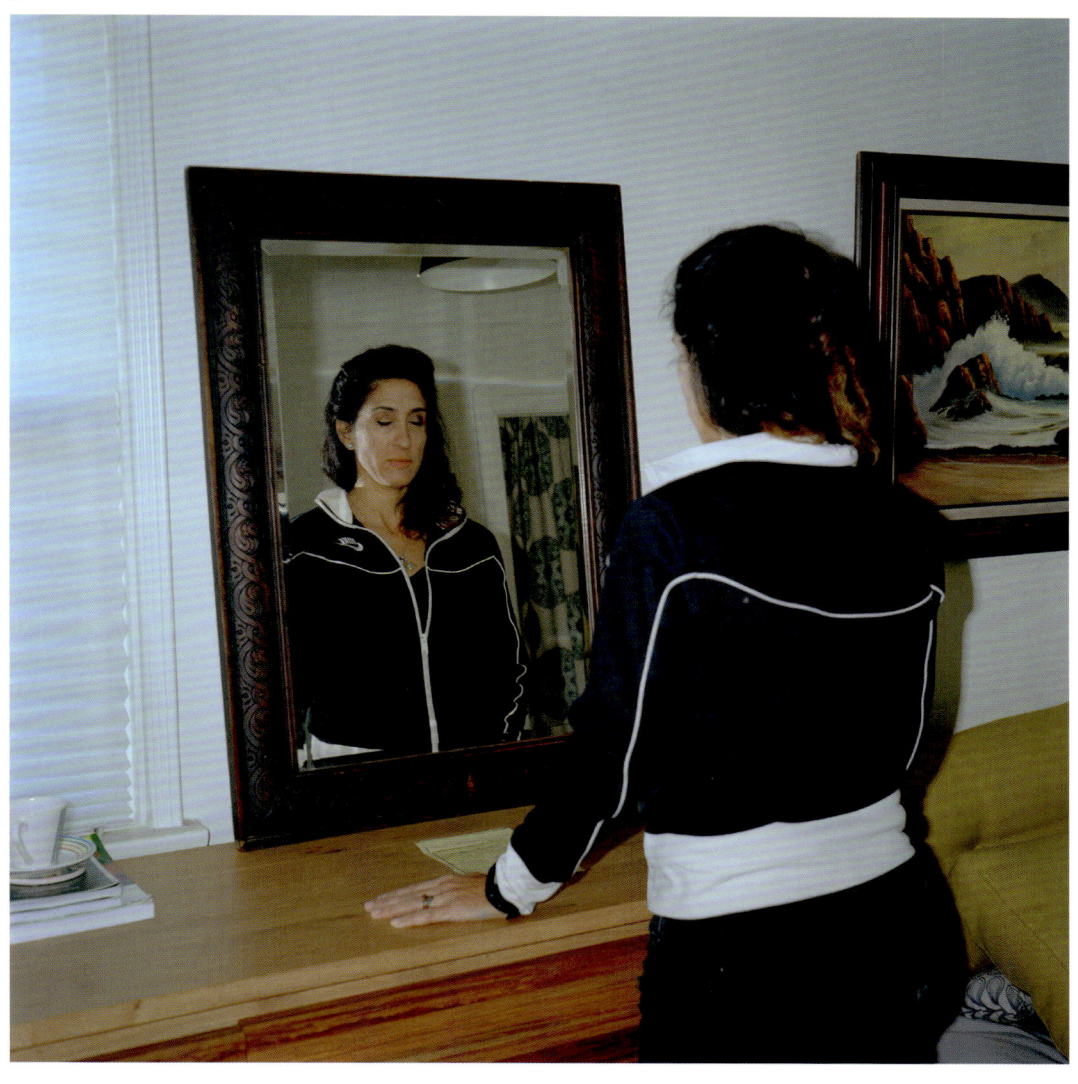

| # | TITLE | TIMESTAMP | MEDIUM | CHAIN | CONTRACT ADDRESS | TOKEN ID | EDITION SIZE |
|---|---|---|---|---|---|---|---|
| 01, 02 | **Twin Flames** | 02-05-2021 18:50:00 | Photograph | ETH | 0x495f947276749Ce646f68AC8c248420045cb7b5e | 0–5500...2033 | 1/1 of 100 |

EDITIONS ILLUSTRATED: (01) #49 – Alyson & Courtney Aliano (minted on 0x3c28de567d1412b06f43b15e9f75129625fa6e8c), (02) #83 – Bahareh & Farzaneh Safarani

# JUSTIN AVERSANO

UNITED STATES 1992

02

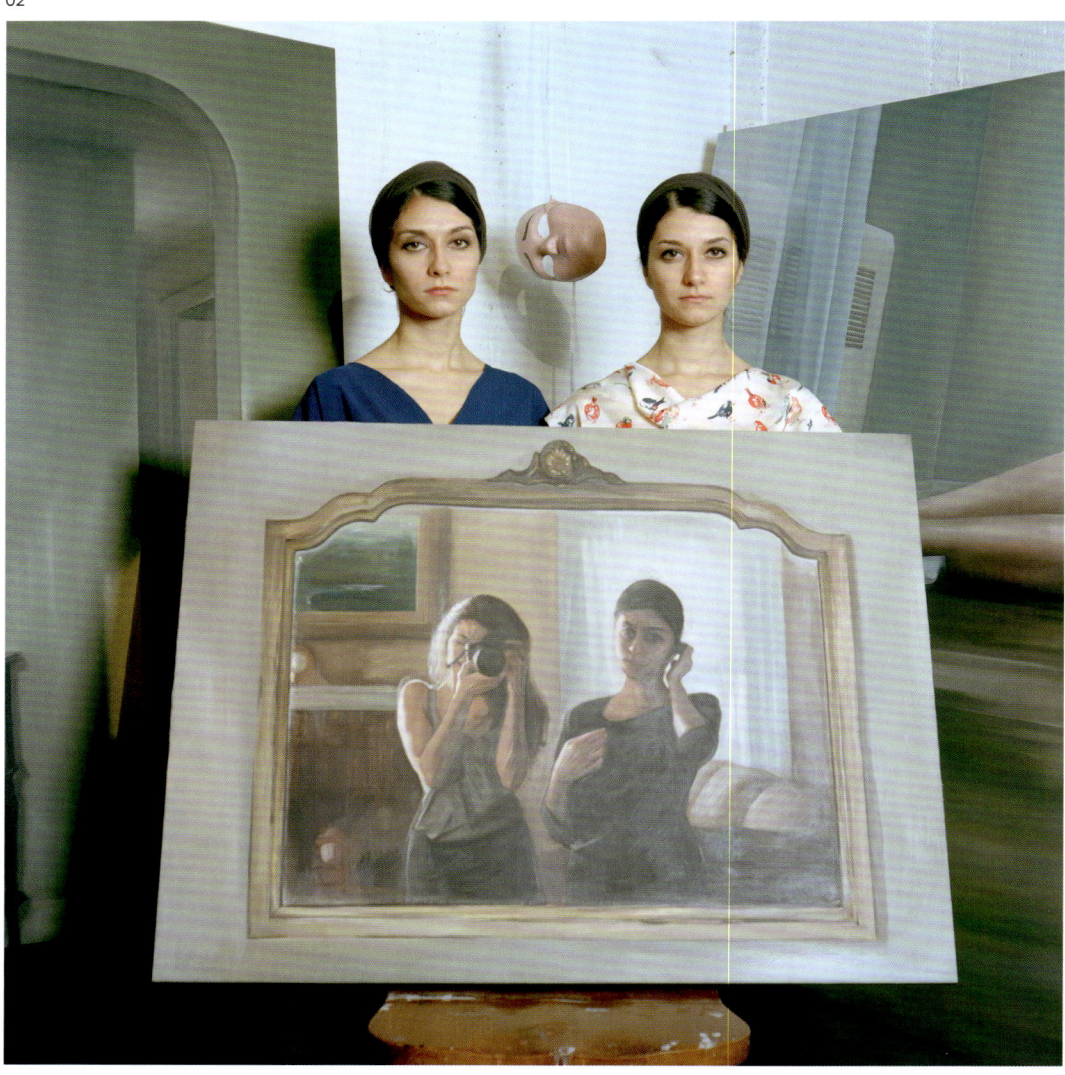

When I first met Justin Aversano in May 2019, neither he nor I had any idea what an NFT was. Few did. We knew photography, however. Justin had just opened his *Twin Flames* (2017–18) exhibition at Superchief Gallery, New York, which showcased, in gothic candelabra fashion, his now legendary art photography series of the same name. Justin and I also knew loss; specifically the loss of a twin.

For *Twin Flames*, Aversano, a School of Visual Arts (BFA) graduate in photography, traveled to multiple continents over the course of two years (2017–18) to photograph over one hundred sets of twins, leaving him with a hundred unique images. In 2014, before embarking on the series, Aversano lost his mother to a long battle with ovarian cancer. Before she passed, she confirmed that Justin had lost his fraternal twin sister, Alessia, in utero. Justin was left mostly in the dark regarding this loss, then burdened with it,

just as he was forced to begin grieving the passing of his mother. *Twin Flames* was the cosmic ceremony Justin devised to address his compounded sense of grief, guilt, love, life, and loss.

Like Andy Warhol's (1928–1987) *Soup Cans* (1962), which were never sold piecemeal, Justin and I understood there was something special about the full collection of 100 chromogenic *Twin Flames* prints, each 41 × 50.8 centimeters. On Valentine's Day of 2021, after two years of attempting to sell the full analog collection, as the world reckoned with a pandemic and social unrest, Justin minted and sold the full series on OpenSea, making it the first significant, complete art photography set sold in Web3.

**KURT MCVEY**
GUEST WRITER AT *THE NEW YORK TIMES*,
*INTERVIEW* MAGAZINE, AND *ARTNET NEWS*

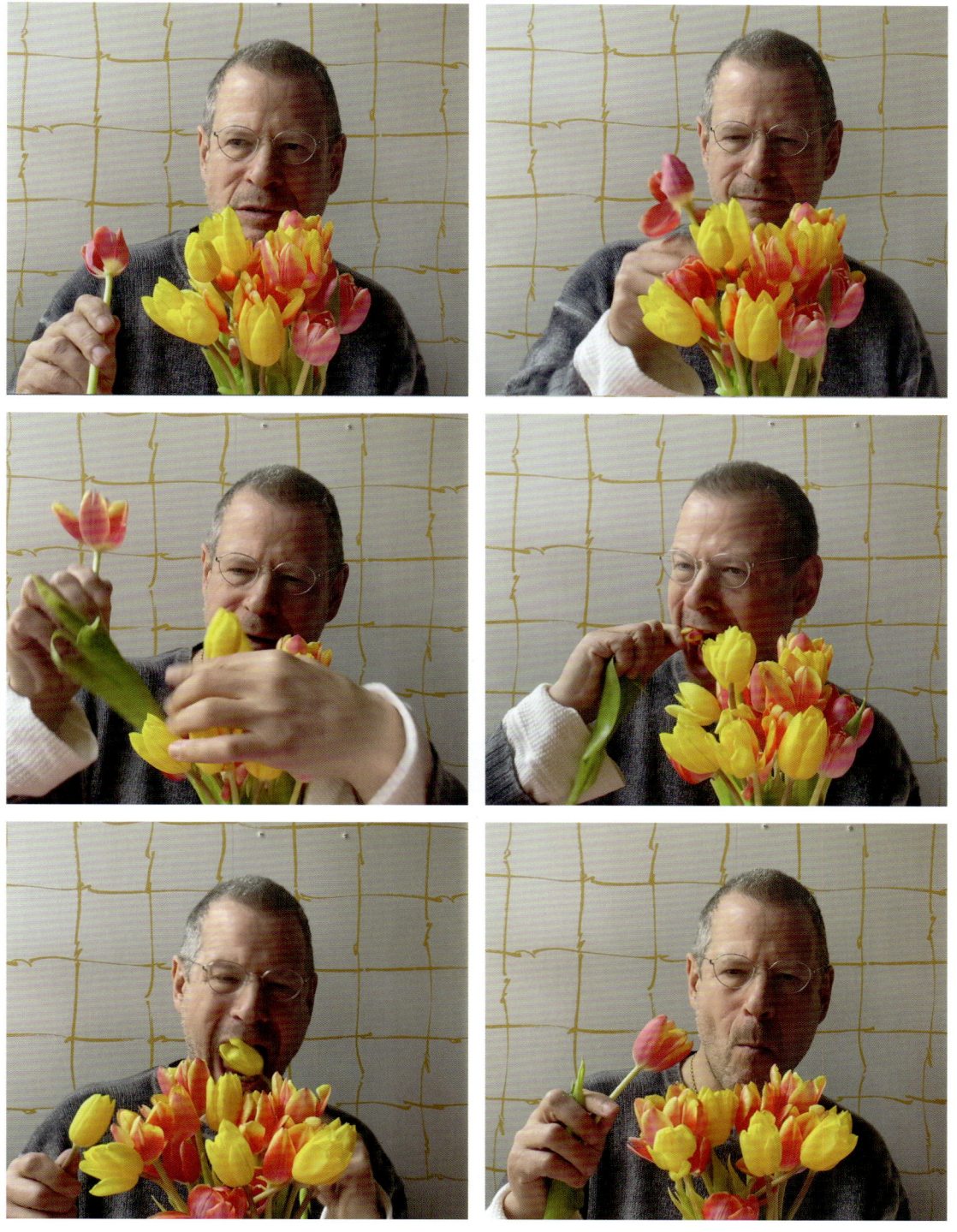

| # | TITLE | TIMESTAMP | MEDIUM | CHAIN | CONTRACT ADDRESS | TOKEN ID | EDITION SIZE |
|---|---|---|---|---|---|---|---|
| 01 | **Eating the bubble** | 05-17-2021 18:41:14 | JPEG, MP4 | ETH | 0xaaddaecf44ac69c8a9aa991eecb20eb325e6b3d8 | 50600010001–50600010050 | 50 |
| 02 | **Branding (Homage to Prince)** | 04-24-2022 13:19:15 | MP4 | ETH | 0x7110b77fd68d2949aa7aaf21666b9d4bb423add5 | 2 | 1/1 |
| 03 | **i tokenized my grandma blanche** | 03-07-2021 01:43:00 | JPEG | ETH | 0x495f947276749ce646f68ac8c248420045cb7b5e | 2127...9073 | 1/1 |

# KENNY SCHACHTER

UNITED STATES 1961

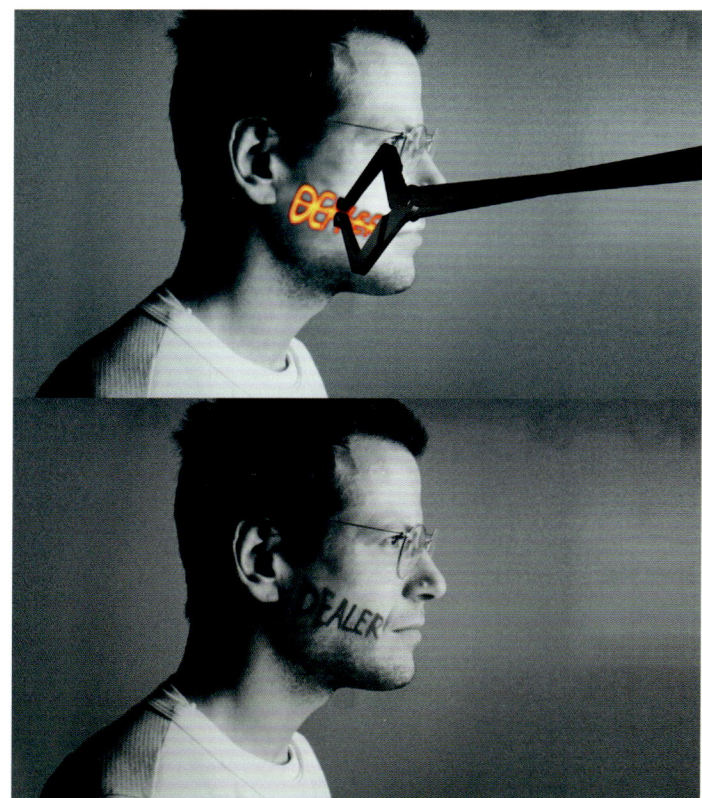

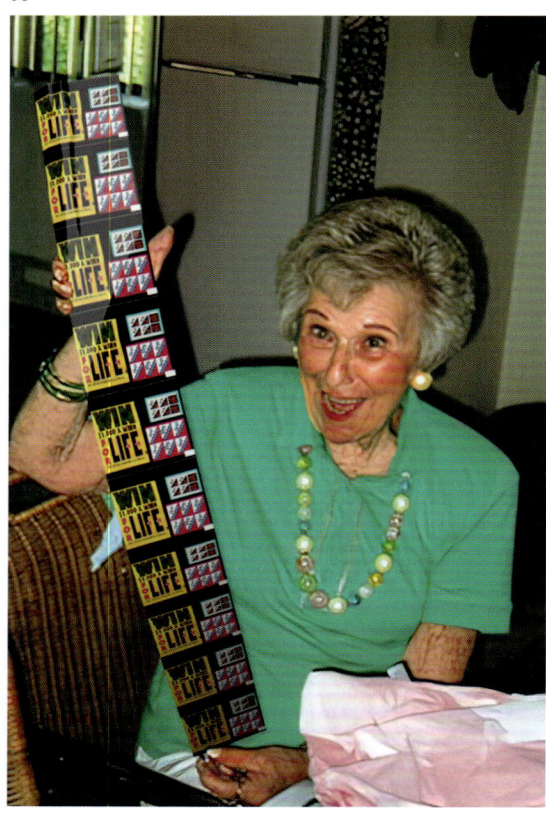

I have been making art, writing, teaching, curating, and dealing since the late 1980s. Having studied philosophy, politics, and law, I'm self-taught in the art arena, chronicling the dissemination of art once it leaves the studio and enters the stream of commerce. I've written on the machinations of the exclusionary traditional art world for *Artnet*, *The Art Newspaper*, *New York Magazine*, and *The Times*, but also first-handedly experienced the capricious practices that seem hell-bent on erecting barriers to entry to all but the chosen few — the only word the art world appears to know is no.

In the face of endless obstacles to getting my art exhibited, I embedded artworks into my writings overcoming the resistance to gaining a foothold into the system. Being seen and heard was one thing, but I had abandoned hope of the elusive thing I am most passionate about — making a living from my own art. That was until the advent of NFTs.

Since I became aware of the phenomenon in 2020, I've widely lectured on the subject (from Harvard University to the University of Zurich), taught an NFT class at New York University, guested on dozens of podcasts including *Talk Art* and *Time Sensitive*; and participated in numerous NFT related documentaries. Just shy of 60, I was empowered by minting my own artworks on sites such as Nifty Gateway, SuperRare, KnownOrigin, and Foundation, among others. NFTs have upended the historical art market dynamic and are undoubtedly here to stay — see my video *Eating the Bubble* (2021) where I devoured a dozen tulips illustrating the fact that even after the economic hype abated for the tulip craze in the 17th century, our love for the flower still persists.

NFTs have enabled artists to take the reins and have a direct impact in marketing their own works.

**KENNY SCHACHTER**
ARTIST, CURATOR, TEACHER,
WRITER, AND CRITIC AT *ARTNET*

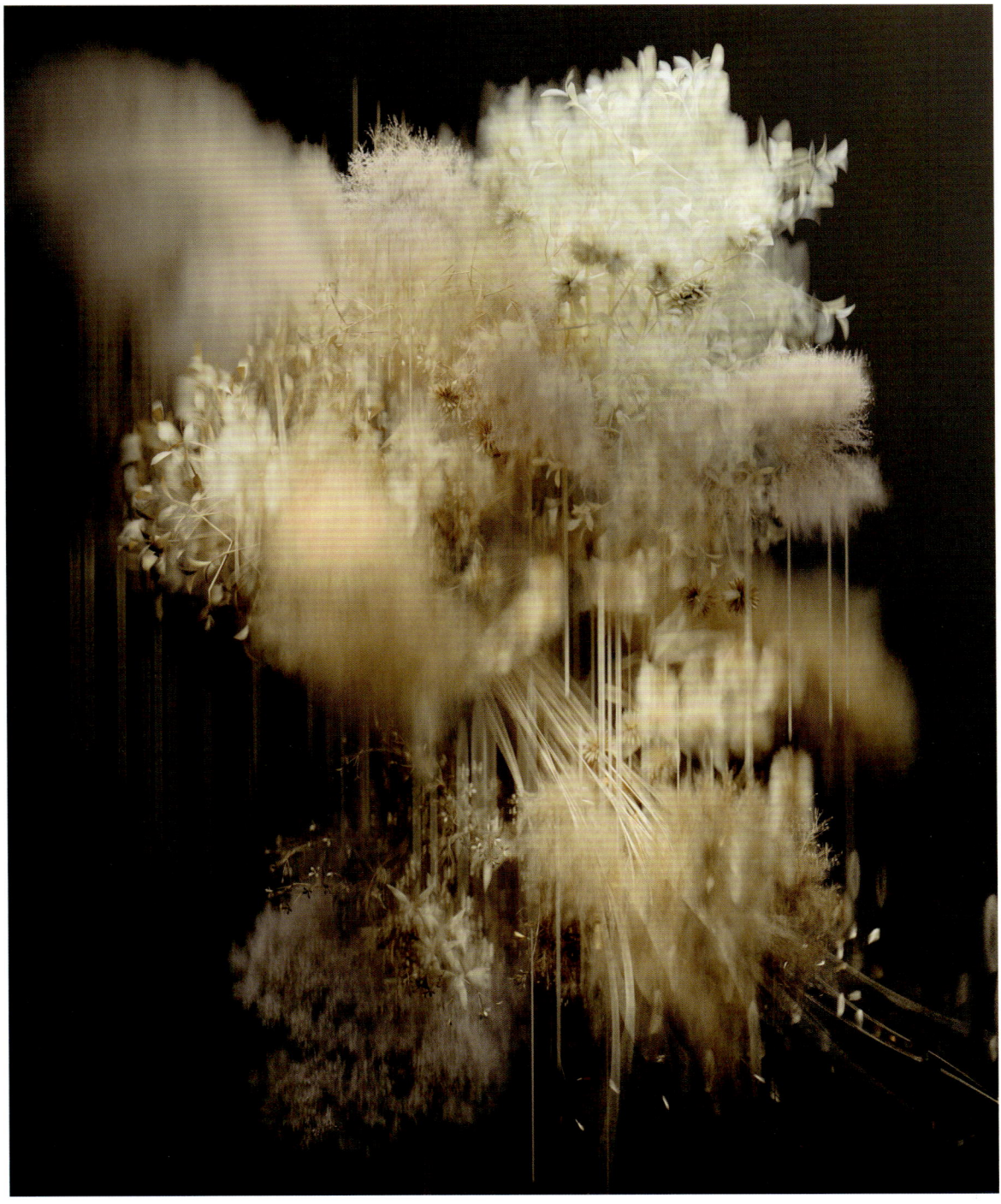

| # | TITLE | TIMESTAMP | MEDIUM | CHAIN | CONTRACT ADDRESS | TOKEN ID | EDITION SIZE |
|---|---|---|---|---|---|---|---|
| 01 | **Gold Pollen** | 02-25-2022 23:32:33 | Custom made 3D digital software | ETH | 0xe0cb74ce662778ea72bb2dbd4775043e-5aedb582 | 81000200001–81000200007 | 7 |
| 02 | **Hortensia Chair** | 11-27-2020 20:43:19 | Custom made 3D digital software | ETH | 0xb932a70a57673d89f4acffbe830e8ed7f75fb9e0 | 16668 | 1/1 |

02

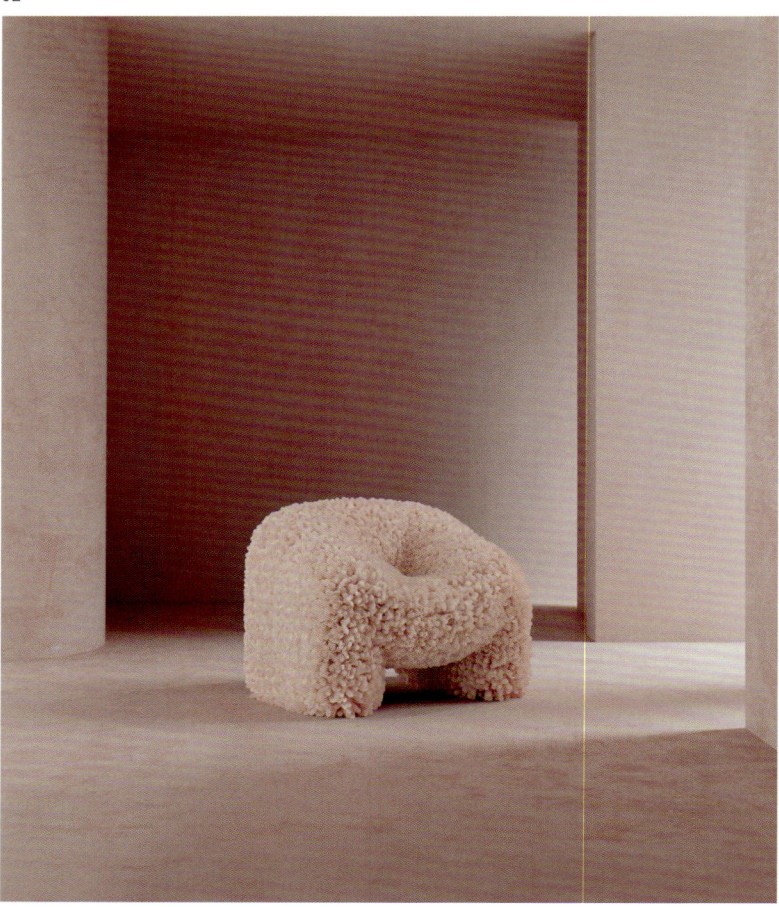

In February 2021 (ancient history in the digital world), Andrés Reisinger astonished onlookers with an online auction called *THE SHIPPING* — ten pieces of virtual furniture, each associated with an NFT. The sale was a great success and immediately became a talking point. The design community pronounced itself collectively baffled. How was it possible to sell an immaterial chair? Why would anyone want to buy one, and what exactly did they end up owning?

People learned quickly enough. Reisinger's sale was an early wave of what is now an ocean-sized NFT marketplace. It also pointed to other horizons, most importantly in his own creative practice. He has deftly navigated between the spheres of analog and virtual production, creating densely allusive objects and cinematic scenarios for them to occupy, all with artisanal care. Some works in his oeuvre have traversed a whole range of immaterial and physical incarnations.

The *Hortensia Chair* (2019), for example, was a viral hit online when Reisinger first posted it in July 2018. Though it was explicitly intended to be impossible — it was after all made of hydrangea petals — he immediately began receiving orders for "real" chairs, which he could of course not fulfill. Every aspect of Reisinger's career has destabilized expectations about what is real and what is not; though, it is more helpful to think about different registers of reality, and the interrelations between them. And so *Hortensia Chair* went on an unlikely journey, first being made in a limited run of prototypes (in partnership with Julia Esqué) and then serially by furniture company MOOOI. In early 2022, Reisinger released his *Pollen* series, allowing collectors of *Hortensia Chair* to "pollinate" their NFT, creating season specific editions and one-of-ones of the work.

That's just one example of how Reisinger is deploying design to demonstrate that the virtual can be a limitless space of operation. It's an inviting world, and so easy to enter: all we have to do is believe.

**GLENN ADAMSON**
CURATOR AT THE CHIPSTONE FOUNDATION AND AUTHOR;
PREVIOUSLY DIRECTOR OF
THE MUSEUM OF ARTS AND DESIGN, NEW YORK;
HEAD OF RESEARCH AT
THE VICTORIA & ALBERT MUSEUM, LONDON

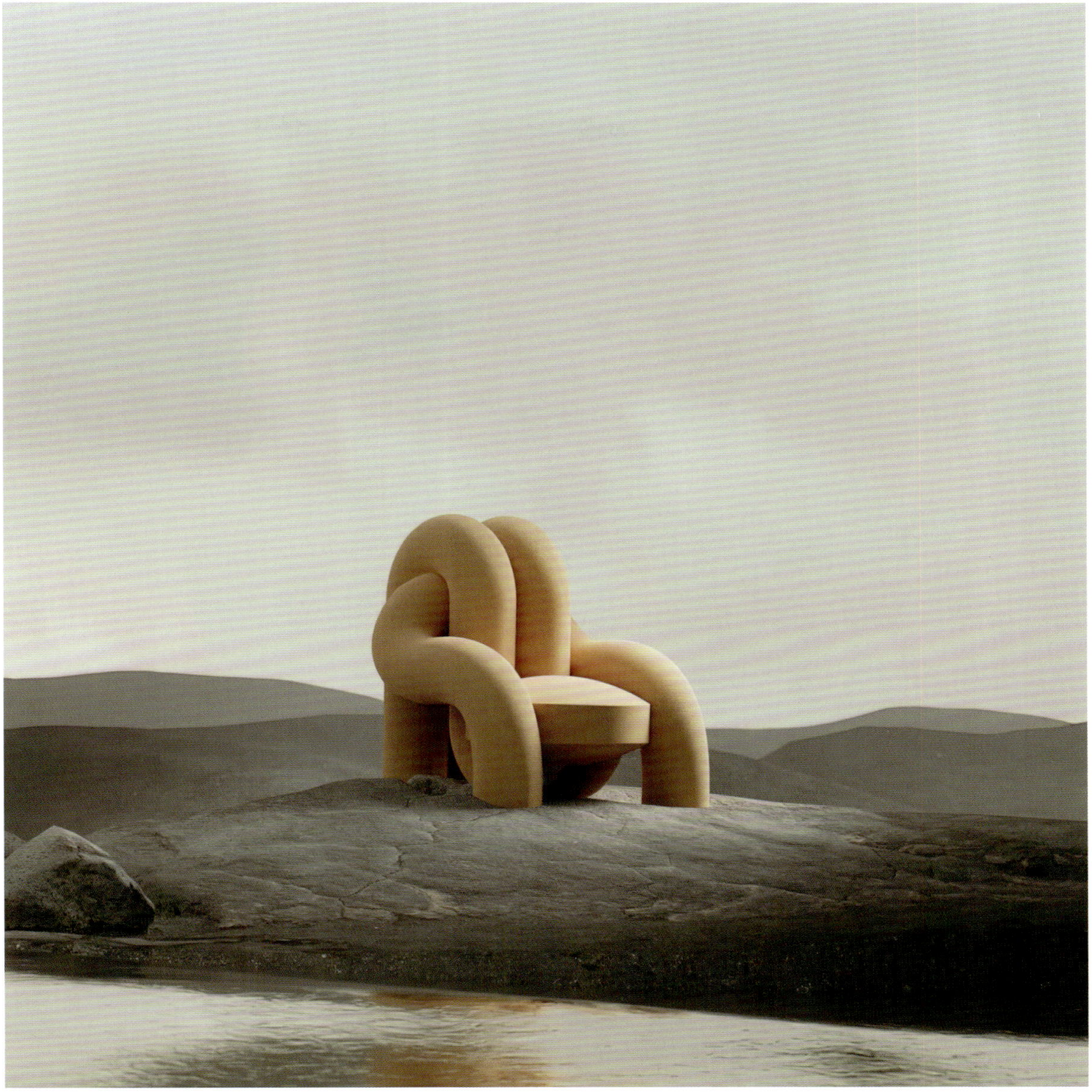

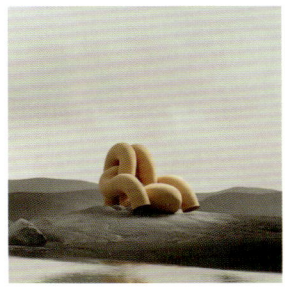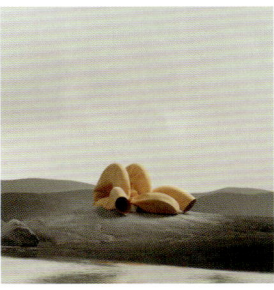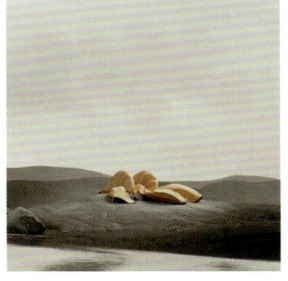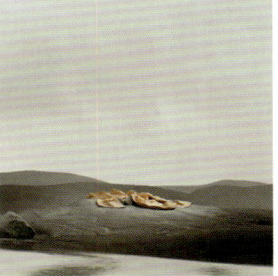

| # | TITLE | TIMESTAMP | MEDIUM | CHAIN | CONTRACT ADDRESS | TOKEN ID | EDITION SIZE |
|---|-------|-----------|--------|-------|------------------|----------|--------------|
| 03 | **Tangled** | 02-18-2021 06:09:11 | Custom made 3D digital software | ETH | 0x9f8371fe1fda39d76684be54fd4605f4932d6755 | 25900050001 | 1/1 |
| 04 | **Complicated Sofa** | 02-18-2021 06:14:14 | Custom made 3D digital software | ETH | 0x9f8371fe1fda39d76684be54fd4605f4932d6755 | 25900060001–25900060003 | 3 |

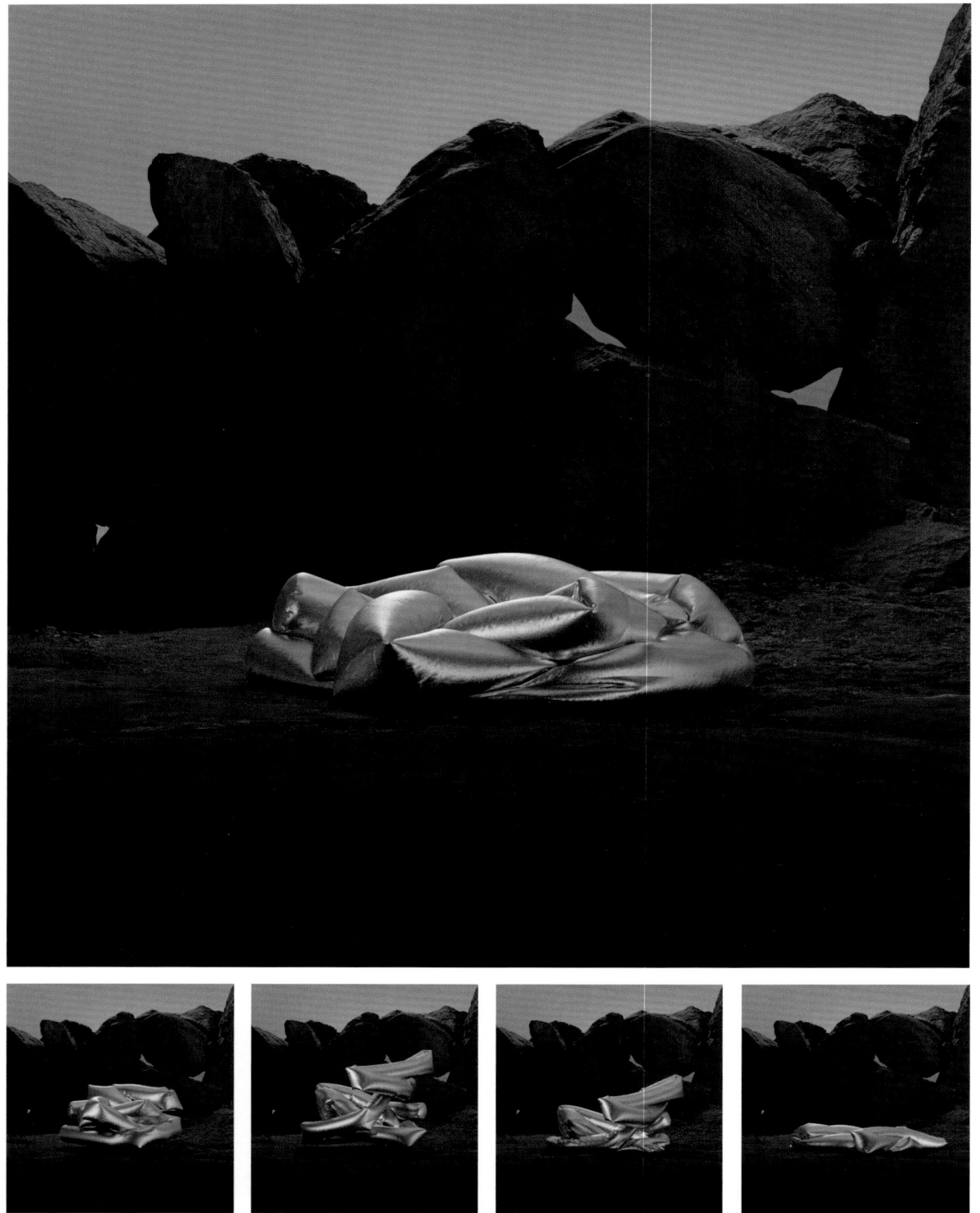

MICHAEL BOUHANNA
JEHAN CHU

# ON COLLECTING
## From the Wunderkammer to the Wallet

*Marly stared. Box of plain wood, glass-fronted. Objects …*
*"Cornell," she said, her tears forgotten. "Cornell?" She turned to Virek.*
*"Of course not. The object set into that length of bone is a Braun biomonitor.*
*This is the work of a living artist."*
*"There are more? More boxes?"*
*"I have found seven. Over a period of three years. The Virek Collection,*
*you see, is a sort of black hole."*

William Gibson
*Count Zero*, 1986

In this essay, Michael Bouhanna begins with an intertwining of the histories of collecting and the history of the disruption of finance, while also exploring the idea of the wunderkammer as a historical antecedent to the NFT wallet. This is followed by Jehan Chu's examination of the collecting landscape in digital art and NFTs from the 1960s to today, through discussions with key collectors and data analysis.

**08.00**
Simon de la Rouviere
*This Artwork Is Always on Sale*, 03-21-2019 21:14:06
Solidity, GIMP, Adobe Photoshop
Ethereum, 0x2b4fa931adc5d6b58674230208787a3df0bd2121, 42

The disruption of traditional collecting practices brought about by NFTs has been widely noted. A practice that has long-prized privacy, subtlety, and information asymmetry is now being played out in the hyper-transparent contexts of the blockchain. The private has turned public and then private again, as the transparency the blockchain affords the public is balanced with the anonymity the same technology affords the collector (if they so wish). Liquidity, automation, rapid financialization, copy trading, and the attention algorithms of Twitter have upended a culture that prized the slow forming of consensus through long-standing often dynastic commercial galleries and wider institutional networks. Collectors not only operate differently, with a different set of tools, but they are a markedly different group of individuals. They have different priorities, different aesthetic and intellectual reference points, and different values, raised largely through philosophies of crypto, the literature of science fiction, and the aesthetics of gaming. And yet through all these differences, the act of collecting at its core has largely remained the same, indeed, if anything it has resurrected older models of collecting that stretch back to the Renaissance. Within the context of this new decentralized class of collectors, this essay will illustrate a strong historical relationship between the history of collecting and the history of disruption in finance — of which crypto is just the latest incarnation. The collecting practices and specifically the motivations of historically disruptive banking families and entrepreneurs will also be shown to resonate with those of the current rising class of decentralized buyers. Later, the NFT wallet will be compared with the 16th-century concept of the *wunderkammer*, provoking new ways of considering the NFT collection, its horizontality, and its specificities. From here, NFT collecting will be placed within the histories of digital art collecting back through the 1960s before embarking on a data-driven approach to understanding the trends, issues, and benefits of NFT collecting today and into the future.

## A History of Collecting and the Disruption of Finance

Though many art collectors today are used to the long established ecosystem of galleries providing access to sought after artists, this structure is relatively recent. Throughout the Middle Ages, the predominant patron of the arts was the Catholic Church, which commissioned artists to reinforce its divinity and inspire the awe and support of its congregation. The emergence of a new powerful class of merchants and banking families in Northern Italy around the time of the Renaissance led to a partial decentralization of this system. This was eventually accelerated by the Reformation and the growing secularization of art. Early examples of this change include Enrico Scrovegni (d. 1336), a moneylender from Padua and famous patron of Giotto (ca. 1267–1337) who he commissioned to paint magnificent frescoes in the Scrovegni Chapel in around 1300. Scrovegni's motives were typical of the time. His father, Reginaldo, is described as trapped in hell in Dante's *Inferno* for committing the crime of usury. A public demonstration of Enrico Scrovegni's piety, he appears himself in the *Life of the Virgin* (1303–1305) over the entrance door presenting a model of the chapel to the Virgin [08.01]. This very literal representation shows how the commission was a gift intended to buy Scrovegni out of the same fate as his father.[1] The lavishly decorated chapel also furthered Scrovegni's social ambitions, and in his lifetime, he built a palace and married into nobility.

The Medici, Strozzi, Sassetti, and Pazzi were among the major banking families that, after 1400, turned Florence into one of the richest cities in the world and a global center for cultural innovation. Much like Scrovegni, their religious patronage was planned with the afterlife in mind. However, they also extended their preoccupations towards secular scholarship and, inspired by ancient civilizations and in fierce competition with each other, financed a new age of art production that revived antiquity, making it the dominant aesthetic of their time. Through these activities, these wealthy patrons formed networks with the leading humanist intellectuals of their day.[2] These associations lent the families greater respectability, which was crucial for their involvement not just in business but in civic affairs — the source of much of their political power.[3]

The Medicis' incomparable wealth arose from their popularization of double-entry bookkeeping, a model that would spread to the Dutch Republic in around 1600 and, in the same century, to England. A major disruption of finance at the time, it was an essential tool for calculating profit and loss and became the basis of modern capitalism.[4] Nearly half a millennium later, it would be blockchain that would usher in a similiarly transformative way of accounting for value and popularize the idea of triple-entry accounting, in which the third entry system would stand for the immutability of the blockchain itself. Cosimo de' Medici (1389–1464) established the Medici family as effective rulers of Florence, a tactically tricky position considering that the state was a republic.[5] In public, therefore, he was wary of conspicuous consumption, but in private he would have been keen to impress both confidants

[1] Laura Jacobus, "Piety and propriety in the Arena Chapel," *Renaissance Studies*, Vol. 12, No. 2 (1998): 177–178.

[2] Bonnie A. Bennett, *Donatello* (New York: Phaidon Press, 1984), 78.

[3] Mark Jurdjevic, "Civic Humanism and the Rise of the Medici," *Renaissance Quarterly*, Vol. 52, No. 4 (Winter, 1999).

[4] Jacob Soll, *The Reckoning: Financial Accountability and the Rise and Fall of Nations* (New York: Basic Books, 2014), xiv.

[5] Robert Dalton Bryant, *The Medici and a Florentine Plutocracy in the Quattrocento* (United States: Georgia Southern University, 2020).

08.01

Detail of Enrico Scrovegni offering to Mary the chapel that he built
Giotto di Bondone, *Life of the Virgin*, 1303–05
Fresco
Scrovegni Chapel, Padua, Italy

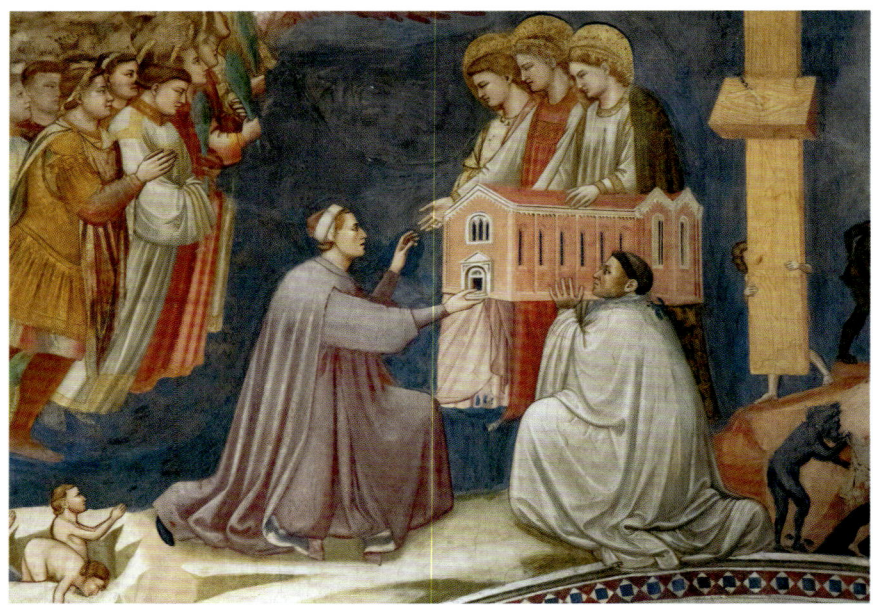

and rivals. In the 1440s, he likely commissioned Donatello (ca. 1386–1466) to produce an elegant small-scale bronze statue of David from the biblical tale of David and Goliath. Placed in the central courtyard of the Medici palace, it was a subtle allegory of the family's formidable strength. The first freestanding male nude since antiquity with an alluring realism — the writer and historian Giorgio Vasari (1511–1574) once described the work as "so natural in its liveliness and its softness that it seems impossible to artists that it was not crafted from life."[6] *David* broke with medieval sculptural tradition and is a landmark work of the Early Renaissance, forever reminding us of Cosimo's great erudition.[7] It is art, not finance, that affords historical immortality, and because of works like these the Medici name lives on, associated not so much with their disruptions of finance but their rich patronage of culture.

Founders of the first major international private bank, the five sons of Mayer Amschel Rothschild (1744–1812), who started out in banking by handling the finances of the Crown Prince Wilhelm of Hesse in Frankfurt in the 1760s, spread the family business to London, Paris, Vienna, and Naples.[8] Continuing to work in close cooperation, the Rothschilds' speciality and major disruptions were in creating large private lending markets to governments and in turn the seeding of European industrialization through efficient and apolitical private capital. History often rhymes, and one can see in the nascent world of DeFi, with its increasing liquidity and efficiencies, that cryptocurrencies bring similar hallmarks of financial disruption that the Rothschilds built their cultural foundation on nearly 300 years ago.

Each branch of the Rothschilds became notable collectors, and Ferdinand de Rothschild (1839–1898) is exemplary in his cultivation of the so-called "le goût Rothschild" — highly opulent interiors inspired by 18th-century France. Channeling the splendor and sophistication of the *ancien régime*, the look became a hallmark aesthetic of the American Gilded Age and was adopted by families like the Vanderbilts, Astors, and Rockefellers, speaking to the considerable power and respect commanded internationally by the Rothschilds.[9] The daughter of August Belmont, who represented the Rothschilds in the United States during the 1800s, married into the Vanderbilt family. Ferdinand filled his stately château-style house Waddesdon Manor with French furniture, gilt boxes, Dutch Golden Age paintings, Sèvres porcelain, and portraits like Gainsborough's *Pink Boy* (1782). He was lampooned by the press for his extravagant purchase of Marie-Antoinette's desk for £6,000, but Ferdinand never considered these kinds of cultural objects to be merely gratuitous decorations.[10] "Newly formed collections are generally more accessible," he once said.[11] "They contribute, not a little, to dignify their new residence; they attract more enlightened and intelligent portions of society, who, in their turn, attract the fashionable throng. Thus brilliant gatherings are formed [...] [which] may lead to the social and political development of a future age."[12] Ferdinand

[6] A. Victor Coonin, *Donatello and the Dawn of the Renaissance* (London: Reaktion Books, 2019).

[7] Joachim Poeschke, *Donatello and His World: Sculpture of the Italian Renaissance* (New York: Harry N. Abrams, 1993), 42.

[8] "Mayer Amschel Rothschild (1744–1812)," *The Rothschild Archive*, accessed June 22, 2022, https://family.rothschildarchive.org/people/21-mayer-amschel-rothschild-1744-1812.

[9] "Le Goût Rothschild," *The Rothschild Archive*, accessed June 22, 2022, https://www.rothschildarchive.org/family/family_collections/le_gout_rothschild.

[10] Pippa Shirley, "The Rothschilds as Collectors," March 1, 2013, Money for the Most Exquisite Things: Bankers and Collecting from the Medici to the Rockefellers Symposium at Frick Collection's Art Reference Library, video recording.

[11] Ellie Miles, "Redisplaying the Waddesdon Bequest," Lecture, British Museum, June 11, 2015.

[12] Ibid.

Domenico Remps
*Cabinet of Curiosities*, 1690
Oil on canvas, 99 × 137 cm
Opificio delle Pietre Dure, Florence, Italy

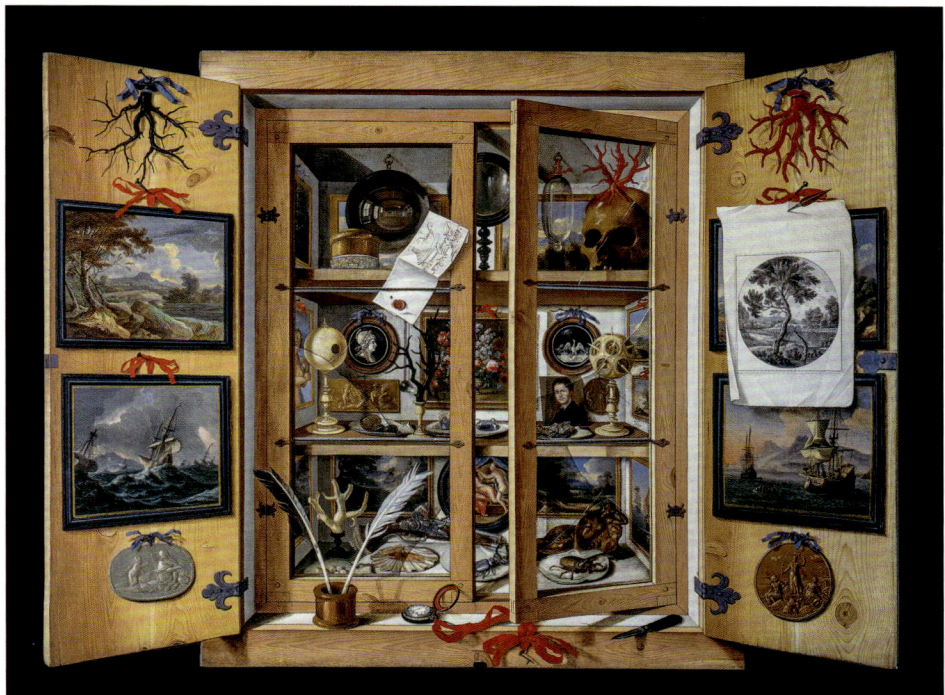

had a strong sense of art's soft power and social influences, and each object he bought was a conversation piece around which social, political, and reputational engagement was to be conducted.

## The NFT Wallet as Wunderkammer

Perhaps the best historical precedent for NFT collecting can be seen in the *wunderkammer*, or cabinet of curiosities, which emerged in the 16th century and would contain strange or exotic artifacts such as specimens, fossils, maps, relics, antiquities, and fanciful objects or "oddities," alongside contemporary painting, sculpture, and publications of the time.[13] Much like with NFTs, many of these objects were related to emerging disciplines and technologies like archaeology, natural history, biology, geography, and astrology, with their collectors bringing objects back from foreign lands and new territories only just starting to be explored. Together, they heralded the dawn of a newly enlightened age of science and technology.

One *wunderkammer* of particular world renown, created by the Holy Roman Emperor Rudolf II (1552–1612), attempted to capture the entire knowledge of its day. This collection of automatons, clocks, and scientific instruments was the basis for the Kunsthistorisches Museum in Vienna.[14] A trompe l'oeil depiction of a *wunderkammer* **[08.02]** produced in around 1690 by Domenico Remps (1620–ca. 1699) captures the depth of the cabinet of curiosities as a three-dimensional enclosed space that, encased in glass, anyone is able to peer into. The idea is echoed in the inherent transparency of the NFT collection, encased within a wallet, for anyone to see online. The cabinet contains globes, artworks, insect specimens, coral, a skull, vials, notes, and other objects waiting to be picked up and turned over. We can clearly see the effect of placing these assorted items in conversation with each other but with no particular order, freeing the viewer to bring their own subjective interpretation.

While the 16th-century European collector was collecting during the Age of Exploration — a period of new contact with Asia, Africa, and the Americas, today the NFT collector finds themself surrounded by new unexplored digital territories of the blockchain and metaverse. The *wunderkammer*, like the NFT wallet or collection, was nonhierarchical in its focus, allowing for a broader, more populist definition of cultural objects, unlike 20th-century collecting practices, paintings were placed indiscriminately next to objects of

[13] "Cabinet of Curiosities," British Library, accessed June 22, 2022, https://www.bl.uk/learning/timeline/item107648.html.
[14] "Kunstkammer Wien: The Cradle of the Museum," Kunsthistorisches Museum Wien, accessed June 20, 2022, https://www.khm.at/en/visit/collections/kunstkammer-wien.

08.03
Joseph Cornell
*Les Constellations Voisines du Pôle*, ca. 1950s
Mixed media and assemblage, 45.7 × 30.5 × 12.7 cm
Newark Museum, New Jersey, United States

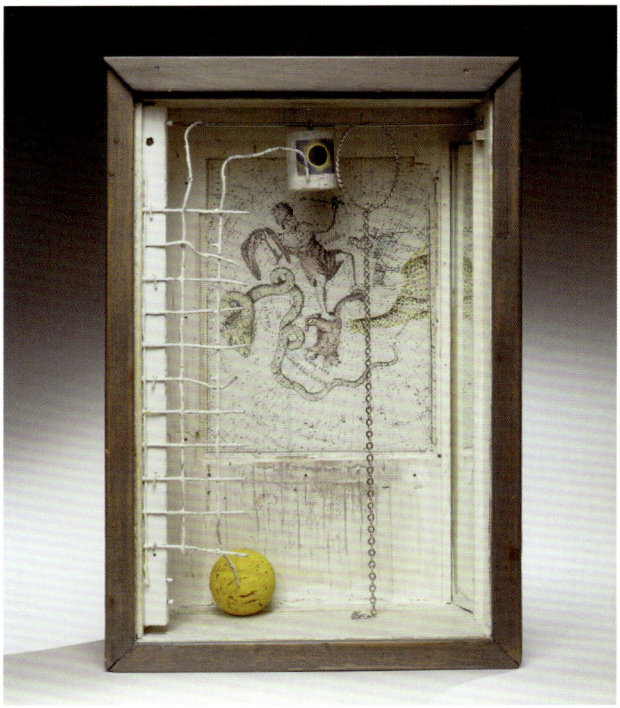
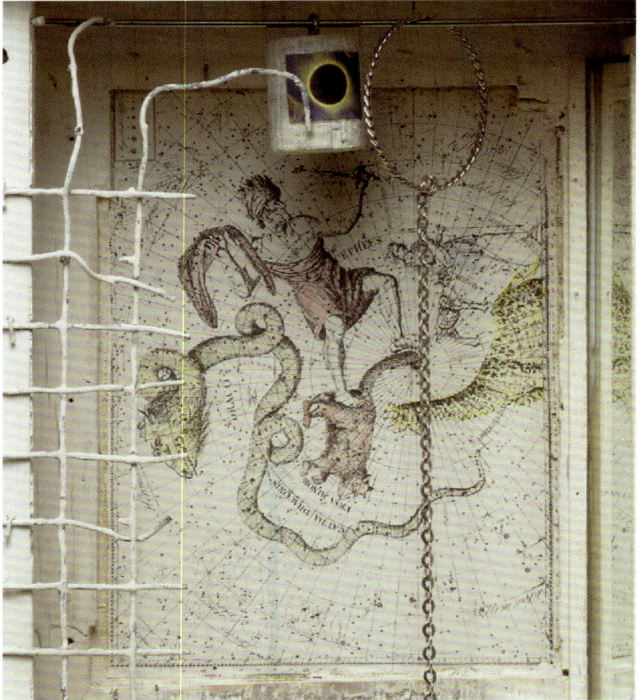

natural history or scientific tools. A great many categories of objects can now be acquired as NFTs and held indiscriminately within one wallet, including historic and contemporary algorithmic artworks, including those by Vera Molnár and Tyler Hobbs, 3D sculptural renderings, explorations in AI and GANs, algorithmically generated music, POAPs (Proof of Attendance Protocols), land parcels across multiple metaverses, internet memes like Nyan Cat or Trollface, and other digital cultural objects like manuscripts, as in the case of Tim Berners-Lee's source code for the internet, social media ephemera, like Jack Dorsey's first ever tweet and even viruses-cum-artworks, like *Kudzu* (2021). As Wolfram Koeppe notes regarding the *wunderkammer*, "the taste for the utterly abnormal, for bizarre oddities, like the unusually large or the unusually small, for extravagantly exotic shapes and unknown origins or artistic virtuosity" was "cultivated to an extreme degree during this period."[15] The same could be said of NFTs today.

The relationship between the *wunderkammer* and the NFT wallet finds its place also in the 20th-century science fiction of William Gibson and the surreal assemblage boxes of Joseph Cornell (1903–1972) **[08.03]**. Gibson's *Count Zero* (1986), which was inspired by Cornell's boxes (themselves a form of contemporary *wunderkammer* and/or artistic antecedent to the NFT wallet), revolves around the narrative of Virek, a mysterious and fabulously wealthy collector, obsessed with locating the creator of art installation boxes that he has acquired. Virek believes this is crucial to him making his next evolutionary step to humanity's next form. This blend of science fiction, mysterious wealth, eccentric collecting practices, and art boxes with transparent glass fronts is a prescient foretelling of the NFT collecting practices today.

While anchored by a deeply intellectual engagement in humanism, irreverence, absurdity, and playfulness sit equally at the heart of the *wunderkammer*. Much like the importance and immutability of provenance to the NFT collection, *wunderkammers* were also some of the first major collections to be well recorded, archived, and provenanced through catalogs and taxonomies. The later collection of Olaus Wormius (1588–1654) was cataloged with an unusual amount of precision in *Museum Wormianum: seu historia rerum rariorum* (1655) **[08.04, 08.05]**, making use of Gutenberg's invention of the printing press — itself a conceptual antecedent for blockchain ledgers. References to narwhal tusks reputed to be unicorns' horns, mythical objects such as a giant's head, and a Scythian lamb — a fern that is part plant, part

15 Wolfram Koeppe, "Collecting for the Kunstkammer," *Heilbrunn Timeline of Art History* (New York: The Metropolitan Museum of Art, 2000), http://www.metmuseum.org/toah/hd/kuns/hd_kuns.htm.

G. Wingendorp, double-page engraved plate showing the interior of the museum in
Ole Worm, *Museum Wormianum seu Historia Rerum Rariorum* [...] (Leiden, Elszevier 1655)

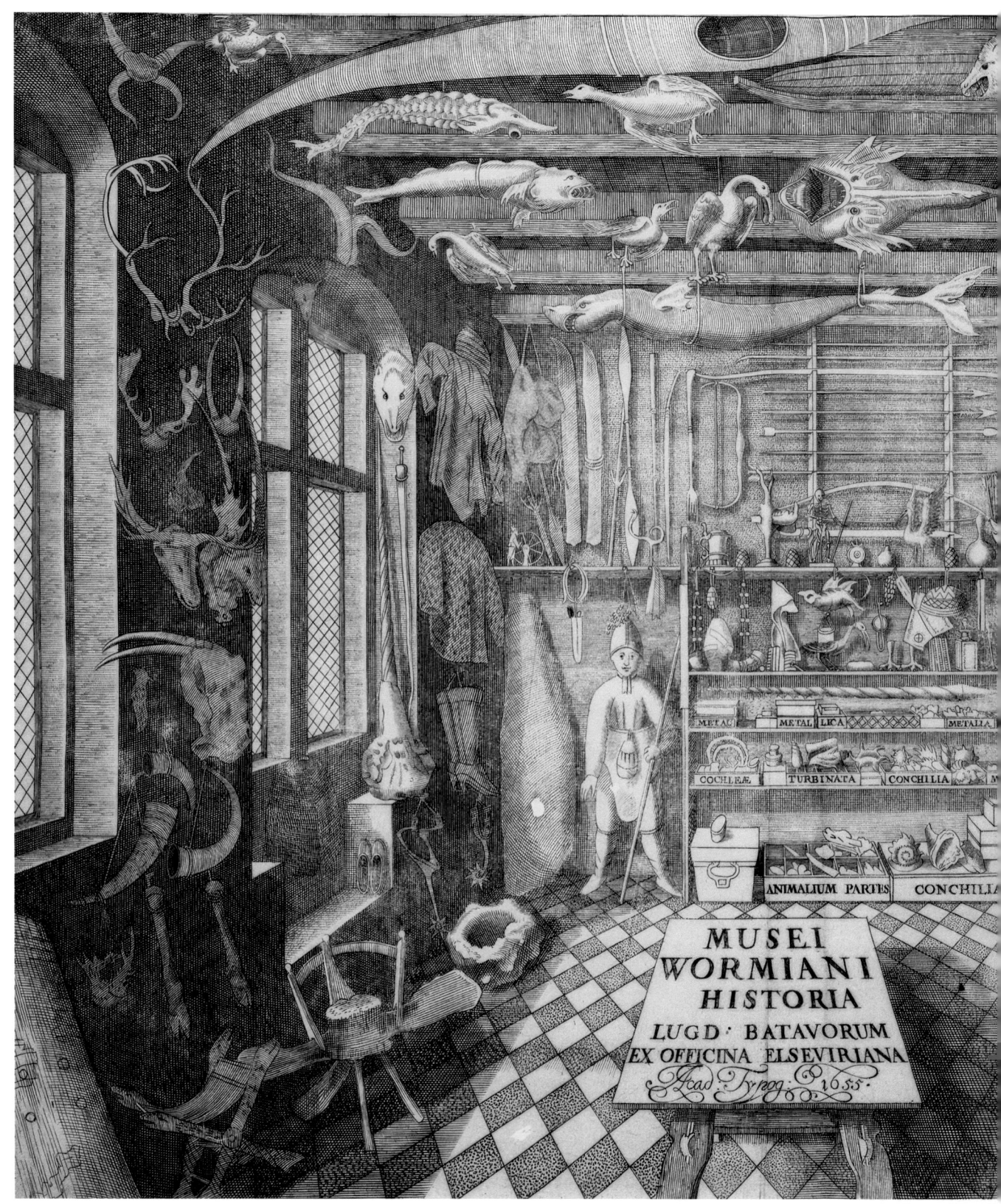

METALL | METALLICA | METALLIA
COCHLEÆ | TURBINATA | CONCHILIA
ANIMALIUM PARTES | CONCHILIA

MUSEI
WORMIANI
HISTORIA
LUGD: BATAVORUM
EX OFFICINA ELSEVIRIANA
Acad Typog. 1655.

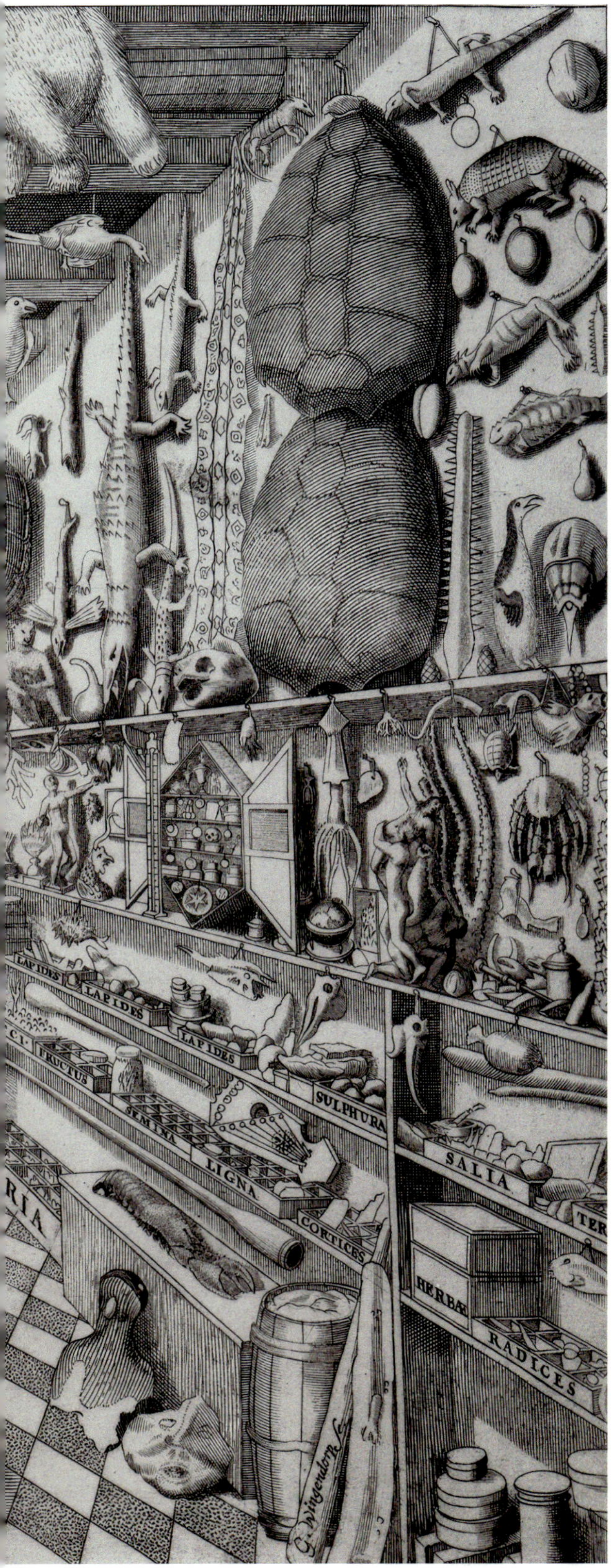

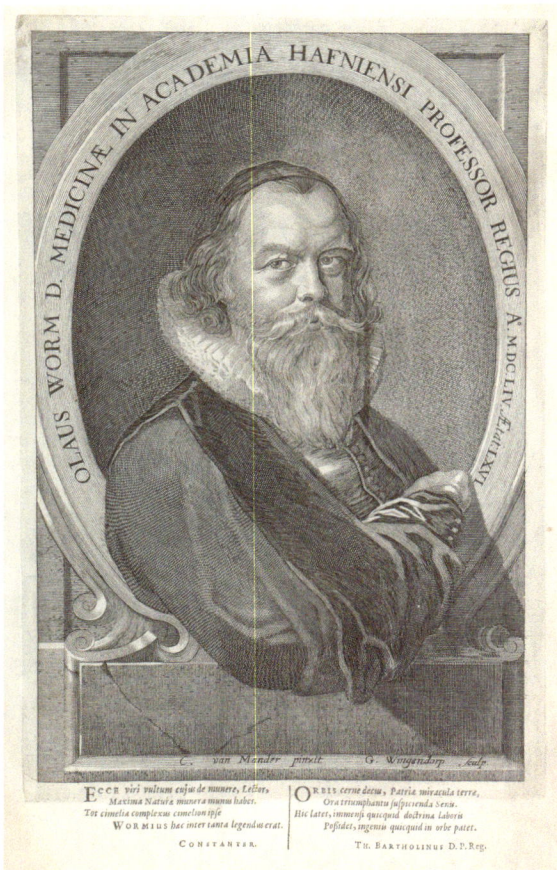

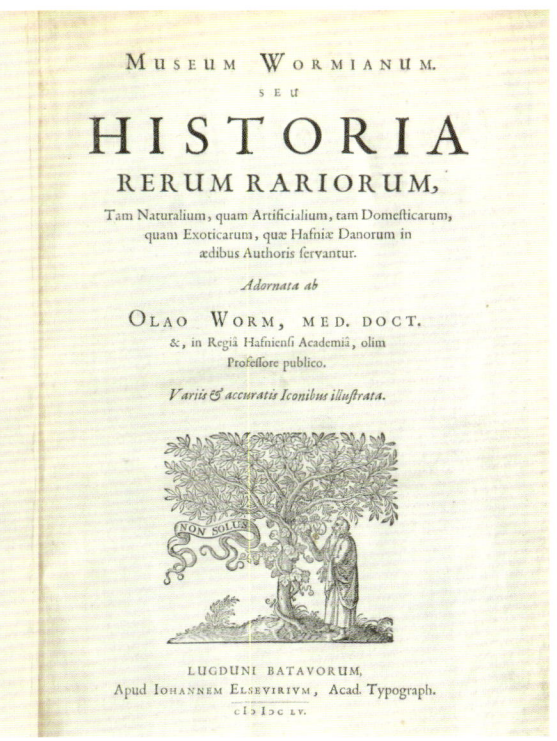

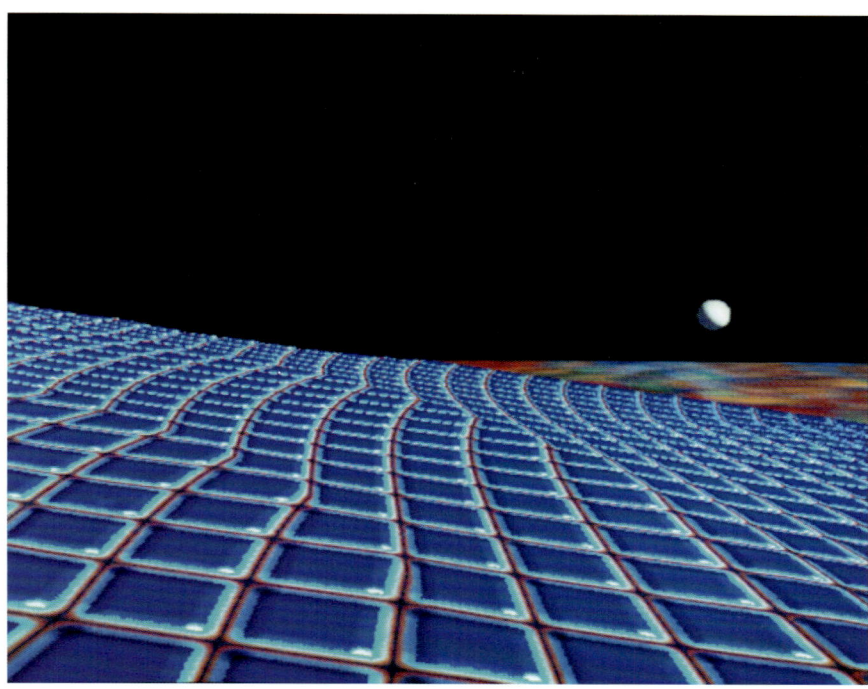

lamb — give flavor to the exotic natures of *wunderkammers* where contemporary memes are now supplanted by 17th-century beliefs in the magical and mystical.[16]

Tracing the history of these collectors and their *wunderkammers*, we see many parallels with today's rising class of decentralized collectors. In previous centuries, the rising disruptors of finance used art to establish themselves within new circles of thought and discourse, as was the case for Cosimo de' Medici in 15th-century Florence. Today, crypto collectors are establishing a new worldview through cultural principles of decentralization, transparency, increased liquidity, and financialization, an anti-elitist and global view of access to systems of culture and finance. The importance of digital culture and assets are all reflected in the collecting practices of this new decentralized class of collectors. Patrons of the past were often instrumental in introducing new movements or styles, from Medici's support of the Renaissance's revival of antiquity to the frequent imitations of Rothschild interiors. Collectors like David Rockefeller (1915–2017) weren't deterred by the criticisms provoked by more challenging work, many of which echo those leveled against NFTs today. "The conventional notions of art have changed, and a lot of things done today are considered works of art that would have been rejected in the past," Rockefeller once said.[17]

### A History of Digital Art Collecting (1969–2010)

Such collecting practices have also been prominent in the canon of digital and computer art long before the inception of NFT technology. For over half a century, numerous collections — both public and private — have been built around digital or computer art. While the benefits of hyper-liquidity, file security, and provenance immutability afforded by the blockchain were nonexistent at the time, the appreciation and desire to collect important pre-tokenized digital works was not different to many NFT collectors today.

The Victoria and Albert Museum (V&A) in London has been building one of the world's most extensive collections of digital art since 1969, ranging from early experiments with analog computers and mechanical devices to contemporary digital artworks.[18] The museum initially began collecting digital art as a response to society's rising interest in how technology could reshape modern life and culture, a narrative that would undoubtedly translate to many NFT collectors today as they look to collect the cultural foundations of the blockchain era.[19] One historical example of this in the museum's collection is the work of

[16] Tiffany Jenkins, *Keeping Their Marbles: How the Treasures of the Past Ended Up in Museums...and Why They Should Stay There* (Oxford: Oxford University Press, 2016).

[17] David Rockefeller, Interview with *The Art Newspaper* via *Forbes*, "David Rockefeller on Art," *Forbes*, March 05, 2003, https://www.forbes.com/2003/03/05/cx_0305conn.html?sh=707107761e87.

[18] Pita Arreola, Corinna Gardner, and Livia Turnbull of the Victoria & Albert Museum, interview with the author, August 10, 2022.

[19] Ibid.

08.07
David Em
*Aku*, 05-10-1978
DEC PDP 11/55, Evans & Sutherland Picture System 2 and 8-bit frame buffer
The Victoria and Albert Museum, London, United Kingdom

08.07
David Em
*Aku*, 05-10-1978
DEC PDP 11/55, Evans & Sutherland Picture System 2 and 8-bit frame buffer
The Victoria and Albert Museum, London, United Kingdom

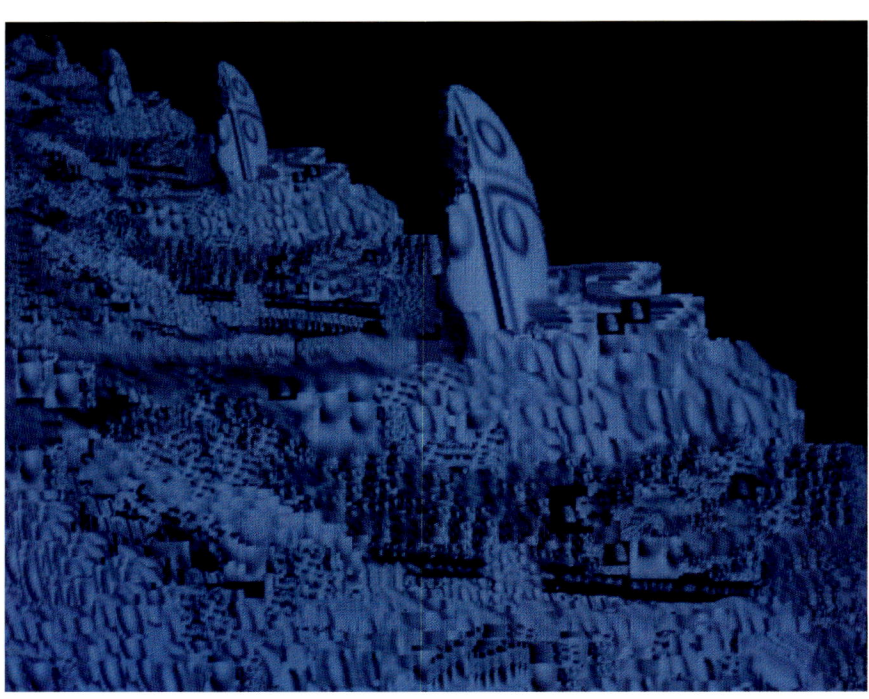

[20] NASA's Jet Propulsion Laboratory has maintained its neo-patronage-like role for digital artists, even striking collaborations with leading figures in the NFT space such as Refik Anadol. With the agency's 60-year-old publicly available space exploration archives at his disposal, in 2018 Anadol created a series of complex data sculptures from some of the most advanced datasets in NASA's history. Despite collaborating nearly half a century apart, both Anadol and Em represent a core development in the role of the institution as a hotbed for creative practice.

[21] Digital Art Museum, *Biography of David Em*, accessed September 3, 2022, https://dam.org/museum/artists_ui/artists/em-david/.

[22] David Em, interview with the author, October 12, 2022.

[23] The disparity between major institutions collecting digital art and their high level of engagement when sparking critical conversation is not necessarily one of rejection nor hesitation. Rather, time-based media art, in many cases, poses far more complexities in its preservation and display than forms of physical art. Unlike in the NFT space where images are stored either on-chain or on decentralized cloud servers, many traditional time-based media artworks exist only once they are installed. Not only does this raise questions surrounding the works originality and identity, but further issues are faced with the ever-updating technological world we live in as these once-new devices and file types become outdated and obsolete.

[24] David Em, interview with the author.

American artist David Em. It is Em's explorative and experimental approach, through the implementation of cutting-edge science and technology in his practice, that makes him such an emblematic part of the V&A's collection. During Em's spell as the artist in residence at NASA's Jet Propulsion Laboratory from 1976 to 1988, he became the first artist to produce a navigable virtual world.[20] For his works *Approach* (1979) **[08.06]** and *Aku* (1978) **[08.07]**, Em harnessed NASA's software for creating 3D simulations of spacecraft trajectories to construct complex digital compositions, years ahead of their time.[21] These important early and disruptive examples of computer art lent institutional acceptance to those who "were not initially accepted as true artists by the wider commercial art world," Em notes.[22] The collecting practices of the V&A have also been mirrored at the San Francisco Museum of Modern Art (SFMOMA), which established the first new media department in the United States in 1987, and the Whitney Museum of American Art which launched their online digital art commission platform Artport in 2001. Elsewhere in Europe, institutional collections such as at the ZKM | Center for Art and Media Karlsruhe, founded by its first director, Heinrich Klotz (1935–1999), in the early 1990s, now counts as one the largest digital art collections in the world. While these important collections suggest a deep institutional engagement in the history of digital art, they are, when viewed in comparison with mainstream museum collections, both still marginal and niche.[23] These significant collections of digital art are either the product of bequests or an art-adjacent curatorial focus allowing for the inclusion of digital art (the V&A), specialized digital art institutions (ZKM), or even perhaps a reflection of local tech scenes (SFMOMA).

Digital art collecting practices have also been prominent on a private level too. One figure whose contributions should not be overlooked was the life work of American collector, art historian, and archivist of computer art, Patric Prince (1942–2021) **[08.08]**. Prince's collection of around 200 works, including Em's *Aku*, has since been donated to the V&A, where they constitute some of the most important digital and computer artworks in the museum's collection. While collecting the work of artists using countless forms of digital media, one of Prince's greatest contributions to the medium was her role in curating and organizing some of the first consistent programming of exhibitions of digital art, most notably the SIGGRAPH retrospectives of the 1980s **[08.09]**. As an artist working at the time, Em expresses how a lack of real infrastructure for showing digital art meant that artists were, to many extents, cut off from those working and collecting in the traditional art world.[24] It was SIGGRAPH that

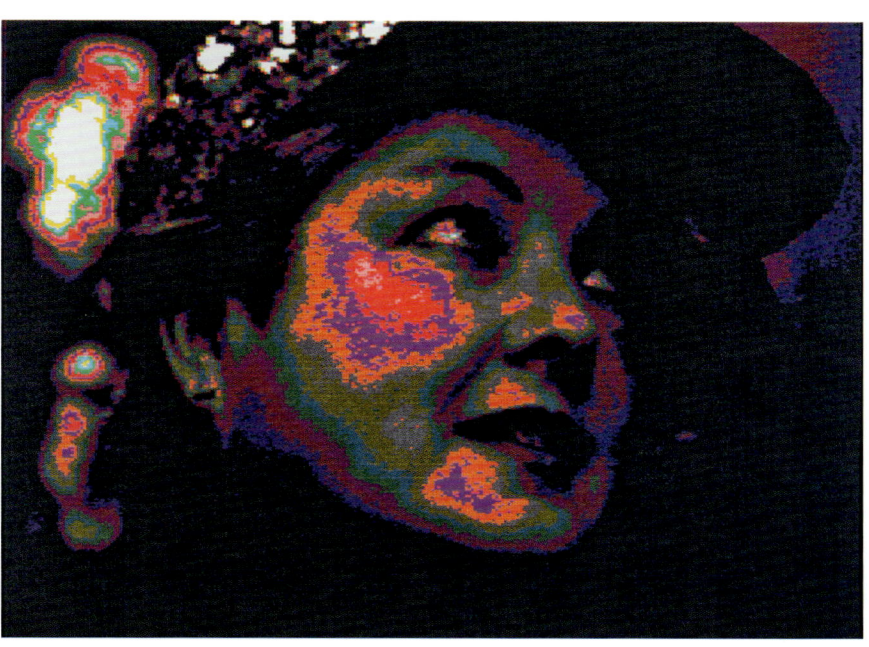

offered a hub for this early digital scene. For one week each year bringing together a decentralized community of artists, technologists, and institutions; it is in many ways no different to large-scale NFT conferences today. Along with her collaborators, Prince substantiated an academic grounding for the interaction of these new technologies with artistic practice, with SIGGRAPH ultimately becoming "one of the principal nodes for computer art."[25] By leveraging her role as a collector, Prince facilitated a wider framework for the curation and understanding of computer and digital art.

In the context of collecting both digital art and NFTs, few collectors, if any, are as relevant as Anne and Michael Spalter. The Anne and Michael Spalter Digital Art Collection (Spalter Digital) **[08.10]** is one of the world's largest private collections of algorithmic, digital, and computer art, comprising over 1,200 works. From early pioneers of the 1950s like Ben Laposky to contemporary leaders in the NFT space such as Dmitri Cherniak and Erick Calderon, the Spalters offer the quintessential bridge between traditional forms of collecting and that in the age of NFTs. Speaking of this bridge, the Spalters profess how "the embracing of generative art, seismically advanced thanks to NFTs, has put a spotlight on what we have considered a key piece of the canon of art history for decades."[26] The Spalters see NFTs, and on-chain generative art specifically, as the "natural extension" of their enduring mission to "preserve and advance generative and digital art."[27] Over the last two decades, they have lent works to institutions including the MoMA, V&A, Museum of Fine Arts in Boston, the Kitchen, Fondazione Bevilacqua, Daelim Museum, deCordova Sculpture Park and Museum, Venice Biennale, and the Espace de l'Art Concret, providing a blueprint for the institutional adoption of NFTs within their programming in the future. Through the legacies of both Prince and Anne Spalter, it should also be noted the key historical role women have played in this history.

### Collecting and the Psychology of Crypto

In comparison to Web 2.0, the very idea of crypto is an exercise in collecting not culture but tokens. The philosophy of HODLing showcases that anyone in crypto is a collector, owning bitcoin is collecting, owning Dogecoin is collecting. The idea of "not your key, not your coins," that sits at the basis of crypto, has provided fertile psychological ground for the transition to art collecting. The idea of absolute ownership, and enjoyment through ownership, sits at the heart of crypto psychology. While Web 2.0 prized the value of the network, the Web3 world prizes the value of immutable assets. Equally important to this notion of collecting are the roles of

[25] Sophie Le-Phat Ho, "Parallel Evolution: the Patric Prince Collection and SIGGRAPH," *The Computer Arts and Technocultures Project*, The Computer Arts Society, London, England, accessed August 4, 2022, https://www.docam.ca/techwatch/fiche3.php?id=85.
[26] Anne and Michael Spalter, interview with the author, July 15, 2022.
[27] Ibid.

**08.09**
ACM SIGGRAPH exhibition catalog cover, August 18–22, 1986
13th Annual Conference on Computer Graphics and Interactive Techniques, Dallas, United States

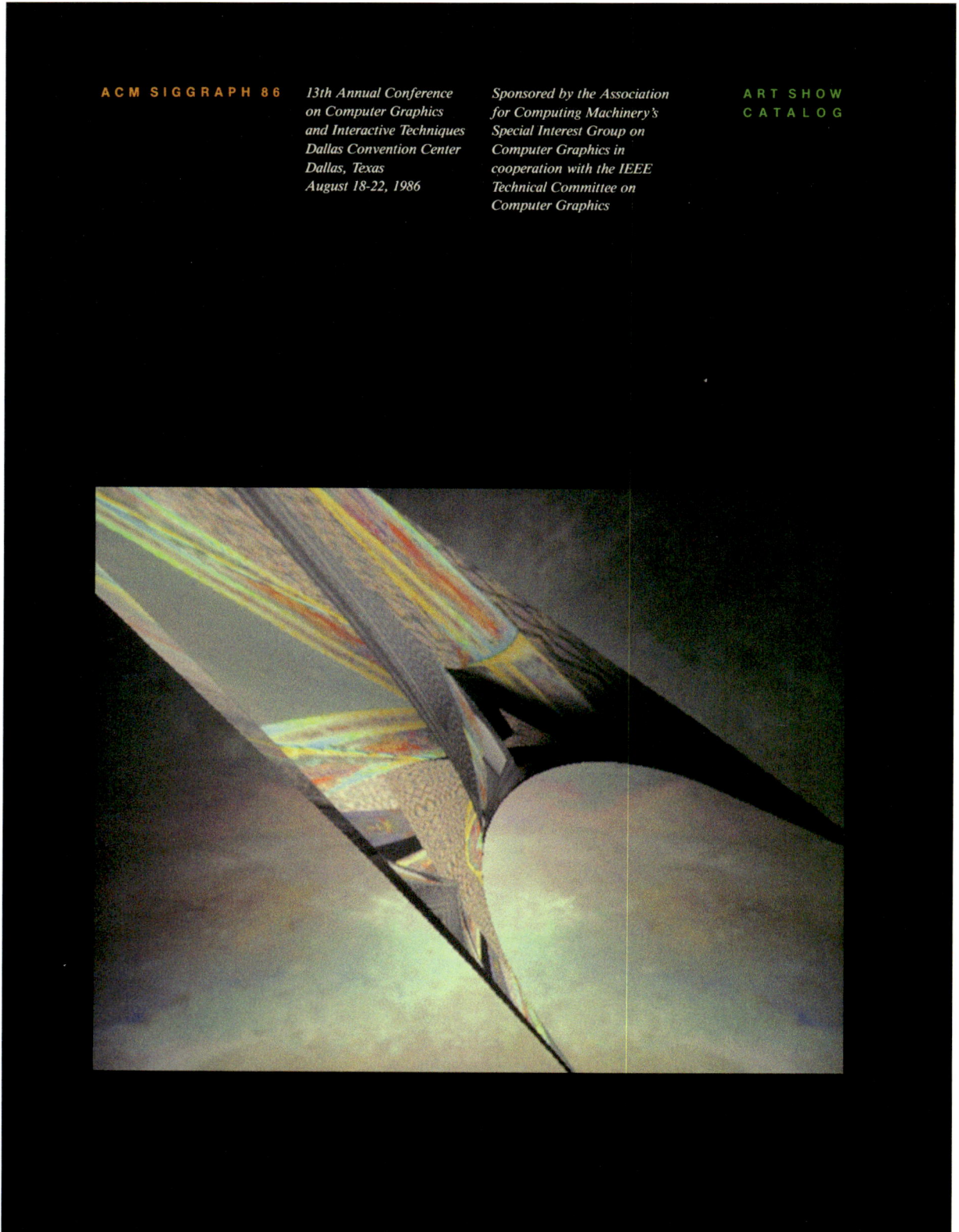

ACM SIGGRAPH 86

*13th Annual Conference
on Computer Graphics
and Interactive Techniques
Dallas Convention Center
Dallas, Texas
August 18-22, 1986*

*Sponsored by the Association
for Computing Machinery's
Special Interest Group on
Computer Graphics in
cooperation with the IEEE
Technical Committee on
Computer Graphics*

ART SHOW
CATALOG

**08.10**
Frieder Nake
*Walk through Raster*, 1967
Algorithmic drawing executed by digital computer Telefunken TR4,
in combination with drawing machine
Zuse Graphomat Z64, 50.8 × 50.8 cm
Anne and Michael Spalter Collection, Rhode Island, United States

Manfred Mohr
*P-021 Band Structure*, 1970
Plotter drawing in ink on tracing paper, 39.4 × 39.4 cm
Anne and Michael Spalter Collection, Rhode Island, United States

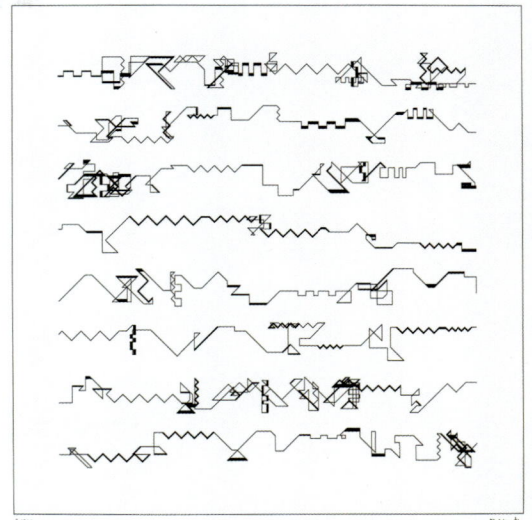

Vera Molnár
*Interstices (Gaps)*, 1983
Plotter drawing on paper, 29.2 × 40.5 cm
Anne and Michael Spalter Collection, Rhode Island, United States

Frieder Nake
*Matrizenmultiplikation (Matrix Multiplication) Serie 19 Blatt 5*, 1967
Algorithmic drawing executed by digital computer Telefunken TR4,
in combination with drawing machine
Zuse Graphomat Z64, 47.6 × 47.6 cm
Anne and Michael Spalter Collection, Rhode Island, United States

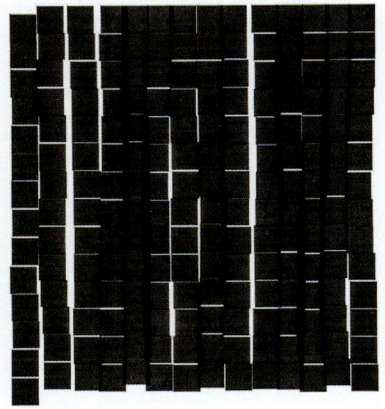

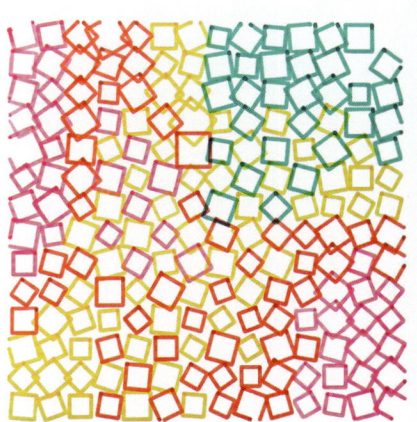

**08.11**
Avatar of Beauty and the Punk
Larva Labs, *CryptoPunks #2491*, 2017
Generative pixel art
Ethereum, 0xb4...3bbb, 2491

**08.12**
Avatar of Benny Gross
Taproot Wizards,*Taproot Wizard #2059*, 2023–ongoing
Adobe Photoshop and proprietary code
Bitcoin, Inscription 149,909

**08.13**
Avatar of Pablo Rodriguez-Fraile
Andrea Bonaceto, *PABLO*, 07-19-2021 17:46:15
Vector artwork
Ethereum, 0x54...8ab1, 64600010001

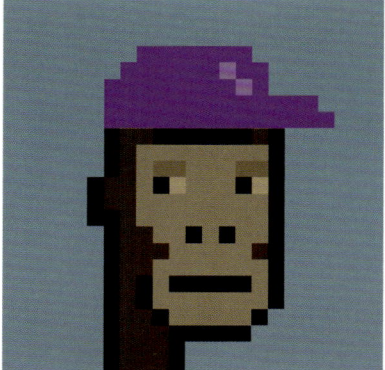

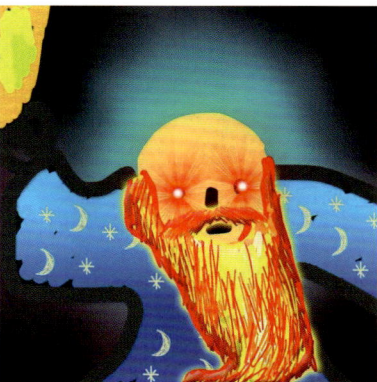

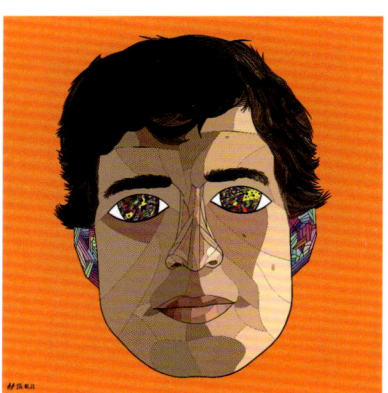

speculation and trade that we will go on to explore later. The volatility of NFTs is both a function of the medium and also the very nascent belief systems around both crypto and NFTs, still only 14 years old for crypto, and in its modern sense, 3 to 4 years old for NFTs. The volatility of this consensus building suggests unknown future outcomes and the early forming of a cultural basis. Indeed, it took nearly a century following the invention of photography for the medium to receive its first museum exhibition in the United States. The 1910 Albright Art Gallery show in Buffalo was an early demonstration in photography as a form of artistic expression during a time when the majority regarded cameras as tools for documentary. While the NFT space has moved much faster today towards acceptance, we must remind ourselves in discussions around volatility and trade that we are still at the very beginning of this medium.

### "Patronage" in the NFT Space

Who, then, are today's emerging NFT patrons? Before exploring such a question it is important to distinguish the development of the term *patron* from its authoritative feudal origins laid out in the earlier parts of this essay to its current relationship with NFTs. While many of the traditional patrons covered in this essay, like Scrovegni, possessed a commanding rule over an artist's subject matter, in many cases for pious motives, in current times it is the restoration of a more direct relationship between artist and collector, mediated by larger and more horizontal platforms than gallery structures, that has seen a revival of the term in the NFT space. This relationship between artist and collector mediated by social media, the horizontal platform, and the transparency of the blockchain is creating new typologies of relationships in art, and even new conceptual strategies for art-making itself. Yet, to present the NFT space as solely a new bedrock for benevolent patronage would be to disregard the equal importance of speculation and trade that has been so central to the recent history of NFT collecting.

The benefits of this new model are many. The transparency of the blockchain underpins the idea that NFT collecting can be treated as a "public good" — where the collector, through ownership, is allowing the public visibility of the work forever following minting. This balance between private ownership and public consumption is perhaps one of the most important and disruptive innovations in the collecting of art that NFTs have brought about. More broadly, participation within this system gives economic sustenance to the blockchains and decentralized file servers that NFTs use for their preservation, making collecting *and* trade vital parts of the overall system's sustainability. This new form of direct patronage also brings about direct co-benefits. Collectors of all levels and types can participate and develop a relationship with artists directly through social media, transacting without waitlists on the blockchain. With it presents a loss of friction of the exclusive age of traditional art world hierarchies and gallery waiting lists. These flattened-out distribution systems, afforded by Web3, have allowed artists to coordinate across Discord and Twitter to a global pool of collectors in real time reaching all spectrums of the market.

Collectors are also increasingly operating not just as end-receivers but as publishers and promoters. Projects such as Pablo Rodriguez-Fraile's Aorist was an early attempt at a hybrid approach between the gallery and platform system. Ryan Zurrer's 1of1, as will be discussed

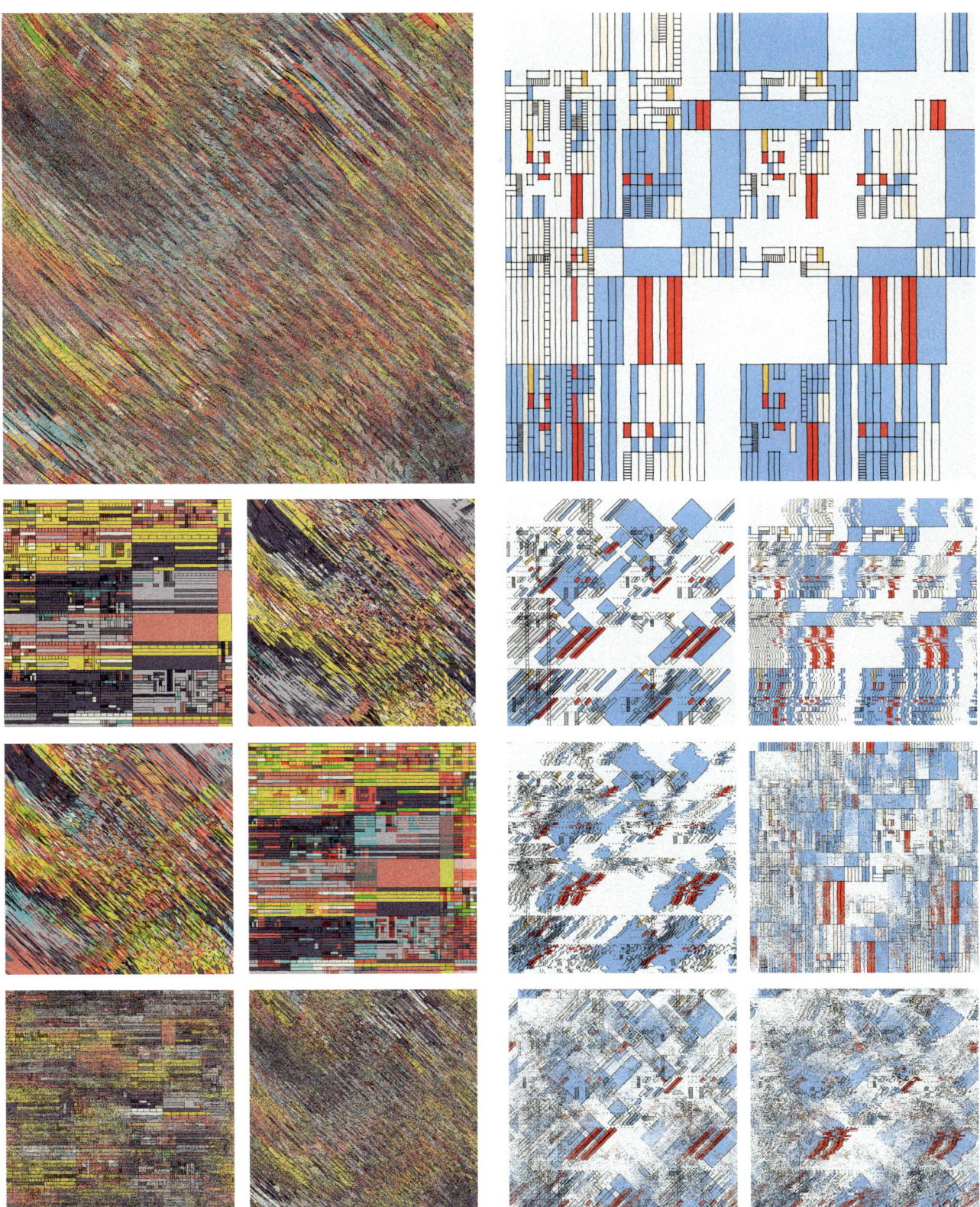

**08.15** (above)
Screenshots of Tyler Hobbs and Indigo Mané's *QQL*
(2022) control panels at qql.art

**08.16** (below)
Tyler Hobbs and Indigo Mané
*QQL #117 & #8*, 2022
JavaScript, p5.js, Solidity
Ethereum, 0x845dd2a7ee2a92a0518ab2135365ed63fdba0c88, 117 & 8

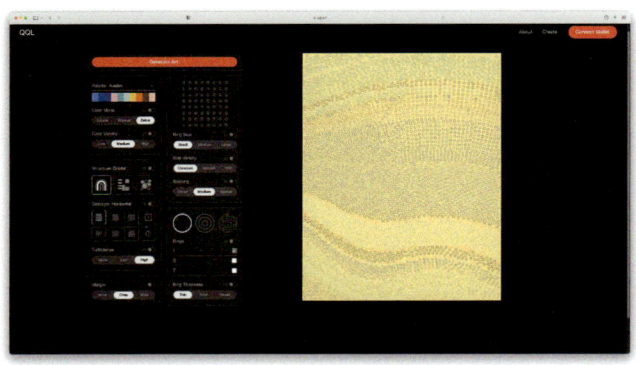

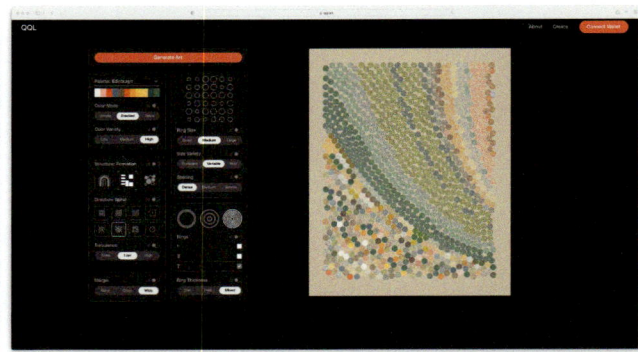

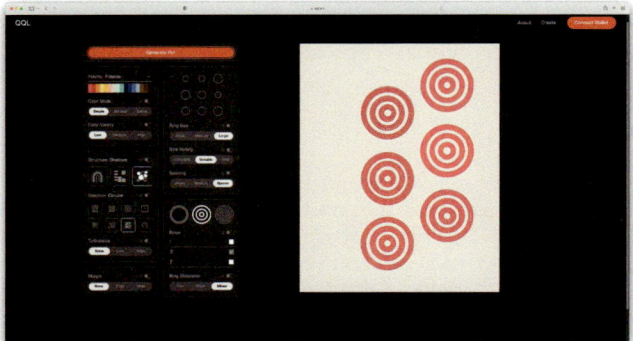

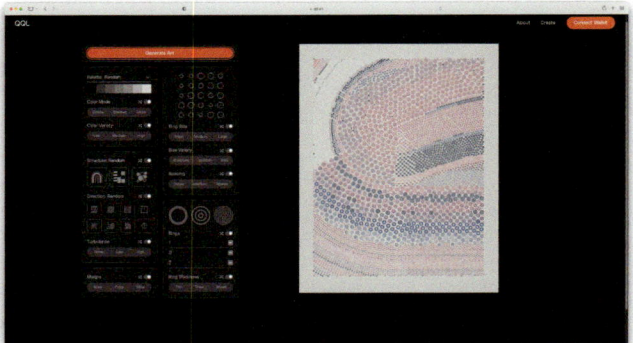

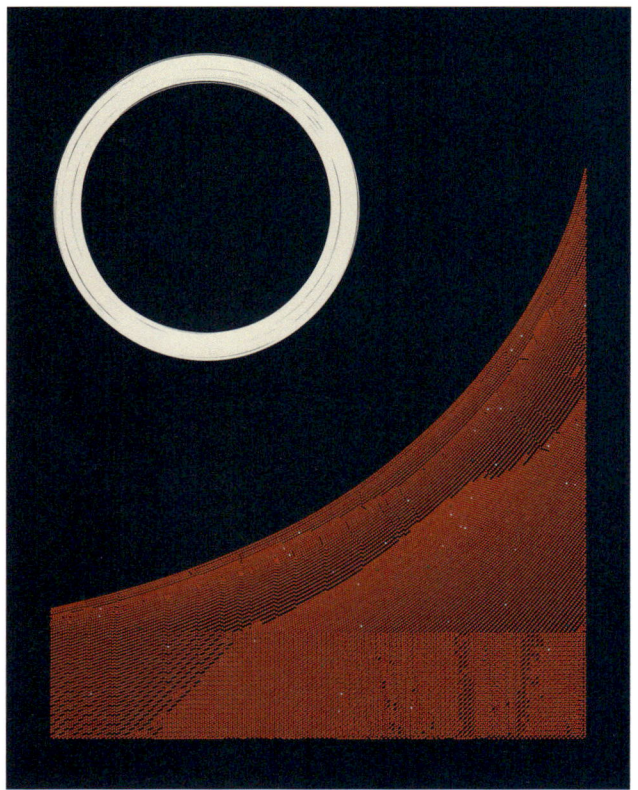

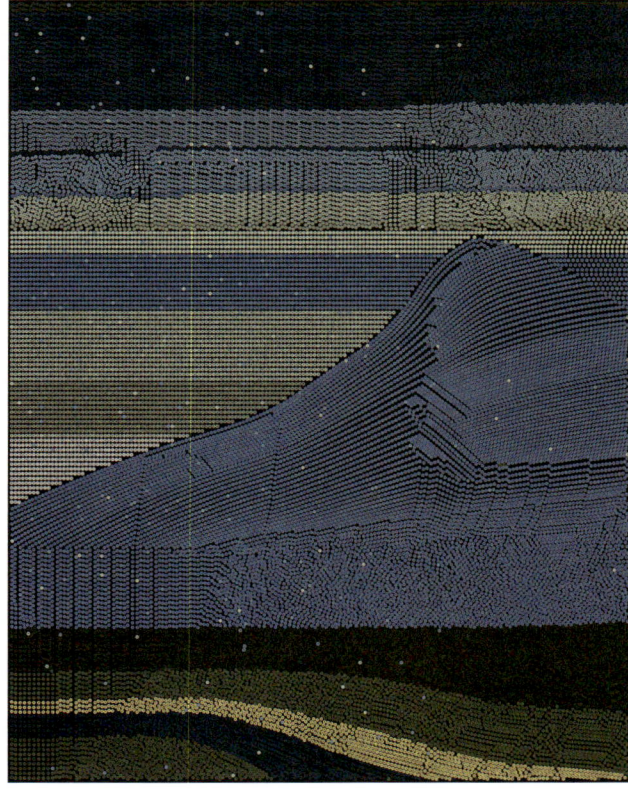

later, are seeing noted collectors use their collection and thought leadership to supplant the gallerist as tastemaker. This practice of collecting as the basis for a business platform is mirrored elsewhere, notably across Twitter. Prominent collectors, often but not always pseudonymous, from gmoney.eth, Beauty and the Punk **[08.11]**, Pranksy, Seedphrase to WhaleShark and j1mmy.eth were among the first to have built and monetized large social media followings around their collections. Often these collections are built around an avatar, such as @punk2476, @punk6529, @punk4156. Of course, there are other collectors, such as 55FAF0, who operate anonymously without any social media footprint.[28] Despite their enigmatic nature, 55FAF0 has quietly amassed one of the most highly regarded collections of NFTs in the world. Collectors are also building relationships with institutions. The omnipresent collector and community champion Benny Gross **[08.12]** sits on the digital art acquisition committee at the Whitney, while Jehan Chu founded a similiar committee at LACMA. The development in 2025 of the Infinite Node Foundation by Micky Malka and Becky Kleiner, seeded with a $25 million donation to preserve, educate on, and exhibit digital art, points to an increasing maturity of NFT collecting practices. The more direct model to art collecting has also been deemed to present certain negative aspects too. While Rodriguez-Fraile **[08.13]** sees patronage as "critical" in the NFT space, he recognizes the issues of scalability present in maintaining a direct relationship between collector and artist, unmediated by the gallery space.[29] Interestingly, he notes that the decentralized ethos of the NFT space can be "counterproductive to the growth and maturity of digital art" as there is an increasing expectation that artists occupy the role of "entrepreneurs and expert accountants, social media gurus, strategists, etc."[30]

## The Artist's Response

Yet, the direct interactions between artist and collector are also changing models of art-making itself, with artists using code to provide personalized and co-creative experiences to larger bodies of collectors that they can't service personally. In Landline Art's *Sedimentary Dissolution* (2021) **[08.14]**, the artist provides 20 different versions of each work per mint for the collector to explore. Each of these 20 original versions may be further manipulated with keystroke functions such as toggling on and off "erosion" or "RGB dissolution," allowing the collector creative agency in the production and visualization of the work.[31] Other artists have employed similar mechanisms in their work, most recently Tyler Hobbs and Indigo Mané's *QQL* (2022) **[08.15, 08.16]**, "an experiment in generative collaboration" between artist and collector, whereby the final outcome of the series was dictated by the curaotiral decisions of its collectors.[32] By publishing *QQL*'s generative algorithm and the tools to interact with it, the artists pushed their collectors "to take agency to become co-creator" such that "the collector is now the curator."[33]

## Membership, Access, and Exclusivity: Collecting and the Collective

Collectors are also collectivizing, primarily through DAOs but also through membership clubs like PROOF Collective, financialized products such as Ryan Zurrer's 1of1, and global communities like Bright Moments. PROOF Collective **[08.17]** was a token-gated members' club of 1,000 collectors and artists, disrupts traditional art advisory with a Web3 approach, emphasizing community and hive-mind decision-making.[34] Members, driven by drops like "Grails," are given gated access to works by leading artists, such as Larva Labs **[08.18]**. Other approaches to access can be seen in Ryan Zurrer's 1of1 collectors club, a highly curated, performance-driven blue-chip NFT collection managed by a streamlined body of leading professionals. Collectors participate through fractionalization within the venture structure, combining ownership, collecting, and investment into one project. In a similar vein, Bright Moments, founded by Seth Goldstein in 2021, has pioneered the concept of in-person minting-as-experience — otherwise known as live minting — bringing physical space and human connection to bear on an otherwise digital medium. Bright Moments traversed cities around the globe — from Venice Beach to Tokyo — with a flexible drop-ship model to cultural production. Just as PROOF Collective and 1of1 have left their mark on the NFT landscape, Bright Moments underscores the vital role of hub-and-spoke networks within decentralized communities. All these structures, from the exclusivity of PROOF to the financialization and institutionalization of 1of1, and the community approach of Bright Moments, suggest that traditional collecting structures are being layered into the NFT space as it matures. While fundamentally more decentralized and innovative in approach, some of these models, if not managed correctly, also risk returning to the same models of priority and access that the original tenets of crypto and NFTs attempted to move away from.

[28] 55FAF0 is the popularized nickname and abbreviation for wallet: 0x55FaF0e5E6e532b1C5799 bDEec1A0F193E54a92D

[29] Pablo Rodriguez-Fraile, interview with the author, July 20, 2022.

[30] Ibid.

[31] Landlines Art, "Sedimentary Dissolution," *fxhash*, January 22, 2022, https://www.fxhash.xyz/generative/slug/sedimentary-dissolution.

[32] Tyler Hobbs, "QQL," *Vimeo*, September 13, 2022, https://vimeo.com/749223222.

[33] Tyler Hobbs and Indigo Mané, "About," *QQL*, accessed November 1, 2022, https://qql.art/about.

[34] Justin Mezzell, interview with the author, July 20, 2022.

08.17
PROOF
*PROOF Collective*, 12-09-2021 19:33:36
Adobe Illustrator, Figma
Ethereum, 0x08D7C0242953446436F34b4C78Fe9da38c73668d, 0–999

08.18
Larva Labs
*Protoglyph*, 03-03-2022 23:15:29
Solidity
Ethereum, 0xb6329bd2741c4e5e91e26c4e653db643e74b2b19, 20

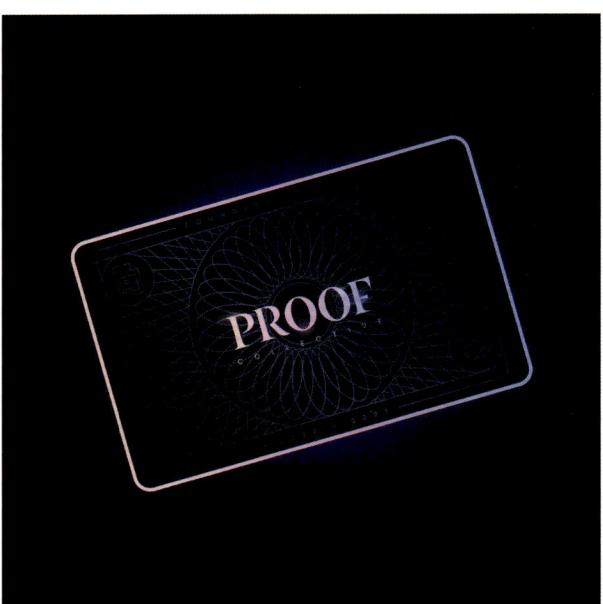

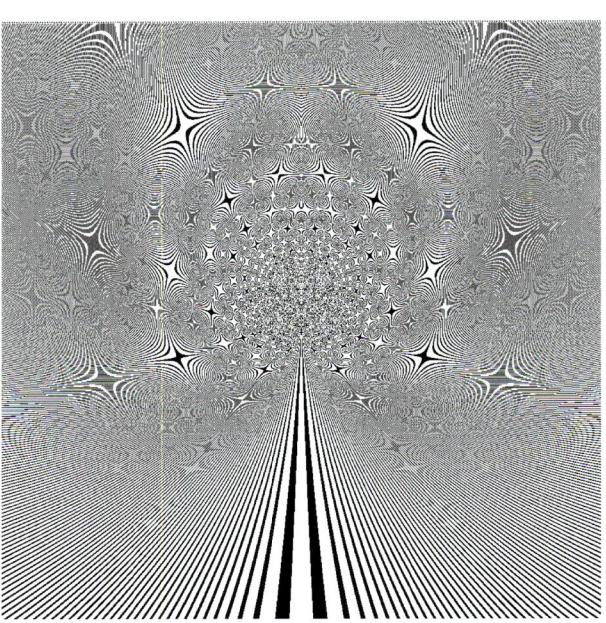

## Speculation and Trade: Rethinking the Culture of Collecting for Better and Worse

Alongside patronage, speculation and trade are inherent and vital aspects to the system, where these three types of collecting practices are intermixed to create a new form of cultural spectacle. The demonization of speculation and trade is a byproduct of overlaying of traditional collecting cultures, as defined by galleries for their own economic gain, onto this new system. Writing in 1971, the same year as Seth Siegelaub's *The Artist's Reserved Rights Transfer And Sale Agreement*, Frieder Nake bemoaned the power of the dealer writing in "There Should Be No Computer Art": "The dominating and most important person in the art world today is the art dealer, he determines what is to be sold and what is not. It is the art dealer who actually created a new style, not the artist."[35] Systems are never perfect, the elite system of the gallery model that solves for few artists, and even for those renegotiates power into the hands of dealers, has found itself up against a freer, more horizontal, global system on the blockchain. Replacing the figure of the reputational dealer with the hyper-liquidity of the market gives way to natural byproducts of trade and speculation. In this sense, trade in the NFT space can be seen as a real-time evaluation of consensus by larger market majorities taking in various evolving data points — be they exhibitions, criticism, or respected collections acquiring work transparently on the blockchain. As previously stated, volatility is a by-product of both crypto economics and the space's immaturity.

An examination of the etymology of the word *speculation* opens up a number of fruitful avenues to consider the contemporary role of this practice inherent in NFTs. Beginning in the late 14th century in Old French, the term *speculacion* was associated with "intelligent contemplation, consideration; act of looking" and "close observation, rapt attention."[36] Derived directly from the Late Latin *speculationem* meaning "contemplation, observation," and *speculari* "examine, explore" from *spectare* "to look at, view," by the 15th century the term had evolved to mean "the pursuit of the truth."[37] It was only in the 18th century that it came to suggest the idea of taking on a higher risk for outsized return. In long-form algorithmic art through platforms such as Art Blocks where the collector must mint in order to view a work, the 16th-century idea of speculation as an "instrument for rendering a part accessible to observation," comes into focus anew. The transition of code from text to image is carried out not by the artist, but the collector, where their unique hash indelibly marks the output of the work. It is here we see the idea of NFT collecting, and its speculative agenda, as a public good. The work *requires* the collector's speculation to be born.

[35] Frieder Nake, "There Should Be No Computer Art," *Bulletin of the Computer Arts Society*, October 1971, 18–19, https://dam.org/museum/essays_ui/essays/there-should-be-no-computer-art/.
[36] "Speculation," Online Etymology Dictionary, accessed November 5, 2022, https://www.etymonline.com/word/speculation.
[37] Ibid.

08.19
MetaKovan's avatar by Silvio Vieira
*Contemplation (of Creation)*, 02-05-2020 23:33:29
Blender, Adobe Photoshop
Ethereum, 0xb932a70a57673d89f4acffbe830e8ed7f75fb9e0, 7739

08.20 ▶
Harm van den Dorpel
*Event Listeners*, 2015
OSX Screensaver
MAK – Museum of Applied Arts, Vienna

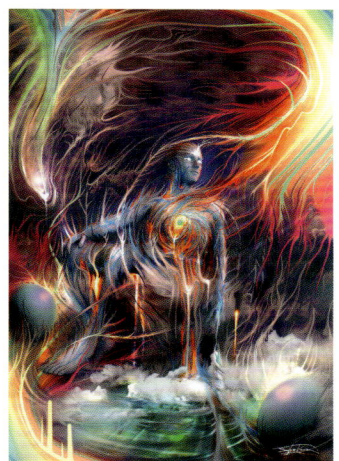

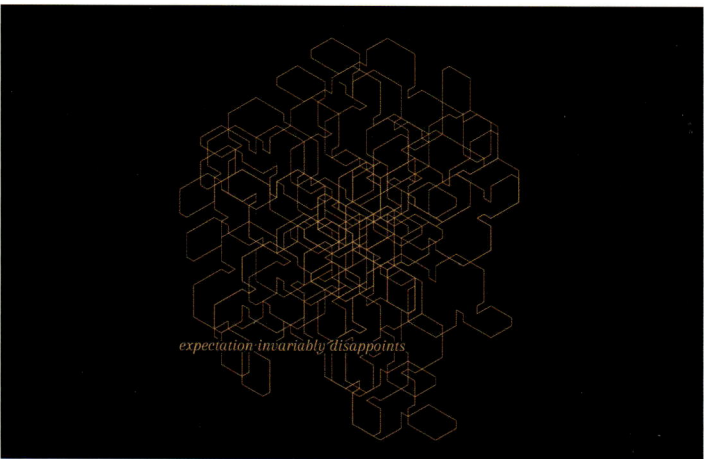

While the attention economy infects every artists' practice on the blockchain, the notion of speculation as "close observation or rapt attention" is foregrounded best by Kevin Abosch's *1111* (2021) in which he continually asked collectors to "PAY ATTENTION" during the life cycle of the launch. Indeed, the very phrase itself, the notion of paying with attention is perhaps the best distillation of crypto and NFT economics. If NFTs speak the language of market-based speculation as a way of looking or sorting, then capitalism has fully supplanted the middleman as the ink with which our on-chain cultural history is being written, for better and worse.

In a system that works to ensure a greater level of control around artist resale royalties (although not by any means complete), a steady level of speculation and trade is healthy to both the artist and collector. Yet, as a result of the crypto economy's high levels of volatility, the NFT space has become one dominated by flippers and traders, whereby profiting is the major motive behind the acquisition and resale of work. Further still, here we see the effects of a market that remains deeply tied to the fluctuations of the wider, much larger crypto economy. OpenSea volume is significantly negatively correlated with the volatility of Ethereum, which implies that when Ethereum volatility rises, OpenSea volumes drop. Or alternatively, when Ethereum volatility decreases, OpenSea volumes rise.[38] This financialization of art can be seen best in recent surveys, 82% of NFT buyers said that value potential was their most important motivation, while 67% said that it was their passion for art.[39] Over a third, 39%, of NFT buyers said that social impact and patronage was a key motivation for them, and 38% said that the social and community aspect of buying NFTs was important to them. While a much larger 96% of male buyers said they had bought art for investment reasons, and 58% for their passion for digital art, against 67% and 76% for female buyers.[40]

In his prescient 1967 work *Society of the Spectacle*, Guy Debord observes the spread of commodity images by the mass media produces "waves of enthusiasm for a given product" resulting in "moments of fervent exaltation similar to the ecstasies of the convulsions and miracles of the old religious fetishism."[41] NFTs are, in their commodification of the mass-media spectacle, a theoretical endpoint for Debord's Situationist writings. The combination of patronage, speculation, and trade inflected by the mass media has created volatile but decidedly more open markets.

## The Global Footprint of NFT Collecting

NFTs have shifted the concentration of power in collecting away from specific locations, where access to the best work has for a long time required physical proximity to galleries and strong local art scenes. The online native nature of NFT collecting has transformed collecting into a global pursuit. A 2021 market report by Cointelegraph highlighted this international footprint in how, "like conventional cryptocurrency, NFTs have achieved global popularity, with no [continent] making up more than 40% of monthly web visits since March 2021."[42] By the end of 2021, Central and Southern Asia accounted for ~30% of monthly web visits to

[38] Nathan Thompson, "NFT Buying Behavior: A Surprising Trend," *Tech in Asia*, March 22, 2022, https://www.techinasia.com/nft-buying-behavior-surprising-trend.

[39] Hiscox and ArtTactic, "Hiscox online art trade report 2021," *Hiscox*, 2021, 20, https://www.hiscox.co.uk/sites/default/files/documents/2022-04/21674b-Hiscox_online_art_trade_report_2021-part_two_1.pdf.

[40] Ibid.

[41] Guy Debord, "Unity and Division Within Appearance," *The Society of the Spectacle*, Thesis 67, 1967.

[42] Chainanalysis, "The 2021 NFT Market Report," *Chainanalysis*, 2021, 3.

NFT platforms, followed by North America at just above 20%, Western Europe and Latin America at ~15%, followed by Eastern Asia (~7%), Middle East (~5%), Eastern Europe (~5%), and finally Africa (~3%).[43] One figure who embodies these globalized narratives is Vignesh Sundaresan, widely known as MetaKovan [08.19] — the collector of Beeple's *EVERYDAYS: THE FIRST 5000 DAYS*, purchased for $69 million in March 2021. In his own words, as a "representative of a developing country," MetaKovan is driven to use his newfound reputation as a well-known NFT collector "to create networks to transmit this cultural knowledge to developed countries," with a specific focus on the Indian subcontinent.[44] Aside from the price paid for *EVERYDAYS: THE FIRST 5000 DAYS* and the experimental trajectory of the associated B20 project, the purchase catapulted the NFT space into the cultural mainstream, acting as the major tipping point in the economic and cultural history of NFTs. It should be seen as a dividend that lifted the whole community, spearheading billions of dollars of flows to artists. This 0 to 1 recalibration may well be Sundaresan's lasting legacy.

## NFTs and Public Collections

The fabric of the blockchain has also allowed for the articulation of this new art history to be governed by new institutions, rather than in more traditional public collecting spheres. Take the Museum of Crypto Art (MOCA), founded by Colborn Bell and Pablo Rodriguez-Fraile (who has since left). Bell expresses how the museum seeks "to focus on the aggregated power of each individual contributing to a larger movement."[45] Allocating its $MOCA token to the community, the museum operates with a decentralized curation approach, "flattening individual biases for a more egalitarian and representative creative voice within crypto art."[46]

Traditional public art institutions and museums have slowly begun venturing into the space. In 2015, the MAK – Museum of Applied Arts, Vienna, became the first museum to acquire a blockchain registered work, purchasing Harm van den Dorpel's *Event Listeners* (2015) [08.20] with bitcoin.[47] Since the MAK acquisition, numerous other museums have begun entering the NFT and blockchain space with a spectrum of strategies. In 2019, the Whitney Museum of American Art in New York commissioned *Public Key/Private Key* by Jennifer and Kevin McCoy, a work that uses the blockchain to explore the market life of artworks under museum ownership.[48] More recently, the ICA Miami acquired two *CryptoPunks* both through donations. In early 2023, SFMOMA obtained its first NFT, Lynn Hershman Leeson's *Final Transformation #2* (2022), also a donation. Both Centre Pompidou in Paris and Los Angeles County Museum of Art (LACMA) announced the acquisition of numerous NFTs into their collections in February 2023, including Jonas Lund's *Smart Contract Burn — Hoarder* (2021) [08.21] and *Ringer #962* (2021) by Dmitri Cherniak. Each institution also acquired a *CryptoPunk*. Following a show at the Castello di Rivoli in Italy with Francis Bacon, Beeple's *Human ONE* (2021) continued its global tour at M+ in Hong Kong, led by 1of1, suggesting the start of traveling institutional programming. The majority of works are being donated, and more needs to be done to secure larger acquisiton budgets. In late 2024 and early 2025, the Toledo Museum of Art purchased Yatreda's *Abyssinian Queen* (2024), while the Centre Pompidou acquired Robert Alice's *382181_ Garden City* (2023). In a world where museums can feasibly hold millions of NFTs and collectors are incentivized to donate works, more pressure needs to be placed on institutions to participate financially, helping to fund artistic practices, and validating against their only limit — budget.

Museums are also exploring ways they can create future liquidity from their collections without deaccessioning works. MoMA's collaboration with Refik Anadol, in which the artist accessed data from the museum collection for a series of AI NFTs, saw the museum earn 17% of all primary sales and 5% of secondary sales — providing them with a small but longtail ongoing revenue stream. Alongside MoMA, Jean-Sébastien Beaucamps and Marlène Corbun at laCollection have pioneered deeper commercial collaborations with institutions, most notably with the British Museum, where they helped monetize their collection of Hokusai prints into a seven-figure revenue stream. Elsewhere, the Uffizi Gallery and Hermitage Museum employed NFTs as a mechanism for raising funds during COVID-19. Digital reproductions of the Uffizi's *Doni Tondo* (1505–06) by Michelangelo, or Leonardo da Vinci's *Madonna Litta, Judith* (ca. 1490s) at the Hermitage raised €240,000 and $444,000 respectively.[49] While these two last examples were met with mixed reactions from the public, they provide exciting avenues for museums to explore, both from a community engagement and fundraising point of view.

## The Future of Collecting NFTs

Through amassing collections of NFTs and crypto art large and small, collectors of all levels are helping to propagate a new cultural history around the blockchain. It is of note that

[43] Ibid.

[44] Ibid.

[45] Colborn Bell, interview with the author, July 26, 2022.

[46] Ibid.

[47] MAK – Museum of Applied Arts, Vienna, "MAK purchases digital art work by Harm van den Dorpel with Bitcoin," *MAK*, April 23, 2015, https://www.mak.at/jart/prj3/mak/data/uploads/downloads/presse/2015/Harm_van_Dorpel_e.pdf.

[48] Jennifer and Kevin McCoy, "Public Key / Private Key," *Mccoyspace*, 2019, https://dev.mccoyspace.com/project/121/.

[49] Controversially, the Uffizi Gallery only made €70,000 from the €240,000 sale, while Cinello — the tech company who reproduced the works — took the majority of the proceeds. Following this, the Italian government went as far as asking institutions like the Uffizi to temporarily cease contracts with NFT providers. Dorian Batycka, "Italy Instructs Museums to Halt Contracts With NFT Companies, Citing 'Unregulated' Terms That Could Affect the Country's Cultural Heritage," *Artnet News*, July 11, 2022, https://news.artnet.com/market/cinello-nft-michaelangelo-2145003.

Smart Burn Contract #11

The Owner of    This NFT

May not    ~~Must~~    ~~May only~~

SELL ANY WORKS FROM THEIR
COLLECTION.

~~Once a month~~    ~~Once~~

~~For a month~~    ~~For a year~~

Continuously    In perpetuity

Documentation to be provided at https://smart-contracts.host
to avoid having this NFT burned.

the first killer app for crypto has been art, and strikes as a strong raisonne d'etre for art's farsighted ability to see beyond the present. For many people, art was the driving force for their first interactions with the blockchain. Unlike Web 2.0 in which digital content was free, as discussed, the psychology of collecting and consensus-building is innate to crypto — and provides fertile psychological ground for a sustained collecting of blockchain-based art. Even the principle of trading cryptocurrencies itself is a form of auction that takes place continually. Auction houses (not galleries) were the earliest institutions in the traditional art world to legitimize NFTs, introducing them to more traditional collector groups, where their rarified air is also complemented with a capitalist yet democratic auction mechanism. The arrival of the major auction houses in 2020, led by both Christie's and Sotheby's, represented the start of a cross-pollination between the traditional art world and the NFT space. Elsewhere the development of more curated platforms such as Feral File, *Outland*, Verse, and Fellowship speaks to a more sophisticated market for collecting. The end of the first major boom in NFTs has flushed-out of speculation. What is left will be the seeds of a more structured and dedicated group of collectors, where volatility will decline as both the NFT and crypto spaces mature. More traditional models are also sprouting up, both Nguyen Wahed and HEFT have created traditional gallery spaces in New York with rigorous programming. Elsewhere, collectors are trading between themselves, advised and brokered by trusted experts such as Eli Scheinman. The increased attention on museums adapting to life in the digital age will spark growing NFT collections and programming. In 2022, shows such as Tina Rivers Ryan's *Peer to Peer* at Buffalo AKG Art Museum and MoMA's *Refik Anadol: Unsupervised* **[08.22]** present exciting steps forward in the programming of NFTs at major global institutions. Further still, the royalties earned by the museum from Anadol's *Unsupervised — MoMA Dreams* series offers an early insight into how NFTs can bring new commercial opportunities to traditional establishments. As we have seen with the generative projects of Landlines Art and the *QQL* series, artists will engage with more dynamic mechanisms, playing with the game theory of collectors and collector psychology. The blockchain will be further abstracted away over time, lowering technical barriers to entry.

Yet perhaps the most exciting future for NFT collecting is far away from the traditional models of the wealthy (crypto) patron, the traditional art world system, and the major institutions cautiously engaging in the space. NFTs are starting to broaden the scope of who identifies as a collector, speaking to a younger digitally native generation, across multiple geographies. Code-based algorithmic works, in larger edition sizes, will allow for lower price points and none of the overheads associated with traditional art. People will be able to engage in global conversations around culture through horizontal platforms, building their own digital *wunderkammers* across geographies and time zones. Fractionalization will give a much larger majority access to ownership of important and valuable artworks — digital or physical. Increased liquidity will allow NFTs to generate yield creating more self-sustaining collections. Avatar projects will bring portraiture to much larger publics, lowering barriers to more traditional forms of collecting. This more popular engagement in NFT collecting with general publics across the world will broaden arts appeal further and be perhaps NFTs' greatest legacy.

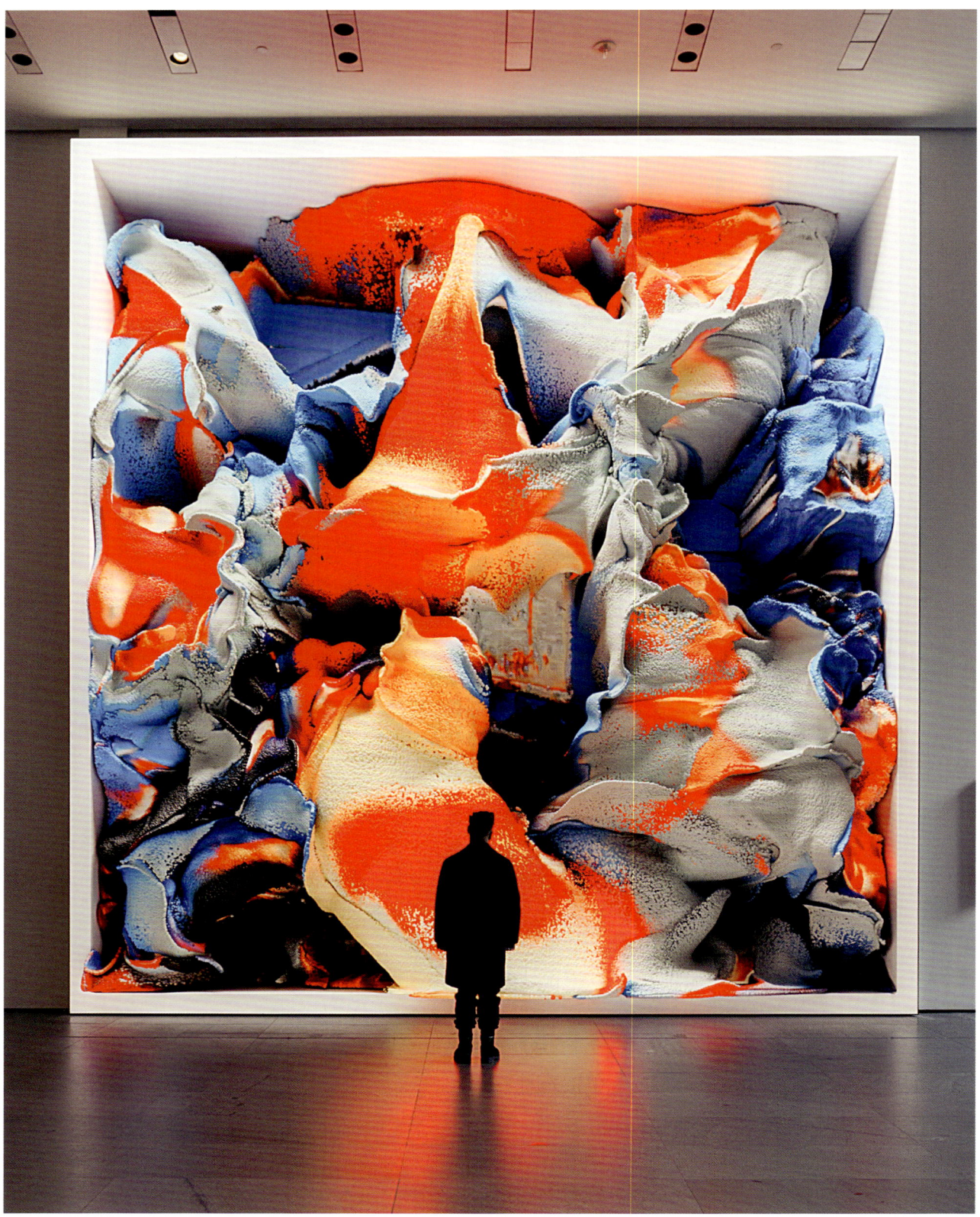

01

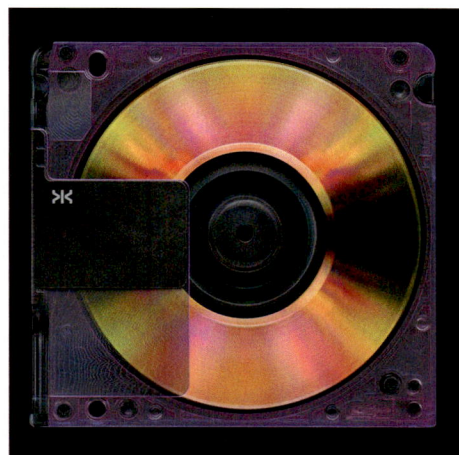

02

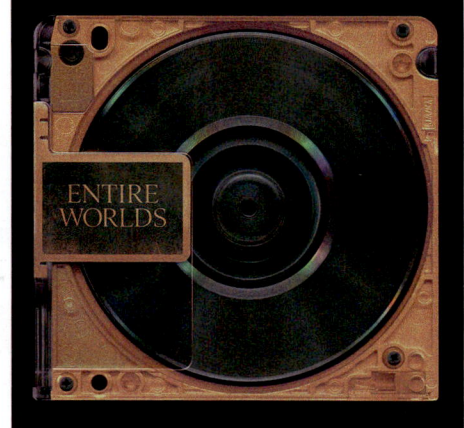

03

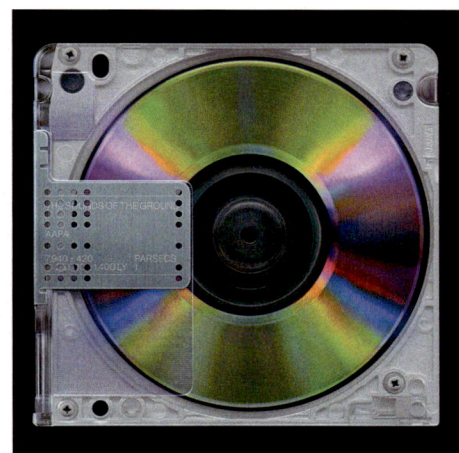

04

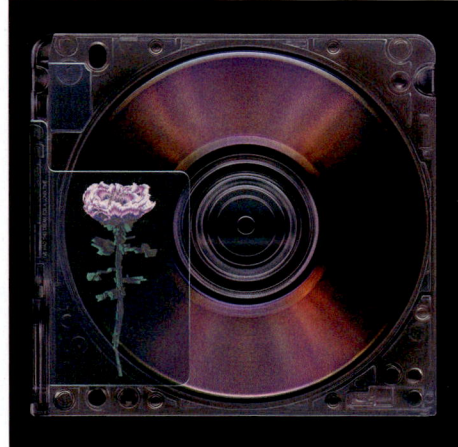

05

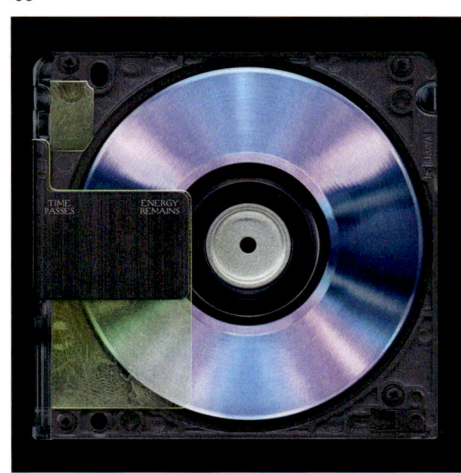

06

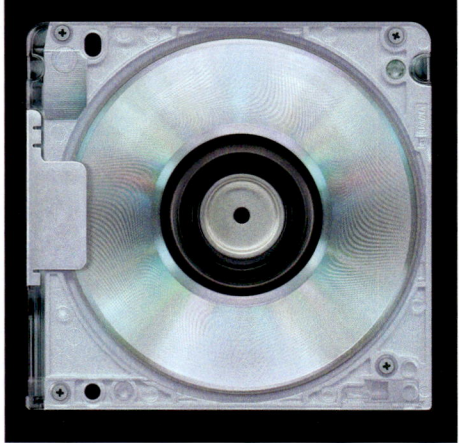

| # | TITLE | TIMESTAMP | MEDIUM | CHAIN | CONTRACT ADDRESS | TOKEN ID | EDITION SIZE |
|---|---|---|---|---|---|---|---|
| 01–06 | **Tombs [CMYK Reproductions]** | 09-07-2022 22:13:29 | Adobe Photoshop, Adobe Illustrator | MULTI | 0x185e8a578bf6896e3988e7c38a6a23889ca2af9f (Tomb Index address, series spread over 20 different contracts) | Various | 1/1 of 177 |
| 07 | **Exodus II** | 06-02-2021 22:07:29 | Pangram Haiku | ETH | 0x76e422de0ce8842ebe837bc7ab6984b4fff88055 | 1–19 | 1/1 of 19 |

EDITIONS ILLUSTRATED: (01) CLVIII–IX–SECTOR (02) LX – ENTIRE WORLDS, (03) LXVIII–EARTH, (04) LXII–REPLICA, (05) XCVII–ENERGY REMAINS, (06) VIII–ORIGIN, (07) XI – Quadratic Empire

07

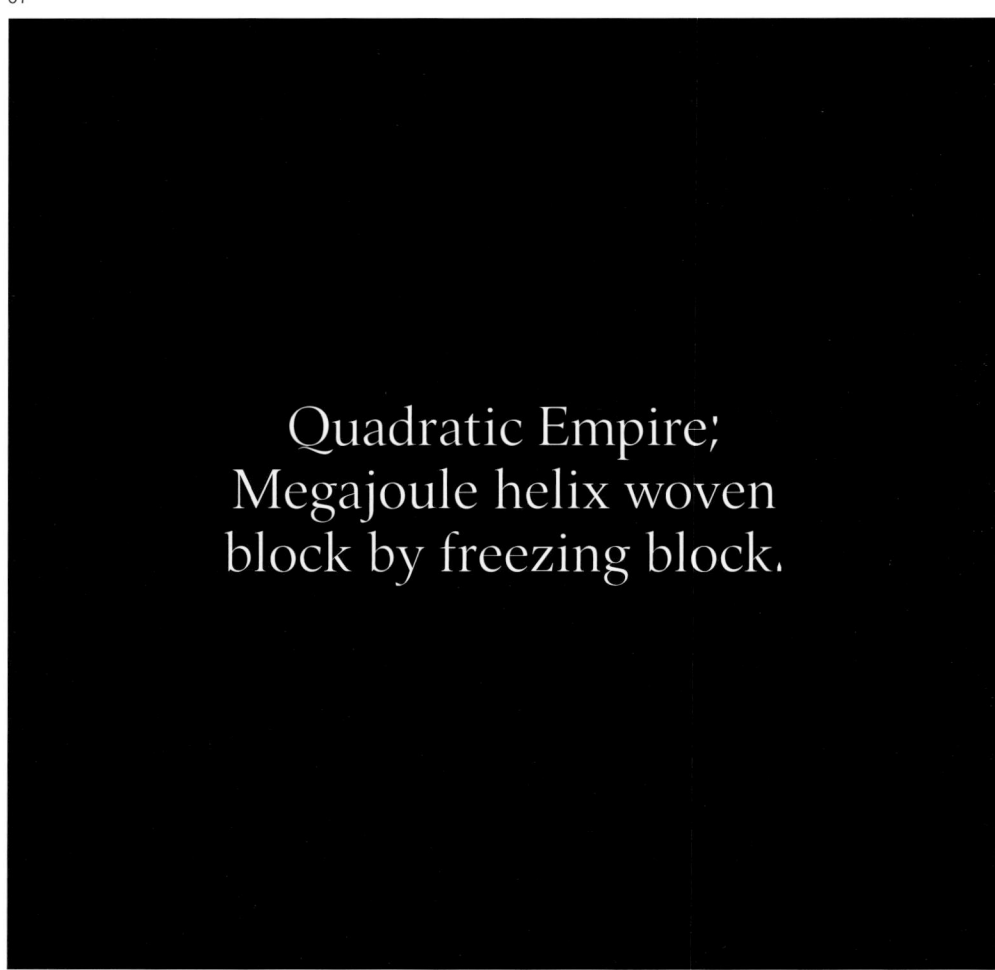

Quadratic Empire;
Megajoule helix woven
block by freezing block.

David Rudnick's conceptual poetry cycle is titled *Exodus II* (2021), and its imagery is often suitably biblical. But it also trades in contemporary technology, with evocations of "hacked Amazon" and "pixels liquidized." Rudnick employs the haiku, a Japanese form that was adapted by the Imagists and further popularized by American Beat poets. Rudnick has assigned himself another formal challenge: each poem in *Exodus II* must contain all 26 letters of the alphabet. This constraint seems to impact the selection of images and words more than any thematic concern. To get those Xs and Zs Rudnick must delve into history and specialized vocabularies, often religious and geological. But there is a kabbalistic quality to Rudnick's method — the idea that each grapheme holds a powerful connection to meaning.

Written in 2010 and 2011, these poems became NFTs a decade later. The blockchain is an apt home for *Exodus II*, another kind of faith-based textual system, where the alphanumeric codes of hashes are endowed with the power to render trust meaningless and make value from the ether. Rudnick released the token-poems with the online gallery Folia through an unusual timed auction: they become available to mint automatically, for a limited period of 40 years. If no one claims the token, it will be minted to the author's wallet. Each poem is thus a voice in the wilderness, inscribed in the blockchain, ephemeral and permanent.

Building on his interest in sign and signifier, David Rudnick's newest project the *Tomb* series (2022), uses the design of optical data disks to create trans-substantive links between archaic physical means of data storage and the immaterial world of Web3. The series consists of 177 individual *Tombs*, drawn only using the trackpad of a 2012 Apple MacBook Pro within Adobe Photoshop and Illustrator CS3, that enclose individual characteristics and components. Though *Tombs* are owned by individuals, their buried treasures can be "recovered" — or excavated — by other creators, and enriched with new content, so as to fuel community-based curation and cultural production.

**BRIAN DROITCOUR**
EDITOR-IN-CHIEF AT OUTLAND

01

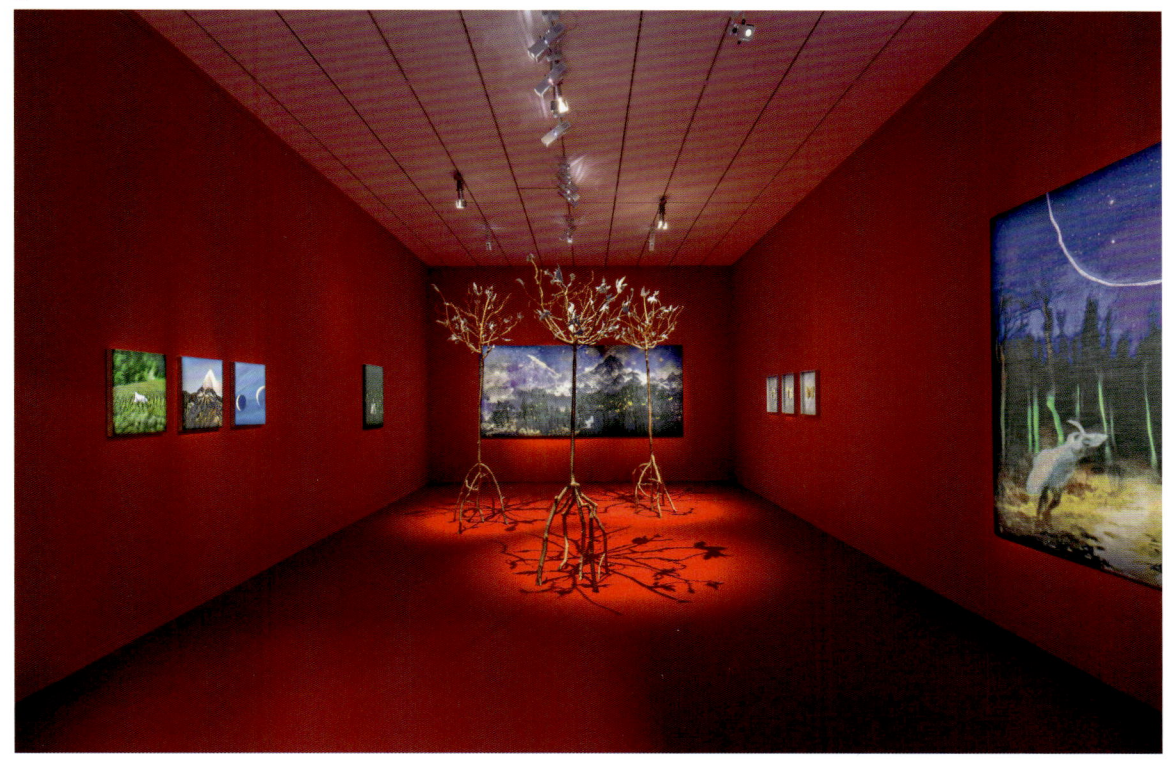

02

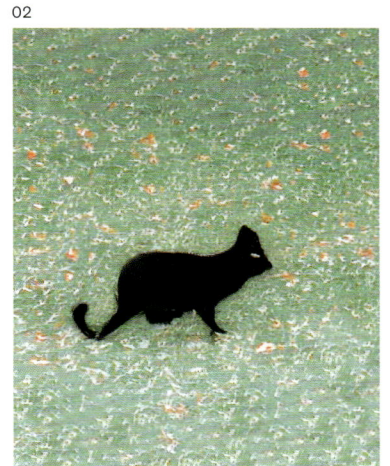

03

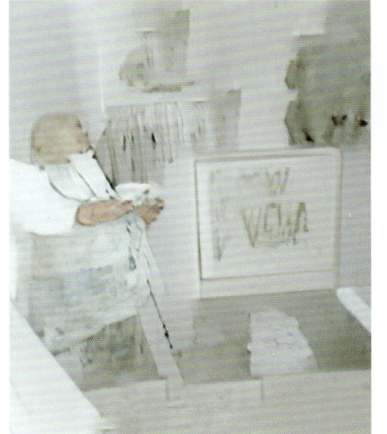

04

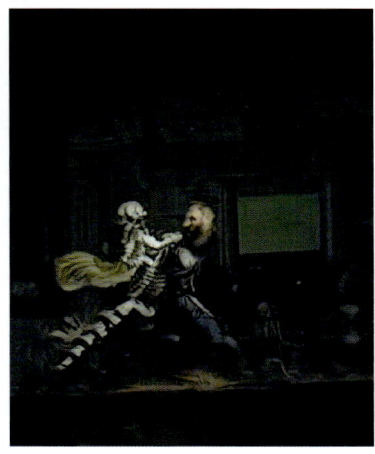

| # | TITLE | TIMESTAMP | MEDIUM | CHAIN | CONTRACT ADDRESS | TOKEN ID | EDITION SIZE |
|---|---|---|---|---|---|---|---|
| 01 | *Installation view of la traversée de la forêt, macLYON* | | | | | | |
| 02 | *an extremely intelligent black cat waiting for a bearded man in a flower meadow* | 05-29-2021 00:51:23 | Adobe Photoshop | ETH | 0x46c31b6b330c4522d6b37cb3cecdf2da9ff46f61 | 46 | 1/1 |
| 03 | *a working session in the atelier of Vera Molnár* | 05-29-2021 00:51:16 | Adobe Photoshop | ETH | 0x46c31b6b330c4522d6b37cb3cecdf2da9ff46f61 | 45 | 1/1 |
| 04 | *a bearded man dancing with death* | 05-29-2021 00:12:56 | Adobe Photoshop | ETH | 0x46c31b6b330c4522d6b37cb3cecdf2da9ff46f61 | 16 | 1/1 |

EDITIONS ILLUSTRATED: (01) Bronze sculptures, Aubusson tapestries, oil paintings from *le travail des rêves*, all derived from AI-generated images. Exhibition on view, March 7–July 13, 2025

05

eleven thousand days

I have already experienced almost every pleasure
        and disappointment,
every happiness
        and every suffering
            that I will ever know,

and     every     day     is     the     same.

06

last night before the ascent

far within me, where the memory of what I am is still unclouded,
a little child is waking up
and making an old man's mask weep

though I have been idle for a moment, I am not yet asleep

the sound of the sea in a shell
a dark bird in a child's ear
a breath in a whisper
the word that is not spoken
the unsaid word that is the word that is said
    the light that is not seen
    the light that cannot be seen
because it is too bright to be seen and would blind        the eyes
if it were seen
    the light that is not seen
    the light that is seen.

Depicting dreams has long bordered on the absurd. Abstract, fragmented, and fleeting, dreams begin in one person; when shared, they edge closer to grounded existence. This act of sharing emphasizes the intimacy of dreams and makes them feel more grounded.

In *le travail des rêves*, released in 2024 as part of Bright Moments in Paris, aurèce vettier — an art entity founded in 2019 by Paul Mouginot — invites viewers into a poetic dreamscape. The work encourages immersion in memories spanning from childhood to the present. Guided by titles, viewers are still left with room for interpretation. In *The Poetics of Space* (1954), Bachelard suggests that "works of art are the by-products of this existentialism of the imagining being." This idea resonates with *le travail des rêves* and the wider work of aurèce vettier. The series emerges from this existentialist pursuit, offering poetic visuals that reflect both light and dark memories — and what it means to be human.

aurèce vettier's practice revolves around two axes: sur-nature, an artificial reimagining of botanical forms using AI trained on herbarium sheets; and sur-reality, a long-term investigation into dreams, where recollections and subconscious fragments are translated into algorithmic images. *le travail des rêves* draws on personal archives — family photographs, digital traces, and memories — to create dreamlike AI-generated settings reinterpreted through NFTs, poetry, oil paintings, tapestries, and bas-reliefs.

These axes converged in the 2025 exhibition at macLYON, as part of aurèce vettier's *Echoes of the Past, Promises of the Future*, where large-scale works formed a hybrid landscape — part memory, part fiction — exploring AI's role in shaping mythologies and future visual languages.

By merging AI and traditional craft, and using algorithms interpretively, aurèce vettier creates a personal dreamscape that only he can make.

**STINA GUSTAFSSON**
INDEPENDENT CURATOR AND ARTISTIC DIRECTOR AT
DEPARTMENT OF DECENTRALIZATION

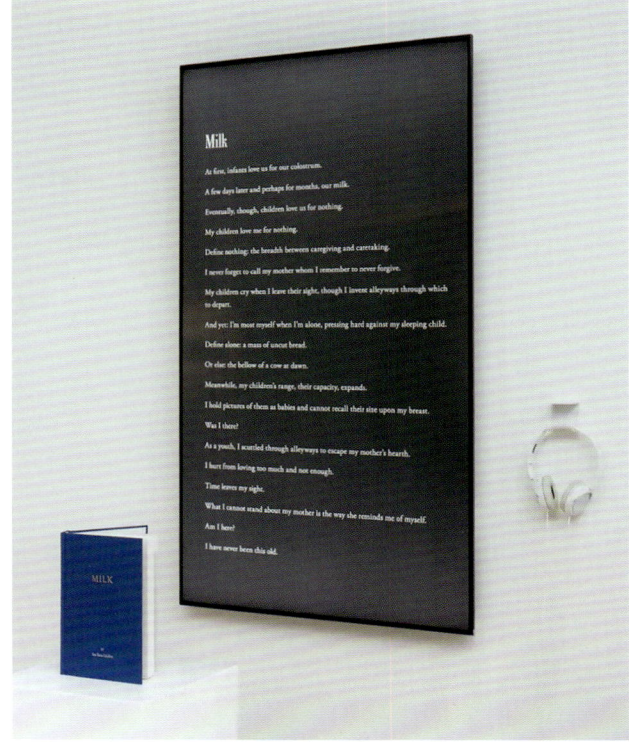

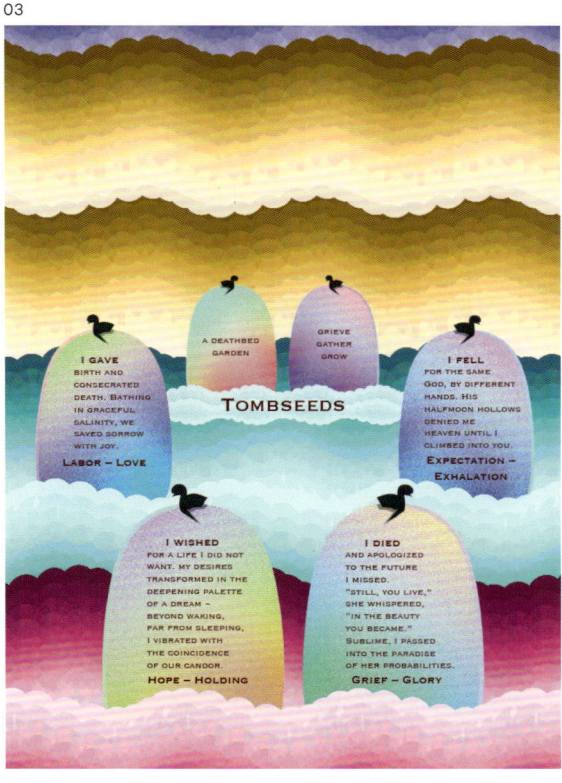

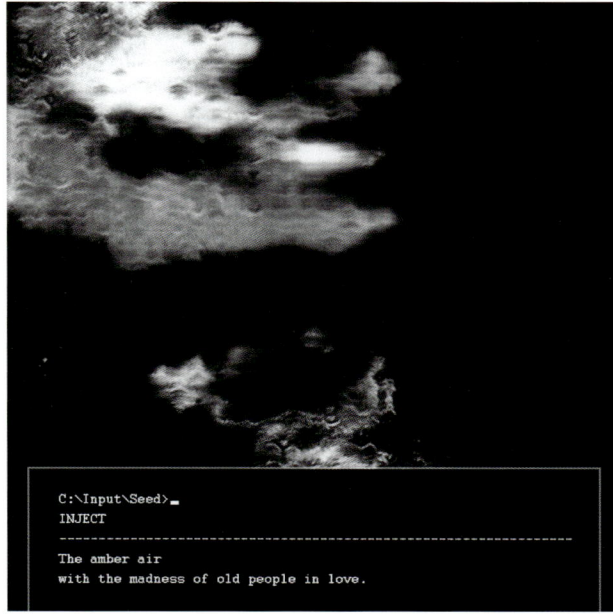

| # | ARTIST | TITLE | TIMESTAMP | MEDIUM | CHAIN | CONTRACT ADDRESS | TOKEN ID | EDITION SIZE |
|---|--------|-------|-----------|--------|-------|------------------|----------|--------------|
| 01 | Sasha Stiles | **Fragment 1** | 11-01-2021 03:21:42 | Media-rich textblock with AI-generated language | XTZ | KT1RJ6PbjHpwc3M5r-w5s2Nbmefwbuwbdxton | 495965 | 1/1 |
| 02 | Ana María Caballero | **Milk** | 01-04-2024 13:59:35 | Physical book, mp4 | ETH | 0x7CDe13f6289A5dF-B77424Aa3EdD83fFddC46D354 | 34 | 1/1 |
| 03 | Elizabeth Sweet | **Tombseeds** | 08-08-2022 13:28:14 | Javascript, CSS, Adobe Photoshop | XTZ | KT1MKvjmjAJaz735R7KCvPH-QHdDJtm5Tm88S | 1 | 1/1 of 10 |
| 04 | Kalen Iwamoto & Rose Jackson | **inject (from the Seeds and Ashes series)** | 03-31-2022 06:37:44 | Text & Image (GAN trained on artist's work; AI text) | XTZ | KT1QiZK4JxYMyJc9pMoM63D-ZLtiVKSZvkgcz | 22 | 1/1 of 10 |
| 05 | theVERSEverse | Mission Statement | | | | | | |

# theVERSEverse

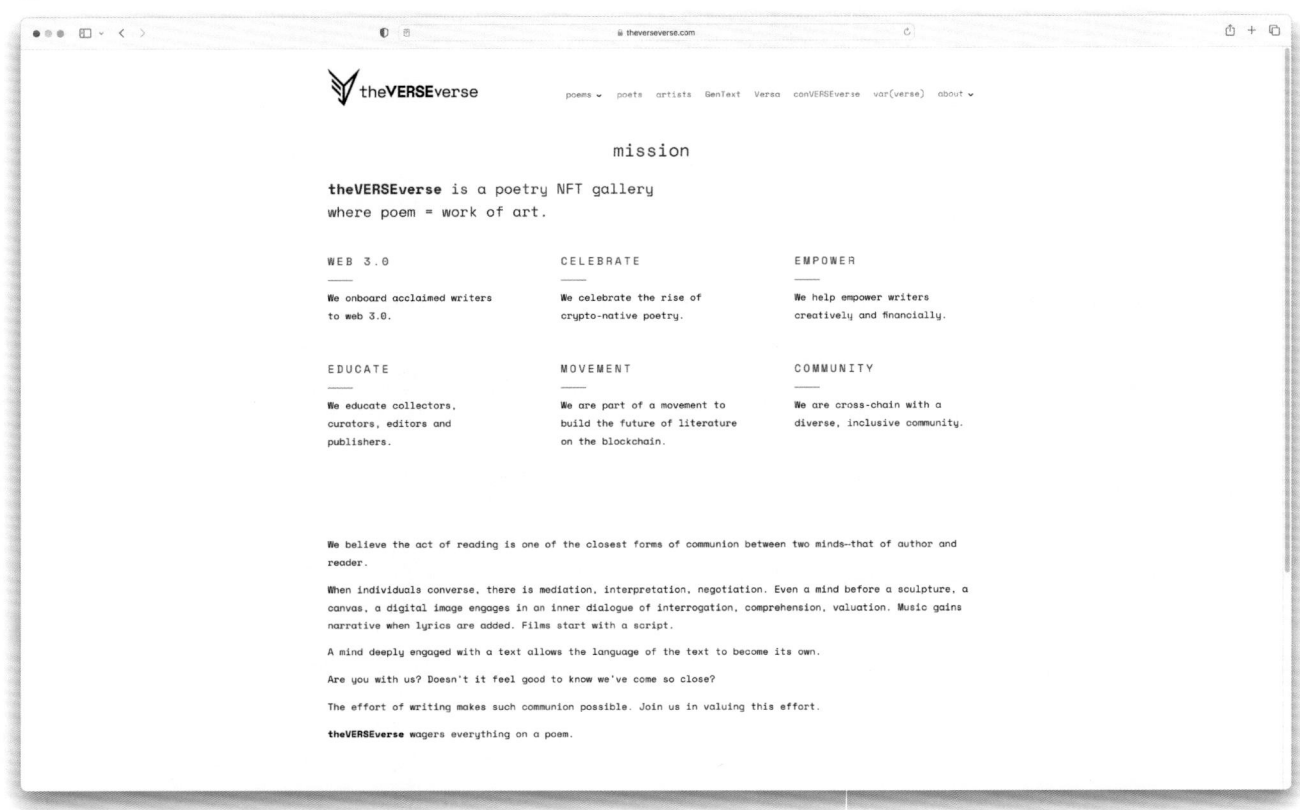

Founded in late 2021 by Ana Maria Caballero, Kalen Iwamoto, and Sasha Stiles — launched with artistic advisor Gisel Florez, and later joined by Elisabeth Sweet — theVERSEverse is a literary collective and digital poetry gallery. The collective seeks to redefine and reconsider how poetry is experienced, valued, and collected.

At its core, theVERSEverse asserts that every poem is a work of art. Not just metaphorically, but in form, in function, and in how it culturally circulates in the world. As poetry is often revered but rarely resourced, theVERSEverse advocates and stewards for its deeper engagement.

theVERSEverse upholds avant-garde traditions while embracing contemporary technologies such as computation, AI collaboration, and web3 publishing. Here, they challenge and investigate historical experimentation in language. The collective's curatorial and artistic projects, such as *POEME OBJKT / POEME SBJKT*, *GEN TEXT*, *VERSA*, *POESÍA DE PROTESTA*, and *FERALVERSE*, build on the lineage of experimental poetics: from Dada and Oulipo to concrete poetry and net art.

theVERSEverse create and exhibit works that turn poetry into experiences and digital artifacts. By moving verse beyond the page and across media, poetry enters dialogue with both physical and virtual space, challenging how meaning and resonance can endure as artistic form. In collaborations with such partners as the Estate of Allen Ginsberg, the Francisco Carolinum Museum, MAD Arts Museum, the Tezos Foundation, and Sudowrite, the collective explores poetry as conceptual gesture, sensorial object, performative act, and collectible artifact.

As a space for poetic innovation, theVERSEverse invokes unprecedented verses and muses on the past, present, and future of language. They provide a foundation for constant evolution and conversation on poetry's role, function, and form.

**ABIGAIL MILLER**
DIGITAL ART LEAD, AVANT ARTE

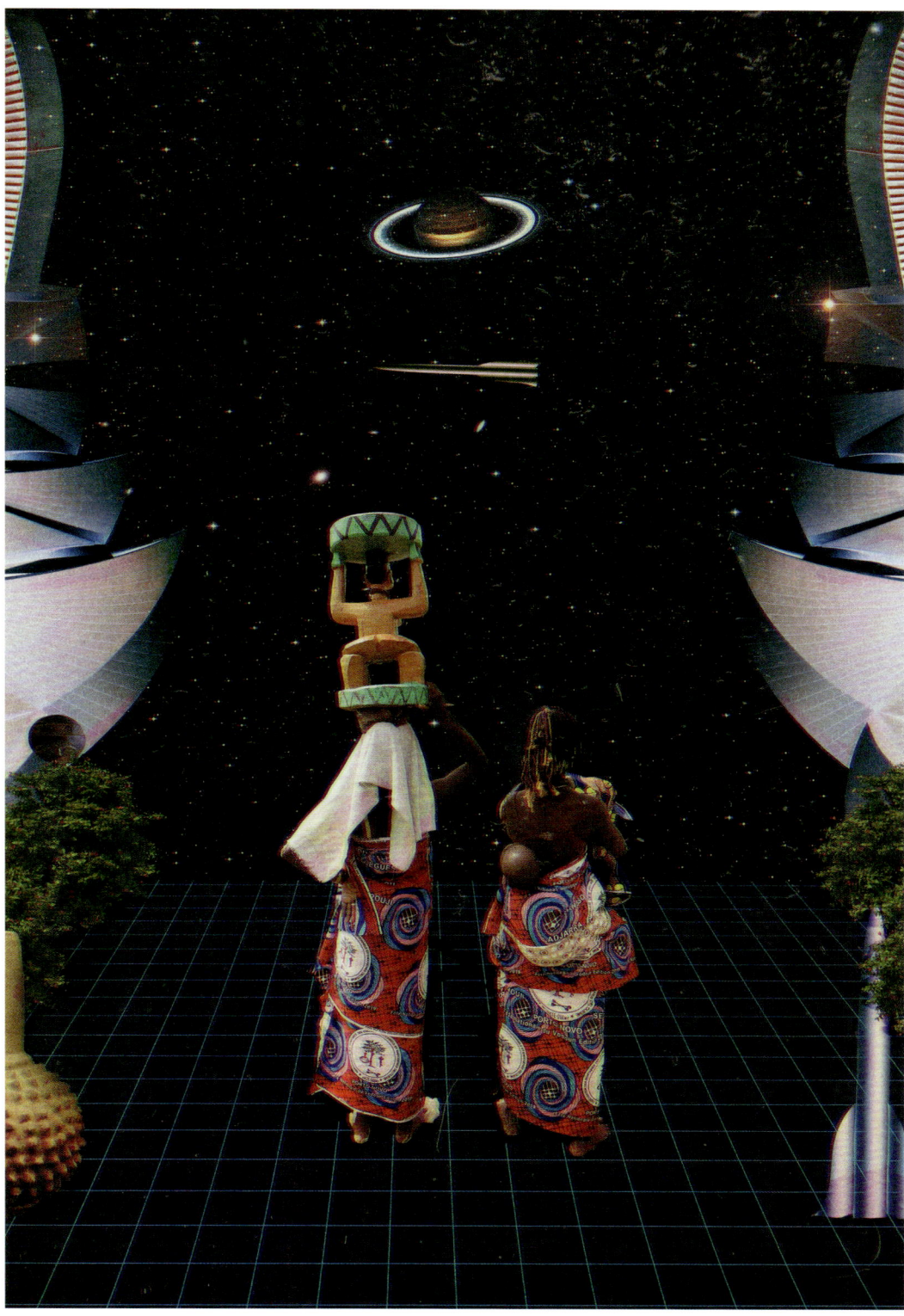

| # | TITLE | TIMESTAMP | MEDIUM | CHAIN | CONTRACT ADDRESS | TOKEN ID | EDITION SIZE |
|---|-------|-----------|--------|-------|------------------|----------|--------------|
| 01 | **Carrying Culture Into Unknown Planes** | 12-13-2021 07:01:18 | Adobe Photoshop | ETH | 0x9f5624edffda435300e-281536ac6852d6c21f371 | 5 | 1/1 |
| 02 | **Intergalactic Afroverse** | 10-24-2021 14:27:01 | Adobe Photoshop | ETH | 0x495f947276749ce646f-68ac8c248420045cb7b5e | 2852...2260 | 20 |

02

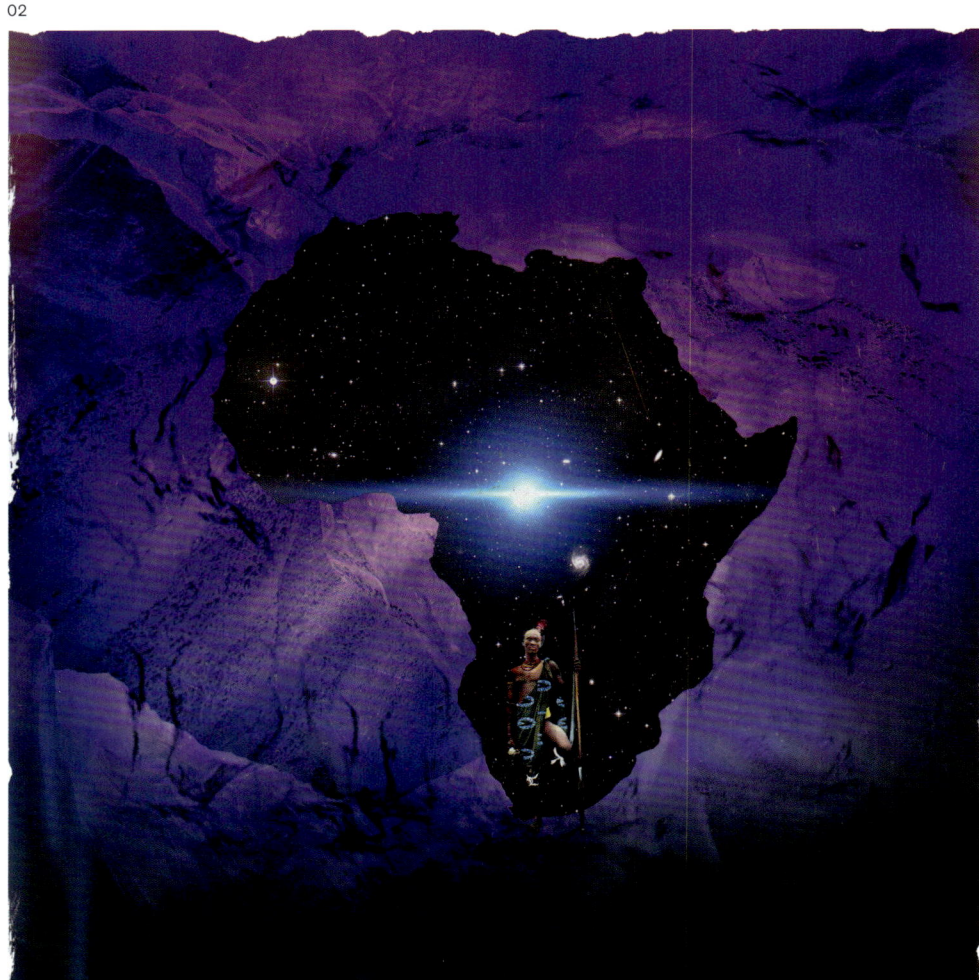

Isaac Opoku's (aka Afroscope) exploratory journey and self-discovery as a creative soul began through several visits and conversations with two co-founders of Nubuke Foundation, myself and Kofi Setordji about ten years ago. At the time it seemed that there did not yet exist opportunities for his multilayered, experimental ideas, thoughts, and work to be expressed, experienced, or even accepted. That could also be attributed to him veering away from the field of economics and statistics, which he studied at university. In his practice, he boldly engages with materials, historical and cultural texts, motifs, and religion from his native Ghana and other African cultures, and employs technology, code, and AI to extrapolate these themes in different realms. His works are like open books, led by his unconventionally long storyboards on Instagram, a natural turn for an artist who could hardly contain or encapsulate his ideas or expression on the traditional canvas. An incredible optimist, Isaac's works have evolved into the digital, VR, and AI platforms, representing African artists showcasing in the NFT community. His works speak to his positive outlook and dreams by creating realities that viewers can escape to.

In *Carrying Culture Into Unknown Planes* (2021) for instance, the superposition of traditional characters on the verge of an infinite plane doesn't instigate fear but instead suggests a sublime and inspiring venture into the unknown, whether it be the universe around us or the untapped potential of the metaverse. Isaac's exploration and use of digital technology is a reflection of his views about how technology can be employed to transform and improve the lives of the average Ghanaian citizen, taking away drudgery and repetitive tasks and replacing it with futuristic applications that can be used by all strata of society in a meaningful and impactful way. In 2022, Isaac was selected to represent Ghana in the 59th Venice Biennale. He is one of the first alumni of the Nubuke Foundation's artist development program, YGA.

**ODILE TEVIE**
DIRECTOR & CO-FOUNDER OF NUBUKE
FOUNDATION, ACCRA, AND COLLECTOR

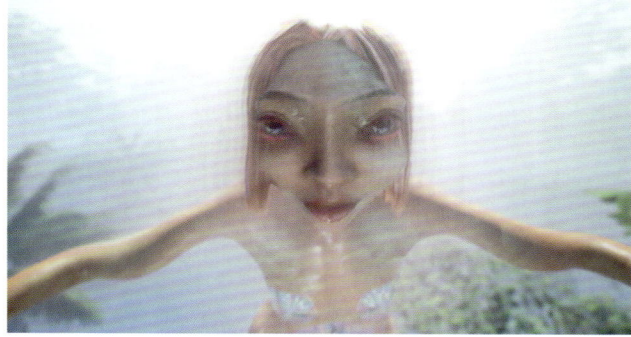 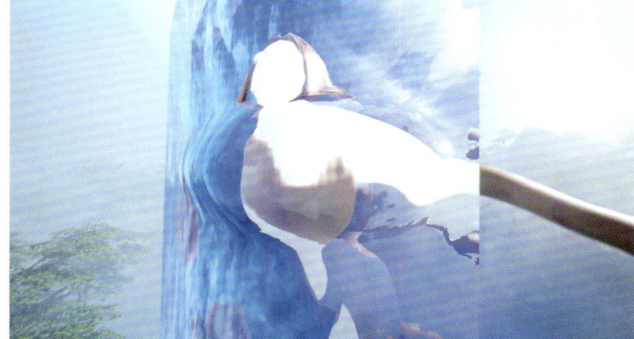

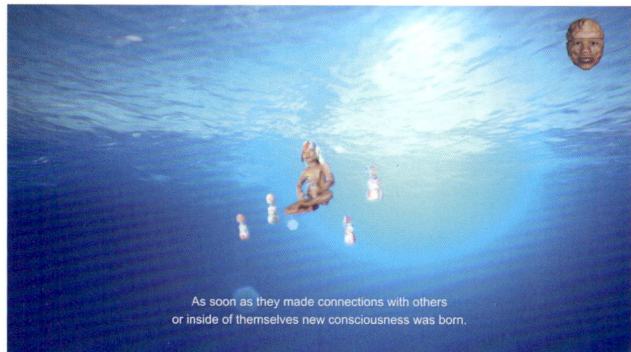 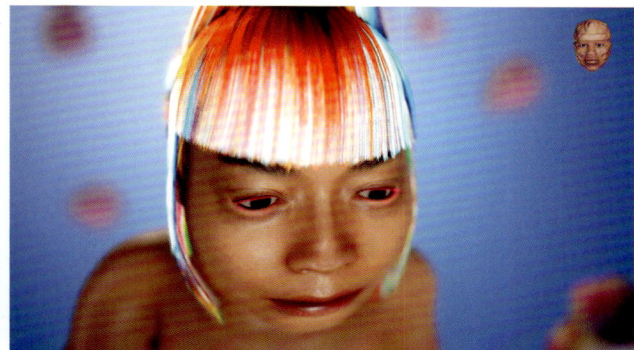

As soon as they made connections with others
or inside of themselves new consciousness was born.

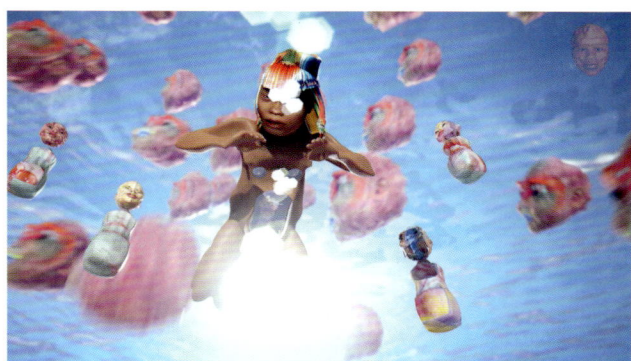 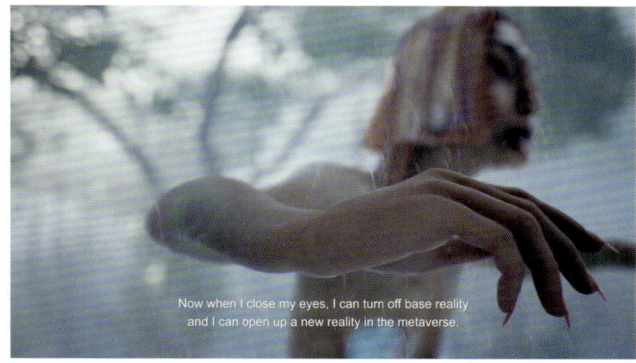

Now when I close my eyes, I can turn off base reality
and I can open up a new reality in the metaverse.

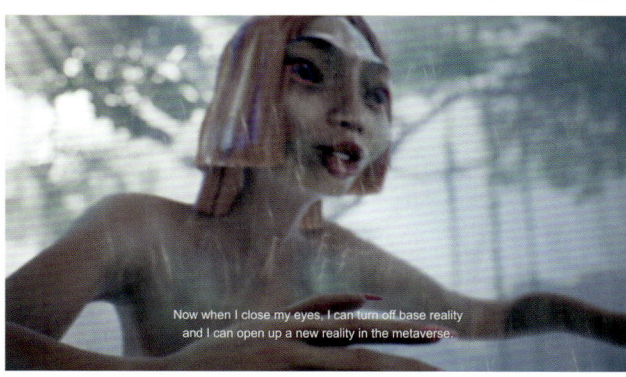 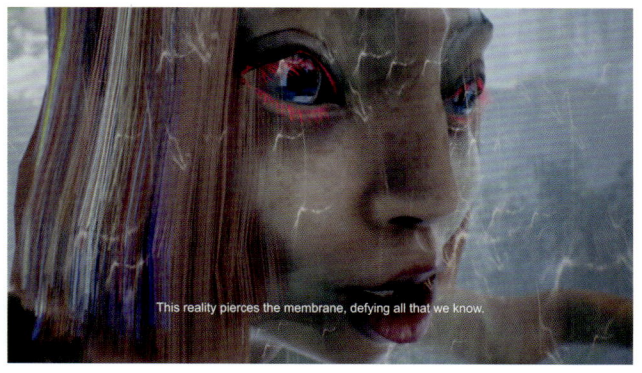

Now when I close my eyes, I can turn off base reality
and I can open up a new reality in the metaverse.

This reality pierces the membrane, defying all that we know.

| # | TITLE | TIMESTAMP | MEDIUM | CHAIN | CONTRACT ADDRESS | TOKEN ID | EDITION SIZE | COLLABORATORS |
|---|---|---|---|---|---|---|---|---|
| 01 | **Dream Time Life Simulation** | 05-06-2021 10:21:53 | Unreal Engine 4, Character Creator, Blender, Adobe Substance 3D Painter, iClone Animation Software, MP4 | ETH | 0x3b3ee1931dc30c19573-79fac9aba94d1c48a5405 | 34725 | 1/1 | – |
| 02 | **Wisdoms for Love 3.0** | 03-25-2021 11:14:00 | Unreal Engine 4, Blender, Character Creator, iClone, Adobe Substance 3D Painter, PNG (from web-based game) | ETH | 0x495f947276749ce646f-68ac8c248420045cb7b5e | 6334...4961 | 1/1 | Obso1337, Ryan Vautier, Sakeema Crook |

# KEIKEN

02

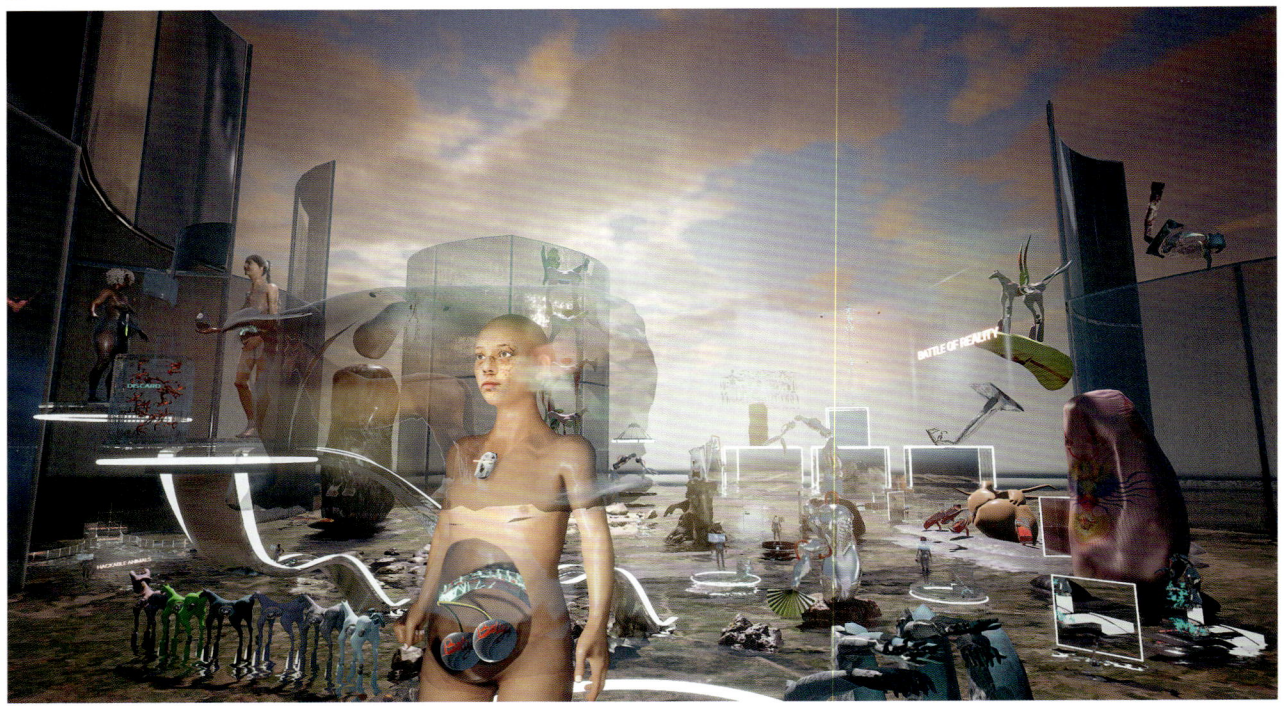

Keiken is an artist collective, co-founded by Tanya Cruz, Hana Omori, and Isabel Ramos. Their practice builds and reimagines metaverses as spaces for rehearsing possible futures. Using gaming strategies, installation, and extended reality (XR) they think through blockchain's affordances as a social apparatus. In an ethereal backdrop with soothing sounds, two voices guide us through *Wisdoms for Love* (2021), a labyrinth of metaphorical decisions. In navigating these forking paths, players obtain Wisdom Tokens (NFTs) that decide on their fate through Moral Contracts (smart contracts). Assets like *Suffering Truth* (2021) or *Cosmoscentric Bowl* (2021) are the currency that condition your life value and, in turn, transform this notion in a practice far away from the reality of market relations. This NFT collection is conceived as tools for growth that determine wealth in this game, and they are given for free at the end. In this way, Keiken questions traditional forms of exchange, and propose tokenomics as a blueprint for a new social construct. This immersive world-building experience embodies the practice of blockchain and gamifies it, allowing the audience to experience alternative social imaginaries grounded in nonmarket values. This digital world-building is not only critical, but it makes it possible to experience an unwritten future that breaks apart from the ritual of capitalism.

In 2019, *Feel My Metaverse* reflected on the tensions between the corporate imaginings of a digitally mediated future and its economic and ecological repercussions and social disparities. The metaverses crafted by Keiken are analytical devices conveying alternative value systems. In this way, they rethink them as sites of struggle in lieu of escapism, where blockchain affordances become the infrastructures of alternative social imaginaries.

**BARBARA CUETO**
DIGITAL CURATOR AT C/O BERLIN

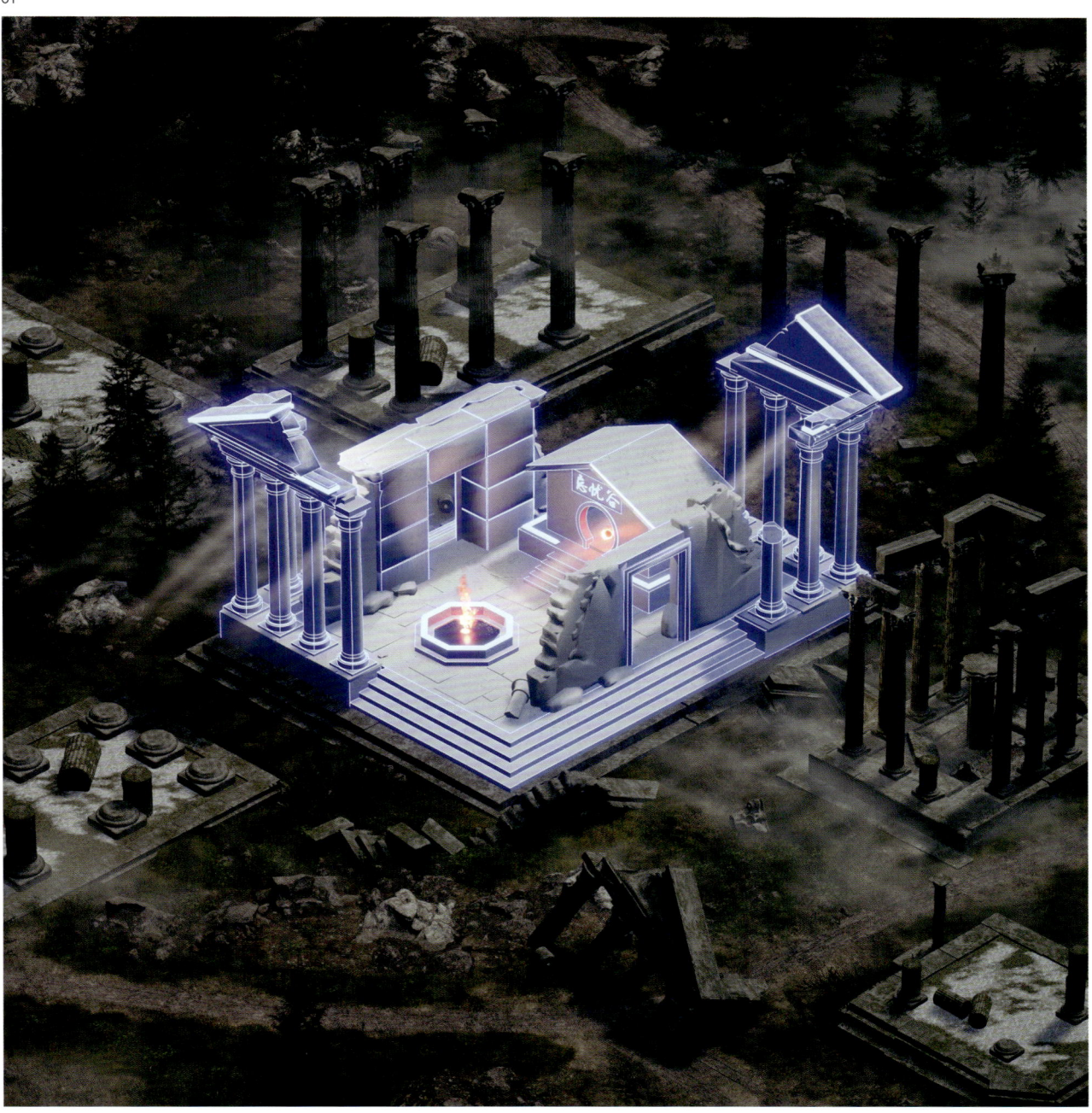

| # | TITLE | TIMESTAMP | MEDIUM | CHAIN | CONTRACT ADDRESS | TOKEN ID | EDITION SIZE |
|---|---|---|---|---|---|---|---|
| 01–03 | **Nepenthe Valley** | 03-09-2022 10:00:00 | Unreal Engine, Rhino3D, Ableton Live | SOL | (01) 6esmnymcm7517225am8kscxhnixtczs5a4sxx3dhv11j (02) gjksutyvm9vneavqbov2emahad8ckexnw8g7irs2qwfs (03) fygcejenncpgugmzdrchy8fojohmxrgudvuxgykqg1jd" | NV01-NV12 | NV01-NV08 in editions of 111, NV09-N12 in editions of 1111 |

EDITIONS ILLUSTRATED: (01) The Lodge (Map) (02) The Spring (Postcard) (03) The Lodge (Postcard)

# LAWRENCE LEK
## MALAYSIA 1982

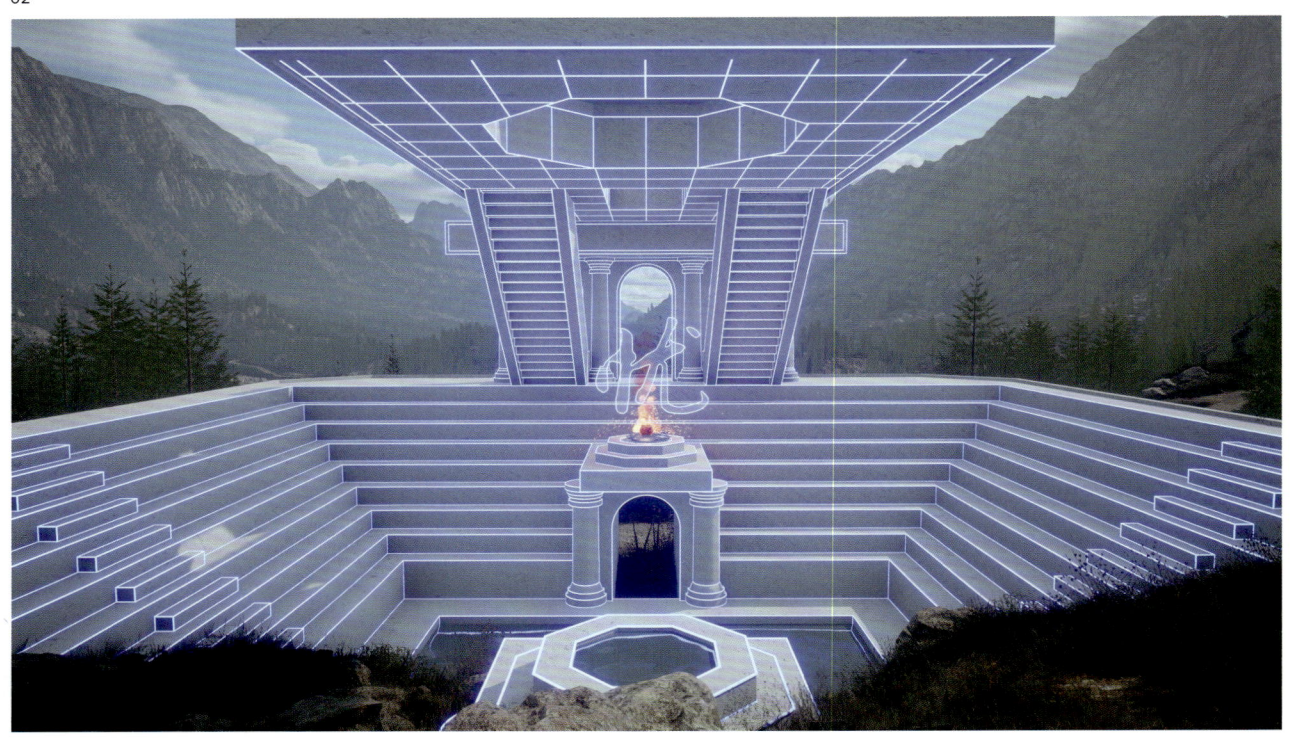

It began as an experience. An imagined chill-out club. Mirrored walls outlined in neon, a tropical island that is eternally in golden hour. You glide through glittering waters to the soothing of ambient music. Your existence activates a message, "You came here to forget. Don't you remember?"

*Nepenthe Valley* (2021), a sonic environment set in the near future where entertainment has become fully automated, turns a sharp eye towards the culture of wellness in an era of existential anxiety and environmental collapse. In 2021, the sound installation debuted at the 34th Ljubljana Biennial, setting the stage for the emerging world of *Nepenthe Valley*.

Building virtual worlds to reimagine the future has long driven the works of London-based, Malaysian Chinese artist Lawrence Lek, known for his ongoing series of CGI films, soundtracks, and virtual worlds, often set within a Sinofuturist universe. Whereas Lek's signature video-essay *Sinofuturism (1839–2046 AD)* (2016) marks its birth by the Opium War, *Nepenthe Valley* — named after the medicine for forgetting from Homer's *Odyssey* — is a timeless, virtual landscape devoid of geopolitical specificity. The shining ruins present an uncanny warping of past and future, inviting us into an alluring, collective dream for the metaverse. *Nepenthe Valley* exists as an episodic open-world game that originated as a collection of NFTs presented in March 2022 by HORIZONS — a platform by new media collective SO-FAR and virtual gallery AORA. Designed with the utility to unlock secret locations and elixirs in the game, each of the launch NFTs relates to a distinct location, architecture, and soundscape of the *Valley*. Ultimately, it is a radical experiment in collective world-building and memory-making. NFT collectors are invited to activities exploring healing and identity in Web3, which in turn, explores our existence in real life. What can we remember when our bodies enter the virtual realm?

After all, "Don't you remember? You came here to forget."

**JINJIN**
POET, ARTIST, AND CO-FOUNDER OF CHAOS

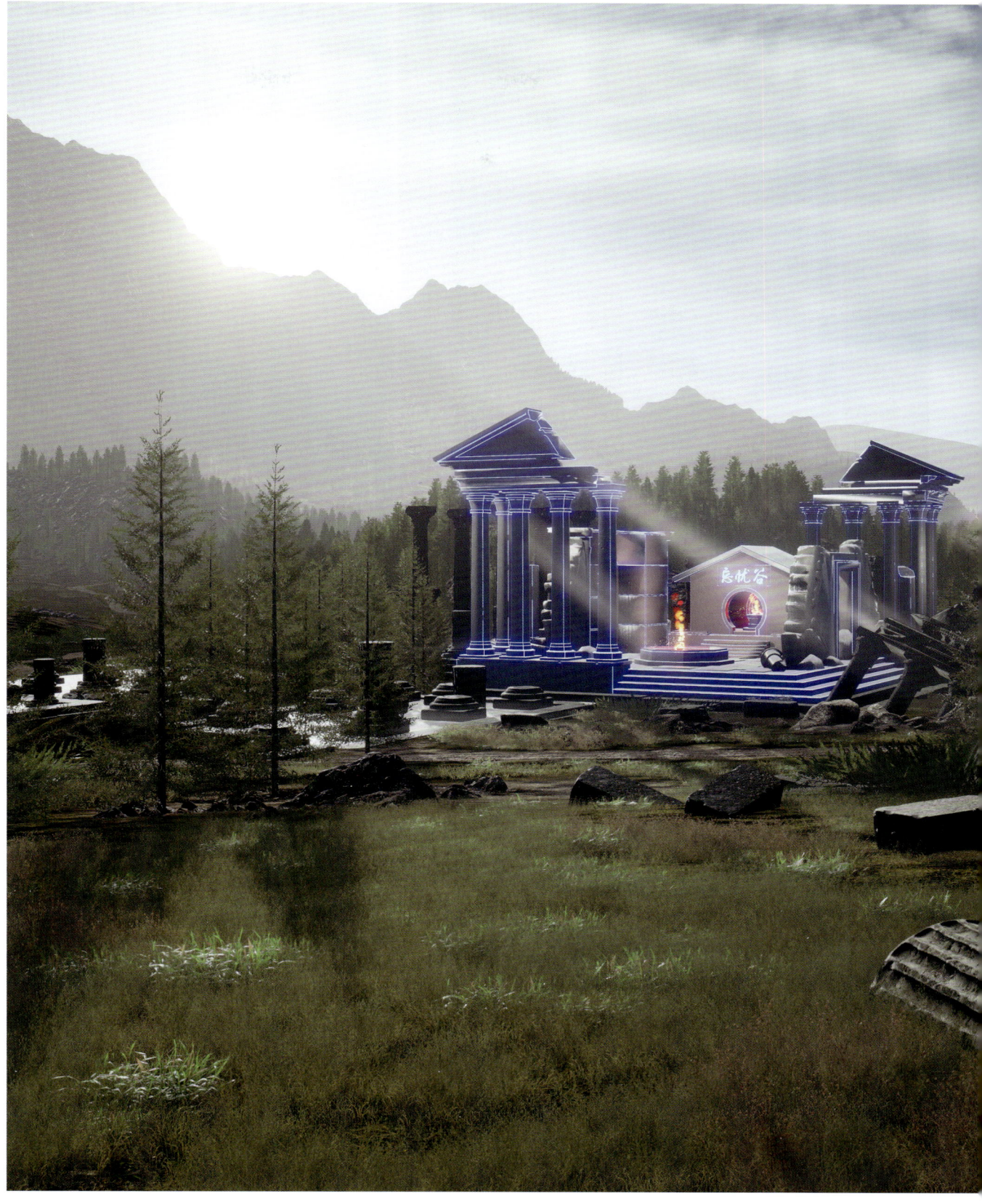

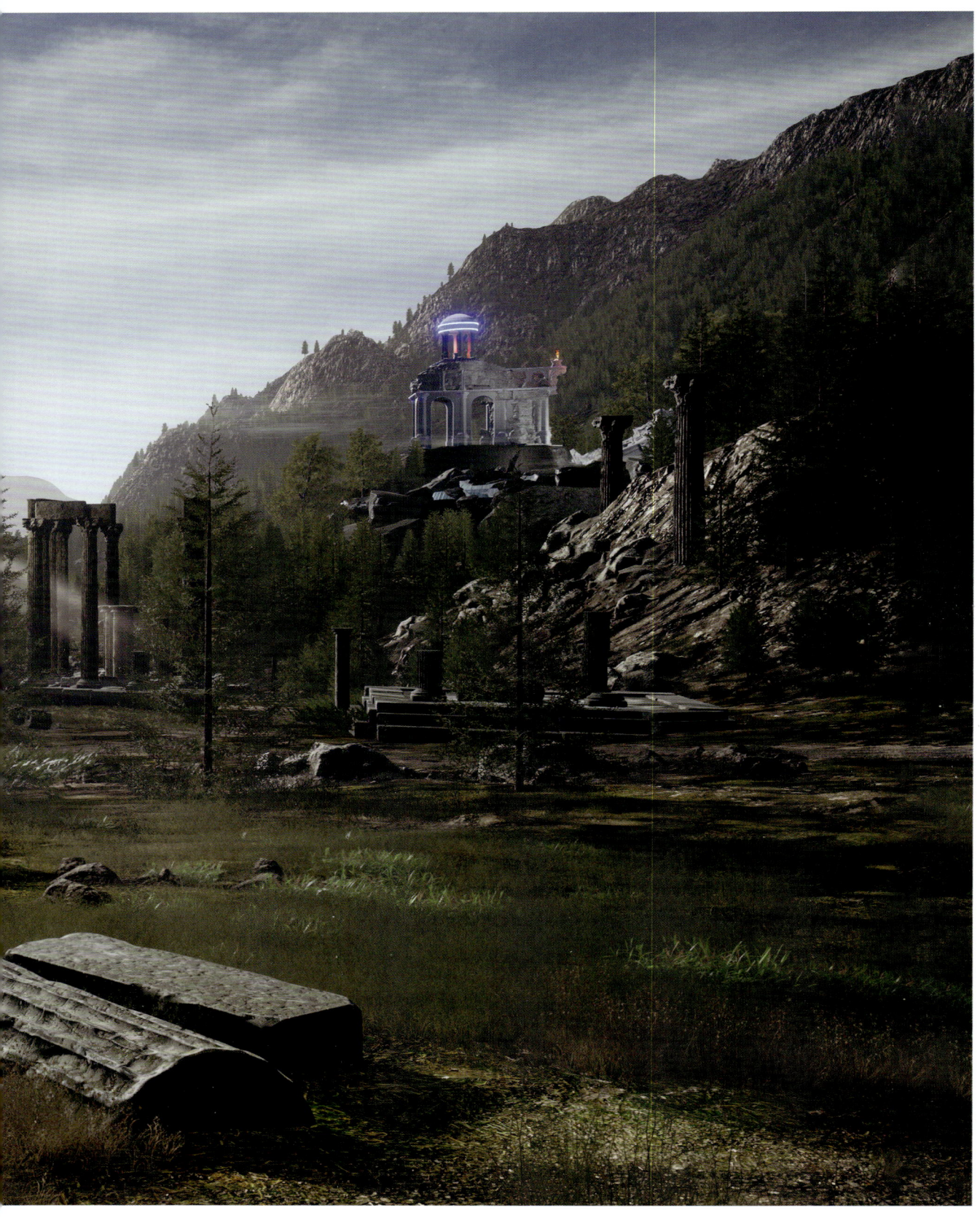

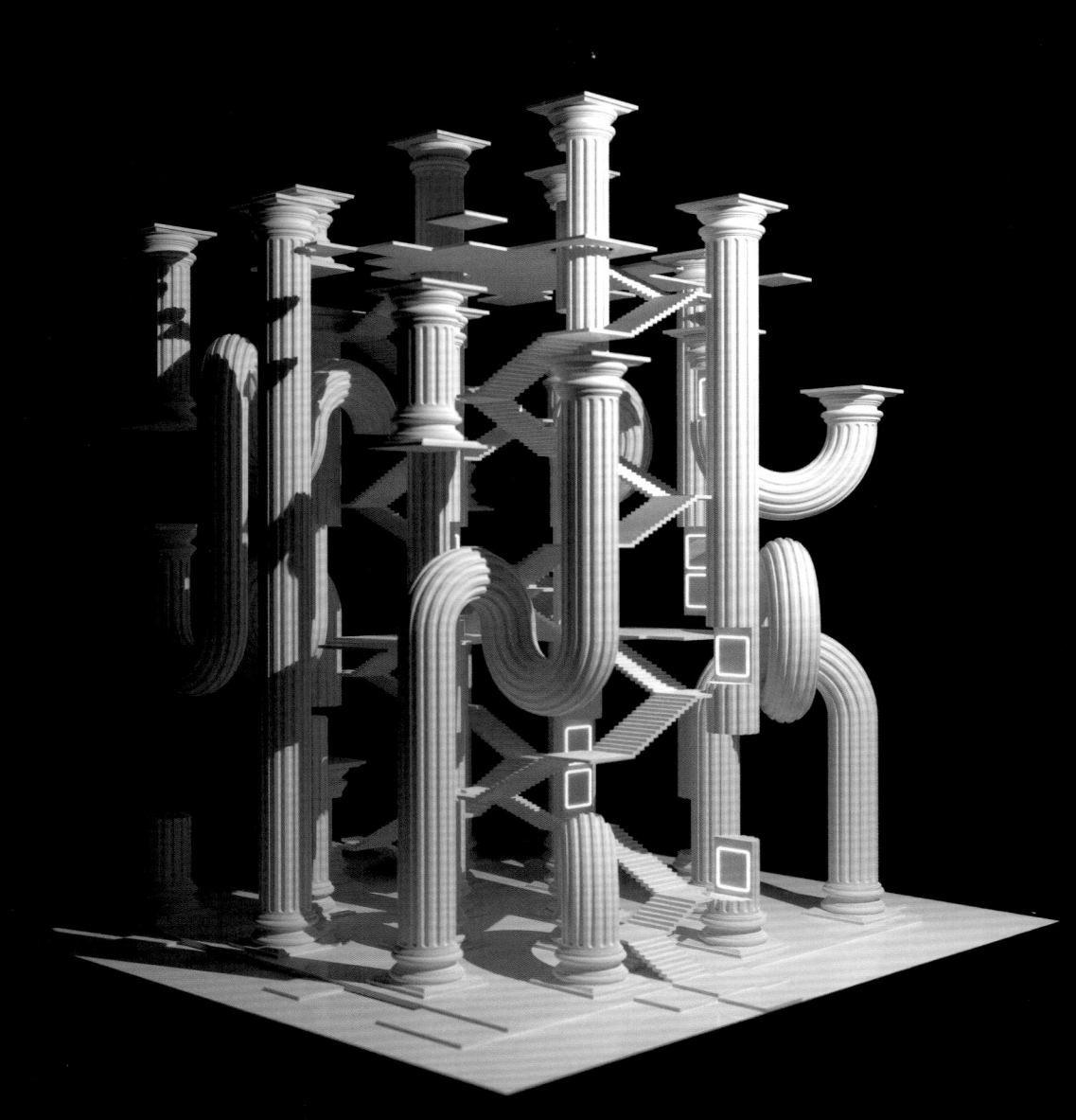

*OUTLAND* IN
CONVERSATION WITH
HANS ULRICH OBRIST

# ON THE METAVERSE

Welcome to the Fun Palace: Curating & Exploring Native Digital Worlds

*No need to look for an entrance, just walk in anywhere.*

*Choose what you want to do [...] try starting a riot or beginning
a painting, or just lie back and stare at the sky.*

*What time is it? Any time of day or night,
winter or summer — it really doesn't matter.*

*A university of the streets [...] a playground for adults,
built like a big shipyard with no walls.*

*A laboratory of fun.*

Joan Littlewood and Cedric Price
Collected statements on the Fun Palace (1964–1966)

**09.00**
UntitledXYZ
MOCΔ *ROOMs* (2021–ongoing)
3D interactive models
Ethereum, 0x1b8aB0b410f54aE0a24320e6188E3Ec20A6c609a, 0–∞

At one point in *Snow Crash*, the 1992 novel in which Neal Stephenson introduced the concept of the metaverse as a network where people could interact in virtual space via virtual bodies, the protagonist encounters a software-based entity known as the Librarian, who shares some esoteric knowledge. The *nam-shub* was a key element of ancient Sumerian science and magic, the Librarian explains. It was an incantation that shapes the world. The protagonist instantly draws an analogy between the nam-shub and code, which in the metaverse is text with the power to transform bodies, things, and places.

The performative force of code is a fact of software in general, but for the blockchain — still far from being conceived when Stephenson wrote *Snow Crash* — the textual magic of code seems even more powerful. Blocks of code are permanent as cuneiform etched in stone. They can make and ruin fortunes, enact irreversible decisions. NFTs will play important roles in the metaverse that is now taking shape, and not only as works of art decorating its shared spaces.

One of the earliest instances of the blockchain-based metaverse, Decentraland, launched in 2017. Parcels of land there are traded as NFTs; sales are mediated by an in-world currency ($MANA). The economy recalls that of *Second Life*, where virtual property and services were bought and sold for Linden dollars. But in Decentraland everything is recorded on the blockchain. Last year a number of brands purchased plots to throw launch events and fashion shows. Art was sold there, too. Sotheby's built a replica of its Bond Street headquarters to display the works included in its June 2021 *Natively Digital* auction. König Galerie re-created the refurbished brutalist church of its Berlin location in Decentraland with aid from artist Manuel Rossner, who incorporated his own 3D digital sculptures as interventions in the virtual architecture. *THE ARTIST IS ONLINE*, König's first NFT show, opened there in March 2021 **[09.01]**. Cryptovoxels is another blockchain-based 3D world, one where everything is built from volumetric pixels, like in *Fortnite*. The Francisco Carolinum in Linz, Austria, bought parcels of land in Cryptovoxels to host a virtual companion to *Proof of Art: A Brief History of NFTs* **[09.02]**, a 2021 museum survey that linked the current activity in blockchain-based art to historic innovations by artists like Nam June Paik (1932–2006) and Lynn Hershman Leeson. Fingerprints DAO also built a museum to display its collection of conceptual blockchain art in Cryptovoxels. The platform's advantage over Decentraland is faster loading times: it takes a lot of memory to render 3D worlds from the blockchain to the browser, and the uniformity of voxels speeds things up. Computing power remains the major obstacle to developing the metaverse; it's the reason why virtual exhibitions rarely imagine new ways to display art, limiting themselves instead to be pale shadows of the white cube.

Besides Decentraland and Cryptovoxels, there are other worlds that can be used for curating exhibitions, like Somnium Space; worlds designed specifically for displaying NFT art, like Rare Rooms; and game worlds like *Axie Infinity* and *Star Atlas* that could potentially be hijacked for artistic interventions, as *Fortnite* and *World of Warcraft* have been. The Museum of Crypto Art, a collection that has built a site for virtual display in Somnium Space **[09.03]**, has also developed a project called *ROOMs* **[09.00]**. These NFTs are modular virtual galleries where collectors can arrange their works and port them into various metaverse applications, in order to show their collections in multiple locations, on multiple blockchains, simultaneously. It's an initiative that seeks to make good on Web3's promise of interoperability—a use of decentralized protocols that free NFTs from proprietary formats and siloed corporate limitations. LaTurbo Avedon, an artist who has been working with virtual worlds for over a decade, launched a project in 2021 called *Materia*. Still in its early stages, *Materia* **[09.04, 09.05]** is intended to eventually become an artist-run metaverse, built from the ground up with community input. Avedon has released a series of NFTs on different marketplaces, which collectors can purchase and "socket," connecting them with one another in ways that determine the cosmology and material structure of the world to come. Avedon's approach hints at how the metaverse demands a different way of thinking about NFTs than the one most widespread now. They are not merely artworks, or receipts for artworks; they can be elements in a system of permissions and connections that define a virtual environment. By starting with these building blocks, Avedon demonstrates how people can realize the potential of Web3 and work together to create the worlds they want to see, rather than relying on tech giants and other powerful entities to set the terms for the metaverse. These more utopian goals, and Avedon's implementations of them, can be contrasted with the longer historical timelines of land claims and colonization of new territories that Simon Denny explores in his work *Metaverse Landscapes* (2022–ongoing) **[09.06]**. Hijacking the landscape traditions such as the 19th-century American tradition of "manifest destiny" where picturesque view painters would paint landscapes that helped naturalize different kinds of ownership claims (often of disputed lands), Denny's physical and digital work recast these issues within the politics of the metaverse. Refiguring Decentraland parcels into paintings and recording their

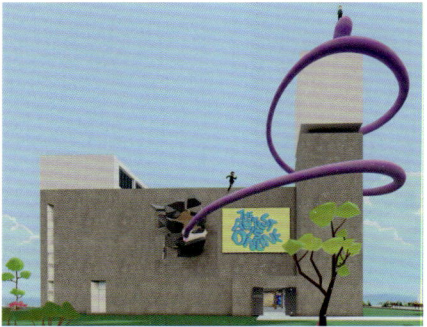
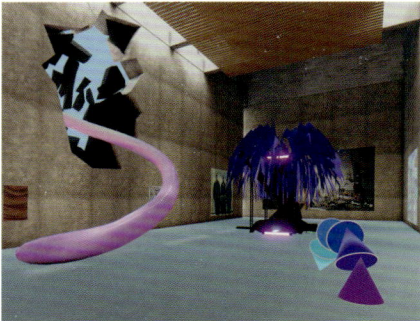
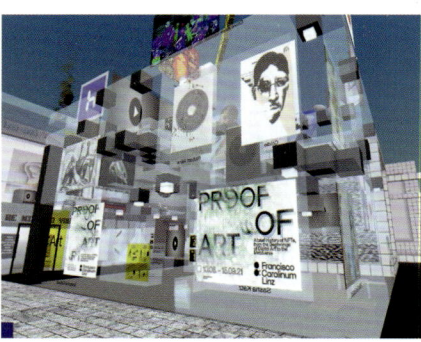
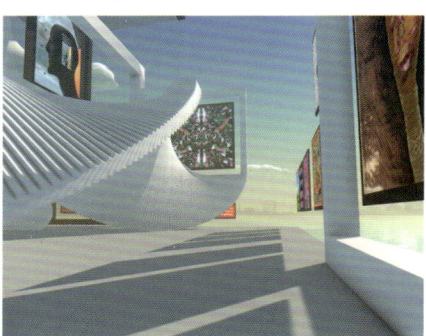

ever-changing ownership structures via NFTs, Denny presents a counterpoint to the hype surrounding a free and open metaverse, drawing attention to the capitalist colonization of this new "free" territory. Taken together, both Avedon's *Materia* and Denny's *Metaverse Landscapes* suggest the forking roads the current Web3 metaverse ecosystems can take.

Below, curator Hans Ulrich Obrist speaks with Jason Li, founder and CEO of *Outland*, and Christopher Y. Lew, *Outland*'s chief artistic director, about the speculative possibilities of the metaverse, and what they could mean for art and cultural institutions. As artistic director at the Serpentine Galleries, Obrist has led an ambitious program to show virtual reality, mixed reality, and other mediums laying the groundwork for the visual culture of the metaverse. He also established Future Art Ecosystems, an initiative that publishes annual reports surveying the landscape of artists working with new technologies and how they are changing the relationships between art, institutions, and audiences. *Outland* is an online magazine for digital art that launched in November 2021, publishing criticism and conversations to develop the discourse around art and Web3 while also commissioning NFT projects. The following conversation expands the framework for thinking about art and NFTs, anticipating how NFTs can take on new roles in the metaverse to impact interpersonal and institutional behaviors. Obrist, Li, and Lew discuss the intellectual histories that set the tone for Web3 and provide the vocabulary for defining and critiquing it. They consider artists of generations past who engaged with the concepts and methods of science fiction to understand how young artists today are doing the same to influence the direction of the metaverse's development. They think about how the metaverse already exists now, in the overlapping networks of Web 2.0 and Web3. And they come to a consensus that the best possible metaverse is a multiverse of many virtual worlds, one that gives artists and users the agency to determine how their virtual selves can live and interact. When the hero of *Snow Crash* learns that the Sumerian demigod Enki created a nam-shub that ripped society away from centralized control, he muses: "Maybe Babel was the best thing that ever happened to us."

**BRIAN DROITCOUR**
EDITOR-IN-CHIEF AT *OUTLAND*

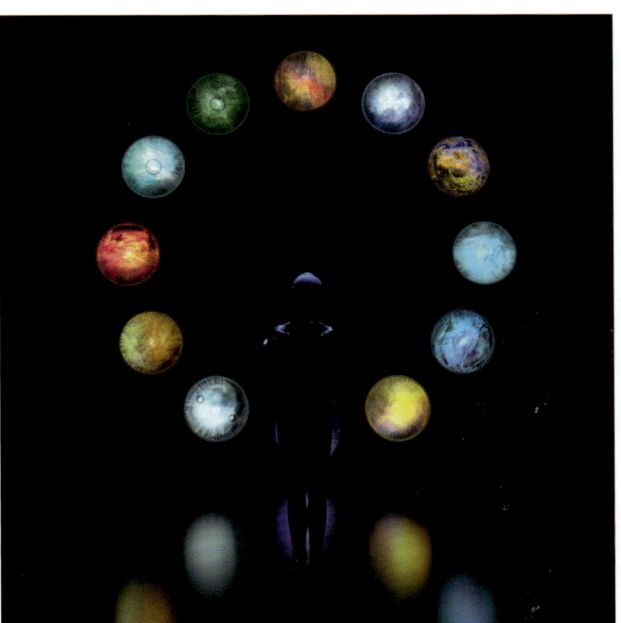

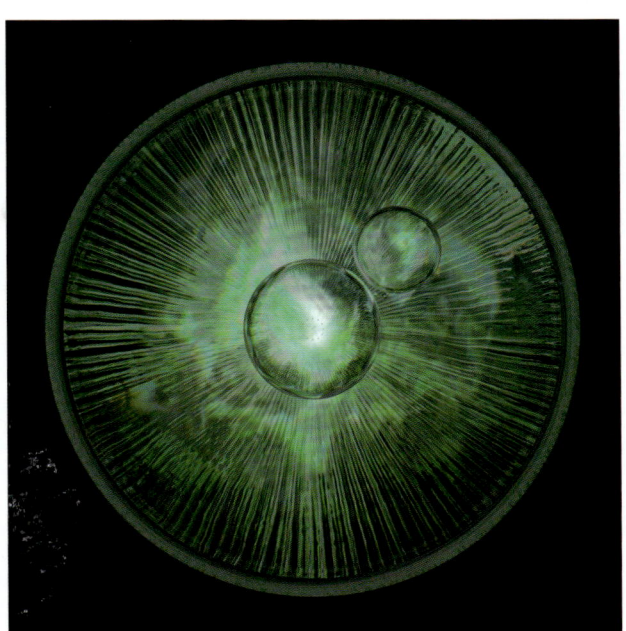

**CHRISTOPHER Y. LEW:** Much of the language around the metaverse comes out of science fiction, particularly cyberpunk. We've moved from the cyberspace of William Gibson's *Neuromancer* (1984) and now we're getting to the metaverse of Neal Stephenson's *Snow Crash*. I've been thinking about a few artists that I've been in dialogue with for many years that are very influenced by science fiction. Sophia al-Maria coined the term *Gulf Futurism* with Fatima al-Qadiri. That framework used the language of science fiction to talk about the rapidly developing cities of the Gulf, and how quickly Bedouin families like al-Maria's ended up in these futuristic cities that seemingly appeared overnight. Science fiction has demonstrated how to take the concerns of today and project them into the future in order to understand the present. But they're also looking at the future from this moment in order to influence what that future can be and not leave it up to giant corporations to make those decisions. That perspective can be very empowering for artists.

**HANS ULRICH OBRIST:** Philippe Parreno urged me to read *Snow Crash* back in the late '90s. It was actually Bruce Sterling who got me on the internet. I was at a conference with him in 1994 and he couldn't understand why I wasn't online. He sent me to the cyber cafe to open my first email account. At that time, very few people in the art world were on email.

The first show Philippe and I did together was *Alien Seasons* at the Musee de l'Art Moderne de la Ville de Paris in 2002. We invited the futurist Jaron Lanier to collaborate. He's relevant for many of the things being discussed now. At a restaurant in Paris, he drew a cuttlefish, an animal that communicates almost post-symbolically because its skin is like a projection surface for film, with permanently changing colors and patterns. The cuttlefish not only became the guide through the exhibition, but whenever cuttlefish popped up, other aspects of the show were activated. I connected this whole idea of the virtual in Lanier to the virtual in Deleuze.

**LEW:** There are clear connections between those two generations. Lanier worked on early virtual reality, the promise of which is being delivered today, but for over a decade he has been writing books about the repercussions and dangers of that technology.

**OBRIST:** Dominique Gonzalez-Foerster's exhibition *Alienarium 5*, at the Serpentine in 2022, was a speculative environment that invites us to imagine possible encounters with extra-terrestrials. The show culminates many decades of her interest in science fiction. The show involves a collaboration with a musician and a perfumier. She transformed the Serpentine into this multisensory, otherworldly environment.

**09.06**
Simon Denny
*Metaverse Landscape 4: Decentraland Parcel 40, -96*, 2022
UV print and oil on canvas, wood, MDF, Plexiglas, Ethereum paper wallet, dynamic ERC-721 NFT, 127.4 × 122.4 × 6.2 cm, framed
Ethereum, 0x2A86C5466f088caEbf94e071a77669BAe371CD87, 11162024661369549010673884926386277492224414022536721016537738937911654701 6263

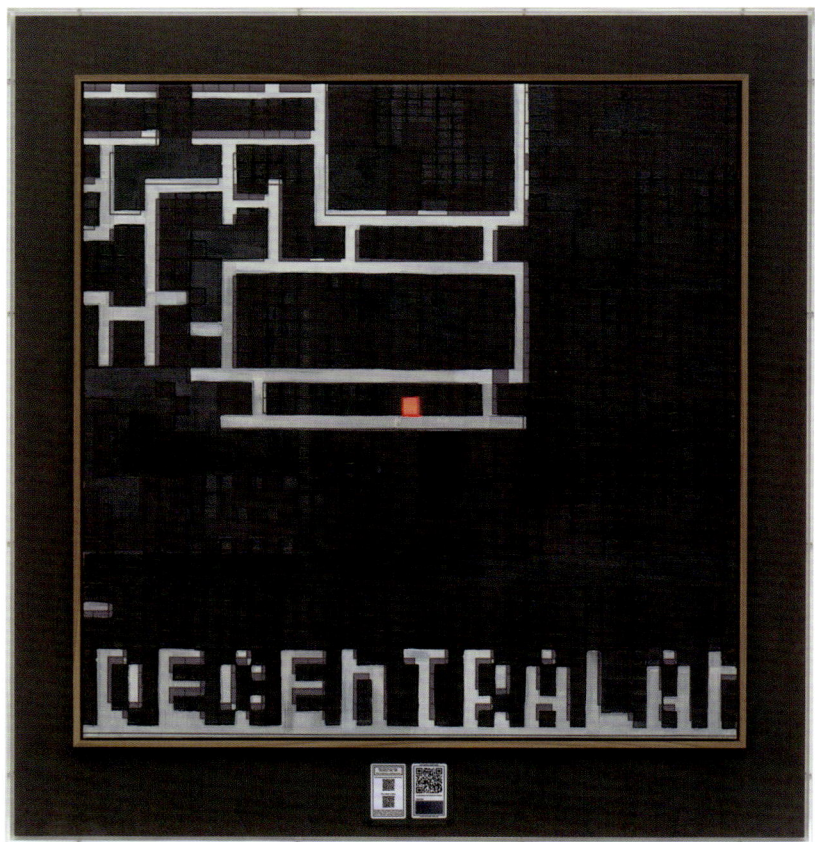

There's a VR piece that offers alternative forms of connection through extraterrestrial embodiment. You go from the 360-degree panorama, which is a big collage that uses outer space as a framework, to these encounters. It's about welcoming visitors into a world of expanded possibility. It's the opposite of *War of the Worlds*. *Alienarium 5* alludes to the metaverse's potential as a place where artists can create total environments for exploring other forms of existence.

Artists have played such an important role in contributing to the evolution of virtual environments. It raises its question: Should cultural institutions take part in building the metaverse? That's what the Serpentine does with our Future Art Ecosystems (FAE). The purpose of Future Art Ecosystems is to provide analytical and conceptual tools and strategic guidance for the construction of 21st-century cultural infrastructure: the systems that would support art and advanced technologies as a whole, and be responsive to a broader societal agenda. The core team responsible for the production of FAE2 includes the Serpentine R&D Platform (Alex Boyes, Tamar Clarke-Brown, Victoria Ivanova, Eva Jäger, Ben Vickers, and Kay Watson). We have published two reports so far, and the second is about art in the metaverse. We tried to get away from this very restrictive binary of physical and digital. We take a holistic approach, where the physical gallery is no longer at the center, but part of an integrated narrative. Indeed, many NFT artists are straddling the physical and digital worlds perhaps because there doesn't yet exist decentralized or centralized metaverse spaces at scale that the public is engaging with.

**JASON LI:** Meta Art, formerly called Facebook Open Art, is partnering with organizations like ICA San Francisco, the New Museum, and the Park Avenue Armory to present events and exhibitions. They also host a six-month artist residency at their headquarters, giving artists access to their new technologies, like Horizon Worlds, a free VR virtual world game. That platform isn't fully built out yet. The avatars and architecture still look very cartoonish.

**09.07**
Installation view of *FREEPORT*
EPOCH Gallery
June 12–October 8, 2021

**09.08**
Installation view of *REPLICANTS*
EPOCH Gallery
October 9–January 14, 2022

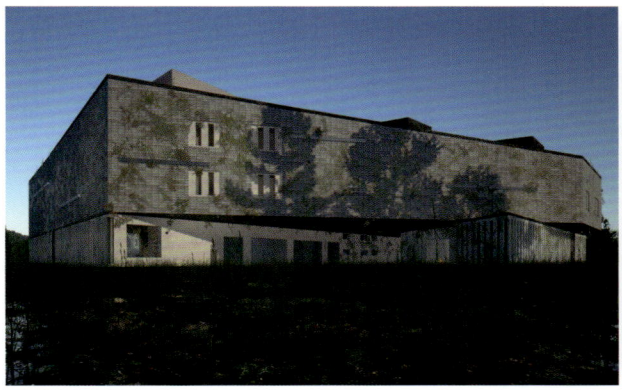
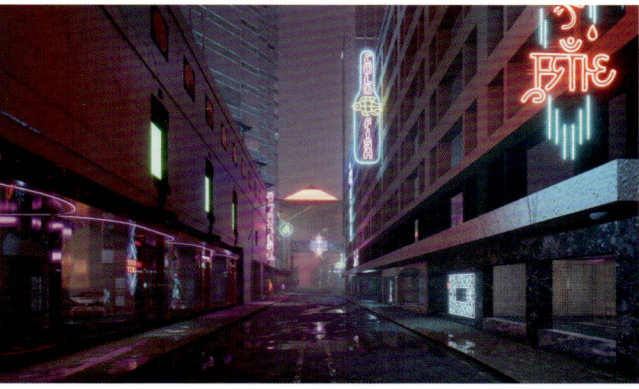

They're hoping artists can help move it forward. In terms of software, there are numerous opportunities for pluralism in the metaverse. Hardware is the major bottleneck. Oculus is the most widely used VR headset on the market. But still it has huge technological limitations. It's very uncomfortable to wear for long periods of time, and there is no way to process two-handed gestures. Meanwhile, platforms like Spatial are offering software for artists to build their own networks. They're trying to avoid a situation where the metaverse is run like a Web 2.0 platform.

**OBRIST:** I had long conversations a couple of years ago with Tim Berners-Lee about the invention of the World Wide Web in 1989. It was meant to be for everyone. He feels the idea is threatened now because the spaces of social media are commercialized, and the internet can't be accessed for free without submitting to surveillance. That's the main concern with the possibility of one company owning the metaverse as a monopoly.

Art engaging with technology continues the legacy of Berners-Lee. We did a show with Sondra Perry, who makes work about Black American experiences and the ways in which technology and identity are entangled, using digital tools like green-screen technology, 3D avatars, and found footage. Perry has said she's interested in thinking about how Blackness shifts and morphs to combat oppression and surveillance. Net neutrality is at the core of her work. It's based on ideas of collective production. She uses open-source software to edit the work and then releases it digitally for use in galleries and classrooms while actually making all the work available for free online. Another artist who comes to mind in this context is Sarah Friend. Her practice takes a very subversive approach to working with the blockchain. In Friend's work *Lifeforms* (2021), for example, the value of an NFT is dependent on being passed on to other people, otherwise the NFTs will disappear. The lack of permanence to the work suggests avenues to a more spontaneous and incidental metaverse experience, where interpersonal relationships, not ownership, sit at the core of metaverse-mediated public spaces. What will be crucial for the future of art on the blockchain and in decentralized metaverses is an increase in diversity and accessibility. As with all art and the making thereof, it should be for all and accessible to everyone. Limiting such access creates exclusionary domains which are limiting the possibilities of creating — especially within a realm that has the potential to be so vast.

**LEW:** In much of his writing, Jaron Lanier talks about the lock-in effect of protocols. At a certain point these things get prescribed, and then it's virtually impossible to change them. One of his examples is MIDI. It's a music technology developed in the early 1980s for keyboard players that didn't account for how notes could be played on other instruments. What had been designed for a narrow application was adopted as a universal standard for a wide range of digital instruments and ended up locking out other modes of expression. The metaverse has so much potential. Will corporations create new walled gardens? Or will artists and others who are upholding the legacies of pioneers of the internet prevail and create a more open internet? What will intentionally and unintentionally be locked in or out of these new systems?

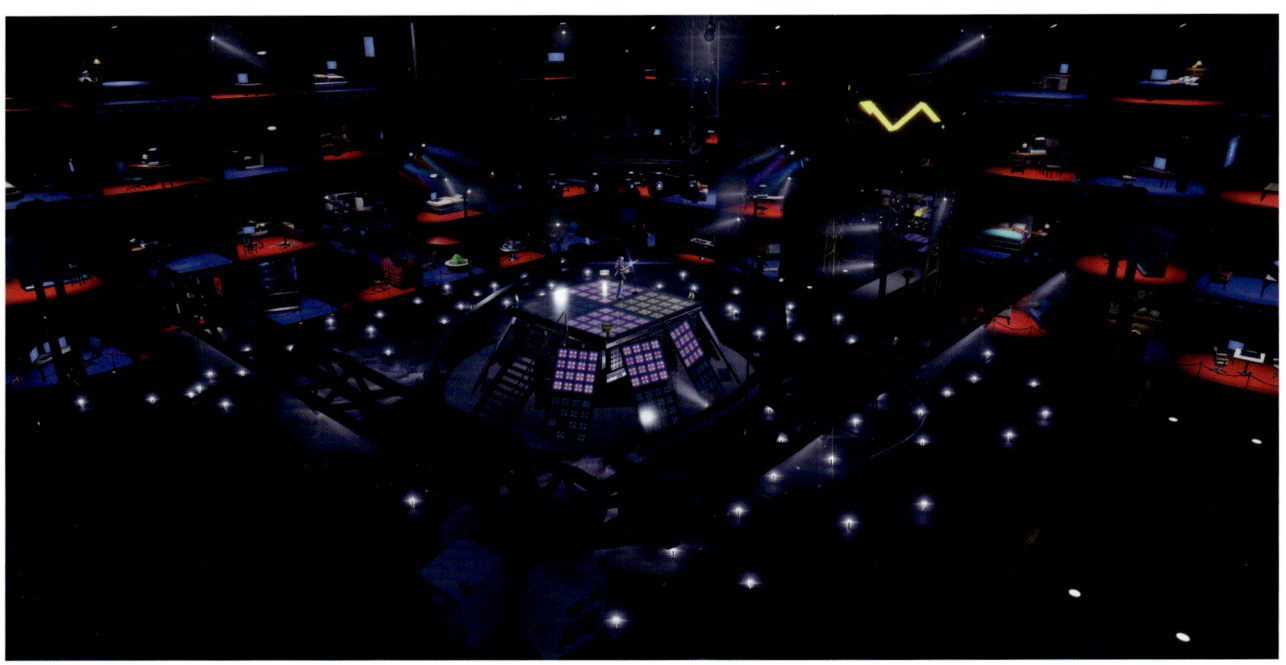

For his EPOCH Gallery project **[09.07, 09.08]**, Peter Wu+ creates virtual worlds to present exhibitions, in environments based on a street in Hong Kong or a freeport in Luxembourg. These immersive environments become critical contexts for works by other artists. The whole show is sold as an NFT, rather than minting individual works. It keeps each exhibition intact, though in the process it creates a closed system that isn't to be changed.

**OBRIST:** That's interesting. Other artists have built out virtual exhibition environments, too. LaTurbo Avedon built a replica of the permanent venue for the Manchester International Festival in *Fortnite* **[09.09]**. It was the first time we could experience an institution virtually before it opened to the public in the physical world. *KAWS: New Fiction* (2022) functioned in parallel at the Serpentine and in *Fortnite*. We had a much younger audience in the galleries and up to ten million people per day online. The exhibition's success shows the importance of combining physical and virtual experiences and the potential exciting scope for art in the metaverse. Artists like Refik Anadol, for example, are taking the potential of NFTs to a new level by literally altering physical buildings digitally and linking these works to NFTs. Anadol's studio will take apart buildings layer by layer and remake them digitally to change the experience of them completely into mixed reality. This idea of remaking architecture digitally using AI and machine learning to create speculative and digitally native architectures is an important roadmap for metaverse builders. It would be a missed opportunity to build out metaverse environments using the same physically rooted architectural syntax that are based on the laws of physics coming out of a millennia old post-and-lintel system. Building out virtual worlds to create spaces that people really inhabit is the first opportunity to entirely reinvent architectural languages ungoverned by gravity.

**LI:** Examples like EPOCH Gallery and *Fortnite* installations bring out the distinction between proprietary systems, where there's a walled community run by one company, and interoperable systems, where you can move assets between different spaces. Interoperability is one of the main principles of Web3. There are startups working to build a zero layer, a fundamental protocol that allows you to transfer NFTs among different blockchains. It will let you go on different platforms to show your NFTs or take part in various activities using them.

But I believe Meta would want to keep everything inside their ecosystem. That would work the best for them, financially. I don't see how they can make any fundamental changes without tearing down their whole business model, which revolves around getting data from

**09.10** (from left to right) ▶
Mathcastles
*Terraforms Level 7 at {23, 20}, Level 11 at {20, 23}, Level 6 at {22, 9} & Level 12 at {10, 11},* 2021
Solidity
Ethereum, 0x4E1f41613c9084FdB9E34E11fAE9412427480e56, 940, 2368, 7024 & 7359

**09.11** (bottom left and below)
Screenshots of the Hypercastle Explorer, a community project led by Matthew Schell to build a Unity game engine based 2D and 3D explorer of Mathcastles, *Terraforms,* 2021

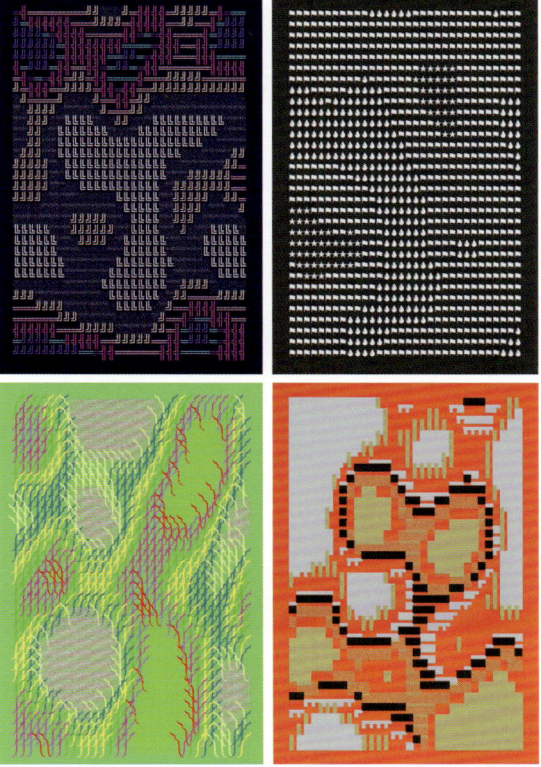

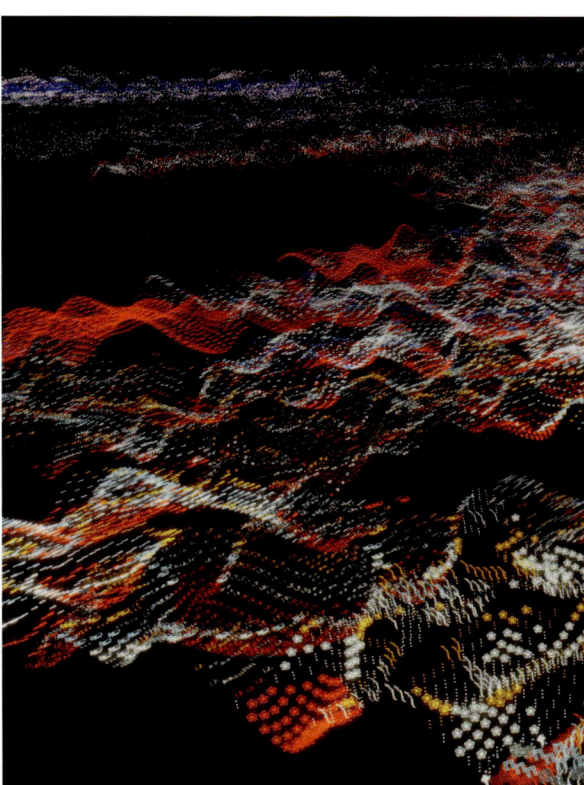

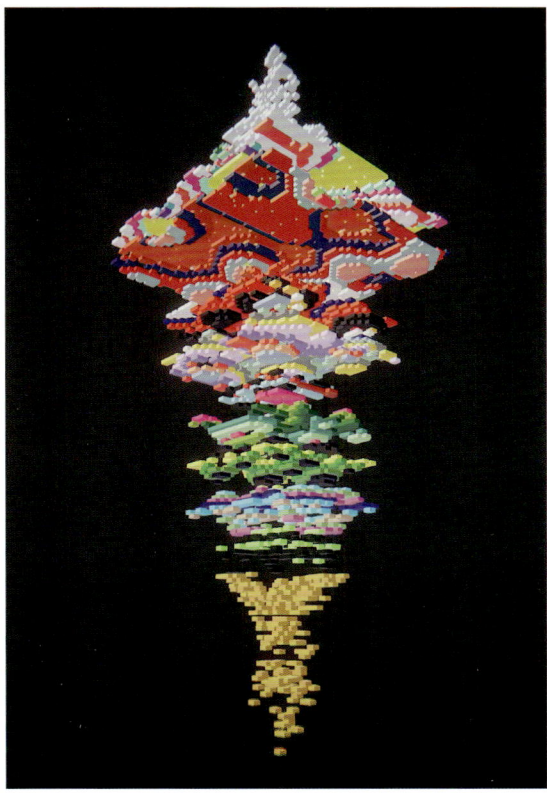

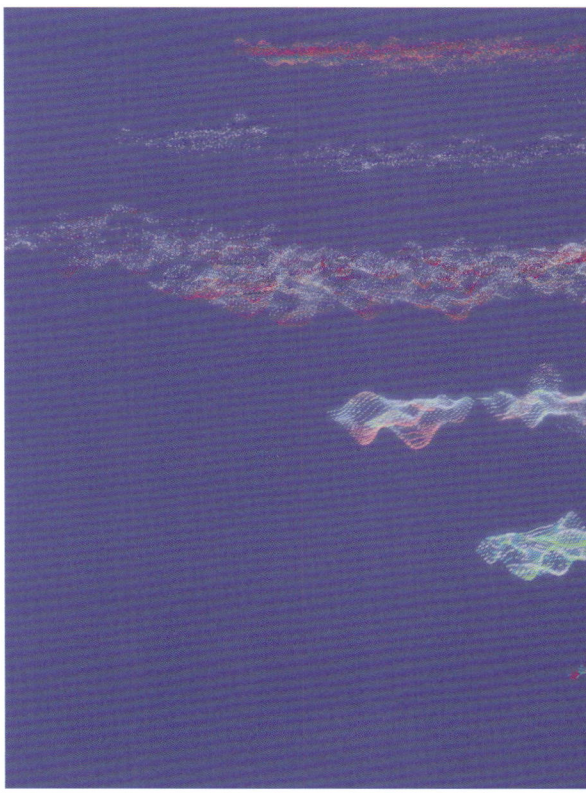

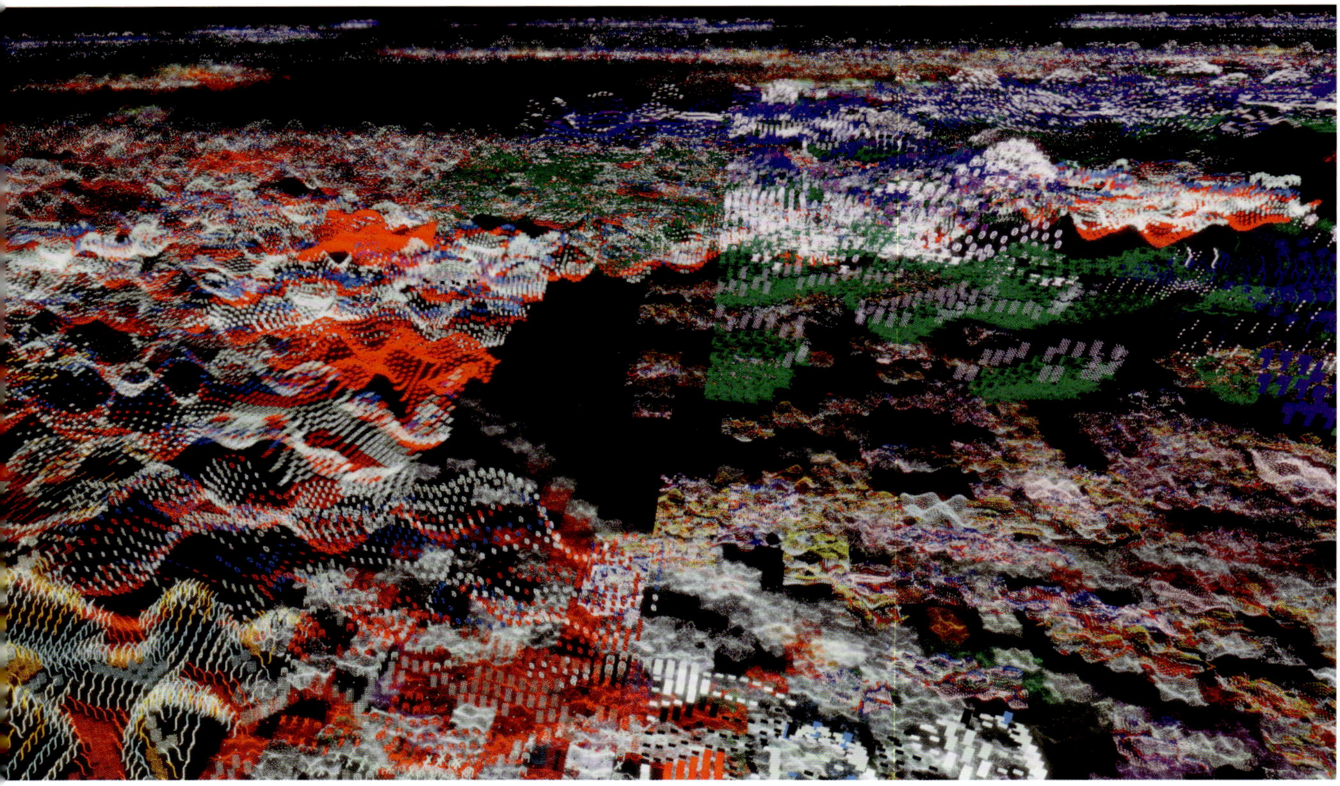

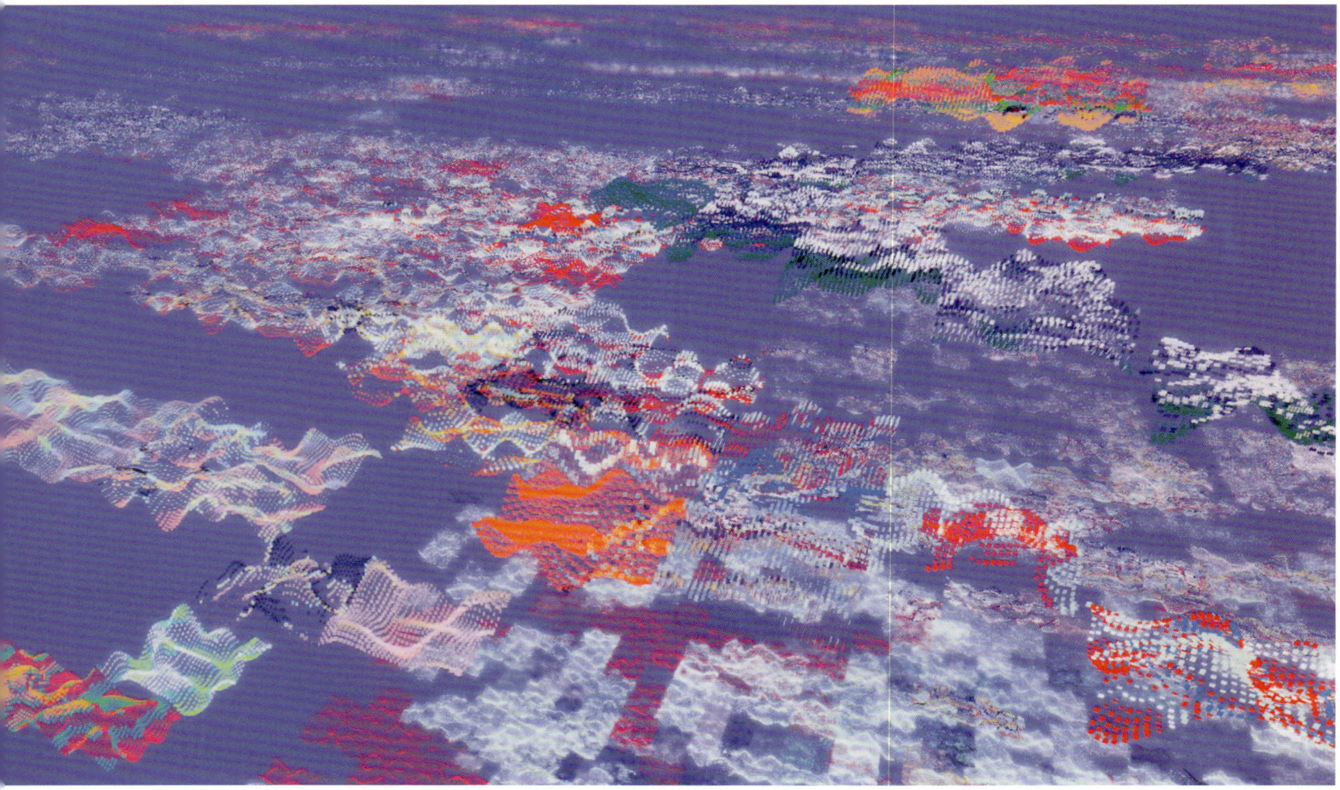

Angela Washko
*The Council on Gender Sensitivity and Behavioral Awareness in World of Warcraft*, 2012–16
Virtual performance in *World of Warcraft*

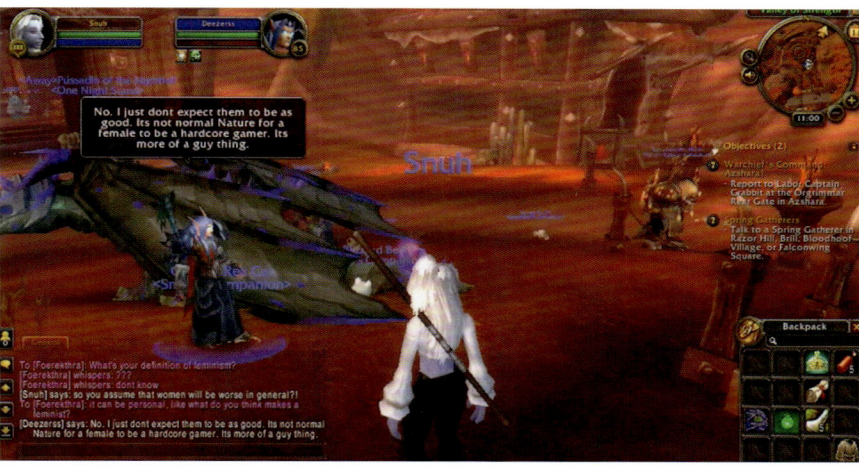

users. The idea of the metaverse and Web3 is giving data back to users. That's quite contradictory for them. Other platforms, like Decentraland, sound very sexy and attractive. But I don't think they've ever had more than 2,000 people online at the same time. Their existence is almost like MySpace. True innovators often end up dying out. One of the most innovative projects in the NFT space is Mathcastle's *Terraforms* (2021) **[09.10]** project, in which 10,000 generative NFTs were encoded within invisible 3D height mapping data both within each individual NFT and then within the network of 10,000 to produce an architecture called the Hypercastle **[09.11]**. All the visualization and development of the Hypercastle has been produced by the community owners of the *Terraforms* project. It is also important to note that the Hypercastle is a speculative architecture in the way that other "metaverse" architectures are always hamstrung by a Cartesian geometry. The result is a digitally native architecture, owned in an NFT native way, where the Hypercastle is owned, visualized, and built by the NFT owners. It's an exciting model.

As of now, Twitter and Discord are the largest exhibition platforms for NFTs, especially PFP projects. A lot of the crypto talk back in 2011 and 2012 started on Twitter. It's a text-based platform, so it's a good place to find explanations and analyses of the crypto market. Weirdly, as visual as NFTs are, Twitter became the headquarters of this whole movement, because the major NFT collectors are long-time Twitter users. Interestingly, when comparing social media platforms with blockchain architectures, Twitter as a structure is by far the closest from a user-interface perspective. Blockchains and Twitter are both text-based platforms, where text is archived and timestamped in chains of comments and quotes. Images are linked crucially below text in the hierarchy (unlike Instagram which leads with the image), which is the same structure for the blockchain, where the ledger records the text or hyperlink to the decentralized file server. In this sense, Twitter can be seen as a more engaging proxy for interacting with the blockchain itself. Perhaps this is a subliminal reason, amongst many others, for Twitter's supremacy as the current virtual town square or "metaverse" for blockchain-based art and cultural dialogue.

**OBRIST:** I think Twitter is the space where the NFT discussion is happening because of how it gamifies communication. Gamified systems are everywhere in modern life. Very often our desires are shaped by incentives and systems we are not aware of, and we might start playing games we don't even want to play. We play the game, but the game plays us. The idea of worldbuilding is significant for understanding the metaverse and how art can shape it, but so is the connection between games and agency. We're getting more and more stuck in this quantified world. And I think that's where art can liberate us.

**LEW:** Gaming shifts you away from a single subjectivity, too, which lets you open up to something beyond your own identity. It makes me think about the popularization of avatars, whether that's through PFP NFTs or the whole-body avatars envisioned for the metaverse. I'm curious to hear your thoughts on that, Jason — how PFPs are being adopted now and how that relates to the idea of gamification.

09.13
Lawrence Lek's *Nepenthe Zone* (2021) exhibited at *Worldbuilding: Gaming and Art in the Digital Age*, curated by Hans Ulrich Obrist, June 4, 2022–December 10, 2023, Julia Stoschek Collection, Düsseldorf, Germany

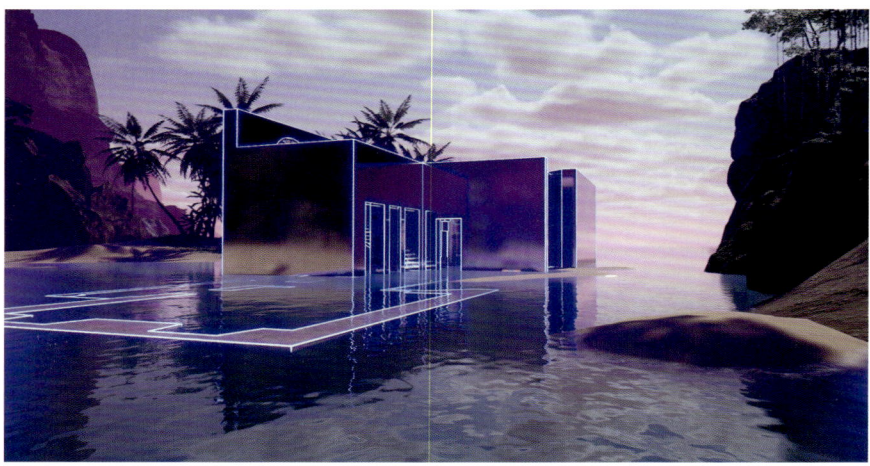

**LI:** What people in the NFT business call utility is a kind of gamification. It means giving people incentives and perks to collect and hold tokens. *Moonbirds* (2022), a collection of 10,000 PFPs from PROOF, came out after the blue-chip PFP projects but managed to garner high prices because of what they offered to holders. If you "nest" your *Moonbird*, or register it with PROOF, you'll accrue benefits as a member of a private club. The longer it nests, the more perks you get. We released James Jean's project *Fragments* (2022), where the NFTs are attached to a physical pagoda he is building as well as a virtual pagoda. People who are holding onto the *Fragments* for this chapter will have the key to enter the next chapter. We suggested adding gamifying factors at the design stage. It's an experiment for artists as well as for us and the collectors.

Some NFT projects focus exclusively on gamification. It's almost like what people call play-to-earn games. People go to them purely for financial reasons. It's a very speculative environment. NFTs are still new at this stage, and different concepts will attract other kinds of people. But I agree with Hans Ulrich that the gaming environment is the backbone of the metaverse, and we need to figure out how to use elements of gamification in ways that are sustainable.

There are many examples of gamified projects that will just become very popular for a month at most. Then the whole system goes down in a death spiral. Once the token value in that gamified system goes down, there are fewer transactions, fewer collectors, more sellers. So those projects need to keep creating hype to draw people in. *Axie Infinity* is a *Pokémon*-like game where you fight different paths to earn tokens. It's one of the largest projects — if not the largest — project in the whole space but it lost a lot of value this year. In the long run if the metaverse has to be built on a gaming environment, we'll need healthier, more organic systems of gamification.

**LEW:** The way text-heavy platforms Twitter and Discord have been adopted by Web3, as opposed to image-based platforms like Instagram, reminds me of how back in the day of dial-up modems, I would play MUDs, or multi-user dungeons, online spaces riffing on *Dungeons & Dragons* and other role-playing games. With only text it felt really immersive and deeply interactive. That's the type of thing that I would like to see, whatever comes of the metaverse: that enriched sense of community. MUDs are games, but half the time it felt like people were just there to hang out and socialize, agnostic to whatever gaming system that was there.

**OBRIST:** Multiplayer games are ultimately about the relationship between players. A game can show political action and moral transformation, which of course is interesting in relation to socially transformative art — staging direct interventions into society and politics through multiplayer games. Angela Washko staged performances inside the massively multiplayer online role-playing game *World of Warcraft* from 2012 to 2016 **[09.12]**, consisting of conversations with other players about feminism. She started the project to address the misogyny and discrimination she experienced in the game. Gaming holds great potential for political action. In 2021, 2.8 billion people — almost a third of the world's population — were playing

Danielle Brathwaite-Shirley
*WE CAN'T DO THIS ALONE*, 2022
Live performance
Camberwell Studios, London, United Kingdom

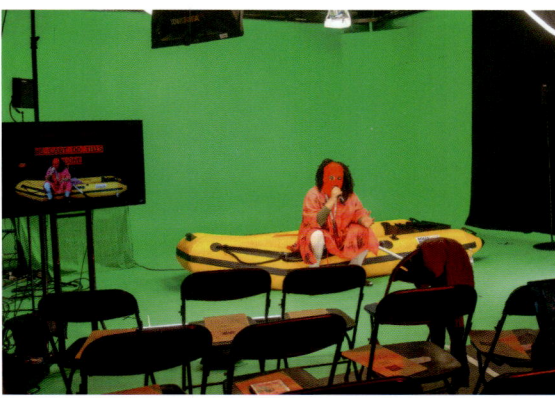
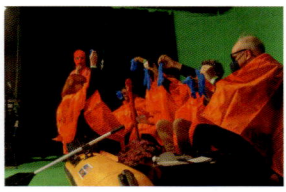
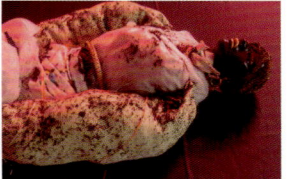

video games. What was once a niche pastime has become the biggest mass phenomenon of our time, bigger than the music and film industry together.

Gaming is becoming to our time what movies were to the 20th century and what novels were to the 19th century. It's not completely new. Artists are always early. Decades ago artists began to already feel that these game technologies would be important for the infrastructure of the 21st century. You can see how artists like Peggy Ahwesh or Sturtevant (1924–2014) integrated the visual language of games, how they appropriated or subverted existing video games, and criticized the often discriminatory and stereotypical depictions you find in mainstream games. Of course at that time it was basically just a small insular group of engineers who completed these games and that made it very non-inclusive. Today, of course, more people have access to the tools of making games. And that means that it's very different from Hollywood. There's a really interesting book by Anna Anthropy called *Rise of the Videogame Zinesters* (2012). "What I want from video games is a plurality of voices, I want games to come from a vital set of experiences and present a vital range of perspectives," she says. "I can imagine — and you are invited to imagine it with me — a world in which digital games are not manufactured for the same small audience, but one in which games are authored by you and me for the benefit of our peers." And you can extrapolate that to the metaverse because we don't want a monopoly. We want a plurality of voices. We want experiences that aren't manufactured for a homogenized audience — we want a true polyphony or inclusivity.

**LEW:** Anthropy has what I read as a very Gen X, indie mindset that could come back in Web3. She's thinking about individual makers creating small-form games, as opposed to these huge companies and teams that are making what feel like blockbuster movies. But I wonder if we're connecting games to the metaverse because of our own myopia. We just don't know anything else. I'm thinking about the advent of photography and the Pictorialists, who were making images that looked like paintings, trying to mimic a previous form. Maybe we don't recognize what that new form of art in the metaverse is. While the technological underpinnings are close to gaming engines, we can't envision what the next step could be.

**OBRIST:** At my exhibition *Worldbuilding: Gaming and Art in the Digital Age* at the Julia Stoschek Collection in Düsseldorf about half of the works are recorded experiences of games **[09.13]**. And half are actually games — action games, multiplayer games, one person games, and so on. The show becomes a situation where people can play these games. At a museum, immersive installations can become part of the game. They create surroundings that players can't have at home, integrating physical space in the experience of the game. Rauschenberg always said that we need to think more about time in relation to art. There's so much talk about space but time has been neglected. It's astonishing how little time people spend in front of art at exhibitions. It differs from statistic to statistic, but it's always shockingly low. Meanwhile over the last couple of weeks, I've spent about 20 hours with *Elden Ring*. A friend said he's played it for a hundred hours. We really spend a lot of time with games. The video games industry has spent decades developing, prototyping, and operationalizing the technologies for the creation of hybrid digital-physical experiences that involve bodily interaction and avatars; digital spatial experiences

**09.15**
Gabriel Massan featuring Castiel Vitorino Brasileiro, Novíssimo Edgar, LYZZA
*Third World: The Bottom Dimension*, 2023
Video game

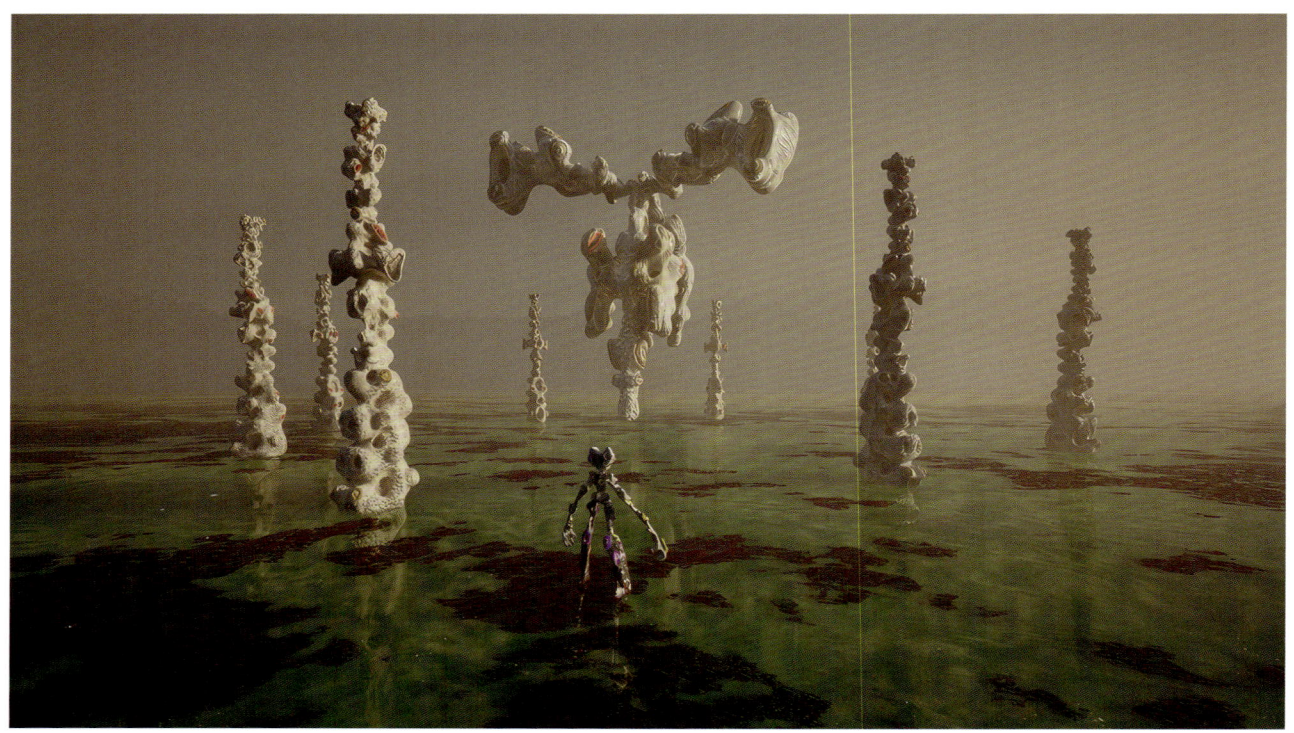

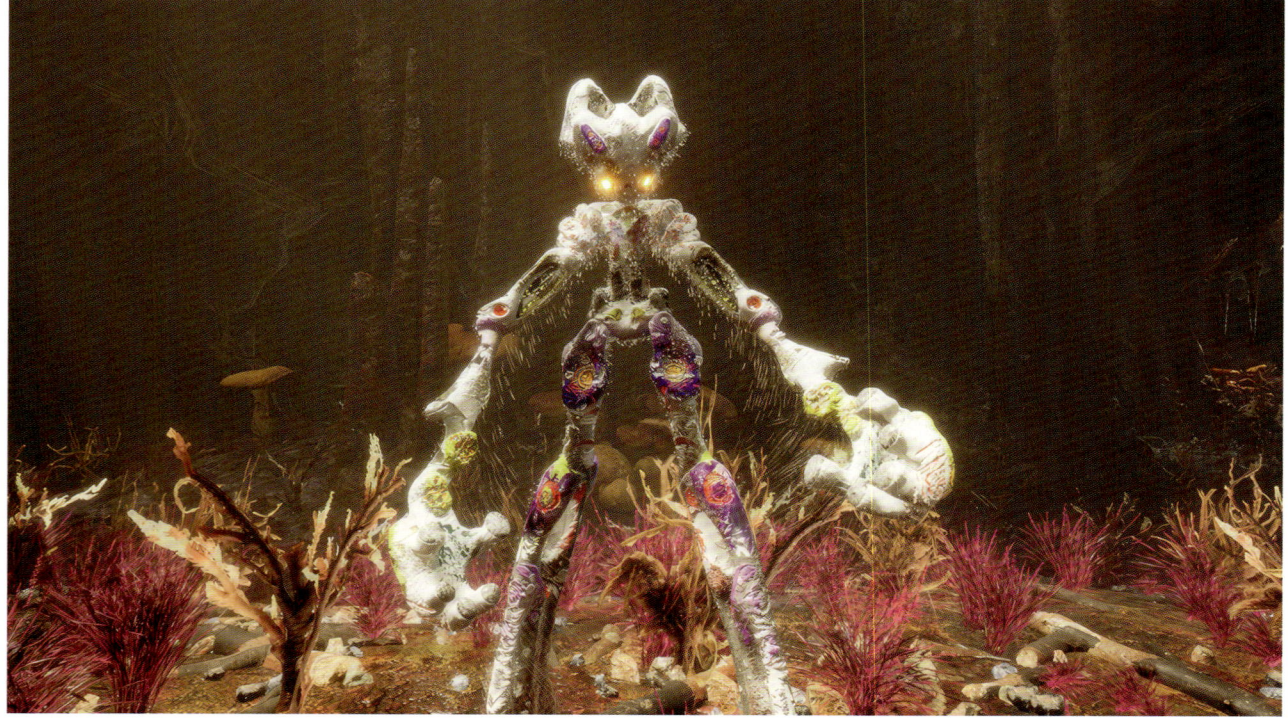

**09.16**
Cedric Price
*Drawing for the Fun Palace project brochure*, 1964
Photomechanical print, 36.2 × 59.6 cm

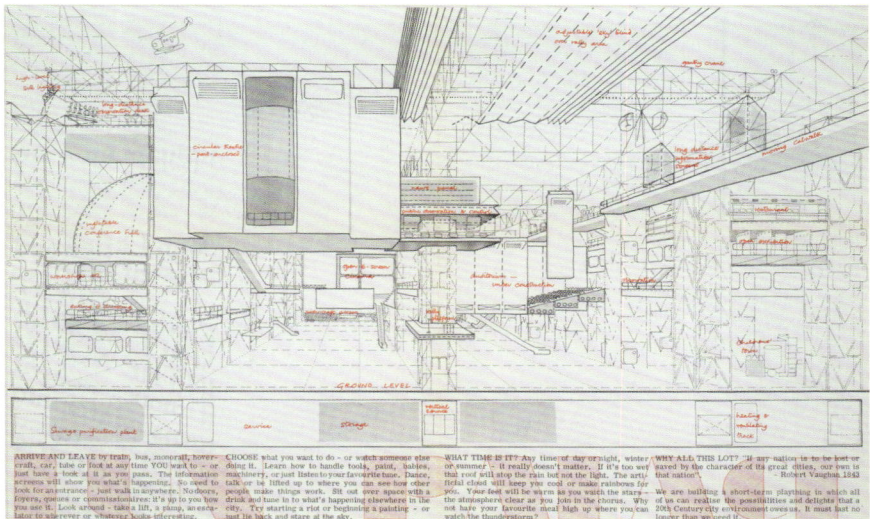

that are seemingly unlimited in scale and imagination; and facilitation of multiparty, real-time interactions with other users and the digital environment. Game technologies are becoming the fundamental infrastructure for the metaverse — an ecosystem of virtual worlds that is likely to transform the internet and may become the gateway to a spatial web. Danielle Brathwaite-Shirley is an amazing, unusually prolific artist and archivist and game designer whose work centers on Black trans people. As she designs and builds physical and virtual worlds, she's thinking about interactivity, how the viewer is implicated in the way each work progresses and is experienced **[09.14]**. Her work shows how play can affirm and build community. It provides a model for an inclusive and impactful approach to the metaverse. Another great example is the practice of Gabriel Massan **[09.15]**. Massan is a multidisciplinary digital artist, combining storytelling and world-building techniques to create digital worlds and sculptures that alternatively simulate and narrate situations of inequality within the Black-Indigenous Latin American experience. We are working at the Serpentine with Massan and a team of collaborators on, what Massan describes as, a "consciousness-raising game that explores Black-Indigenous Brazilian experiences."

**LEW:** Artists have found compelling ways to translate the individual gaming experience to the more public form of a gallery. Feng Mengbo's *Long March: Restart* (2010) emphasizes the immersive aspect of the experience, making it different than playing a traditional video game alone in front of your TV. His work is a multichannel installation with floor-to-ceiling images. It really feels like you're in the game, holding a cordless controller and walking along with the side scroller in order to keep up with the figure that you're playing. *Q4U* (2002), Feng's early hack that modified the popular first-person shooter game *Quake*, did something totally different. He replaced the enemies with images of himself holding a video camera to raise the specter of pervasive surveillance. But the physical experience was something I was thinking about when I was co-organizing the 2017 Whitney Biennial. Mia Locks and I invited Porpentine Charity Heartscape to take part, and her games are really intimate experiences written in HTML. They're interactive narratives, and players have to choose different paths. How do you make that into a more public experience? Certainly people could sit at a station and play. But we also projected the screen from one station onto a large wall, so visitors could watch someone play and make decisions. It's important for an exhibition to create a shared experience that you can't have when you're playing a game at home. It's that kind of sociality that leads to community formation. There's a similar potential for what the metaverse can do to bring people together.

**OBRIST:** Ben Vickers, who started the art and technology program at the Serpentine, always said: Can we network an existing institution, or do we just need a new institution? Of course I think the answer is both/and instead of either/or. I hope that our Future Art Ecosystems reports show how one can actually network an existing institution at the Serpentine,

**09.17**
Aerial view of the 6529 Museum District in the Open Metaverse.
Accessed via oncyber.io/6529om, October 20, 2022

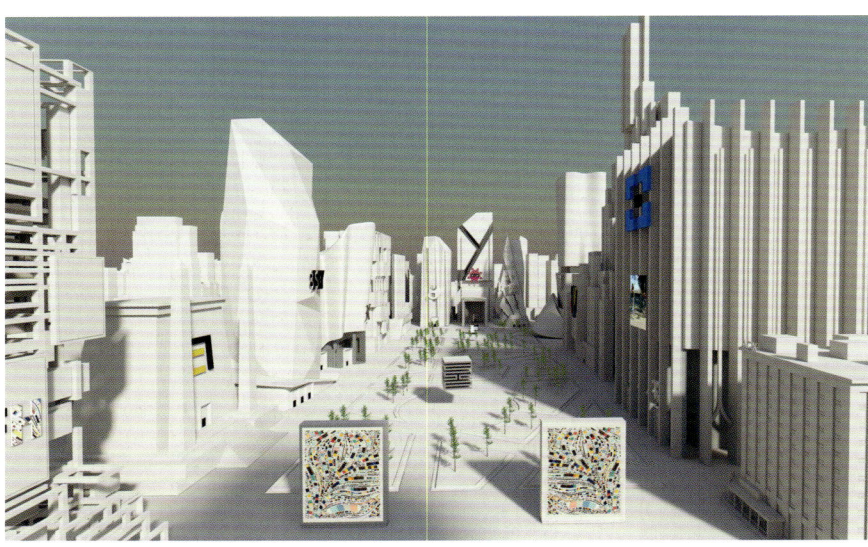

and that's what our digital projects and mixed-reality projects are trying to do. Of course that raises the question of what a completely new institution from scratch for this age would look like.

Joan Littlewood (1914–2002), a pioneer of street theater, and the architect and urbanist Cedric Price (1934–2003) — it's very important to credit them both because very often only Cedric is named — dreamt of a space they called the Fun Palace where people in the community could come together to celebrate art and science and culture. You could choose what you wanted to do. You could watch someone else doing it. And that's what happens at a gaming exhibition — you can learn how to play a game by watching others do it.But the idea of the Fun Palace **[09.16]** was that you could learn how to handle tools, listen to your favorite tune, dance, talk, or watch how other people make things work. You could just lie back and stare at the sky.

The inspiration came from traditional pleasure gardens, which were for the community as a whole. Cedric and Joan wanted a laboratory of fun, a university of the streets. Cedric collaborated with Gordon Pask who was one of the great cyberneticians of that time. I think the vision for the Fun Palace has a lot to do with cybernetics. When I met with Cedric and we started to have these conversations about the Fun Palace, I wanted to know more about cybernetics. I went to see this last surviving pioneer of the cybernetic movement, Heinz von Foerster (1911–2002). He believed that scientists were like artists. He worked in the mid-1940s with Norbert Wiener (1894–1964), and then in the 1960s, he founded the field of second-order cybernetics in which the observer is understood as part of the system itself, not an external entity. This legacy could be seen as an alternative intellectual history of the blockchain — one that is less focused on the libertarian drive to make public institutions obsolete and allow technology-based self-determination, and instead concerned with building the groundwork for effective collaboration and mutual support. Von Foerster summed up the lessons of cybernetics as learning to think in circles. It's very interesting to think about how a circular art organization would work.

**LEW:** We're at an inflection point where people are asking what role institutions should play in society and what is appropriate or necessary right now. As new territories in which an increasing portion of social and cultural interaction will be mediated, metaverse organizations need to be nimble and responsive to this. Places such as 6529's Open Metaverse **[09.17]**, which is free for anyone to access and take part in building, offer new alternatives and visions. That's the spirit of pluralism and portability — the qualities of an ideal metaverse — that we're all hoping will be instilled in the future we are collectively creating.

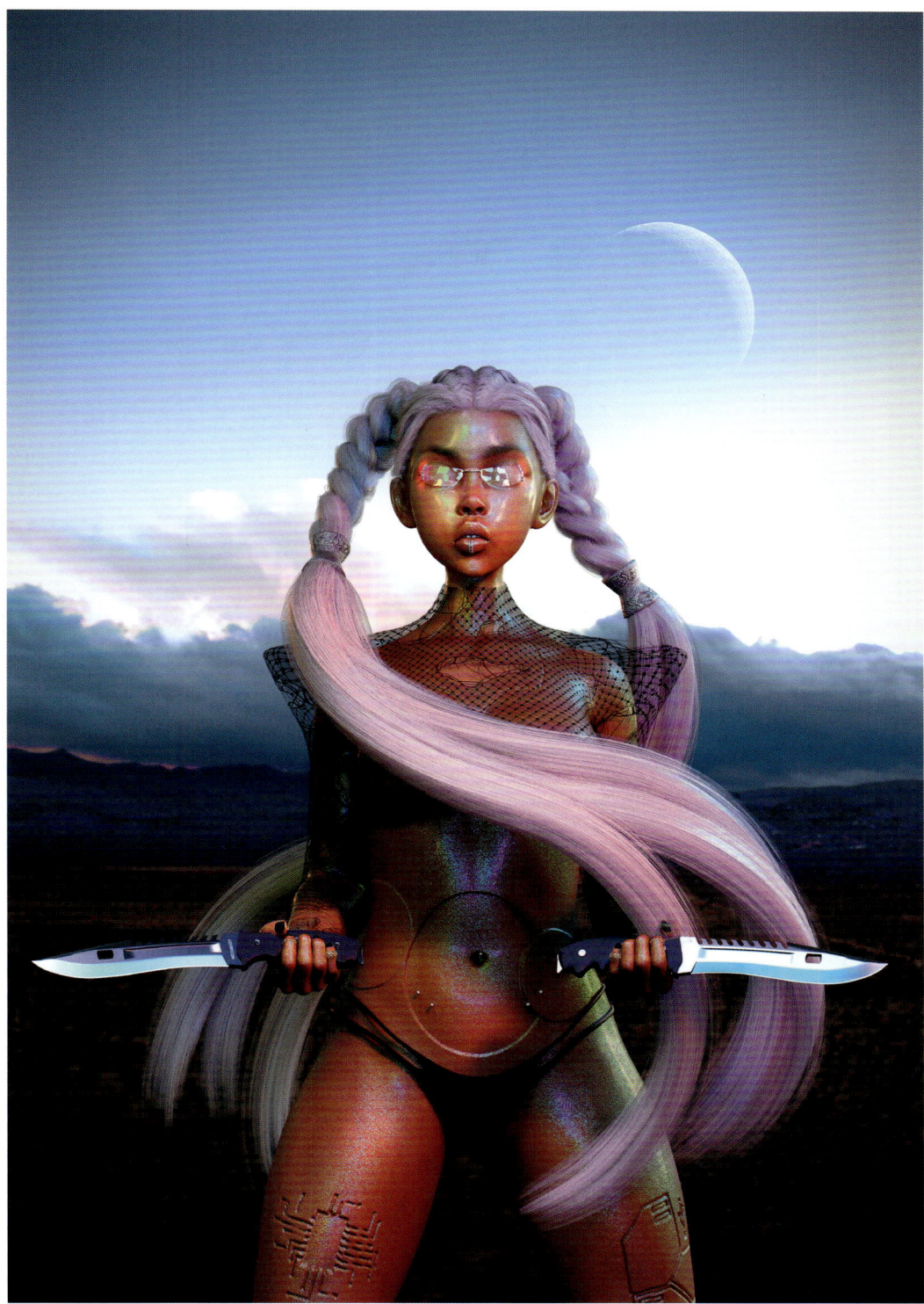

| # | TITLE | TIMESTAMP | MEDIUM | CHAIN | CONTRACT ADDRESS | TOKEN ID | EDITION SIZE |
|---|-------|-----------|--------|-------|------------------|----------|--------------|
| 01 | **Two of Swords 2019** | 11-15-2021 04:05:13 | Daz 3D, Adobe Photoshop | ETH | 0x3b3ee1931dc30c195737-9fac9aba94d1c48a5405 | 107876 | 1/1 |
| 02 | **Creation of My Metaverse (Between this World and the Next)** | 05-28-2021 09:26:08 | Daz 3D, Cinema 4D, Octane Render, Adobe Photoshop, Fresco | ETH | 0x6c326e329963f30f7501-36f822cae928fb1f805c | 0 | 1/1 |

# SERWAH ATTAFUAH

AUSTRALIA 1998

02

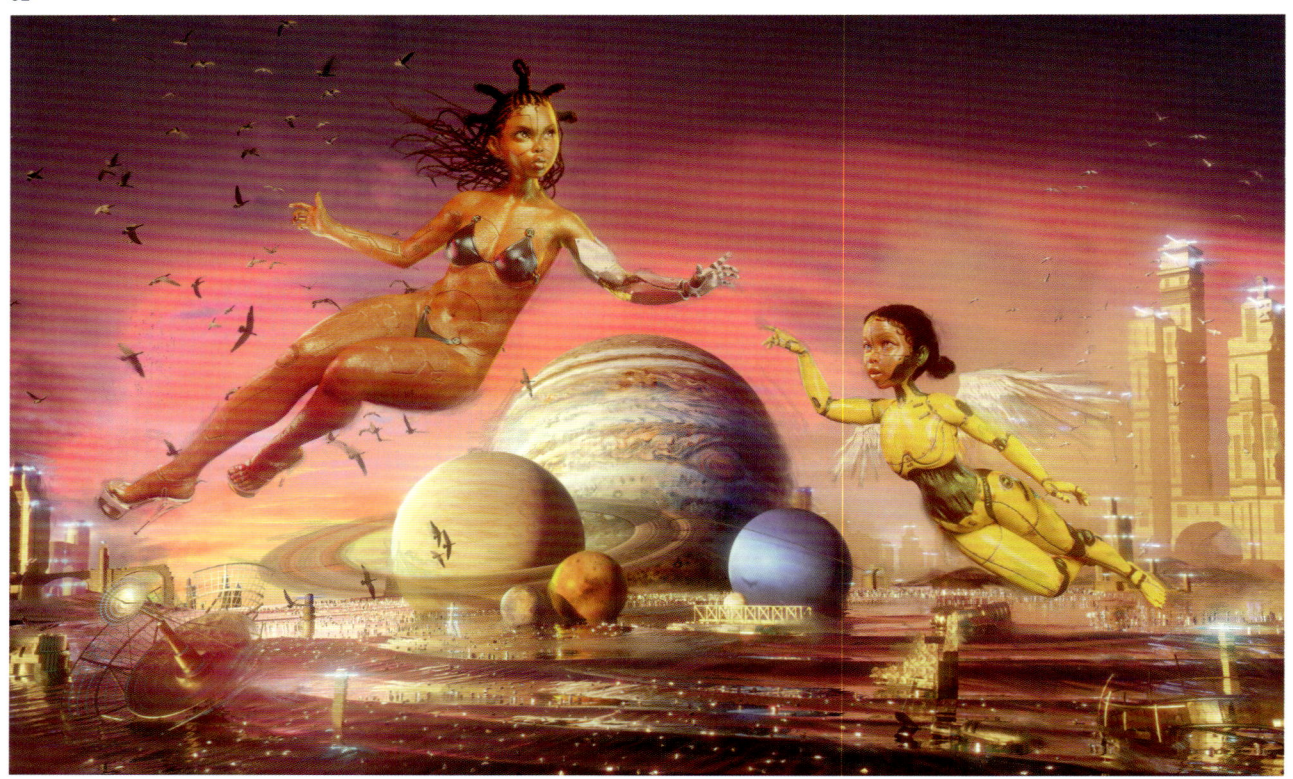

You can immediately identify a work by Serwah Attafuah when you see it. Each piece is its own techno-surreal dreamscape. Serwah is able to bring together a variety of physical and digital mediums and genres into something that is singularly iconic and evocative of a new world. She started her practice as an oil painter, going on to study costume design and prosthetics at TAFE in Sydney. After realizing that those mediums didn't hold her interest, she searched for a way to create that was completely her own. She focused on 3D art and animation, teaching herself to use tools like Blender, Daz, and Iray. Simultaneously, she founded an anti-colonial death metal band and went on to play with some punk and hardcore groups. Serwah is heavily influenced by Afrofuturism, renaissance portraiture, early cyberpunk literature, and her Ghanaian and Italian heritage.

I was initially drawn to Serwah's work because of her ability to seamlessly integrate those disciplines into something net-new while also incorporating aspects of herself into her visual reality.

You see her figures navigate these futuristic spaces, drawing from stories that are both personal and shared in our collective imagination. I relate to these stories and Serwah's own origin story as an autodidactic, genre-bending artist.

*Untitled 2020 (Cinderella)* (2021) was made in response to the 2020 Australian bushfires, which was a frightening experience for Serwah, being based in West Sydney. While making the work, she was also going through a breakup and experiencing depression. Set in a lush expanse dotted with stone pillars and towers, the figure embodies the emotions — the fear, the sadness, the isolation — of that moment. Serwah masterfully orchestrates Afrofuturistic depictions of alternative worlds while still drawing strong parallels to our current realities.

**KAYVON TEHRANIAN**
CEO & CO-FOUNDER OF FOUNDATION

03

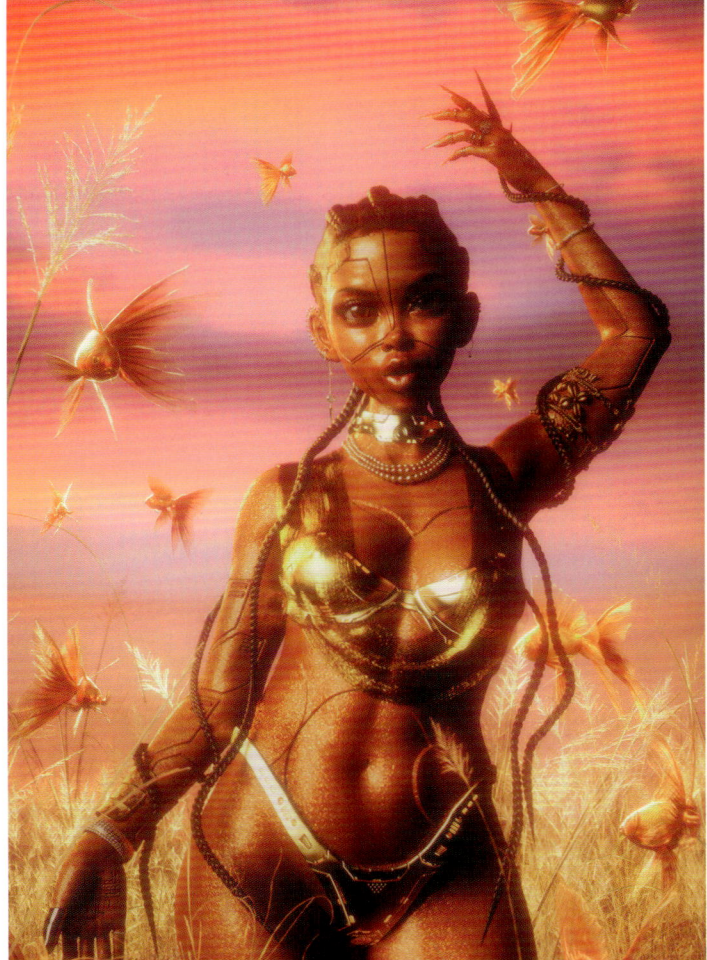

04

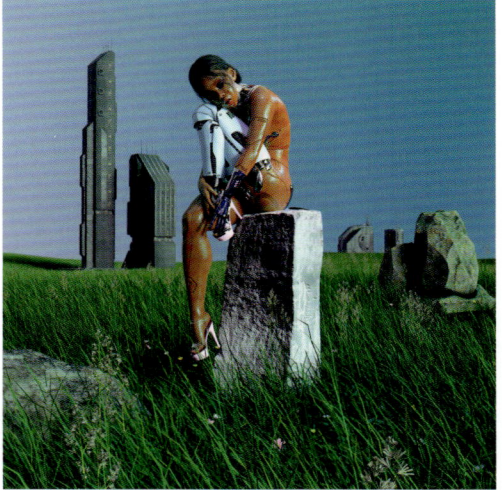

05

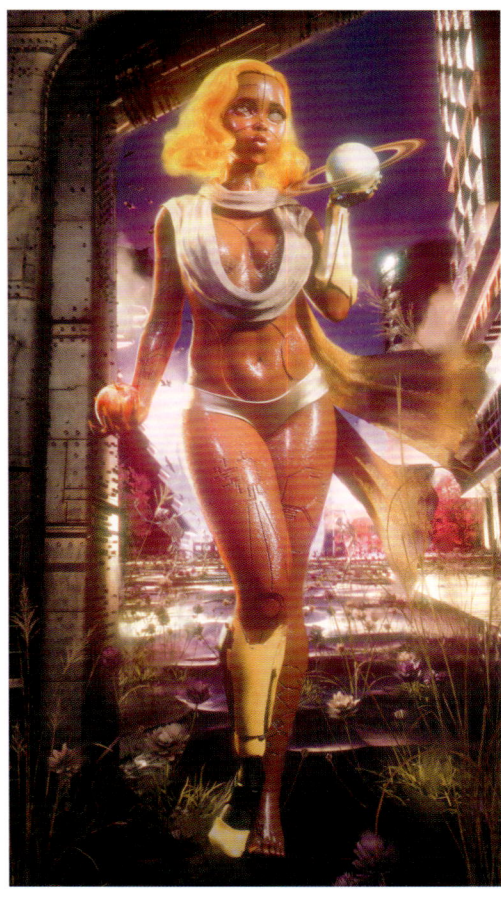

| # | TITLE | TIMESTAMP | MEDIUM | CHAIN | CONTRACT ADDRESS | TOKEN ID | EDITION SIZE |
|---|-------|-----------|--------|-------|------------------|----------|--------------|
| 03 | **PRELUDE 2022** | 01-23-2022 22:27:40 | Daz 3D, Cinema 4D, Octane Render, ZBrush, Adobe Photoshop, Maya | ETH | 0xb932a70a57673d89f4-acffbe830e8ed7f75fb9e0 | 31941 | 1/1 |
| 04 | **Untitled 2020 (Cinderella)** | 04-14-2021 03:59:46 | Daz 3D, Adobe Photoshop | ETH | 0x3b3ee1931dc30c19573-79fac9aba94d1c48a5405 | 24075 | 1/1 |
| 05 | **Perpetuity 2021** | 12-17-2021 01:11:48 | Daz 3D, Cinema 4D, Octane Render, Adobe Photoshop, Fresco | ETH | 0x3b3ee1931dc30c195737-9fac9aba94d1c48a5405 | 119758 | 1/1 |
| 06 | **Consensual Hallucinations 2021** | 03-17-2021 03:58:44 | Daz 3D, Adobe Photoshop | ETH | 0x3b3ee1931dc30c19573-79fac9aba94d1c48a5405 | 8831 | 1/1 |

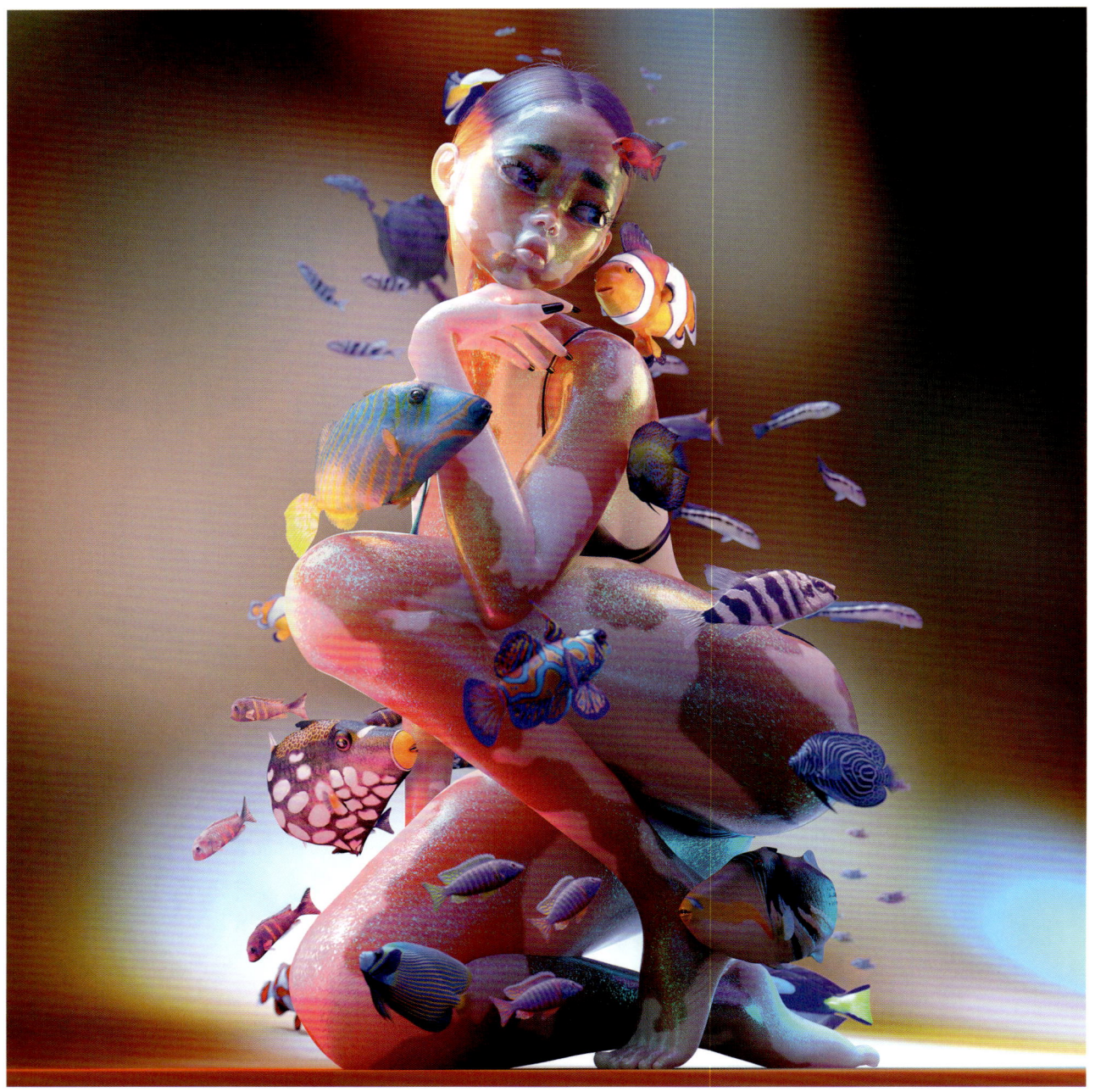

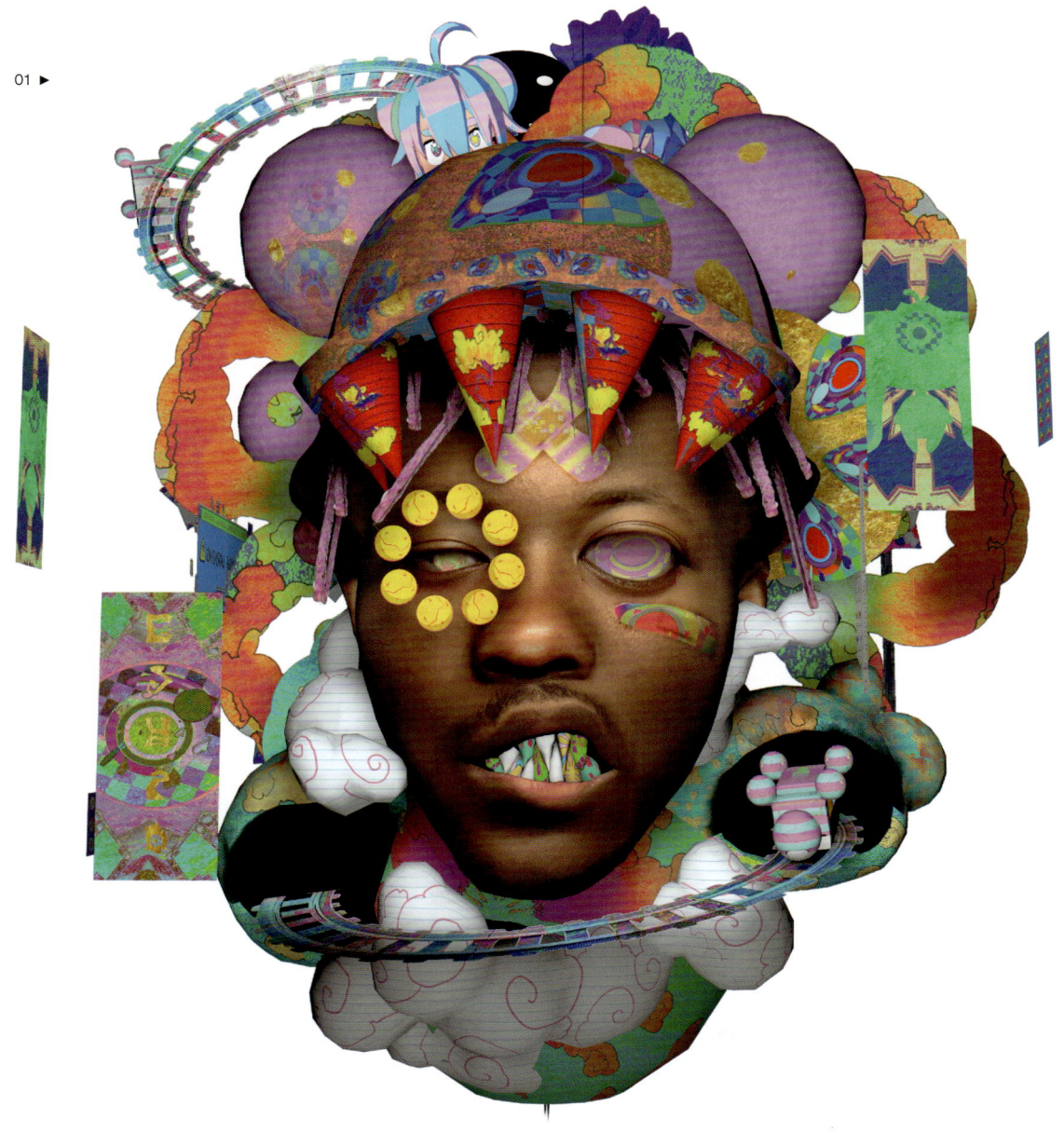

| # | TITLE | TIMESTAMP | MEDIUM | CHAIN | CONTRACT ADDRESS | TOKEN ID | EDITION SIZE |
|---|---|---|---|---|---|---|---|
| 01 | --★ ꜱ3lfⓘ pörⒸrⓐjⒸ ★-- **AR Self portrait** | 07-28-2021 17:25:05 | Cinema 4D, Adobe Photoshop, Substance Painter | ETH | 0x3b3ee1931dc30c1957379fac9aba94d1c48a5405 | 65449 | 1/1 |
| 02 | **THE FUTRUE .01** | 03-06-2021 03:58:21 | Cinema 4D, Adobe Photoshop, FL Studio, Substance Painter, Marvelous Designer | ETH | 0x3b3ee1931dc30c1957379fac9aba94d1c48a5405 | 3917 | 1/1 |

# OSEANWORLD

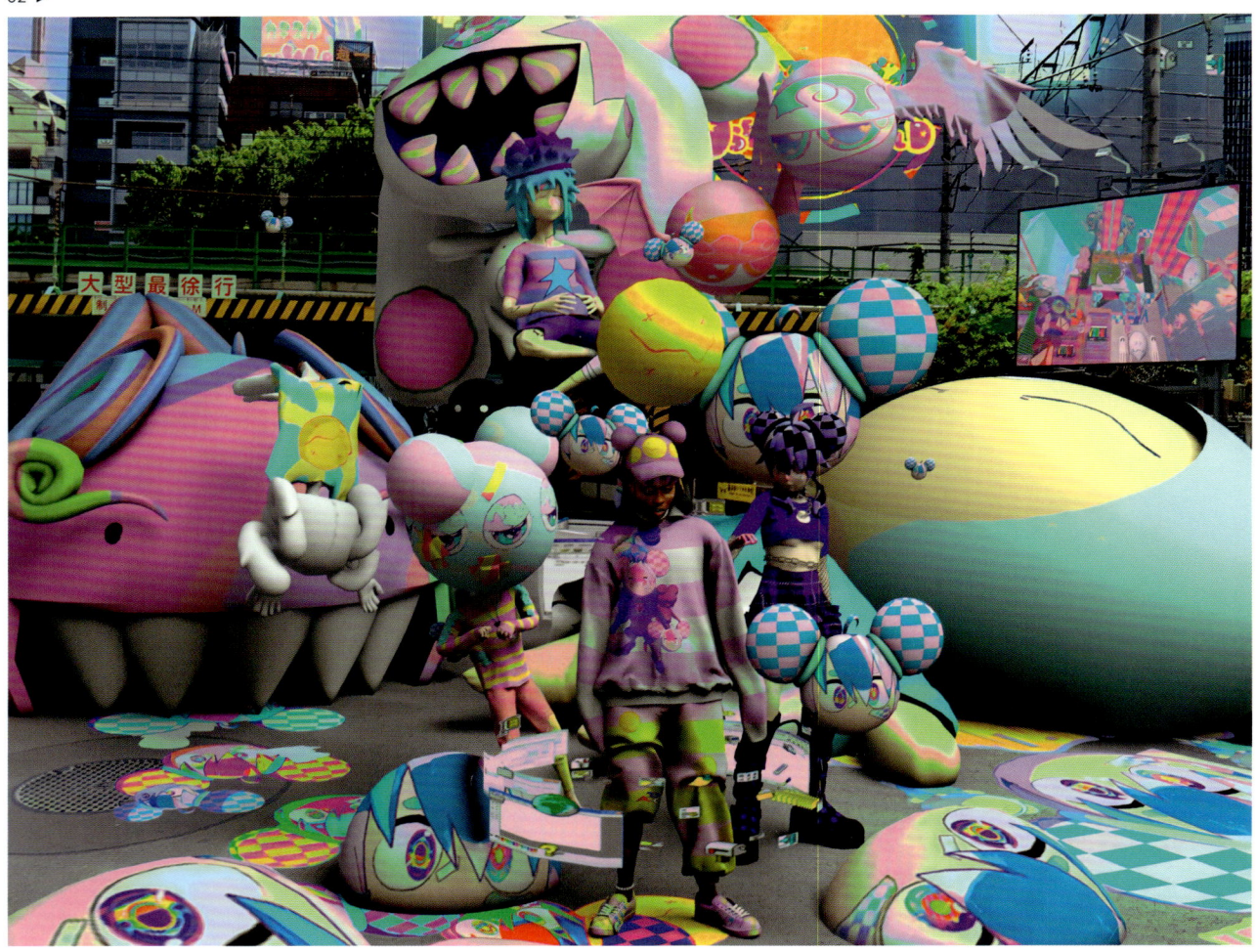

From the metaphorically accurate super-heated melting pot of Little Five Points, Atlanta, Oseanworld rightfully inherits the confluence of immersive animative experiences and rap culture that make the area such a creative hub. He creates instantly recognizable characters to thrive in the Osean world universe, including Yameii, Choice, Doom Doom, and Saddboy, all of whom feature in Osean's first NFT, *FUTRUE .01* (2021). In this work the characters populate the artist's neon-filled cyberpunk world, presented to us as a flashing, futuristic stage set. The work, complete with electronic sound effects and a robotically rhythmed viewpoint, fully immerses the viewer in the artist's hypnotic, yet electrifying landscape.

Osean's characters have a way of transgressing borders between the virtual and the physical. One can find Yameii's story in Osean's manga, clothing line, or in real life as a hologram at sold-out shows where she performs alongside Doom Doom, a monster. In *Cyberspace* (2020), you can find her in animated videos such as "Heartless," where she performs in a strobing, computer-generated city over a beat of trunk-speaker-crushing bass that is undeniably Atlanta.

Osean's interdisciplinary, multi-character storytelling evokes a presence not felt since the mid-aughts when seemingly opposing mediums and cultures began to merge. Gorillaz released their proto-metaverse, Kong Studios, where fans could navigate a bandwide canon story line involving a click-to-explore game, years of music videos and blogs. On another continent, but banded together by fiberoptic cables, Murakami creates the Dropout Bear for Kanye West, and the late MF DOOM opines on the rapper economy in blurbs lodged between anime and cartoons on late-night programming.

Yameii and the whole of Oseanworld can appear anywhere, at any moment in time, and be aesthetically cogent as characters and as a message representing decades of technological and cultural development. Osean succeeds in the most vital delivery of NFTs: to deliver works that look and sound the way that the internet feels.

**GARRETTE FURO**
CO-FOUNDER OF ATOMIC FORM, DEGENERATE

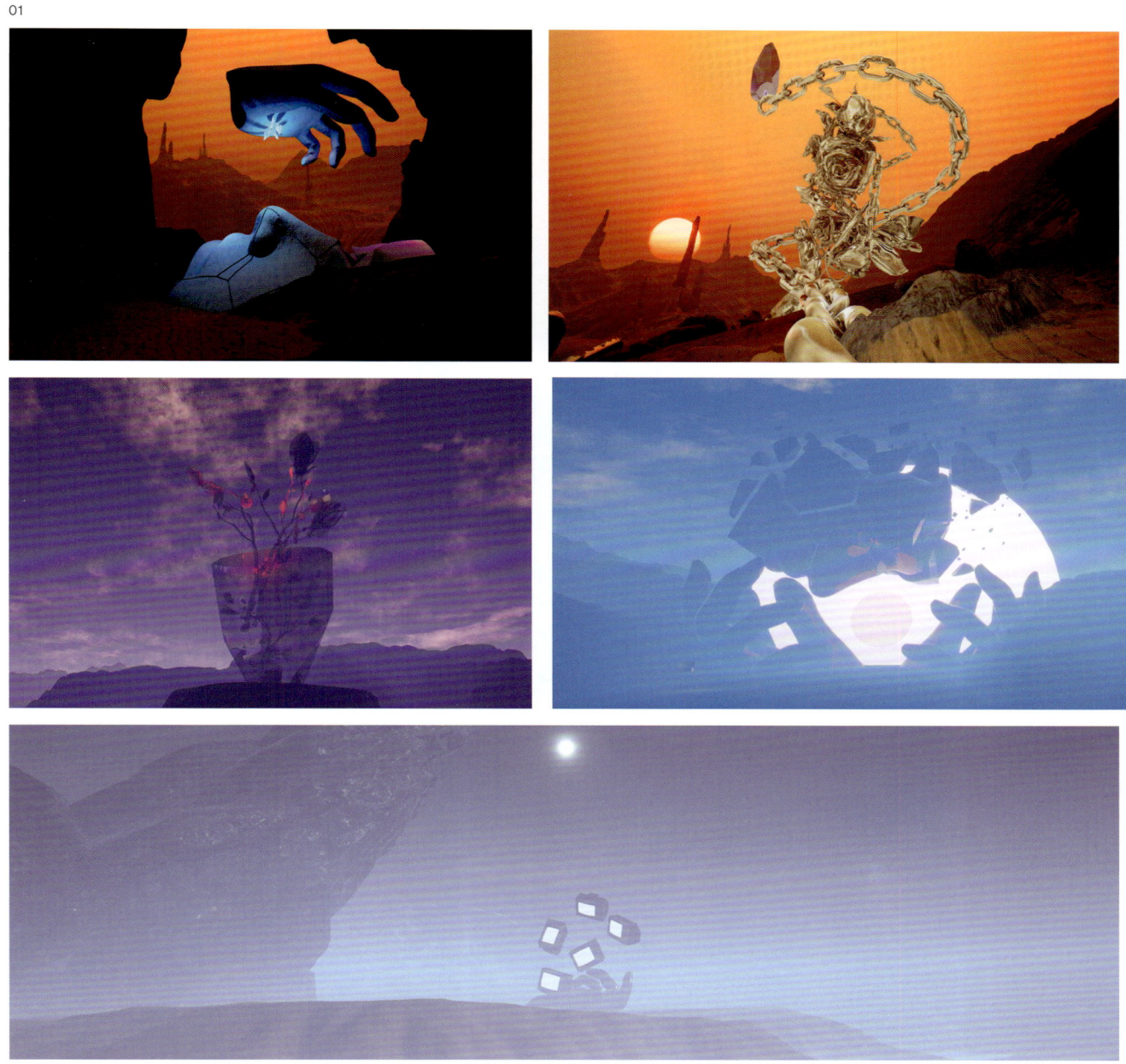

| # | TITLE | DATE | MEDIUM |
|---|-------|------|--------|
| 01 | **LVCIDIA//** | 2022 | Unreal Engine |

# FVCKRENDER
CANADA 1991

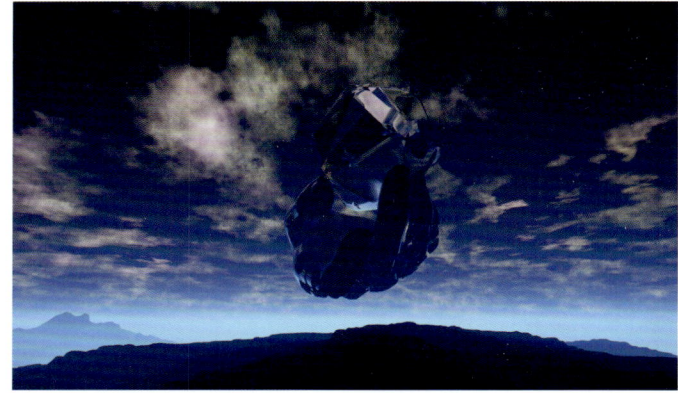 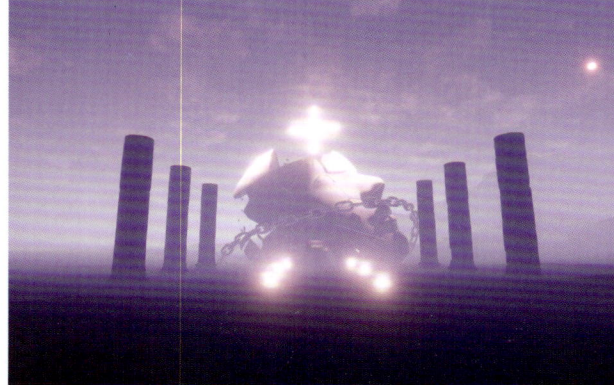

 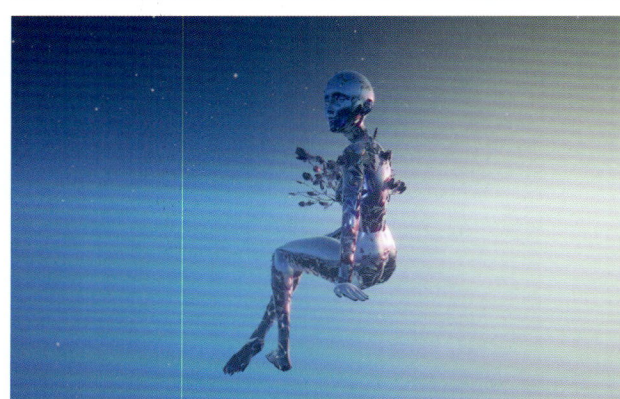

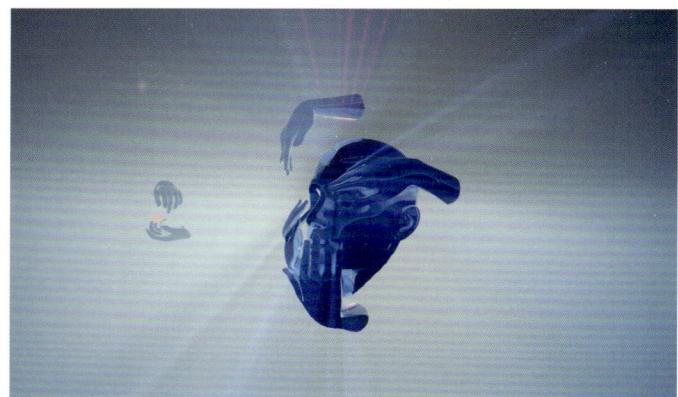 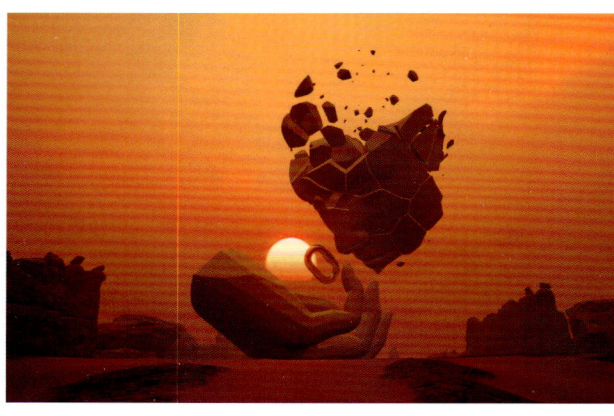

My first encounter with Frédéric Duquette's (aka FVCKRENDER) work was during the release of the FVCKRENDERVERSE//. I remember being blown away by the immersiveness of the world that Fred had created, it was a surreal and visceral experience. Seeing the large-scale art in a digitally native setting made me realize just how beautiful 3D art could be and more importantly it provided a vision for what the future of NFTs in Web3 could be. I immediately knew that Fred was going to be an iconic artist. Since then, Fred and I have become good friends and collaborators on many projects. I've learned that his creativity and passion come from a place of love for his work and the people that surround him. One of the things that I love about Fred is his willingness to

experiment and try something new. He is always willing to push the bounds of what digital art can be, all while adding a layer of fun and expressiveness to his art, making Fred's work unique. It has been incredible to watch Fred's journey as an artist, from doing commercial work to having his work be sold at renowned auction houses such as Christie's and Sotheby's. Fred is an artist who is truly ahead of his time. I hope others will come to see just how impactful Fred's work has been on the digital art ecosystem.

**RICHERD**
CO-FOUNDER OF MANIFOLD.XYZ

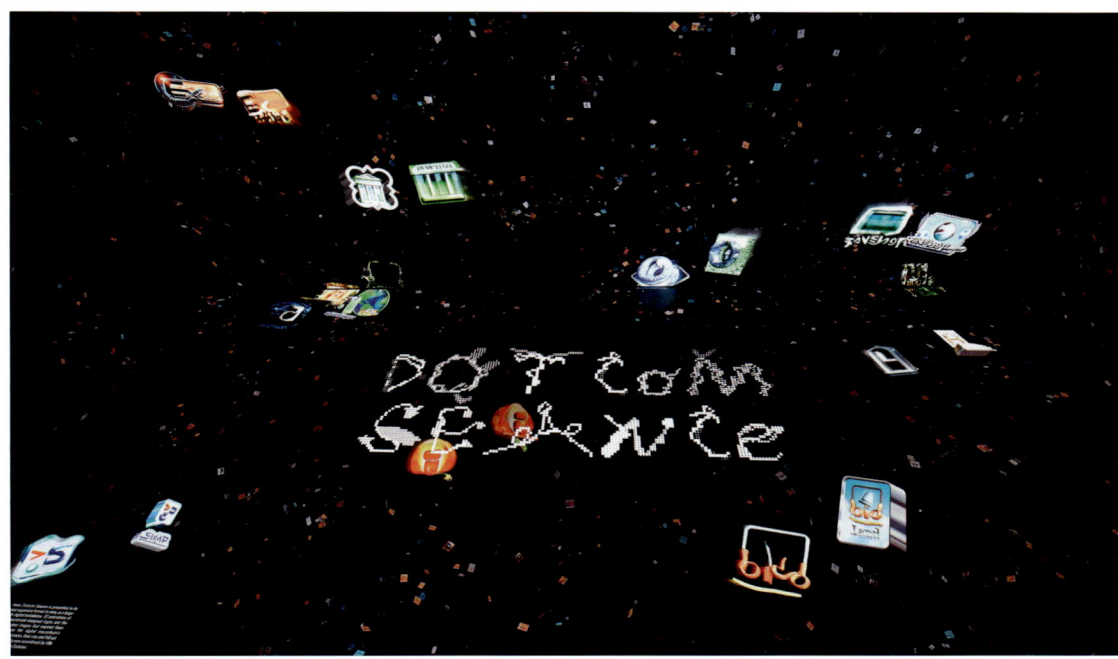

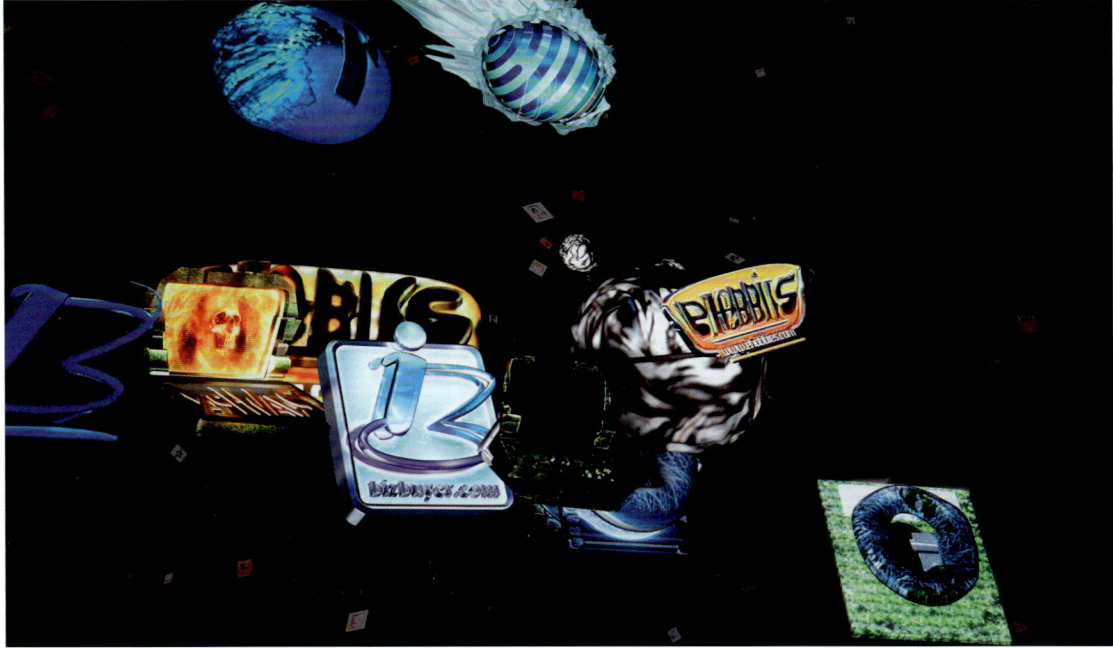

| # | TITLE | TIMESTAMP | MEDIUM | CHAIN | CONTRACT ADDRESS | TOKEN ID | EDITION SIZE | COLLABORATORS |
|---|---|---|---|---|---|---|---|---|
| 01–04 | **DotCom Séance** | 12-17-2021 08:32:33 | Diffusion, CLIP, Adobe Creative Suite | ETH | 0x6ca044fb1cd505c1db4 ef7332e73a236ad6cb71c | 1–21 (Twardowski), 201-2133 (Cosmographia, 460 minted) | 1/1 of 511 | Guile Twardowski, Cosmographia |

EDITIONS ILLUSTRATED: (02) funbug.com, (03) iharvest.com, (04) cashwars.com (Above illustrations designed by Guile Twardowski with a suite of hidden text-to-image logo-NFTs by Cosmographia below)

02

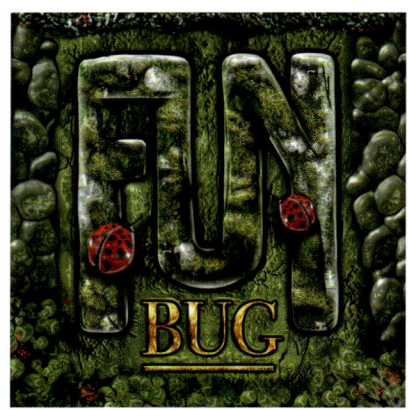

03

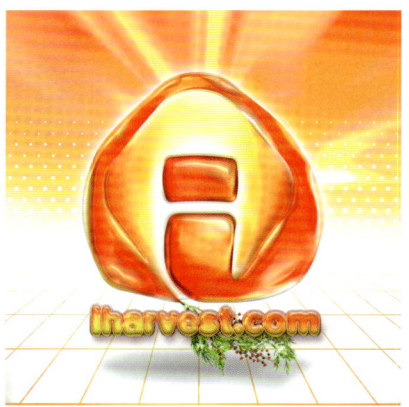

04

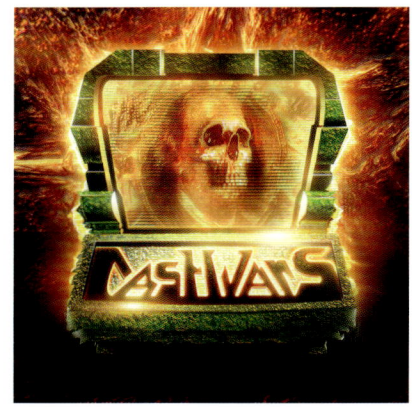

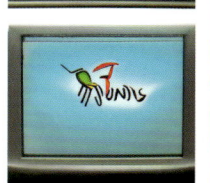
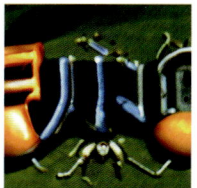
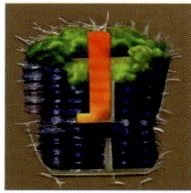

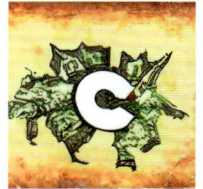
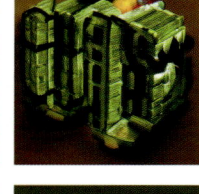

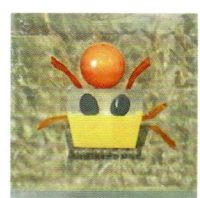
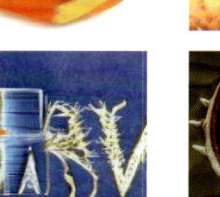
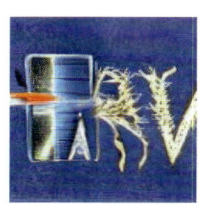
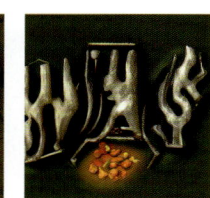

Simon Denny creates conceptual installations that explore how digital information gives form to the ideologies of corporations and governments. His 2016 show at Petzel Gallery, *Blockchain Future States*, highlighted the economic and political models driving the adoption of this then-nascent tool. Two years later, he helmed the curation of *Proof of Work* (2018), the first museum exhibition devoted to art made on and about the blockchain. Its 2021 sequel, *Proof of Stake: Technological Claims*, questioned what it means to define ownership as a technological system.

Denny did not make any NFTs himself until 2019, when he released his rendering of Amazon's patented *Worker Cage* on left gallery. For his 2021 series *NFT Mine Offset*, he acquired second-hand Ethereum mining computers from eBay, hiring a gaming illustrator to produce models of them for short videos auctioned on SuperRare; he also donated the miners to climate prediction.net, a nonprofit that uses powerful computers to model climate change. The series is less an indictment of the environmental costs of NFTs (or the pretenses of carbon offsetting) than a demonstration of how NFTs accrue value while circulating within overlapping systems: Web 2.0 and Web3, art and finance, energy grids and social networks, physical machines and virtual spaces.

Denny's 2022 project *DotCom Séance* resurrected failed Web 1.0 companies like cashwars.com as ENS domains. For each, collectors could mint either a new "cosmic logo" generated by text-to-image AI or an interpretation of that logo by Guile Twardowski, artist of the *CryptoKitties* (2017). The séance suggests that NFTs are the ghosts of the dotcom bubble, while pointing to the irrational beliefs in supernatural forces undergirding new technologies and free markets alike. Ultimately, Denny's NFTs remind us that art always has been alchemical — turning marble to flesh and canvases to gold — and that "immutable" records are in fact complex series of material and symbolic exchanges.

**TINA RIVERS RYAN**
ASSOCIATE CURATOR AT BUFFALO AKG ART MUSEUM,
ART HISTORIAN, AND DIGITAL ART CRITIC

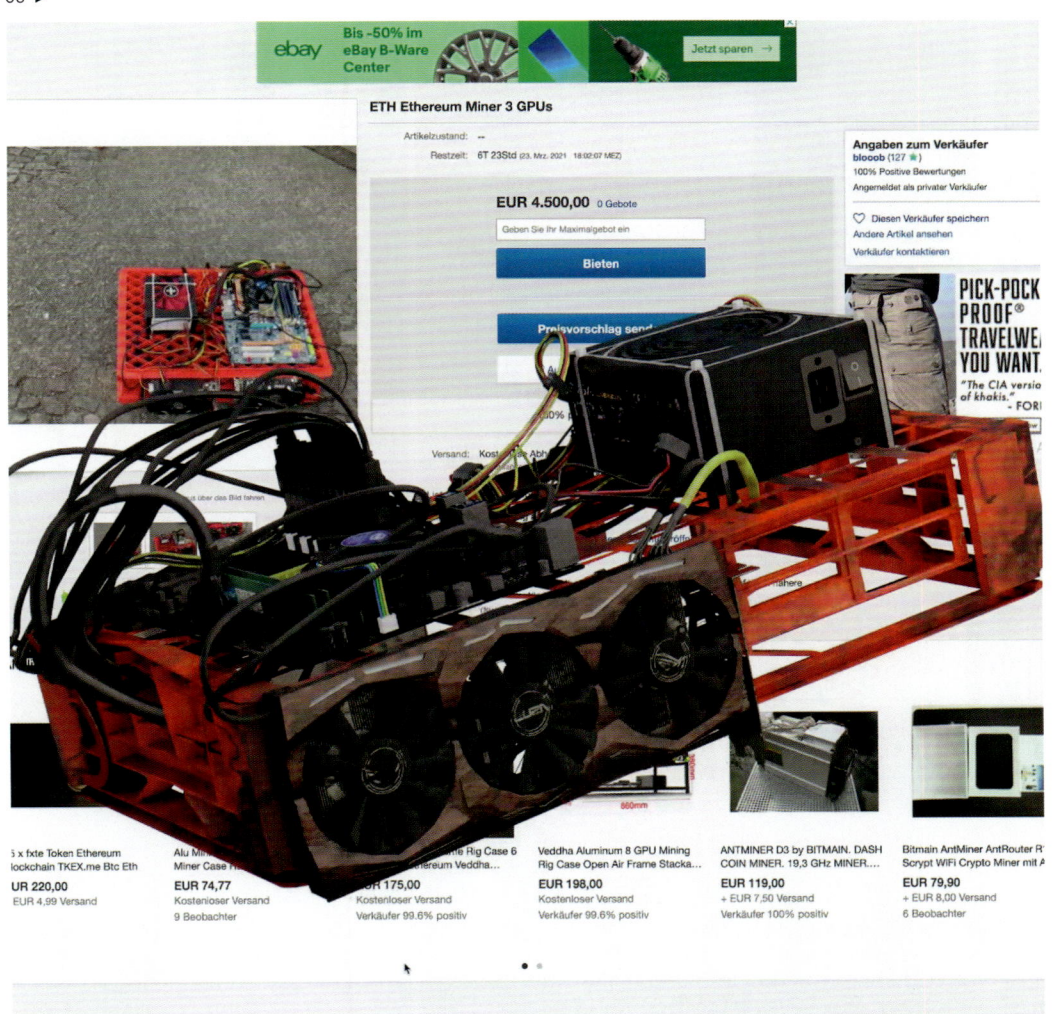

Weitere passende Anzeigen

| # | TITLE | TIMESTAMP | MEDIUM | CHAIN | CONTRACT ADDRESS | TOKEN ID | EDITION SIZE |
|---|-------|-----------|--------|-------|------------------|----------|--------------|
| 05 | **NFT Mine Offset: ETH Ethereum Miner 3 GPUs** | 04-29-2021 21:20:42 | MP4 | ETH | 0xb932a70a57673d89f4a-cffbe830e8ed7f75fb9e0 | 24095 | 1/1 |
| 06 | **Metaverse Landscape 37: The Sandbox Land (-135, -34)** | 05-22-2023 18:20:35 | Oil on canvas, UV print, ETH paper wallet, dynamic ERC-721 NFT | ETH | 0×42ced6954870f4a-17f3a4658d06f63c79de6f7ea | 31 | 1/1 |

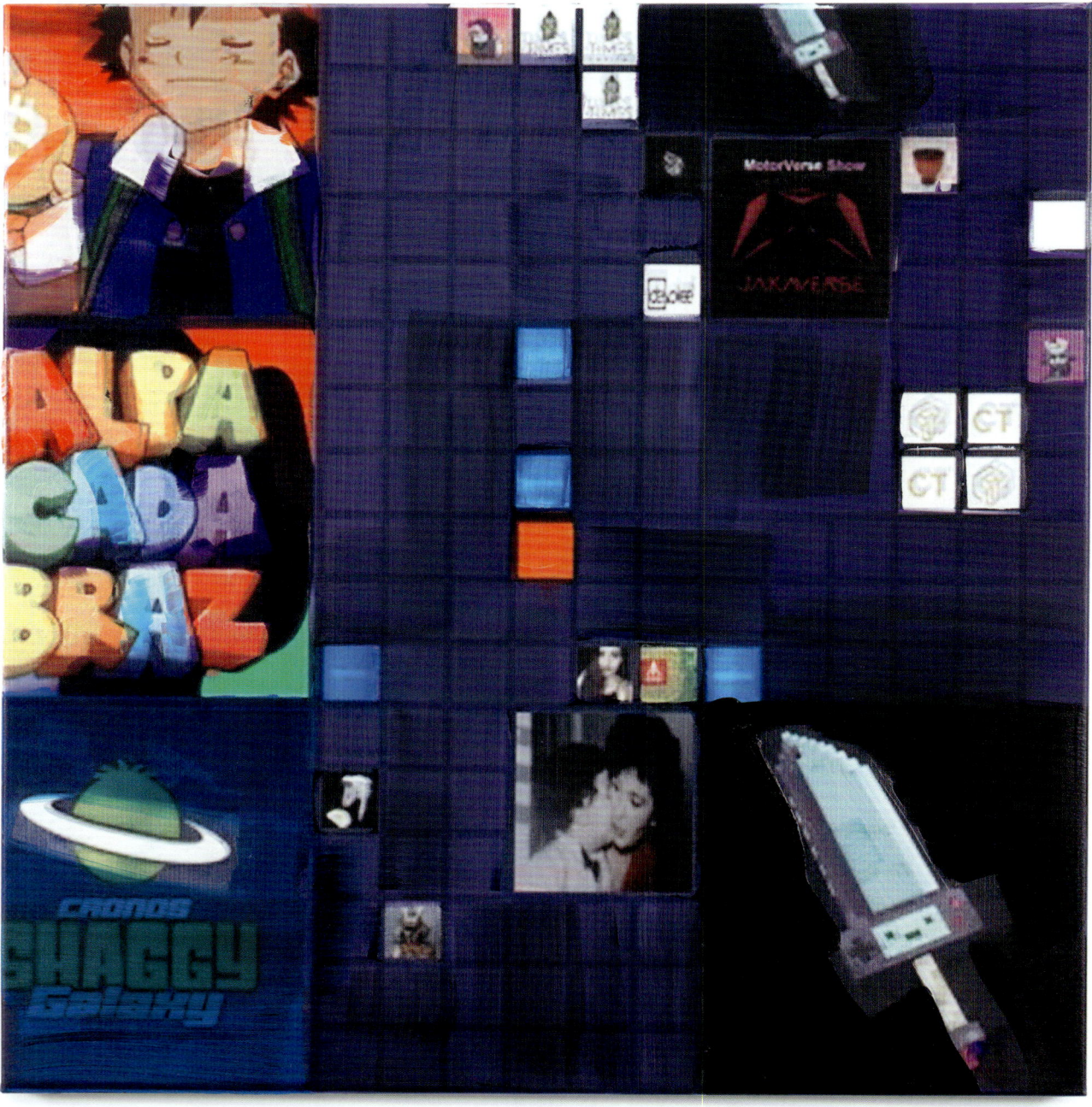

| # | TITLE | TIMESTAMP | MEDIUM | CHAIN | CONTRACT ADDRESS | TOKEN | EDITION SIZE |
|---|---|---|---|---|---|---|---|
| 01 | **Checks** | 01-03-2023 05:28:35 | Onchain SVG / Solidity | ETH | 0×34eEBEE6942d8Def3c125458D1a86e0A897fd6f9 | 1-16031 | Reducing from 16,031 |
| 02 | **Opepen Edition** | 01-08-2023 7:21:11 | Multiple (Work in Progress) | ETH | 0×6339e5E072086621540D0362C4e3Cea0d643E114 | 1-16000 | 1/1 of 16000 |

# JACK BUTCHER

02 ▶

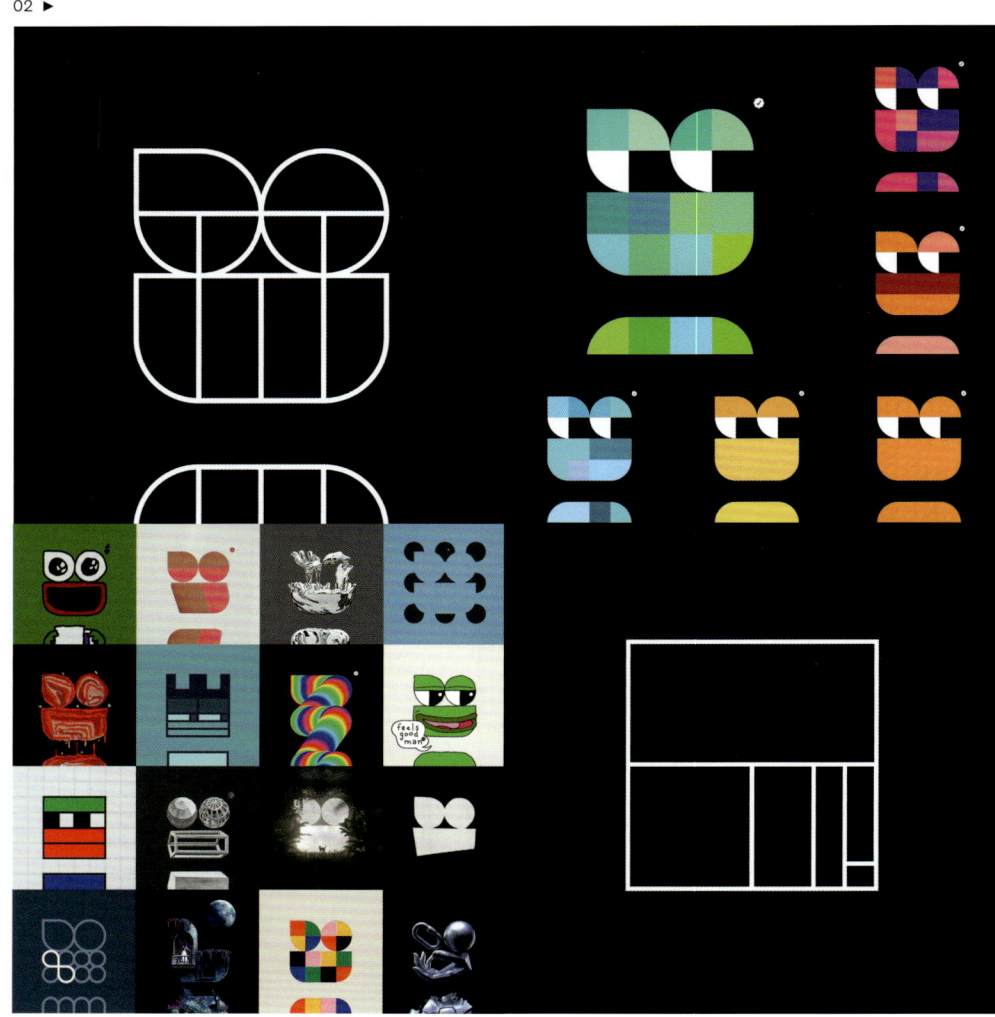

In the fast-evolving landscape of digital art and NFTs, Jack Butcher stands out as an artist who has fundamentally redefined how we interact with digital ownership, dynamic art, and immutable artifacts. His work doesn't just exist on the blockchain; it lives, evolves, and breathes because of it.

Most artwork uses the blockchain as merely a certificate of ownership, a mechanism to trade digital files. Jack's artwork, particularly *Checks* and *Opepen*, uses NFTs as a canvas, a medium, and a system for exploring value, identity, and the very nature of participation.

*Checks*, for example, started as a minimalist exploration of Twitter's verification culture but evolved into a self-referential, community-driven exercise in decentralization. The project played with concepts of scarcity, replication, and mutability, allowing holders to burn and merge their NFTs, actively reshaping the supply and narrative of the collection. *Opepen* is another dynamic masterpiece in the making — a system that unfolds over time, driven by collector participation. Instead of dropping a fixed set of images, Butcher created a framework where editions are revealed in waves, making ownership feel like being part of an evolving artwork. It's a perfect example of how he turns NFTs into interactive experiences rather than static assets, reinforcing that digital art can be fluid, participatory, and ever-changing.

In many ways, this work has rewritten our expectations of what NFTs can be. While early digital artists focused on immutability as a virtue — creating permanent, untouched works—Jack's work embraces programmability and change, turning art into an interactive, living entity — a broad concept we've only begun to explore.

**BEEPLE**
ARTIST

```solidity
/**
 *SUBMITTED FOR VERIFICATION AT ETHERSCAN.IO ON 2017-11-28
*/

PRAGMA SOLIDITY ^0.4.11;


/**
 * @TITLE OWNABLE
 * @DEV THE OWNABLE CONTRACT HAS AN OWNER ADDRESS, AND PROVIDES BASIC AUTHORIZATION CONTROL
 * FUNCTIONS, THIS SIMPLIFIES THE IMPLEMENTATION OF "USER PERMISSIONS".
*/
CONTRACT OWNABLE {
  ADDRESS PUBLIC OWNER;


  /**
   * @DEV THE OWNABLE CONSTRUCTOR SETS THE ORIGINAL `OWNER` OF THE CONTRACT TO THE SENDER
   * ACCOUNT.
   */
  FUNCTION OWNABLE() {
    OWNER = MSG.SENDER;
  }


  /**
   * @DEV THROWS IF CALLED BY ANY ACCOUNT OTHER THAN THE OWNER.
   */
  MODIFIER ONLYOWNER() {
    REQUIRE(MSG.SENDER == OWNER);
    _;
  }


  /**
   * @DEV ALLOWS THE CURRENT OWNER TO TRANSFER CONTROL OF THE CONTRACT TO A NEWOWNER.
   * @PARAM NEWOWNER THE ADDRESS TO TRANSFER OWNERSHIP TO.
   */
  FUNCTION TRANSFEROWNERSHIP(ADDRESS NEWOWNER) ONLYOWNER {
    IF (NEWOWNER != ADDRESS(0)) {
      OWNER = NEWOWNER;
    }
  }

}




/// @TITLE INTERFACE FOR CONTRACTS CONFORMING TO ERC-721: NON-FUNGIBLE TOKENS
/// @AUTHOR DIETER SHIRLEY <DETE@AXIOMZEN.CO> (HTTPS://GITHUB.COM/DETE)
CONTRACT ERC721 {
    // REQUIRED METHODS
    FUNCTION TOTALSUPPLY() PUBLIC VIEW RETURNS (UINT256 TOTAL);
    FUNCTION BALANCEOF(ADDRESS _OWNER) PUBLIC VIEW RETURNS (UINT256 BALANCE);
    FUNCTION OWNEROF(UINT256 _TOKENID) EXTERNAL VIEW RETURNS (ADDRESS OWNER);
    FUNCTION APPROVE(ADDRESS _TO, UINT256 _TOKENID) EXTERNAL;
    FUNCTION TRANSFER(ADDRESS _TO, UINT256 _TOKENID) EXTERNAL;
    FUNCTION TRANSFERFROM(ADDRESS _FROM, ADDRESS _TO, UINT256 _TOKENID) EXTERNAL;

    // EVENTS
    EVENT TRANSFER(ADDRESS FROM, ADDRESS TO, UINT256 TOKENID);
    EVENT APPROVAL(ADDRESS OWNER, ADDRESS APPROVED, UINT256 TOKENID);

    // OPTIONAL
    // FUNCTION NAME() PUBLIC VIEW RETURNS (STRING NAME);
    // FUNCTION SYMBOL() PUBLIC VIEW RETURNS (STRING SYMBOL);
    // FUNCTION TOKENSOFOWNER(ADDRESS _OWNER) EXTERNAL VIEW RETURNS (UINT256[] TOKENIDS);
    // FUNCTION TOKENMETADATA(UINT256 _TOKENID, STRING _PREFERREDTRANSPORT) PUBLIC VIEW RETURNS (STRING INFOURL);

    // ERC-165 COMPATIBILITY (HTTPS://GITHUB.COM/ETHEREUM/EIPS/ISSUES/165)
    FUNCTION SUPPORTSINTERFACE(BYTES4 _INTERFACEID) EXTERNAL VIEW RETURNS (BOOL);
}


// // AUCTION WRAPPER FUNCTIONS


// AUCTION WRAPPER FUNCTIONS
```

MARÍA PAULA FERNÁNDEZ
SIMON DENNY
ADINA GLICKSTEIN

# ON BUILDING

"It's Time to Build": A History of NFT Infrastructure

*Currency is the least interesting thing you
could build with this technology.*

Anil Dash and Kevin McCoy's Monegraph
Presentation for Rhizome Seven on Seven, 2014

## Introduction: Critics and Hackers

At the beginning of the coronavirus pandemic, on April 18, 2020, Marc Andreessen **[10.01]** penned a blog post decreeing that, in the wake of this black swan disaster, the "Time to Build" was upon us. His injunction — take the initiative to create new structures that actively address the lack of ingenuity and pragmatism in private and public sectors alike — came from a firsthand conviction that critique is best served by actively making anew. In 1992, Andreessen, then an undergraduate on the brink of his BS in Computer Science, co-developed Mosaic, one of the first user-friendly web browsers. Mosaic evolved into Netscape, marking the start of the commercial internet and ushering in Web 1.0 as we know it. Fast-forward to 2022 and Andreessen's firm, a16z, is one of the most notorious (and foresighted) venture capitalists on Sand Hill Road, boasting a portfolio stacked with many of the Web 2.0 platform giants that organize most of our browsing hours today, alongside numerous major players in the emerging world of Web3. Fear him, disagree with him, or respect him, Andreessen's philosophy has long been coupled with action; as a hacker, an instigator, and a builder, he embodies the ethos he promotes.

This emphasis on building, which lends its title to this essay, harmonizes with the history of Web3, where critique often takes the shape of creation. The artist-researcher-theorist Jaya Klara Brekke has outlined the figure of the "hacker-engineer" as a central protagonist in the infrastructural development of Web3 technologies, grounding the making of contemporary digital network economies in cypherpunk and hacker lineages.[1] This holds true in the NFT space, where new possibilities for making and distributing digital art have come to light through an iterative, decentralized process, as much as anywhere else in Web3. At the most basic, blockchains of all kinds offer the potential to serve as public, immutable ledgers maintained by the people using them rather than being overseen by a top-down authority — whether that be a state or a bank, or, in the cultural fields, an auction house or a gallery. And as Brekke's observation stresses, hacking and building are deeply intertwined; not so much opposed categories as pieces of the same process.

Building, conceived of in this way, takes the form of a critical gesture. It heeds Andreessen's call to bring the worlds we want to see into existence, no matter our technical background; to make new things instead of just commenting on the extant system from some imagined position of intellectual remove. The role of critique underwent a similar shift at a critical point of art-historical inflection long before Web3. In 1968, Lucy Lippard and John Chandler wrote that, following the conceptual turn, the role of criticism must be recast: "Judgment of ideas is less interesting than following ideas through […]. If the object becomes obsolete, objective distance becomes obsolete."[2] As the "art object" grows increasingly immaterial, they argue, critique ought to become more tangible, more focused on advancing new ideas through practice.

NFTs, of course, are not "immaterial" — they are made of software, files, and networks, all of which take physical forms; they have a spatial, material, and carbon footprint.[3] Nevertheless, pieces of their origin story could be situated in the history of conceptual art that Lippard and Chandler established (as indeed they are elsewhere in this book), and the unexpected resonance between these art historians' observations and Andreessen's call to build is revealing. The infrastructural history of NFTs has been shaped by the active efforts of interested parties — artists, technologists, and people working across the two. Through their collective, dynamic work, existing technology has been reshaped to new ends, the field of future possibility broadened in the process.

A note on methodology: to reflect on the emergence of NFT infrastructure — and to show how it came to exist through the labor of communities and networks — is necessarily to set forth some kind of timeline. This is a pragmatic choice, enabling us to suggest that these developments often happened in conversation with each other, building on — knowingly or not; critically or in homage to — the projects that came before.[4] It's not our goal to identify what constituted the first "true" NFT project. That question is hotly contested, and is also beyond the scope of this essay. Likewise, the precise dates of new infrastructural developments — especially in the Ethereum ecosystem, and wherever else community proposals and review processes are concerned — can be amorphous.[5] Rather than staking a claim about which of the numerous inventive and prescient early tokenized artworks was the earliest, the most significant, or the truest to NFTs' present form, we offer a (necessarily selective) historical sketch of the infrastructure that underlies them. And in an effort to be sensitive to length constraints, we don't define much terminology in this text, but a helpful inventory of terms can be found in the Glossary.

Similarly, we've chosen to limit our scope primarily to the (pre)history of NFTs on the Bitcoin and Ethereum blockchains, as these have been the historic locus of infrastructural development. Rich and varied NFT art ecosystems exist on other, newer chains including

[1] Jaya Klara Brekke, "Hacker-Engineers and Their Economies: The Political Economy of Decentralized Networks and 'Cryptoeconomics,'" *New Political Economy*, 26, 2020, https://doi.org/10.1080/13563467.2020.1806223.

[2] Lucy Lippard and John Chandler, *Six Years: The Dematerialization of the Art Object from 1966 to 1972* (New York: Praeger, 1973), 49.

[3] Artists, researchers, and technologists like Joanie Lemercier have extensively explored the environmental toll of the Ethereum blockchain, mostly around the carbon expenditure of its current validation mechanism, proof of work. As of this writing, proof-of-work is widely understood to be a temporary solution and on its way out. A shift to a less-taxing alternative, proof of stake, is expected by 2022. For an overview of the environmental problems with proof of work see Joanie Lemercier, "The problem of (Ethereum) CryptoArt," Joanie Lemercier Studio, February 17, 2021, https://joanielemercier.com/the-problem-of-cryptoart/.

[4] It's worth noting that the emergence of contemporary NFT infrastructure was propelled by people working on similar projects in parallel and complementary, while not explicitly interrelated, ways. Numerous artists and tech founders were interviewed as part of the research leading up to this essay, and most of them saw retrospective connections between their work and others', but overwhelmingly claimed to have little awareness of similar initiatives in the landscape at the time. In short: the history itself has unfolded in a decentralized manner.

[5] In the interest of factual accuracy, we have opted to give months and years, rather than specific dates, when the exact timing of a project or development is unclear in the historical record.

**10.01**
A profile picture used by Marc Andreessen on Twitter
Beeple
*CHARLIE RED* (from *THE EVERYDAYS*, 2007–ongoing), June 17, 2021
Cinema 4D, Octane Render, Adobe Photoshop

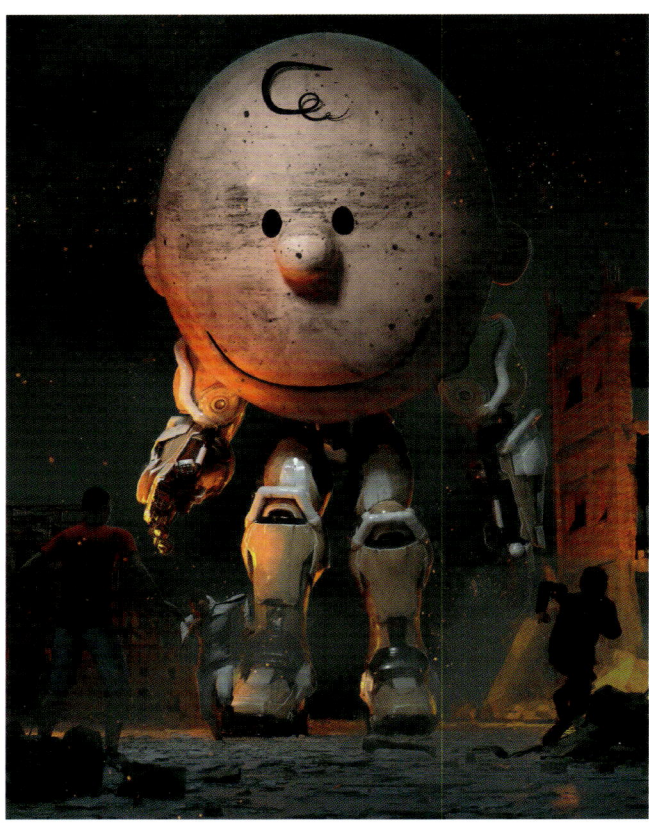

Solana, Algorand, and perhaps most notably Tezos. Tezos in particular has been home to a number of platforms and organic communities, often prolific and artist-run, like 2021's Hic Et Nunc and 2022's fxhash, and is rapidly gaining prominence in the ever-evolving space. Still, the earlier histories of "building" that we outline here, especially around the establishment of token standards, were largely centered on Bitcoin and Ethereum.

And why choose to focus on infrastructure in the first place? As media anthropologist Brian Larkin has argued, attending to infrastructure can allow us to understand "how the political can be constituted through different means," as both technologies and the relations between them give ways to particular fantasies, ideologies, and desires.[6] Bitcoin and Ethereum, with their distinct yet entwined communities and histories, offer a window into how the landscape of NFTs as we know them today came into being through entangled cybernetic loops: artists, technologists, and people in between iterating towards a future perpetually under construction.

### Bitcoin (Im)Purism

The history of hacker-engineers and artistic innovators paving the way towards NFTs traces back nearly as far as the advent of the blockchain itself. In 2012, four years after the Bitcoin network's initial launch, Yoni Assia, Lior Hakim, Meni Rosenfeld, Rotem Lev, and Vitalik Buterin (who was, at the time, a secondary school student writing for *Bitcoin Magazine*) authored a whitepaper that outlined a protocol for experimenting with colored coins, or ways of adding information to Bitcoin transactions, "coloring" tokens — specifically, the "unspent transaction output," or UTXO — to represent a connection to other assets **[10.02]**.[7]

In a slightly different vein, Counterparty, an open-source project initially designed as a peer-to-peer financial platform on top of the Bitcoin blockchain, made it possible for users to create, name, and issue their own tokens. Launched in 2014 **[10.03]**, it created the possibility of "broadcasting," or publishing text and data through Bitcoin transactions. Like any Bitcoin

[6] Brian Larkin, "The Politics and Poetics of Infrastructure," *Annual Review of Anthropology*, Vol. 42, October 2013, 329.
[7] Foreshadowing a contemporary line of critique against NFTs: these coins' relationship to the physical goods they represented only existed insofar as the people trading them agreed to enforce it.

```
pk = PUBLIC KEY
extended_ripemd = `0x73`+RIPEMD-160(SHA-256(pk))
checksum = first 4 bytes of SHA-256(SHA-256(extended_ripemd))
Testnet Colored Coin Address = Base58check(extended_ripemd+checksum)
```

block, each Counterparty broadcast is timestamped, browsable, and permanently stored on the ledger.[8] In an innovative turn that prefigured Ethereum's system of housing smart contracts on a public blockchain, Counterparty consisted of a single smart contract deployed as node software, with input parameters written on-chain using unspendable outputs in standard Bitcoin transactions. Adam Krellenstein, one of Counterparty's co-founders, explained in an email to the authors of this essay that the idea came from initiatives around the same time like Mastercoin, which sought to build a distributed financial system using Bitcoin with additional affordances for different kinds of assets.[9] Art and digital collectibles quickly became one such asset class, and are still traded on Counterparty's decentralized exchange (DEX) today, though in relatively smaller volume than on Ethereum.

Counterparty broadcast tokens formed the basis for projects like JP Janssen's *OLGA* — a work discussed further in this book's first chapter, "On Quantum" — which, in June 2014, constituted one of the first 1/1 token issuances, in an early attempt at making unique and ownable blockchain-based art. Counterparty also lent itself to fungible-token-based artworks like NILICoins [10.04], where Israeli artist Nili Lerner issued 11 tokens, describing them as "art coins/tokens." The series consists of seven brand name tokens issued as appropriation art, including Coca-Cola Coin [ICOKE] and Disney Coin [IDISNEY], whilst another coin in the series, NILI [NILI], is described as a token backed by the value of the artist's existing physical artwork. Lerner announced the project on a BitcoinTalk forum in September of 2014, where it was met with modest excitement. The prevailing response amongst BitcoinTalk commenters, though, was chagrin — "So the fact is that you, as an artist, are short of money. You wanna find some in the crypto world?" — illustrating the Bitcoin community's hesitancy towards projects that used the blockchain for anything other than cryptocurrency trading (and perhaps equally, the perils of being too prescient, i.e., early to market).[10]

Roughly contemporaneous with these Counterparty experiments, in May 2014, Anil Dash and Kevin McCoy debuted Monegraph at Rhizome's fourth annual Seven on Seven conference, held at New York's New Museum. A prototype for registering ownership of digital artworks, it heeded questions born from post-internet art — prominent at the time among younger artists inspired by earlier net and browser art, attempting to expand the container for internet-reflexive and digital work to a "protocol" or format that could hold both financial and canonical value.[11] Rather than focusing on the art object in an exhibition context as many post-internet artists did, Dash and McCoy looked to nascent, natively digital technology.

Monegraph piggybacked on the Namecoin blockchain, an early Bitcoin fork; fashioned similarly to predecessors like Counterparty, it harnessed the potential of storing small amounts of extra information in regular transactions. The on-chain component of a Monegraph claim consisted of a key including a numerical hash, forming a sort of "signature" corresponding to each digital file. Through this unique, traceable key, each artwork's chain of ownership could be established and tracked through its record on the blockchain. In connection with a key, each Monegraph claim included a URL pointing to the digital work itself, along with an assertion of the title to the work in plain, readable language. Forgoing wallets, it harnessed Twitter tie-ins for its identity-verification layer. And in a sideswipe at the purists who saw crypto as strictly a financial medium, one slide of Dash and McCoy's presentation proclaimed: "Currency is the least interesting thing you could build with this technology."

Foresighted as it may have been, Monegraph's creators insist that they did not invent NFTs as we presently understand them. "By doing a public, visible demonstration, we took the most likely path of preventing the technology from harming artists by removing the ability for others to patent it later in an exploitative way," Dash reflected in 2021, emphasizing Monegraph's origins "in a context of a nonprofit, artist-centered demonstration held at a museum."[12] Again, the question of who — or what — "invented" NFTs is less important than the ecosystem that facilitated their development, and the recognition that their underlying infrastructure was produced through a process of hacking and ad-hoc iteration: communities, networks, and artists taking the responsibility to create new tools themselves, usable by their own hands.

[8] Counterparty, "Counterwallet," accessed May 20, 2022, https://counterparty.io/docs/faq-counterwallet/.

[9] In contrast to Mastercoin, which raised around 5,120 bitcoin, worth approximately $500,000 at the time, with an ICO, or "initial coin offering," Counterparty distributed its native currency, XCP, using "proof-of-burn": the developers, just like everyone else who wanted to acquire the tokens, had to get them by sending the corresponding amount of bitcoin to an unrecoverable wallet address. In this sense, Counterparty embodied the spirit of decentralization from the outset: risk was distributed equally across its founders and devs, who obtained XCP by destroying bitcoins just like the rest of the protocol's early adherents. An ICO would also have situated whoever held the money from the sale as a single potential point of failure — so the early decision to fund Counterparty with proof-of-burn also set it up for longevity, which could help explain the fact that it's still in use today.

[10] The BitcoinTalk forum where Lerner launched NILIcoins is also marked with a warning: "One or more bitcointalk.org users have reported that they strongly believe that the creator of this topic is a scammer. (Login to see the detailed trust ratings.) While the bitcointalk.org administration does not verify such claims, you should proceed with extreme caution" (Nili Lerner, "[NILI] NILIcoins Art-Coins," Bitcoin Forum, https://bitcointalk.org/index.php?topic=782161.0).

[11] In a Twitter Spaces conversation moderated by Robert Alice on June 7, 2022, McCoy commented on the visibility of post-internet art at this time in New York. He cited his academic relationship, while teaching at NYU, with prominent post-internet artist Brad Troemel — particularly Troemel's work on Silk Road and physical Bitcoin tokens — as one factor having lead him to look deeper into the potential of bringing art and blockchains into meaningful technical synthesis.

[12] Anil Dash, "On 'Inventing NFTs' and How We Don't Have Any Good Way to Talk about Tech." Anil Dash, Nov 21, 2022, https://anildash.com/2021/11/14/i-didnt-invent-nfts-but-we-dont-really-have-any-other-way-to-talk-about-tech/.

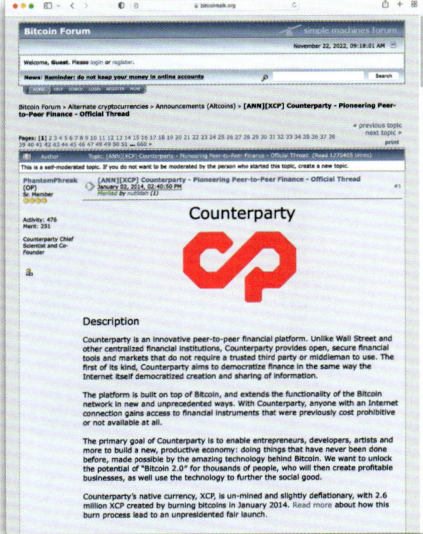

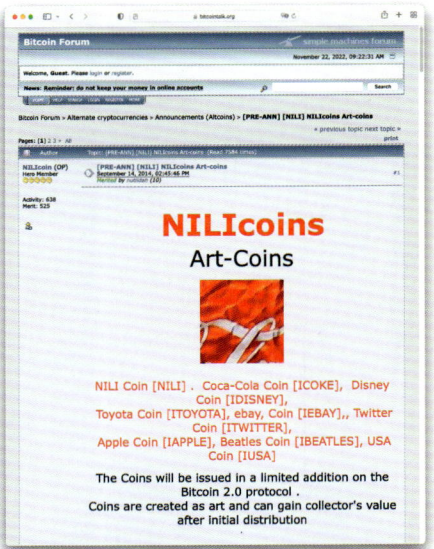

## Selling Bits of Cultural IP

The idea of buying and selling bits of cultural IP, often hinging on in-group knowledge, of course predated the blockchain through media like trading card games; and the advent of Bitcoin, conferring demonstrable digital scarcity to secure these exchangeable assets' status as "rare," fueled their development even further. An exemplary case of the union between niche memes and digital scarcity came in September of 2016 with the advent of rare pepes, Bitcoin-secured cards bearing the figure of the infamous cartoon frog, capitalizing on the speculative trade of dank memes in imaginary Reddit markets (such as /r/MemeEconomy). While rare pepes are also discussed elsewhere in this book, in "On Quantum" and "On Crypto Art," their infrastructural history warrants specific attention. Unlike the Spells of Genesis trading cards before them, which were situated within a larger game world, rare pepes did not exist inside a game — the market itself was the game. Users could submit their own cards, complete with original artwork; the forum for frog-exchange thus became a community, centered not just on cards' exchange, but on their creation. Rare Pepe Wallet, which hit the scene on September 15, 2016, offered an accessible user interface for the purchase and sale of these cards, and could be seen as a progenitor to the NFT marketplaces of today. It also pioneered the idea of access tokens, enabling the holders of certain pepe cards to unlock gated bonus content. Rare Pepe Wallet is still in operation half a decade later, and rare pepes are traded on Counterparty to this day.[13]

Other projects around that time also harnessed Bitcoin's potential to verify scarcity and provenance for less memetic ends. Ascribe set out to create blockchain-based certificates of authenticity for artworks **[10.05]**. Its founders Trent and Masha McConaghy came from artificial intelligence / machine learning and curatorial backgrounds respectively; the protocol was created, starting in 2013, in conversation with an array of artists producing digital work — Harm van den Dorpel and Constant Dullaart helped develop the beta — in an attempt to cure the widespread "online attribution problem." While digital art had, by the early 2010s, attained major recognition in the offline art world, issues around its transfer, exhibition, and provenance still needed to be reckoned with: how could artists securely show, sell, and license their digital-born work?[14] There had to be a better way, and by the McConaghys' assessment, it began with Bitcoin. Officially launched in 2015, Ascribe marketed itself as a way of registering provenance and IP on the Bitcoin blockchain. It boasted a wider range of sales actions than Counterparty, many of which were inherited from the legacy art market: with Ascribe, artists could make and register editions, and buyers (whether individuals or institutions) could consign and borrow the works they owned.

As one early employee explained, they weren't really interested in developing a new market — rather, they were curious about how the blockchain, with its public and immutable ledgers, could create more transparency in the existing one. Ascribe thus stands out as

[13] Unlike other early Bitcoin-based initiatives coming directly out of the art world, the pepe trade has been celebrated by the Bitcoin community. At least one pepe trading card experiment on Ethereum, called "Peperium," was proposed on online forums, but never managed to take off. This might invite conclusions about the ideological landscape of Bitcoin vs. Ethereum, in step with research carried out by Lana Swartz and Ann Brody, both of whom conclude that Ethereum is more aligned with cypherpunk libertarianism and "infrastructural mutualism" while Bitcoin slants towards a post-Randian crypto anarchism. See Lana Swartz, "What Was Bitcoin, What Will It Be?" *Cultural Studies*, Vol. 32, 2018; Ann Brody and Stéphane Couture, "Ideologies and Imaginaries in Blockchain Communities," *Canadian Journal of Communication*, Vol. 46, No. 3, 2021.

[14] The Ascribe whitepaper summarizes these challenges by asking, among other questions: Was Molly Soda really just supposed to sell webcam videos on a flash drive? See Trent McConaghy and David Holtzman, "Towards an Ownership Layer for the Internet," *Ascribe*, June 24, 2015, https://cryptochainuni.com/wp-content/uploads/ascribe-whitepaper-Towards-An-Ownership-Layer.pdf.

**10.05**
Ascribe's Certificate of Authenticity for
Tintin Cooper, *Kiss (#02/25)*, 2015
GIF
Bitcoin, 16DZphH3M9AKpwMbgnUVygsyvdBT8yK9n3

**10.06**
Code from Ascribe's SPOOL protocol released on
GitHub in 2015
by Dimitri de Jonghe and Trent McConaghy

**10.07**
Screenshot of tweet by the Department
of Decentralization about Coinbase
attempting to trademark "buidl,"
December 6, 2018

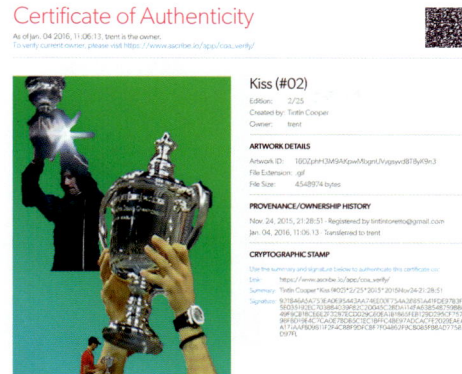

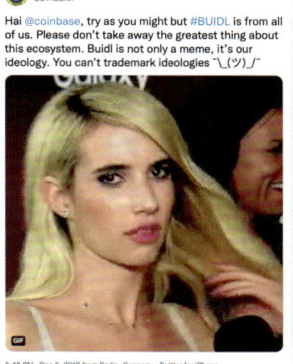

an embodiment of the "hacker-engineer" ethos which, per Brekke's figuration, sees blockchain tech as a way of fighting the centralized control of information and to intervene in the infrastructure that shapes existing economic flows. Hacked together in a way that Tim Daubenschütz, one of the developers behind Ascribe, recalls as "extremely avant-garde," the platform elegantly addressed the critical issue of establishing provenance for works that live and circulate online — but it never quite found its niche.[15] Some who were involved at the time suspect that this was because legacy institutions feared the market transparency that it sought to guarantee; others suspect that it, like several prescient projects before it, was simply too early to market.

In either case, Bitcoin was ill-equipped to handle Ascribe, and it was sometimes met with outright hostility in the crypto community. On a technical level, Ascribe capitalized on a standardized function called OP_RETURN, which enables a user-defined sequence of up to 40 bytes to be written onto the blockchain. This allowed for things like links — pointing to images and longer texts living off-chain — to be stored in Bitcoin transactions. Daubenschütz wrote about the project in a recent newsletter for NFT curation protocol JPG.space: "Ascribe was built on Bitcoin [...] by signing up via email and password, a hierarchical deterministic wallet was derived from the federation wallet; all ownership transactions were stored in an inventive protocol called SPOOL, the "Secure Public Online Ownership Ledger"**[10.06]**.[16] Similar to the well-known ERC-721 NFT standard, the SPOOL encodes ownership information on-chain; but it was a hell of a mess as Bitcoin really wasn't meant for any of this."[17] Indeed, issues occasionally arose with Bitcoin validator nodes rejecting the transactions for containing too much data; some hardcore Bitcoin purists even called OP_RETURN transactions "spammy" or blamed them for bloating the network.[18] This hostility towards the grafting of different types of assets onto Bitcoin transactions has recently softened somewhat: following the Taproot upgrade in November 2021, a protocol called Ordinals makes it possible to inscribe digital assets on a "satoshi," the lowest denomination of a bitcoin. This has facilitated the creation of what are essentially Bitcoin NFTs — many of which, as of this writing, deal in familiar motifs like Apes, Rocks, and Punks. However, Ordinals have still caused "uproar over the prospect of ubiquitous internet memes... clogging up the blockchain" in certain circles, recalling the pushback faced by Ascribe.[19]

## Ecosystems of Many Interworking Parts

Around the time that this all was unfolding in the Bitcoin space, the blockchain that undergirds NFTs as we know them today made its way into the world. Ethereum — proposed by Vitalik Buterin in 2013, crowdfunded in 2014, and inaugurating its "Frontier Phase" on July 30, 2015 — offered smart contracts as a native functionality, weaving the capacity to store and execute self-enforcing code directly into its blockchain. While Bitcoin affords for some limited smart contract functions, Ethereum was built with a more expansive vision in mind. Its programming language, Solidity, is geared towards Turing-complete operations, unlike Bitcoin's programming language, SCRIPT, which is tailored to monetary transactions. These infrastructural differences entailed cultural differences in turn. Crypto-culture researcher Ann

[15] Tim Daubenschütz, interview with authors, April 8, 2022.
[16] Dimitri de Jonghe and Trent McConaghy, "SPOOL Protocol," GitHub, March 14, 2015, https://github.com/ascribe/spool/blob/master/README.md.
[17] Tim Daubenschütz, "The JPG Newsletter with My Friend Tim as Special Guest," JPG, April 8, 2022, https://jpg100.substack.com/p/the-jpg-newsletter-with-my-friend.
[18] Reactions like this one were common across the #bitcoin IRC channels in the mid-2010s.
[19] David Pan, "Bitcoin Will Be Fine With Monkey JPEGs, Creator of NFT Protocol Says," Bloomberg, February 20, 2023, https://www.bloomberg.com/news/articles/2023-02-19/what-are-ordinals-and-can-donald-trump-nfts-boost-bitcoin-btc-blockchain/.

10.08
Screenshot of tweet by Simon de la Rouviere about an early "standardised token/coin contract," July 15, 2015

10.09
Screenshot from video documentation of Simon de la Rouviere's Tokens talk at Devcon1, 2015

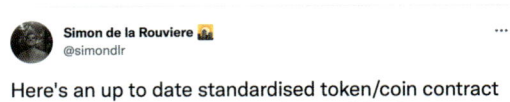

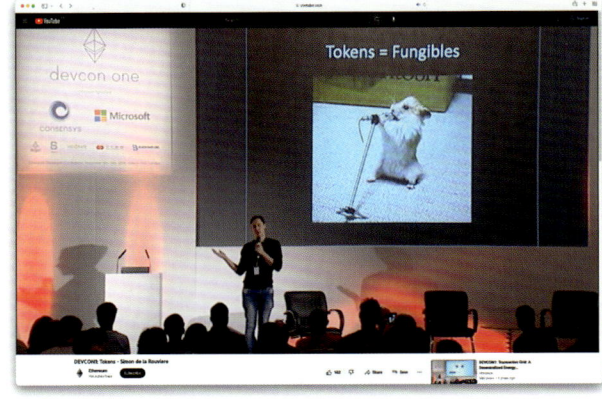

Brody suggests that Ethereum's design as a virtual machine opens it up to a broader range of ideological orientations; its "world computer" imaginary positions it in line with what Lana Swartz calls "infrastructural mutualism" — a perspective that sees cryptocurrencies as a conduit to freedom of information and decentralization, not just decentralized finance, in step with the cypherpunk values that Brekke locates in the figure of the hacker-engineer. Drawing on earlier writing by Gabriella Coleman, Brody highlights the affinity for "tinkering" in the Ethereum ecosystem; borrowing Christopher Kelley's formulation of the "recursive public," she explains how the network's creation through feedback shapes its own means of existence.[20]

Ethereum's openness and programmability, along with its community-driven development process, necessitated the adoption of universal token standards — certain commonly agreed-upon specifications around how tokens are created and deployed — to ensure compatibility between different developments across the blockchain. In Ethereum's case, the ERC, or "Ethereum Request for Comments," is the most basic application-level standard. The protocol for creating ERCs to facilitate the definition of future standards was laid out by a community of developers — not Ethereum employees, but hobbyists and dApp-designing dreamers — in the network's early days. "What's unique about blockchains like Ethereum," Dieter Shirley, CTO of Dapper Labs, tells us, "is that they aren't just pieces of software, but ecosystems of many interworking parts."[21] Community proposals can submit ideas for improving those parts, but they can also introduce new parts altogether.

Like Bitcoin, Ethereum's code is open source, meaning no single entity owns or controls it, and developers are encouraged to "fork" code, reuse existing functionality, and iterate on what others have already built. Crucial to recognize, the same open-source spirit runs through the proposal process through which the protocol itself has been architected and elaborated. Not only the code, but the procedure for submitting and formalizing it, are developed by interested individuals on public fora, and have been from the outset.[22] As the "recursive public" builds (or "buidls," as the meme goes **[10.07]**), new possibilities, each with the potential to reshape the network, come into being.

Original proposals for "standardized contract APIs," as they were conceived of around the time of the Frontier launch, focused on "coins" rather than "tokens," aiming to provide basic and universal functionality for transferring and spending tokens within smart contracts. The first "coin standards" were discussed at Devcon1 in London, and the debate around their specifications continued in a GitHub "gist" (or online code snippet) created by Fabian Vogelsteller. Joseph Chow proposed ERC-19, an early coin standard that was abandoned in favor of Vogelsteller's thread, EIP-20, which eventually, in November 2015, became the ERC-20 token, the fungible token standard still widely in use today. ERC-20 formed the minimal technical standard for all Ethereum smart contracts; to this day, all other Ethereum tokens building beyond it must follow the rules that it defines.[23]

The process of proposing and formalizing new token standards continued following ERC-20, unfolding through a similar process to the advent of ERC-20. Ethereum Improvement Proposals, or EIPs, are submitted as draft standards and presented in a GitHub repository for review and discussion **[10.08]**. They're shared widely to gather community interest, circulating

[20] Ann Brody and Stéphane Couture, "Ideologies and Imaginaries in Blockchain Communities," *Canadian Journal of Communication*, Vol. 46, Issue 3, 2021, 545.
[21] Dieter Shirley, email to authors, April 11, 2022.
[22] Anyone with a GitHub account can, in theory, contribute to Ethereum. The various possible ways to contribute, including working on open issues and adding developer tools, are outlined on https://ethereum.org/en/contributing/, along with the names and PFPs of the community members who have contributed so far. There are 770 as of this writing, in April 2022.
[23] For the real heads: ERC-20 outlines six basic coding functions central to token implementation, which must be uniform across all tokens in the Ethereum ecosystem: totalSupply, balanceOf, allowance, transfer, approve, and transferFrom. See Ethereum Foundation, "ERC-20 Token Standard." Ethereum.org, August 15, 2022, https://ethereum.org/en/developers/docs/standards/tokens/erc-20/.

**10.10**
Screenshot of tweet by Manuel Aráoz announcing
Decentraland testnet launch, March 15, 2017

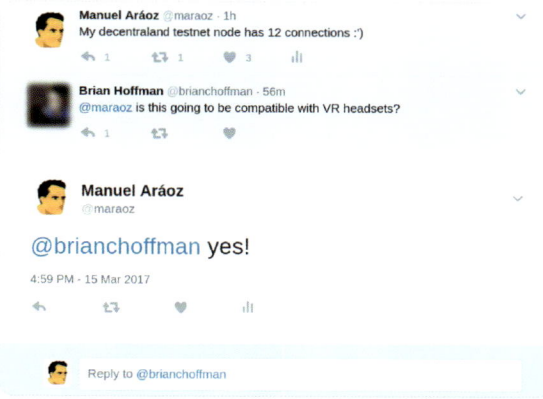

**10.11**
Screenshot from GitHub, EIP-20, comment by obscuren, November 20, 2015

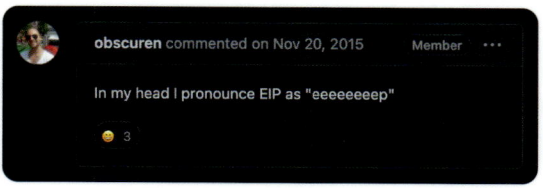

**10.12**
Screenshot of tweet by Linda Xie about ETHDenver, February 19, 2018

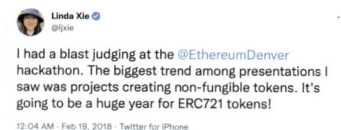

on Web 2.0 social media like Reddit, Twitter, and Discord. After feedback and revision, if they make the cut, they're eventually pronounced "FINAL" through an "ALL CORE DEVS CALL" that achieves rough consensus. The proposals are then recognized as numbered ERCs, and accepted as standards for the Ethereum community to implement across their projects.[24] Simon de la Rouviere, who led the standards panel at Devcon1 **[10.09]**, explains that "An EIP is a document created by the community that formalizes a specific way to improve Ethereum [...] It's important as a tool to gather, form, discuss, and formalize improvements and changes to the ecosystem."[25] Billy Rennekamp offers a similar explanation of the EIP process, adding that "it's basically a way for engineers to discuss standardizing a way to do something with software so that everyone does it the same way [...] it makes it possible to have predictable interactions." He continues, "Because Ethereum and other blockchains are operated by a large number of third parties, there's no possibility of enacting change from a singular actor. It is the 'populus' that must agree to enact the idea in the end."[26]

The hacker-engineer ethos that animated Ethereum's early development also resonated with technologists like John Watkinson and Matt Hall, who, working under the name Larva Labs, released *CryptoPunks* on June 23, 2017. *CryptoPunks* — discussed at length in "On Avatars" — comprised a script that generated 10,000 8-bit pixel art characters with random combinations of features; each Punk is unique, though at the time of the project's release, there was not yet a formal standard for non-fungible Ethereum tokens. *CryptoPunks'* token infrastructure built on ERC-20, the primary accepted standard at the time, but foretold the market for non-fungible tokens that would come soon after. In parallel, the first virtual worlds on Ethereum, like Decentraland, were being built. First successfully deployed to a testnet in 2017 **[10.10]**, and launched publicly in 2020, Decentraland — developed by Manuel Araoz, who had shipped the Bitcoin-based registry service Proof of Existence in 2013 — created an environment, like the game-worlds of early XTP-based trading card projects before it, where ownable digital assets had evident value.

By autumn of 2017, the idea of creating a new standard for unique tokens was still early and relatively niche, despite *CryptoPunks'* successful sale.[27] Building on the emerging idea, Dieter Shirley opened the conversation towards EIP-721 **[10.11, 10.12]** (which William Entriken, Jacob Evans, and Nastassia Sachs would later contribute to). "When I proposed EIP-721 (which then became ERC-721), the notion of non-fungible tokens was nascent at best," Shirley recalls.[28] At that moment, there was little interest in establishing an official standard for non-fungible tokens, even despite the history of art-related Bitcoin initiatives that testified to the utility of unique, verifiable ownership and provenance. The proposal to create a non-fungible token standard needed a visible justification; it had to map to something meaningful for the Ethereum community to comprehend its utility and importance.

This landmark moment of consolidating meaning came, timed to a bullish crypto market in November 2017, in the form of a cat game. Why bother architecting a new standard for unique, ownable tokens? The allure of trading and breeding genetically distinct cartoon felines proved one compelling reason. Developed by Dapper Labs and illustrated by Guile Twardowski **[10.13]**, *CryptoKitties* set forth a fun and understandable use case for non-fungible tokens: its breeding mechanic was singularly feasible thanks to unique tokens and immutable ledgers, and in demonstrating this possibility, it pioneered a new kind of networked community. The *CryptoKitties* "White Pa-Purr" touches on the appeal of digital collectibles

[24] The list of accepted token standards is maintained at https://eips.ethereum.org/erc.
[25] Simon de la Rouviere, email to the authors, April 9, 2022.
[26] Billy Rennekamp, Telegram chat with the authors, April 10, 2022.
[27] Larva Labs' website states that *CryptoPunks* served as "the inspiration for the ERC-721 standard"; this claim is subjective and tough to evaluate, but one could easily cast it in gentler terms and note that the Punks crucially shaped the thought-space surrounding digital collectible art assets. See "*CryptoPunks*," Larva Labs, accessed April 11, 2022, https://www.larvalabs.com/cryptopunks.
[28] Shirley, email to authors, April 11, 2022.

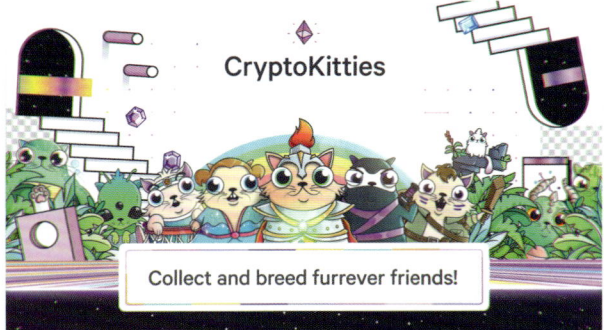

**CryptoKitties**

Collect and breed furrever friends!

**ArtReview**

**Power 100**

1    **ERC-721**
     **Non-Human Entity - The specification for the 'non-fungible token'**
     1 in 2021

that earlier Bitcoin projects like Counterparty and Ascribe helped establish, updated to suit the affordances of the more programmable Ethereum blockchain. On a technical level, *CryptoKitties* operated on an early version of the ERC-721 standard, which one of its creators, Dieter Shirley, had helped to author.[29]

NFTs as we know them today are more or less in line with the model that *CryptoKitties* exemplified, adhering to the ERC-721 token standard. ERC-721 NFTs are comprised of three main components: a smart contract, a numeric identifier, and metadata typically including a name, a description, and a location pointing to the digital asset that the token represents. Wilkins Chung, the co-founder of Manifold, offers a good technical run-through of how it all fits together: The smart contract serves as a ledger, collecting the record of ownership that comprises the NFT's provenance. The smart contract and identifier guarantee that the token is provably unique, and the contract contains the functions necessary to look up the metadata — which can be stored on-chain or off-, in another file system like IPFS, a file storage blockchain like Arweave, or good old Amazon Web Services.[30] This setup is true for NFTs on all Ethereum Virtual Machine (EVM)–based blockchains; it is also the case for NFTs on Tezos (which follow the TZIP-12 token standard).[31]

### Crypto Art and the Market(place)

Following *CryptoKitties*' smash success came a Cambrian explosion of NFTs that further proved its central assertion: NFTs create a visible purpose for smart contracts beyond cryptocurrency. Between 2018 and the present, the number of innovative NFT projects worth remarking on is too great to even begin to gloss here.[32] Most of these (at least the ones on Ethereum) have sat on the same token infrastructure that *CryptoKitties* established. With a dramatic ascent in the summer of 2021 as blockbuster NFT sales rocked the legacy art world, ERC-721 even topped the year's ArtReview Power 100 **[10.14]**, outranking the likes of Larry Gagosian and David Zwirner on the publication's annual list of the most influential people (or in this case, nonhuman entities) in contemporary art.

The infrastructure of the NFT space has not stopped evolving since then. Since ERC-721, a handful of new standards have been proposed and approved by the community, if not yet widely adopted — including ERC-1155, a hybrid encompassing features of both fungible and non-fungible tokens, and ERC-223 and ERC-777, both of which attempt to address design flaws in ERC-20 that make it possible to send tokens unrecoverably to a smart contract.[33] The primary locus of infrastructural innovation has, by and large, shifted away from defining new kinds of tokens. Rather, the movement has been towards the creation of new tools and marketplaces that empower creators by offering user-friendlier ways of interacting with smart contracts. These aim to grant artists more creative control over how their work is presented and experienced, in addition to broadening the audience that can access it or find it meaningful.[34]

Some of the sales platforms that have emerged in this explosive moment, like the curated marketplace SuperRare, launched in April 2018, replicated the sales mechanics of the legacy art world. But in certain critical ways, it also diverged, opening the door to a generation of crypto-native artists. (The original creator of an NFT sold on SuperRare is entitled to 10% of secondary sales, for instance — a practice infamously hard to enforce and far from

[29] n.b. *CryptoKitties* launched before the final proposal for ERC-721 was accepted; it uses v0 of the token standard, not the community-formalized v1, which came in January 2018. See the *CryptoKitties* Team, "*CryptoKitties*: Collectible and Breedable Cats Empowered by Blockchain Technology; White Pa-Purr, V3" Axiom Zen, 2017.
[30] Wilkins Chung, email to authors, April 13, 2022.
[31] Solana functions differently than these blockchains: its NFTs come out of a singular Solana Token Program, which enables the minting, transferring, and burning of both fungible and non-fungible tokens; instead of deploying a new smart contract for each new token, actions are carried out by sending an instruction to the token program. See "A Solana Cluster | Solana Docs," Solana, accessed April 11, 2022, https://docs.solana.com/cluster/overview.
[32] Of course, many of these projects are explored in depth throughout *On NFTs*.
[33] Ethereum Foundation, "Token Standards," Ethereum.org, accessed June 14, 2022, https://ethereum.org.
[34] Perhaps this turn towards marketplace innovation has underscored another axiom: contemporary art is inextricable from markets. This fact, often only hesitantly acknowledged at best in the legacy art scene, is a fundamental part of this new world: NFTs don't so much financialize art as highlight how art has always been financialized.

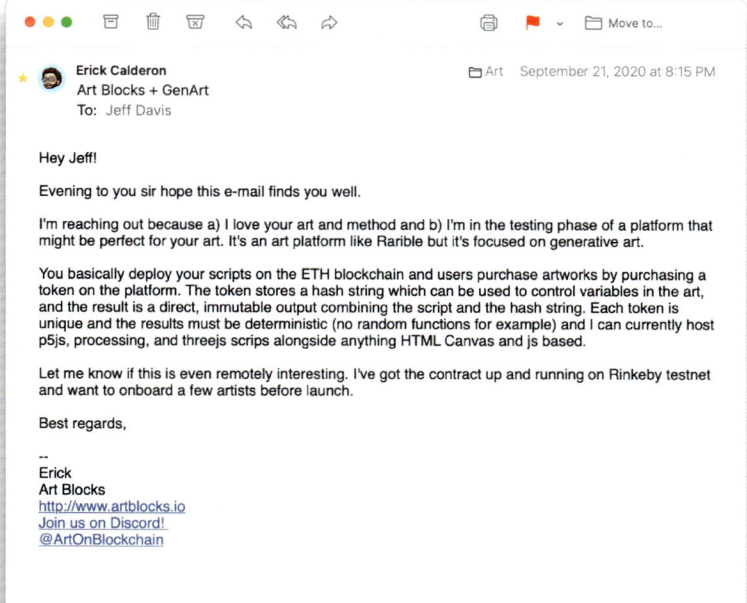

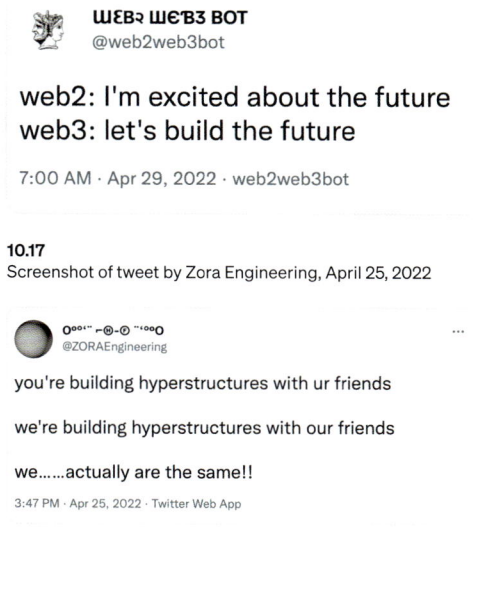

standard in the offline art world.) Others, like OpenSea, which began in December of the previous year, are less precisely tailored to art but have created a vibrant economy for all kinds of digital collectibles. A vast majority of Ethereum NFTs index to OpenSea, and many websites, including JPG.space and various aggregators, pull from the OpenSea API. It's therefore the largest secondary market discovery platform for Ethereum (along with other chains like Polygon, Klatyn, and Solana); its nearly comprehensive range makes it a popular price indicator and a point of reference for other marketplaces. Minting is completely open (for better or worse), meaning that anyone with enough ether in their wallet to pay gas fees can list an NFT of their own. But it's also, crucially, centralized. NFTs minted on OpenSea are locked into the platform, and works can be taken down at any time for any reason. These drawbacks have catalyzed a litany of projects that, in various ways, attempt to break free from the OpenSea API.

One alternative came in the form of Art Blocks, a marketplace launched in 2020 specifically for generative art, appealing to creative technologists and software-literate collectors. Art Blocks founder Erick Calderon, a practicing artist himself, reached out to software artist Jeff Davis (who is now the platform's Chief Creative Officer) **[10.15]** after discovering his work on the NFT marketplace Rarible. The two shared a hunch that ERC-721 NFTs were perfectly suited to capturing the outputs of code-based art, as each randomly generated work could be associated with an equally unique token, making something permanent and traceable out of the notoriously ephemeral medium.[35] Calderon cites *CryptoPunks* as inspiration, seminal in demonstrating the synergy between randomly generated code-based art — historically difficult to preserve or market — and blockchain technology. Other boutique publishing platforms like Folia, which launched in February 2021, have also emerged to give artists greater agency over their smart contracts and offer a more bespoke front-end exhibition interface. Foundation also emerged in February 2021, with a similar structure to SuperRare. It resonated with the offline art world thanks to curator Lindsay Howard's touch; like SuperRare, though, it distinguishes itself from the legacy art world by guaranteeing artists a cut of all future secondary sales on its platform.

### Conclusion: Maintaining Decentralization and Creative Sovereignty

Beyond this profusion of (admittedly centralized) marketplaces, it is readily becoming possible for creators to design and deploy on their own, generating new possibilities for NFT exhibitions and sales that push against the Web 2.0-esque tendency towards platform

[35] Jeff Davis and Erick Calderon, interview with the authors, April 5, 2022.

monopoly **[10.16]**. The block explorer EtherScan, founded in 2015, makes deals from all marketplaces transparent and searchable, displaying public information about transactions carried out across the Ethereum blockchain. While not a marketplace itself, EtherScan does allow minting directly from smart contracts — a feature that projects like *Loot* (2021) took advantage of by cleverly enabling people to claim NFTs freely using the block explorer's inbuilt "write contract" function.

It's also common to build one's own marketplace as an interface for minting and selling — but this can be prohibitively challenging for creators who aren't comfortable writing their own smart contracts in Solidity. However, these barriers to accessibility are lowering thanks to projects like (the a16z-funded) Manifold, which launched Manifold Creator, an open-source smart contract, in May 2021, followed by Manifold Studio, a friendly user interface for minting with it, that December. Striving to do away with the idea of an intermediary platform altogether — their mantra, co-founder Wilkins Chung tells us, is "the creator is the platform" — Manifold's tools make it possible for artists who don't know how to code in Solidity to customize the smart contracts behind their NFTs.

"There are a significant number of 'public utilities' that need to exist for the NFT ecosystem to prosper and maintain decentralization and creative sovereignty," Chung explained to us in an email interview. Another such utility, Zora, launched in a similar spirit shortly before Manifold Creator, in January 2021. Together, platforms like these have heralded a re-decentralization of the NFT ecosystem. NFTs minted with the Zora protocol can be bought and sold across platforms, rather than being locked into the marketplace of their creation; being as it is a protocol rather than a conventional marketplace, the platform takes no fees and allows artists to set their preferred percentage cut for secondary sales.

Zora founder Jacob Horne has since elaborated the idea of "hyperstructures," or free and permissionless crypto protocols that can run in perpetuity without charging user fees or relying on intermediaries **[10.17]**. Hyperstructures resonate with the original vision of dApps that Gavin Wood laid out in his seminal 2014 blog post, "What Web 3.0 Looks Like" — secure, open, trustless, and interoperable systems for communication — and further advance the lineage of hacker-engineering, especially with their emphasis on business models that do not rely on the extraction of user data as a source of value.[36] "The nature of the medium of token ownership and unstoppability means we no longer need to extract profits to realize value creation," Horne explains.[37] Some companies building Web3 protocols have more explicitly shifted to adopt this approach in early 2022, including Fractional, Verse, and 0xSplits.[38]

Standing by the claims and tenets of Web3 rhetoricians, the next innovations in NFT infrastructure must continue to elaborate the values — non-extractive revenue models, permissionlessness, unstoppability, and censorship resistance — that animate projects like these. The obligation to speculate towards better futures, to build as a form of critique, recurs across Wood's and Horne's writing; it echoes Andreessen; it resonates with Chandler and Lippard. Perhaps it will catalyze the next cycle in this entangled, open-source loop. The infrastructural innovation that enabled NFTs — and the cascade of hyperstructures that they have made possible — is a polyphonic history, its hacker protagonists continually shaping the ever-expanding field. This brief overview of that history is partial and contingent, as any timeline will necessarily be. It's not closed, nor teleological, and others can and ought to be created. Like the infrastructural development of NFTs itself, this history is replete with open-source processes, underpinned by building and hacking that allow new forms of culture to emerge and proliferate. This iterative, collective process must be represented as complex and visible, foregrounded in the forums (like this one) where canons of digital art are built and rebuilt.

[36] Gavin Wood, "ÐApps: What Web 3.0 Looks Like," April 17, 2014, https://gavwood.com/dappsweb3.html.
[37] Jacob Horne, "Hyperstructures," Personal Blog, jacob.energy, January 16, 2022, https://jacob.energy/hyperstructures.
[38] Fractional (fractional.art) enables people to buy and sell fractionalized shares of NFTs; Verse (verse.xyz) self-described as a "hyperexchange protocol," and 0x Splits (0xsplits.xyz) is a protocol for splitting on-chain income.

Short Sword
Divine Robe of the Fox
Hood
Plated Belt
Divine Slippers
Chain Gloves
Necklace
Titanium Ring

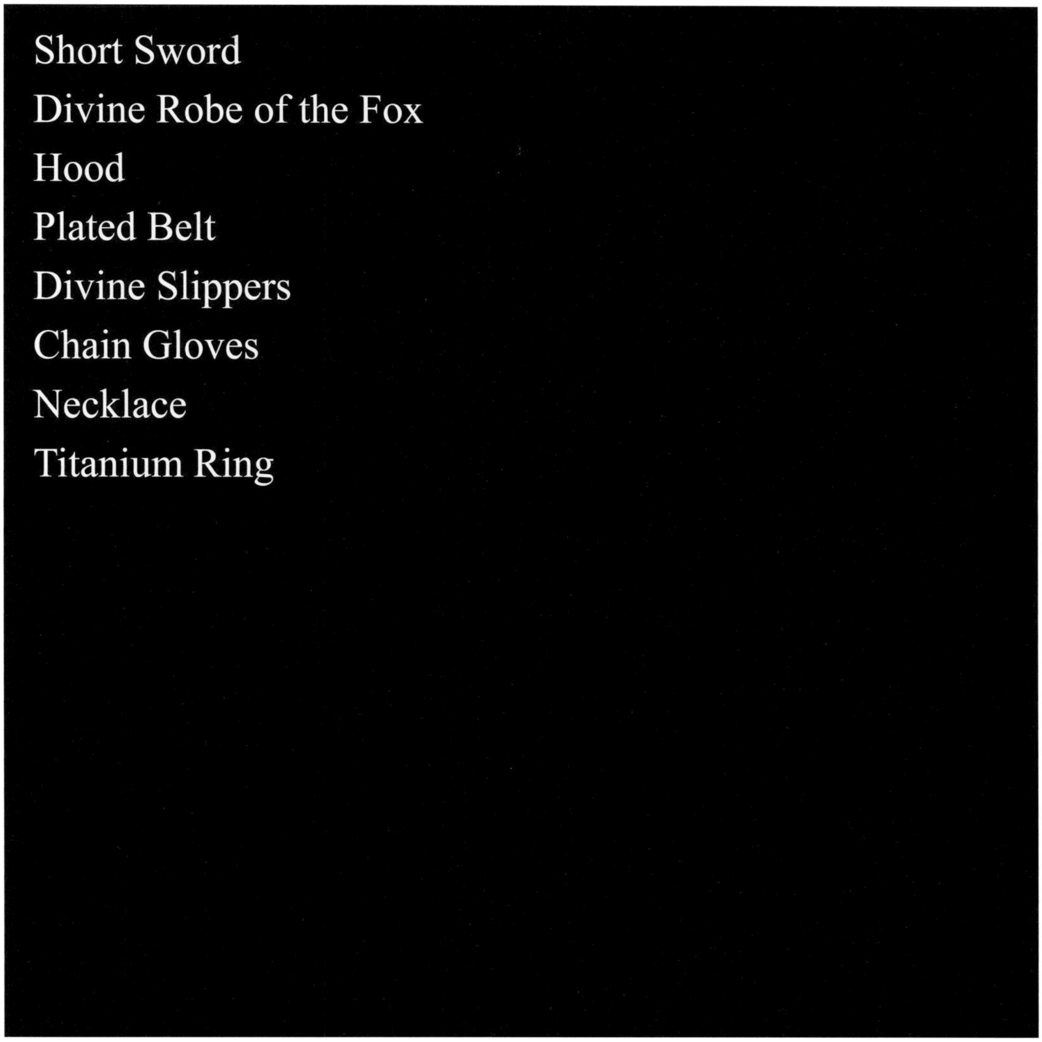

| # | TITLE | TIMESTAMP | MEDIUM | CHAIN | CONTRACT ADDRESS | TOKEN ID | EDITION SIZE |
|---|---|---|---|---|---|---|---|
| 01–05 | **Loot (for Adventurers)** | 08-27-2021 17:47:24 | Text, SVG, Solidity | ETH | 0xff9c1b15b16263c61d017ee9f65c50e4ae0113d7 | 1-7779 | 1/1 of 7,779 |

EDITIONS ILLUSTRATED: (01) #748, (02) #1, (03) #3043, (04) #4765, (05) #1370

# DOM HOFMANN

02

"Grim Shout" Grave Wand of Skill +1
Hard Leather Armor
Divine Hood
Hard Leather Belt
"Death Root" Ornate Greaves of Skill
Studded Leather Gloves
Necklace of Enlightenment
Gold Ring

03

Tome
Hard Leather Armor of Anger
"Woe Grasp" Hood of the Twins +1
"Rage Shout" Sash of Protection +1
Demonhide Boots of the Fox
"Sorrow Bite" Silk Gloves of the Fox +1
Amulet of Titans
Titanium Ring of the Twins

04

Katana
Divine Robe of Rage
War Cap of the Twins
Silk Sash
Linen Shoes
Ornate Gauntlets
Necklace
Bronze Ring

05

"Maelstrom Sun" Tome of Fury
Divine Robe of Perfection
"Cataclysm Moon" Leather Cap of Rage +1
Leather Belt
Hard Leather Boots of Perfection
Ornate Gauntlets
Amulet
Silver Ring

By the age of 12, Dom was deeply drawn to all the visual aspects of a computer and what it could display. Having already learned how to reassemble a computer at an earlier age, he learned programming because he wanted to be able to put things on his screen. Digital art became his gateway to programming.

Dom and I met in 2014. He had just moved on from Vine, an early video sharing platform Dom co-founded with 200 million active users at its peak. He has since worked on projects that time and again centered community, not just in the creation of a space but by facilitating ownership for those participating. As a writer myself, whose only medium has ever been words, Dom's ability to conjure worlds and connectivity through emerging technology — at times almost indescribable to me — is the essence of his work *Loot* (2021).

*Loot* explores the concept of trustless collaborative world-building, employing Solidity as the sole medium. It was originally released to the public domain as a collection of 8,000 procedurally generated "bags," each of which contains a list of gear appropriate for an archetypal fantasy adventurer. Importantly, each bag is described and depicted solely by text. Stats, images, and other functionality are intentionally omitted for others to interpret, which has allowed the project to act as the initial building block and prompt for an infinitely expansive fictional universe.

Similar in sensibility to folk art for its community-oriented nature, *Loot* started a movement around composability and bottom-up world-building, challenging the idea of what an NFT encompasses and its ability to function as a decentralized building block around which whole worlds are created not by individuals but by communities.

**TASNIM AHMED**
WRITER AND WIFE OF DOM HOFMANN

# LOOT #748

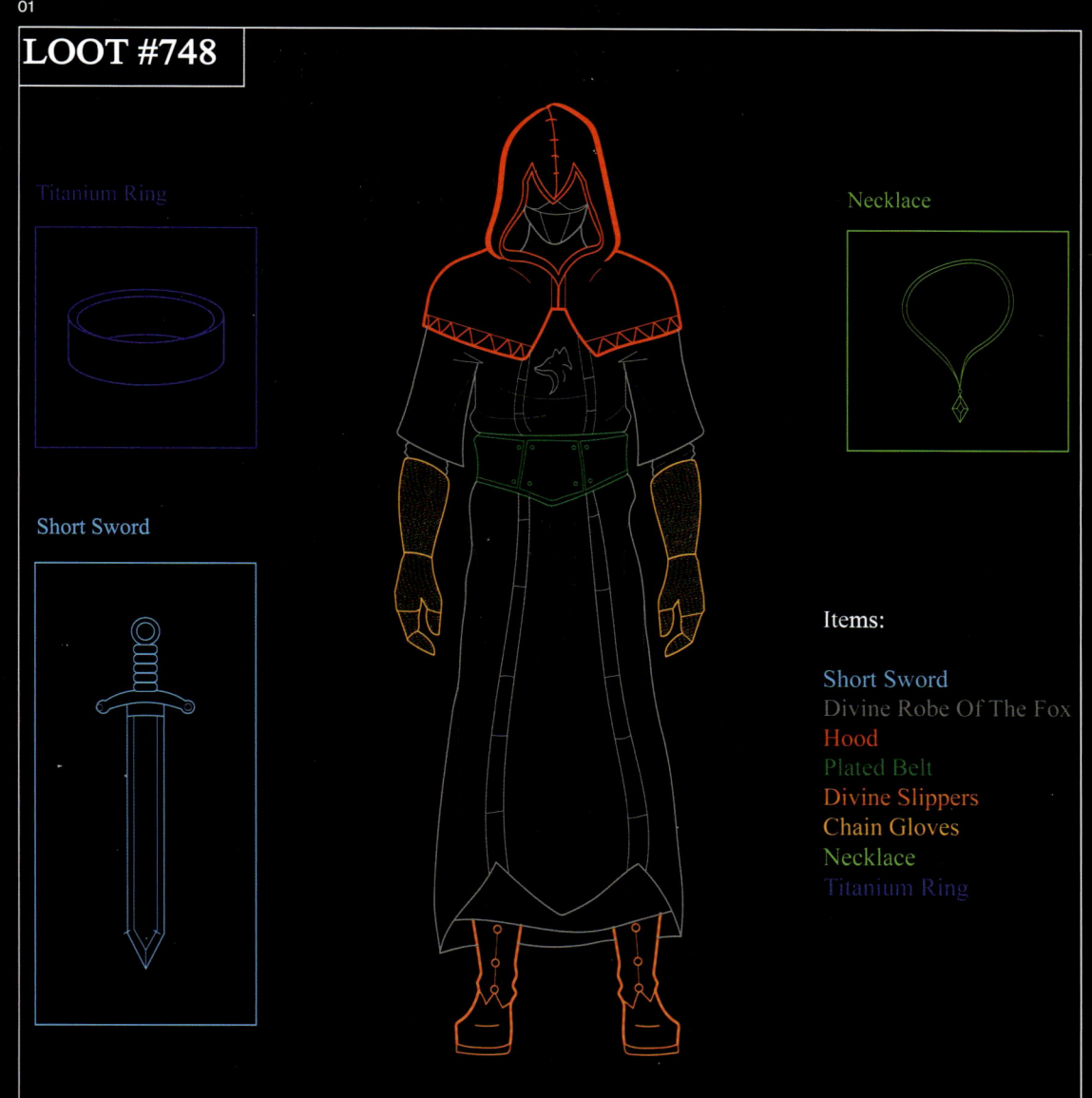

Titanium Ring

Necklace

Short Sword

Items:

Short Sword
Divine Robe Of The Fox
Hood
Plated Belt
Divine Slippers
Chain Gloves
Necklace
Titanium Ring

| # | TITLE | TIMESTAMP | MEDIUM | CHAIN | CONTRACT ADDRESS | TOKEN ID | EDITION SIZE |
|---|-------|-----------|--------|-------|------------------|----------|--------------|
| 01 | **An Artistic Impression of Loot #748** | – | – | – | – | 1–1616 | – |
| 02, 03 | **The Eye (for Adventurers)** | 08-27-2022 17:48:18 | On-chain library | ETH | 0xb8a51862964f77025abb65e2c6a39ee8070c8ed4 | 1–1616 | 1/1 of 1,616 |

EDITIONS ILLUSTRATED: (02) Lost Order of Chad – Encyclopedia Entry by Pinky (03) The Eye by Devon H. Dolan

# LOST ORDER OF CHAD
## ENCYCLOPEDIA ENTRY

There are many paths that a warrior may walk.

Some choose to master a weapon, whereas others forge their bodies and souls into a weapon.

These masters are the ones whose names and feats you know well. The Epic of Talius and the Phoenix Tear to cure his dying wife of an unstoppable plague, or even the feats of the Emperor, sundering the universe to create a Portal to Plouton with his Armageddon Bender Wand.

Their possessions remain forever inscribed with the feats they achieved, the Divines themselves taking note of mere mortals. The sheer powers that these items wielded ranged from a curious trick to outright mindboggling destruction as if the stars themselves had been called to battle.

Often, the weapon itself was enough of a deterrent to any would-be bandit or thief, for of the millions of weaponry, enchanted jewelry and armors, only a few would achieve such greatness, and the owners of them would treat their loss as they would that of a family member. A wand would be thought lost to time or battle, and then mysteriously find itself in the path of a novice magic user who had suffered unjustly under a cruel regime. Some of the greatest Mages stories begin with the slightest of observations, but the truly heroic, the ones whose names you hear in any tavern tale, every last one suffered the greatest of loss or grievous mistreatment.

The Divines play with mortals as the elderly play bones, betting on the deaths, adultery, and whatever other drama that may amuse them, and these great weapons and armors would often be a focus for their scheming.

Those who study the blade often find themselves receiving a more practical lesson than they desired, in the shape of an arrow or warhammer. A Katana wielded by a Bladedancer follower of other Orders, particularly the more esoteric or sedentary ones, is often found later sticking out of their bodies as a cruel jest by their victorious foes. A Brother trains their mind, body, and soul to be a lethal combination of brute force and speed, their prowess in the application of force second to none but the Sisterhood, although they specialize in the application of that force from a distance, and with decidedly less collateral damage. The greatest Weapons and Armor of Plouton have long since been eclipsed by what we have found here, in the new world of Realms. Even our Emperor's most sacred belongings only scratch the surface compared to the Order of Brilliance Head Armory, and indeed that is where they lie now. The Armageddon Bender Wand

A Divine Swordsman is a blessing (or curse!) on the battlefield, but for a scouting team?

No, their strengths would only see them fall behind or meet an untimely demise in the back alleys of a foreign town.

Of all the greatest warriors, hunters, and mages of the Realms, a scant thousand or so can lay claim to more than one legendary or mythical item. The mightiest of foes to face on any battlefield and armies of one, capable of decimating a regiment with but one swing of a mighty axe, or a particularly destructive spell.

# THE EYE

When knowledge is preserved, so is our history, and with it, humanity.

When adventurers walked freely amongst the realms, they sought story. It was fundamental.

"As through shared narrative, all our truths are revealed," twas the motto in the County of Prefixes.

To learn about our world, we must reflect upon its past. To learn about its people, we must inhabit the imagined, and interact ensemble. Together, as all these events shape us. We envision and uphold its future.

At the Town Square, crowds gathered in delight as the Lorators regaled story in grand ceremony. It was their duty. But with each pass of an oral performance, the lore itself shifted ever so slightly. Memory can only be so strong.

And with this, the Historians were entertained by opportunity. They devised a plan. In arms, they forged a device to preserve story; to advance civilization. It was learned from the fable of the Fox: progress waits for no one.

They called it The Eye.

Only so few were manufactured, and collected by sacred hands, by those who appreciate the tradition the Lorators beget. It was Codified by its collectors. A missing item from the Mage class, its power unrivaled. And through the call of the Scrolls, the Historians motivated the community, in bounty and bag, for credited accounts of their lives – for all to decipher, enjoy, and expand upon.

These legends were enshrined, archived, in The Eye – our immutable, illuminating record of runes.

The Eye, a time capsule, will stand the test of time. It is all that will remain, its contents knowingly kept. It will persist through the ages, the generations, and contain inscriptions from the Orders.

For all to see. For all to use. For all to share. To be rediscovered, forevermore. In its Higher Greatness, we prevail.

As an adventurer progresses in their experience and training, they may be able to wield weapons that they could not in years past, or armor that would have previously restricted their mobility too much. A seasoned veteran adventurer with poor quality equipment (it happens to the best of us!) is still easily capable of putting a hot-blooded youth in their place.

In my years of studying this phenomenon, the most consistent source of growth has appeared to be immersion in dangerous situations and triumph (or perish!). These tribulations affect item and wielder alike, with the greater the struggle or loss being correlated to the power gained.

The atrocities committed by power-hungry despots and tyrants are what lead to some of the names of the less savory historic items that we all know and hate. Should a bearer of these items be spotted, it should be reported to the Order High Command at utmost haste.

## About *Loot*

As discussed by Tasnim Ahmed, *Loot*, created by Dom Hofmann, has introduced a new model to the NFT space by using meta-data as the foundation for decentralized building. Importantly, because traits are stored on-chain, other projects can employ and build upon *Loot* for their own ecosystems. As these derivatives have flourished since *Loot*'s inception, they have collectively become known as the "Lootverse." The following images and texts are examples of how communities have interpreted and interacted with *Loot* to build the foundations of this new online world.

The first example of *Loot*'s potential is shown in the artist interpretation of the highly sought-after *Loot #748* and its unique

Divine Robe of the Fox trait. This image illustrates how *Loot* can be used as the foundation for games or character creation by developers.

With each NFT forming an on-chain library, *The Eye (for Adventurers)* is a *Loot* derivative that allows community members to publish mythological stories about the origins and tales of the Lootverse. The project has led to a rich, yet decentralized building of lore around *Loot*, forming a collaborative storytelling community. As with all of the tales in *The Eye*, the two texts illustrated exist entirely on-chain.

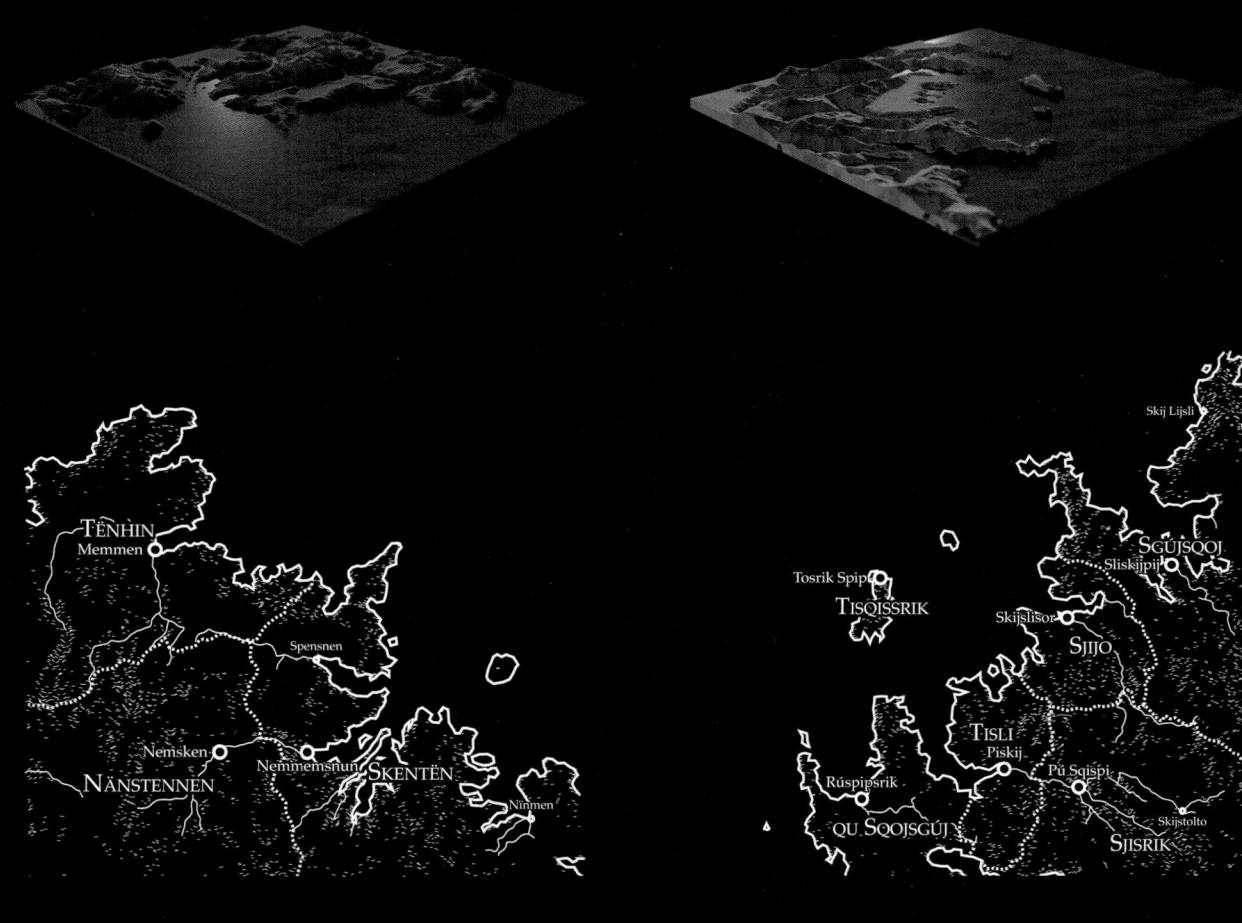

| # | TITLE | TIMESTAMP | MEDIUM | CHAIN | CONTRACT ADDRESS | TOKEN ID | EDITION SIZE |
|---|-------|-----------|--------|-------|------------------|----------|--------------|
| 04–07 | **Realms (for Adventurers)** | 08-31-2021 18:37:58 | On-chain land parcels | ETH | 0x7afe30cb3e53dba6801aa0ea647a0ecea7cbe18d | 1–8000 | 1/1 of 8,000 |

EDITIONS ILLUSTRATED: (04) Hemmemskän, (05) Stolsli, (06) Aunomim, (07) 'ilh'ilhmil

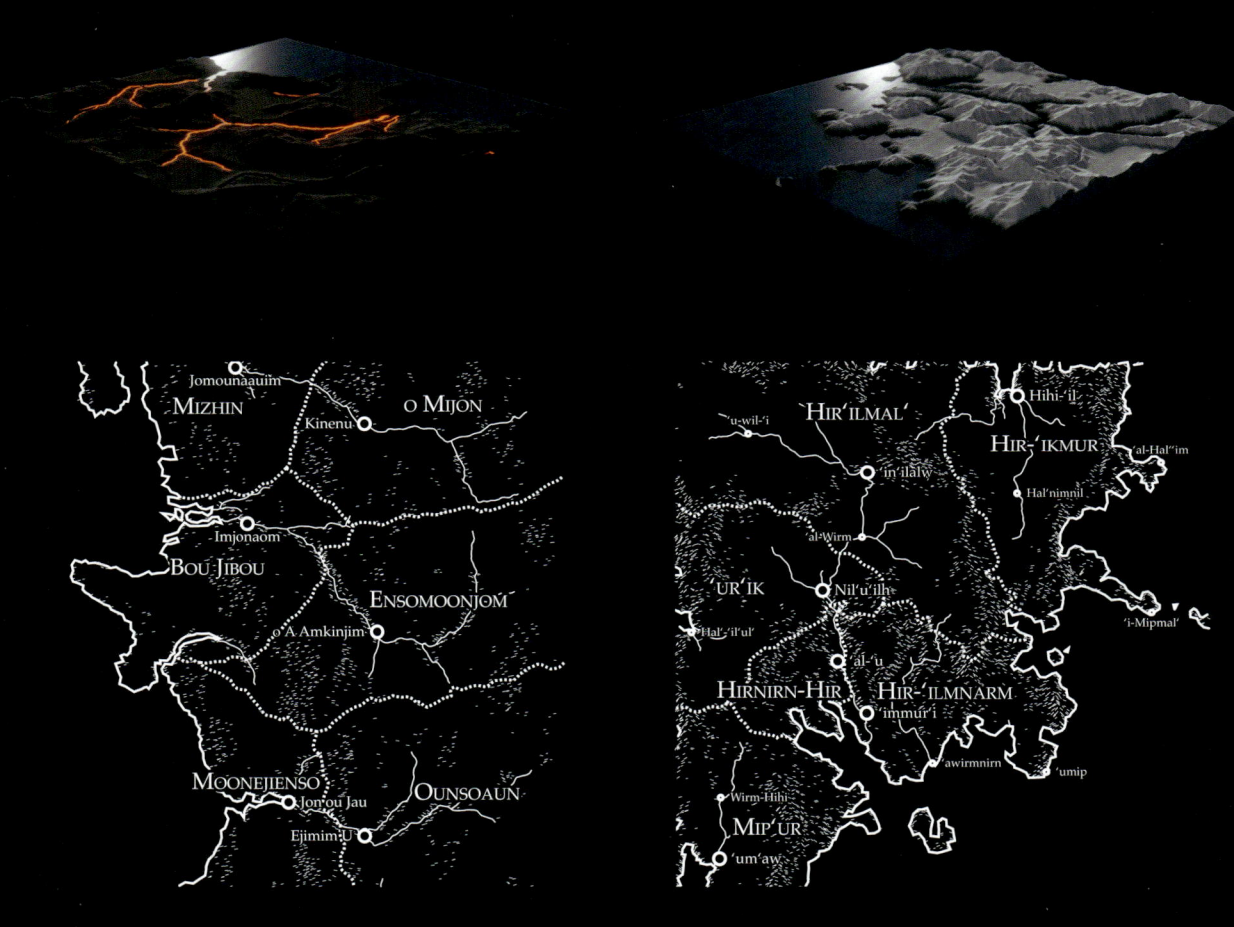

*Realms (for Adventurers)* aims to be one of the most advanced *Loot* derivatives, with a MMOCCG (massively multiplayer on-chain composable game) in development. Each of the 8,000 unique, procedurally generated *Realms* includes a map with regions, cities, rivers, harbors, and topography from the land plot. Delving further, every *Realm* contains at least one, and up to seven, of the 22 different resources discovered in the Lootverse, from common assets like wood, to the rarer luxuries of sapphire or Dragonhide.

Starting out as 2D SVG maps, *Realms* has been developed into high-fidelity 3D land plots, highlighting the progressive expansion of the ecosystem.

Given *Loot*'s release in 2021, the sheer scope of interpretations and active building in this short timeline — around just eight unique lines of text — stands as a testament to the community-driven nature of the NFT space.

| # | TITLE | TIMESTAMP | MEDIUM | CHAIN | CONTRACT ADDRESS | TOKEN ID | EDITION SIZE |
|---|---|---|---|---|---|---|---|
| 01 | **ChainFace** | 01-19-2020 23:21:59 | Solidity | ETH | 0x91047abf3cab8da5a9515c8750ab33b4f1560a7a | 0–9999 | 1/1 of 10,000 |
| 02 | **ChainFaces Arena** | 01-01-2022 00:01:05 | Solidity | ETH | 0x93a796b1e846567fe3577af7b7bb89f71680173a | 0–26968 | 1/1 of 26,969 |
| 03–06 | **Squiggly** | 10-02-2020 18:59:36 | Solidity | ETH | 0x36f379400de6c6bcdf4408b282f8b685c56adc60 | 0–99 | 1/1 of 100 |

EDITIONS ILLUSTRATED: (01) With further editions of the same series, various, (02) With further editions of the same series, various, (03) #89, (04) #98, (05) #17, (06) #2

# NATE ALEX

03

04

05

06

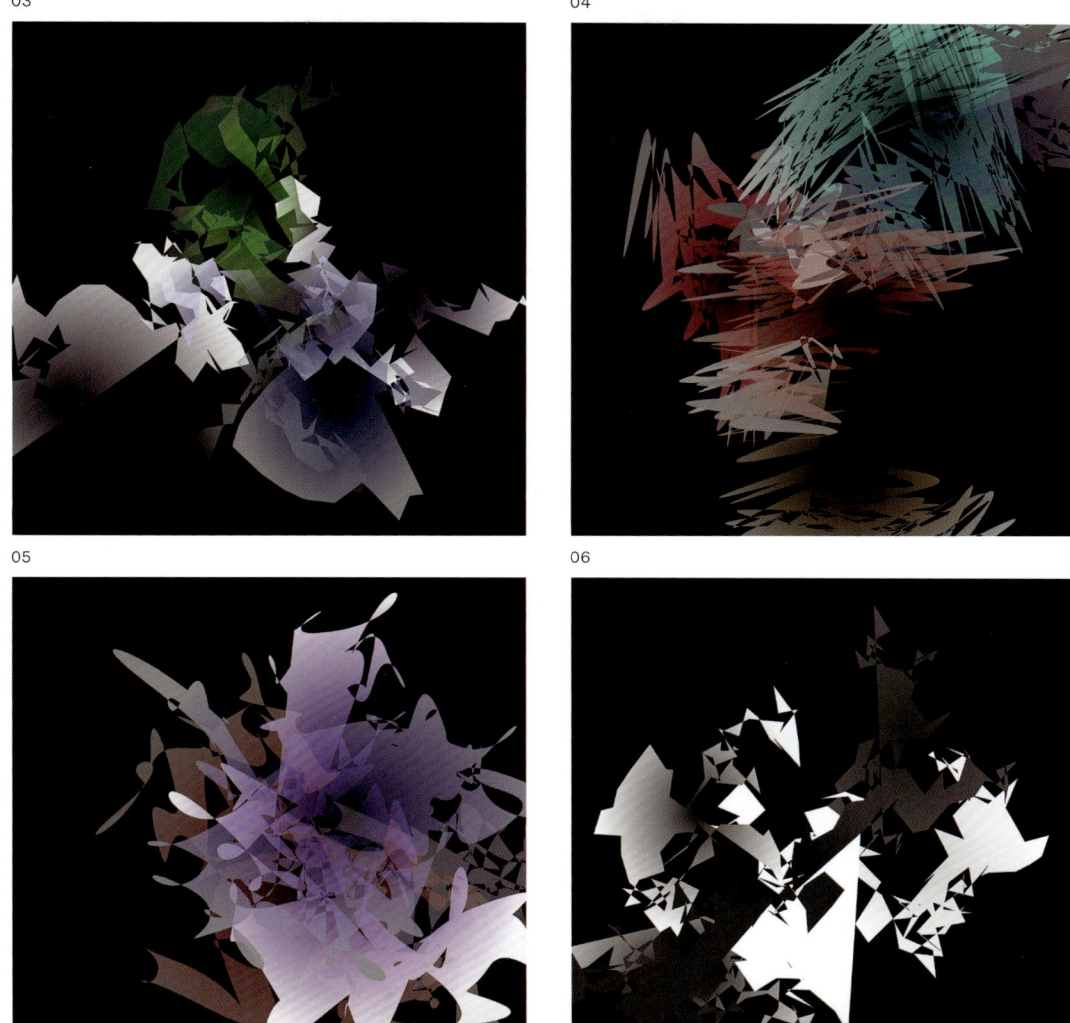

I first came across S*quiggly* (2020) in late October 2020. It was one of the first projects I got interested in when I entered the space. The random patterns generated by the work's Bezier curve algorithm form compositions that reference early computer art in their radical looseness and raw, disruptive compositional variation. Like the pioneer Ben Laposky, who made organic shapes from an oscilloscope, Nate uses the specificity of his medium — the blockchain — to create unique on-chain generative works. *Squiggly* is as much an experiment in art as it is one in technology.

The really amazing thing about Nate is his continuous drive to push boundaries. I know he will downplay his creative abilities when you speak to him, but he is the true definition of a creative. Code is art. And his ability to really extend what is possible with the technology is what makes him one of the leading technical and conceptual disruptors in the space.

As his friend and collector, I have had the pleasure of talking to him throughout the years and really watching the things he has done. We actually met for the first time in person about a year and a half after our first conversations, and it was like we were long lost friends that picked up right where we left off.

When art historians look back at the beginning of the NFT movement, I believe Nate Alex will be seen as a pivotal figure, for his ability to both innovate and in the platform he has built for himself, to educate too. I am very honored to have his work in my collection and look forward to all the things he does in the future.

**GMONEY**
FUTURIST, DISRUPTOR, APE

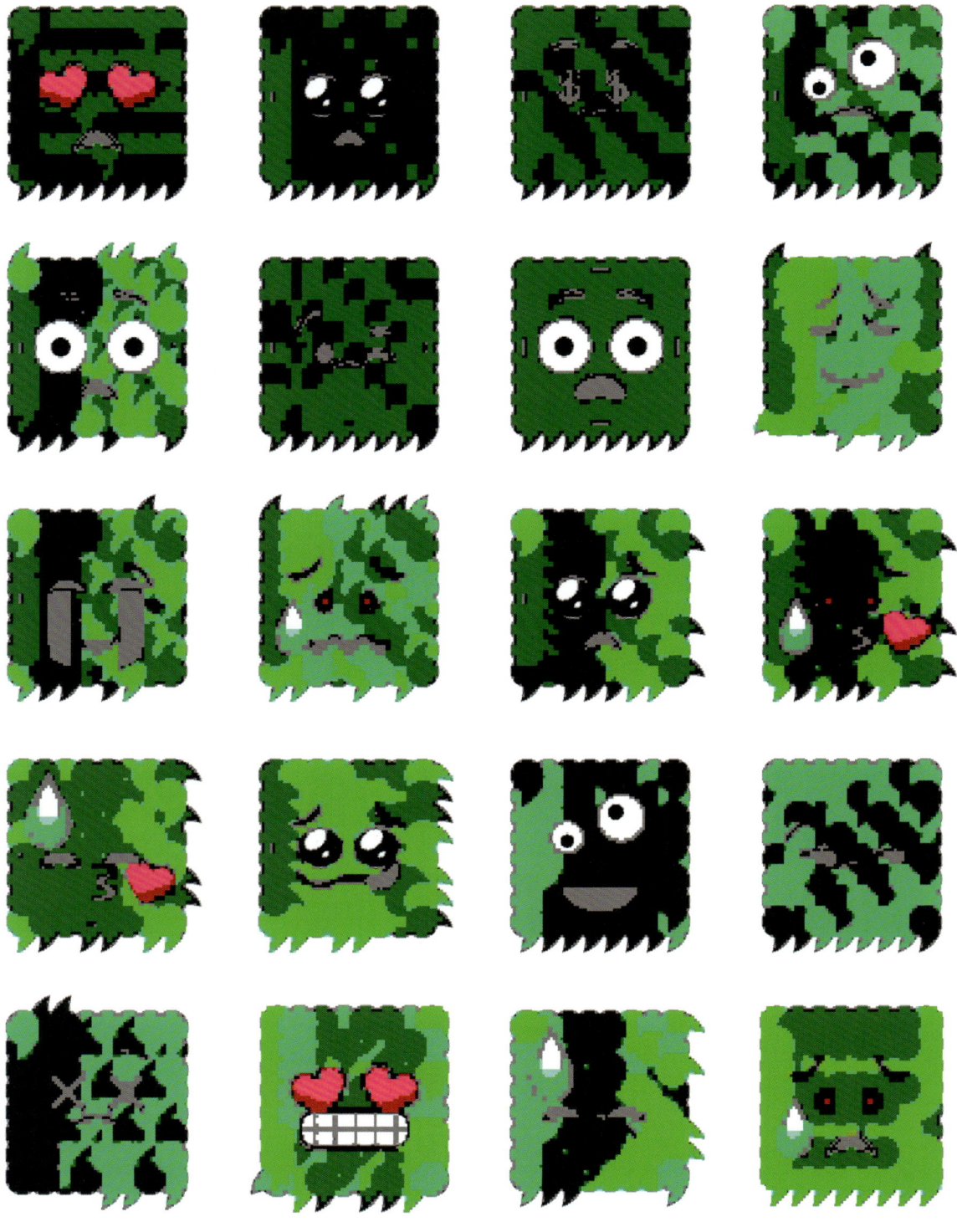

| # | TITLE | TIMESTAMP | | MEDIUM | CHAIN | CONTRACT ADDRESS | | TOKEN ID | EDITION SIZE |
|---|---|---|---|---|---|---|---|---|---|
| 01, 02 | **Kudzu** | 04-19-2021 22:31:16 | | JavaScript, Canvas | ETH | 0x9d413b9434c20c73f509505f7fbc6fc591bbf04a | | 71694–∞ | 1/1 of ∞ |

EDITIONS ILLUSTRATED: (01) Various, (02) Map created by Burak Arikan

# KUDZU

02

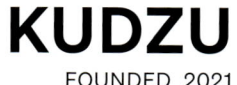

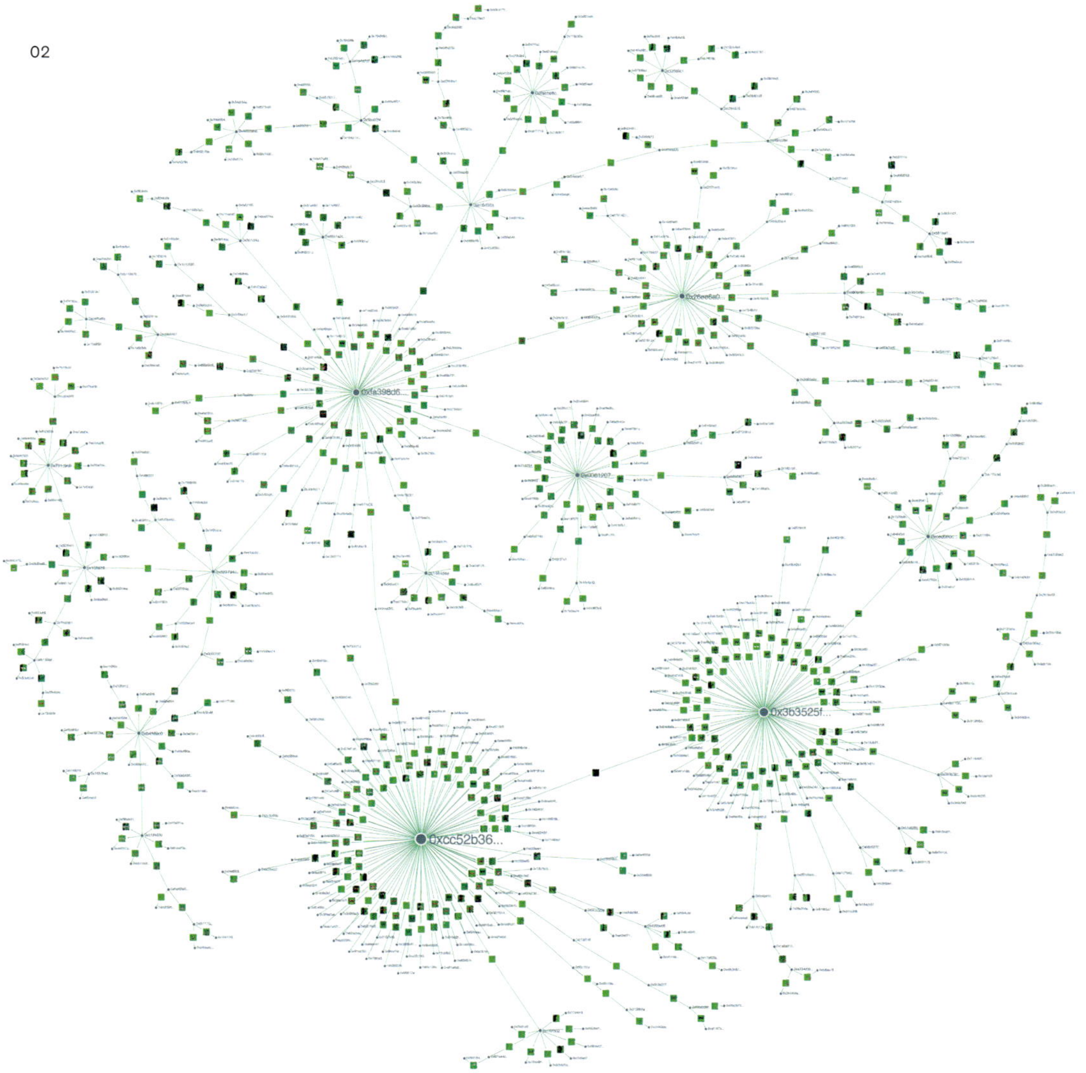

Folia is an independent NFT gallery and artist collective presenting tokenized digital editions. Folia takes a collaborative approach, frequently working with artists who have established digital practices to create new works using the blockchain as artistic medium.

*Kudzu* (2021) is a socially transmitted NFT virus created by Folia members Billy Rennekamp, Dan Denorch, Everett Williams, and Sam Hart. The name is borrowed from the green climbing vine native to East Asia and considered an invasive weed elsewhere in the world.

The *Kudzu* smart contract uses a modified transfer function to mint a new NFT to the recipient, rather than moving the token from the sender's account. While adhering to the ERC-721 standard, the augmented NFT is nontransferrable and confers a

tokenized right to create new NFTs for any destination address. Addresses may only be infected once, assigning each a unique *Kudzu* avatar, or PFP. A small segment of the token ID is reserved as the viral chromosome, allowing *Kudzu* to pass one facial trait to recipients, along with one random gene. As *Kudzu* spreads, the variegated body evolves and becomes more complex.

The viral artwork was created as an unlimited edition in the hopes that the entire Ethereum blockchain may one day be covered in green. Spread the *Kudzu*.

**SAM HART**
EARLY BLOCKCHAIN ARTIST AND CURATOR

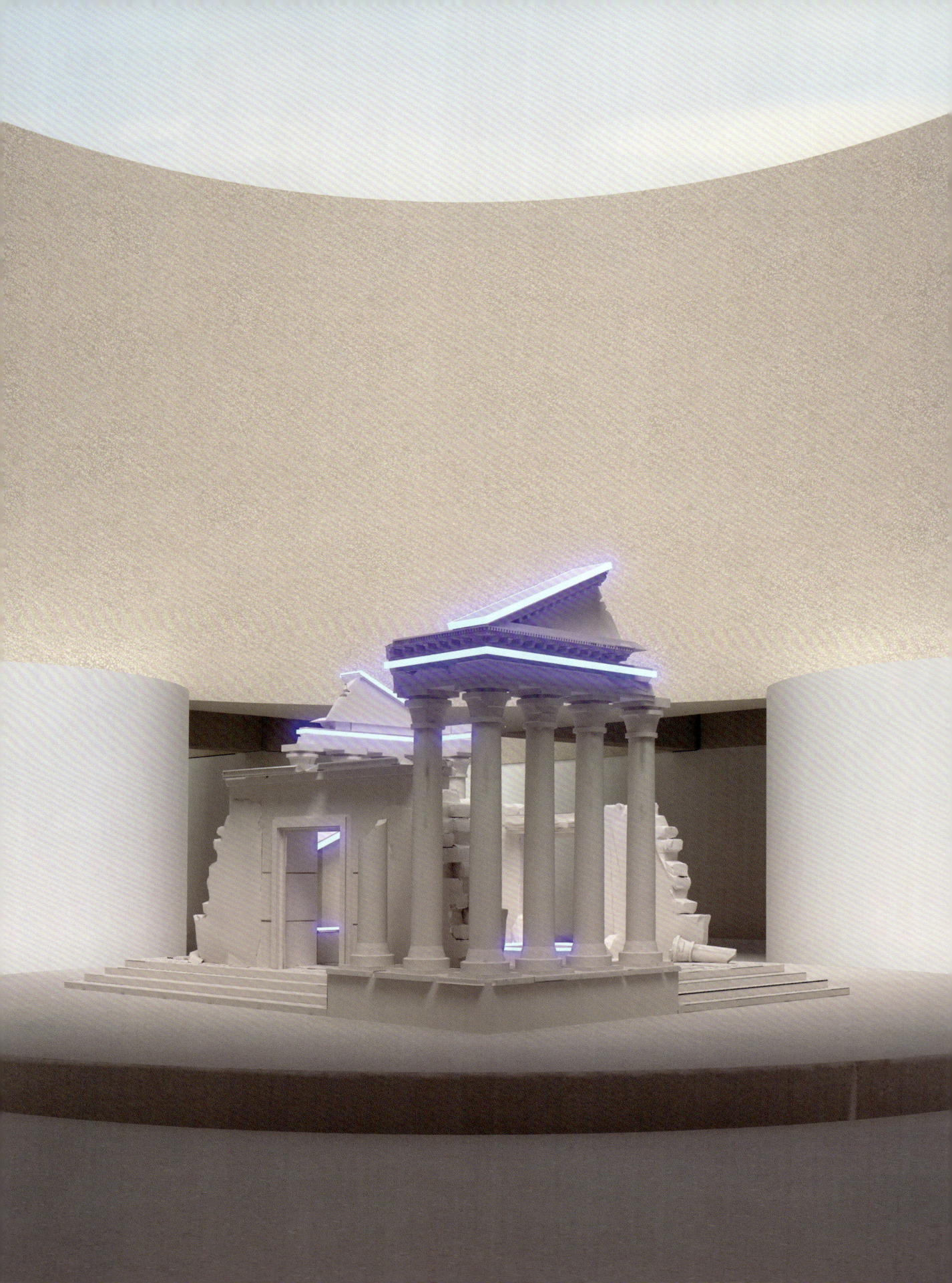

COLLECTED BY THE COMMUNITY
COLLATED BY ROBERT ALICE

# EXHIBITION HISTORY

*Special thanks to*
Ana Bambic Kostov
aurèce vettier
Brendan Dawes
Brian Droitcour
Casey Reas
Christina J. Chua
Clara Peh
David Em
Eleonora Brizi
Georg Bak
India Price
Jeff Davis
Jonas Lund
Lawrence Lek
Linda Dounia
María Paula Fernández
Martin Lukas Ostachowski
Matt Kane
Micol Ap
Nicolas Sassoon
Osinachi
Qinwen Wang
Rachel Greene
Refik Anadol
Rhea Myers
Sarah Meyohas Studio
Serwah Attafuah
Simon Denny
Studio Sarah Friend
Tina Rivers Ryan

This exhibition history attempts to showcase the most important and influential shows that have shaped the contemporary NFT scene. Beginning with important digital art exhibitions from the 1960s, the timeline demonstrates that galleries and institutions were already showing an interest in artists working in digital mediums early on. The emergence of online shows in the 1990s, at the impulse of institutions and artists alike, signal explorations of web-specific mediums of display; a practice that only intensified after the emergence of NFTs and the normalization of metaverse platforms.

From 2018 onwards, starting with the seminal *RARE AF* exhibition in New York, NFT-specific exhibitions appeared all over the world. Sometimes creating their own physical or digital establishments and fairs through partnerships with platforms, and progressively making their way into the fabric of the mainstream art world, gaining institutional recognition with representations at Art Basel, at the Venice Biennale, and in major museums like the Hermitage and the Uffizi. The list compiled here records a total of 242 exhibitions — 43 digital, 174 physical, and 25 hybrid — spread over 27 countries, one micronation, and six continents.

In order to compile this list, Robert Alice and their studio reached out to friends, artists, curators, historians, and platforms and in turn their networks in order to try to broadly cover all facets of the NFT space. The research allowed the studio to take note of some of the shortcomings of metaverse shows in their current form. Few of the temporary shows have been well documented or archived, making information significantly more difficult to access and last in perpetuity. Please also note that while the timeline stopped in 2022, for this second edition we have decided to illustrate it with exhibitions between 2023–2025 in an attempt to bring it up to date visually.

**11.00**
Lawrence Lek
*Nepenthe Valley*, 2022
Still from Horizons Gallery

**11.01**
Installation views of *Computer-Generated Pictures*, curated by Howard Wise, Howard Wise Gallery, New York, United States, 1965

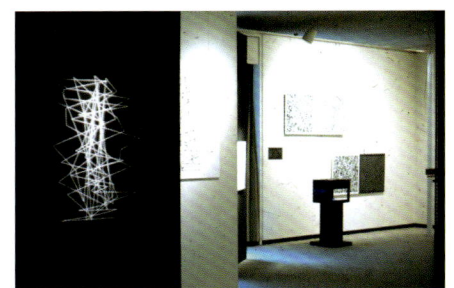
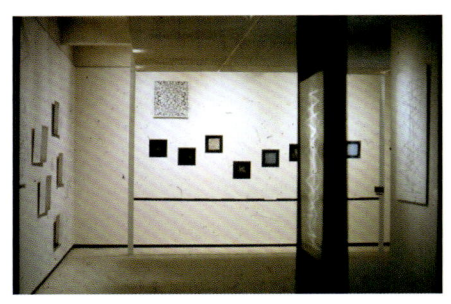

| | CURATOR(S) | EXHIBITION TITLE | INSTITUTION(S)/COMMERCIAL | LOCATION | TYPE OF EVENT | OPEN DATE | END DATE |
|---|---|---|---|---|---|---|---|
| 1 | Max Bense, Siegfried Maser | Computergrafik | Studiengalerie der TH Stuttgart | Stuttgart, Germany | Physical | 02-05-1965 | 02-19-1965 |
| 2 | Howard Wise | Computer-Generated Pictures | Howard Wise Gallery | New York, USA | Physical | 04-06-1965 | 04-24-1965 |
| 3 | Jasia Reichardt | Cybernetic Serendipity | Institute of Contemporary Arts | London, UK | Physical | 08-02-1968 | 10-20-1968 |
| 4 | Dirnitrije Basicevic, Boris Kelemen, Matko Mestrovic, Abraham André Moles, Ivan Picelj | Tendencies 4: Computers and Visual Research | Museum of Contemporary Art Zagreb | Zagreb, Yugoslavia (modern-day Croatia) | Physical | 08-03-1968 | 08-30-1969 |
| 5 | Experiments in Art and Technology | Some More Beginnings : Experiments in Art and Technology | Brooklyn Museum | New York, USA | Physical | 11-25-1968 | 01-05-1969 |
| 6 | Pontus Hultén | The Machine as Seen at the End of the Mechanical Age | Museum of Modern Art | New York, USA | Physical | 11-27-1968 | 02-09-1969 |
| 7 | Maurice Tuchman | Art and Technology | LACMA | Los Angeles, USA | Physical | 1969 | No Record |
| 8 | Jorge Glusberg | Arte y Cibernética | Centro de Estudios de Arte y Comunicación | Buenos Aires, Argentina | Physical | 1969 | No Record |
| 9 | Computer Arts Society | Event One | Royal College of Art | London, UK | Physical | 03-29-1969 | 03-30-1969 |
| 10 | Howard Wise | TV as a Creative Medium | Howard Wise Gallery | New York, USA | Physical | 05-17-1969 | 06-14-1969 |
| 11 | Beryl Phyllis, Korot Gershuny, Michael Shamberg, Ira Schneider | Radical Software Vol. I, no. 1 | Radical Software, Raindance Corporation | New York, USA | Physical | 06-01-1970 | 1974 |
| 12 | Kynaston McShine | Information | Museum of Modern Art | New York, USA | Physical | 07-02-1970 | 09-20-1970 |
| 13 | Jack Burnham | Software | Jewish Museum | New York, USA | Physical | 09-16-1970 | 11-08-1970 |
| 14 | Manfred Schneckenburger | Nam June Paik's TV Garden (1974) at Documenta 6 | Documenta 6 | Kassel, West Germany | Physical | 06-24-1977 | 10-02-1977 |
| 15 | Hubert Bognermayr, Herbert W. Franke, Hannes Leopoldseder, Ulli A. Rützel | 1st Ars Electronica | Brucknerhaus | Linz, Austria | Physical | 09-18-1979 | 09-21-1979 |
| 16 | Jean-François Lyotard, Thierry Chaput | Les Immateriaux | Centre Pompidou | Paris, France | Physical | 03-28-1985 | 07-15-1985 |

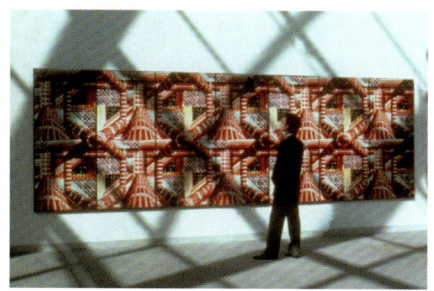

| ARTIST(S) INVOLVED | SUGGESTED BY |
|---|---|
| Georg Nees | Tina Rivers Ryan |
| Bela Julesz, A. Michael Noll | Tina Rivers Ryan |
| Jeffrey Steele, Bridget Riley, Charles Csuri, Fujio Niwa, Gordon Pask, Wen Ying Tsai | Studio Robert Alice, Rachel Greene |
| Frieder Nake, Jane Moon, Kerry Strand, John Szabo +... | Studio Robert Alice |
| Ralph Morrill, Norton Wise +... | Tina Rivers Ryan |
| Giacomo Balla, Umberto Boccioni, Alexander Calder, Marcel Duchamp, Max Ernst, Lyonel Feininger, Rube Goldberg, El Lissitzky, Man Ray, Francis Picabia, Vladimir Tatlin, Jean Tinguely +... | Studio Robert Alice |
| Stephen Antonakos, Avigdor Arikha, Michael Asher, John Baldessari, Iain Baxter, Larry Bell, Max Bill +... | Tina Rivers Ryan |
| Jorge Glusberg, Luis F. Benedit, Antonio Berni, Eduardo Mac Entyre, Osvaldo Romberg, Miguel Ángel Vidal +... | Tina Rivers Ryan |
| Alan M. France, R. John Lansdown, Malcolm Le Grice, John Lifton, George Mallen, Alan Sutcliffe, Beverly Rowe, Jasia Reichardt, Robert Parslow, Ian Pickering, Alan Mayne | Studio Robert Alice |
| Nam June Paik, Charlotte Moorman, Paul Ryan, Ira Schneider, Frank Gillette, Eric Siegel, Serge Boutourline, Earl Reiback, John Seery, Thomas Tadlock, Aldo Tambellini, Joe Weintraub | Rachel Greene |
| Ira Schneider, Davidson Gigliotti +... | Rachel Greene |
| Vito Acconci, Carl Andre, Siah Armajani, Keith Arnatt, Art & Language Press, Art & Project, Richard Artschwager, David Askevold, Terry Atkinson, David Bainbridge, John Baldessari, Michael Baldwin, Barrio, Robert Barry, Frederick Barthelme, Bernhard and Hilla Becher, Joseph Beuys, Mel Bochner, Bill Bollinger, George Brecht, Stig Broegger, Stanley Brouwn, Daniel Buren, Victor Burgin, Donald Burgy, Ian Burn, Mel Ramsden, James Lee Byars, Jorge Luis Carballa, Christopher Cook, Roger Cutforth, Carlos D'Alessio, Hanne Darboven, Walter de Maria, Jan Dibbets, Gerald Ferguson, Rafael Ferrer, Barry Flanagan, Group Frontera, Hamish Fulton, Gilbert and George, Giorno Poetry Systems, Dan Graham, Hans Haacke, Ira Joel Haber, Randy Hardy, Michael Heizer, Hans Hollein, Douglas Huebler, Robert Huot, Peter Hutchinson, Richards Jarden, Stephen Kaltenbach, On Kawara, Joseph Kosuth, Christine Kozlov, John Latham, Barry Le Va, Sol LeWitt, Lucy R. Lippard, Richard Long, Bruce McLean, Cildo Campos Meirelles, Marta Minujin, Robert Morris, N. E. Thing Co., Bruce Nauman, New York Graphic Workshop, Stephen Lawrence, Group OHO, Helio Oiticica, Yoko Ono, Dennis Oppenheim, Panamarenko, Giulio Paolini, Paul Pechter, Giuseppe Penone, Adrian Piper, Michelangelo Pistoletto, Emilio Prini, Alejandro Puente, Markus Raetz, Yvonne Rainer, Klaus Rinke, Edward Ruscha, J. M. Sanejouand. Richard Sladden, Robert Smithson, Keith Sonnier, Ettore Sottsass jr., Erik Thygesen, John Van Saun, Guilherme Magalhaes Vaz, Bernar Venet, Jeffrey Wall, Lawrence Weiner, Ian Wilson | Rachel Greene |
| Vito Acconci, David Antin, Architecture Group Machine M.I.T., John Baldessari, Robert Barry, Linda Berris, Donald Burgy, Paul Conly, Agnes Denes, Robert Duncan Enzmann, Carl Fernbach-Flarsheim, John Godyear, Hans Haacke, Douglas Huebler, Joseph Kosuth, Nam June Paik, Alex Razdow, Sonia Sheridan, Evander D. Scjhley, Theodosius Victoria, Laurence Weiner | Rachel Greene |
| Nam June Paik | Studio Robert Alice |
| Jacov Agam, Ed Emshwiller, Catherine Ikam, Tatsuo Miyajima, Toshio Iwai, Jeffrey Shaw, Dick Groeneveld +... | Studio Robert Alice |
| Alvar Aalto, John Anselmo, Giacomo Balla, Robert Barry, Larry Bell, Stephen Benton, Jean Louis Boissier, Jean Claude Bourdier, Jacques Elie Chabert, Chardin, Robert Delaunay, Sonia Delaunay, Frederic Develay, Marc Denjean, Cesar Domela, Marcel Duchamp, Peter Eisenman, Claudine Eizykman, Guy Fihman, Dan Flavin, Lucio Fontana, Jean-Charles Francois, Dan Graham, Nathalie Goncharova, Zaha Hadid, Denis Horuath, Dominique Horvilleur, Illegal Command, Yves Klein, Joseph Kosuth, Rem Koolhaas, Thierry Kuntzel, Michael Larionov, Kasimir Malevich, Piero Manzoni, John Paul Martin, Quentin Metsys, Laszlo Moholy-Nagy, Jacques Monory, Sam Moree, Francois Morellet, Camille Philibert, Philippe Puicouyoul, Georges Seurat, takis, Doug Tyler, Simon Vouet, Piet Zwart, Andy Warhol | Studio Robert Alice, aurèce vettier |

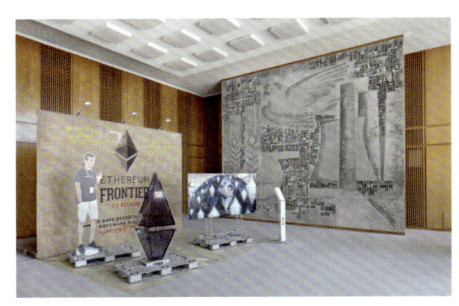

**11.04**
Installation view from Simon
Denny, *Blockchain Visionaries*
[with Linda Kantchev],
Berlin Biennale, Germany, 2016

| | CURATOR(S) | EXHIBITION TITLE | INSTITUTION(S)/COMMERCIAL | LOCATION | TYPE OF EVENT | OPEN DATE | END DATE |
|---|---|---|---|---|---|---|---|
| 17 | Cynthia Goodman, International Business Machines Corporation, National Endowment for the Arts, Everson Museum of Art | Digital Visions: Computers and Art | Everson Museum of Art | New York, USA | Physical | 09-17-1987 | 11-08-1987 |
| 18 | Nagoya City Art Museum, Nagoya Science Museum, The Chunichi Shimbun, The Council for the International Biennale in Nagoya | 1st Artec Biennale | International World Design Exposition | Nagoya, Japan | Physical | 07-06-1989 | 11-26-1989 |
| 19 | Douglas Davis | The World's First Collaborative Sentence | Lehman College Art Gallery | New York, USA | Physical / Digital | 12-07-1994 | Ongoing |
| 20 | Tamas Banovich, Ken Coupland | Can You Digit? | Postmasters Gallery | New York, USA | Physical | 03-16-1996 | 04-13-1996 |
| 21 | San Francisco Museum of Modern Art | 010101: Art in Technological Times | San Francisco Museum of Modern Art | San Francisco, USA; Online | Physical / Digital | 03-03-2001 | 07-08-2001 |
| 22 | – | Bitstreams | Whitney Museum of American Art | New York, USA; Online | Physical / Digital | 03-22-2001 | 07-10-2001 |
| 23 | Bitforms Gallery | Transmission (Undeciphered) | Bitforms Gallery | San Francisco, USA | Physical | 11-15-2001 | 12-02-2001 |
| 24 | Gerfried Stocker | Code – The Language of Our Time | Prix Ars Electronica | Linz, Austria | Physical | 09-06-2003 | 09-11-2003 |
| 25 | Marius Watz | Generative X, Between Art and Code | Norwegian National Museum | Oslo, Norway | Physical | 09-23-2005 | 10-16-2005 |
| 26 | Wulf Herzogenrath, Barbara Nierhoff-Wielk | Ex Machina – Frühe Computergrafik bis 1979 | Kunsthalle Bremen | Bremen, Germany | Physical | 06-17-2007 | 08-26-2007 |
| 27 | Debora Wood, Paul Hertz | Imaging by Numbers | Block Museum of Art | Illinois, USA | Physical | 01-18-2008 | 04-06-2008 |
| 28 | Miltos Manetas, Jan Åman | The Embassy of Piracy | Internet Pavilion, Venice Biennale | Venice, Italy; Online | Physical / Digital | 06-03-2009 | 11-22-2009 |
| 29 | Rhea Myers | Digital Pioneers | Victoria and Albert Museum | London, UK | Physical | 12-07-2009 | 04-25-2010 |
| 30 | Aram Bartholl | Speed Show Vol. 1 : TELE-INTERNET | Speed Shows | Berlin, Germany | Physical | 06-11-2010 | 06-11-2010 |
| 31 | Rafaël Rozendaal, Anne de Vries | BYOB (Bring your own Beamer) | Bureau Friederich Projectstudio | Berlin, Germany | Physical | 07-20-2010 | 07-20-2010 |
| 32 | George Fifield | Drawing with Code | DeCordova Museum and Sculpture Park | Lincoln, USA | Physical | 01-29-2011 | 04-24-2011 |
| 33 | Kelani Nichole | New Sculpt | TRANSFER Gallery | New York, USA | Physical | 07-20-2013 | 08-10-2013 |
| 34 | Lindsay Howard | Paddles ON! | Phillips, Tumblr | New York, USA | Physical | 10-05-2013 | 10-12-2013 |
| 35 | Kelani Nichole | NET VVORTH | TRANSFER Gallery | New York, USA; Online | Digital | 12-14-2013 | 12-14-2013 |

**11.05**
The Rare Digital Art Festival (RARE
AF), New York, United States, 2018

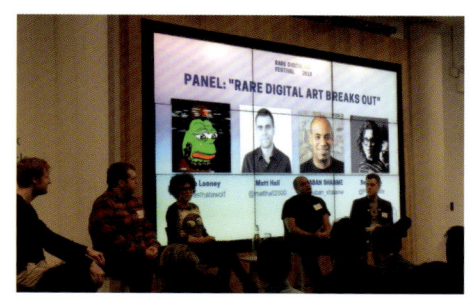

| ARTIST(S) INVOLVED | SUGGESTED BY |
|---|---|
| Andy Warhol, David Hockney, Jennifer Bartlett, Larry Rivers, Philip Pearlstein +... | Tina Rivers Ryan |
| Klaus Basset, Willi Plöchl, Christian Cavadia, Dr. Helmut von Falser, Peter Vogel, Prof. Otto Beckmann, Oskar Beckmann, Dr. Paul Jenewein, Ludwig Rehberg +... | Studio Robert Alice |
| Douglas Davis +... | Studio Robert Alice, Rachel Greene |
| Erik Adigard, M.A.D, Laurence Arcadias, Aufuldish & Warinner, Kevin Sawad Brooks, Ursula Endlicher, Tirtza Even, Ken Feingold, Ebon Fisher, Perry Hoberman, Brad Johnson, Craig Kalpakjian, Alan Keahey, George Legrady, Stephen Linhart, Gerard Lynn, Mark Madel, Lev Manovich, Thomas Miller, post tool design, pixelpeppy, Erwin Redl, bigtwin, Terbo Ted +... | Christina J. Chua |
| Lee Bul, Roxy Paine +... | Studio Robert Alice |
| Jeremy Blake, Leah Gilliam, LOT/EK, DJ Spooky That Subliminal Kid, Jim O'Rourke, Paul Pfeiffer, Marina Rosenfeld, Elliott Sharp, Diana Thater, Pamela Z +... | Studio Robert Alice |
| Casey Reas | Christina J. Chua |
| Richard Kriesche, Roman Verostko, Casey Reas, Fiona Raby, Marc Canter, Hiroshi Ishii Oliver Fritz, Joachim Sauter, Libeskind, Scott deLahunta | Casey Reas |
| Casey Reas, Ben Fry, Martin Wattenberg, Golan Levin +... | Studio Robert Alice |
| Charles Csuri, Roland K. Fuchshuber, Karl Gerstner, Theo Goldberg, Mila Gravenhorst, Julius Guest, Sozo Hashimoto, Ernst Havlik, Grace C. Hertlein, Kurt Ingerl, Mihail Jalobeanu, Gerhard F. Kammerer, Wolfgang Kiwus, Miroslav Klivar, Kenneth C. Knowlton, William J. Kolomyjec, Peter Kreis, Ernst Otto Krämer, Ruth Leavitt, Tony Longson, Aaron Marcus, Tomislav Mikulic, Manfred Mohr, Vera Molnár, Frieder Nake, Georg Nees, A. Michael Noll, R.D.E. Oxenaar, Sylvia Roubaud, Annamaria Sala, Marzio Sala, Reiner H. Schneeberger, Ernst Schott, Lillian F. Schwartz, Chihaya Shimomura, Bruno Sonderegger, Norton Starr, Rolf Wölk, Edward Zajec, Vilko Žiljak | Georg Bak |
| Ben Laposky, Herbert W. Franke, Manfred Mohr, Edward Zajec, David Em, Lane Hall, Roman Verostko, Joshua Davis, C.E.B. Reas | Tina Rivers Ryan |
| Miltos Manetas, Rafaël Rozendaal, Petra Cortright, Martijn Hendriks, Harm van den Dorpel, Sinem Erkas, Elna Frederick, Parker Ito, Oliver Laric, Guthrie Lonergan, Pascual Sisto, Aleksandra Domanovic, Christian Wassmann, AIDS-3D | Studio Robert Alice |
| Ben Laposky, Charles Csuri, Paul Brown, Harold Cohen | Tina Rivers Ryan |
| Jon Cates, Constant Dullaart, Dragan Espenschied, JODI, Geraldine Juarez, Tobias Leingruber, Olia Lialina, Moddr, Johannes P Osterhoff, Evan Roth, Ralph Schulz, Paul Slocom | Studio Robert Alice |
| AIDS-3D, Alexandra Domanovic, Andreas Angelidakis, Andrew Keaton, Angelo Plessas, Anne de Vries, Billy Rennekamp, Constant Dullaart, Dafna Maimon, Darri Lorenzen, Emile Zile, Hayley Silverman, Helga Wretman, Jaime Whipple, Juliette Bonneviot, Kari Altmann, Katja Novitskova, Kinga Kielczynska, Lindsay Lawson, Mike Ruiz, Oliver Laric, Rafaël Rozendaal, Spiros Hadjidjanos, Timur Si-Qin, Voin de Voin, Wojciech Kosma | Studio Robert Alice |
| Yoshiyuki Abe, Manuel Barbadillo, Desmond Paul Henry, Jean-Pierre Hébert, Sture Johannesson, Hiroshi Kawano, Kenneth C. Knowlton, Ben F. Laposky, Manfred Mohr, Vera Molnár, Frieder Nake, Georg Nees, Lillian F. Schwartz, Stan VanDerBeek, Roman Verostko, Mark Wilson, Edward Zajec | Matt Kane |
| LaTurbo Avedon | Tina Rivers Ryan |
| Silvia Bianchi, Ricardo Juárez, Petra Cortright, Alexandra Gorczynski, Joe Hamilton, Ilja Karilampi, Brenna Murphy, Aude Pariset, Sabrina Ratté, Casey Reas, Rafaël Rozendaal, Nicolas Sassoon, Molly Soda, Kate Steciw, Mark Tribe, Clement Valla, Addie Wagenknecht, Jamie Zigelbaum | Casey Reas |
| Daniel Temkin | Tina Rivers Ryan |

**11.06**
*Virtual Niche* poster, curated by
Qinwen Wang, UCCA, Beijing,
China, 2021

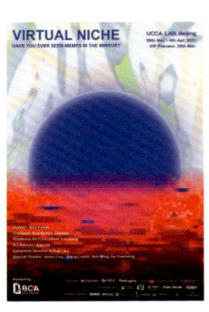

| | CURATOR(S) | EXHIBITION TITLE | INSTITUTION(S)/COMMERCIAL | LOCATION | TYPE OF EVENT | OPEN DATE | END DATE |
|---|---|---|---|---|---|---|---|
| 36 | Erik H Rzepka, Wesley Yuen | Computers and Capital: The Rise of Digital Currency | CoinFest 2014 | Vancouver, Canada | Physical | 03-13-2014 | 03-16-2014 |
| 37 | Willa Köerner, Jenny Sharaf | Proof of Work | The Sub | San Francisco, USA | Physical | 03-24-2014 | 03-24-2014 |
| 38 | Kevin McCoy & Anil Dash | Seven on Seven Conference | New Museum | New York, USA | Physical | 05-03-2014 | 05-03-2014 |
| 39 | Jenna Lash | Monetary Series | Bitcoin Center NYC | New York, USA | Physical | 05-09-2014 | 09-01-2014 |
| 40 | – | Opening Times | Seventeen Gallery | Online | Digital | 06-01-2014 | 09-01-2014 |
| 41 | Lindsay Howard | Paddles ON! | Phillips, Tumblr | London, UK | Physical | 07-03-2014 | 07-03-2014 |
| 42 | – | The Darknet: From Memes to Onionland. An Exploration | Kunst Halle Sankt Gallen | St. Gallen, Switzerland | Physical | 10-18-2014 | 01-11-2015 |
| 43 | Lucy Hunter, R Lyon | Bitchcoin | Where Gallery | New York, USA | Physical | 02-15-2015 | No Record |
| 44 | Espacio Byte | Automatic-0 – Poetics of Generativity | Espacio Byte | Espacio Byte, Online | Digital | 10-01-2015 | Ongoing |
| 45 | Ruth Catlow | The Human Face of Cryptoeconomies | Furtherfield | London, UK | Physical | 10-17-2015 | 11-22-2015 |
| 46 | Lisa Spellman | Stock Performance | 303 Gallery | New York, USA | Physical | 01-08-2016 | 02-06-2016 |
| 47 | Omar Kholeif | Electronic Superhighway (2016–1966) | Whitechapel Art Gallery | London, UK | Physical | 01-29-2016 | 05-15-2016 |
| 48 | Gray Area Foundation for the Arts, Research at Google | DeepDream: The Art of Neural Networks | Grey Area Foundation for the Arts | San Francisco, USA | Physical | 02-26-2016 | 02-27-2016 |
| 49 | Ruth Catlow | Furtherfield Showcase: Art and the Blockchain | Digital Catapult Centre | London, UK | Physical | 03-28-2016 | 04-26-2016 |
| 50 | Simon Denny | Blockchain Visionaries | 9th Berlin Biennale | Berlin, Germany | Physical | 06-04-2016 | 09-18-2016 |
| 51 | Simon Denny | Blockchain Future States | Petzel Gallery | New York, USA | Physical | 09-22-2016 | 10-22-2016 |
| 52 | Georg Bak | Thinking in Algorithms | Scheublein + Bak | Zürich, Switzerland | Physical | 09-22-2016 | 10-25-2016 |
| 53 | Avant | Øx | Avant.org, Ethereal Summit | New York, USA | Physical | 05-20-2017 | 05-20-2017 |
| 54 | – | In Character | San Francisco Museum of Modern Art | San Francisco, USA | Physical | 06-03-2017 | 01-01-2018 |
| 55 | – | qubibi | MuDA | Zürich, Switzerland | Physical | 09-09-2017 | 01-28-2018 |

11.07
Installation view of *Virtual Niche*,
curated by Qinwen Wang, UCCA,
Beijing, China, 2021

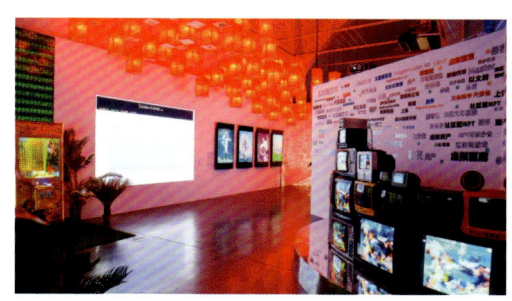

| ARTIST(S) INVOLVED | SUGGESTED BY |
|---|---|
| Jon Cates, Ellectra Radikal, FELT, Giselle Zatonyl, Matt Tecson, Roger Grandlapin, Kutay Cengil, Systaime, Devon Hatto, Adam Braffman, Nicolas Koroloff, Dominik Podsiadly, Chimerik. Miyö Van Stenis, ASS Rain, Robert B. Lisek | Rhea Myers |
| Alexandra Gorczynski, Doug Garth Williams, Laura Hyunjhee Kim, Anthony Discenza, Labanna Babalon, Chris Corrente, Lola Thompson, David Horwitz, Hilary Pecis, Molly Soda, Simon Pyle, David Kim | Martin Lukas Ostachowski |
| Jennifer & Kevin McCoy | Martin Lukas Ostachowski |
| Jenna Lash | Martin Lukas Ostachowski |
| Nicolas Sassoon | Nicolas Sassoon |
| Alexandria McCrosky, Amalia Ulman, Evan Roth, Hannah Perry, Harm van den Dorpel, Heather Phillipson, James Bridle, Jeanette Hayes, Jonas Lund, Laura Brothers, Luis Hidalgo, Maja Cule, Majed Aslam, Michael Manning, Michael Staniak, Oliver Sutherland, Quayola, Sara Ludy, Sophie Kahn, Yung Jake, Yuri Pattison | Casey Reas |
| !Mediengruppe Bitnik, Anonymous, Cory Arcangel, Aram Bartholl, Heath Bunting, Simon Denny, Eva and Franco Mattes, Seth Price, Robert Sakrowski, Hito Steyerl, Valentina Tanni | Simon Denny |
| Sarah Meyohas | Sarah Meyohas Studio |
| Holger Lippmann, Mark Nystrom, Federico Marino, Krzysztof Syruć, Yancy Way, Rhea Myers, mad-as.hell, Stanza | Rhea Myers |
| Émilie Brout, Maxime Marion, Shu Lea Cheang, Sarah T Gold, Jennifer Lyn Morone, Rhea Myers, Paula Crutchlow, Dr. Ian Cook, Dan Hassan, Brett Scott | Rhea Myers |
| Sarah Meyohas | Sarah Meyohas Studio |
| Jacob Appelbaum, Cory Arcangel, Roy Ascott, Jeremy Bailey, Judith Barry, Wafaa Bilal, Zach Blas, Olaf Breuning, James Bridle, Heath Bunting, Bureau of Inverse, Technology (B.I.T.), Antoine Catala, Aristarkh Chernyshev, Petra Cortright, Vuk Ćosić, Douglas Coupland, CTG (Computer Technique Group), Cybernetic Serendipity, Aleksandra Domanović, Constant Dullaart, Experiments in Art and Technology (E.A.T.), Harun Farocki, Joana Hadjithomas, Khalil Joreige, Celia Hempton, Camille Henrot, Gary Hill, Ann Hirsch, Nancy Holt, Richard Serra, JODI, Eduardo Kac, Allan Kaprow, Hiroshi Kawano, Mahmoud Khaled, Oliver Laric, Jan Robert Leegte, Lynn Hershman Leeson, Olia Lialina, Tony Longson, Rafael Lozano-Hemmer, Jonas Lund, Jill Magid, Eva and Franco Mattes, Model Court, Manfred Mohr, Vera Molnár, Mouchette, Jayson Musson, Frieder Nake, Joshua Nathanson, Katja Novitskova, Mendi, Keith Obadike, Albert Oehlen, Trevor Paglen, Nam June Paik, Jon Rafman, Evan Roth, Thomas Ruff, Alex Ruthner, Jacolby Satterwhite, Lillian F. Schwartz, Peter Sedgley, Taryn Simon, Frances Stark, Hito Steyerl, Sturtevant, Martine Syms, Thomson and Craighead, Ryan Trecartin, Amalia Ulman, Stan VanDerBeek, Steina and Woody Vasulka, Addie Wagenknecht, Lawrence Weiner, Ulla Wiggen, The Yes Men, YOUNG-HAE CHANG HEAVY INDUSTRIES | Jonas Lund |
| Mike Tyka, Memo Akten, Mario Klingemann, Josh Nimoy, James "Pouff" Roberts, Samim Winiger, Jessica Brillhart, Doug Fritz, Alexander Mordvintsev, Michael Ishigaki, Ross Goodwin | Refik Anadol |
| Rhea Myers, Okhaos, Émilie Brout, Maxime Marion | Martin Lukas Ostachowski |
| Simon Denny | Simon Denny |
| Simon Denny | Studio Robert Alice |
| Heather Dewey-Hagborg, Alfons Eggert, Herbert W. Franke, Philipp Goldbach, Hein Gravenhorst, René Groebli, Heinrich Heidersberger, Gottfried Jäger, Hans Jenny, Susan Morris, Michael Reisch, Adrian Sauer, Benjamin Heidersberger | Georg Bak |
| Sam Hart, Melanie Hoff, Nora Khan, Lars TCF Holdhus, Rhea Myers, Simon Denny, FOAM | Rhea Myers, Brian Droitcourt |
| Nam June Paik | Studio Robert Alice |
| qubibi | aurèce vettier |

| | CURATOR(S) | EXHIBITION TITLE | INSTITUTION(S)/COMMERCIAL | LOCATION | TYPE OF EVENT | OPEN DATE | END DATE |
|---|---|---|---|---|---|---|---|
| 56 | Julian Oliver | Harvest | Konstmuseet i Skövde | Skövde, Sweden | Physical | 09-14-2017 | 11-14-2017 |
| 57 | Fernando Schrupp | Demo Day | Kunstraum LLC | New York, USA | Physical | 09-24-2017 | 10-29-2017 |
| 58 | – | Cloud of Petals | Red Bull Arts | New York, USA | Physical | 10-12-2017 | 12-10-2017 |
| 59 | Peter Weibel, Lívia Nolasco-Rózsás, Yasemin Keskintepe, Blanca Giménez | Open Codes. Die Welt als Datenfeld ("The World as a Data Field") | ZKM Center for Art and Media | Karlsruhe, Germany | Physical | 10-20-2017 | 06-02-2019 |
| 60 | Max Dovey | Breath (BRH) Respiratory Mining | Neon Digital Art Festival | Dundee, UK | Physical | 10-28-2017 | 10-28-2017 |
| 61 | Clare Brennan, Sarah Cook, Mark Daniels, Donna Holford-Lovell | Media Archaeology: Excavations, Neon Festival | West Ward Works | Dundee, UK | Physical | 11-09-2017 | 11-12-2017 |
| 62 | Anika Meier, Sabrina Steinek. | Virtual Normality: Women Net Artists 2.0 | Museum der bildenden Künste | Leipzig, Germany | Physical | 01-12-2018 | 04-08-2018 |
| 63 | Joe Looney, Rare Art Labs, Tommy Nicholas | Rare AF 1 | Rare Art Labs, Tommy Nicholas | New York, USA | Physical | 01-13-2018 | 01-13-2018 |
| 64 | Simon Denny | Games of Decentralized Life | Galerie Buchholz | Cologne, Germany | Physical | 04-18-2018 | 06-16-2018 |
| 65 | – | ClickMine, Ethereal Summit | Knockdown Center | New York, USA | Physical | 05-11-2018 | 05-12-2018 |
| 66 | – | Ethereal Summit 2018 | Ethereum Foundation | New York, USA | Physical | 05-11-2018 | 05-12-2018 |
| 67 | Victoria Kondrashova, Dmitry Ozerkov | Innovation as Artistic Technique | The State Hermitage Museum | St. Petersburg, Russia | Physical | 05-25-2018 | 06-05-2018 |
| 68 | – | Coder le Monde Mutations / Créations 2 | Centre Pompidou | Paris, France | Physical | 06-15-2018 | 08-27-2018 |
| 69 | Omar Kholeif | I Was Raised on the Internet | MCA Chicago | Chicago, USA | Physical | 06-23-2018 | 10-14-2018 |
| 70 | January Parkos Arnall, Christy LeMaster | Prime Time: F00TW3RK – GIF Party | MCA Chicago | Chicago, USA | Physical | 06-30-2018 | 06-30-2018 |
| 71 | – | Chance and Control: Art in the Age of Computers | Victoria and Albert Museum | London, UK | Physical | 07-07-2018 | 11-18-2018 |
| 72 | Thomas Webb | Strangers | Woodbury House | London, UK | Physical | 07-18-2018 | 07-19-2018 |
| 73 | – | Distributed Systems | Gray Area | San Francisco, USA | Physical | 07-26-2018 | 08-03-2018 |
| 74 | Sam Hart, Sarah Hamerman | Secrets | San Francisco Mint | San Francisco, USA | Physical | 08-01-2018 | 08-02-2018 |
| 75 | Simon Denny | Proof of Work | Schinkel Pavillon | Berlin, Germany | Physical | 09-08-2018 | 12-20-2018 |
| 76 | Christiane Paul, Carol Mancusi-Ungaro, Melva Bucksbaum, Clémence White | Programmed: Rules, Codes and Choreographies in Art | Whitney Museum of American Art | New York, USA | Physical | 09-28-2018 | 04-14-2019 |
| 77 | Pascal Boyart | Bitcoin Art (r)evolution | Bitcoin Art (r)evolution | Paris, France | Physical | 09-28-2018 | 10-05-2018 |
| 78 | Trevor Jones | The Art of Blockchain | Dundas Street Gallery | Edinburgh, UK | Physical | 10-22-2018 | 10-26-2018 |
| 79 | Shiva Lynn Burgos, Georg Bak, Alisa Phommaxahay | Binary / Non-Binary | Geste Paris | Paris, France | Physical | 11-06-2018 | 12-01-2018 |

| ARTIST(S) INVOLVED | SUGGESTED BY |
|---|---|
| Julian Oliver | Martin Lukas Ostachowski |
| Aram Bartholl, Émilie Brout, Maxime Marion, Ursula Damm, Eteam, Nathaniel Faulkner, Esther Hunziker, Eduardo Kac, Marc Lee, Claudia Maté, Jennifer & Kevin McCoy, Rhea Myers, Andrew Nunes, Nicholas O'Brien, Alexander Reben, Daniel Temkin, Ubermorgen, Michel Winterberg | Rhea Myers |
| Sarah Meyohas | Sarah Meyohas Studio |
| Harm van den Dorpel, Simon Denny | Simon Denny |
| Max Dovey | Martin Lukas Ostachowski |
| Morehshin Allahyari, Nicky Bird, Verity Birt, Ele Carpenter, Joseph DeLappe, Rhoda Ellis, Adam Lockhart, Sarah Friend, Claire Hentschker, Olia Lialina, Patrick Lichty, William Miller, Elke Reinhuber, VOID | Studio Sarah Friend |
| Signe Pierce, Molly Soda, Leah Schrager, Refrakt, Nicole Ruggiero, Stephanie Sarley, Arvida Byström, Nakeya Brown, Juno Calypso, Izumi Miyazaki, LaTurbo Avedon | Studio Robert Alice |
| Matt Hall, Joe Looney, Mack Flavelle, Bea Ramos, Shaban Shaame, Vladimir Vukicevic, Kilian Kunst, Yehudit Mam, Kieran Farr, Jessica Angel | Studio Robert Alice |
| Simon Denny | Martin Lukas Ostachowski |
| Sarah Friend | Studio Sarah Friend |
| Osinachi, Don Jazzy +... | Coldie |
| Kevin Abosch +... | Martin Lukas Ostachowski |
| Alisa Andrasek, Andrea Branzi, EZCT Architecture & Design Research, Mishka Henner, Gottfried Honegger, Vera Molnár, Neri Oxman | Georg Bak |
| Sophia Al-Maria, American Artist, Anna Anthropy, Cory Arcangel, Jeremy Bailey, Zach Blas, Nate Boyce, Ingrid Burrington, Cao Fei, Antoine Catala, Jon Chambers, Shu Lea Cheang, Ian Cheng, Chris Collins, Petra Cortright, Douglas Coupland, Simon Denny, DIS, Aleksandra Domanović, Stan Douglas, Constant Dullaart, E. Jane, Lizzie Fitch, Ryan Trecartin, John Gerrard, Goldin+Senneby, Óscar González-Díaz, Matthew Angelo Harrison, Erin Hayden, Porpentine Charity Heartscape, Mashaun Ali Hendricks, Femke Herregraven, Shawné Michaelain Holloway, Joel Holmberg, Juliana Huxtable, Oliver Laric, Rafael Lozano-Hemmer, Sara Ludy, Rachel Maclean, Eva and Franco Mattes, Takeshi Murata, Jayson Musson, Mendi, Keith Obadike, Laura Owens, Trevor Paglen, Heather Phillipson, Angelo Plessas, Jon Rafman, Sean Raspet, Tabita Rezaire, Tabor Robak, Evan Roth, Jacolby Satterwhite, Ben Schumacher, Bogosi Sekhukhuni, Elias Sime, Daniel Steegman Mangrané, Hito Steyerl, Christopher Kulendran Thomas, Thomson & Craighead, Josh Tonsfeldt, Francis Tseng, Amalia Ulman, Harm van den Dorpel, Artie Vierkant, Andrew Norman Wilson, Young-Hae Chang Heavy Industries | Matt Kane |
| The Era, Jana Rush, Sky Heyn Cubacub, the Radical Visibility Collective | Matt Kane |
| Frieder Nake, Vera Molnár, Manfred Mohr, Harold Cohen, Roman Verostko, Casey Reas | Georg Bak |
| Thomas Web | Studio Robert Alice |
| Andrew Newman, Cassie Thornton, Christoph Wachter, Mathias Jud, Claire L. Evans, Cullen Miller, DISNOVATION.ORG, Gabriel Dunne, Grayson Earle, Harm van den Dorpel, Maria Roszkowska, Matt Liston, Max Hampshire, Nicolas Maigret, Primavera De Filippi, RIAT, Rhea Myers, Sarah Friend, Simon Denny, #NEWPALMYRA | Brian Droitcour |
| Rhea Myers | Brian Droitcor, Rhea Myers |
| CryptoKitties, Aria Dean, Distributed Gallery, Harm van den Dorpel, FOAM (Ryan John King, Ekaterina Zavyalova, Nick Axel, Kristoffer Josefsson), Sarah Hamerman, Sam Hart, Decentralized Autonomous Kunstverein (Nick Koppenhagen, Wesley Simon), Kei Kreutler, left gallery (Harm van den Dorpel, Paloma Rodríguez Carrington), Wayne Lloyd, Mark Lombardi, Jonas Lund, Rhea Myers, Hayal Pozanti, Billy Rennekamp, Jason Rohrer, Miljohn Ruperto, Ulrik Heltoft, 0xΩ (Avery Singer, Matt Liston), terra0 (Paul Seidler, Paul Kolling, Max Hampshire), Georgia Hansford, Louis Center, Gregor Finger | Studio Robert Alice |
| Josef Albers, Cory Arcangel, Tauba Auerbach, Jonah Brucker-Cohen, Jim Campbell, Ian Cheng, Lucinda Child, Charles Csuri, Agnes Denes, Alex Dodge, Charles Gaines, Philip Glass, Frederick Hammersley, Channa Horwitz, Donald Judd, Joseph Kosuth, Shigeko Kubota, Marc Lafia, Barbara Lattanzi, Lynn Hershman Leeson, Sol LeWitt, Manfred Mohr, Mendi & Keith Obadike, Nam June Paik, William Bradford Paley, Paul Pfeiffer, Casey Reas, Earl Reiback, Rafaël Rozendaal, Lillian Schwartz, James L. Seawright, John F. Simon Jr., Steina, Mika Tajima, Tamiko Thiel, Cheyney Thompson, Joan Truckenbrod, Siebren Versteeg, Lawrence Weiner | Georg Bak |
| Andy Bauch, Coin Artist, Josie Bellini, Nanu Berks, Mark Bern, Yosh, Pascal Boyart, Yom de Saint Phalle, Choq, Youl, Ilies Issiakhem | Martin Lukas Ostachowski |
| Trevor Jones | Martin Lukas Ostachowski |
| Constantin Brancusi, Frederick Sommer, Pierre Molinier, Hiroshi Sugimoto, Ned & Shiva Productions, Francis Ruyter, Olaf Nicolai, Tom Butler, Ghost of a Dream, Zean Cabangis, Elger Esser, CJ Heyliger, Susan Morris, Rhea Myers, Nicolas Schöffer | Georg Bak |

| | CURATOR(S) | EXHIBITION TITLE | INSTITUTION(S)/COMMERCIAL | LOCATION | TYPE OF EVENT | OPEN DATE | END DATE |
|---|---|---|---|---|---|---|---|
| 80 | Georg Bak | Perfect and Priceless: Value Systems on the Blockchain | Kate Vass Galerie | Zürich, Switzerland | Physical | 11-16-2018 | 01-11-2019 |
| 81 | Julian Stadon | Blockchain Aesthetics | University of Hertfordshire | Hertfordshire, UK | Physical | 12-10-2018 | 12-11-2018 |
| 82 | Caroline Vossen, Albertine Meunier | Infinite Skulls | Avant-Galerie Vossen | Paris, France | Physical | 02-07-2019 | 02-11-2019 |
| 83 | NFT.NYC | NFT.NYC | NFT.NYC | New York, USA | Physical | 02-19-2019 | 02-19-2019 |
| 84 | Jennifer & Kevin McCoy | Public Key/Private Key | Whitney Museum of American Art | New York, USA | Physical | 03-05-2019 | 11-04-2019 |
| 85 | Office Impart, Anne Schwanz | Behind the Screen | Kindl Contemporary | Berlin, Germany | Physical | 03-10-2019 | 07-21-2019 |
| 86 | Casey Reas, Iris Long, Carol Sabbadini | a2p | Bitmark | Bitmark, Online | Digital | 04-05-2019 | 04-28-2019 |
| 87 | Rhea Myers | Rare AF 2 | Bushwick Generator | New York, USA | Physical | 05-18-2019 | 05-18-2019 |
| 88 | Jason Bailey, Georg Bak | Automat und Mensch | Kate Vass Galerie | Zürich, Switzerland | Physical | 05-29-2019 | 10-15-2019 |
| 89 | Baden Pailthorpe, Denise Thwaites | Blocumenta | Art Space | Sydney, Australia | Physical | 06-15-2019 | 07-07-2019 |
| 90 | – | iDAF International Digital Art Festival | Federation House | Manchester, UK | Physical | 06-26-2019 | 06-27-2019 |
| 91 | Martin Lukas Ostachowski | Tropopause Contemplation – Blockchain Technology and Inclusive Decentralization | Centre Culturel et Communautaire Françoise-Dunn | Quebec, Canada | Physical | 09-06-2019 | 09-28-2019 |
| 92 | María Paula Fernández, Stina Gustafsson | Crypto Grows on Trees | Devcon V | Osaka, Japan | Physical | 10-08-2019 | 10-11-2019 |
| 93 | – | Strobe Warnings | Dimension Gallery | Cryptovoxels, Online | Digital | 11-01-2019 | Ongoing |
| 94 | Max Osiris | Crypto Art Show | Innerspace Gallery | Los Angeles, USA | Physical | 11-09-2019 | 11-09-2019 |
| 95 | Danky.art | Inaugural Group Show | Dimension Gallery, The Rose Nexus | Cryptovoxels, Online | Digital | 11-11-2019 | Ongoing |
| 96 | Jake Johns, Jamie Ekkens | A New Medium | Zhu Bing Ren Copper Gallery | Shanghai, China | Physical | 11-15-2019 | 11-15-2019 |
| 97 | Jason Bailey, Anne Bracegirdle, Serena Tabacchi | DADA at Late Tate | Tate Modern | London, UK | Physical | 11-29-2019 | 11-29-2019 |
| 98 | – | Kate Vass at CADAF | CADAF, Kate Vass Galerie | Miami, USA | Physical | 12-05-2019 | 12-08-2019 |
| 99 | Anika Meier | Link in Bio: Art After Social Media | Museum der bildenden Künste | Leipzig, Germany | Physical | 12-17-2019 | 03-15-2020 |
| 100 | – | Existence as Protest | Kate Vass Galerie | Zürich, Switzerland | Physical | 03-03-2020 | 06-30-2020 |
| 101 | Coldie | Get Out (While You Stay In) Art Show | Citadel 6.15 | Cryptovoxels, Online | Digital | 03-27-2020 | 03-29-2020 |

| ARTIST(S) INVOLVED | SUGGESTED BY |
|---|---|
| Nicolas Maigret & Maria Roszkowska, Larva Labs, Grayson Earle, Rhea Myers, Kevin Abosch, Ai Weiwei, terra0, Cullen Miller, Gabriel Dunne, César Escudero Andaluz, Martin Nadal, Ed Fornieles, Harm van den Dorpel, Distributed Gallery, Sarah Friend | Studio Robert Alice |
| Tiare Ribeaux, Donald Hanson, Heather Dewey Hagborg, Erik Zepka, Heath Bunting, Pierre Proske, Varvara and Mar, Julian Stadon, Branger_Briz, Rhea Myers, Mez Breeze | Martin Lukas Ostachowski |
| Robbie Barrat, Ronan Barrot | aurèce vettier |
| Larva Labs, Eve Sussman, Beatriz Helena Ramos | Studio Robert Alice |
| Jennifer & Kevin McCoy | Martin Lukas Ostachowski |
| Constant Dullaart, Jonas Lund, !Mediengruppe Bitnik, Gonzalo Reyes Araos, Tristan Schulze, Addie Wagenknecht, Julia Weißenberg | Jonas Lund |
| Casey Reas, Stalgia Grigg, Jeremy Couillard, Kevin McCoy, Kristin McWharter, Dina Kelberman, Chris Coleman, Refik Anadol, Sam Lavigne, DAHN GIM, Allison Parrish, Alejo Duque, Alvaro Lacouture, Santiago Echeverry, Baoyang Chen, Ye Funa, Taeyoon Choi, Cassie McQuater, David Medina, SALIM, Pu Yingwei, LoVid, A.M. Darke, R. Luke Dubois, Golan Levin, Tian Xiaolei, Quiasma, Carmen Gil Vrolijk, Shi Zheng, Chen Zhe, Hye Min Cho, He Zike, Barthélemy Antoine-Lœff, Memo Akten, Lisa Chang Lee, Cao Shu, chenchenchen, Qiu Siyao, Deng Hanbin, Payne ZHU, Chen Zhou, Weiyi Li, linke waco, Xinhao Cheng, Laura Colmenares Guerra, Angela Washko, Sarah Rosalena Brady, aaajiao, Mario Klingemann, flower, Silvia Mangosio, Artificio, Victor David, Animal Charm, Jody Zellen, Antonia Bustamante, Tega Brain, Curime Batliner, Angelo Iannone, Juan Pablo M Begué, Santiago Camargo, Katie Torn, Carol Sabbadini, Sofia Crespo, Marina Zurkow, Siebren Versteeg, Mariela Yeregui, GUO Cheng, Liu Yi, Wa Liu, Iris Long Xingru, WRONG | Casey Reas |
| DADA, SuperRare, KnownOrigin, RadiCards, Snark.Art, Rare Art Labs, OpenSea, Ujo Music, Codex, Bounties Network, Artolin, PixEOS, Larva Labs, Nifty.Supply, Creative Crypto, Bitcorn, Counterparty, Non-Fungible Alliance, Blockchain Art Collective, Furtherfield, CryptoKaiju, Makersplace, BlockCities, Rare Pepe Foundation | Rhea Myers |
| Herbert W. Franke, Gottfried Jäger, Desmond Paul Henry, Nicolas Schöffer, Georg Nees, Manfred Mohr, Roman Verostko, Vera Molnàr, Frieder Nake, Harold Cohen, Gottfried Honegger, Cornelia Sollfrank, John Maeda, Casey Reas, Jared Tarbell, Memo Akten, Mario Klingemann, Manolo Gamboa Naon, Alexander Mordvintsev, Helena Sarin, David Young, Anna Ridler, Tom White, Sofia Crespo, Matt Hall, John Watkinson, Primavera de Filippi, Robbie Barrat, Kevin Abosch, Harm van den Dorpel, Benjamin Heidersberger | Georg Bak |
| Jonas Lund, terra0, Dara Gill, Jess Herrington, Anna Madeleine, Gwen Taualai | Jonas Lund |
| Mario Klingemann, Dejha Ti, Ania Catherin, Reece McDowell, Megan Cowley, Neon, Guy Warley, Peter Bock, Stan Ragets, Yura Miron, Brad Damico, Andres Senn, Gala Mirissa, Greg Fiut, Minju Kim, Graceland, artonymousarti, fakt, HEXOx6C, MuirMcNeil, Serste, Indolestic, Adrian Le Bas, Ophelia Fu, Javier Arrés, Ladislas, Chachignot, Bård Ionson, Brandi Kyle, Paolo Leone, Marko Zubak, Hackatao, Elyse McVicker, Travis LeRoy Southworth, Marquise Sims, onefallart, Charlie Harney, Ernesto Romano, Jake Brukhman, Jsf, Goh Uozumi, Musical Blockchain, Martin Lukas Ostachowski, Coldie, GusGG, Skrew Studio, Somewan, John Luce lockett, Jonathan Lansey, Lee Holland, Stina Jones, BBC Creative, Art with Flo, drewmadestuff, Zyralynn, Sarah Martin, Benjamin lee, daveyjose | Martin Lukas Ostachowski |
| Martin Lukas Ostachowski | Martin Lukas Ostachowski |
| Sarah Friend, Arkadiy Kukarkin, Tarun Chitra, Reese Donohue, Sarah Meyohas, Social Dist0rtion Protocol | Studio Sarah Friend |
| Matt Kane | Matt Kane |
| Max Osiris, Lucho Poletti, Brekkie von Bitcoin, Coldie, Ilan Katin, BlackboxDOTart, Brandi Kyle, Brad Damico, Mattia Cuttini, Oficinas TK | Martin Lukas Ostachowski |
| Connie Digital, Yuma Kishi, William D. Higginson, Ruttger van der Tas, Ryan Seslow +... | Matt Kane |
| ROBNESS, Kendall Rogers, Jake Johns, Pradnya Kapshikar, Jamey Braden, Emma Kearney, An Xu, Yura Miron, Max Osiris, Francesco Casolari, Katharina Lehmann, Ricky Chan, the MLB, Aga Kalhas, Jinwoo Lee, Brad Damico, Lawrence Lee, Andrew Cole, Andrew Francisco, Zhu Ren Bing | Martin Lukas Ostachowski |
| Ophelia Fu, Ilan Katin, Daveed, Simon Wairiuko, Isa Kost, Moxarra González, Javier Errecarte, Otro Captore, Raul Avila, Lissette San Martín, Joe Chiappetta, Boris Z. Simunich, Alex Henry, Serste, Vanesa Stati, Massel Quispe, Mar Espi, Boris Toledo, Marko Zubak, Cromomaniaco, Beatriz Ramos | Studio Robert Alice |
| Jared Tarbell, Memo Akten, Manolo Gamboa Naon, Espen Kluge, Helena Sarin, Desmond, Paul Henry, David Young, Sofia Crespo, Tom White, Cornelia Sollfrank, Larva Labs, Rhea Myers, Ed Fornieles | Rhea Myers |
| Thomas Albdorf, Lisette Appeldorn, Jeremy Bailey, Cibelle Cavalli Bastos, Viktoria Binschtok, Aram Bartholl, Arvida Byström, Nadja Buttendorf, Petra Cortright, Filip Custic, Stine Deja, Marie Munk, Chris Drange, Constant Dullaart, Hannah Sophie Dunkelberg, Anna Ehrenstein, Oli Epp, Séamus Gallagher, Tom Galle, Adam Harvey, Lauren Huret, Johanna Jaskowska, Andy Kassier, Hanneke Klever, Florian Kuhlmann, Lynn Hershman Leeson, Brandon Lipchik, Jonas Lund, Echo Can Luo, Ines Marzat, Jillian Mayer, Florian Meisenberg, Anna K.E., Rosa Menkman, Marisa Olson, Andy Picci, Sebastian Schmieg, Leah Schrager, Kristina Schuldt, Thomas Webb, Selam X, Steffen Zillig | Studio Robert Alice |
| Osinachi | Osinachi |
| Async, Obaki AI, Fractal Encrypt, CryptoMotors, Roses, Age of Chains, Rah Crawford, Avastars, Upheaver, Coldie, Eburgami, Josie, Bigcomicart, JOY, Jason Bailey, Matt Kane, Trevor Jones, Lucho Polleti, Rutger Van Der Tas, n0shot, Jsf, Conlan, DADA, Hackatao, Hex6c, Obvious, Giant Swan, Twisted Vacancy, giselx, ROBNESS, Ekaitza, GusGG, Yonat Vaks, Johnny Dollar, Nelly Baksht, Tom Badley, RYR, Tommy, Ryan Seslow, mlibty, Alotta Money, Sparrow, Pascal Boyart, Pak, Martin Lukas Ostachowski, Shortcut, jivinci, Van, VESA, Opheliafu, Martin Fischer, Espen Kluge, Robbie Barrat, Chief Monkey, Pindar Van Arman, Hackatao, Yura Miron, Primal Cypher, XCOPY | Matt Kane |

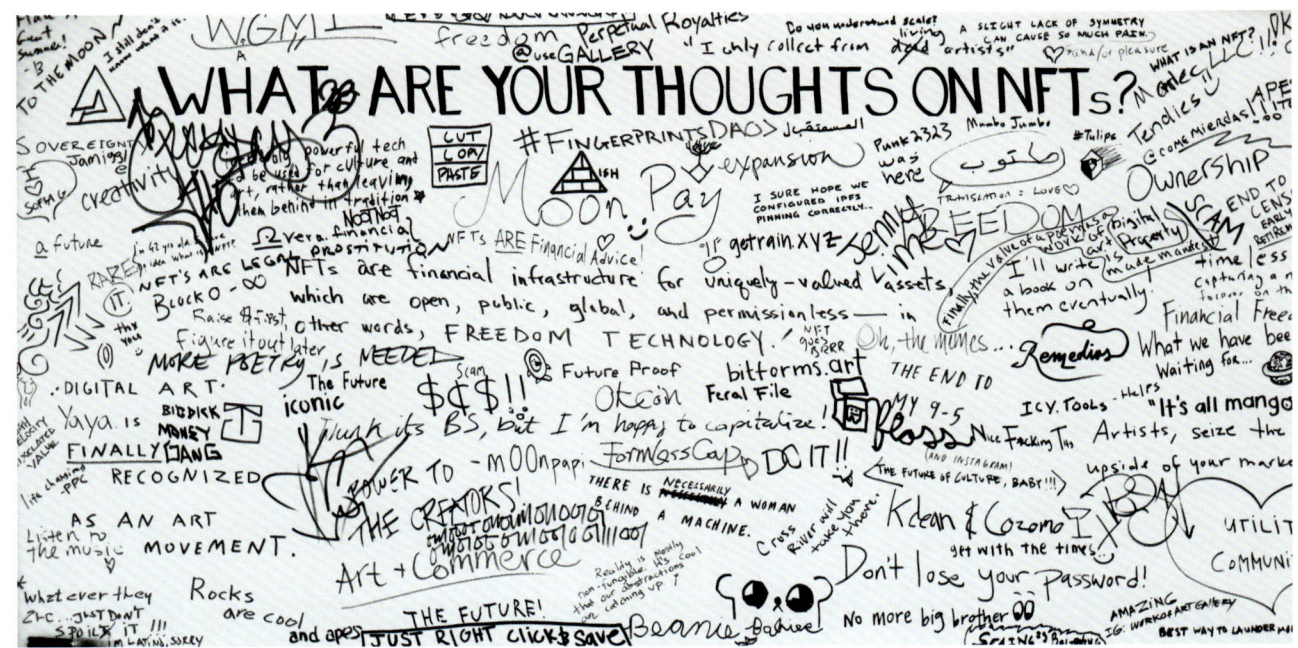

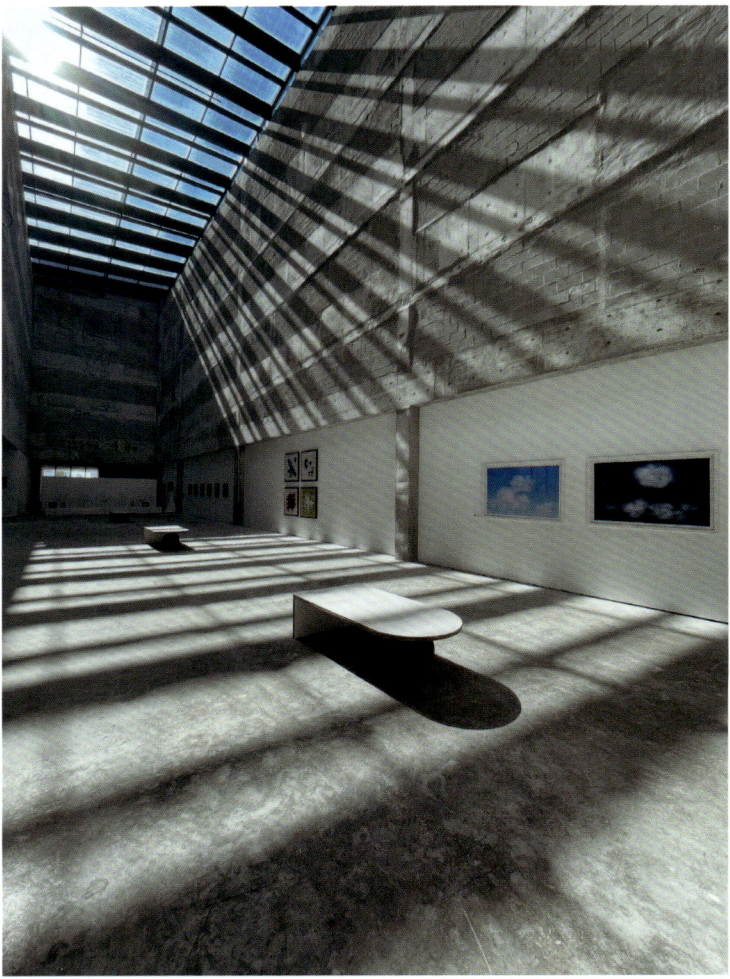

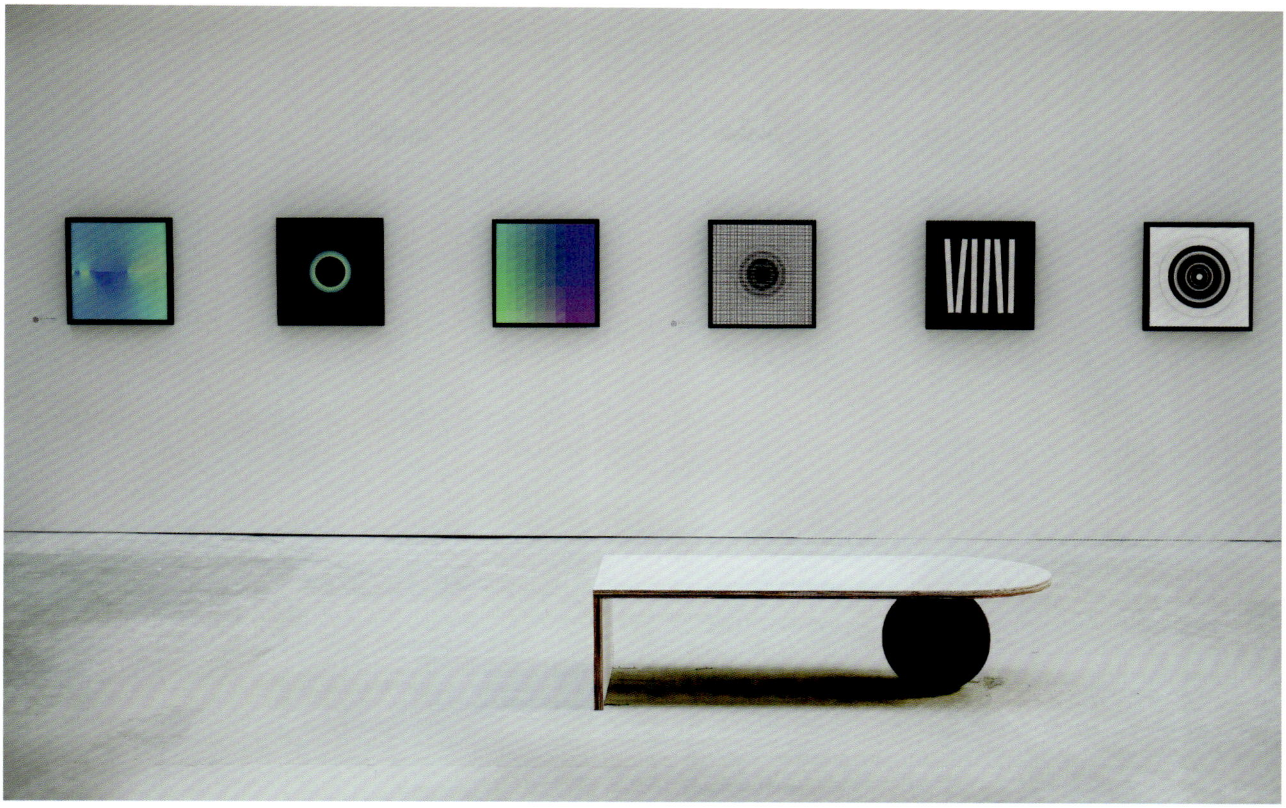

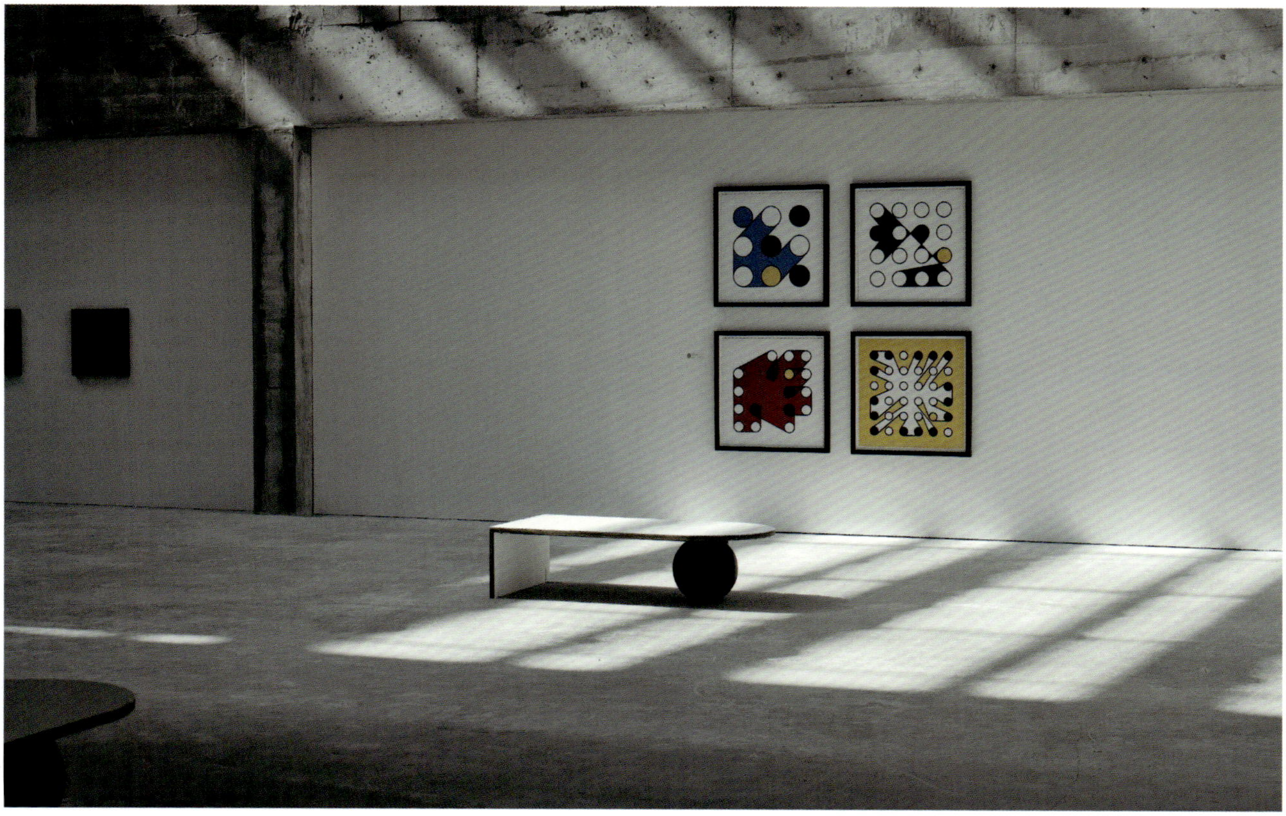

| | CURATOR(S) | EXHIBITION TITLE | INSTITUTION(S)/COMMERCIAL | LOCATION | TYPE OF EVENT | OPEN DATE | END DATE |
|---|---|---|---|---|---|---|---|
| 102 | Faith Holland, Lorna Mills, Wade Wallerstein | Well Now WTF! | Silicon Valet | Online | Digital | 04-04-2020 | Ongoing |
| 103 | SuperRare | SuperRare Birthday Party | SuperRare SpaceStation | Cryptovoxels, Online | Digital | 04-24-2020 | 05-23-2020 |
| 104 | BI Xin, CAO Jiamin | Crypto Manifold | Chronus Art Centre | Shanghai, China | Physical | 06-27-2020 | 10-10-2020 |
| 105 | Angie Taylor | SHE ART | London Gallery | Cryptovoxels, Online | Digital | 09-11-2020 | Ongoing |
| 106 | – | Block 21 (42.36433° N, -71.26189° E) | Christie's, Async Art | Christie's New York, USA; Online | Physical / Digital | 10-01-2020 | 10-06-2020 |
| 107 | Eleonora Brizi | Renaissance 2.0 2.0 | Complesso Museale | Rome, Italy | Physical | 10-20-2020 | 10-30-2020 |
| 108 | Lindsay Howard | Collect Digital Art | Foundation | Foundation, Online | Digital | 10-27-2020 | No Record |
| 109 | Herman Marigny IV, Brandon Bailey, Martel Campbell, Kris Stith, Micheal McElveen, Andre "Angie C" Chandler, Alexys Taylor, Stephanye Watts, Cee Sando, Ameer Carter, Jason Woodberry, Micah Johnson, Lady Phoenix, Tiffany Heacock, Markisha Allen, Mariah Scott, Cuy Sheffield, Michael J. Ewing, Toye Adenekan | Beyond Provenance: Speculative $Black Futures on the Blockchain | One / Off | Cryptovoxels, Online | Digital | 12-28-2020 | Ongoing |
| 110 | Caroline Vossen | From Tulip to Crypto Daisy | L'Avant Galerie Vossen | Paris, France | Physical | 01-09-2021 | 05-01-2021 |
| 111 | Sats Moon | Future Art – An Immersive Rare Digital and Crypto Art Show | Paddington Town Hall | Sydney, Australia | Physical | 01-15-2021 | 01-17-2021 |
| 112 | World of Women, Codegreen, Dani Ton | Women & Climate | SuperRare, World of Women, Code Green, World Economic Forum Group Auction | SuperRare, Digital Auction of Davos, Online | Digital | 01-24-2021 | 01-24-2021 |
| 113 | Serena Tabacchi, Marie Chatel | Abstract Art in the Age of New Media | Museum of Contemporary Digital Art, University College London, Hobs3D | Online | Digital | 02-08-2021 | 03-09-2021 |
| 114 | Ry David Bradley, Hanna Hansdotter | Once Twice | The Hole, SuperRare | New York, USA; Decentraland, Online | Physical / Digital | 02-19-2021 | 03-28-2021 |
| 115 | – | EVERYDAYS: THE FIRST 5000 DAYS | Christie's, Makersplace | Christie's, Online | Digital | 02-25-2021 | 03-11-2021 |
| 116 | Makersplace, Universe Contemporary, WOCA, DADA | Venus of Metaverse | Zardoz Gallery, Studio Pearl, One BC Galleries, Joy Multiplication, Perla Gallery, Narra Gallery, ChiccArt, Tara Digital Collective | Cryptovoxels, Decentraland, Artsy, Online | Digital | 03-13-2021 | 04-04-2021 |

| ARTIST(S) INVOLVED | SUGGESTED BY |
|---|---|
| A Bill Miller, Ad Minoliti, Adrienne Crossman, Alex McLeod, Alice Bucknell, Alma Alloro, Ambar Navarro, Andres Manniste, Anne Spalter, Anneli Goeller, Anthony Antonellis, Antonio Roberts, Ben Sang, Benjamin Gaulon, Bob Bicknell-Knight, Carla Gannis, Casey Kauffmann, Casey Reas, Cassie McQuater, Chiara Passa, Chris Coleman, Chris Collins, Cibelle Cavalli Bastos, Claudia Bitran, Claudia Hart, Clusterduck Collective, Daniel Temkin, Devin Kenny, Morgan Green, Diego Ortega, Don Hanson, Dominic Quagliozzi, Elektra KB, Ellen.Gif, Eltons Kuns, Emilie Gervais, Emily Mulenga, Erica Lapadat-Janzen, Erica Magrey, Erin Gee, Eva Davidova, Eva Papamargariti, Everest Pipkin, Exonemo, Faith Holland, Felt Zine, Francoise Gamma, Graham Akins, Guido Segni, Hannah Neckel, Haydiroket, Hyo Myoung Kim, Ian Bruner, Jan Robert Leegte, Janet.40, Jason Isolini, Jazmin Jones, Jenson Leonard, Jeremy Bailey, Jillian McDonald, Juan Covelli, Kamilia Kard, Katherine Sultan Erminy, Keiken, George Jasper Stone, Kid Xanthrax, LaJuné McMillian, Laleh Mehran, LaTurbo Avedon, Laura Gillmore, Laura Hyunjhee Kim, Lauryn Siegel, Libbi Ponce, Lilly Handley, Lior Zalmanson, Lorna Mills, LoVid, Mara Oscar Cassiani, Mark Dorf, Mark Klink, Maurice Andresen, Maya Ben David, Miguel Martin, Molly Erin McCarthy, Molly Soda, Mohsen Hazrati, Nicolas Sassoon, Nicole Killian, Off Site Project, Olia Svetlanova, Olivia Ross, Ophélie Demurger, Pastiche Lumumba, Peter Burr, Petra Cortright, Pinar Yoldas, Rachel Rossin, Rafia Santana, Rah Eleh, Rick Silva, Rita Jiménez, Rodell Warner, Rosa Menkman, Ryan Kuo, Ryan Trecartin, Santa France, Sara Ludy, Sebastian Schmieg, Shana Moulton, Shawné Michaelain Holloway, Snow Yunxue Fu, Solimán Lopez, Surabhi Suraf, Stacie Ant, Sydney Shavers, Terrell Davis, Theo Triantafyllidis, Tiare Ribeaux, Tobias Williams, Travess Smalley, Tyler Kline, Wednesday Kim, Will Pappenheimer, Yidi Tsao, Yoshi Sodeoka, Ziyang Wu | Studio Robert Alice |
| XCOPY +... | Matt Kane |
| !Mediengruppe Bitnik, CHEN Baoyang, Simon Denny, Grayson Earle, Sarah Friend, Marija Bozinovska Jones, Paul Kolling, Max Hampshire, Paul Seidler, Matthias Tarasiewicz, Lina Theodorou, Rhea Myers | Rhea Myers |
| Josie Bellini, Liza Grace, thesarashow, Vyannka, Vanesa Stati, mel duARTE, BlackBoxDotArt, Gala Mirissa, Daira, CrypticFauna, Miss Al Simpson, Silje Thorn, VK Crypto, CECHK, kristyglas, Indrani Mitra, Stina Jones, Lapin Mignon, Etta Tottie, Combugnera, Hivemindlife, Cicatriciebaci, thebadlament, Kitty Bast, Marah Gemx, Bárbara Bezina, Giselx, Angie Taylor, oculardelusion, Stellabelle, Vivienne Scardovelli, Jilt, LUVRWorldwide, y0b, Mehak Jain, Ann Ahoy, Heresy, daniella_doodles, placeofmany, squirterer, Aksana Zasinets, Lulu xXX, Inês Merino, Mafj, Margaretza Rosswarth, blacksneakers, BrightLight, Nelly Baksht, Katy Arrington, soulinearte, Camo L | Studio Robert Alice |
| Robert Alice | Studio Robert Alice |
| Ai Weiwei, Ania Catherine, Dejha Ti, Sofia Crespo, Dada, Richard Garet, Giant Swan, Hackatao, Matt Kane, Amay Kataria, Lili & Honglei, Penelope, Ben Snell, Maria Svarbova, Jennifer A. T. Tran, Jason Yung, The Jade Project | Studio Robert Alice, Eleonora Brizi |
| Serwah Attafuah, Jon Burgerman, Zach Lieberman, Pearlyn Lii, Jonathan Monaghan, Signe Pierce, Sarah Zucker | Serwah Attafuah |
| Yanga, Jourdaine Graffie, Jaheel Dowdy, Vakseen +... | Studio Robert Alice |
| Allbi, Bananakin, Robbie Barrat, Ronan Barrot, Louise Belin, Bleh, Fernando Botero, Bady Dalloul, Jade Dalloul, DataDada, Norman Harman, Denis Laget, Prosper Legault, Lulu xXX, Albertine Meunier, Denis Monfleur, Mona Oren, Paul Rebeyrolle, Anna Ridler, ROBNESS, Milène Sanchez, Sylvie Tissot | Studio Robert Alice |
| FEWOCiOUS, XCOPY, Twisted Vacancy, Miss AL Simpson, Sarah Zucker, neurocolor, ROBNESS, LuluxXX, Burst, Wrong Bedroom, Neon, Gary Cartlidge, Max Osiris, Norman Harman, msp4rrow, Hexosis, X89, PI Slices | Studio Robert Alice |
| Alexa Meade, Amber Vittoria, Donglu Yu, Elise Swopes, Inna Modja, izzako, lanadenina, marjan, Serwah Attafuah, Shavonne Wong, Yam K, zhuk | Serwah Attafuah |
| Banz & Bowinkel, Robbie Barrat, Maurice Benayoun, Gordon Berger, Mathieu Merlet-Briand, Mattia Cuttini, Damjanski, Brendan Dawes, Chris Dorland, Snow Yunxue Fu, Shohei Fujimoto, Darcy Gerbarg, Gibson / Martelli, Kjetil Golid, Bård Ionson, Joanne Hastie, Markos Kay, Mario Klingemann, Arnaud Laffond, Sara Ludy, Manfred Mohr, Casey Reas, Alex Reben, Aaron Scheer, Yoshi Sodeoka, Harrison Willmott, David Young | Martin Lukas Ostachowski |
| Ry David Bradley, Hanna Hansdotter | Martin Lukas Ostachowski |
| Beeple | Studio Robert Alice |
| Mar E, Dawnia Darkstone, Flavia Ceccarelli, Helena Sarin, Iren Lesik, SorrellCK, Marina Victoria, Ruth Allen, Jessica Esch, Claire Noelle, Grace Ng, Ina Vare, Juliette Grimaldi, LUVRworldwide, Moyosore Briggs, Orla in Berlin, Stina Jones, Ceren Yuzgul, Luisa Espiñeira, Nadia Forkosh, Myra, lulu xXX, squirterer, Inês Merino, Amber Vittoria, Anna Zhilyaeva, Shu Lea Cheang, Katy Arrington, black sneakers, Vision Vandal, Silvana Delbo, Hackatao, Eleven, Cyber Shakti, Shin Oh, Ruth Allen, Isa Kost, Barbara Tosti, Serste, Cristiana Vettor, Vanesa Stati, Beryl Bilici, Gala Mirissa, Alexandra Rubio, Greta Brat, Hola Lou, Nika Danny, Gerdana Neis, Pirate Sheep, Blanca Gervilla Martinez, AfrOdita, The Cetacean Goddess, Veronika Vajdova, Kristy Glas, Kitty Bast, BlackBoxDotArt, Maria Garcia, Beatriz, Sparrow, Stellabelle, Thebadlament, Angie Taylor, Kristy Glas, Laura Bench, CrypticFauna, lesCogumelos, hairofmedusa, Gerdana Neis, Karen Frances Eng, Mehak Jain, Mrs Kitols, Alena, EM!, Laura Camellini, Kathrina Rupit, Beryl Bilici, Jenny Mandl, Eko, Orabelart, Claire Silver, Veronika Vajdova, Bárbara Bezina, Cryptoyuna, Voke, Indrana Mitra, Maria Menshikova, Yana Tselinki, Dunja Jung, Abbey Orsler, Tansie Stephens, Sofia Ramirez, Ann Ahoy, Angel, Ally Grimm, Alejandra Her, Lapin Mignon, Sarah PU51FLY, Joëlle, Tosca, Melyjta, artonomous, Luna Ikuta, Sarah Zucker, Orfhlaith Egan, Alejandra Herrera, Valentina Loffredo, Mahima Chaudhury, Kristy Glas, Shirley Gong, Hilal Yasti | Studio Robert Alice |

**11.09**
DADA at Tate Late, Tate Modern,
London, United Kingdom, 2019

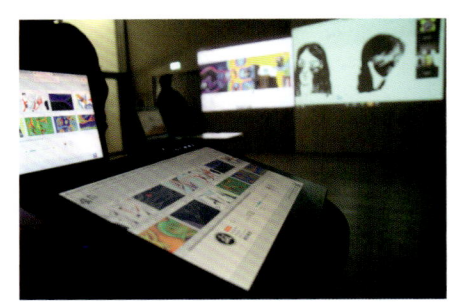

| | CURATOR(S) | EXHIBITION TITLE | INSTITUTION(S)/COMMERCIAL | LOCATION | TYPE OF EVENT | OPEN DATE | END DATE |
|---|---|---|---|---|---|---|---|
| 117 | Jonathan Goodman | High on Collage | Trigonal Gallery | Artsy, Online | Digital | 03-16-2021 | 04-19-2021 |
| 118 | Silicon Valet | Believe in Us But Not Too Much | New Art City | Online | Digital | 03-17-2021 | Ongoing |
| 119 | Greg Mike | Chain Reaction | ABV Gallery | Atlanta, USA | Physical | 03-20-2021 | 03-28-2021 |
| 120 | – | THE ARTIST IS ONLINE | König Galerie | Berlin, Germany; Decentraland, Online | Physical / Digital | 03-21-2021 | 04-21-2021 |
| 121 | Casey Reas | Social Codes | Feral File | Online | Digital | 03-24-2021 | Ongoing |
| 122 | Ed Zipco | Season One Starter Pack | Superchief Gallery | New York, USA | Physical | 03-25-2021 | 05-25-2021 |
| 123 | Sun Bohan | Virtual Niche: Have You Ever Seen Memes in the Mirror? | UCCA Lab | Beijing, China | Physical | 03-26-2021 | 04-04-2021 |
| 124 | Wade Wallerstein | Pieces of Me | Transfer Gallery, Left.Gallery | Online | Digital | 04-01-2021 | Ongoing |
| 125 | Aaron Mulligan, Lucía Rodríguez | Crystal Tokyo | JuiceBox | Online | Digital | 04-04-2021 | Ongoing |
| 126 | Daniel Heiss, Margit Rosen | CryptoArt It's Not About Money | ZKM Centre for Art and Media | Karlsruhe, Germany | Physical | 04-07-2021 | 07-18-2021 |
| 127 | Max Moore | The Fungible | Sotheby's, Nifty Gateway | Nifty Gateway, Online | Digital | 04-12-2021 | 04-14-2021 |
| 128 | gmoney | Pixelated | SaveArtSpace | Miami, USA | Physical | 04-12-2021 | 05-10-2021 |
| 129 | Simonida Pavicevic | Matter and Form | HOFA Gallery, Rarible, KnownOrigin, MarkersPlace | London, UK | Physical / Digital | 04-29-2021 | 05-29-2021 |
| 130 | Kenny Schachter | Breadcrumbs: Art in the Age of NFTism | Galerie Nagel Draxler | Cologne, Germany | Physical | 05-12-2021 | 08-21-2021 |
| 131 | Lady PheOnix | Proof of Sovereignty | Christie's | New York, USA | Physical | 05-25-2021 | 06-03-2021 |
| 132 | Mila Askarova | .ext | Gazelli Art House | London, UK | Physical | 05-26-2021 | 07-01-2021 |
| 133 | Du Xiyun, Qin Jianqin | A Realistic Shocking of the Virtual Authenticity | CryptoArt.Ai | Shanghai, China | Physical | 05-29-2021 | 06-06-2021 |
| 134 | John Anderson | DigitWork – NFTs – Is It Art? | DigitWork | Online | Digital | 06-01-2021 | Ongoing |
| 135 | Robert Alice, Max Moore, Michael Bouhanna | Natively Digital | Sotheby's | London, New York, Hong Kong, Online | Physical / Digital | 06-03-2021 | 06-10-2021 |

**11.10**
Installation views of
*Breadcrumbs: Art in the age
of NFTism*, curated by Kenny
Schachter, Nagel Draxler,
Cologne, Germany, 2021

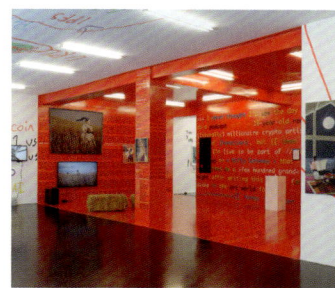 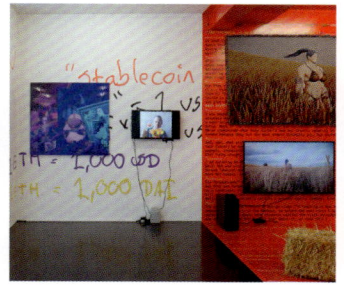 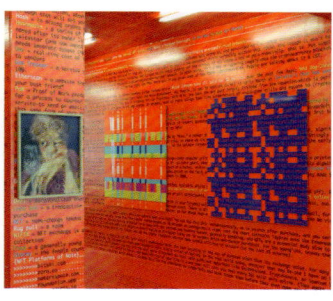

| ARTIST(S) INVOLVED | SUGGESTED BY |
|---|---|
| Jesse Lappin | Studio Robert Alice |
| Adrian Pijoan | Studio Robert Alice |
| Aches, Alex Ness, Baiege, Ben Johnston, Blake Kathryn, Crankdat, Fvckrender, Gmunk, Greg Mike, Lucas Beaufort, Matt Gondek, Michael Reeder, MRE, Nychos, Persue, Serial Looper, Six N Five, Steven Baltay, Victor Mosquera, Wolfdog | Studio Robert Alice |
| Olive Allen, LaTurbo Avedon, Giulia Banz, Friedemann Bowinkel, Ry David Bradley, Damjanski, Maja Djordjevic, Ben Elliot, Rachel de Joode, Keiken, Nik Kosmas, Mario Klingemann, Zach Lieberman, Jonas Lund, Andy Picci, Manuel Rossner, Kenny Schachter, Aaron Scheer, Emma Stern, Anne Vieux, Addie Wagenknecht, Thomas Webb, John Yuyi | Jonas Lund |
| Andrew Benson, Dmitri Cherniak, LIA, Raven Kwok, Anna Carreras, Manolo Gamboa Naon, Maya Man, Frederik Vanhoutte, Saskia Freeke, Dave Whyte | Casey Reas, Studio Robert Alice |
| Swoon, Ondrej Zunka, Ellen Sheidlin, Saturno, Clams Casino, Lauren YS, Ron English, Daniel Johnston, Clutter, JJ Villard, Lourdes Leon, FaithXLVII, Sarah Nicole Francois, Em.1t, Justin Aversano, Alex Schaffer, Princess Nokia, Hood By Air, James Jirat Patradoon, Hoxxoh, Equinox, 1010, Mashkow, Logan Hicks, Synchrodogs, Ahol Sniffs Glue, Mat Brown, Ho99o9, Ruby 9100M, Aerosyn Lex Maestrovic, Nick Eays, Devin Oktar Yalkin, Moon Patrol, Yuen Hsieh, Snipe1, NudeRobot, Lionolin, Ghostshrimp, Francesco Lo Castro, C.Finley, Voja, Ka5sh, Jason Ebayer, Pol Kurucz, Julian Llouve, To The Moon, Ian Valentine, Vyle, Nusi Quero, Axel Void, Vague Sadan, Will Carsola, El Popo Sangre, David Heo, 404.zero, Robert Seven Connett, Baghead, Flavio Carvalho, Radimir, Gian Galang, Sickid, Robot Moonjuice, Entes93, Sho Konishi, Chrome Destroyer, Coby Kennedy, Dondi, Falreng, Newk3d, Lilkool, Boldtron +... | Studio Robert Alice |
| Alida Sun, Alotta Money, Artonomous, Bronwyn Lundberg, Beeple, Tiger Cai, Baoyang Chen, Ellwood, Celyn Bricker, Dabeiyuzhou, deadmau5, Mad Dog Jones, FEWOCiOUS, Hipworth, CryptoZR, June Liu, Maalavidaa, Marble Mannequin, Mario Klingemann, mbsjq, Pak, Refik Anadol, Reva, Robbie Barrat, Robert Alice, Sun Bohan, Suryanto, Sun Yitian, Wu Jianan, Wang Weisi, Creators of First Supper (Alotta Money, Blackboxdotart, Coldie, Connie Digital, Hackatao, Josie Bellini, Matt Kane, Mlibty, Rutger van der Tas, Shortcut, TwistedVacancy, VansDesign, XCOPY) | Studio Robert Alice |
| Ryan Kuo, LaJuné McMillian, Krist Wood, Cassie McQuater, Olia Svetlanova, Tiare Bibeaux, Jody Stillwater, Casey Kauffmann, Mark Sabb, Devon Moore, Laturbo Avedon, Danielle Braithwaite-Shirley, Claudia Mate, Stacie Ant, Faith Holland, Serwah Attafuah, Alice Yuan Zhang, Carla Gannis, Aaajiao, Lorna Mills, Kumbirai Makumbe, Auriea Harvey, Eva Papamargariti, E. Jane, Wednesday Kim, Francoise Gamma, Sara Ludy, Theo Triantafyllidis, Molly Soda, Fakeshamus, Marisa Olson, Keiken, Lawrence Lek, Moreshin Allahyari, Zach Blas, Alfredo Salazar-Caro, Travess Smalley, Kim Laughton, Claudia Hart, Julieta Gil, Isaac Kuraki, Rafia, Sydney Shavers, Rick Silva, Rosa Menkman, Olivia McKayla Ross, QianQian Ye | María Paula Fernández |
| Nichole Shinn, Serwah Attafuah, Laura Noguera, Erykah Townsend, Lucía Rodríguez, Kasey Edgerton, Adina Glickstein, Eric Edvalson, Evelyn Haupt, Julianne Aguilar, Zak Alexander Rose, Lois Hopwood | Serwah Attafuah |
| Bryan Brinkman, Daniel Calderon, Dmitri Cherniak, Jeff Davis, Gerard Ferrandez, Guile Gaspar, Kjetil Golid, John Watkinson, Matt Hall, Aaron Penne, Erick Snowfro, and Hideki Tsukamoto | Studio Robert Alice |
| Pak | Studio Robert Alice |
| Larva Labs | Studio Robert Alice |
| Gregory Siff, Jan Kaláb, Vladinsky, Zhuang Hong-Yi, Jason Sims, Romina Ressia, Katya Zvereva, Loribelle Spirovski, Bran Symondson, Mary Ronayne, Chris Lizarraga, Ilhwa Kim, Marie Soliman, Noman, Aleksandr P, Derrick Santini, Darian Mederos | Studio Robert Alice |
| Kevin Abosch, Olive Allen, Darren Bader, Eva Beresin, Tracey Emin, Sarah Friend, Rulton Fyder, Rhea Myers, Osinachi, Max Osiris, DotPigeon, Anna Ridler, ROBNESS, Koichi Sato, Kenny Schachter, Theo Triantafyllidis | Rhea Myers |
| Nam June Paik, Jenny Holzer, Ash Thorp, Auriea Harvey, Urs Fischer, Gucci, Jeron Braxton, Raf Grassetti, Gmunk, Joshua Davis, Gerald Laing, Tamiko Thiel, Claudia Hart, Coin Artist, Josie Bellini, Ix Shells | Studio Robert Alice |
| Brendan Dawes, Claudia Hart, Tupac Martir | Brendan Dawes, India Price |
| Beeple, Pak, Hackatao, Ouchhhh, Marcelo Cantu, Max Mao, Jon Noorlander, Suryanto, Jonathan Nash, Andreas, chmiel_art, marc0matic, Shindo, yellosesame, Charles Cheong, CornelSwoboda, etienecraus, Glass Crane, mbsjq, Zhang Huan, Aimo Yang, VJ Elephant, Song Ting, Wang Ke, Xin Qi | Studio Robert Alice |
| Daniel Ambrosi, John Anderson, Sean Mick, Anne Spalter, Matt Kane, James Fox, Richard Garet, Burst | Matt Kane |
| Kevin McCoy, Rhea Myers, Art Blocks, Pak, Larva Labs, Robert Alice, Ryoji Ikeda, Simon Denny, Anna Ridler, Mario Klingemann, LaJuné McMillian, Don Diablo, Sarah Zucker, Lethabo Huma, Serwah Attafuah, Fvckrender, Oseanworld, XCOPY, Mad Dog Jones, Ikaro Cavalcante, Brendan Dawes, Casey Reas, Sara Ludy, Addie Wagenknecht, Terra0, Matt Kane, Justin Aversano | Jeff Davis |

**11.11**
Installation views of *Proof of Art: A Brief History of NFTs*, curated by Jesse Damiani, Fabian Müller, and Markus Reindl, Cryptovoxels and Francisco Carolinum, Linz, Austria, 2021

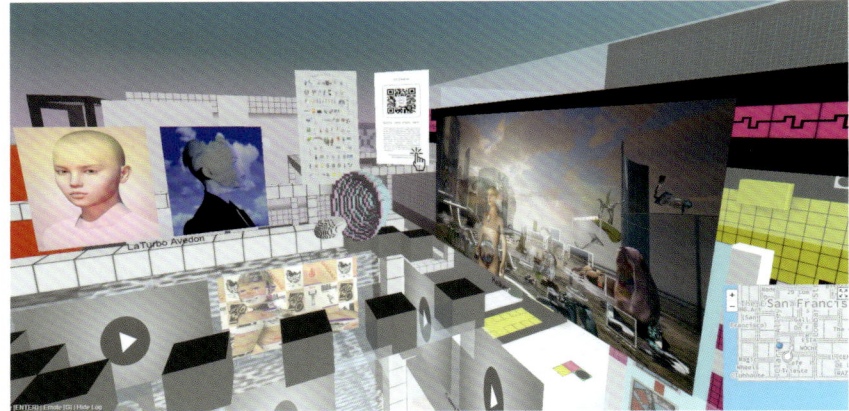

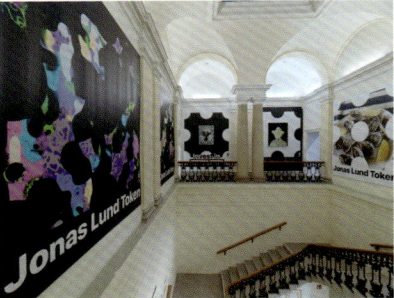

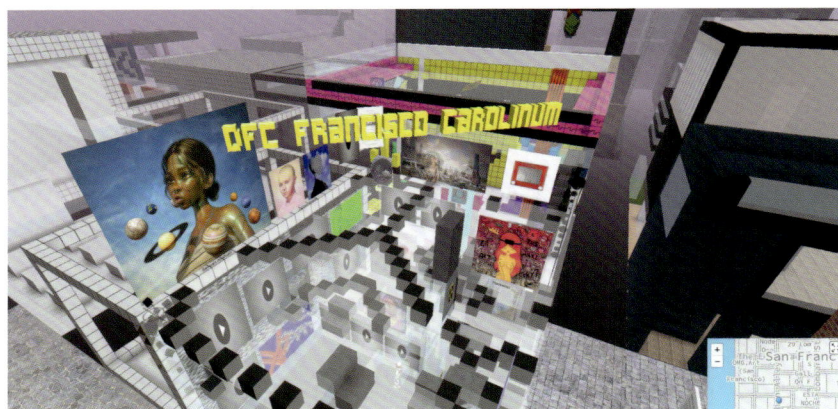

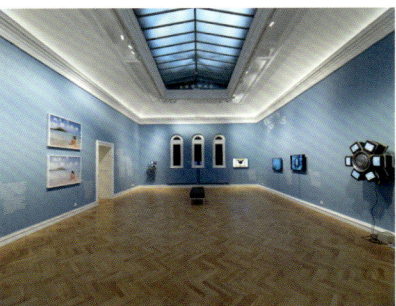

**11.12**
Installation view of *Pixelated*, curated by SaveArtSpace, Miami and New York, United States, and London, United Kingdom, 2021

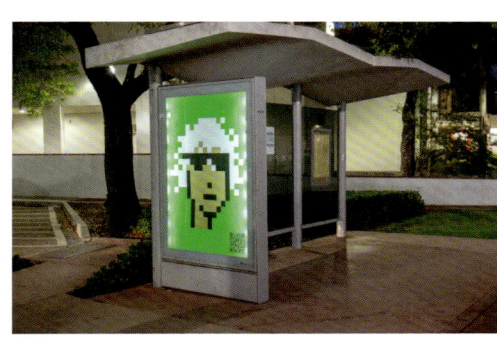

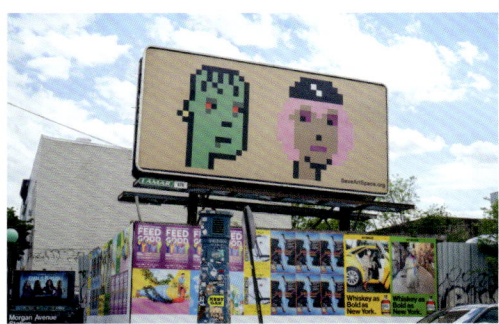

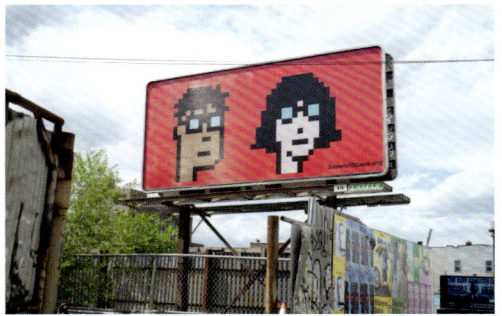

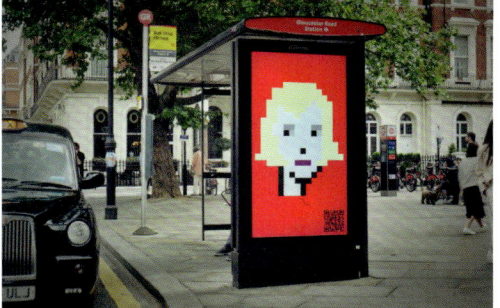

**11.13**
Installation views of *NFT: Poétiques de l'immatériel: du certificat à la blockchain*, curated by Marcella Lista and Philippe Bettinelli, Centre Pompidou, Paris.
Exhibition features selections from the museum's collection, announced February 2023.

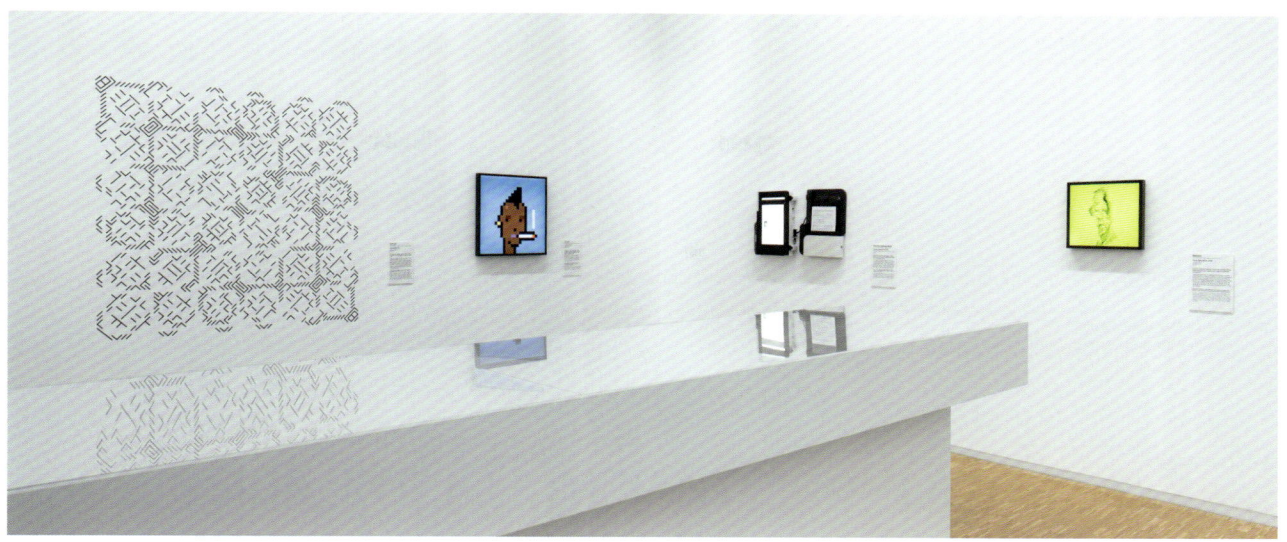

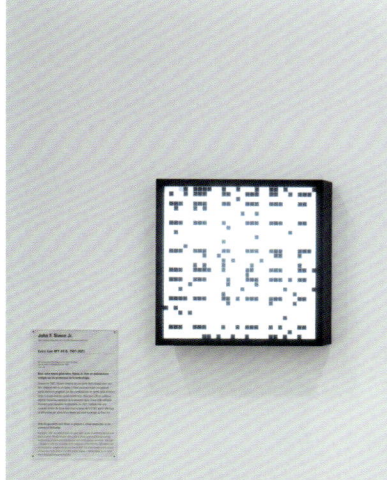

## NFT
### Poétiques de l'immatériel
### du certificat à la blockchain

Cette présentation réunit l'ensemble des œuvres relatives à la blockchain qui ont été récemment acquises par le Musée national d'art moderne. Elle reflète la diversité des cultures artistiques qui est le propre du paysage du Web3, croisant les champs de l'art numérique, du crypto art et d'un art contemporain qui aborde les particularités de l'économie décentralisée.

Associant un certificat d'authenticité et un registre comptable dans une « chaîne de blocs » numérique sécurisée, le NFT (ou jeton non fongible) semble répondre aux interrogations posées dès le 20ᵉ siècle par l'authentification et la circulation d'œuvres immatérielles. Ce support de diffusion et de transaction est devenu en quelques années l'objet de réflexions artistiques précises, où s'exposent nouvellement les imbrications de l'art et de l'économie. Certains artistes adoptent la technologie dite *on-chain* en codant l'œuvre à même la chaîne de blocs du NFT, défi qui s'inscrit dans la continuité des expérimentations de l'art génératif. Chez d'autres, le NFT pointe vers une œuvre numérique autonome, ou *off-chain*.

Les stratégies critiques des artistes ici exposés touchent aux formes masquées de la finance, à l'écologie, au droit d'auteur, à la fabrication artificielle de la rareté à l'ère du numérique, à la critique institutionnelle. Un choix d'œuvres et de documents du siècle passé – certificats, protocoles et leurs détournements – leur fait écho, témoignant d'une riche lignée de réflexions conceptuelles quant aux cadres juridique et économique des œuvres immatérielles.

## NFT
### Poetics of the immaterial
### from certificates to blockchains

This presentation brings together all the blockchain-related works recently acquired by the Musée national d'art moderne. It reflects the diversity of artistic cultures that is specific to the landscape of Web3, blending digital art, crypto art and contemporary art that deals with the particularities of the decentralised economy.

Combining a certificate of authenticity and an accounting ledger in a secure digital "blockchain", NFTs (or Non Fungible Tokens) seem to respond to the questions raised since the 20th century concerning the authentication and circulation of immaterial works. In just a few years, these supports for dissemination and transaction have become the subject of precise artistic reflections in which the interweaving of art and the economy are newly exposed. Some artists adopt the technology known as "on-chain" by coding the work to the NFT blockchain, a challenge that forms part of the ongoing experiments of generative art. For other, NFTs point toward an autonomous or "off-chain" digital work.

The critical strategies of the artists exhibited here relate to the masked forms of finance, to ecology, copyright, the artificial fabrication of rareness in the digital era, and institutional critique. It is reflected in a choice of works and documents from the last century – certificates, protocols and their reappropriation – testifying to a rich line of conceptual thought with regard to the legal and economic frameworks of immaterial works.

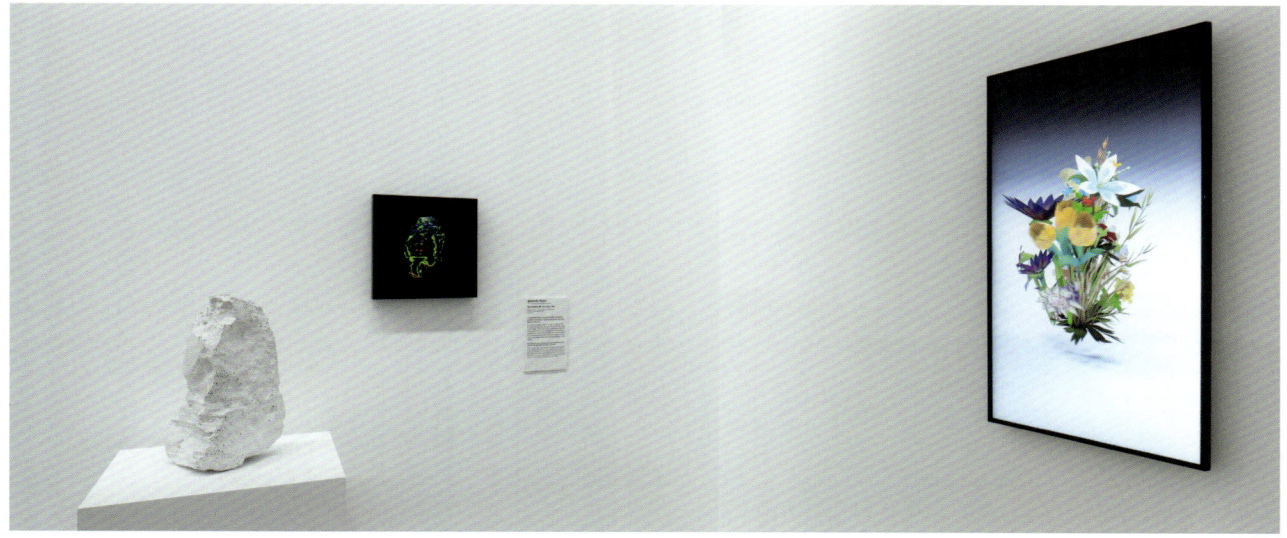

**11.14**
Installation view of *Venus of the Metaverse*, curated by Makersplace, Universe Contemporary, WOCA, and DADA, Online, 2021

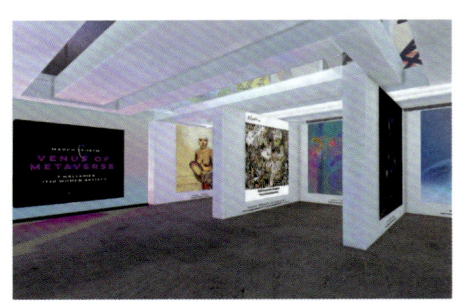

| | CURATOR(S) | EXHIBITION TITLE | INSTITUTION(S)/COMMERCIAL | LOCATION | TYPE OF EVENT | OPEN DATE | END DATE |
|---|---|---|---|---|---|---|---|
| 136 | Jesse Damiani, Fabian Müller, Markus Reindl | Proof of Art: A Brief History of NFTs | Francisco Carolinum | Linz, Austria | Physical / Digital | 06-11-2021 | 09-12-2021 |
| 137 | Outland art | Freeport | Epoch Gallery | Online | Digital | 06-12-2021 | 10-01-2021 |
| 138 | Diana Sinclair | The Digital Diaspora | Superchief Gallery | New York, USA | Physical | 06-18-2021 | 06-20-2021 |
| 139 | – | CryptOGs: Pioneers of Crypto Art | Bonhams, SuperRare | Bonhams, Online | Digital | 06-21-2021 | 06-30-2021 |
| 140 | – | Salon Solaire | Suns.Works | Zürich, Switzerland | Physical | 06-21-2021 | 08-08-2021 |
| 141 | Ryan Stanier | The Other Art Fair Los Angeles | ROW DTLA | Los Angeles, USA | Physical | 06-24-2021 | 06-27-2021 |
| 142 | Matt Kane | Share The Light I: A Pop-Up Roof Exhibition | Matt Kane Personal Collection | Cryptovoxels, Online | Digital | 06-24-2021 | Ongoing |
| 143 | Blockchain Art Exchange | CrypTOKYO | UltraSuperNew Gallery | Tokyo, Japan | Physical | 06-26-2021 | 07-22-2021 |
| 144 | Rick Silva | Fragments of a Hologram Rose | Feral File | Feral File, Online | Digital | 06-29-2021 | Ongoing |
| 145 | Crypto Art Week Asia | Crypto Art Week Asia | Crypto Art Week Asia | Berlin, Germany; Singapore; Osaka, Tokyo, Japan; Seoul, South Korea; Hong Kong; Hangzhou, China; Decentraland, Cryptovoxels, Second Life, Somnium Space, Cyber, Online | Physical / Digital | 07-09-2021 | 07-17-2021 |
| 146 | Louis Ho | Only Losers Left Alive (Love Songs for the End of the World) – Part One | YEO Workshop | Singapore | Physical | 07-10-2021 | 07-31-2021 |
| 147 | Christopher Clary, Pearlyn Lii | NFS NSFW NFT | New Inc, Rhizome, New Art City | Online | Digital | 07-15-2021 | Ongoing |
| 148 | Anika Meier, Johann König | ON THIS DAY | König Galerie | Berlin, Germany; Decentraland, Online | Digital | 07-18-2021 | 08-27-2021 |
| 149 | Max Kulchinsky | MetaPhysical | DorDor gallery | New York, USA | Physical / Digital | 07-23-2021 | 07-24-2021 |
| 150 | Ali Sabet | Stratosphere NFT Art International | STRATOSPHERE DAO | Beijing, China | Physical / Digital | 07-24-2021 | 08-02-2021 |
| 151 | JPG | Deep Time | JPG Protocol | Online | Digital | 07-28-2021 | No Record |
| 152 | Cheng Xue, REVA | NFT ART WEEK | Neal Digital, Stratosphere DAO | Beijing, China | Physical | 07-31-2021 | 08-06-2021 |

**11.15**
Installation view of *Natively Digital: A Curated NFT Sale*, curated by Robert Alice and Sotheby's, Decentraland (Soho 52,83), 2021

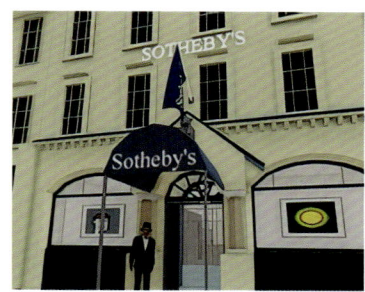

**11.16**
Installation views of Robert Alice's *Block 34 (51.895167° N, 1.4805° E) (2019–)*, Principality of Sealand, 2021

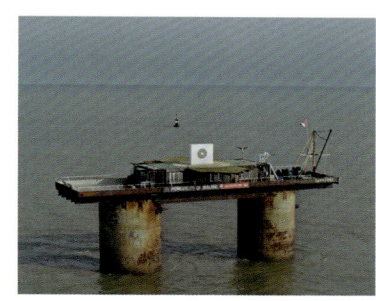

| ARTIST(S) INVOLVED | SUGGESTED BY |
|---|---|
| !Mediengruppe Bitnik, Kevin Abosch, Ai Wei Wei, Refik Anadol, Nancy Baker Cahill, Blake Kathryn, Cryptowiener, Simon Denny, Harm van den Dorpel, Constant Dullaart, Primavera de Filippi, Finest Rares (Jason Rosenstein), Herbert W. Franke, Sarah Friend, Fvckrender, Keiken, Larva Labs, Lynn Hershman Leeson, Nili Lerner, Jonas Lund, Marjan Moghaddam, Sarah Meyohas, Rhea Myers, Nam June Paik, Anna Ridler, Mark Sabb, Terra0, Claudia Hart, Addie Wagenknecht, Sasha Katz, Gisel X Florez, CryptoYuna, Helena Sarin, kyt, lulu xXX, Flufflord, VXN, Joaquina Salgado, Serwah Attafuah, Krista Kim, Ix Shells, Grimes x Mac, Hackatao, LaTurbo Avedon, REEPS100, Trung Bao, Ness Nissla, kai, Chris Torres, Coldie, Alexander Reben, Olive Allen, Mario Klingemann, SIRSU, Robert Alice, Robert Gallardo, Casey Reas, Hideki Tsukamoto, Kenny Schachter, Matt Kane, Carlos Marcial, Keiken | Studio Robert Alice |
| Neïl Beloufa, Sarah Rosalena Brady, Alice Bucknell, Juan Covelli, Alexandra Koumantaki, Amanda Ross-Ho, Hirad Sab | Brian Droitcour |
| blacksneakers, Dada Boipelo, Em0n33y, Ix Shells, Jae, Kai Morton, LATASHÁ, JAH., Lomedia, LUZ, Lyonna Lyu ::, Nicholas-Constantine Cephas, Moonsundiamond, Serwah Attafuah, Moyosore Briggs, tyl000rd, Yosnier +… | Studio Robert Alice |
| Coldie, XCOPY, Matt Kane, Sarah Zucker, Osinachi, Alotta Money, Miss Al Simpson, Mattia Cuttini, Janne | Matt Kane |
| Brigham Baker, Bonnie Camplin, Sarah Friend, Raphael Hefti, Paulo Kapela, Mickael Marman, Luigi Ontani, Tabitha Swanson, Una Szeemann | Studio Sarah Friend |
| Jessica Carranza , Ricardo Cobian, Aaron Haxton, Abby Masoumi, Abby Elizabeth, Adrien Saporiti, Alejandro Áboli, Alex Selkowitz, Amanda Flowers, Anna R. Wingfield, Boris Giulian +… | Matt Kane |
| Brandon Walsh, Vida Vakil, Tierras Raras, JABean, Martin Lukas Ostachowski, xibot, Obxium, Colin.eth, Skeen, Corrosive, Second Realm, Ann Ahoy, Maxwell Step, Les Dore, rabanheidr, sgt_slaughtermelon, MaxXx Osiris, Jay Delay, shaollin shoppe, Ilan Katin, Maria Garcia, BigComicArt, Shortcut, Artnome, Bård Ionson, ROBNESS, VESA, SamJ, Moxarra Gonzalez, Godfrey Meyer, Stina Jones, Rutger van der Tas, Thato, UrBen, DAHNKE, Barbara Tosti, Sparrow, Phulusho, Panther Xita, Larence Lee, Helena Sarin, artonymous artifakt, abysms, oficinastk, Rhyolight, Norman Harman, Manards, twoclicks, Miss Al Simpson, Paulius Uza, Lipsmak, jivinci | Matt Kane |
| Yasumasa Yonehara, Tetsuzo Okubo, Ichi Hatano, Maxim, Beeple, ROBNESS, Botchy-Botchy +… | Martin Lukas Ostachowski |
| Andrew Thomas Huang, Brandon Blommaert, Ido Radon, Kim Laughton, kyttenjanae, Lawrence Lek, Nate Boyce, Peter Burr, Rosa Menkman, Sabrina Ratté, Sara Ludy | Lawrence Lek |
| NUMOMO, radarboy3000, Mantravine, Mischief Makers, Faris Nasir, Rare Scrilla +… | Studio Robert Alice |
| Chok Si Xuan, Mark Chua, Lam Li Shuen, Hamkah Latib, Victoria Hertel, Paradise Now, Sarah Isabelle Tan, Brandon Tay, XUE | Christina J. Chua |
| Itziar Barrio, Christopher Clary, Johanna Flato, Nahee Kim, Pearlyn Lii, Mark Ramos, Lula Mebrahtu, Ricardo Miranda Zúñiga, Bhavik Singh, Yeseul Song, Ziyang Wu | Brian Droitcour |
| Jonas Lund | Jonas Lund |
| blacksneakers, Sean Williams, Noah Kocher, mew.psd, Soulo Saint, Sophie Sturdevant, Squibs, Bobbi Cai, Dillon ATM, Max Kulchinsky | Martin Lukas Ostachowski |
| Abbey orsler, Abdulla BinHindi, Aghdas Karbassi, Ah-Yun Chae, Ahmed Arfeen, Aimua Ogboghodor, Ain Namseo +… | Martin Lukas Ostachowski |
| Kevin Abosch, Alexis André, Jason Bailey, Robbie Barrat, 0xDEAFBEEF, Elena Dorfman, Harm van den Dorpel, Micah Johnson, Tywen Kelly, Larva Labs, Sara Ludy, Mad Dog Jones, Ezra Miller, Helena Sarin, Anne Spalter, Clement Valla, Sarah Zucker | María Paula Fernández |
| Ali Sabet, Mr. Misang +… (500+) | Studio Robert Alice |

**11.17**
Installation views of Sam Spratt's *The Monument Game*, presented by 1of1, at the Docks Cantiere Pietro Cucchini, Venice, April 17–June 21, 2024

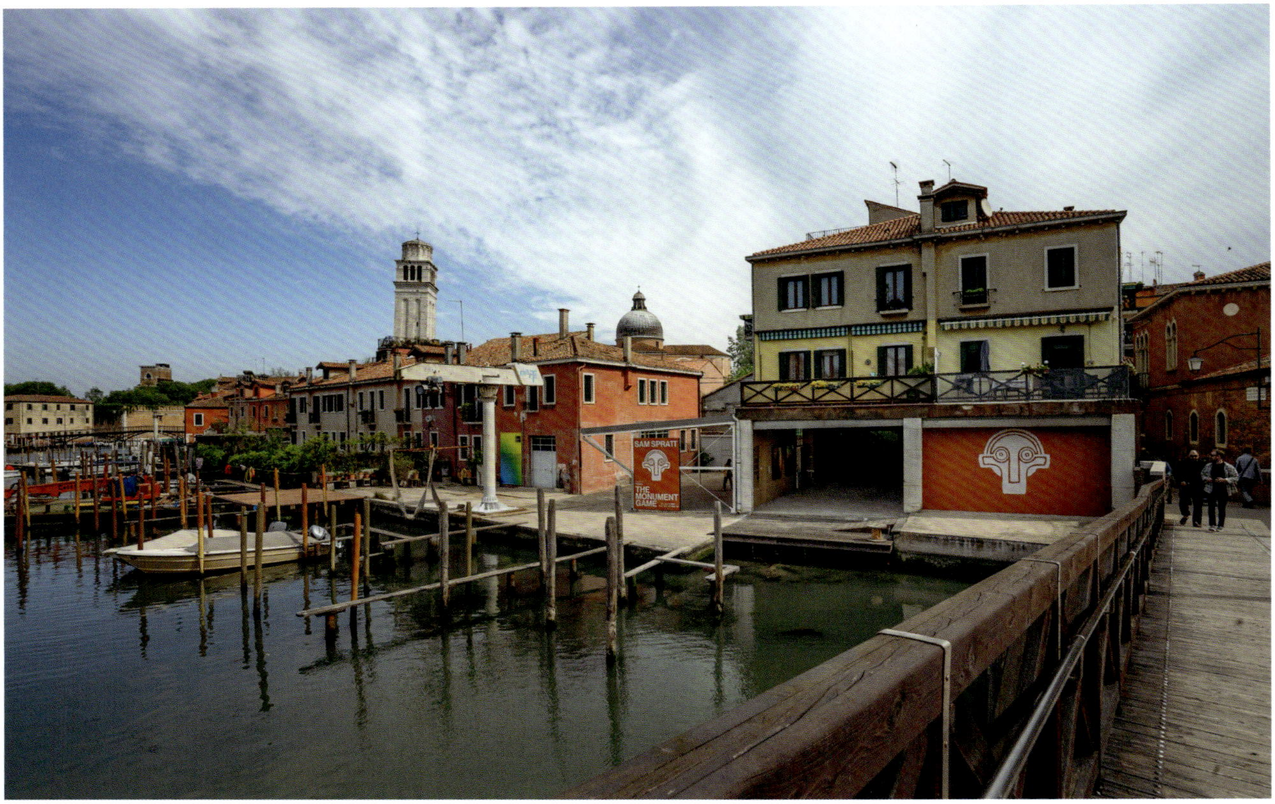


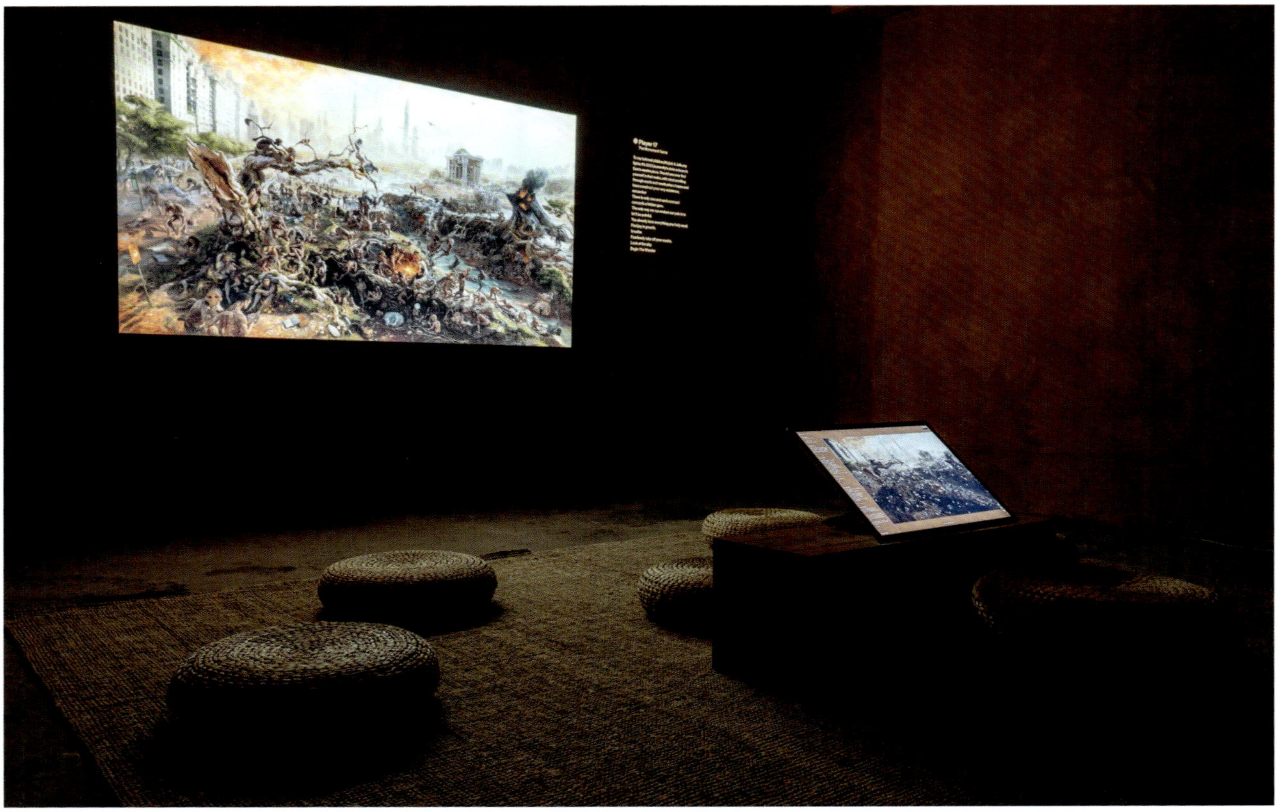

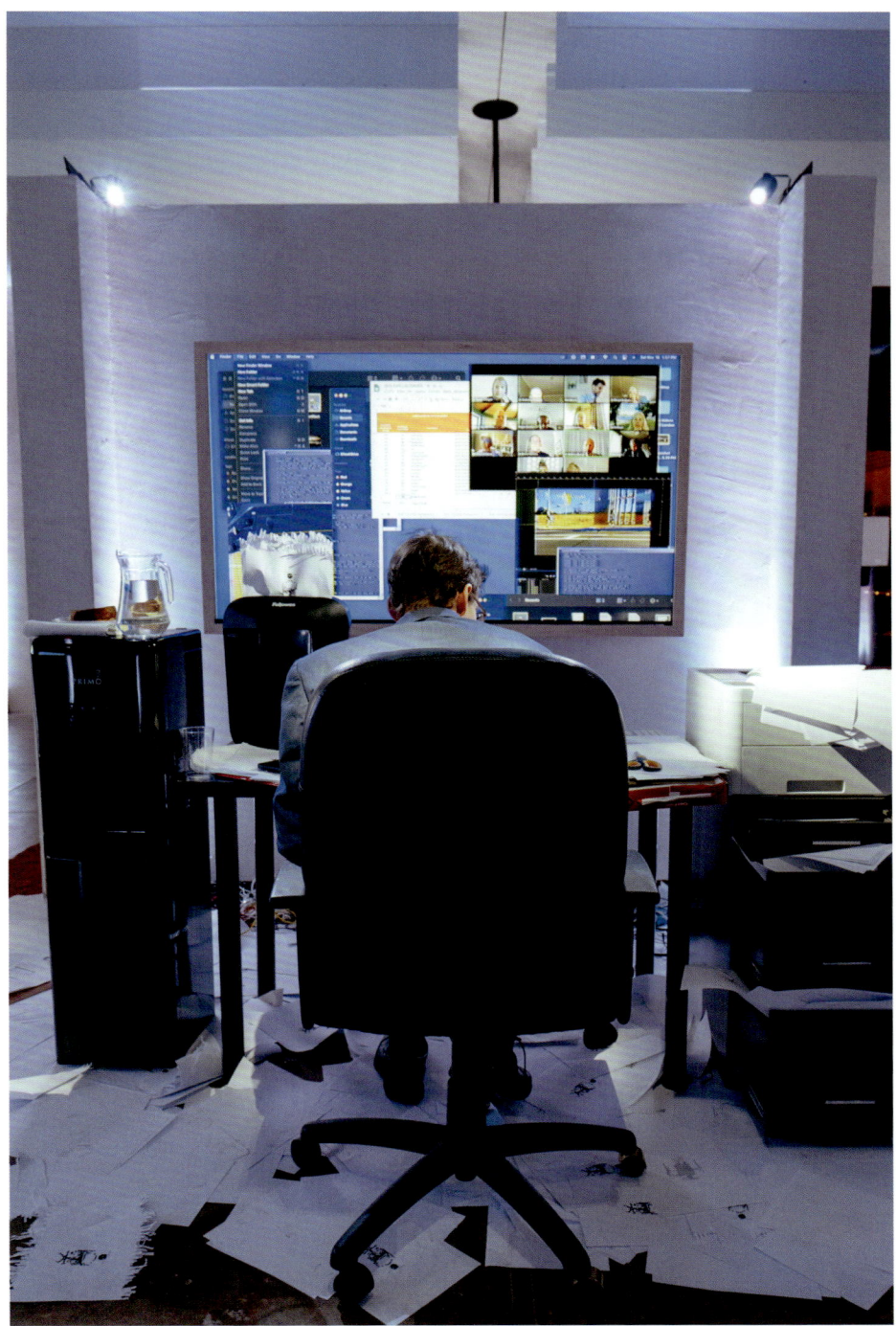

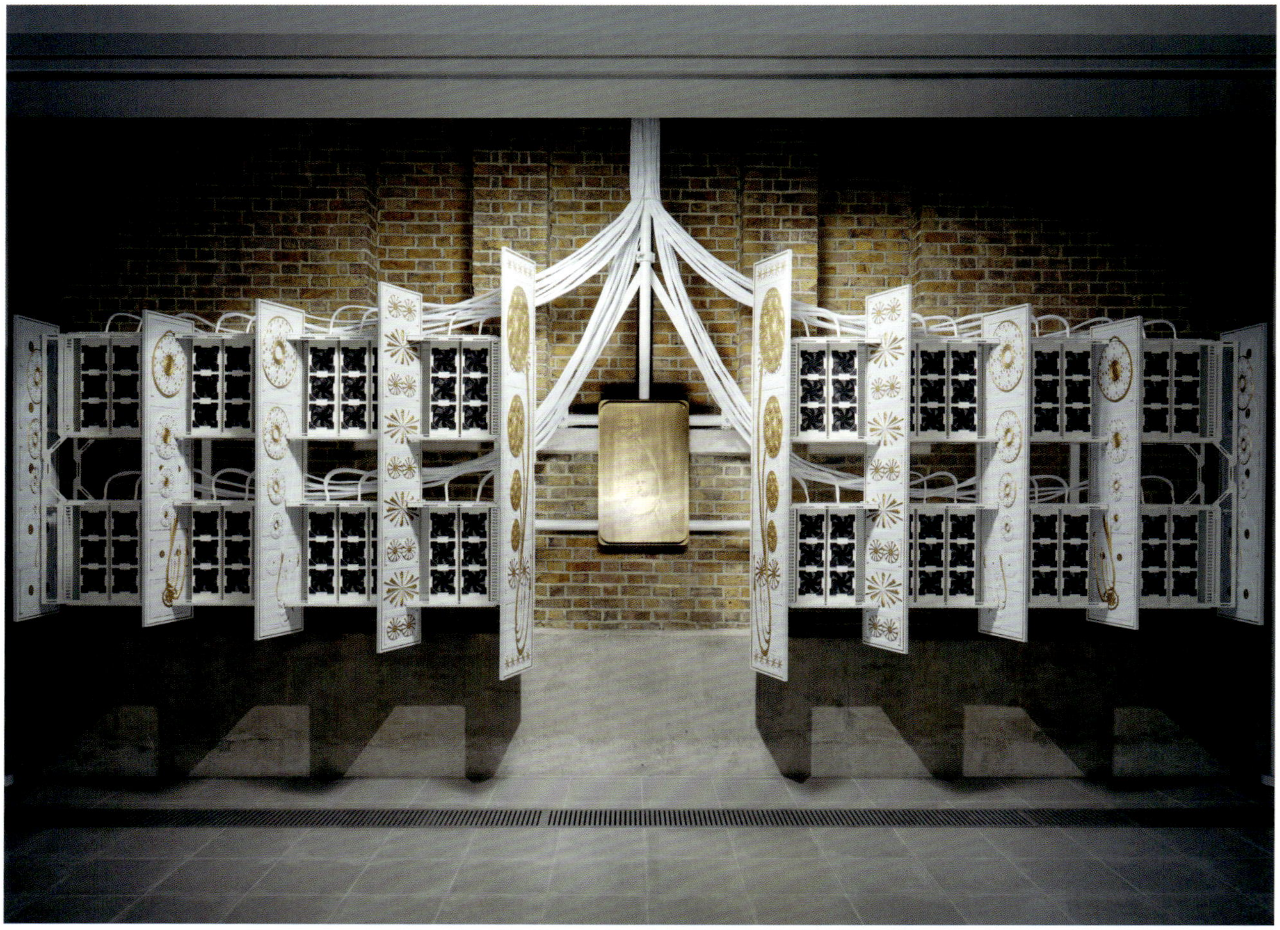

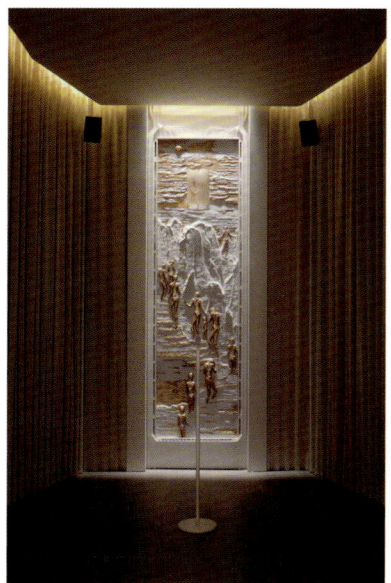

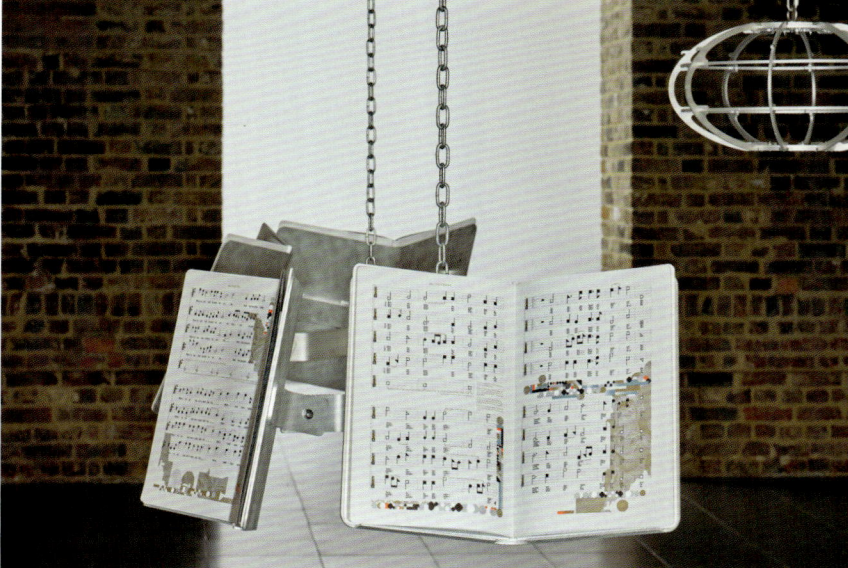

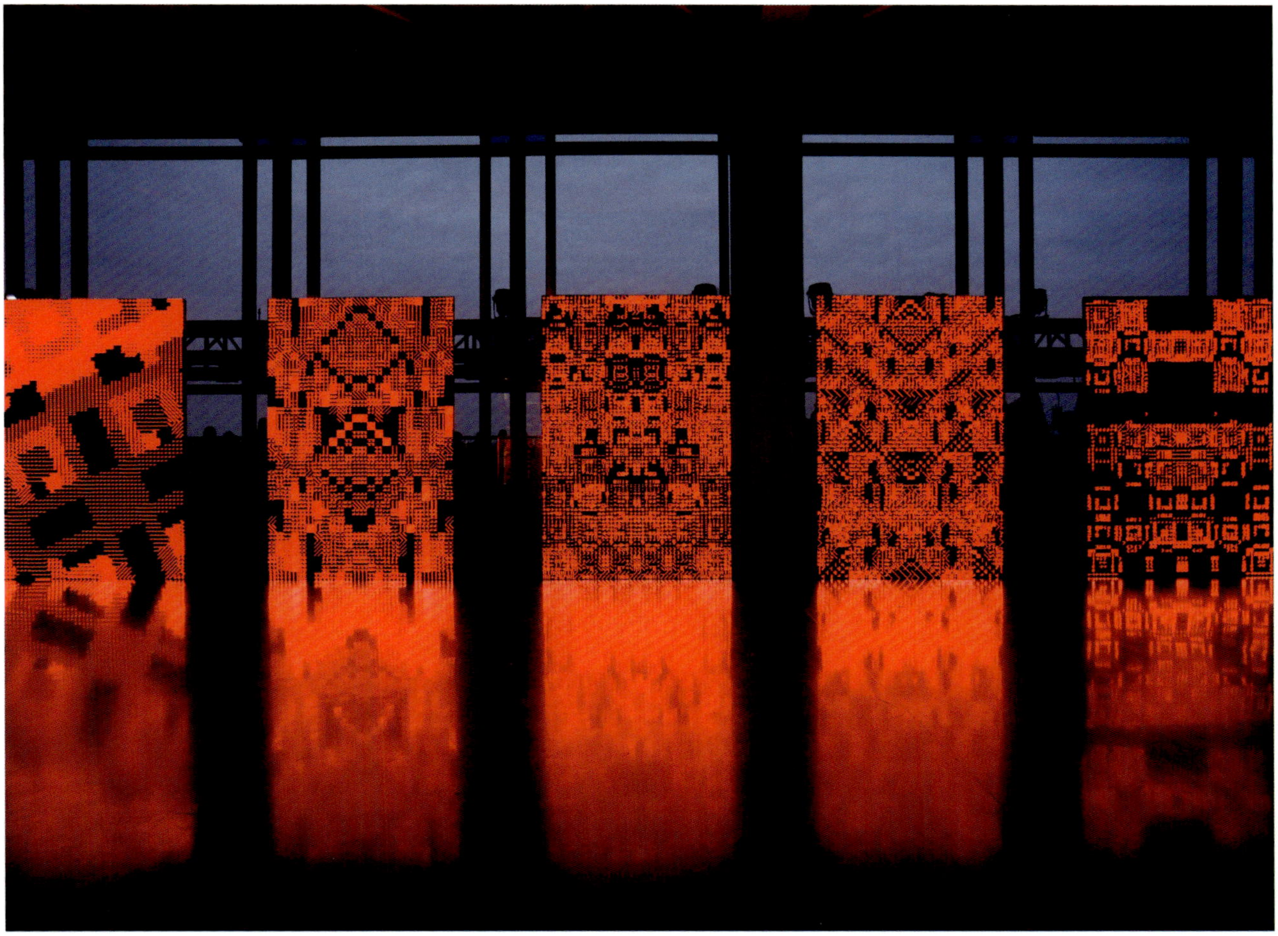

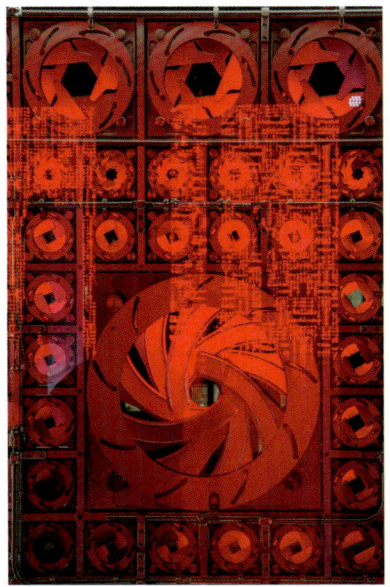

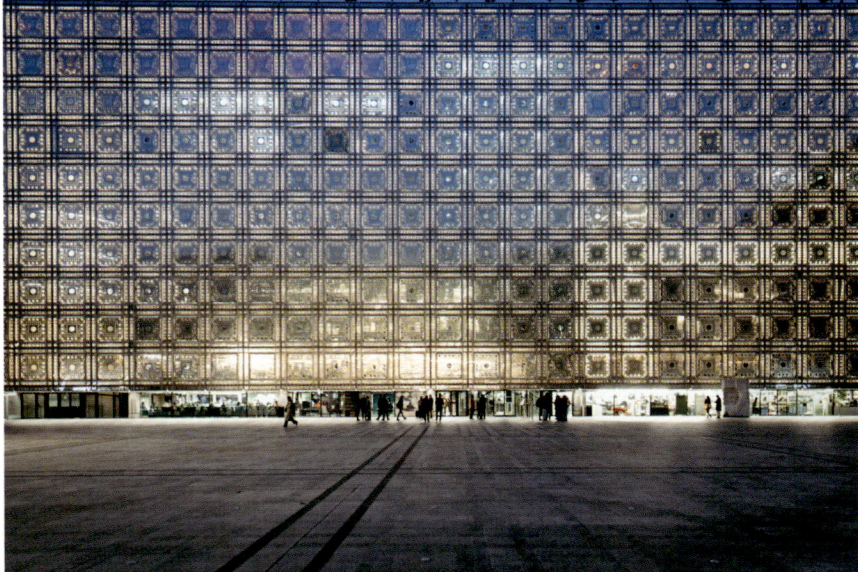

| | CURATOR(S) | EXHIBITION TITLE | INSTITUTION(S)/COMMERCIAL | LOCATION | TYPE OF EVENT | OPEN DATE | END DATE |
|---|---|---|---|---|---|---|---|
| 153 | Louis Ho | Only Losers Left Alive (Love Songs for the End of the World) – Part Two | YEO Workshop | Singapore | Physical | 08-07-2021 | 08-29-2021 |
| 154 | Danielle Paterson | Non-Fungible Bodies: Modified, Adorned, Digitized | Postmasters Blockchain Gallery | New York, USA | Physical | 08-22-2021 | 08-25-2021 |
| 155 | Simon Denny | Proof of Stake – Technological Claims | Kunstverein in Hamburg | Hamburg, Germany | Physical | 09-04-2021 | 11-14-2021 |
| 156 | Kenny Schachter | NFTism: No Fear in Trying | Unit London | London, UK | Physical | 09-11-2021 | 09-25-2021 |
| 157 | – | Contingent Systems | Illingworth Kerr Gallery | Calgary, Canada | Physical | 09-16-2021 | 11-20-2021 |
| 158 | Kenny Schachter | Crypto Kiosk at Art Basel | Galerie Nagel Draxler | Basel, Switzerland | Physical | 09-21-2021 | 09-26-2021 |
| 159 | Robert Alice | Portraits of a Mind | Sealand | Principality of Sealand | Physical | 09-25-2021 | 09-28-2021 |
| 160 | Mintverse, Neal Digital | Generative Art and the Future | Poly China (Auction house) | Shenzhen, China | Physical | 09-26-2021 | 09-27-2021 |
| 161 | Max Moore, Michael Bouhanna | Machine Hallucinations – Space – Metaverse | Sotheby's | Hong Kong | Physical / Digital | 09-30-2021 | 10-04-2021 |
| 162 | Bitforms Gallery | A Generative Movement | Bitforms Gallery | San Francisco, USA | Physical | 10-02-2021 | 02-05-2022 |
| 163 | Daria Borisova | Different Shades of Water | 1-54, Christie's | London, UK | Physical | 10-05-2021 | 10-19-2021 |
| 164 | Filippo Lorenzin | Liminal Territories | pal project | Paris, France | Physical | 10-05-2021 | 11-20-2021 |
| 165 | Anika Meier, Johann König | Global Gallery | König Galerie, Porsche | New York, USA; Seoul, South Korea; Tokyo, Japan; Madrid, Spain; Berlin, Germany | Physical | 10-07-2021 | Ongoing |
| 166 | Eleonora Brizi | Beyond the Void: Hakatao, Fontana | Ca' la Ghironda Museum in Collaboration With Zanini Art Gallery | Bologna, Italy | Physical | 10-17-2021 | 11-14-2021 |
| 167 | Hiroki Yamamoto | NFT in the History of Contemporary Art | SBI Art Auction | Tokyo, Japan | Physical | 10-30-2021 | 10-30-2021 |
| 168 | Postmasters gallery | Gas Station | Postmasters Blockchain Gallery | New York, USA; Online | Physical / Digital | 11-01-2021 | 11-03-2021 |
| 169 | Neal Digital | CAFA NEAL Lab Global NFT Art Global | CAFA, Neal Digital | Beijing, China | Physical | 11-01-2021 | 01-02-2022 |
| 170 | Osinachi, Maurica Chapot, Ayo Lawson | "RÉLOADING..." | ART X Lagos, SuperRare | Lagos, Nigeria; SuperRare, Online | Digital | 11-04-2021 | 11-21-2021 |
| 171 | NFT.NYC | GN NFT | NFT.NYC | New York, USA | Physical | 11-04-2021 | 11-04-2021 |
| 172 | Ali Sabet | META MENA | Emergeast, Known Origin | Online | Digital | 11-07-2021 | Ongoing |
| 173 | Clara Peh | Right Click + Save | Le Freeport Singapore | Singapore, Online | Physical / Digital | 11-07-2021 | 11-14-2021 |
| 174 | Dimitri Ozerkov, Anastasia Garnova | The Ethereal Aether | Hermitage Museum | St. Petersburg, Russia; Online | Digital | 11-10-2021 | 12-10-2021 |
| 175 | Shen Ruijun, Marie Martraire, Shona Mei Findlay | If Time Is Money, Are ATMs Time Machines | Kadist, Golden Eagle Art Museum | Nanjing, China | Physical | 11-10-2021 | 03-08-2022 |
| 176 | Ellen Xu | Shenzhen NFT Art Week | Neal Digital | Shenzhen, China | Physical | 11-17-2021 | 11-22-2021 |
| 177 | Alexis de Bernede, Marius Jacob-Gismondi | Opus Sectile, from hard stone marquetry to aurèce vettier | Darmo Art | Paris, France; Online | Physical / Digital | 11-17-2021 | 12-19-2021 |

| ARTIST(S) INVOLVED | SUGGESTED BY |
|---|---|
| Georgette Goh, Geraldine Lim, Juria Toramae, Masuri Mazlan, Samuel Xun, Sarah Isabelle Tan, Mark Chua, Lam Li Shuen, Victoria Hertel | Christina J. Chua |
| Araya, Julia Brunson, Gregory Coscia, John Novotny, Emily Omesi, Haley Peacock, Murrie Rosenfeld | Christina J. Chua |
| Robert Alice, Mel Chin, Joshua Citarella, Simon Denny, Fang Di, Stephanie Dinkins, DISNOVATION, Sarah Friend, Isa Genzken, Holly Herndon, Mathew Dryhurst, Femke Herregraven, Mike Kelley, Josh Kline, Paul Kolling, Agnieszka Kurant, James Luna, Karamia Müller, New Red Order (Zack Khalil, Adam Khalil, Jackson Polys), Yuri Pattison, Timur Si-Qin, Jaune Quick-to-See Smith, Krista Belle Stewart, Paul Thek, Luke Willis Thompson, Prateek Vijan, Beecoin | Simon Denny |
| Jermey Olson, Caio Tombly, Rewind Collective, Olive Allen, Ix Shells +... | Studio Robert Alice |
| FRAUD (Francisco Gallardo, Audrey Samson), Sarah Friend, LA Birdwatchers (Suzanne Kite, Aljumaine Gayle, Nicholas Shapiro, Ladan Mohamed Siad), Helen Knowles, Lauren Lee McCarthy, Anna Ridler, Stephanie Syjuco, ZZYW | Studio Sarah Friend |
| Kevin Abosch, Olive Allen, Sarah Friend, Osinachi, DotPigeon, Anna Ridler, Kirsi Mikkola, Kenny Schachter, Theo Triantafyllidis | Studio Robert Alice |
| Robert Alice | Studio Robert Alice |
| Brendan Dawes, Gene Kogen, Moses, REVA, Baiwei, Cindy Ng, Sun Yuqian +... | Brendan Dawes |
| Refik Anadol | Refik Anadol |
| Refik Anadol, Daniel Canogar, LIA, Rafael Lozano-Hemmer, Manfred Mohr, Casey Reas, Siebren Versteeg, Marina Zurkow | Christina J. Chua |
| Osinachi | Osinachi |
| Rosana Antolí, Robbie Barrat, Jim Campbell, Carla Gannis, Guildor, Auriea Harvey, Luna Ikuta, Jono, Sasha Katz, Yuma Kishi, Paul Pfeiffer, Jan Robert Leegte, Helena Sarin, Edgar Sarin, aurèce vettier | aurèce vettier |
| Andy Picci, Auriea Harvey, Friedemann Banz, Giulia Bowinkel, Ben Elliot, John Yuyi, Jon Burgerman, Jonas Lund, kennedy+swan, Manuel Rossner, Nicole Ruggiero, Junuwana | Jonas Lund |
| Hakatao, Fontana | Eleonora Brizi |
| Serwah Attafuah, Lu Yang, Yu-Ki Yuki, Kenny Schachter, Sputniko!, Takakura Kazuki, UuDam Tran Nguyen, David Oreilly | Studio Robert Alice |
| Olive Allen, John Yuyi, Tianzhuo Chen, Shamus Clisset, Vuk Cosic, Mark Dorf, Harm van den Dorpel, Claudia Hart, LoVid, Miltos Manetas, Jennifer & Kevin McCoy, Alex Mcleod, Kenny Schachter, Carl Skelton, Ubermorgen, Eddo Stern, Pussykrew | Christina J. Chua |
| Alotta Money, Alida Sun, Brendan Dawes, Matt Kane, Coldie +... | Matt Kane |
| Abdulrahman Adesola Yusuf, Idris Veitch, Linda Dounia, Mucyo Daniel Dylan (MDD), Niyi Okeowo, Nyahan Tachie-Menson, Moonsundiamond, PR$DNT HONEY, Thapelo Keetile, Youssef El Idrissi | Linda Dounia |
| 0xDEAFBEEF, Dmitri Cherniak, EulerBeats, Ix Shells, PplPleasr, Serwah Attafuah, Shl0ms, Tyler Hobbs, XCOPY, Sarah Meyohas, Larva Labs, Metaliths | Serwah Attafuah |
| Muhcine Ennou, Mays Al Moosawi, Mazyar Kamkar, M Smart, Muhcine Ennou, Amelia Hadouchi, Beya Khalifa, Farbod Mehr, Sasan Nasernia, Rabee Baghshani, Parham Ghalamdar, Nic Courdy, Keyvan Shovir, Parsa Mostaghim, Dear Nostalgia, Parin Heidari, Nour Hage | Studio Robert Alice |
| Robert Alice, Sarah Meyohas, Tyler Hobbs, Andy Warhol, Refik Anadol, rare pepes, Dmitri Cherniak | Clara Peh, Christina Chua |
| Kevin Abosch, Refik Anadol, Domenico Barra, hex6c, Roberto Ranon, Prof. Alberto Policriti, Marco Brambilla, Nancy Baker Cahill, Shu Lea Cheang, Mat Collishaw, CryptoKitties, Cybercars, Darkzuu, Simon Denny, Mr Doodle, espina, Urs Fischer, Mihai Grecu, Hackatao, Claudia Hart, Tommy Hartung, Zhang Huang, Michael Joo, Danil Krivoruchko, Krista Kim, Volkmar Klien, Larva Labs, LIA, Lirona, Soliman Lopez, Kevin McCoy, Jonathan Monaghan, ROBNESS, Rafaël Rozendaal, Simon de La Rouivere, Snowfro, Eve Sussman, terra0, Siebren Verstieg, Robert Wilson | Studio Robert Alice |
| Julian Abraham, Walead Beshty, Rossella Biscotti, Javier Castro, Ian Cheng, Heman Chong, Duto Hardono, Matt Kane, Ayoung Kim, Taiyo Kimura, Li Lang, Liu Yu, Cinthia Marcelle, Adriana Martínez, Kate Mitchell, Amor Muñoz, Diana Fonseca Quiñones, Shang Yixin, Song Dong, Mungo Thomson, Wang Jianwei, Luka Yuanyuan Yang | Matt Kane |
| Krista Kim, Brendan Dawes, Ivona Tau, Ou Yang, Tom Gerrard, Gene Cogan, Cindy NG, Chewy Stoll, MuLei, Sunyuqian +... | Studio Robert Alice |
| aurèce vettier | aurèce vettier |

| | CURATOR(S) | EXHIBITION TITLE | INSTITUTION(S)/COMMERCIAL | LOCATION | TYPE OF EVENT | OPEN DATE | END DATE |
|---|---|---|---|---|---|---|---|
| 178 | – | NFT: Illuminated | Vicinity, The Galeries | Sydney, Australia | Physical | 11-18-2021 | 01-05-2022 |
| 179 | Gordon Berger, Ghost Agent | Cryptographics – The Beginning of Blockchain Generative Art | Cryptovoxels | Cryptovoxels, Online | Digital | 11-20-2021 | Ongoing |
| 180 | Feng-Yi Chu | Dear Block Chen | Solid Art | Taipei, Taiwan | Physical | 11-20-2021 | 01-15-2022 |
| 181 | Lucas Samaras | XYZ | Pace Verso | Pace Gallery, Online | Digital | 11-22-2021 | Ongoing |
| 182 | Piergiulio Lanza (DART) Alessandro Brunello, Alan Tonetti, Serena Tabacchi | DART2121 Crypto Art is Now | Dynamic Art Museum | Milan, Italy | Physical | 11-23-2021 | 02-06-2022 |
| 183 | Catherine Lebrun | Digital Reflection | Subtile | Luxembourg | Physical | 11-25-2021 | 12-12-2021 |
| 184 | Clitsplash | Erotika | Miami Art Week, Arium, KnownOrigin, Playground, FeministArt | Miami, USA; Online | Physical / Digital | 11-29-2021 | 12-08-2021 |
| 185 | Casey Reas | Graph | Feral File | Feral File, Online | Digital | 11-30-2021 | Ongoing |
| 186 | SuperRare, BlockParty, Ronnie K. Pirovino, SeedPhrase, 33NFT | The Gateway | NFT Now, Christie's | Miami, USA | Physical | 12-02-2021 | 12-03-2021 |
| 187 | Tezos | Humans + Machines: NFTs and the Ever-Evolving World of Art | Art Basel Miami Beach | Miami, USA | Physical | 12-02-2021 | 12-04-2021 |
| 188 | Angel Darmella E'Stash | Zoratopia IRL | Zora | Miami, USA | Physical | 12-03-2021 | 12-03-2021 |
| 189 | Sofia Garcia, Kate Hannah | The Digital | ARTXCODE, Miami Art Week | Miami, USA | Physical | 12-03-2021 | 12-05-2021 |
| 190 | Unit London | Transformations | Unit London | London, UK | Physical | 12-07-2021 | 01-08-2022 |
| 191 | Jesse Damiani, Sinziana Velicescu | Color :: Field | Vellum LA | Los Angeles, USA | Physical | 12-09-2021 | 01-16-2022 |
| 192 | Merlina Rañi, CryptoARG, Carla Chmiel, Lucía López, Sandro | No Existe Tierra Más Allá | Crypto Argentina Collective | Buenos Aires, Argentina | Physical | 12-10-2021 | 12-11-2021 |
| 193 | The Columns Gallery | Material Sense | The Columns Gallery | Singapore | Physical | 12-14-2021 | 01-06-2022 |
| 194 | Bnoiit C, Kevin Abosch, Albertine Meunier | Crypto Art Revolution | French Museum of Crypto Art | Paris, France; Online | Physical | 12-14-2021 | 12-16-2021 |
| 195 | Domenico Quaranta | For Your Eyes Only | Feral File | Feral File, Online | Digital | 12-16-2021 | Ongoing |
| 196 | Cyber Shakti, Amrit Pal Singh, Indrani Mitra, Mehak Jain, A Nadamel, Cyber Shakti, Jatin Pathi, Prasad Bhat and Melvin Thambi, Shivani Mitra, Barthazian | DAZE | Lokayata Art Gallery, Crypto Art India Collective | New Delhi, India | Physical | 12-18-2021 | 12-19-2021 |
| 197 | Max Haarich, Gleb Divov | TeleNFT | SAT.1 Teletext, Museum Franciscum Carolinum | Linz, Austria; Online | Physical / Digital | 01-11-2022 | Ongoing |
| 198 | Kenny Schachter, Daniel Heiss | Metadada | Galerie Nagel Draxler | Cologne, Germany | Physical | 01-14-2022 | 04-16-2022 |
| 199 | Anna Seaman | 50 NFTs Celebrating 50 Years of the UAE | Morrow Collective, Dubai Culture | Cryptovoxels, Online | Digital | 01-15-2022 | 02-15-2022 |
| 200 | Daniel Birnbaum | KAWS: New Fiction | Serpentine North Gallery, Acute Art, Fortnite | London, UK; Online | Physical / Digital | 01-18-2022 | 02-27-2022 |
| 201 | Jesse Damiani, Sinziana Velicescu | Elsewhere is a Negative Mirror | Vellum LA | Los Angeles, USA | Physical | 01-20-2022 | 02-13-2022 |
| 202 | Sydney Xiong, Marisa Kayyem | Second Lives | APENFT Art Museum, Live Art | Cryptovoxels, Online | Digital | 01-25-2022 | Ongoing |

| ARTIST(S) INVOLVED | SUGGESTED BY |
| --- | --- |
| Aldous Massie, Bianca Beers, David Porte Beckefeld, James Jirat Patradoon, Jonathan Puc, Lucius Ha, Rel Pham, Serwah Attafuah | Serwah Attafuah |
| Gordon Berger, Ghost Agent +... | Studio Robert Alice |
| Kevin Abosch, Lans King, Martin Lukas Ostachowski, Nai-Ren Chang, Tzu-Tung Lee, Winnie Soon, Yi-Chun Lin, Iololol (Xia Lin, Sheryl Chang), Rexy Tseng, Aluan Wang, Jui-Lan Yao | Studio Robert Alice |
| Lucas Samaras | Studio Robert Alice |
| Beeple, Yuga Labs, Larva Labs, Kevin Abosch, Alessandro Bavari, Alessio De Vecchi, Raf Grassetti +... | Studio Robert Alice |
| Phillip Fotheringham-Matt | Studio Robert Alice |
| Cymoonv, Cesar Saavedra, La Salò, Natalie Shau, Serwah Attafuah, Jose Nazabal, Sasha Katz, Yulia Shur, Looping Lovers, Ellen Sheidlin, Almendra Bertoni, Nina Hawkins | Serwah Attafuah |
| Aleksandra Jovanić, Iskra Velitchkova, James Merrill, Julien Gachadoat, Licia He, Tyler Hobbs | Casey Reas |
| Andre Oshea , Ash Thorp, Baeige, Blake Kathryn, Chad Knight, Coldie, Snoop Dogg, Cory, Van Lew, Dave Krugman, Defaced, DotPigeon, Emonee LaRussa, Fabio Giampietro, Federico Clapis, FriendsWithYou, FVCKRENDER, Helena Sarin, JENISU, Joshua Davis, KEELEY, Krista Kim, Lushsux, MADSTEEZ, Matt Kane, Olive Allen, Otherworld, Sarah Zucker, Skygolpe, Victor Mosquera, WhIsBe +... | Matt Kane |
| A.L Crego, Anna Lucia, Auriea Harvey, Bees & Bombs, Eko33, Ganbrood, Helena Sarin, Henrik Uldalen, Iskra Velitchkova, Joanie Lemercier, Kelly Richardson, Kevin Abosch, Lia Something, Linda Dounia, Mario Klingemann, Matt DesLauriers, Memo Akten, mumu the stan, P1xelfool, Polyhop, Qubibi, SUTU, Taís Koshino, Universal Everything, Zach Lieberman | Studio Robert Alice, Micol Ap |
| Wata, Sophie Sturdevant, Mikael Moore, FaithLove, Sian Morson, Alex Siber, FeltZine, Abieyuwa, Klara Vollstaedt, HVND SU, Lomedia | Serwah Attafuah |
| Aaron Penne, Boreta, Alexis André, Ansh Kumar, Casey Reas, Dmitri Cherniak, Hideki Tsukamoto, Ix Shells, Jake Rockland, Jason Ting, Jeff Davis, Kaylla Torres, Matt DesLauriers, Michael Connolly, Minne Atairu, Monica Rizzolli, Sarah Ridgley, Snowfro, Stefano Contiero, Lazlo Lissitzky, Tyler Hobbs. | Jeff Davis |
| Chad Knight, Serwah Attafuah, Tyler Hobbs, Brendan Dawes, Marjan Moghaddam, Jason Seife, Ellen Shiedlin, Jon Burgerman, Unskilled Worker, Jonathan Quintin, Maxim Zhestkov, Ix Shells | Studio Robert Alice |
| Andy Gilmore, Ix Shells, LIA, Zach Lieberman, Nicolas Sassoon, Alida Sun, Anne Vieux, Zouassi | Studio Robert Alice |
| Afr0dita , Astrosuka + Sofja, Basseado, Crypt0Baby, Federico Bona, Frenetik Void, Faktor, Falko, Gabriel Rud, Guido Corallo, Hilen Godoy, Joaquin Vismarax, Kamil Jauregui, Kazwes, Lenny Forster, Lobatus, Lolo Armdz, Lucas Aguirre, Lulú, Luran, Luxi, Mardeformas, Nana Schlez, Okytomo, Parts Labour, TheInternetOffice + Daira, Tierras Raras, Ver Clausi, VXN | Martin Lukas Ostachowski |
| Han Yajuan, Jeon Byeong Sam, Arabelle Zhuang, Ernest Wu, Serwah Attafuah, Shavonne Wong, Tristan Lim | Studio Robert Alice |
| Bård Ionson, Pascal Boyart, XCOPY, Miss Al Simpson, ROBNESS +... | Martin Lukas Ostachowski |
| Morehshin Allahyari, Sara Bezovšek, Émilie Brout, Maxime Marion, Anna Carreras, Petra Cortright, Francoise Gamma, Theodoros Giannakis, Kamilia Kard, Jonas Lund, Lev Manovich, Petros Moris, Katja Novitskova, Jon Rafman | Jonas Lund |
| Cyber Shakti, Amrit Pal Singh, Indrani Mitra, Mehak Jain, A Nadamel, Jatin Pathi, Prasad Bhat, Melvin Thambi, Shivani Mitra, Barthazian | Studio Robert Alice |
| Bloom Jr., U. Dresemann, Protostyle, Claudie Linke, Gleb Divov, Jarkko Räsänen, Juha van Ingen, Mamadou Sow, Max Haarich, Nissla, NUMO, Mario Klingemann, Sp4ce, tius, Michael Jathe | Martin Lukas Ostachowski |
| Kenny Schachter | Studio Robert Alice |
| Khalid Al Banna, Alia AlGaoud, Dalal Ahmed | Studio Robert Alice |
| KAWS | Studio Robert Alice |
| Saks Afridi, Kirk Finkel, Vince Fraser, Mari.K, Le Fawnhawk, DeepLight Labs, Nate Mohler, Kristen Roos, Sabrina Ratté, Nicolas Sassoon, Thato Tatai | Studio Robert Alice |
| Beeple, FEWOCiOUS, Pak, WMD Studios, Lil E, Jansword Zhu, Verdi Jackson, Kong, Allyn Belfred, Chengcheng Shi, Ron Guetta, HUIHUAN, Pandalifa, Jansword Zhu, LOVEBEING, Zhang Hui, Zhao Xuetong, RocketHand Studio | Studio Robert Alice |

**11.21**
Installation view of
*DYOR*, curated by Nina
Roehrs, Kunsthalle Zürich,
Switzerland, 2022

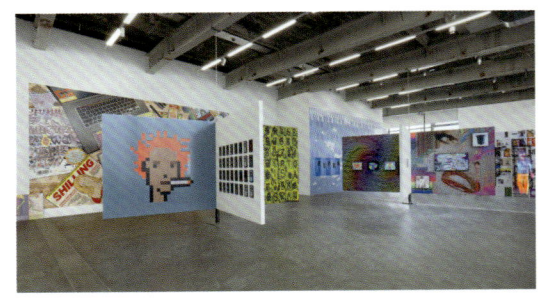

| | CURATOR(S) | EXHIBITION TITLE | INSTITUTION(S)/COMMERCIAL | LOCATION | TYPE OF EVENT | OPEN DATE | END DATE |
|---|---|---|---|---|---|---|---|
| 203 | Edoardo Durante, Pietro Massouda, Stella Stone | SUI GENESIS: Digital Shaping | Reasoned Art & Lava Club | Milan, Italy | Physical | 01-27-2022 | 02-05-2022 |
| 204 | Galloire art | I'm Not a Robot | Galloire Art | Dubai, UAE; Online | Physical / Digital | 01-31-2022 | 02-28-2022 |
| 205 | Peter Wu, LACMA Art + Technology Lab | ECHOES | EPOCH Gallery | Online | Digital | 02-04-2022 | 05-13-2022 |
| 206 | Adam Lindemann | Snowfro: Chromie Squiggles | Venus Over Manhattan, Infinite Objects | New York, USA | Physical | 02-12-2022 | 02-26-2022 |
| 207 | DropIt | DropIt | DropIt, Melbourne Art Fair | Melbourne, Australia | Physical | 02-17-2022 | 02-20-2022 |
| 208 | Pace, Art Blocks | Cosmic Reef | Pace, Art Blocks at Frieze LA | Los Angeles, USA | Physical | 02-17-2022 | 02-20-2022 |
| 209 | Jesse Damiani, Sinziana Velicescu | The Decentralized Unicists: A Botto Solo Show | Vellum LA | Los Angeles, USA | Physical | 02-17-2022 | 03-06-2022 |
| 210 | Vertical Crypto Art | ART & NFT: The Digital Roots LA | VerticalCrypto Art, Tezos, Rarible | Los Angeles, USA | Physical | 02-17-2022 | 02-23-2022 |
| 211 | Robert Sakrowski | NfTNeTArT – From Net Art to Art NFT | Panke Gallery, Office Impart | Berlin, Germany | Physical | 02-19-2022 | 03-26-2022 |
| 212 | Daria Borisova | Block Party: Encountering NFTs in the Middle East | Christie's, Art Dubai Week | Dubai, UAE | Physical | 03-07-2022 | 03-29-2022 |
| 213 | The 721 | The Icons of Crypto Art | The 721, Dubai Design District | Dubai, UAE | Physical | 03-08-2022 | 03-13-2022 |
| 214 | Jenn Ellis | Nepenthe Valley | AORA, SO-FAR, Horizons Space | Online | Digital | 03-09-2022 | Ongoing |
| 215 | David Porte Beckefeld | Satellite | Twenty Twenty Six | Bondi, Australia | Physical | 03-10-2022 | 04-03-2022 |
| 216 | Artnet | Feels Rare Man | ArtNFT | Online | Digital | 03-11-2022 | 03-22-2022 |
| 217 | Cosmo Lindsay, Breagha Campbell, Alex Everett | Network Effects | Serpentine Future Contemporaries | London, UK | Physical | 03-15-2022 | 03-15-2022 |
| 218 | Chris Fussner | Art Dubai Digital | Art Dubai | Dubai, UAE; Online | Physical / Digital | 03-16-2022 | 03-19-2022 |
| 219 | ROBNESS | #TRASHART – NFT GARBOLOGY | Avant Galerie Vossen | Paris, France | Physical | 03-26-2022 | 03-28-2022 |
| 220 | Transfer | Pieces of Me | Left.Gallery | Online | Digital | 04-01-2022 | Ongoing |
| 221 | institut., VerticalCryptoArt, Breezy, ARTPOOL, Jose Ramos, Ephemeral Ethernal | Non Fungible Conference | NFC Summit | Lisbon, Portugal | Physical | 04-04-2022 | 04-05-2022 |

**11.22**
Installation views of *Beeple: Uncertain Future*, Jack Hanley Gallery, New York, United States, 2022

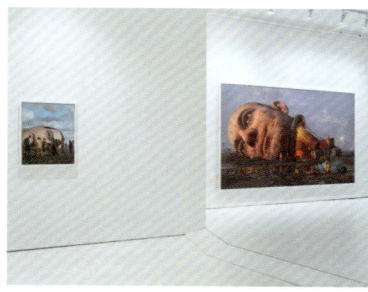

**11.23**
Installation views of Leo Villareal's *Cosmic Bloom* (2022), Outland, London, United Kingdom, 2022

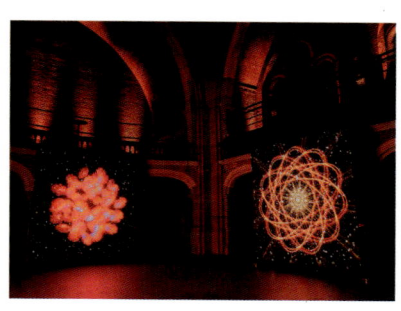

| ARTIST(S) INVOLVED | SUGGESTED BY |
|---|---|
| Waarp, Hardmetacore, Paola Pinna, Joe Karava | Martin Lukas Ostachowski |
| Jonas Lund, Daniel Canogar, Addie Wagenknecht, Anne Spalter, Xavi Sole Mora, Jonathan Monaghan | Studio Robert Alice |
| Lukas Avendaño, EYIBRA, NNUX, Oswaldo Erreve, Jacqueline Kiyomi Gork, Rhett LaRue, Lawrence Lek, Jen Liu, Ronald Rael, Virginia San Fratello, Sarah Rara | Lawrence Lek |
| Snowfro | Studio Robert Alice |
| Serwah Attafuah +... | Serwah Attafuah |
| Leo Villareal | Jeff Davis |
| Botto | Studio Robert Alice |
| Ania Catherine, Dejha Ti, Brendan Dawes, Henrik Uldalen, ivona Tau, Jesse Draxler, Joëlle, Lucas Aguirre, Maria Gudjohnsen, Mario Klingemann, Marjan Moghaddam, Miss AL Simpson, neurocolor, Nicole Ruggerio, Pindar van Arman, ROBNESS, SamJ, Kate the Cursed, Sofia Crespo, Entangled Others, Yinka Ilori | Micol Ap |
| Kim Asendorf, LaTurbo Avedon, Sarah Friend, LIA, Jonas Lund, Rhea Myers, Rafaël Rozendaal, Cornelia Sollfrank, Harm van den Dorpel | María Paula Fernández, Rhea Myers |
| Justin Aversano, José Delbo, Trevor Jones, Osinachi, Rewind Collective, Nicole Ruggiero, Sarah Zucker | Osinachi, Studio Robert Alice |
| Alotta Money, Artonymous Artifakt, Bård Ionson, Carlos Marcial, Coldie, Connie Digital, Gary Cartlidge, Gisel Florez, Gremplin, Hackatao, Hex6c, Jake, Jivinci, Josie Bellini, Killer Acid, Kristofer Robins, Kristy Glass, Larva Labs, Lumps, Mason, London, Matt Kane, Mattia Cuttini, Max Osiris, Miss Al Simpson, XCOPY +... | Studio Robert Alice |
| Lawrence Lek | Christina J Chua |
| Jonathan Zawada, Serwah Attafuah, David McLeod, BossLogic, LIRONA, Mikaela Stafford, Chris Golden, Jessica Ticchio, Yambo, Trevor Jones, Beeple | Serwah Attafuah |
| Various Artists (rare pepes) | Studio Robert Alice |
| Osinachi, Iskra Velitchkova, Ix Shells, qubibi, Sarah Meyohas, Robert Alice | Studio Robert Alice |
| Martha Fiennes, Raghava KK, Refik Anadol, Krista Kim | Ana Bambic Kostov, Christina Chua |
| ROBNESS, Aleksandraart, Anonymous Nobody, Aprilyfu, Barbara Tosti, BigComicArt, Bitjamin, BnoiitC, CECHK, CK Travelling, Collin, Crypto-Art-House, Cryptomatic, Cryptophobia, Cryptotonya, CryptoYuna, Cypherpunk Now, Darkfarms, DeeperLab, Desultor, Empress Trash, Eric P. rhodes, ETHwords, Ferris Bullish, Ftr Saroth, Galavis, Gary Cartlidge, GT Sewell, Harv, Iambonkers, iHODL, JayDelay, Jivinci, Johnny Dollar, Kamisama, KBO Metaverse, Lambie, Lapin Mignon, Lulu xXX, MajorArt, Marcotic, Mattia Cuttini, Max Capacity, Max Trash, Maxosiris, Meunier Albertine , Miusoph, Mjfellowactuary, Neurocolor, NFTBox, Nino Arteiro, Norman Harman, Obxium, Ooakosimo, Opennft, Osiris Orion, Prosper Legault, Rare Designer, Rare Scrilla, Reviiser, Richard Dixon, Ronan Barrot, Squintdev, Stellabelle, Sugarclub, Suryanto Sur, The Druid, The Perfessor, Twerky Club, Ulysses, Wizardx, Xibot, YRDGZ | Martin Lukas Ostachowski |
| aaajiao, Moreshin Allahyari, Serwah Attafuah, Stacie Ant, LaTurbo Avedon, Zach Blas, Danielle Brathwaite-Shirley, Shamus Clisset, Harm van den Dorpel, Francoise Gamma, Carla Gannis, Julieta Gil, Claudia Hart, Auriea Harvey, Faith Holland, E. Jane, Huntrezz Janos, Isaac Kariuki, Casey Kauffmann, Keiken, obso1337, Wednesday Kim, Ryan Kuo, Kim Laughton, Lawrence Lek, Kristin Lucas, Sara Ludy, Kumbirai Makumbe, Claudia Maté, LaJuné McMillian, Cassie McQuater, Rosa Menkman, Lorna Mills, Marisa Olson, Eva Papamargariti, Pussykrew, RaFia, Tiare Ribeaux, Jody Stillwater, Olivia McKayla Ross, Mark Sabb, Devon Moore, Alfredo Salazar-Caro, Sydney Shavers, Rick Silva, Travess Smalley, Molly Soda, Olia Svetlanova, Theo Triantafyllidis, Krist Wood, Qianqian Ye, Alice Yuan Zhang | Serwah Attafuah |
| – | Studio Robert Alice |

| | CURATOR(S) | EXHIBITION TITLE | INSTITUTION(S)/COMMERCIAL | LOCATION | TYPE OF EVENT | OPEN DATE | END DATE |
|---|---|---|---|---|---|---|---|
| 222 | Bright Moments | Bright Moments – Berlin Collection | Bright Moments, Kraftwerk | Berlin, Germany | Physical | 04-06-2022 | 04-24-2022 |
| 223 | Sydney Xiong | Digital Wanderlust | CHAO Art Center | Beijing, China | Physical | 04-08-2022 | 04-13-2022 |
| 224 | GAZELL.iO | ORDER & LAGOS | GAZELL.iO, Gazelli Art House | London, UK | Physical | 04-08-2022 | 05-07-2022 |
| 225 | Robert Alice | 0:14. A Selection of Early NFTs | Decentral Art Pavillion | Venice, Italy | Physical | 04-20-2022 | 06-20-2022 |
| 226 | Florencia S.M. Brück, Javier Krasuk, Diego Lijtmaer, Simone Furian | Decentral Art Pavilion | Decentral Art Pavillion | Venice, Italy; Online | Physical / Digital | 04-20-2022 | 06-20-2022 |
| 227 | Jan Robert Leegte, Stina Gustaffson | Art and the Blockchain | Former SMBA, Eth Devcon | Amsterdam, the Netherlands | Physical | 04-21-2022 | 04-23-2022 |
| 228 | Paul Emmanuel Loga Mahop, Sandro Orlandi Stagl | The Times of the Chimera | Cameroon Pavilion, Venice Biennale, Global Crypto Art DAO | Venice, Italy | Physical | 04-22-2022 | 11-27-2022 |
| 229 | Eric Abdykalykov | Gates of Turan | Kyrgyz Pavilion, Venice Biennale, ILGERI | Venice, Italy | Physical | 04-22-2022 | 11-27-2022 |
| 230 | Refik Anadol | Living Architecture: Casa Batlló | Casa Batlló | Barcelona, Spain | Physical | 05-07-2022 | 05-07-2022 |
| 231 | VerticalCryptoArt | ART&NFT: The Digital Roots NYC | VerticalCrypto Art, Tezos | New York, USA | Physical | 05-16-2022 | 05-16-2022 |
| 232 | An Rong, Nika Bar-On Nesher | Visions From Remembered Futures | SuperRare Gallery | New York, USA | Physical | 05-19-2022 | 06-08-2022 |
| 233 | Sats Moon, Potbelleez, Dave Goode | Future Art is Vivid | Future Art | Sydney, Australia | Physical | 05-27-2022 | 05-27-2022 |
| 234 | Mbogi ya NFT | Kenya NFT Summit | iHUB | Nairobi, Kenya | Physical | 06-05-2022 | 06-05-2022 |
| 235 | Freda Fiala, River Lin | The Non-Fungible Body | OK Center for Contemporary Art Austria | Linz, Austria | Physical | 06-17-2022 | 06-19-2022 |
| 236 | Cozomo de' Medici | The Medici Collection | Times Square | New York, USA | Physical | 06-20-2022 | 06-26-2022 |
| 237 | Bright Moments | Bright Moments – London Collection | Bright Moments | London, UK | Physical | 06-30-2022 | 07-30-2022 |
| 238 | VerticalCryptoArt | Proof of People – NFT Festival for Art & Culture | VerticalCrypto Art, Tezos | London, UK | Physical | 07-06-2022 | 07-08-2022 |
| 239 | Georg Bak | Ex-Machina: A History of Generative Art | Phillips London | London, UK | Physical / Digital | 07-11-2022 | 08-05-2022 |
| 240 | Albertine Meunier, Benoit Couty, Thuy-Tien Vo | NFT Revolution | 0x4rt, Next World Forum | Riyadh, Saudi Arabia | Phyiscal | 09-07-2022 | 09-08-2022 |
| 241 | Abigail Miller, Unit London, AOI | In Our Code | Unit London in partnership with AOI | London, UK | Phyiscal | 09-13-2022 | 10-16-2022 |
| 242 | Emily May | NFTUK | NFTUK, FLANNELS, W1 Curates | London, UK | Phyiscal | 09-15-2022 | 09-15-2022 |

| ARTIST(S) INVOLVED | SUGGESTED BY |
|---|---|
| Boreta, Holger Lippmann, Alida Sun, Gabriel Massan, MPKOZ, Jeff Davis, Loren Bednar, Jason Ting, Ellie Pritts, Casey Reas | Jeff Davis |
| Andrés Reisinger, Beeple, Benjamin Bardou, Deadmau5, Mad Dog, Jones, Ellwood, FEWOCiOUS, Keiken, Kenny Schachter, Lil E, Mitchell F. Chan, Obvious, Pak, Refik Anadol, Robbie Barrat, Sanji Yang, Urs Fisher, Wang Xing, Wu Ziyang, Zhu Jianchen | Studio Robert Alice |
| Arclight | India Price |
| Rhea Myers, Kevin McCoy, Sarah Meyohas, Mitchell F Chan, Dan Kaminsky, Hal Finney, Snowfro, Larva Labs, XCOPY, Simon Denny | Studio Robert Alice |
| Alida Sun, Ana Carreras, Botto, Bruce Gilden, Coldie, Cristina de Middel, Kjetil Golid, Lia, Matt Deslauries, Robert Alice, ROBNESS, Sean Mundy, XCOPY | Ana Bambic Kostov, Jeff Davis |
| Rafaël Rozendaal, Harm van den Dorpel, Joan Heemskerk, Jonas Lund, Manuel Rossner, Lorna Mills, Adrian Le Bas, Kim Asendorf, Auriea Harvey, Jan Robert Leegte, Sabrina Ratté, Wyne Veen, Sarah Friend, Constant Dullaart | Jonas Lund |
| Francis Nathan Abiamba, Angéle Etoundi Essamba, Justine Gaga, Salifou Lindou, Shay Frisch, Umberto Mariani, Matteo Mezzadri, Jorge R. Pombo, NFT (Kevin Abosch, João Angelini, Marco Bertin, Cryptoart Driver, Lana Denina, Alberto Echegaray Guevara, Genesis People, Joachim Hildebrand, Meng Huang, Eduardo Kac, Giulia Kosice, Julio Le Parc, Marina Nuñez, Miguel Soler-Roig, Miguel Ángel Vidal, Burkhard von Harder, Gabe Weis, Clark Winter, Shavonne Wong, Wang Xing, Alessandro Zannier, ZZH | Studio Robert Alice |
| Firouz Farman Farmayan | Studio Robert Alice |
| Refik Anadol | Studio Robert Alice |
| Damjanski, Helena Sarin, Jana Styblova, Leander Herzog, Lia Something, Linda Dounia, Loren Bednar, Nicolas Sassoon, P1xelfool, Rose Jackson, Skye Nicolas | Micol Ap |
| ACK, Blake Kathryn, Botto, Dangiuz, David Bianchi, Federico Clapis, jarvinart, Krista Kim, MadMaraca, Maskarade, mgxs, NessGraphics, Reuben Wu, Vintagemozart, XSULLO, Zomax | Studio Robert Alice |
| Sarah Zucker, Goldie, EM!, Giant Swan, marc-o-matic, Robson, Serwah Attafuah +... | Serwah Attafuah |
| Zollz, Donde, Sinatra Chumo, Native Nairobi, Wanji Gallery, vandemlau, Paul Kinuthia, The Puggerfly, DesignCentral.ke , Kionii, Matthew Matete, Metagrapher, Majic, MVNSA, Isaac Gitau, Katenje, Sweet Taboo, Dada Boipelo, The Dadas, Y-9A, mosinhio_ art of madness, Sanny Muthoni, Independent Miner, Kacii Eleven, AISU, Youngkevarts, Manjahi Njoroge, afronftlab, Ruiru Vibration, GALACTIC ZEBRA, Sherie Margaret Ngigi, May, Kiggs, Hind Abuelgasim, Tim.Earth, Pichacraft, monk with an afro, Astral Giraffes, isota | Studio Robert Alice |
| Cibelle Cavalli Bastos, Marita Bullmann, Yun-Chen Chang, Beatrice Didier, Jan Hakon Erichsen, Maria Kulikovska, David Henry Nobody Jr, Sara Lanner, Sajan Mani, Boris Nieslony, Yiannis Pappas, Jianan Qu, Xavier Le Roy, Sarah Trouche, Rong Xie | Martin Lukas Ostachowski |
| Rata Yonqui, Justin Aversano, XCOPY, Botto, ScamArt, Dom Qwek, Sam Spratt, Claire Silver, Des Lucréce, Heart You, VincentVanDough, Lana Denina, Mindzeye, rare pepes, Visithra, Apocalypse Art, Cem Hasimi, Tyler Hobbs, Adam Swaab, DeeKay Motion, Yam Karkai, What is real?, Scamart, Coldie, Haru Komoda, Heart You, Ryan Talbot, Jenni Pasanen, Luis Ponce, Michele Petrelli, Monica Rizzoli, Heidi Klum | Studio Robert Alice |
| Nicolas Sassoon, Jeff Davis, Sputniko, Matt DesLauriers, Thomas Lin Pedersen, Emily Xie | Studio Robert Alice |
| Agoria, Andrés Zighelboim, Angie Taylor, Anna Lucia, Anubis3100, Bas Uterwijk, BoryaXYZ, Brendan Dawes, Bruce – Studio Yorktown, Buppy Preath, Cadie Desbiens, CGcortex, Chabeli Farro, Cyber Baat, DRESS X, Elizabeth Bigger and Luis Fraguada, ertdfgcvb, Frederik Vanhoutte, ganchitecture, Henrikau, Iness Rychlik, Iskra Velitchkova, Joe Pease, Joëlle, KARBORN, Kevin Absoch, Kim Asendorf, Lisa Orth, Lumps, Marcelo Sorario, Mario Klingemann, Matthew Hawtin & Murat Atimtay, Matthew Plum Fernandez, Miss Al Simpson, Molly O'Brien, Nancy Baker Cahill, Neurocolor, Norman Harman, Omer Agustoslu, Operator, Pascal Boyart, Patricia Infinity, Paul Reid, qubibi, RED DAO, Robert Alice, ROBNESS, Rudxane, Sable Raph, Sam J, Sarah Friend, SkyGolpe x Jesse Draxler, Sofia Crespo, Sofia Crespo & Feileacan, Sutu "Neonz AR," Sutu "SutuVerse," Vector Meldrew, Yazid | Studio Robert Alice |
| Vera Molnár, Hebert W. Franke, Gottfried Jäger, Dmitri Cherniak, Snowfro, Distributed Gallery | Georg Bak |
| Reem Al Faisal, Mad Maraca, Adra Kandil, BlackBox.Art, Abdoulaye Barry, Juan José López, Ralph Khoury, Stellabelle, Gary Cartlidge, Joern Bielewski, XCOPY, Oficinas TK, Mattia Cuttini, Max Osiris, Jivinci, Alotta Money, Pascal Boyart, Jessy Jeanne, Robbie Barrat, MarkTheHabibi, Bard Ionson, FARAH, Matt Kane, crashblossom, Kevin Abosch, Etienne De Crecy, Neil Boufa, HamadsWorld, Fabiano Speziari, Bager Kaya, Norman Harman, Anne Spalter, luluxxx, Stephan Breuer, Magda Americangangsta, abysms, MAXCAPA.CITY, TokenAngels, ROBNESS, Muhcine, Noonie, Albertine Meunier, Ferris Bullish, Nahiko, ARC | Studio Robert Alice |
| Casey Reas, Helena Sarin, Ix Shells, Zach Lieberman, Krista Kim, Sofia Crespo, Emily Xie, Che-Yu Wu, William Mapan, Iskra Velitchkova, Tyler Hobbs | Studio Robert Alice |
| B Kyle, Jake Farmer, Zakalwe_x, Vector Meldrew, OgiWorlds, Numan Khan, Leimai Lemaow, Piano And The Fox, Stephy Fung, Gordon Berger, Meg Thorpe, XCOPY, S.Rodan, Evi, Ani + Pinxx, On Thin Ice, Janice Mascarenhas, David Lisser, Moyosore Briggs, Graceland London, Flower Blocks, Yuqian Sun (Cheesetalk), Saucebook, Defaced, Becka, Siddiqa Juma, Saira Jamieson, swolfchan, Gxng Yxng, Lewis Osborne, Meelo, The Immersive KIND x Ivan Svanberg, Ella, GRAIN DEVIL, Jo Ho, Cybr Magazine, rubahitam, J Cabo, Bad Oats, Random Freaks, Rayan Elnayal, Shakka, qfilmstv, Jessica Wild Child, Trevor Jones, RSTLSS, Mila Loli, Bill Elis, Whisbe, Maxim Zhestkov, Voice Gems | Studio Robert Alice |

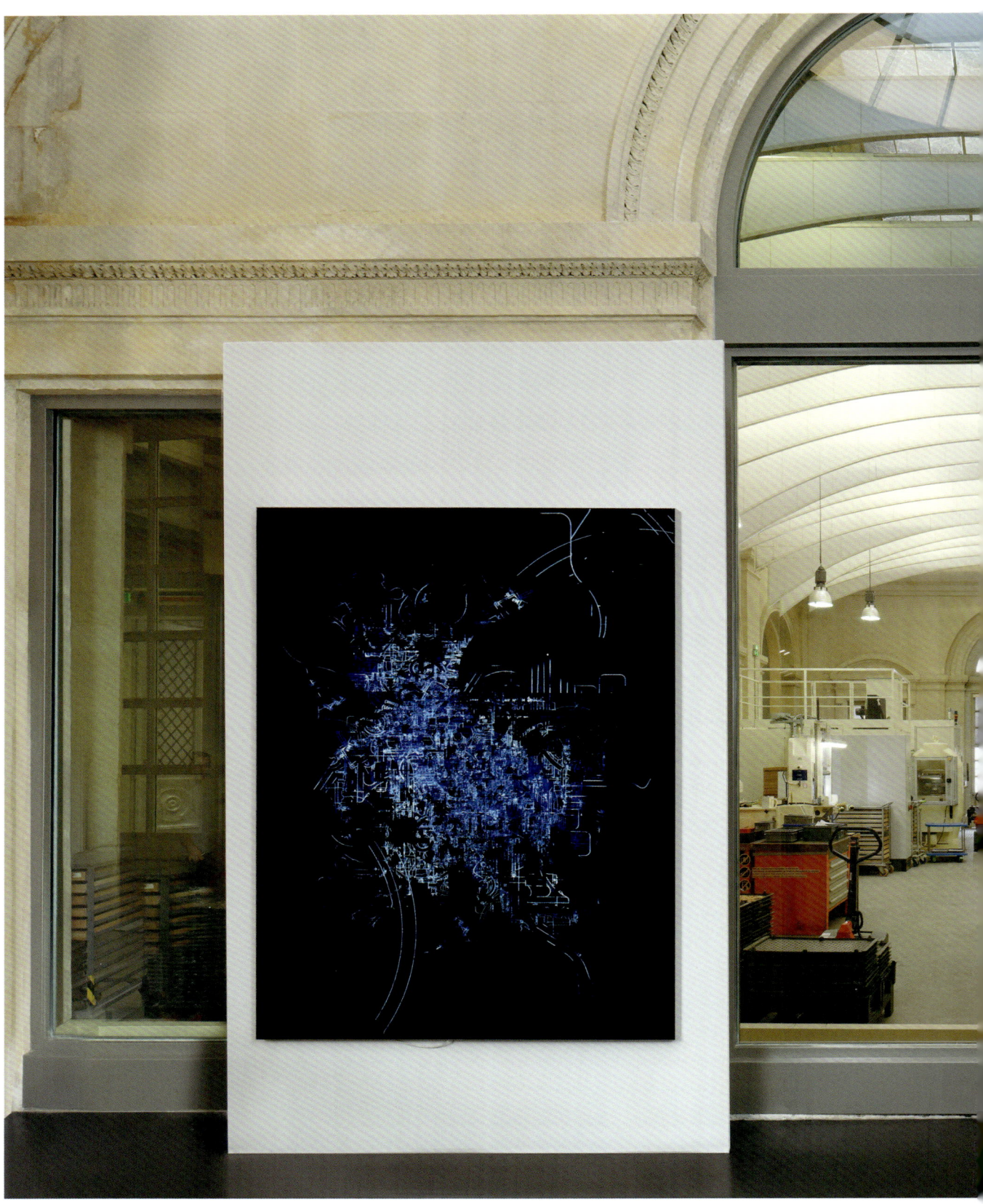

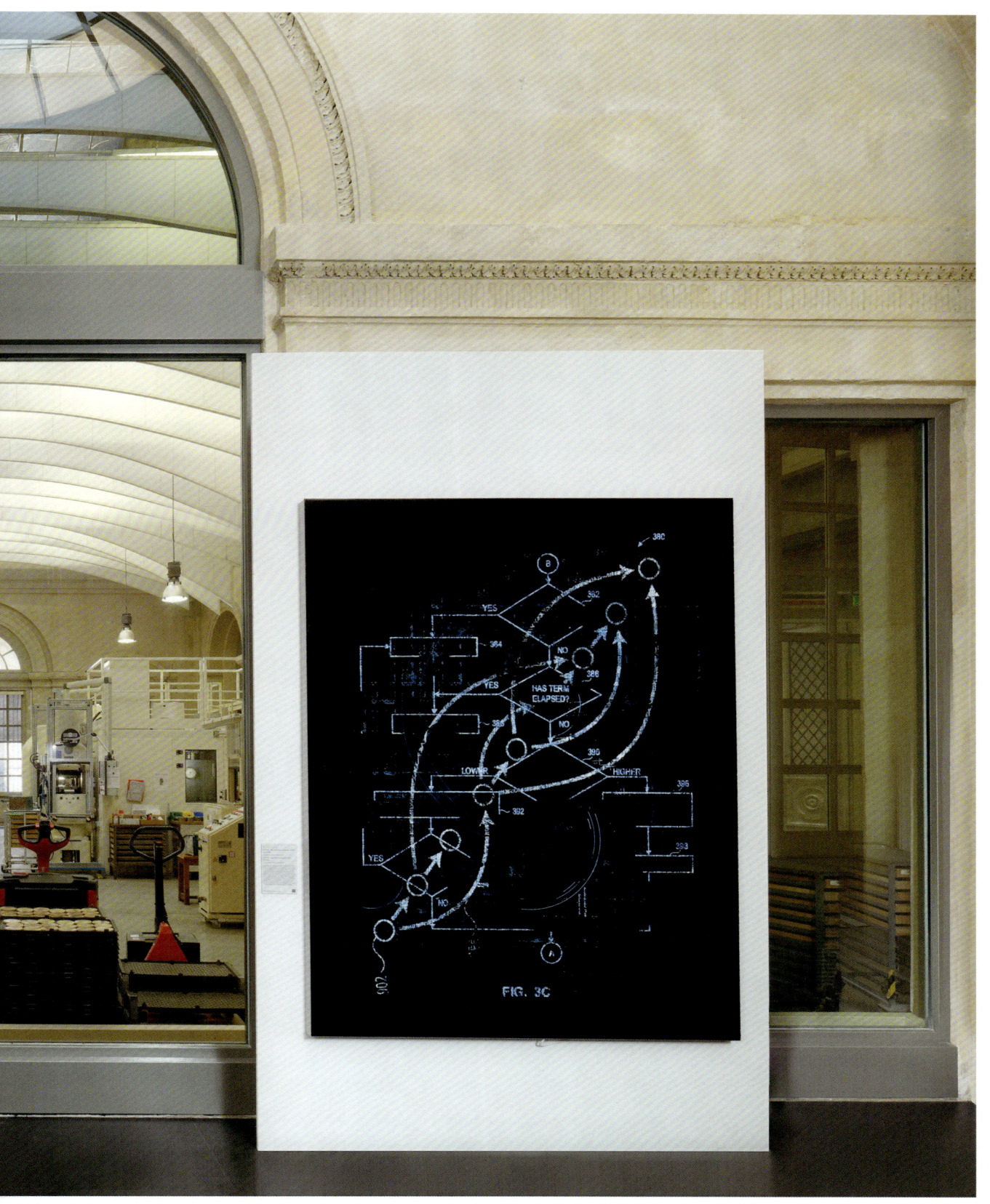

# QR CATALOGUE

The *On NFTs QR Catalogue* is a supplementary resource created to streamline your interaction with the video and dynamic artworks featured in *On NFTs*. Using the QR codes, you will be directed to the precise decentralized online hosting locations of these works. This allows you to immediately access and immerse yourself in the original media as envisioned by the artists themselves. In addition to the video and dynamic artworks, you will also have access to other videos, lectures, and historical pieces.

In this catalogue, each entry includes the artist's name, title of the work, page number, figure number, a thumbnail, and a QR code. These correspond to the entries in the main section of this publication that are marked with a "play" symbol (►), signifying videos and dynamic illustrations. Using your smartphone's camera feature, you can scan the QR codes to access the associated online file and enable seamless media streaming. Over the following pages, you can explore the more than 180 videos and dynamic NFT artworks as their creators intended, adding another dimension to your experience of this publication and understanding of the artistic landscape of NFTs.

►
**XCOPY**
*Nullwave*
GIF
Ethereum, 0×41a322b28d0ff354040e2cbc676f0320d8c8850d

**KEVIN MCCOY**
*Quantum*
p. 036, #01; pp. 060, 01.00; pp. 066, 01.04

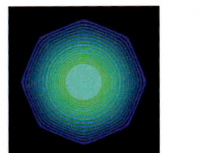 

**KEVIN MCCOY**
*Cars*
p. 037, #02

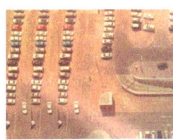 

**KEVIN MCCOY**
*Primordial Loop*
p. 038, #03

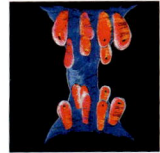 

**KEVIN MCCOY**
*Quantum Leap Primordial Star 1*
p. 039, #04

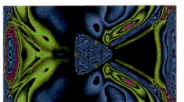 

**SARAH MEYOHAS**
*Bitchcoin*
p. 041, #10

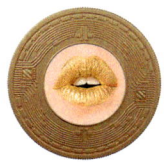 

**SARAH MEYOHAS**
*Cloud of Petals*
p. 043, #12
Artwork trailer on Vimeo

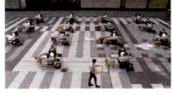 

**ANNA RIDLER**
*BlackTulip*
p. 049, # 02

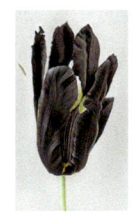 

**RARE PEPE CARDS, INDELIBLE**
*JIHANWU*
p. 050, #09

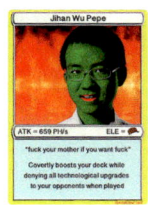 

**CURIO CARDS, ROBEK WORLD**
*The Barbarian*
p. 052, #23

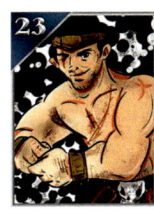 

**CURIO CARDS, THOROS OF MYR**
*Eclipse*
p. 053, #30

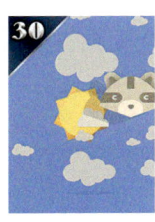 

**RHIZOME**
Seven on Seven 2014: Kevin McCoy & Anil Dash
p. 062, 01.01
Lecture on Vimeo

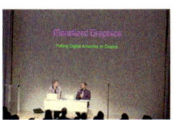 

**JOHN WHITNEY**
*Permutations*
p. 067, 01.05
For US Licensing please contact canyoncinema.com

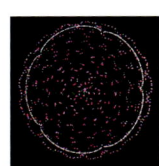 

**XCOPY**
*DE$CENT*
p. 075, 01.17
Unofficial artwork link, original lost on Ascribe

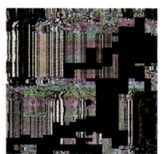 

**XCOPY**
*data_lords*
p. 080, #01

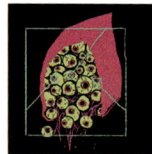 

**XCOPY**
*MUTATIO, 03-19-2024 15:20:53*
p. 077, 1.19

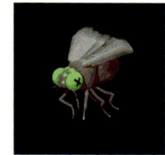 

**XCOPY**
*Right-click and Save As guy*
p. 081, #02

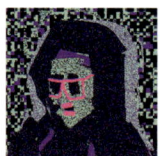 

**XCOPY**
*All Time High in the City*
pp. 082, 083, #03

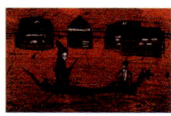 

**XCOPY**
*A Coin for the Ferryman*
p. 084, #04

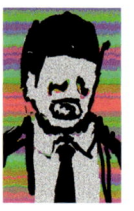 

**XCOPY**
*Nullwave*
p. 085, #05

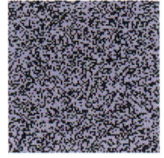 

**XCOPY**
*The Doomed*
p. 085, #06

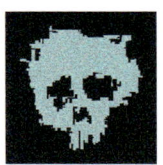 

**XCOPY**
*MAX PAIN*
p. 085, #07

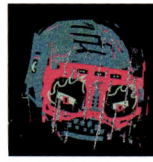 

**XCOPY**
*ART HISTORY: VOLUMES I–X*
p. 085, #08

**SARAH ZUCKER**
*Caryatid: Wink*
p. 086, #01

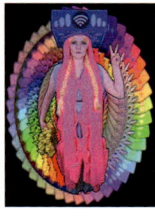 

**SARAH ZUCKER**
*Caryatid: Recursion*
p. 086, #02

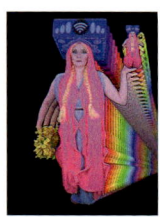 

**SARAH ZUCKER**
*Caryatid: Vision*
p. 086, #03

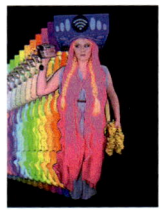 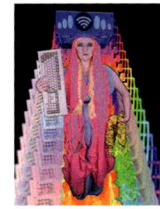

**SARAH ZUCKER**
*Caryatid: Thought*
p. 086, #04

 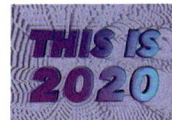

**SARAH ZUCKER**
*THIS IS 2020*
p. 087, #05

**SARAH ZUCKER**
*Space Loaf*
p. 087, #06

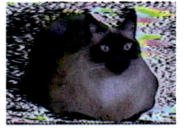 

**SARAH ZUCKER**
*Self Transcending*
p. 087, #07

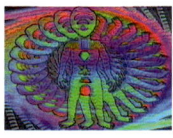 

**SARAH ZUCKER**
*Most Everyone's Mad Here*
p. 087, #08

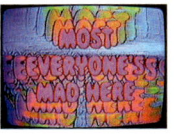 

**ROBNESS**
*64 GALLON TOTER*
p. 093, #03

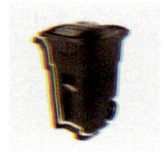 

**HACKATAO**
*It's SCAM–Left*
p. 094, #01

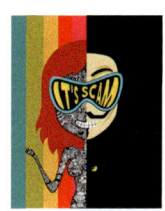 

**HACKATAO**
*Girl Next door*
p. 095, #02

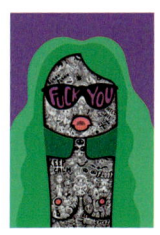 

**AILADI**
*I adopted a fly*
p. 098, #01

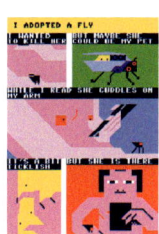 

**AILADI**
*The lizard*
p. 098, #02

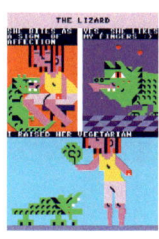 

**AILADI**
*Ticchettio*
p. 098, #03

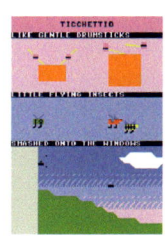 

**AILADI**
*Grandma*
p. 098, #04

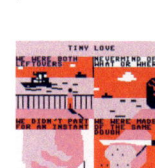

**AILADI**
*Tiny Love*
p. 099, #05

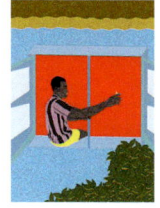

**OSINACHI**
*Man in the Window*
p. 102, 02.00

**OSINACHI**
*Nduka's Wedding Day*
p. 108, 02.05

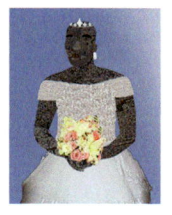

**CARLOS MARCIAL**
*Here Comes Fiat*
p. 110, 02.06

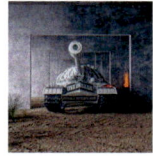

**SARAH ZUCKER**
*You Can Save This*
p. 111, 2.07

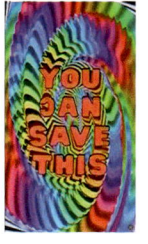

**ROBNESS**
*Cryptophecies*
p. 111, 2.08

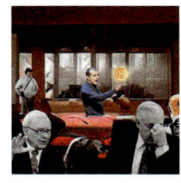

**OSINACHI**
*Resignation*
p. 118, #01

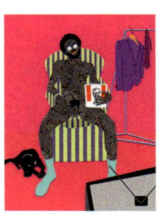

**OSINACHI**
*Two Generals at War I*
pp. 122, 123, #04

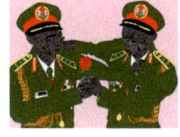

**ROBERT ALICE**
*H15715_The Imperfect Librarian*
p. 124, #01

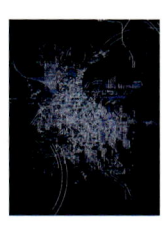

**ROBERT ALICE**
*Portraits of a Mind: Block 34*
*(51.895167° N, 1.4805° E)* p. 125, #04

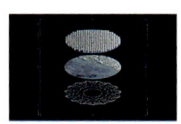

**RUTHERFORD CHANG**
*Block 839969 from CENTS*
p. 127, # 02

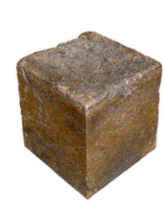

**MATT KANE**
*Gazers #29*
p. 128, #01

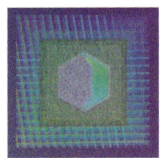 

**MATT KANE**
*Gazers #225*
p. 128, #02

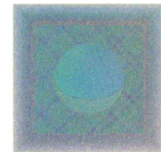 

**MATT KANE**
*Gazers #59*
p. 128, #03

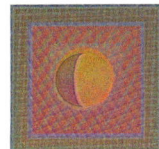 

**MATT KANE**
*Gazers #88*
p. 128, #04

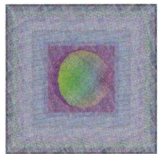 

**MATT KANE**
*CRYPTOART MONETIZATION GENERATION*
p. 129, #05

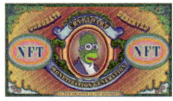 

**ERICK CALDERON**
*Chromie Squiggle #8110*
p. 130, #01

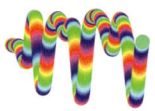 

**ERICK CALDERON**
*Chromie Squiggle #8099*
p. 131, #02

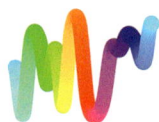 

**DANIEL CALDERON**
*Gen 3 #315*
p. 134, #01

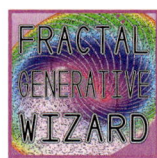 

**DANIEL CALDERON**
*Gen 3 #55*
p. 137, #04

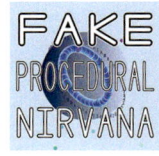 

**CASEY REAS**
*There's No Distance 2.1*
p. 143, #05

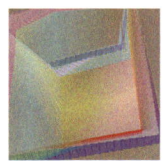 

**CASEY REAS**
*CENTURY #316*
pp. 144, 145, #06
First edition in tile

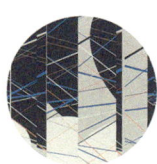 

**ANNA CARRERAS**
*Ganxillo*
p. 161, #03

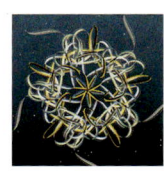 

**ANNA CARRERAS**
*Arrels*
pp. 162, 163, #04

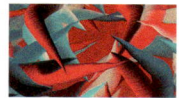

**DARIEN BRITO**
*Pigments #356*
p. 199, #05

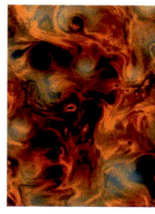

**DARIEN BRITO**
*Pigments #788*
p. 199, #06

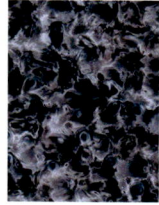

**LIA**
*Sync [var. 04]*
p. 225, #09

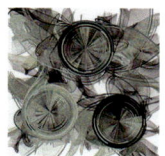

**RAFAËL ROZENDAAL**
*Endless Nameless #100*
p. 228, #01

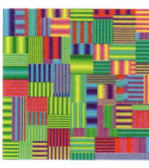

**RAFAËL ROZENDAAL**
*Endless Nameless #66*
p. 229, #02

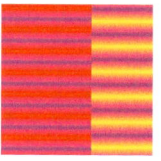

**RAFAËL ROZENDAAL**
*Dive #14*
p. 230, #03

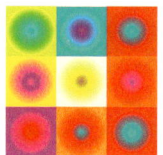

**RAFAËL ROZENDAAL**
*Dive #184*
p. 231, #04

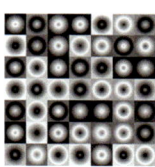

**IX SHELLS**
*Dreaming at Dusk*
p. 233, #02

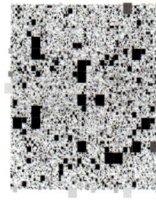

**YOSHI SODEOKA**
*Wetware Vegetation*
p. 238, #01

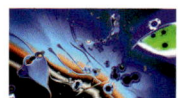

**YOSHI SODEOKA**
*Wetware Medulla*
p. 238, #02

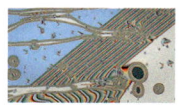

**YOSHI SODEOKA**
*Wetware Mutation*
p. 238, #03

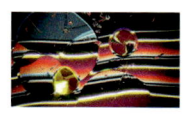

**YOSHI SODEOKA**
*Wetware–Bacteria WTWR–BCTR \*\*\*083-3GD*
p. 239, #04

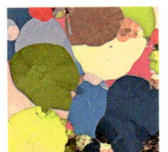 

**AARON PENNE & BORETA**
*Rituals–Venice #117*
p. 240, #01

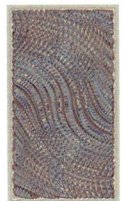 

**AARON PENNE & BORETA**
*Rituals–Venice #866*
p. 241, #02

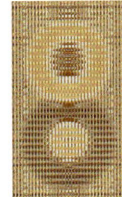 

**AARON PENNE & BORETA**
*Rituals–Venice #3*
p. 241, #03

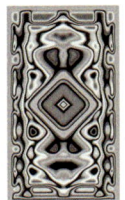 

**AARON PENNE & BORETA**
*Rituals–Venice #680*
p. 241, #04

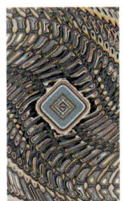 

**AARON PENNE & BORETA**
*Rituals–Venice #56*
p. 241, #05

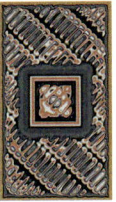 

**AARON PENNE & BORETA**
*Rituals–Venice #567*
p. 241, #06

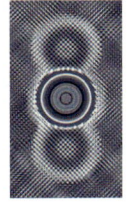 

**AARON PENNE & BORETA**
*Rituals–Venice #907*
p. 241, #07

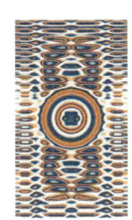 

**0XDEAFBEEF**
*Entropy #148*
p. 244, #01

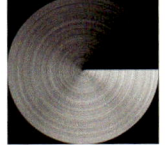 

**0XDEAFBEEF**
*Glitchbox #182*
p. 245, #02

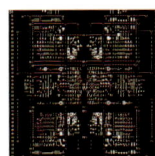 

**0XDEAFBEEF**
*Transmission #139*
pp. 246, 247, #03

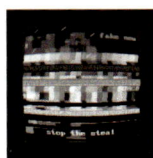 

**LEANDER HERZOG**
*Infinite Garden*
p. 248, 249, #01–06

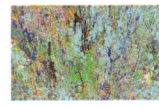 

**KIM ASENDORF**
*PXL DEX*
p. 250, # 01–04

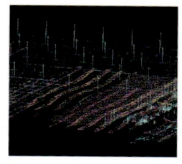 

**KIM ASENDORF**
*Monogrid*
p. 251, # 05

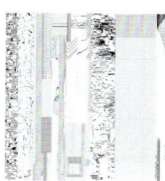 

**HARM VAN DEN DORPEL**
*Markov's Dream: Orb (lite) #69*
p. 253, #02

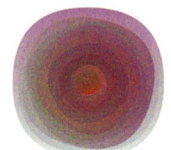 

**HARM VAN DEN DORPEL**
*Markov's Dream: Orb (lite) #71*
p. 253, #03

**HARM VAN DEN DORPEL**
*Markov's Dream: Orb (lite) #72*
p. 253, #04

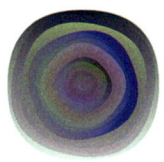 

**HARM VAN DEN DORPEL**
*Markov's Dream: Orb (lite) #74*
p. 253, #05

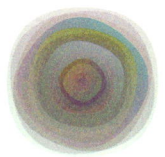 

**HARM VAN DEN DORPEL**
*Markov's Dream: Orb (lite) #62*
p. 253, #06

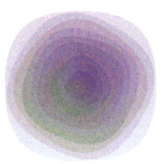 

**HARM VAN DEN DORPEL**
*Markov's Dream: Orb (lite) #63*
p. 253, #07

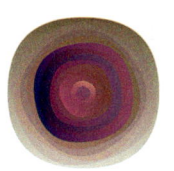 

**HARM VAN DEN DORPEL**
*Markov's Dream: Orb (lite) #53*
p. 249, #08

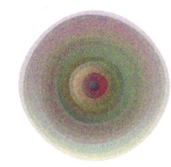 

**HARM VAN DEN DORPEL**
*Markov's Dream: Orb (lite) #93*
p. 253, #09

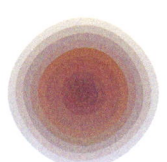 

**HARM VAN DEN DORPEL**
*Markov's Dream: Orb (lite) #95*
p. 253, #10

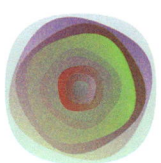 

**DIVERGENCE**
*Buddhabrot*
p. 258, #01

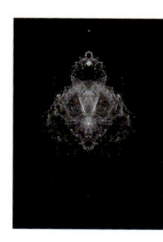 

**0XDEAFBEEF**
*Synth Poems #17*
p. 271, 04.07

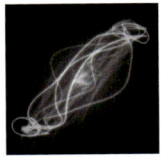 

**MAD DOG JONES**
*Replicator Gen 1*
p. 280, #01

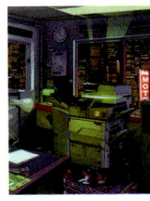 

**MAD DOG JONES**
*Replicator Gen 5*
p. 281, #02

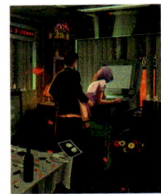 

**MAD DOG JONES**
*Replicator Gen 7*
p. 281, #03

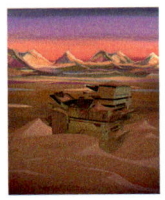 

**PAK**
*Five Hundred Cubes*
p. 282, #01

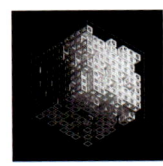 

**PAK**
*A Cube*
p. 283, #02

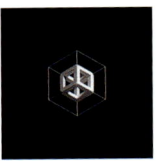 

**PAK**
*Rubik's Lure*
p. 286, #20

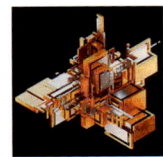 

**PAK**
*Metarift*
p. 287, #21

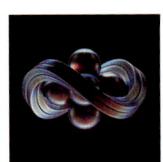 

**SHL0MS**
*Car*
p. 288, # 01

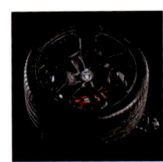 

**ANDREAS GYSIN**
*svg4.svg, Code is dust*
pp. 290, 291, #01, 02

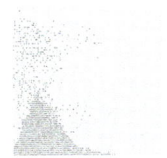 

**ANDREAS GYSIN**
*svg.svg, Code is form*
pp. 292, 293, #03

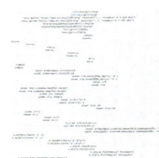 

**ANDREAS GYSIN**
*svg2.svg, Code is wings*
pp. 292, 293, #04

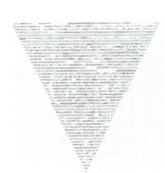 

**ANDREAS GYSIN**
*svg3.svg, Code is tower*
pp. 292, 293, #05

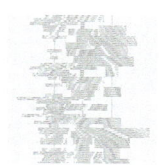 

**ANDREAS GYSIN**
*svg6.svg, Code is alive*
pp. 292, 293, #06

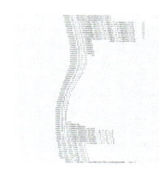 

**JOSHUA DAVIS**
*the V01D / 007-001 / Jana Stýblová*
p. 299, #03

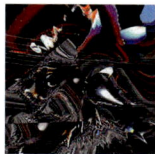 

**EZRA MILLER**
*Solvency #223*
p. 296, #01

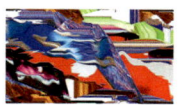 

**EZRA MILLER**
*Solvency #287*
p. 296, #02

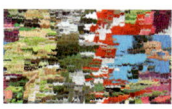 

**EZRA MILLER**
*Silk Road #811*
p. 297, #03

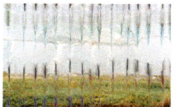 

**EZRA MILLER**
*Silk Road #377*
pp. 298, 299, #04

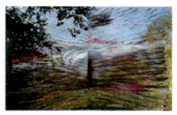 

P1xelfool
*gämma 10+1*11*
p. 300, #01

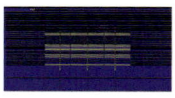 

**P1XELFOOL**
*gämma 2+1*11*
p. 300, #02

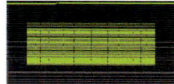 

**P1XELFOOL**
*gämma 9+1*11*
p. 301, #03

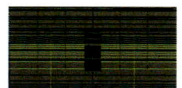 

**P1XELFOOL**
*gämma 2+2*11*
p. 301, #04

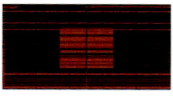 

**NICOLAS SASSOON**
*RIFT*
p. 304, #01

**NICOLAS SASSOON**
*HOLOGLASS*
p. 305, #02

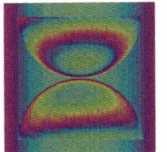 

**NICOLAS SASSOON**
*PLANETS[♂]*
pp. 306, 307, #03

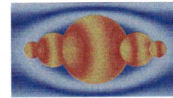 

**SARA LUDY**
*Astral Garden*
p. 308, #01

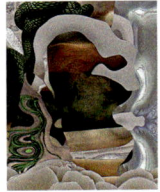 

**BRENDAN DAWES**
*Moments Spent With Others*
p. 310, #01

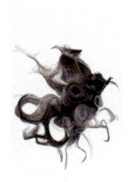 

**ASH THORP**
*Degradation*
p. 312, #01

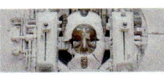 

**ASH THORP**
*Interlinked*
p. 313, #02

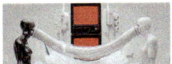 

**ASH THORP**
*Product Placement*
p. 313, #03

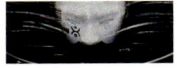 

**BEEPLE**
*GIGACHAD*
p. 314, #01

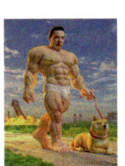 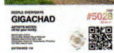 

**BEEPLE**
*GOOGLE DATA COLLECTION 2098*
p. 315, #02

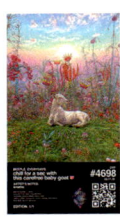 

**BEEPLE**
*CHILL BABY GOAT*
p. 315 #03

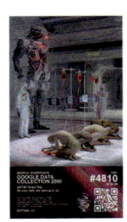 

**BEEPLE**
*Human ONE*
pp. 322, 323, #05

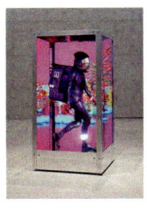 

**BEEPLE**
*REBIRTH*
p. 328, 05.01

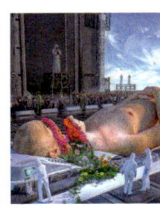 

**REFIK ANADOL**
*Living Architecture: Casa Battló*
p. 332, 05.07

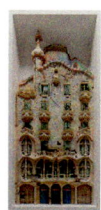 

**BRENDAN DAWES**
*The Art of Cybersecurity*
p. 336, 05.16

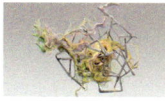 

**ERICK CALDERON**
*Chromie Squiggle*
p. 344, 05.33

**LORNA MILLS**
*Dolphin Date*
p. 356, #01

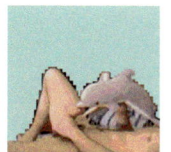 

**LORNA MILLS**
*I Don't Smoke Coach*
p. 356, #02

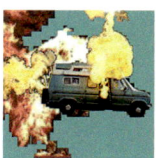 

**LORNA MILLS**
*Twin Cheeks*
p. 356, #03

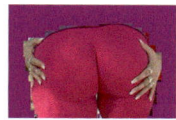 

**LORNA MILLS**
*Whorey Potter and the Socerer's Dick*
p. 356, #04

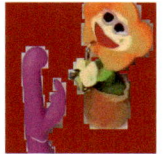 

**LORNA MILLS**
*Wedding Day at Troldhaugen*
p. 357, #05

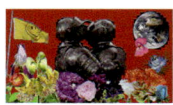 

**AURIEA HARVEY**
*Minoriea Bust v1-dv2 (Sovereign)*
p. 358, #01

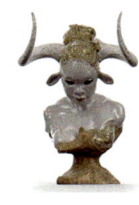 

**KATHERINE FRAZER**
*Magic Move 1*
p. 363, #02

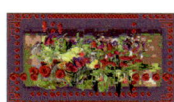 

**CIBELLE CAVALLI BASTOS**
*Bença [Blessings]*
p. 367, #13

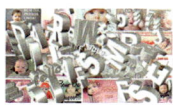 

**MARIO KLINGEMANN**
*Monday?*
p. 368, #01

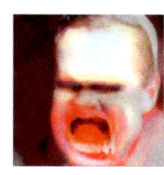 

**ANNE SPALTER**
*THE WONDER OF IT ALL*
p. 371, #02

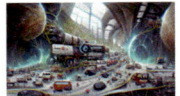 

**SOFIA CRESPO**
*[[seed_of_seeds]]*
p. 374, #01

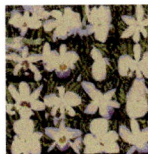 

**SOFIA CRESPO**
*hideseek_hope_9078*
p. 375, #02

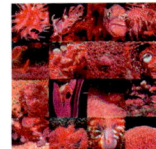 

**REFIK ANADOL**
*Machine Hallucinations: Coral Dreams*
p. 381, #02

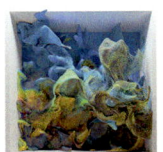 

**REFIK ANADOL**
*Machine Hallucinations – Space: Metaverse*
pp. 384, 385, #05

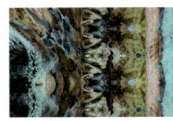 

**MOREHSHIN ALLAHYARI**
*Moon-faced*
pp. 386, 387, #01–03

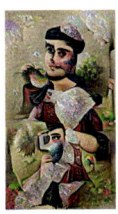 

**HOLLY HERNDON & MAT DRYHURST**
*Crossing the Interface (DAO) VI*
p. 389, #02

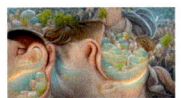 

**HOLLY HERNDON & MAT DRYHURST**
*Crossing the Interface (DAO) X*
p. 389, #03

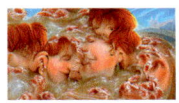 

**HOLLY HERNDON & MAT DRYHURST**
*Crossing the Interface (DAO) VIII*
p. 389, #04

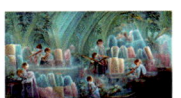 

**HOLLY HERNDON & MAT DRYHURST**
*Crossing the Interface (DAO) XIII*
p. 389, #05

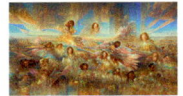 

**RIMBAWAN GERILYA**
*Solitary Grave II*
p. 394, #01

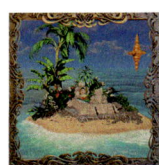 

**RIMBAWAN GERILYA**
*Sacred Border (Batas Suci)*
p. 395, #02

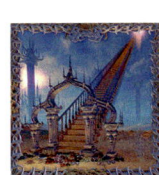 

**RINIIFISH**
*My Hell / M7 Planet*
p. 396, #01

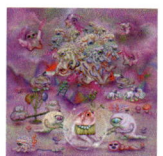 

**RINIIFISH**
*Heart Throb / M7 Planet*
p. 397, #02

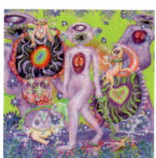 

**PHILIPPE PARRENO**
*Anywhere Out of the World*
p. 413, 06.08
Artwork on Vimeo

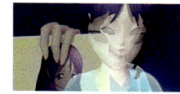 

**SPUTNIKO!**
*Menstrualverse*
p. 426, 06.29

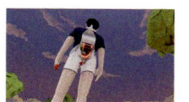 

**LINDA DOUNIA**
*Proof of Zen*
p. 462, #01

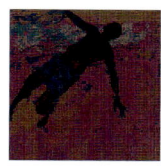 

**DADA BOIPELO**
*The crowd*
p. 465, #02

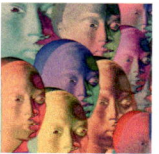 

**PUSSY RIOT**
*DRINK MY BLOOD*
p. 467, #02

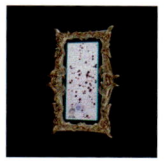 

**URS FISCHER**
*CHAOS #3 Kibitzer*
p. 472, #01

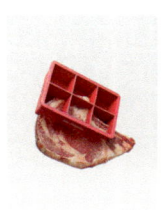 

**URS FISCHER**
*CHAOS #93 Resistance*
p. 472, #02

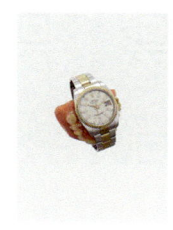 

**URS FISCHER**
*CHAOS #154 Western*
p. 472, #03

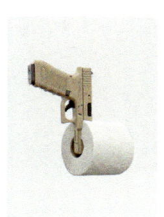 

**URS FISCHER**
*CHAOS #200 Semiotics*
p. 472, #04

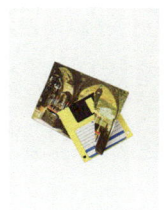 

**URS FISCHER**
*CHAOS #1 Human*
p. 473, #05

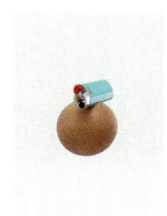 

**URS FISCHER**
*CHAOS #273 Thespian*
p. 473, #06

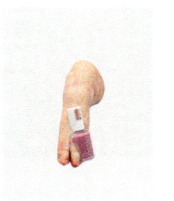 

**URS FISCHER**
*CHAOS #501*
pp. 474, 475, #07
Artwork on Vimeo (unminted at time of publication)

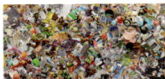 

**YATREDA**
*Queen of Sheba*
p. 482, #01

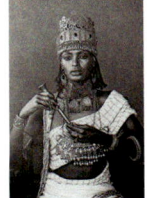 

**YATREDA**
*Royal Armada of Aethiopia*
p. 483, #02

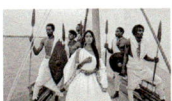 

**YATREDA**
*Arsi Oromo, Devotion:*
*Movement of the Ancestors*
p. 484, #03

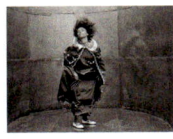 

**YATREDA**
*King Lalibela –*
*Rock-hewn: Kingdoms of Ethiopia*
p. 484, #04

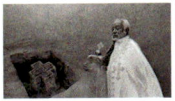 

**YATREDA**
*Medusa: Andromeda of Aethiopia*
p. 485, #05

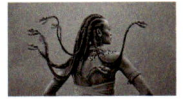 

**YATREDA**
*Amhara, Lion's Roar:*
*Movement of the Ancestors*
p. 485, #06

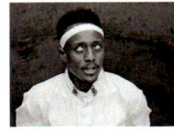 

**KENNY SCHACHTER**
*Eating the bubble*
p. 488, #01

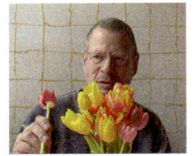 

**JOE PEASE**
*Everything is Temporary*
p. 476, # 01

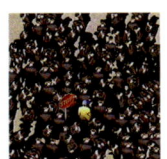 

**JOE PEASE**
*Open the Floodgates*
p. 477, # 02

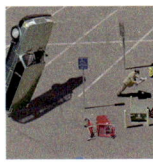 

**KENNY SCHACHTER**
*Branding (Homage to Prince)*
p. 489, #02

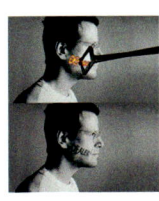 

**ANDRÉS REISINGER**
*Gold Pollen*
p. 490, #01

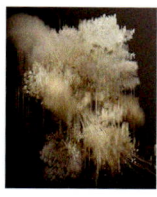

**ANDRÉS REISINGER**
*Tangled*
p. 492, #03

**ANDRÉS REISINGER**
*Complicated Sofa*
p. 493, #04

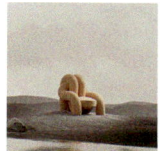

**HARM VAN DEN DORPEL**
*Event Listeners*
p. 512, 08.20

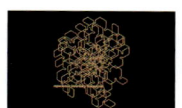

**THEVERSEVERSE**
*Sasha Stiles, Fragment 1*
p. 520, # 01

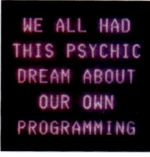

**KEIKEN**
*Dream Time Life Simulation*
p. 524, #01

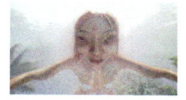

**MATHCASTLES**
*Terraforms Level 7 at {23, 20}*
p. 538, 09.10

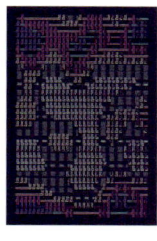

**ANGELA WASHKO**
*The Council on Gender Sensitivity and Behavioral Awareness in World of Warcraft*
p. 540, 09.12, Artwork on artist's website

**OSEANWORLD**
*-- ★ ꜱɜꞁꜰⓞ pörȼrɐjȼ ★-- AR Self portrait*
p. 550, #01
3D artwork file

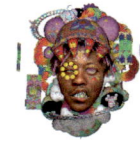

**OSEANWORLD**
*THE FUTRUE .01*
p. 551, #02

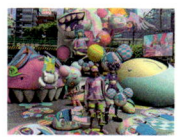

**SIMON DENNY**
*NFT Mine Offset: ETH Ethereum Miner*
*3 GPUs*
p. 556, #05

**JACK BUTCHER**
*Opepen Edition*
p. 559, # 02

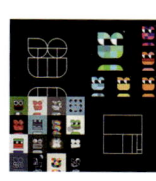

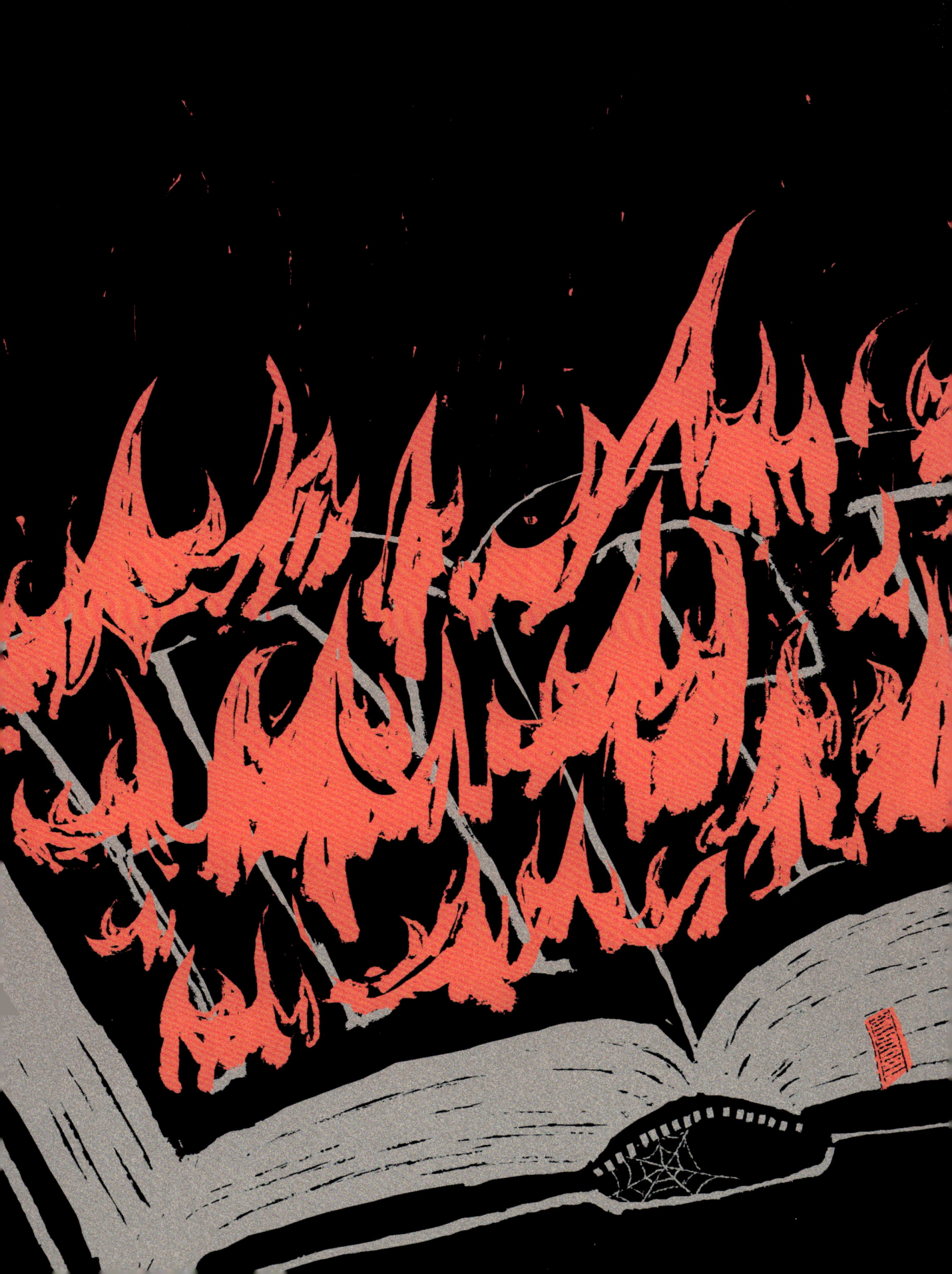

# ENDMATTER

# GLOSSARY

## 1/1 Art
Expression | A unique work of art that has been issued in an edition of one.

## 1/1 of X
Expression | A unique artwork within a collection of X pieces, often used to describe PFP or algorithmic art NFTs. For example, *CryptoPunks* are 1/1 of 10,000 and *Fidenzas* are 1/1 of 999.

## A

### Airdrop
Noun | The practice of sending cryptocurrency or NFTs, usually for free, to a number of predetermined wallet addresses. Airdrops are often used as a loyalty benefit to NFT holders, or to generate attention for new NFT projects by rewarding the purchase of certain NFTs, or sharing relevant content on social media.

### Algorist
Noun | An artist who uses algorithmic processes in their work. Jean-Pierre Hébert and Roman Verostko initially coined the term in 1995 to define the movement.

### Algorithm
Noun | A set of step-by-step instructions or rules that a computer follows to perform a specific task or solve a particular problem.

### Algorithmic Art
Noun | A subset of generative art, art generated by a computational algorithm.

### Alpha
Noun | A term borrowed from the finance community indicating the hierarchy in performance, authority, or knowledge. Having "alpha" typically refers to an individual or group with a competitive trading advantage.

### AMA
Abbreviation | Short for "Ask Me Anything," used by people to invite questions during live or preplanned Q&A sessions. Many crypto and NFT projects hold AMA sessions to maintain engagement with the community and encourage participation in their project.

### Anti-Dump, *also* Anti-Dumping Policy
Noun | A policy or set of rules that protects crypto or NFT investors from falling prey to pump and dump schemes. Such policies may limit the size of buy orders to prevent rapid price inflation, or put in place a cooling-off period and increased tax after each sale to regulate price volatility and prevent whales from trading large amounts of tokens in a single transaction.

### Apeing, *also* Aped
Verb | To speculatively invest large sums of money into (new) crypto projects or tokens with little prior research or due diligence. Apeing is usually the product of Twitter hypes or virality. The expression originates in the "apes together strong" meme and hints at the collective understanding (or delusion) of value. Apes have become an important symbol of NFTs following the popularization of *CryptoPunks* (of which 24 are apes) and Bored Ape Yacht Club's ape-themed PFPs.

### API
Abbreviation | Short for "Application Programming Interface," a set of routines, protocols, and tools for building and integrating application software. APIs allow different software applications to interact, for example, by determining how one software will respond to data or actions from another software. APIs form the backbone of the new digital economy.

### AR
Abbreviation | Short for "Augmented Reality," an interactive experience of a real-world environment or item that has been complemented with computer-generated elements, such as sound, visuals, or smells.

### Art Blocks
Noun | A digital art platform on the Ethereum blockchain that is used to produce, sell, and store algorithmic art, involving collectors in the artist's creative process.

### Arweave
Noun | A decentralized storage protocol that uses a blockchain-like technology, known as blockweave, to store applications, documents, and data across a distributed network.

### ASCII
Abbreviation | Short for "American Standard Code for Information Interchange," ASCII is a character encoding standard for electronic communication comprising just 128 characters.

### ASCII Art
Noun | Art that is created using ASCII characters. Kenneth Knowlton (1931–2022) was an early pioneer of the technique, while *ASCII BERNANKE* (2011) by Dan Kaminsky was one of the first artworks to be registered on the blockchain, which also used ASCII characters.

### Ascribe
Noun | Started in 2013 and discontinued in 2017, an early protocol that used the Bitcoin blockchain to allow digital artists to record their intellectual property.

### Asset-Backed Tokens
Noun | A token that is linked to a tangible or intangible object of economic value. This is a way of digitizing claims on an asset and recording the relevant data on a blockchain.

### Astroturfing
Verb | To present marketing, public relations, or otherwise sponsored content in the guise of genuine and unprompted views of community members.

### ATH
Abbreviation | Short for "All-Time-High," a cryptocurrency or cryptoasset's historical peak, for instance, in price or market capitalization.

### ATL
Abbreviation | Short for "All-Time-Low," a cryptocurrency or cryptoasset's historical low point, for instance, in price or market capitalization.

### Auction
Noun | A public sale where potential buyers submit bids and the asset in question is sold to the highest bidder. In the art world, auctions are not only important social events but set the tone for the art market, indicating trends and benchmark values. While increasingly offered at traditional auction houses, NFTs are usually auctioned on online platforms.

### Avatar
Noun | Avatar is an idea within Hinduism and comes from the Sanskrit word *avatara*, meaning "descent." It denotes the incarnation of a powerful deity on Earth. While first popularized in gaming, in the crypto space avatars are unique digital portraits used as pseudononymous identities, usually from the shoulders up and often used as PFPs.

### AWS
Abbreviation | Short for "Amazon Web Server," a cloud service offered by Amazon that provides distributed computing processing capacity and software tools.

## B

### Bag, *also* Your Bags
Noun | Crypto slang for someone's crypto portfolio, typically used in reference to large cryptocurrency or NFT holdings.

### Baking
Verb | The transaction verification method to create a new block on the Tezos blockchain.

### Bear Market / Bearish
Expression | Refers to a market that experiences prolonged price decline, usually by 20% from recent highs. Investor confidence is low and there is widespread pessimism in the market. Bearish is someone who believes price will decline for a period of time.

### Big Tech
Noun | The biggest, most dominant corporations in the information technology industry worldwide, namely "The Big Five" such as Amazon, Apple, Google, Meta (Facebook), and Microsoft.

## Bitcoin (BTC)

Noun | The best-known decentralized digital currency that was founded by a mysterious entity named Satoshi Nakamoto in 2009. The bitcoin cryptocurrency runs on the Bitcoin blockchain and functions as a peer-to-peer payment mechanism with no central authority. Its transactions are verified by a proof-of-work algorithm and recorded in a publically distributed ledger called a blockchain. New coins can be generated through mining, however, thanks to its technologically imposed scarcity, the supply of bitcoin is capped at 21 million coins.

## Block

Noun | An immutable data structure that stores the record of transactions on a blockchain. A blockchain is made up of a chronological string of blocks. When one block is filled with transactions and then validated the block is closed and a new block created. This process can carry on ad infinitum.

## Block Height

Noun | The distance from the genesis block (Block 0 or Block 1, depending on the blockchain) in number of blocks.

## Block Size

Noun | The amount of data that is able to be stored in a block.

## Block Time

Noun | The amount of time taken to generate a new block.

## Blockchain

Noun | The specific architecture of distributed ledger technology that underpins the mechanism behind cryptocurrencies and NFTs. As a decentralized digital database, it can be viewed and operated from multiple locations and devices without a central authority. Information is stored in units of data ("blocks") that are linked to one another to form the append-only database ("chain"). Each authorized entity of the network ("node") holds an identical copy of the blockchain, which is updated whenever new information is added to the ledger. This allows for impeccable audit trails, complete transparency, and real-time tracking of any transactional activity in the network.

## Blue Chip

Expression | Originally denoting a recognized, well-established, and financially sound company with a strong market presence. In the art world, blue chip refers to something that is of the highest quality or someone (a person or institution), who is world renowned, usually in reference to the strength of that given artist's, or artwork's, market in holding and increasing its value.

## Bot

Noun | An automated computer program that performs predetermined tasks online such as cryptocurrency trading, chatting with users, or sending spam.

## Bridge

Noun | A connection between two blockchains that allows for the transfer of data or tokens.

## BSC

Abbreviation | Short for "Binance Smart Chain," a more centralized blockchain developed by Binance, a large cryptocurrency exchange company, to compete with Ethereum. It proposes fast transactions, smart contract functionality, and EVM compatibility.

## BTD / BTFD

Abbreviation | Short for "Buy the (Fucking) Dip," an enthusiastic encouragement to buy a cryptocurrency or NFT following a price dip in the hope of a rapid value increase.

## BUIDL

Verb | A mispelling of "build" extrapolated from the crypto in-joke HODL / HOLD (see HODL). BUIDL is a mentality, and an incitation to build useful projects in the crypto space, especially in market downturns.

## Bull Market / Bullish

Expression | Refers to a time of rapid growth in the market. Where investor sentiment is positive and there is widespread optimism. Bullish refers to someone who is optimistic and confident prices will increase.

## Burn

Verb | The act of removing a token from circulation by sending it to a defunct or inaccessible wallet address.

## Buying on Secondary

Expression | Buying secondhand from a platform rather than minting at the original drop.

# C

## CC0

Abbreviation | Short for "Creative Commons Zero," is a licensing system, first launched by Creative Commons in 2009, by which creators, such as artists, waive any and all copyright in their work, thereby placing it into the public domain for anyone to freely use, adapt, and capitalize on. Examples of CC0 NFTs include *Nouns*, *CrypToadz*, and *Blitmaps*.

## Centralized

Adjective | A centralized system is one that is governed and administrated by a principal authority. For example, this is the case for most social media platforms. A blockchain can be centralized if it is private rather than public and managed by a single group or organization, for example, the Ripple cryptocurrency.

## Code

Noun | Code is a set of program instructions. A developer writes code (a combination of words and numbers) to instruct a machine to execute a set of instructions.

## Code Is Law

Expression | The belief that the capability of code acts as the digital rule, in that intentional features and unintentional "bugs" are indistinguishable, as the execution of the code is what defines the outcome.

## Coinbase

Noun | The largest American cryptocurrency exchange by trading volume, founded in 2012 by Brian Armstrong.

## Cold Wallet

Noun | An offline cryptocurrency wallet, such as a hardware wallet. Cold wallets are more secure than hot wallets.

## Collectible

Noun | An object that is considered to have value and usually exists in a limited quantity. The value of crypto collectibles, i.e., NFTs, often depends on their rarity.

## Conceptual Art, *also* Conceptualism

Noun | A form of art that focuses on the idea or concept of a work, rather than its execution, embodiment, or aesthetics. Though pioneered in the early 20th century, the term usually refers to art made in the 1960s and 1970s when the movement gained traction.

## Consensus Mechanism

Noun | A technology based on game theory that dictates how data and transactions are validated without a central administrator on a blockchain. The most well-known consensus mechanisms are proof of work and proof of stake.

## Contemporary Art

Noun | Art of any style or medium that is produced by artists of modern-day society, which is often broadly interpreted and can mean art made between the 1960s and the present day.

## Cope

Verb | Taking an overly cautious approach due to repercussions of previous apeing and thereby missing out on a promising token.

## Copy Cat

Noun | An NFT project that copies a popular project, often to feed off their hype.

## Counterparty

Noun | Launched in 2014, a platform built on top of the Bitcoin blockchain, allowing users to create, name, and issue their own tokens.

## Crypto, *also* Cryptocurrency

Noun | A digital currency that is run by blockchain technology.

## Crypto Asset

Noun | A digital asset that is underpinned by blockchain technology, for example cryptocurrencies or NFTs.

## Cryptography

Noun | A mathematical method of encrypting secure communication that can conceal and reveal information with varying levels of difficulty.

## Cryptography Mailing List

Noun | A mailing list devoted to cryptographic technology and its political impact. It was here where Satoshi Nakamoto first published the Bitcoin whitepaper.

**Cryptovoxels**
Noun | An Ethereum-based metaverse platform launched in 2018. See *Metaverse*.

**Cybernetics**
Noun | The science of control and communications in the animal and machine, as defined by Norbert Wiener in *Cybernetics*, 1948.

**Cyberpunk**
Noun | A science fiction subgenre that revolves around a somewhat dehumanized integration of future urban society and technology. Neal Stephenson's *Snow Crash* from 1992 is one of the most popular novels in the cyberpunk genre.

**Cyberspace**
Noun | Coined by William Gibson in "Burning Chrome" from 1982, refers to the interconnectivity of computing technologies.

**Cypherpunk**
Noun | A cypherpunk is an individual who advocates mass adoption of strong cryptography and privacy-enhancing technology to enact social and political change. Cypherpunk came out of the Cypherpunk Mailing List and has been an active community since the 1990s.

# D

**Dada**
Noun | Dada was a nihilistic and anti-aesthetic art movement that was born out of the horrors of the First World War. The art was often nonsensical or satirical.

**Dank**
Adjective | Or "Dankness" (noun) the quality or state of possessing a high calibre of meme content.

**DAO**
Abbreviation | Short for "Decentralized Autonomous Organization," a digital association or cooperative on the blockchain where token-holding members vote on decisions that are subsequently executed via smart contracts.

**dAPI**
Abbreviation | Short for "Decentralized API," which are API services that are interoperable through blockchain technology, thereby allowing the apps' underlying smart contracts to access API data while maintaining the system's security assurances.

**dApps**
Abbreviation | Short for "Decentralized Applications," which are applications (apps) that are powered by smart contracts and can operate autonomously on decentralized networks, such as Ethereum. OpenSea, for example, is a dApp that provides a marketplace to NFT users.

**Dark Web**
Noun | A subset of the deep web (about 0.01%) that contains online content existing on darknets, i.e., computer networks that use the internet but require specific software, configurations, and authorization to access, allowing users to communicate and/or conduct business anonymously. Many dark web marketplaces transact with cryptocurrencies given the censorship they offer, such as Silk Road (2011–2013).

**Decentraland**
Noun | An Ethereum-based metaverse platform launched in 2020. See *Metaverse*.

**Decentralized**
Adjective | In a decentralized system, administration and decision-making are shared among constituent members, making it more horizontal and secure, though often slower, than centralized systems. Notably, the idea of decentralized networks, such as P2P file-sharing services, has been around since the turn of the millennium and predates blockchain technology.

**Ded**
Abbreviation | Short for "Dead," a way to reply to something so funny that you have figuratively died of laughter.

**Deep Web**
Noun | A term coined by computer scientist Michael K. Bergman in 2001, referring to the part of the World Wide Web that cannot be found or accessed through standard web search engines.

**DeFi**
Abbreviation | Short for "Decentralized Finance," referring to financial services that take place on a blockchain and where, unlike in tradition finance, no single entity has control over the money and activity. Loans, interest, and derivatives are all controlled and implemented by smart contracts.

**Degen**
Abbreviation | Short for "Degenerate," a terms to describe people who tend to make risky or poor bets. In the NFT space, it may be used to scold someone for apeing.

**Delist**
Verb | To remove an NFT listing from a marketplace.

**Derivatives**
Noun | Crypto projects derived from popular projects. The topic of their value is divisive within the NFT community.

**Devs**
Abbreviation | Short for "Developers," specifically those working on a crypto or NFT project.

**DEX**
Abbreviation | Short for "Decentralized Exchange," a P2P marketplace where transactions are made directly between traders without the need for a middleman.

**Diamond Hands**
Noun | Someone who, unlike paper hands, does not panic sell their assets and holds on to them despite price volatility or FUD.

**Digital Art**
Noun | Art made or displayed with digital technologies.

**Digital Asset**
Noun | An asset in digital form or digital representation of an asset.

**Discord**
Noun | An online messaging and social media platform released in 2015, mainly used by the gaming, crypto, and NFT communities for private or public communication on updates, trends, and projects.

**DLT**
Abbreviation | Short for "Distributed Ledger Technology," a decentralized database that relies on its network to review and approve newly added data, e.g., transactions. While blockchain is a type of DLT, not all DLT comes in the form of blockchain. For instance, DLT does not necessarily have a block structure, or chronological chain sequence.

**Doxing, *also* Doxxed**
Verb | To publish private identifying information about someone or oneself online. When an individual in the NFT space is doxxed, this usually means that the identity behind their Twitter alias or wallet address is disclosed, with or without their permission.

**Drop**
Noun | The initial release of an NFT project.

**Dump, *also* Dumping**
Noun/Verb | A rapid drop in the value of a coin due to irregular selling activity and usually caused by a whale selling their tokens (at market price or below) in an attempt to profit from a recent price increase.

**Dutch Auction, *also* Descending Price Auction**
Noun | A bidding technique where the price of the asset offered for sale is lowered in intervals until a buyer is found or the collection sells out. The starting price is sometimes determined by taking bids prior to the auction to identify the asset's ceiling price.

**DYOR**
Abbreviation | Short for "Do Your Own Research," an encouragement to conduct due diligence prior to investing in a crypto or NFT project, often used cynically by more experienced participants when asked NFT-related questions by inexperienced or new market participants.

# E

**Edition Number**
Noun |The total size of edition of NFTs, or the number of a particular work within the edition.

## EIP

Abbreviation | Short for "Ethereum Improvement Proposals," a tool by which network upgrades and application standards for the Ethereum blockchain can be proposed, peer-reviewed, and proved by community members. An EIP contains the technical descriptions, such as protocol specification, APIs, and contract standards, for the potential new standard.

## ENS

Abbreviation | Short for "Ethereum Name Service," a system on the Ethereum blockchain that connects wallet addresses to human-readable names, usually ending with the name suffix .eth, for example Alice.eth. Crypto users often buy ENS addresses to facilitate public identification for public entities or identities.

## ERC-20

Abbreviation | Short for "Ethereum Request for Comment 20," it was proposed by Fabian Vogelsteller in November 2015. It is a token standard for fungible tokens that implements an API for tokens within smart contracts.

## ERC-721

Abbreviation | Short for "Ethereum Request for Comment 721," an ERC for NFTs ensuring that each token is unique. The ERC-721 is the most widely used token standard for creating NFTs on Ethereum.

## ERC-1155

Abbreviation | Short for "Ethereum Request for Comment 1155," the ERC that enables the use of a single smart contract to represent a class of assets, such as NFT collections, rather than each token or asset individually. This allows for more efficient trades and bundling of transactions.

## Escape Velocity

Noun | In physics, escape velocity signifies the minimum speed required for a body to escape from a gravitational center of attraction. In the NFT or crypto realm, it is used to describe the critical point, such as a certain price, from where a token's value will rise dramatically, and/or more broadly the breaking away from the traditional financial system.

## Escrow

Noun | A legal arrangement by which a third party temporarily holds assets or cash until a deal is completed or a predecided condition is met.

## ether, also ETH or Ξ

Abbreviation | The native currency of the Ethereum blockchain.

## Ethereum

Noun | A blockchain that, thanks to its numerous programmable features, has a wide variety of (potential) uses, including the ether cryptocurrency, secondary ERC-20 cryptocurrencies, dApps, blockchain-based software, and DAOs. Ethereum is the most widely used blockchain in Web3.

## Ethereum 2.0, also ETH2

Noun | A set of upgrades to Ethereum that rolled out on September 6, 2022, allowing for it to be faster, less expensive, and more scalable. Most significantly, ETH2 migrated the blockchain from the proof-of-work to the proof-of-stake consensus mechanism.

## Etherscan

Noun | A block explorer that allows one to search the Ethereum blockchain.

## EVM

Abbreviation | Short for "Ethereum Virtual Machine," a platform where developers can create dApps on Ethereum and where all Ethereum accounts and smart contracts live. EVM acts like a decentralized computer with millions of executable projects and forms the bedrock of Ethereum's operating structure.

## Exchange

Noun | A marketplace to trade cryptocurrencies.

# F

## Few

Abbreviation | Short for "Few people understand," a way to comment on an underrated or underestimated event, token, or person in the NFT or crypto space.

## Fiat Currency

Noun | A government-issued currency not backed by any commodity. This is the case for most national currencies in the post–Bretton Woods era.

## Flip / Flipping

Verb | The act of buying something at a low price and selling it quickly for profit.

## Floor, also Floor Price

Noun | The lowest available price in an NFT collection on the secondary market.

## Floor Is Lava

Expression | The expression given when an NFT project is being bought up quickly, often by whales, resulting in the floor price rising rapidly.

## FML

Abbreviation | Short for "Fuck My Life," an expression of discontent or frustration with a situation.

## FOMO

Abbreviation | Short for "Fear Of Missing Out," which usually refers to rash and imprudent decisions based on following a trend or rumor. FOMO is often the root cause of apeing. The term originated on social media.

## Fork

Noun | A permanent change made to a blockchain's underlying protocol or basic set of rules, for instance, to add new features or fix bugs, or the emergence of a new, divergent branch of a blockchain, creating two new chains. In some instances, forks can be short-lived, for example to quickly reach consensus in the distributed system.

## Fractional Ownership

Noun | Where the ownership of an asset, such as an NFT, is divided between several parties who each can only sell on their respective shares.

## Fren

Expression | Crypto slang for "Friend," a polite way to address fellow community members.

## FUD

Abbreviation | Short for "Fear, Uncertainty, and Doubt," which refers to pessimistic views, usually online or in the media, about the future outlook of a token or project. Often there is the perception that they are fake news, or written with dubious intentions.

## FUDster

Expression | A reproachful nickname for someone who spreads (sometimes misleading or false) FUD to influence perception of a token, project, or the market in general.

## Fungible Tokens

Noun | Tokens that are interchangeable, such as cryptocurrencies.

## fxhash

Noun | An open platform to create and collect generative NFTs on the Tezos blockchain, founded by ciphrd in November 2021.

# G

## Game Theory

Noun | The study of mathematical models conceiving the interactions between competing rational players, often used to weigh up risks and rewards for each player depending on the other player's actions. Game theory is a fundamental mechanism underlying blockchain technology and allows cryptocurrencies to ensure the reliability of distributed databases.

## GAN

Abbreviation | Short for "Generative Adversial Network," a form of deep learning that generates new and realistic content from a dataset.

## Gang Gang

Expression | Another way to say "I'm with you," for instance, to express approval of a statement or agree to a suggested plan.

## Gas, also Gas Fee

Noun | The cost of a transaction on a blockchain network which is ultimately paid to the miners to compensate for the computing energy required to process and validate transactions. The fee is determined by the respective level of network traffic and the desired speed, rather than the value of the transaction. Gas is usually paid in the blockchain's native cryptocurrency.

## Gas War

Noun | A process whereby potential buyers compete in outbidding each other to achieve faster transactions and thus priority on newly launched NFT collections whose demand exceeds its supply. Gas wars are common during popular NFT drops.

**Gen Z,** *also* **Generation Z** *or* **Zoomers**
Expression | The generation born roughly between 1996 (subject of extensive online debate) and 2010. Gen Z grew up on Web 2.0 and social media, which is why they now control the memes with their dark, existentialist humor. As digital natives, many Gen Zs feel right at home in the crypto and NFT space.

**Generative Art**
Noun | Also "Gen Art." An umbrella term that refers to any artwork created by rules or a system, and can therefore be completed independently from the artist. Generative art has been conceptually significant since the early 20th century, but became increasingly widespread with the development of new technologies, see *Algorithmic Art.*

**Genesis Block**
Noun | The first block of a blockchain.

**Genesis Work**
Noun | An artist's first NFT or the first NFT minted in a series.

**GIF**
Abbreviation | Short for "Graphics Interchange Format." A GIF is a file format that supports looped videos. The term is often used as a metonymy for the videos themselves, and is known to divide the online community over its pronunciation — with a hard or a soft *g*.

**GitHub**
Noun | A social network for software developers to collaborate and share open-source projects.

**Glitch Art**
Noun | The practice of employing digital or analog errors within one's work to create distorted aesthetics. Such can be achieved by corrupting digital files, manipulating digital devices, or artificially rendering glitch-like aesthetics onto a work. Notable "Glitch Art" artists include XCOPY and Dawnia Darkstone.

**GM**
Abbreviation | Short for "Good Morning," a common greeting in the crypto space, especially on crypto Twitter. Its history is unknown.

**GN**
Abbreviation | Short for "Good Night," on crypto Twitter, an indication to peers that you are logging off.

**GOAT**
Abbreviation | Short for "Greatest Of All Time," a show of respect and homage to a fellow community member.

**Governance Tokens**
Noun | A token that providers the owner with voting rights in a democratic system for collective decision-making, such as a DAO.

**GPT-3**
Noun | An advanced artificial intelligence system with an autoregressive language model that uses deep learning to produce human-like text. Following an initial text prompt, GPT-3 will produce further text that continues the prompt.

**GPU**
Abbreviation | Short for "Graphics Processing Unit," a computer chip (or processor) originally designed to allow and accelerate graphics rendering, i.e., the creation of 3D images on a computer. GPU's ability to process many pieces of data simultaneously has made it an efficient tool in mining cryptocurrencies.

**Gwei,** *also* **Nanoether** *or* **Nano**
Noun | A denomination of ETH denoting the ninth power of the fractional ETH, i.e., 0.000000001 ETH. It is a portmanteau of "giga" and "wei," wei being the smallest denomination of Ethereum.

# H

**Hacker**
Noun | An individual/group who uses computer, networking, or other skills to overcome technical problems. This term can also mean someone who uses these abilities to illegally gain unauthorized access to others networks and systems.

**Halving**
Noun | As miners complete the proof of work and new blocks are added to the Bitcoin blockchain, a certain amount of bitcoin is released for each block to reward the miners for sustaining the network's security. As the number of bitcoin is finite (21 million), the block reward paid to miners for validating the block is halved every 210,000 blocks (~4 years) to ensure this cap is kept. With Bitcoin, the supply started at 50 BTC per block, at time of publishing it is at 6.25 BTC.

**Hash**
Noun | A hash is a fixed-length digest of a message which is the result of an encryption algorithm.

**HEN**
Abbreviation | Short for "Hic et Nunc." A low-cost and environmentally friendly marketplace for art built on top of the Tezos blockchain. HEN was shut down by its founder in November 2021 but was resurrected only a few weeks later by the community. It is now known as OBJKT.

**HODL**
Abbreviation | Short for "Hold On for Dear Life," a passive investment strategy by which someone holds on to an asset for a very long time, regardless of any change in the price or market. The term originates in a typo from a Bitcoin forum back in 2013 that was subsequently re-interpreted and widely spread as a text meme.

**Hot Wallet**
Noun | An online cryptocurrency wallet, such as MetaMask, typically less secure than a cold wallet.

# I

**I See What You Did There**
Expression | A way to respectfully acknowledge or commend a smart move by a friend, competitor, or collaborator in the NFT space.

**ICO**
Abbreviation | Short for "Initial Coin Offering," the crypto industry's equivalent to an initial public offering (IPO). ICOs are a way for companies or projects to raise funds through a crowdsale of their token.

**Immutability**
Noun | A core principle of a blockchain, immutability is the inability for a record or piece of data to be changed.

**Inflation**
Noun | A general increase in prices of virtual assets and fall in the purchasing value of a cryptocurrency.

**Intermediary,** *also* **Middleman**
Noun | A person or entity positioned between different parties who brokers an agreement or carries out business on a party's behalf, usually in return for a cut of the sales price. In the art world, this is often an agent or gallerist. While blockchain offers the possibility of middleman-free transactions, many NFT sales are still brokered by third parties.

**Interoperability,** *also* **Cross-Chain Interoperability**
Noun | Technology that enhances the interconnection between blockchain networks, for instance through token standards, so that data or assets can be viewed and moved across multiple ecosystems, such as wallet providers, marketplaces, and metaverses.

**IP**
Abbreviation | Short for "Intellectual Property," intangible property which is usually a creation of human intellect. This includes inventions, literary and artistic works, designs, symbols, and names or images used in commerce. A number of international and domestic legal instruments allow creators to protect their IP from being used or copied.

**IP Address**
Abbreviation | Short for "Internet Protocol Address," a unique numeric identifier for each device connected to the internet or a local network.

**IPF,** *also* **IPFS**
Abbreviation | Short for "Interplanetary File System," a decentralized P2P file storage system created by Juan Benet in 2015 where data is stored across multiple locations instead of one single-host server. Many off-chain NFTs use IPFS to store their metadata.

**IRL**
Abbreviation | Short for "In Real Life," synonym of meatspace, i.e., the real world as opposed to digital space.

**IYKYK**
Abbreviation | Short for "If You Know, You Know," similar to "few," implying that a statement or event will make sense to a connoisseur only.

## J

### JPEG

Abbreviation | Short for "Joint Photographic Experts Group," a standard format for containing lossy and compressed image data, most commonly used for the storage and transmission of digital photographs. While many (but not all) NFTs are linked to JPEGs, the community sometimes uses the term synonymously to "NFT," mocking those who cannot tell their JPEGs from their GIFs.

## K

### Kinetic Art

Noun | Born in the early 20th century but gaining traction especially in the 1950s and '60s, art that uses movement, either from the viewer or from the object, in order to create its effect.

### KOL

Abbreviation | Short for "Key Opinion Leader," an influencer whose social status and/or online following is large enough that they are able to impact other community members' decision-making, or steer market trends.

### KYC

Abbreviation | Short for "Know Your Customer," a process of verifying someone's identity by way of identification documents, photos, and/or personal information, before entering into a commercial relationship with them. KYC is one of the key components of anti–money laundering measures.

## L

### Larva Labs

Noun | A US-based mobile software company set up by Matt Hall and John Watkinson, known for creating *CryptoPunks* and *Autoglyphs*.

### Layer 2

Noun | A Layer 2 is a scaling solution that works on top of an underlying Layer 1 blockchain protocol (e.g., Ethereum). Layer 2 inherits the security of the underlying blockchain it is built on, but improves scalability, transaction speed, and efficiency.

### LFG

Abbreviation | Short for "Let's Fucking Go," an expression of excitement, especially regarding rising prices. The hubris of the term is encapsulated best by the Luna Foundation Guard, set up by Do Kwon, and the subsequent collapse of the Terra/Luna blockchain ecosystem in just three days.

### Limited Edition

Noun | An asset, such as a collectible, of which there is a finite number of copies, such as an NFT collection where the amount of NFTs that are available to be minted is capped.

### Liquidity Pool

Noun | A crowdsourced collection of tokens that is locked in a smart contract as an assurance of liquidity in order to facilitate trade on a decentralized exchange.

### Looks Rare

Expression | An ironic way of saying that something does not look rare and is therefore unlikely to be of value in the NFT space.

### Love to See It / Hate to See It

Expression | A way to voice (dis)approval of a community member's actions or an event. Can be used earnestly or sarcastically.

## M

### Mail Art

Noun | Also known as "postal art," a practice that emerged in the 1960s and that consists of sending small works of art by the post in order to counter the elitist modes of display of the traditional art world.

### Marketplace

Noun | An NFT marketplace is a (decentralized) platform where people can buy, sell, and trade NFTs.

### Maxi

Expression | Derived from "Bitcoin Maximalist," which refers to the believers in the supremacy of bitcoin over other cryptocurrencies. An NFT Maxi, is someone who believes that NFTs will cater to all the creators', collectors', and other community members' needs in the future.

### McDonald's

Noun | The back-up career plan for all the market participants (moonboys) who are not going to make it (NGMI). Best used ironically in reference to oneself.

### Meatspace

Noun | Real (physical) life, as opposed to digital space.

### Meme

Noun | A photograph, drawing, screenshot, or graphic, often accompanied by a short text, used for humorous online commentary and usually created with the intention to be shared (and go viral). Many famous memes, such as rare pepe and Doge, have been turned into NFTs. The term was coined by the biologist Richard Dawkins in 1976 as a cultural parallel to biological genes.

### Metadata

Noun | Data that provides information about other (higher order) data, such as descriptive information about a resource, which helps to sort and identify attributes of the data it describes.

### MetaMask (MM)

Noun | A free browser extension wallet and mobile app, which allows users to store, manage, transfer, and swap cryptocurrency and NFTs.

### Metaverse

Noun | A network of immersive, interoperable virtual worlds with real-time economies and interactions, such as gaming experiences or digital events. The idea was first explored in Neal Stephenson's 1992 novel *Snow Crash*.

### Migration

Noun | The transfer of a token from one blockchain to another.

### Millennials, *also* Gen Y *or* Generation Y

Expression | The generation born roughly between the early 1980s and mid-1990s, often characterized by wearing skinny jeans, using the cry-laugh emoji, and putting hashtags in their social media posts. As the first digitally native generation, millennials are the OG meme creators, online influencers, and crypto geeks.

### Mining

Verb | The process of verifying and approving new transactions on a blockchain in line with the governing consensus mechanism, normally proof of work, which is rewarded by an award, such as a coin (hence the term "mining cryptocurrency"). Proof-of-work mining usually requires sophisticated hardware and enormous computational energy.

### Minnow

Noun | Also a "Fish." As opposed to a whale, someone who has a small amount of crypto assets.

### Mint

Noun or Verb | "To mint" is the act of initially issuing an NFT on the blockchain. Once minted, the NFT is available for (public) consumption and can be viewed and traded on a marketplace. A newly issued NFT can also be referred to as a "mint." Once an NFT has been minted, it can't be deleted or erased from the blockchain.

### MMO / MMORPG

Abbreviation | Short for "Massively Multiplayer Online Game" and "Massively Multiplayer Online Role-Playing Game," an online game that features a large number of players on the same server.

### Mods

Abbreviation | Short for "Moderators," users who maintain the upkeep of social media channels by creating engagement and monitoring spam.

### Monegraph

Noun | Portmanteau of "monetized graphics," created by Kevin McCoy and Anil Dash at Rhizome's 2014 Seven on Seven conference, a blockchain-based solution to verify the uniqueness and provenance of digital artworks.

### Moonboy

Noun | Someone who blindly invests in a shitcoin or unpromising NFT project, expecting it to moon against all reason.

### Mooning, *also* Moon

Verb | A financial term to describe the exponential growth of an asset's value, particularly a cryptocurrency, with the humorous suggestion that participants would ride the graph so high that they would reach the moon.

**Multisig**
Abbreviation | Short for "Multi-Signature Wallet." A wallet that requires more than one signature for a transaction before funds are moved, adding extra security. The wallets are regularly used in DAOs, where wallets have multiple owners.

# N

**Namecoin**
Noun | An early Bitcoin fork. *Quantum* (2014), widely regarded as the first NFT, was originally minted on Namecoin.

**Net Art**
Noun | Born in the late 1990s, net art refers to artworks made on and for the internet.

**NFA**
Abbreviation | Short for "Not Financial Advice," a useful disclaimer when sharing opinions about crypto.

**NFT**
Abbreviation | Short for "Non-Fungible Token," a cryptographic token that exists on a blockchain and represents (ownership of) an asset, often a digital file, such as photos, videos, music, or avatars. Each NFT has its own identification code and metadata which makes it unique and non-interchangeable. For a more decentralized definition of NFT, please see "NFTs are..."

**NFT Archaeologist**
Noun | An individual who actively researches on- and off-chain data in the hope of discovering forgotten or overlooked projects and histories of the blockchain.

**NGMI**
Abbreviation | Short for "Not Gonna Make It," a way to scold oneself for poor decision-making regarding a crypto or NFT trade, and/or express general pessimism about the market, as opposed to the belief that they are GMI or that WAGMI.

**Nifty Gateway**
Noun | A popular NFT marketplace for curated drops and collections, founded in 2018 by Duncan and Griffin Cock Foster.

**Node**
Noun | An active participant in the securing of a blockchain network, either as a miner (proof of work) or a validator (proof of stake). It usually refers to a computer connected to the respective network that can execute certain functions like creating, receiving, or sending information.

**Non-Custodial Wallet**
Noun | A cryptocurrency wallet where users have full control over their assets and private keys rather than storing them on a centralized exchange.

**Noob**
Expression | A sarcastic term for inexperienced "newbies" or "normies," i.e., newcomers, in the crypto space.

**NSFW**
Abbreviation | Short for "Not Safe For Work" or "Not Suitable For Work," used to warn someone that the contents of a website or attachment should only be looked at in private.

# O

**Off-Chain**
Adjective | Something that happens or is recorded outside the blockchain.

**Off-Chain Metadata**
Noun | Metadata that is stored externally to a token. Given high network storage costs of blockchains, most NFTs use off-chain decentralized servers to store their metadata.

**OG**
Abbreviation | Short for "Old Guard" or "Original Gangster." It refers to trendsetters, or in the NFT space, early members of the community who are highly respected or admired.

**OK Boomer, *also* Okay Boomer**
Expression | A cynical way to disagree with someone from the Baby Boomer generation, i.e., born roughly between 1946 and 1965, or anyone ever so slightly older or less tech-savvy than yourself. Often used in memes.

**On-Chain**
Noun | Something that happens, lives, or is recorded on a blockchain, such as a token, transaction, or contract.

**On-Chain Metadata**
Noun | Metadata stored on a blockchain, i.e., directly incorporated into a smart contact.

**Open Edition**
Noun | An NFT collection for which any number of editions may be minted, either indefinitely or during a limited period of time.

**Open Source**
Noun | Data, programs, code, or other information that is publicly available for use or modification by others to encourage transparency and collaboration.

**OpenSea**
Noun | A leading decentralized P2P NFT marketplace on the Ethereum blockchain, founded by Devin Finzer and Alex Atallah in 2017.

**Oracle**
Noun | A third-party service, such as an agent or code, that feeds information into a smart contract, thereby bridging the blockchain with the real world.

**Orphan / Orphaned Block**
Noun | Originally, a block whose parent block is unknown. The meaning of the term has evolved to designate a block that has not been accepted into the blockchain.

# P

**P2E, *also* GameFi**
Abbreviation | Short for "Play to Earn" / a portmanteau of "Game Finance," blockchain-based games where users can earn financial rewards by performing in-game tasks.

**P2P**
Abbreviation | Short for "Peer-to-Peer," a direct interaction between parties on a decentralized network where no intermediary is required or interferes.

**Paper Hands**
Noun | Someone who, unlike diamond hands, panic sells or undervalues their assets.

**Performance Art**
Noun | Artworks that are created through discrete performances by the artist using their body (or others) as a medium. The roots of performance art stretch back to Dada cabaret and Futurist productions in the 1910s. A smart contract can be seen as a participant or performative agent, and is a new form of digital performance art that can evolve in perpetuity and on a much larger scale on the blockchain.

**Permissionless**
Adjective | A blockchain that anyone can use without authorization from a third party.

**PFP**
Abbreviation | Short for "Profile Picture," an image or avatar, such as a *CryptoPunk* or Bored Ape NFT, that is shown on someone's social media profile. Increasingly defining people's digital identity, PFPs often imply status and association with a certain community.

**Phishing**
Verb | Posing as a legitimate entity to scam internet users out of sensitive information.

**Pixel**
Noun | A single-colored square that constitutes the smallest element in a digital image. The more pixels there are in an image, the higher the resolution.

**PNG**
Abbreviation | Short for "Portable Network Graphics," a commonly used image format.

**POH, *also* PoH**
Abbreviation | Short for "Proof of History," a blockchain consensus mechanism used on the Solana blockchain (together with proof of stake) that cryptographically verifies the time passed between two events. This allows the verification of data to be broken down into several sequences which the nodes (or verifiers) can stream in real time rather than waiting to fill an entire block and send it to the network at once.

**POS, *also* PoS**

Abbreviation | Short for "Proof of Stake," a blockchain consensus mechanism first introduced in 2012, by which miners validate transaction bundles, i.e., blocks, by staking their coins into a special wallet as collateral and subsequently review the transaction history on their computers. While POS requires substantially less computing power than POW, its algorithm is criticized for distributing mining power according to the share of coins that a user holds, thereby advantaging those with more liquidity and amplifying existing wealth structures. It is also seen as less secure.

**Post-Internet Art**

Noun | An art movement whereby works are derived from the internet or its effects on aesthetics, culture, and society.

**POW, *also* PoW**

Abbreviation | Short for "Proof of Work," a consensus mechanism, the idea of which dates back to 1999. On a blockchain, the first miner to solve an extremely complex mathematical problem gets to approve a transaction bundle, i.e., a block, in return for a reward, usually a coin. While POW is a widespread, more secure consensus mechanism, it is often criticized for its enormous energy footprint caused by the required computing power.

**Pre-Mine**

Verb | The process of creating some or all of a token's initial supply prior to its public launch.

**Presale**

Verb | A funding method used by companies and project developers to raise capital through an initial sale (such as an ICO). Where private investors and early adopters can buy the token, or for NFTs this can often be through a whitelist, before its public release.

**Primary Market**

Noun | A market where original owners, for instance artists, sell their creations for the first time.

**Private Blockchain**

Noun | A centralized blockchain controlled by an organization and where participants are regulated.

**Private Key**

Noun | This is a variable in cryptography that is used with an algorithm to encrypt and decrypt data. It is used to sign transactions and prove ownership of a blockchain address in cryptocurrency terms.

**Probably Nothing**

Expression | An ironic substitute for "probably something," describing an event that is likely to impact the NFT space.

**Processing**

Noun | An open-source programming language and sketchbook developed by Casey Reas and Ben Fry in 2001, focused on developing visual arts and design through computer programming.

**Protocol**

Noun | A protocol is a set of rules defined by a set of assumptions to achieve a specific goal. This usually involves consensus, transaction validation, and network participation on a blockchain.

**Provenance**

Noun | The history of a work of art, used to prove authenticity and legitimate acquisition and usually derived from sales records, collection inventories, catalogues raisonnés. The blockchain is the first immutable provenance system in the world.

**Public Blockchain**

Noun | A blockchain that can be accessed and used by everyone, such as Bitcoin and Ethereum.

**Public Key**

Noun | A public key is a series of alphanumeric characters that can be used to encrypt plain text to a ciphertext. It is also the public address that owners use to receive transactions. The key can be used to view the entire contents of any wallet, although this doesn't reveal personal details of that account holder.

**Pump and Dump**

Expression | A fraud scheme whereby an investor (whale) purchases a large quantity of tokens to artificially inflate the price and subsequently dumps them at a profit. This can also be enacted by the founders of a project.

# Q

**QR Code**

Noun | A machine-readable label consisting of a pixel grid that links to a discrete URL.

# R

**Rarities**

Noun | A label or cataloged trait that allows NFT collectors to understand the intended or unintended hierarchies within a collection of NFTs, these are increasingly becoming part of an artist's conceptual groundwork when making an NFT project.

**Reddit**

Noun | A social media platform founded in 2005 where users can form communities and exchange information about topics of interest.

**REKT**

Expression | Crypto Twitter slang for "wrecked," borrowed from the gaming community where it describes the state of someone who was destroyed or ruined, in the NFT space it refers to a bad loss in trade or unfortunate development of one's portfolio.

**Render**

Verb | A computer image created from 2D or 3D models, typically of a realistic or photorealistic aesthetic.

**Reveal**

Noun | Revealing the type or aesthetics of an NFT after it is minted, depending on the collection, this may be immediately after the item is minted or with a delay, which could be 24 hours or longer.

**RGB**

Abbreviation | Short for "Red, Green, and Blue," RGB refers to a system representing the colors used on a digital display screen. Red, green, and blue can be combined in various proportions to obtain any color in the visible spectrum.

**Right Click Save As**

Expression | The action to perform in order to save a file onto your computer. An expression used to discredit NFTs by attempting to demonstrate their fungibility.

**Ring Signature**

Noun | A digital transaction that can be performed by any member of a set of users that each have the keys. It lets the sender know someone from the set of users signed it but not who, which means they can't spend funds unless the other signers provide their approval also.

**Roadmap**

Noun | A nonbinding document that lays out the goals, milestones, and strategies of an NFT project to demonstrate the project's potential and align the creator's expectations. Roadmaps are generally desirable in PFP projects but insulting to ask for in art projects.

**Royalties**

Noun | A payment made in return for the ongoing use of someone's intellectual property. In the art world, royalties usually provide artists with a share in the sale proceeds of secondary sales. Royalties can be written into the smart contract of NFTs (typically set at 10%), thus allowing the artist to earn income from all future sales of the work.

**Rug / Rug Pull**

Noun | A scheme where, immediately after a seemingly legitimate project's launch, the developers disappear with all of the funds, leaving the investors with worthless tokens. Due to the lack of regulation in the space, rug pulls are common, so DYOR.

# S

**Salt**

Noun | From "salty," i.e., being upset over something, salt is what you may feel when you are coping.

**Satoshi**

Noun | A satoshi is the smallest fraction of bitcoin (0.00000001 BTC). The denomination is named after Satoshi Nakamoto — the pseudonym of the person(s) who developed Bitcoin.

**Satoshi Nakamoto**

Noun | Satoshi Nakamoto (born April 5, 1975) is the pseudonymous creator of Bitcoin, the first decentralized cryptocurrency. The identity of Satoshi remains unknown, but their 2008 Bitcoin whitepaper was the major breakthrough for the development of blockchain technology.

**Scarcity**

Noun | Refers to the amount of a specific project or item that is available at any given time. NFTs have offered (artificial) digital scarcity for the first time.

**Schelling Point**
Noun | A game theory concept introduced by Thomas Schelling describing a solution that different people in a similar situation tend to choose by default in the absence of communication. In the NFT space, it describes the platforms and tokens that will ultimately be the most successful because they are perceived by the community to be the most promising.

**Script**
Noun | A series of instructions to be executed by a program.

**Secondary Market**
Noun | A market where investors or collectors, i.e., secondary owners, can resell their assets.

**Seed Phrase**
Noun | A series of randomly generated words, usually comprising sets of 12 or 24, that are the master key to accessing all private keys associated with a wallet. This is also known as a recovery phrase, needed to grant access to your crypto-currency wallet if your private key is deleted or lost.

**Seems Legit**
Expression | A way to proclaim that a project appears legitimate and/or promising (if used seriously) or sus (if used ironically).

**Ser / Mam**
Expression | Crypto slang for "Sir" / "Ma'am," a polite way to address a fellow community member.

**Sharding**
Verb | The act of splitting a blockchain network into multiple parts, or shards, in order to allow scalability.

**Shilling**
Verb | To enthusiastically promote one's own token or project, often with a false pretense of sincerity, to encourage others to invest, and/or create FOMO. While the NFT art community is heavily financialized, shilling is generally frowned upon.

**Shitcoin**
Expression | A cryptocurrency with little or no value, often identifiable by their unsound whitepaper (or absence thereof), low market capitalization, and an excessive supply of tokens.

**Smart Contract**
Noun | A computer protocol governed by "if/when … then" statements that executes itself once certain predetermined conditions are met, generally used to mint or transfer NFTs. Smart contracts allow for the programmatic enforcement of an agreement, such as the payment of royalties upon every sale of an asset without the need for an intermediary, and create an irreversible, immutable record on the blockchain. Smart contracts can be but are not necessarily legally enforceable contracts.

**Solana, *also* SOL**
Noun | Solana is a blockchain that supports the SOL cryptocurrency and is popular among NFT creators due to its unique combination of POH and POS consensus mechanisms which makes it quicker, cheaper, and more sustainable than many other cryptocurrencies. As of time of writing, side effects are occasional downtimes and a higher degree of centralization.

**Solidity**
Noun | A programming language used to create smart contracts for programs running on Ethereum Virtual Machine.

**Source Code**
Noun | A high-level code readable by humans, written using a computer programming language. The goal of the code is to set exact rules and specifications for the computer, that can then be translated into the machine's language.

**Spam**
Noun | Unwanted digital promotional content, often in large quantities. The use of the term originates from an eponymous Monty Python sketch from 1972 where Spam — a type of canned meat — becomes progressively omnipresent.

**Stable Coin**
Noun | A cryptocurrency that is pegged to another (usually fiat) currency. They aim to provide low volatility and an index of the underlying asset. Stablecoins can either be backed or algorithmic in nature.

**Staking**
Verb | The process of locking up currencies in a wallet in order to earn rewards. In the case of proof-of-stake currencies, this also serves to validate transactions.

**Standardization**
Noun | Standardization is about building a common, reusable, inheritable standard relevant to all non-fungible tokens. These may include simple primitives such as ownership, transfer, and simple access control.

**Surrealism**
Noun | Surrealism was an international artistic movement, led and co-founded by André Breton (1896–1966) in 1924, that explored the workings of the mind, focusing on the irrational, unconscious, and dream states.

**Sus**
Abbreviation | Short for "Suspect" or "Suspicious," often used to describe an untrustworthy person or activity, such as a potential pump and dump scheme.

**SVG, *also* SVG File**
Abbreviation | Short for "Scalable Vector Graphics," a standard graphics file type using Extensible Markup Language (XML), i.e., text, to render images on the internet in any size or resolution.

**Sweep the Floor, *also* Floor Sweeping**
Expression | The act of buying all floor price NFTs in a collection.

**Szn**
Abbreviation | Short for "Season," this refers to the market cycle, usually in references to a bull market.

# T

**Tezos (XTZ)**
Noun | A proof-of-stake cryptocurrency that became popular in early 2021, especially within the artistic community, due to its low gas fees and more environmentally friendly transaction mechanism.

**This Is the Way**
Expression | A catchphrase from the Disney+ Star Wars television series *The Mandalorian* where it signified shared aspirations and a strongly bonded community. In the NFT space, it is used to commend courteous or generally positive behavior.

**Timestamp**
Noun | The recorded time of a transaction on a blockchain.

**Token**
Noun | Any singularly instantiated digital asset that is transferred between two people is called a token. BTC is the token of Bitcoin. Some tokens, called stablecoins, follow the price of fiat currencies. Others, called NFTs, can represent collectables or artworks.

**Token ID**
Noun | A token ID is a unique identifier for a particular NFT on a smart contract.

**Token Standards**
Noun | A set of rules that are integrated in a token's smart contract to ensure its compatibility with different blockchain protocols and allow different assets to coexist in the same ecosystem. Typically, they define how a token can be transferred and how to keep a consistent record on the underlying blockchain's network.

**Tokenomics, *also* Token Economics**
Noun | The science and study of the token economics. It covers all aspects of the rules that govern a cryptocurrency's issuance, supply, management, and even token burning.

**Tradeability**
Noun | Tradeability is the feature of free trade on an open marketplace. Open marketplaces allow users to sell items outside their original environments and take advantage of sophisticated trading capabilities. Tradeability represents a shift from a closed economy to an open, free-market economy.

**Trading Cards**
Noun | Collectible cards with particular traits and characteristics that dictate their value. Trading cards originated as physical goods, often representing athletes or famous fictional characters, but made their way early into the cryptospace with Spells of Genesis and rare pepes.

**Transaction Fee**
Noun | A variable payment that is charged to users performing a transaction. This fee is required in order to process transactions on the blockchain.

**Turing Complete**

Adjective | Refers to a general-purpose computer or computing language that can solve any computational problem given enough time, memory, and the necessary instruction set. The term can be used to describe modern programming languages, e.g., C++, Python, JavaScript, etc.

# U

**Up Only**

Expression | A phrase to express excitement and optimism about a token or project, usually referring to price.

**URL**

Abbreviation | Short for "Uniform Resource Locator," also known as a web address, a URL is the location of a web page on the internet.

**Utility Token**

Noun | A token that is specifically designed to help people use something, such as the governance token of a project.

**Utility-Focused NFTs**

Noun | An NFT that adds value to its ownership other than its art and price by building uses and incorporating benefits via airdrops or exclusive rewards, to add value to owners.

# V

**Valhalla**

Noun | In Norse mythology, a majestic hall where warriors dwell and battle in the afterlife. In the crypto space, used as a synonym for heaven.

**Vaporware**

Expression | A cryptocurrency project that has been widely advertised, but has not been deployed.

**Vault**

Noun | A vault is a long-term store of crypto assets, that is usually a cold wallet.

**Verified Contract**

Noun | A public contract that is able to be studied, read, and have its code audited. Verified contracts are used widely for transactions in need of higher levels of trust. Ideally, they are audited by third parties.

**Volatility**

Noun | A measure to describe the variation of an asset's trading price over a given period of time.

**VR**

Abbreviation | Short for "Virtual Reality," an immersive technology that simulates an artificial three-dimensional environment.

# W

**WAGMI**

Abbreviation | Short for "We All Gonna Make It," an exclamation of optimism about a coin, NFT, or the general state of the market, as opposed to the fear that you are NGMI.

**Wallet**

Noun | An application that is used to store, send, or receive cryptocurrency. The wallet allows users to store the passkeys with which they sign their transactions and provides the interface to access their crypto.

**Web 1.0**

Noun | The first years of the internet (1990s to the early to mid-2000s), sometimes referred to as the "read-only" web due to limited interactivity.

**Web 2.0**

Noun |The internet today, characterized by more user participation than Web 1.0, social media, and private centralized platforms. Unlike in a decentralized Web3, Web 2.0 is mainly governed by Big Tech who own and control most of the data.

**Web 3.0**

Noun | Also known as the Semantic Web, it is a continuation from Web 1.0 and Web 2.0, whereby a shared common framework allows for the connectivity of data across different platforms and applications. While they overlap in theory and practice, this is not to be confused with blockchain-based Web3.

**Web3**

Noun | The blockchain-anchored web set within a decentralized online ecosystem. Web3 holds the concepts of security, decentralization, and personal sovereignty at its core, returning power to users in the form of ownership of all manner of assets (digital goods, identities, and personal data) through blockchain technology, cryptocurrencies, and NFTs.

**WebGL**

Abbreviation | Short for "Web Graphics Library," a JavaScript API for rendering 2D and 3D graphics within any compatible web browser without the assistance of a plug-in.

**Wen Moon?** *also* **Wen Lambo?**

Expression | A phrase used to ask (ironically) when the value of their crypto or NFTs will skyrocket — to the moon, or high enough so they can afford to buy a Lamborghini.

**WETH**

Abbreviation | Short for "Wrapped Ethereum," an ERC-20 token that is directly pegged to ETH 1:1. WETH can be used on dApps that ETH is not compatible with.

**Whale**

Noun | Someone with a holding in crypto or NFTs large enough to single-handedly manipulate the market and indicate future trends. Whales only surface rarely.

**Whitelist**

Noun | A select few who have early access to an NFT drop.

**Whitepaper**

Noun | An official technical document released by crypto developers in order to explain their concept. See, for instance, Satoshi Nakamoto's 2008 Bitcoin whitepaper.

**Wrapped Tokens**

Noun | A token that represents an NFT or cryptocurrency from another token standard or blockchain that is worth the same as the original. When you wrap an NFT you exchange its set of standards for token interaction with another set of standards. Wrapping tokens can be an effective way of giving older tokens improved functionality, such as enabling pre-ERC-721 NFTs the ability to be traded on platforms like OpenSea.

# X

**XCP**

Noun | The native token of Counterparty. It is a technical necessity to add advanced features to Counterparty, which by nature require a protocol-aware currency. Bitcoin can only be aware of BTC, while Counterparty can be aware of both BTC and XCP itself. This makes it possible to trade in a decentralized manner, escrow funds, and harness the full potential of programmable money.

# Y

**YOLO**

Abbreviation | Short for "You Only Live Once," an incitation to act in the present without thinking too much.

# BIBLIOGRAPHY

## 00 INTRODUCTION

Cascone, Sarah. "Depressing New Report Finds That Women Artists Accounted for Just 16 Percent of NFT Sales Over the Past 21 Months." *Artnet,* November 5, 2021. https://news.artnet.com/market/nft-sales-just-16-percent-women-2030490.

Catlow, Ruth, Marc Garrett, Nathan Jones, and Sam Skinner. *Artists Re:Thinking the Blockchain.* London: Torque Editions, 2017.

Geczy, Adam. "What can Adorno and Walter Benjamin teach us about NFTs & Art." *its(t) artswithadam* (blog), 2021. https://www.itstartswithadam.com/blog/what-can-adorno-amp-walter-benjamin-teach-us-about-nfts-amp-art.

Marlinspike, Moxie. "My First Impression about Web3." *Moxie.org* (blog), January 7, 2022. https://moxie.org/2022/01/07/web3-first-impressions.html.

## 01 ON QUANTUM

Assia, Yoni, Vitalik Buterin, Lior Hakim, Meni Rosenfeld, and Rotem Lev. "Colored Coins Whitepaper." *eToro*, 2013. https://www.etoro.com/wp-content/uploads/2022/03/Colored-Coins-white-paper-Digital-Assets.pdf.

Baudrillard, Jean. *Simulation and Simulacra.* Translated by Shelia Faria Glaser. Michigan: University of Michigan Press, 1994.

Benjamin, Walter. "The Work of Art in the Age of Mechanical Reproduction." Translated by Henry Zohn. In Hannah Arendt (ed.). *Illuminations.* New York: Schocken Books, 1969.

Buist, Kevin. "What's Their Game?" *Outland*, December 9, 2021. https://outland.art/blitmap-loot-ectogames/.

Franceschet, Massimo, Giovanni Colavizza, T'ai Smith, Blake Finucane, Martin Lukas Ostachowski, Sergio Scalet, Jonathan Perkins, Sebastián Hernández, and James Morgan. "Crypto Art: A Decentralized View." *Leonardo*, Vol. 54, No. 4, 2021. https://doi.org/10.1162/leon_a_02003.

Frye, Bryan L., and Primavera De Filippi. "In Conversation: Bryan L. Frye & Primavera de Filippi." *Outland*, April 5, 2022. https://outland.art/brian-frye-primavera-de-filippi/.

Geczy, Adam. "What can Adorno and Walter Benjamin teach us about NFTs & Art." *its(t) artswithadam* (blog), 2021. https://www.itstartswithadam.com/blog/what-can-adorno-amp-walter-benjamin-teach-us-about-nfts-amp-art.

Grant, Daniel. "Collector Files Lawsuit Over Lost Paperwork." *Artnews*, 2012. https://www.artnews.com/art-news/news/collector-files-lawsuit-over-lost-lewitt-paperwork-578/.

Greer, David. "Quantum." *Mccoyspace*, 2021. https://www.mccoyspace.com/project/125/.

Groys, Boris. *On the New.* München: Carl Hanser Verlag, 1992.

Holmes, Helen. "Kenny Schachter, NFT-Whisperer, on the Pleasures of Embracing the Digital Deluge." *The Observer*, December 6, 2021. https://observer.com/2021/06/kenny-schachter-nft-cryptocurrency-rarible/.

Indrisek, Scott. "Pepe the Frog's Creator, Matt Furie, Is Trying to Save His Lovable Stoner Frog from the Alt-Right." *Artsy*, July 13, 2017. https://www.artsy.net/article/artsy-editorial-pepes-creator-save-lovable-stoner-frog-alt-right.

Joselit, David. *After Art*. Princeton: Princeton University Press, 2013.

Larmagnac-Matheron, Octave. "NFTs: A Digital Antifungal?" *Philonomist*, March 25, 2021. https://www.philonomist.com/en/article/nfts-digital-antifungal?check_logged_in=1.

Ludel, Wallace. "Sotheby's and Artist Kevin McCoy sued over sale of early NFT." *The Art Newspaper*, February 4, 2022. https://www.theartnewspaper.com/2022/02/04/sothebys-kevin-mccoy-lawsuit-quantum-nft.

Marlinspike, Moxie. "My First Impression about Web3." *Moxie.org* (blog), January 7, 2022. https://moxie.org/2022/01/07/web3-first-impressions.html.

Myers, Rhea. "Regarding Quantum." *Rhea.art* (blog), accessed July 25, 2022. https://rhea.art/regarding-quantum.

Qadir, Sal, and Gabe Parker. "NFT Royalties: The $1.8bn Question." *Galaxy*, October 21, 2022, https://www.galaxy.com/research/insights/nft-royalties/.

Rhizome. "Seven on Seven 2014: Kevin McCoy & Anil Dash." *Vimeo*, 2014. https://vimeo.com/96131398.

Veal, Clare. "Bringing the Land Foundation Back to Earth: A New Model for the Critical Analysis of Relational Art." *Journal of Aesthetics & Culture*, Vol. 6, No. 1, 2014. https://doi.org/10.3402/jac.v6.23701.

Vierkant, Artie. *The Image Object Post-Internet.* 2010. https://jstchillin.org/artie/pdf/The_Image_Object_Post-Internet_a4.pdf. Winkelmann, Mike. "About." *Beeple-Crap*, accessed June 29, 2022. https://www.beeple-crap.com/about.

Youngblood, Gene. *Expanded Cinema*. New York: E.P. Dutton & Company, 1970.

## 02 ON CRYPTO ART

Bailey, Jason. "Have NFTs Lost Their Way." *Right Click Save*, January 31, 2022. https://www.rightclicksave.com/article/have-nfts-lost-their-way.

Bailey, Jason. "What is CryptoArt?" *Artnome*, January 19, 2018. https://www.artnome.com/news/2018/1/14/what-is-cryptoart.

Berks, Nanu. "NFTs." *Nanuberks.com*, accessed June 8, 2022. https://www.nanuberks.com/nfts/.

Chan, Mitchell. "NFTs, Generative Art, and Sol LeWitt." *Medium*, July 26, 2021. https://medium.com/@mitchellfchan/nfts-generative-art-and-sol-lewitt-e99a5fa2b0cb.

Cryptograffiti. "About." *Cryptograffiti.com*, accessed June 8, 2022. https://cryptograffiti.com/pages/about-us.

DanStone. "Inside NFTs: Nanu Berks." *Global Coin Research*, April 27, 2021. https://globalcoinresearch.com/2021/04/27/inside-nfts-nanu-berks/.

Estorick, Alex. "Algorithmic Violence and the Politics of Data: The Work of Mimi Onuoha and Gretchen Andrew." *Flash Art Online*, December 11, 2020. https://flash---art.com/2020/12/algorithmic-violence-and-the-politics-of-data-the-work-of-mimi-onuoha-and-gretchen-andrew/.

Estorick, Alex, Kyle Waters, and Chloe Diamond. "In Search of An Aesthetics of Crypto Art." *Artnome*, April 10, 2021. https://www.artnome.com/news/2021/4/10/in-search-of-an-aesthetics-of-crypto-art.

Fraiberger, Samuel P., Roberta Sinatra, Magnus Resch, Christoph Riedl, and Albert-László Barabási. "Quantifying Reputation and Success in Art." *Science*, November 8, 2018. https://www.science.org/doi/abs/10.1126/science.aau7224.

Mam, Yehudit. "Yehudit Mam: About." *Medium*, accessed June 8, 2022. https://grandenchilada.medium.com/about.

Marcial, Carlos, and Richard Entrup. "How NFTs Changed the Art World." *Right Click Save*, February 25, 2022. https://www.rightclicksave.com/article/how-nfts-changed-the-art-world.

Pentcheva, Bissera. *The Sensual Icon: Space, Ritual, and the Senses in Byzantium*. Pennsylvania: The Pennsylvania State University Press, 2010.Ramos, Beatriz Helena. "Rare Digital Art Festival #1 Anniversary: DADA." *Right Click Save*, February 14, 2022. https://www.rightclicksave.com/article/rare-digital-art-festival-anniversary-dada.

Zucker, Sarah. "Artist Sarah Zucker." *Art Sense*, Ep. 17, Apple Podcasts, accessed June 8, 2022. https://podcasts.apple.com/us/podcast/ep-17-artist-sarah-zucker/id1574394526?i=1000539042134.

## 03 ON ALGORITHMIC ART

Assis, Michael. "On the Artist and Long-Form Generative Art." *Right Click Save*, May 13, 2022. https://www.rightclicksave.com/article/on-the-artist-and-long-form-generative-art.

Bailey, Jason. "Autoglyphs, Generative Art Born on the Blockchain." *Artnome*, April 8, 2019. https://www.artnome.com/news/2019/4/08/autoglyphs-generative-art-born-on-the-blockchain.

Bailey, Jason. "Why Love Generative Art?" *Artnome*, August 26, 2018. https://www.artnome.com/news/2018/8/8/why-love-generative-art.

Bentson, Patricia. "Algorithmic Art." *Leonardo* (blog), June 19, 2014. https://leonardo.info/blog/2014/06/19/algorithmic-art?gclid=Cj0KCQjwsdiTBhD5ARIsAIpW8CLLBbdr3MdtqDd0FzckIFzi159OmkrxaRYy25LXebJSVDVvusTvJDQaAnw_EALw_wcB.

Boden, Margaret, and Ernest Edmonds. "What Is Generative Art?" *Digital Creativity*, Vol. 20, 2009.

Caplan, Lindsay. "The Social Conscience of Generative Art." *ARTnews.com*, January 3, 2020. https://www.artnews.com/art-in-america/features/max-bense-gustav-metzger-generative-art-1202674265/.

Edwards, Benj. "The Never-before-Told Story of the World's First Computer Art (It's a Sexy Dame)." *The Atlantic*. Washington: Atlantic Media Company, January 24, 2013. https://www.theatlantic.com/technology/archive/2013/01/the-never-before-told-story-of-the-worlds-first-computer-art-its-a-sexy-dame/267439/.

Franke, Herbert W. "Computers and Visual Art." *Leonardo*, Vol. 4, No. 4, 1971.

Franke, Herbert W. "Oszillogramm." *SIGGRAPH*. accessed April 28, 2022. https://digitalartarchive.siggraph.org/artwork/herbert-w-franke-oszillogramm/.

Galanter, Philip. "What is Generative Art? Complexity Theory as a Context for Art Theory." 6th Generative Art Conference, 2003.

Galanter, Philip. "Generative Art Theory." In Christian Paul (ed.). *A Companion to Digital Art*. New Jersey: Wiley-Blackwell, 2016.

Hobbs, Tyler. "The Rise of Long-Form Generative Art." *Tyler Hobbs Essays*, August 6, 2021. https://tylerxhobbs.com/essays/2021/the-rise-of-long-form-generative-art.

Klütsch, Christoph. "Computer Graphic-Aesthetic Experiments between Two Cultures." *Leonardo*, Vol. 40, No. 5, 2007.

Klüver, Billy, and Robert Rauschenberg. "Founders of E.A.T." *E.A.T. News*, Vol. 1, No. 2, June 1, 1967. https://www.experimentsinartandtechnology.org/forming-the-organization.

Laposky, Ben F. "Electronic Abstractions: An Exciting 20th Century Art Form." The Sioux City Art Center, 1960.

Lewitt, Sol. "Paragraphs on Conceptual Art." *Artforum*, Vol. 5, No. 10, Summer 1967.

Maeda, John. *Design by Numbers*. Cambridge, MA: MIT Press, 2001.

Mason, Catherine. "Cybernetic Serendipity: History and Lasting Legacy." *Studio International*, March 11, 2018. https://www.studiointernational.com/index.php/cybernetic-serendipity-history-and-lasting-legacy.

Marraccini, A.V. "On The New Evolution of Generative Art." *Right Click Save*, February 11, 2022. https://www.rightclicksave.com/article/on-the-new-evolution-of-generative-art.

McCoy, Kevin. "Quantum." *Mccoyspace*, accessed July 8, 2022. www.mccoyspace.com/project/125/.

Mohr, Manfred. "Demonstration Plot from show May 11–June 6, 1971." *Computer Graphics, Une Esthétique Programmée, ARC – Musée d'Art Moderne de la Ville de Paris 1971*, 2011. http://www.emohr.com/paris-1971/demo.html.

Nake, Frieder. "Paragraphs on Computer Art, Past and Present." In Francesca Franco, Nick Lambert, and Jeremy Gardiner (ed.). *CAT'10: Proceedings of the 1st International Conference on Ideas before Their Time: Connecting the Past and Present in Computer Art*. London: British Computer Society, 2010.

Noll, A. Michael. "Early Digital Computer Art at Bell Telephone Laboratories, Incorporated." *Leonardo*, Vol. 49, No. 1, 2016. https://ethw.org/First-Hand:Early_Digital_Art_At_Bell_Telephone_Laboratories,_Inc#.

Noll, A. Michael. "Human or Machine: A Subjective Comparison of Piet Mondrian's 'Composition with Lines' and a Computer-Generated Picture." *The Psychological Record*, Vol. 16, No. 1, January 1966.

Noll, A. Michael. "The Beginnings of Computer Art in the United States: A Memoir." *Leonardo*, Vol. 27, No. 1, 1994.

Processing Foundation. "A Modern Prometheus." *Medium*, May 29, 2018. https://medium.com/processing-foundation/a-modern-prometheus-59aed94abe85.

Rivers Ryan, Tina. "McLuhan's Bulbs: Light Art and the Dawn of New Media." PhD diss., New York: Columbia University, 2016. https://doi.org/10.7916/D82V2G52.

Taylor, Grant. "Routing Mondrian: The A. Michael Noll Experiment." *FOUND – SAMPLED – STOLEN – STRATEGIES OF APPROPRIATION IN NEW MEDIA*, Vol. 8, No. 2, Fall 2012. http://median.newmediacaucus.org/routing-mondrian-the-a-michael-noll-experiment/.

Verostko, Roman. "The Algorists." accessed April 28, 2022. http://www.verostko.com/algorist.html.

## 04 ON CHAIN

Bourriaud, Nicolas. *Relational Aesthetics*. Dijon: Les Presses du réel, 2002.

Burnham, Jack. In Melissa Ragain (ed.). *Dissolve into Comprehension: Writings and Interviews, 1964–2004*. Cambridge, MA: The MIT Press, 2015.

Connor, Michael. "What's Postinternet Got to Do with Net Art?" *Rhizome*, November 1, 2013. https://rhizome.org/editorial/2013/nov/01/postinternet/.

Drexler, Eric K., and Mark S. Miller. In Bernardo Huberman (ed.). *The Ecology of Computation*. Amsterdam: Elsevier Science Publishers, 1988.

Entriken, William, Dieter Shirley, Jacob Evans, and Nastassia Sachs. "EIP-721: Non-Fungible Token Standard." Ethereum.org, 2018. https://eips.ethereum.org/EIPS/eip-721.

Krauss, Rosalind. In Hal Foster et al. (eds.). *Art since 1900: Modernism, Antimodernism, Postmodernism*. London: Thames & Hudson, 2005.

LeWitt, Sol. "Paragraphs on Conceptual Art." *Artforum*, Vol. 5, No. 10, Summer 1967.

McLuhan, Marshall. *Understanding Media: The Extensions of Man*. New York: McGraw-Hill, 1964.

Nakamoto, Satoshi. *Bitcoin: A Peer-to-Peer Electronic Cash System*. 2008. https://bitcoin.org/bitcoin.pdf.

Szabo, Nick. "Formalizing and Securing Relationships on Public Networks." *First Monday*, Vol. 2, No. 9, September 1997.

Szabo, Nick. "Smart Contracts." 1994. https://web.archive.org/web/20160323035617/szabo.best.vwh.net/smart.contracts.html.

## 05 ON PROCESS

—

## 06 ON AVATARS

Abbruzzese, Jason. "This ethereum-based project could change how we think about digital art." *Mashable*, June 16, 2017.

Avedon, LaTurbo. "Conversations | Exhibiting in the Metaverse." ArtBasel (panel), June 18, 2022.

Binance. "Global Crypto Index 2021." January 28, 2021. https://research.binance.com/static/pdf/Global_Crypto_Index_2021.pdf.

Chan, Mitchell F. "Punks and Sellouts." *Outland*, March 18, 2022. https://outland.art/yuga-labs-cryptopunks-sale/.

Farmer, F. Randall. "Lucasfilm's Habitat Promotional Video." YouTube, May 17, 2008. https://www.youtube.com/watch?v=VVpulhO3jyc.

Financial Conduct Authority. "Cryptoasset consumer research 2020." June 30, 2020. https://www.fca.org.uk/publication/research/research-note-cryptoasset-consumer-research-2020.pdf.

Garriott, Richard. "Coining Term 'Avatar': The origins of the term 'avatar' in games." *CRITICAL PATH*, interview from 2010, published July 29, 2016. https://www.criticalpathproject.com/video/coining-term-avatar/.

Gemini. "Global State of Crypto Report." April 4, 2022. https://www.gemini.com/state-of-us-crypto.

Gibson, William. *Neuromancer*. New York: Berkley Publishing Group, 1989.

Green, Raquel, Paul H. Delfabbro, and Daniel L. King. "Avatar Identification and problematic gaming: The role of self-concept clarity." *Addictive Behaviors*, Vol. 113, 2021. https://doi.org/10.1016/j.addbeh.2020.106694.

Hall, Matt. "CryptoPunks — Interview with Co-Founder Matt Hall." *Art Market Guru*, January 6, 2019. https://www.artmarket.guru/le-journal/interviews/cryptopunks-matt-hall/.

Hall, Matt, and John Watkinson. "Yuga Labs Acquires CryptoPunks and Meebits." *Larva Labs* (blog), March 11, 2022. https://www.larvalabs.com/blog/2022-3-11-18-0/yuga-labs-acquires-cryptopunks-and-meebits.

Hao, Karen. "The first rule of being a woman in crypto is you do not talk about being a woman in crypto." *Quartz*, July 31, 2018. https://qz.com/1262167/the-first-rule-of-being-a-woman-in-crypto-is-you-do-not-talk-about-being-a-woman-in-crypto/.

Harmon, Leon D. "The Recognition of Faces." *Scientific American*, Vol. 229, No. 5, 1973.

Klimmt, Cristoph, Dorothée Hefner, and Peter Vorderer. "The video game experience as 'true' identification: A theory of enjoyable alterations of players' self-perception." *Communication Theory*, Vol. 19, 2009. https://doi.org/10.1111/j.1468-2885.2009.01347.x.

Miller, Mark R., Fernanda Herrera, Hanseul Jun, James A. Landay, and Jeremy N. Bailenson. "Personal identifiability of user tracking data during observation of 360-degree VR video." *Scientific Reports*, Vol. 10, 2020. https://doi.org/10.1038/s41598-020-74486-y.

Park, Don. "Identicon and Robohash." *Don Park's Weekly Habit* (blog), July 30, 2011. https://blog.docuverse.com/2011/07/30/identicon-and-robohash/.

Parrinder, Geoffrey. *Avatar and Incarnation: The Divine in Human Form in the World's Religions*. London: Oneworld Publications, 1997.

Rheingold, Howard. "Slice of Life in My Virtual Community." *Global Networks-a Journal of Transnational Affairs*, August 11, 1993.

Russell/SYBASE, Ryan. "[crypto] Avatar Protection?" cryptoanarchy.wiki, December 4, 1996. https://mailing-list-archive.cryptoanarchy.wiki/archive/1996/12/d5e950886cdb96294bba25d-6981d3138c5ba31fec5a3081b9cd2aa1327c67ece/.

Saucier, Luc. "Annlee Association Articles, Assignment of Rights Contract Governing the Author of Annlee." In Pierre Huyghe and Philippe Parreno (ed.). *No Ghost Just A Shell*. Eindhoven: Van Abbemuseum, 2003.

Scarborough, James K., and Jeremy N. Bailenson. "Avatar Psychology." In Mark Grimshaw (ed.). *The Oxford Handbook of Virtuality*. Oxford: Oxford University Press, December 2013. https://doi.org/10.1093/oxfordhb/9780199826162.013.033.

Stephenson, Neal. *Snow Crash*. New York: Bantam Books, 1993.

Tanner, Marcia. "No Ghost Just a Shell." *Stretcher*, 2003. https://www.stretcher.org/features/no_ghost_just_a_shell/.

Tufte, Edward. *Envisioning Information*. Cheshire, Connecticut: Graphics Press, 1990.

Van Looy, Jan, Cédric Courtois, and Melanie De Vocht. "Player identification in online games: Validation of a scale for measuring identification in MMORPGs." *Media Psychology*, Vol. 15, No. 2, 2012. https://doi.org/10.1145/1823818.1823832.

Wilf, Steven. "What We Talk About When We Talk About Fictional Characters (and Copyright)." *Critical Analysis of Law*, Vol. 7, No. 1, 2020.

Wolff, Rachel M. "We bought a virgin: The Issue of the Artist in No Ghost Just A Shell." *Shift: Graduate Journal of Visual and Material Culture*, Vol. 4, 2011.

Yee, Nick, Jeremy N. Bailenson, and Nicolas Ducheneaut. "The Proteus Effect: Implications of Transformed Digital Self-Representation on Online and Offline Behavior." *Communication Research*, Vol. 36, No. 2, April 2009. https://doi.org/10.1177/0093650208330254.

## 07 ON DAOS

Beni, Gerardo. "The concept of cellular robotic system." *Proceedings IEEE International Symposium on Intelligent Control 1988*, August 24, 1988.

Botto. "Botto's Art Engine." *Docs*, 2021. https://docs.botto.com/details/bottos-art-engine.

Bruner, Raise. "Ukraine Received More Than $30M in Crypto Donations. Here's Where It's Going." *TIME*, March 1, 2022. https://time.com/6153320/crypto-ukraine-charity/.

Buterin, Vitalik. "Bootstrapping a Decentralized Autonomous Corporation: Part I." *Bitcoin Magazine*, September 19, 2013. https://bitcoinmagazine.com/technical/bootstrapping-a-decentralized-autonomous-corporation-part-i-1379644274.

Cyber Baat. "The Cyber Baat Fundraiser." *Mirror*, February 1, 2022. https://mirror.xyz/cyberbaat.eth/P6b9unXXdg-TiQ08EHKVTKNufNrH_IcVOK1d_spM8Xs.

Gottsegen, Will. "New DAO Raises $3M in ETH for Ukrainian Army." *CoinDesk*, February 27, 2022. https://www.coindesk.com/tech/2022/02/27/new-dao-raises-3-million-in-eth-for-ukrainian-army/.

Hamill, Susan Pace. *The Origins Behind the Limited Liability Company*. Ohio: Ohio St. L. J. 1459/1463, 1998.

Larimer, Dan. "Overpaying for Security." *LTB Network*, September 7, 2013. https://letstalkbitcoin.com/is-bitcoin-overpaying-for-false-security#.UjtiUt9xy0w.

Locke, Taylor. "The original 'Doge' meme sold as an NFT for $4 million–now you can own a piece of it for less than $1." *CNBC*, September 1, 2021. https://www.cnbc.com/2021/09/01/fans-can-buy-a-fraction-of-original-doge-meme-nft-owned-by-pleasrdao.html.

MOCΔ. "MOCΔ Art Collections." *Notion*, 2022. https://museumofcrypto.notion.site/M-C-Art-Collections-17fedaf714674e748539ea19cce6b19c.

MOCΔ. "MOCΔ Community Collection." *Medium*, November 16, 2021. https://museumofcryptoart.medium.com/m-c-community-collection-a3da46380a0b.

MOCΔ. "MOCΔ Governance & Points." *Notion*, 2022. https://www.notion.so/M-C-Governance-Points-98b922b68a5d449886da6edf5ceff5ae.

Nelson, Danny. "NSA Whistleblower Edward Snowden Sells NFT for $5.4M." *Coindesk*, April 16, 2021. https://www.coindesk.com/markets/2021/04/16/nsa-whistleblower-edward-snowden-sells-nft-for-54m.

Pace Hamill, Susan. *The Origins Behind the Limited Liability Company*. Ohio: Ohio St. L. J. 1459/1463, 1998.

Patel, Nilay. "From a Meme to $47 Million: ConstitutionDAO, Crypto, and the Future

of Crowdfunding." *The Verge*, December 7, 2021. https://www.theverge.com/22820563/constitution-meme-47-million-crypto-crowdfunding-blockchain-ethereum-constitution.

Roberts, Daniel. "What DAOs Can Do: $6.75M in Ethereum for Ukraine." *Decrypt*, March 5, 2022. https://decrypt.co/94386/ukraine-dao-millions-in-ethereum-shows-what-dao-can-do.

Rodrigues, Usha R. *Law and the Blockchain*. Iowa: Iowa L. Rev. 679/707, 2019.

Rohr, Jonathan, and Aaron Wright. *Blockchain-Based Token Sales, Initial Coin Offerings, and the Democratization of Public Capital Markets*. California: Hastings L. J. 463, 2019.

Spike, Sam. "Fingerprints DAO." *JPG*, accessed August 4, 2022. https://jpg.space/samspike/exhibition/Fingerprints-DAO.

The SuperRare DAO. "The SuperRare Network." *Docs*, 2022. https://docs.superrare.com/the-superrare-dao.

Thomson, Janice E. *Mercenaries, Pirates, and Sovereigns: State-Building and Extraterritorial Violence in Early Modern Europe*. New Jersey: Princeton University Press, 1996.

Toppin, Jamel. "DAO's Aren't a Fad — They're a Platform." *Forbes*, February 3, 2022. https://www.forbes.com/sites/jeffkauflin/2022/02/03/daos-arent-a-fad-theyre-a-platform/. Werner, Walter. *Corporation Law in Search of Its Future*. New York: Columbia L. Rev. 1611, 1981.

Wright, Aaron. "The Rise of Decentralized Autonomous Organizations: Opportunities and Challenges." *Stanford Journal of Blockchain Law & Policy*, June 30, 2021. https://stanford-jblp.pubpub.org/pub/rise-of-daos/release/1.

Wright, Aaron, and Primavera De Filippi. *Blockchain and the Law: The Rule of Code*. Massachusetts: Harvard University Press, 2018.

Wright, Keira. "PleasrDAO adds $4M 'OG NFT' Wu-Tang Clan album to its collection." *Cointelegraph*, October 21, 2021. https://cointelegraph.com/news/pleasrdao-adds-4m-og-nft-wu-tang-clan-album-to-its-collection.

## 08 ON COLLECTING

Batycka, Dorian. "Italy Instructs Museums to Halt Contracts With NFT Companies, Citing 'Unregulated' Terms That Could Affect the Country's Cultural Heritage." *Artnet*, July 11, 2022. https://news.artnet.com/market/cinello-nft-michaelangelo-2145003.

Bennett, Bonnie A. *Donatello*. New York: Phaidon Press, 1984.

Bryant, Robert Dalton. *The Medici and a Florentine Plutocracy in the Quattrocento*. Georgia: Georgia Southern University, 2020.

Chainanalysis. "The 2021 NFT Market Report." *Chainanalysis*, 2021.

Coonin, A. Victor. *Donatello and the Dawn of the Renaissance*. London: Reaktion Books, 2019.

Debord, Guy. "Unity and Division Within Appearance." *The Society of the Spectacle*, Thesis 67, 1967.

Digital Art Museum. "David Em" *Digital Art Museum (DAM)*, accessed September 3, 2022. https://dam.org/museum/artists_ui/artists/em-david/.

Hiscox and ArtTactic. "Hiscox online art trade report 2021." *Hiscox*, 2021. https://www.hiscox.co.uk/sites/default/files/documents/2022-04/21674b-Hiscox_online_art_trade_report_2021-part_two_1.pdf.

Hobbs, Tyler. "QQL." *Vimeo*, September 13, 2022. https://vimeo.com/749223222.

Hobbs, Tyler, and Indigo Mané. "About." *QQL*, accessed November 1, 2022. https://qql.art/about.

Honour, Hugh, and John Fleming. *A World History of Art*. London: Macmillan, 1982.

Jacobus, Laura. "Piety and propriety in the Arena Chapel." *Renaissance Studies*, Vol. 12, No. 2, 1998.

Jenkins, Tiffany. *Keeping Their Marbles: How the Treasures of the Past Ended Up in Museums ... and Why They Should Stay There*. Oxford: Oxford University Press, 2016.

Jurdjevic, Mark. "Civic Humanism and the Rise of the Medici." *Renaissance Quarterly*, Vol. 52, No. 4, Winter, 1999.

Koeppe, Wolfram. "Collecting for the Kunst-kammer." *Heilbrunn Timeline of Art History*. New York: The Metropolitan Museum of Art, October 2002. http://www.metmuseum.org/toah/hd/kuns/hd_kuns.htm.

Kunsthistorisches Museum Wien. "Kunst-kammer Wien: The Cradle of the Museum." *Kunsthistorischen Museum Wien*, accessed June 20, 2022. https://www.khm.at/en/visit/collections/kunstkammer-wien.

Le-Phat Ho, Sophie. "Parallel Evolution: the Patric Prince Collection and SIGGRAPH," *The Computer Arts and Technocultures Project*. The Computer Arts Society, London, accessed August 4, 2022, https://www.docam.ca/techwatch/fiche3.php?id=85.

MAK – Museum of Applied Arts, Vienna. "MAK purchases digital art work by Harm van den Dorpel with Bitcoin." *MAK*, April 23, 2015. https://www.mak.at/jart/prj3/mak/data/uploads/downloads/presse/2015/Harm_van_Dorpel_e.pdf.

McCoy, Jennifer, and Kevin McCoy. "Public Key / Private Key." *Mccoyspace*, 2019. https://dev.mccoyspace.com/project/121/.

Mellow, James, R. "The Stein Salon Was the First Museum of Modern Art." *The New York Times*, December 1, 1968. https://archive.nytimes.com/www.nytimes.com/books/98/05/03/specials/stein-salon.html?scp=71&sq=catholic%2520museum&st=cse.

Miles, Ellie. "Redisplaying the Waddesdon Bequest." British Museum (lecture), June 11, 2015.

MOCΔ. "$MOCA Token." *Medium*, May 26, 2021. https://museumofcryptoart.medium.com/moca-token-e84a22b9b39e.

Nake, Frieder. "There Should Be No Computer Art." *Bulletin of the Computer Arts Society*, October 1971. https://dam.org/museum/essays_ui/essays/there-should-be-no-computer-art/.

Poeschke, Joachim. *Donatello and His World: Sculpture of the Italian Renaissance*. New York: Harry N. Abrams, 1993.

Rockefeller, David. "David Rockefeller on Art." Interview with the *Art Newspaper* via *Forbes*, March 5, 2003. https://www.forbes.com/2003/03/05/cx_0305conn.html?sh=707107761e87.

Shirley, Pippa. "The Rothschilds as Collectors." *The Frick Collection*. YouTube, March 1, 2013. https://www.youtube.com/watch?t=5&v=ukfvlU1mZPM&feature=emb_imp_woyt.

Soll, Jacob. *The Reckoning: Financial Accountability and the Rise and Fall of Nations*. New York: Basic Books, 2014.

The British Library. "Cabinet of Curiosities." *BL.uk*, accessed June 22, 2022. https://www.bl.uk/learning/timeline/item107648.html.

The Rothschild Archive. "Le Goût Rothschild." *Rothschild Family Archive*, accessed June 22, 2022. https://www.rothschildarchive.org/family/family_collections/le_gout_rothschild.

The Rothschild Archive. "Mayer Amschel Roth-schild (1744–1812)." *Rothschild Family Archive*, accessed June 22, 2022. https://family.rothschildarchive.org/people/21-mayer-amschel-rothschild-1744-1812.

Thompson, Nathan. "NFT Buying Behavior: a Surprising Trend." *Tech in Asia*, March 22, 2022. https://www.techinasia.com/nft-buying-behavior-surprising-trend.

## 09 ON THE METAVERSE

—

## 10 ON BUILDING

Brekke, Jaya Klara. "Hacker-Engineers and Their Economies: The Political Economy of Decentralised Networks and 'Cryptoeconomics'." *New Political Economy*, Vol. 26, No. 4, July 4, 2021. https://doi.org/10.1080/13563467.2020.1806223.

Brody, Ann, and Stéphane Couture. "Ideologies and Imaginaries in Blockchain Communities: The Case of Ethereum." *Canadian Journal of Communication*, Vol. 46, No. 3, September 9, 2021.

https://doi.org/10.22230/cjc.2021v46n3a3701.

Counterparty. "Counterwallet: Broadcast | Counterparty." April 5, 2015. https://counterparty.io/docs/broadcast/.

Dash, Anil. "On 'Inventing NFTs' and How We Don't Have Any Good Way to Talk about Tech." *Anildash.com* (blog), November 14, 2021. https://anildash.com/2021/11/14/i-didnt-invent-nfts-but-we-dont-really-have-any-other-way-to-talk-about-tech/.

Daubenschütz, Tim. "The JPG Newsletter with My Friend Tim as Special Guest: On Ascribe, Jpegs, Quadratic Voting, and Non-Transferrable Non-Fungible Tokens." *JPG — the on-Chain Curation Protocol* (blog), April 8, 2022. https://jpg100.substack.com/p/the-jpg-newsletter-with-my-friend.

De Jonghe, Dimitri, and Trent McConaghy. "SPOOL Protocol." *GitHub*, March 14, 2015. https://github.com/ascribe/spool/blob/master/README.md.

Ethereum Foundation. "ERC-20 Token Standard." *Ethereum.org*, accessed August 15, 2022. https://ethereum.org/en/developers/docs/standards/tokens/erc-20/.

Ethereum Foundation. "Token Standards." *Ethereum.org*, accessed June 14, 2022. https://ethereum.org/en/developers/docs/standards/tokens/.

Horne, Jacob. "Hyperstructures." *Jacob.energy* (blog), January 16, 2022. https://jacob.energy/hyperstructures.

Jonghe, Dimitri de, and Trent McConaghy. "SPOOL Protocol." *GitHub*, March 14, 2015. https://github.com/ascribe/spool#spool.

Larkin, Brian. "The Politics and Poetics of Infrastructure." *Annual Review of Anthropology*, Vol. 42, No. 1, October 21, 2013. https://doi.org/10.1146/annurev-anthro-092412-155522.

Larva Labs. "CryptoPunks." Larva Labs. https://www.larvalabs.com/cryptopunks.

Lemercier, Joanie. "The problem of (Ethereum) CryptoArt." *Joanie Lemercier Studio*, February 17, 2021. https://joanielemercier.com/the-problem-of-cryptoart/.

Lerner, Nili. "[NILI] NILIcoins Art-Coins." *Bitcoin Forum*, September 14, 2014. https://bitcointalk.org/index.php?topic=782161.0.

Lippard, Lucy, and John Chandler. *Six Years: The Dematerialization of the Art Object from 1966 to 1972*. New York: Praeger, 1973.

McConaghy, Trent, and David Holtzman. "Towards An Ownership Layer for the Internet." ascribe GmbH, June 24, 2015. https://cryptochain-uni.com/wp-content/uploads/ascribe-whitepaper-Towards-An-Ownership-Layer.pdf.

Rhizome. "Seven on Seven 2014: Kevin McCoy & Anil Dash." *Rhizome*, 2014. https://rhizome.org/editorial/2014/may/03/seven-on-seven-2014.

Solana. "A Solana Cluster | Solana Docs." *Solana Docs*, accessed April 11, 2022. https://docs.solana.com/cluster/overview.

Swartz, Lana. "What Was Bitcoin, What Will It Be? The Techno-Economic Imaginaries of a New Money Technology." *Cultural Studies*, Vol. 32, No. 4, July 4, 2018. https://doi.org/10.1080/09502386.2017.1416420.

The CryptoKitties Team. "CryptoKitties: Collectible and Breedable Cats Empowered by Blockchain Technology; White Pa-Purr, V3." *Axiom Zen*, 2017.

Wood, Gavin. "ÐApps: What Web 3.0 Looks Like." *Gavwood.com* (blog), April 17, 2014. https://gavwood.com/dappsweb3.html.

# IMAGE CREDITS

**ARTIST CREDITS** // **0xDEAFBEEF** // © Courtesy of Tyler de Witt; **Aaron Penne & Boreta** // Courtesy of Aaron Penne x Boreta; **Afroscope** // © Courtesy of Afroscope (Nana Opoku); **AILADI** // Courtesy of Ailadi; **Andreas Gysin** // © Courtesy of ertdfgcvb; **Andrés Reisinger** // © Courtesy of Andrés Reisinger; **Anna Carreras** // Courtesy of Anna Carreras ; **Anna Ridler** // Courtesy of Anna Ridler; **Anne Spalter** // Courtesy of Anne Spalter; **Arclight** // Courtesy of Arclight; **Ash Thorp** // Courtesy of ALT Creative, Inc.; **aurèce vettier** // Courtesy of aurèce vettier, and Romain Darnaud / © VG Bild-Kunst, Bonn 2025; **Auriea Harvey** // © Courtesy of Auriea Harvey; **Beeple** // Mike Winkelmann; **Botto** // Courtesy of BottoDAO; **Brendan Dawes** // Courtesy of Brendan Dawes; **Casey Reas** // Courtesy of Casey Reas; **Cibelle Cavalli Bastos** // Courtesy of Cibelle Cavalli Bastos; **Coldie** // © Courtesy of Coldie; **CryptoKitties** // Dapper Labs, Inc.; **Curio Card 1, 18** // Creative Commons (Artwork by Phneep); **Curio Card 17–19** // Courtesy of Luis Buenaventura; **Curio Card 2–10, 14, 15, 20** // Creative Commons (Artwork by Phneep); **Curio Card 21–23** // © Courtesy of Robek World; **Curio Card 24–26** // Courtesy of Daniel Ari Friedman; **Curio Card 27–29** // © Marisol Vengas | Max Infeld; **Curio Card 30** // Creative Commons (Artwork by Thoros of Myr); **DADA** // © 2017, 2018, 2019, 2020 DADA; **Dada Boipelo** // Courtesy of Dada Boipelo; **Damien Hirst** // © Damien Hirst and Science Ltd. All rights reserved / VG Bild-Kunst, Bonn 2025; **Daniel Calderon** // Courtesy of DCA (Daniel Calderon Arenas); **Darien Brito** // © Courtesy of Darien Brito; **David Rudnick** // Courtesy of David Rudnick; **divergence** // Courtesy of divergence; **Dmitri Cherniak** // Courtesy of Dmitri Cherniak; **Dom Hofmann** // Courtesy of Dominik Hofmann / The Eye (for Adventurers) courtesy of OpenQuill.Foundation; **Emily Xie** // Courtesy of Emily Xie; **Erick Calderon** // Courtesy of Erick Calderon; **Etherpoems** // RAVENS EYE; © Courtesy of aurèce vettier / © VG Bild-Kunst, Bonn 2025; **EtherRocks** // Public Domain; **Ezra Miller** // Courtesy of Ezra Miller; **FEWOCiOUS** // Courtesy of FEWOCiOUS, © 2021 FEWOCiOUS, All Rights Reserved; **fingacode** // Courtesy of fingacode; **FVCKRENDER** // Courtesy of FVCKRENDER; **Hackatao** // © Courtesy of Hackatao; **Harm van den Dorpel** // Harm van den Dorpel; **Helena Sarin** // Courtesy of Helena Sarin, Neural Bricolage; **Herbert W. Franke** // Archive „art meets science"; **Holly Herndon & Mathew Dryhurst** // Courtesy of Holly Herndon & Mathew Dryhurst; **Iskra Velitchkova** // Courtesy of Iskra Velitchkova; **Ix Shells** // © Courtesy of Itzel Yard; **Jack Butcher** // © Courtesy of Jack Butcher / © VG Bild-Kunst, Bonn 2025; **Jan Robert Leegte** // Jan Robert Leegte; **Jeff Davis** // © Courtesy of Jeff Davis; **Joe Pease** // joepease 2024; **Jonas Lund** // Courtesy of Jonas Lund; **Joshua Davis** // Courtesy of Joshua Davis / PrayStation; **Justin Aversano** // Courtesy of Justin Aversano; **Katherine Frazer** // © Courtesy of Katherine Frazer; **Keiken** // (Courtesy of Keiken and Daata); Courtesy of Keiken, obso1337, Ryan Vautier and Sakeema Crook; **Kenny Schachter** // Courtesy of Kenny Schachter; **Kim Asendorf** // © Kim Asendorf; **Kevin Abosch** // © Courtesy of Studio Kevin Abosch; **Kevin McCoy** // © Courtesy of Kevin McCoy; **Kudzu** // © Courtesy of Folia; Courtesy of Burak Arikan; **Larva Labs** // #5938, #6900, #7035 George McDonaugh; #4776 Kenshiro, #2098 Miguel Faus, #6287 J Widmann, #7307, #2215 heygareth; #5046 Galbraith, #4633 Punk 4633, #8219 gmoney.eth, #6013 Punk 6013, #1478 Erick "Snow-fro" Calderon, #9810 ashdre, #4150 Fanny Lakoubay, #3128 thefunnyguys, #6360 @Balon_art, #8472, #5017, #3831 Cozomo de' Medici; #6046 @richerd; #1, #119, #144, #146, #147, #149, #152, #156, #157, #163, #166, #170, #174, #188, #194, #248, #274, #293, #304, #362, #369, #373, #393, #395, #472, #484, #495, #515, #523, #539, #558, #594, #595, #601, #623, #655, #656, #657, #673, #676, #687, #710, #711, #744, #754, #808, #823, #824, #828, #833, #835, #837, #840, #873, #882, #885, #887, #889, #890, #892, #895, #899, #902, #911, #932, #933, #935, #941, #942, #946, #947, #953,

# EDITOR'S THANKS

Cosmo Lindsay for the being the nervous system of this book and its heartbeat; Marlene Taschen for steering the boat with a constant smile and a strawberry milkshake; Benedikt Taschen for a drive and lunch I won't forget; Fernando Gutiérrez and Alex Bassett for giving vision to words and that timeline; Camille Beckmann, Mia Stern, Gabrielle Schwarz, Jack Spurrier, Allison McCafferty, Igor Bojczuk, and the terrier Robbie Cleave for making it a reality and a day-to-day pleasure; Clara Metter for your steadfast support; Jehan Chu for opening the first door; Peter Fetterman for opening this one; Vivian Brodie for taking a chance; Rudy Capildeo for watching over the ink; the team at Sandbox for keeping the lights on; Kathrin Murr for your patience; Frank Goerhardt and Thomas Grell for making the digital physical and being our Gutenberg; Thea Miklowski for finding 4,715 Easter eggs; Daniel Shiu for laying one more; James Parker Healy and Michael Villere for winning all the bets; Osinachi for your knowledge of the African continent; Christina J. Chua, Clara Peh, and Qinwen Wang for your support across Asia; Metakovan and the team at Metapurse for your understanding of the Indian subcontinent; Tina Rivers Ryan for your vast historical grounding; Anne and Michael Spalter and Bryan Smith Art Services for providing emails galore and always being a heartbeat away; Teeto, JonJons, and Bartress for keeping the fourth in check; Noodles and Ernitta for always being at the end of the line; Dolly for riverside smiles; F&P for being F&P; BBAG for being the hub that you are; Spirries for involving me; to Lewis Blackwell for his council, encouragement, and reminding me of Arts Club sessions with Warrick; to Lucy Brownridge for going above and beyond with friendly advice; Lawrence Tilli for those earliest of conversations; Nansen for giving us eyes and ears onto the blockchain; Adina Glickstein for being a second pair of eyes; Stefan Dalal for making those introductions; Adam McBride for filling in the gaps; Joe Looney for diving deep into Counterparty history; On Kawara and Roman Opalka for showing us how it could be done; Satoshi for getting it done.

To all my collectors whose support I deeply value and most importantly to all the artists, contributors, writers, researchers, and conversations that have made and informed this project — thank you so much for your time.

And lastly, to the NFT space, see you again in a few years time.

R.A.

**Generative Endpapers (front and back)**
Robert Alice
Outputs from *Source [On NFTs]*, 2024
Text, Natural Language Processing, p5.js
0×5e5551ff74c8f5bd3aaae8801aed0d579ddb470c, 1-125

Commissioned by TASCHEN, these endpapers are outputs from a generative algorithm. Made entirely out of text, the endpapers explore text as the fundamental substrate of both NFTs and blockchains. Veering from order to chaos, legibility to abstraction, the algorithm speaks to both the chaotic nature of history in a post-truth world and the blockchain as a site for digital graffiti. Trained on 30 key texts that have influenced *On NFTs*, the algorithm uses machine learning to collide key words from these historical texts. The resultant strings of concrete poetry are the pigment to the artwork and found in the metadata to each NFT. Launched at Christie's New York as part of the launch of *On NFTs*, outputs from the algorithm are held in the libraries of the Centre Pompidou and LACMA.

© 2025 TASCHEN GmbH
Hohenzollernring 53, D–50672 Köln
www.taschen.com

Design:
Fernando Gutiérrez, London
Cover design:
Zak Group, London
Endpapers:
Robert Alice, London
NFT & Web3 development:
Digital Practice (www.digitalpractice.art), New York
Editorial coordination:
Cosmo Lindsay, London, and Kathrin Murr, Cologne

ISBN 978-3-8365-9345-8
Printed in Italy

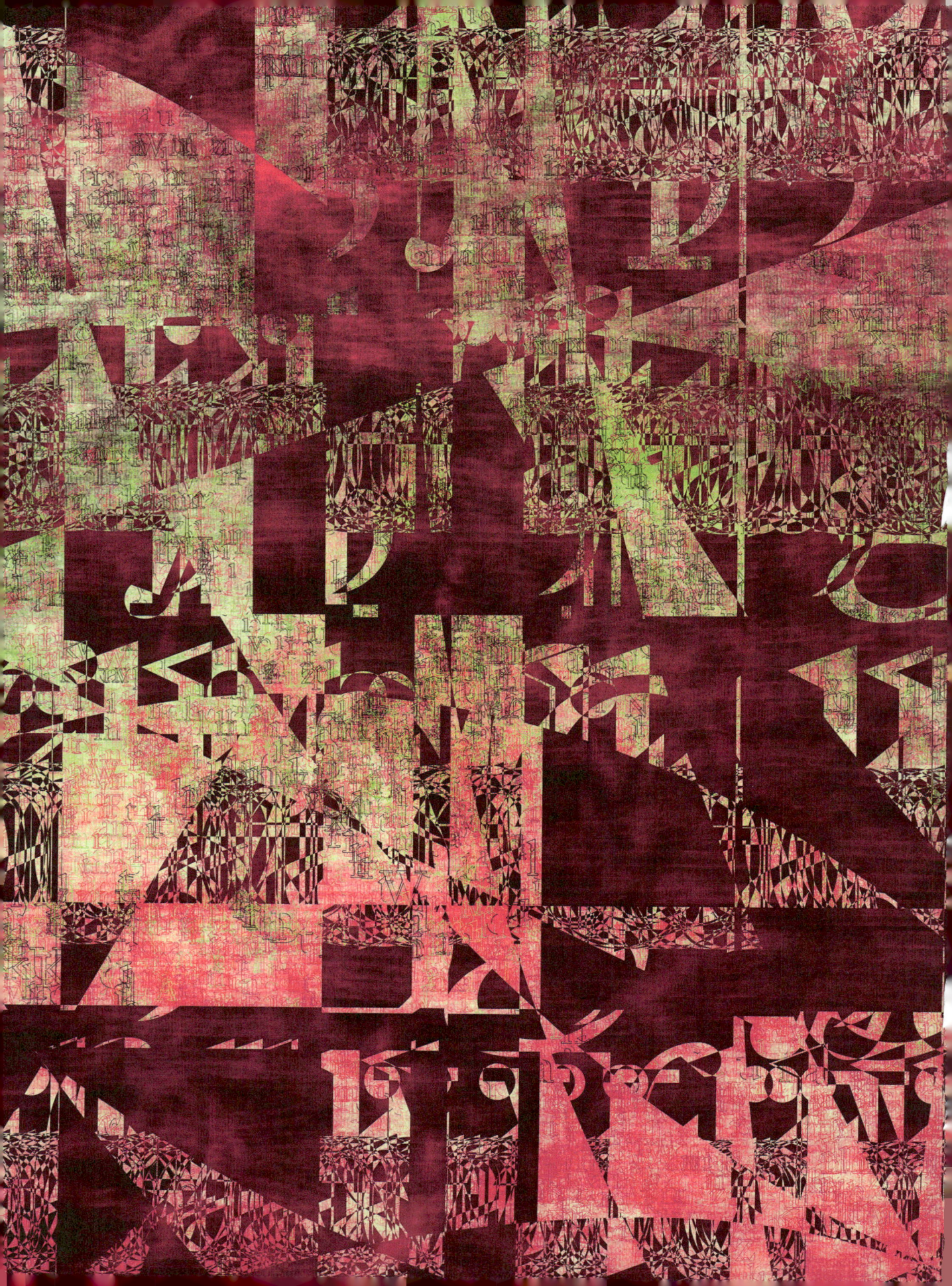